The **Rough Guide** to

Tuscany & Umbria

written and researched by

Tim Jepson, Jonathan Buckley and Mark Ellingham

ROUGH
GUIDES

NEW YORK · LONDON · DELHI

www.roughguides.com

Contents

The Palio colour section
following p.344

The great outdoors
colour section following
p.504

◀◀ Cypress trees and umbrella pines, Val d'Orcia ◀ Giambologna's Oceano, the Bargello, Florence

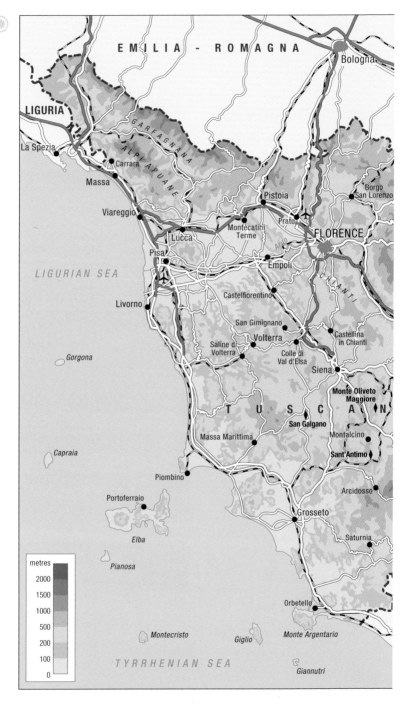

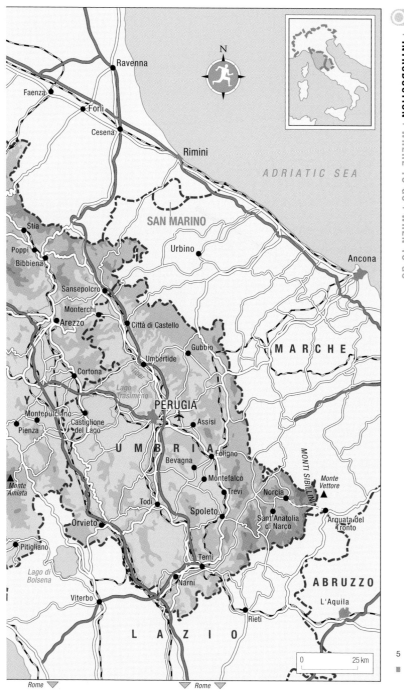

Introduction to

Tuscany & Umbria

Tuscany and Umbria harbour the classic landscapes of Italy, familiar from a thousand Renaissance paintings, with their backdrop of medieval hill-towns, rows of cypress trees, vineyards and olive groves, and artfully sited villas and farmhouses. It's a stereotype that has long held an irresistible attraction for northern Europeans. Shelley referred to Tuscany as a "paradise of exiles", and ever since his time the English, in particular, have seen the region as an ideal refuge from a sun-starved and overcrowded homeland.

The expatriate's perspective may be distorted, but the central provinces – especially in Tuscany – are indeed the essence of Italy in many ways. The national language evolved from Tuscan dialect, a supremacy ensured by Dante, who wrote the *Divine Comedy* in the vernacular of his birthplace, Florence. Other great Tuscan writers of the period – Petrarch and Boccaccio – reinforced its status, and in the nineteenth century Manzoni came to Tuscany to purge his vocabulary of any impurities while working on *The Betrothed*, the most famous of all Italian novels. But what makes this area pivotal to the culture not just of Italy but of all Europe is, of course, the **Renaissance** period (see box, p.8), whose masterpieces of painting, sculpture and architecture are an intrinsic part of any tour. The name by which we refer to this extraordinarily creative era was coined by a Tuscan, Giorgio Vasari, who wrote in the sixteenth century of the "rebirth" of the arts with the humanism of Giotto and his successors.

Palazzo dei Priori, Perugia

Nowadays Tuscany and Umbria are among the wealthiest regions of the modern Italian state, a prosperity founded partly on agriculture and tourism, but largely on their industrial centres, which are especially conspicuous in the Arno valley. Nonetheless, both Tuscany and Umbria are predominantly **rural**, with great tracts of land still looking much as they did half a millennium ago. Just as the hill-towns mould themselves to the summits, the terraces of vines follow the lower contours of the hills and open fields spread across the broader valleys, forming a distinctive balance between the natural and human world.

Fact file

Tuscany

• **Tuscany** (Toscana) has a population of around 3.5 million, with some 400,000 in Florence, its capital.

• It is bordered by the **sea** to the west, and by the Apennine **mountains** to the east; in the north lie the Alpi Apuane (where Monte Prado reaches 2054m), while in the south rises Monte Amiata. South of Livorno lies the coastal **plain** of the Maremma. Tuscany has more **woodland** than any other Italian region.

• Tourism is a major contributor to the region's **economy**, as are agriculture (especially beef, wine and olive oil) and textile production, which is concentrated in the Arno valley and Prato.

Umbria

• **Umbria** is the only landlocked region of the Italian peninsula. Of its 900,000 **population**, 150,000 live in Perugia, the capital.

• The **terrain** is gentler than Tuscany, but the Apennines run along the eastern border, where, in the Sibillini mountains, Monte Vettore reaches 2476m just over the border in Marche. Some thirty percent of Umbria is woodland.

• Perugia manufactures food and clothing, and factories dot the Vale of Spoleto, but the major **industries** (steel, chemicals, textiles, paper and food) are in the south, around Terni. Traditional **crafts** are also significant, especially pottery.

Where to go

Florence was the most active centre of the Renaissance, flourishing through the patronage of the all-powerful Medici and a multitude of religious bodies and guilds, whose merchants and manufacturers laid the foundations of the city's prosperity. Every eminent artistic figure from Giotto onwards is represented here, in an unrivalled gathering of churches, galleries and museums.

Although Florence tends to take the limelight today, the historic rivalry between the towns of both provinces – an important factor in a region whose inhabitants feel a strong loyalty to their home town – ensured that pictures and palaces were sponsored by everyone who could afford them. Exquisite Renaissance works adorn almost every place of any size from the Tuscan coast to the Apennine slopes of eastern Umbria, while

Renaissance art

Tuscany was the powerhouse of what has come to be known as the Renaissance, and the city of Florence is the supreme monument to European civilization's great leap into modernity. Buildings by the likes of Brunelleschi and Alberti, the architects who reinvented the style of ancient Rome, still adorn the fabric of the city, while within its churches you can admire paintings and sculptures by artists who put the study of humanity back at the centre of western art: Donatello,

Masaccio, Botticelli, Uccello, Ghirlandaio, Michelangelo, and the greatest of their forerunners, Cimabue and Giotto. The city's museums contain an astounding abundance of masterpieces, with the galleries of the Uffizi constituting the world's richest showcase of Renaissance art. But almost every sizeable town in central Italy commissioned works during this period that have proved to be of durable fascination – as in the stunning fresco cycles in Arezzo (Piero della Francesca), Orvieto (Luca Signorelli), Siena (Pinturicchio), San Gimignano (Benozzo Gozzoli), Montefalco (Gozzoli again), Perugia (Perugino) and Prato (Fra Filippo Lippi), to name only a few.

the largest towns can boast artistic projects every bit as ambitious as those to be seen in Florence (see box opposite).

Moreover, the art of the Renaissance did not spring out of thin air: both Tuscany and Umbria can boast a cultural lineage that stretches back unbroken to the time of Charlemagne and even beyond. **Lucca** is one of the handsomest Romanesque cities in Europe, and **Pisa** – whose Campo dei Miracoli, with its Leaning Tower, is one of Europe's most brilliant monumental ensembles – is another city whose heyday came in the Middle Ages. **Siena**'s red-brick medieval cityscape, arranged around its fabulous scallop-shaped Campo, makes a refreshing contrast with the darker tones of Florence, while a tour through Umbria can seem like a procession of magnificent ancient hill-towns. The attractions of **Assisi** (birthplace of St Francis), **Spoleto** and the busy provincial capital of **Perugia** are well known, but other Umbrian towns remain more obscure – such as **Gubbio** and the backwater

Saints

Florence has St Peter Martyr and the more obscure St Giovanni Gualberto; Siena has St Catherine, joint patron of Italy, and St Bernardino, patron saint of advertising… but Tuscany's roll-call of the holy is meagre compared to that of its neighbour, the so-called *terra dei santi* ("land of the saints"). Umbria's towns and villages are littered with shrines to holy men and women, none more peculiar than those of Montefalco, where a trio of mummified bodies are the object of veneration. St Francis of Assisi lies in the greatest of Umbria's pilgrimage churches, a short distance from the resting-place of his devout companion, St Clare. The founder of western monasticism, St Benedict, hailed from Norcia, not far from the hometown of St Rita, patron saint of the impossible. And just outside Terni, there's a pilgrimage site dedicated to St Valentine, thought to have been born there. The one Umbrian saint who could be said to rival the fame of Francis, Valentine differs from him in one crucial respect: in all likelihood, he didn't exist.

delights of **Bevagna** and **Todi**. Many of the Umbrian towns retain a fair showing of their ancient past, too, with Etruscan and Roman walls and tombs to be seen on sites left undisturbed for centuries.

The variety of **landscape** within this comparatively small area is astounding. A short distance from central Florence spread the thickly wooded uplands of the **Mugello** and the **Casentino**, while Lucca is a springboard for the **Alpi Apuane**, whose mountain quarries have supplied Europe's masons with pure white marble for centuries. Along the Tuscan shoreline the resorts are interspersed by some of Italy's best-kept wildlife reserves, including the fabulous **Monti dell'Uccellina**, the last stretch of

Regional wines

Until recently, **wine** in Tuscany and Umbria had been made more or less the same way for centuries – in small quantities, by small producers, and using old-fashioned techniques and two robust and workaday grape varieties (Sangiovese and Trebbiano). Much – apart from the ubiquitous Chianti – was made for local consumption, and quality, to put it mildly, was variable.

Then came **Denominazione d'Origine Controllata (DOC)**, a state-inspired, countrywide system aimed at bringing order to Italy's many thousands of wines. For a while it worked, and quality improved. Then, like most Italian bureaucratic initiatives, it ran into trouble: virtually every wine of note had a DOC listing, and the label ceased to mean very much at all. Enter (in 1980) **DOCG**, where the quality of far fewer wines (Brunello di Montalcino, Vino Nobile di Montepulciano and Chianti in Tuscany, and Sagrantino in Umbria) was *garantita* – guaranteed.

Both systems, however, impose strict production controls, and in the last twenty years or so, many younger, more experimental producers have disdained both classifications. Instead, they have introduced modern, New World production methods and "foreign" grape varieties, especially the Cabernets and Pinor Noirs of France. The result has been the so-called "**Super Tuscans**", often sublime (and hugely expensive) wines, many from the Bolgheri region in the Maremma, and usually marketed under the most humble classification of all, Vino da Tavola – table wine.

virgin coast in the whole country. Out in the **Tuscan archipelago**, the island of **Giglio** is relatively unspoilt by the sort of tourist development that has infiltrated – though certainly not ruined – nearby **Elba**. The pastoral archetype is perhaps most strikingly subverted in the deep south of the province, where the agricultural hinterland of Siena soon gives way to the bleak **crete** and the sulphurous pools of **Saturnia**.

Landlocked Umbria may not be as varied as its neighbour, but the wild heights of the **Valnerina**, the **Piano Grande**'s prairie-like expanse and the savage peaks of the **Monti Sibillini** all contrast with the tranquil, soft-contoured hills with which the region is most often associated.

When to go

Midsummer in central Italy is not as pleasant an experience as you might imagine: the heat can be stifling, and from May to September you'll require luck to find accommodation in all but the most out-of-the-way spots. If at all possible, the month to avoid is **August**, when the great majority of Italians take their holidays. As a result many town restaurants and some hotels are closed for the entire month and the beaches are jammed solid. As the standard Italian idea of an enjoyable summer break is to spend a few weeks towel-to-towel on the sand, Umbria escapes the worst of the rush, but the problem of limited opening remains.

Florence throughout the summer is such a log jam of tour groups that the major attractions become a purgatorial experience: a two-hour queue for the Uffizi is not unusual. To enjoy a visit fully, go shortly **before Easter** or in the **late autumn** – times of the year that are the best for Tuscany and Umbria as a whole, as the towns are quieter and the countryside is blossoming or taking on the tones of the harvest season. The Umbrian climate varies slightly from Tuscany's, chiefly because of its distance from the sea; temperatures in summer are fractionally higher, while the hill-top position of many towns can make them surprisingly windy and cool at other times. **Winter** is often quite rainy, but the absence of crowds makes this a good option for the cities on the major art trails. Bear in mind, however, that the high altitude of much of the region means many roads are impassable in midwinter, and in places

▲ Florentines drinking in the summer sunshine

like the upper Casentino or the Sibillini the snow might not melt until March or even April.

It's always worth checking when each town has its **festivals** or pilgrimages. Accommodation is always tricky during these mini-peak seasons, but some of the festivities are enjoyable enough to merit planning a trip around. Many have been crucial to their town's image for centuries – the most celebrated of these being the Siena **Palio**, a hell-for-leather horse race round the central square. The frenzy of Gubbio's semi-pagan **Corsa dei Ceri** almost matches it, as does the passionate commitment of Florence's **Calcio Storico**, a football match in medieval attire with no holds barred. Costumed **jousts** and other martial displays are a feature of several festive calendars, notable examples being the jousts in Pistoia and Arezzo and the twice-yearly **crossbow competitions** between Gubbio and Sansepolcro. **Holy days** and **saints' days** bring in the crowds in equal numbers, with Assisi leading the way as the most venerated site.

Local produce

Simplicity remains the defining characteristic of the cuisine of Tuscany and Umbria. Complicated sauces play no part in the classic recipes of these regions: here it's all about top-quality local produce, brought to the table with a minimum of intervention. A swift grilling, a drizzle of olive oil, a light garnish of herbs – that's all the enhancement deemed necessary for a cut of prime Tuscan beef or Umbrian pork. Vegetables tend to feature as side dishes and starters (the thick bean soup called *ribollita* is a signature Tuscan creation), and spinach and artichokes are staples of most menus, as are Umbrian truffles in the autumn. As for wine, you're spoiled for choice; see the Regional wines box on p.10.

Among the innumerable **arts festivals**, the highest profiles are achieved by the contemporary arts extravaganza in Spoleto, the Umbria Jazz festival in Perugia and the Maggio Musicale in more conservative Florence – but as with the more folkloric events, even the smallest towns have their cultural season. Finally, there's scarcely a hamlet in Tuscany or Umbria that doesn't have a **food** or **wine** festival, the region seeming to find an excuse to celebrate almost everything that breathes or grows. Attracting mainly just the locals and often lasting for just a day, these events place less stress on the hotels, though it might be a good idea to book a room if you're dropping by; fountains running with wine and other such excesses are pretty common.

Tuscany and Umbria temperatures

The table shows maximum and minimum daytime temperatures.

	January		April		July		October	
	Min	Max	Min	Max	Min	Max	Min	Max
Florence								
°C	1	10	8	19	17	31	10	21
°F	34	50	46	66	62	88	50	70
Livorno								
°C	2	11	7	18	16	29	11	21
°F	35	51	45	64	61	84	51	70
Perugia								
°C	0	9	5	17	15	30	9	20
°F	32	48	41	63	59	86	48	68

things not to miss

It's not possible to see everything that Tuscany and Umbria have to offer in one trip – and we don't suggest you try. What follows is a selective taste of the regions' highlights: great places to visit, outstanding buildings, spectacular scenery and unforgettable events. They're arranged in five colour-coded categories, which you can browse through to find the very best things to see and experience. All entries have a page reference to take you straight into the guide, where you can find out more.

01 Assisi Page **522** ●Morning mist settles in the Vale of Spoleto below Assisi, birthplace of St Francis and one of the most beautiful of Umbria's many hill-towns.

02 **San Gimignano** Page **364** • San Gimignano is one of the best-preserved medieval towns in Italy. Fifteen of the original 72 towers built in the Middle Ages survive.

04 **Spoleto** Page **565** • The facade of Spoleto's cathedral owes its charm to the restrained combination of Romanesque and Renaissance elements.

03 **Corsa dei Ceri** Page **511** • Processions, pageants and a race between three teams bearing the *ceri*, or candles, mark the Corsa dei Ceri, held in the Umbrian town of Gubbio each year on May 15.

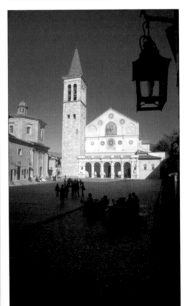

05 **Piazza del Duomo** Page **72** • Florence's cathedral square is a stupendous ensemble of religious architecture.

06 **Barga, Alpi Apuane** Page **252** • The village of Barga, known for its sublime cathedral and summer music festival, is set in the shadow of the Orrecchiella and Alpi Apuane mountains.

07 Monti dell'Uccellina Page **305** • The protected environment of the Monti dell'Uccellina in the Maremma is one of the last pristine stretches of coastline in Italy.

09 Pienza Page **407** • The Duomo and Piazza Pio II form the centrepiece of Pienza, designed as a Utopian Renaissance city in the fifteenth century.

08 Santa Croce, Florence Page **138** • The Cappella Pazzi, in the cloisters of Santa Croce, is the gold standard of Renaissance church architecture.

17

10 **Santa Maria Novella, Florence** Page **112** • One of Florence's key churches, Santa Maria Novella, has a hybrid Romanesque and Renaissance facade and frescoes by Andrea di Firenze, Uccello, Masaccio, Ghirlandaio and Filippino Lippi.

11 **Pisa** Page **263** • Pisa's Campo dei Miracoli is the stage for more than just the Leaning Tower: you'll find the city's cathedral here, as well as the magnificent baptistery and the beautiful cemetery known as the Camposanto.

12 Orvieto Page **621** • Umbria's most striking hill-town crowns a dramatic volcanic outcrop, and is dominated by one of Italy's finest cathedrals.

14 Lucca Page **228** • From the thirteenth-century facade of San Michele in Foro the archangel Michael gazes over the centre of the graceful small city of Lucca.

13 Sant'Antimo Page **401** • Splendid and serene, Sant'Antimo is one of several working abbeys set in the glorious countryside south of Siena.

15 Museo Civico, Sansepolcro Page **452** • Piero della Francesca's mighty *Resurrection* brings visitors from all over Europe to the small town of Sansepolcro.

16 Cortona Page **459** • With barely a single level street in the *centro storico*, Cortona is the hilliest of hill-towns.

18 Tuscan wine Page **40** • Some of Italy's finest vintages can be sampled in the wine bars of Tuscany and Umbria.

19 Ice cream Page **36** • Until you've sampled *gelato*, you don't know just how good ice cream can be.

17 San Lorenzo, Florence Page **118** • Brunelleschi, Donatello and Michelangelo all contributed to the construction and adornment of the parish church of the Medici.

20 **Piano Grande** Page **591** • The Piano Grande, an extraordinary upland above Norcia, is the most striking feature of the Sibillini mountains, part of the Apennine chain in eastern Umbria.

21 **The crete** Page **389** • The almost bare, clay hills of the *crete* south of Siena make up one of Tuscany's most beautiful and distinctive landscapes. In summer the fields blaze with poppies, sunflowers and ripening wheat.

21

22 **The Casentino** Page **454** • Leave the crowds behind in the lush wooded hills of the Casentino.

23 **Volterra** Page **375** • The brooding hill-town of Volterra has an impressive Etruscan, Roman and medieval heritage.

23

24 **Duomo, Siena** Page **334** •Siena's Romanesque-Gothic cathedral is filled with art, including a beautiful fresco cycle by Pinturicchio.

25 **Piazza Grande, Arezzo** Page **447** • Renowned for the frescoes in the church of San Francesco, Arezzo also boasts one of the most impressive main squares in Tuscany.

27 **The Uffizi** Page **92** •
Botticelli's *Birth of Venus* is just one masterpiece amid dozens in the galleries of the Uffizi.

26 **The Fontana Maggiore, Perugia** Page **479** • The ornately sculpted Fontana Maggiore has survived for over 800 years at the heart of Perugia, Umbria's lofty regional capital.

Basics

Basics

Getting there

The main airports serving Tuscany and Umbria are at Pisa, Rome and Bologna, though the smaller ones at Florence, Perugia and Ancona can also be useful. From the UK and Ireland, competitive prices for charter, no-frills or scheduled flights with major carriers outweigh the inconvenience of the long rail journey. Flights from Canada, North America and Australasia mostly come into Rome (or, less conveniently, Milan), with one airline flying to Pisa from the US. From down under, you may find it cheaper to fly to London and get a budget onward flight from there.

Airfares depend on the **season**, with the highest being around Easter, from June to August, and from Christmas to New Year; fares drop during the "shoulder" seasons – September to October and April to May – and you'll get the best prices during the November-to-March low season (excluding Christmas and New Year). It is generally more expensive to fly at weekends; prices quoted below assume midweek travel. You can often cut costs by going through a **discount flight agent** who may also offer special student and youth fares and a range of other travel-related services such as travel insurance, rail passes, car rentals, tours and the like.

Flights from the UK and Ireland

The biggest **budget airlines** serving Pisa from the UK are Ryanair, flying from London Stansted, Bournemouth, East Midlands, Liverpool, Edinburgh and Glasgow, and easyJet, flying from Gatwick, Luton and Bristol. In the summer, Jet2 flies from Manchester, Leeds, Newcastle and Bradford, and Thomsonfly from Gatwick, Coventry, Leeds and Manchester. If you book well in advance you can sometimes find **fares** for as little as £25 return for off-peak flights, though these rock-bottom prices tend to apply only to early-morning or late-evening flights. For more reasonable flight times, prices are £100–150 return in summer, as long as you make your reservation well in advance: book any less than two weeks before departure, and you'll pay as much as for a seat on a full-service airline. You may

also find **charter flight** bargains in high season: it's worth checking with a specialist agent or scouring the classified section of the weekend newspapers for last-minute deals.

Of the **full-service airlines** in the UK, British Airways serves **Pisa** several times daily out of London Gatwick and Manchester, and Alitalia flies via Milan or Rome. A return flight with Alitalia or BA from London to Pisa in low season can cost around £100, with prices from £150 to £300 in high season. Note, however, that at the time of writing, the future of Alitalia was unclear. Keep your eyes open for special offers, which have become more numerous in the wake of competition from the no-frills outfits. Meridiana is currently the only airline with non-stop flights from Gatwick to Florence Perétola; their tickets tend to be more expensive than anyone else's – from £150 off-peak, £200 in summer.

BA also operates regular flights to **Bologna** Marconi from London Gatwick. This is generally a cheaper option than flying to Pisa, and because Bologna is a less popular destination you can often find seats when the Pisa flights are sold out. Bologna airport is a shuttle-bus ride from Bologna train station, from where Florence is an hour's train ride away. (Forlì airport, the point of arrival for Ryanair flights to Bologna, is a good deal more distant and will add an extra hour to your journey.)

Where regular, scheduled flights to Umbria are concerned, flying into **Rome** is simplest, with an onward journey by road or rail of around two hours to Perugia or Spoleto, three hours to Florence. **Fiumicino**, the common name for Rome's Leonardo da Vinci airport, is about 30km west of the city centre, from where a half-hourly train takes thirty minutes to reach Stazione Termini, Rome's principal station. Many charter flights and no-frills airlines use Rome's smaller **Ciampino** airport, southeast of the city, from where regular coaches make the forty-minute trip to Stazione Termini. The tiny airport at **Perugia** has Ryanair flights from Stansted and easy travel links to the city and the region. The east-coast port of **Ancona** is another possibility, with a shuttle bus from the airport to the main train station for onward travel into Umbria.

From Dublin, Aer Lingus has two flights a week to Bologna (Marconi) and daily services to Rome Fiumicino; Alitalia also has regular flights (via Paris) to Bologna and Rome. You can find high-season return deals for €200 or lower if you book early, but prices in high season can rise to more than €500. In high season Ryanair flies from Dublin to Pisa daily for around €150; otherwise you could pick up a Ryanair flight from Dublin or Shannon to Stansted and catch a Pisa plane from there.

There are no direct flights from Northern Ireland; **from Belfast**, the cheapest option is to buy an easyJet ticket to London and an onward flight to Pisa.

Flights from the US and Canada

The only **direct service** between North America and Tuscany (and thus northern Umbria) is offered by Delta, which flies from New York JFK to Pisa five times a week. Otherwise, there are plenty of flights **from the US and Canada** to Rome or Milan Malpensa, from where you can pick up an onward train to Pisa or Florence. Alitalia and Delta have daily flights to Milan from New York, Miami, Chicago and Boston, and to Rome from New York; note that at the time of writing, however, the future of Alitalia was unclear. Other options to Rome include American Airlines from Chicago, and Alitalia and Air Canada from Toronto (usually with a connection in Europe en route). Many European carriers also fly from major US and Canadian cities (via their capitals) to Rome,

Milan and Pisa. The cheapest return fares to Rome from New York in low season are around $750, rising to $1500 during the summer.

Flights from Australia and New Zealand

There are no direct flights to Italy **from Australia or New Zealand**, but plenty of airlines fly to Rome via Asian hubs. Round-trip fares from Sydney with the major airlines (Alitalia, Qantas, Japan, Singapore or Malaysian) start at around A$2000 in low season, rising to upwards of A$3500 in high season. From New Zealand you can expect to pay from around NZ$2200 in low season to NZ$3500 in high season.

Trains

Travelling **by train** to Italy won't save any money, but the beauty of train travel is that you can break up your journey en route. The choice of routes and fares is hugely complex, but the most direct route is to take the Eurostar from London to Paris, then pick up the "Palatino" overnight service from Paris to Florence, via Milan (ⓦwww.artesia.eu), or take the high-speed TGV from Paris to Milan, and change there for Florence; total journey time is around 14–18 hours, and with some online research you can put together a one-way ticket for a little over £100 in low season, though peak prices can go as high as £250. Discounts for under-26s are sometimes available and advance booking is essential. If you're planning to include Italy as part of a longer European trip you could invest in a **rail pass** – the Rail Europe website is a useful source of information.

Rail contacts

European Rail ⓦ www.europeanrail.com. Independent specialist in European rail travel.
Eurostar ⓦ www.eurostar.com.
InterRail ⓦ www.interrail.net.
Rail Europe ⓦ www.raileurope.co.uk. Information on international train travel, including tickets and passes.
The Man in Seat 61 ⓦ www.seat61.com. An excellent site, packed with useful tips.
Trainseurope ⓦ www.trainseurope.co.uk. Another good agency for European rail tickets.

Fly less – stay longer! Travel and climate change

Climate change is perhaps the single biggest issue facing our planet. It is caused by a build-up in the atmosphere of carbon dioxide and other greenhouse gases, which are emitted by many sources – including planes. Already, **flights** account for three to four percent of human-induced global warming: that figure may sound small, but it is rising year on year and threatens to counteract the progress made by reducing greenhouse emissions in other areas.

Rough Guides regard travel as a **global benefit**, and feel strongly that the advantages to developing economies are important, as are the opportunities for greater contact and awareness among peoples. But we also believe in travelling responsibly, which includes giving thought to how often we fly and what we can do to redress any harm that our trips may create.

We can travel less or simply reduce the amount we travel by air (taking fewer trips and staying longer, or taking the train if there is one); we can avoid night flights (which are more damaging); and we can make the trips we do take "climate neutral" via a carbon offset scheme. **Offset schemes** run by climatecare.org, carbonneutral .com and others allow you to "neutralize" the greenhouse gases that you are responsible for releasing. Their websites have simple calculators that let you work out the impact of any flight – as does our own. Once that's done, you can pay to fund projects that will reduce future emissions by an equivalent amount. Please take the time to visit our website and make your trip climate neutral, or get a copy of the *Rough Guide to Climate Change* for more detail on the subject.

www.roughguides.com/climatechange

Airlines, agents and operators

Online booking

ⓦ www.expedia.co.uk (UK), ⓦ www.expedia.com (US), ⓦ www.expedia.ca (Canada)
ⓦ www.lastminute.com (UK)
ⓦ www.opodo.co.uk (UK)
ⓦ www.orbitz.com (US)
ⓦ www.skyscanner.net (UK)
ⓦ www.travelocity.co.uk (UK), ⓦ www.travelocity .com (US), ⓦ www.travelocity.ca (Canada), ⓦ www .travelocity.co.nz (NZ)
ⓦ www.travelonline.co.za (SA)
ⓦ www.zuji.com.au (Australia)

Airlines

Aer Lingus Republic of Ireland ☎ 0818/365 000, NZ ☎ 1649/3083355, SA ☎ 1-272/2168-32838, UK ☎ 0870/876 5000, US & Canada ☎ 1-800/ IRISH-AIR; ⓦ www.aerlingus.com.
Air Canada US & Canada ☎ 1-888/247-2262, UK ☎ 0871/220 1111, Republic of Ireland ☎ 01/679 3958, Australia ☎ 1300/655 767, NZ ☎ 0508/747 767; ⓦ www.aircanada.com.
Alitalia US ☎ 1-800/223-5730, Canada ☎ 1800/361-8336, UK & Ireland ☎ 0871/424 1424, NZ ☎ 09/308 3357, SA ☎ 11/721 4500; ⓦ www .alitalia.com.

American Airlines US ☎ 1-800/433-7300, UK ☎ 020/7365 0777, Republic of Ireland ☎ 01/602 0550, Australia ☎ 1800/673 486, NZ ☎ 0800/445 442; ⓦ www.aa.com.
British Airways US & Canada ☎ 1-800/AIRWAYS, UK ☎ 0844/493 0787, Republic of Ireland ☎ 1890/626 747, Australia ☎ 1300/767 177, NZ ☎ 09/966 9777, SA ☎ 114/418 600; ⓦ www .ba.com.
Delta US & Canada ☎ 1-800/221-1212, UK ☎ 0845/600 0950, Republic of Ireland ☎ 1850/882 031 or 01/407 3165, Australia ☎ 1300/302 849, NZ ☎ 09/9772232; ⓦ www.delta.com.
easyJet UK ☎ 0905/821 0905, ⓦ www.easyjet.com.
Jet2 UK ☎ 0871/226 1737, Republic of Ireland ☎ 0818/200 017; ⓦ www.jet2.com.
Meridiana UK ☎ 0845/355 5588, ⓦ www .meridiana.it.
Ryanair UK ☎ 0871/246 0000, Republic of Ireland ☎ 0818/303 030; ⓦ www.ryanair.com.
Thomsonfly UK ☎ 0871/231 4869, ⓦ www .thomsonfly.com

Agents and operators

Abercrombie & Kent US ⓦ www .abercrombiekent.com. Deluxe village-to-village hiking and biking tours, as well as rail journeys.
ATG-Oxford ⓦ www.atg-oxford.co.uk. Excellent and long-established specialist in group or flexible

self-guided walking and cycling holidays, with luggage transported between hotels.

CIT Australia www.cittravel.com.au. Italian specialists, with packages to Florence and elsewhere.

Citalia UK www.citalia.com. Long-established company offering city-break packages in three- and four-star hotels.

Flight Centre Australia www.flightcentre .com.au, www.flightcentre.co.nz. Specializes in discount airfares and holiday packages.

Italiatours UK www.italiatours.co.uk, US www.italiatours.com. Package deals, city breaks and specialist Italian-cuisine tours. Also offers tailor-made itineraries and can book local events and tours.

Kirker Holidays UK www.kirkerholidays.com. Independent operator renowned for excellent city- and short-break deals to Tuscany.

Martin Randall UK www.martinrandall.com. One of the best operators in the sector: imaginative art, music and cultural tours ranging from three to twelve nights, including Piero della Francesca,

Florence & Siena and Florence Revisited (lesser-known sights and private palaces).

North South Travel UK www.northsouthtravel .co.uk. Friendly, competitive travel agency, offering discounted fares worldwide. Profits are used to support projects in the developing world, especially the promotion of sustainable tourism.

STA Travel UK www.statravel.co.uk, US www.statravel.com, Australia www.statravel .com.au, NZ www.statravel.co.nz. Worldwide specialists in low-cost flights and tours for students and under-26s, though other customers welcome. Also offers student IDs, travel insurance, car rental, rail passes and more.

Sunvil Holidays UK www.sunvil.co.uk. City breaks and hotel and villa packages, but especially strong on tailor-made fly-drive packages in three- to five-star hotels.

Trailfinders Australia www.trailfinders.com.au. One of the best informed and most efficient agents for independent travellers.

Getting around

Use of a car is a major advantage if you want to travel extensively around Tuscany and Umbria. You can still get to all the major places by public transport, but away from main routes services can be slow and sporadic. In general, trains are more convenient for longer journeys, buses for local routes. Throughout the guide, the "Travel details" section, at the end of each chapter, lists local bus and train information.

By car

Travelling **by car** in Italy is relatively painless. The roads are generally good, the motorway (autostrada) network comprehensive and Italian drivers rather less erratic than their reputation suggests. The major motorways are **toll-roads**, on which you take a ticket as you join and pay as you exit. **Speed limits** are 50kph in built-up areas, 90kph on minor roads outside built-up areas, 110kph on main roads (dual carriageways), and 130kph on nearly all motorways (a few stretches have a 150kph limit). Note that in wet weather, an 80kph limit applies on minor roads, 90kph on main roads and 110kph on motorways. If you **break down**, dial ☏116

at the nearest phone and tell the operator (who will sometimes speak English) where you are, the type of car and your number plate; the Automobile Club d'Italia (ACI) will send someone out to fix your car – at a price, so you might consider getting cover with a motoring organization in your home country before you leave.

Car rental is pricey, with a Fiat Punto (a standard "subcompact" model) costing more than €300 per week with unlimited mileage. There are plenty of companies at Pisa airport and in the major cities, but it works out cheapest to book before leaving. Most firms will only rent to drivers over 21 who have held a licence for at least a year.

Bringing **your own vehicle**, you need a valid full driving licence (with paper counterpart if you have a photocard licence) and an international driving permit if you are a non-EU licence-holder. It's compulsory to carry your car documents and passport while you're driving: you may be required to present them if stopped by the police – not an uncommon occurrence.

By train

The **train** service offered by Italian State Railways (Trenitalia, but still often referred to as Ferrovie dello Stato, or FS; ⓦwww .trenitalia.com) between major towns and cities is relatively inexpensive, reasonably comprehensive and – despite its reputation – fairly efficient. For extensive train travel in Tuscany and Umbria, however, bear in mind that although cities such as Florence and Pisa have centrally located stations, many towns do not; usually, stations are a good bus ride away from town centres, even at important, heavily visited places such as Siena and Montepulciano. To add insult to injury, you'll often find the vagaries of timetables and routings forcing you to change trains in otherwise dull little towns such as Teróntola or Orte. In addition, some places (Gubbio, the Chianti district, and whole swathes of southern Tuscany and eastern Umbria) are inaccessible by train.

There are various categories of train, the quickest of which are the **Eurocity** services (EC), which connect major cities across Europe, perhaps stopping at only two or three places in each country. **Eurostar Italia** (ES) runs between major cities and is faster and more efficient than **Intercity** (IC) trains and Intercity Plus trains (which claim better service and improved carriage interiors). You need to reserve for all these services, and pay a supplement of about thirty percent of the ordinary fare. There are no supplements

for the **Espresso** (EX), medium-fast trains that stop at major towns and cities, **Interregionali** (IR), similar to the Espresso, but usually with more stops, or **Regionali** (Reg), slow trains that generally stop at every station.

At train stations, separate **timetables** are used for departures (*partenze* – usually yellow) and arrivals (*arrivi* – usually white); be careful not to confuse the two. Pay attention to the timetable **notes**, which may specify the dates between which some services run ("*si effetua dal ... al ...*"), or whether a service is seasonal (*periodico*). The term *giornaliero* means the service runs daily, feriali from Monday to Saturday, *festivi* on Sundays and holidays only. Florence's main station has a large information centre.

In addition to the routes operated by FS, there are a number of privately run lines, often using separate stations, though charging similar fares; where a private line uses an FS station (such as at Arezzo or Terni), there may often be a separate ticket counter.

Tickets and fares

Fares are calculated by the kilometre: a return fare (*andata e ritorno*) is exactly twice that of a single (*andata*). A ticket (*biglietto*) can be bought from a station ticket office (*biglietteria*), online at ⓦwww.trenitalia.com, from ticket machines at the station, some travel agents and sometimes from station news kiosks or bars (for short trips). All tickets must be **validated** just before travel (see box below): once validated, tickets for journeys up to 200km are valid for six hours, over 200km for 24 hours. Children aged 4–12 pay half price; under-4s travel free.

Train services in Tuscany and Umbria

Florence is the centre of the Tuscan rail network. Two lines run westwards from the

Ticket machines

All stations have small yellow machines at the end of the platforms or in ticket halls in which you must **stamp your ticket** before boarding the train; however, don't stamp the return portion of your ticket until you embark on the return journey. If you don't validate your ticket, you become liable for an on-the-spot fine.

city, one of them passing through **Prato**, **Pistoia**, **Montecatini** and **Lucca** on its way to the coast at **Viareggio**, the other going through **Empoli** and **Pisa** before reaching the sea at **Livorno**. From Lucca, a picturesque line runs through the Garfagnana to **Aulla**, providing access to the Lunigiana region and connections to La Spezia and Milan. To the east, a line rises through the **Mugello** district and then loops out of Tuscany towards Faenza, roughly parallel to the route through the mountains to Bologna.

South of Florence, mainline trains follow the River Arno to **Arezzo**, then south past **Cortona** to **Chiusi**, **Orvieto** and Rome. From Arezzo, a private line branches up into the Casentino region. Just beyond Cortona, **Terontola** marks the junction for the branch line east to **Perugia**, the fulcrum of Umbria's network; several trains a day run directly from Florence to Perugia and on to **Foligno** and **Spoleto**. Trains also run directly from Florence to **Siena** – sometimes with a change at Empoli – although the direct bus journey is quicker and easier. From Siena, train routes continue southeast to Chiusi, and southwest to **Grosseto**.

Mainline trains from Rome to Genoa run along – or just inland from – the Tuscan coast, on a route linking **Orbetello**, Grosseto, Livorno, Pisa, Viareggio and the resorts of the Versilia coast, principally Massa and **Carrara**. At **Cecina**, near Livorno, there's a spur inland to within a few kilometres of **Volterra**, where the line abruptly ends.

All Umbria's major towns, with the exception of Gubbio, are easily accessible by train. In the west, the **Rome–Florence** route is the main artery, with branch-line connections throughout the region. Most of the high-speed services between the two cities stop at no Umbrian stations other than **Orvieto**; you'll probably have to change onto a slower train in order to reach the junction towns of Orte (for Narni and Spoleto), Chiusi (for Siena) or Teróntola (for Perugia and Assisi).

From **Orte** just over the Lazio border in the south, trains run through the heart of Umbria via **Narni**, **Terni** (terminus of the FCU line; see below), **Spoleto**, **Foligno** and **Gualdo Tadino** on their way to Ancona

on the coast. From Teróntola on the Rome–Florence line, trains head east along the northern shore of Lago Trasimeno to **Perugia**, and on to **Assisi** and **Spello**, meeting the Rome–Ancona route at Foligno. Perugia lies midway along the **Ferrovia Centrale Umbra** (FCU), a private railway that fills some crucial gaps left by the state network, linking the city with **Terni** and **Todi** in the south, and **Città di Castello** and **Sansepolcro** in the north. Services are frequent, though buses often replace trains over certain sections. A couple of trains daily also run from both Rome and Florence direct to Perugia.

By bus

If you're limited to public transport and want to get to know Tuscany and Umbria thoroughly, sooner or later you'll have to use regional **buses** (autobus or pullman). There are dozens of different bus companies, all of which are under joint public and private ownership. Some of the companies operate solely on local routes, others run nationwide between major cities; almost everywhere has some kind of bus service, but schedules can be sketchy, and are drastically reduced – sometimes nonexistent – on Sundays. Bear in mind also that in rural areas schedules are often designed with the working and/or school day in mind, meaning a frighteningly early start if you want to catch the sole bus out of town and perhaps no buses at all during school holidays.

In larger towns, the **bus terminal** (autostazione), where you can buy tickets and pick up timetables, is usually very close to the train station; in smaller towns and villages, most buses pull in at the central piazza, which may have a newsstand selling bus tickets (if not, you can buy tickets on the bus).

City buses are always cheap, usually in the region of €1 for a ticket, valid either for a single journey or for any number of journeys within a set period (typically 40–60min). You must always buy a ticket before getting on the bus, from local *tabacchi* or the kiosks at bus terminals and stops; and you must validate them in the machine inside the bus. In most cities there are regular ticket checks, with hefty spot-fines for offenders.

By bike or motorbike

Cycling is seen in Italy as a sport rather than a way of getting around: on a Sunday you'll see plenty of people out for a spin on their Campagnolo-equipped machines, but you'll not come across many luggage-laden tourers. Only in major towns will you find a shop stocking spares for non-racing bikes, so make sure you take a supply of inner tubes, spokes and any other bits you think might be handy. It's possible to rent bikes in major towns, but **mopeds** and **scooters** are easier to find: expect to pay around €60–70 a day. Crash helmets are compulsory.

Accommodation

Accommodation is a major cost in Tuscany and Umbria, where prices of hotels tend to rise annually, as there's huge demand. There are few really inexpensive hotels, at least in the major Tuscan centres, and only a scattering of hostels.

Accommodation in Italy is strictly regulated. All hotels are **star-rated** from one to five; prices are officially registered for each room and must be posted at the hotel reception and in individual rooms (usually on the back of the door). A star rating can give a good idea of the facilities to expect – a two-star hotel, for example, will always have rooms with a private bathroom: in a one-star, you may have to share a bathroom down the corridor. Ask to see a variety of rooms if the first you're shown is too expensive or not up to scratch; there may be cheaper rooms available. Most tourist offices carry full **lists of hotels** and other accommodation such as B&B and agriturismo options. They may be able to help you find a room at short notice, but few have dedicated accommodation services.

In high season it is essential to **book rooms in advance**; for Florence and Siena, this is advisable at any time of year. The same applies during religious holidays (notably Easter) in towns such as Assisi, and anywhere where a festival is taking place. Always establish the full price of your room – including breakfast and other extras (tax and service charges are usually included) – before you accept it. It's often a good idea to call or email a day or so before arrival to **confirm your booking**. If you're going to be arriving late in the evening, it's even worth another call that morning to reconfirm.

Hotels

Hotels in Italy are known by a variety of names. Most are simply tagged **hotel** or **albergo**. Others may be called a **locanda**, a

Accommodation price codes

Throughout this guide, all accommodation prices have been graded with the codes below, indicating the least you can expect to pay for a **double room in high season**.

❶ €60 and under
❷ €61–80
❸ €81–100
❹ €101–130
❺ €131–160
❻ €161–200
❼ €201–250
❽ €251–300
❾ €301 and over

name traditionally associated with the cheapest sort of inn, but now sometimes rather self-consciously applied to smart new hotels. A **pensione** was also traditionally a cheap place to stay, though the name now lacks any official status: anywhere still describing itself as a *pensione* is probably a one-star hotel.

The star system gives you an idea of what you can expect from a hotel, though it's essential to realize the system is based on an often eccentric set of criteria relating to facilities (say, a restaurant or an in-room TV) rather than notions of comfort, character or location. A three-star, for example, must have a phone in every room: if it hasn't, it remains a two-star, no matter how magnificent the rest of the hotel.

One-star hotels in tourist towns in high season tend to start at about €50 for a double room without private bath; **two-star** hotels cost upwards of €80 for an en-suite double; **three-star** places are rarely cheaper than €100. **Four-star** hotels are a marked step up: everything has more polish, and in rural four-stars you'll probably get a swimming pool; €150–200 is the typical range here (though some establishments are much pricier), while for a deluxe **five-star** (rare outside the major centres) you should expect to pay more than €250 a night. Prices in Florence and Siena, and to a lesser extent Perugia, Assisi and Orvieto, are much higher than anywhere else in the region: you can pay around €100 for an en-suite one-star room in peak season, while €500 per night is far from rare in the five-stars.

In the more popular cities, especially Florence, it's not unusual for hotels to impose a **minimum stay** of three nights in summer. Note also that single rooms nearly always cost far more than half the price of a double, although kindlier hoteliers – if they have no singles available – may offer you a double room at the single rate.

Self-catering

High hotel prices in much of Tuscany and Umbria make **self-catering** an attractive proposition. Many package companies offer self-catering as an alternative to hotel accommodation, but better selections of apartments are provided by specialist agents such as those listed below.

Travelling with a group of people, or even just in a pair, it's worth considering renting a **villa** or **farmhouse** for a week or two. These are not too expensive if you can split costs, are of a consistently high standard, and often enjoy marvellous locations.

Property rental companies

Bridgewater's Ⓦ www.bridgewater-travel .co.uk. A company with over 25 years' experience of apartments in Florence and Siena, and of *agriturismo* and villas across Tuscany and Umbria.
Carefree Italy Ⓦ www.carefree-italy.com. Farmhouses and villas, often in shared complexes; also has a range of small hotels and city apartments.
Cottages to Castles Ⓦ www.cottagestocastles .com. Numerous Tuscan and Umbrian cottages, villas and apartments.
Cuendet Ⓦ www.italianlife.co.uk. Database of hundreds of properties across both regions.

Agriturismo

An increasingly popular accommodation option is **agriturismo**, a scheme whereby farmers rent out converted barns and farm buildings. Usually these comprise a self-contained flat or building, though a few places just rent rooms on a bed-and-breakfast basis. This market has boomed in recent years, and while some rooms are still annexed to working farms or vineyards, many are smart, self-contained rural vacation properties. Attractions may include home-grown food, swimming pools and a range of activities, from walking and riding to archery and mountain biking. Many *agriturismi* have a **minimum-stay requirement** of one week in busy periods.

Tourist offices keep lists of local properties, or you can search one of the growing number of *agriturismo* websites – there are hundreds of properties at Ⓦ www.agriturismo.com, Ⓦ www.agriturismo.net, Ⓦ www.agriitalia.it and Ⓦ www .agriturist.it.

CV Travel Ⓦ www.cvtravel.co.uk. A long-established, high-end company with a reputation for securing the most sumptuous properties in Tuscany and Umbria.

Holiday Rentals Ⓦ www.holiday-rentals.co.uk. This site puts you directly in touch with the owners of scores of Tuscan and Umbrian properties.

IST Italian Breaks Ⓦ www.italianbreaks.com. A good range range of villas and apartments.

Owners' Syndicate Ⓦ www.ownerssyndicate .com. Leading operator, with properties in Tuscany and Umbria.

To Tuscany Ⓦ www.to-tuscany.com. Offers a large number of properties, in all price ranges.

Traditional Tuscany Ⓦ www.traditionaltuscany .co.uk. Offers B&B in Florentine palaces and on working farms and vineyards, plus a selection of villas and converted farms.

Tuscan Holidays Ⓦ www.tuscanholidays.co.uk. A small company with around 130 carefully selected properties in Tuscany, many with pools.

Veronica Tomasso Cotgrove Ⓦ www.vtcitaly .com. Carefully chosen villas and apartments, including some huge properties.

Bed and breakfast

Legal restrictions used to make it very difficult for Italian home-owners to offer **bed and breakfast** accommodation, but in 2000 the law was relaxed, and now there are hundreds of B&Bs in Tuscany and Umbria, with the greatest concentration in Florence and the main tourist towns. Prices at the lower end of the scale are comparable to one-star hotels, but one unexpected consequence of the change in the law has been the emergence of upscale B&Bs in castles, palaces and large private homes. Tourist offices and local websites often carry lists of B&Bs, and Ⓦ www.bed-and-breakfast.it is another useful resource. In addition to registered B&Bs you'll also find "**rooms for rent**" (*affittacamere*) advertised in some towns. These differ from B&Bs in that breakfast is not always offered, and they are not subject to the same regulations as official B&Bs;

nearly all affittacamere are in the one-star price range.

Hostels and student accommodation

Most hostels belong to the **Hostelling International (HI)** network (Ⓦ www.hihostels .com), and strictly speaking you need to be an HI member to stay at them. Many, however, allow you to join on the spot, or simply charge you a small supplement. Whether or not you're an HI member, you'll need to **book ahead** in the summer months. The most efficient way to book at main city hostels is using HI's own online booking system; for more out-of-the-way locations, contact the hostel direct.

Religious organizations

Religious organizations all over Tuscany and Umbria offer cheap accommodation in lodgings annexed to **convents** or **monasteries**, or in pilgrim hostels. Most offer rooms with and without bathroom; only a few have dorm rooms with bunks. Some accept women only, others families only or single travellers of either sex. Most have a curfew, but few, contrary to expectations, pay much heed to your coming and going. Virtually none offers meals.

Camping

There are surprisingly few **campsites** in rural Tuscany and Umbria, but camping is popular along the coast, where the sites are mostly on the upmarket side. Prices in high season tend to start from around €10 per person, plus €15 per pitch, though some of the smaller sites may be a little cheaper. If you're camping extensively, it's worth checking Italy's informative camping website, Ⓦ www .camping.it, for details of sites and booking facilities.

Food and drink

The traditional dishes of Tuscany are Italy's most influential cuisine: the ingredients and culinary techniques of the region have made their mark not just on the menus of the rest of Italy but also abroad. Umbrian cooking may not be accorded quite the same degree of reverence, but its produce is of equally high quality, with its truffles and ham being especially prized. And wine has always been central to the area's economy and way of life, familiar names such as Chianti and Orvieto representing just a portion of the enormous output from Tuscan and Umbrian vineyards.

Breakfast and snacks

Most Italians start their day in a bar, their **breakfast** (*prima colazione*) consisting of a coffee and the ubiquitous *cornetto* or brioche – a jam-, custard- or chocolate-filled croissant. Unfilled croissants can be hard to find; ask for *un cornetto semplice*.

At other times of the day, **sandwiches** (*panini*) can be pretty substantial, a filled roll for two or three euros. Sandwich bars (*paninoteche*) can be found in many larger towns; grocers' shops (*alimentari*) will often make sandwiches to order. Bars may offer *tramezzini*, ready-made sliced white bread with mixed fillings.

There are a number of options for **takeaway food**. It's possible to find slices of pizza (*pizza al taglio* or *pizza rustica*) pretty much everywhere – buy it by weight (an *etto* is 100g). You can get pasta, chips and even hot meals in a **tavola calda**, a sort of snack bar that's at its best in the morning when everything is fresh. The speciality in a **rosticceria** is usually spit-roasted chicken, alongside fast food such as pizza slices, chips and burgers.

All across Italy, **pizza** comes thin and flat, not deep-pan. Most are cooked in the traditional way, in wood-fired ovens (*forno a legna*): they arrive blasted and bubbling on the surface, and with a distinctive charcoal taste. **Pizzerias** range from a stand-up counter selling slices (*al taglio*) to a fully fledged sit-down restaurant.

Other sources of snacks are **markets**, some of which sell take-away food, including *focacce*, oven-baked pastries topped with cheese or tomato or filled with spinach, fried offal or meat; and *arancini* or suppli, deep-fried balls of rice filled with meat (*rosso*) or butter and cheese (*bianco*). **Supermarkets**, too, are an obvious stop for a picnic lunch.

Restaurants

Traditionally, Tuscan and Umbrian **restaurant** meals (lunch is *pranzo*, dinner is *cena*) are long and pretty solid affairs, starting with an antipasto, followed by a risotto or a pasta *primo*, leading on to a fish or meat *secondo*, cheese, and finished with fresh fruit and coffee. Even everyday meals are a miniaturized version of this. Modern minimalism has

---

Ice cream

Italian **ice cream** (*gelato*) is justifiably famous: a cone (*cono*) or "cup" (*coppa*) are indispensable accessories to the evening *passeggiata*. Most bars have a fairly good selection, but for real choice go to a **gelateria**. There's no problem locating the finest in town: it's the one that draws the crowds. There's usually a bewildering array of flavours (*gusti*) to choose from, but often the basics – chocolate, strawberry, vanilla – are best. Unless you plump for the smallest size you'll usually be able to choose a combination of two or three. You may be asked if you want a squirt of cream (*panna*) on top – it's usually free.

made inroads into the more expensive restaurants, but the staple fare at the majority of places is exactly what it might have been a century ago. **Vegetarians** generally manage fine: there are plenty of meat-free pasta, pizza and salad options to choose from. Beware vegetable soups, however, which may be made with meat stock.

Restaurants are most commonly called either **trattorie** or **ristoranti**. Traditionally, a trattoria is a cheaper and more basic purveyor of home-style cooking (*cucina casalinga*), while a ristorante is more upmarket, with aproned waiters and table-cloths. These days, however, there's a fine line between the two, as it's become rather chic for an expensive restaurant to call itself a trattoria. It's in the rural areas that you're most likely to come across an old-style trattoria, the sort of place where there's no written menu (the waiter will simply reel off a list of what's available) and no bottled wine (it comes straight from the vats of the local farm). A ristorante will always have a written menu and a reasonable choice of wines, though even in smart places it's standard to choose the ordinary house wine. In popular tourist towns, notably Florence, you may well find restaurants unwilling to serve anything less than a full meal: no lunchtime restraint of a pasta and salad allowed.

Osterie used to be old-fashioned places specializing in home cooking, though recently the osteria tag more often signifies a youngish ownership and clientele, and adventurous foods. Other types of restaurant include **spaghetterie** and **birrerie**, bar-restaurants that serve basic pasta dishes, or beer and snacks.

The menu and the bill

The cheapest – though not the most rewarding way – to eat in city restaurants is to opt for a set-price **menù turistico**. This will give you a first course (pasta or soup), main course, dessert (usually a piece of fruit), half a litre of water and a quarter litre of wine per person. Beware the increasingly common *prezzo fisso* menu, which excludes cover, service, dessert and drinks.

Working your way through an Italian menu is pretty straightforward. The **antipasto** (literally "before the meal") generally consists

There's a detailed **menu reader** of Italian terms on pp.685–691.

of cold cuts of meat, seafood and cold vegetable dishes. The next course, il primo, consists of soup or a risotto, polenta or pasta dish. This is followed by il secondo – the meat or fish course, usually served alone, except for perhaps a wedge of lemon or tomato. Watch out when ordering fish or Florence's famous *bistecca alla fiorentina*, which will usually be served by weight: 250g is usually plenty for one person, or ask to have a look at the fish before it's cooked. Anything marked S.Q. or hg means you are paying by weight: hg stands for a hectogram (*etto* in Italian) – 100g, or around 4oz. Vegetables (**il contorno**) and salads (**insalata**) are ordered and served separately.

For afters, you nearly always get a choice of fresh fruit (*frutta*) and desserts (**dolci**) often ice cream or homemade flans (*torte*). At the end of the meal, ask for the bill/check (**il conto**). In many *trattorie* this amounts to no more than an illegible scrap of paper, and if you want to be sure you're not being ripped off, ask for a receipt (*ricevuta*), something all bars and restaurants are legally bound to provide anyway. Almost everywhere you'll pay a **cover charge** (*pane e coperto* or just *coperto*), on top of your food, of €1–1.50 per head. As well as the *coperto*, **service** (*servizio*) will often be added, generally about ten percent; if it isn't, you should perhaps **tip** about the same amount.

Tuscan cuisine

The most important ingredient of Tuscan cooking is **olive oil**, which comes into almost every dish – as a dressing for salads, a medium for frying, or simply drizzled over vegetables and into soups and stews just before serving. Olive-picking begins around November, before the olives are fully ripe; the oil produced from the first pressing is termed *extra vergine*, the purest and most alkaline, with less than one-percent acidity. The quality of the oil declines with subsequent pressings.

The biggest influences on Tuscan cooking are the simple rustic dishes of **Florence**, the most famous of which is *bistecca alla fioren-tina*, a thick T-bone steak grilled over charcoal, usually served rare. The meat for true Florentine *bistecca* comes from the Valdichiana area south of Arezzo, from an animal no more than two and a half years old. You'll find a lot of "hunters' dishes" (*cacciatore*), most commonly *cinghiale* (wild boar) and *pollo* (chicken). The Florentines are also fond of the unpretentious *arista*, roast pork loin stuffed with rosemary and garlic, and of *pollo alla diavola*, a flattened chicken marinated with olive oil and lemon juice or white wine, then dressed with herbs before grilling.

Each major Tuscan town has its culinary specialities, a vestige of the days when the region was divided into city states. **Pisa's** treats include black cabbage soup, new-born eels (*cieche*) fried with garlic and sage, and *torta coi bischeri*, a cake filled with rice, candied fruit, chocolate, raisins and pine nuts, and flavoured with nutmeg and liqueur. Many of the specialities of **Siena** date back to the medieval period, including *salsicce secche* (dried sausages) and *panforte di Siena*, a celebrated spicy cake of nuts and candied fruit. **Arezzo** has *acquacotta*, a soup of fried onion, tomato and bread, mixed with egg and cheese.

Everywhere in the province, **soups** are central to the cuisine, the most famous being *ribollita*, a thick vegetable concoction traditionally including leftover beans (hence "reboiled"). *Pappa al pomodoro* is a popular broth with bread, tomatoes and basil cooked to a sustaining stodge. White cannellini **beans** are the favourite vegetables, boiled with rosemary and doused with olive oil, or cooked with tomatoes (*all'uccelletto*). Also typically Tuscan is **spinach**, which is served as a side vegetable, in combination with omelettes, poached eggs or fish, mixed with ricotta to make gnocchi, or as a filling for *crespoline* (pancakes). Spinach and green beans are often eaten cold, usually with a squeeze of lemon.

Wild chestnuts are another staple: there's a long tradition of specialities based on dried chestnuts and chestnut flour, such as the delicious *castagnaccio* (chestnut cake), made with pine nuts, raisins and rosemary. Sheep's milk pecorino is the most widespread Tuscan **cheese**, but the most famous is the oval marzolino from the Chianti region, which is often grated over meat dishes.

Dessert menus will often include *cantuccini*, hard biscuits which are dipped in a glass of Vinsanto, or *zuccotto*, a brandy-soaked sponge cake filled with cream mixed with chocolate powder, almonds and hazelnuts – like tiramisù elsewhere in Italy.

Umbrian cuisine

Umbria's cooking also relies heavily on rustic staples – pastas and roast meats – and tends to be simple. Umbria is, however, the only region in Italy apart from Piemonte to offer **truffles** in any abundance (see box, p.589). Traditionally the white truffle is the most highly prized on account of its aroma, but locals swear by the Umbrian grey-white (*bianchetto*) variety and the black truffle that's most common to the area around Spoleto and Norcia. You're most likely to come across them with tagliolini (a super-fine thread of pasta that enables you to taste the truffle), as a modest sprinkling over a dish of tagliatelle or meat, or on crostini – at a price that prohibits overindulgence.

Meat, and in particular **pork**, is the staple of the Umbrian main course, usually grilled or roasted. The region's small, free-range black pigs are famous, and have lately been joined by wild boar (*cinghiale*) – apparently emigrés from Tuscany, now reproducing at a prodigious rate. **Norcia** is the heart of pig country, with a superb selection of all things porcine, though other towns boast their own specialities. **Città di Castello** produces a *salame* made with spices and fennel seed; **Cascia** and **Preci** are known for their mortadella; **Foligno** has a distinctive dry *salame*; and **Gualdo Tadino** does a special sausage, the *soppressata*. Also look out for the extraordinary fruit-and-nut-flavoured *salame mezzafegato*. Endemic to the region is *porchetta*, roast suckling pig stuffed with herbs and spices and eaten sliced in crusty white rolls. It's an Umbrian concoction that has spread through most of central Italy, available as a snack from markets and roadside stalls. Other specialities are the lentils of **Castelluccio**, the beans of **Trasimeno**, the peas from **Bettona**, and the celery and cardoons from around **Trevi**. Umbrian **olive oil**, though not as hyped as the Tuscan oils, has a high reputation, especially that from around Trevi and Spoleto.

Game may crop up on some menus, most often as pigeon, pheasant or guinea fowl. It's not unknown to be offered *tordo* (thrush), usually as a paté; other songbirds are hunted, often illegally, but they're unlikely to find their way into a restaurant. Despite Umbria's lack of a coast, some restaurants make the effort to bring in fresh **fish**, and there's a reasonable selection available close to lakes and mountain rivers. **Cheeses** follow the usual variations, with the only genuine one-offs to be found in the mountains around Norcia and Gubbio.

Perugino **chocolate** is outstanding, but it's available throughout Italy. One genuine novelty are the white **figs** of Amelia, mixed in a tooth-rotting combination of almonds and chocolate.

Drinking

Drinking is essentially an accompaniment to food: there's little emphasis on drinking for its own sake. Locals sitting around in bars or cafés – whatever their age – will spend hours chatting over one drink. And even in bars, most people you see imbibing one of the delicious Italian grappas or brandies will take just one, then be on their way. The snag is that, since Italians drink so little, prices can be high.

Bars are often very functional, brightly lit places, with a chrome counter, a Gaggia coffee machine and a picture of the local football team on the wall. There are no set licensing hours and children are always allowed in. People come to bars for ordinary drinking – a coffee in the morning, a quick beer, or a cup of tea – but don't generally idle away the day or evening in them. In some more rural places it's difficult to find a bar open much after 9pm. It's nearly always cheapest to drink **standing** at the counter (there's often nowhere to sit anyway), in which case you often pay first at the cash desk (*cassa*), present your receipt (*scontrino*) to the barperson and give your order; sometimes you simply order your drink and pay as you leave. There's always a list of prices (*listino prezzi*) behind the bar. If there's waiter service, you can **sit** where you like, though bear in mind that to do this means your drink will cost perhaps twice as much, especially if you sit outside on the terrace. These different prices for the same drinks are shown on the price list as bar, tavola and terrazza.

Coffee, tea and soft drinks

One of the most distinctive smells in an Italian street is that of fresh **coffee**, usually wafting out of a bar. The basic choice is either small and black (espresso, or just *caffè*), or white and frothy (cappuccino). If you want a longer espresso ask for a *caffè lungo* or americano; a double espresso is *una doppia*, while a short, extra-strong espresso is a *ristretto*. A coffee topped with un-frothed milk is a *caffè latte*; with a drop of milk it's *caffè macchiato*; with a shot of alcohol it's *caffè corretto*. Although most places let you help yourself to sugar, a few add it routinely; if you don't want it, you can make sure by asking for *caffè senza zucchero*. Many places also now sell decaffeinated coffee (ask for the brand-name Hag, even when it isn't). In summer you might want to have your coffee cold (*caffè freddo*); for a real treat, ask for *caffè granita*, cold coffee with crushed ice, usually topped with cream. Hot **tea** (*tè caldo*) comes with lemon (*con limone*) as standard, unless you ask for milk (*con latte*); in summer you can drink it cold (*tè freddo*). **Milk** itself is drunk hot as often as cold, or you can get it with a dash of coffee (*latte macchiato*) and sometimes as a milkshake (*frappé*).

There are numerous **soft drinks** (*analcoliche*). A **spremuta** is a fruit juice, usually orange (… *d'arancia*), lemon (… *di limone*) or grapefruit (… *di pompelmo*), fresh-squeezed at the bar, with optional added sugar. A *succo di frutta* is a bottled fruit juice, widely drunk at breakfast. Home-grown Italian cola, Chinotto, is less sweet than Coke – good with a slice of lemon. An excellent thirst-quencher is Lemon Soda (the brand name), a widely available bitter lemon drink.

Tap water (*acqua normale* or *acqua dal rubinetto*) is quite drinkable, and free in bars. **Mineral water** (*acqua minerale*) is a more common choice, either still (*senza gas*, *liscia*, *non gassata* or *naturale*) or sparkling (*con gas*, *gassata* or *frizzante*).

A wine checklist

Tuscan wines

Bianco di Pitigliano Delicate dry white from southern Tuscany.

Bianco Vergine della Valdichiana Soft dry white from south of Arezzo.

Brunello di Montalcino Full-bodied red from south of Siena; one of Italy's finest wines. See also p.401.

Carmignano A dry red produced west of Florence; this area also produces **Vin Ruspo**, a fresh rosé.

Chianti Produced in seven distinct central Tuscan districts. Ranges from the roughest table wine to some of Italy's most elegant reds. See also p.192.

Colline Lucchesi A soft and lively DOC red from the hills east of Lucca.

Galestro A light, dry summer white.

Grattamacco Produced southeast of Livorno, this non-DOC wine comes as a fruity white and a full, dry red.

Montecarlo A full and dry white – one of Tuscany's finest – from east of Lucca.

Montecucco New DOC red from Cinigiano and Civitella Paganico near Grosseto.

Monteregio di Massa Maríttima Another newish DOC red from the Alta Maremma region.

Morellino di Scansano A fairly dry, robust, up-and-coming DOC red, made southeast of Grosseto.

Pomino New DOC from near Rúfina; an excellent red, plus white and Vinsanto.

Rosso di Montalcino A full-bodied DOC, aged less than the great Brunello di Montalcino. See also p.401.

Rosso di Montepulciano Excellent-value red table wine.

Sammarco Big Cabernet wine from the Chianti region.

Sassicaia Full ruby wine from near Livorno made from Cabernet Sauvignon grapes; best left a few years.

Solaia Another Cabernet Sauvignon from the Antinori estate.

Spumante Sparkling wines are a relatively new departure in Tuscany, but vineyards all over the province are now using the *champenoise* or *charmat* method to produce quality vintages.

Beer and spirits

Beer (*birra*) is nearly always a lager-type brew that comes in bottles or on tap (*alla spina*) – standard measures are a third of a litre (*piccola*) and two-thirds of a litre (*media*). Commonest and cheapest are the Italian brands Peroni, Moretti and Dreher, all of which are very drinkable; to order these, either state the brand name or ask for *birra nazionale* – otherwise you may be given a more expensive imported beer. You may also come across darker beers (*birra scura* or *birra rossa*), which have a sweeter, maltier taste and resemble stout or bitter.

All the usual **spirits** are on sale and known mostly by their generic names. There are also Italian brands of the main varieties: the best local brandies are Stock and Vecchia Romagna. A generous shot of these costs about €2, much more for imported stuff or in smart city bars. The home-grown Italian firewater is **grappa**, made from the leftovers of the winemaking process (skins, stalks and the like) and drunk as a *digestivo* after a meal. The best Tuscan varieties are from Montalcino (Brunello) and Montepulciano.

You'll also find **fortified wines** like Martini, Cinzano and Campari. For the real thing, order *un Campari bitter*; ask for a "Campari-soda" and you'll get a ready-mixed version from a little bottle. Lemon Soda and Campari bitter makes a delicious and dangerously drinkable combination. The luridly orange, non-alcoholic Crodino, is also a popular *aperitivo*. You might also try Cynar, an

Tavernelle California-style red from western Chianti.

Tignanello Traditional Sangiovese Chianti, again from Antinori.

Vernaccia di San Gimignano Subtle dry white DOC from the hills of San Gimignano.

Vino Nobile di Montepulciano A full, classy red DOCG from around Montepulciano, south of Siena.

Vin santo Aromatic wine, made from semi-dried grapes and sealed in casks for at least three years. Produced all over Tuscany (and Umbria too), it ranges from dry to sweet, and is often served at dessert.

Umbrian wines

Cabernet Sauvignon di Miralduolo Purplish dry red from Torgiano.

Cervaro della Sala A new white wine, aged in French oak.

Chardonnay di Miralduolo Flowery, dry white from Torgiano, also aged in wood.

Colli Altotiberini A new Tiber valley DOC, best drunk young.

Colli Amerini Another new DOC, best known for its reds.

Colli Perugini Umbria's newest DOC – red, white and rosé.

Colli del Trasimeno Huge area producing reds and whites of ever-rising standard.

Decugnano dei Barbi Rosso Fruity red from near Lago di Corbara.

Montefalco A soft, dry red – Montefalco Rosso – and the more robust Sagrantino di Montefalco, plus Sagrantino Passito, a superb red dessert wine. See also p.556.

Orvieto Umbria's most famous DOC wine, a dry, light white, or a lightly sweet dessert wine (*abboccato*).

San Giorgio A bold, full-bodied red, made in Torgiano.

Solleone Dry, sherry-like aperitif.

Torgiano DOC region southeast of Perugia, producing both red and white wines; look out for the dry, fruity white Torre di Giano, the wood-aged white Torre di Giano Riserva, and the opulent Rubesco Riserva, one of Italy's finest reds.

---

artichoke-based sherry-type liquid often drunk as an aperitif.

There's a daunting selection of **liqueurs**. **Amaro** is a bitter after-dinner drink, and probably the most popular way among Italians to round off a meal. The top brands, in rising order of bitterness, are Montenegro, Ramazotti, Averna and Fernet-Branca. Strega is another drink you'll see in every bar – the yellow stuff in elongated bottles: it's as sweet as it looks but not unpleasant. Also popular, though considered slightly naff in Italy, is *limoncello*, a bitter-sweet lemon spirit.

Wine

Pursuit of **wine** is as good a reason as any for a visit to **Tuscany**. The province

constitutes the heartland of Italian wine production, with sales of Chianti accounting for much of the country's wine exports, and the towns of Montalcino and Montepulciano producing two of the very finest Italian vintages (Brunello and Vino Nobile respectively). Tuscan wines are predominantly based on the local Sangiovese grape, the foundation of heavyweights such as Chianti, Brunello di Montalcino and Vino Nobile di Montepulciano. Traditionally, the best Tuscan wines are reds, but new techniques have boosted the quality of many whites.

Umbria, by contrast, is low-key, except for the white Orvieto – a long-established wine developed by the Etruscans – but is increasingly producing top-quality though as yet little-known wines. The region has only a handful of DOC regions, many producing cheap, serviceable wine that rarely finds its way outside the region. Most are made from similar grapes and in similar ways to the workaday reds of Tuscany; however, innovation is producing ever more interesting high-quality vintages, and there's a trove of little-known wines that repay searching out.

Wine is **very inexpensive**: in some bars you can get a glass of good local produce for as little as €0.50, and table wine in restaurants – often decanted from the barrel – rarely costs more than €6 per litre. Expect to pay from around €10 for a major-name bottle in a restaurant, less than half that from a shop or supermarket.

The media

Local and national newspapers form an essential accompaniment to local bar culture: in small towns, folk are drawn to a bar for a read, not a drink. Television also plays a central role in Italian life: many households have the TV switched on from morning to night, regardless of the poor quality of Italy's numerous local and national channels.

Newspapers

Tuscany's major **newspaper** is the Florence-based *La Nazione*. This is technically a national paper but its sales are concentrated in the central provinces of Italy. It produces local editions, with supplements, including informative entertainments listings, for virtually every major Tuscan town. In Umbria, the leading local paper is the *Corriere dell'Umbria*, with detailed regional and small-town coverage. Of the other nationals, the centre-left *La Repubblica* and right-slanted *Corriere della Sera* are the two most widely read. *L'Unità*, which has evolved from the newspaper of the former Italian communist party, has experienced hard times, even in the party's Tuscan and Umbrian strongholds, but now seems to have regained some lost ground. The most avidly read papers of all are the pink *Gazzetta dello Sport* and *Corriere dello Sport*; essential reading for the serious Italian sports fan, they devote as much attention to players' ankle problems as most papers would give to the resignation of a government. News **magazines** are also widely read in Italy, from *L'Espresso* and *Panorama* to the lighter offerings of *Gente* and *Oggi*. **English and US newspapers** can

be found for two or three times the normal price in all the larger towns and resorts, usually on the day of issue in bigger cities like Florence and Siena.

TV and radio

Italy's three main national **TV** channels are RAI 1, 2 and 3. Silvio Berlusconi's Mediaset runs three additional nationwide channels: Canale 5, Rete 4 and Italia 1. Although all six are blatantly pro-Berlusconi, the degree of sycophancy displayed on the TG4 news has reached such ludicrous heights (newscaster Emilio Fede is variously overcome by tears of joy or despair, depending on the fortunes of Berlusconi) that many Italians now tune in solely for a giggle. Although the stories of Italian TV's stripping housewives are overplayed, the output is generally unchallenging (and sexist) across the board, with the accent on quiz shows, soaps and plenty of American imports. The RAI channels carry less advertising and try to mix the dross with above-average documentaries and news coverage. Numerous other channels concentrate on sport.

The situation in **radio** is even more anarchic, with FM so crowded that you continually pick up new stations whether you want to or not. There are some good small-scale stations if you search hard enough, but on the whole the RAI stations are the most professional. The **BBC World Service** (Ⓦ www.bbc.co.uk) is in English on 648kHz medium wave most of the day; they also broadcast continuously online, as do Voice of America (Ⓦ www.voa.gov) and Radio Canada (Ⓦ www.rcinet.ca).

Festivals

Both Tuscany and Umbria have a plethora of local festivals, with saints' days being the most common excuse for some kind of binge. All cities, small towns and villages have their home-produced saint, whose mortal remains or image are generally paraded through the streets amid much noise and spectacle. There are plenty of other occasions for a festa – either to commemorate a local miracle or historic event, or to show off the local products or artistic talent.

Many festivals happen at Easter, in May or September, or around Ferragosto (Aug 15); dates are detailed below. For **national holidays**, see p.51; for further information on the major festivals, see individual chapters.

Tickets for some cultural festivals – such as the Maggio Musicale in Florence or Spoleto's Festival dei Due Mondi – can be difficult to obtain. If you have no luck with a festival's box office, it may be worth trying **Liaisons Abroad** (Ⓦ www.liaisonsabroad .com), an agency for tickets to major Italian opera and musical events, timed museum tickets, Siena's Palio, Serie A football matches, and more.

Festival calendar

January

Foligno (Jan 24) Festa di San Feliciano; traditional fair.
Trevi (Jan 27) Festa di Sant'Emiliano; torchlit procession.

February

Norcia (3–4 days in Feb) Truffle and sausage festival.
Spello (Feb 5) Olive and bruschetta festival.
Viareggio and **San Gimignano (early/mid-Feb)** Carnevale.
Terni (Feb 14) St Valentine's Day fair.

March

Norcia (March 20–24) Crossbow competition.
Assisi Holy Week celebrations.
Grassina (near Florence), **Gubbio** and **Bevagna** Good Friday processions.
Florence (Easter Sun) Scioppio del Carro; fireworks in Piazza del Duomo.
San Miniato (first Sun after Easter) National kite-flying championships.

April

Montecatini Terme (April 16) Fettunta festival; oil and garlic speciality.
Lucca (April–June) Sacred music festival.
Florence (April–June) Maggio Musicale festival.

May

Terni (May 1) Canta Maggio; parade of illuminated floats.
Assisi (early May) Calendimaggio; spring festival.
Gubbio (May 15) Corsa dei Ceri; candle race.
Foligno (May 15) Giostro della Quintana; medieval joust.
Massa Maríttima (first Sun after May 19) Balestro del Girifalco; crossbow competition.
Cascia (May 21 & 22) Celebrazioni Ritiane; procession in honour of St Rita.
Gubbio (last Sun) Crossbow matches against team from Sansepolcro.
Montespertoli (last Sun) Wine festival.

June

Orvieto and **Spello (early June)** Corpus Domini procession.
Pisa (June 16 & 17) Luminaria torchlit celebration; precedes Regatta di San Ranieri boat race.
Spoleto (June & July) Festival dei Due Mondi; internationally renowned month-long event; classical concerts, film, ballet, street theatre and performance art, staged in the ancient walled town.
Pisa (third Sun) Gioco del Ponte.
Narni (June 20–30) Experimental theatre season.
Florence (week beginning June 24) Festa di San Giovanni; fireworks and the Calcio Storico football game.
Fiesole (mid-June to Aug) Estate Fiesolana; music, cinema, ballet and theatre.
San Gimignano (late June to Oct) Summer festival of music and film.
Bevagna (last week) Mercato delle Gaite; medieval craft fair.
Campello di Clitunno (end June) Trout festival.
Piediluco (end June) Sagra del Pesce.

July

Siena (July 2) Palio horse races, preceded by trial races on June 29 & 30 and July 1.
Torre del Lago (July & Aug) Puccini festival.
Perugia (July & Aug) Umbria Jazz; major jazz event.
Fivizzano (second Sun) Archery contest.
Siena (mid-July) Settimana Musicale.
Gubbio (mid-July to mid-Aug) Spettacoli Classici; classical plays staged in the town's Roman amphitheatre.
Barga (second half July) Opera and theatre festival.
Lucca (third Sun) Festa di San Paolino; torchlit parade and crossbow contest.
Pistoia (July 25) Giostro dell'Orso; jousting.
Le Ghiaie (last week July) Wine festival on Elba.

August

Massa Maríttima (second Sun) Second leg of the crossbow competition.
Montepulciano (second Sun) Food and wine festival.
Città della Pieve (mid-Aug) Festa della Fontana; flooding of the town fountain with wine.
Lucca (Aug 14) Luminaria di Santa Croce; torchlit procession.
Montepulciano (Aug 14–16) Il Bruscello; folkloric song festival.
Cortona (Aug 15) Festa della Bistecca; excessive consumption of local beef.

Florence (Aug 15) Festa del Grillo; fair in the Cascine park.
Orvieto (Aug 15) Festa della Palombella; horse race.
Porto Santo Stefano (Aug 15) Palio Marinaro; parade and rowing race.
Siena (Aug 16) Palio horse races, preceded by trial races on Aug 14 & 15.
Livorno (Aug 17) Palio Marinaro; boat races.
Città di Castello (mid-Aug to early Sept) Chamber music festival.
Arezzo (last two weeks) International choral festival.
Città di Castello (last week) Festival delle Nazioni di Musica da Camera; highly respected festival of chamber music.
Montepulciano (last Sun) Bravio delle Botti; barrel race through town.

September

Todi (ten days in Sept) Arts festival.
Arezzo (first Sun) Giostro del Saraceno; jousting.
Cerreto Guidi (first Sun) Renaissance procession.
Florence (Sept 7) Festa delle Rificolone; torchlit procession.
Prato (Sept 8) Festa degli Omaggi; costumed procession.
Sansepolcro (second Sun) Crossbow matches against Gubbio.
Greve (second Sun) Chianti Classico wine festival.
Foligno (second weekend) Torneo della Quintana; jousting by 600 medieval knights.
Lucca (Sept 14) Festa di Santa Croce/Settembre Lucchese; procession of sacred image and cultural events.
Perugia (last week) Sagra Musicale Umbra; classical music festival, one of the region's most prestigious cultural events.

October

Trevi (Oct 1) Palio dei Terzieri; cart race.
Assisi (Oct 3–4) Festa di San Francesco; major religious festival.
Piediluco (mid-Oct) Wine and chestnut fair.
Umbertide (mid-Oct) Sagra della Castagna; chestnut fair.

November

Perugia (Nov 1–5) Festa dei Ognissanti; All Saints Fair.

December

Siena (Dec 13) Festa di Santa Lucia; pottery fair.
Prato (Dec 25 & 26) Display of Holy Girdle.

Food, wine and arts festivals

Food- and **wine**-inspired festivals are more low-key affairs than the religious and traditional events, but no less enjoyable for that. They generally celebrate the edible speciality of the region to the accompaniment of dancing, music from a local brass band and noisy fireworks at the end of the evening. At Easter and through the summer and autumn there are literally hundreds of such events, most of them catering to locals rather than tourists; for details, ask at tourist offices or check the local newspapers (where you'll find them listed as **sagre**).

The ancient inter-town rivalries across Tuscany and Umbria – encapsulated neatly by the term *campanilismo*, implying that the only things that matter are those that take place within the sound of your village's church bells – find a positive expression in the willingness of local councils to put money into promoting their own **arts festivals**. For the size of the towns involved, the events are often almost ludicrously rich, celebrating the work of a native composer or artist by inviting major international names to perform or direct. Many festivals are given added enjoyment by their location: in summer, open-air performances are often staged in restored ancient amphitheatres, churches or town squares.

Religious and traditional festivals

Many of the local **religious processions** have strong pagan roots, marking important dates on the calendar subsequently adopted and sanctified by the Church. **Good Friday** is also a popular time for processions, with images of Christ on the cross paraded through towns accompanied by white-robed, hooded figures singing penitential hymns. The separate motivations to make some money, have a good time and pay your spiritual dues all merge in the celebrations for a town's **saint's day**, where it's not unusual to find a communist mayor and local bishop officiating side by side.

Umbria has the edge over Tuscany in religious festivities. **Assisi** – with its Franciscan associations – has a disproportionate number of events, the biggest being the Festa di San Francesco (October 3–4), which draws religious leaders and pilgrims from all over Italy. Holy Week in Assisi attracts one of the world's biggest concentrations of nuns, monks and lesser religious fanatics, and Calendimaggio, celebrating Francis's more worldly youth, is also huge, lasting for a week from the first Tuesday in May. In **Cascia**, another of the region's foremost saints, Rita (as popular in some parts of Italy as the Virgin), attracts many thousands of devotees – mainly women – to the torchlight Celebrazioni Ritiane (May 21–22). Also heavily patronized are Corpus Domini in **Orvieto**, celebrated with a costumed procession and a panoply of associated events, and **Gubbio**'s Corsa dei Ceri.

In Tuscany, top honours go to the Palio horse races in **Siena**, which see jockeys careering around the central square in a fiercely contested spectacle (see The Siena Palio colour section). Other towns put on medieval-origin contests, too, though they are somewhat phoney, having been revived recently for commercial ends. Among the most enjoyable are the Gioco di Calcio Storico (see p.172), a rough-and-tumble football game played between the four quarters of **Florence** in June, and the crossbow competitions between teams from **Gubbio** and **Sansepolcro**, held during May and September.

There's also been a revival of **carnival** (*carnevale*), the last fling before Lent, although anarchic fun has generally been replaced by elegant, self-conscious affairs, with costumes and handmade masks – at their most extravagant in **Viareggio**. Carnival usually lasts for the five days before Ash Wednesday; because it's connected with Easter the dates change from year to year.

Outdoor activities

The hills, mountains, lakes and rivers of Tuscany and Umbria offer a wide range of outdoor activities. Some, such as hiking, are potentially outstanding, despite a relative lack of marked paths and good maps in many areas – though some parts of Umbria, southern Tuscany and the Alpi Apuane are well covered. Cycling and riding are also first-rate, and there are good – but limited – opportunities for climbing, caving, fishing, sailing and diving.

Walking

Tuscany and Umbria offer a plethora of **walking** opportunities. The gentle pastoral landscapes of both regions are perfect for easygoing strolls, while the high-mountain terrains of areas such as the Alpi Apuane in Tuscany and Monte Cucco and the Monti Sibillini in Umbria provide the chance for longer and more challenging hikes. Spring is by far the best time to visit, with glorious wildflowers and verdant countryside from mid-April in the lowlands and late May to early June in the mountains. Temperatures are equally kind in September – midsummer is too hot for comfortable hiking – and the weather a touch more reliable, with less chance of rain than in spring, but the landscapes can be sun-scorched.

Hiking in this part of Italy is still in its infancy. You'll find very few marked **trails** or recognized footpaths, and even fewer **maps** of sufficient detail to let you navigate with confidence. One option is to trust the practicalities to the growing number of UK- and US-based walking companies offering guided or self-guided walks.

Certain areas do have marked trails, generally the work of local enthusiasts or the **Club Alpino Italiano** (CAI). Most towns have a CAI office, but these are typically open only for a few hours one day a week: you're better off visiting a local tourist office for details of local trails. Such paths exist in the Alpi Apuane, Orecchiella, Monte Cucco and parts of the Monti Sibillini, as well as in other areas with an active local CAI branch, such as the Val d'Orcia south of Montalcino, parts of Elba, the Casentino, areas around Spoleto and on Monte Subasio above Assisi. Shorter trails can be found in protected parks such as the Monti dell'Uccellina in the Maremma. All CAI paths are indicated by **red and white markers**, and may be numbered, but are often not of sufficient quality to let you follow a route confidently or safely without a map. This is especially true in the mountains, and on long-distance routes, where marking is not as good as in France, Switzerland or the UK.

CAI has also played a part in establishing several **long-distance paths**. These are "Garfagnana Trekking" (a ten-stage walk in the Alpi Apuani and Orecchiella from Castelnuovo del Garfagnana), "Apuane Trekking" (four–eight days from Carrara) and "Piglione Trekking" (three days from Metato in the southern Alpi Apuane). Another major route, the 25-day Grande Escursione Appennica, runs along the crest of the Apennines, part of a much longer, multi-regional route designed to follow the Apennines' crest from north to south.

Other activities

Many of the companies that offer walking tours also offer **cycling** tours, though this is an activity where you can easily strike out alone. Unlike walking, it's also an activity that is extremely popular among Italians, and on Sunday mornings in particular you'll find a lot of fellow enthusiasts on the road.

It's as well to remember that much of Tuscany and Umbria is hilly and that summer temperatures, especially in the afternoon, are off-puttingly high. Also bear in mind that celebrated areas such as Chianti are largely wooded and so not as scenically tempting as the more open reaches of southern Tuscany or the backroads of Umbria. Many minor country roads are gravel-surfaced *strade bianche*: not ideal for long-distance cycling.

Many companies offer **riding** holidays, usually in Chianti or the Maremma, but virtually every rural town and village has at least one stable (*un maneggio* or *club ippico*) where you can take a horse out by the hour, the day or longer. Tourist offices have information on these, and on agriturismo accommodation (see p.34), many of which also offer riding.

Climbing is possible in the Alpi Apuane, where the limestone and marble offer some of the best rock on the Italian peninsula. The finest climbs are on the Procinto, Pizzo d'Uccello, Monte Nona and Pania della Croce, and in winter you can make ice climbs on Pania della Croce and the crests of Pisanino. CAI publish books on climbs in the region, available from larger bookshops in Lucca, Pisa or Florence, and you can pick up local information from CAI offices or the park office in Castelnuovo di Garfagnana (see p.255). In Umbria, there are climbs on Le Lecce and Fossa Secca around Monte Cucco, while the crags around Ferentillo (see p.605) have become one of Italy's leading free-climbing centres.

The karst formations of much of the region offers Italy's best **caving**, especially around Monte Cucco (see p.517), which has some of the world's deepest cave systems and at least twenty pots open to speleologists (some for experts only). There are almost equally good opportunities in the Alpi Apuane, including the Grotta del Vento (see p.254), which is also accessible to non-specialists. CAI offices are the best sources of information.

Italy's best **hang- and para-gliding** is also found on and around Monte Cucco, notably the Val di Ranco, and in the Sibillini above the Piano Grande, where the thermals and steep and treeless slopes provide ideal conditions for both activities.

Fishing and watersports

You can charter boats with guides for saltwater **fishing** from any number of ports on the Tuscan coast. The region's best freshwater fishing (for trout) is on the Nera in the Valnerina (see p.579): the river is well stocked and heavily fished, but comes with a raft of regulations and licence requirements, details of which can be had from the tourist office in Terni, or from the Federazione Italiana Pesca Sportiva (FIPS). Fishing is also possible on lakes Trasimeno and Piediluco.

Sailing and **windsurfing** are common up and down the Tuscan coast, where all the larger resorts have rental outlets for sailboards, catamarans, Zodiacs and the like. You can also rent scuba **diving** and **snorkelling** equipment, or take guided day or night dives, especially around the key diving destinations of Monte Argentario, Elba and smaller islands such as Giannutri.

Travel essentials

Costs

Delicious picnic **meals** can be put together for under €5, and a pizza or plate of pasta in a cheap pizzeria or trattoria will come to around €6 on average. However, in most restaurants in the major tourist centres you'll be lucky to get away with paying €35 a head for a three-course meal with house wine. In almost every restaurant you'll pay a **cover charge** (*coperto*) of €1–1.50 or more a head on top of the cost of your food and drink. As well as the coperto, **service** (*servizio*) will often be added, generally about ten percent; if it isn't, you should tip this amount, and if it is included it's usual to leave a few extra euro – but no more than five percent or so. **Public transport** is good value: the train journey from Florence to Siena (100km), for example, costs around €12 for a second-class return. **Accommodation** in major centres, though, is expensive (see p.34).

Overall, an average minimum **daily budget** for a couple staying in one-star hotels and eating one modest-priced meal out a day would be in the region of €90 per person. In view of the disproportionate cost of single hotel rooms, a person travelling alone can expect this figure to increase by about 25 percent – though not, of course, if staying in a hostel.

Youth/student ID cards soon pay for themselves in savings, principally on entertainment and admission to larger museums and attractions. Full-time students are eligible for the International Student ID Card (**ISIC**); anybody aged 26 or less qualifies for the **International Youth Travel Card**; and teachers qualify for the **International Teacher Card** – all of which carry the same benefits. Check ⓦwww.isiccard.com for details. **Discounts** for under-18s and over-65s are also usually available for major attractions and state museums.

Crime and personal safety

In Florence, the only trouble you're likely to come across are gangs of **scippatori** ("snatchers"), often kids, who operate in crowded streets or markets, train stations and packed tourist sights. As well as handbags, *scippatori* grab wallets, tear off any visible jewellery and, if they're really adroit, unstrap watches. You can **minimize the risk** of this happening by being discreet: wear money in a belt or pouch; don't put anything down on café or restaurant tables; don't flash anything of value; keep a firm

Emergency phone numbers

Police (Carabinieri) ☎112

Any emergency service (Soccorso Pubblico di Emergenza) ☎113

Fire service (Vigili del Fuoco) ☎115

Roadside assistance (Soccorso Stradale) ☎116

hand on your camera; and carry shoulder bags slung across your body. Never leave anything valuable in your car and park in car parks or well-lit, well-used streets.

Italy's reputation for **sexual harassment** of women is based largely on experiences in the south of the country. However, even in the "civilized" north, travelling on your own, or with another woman, you can expect to attract occasional unwelcome attention. There are few things you can do to ward it off. Indifference is often the most effective policy, as is looking as confident as possible, walking with a purposeful stride and maintaining a directed gaze.

In Italy there are several different branches of the **police**, ostensibly to prevent any single branch seizing power. You're not likely to have much contact with the Guardia di Finanza, who investigate smuggling, tax evasion and other finance-related felonies. Drivers may well come up against the **Polizia Urbana**, or town police, who are mainly concerned with traffic and parking offences, and also the **Polizia Stradale**, who patrol motorways.

The **Carabinieri** – the ones Italians are most rude about – are dressed in military-style uniforms and white shoulder belts (they're part of the army), and deal with general crime, public order and drugs control. The **Polizia Statale**, the other general crime-fighting branch, enjoy a fierce rivalry with the Carabinieri, and are the ones to whom you should **report a theft** at their base, the **Questura** (police station). They'll issue you with a *denuncia*, a form which you'll need for any insurance claims after you get home. The Questura is also where you should to go to obtain a visa extension or a *permesso di soggiorno* (permit to stay).

Electricity

The supply is 220V, though anything requiring 240V will work. Most plugs are two round pins: UK equipment will need an adaptor, US equipment a 220-to-110 transformer as well.

Entry requirements

All EU citizens can enter Italy, and stay as long as they like, simply on production of a valid passport. Citizens of the United States,

Canada, Australia and New Zealand need only a valid passport, but are limited to stays of ninety days. All other nationals should consult the relevant embassies about visa requirements. Legally, you're required to **register with the police** within three days of entering Italy, though if you're staying at a hotel this will be done for you. Some policemen are more punctilious about this than ever, though others would be astonished by any attempt to register yourself at the local police station while on holiday.

Italian embassies and consulates abroad

Australia Embassy: 12 Grey St, Deakin, Canberra, ACT 2600 ☎ 02/6273 3333, ⓦ www.ambcanberra .esteri.it. Consulates in Melbourne ☎ 03/9867 5744 and Sydney ☎ 02/9392 7900.
Canada Embassy: 275 Slater St, Ottawa, ON K1P 5H9 ☎ 613/232-2401, ⓦ www.ambottawa.esteri .it. Consulates in Montréal ☎ 514/849-8351 and Toronto ☎ 416/977-1566.
Ireland Embassy: 63–65 Northumberland Rd, Dublin 4 ☎ 01/660 1744, ⓦ www.ambdublino .esteri.it.
New Zealand Embassy: 34–38 Grant Rd, PO Box 463, Thorndon, Wellington ☎ 04/473 5339, ⓦ www .ambwellington.esteri.it.
South Africa Embassy: 96 George Ave, Arcadia 0083, Pretoria ☎ 12/423 0000, ⓦ www .ambpretoria.esteri.it.
UK Embassy: 14 Three King's Yard, London W1Y 2EH ☎ 020/7312 2200, ⓦ www.amblondra.esteri .it. Consulates in Edinburgh ☎ 0131/226 3695 and Manchester ☎ 0161/236 9024.
US Embassy: 3000 Whitehaven St NW, Washington DC 20008 ☎ 202/612-4400, ⓦ www .ambwashingtondc.esteri.it. Consulates in Chicago ☎ 312/467-1550, New York ☎ 212/737-9100 and San Francisco ☎ 415/292-9210.

Embassies and consulates in Italy

Australia Embassy: Via Alessandria 215, 00198 Roma ☎ 06.852.721, ⓦ www.australian -embassy.it.
Canada Embassy: Via G B de Rossi 27, 00161 Roma ☎ 06.445.981, ⓦ www.canada.it.
Ireland Embassy: Piazza di Campitelli 3, 00186 Roma ☎ 06.697.9121.
New Zealand Embassy: Via Zara 28, 00198 Roma ☎ 06.441.7171.
South Africa Embassy: Via Tanaro 14, 00198 Roma ☎ 06.85.25.41, ⓦ www.sudafrica.it.

UK Embassy: Via XX Settembre 80a, 00187 Roma ☎ 06.4220.0001, ⓦ http://ukinitaly.fco .gov.uk. Consulate in Florence: Lungarno Corsini 2 ☎ 055.284.133.
US Embassy: Via V Veneto 119/a, 00187 Roma ☎ 06.46.741, ⓦ www.usembassy.it. Consulate in Florence: Lungarno Vespucci 38 ☎ 055.266.951, ⓦ www.florence.usconsulate.gov.

Gay and lesbian travellers

Attitudes to gay men and women in Tuscany and Umbria are on the whole tolerant, and Florence has a particularly thriving gay scene, but public displays of affection that extend much beyond hand-holding might raise a few eyebrows, especially outside the bigger towns. The national gay organization ARCI-Gay (ⓦ www.arcigay.it) has branches in most big towns; ⓦ www.gay.it has a wealth of information on the scene in Italy. The age of consent in Italy is 18.

Health

If you're arriving in Italy from elsewhere in Europe, North America or Australasia, you don't need any jabs. **EU citizens** are entitled to emergency medical care under the same terms as the residents of the country. As proof of entitlement, British citizens will need a **European Health Insurance Card (EHIC)**, which is free of charge and valid for five years – application forms are issued at UK post offices, or you can apply online at ⓦ www.dh.gov .uk. Note, however, that the EHIC won't cover the full cost of major treatment (or dental treatment), and the high medical charges make travel insurance essential. You normally have to pay the full cost of emergency treatment upfront, and claim it back when you get home (minus a small excess); make very sure you hang onto full doctors' reports, signed prescription details and all receipts to back up your claim.

In an **emergency**, call ☎ 113 and ask for *ospedale* or *ambulanza*, or go to the Pronto Soccorso (Casualty/A&E) section of the nearest hospital. Major train stations and airports often have first-aid facilities.

Italian pharmacists (*farmacie*) are well qualified to give advice on **minor ailments** and to dispense prescriptions; there's generally one open all night in the bigger towns and cities. They work on a rota system, and the address of the one currently open is posted on any farmacia door. If you require a **doctor** (*médico*), ask for help in the first instance at your hotel or the local tourist office. Alternatively look in the Yellow Pages (Pagine Gialle): larger towns will have English-speaking doctors. Follow a similar procedure if you have dental problems. Again, keep all receipts for insurance claims.

Mosquitoes (*zanzare*) can be a nuisance between June and September; most super-markets and pharmacies sell sprays, mosquito coils and after-bite cream.

Insurance

Even though EU health care privileges apply in Italy, you'd do well to take out an **insurance policy** before travelling to cover against theft, loss, illness or injury. Before paying for a new policy, however, it's worth checking whether you're already covered: some all-risks home insurance policies may cover your possessions when overseas, and many private medical schemes include cover when abroad. In Canada, provincial health care plans usually provide partial cover for medical mishaps overseas, while holders of official student/teacher/youth cards in Canada and the US are entitled to meagre accident coverage and hospital in-patient benefits. Students will often find that their student health coverage extends during the vacations and for one term beyond the date of last enrolment.

After checking the possibilities above, you might want to contact a specialist **travel insurance** company, or consider Rough Guides' own travel insurance deal (see box below). A typical travel insurance policy usually provides cover for the loss of baggage, tickets and – up to a certain limit – cash or cheques, as well as cancellation or curtailment of your journey. Most exclude so-called dangerous sports unless an extra premium is paid: in Italy this can mean scuba-diving, windsurfing, trekking or skiing. If you do take medical coverage, ascertain whether benefits will be paid as treatment proceeds or only after you return home, and whether there is a 24-hour medical emergency number. When securing baggage cover, make sure that the per-article limit will cover your most valuable possession. If you need to make a claim, you should keep receipts for medicines and medical treatment, and in the event you have anything stolen, you must obtain an official statement from the police (see p.48).

Internet

Internet cafés are widespread in the larger towns, though many of them are short-lived ventures. The company with the widest network is Internet Train, whose franchises are listed at ⓦ www.internettrain.it. Reckon on paying around €5 for an hour online. It's increasingly common for hotels and even hostels to provide internet access, usually for free; in the more sizeable towns, you'll also come across cafés and bars offering free wi-fi.

Mail

Opening hours of main **post offices** are usually Monday to Saturday 8.30am–7.30pm, although smaller offices are open mornings only (Mon–Fri 8.30am–1.00pm,

Sat 8.30am–noon). You can also buy **stamps** (*francobolli*) in *tabacchi*, and in some gift shops. The Italian postal system is one of the slowest in Europe so if your letter is urgent make sure you send it *posta prioritaria*, which has varying rates according to weight and destination. Letters can be sent **poste restante** (general delivery) to any Italian post office by addressing them "Fermo Posta" followed by the name of the town; your surname should be double-underlined for easier identification, as filing is often diabolical: when picking items up take your passport, and – in case of difficulty – make sure they also check under your middle names and initials.

Maps

The **maps** in this guide should be fine for most purposes, and nearly all tourist offices hand out free maps as well. More detailed maps are produced by a multitude of companies, notably Italy's leading street-plan publisher LAC (Litografia Artistica Cartografica), and the TCI (Touring Club Italiano). The Rough Guide Map: Florence and Siena is printed on waterproof, crease-resistant paper, as is Rough Guides' 1:200,000 Tuscany map, which has all the information you'll need for driving around the area. Otherwise, the widely available TCI 1:200,000 maps (with separate sheets for Tuscany and Umbria) are excellent.

Money

The Italian currency is the **euro** (€), which is composed of 100 cents. You'll usually get the best rate of exchange (*cambio*) from a **bank**. Banking hours vary slightly, but generally are Monday to Friday 8.30am to 1.30pm and 3 to 4.30pm, with some major branches staying open continuously 8.30am to 4.30pm and opening for a couple of hours on Saturday morning. American Express and Travelex offices are open longer hours and in the larger towns you'll find an **exchange bureau** at the train station that stays open late. As a rule, though, the kiosks offer pretty bad rates.

Although it's a good idea to have some cash when you first arrive, **credit and debit cards** can be used either in an ATM

(*bancomat*) or over the counter. MasterCard, Visa and American Express are accepted in most larger city stores, hotels and restaurants, but cash still reigns supreme in much of Italy, so check first before embarking on a big meal out. ATMs are found in even small towns, and most accept all major cards. Remember that all cash advances on a credit card are treated as loans, with interest accruing daily from the date of withdrawal.

Opening hours and public holidays

Most **shops** are open Monday to Saturday from 8/9am until around 1pm, and again from about 3pm until 7/8pm, though in Florence and other main centres, it's become increasingly common for shops to stay open continuously from around 10am to 7.30pm (with slightly shorter hours on Sun). Opening hours for **museums**, **galleries** and **churches** vary and tend to change annually, but only by half an hour or so; we've detailed the current hours throughout the Guide. **Restaurants** typically open for lunch at about 12.30pm and close at 3pm, opening again for dinner at 7/7.30pm. Many close on Sunday evening and Monday at lunch, plus one other day a week.

Everything, except some bars and restaurants, closes on Italy's official **national holidays**, which are: January 1, January 6 (Epiphany), Easter Monday, April 25 (Liberation Day), May 1 (Labour Day), June 2 (Day of the Republic), August 15 (Ferragosto; Assumption), November 1 (Ognissanti; All Saints), December 8 (Immaculate Conception), December 25, December 26.

Phones

Public phone tariffs are among the most expensive in Europe. For national calls, the off-peak period runs Monday to Friday 6.30pm to 8am, then Saturday 1pm until Monday 8am. Area codes are now an integral part of the number and must always be dialled, regardless of where you're calling from. **Phone cards** in various denominations for use in public phones can be bought from many *tabacchi* or stores displaying a Telecom Italian sticker. The **international phone code** for Italy is 39. International **directory**

Calling home from abroad

Note that the initial zero is omitted from the area code when dialling the UK, Ireland, Australia and New Zealand from abroad.

UK international access code + 44 + city code.
Republic of Ireland international access code + 353 + city code.
US and Canada international access code + 1 + area code.
Australia international access code + 61 + city code.
New Zealand international access code + 64 + city code.
South Africa international access code + 27 + city code.

enquiries is on ☏176; an English-speaking operator is on ☏170. Numbers beginning ☏800 are free. The Italian Yellow Pages is at ⓦwww.paginegialle.it.

To use your **mobile phone**, check with your provider whether it will work in Italy and what the charges will be. Technology in Italy is GSM (ⓦwww.gsmworld.com). Unless you have a triband phone, it's unlikely that a mobile bought for use in North America will work elsewhere.

Time

Italy is on Central European Time (CET): 1 hour ahead of London, 6 hours ahead of New York and 8 hours behind Sydney.

Tourist information

Before you leave home, you might want to contact the Italian State Tourist Office (ENIT) for maps and accommodation listings – though you can usually pick up far fuller information from tourist offices in Italy. Details of every town's tourist offices are given in the Guide.

Tuscany and Umbria websites

ⓦ**www.enit.it** Italian State Tourist Board.
ⓦ**www.museionline.it** Links to museums and exhibition sites.
ⓦ**www.terraditoscana.com** Well-designed, informative site covering every aspect of Tuscany from walking and sleeping to wild flowers and local cuisine.
ⓦ**www.turismo.toscana.it** Official website of the Tuscan tourist board.
ⓦ**www.regioneumbria.eu** Official website of the Umbria tourist board.
ⓦ**www.zoomata.com** New ezine with lots of information about Italy today.

Travellers with disabilities

As part of the European Turismo per Tutti (Tourism for All) project – administered in Italy by the national disabled support organization CO.IN – museum, transport and accommodation facilities have improved remarkably in recent years. However, stairs and steps continue to present the most obvious difficulties (restaurants often have their bathrooms downstairs, for instance), while other problems can arise from cars being parked thoughtlessly, and from the sheer distances of car parks from old-town centres. Public transport is becoming more attuned to the needs of disabled travellers, but bus services are still more of a challenge than trains. Another thing to bear in mind – especially in Florence – is that budget hotels often occupy the upper floors of town houses, and may not have lifts; always check before booking.

Travelling with children

Children are adored in Italy and will be made a fuss of in the street, and are welcomed and catered for in bars and restaurants. The only hazards in summer are the heat and sun. The rhythms of the summer climate tend to modify the way you approach the day, and you'll soon find it quite natural to use siesta-time to recover flagging energy, and to carry on past normal bedtimes at night. In high summer, it's not unusual to see Italian children out at midnight, and not looking much the worse for it. You can buy **baby** equipment – nappies, creams and foods – in pharmacies.

See the website ⓦwww.travelforkids.com for more information on child-friendly sights and activities in Italy.

Guide

Guide

Guide

①

Florence

CHAPTER 1 # Highlights

✳ **The Duomo** Climb Brunelleschi's dome, the city's signature building. **See p.73**

✳ **The Uffizi** The world's greatest collection of Italian Renaissance paintings. **See p.92**

✳ **The Bargello** Magnificent sculpture and applied arts collection. **See p.101**

✳ **Santa Maria Novella** Amazing frescoes by Masaccio, Ghirlandaio, Uccello and others. **See p.112**

✳ **San Lorenzo** Crowds flock to see *David* at the Accademia, but the Michelangelos at San Lorenzo are just as remarkable. **See p.118**

✳ **San Marco** Showcase for the devotional art of Fra' Angelico. **See p.128**

✳ **Santa Croce** Giotto's frescoes and Brunelleschi's superb Pazzi chapel. **See p.139**

✳ **Palazzo Pitti** Another top-flight art gallery, and Florence's finest garden. **See p.148**

✳ **Cappella Brancacci** Epoch-defining art in the church of Santa Maria del Carmine. **See p.154**

✳ **Vinai** Stop for a snack at one of Florence's last remaining stand-up wine bars. **See p.167**

▲ Raphael's La Velata, Palazzo Pitti

Florence

S ince the early nineteenth century, **FLORENCE** (**Firenze** in Italian) has been celebrated as the epitome of everything that is beautiful in Italian civilization: Stendhal staggered around its medieval streets in a stupor of delight, the Brownings sighed over its idyllic charms, and E.M. Forster's *A Room with a View* portrayed it as the great antidote to the bloodless sterility of Anglo-Saxon life. And for most modern visitors the first, resounding impressions of the city tend to confirm the myth. The stupendous dome of the cathedral is visible over the rooftops the moment you step out of the train station, and when you reach the Piazza del Duomo the close-up view is even more breathtaking, with the multicoloured **Duomo** rising behind the marble-clad **Baptistery**. Wander from there down towards the River Arno and the attraction still holds: beyond the **Piazza della Signoria**, site of the immense **Palazzo Vecchio**, the water is spanned by the shop-laden medieval **Ponte Vecchio**, with gorgeous **San Miniato al Monte** glistening on the hill behind it.

It has to be said, however, that intensive exploration of the city is not always a stress-free business. The wonders of Florence are known to the whole world, which means that in high season the sheer number of tourists at the major sights is overwhelming – the Uffizi, for instance, is all but impossible to get into unless you've pre-booked your tickets days in advance. And yet, such is the wealth of monuments and artistic treasures here, it's impossible not to find the experience an enriching one. Tuscany was the powerhouse of what has come to be known as the Renaissance, and Florence – the region's dominant political and cultural centre – is the continent's supreme monument to European civilization's major evolutionary shift into modernity. The development of this new

Florentine addresses

Note that there is a double **address** system in Florence, one for businesses and one for all other properties – that, at least, is the theory behind it, though in fact the distinction is far from rigorous. Business addresses are followed by the letter **r** (for *rosso*) and are marked on the building with a red number on a white plate, sometimes with an r after the numeral. The two series are independent of each other, which means that no. 5 may be followed by no. 18r, for example, while no. 120 might be a long way from no. 120r. Properties are numbered according to their relation to the river: if the street is parallel to the Arno, numbers start from the east and proceed west; if the street is perpendicular to the river, the numbering starts from the end nearer the water.

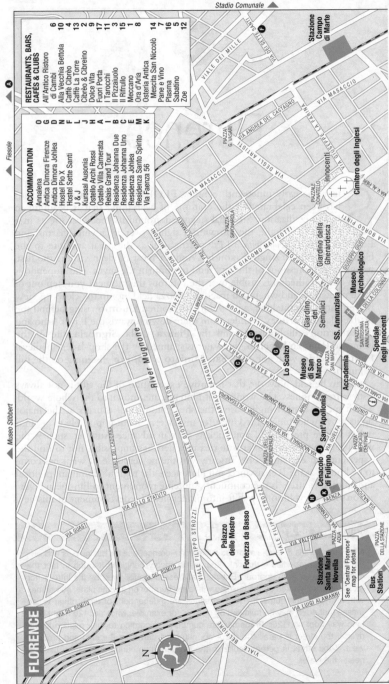

FLORENCE

FLORENCE | 1 | 58

ACCOMMODATION

Annalena	O
Antica Dimora Firenze	G
Antica Dimora Johlea	D
Hostel Pio X	N
Hostel Sette Santi	F
J & J	L
Kursaal Ausonia	J
Ostello Archi Rossi	H
Ostello Villa Camerata	A
Relais Grand Tour	I
Residenza Johanna Due	B
Residenza Johanna Uno	C
Residenza Johlea	E
Residenza Santo Spirito	M
Via Faenza 56	K

RESTAURANTS, BARS, CAFES & CLUBS

All'Antico Ristoro di Cambi	6
Alla Vecchia Bettola	10
Caffè Cibrèo	4
Caffè La Torre	13
Cibrèo & Cibreino	2
Dolce Vita	9
Fuori Porta	17
I Tarocchi	11
Il Pizzaiuolo	3
Il Rifrullo	15
Meccano	1
Ora d'Aria	8
Osteria Antica Mescita San Niccolò	14
Pane e Vino	7
Plasma	16
Sabatino	5
Zoe	12

Stadio Comunale

Stazione Campo di Marte

Fiesole

Museo Stibbert

Palazzo delle Mostre
Fortezza da Basso

River Mugnone

Giardino della Gherardesca

Giardino dei Semplici

Museo di San Marco

Lo Scalzo

Sant'Apollonia

Cenacolo di Fulligno

Accademia

SS. Annunziata

Spedale degli Innocenti

Museo Archeologico

Cimitero degli Inglesi

Stazione Santa Maria Novella

Bus Station

See 'Central Florence' map for detail

Cascine, Central Park &

Prato & Pistoia

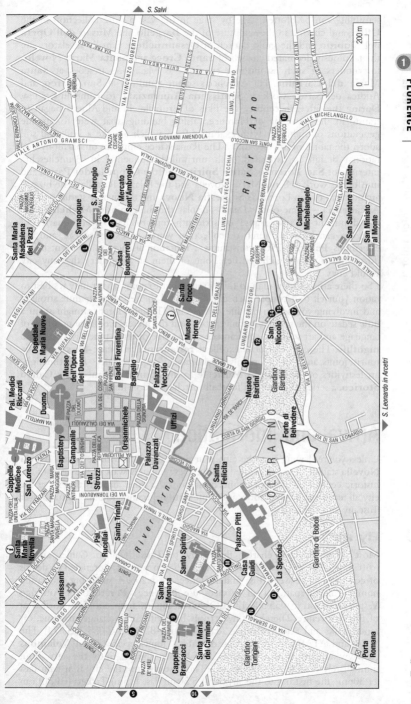

FLORENCE

▲ S. Salvi

▶ S. Leonardo in Arcetri

0 200 m

River Arno

River Arno

VIALE ANTONIO GRAMSCI

VIALE GIOVANNI AMENDOLA

VIA VINCENZO GIOBERTI

VIA DEL GHIBELLINA

VIA PIETRAPIANA BORGO LA CROCE

Santa Maria
Maddalena
dei Pazzi

Synagogue ⓛ

S. Ambrogio

Mercato
Sant'Ambrogio

Casa
Buonarroti

Santa Croce

Museo
Horne

Ospedale
S. Maria Nuova

Museo
dell'Opera
del Duomo

Badia
Fiorentina

Bargello

Pal. Medici
Riccardi

Duomo

Baptistery

Campanile

Orsanmichele

Palazzo
Vecchio

Uffizi

Palazzo
Davanzati

Cappelle
Medicee

San Lorenzo

Pal.
Strozzi

Santa Trinita

Pal.
Rucellai

Santa Maria
Novella

Ognissanti

Santa
Monaca

Santa Maria
del Carmine

Cappella
Brancacci

Santo Spirito

Casa
Guidi

La Specola

Palazzo Pitti

Santa
Felicita

Museo
Bardini

Giardino
Bardini

San
Niccolò

Forte di
Belvedere

O L T R A R N O

Giardino di Boboli

Giardino
Torrigiani

Porta
Romana

Camping
Michelangelo

San Salvatore al Monte

San Miniato
al Monte

PIAZZALE
MICHELANGELO

PONTE SAN NICCOLÒ

PONTE VECCHIO

PONTE S. TRINITA

PONTE
ALLE GRAZIE

PONTE AMERIGO VESPUCCI

VIA DEI SERRAGLI

VIA ROMANA

VIA DE' BARDI

VIA DI SAN LEONARDO

VIALE MICHELANGELO

VIALE GALILEO GALILEI

59

sensibility can be plotted stage by stage in the vast picture collection of the **Uffizi**, and charted in the sculpture of the **Bargello**, the **Museo dell'Opera del Duomo** and the guild church of **Orsanmichele**. Equally revelatory are the fabulously decorated chapels of **Santa Croce** and **Santa Maria Novella**, forerunners of such astonishing creations as Masaccio's frescoes at **Santa Maria del Carmine**, Fra' Angelico's serene paintings at **San Marco**, and Andrea del Sarto's work at **Santissima Annunziata**, to name just a few. During the fifteenth century, the likes of Brunelleschi and Alberti began to transform the cityscape of Florence, raising buildings that were to provide generations of architects with examples from which to take a lead, and still adorn the fabric of the city today. The Renaissance emphasis on harmony and rational design is expressed with unrivalled eloquence in Brunelleschi's interiors of **San Lorenzo**, **Santo Spirito** and the **Cappella dei Pazzi**, and in Alberti's work at Santa Maria Novella and the Palazzo Rucellai. The bizarre architecture of San Lorenzo's **Sagrestia Nuova** and the marble statuary of the **Accademia** – home of the *David* – display the full genius of **Michelangelo**, the dominant creative figure of sixteenth-century Italy. Every quarter of Florence can boast a church or collection worth an extended call, and the enormous **Palazzo Pitti** constitutes a museum district on its own: half a dozen museums are gathered here, one of them an art gallery that any city would envy.

So there are sights enough to fill a month, but to enjoy a visit fully it's best to ration yourself to a couple each day, and spend the rest of your time strolling and involving yourself in the life of the city. Though Florence might seem a little sedate on the surface, its university – and the presence of large numbers of language and art schools – guarantees a fair range of term-time diversions and **nightlife**. The city has some excellent **restaurants** and **café-bars** amid the tourist joints, and there's certainly no shortage of special events – from the high-art festivities of the **Maggio Musicale** to the licensed bedlam of the **Calcio Storico**, a series of costumed football matches held in June.

Arrival and information

Unless you're driving into the city, your point of arrival will be **Santa Maria Novella** station, which is located within a few minutes' walk of the heart of the historic centre: rail and bus connections from the three airports that serve the city all terminate at the station, as do international trains and buses from all over Tuscany and Umbria.

By air

Most scheduled and charter flights fly to **Pisa**'s Galileo Galilei airport (℡050.849.300, Ⓦwww.pisa-airport.com), 95km west of Florence. For details of connections between Pisa and Florence, see p.265. A small but increasing number of international air services use Florence's **Perètola** (or Amerigo Vespucci) airport (℡055.306.1300, Ⓦwww.aeroporto.firenze.it), 5km northwest of the city centre. There's a tiny arrivals hall with an exchange machine, car rental desks and a tourist office (daily 8.30am–8.30pm; ℡055.315.874). The SITA and ATAF bus companies operate a joint service called **Volainbus** (Ⓦwww.ataf.net), which provides half-hourly shuttles into the city from immediately outside the arrivals area. The first bus into the city is at 6am (last 11.30pm), the first out to the airport at 5.30am (last 11pm). Tickets (€4.50) can be bought on board or from machines at the airport and bus station, and the journey takes thirty minutes.

Bologna's Marconi airport (Ⓦ www.bologna-airport.it) – about the same distance from Florence as Pisa – is an alternative gateway. Aerobus shuttles depart every twenty minutes (7.30am–11.45pm) from outside the airport's Terminal A to Bologna's main train station (about 25min; €5 ticket, bought on board), from where regular trains run to Florence's Santa Maria Novella station in about an hour. Note, however, that Ryanair services to Bologna in fact fly to **Forlì airport**, which is more than 60km southeast of Bologna, and very inconvenient for Florence.

By train and bus

Nearly all **trains** arrive at Florence's main central station **Santa Maria Novella**, called "**Firenze SMN**" on timetables. It's located just north of the church and square of Santa Maria Novella, a few blocks west of the Duomo. (A few trains – mostly in the small hours of the morning – use Campo di Marte station, over in the east of the city, from where there are regular buses into the centre.) At SMN station you'll find left-luggage facilities and a 24-hour pharmacy. While in and around the station, you should keep a close eye on your bags at all times: it's a prime hunting ground for pickpockets. Also avoid the concourse's various taxi and hotel touts, however friendly they may appear.

Half a dozen **bus** companies run to Florence from various parts of Tuscany. The main operator is SITA, which has a terminal right opposite the train station at Via Santa Caterina da Siena; all the other companies are based on the eastern side of the station. For addresses and routes, see p.178.

By car

Only residents are allowed to park on the streets in the centre, so you have to leave your **car** in one of the city's main car parks. North of the Arno, the car parks nearest the centre are underneath the train station, just off Piazza della Libertà, and at Piazza Annigoni, near Santa Croce; south of the river the best option is Piazza della Calza, at the southwest tip of the Bóboli gardens. The average rate is €1.50, or around €15 for 24 hours.

If you want to leave your car for a prolonged period, try Piazzale Michelangelo, the nearest substantial **free parking** area to the centre. It's about twenty-minutes' walk to the Piazza della Signoria from here, or a short ride into the centre of town on bus #12 or #13. Watch out for a scam in which

---

Florence websites

Agenzia per il Turismo di Firenze Ⓦ www.firenzeturismo.it. An official tourist board site, useful for information on forthcoming exhibitions and hotel listings.

Firenze.net Ⓦ www.firenze.net. Smart, stylish website, packed with city info and links.

Polo Museale Ⓦ www.polomuseale.firenze.it. Information on Florence's state-owned museums.

The Florentine Ⓦ www.theflorentine.net. The online edition of Florence's English-language local newspaper.

Your Way to Florence Ⓦ www.arca.net/florence.htm. A comprehensive site with news and information on transport, accommodation and opening hours.

bogus car-park attendants direct you into a parking space, thus implying there's a charge: there isn't.

Information

For information about Florence's sights and events, the main **tourist office** is at Via Cavour 1r, five-minutes' walk north of the Duomo (Mon–Sat 8.30am–6.30pm, Sun 8.30am–1pm; ☏055.290.832 or 055.290.833, ⓦwww.firenzeturismo.it). Smaller offices are to be found just off Piazza Santa Croce at Borgo Santa Croce 29r (April–Oct Mon–Sat 9am–7pm, Sun 9am–2pm; Nov–March Mon–Sat 9am–5pm, Sun 9am–2pm; ☏055.234.0444), and opposite the train station, at Piazza della Stazione 4 (Mon–Sat 8.30am–7pm, Sun 8.30am–2pm; ☏055.212.245). All three provide an adequate **map** and various leaflets, including a sheet with opening hours and entrance charges. The office at Via Cavour also handles information on the whole of Florence province, while the office at the station can book accommodation for a fee.

One of the best sources of information on **events** is *Firenze Spettacolo* (ⓦwww.firenzespettacolo.it; €1.80), a monthly, partly bilingual listings magazine available from bookshops and larger newsstands. Also useful is *The Florentine*, a free bi-weekly English-language paper, available at the tourist office, most bookshops and various other spots (listed on ⓦwww.theflorentine.net).

City transport

Finding your way around central Florence is straightforward – it's just ten-minutes' **walk** from Santa Maria Novella to the central Piazza del Duomo, along Via de' Panzani and Via de' Cerretani. You can't miss these roads: stand with your back to the train station and they form the main thoroughfare sweeping away in front of you and to the left. The great majority of the major sights are within a few minutes of the Duomo.

Within the historic centre, walking is generally the most efficient way of getting around, and the imposition of the **zona a traffico limitato (ZTL)** – which

---

The Tramvia

In an attempt to solve the perpetual problem of the management of road and pedestrian traffic in central Florence, the city authorities are building a highly controversial tram network called **Tramvia**, which is intended to consist of three lines: one connecting Santa Maria Novella with Scandicci, to the southwest of the city; the second running from Perètola to Piazza della Libertà, via the station; and the last going from Careggi, to the north of the city centre, all the way to Bagno a Ripoli, in the southeast. Objectors argued from the start that the streets in the centre of Florence are simply too narrow to accommodate tramlines, and their arguments gained force when it was revealed that in order to squeeze the trains past Piazza della Signoria it would be necessary to knock a lump out of the Palazzo Vecchio. That aspect of the masterplan was ditched, and construction of the Tramvia is now going ahead, but – leaving aside the question as to whether Florence is suited to such a system – there are various other tricky local issues to be solved, such as how to run a line past the Duomo without disfiguring this unique urban landscape with a web of overhead cables. At the time of writing, just one line – #1, from Santa Maria Novella to Scandicci – was anywhere near completion. It seems a fair bet that it'll be quite some time before the system is operational.

limits traffic in the centre to residents' cars, delivery vehicles and public transport – has reduced the once unbearable pollution and noise, though many of the central streets are nonetheless so busy that you'll find it hard to believe that any restrictions are in operation.

Buses

Pending completion of the Tramvia (see box opposite), if you want to cross town in a hurry, or visit some of the peripheral sights, your best option is to use one of the frequent and speedy orange ATAF **buses**.

Tickets are valid for unlimited usage within seventy minutes (€1.20), 24 hours (€5) or 72 hours (€12). A **Biglietto Multiplo** gives four seventy-minute tickets for €4.50; better value is the ATAF electronic card ticket called the **Carta Agile**, which comes in two versions – the €10 one is equivalent to ten 70-minute tickets, whereas the €20 card is equivalent to 21. Each Carta Agile can be used by more than one passenger at a time, and is valid for one year. Tickets can be bought from the main ATAF information office in the bays to the east of Santa Maria Novella train station (daily 7am–8pm; ⓦ www.ataf .net), from any shops and stalls displaying the ATAF sign, and from automatic machines all over Florence. Once you're on board, you must **validate** your ticket by stamping it in the machine; there's a hefty on-the-spot **fine** for any passenger without a validated ticket.

Most of the **routes** that are useful to tourists stop by the station, notably #7 (for Fiesole) and #12/13: #13 goes clockwise through Piazzale Michelangelo, San Miniato and Porta Romana (all on the south side of the river), while #12 goes anticlockwise round the same route. In addition to these, small **electric buses** run along four very convenient city-centre routes. Bus #A runs from the station right through the historic centre, passing close by the Duomo and Signoria, then heading east just north of Santa Croce; #B follows the north bank of the Arno; while #C descends from Piazza San Marco, heading south past Santa Croce and across the Ponte delle Grazie on its way to Via Bardi. These three buses follow similar routes on their return journeys. Bus #D leaves the station and crosses the river at Ponte Vespucci; from here it becomes a handy Oltrarno bus, running right along the south bank of the river and, on the return journey, jinking up past Palazzo Pitti, Santo Spirito and the Carmine church on its way back to the Ponte Vespucci.

Taxis

You can't flag down a **taxi** in the street – you have to phone for one (☎ 055.4242, 055.4798, 055.4799 or 055.4390) or go to a taxi rank; key locations include the station, Piazza della Repubblica, Piazza del Duomo, Piazza Santa Maria Novella, Piazza San Marco, Piazza Santa Croce and Piazza Santa Trìnita. If you order a cab by phone, you'll be given the car's code name – usually a town, city or country – and its number, both of which are emblazoned on the vehicle. Italians tend not to order cabs far in advance: simply call a few minutes beforehand. All rides are metered; at the start of the journey the meter should be set at €3.20, or €5.10 if it's a Sunday or public holiday, or €6.40 between 10pm and 6am. Supplements are payable for journeys outside the city limits (to Fiesole, for example), for each piece of luggage placed in the boot (€1), and for phoning for a cab (€1.90). The charge per kilometre is €1.

Accommodation

Accommodation in Florence can be a problem: hotels are plentiful, but demand is almost limitless, which means that prices are high and some hoteliers are less than scrupulous. There's rarely a let-up in the tourist invasion: "low season" is officially the period from mid-November to mid-March (except for Christmas and New Year), plus the weeks from mid-July to the end of August, when millions of Italians head for the beaches or the mountains. Italians might give the city a wide berth in August but foreigners don't, so between March and October you should book your room well in advance or reconcile yourself to staying some distance from the centre. There's a handful of **hostels** and a couple of **campsites** (see p.69 & p.70).

The tourist office at the station can find you a hotel (for a fee), but you'd be ill-advised to roll into town without having somewhere already sorted out. If none of our recommended places has a room, search the listings on the official tourism website: ⓦ www.firenzeturismo.it. Never respond to the touts who hang around the train station: their hotels are likely to be expensive, or remote, or unlicensed private houses.

Accommodation in central Florence is marked on the **map** on pp.66–67, while more outlying places are shown on the map on pp.58–59.

Hotels

Hotel prices in Florence are higher than anywhere else in the country except Venice: one-star establishments in this city cost as much as two-star – even three-star – places elsewhere in Tuscany.

Many hotels in Florence drop their prices considerably in low season – more than fifty percent in some cases; our reviews make it clear what sort of reductions you can expect. Watch out for the hidden extra cost of **breakfast**: some hotels include it in the room price, but many don't; it's nearly always cheaper and usually nicer to eat in a bar or café if you have the option. Prices for rooms may also vary within the same hotel, so if the first price you're quoted seems high, ask if there's anything cheaper. As ever in big cities, **single rooms** are at a premium: you'll do well to get away with less than two-thirds the cost of a double. The maximum cost of a room, plus any charge for breakfast, should be posted on the back of the door; if it isn't, or if you have any other complaints, contact the tourist office. Note that many hotels require a **deposit** to secure booking, which will involve sending credit card details; if a hotel demands a cash deposit, go elsewhere.

City Centre

Alessandra Borgo Santi Apostoli 17 ☎055.283.438, ⓦ www.hotelalessandra.com. One of the best and friendliest of the central two-stars, with 27 rooms (most with bathroom) occupying a sixteenth-century palazzo and furnished in a mixture of antique and modern styles. Used by the fashion-show crowd, so booking is essential in Sept. Doubles start as low as €110 in low season, for rooms with shared bathrooms. ❹

Bretagna Lungarno Corsini 6 ☎055.289.618, ⓦ www.hotelbretagna.net. This one-star riverfront hotel has a superb location and rococo-style breakfast and living rooms. Six of the 24 rooms overlook the Arno, and most of the rest have en-suite bathrooms and a/c. Doubles with shared bathroom are just €50 off-season. ❸

Cestelli Borgo SS Apostoli 25 ☎055.214.213, ⓦ www.hotelcestelli.com. Spotlessly maintained by its young Florentine-Japanese owners, this eight-roomed one-star occupies part of a house that once belonged to a minor Medici, whose bust adorns the facade. The rooms are a good size, and most are en suite. ❸

Gallery Hotel Art Vicolo dell'Oro 5 ☎055.27.263, ⓦ www.lungarnohotels.com. In a small, quiet square a few paces from the Ponte Vecchio, this immensely stylish four-star is unlike any other hotel in central Florence. It has a sleek, minimalist and hyper-modern look – lots of dark wood and neutral colours – and tasteful contemporary art displayed in the reception and all 74 rooms. There's a small but smart bar, a sushi restaurant and an attractive lounge with art-filled bookshelves and comfortable sofas. Doubles normally €300–400, but online deals sometimes offer rooms for as little as €200. ⑨

Helvetia & Bristol Via dei Pescioni 2 ☎055.26.651, ⓦwww.royaldemeure.com. In business since 1894 and favoured by such luminaries as Pirandello, Stravinsky and Gary Cooper, this is now undoubtedly Florence's finest small five-star hotel. The public spaces and 67 bedrooms and suites (each unique) are faultlessly designed and fitted, mixing antique furnishings and modern facilities – such as Jacuzzis in many bathrooms – to create a style that evokes the *belle époque* without being twee. If you're going to treat yourself, this is a leading contender. Doubles start at around €400, without breakfast. ⑨

Hermitage Vicolo Marzio 1/Piazza del Pesce ☎055.287.216, ⓦwww.hermitagehotel.com. Pre-booking is recommended at any time of year to secure one of the 28 rooms in this three-star hotel right next to the Ponte Vecchio, with unbeatable views from some rooms as well as from the flower-filled roof garden. The service is friendly, and rooms are cosy, decorated with the odd antique flourish; bathrooms are small but nicely done. Prices in low season are about half the high-season tariff. ⑥

Torre Guelfa Borgo SS Apostoli 8 ☎055.239.6338, ⓦwww.hoteltorreguelfa.com. Twenty tastefully furnished rooms are crammed into the third floor of this ancient tower, the tallest private building in the city; there are marvellous views from the small roof garden. There are also six cheaper doubles on the first floor (no TV and more noise from the road). Charismatic (if slightly shabby in places), very popular, and quite pricey too – €210–260 for the best room (it has a small terrace), though a room on the first floor costs some €100 less. ⑥

Santa Maria Novella district

Elite Via della Scala 12 ☎055.215.395, ⓦwww .hotelelitefirenze.com. A basic and very inexpensive ten-room two-star run by one of the most pleasant managers in town. Most rooms have private bathrooms; ask for a room at the back – they are somewhat quieter. ③

Grand Hotel Minerva Piazza Santa Maria Novella 16 ☎055.272.30, ⓦwww.grandhotelminerva.com. A big four-star with big rooms, many of them overlooking the piazza. The decor is fairly bland, but the bar and swimming pool on the roof are major pluses. Doubles cost as little as €150, but you're more likely to pay around €200 – still a very good price in this category. ⑨

J.K. Place Piazza Santa Maria Novella 7 ☎055.264.5181, ⓦwww.jkplace.com. One of the most appealing of Florence's designer hotels occupies a fine eighteenth-century building on Piazza Santa Maria Novella. The twenty rooms of this extraordinarily elegant town house have been designed by Michele Bönan in retro-modernist hybrid style, and have DVD players and flat-screen TVs. Doubles €350–500; the gorgeous Penthouse Suite is €800. ⑨

Nizza Via del Giglio 5 ☎055.239.6897, ⓦwww .hotelnizza.com. A smart eighteen-room family-run two star, with helpful staff and very central location. All rooms are en suite, and are better furnished and decorated than many in this category. In low season you might get a room for half the summer rate. ⑤

Station and San Lorenzo districts

Bellettini Via dei Conti 7 ☎055.213.561, ⓦwww.hotelbellettini.com. The warm welcome of owner Signora Gina counts for much in this 27-room two-star; so, too, do her copious breakfasts. Most of the simple rooms have private bathrooms (those without are €40 cheaper); all have TVs and a/c. ⑤

Globus Via Sant'Antonino 24 ☎055.211.062, ⓦwww.hotelglobus.com. The *Globus* has recently been drastically restyled – wenge furniture and natural tones throughout – and is now graded three-star. The 23 a/c rooms start from as little as €70 in off-season. ⑤

Kursaal Ausonia Via Nazionale 24 ☎055.496.324, ⓦwww.kursonia.com. Welcoming and recently refurbished three-star near the station. If you book online, and well in advance, you can pick up a "superior" double (in faux-antique style) for less than €100 in summer; the price of a "standard" room – in which the decor is a bit more functional and bland – can go as low as €55 in low season. ③

Via Faenza 56 Several budget hotels are crammed into this address; note that there is no lift. On the top floor is the *Paola* (☎055.213.682, ⓦwww.albergopaola.com; ②), which is in effect a small hostel, with a four-bed room (with en-suite bathroom) and four six-bed mini-dorms. On

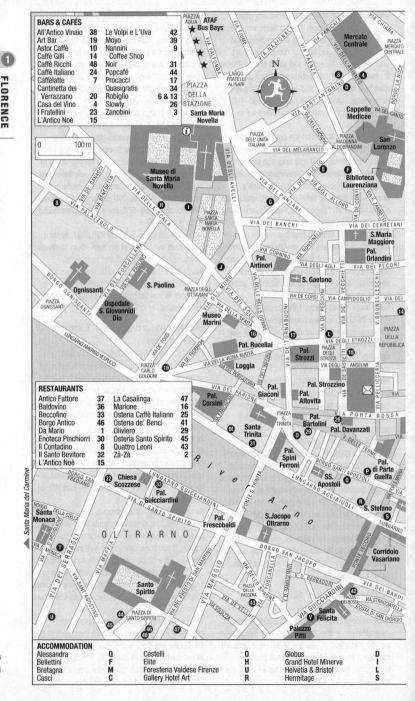

BARS & CAFÉS

All'Antico Vinaio	38	Le Volpi e L'Uva	42
Art Bar	19	Moyo	39
Astor Caffè	10	Nannini	9
Caffè Gilli	14	Coffee Shop	
Caffè Ricchi	48	Noir	31
Caffè Italiano	24	Popcafé	44
Caffèlatte	7	Procacci	17
Cantinetta dei		Quasigratis	34
Verrazzano	20	Robiglio	6 & 13
Casa del Vino	4	Slowly	26
I Fratellini	23	Zanobini	3
L'Antico Noè	15		

RESTAURANTS

Antico Fattore	37	La Casalinga	47
Baldovino	36	Marione	16
Beccofino	33	Osteria Caffè Italiano	25
Borgo Antico	46	Osteria de' Benci	41
Da Mario	1	Oliviero	29
Enoteca Pinchiorri	30	Osteria Santo Spirito	45
Il Contadino	8	Quattro Leoni	43
Il Santo Bevitore	32	Zà-Zà	2
L'Antico Noè	15		

ACCOMMODATION

Alessandra	Q	Cestelli	O	Globus	D
Bellettini	F	Elite	H	Grand Hotel Minerva	I
Bretagna	M	Foresteria Valdese Firenze	U	Helvetia & Bristol	L
Casci	C	Gallery Hotel Art	R	Hermitage	S

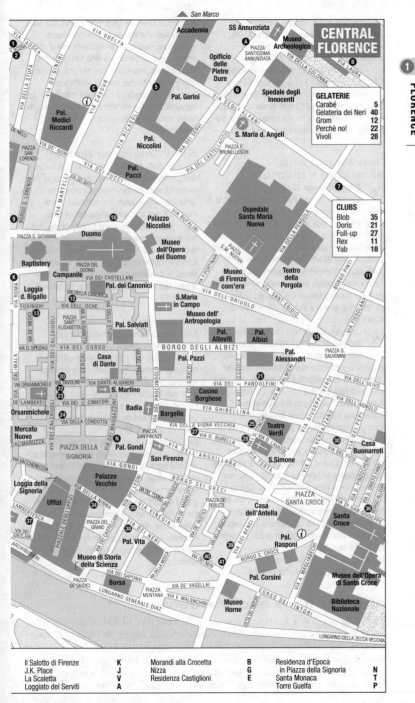

San Marco

CENTRAL FLORENCE

Accademia
SS Annunziata
Museo Archeologico
VIA GUELFA
VIA DELLA COLONNA
VIA LAURA

Opificio delle Pietre Dure
PIAZZA SANTISSIMA ANNUNZIATA

Pal. Gerini
Spedale degli Innocenti

VIA DEGLI ALFANI

S. Maria d. Angeli

PIAZZA F. BRUNELLESCHI

GELERATE

Carabé	5
Gelateria dei Neri	40
Grom	12
Perchè no!	22
Vivoli	28

Pal. Medici Riccardi

Pal. Niccolini

Pal. Pucci

VIA DEI PUCCI

VIA BUFALINI

Palazzo Niccolini

Ospedale Santa Maria Nuova

CLUBS

Blob	35
Doris	21
Full-up	27
Rex	11
Yab	18

Duomo

PIAZZA S. GIOVANNI

Museo dell'Opera del Duomo

PIAZZA S.M. NUOVA

Teatro della Pergola

Baptistery

Campanile

Loggia d. Bigallo

Pal. dei Canonici

Museo di Firenze com'era

S.Maria in Campo

VIA DELL'ORIUOLO

Museo dell' Antropologia

Pal. Salviati

Pal. Altoviti
Pal. Albizi

BORGO DEGLI ALBIZI

Pal. Pazzi

Pal. Alessandri

PIAZZA G. SALVEMINI

Casa di Dante

Casino Borghese

VIA DEI PANDOLFINI

Orsanmichele

S. Martino

Badia

Bargello

VIA GHIBELLINA

Teatro Verdi

Casa Buonarroti

Mercato Nuovo

PIAZZA SAN FIRENZE

San Firenze

S.Simone

Pal. Gondi

PIAZZA DELLA SIGNORIA

VIA DELL'ANGUILLARA

Loggia della Signoria

Palazzo Vecchio

Uffizi

BORGO DEI GRECI

PIAZZA DE' PERUZZI

PIAZZA SANTA CROCE

Casa dell'Antella

Santa Croce

Pal. Vita

Pal. Raspóni

BORGO S. CROCE

Museo di Storia della Scienza

Borsa

PIAZZA MENTANA

Museo Horne

Pal. Corsini

CORSO DEI TINTORI

Museo dell'Opera di Santa Croce

Biblioteca Nazionale

LUNGARNO GENERALE DIAZ

LUNGARNO DELLA ZECCA VECCHIA

Il Salotto di Firenze	K	Morandi alla Crocetta	B	Residenza d'Epoca	
J.K. Place	J	Nizza	G	in Piazza della Signoria	N
La Scaletta	V	Residenza Castiglioni	E	Santa Monaca	T
Loggiato dei Servi	A			Torre Guelfa	P

the same floor is the one-star *Merlini* (☎055.212.848, ⊛www.hotelmerlini.it; ➋), which has ten rooms, most with private bathrooms. On the first floor you'll find the one-star *Armonia* (☎055.211.146, ⓔarmonia1962 @libero.it; ➋), which has seven rooms (none with private bathroom). Also on this floor is the two-star *Azzi* (☎055.213.806, ⊛www.hotelazzi .com; ➍), which is by far the nicest place in the building, with garden views from most of its rooms.

San Marco and Annunziata districts

Casci Via Cavour 13 ☎055.211.686, ⊛www.hotelcasci.com. It would be hard to find a better two-star in central Florence than this 26-room hotel, which occupies part of a building in which Rossini once lived. Only two (sound-proofed) rooms face the busy street: the rest are quiet, clean and neat – and all are well-priced, falling to €100 in off-season. The welcome is warm and the owners are unfailingly helpful and courteous. The big buffet breakfast under the frescoed ceiling of the reception area is a plus, as is free internet access. ➎

Loggiato dei Serviti Piazza Santissima Annunziata 3 ☎055.289.592, ⊛www .loggiatodeiservitihotel.it. This elegant, tasteful and well-priced three-star is situated in one of Florence's most celebrated squares. Its 38 rooms have been incorporated into a structure designed in the sixteenth century in imitation of the Brunelleschi hospital across the square, to accommodate the Servite priests who worked there. Their relative plainness reflects something of the building's history, but all are decorated with fine fabrics and antiques, and look out either onto the piazza or peaceful gardens to the rear: top-floor rooms have glimpses of the Duomo. The five rooms in the nearby annexe, at Via dei Servi 49, are similarly styled, but the building doesn't have the same atmosphere. The website sometimes has discounts of about half the high-season full tariff. ➐

Morandi alla Crocetta Via Laura 50 ☎055.234.4747, ⊛www.hotelmorandi.it.

An intimate three-star gem, whose small size and friendly welcome ensure a home-from-home atmosphere. Rooms are tastefully decorated with antiques and old prints, and vivid carpets laid on parquet floors. Two rooms have balconies opening onto a modest garden; another – with fresco fragments and medieval nooks and crannies – was converted from the site's former convent chapel. In winter there are sometimes special offers as low as €120. ➐

Sant'Ambrogio district

J & J Via di Mezzo 20 ☎055.263.121, ⊛www .jandj.hotelinfirenze.com. The bland exterior of this former fifteenth-century convent conceals a romantic nineteen-room four-star hotel. Some rooms are vast split-level affairs, but all have charm and are furnished with modern fittings and a few antiques. Common areas are decked with flowers, and retain frescoes and vaulted ceilings from the original building. In summer breakfast is served in the convent's lovely old cloister. Doubles around half the high-season tariff in the quietest months. ➑

Oltrarno

Annalena Via Romana 34 ☎055.222.402, ⊛www.hotelannalena.it. Situated a short way beyond Palazzo Pitti (and right by an entrance to the Bóboli gardens), this twenty-room three-star was once owned by the Medici. The best rooms open onto a gallery with garden views, and a sprinkling of antiques lend a hint of old-world charm. Doubles in low season can be as much as €100 below the top rate. ➏

La Scaletta Via Guicciardini 13 ☎055.283.028, ⊛www.lascaletta.com. Some of the rooms in this tidy and recently refurbished sixteen-room two-star give views across to the Bóboli gardens; rooms on the Via Guicciardini side are double-glazed against the traffic. Drinks are served on the rooftop terraces, where you look across the Bóboli in one direction and the city in the other. All rooms are en-suite and nicely decorated in creamy tones. Doubles from only €80 in off-season. ➎

Affitacamere and residenze

To be classified as a hotel in Florence, a building has to have a minimum of seven bedrooms. Places with fewer rooms operate under the title *affitacamere* ("rooms for rent") or *residenze d'epoca* (if occupying a historic building) – though, confusingly, a *residenza d'epoca* might have as many as a dozen rooms. Some *affitacamere* are nothing more than a couple of rooms in a private house (and, though calling themselves "bed and breakfast", may not actually offer breakfast), but several – and most *residenze d'epoca* – are in effect small hotels in all but name, and offer some of the most atmospheric accommodation you can find in Florence. What follows is our pick of the small-scale places to stay; for full listings of accredited *affitacamere*, *residenze* and all other types of accommodation, go to Ⓦ www.firenzeturismo.it. One thing to bear in mind: like the budget hotels, *affitacamere* are often on the upper floors of large buildings, and can usually be reached only by stairs.

City Centre

Residenza d'Epoca in Piazza della Signoria Via dei Magazzini 2 ☏ 055.239.9546, Ⓦ www .inpiazzadellasignoria.com. This luxurious *residenza d'epoca* has ten spacious bedrooms, several of them giving a view of the piazza. The style is antique, but tastefully restrained, and the management is very friendly. ⑧

Il Salotto di Firenze Via Roma 6 ☏ 055.218.347, Ⓦ www.ilsalottodifirenze.it. Six well-appointed rooms (three overlooking Piazza del Duomo). Not a good choice if you're a light sleeper, but the standard of accommodation is high, prices low and the location absolutely central. ⑧

North of the centre

Relais Grand Tour Via Santa Reparata 21 ☏ 055.283.955, Ⓦ www.florencegrandtour.com. The very hospitable owners have done a great job in turning two floors of this old palazzo into a superb guesthouse, with three large bedrooms on the second floor and three suites on the floor above. Each room's decor is unique – one is replete with Neapolitan majolica tiles, another has a gold-leaf wooden ceiling, and a third is loaded with mirrors ("suitable for a couple", as the website has it). ④

🏃 **Residenza Castiglioni** Via del Giglio 8 ☏ 055.239.6013, Ⓦ www .residenzacastiglioni.com. This discreet and hugely stylish hideaway has just half a dozen spacious en-suite double rooms (three of them frescoed), on the second floor of a palazzo very close to San Lorenzo church. Doubles as low as €80 in low season. ⑥

Residenza Johanna Uno Via Bonifacio Lupi 14 ☏ 055.481.896, Ⓦ www.johanna.it. A genteel place that feels very much a "residence" rather than a hotel, hidden away in an unmarked apartment building in a quiet, leafy corner of the city, 5min walk north of San Marco. Rooms are cosy and well kept, and the two *signore* who run the place are as friendly and helpful as you could hope for. The very similar *Residenza Johanna Due* (☏ 055.473.377; same website) is located further out, at Via Cinque Giornate 12, to the north of the Fortezza da Basso. *Johanna Uno* costs in the region of €100–130 a night; *Due* is a little cheaper. ④–⑥

Residenza Johlea Via San Gallo 76 ☏ 055.463.3292, Ⓦ www.johanna.it. Another venture from the people who created the nearby *Residenza Johanna* (see above), offering the same low-cost, high-comfort package. At nearby Via San Gallo 80 you'll find the *Antica Dimora Johlea* (☏ 055.461.185; same website), a plusher version of the *Residenza*, with deluxe doubles for around €125–150, and a pleasant roof terrace. The same team run the similarly upmarket *Antica Dimora Firenze* at Via San Gallo 72 (☏ 055.462.7296; Ⓦ www.anticadimorafirenze.it), which has six very comfortable rooms (some with four-poster beds) in the same price range as the Dimora Johlea. ④–⑥

Oltrarno

🏃 **Residenza Santo Spirito** Piazza Santo Spirito 9 ☏ 055.265.8376, Ⓦ www .residenzasspirito.com. A well-presented *residenza* with two large double rooms overlooking the piazza, both with fantastic frescoed ceilings, and a two-roomed suite. The doubles cost around €120–150; the suite about €100 more. ⑤

Hostels

Foresteria Valdese Firenze – Istituto Gould Via dei Serragli 49 ☏ 055.212.576, Ⓦ www .istitutogould.it. Run by the Waldensian church, this hostel-cum-evangelical college occupies part of a former seventeenth-century palazzo (the doorbell is easily missed). The hostel's 99 beds (in 39 rooms) are extremely popular, so it's wise to book in advance, especially during the academic year. Street-front rooms can be noisy (rear rooms cost a little more), but the old courtyard, terracotta floors and stone staircases provide atmosphere throughout. Prices range from €21 for a bed in a five-bed room to €44 for a single room; nearly all rooms have private bathroom. Check-in Mon–Fri

8.45am–1pm & 3–7.30pm, Sat 9am–1.30pm & 2.30–6pm; reception closed Sun. No curfew.

Hostel Pio X Via dei Serragli 106 ☏055.225.044, ⍉www.hostelpiox.it. One of the cheapest options in town, often booked up by school groups. Don't be put off by the huge picture of Pope Pius X at the top of the steps; the management is friendly and the atmosphere relaxed. Get there by 9am, as the 64 beds are quickly taken. Beds in doubles, triples, quads and quins cost around €18 per person, a few euros more with en-suite bathrooms; minimum stay two nights, maximum five. Midnight curfew; reservations by email only.

Hostel Sette Santi Viale dei Mille 11 ☏055.504.8452, ⍉www.7santi.com. This new hostel occupies a converted convent on a main road just over 1km northeast of the city centre. There are 160 beds in total, some in dorms, but with 32 private rooms with bathroom, plus others with shower or shared bath. Sheets and towels are provided, as is a buffet breakfast. Doubles €40–60, dorm beds around €20. Bus #17 from the station goes past the door; #11 takes you to within one block.

Ostello Archi Rossi Via Faenza 94r ☏055.290.804, ⍉www.hostelarchirossi.com. A 5min walk from the train station, this privately owned guesthouse/hostel is spotlessly clean and decorated with guests' wall-paintings and graffiti. It's popular – the 147 places fill up quickly – and has a pleasant garden and terrace. Single rooms around €30. Dorm beds €20–25, depending on size of dorm (4–9 beds) and whether or not there's an internal bathroom; all prices include breakfast and 30min internet time. Disabled access rooms available. Curfew at 2am for dorms.

Ostello Villa Camerata Viale Augusto Righi 2–4 ☏055.601.451, ⍉www.ostellionline.org. A HI hostel and campsite tucked away in a beautiful park to the northeast of the city, 5km from Santa Maria Novella station. This is one of Europe's most attractive hostels, a sixteenth-century house with frescoed ceilings, fronted by lemon trees in terracotta pots. Doors open at 2pm; if you'll arrive later, call ahead to make sure there's space (bookings by email or fax only). There are 322 dorm beds (€20), and a few two-, three- and four-bed rooms, costing €32.50/€25/€22 per person. Breakfast and sheets are included, but there are no kitchen facilities; dinner costs about €10. Films in English are shown every night. Midnight curfew. Take bus #17b from the train station – it takes about 30min.

Santa Monaca Via Santa Monaca 6 ☏055.268.338, ⍉www.ostello.it. This privately owned hostel in Oltrarno, close to Santa Maria del Carmine, has 115 beds, arranged in dorms with between four and twenty beds. Kitchen facilities (no utensils), washing machines, and a useful notice board with information on lifts and onward travel. Dorm beds €17–20. Check-in 6am–2am; bedrooms have to be vacated between 10am and 2pm. Curfew 2am. It's a 15min walk from the station, or take bus #11, #36 or #37 to the second stop after the bridge.

Campsites

Camping Internazionale Firenze See p.191.
Camping Michelangelo Viale Michelangelo 80 ☏055.681.1977, ⍉www.ecvacanze.it. A 240-pitch site that's always crowded, owing to its superb hillside location in an olive grove overlooking the city centre. Kitchen facilities and well-stocked, if expensive, shop nearby. Take #13 bus from the station. April–Oct.

Camping Panoramico See p.185.
Villa Camerata Viale Augusto Righi 2–4 ☏055.601.451, ⍉www.ostellionline.org. Basic 55-pitch site in the grounds of the *Villa Camerata* HI hostel.

The City

Greater Florence now spreads several kilometres down the Arno valley and up onto the hills north and south of the city, but the major sights are contained within an area that can be crossed on foot in little over half an hour. A short walk from the train station brings you to the **Baptistery**, **Duomo** and the

Florence museum admission

All of Florence's state-run museums belong to an association called **Firenze Musei** (ⓦ www.firenzemusei.it), which sets aside a daily quota of tickets that can be **reserved in advance**. The Uffizi, the Accademia and the Bargello belong to this group, as do the Palazzo Pitti museums (including the Bóboli gardens), the Medici chapels in San Lorenzo, the archeological museum and the San Marco museum.

You can **reserve tickets** (booking fee of €4 for Uffizi and Accademia, €3 for the rest) by phoning ☏055.294.883 (Mon–Fri 8.30am–6.30pm, Sat 8.30am–12.30pm), or through the Firenze Musei website, or at the Firenze Musei booth at Orsanmichele (Mon–Sat 10am–5.30pm), or at the museums themselves, in the case of the Uffizi and Pitti. If you book by phone, an English-speaking operator will allocate you a ticket for a specific hour, to be collected at the museum, again at a specific time, shortly before entry. That's the theory, but in reality the line tends to be engaged for long periods at a stretch. Generally, the under-publicized Orsanmichele booth – which is set into the wall of the church on the Via Calzaiuoli side – is the easiest option. Pre-booking is very strongly recommended at any time of year for the Uffizi (see p.92 for more) and the Accademia, whose allocation of reservable tickets is often sold out many days ahead.

Note that on-the-door admission to all state-run museums is free for EU citizens under 18 and over 65, on presentation of a passport; 18–25s get a fifty percent discount, as do teachers, on proof of identity. Nearly all of Florence's major museums are routinely **closed on Monday**, though some are open for a couple of Mondays each month. In the majority of cases, museum ticket offices close thirty minutes before the museum itself. At the Palazzo Vecchio and Museo Stibbert, however, it's one hour before, while at the Uffizi, Bargello, Museo dell'Opera del Duomo, the dome of the Duomo, the Campanile and Pitti museums it's 45 minutes.

Museo dell'Opera del Duomo; the area south from here to Piazza della Signoria – site of the **Palazzo Vecchio** and the **Uffizi** gallery – is the inner core, into which most of the tourists are packed. A square drawn so that the Duomo and Uffizi stood in the centre of opposite sides would cover many of the best-preserved of Florence's medieval streets and the majority of its fashionable streets.

Immediately north of the Duomo is the San Lorenzo quarter, where market stalls surround one of the city's first-rank churches, in effect the chapel of the Medici dynasty. Within a short radius of here are the monastery of **San Marco**, with its paintings by Fra' Angelico, the **Accademia**, residence of Michelangelo's *David*, and **Piazza Santissima Annunziata**, Florence's most attractive square.

The Uffizi backs onto the Arno river, across which lies the district known as the **Oltrarno**, where the **Palazzo Pitti** and Masaccio's church of **Santa Maria del Carmine** exert the strongest pull, followed by the churches of **Santo Spirito** and the colourful **San Miniato al Monte**.

Close to the eastern side of Piazza del Duomo stands the **Bargello**, the main museum of sculpture; further east, the area around the Franciscan church of **Santa Croce** forms a nucleus of activity. On the western side of the city, directly opposite the train station, the unmissable attraction is **Santa Maria Novella**, Florentine base of the rival Dominican order.

Piazza del Duomo and around

From the train station, all first-time visitors gravitate towards **Piazza del Duomo**, beckoned by the pinnacle of Brunelleschi's dome, which lords it over the cityscape with an authority unmatched by any architectural creation in any other Italian city. Yet even though the magnitude of the **Duomo** is apparent from a distance, the first sight of the church and the adjacent **Baptistery** still comes as a jolt, their colourful patterned exteriors making a startling contrast with the dun-toned buildings around. Each of these great buildings is as remarkable inside as out, and an ascent of the cathedral's **dome** will give you astounding views over the city to the hazy Tuscan hills beyond.

▲ Piazza del Duomo

After exploring the cathedral, you can escape the crowds by climbing the **Campanile**, the Duomo's bell tower, or visit the **Museo dell'Opera del Duomo**, a repository for works of art removed over the centuries from the Duomo, Baptistery and Campanile. With pieces by Donatello, Michelangelo and many others, it's one of the city's two great sculpture collections, the other being the Bargello. On a considerably smaller scale, the **Loggia del Bigallo** contains a tiny museum relating to one of the city's oldest philanthropic institutions, while the **Museo di Firenze com'era** – a short distance east of the piazza – is devoted to the evolution of the Florentine cityscape. If you're in need of a break after this architectural and artistic overload, you could recharge the batteries at one of the cafés on nearby **Piazza della Repubblica**, a square that was planned as a showcase for the capital city of the newly united Italy.

The Duomo

Some time in the seventh century the seat of the Bishop of Florence was transferred from San Lorenzo to Santa Reparata, a sixth-century church which stood on the site of the present-day **Duomo**, or **Santa Maria del Fiore** (Mon–Wed & Fri 10am–5pm, Thurs 10am–3.30pm, Sat 10am–4.45pm, Sun 1.30–4.45pm; first Sat of month closes 3.30pm; free). Later generations modified this older church until 1294, when Florence's rulers were stung into action by the magnificence of newly commissioned cathedrals in Pisa and Siena. Their own cathedral, they lamented, was "crudely built and too small for such a city".

A suitably immodest plan to remedy this shortcoming was ordered from Arnolfo di Cambio, who drafted a scheme to create the largest church in the Roman Catholic world and "surpass anything of its kind produced by the Greeks and Romans in the times of their greatest power". Progress on the project faltered after Arnolfo's death in 1302, but by 1380 Francesco Talenti and a string of mostly jobbing architects had brought the nave to completion. By 1418 the tribunes (apses) and the dome's supporting drum were also completed. Only the dome itself – no small matter – remained unfinished (see p.78).

The exterior

Parts of the Duomo's **exterior** date back to Arnolfo's era, but most of the overblown and pernickety main **facade** is a nineteenth-century simulacrum of a Gothic front. The original facade, which was never more than quarter-finished, was pulled down in 1587 on the orders of Ferdinand I. A competition to produce a new front proved unsuccessful, and for three centuries the cathedral remained faceless. After Florence became capital of the newly unified Italy in 1865, however, no fewer than 92 plans were submitted. The winning entry, by the otherwise obscure Emilio de Fabris, was completed in 1887. To its credit, the new frontage at least retained the original colour scheme and materials, with marble quarried from three different sources: white from Carrara, red from the Maremma and green from Prato.

The cathedral's south (right) side is the oldest part of the exterior – both its side portals deserve a glance – but the most attractive adornment is the **Porta della Mandorla** (number 32 on our plan), on the other side. This takes its name from the almond-shaped frame (or *mandorla*) that contains the grime-streaked relief of the *Assumption of the Virgin* (1414–21), sculpted by Nanni di Banco; the lunette features a mosaic of the Annunciation (1491) to a design by Ghirlandaio.

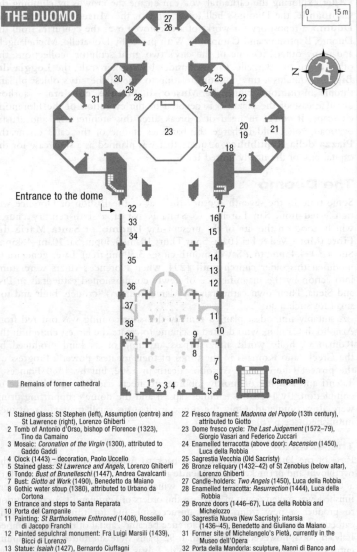

THE DUOMO

0   15 m

Entrance to the dome

Remains of former cathedral

Campanile

1 Stained glass: St Stephen (left), Assumption (centre) and St Lawrence (right), Lorenzo Ghiberti
2 Tomb of Antonio d'Orso, bishop of Florence (1323), Tino da Camaino
3 Mosaic: *Coronation of the Virgin* (1300), attributed to Gaddo Gaddi
4 Clock (1443) – decoration, Paolo Uccello
5 Stained glass: St Lawrence and Angels, Lorenzo Ghiberti
6 Tondo: *Bust of Brunelleschi* (1447), Andrea Cavalcanti
7 Bust: *Giotto at Work* (1490), Benedetto da Maiano
8 Gothic water stoup (1380), attributed to Urbano da Cortona
9 Entrance and steps to Santa Reparata
10 Porta del Campanile
11 Painting: *St Bartholomew Enthroned* (1408), Rossello di Jacopo Franchi
12 Painted sepulchral monument: Fra Luigi Marsili (1439), Bicci di Lorenzo
13 Statue: *Isaiah* (1427), Bernardo Ciuffagni
14 Painted sepulchral monument: Archbishop Pietro Corsino of Florence (1422), Bicci di Lorenzo
15 Stained glass: *Six Saints* (1395), Agnolo Gaddi
16 Bust: Marsilio Ficino (1521), philosopher friend of Cosimo de' Medici, holding a copy of Plato's works
17 Porta dei Canonici: sculpture (1395–99), Lorenzo d'Ambrogio
18 Eight statues of the Apostles (1547–72) against the pillars of the octagon
19 Tribune: each tribune has five chapels; each chapel has two levels of stained glass, most by Lorenzo Ghiberti
20 Frescoes below windows of west and east tribunes: *Saints* (1440), attributed to Bicci di Lorenzo
21 Altar, attributed to Michelozzo
22 Fresco fragment: *Madonna del Popolo* (13th century), attributed to Giotto
23 Dome fresco cycle: *The Last Judgement* (1572–79), Giorgio Vasari and Federico Zuccari
24 Enamelled terracotta (above door): *Ascension* (1450), Luca della Robbia
25 Sagrestia Vecchia (Old Sacristy)
26 Bronze reliquary (1432–42) of St Zenobius (below altar), Lorenzo Ghiberti
27 Candle-holders: *Two Angels* (1450), Luca della Robbia
28 Enamelled terracotta: *Resurrection* (1444), Luca della Robbia
29 Bronze doors (1446–67), Luca della Robbia and Michelozzo
30 Sagrestia Nuova (New Sacristy): intarsia (1436–45), Benedetto and Giuliano da Maiano
31 Former site of Michelangelo's Pietà, currently in the Museo dell'Opera
32 Porta della Mandorla: sculpture, Nanni di Banco and Donatello
33 Painting: *Dante with the Divine Comedy* (1465), Domenico di Michelino
34 Fresco: *SS Cosmas and Damian* (1429), Bicci di Lorenzo; two windows by Agnolo Gaddi
35 Statue (in recess) designed for old cathedral facade: *King David* (1434), Bernardo Ciuffagni
36 Equestrian portrait: *Sir John Hawkwood* (1436), Paolo Uccello
37 Equestrian portrait: *Niccolò da Tolentino* (1456), Andrea del Castagno
38 Bust: *Antonio Squarcialupi* (former cathedral organist, 1490), Benedetto da Maiano
39 *The Prophet Joshua* (1415), Nanni di Bartolo; the head is by Donatello

The two heads in profile either side of the gable may be early works by Donatello.

The interior

The Duomo's **interior** is the converse of the exterior – a vast, uncluttered enclosure of bare masonry. The fourth-largest church in Europe, it once held a congregation of ten thousand to hear Savonarola (see p.130) deliver one of his inflammatory sermons, and the ambience is still more that of a public assembly hall than of a devotional building. Its apparently barren walls, however, hold a far greater accumulation of treasures than at first appears.

The most conspicuous decorations are a pair of memorials to *condottieri* (mercenary commanders). Paolo Uccello's monument to **Sir John Hawkwood** (36), created in 1436, is often cited as the epitome of Florentine mean-spiritedness; according to local folklore – unsupported by any evidence – the mercenary captain of Florence's army was promised a proper equestrian statue as his memorial, then was posthumously fobbed off with this trompe l'oeil version. Perhaps the slight was deserved. Before being employed by Florence, Hawkwood and his White Company had marauded their way through Tuscany, holding entire cities to ransom under threat of ransack. Look back at the entrance wall and you'll see another Uccello contribution to the interior – a **clock** (4) adorned with four rather abstracted Evangelists. It uses the old *hora italica*, common in Italy until the eighteenth century, when the 24th hour of the day ended at sunset.

Andrea del Castagno's monument to **Niccolò da Tolentino** (37), created twenty years later, is clearly derived from Uccello's fresco, but has an aggressive edge that's typical of this artist. Just beyond the horsemen, Domenico di Michelino's 1465 work *Dante Explaining the Divine Comedy* (33) gives Brunelleschi's dome – then only nearing completion – a place scarcely less prominent than the mountain of Purgatory. Dante stands outside the walls, a symbol of his exile from Florence.

Judged by size, the major work of art in the Duomo is the 1572–79 fresco of **The Last Judgement** (23), which fills much of the interior of the dome. At the time of its execution, however, a substantial body of opinion thought Vasari and Zuccari's combined effort did nothing but deface Brunelleschi's masterpiece, and quite a few people today are of the same opinion.

Barriers usually prevent you from getting close to the high altar, so you might not be able to look into the **Sagrestia Nuova** (30), where the lavish panelling is inlaid with beautiful intarsia work (1436–45) by Benedetto and Giuliano Maiano, notably a delicate *Annunciation* in the centre of the wall facing the door. The relief of the *Resurrection* (1442) above the entrance is by Luca della Robbia, his first important commission in the enamelled terracotta for which he became famous. The stunning **sacristy door (29)** created in conjunction with Michelozzo (1445–69) was his only work in bronze. It was in this sacristy that Lorenzo de' Medici took refuge in 1478 after his brother Giuliano had been mortally stabbed on the altar steps by the Pazzi conspirators (see p.76): the bulk of della Robbia's recently installed doors protected him from his would-be assassins. Small portraits on the handles commemorate the brothers.

Across the way, della Robbia's *Ascension* (1450) can be seen above the door of the **Sagrestia Vecchia** (25); it was once accompanied by Donatello's sublime *cantoria*, or choir-loft, now in the Museo dell'Opera del Duomo. Luca della Robbia's equally mesmeric *cantoria*, in the same museum, occupied a matching position above the Sagrestia Nuova.

The Pazzi Conspiracy

The **Pazzi Conspiracy**, perhaps the most compelling of all Florence's murkier acts of treachery, had its roots in the election in 1472 of **Sixtus IV**, a pope who distributed money and favours with a largesse remarkable even by papal standards. Six of his nephews were made cardinals, one of them, the uncouth **Girolamo Riario**, coming in for particularly preferential treatment. Sixtus's plan was that Riario should take over the town of Imola as a base for papal expansion, and accordingly he approached Lorenzo de' Medici for the necessary loan. Aware that Imola was too close to Milan and Bologna to be allowed to fall into papal hands, Lorenzo rebuffed the pope, despite the importance of the Vatican account with the Medici bank, and the family's role as agents for the papacy's alum mines in Tuscany (alum was a vital part of the dyeing industry, and therefore essential to Florence's textile trade). Enraged by the snub, and by Lorenzo's refusal to recognize **Francesco Salviati** as archbishop of Pisa (Sixtus had ignored an agreement by which appointments within the Florentine domain could only be made by mutual agreement), Sixtus turned to the Pazzi, the Medici's leading Florentine rivals as bankers in Rome.

Three co-conspirators met in Rome in the early months of 1477: Riario, now in possession of Imola but eager for greater spoils; Salviati, incandescent at Lorenzo's veto and desperate to become archbishop of Florence; and **Francesco de' Pazzi**, head of the Pazzis' Rome operation and determined to usurp Medici power in Florence. Any plot, however, required military muscle, and the man chosen to provide it, a plain-speaking mercenary called **Montesecco**, proved intensely wary of the whole enterprise: "Beware of what you do," he counselled, "Florence is a big affair." In the end he made his co-operation conditional on papal blessing, a benediction that was readily obtained. "I do not wish the death of anyone on any account," was Sixtus's mealy-mouthed observation, "since it does not accord with our office to consent to such a thing" – yet he knew full well Lorenzo's death was essential if the plot was to succeed. "Go, and do what you wish," he added, "provided there be no killing." **Jacopo de' Pazzi**, the Pazzis' wizened godfather, was also won over by Sixtus's disingenuous support, despite being on good terms with the Medici – indeed, one of his nephews was married to Lorenzo's sister.

Santa Reparata

In the 1960s, remnants of the Duomo's predecessor, **Santa Reparata** (9), were uncovered underneath the west end of the nave, where a flight of steps leads down into the excavation. The remains (admission €3) are extensive, as the nave of the Duomo was built, on the same alignment, several feet above that of the old church, which was thus not fully demolished. Subsequent excavations have revealed a complicated jigsaw of Roman, Paleochristian and Romanesque remains, plus fragments of mosaic and fourteenth-century frescoes. The explanatory diagrams tend to intensify the confusion: to make sense of it all, you'll have to keep referring to the colour-coded model in the farthest recess of the crypt. In 1972, further digging revealed **Brunelleschi's tomb**, an unassuming marble slab so simple that it had lain forgotten under the south aisle. The tombstone's present position is hardly any more glorious (it can be seen, for free, through a grille to the left at the foot of the steps), but the architect does at least have the honour of being one of the very few Florentines to be buried in the Duomo itself.

The dome

Climbing the **dome** (Mon–Fri 8.30am–7pm, Sat 8.30am–5.40pm; €6) is an amazing experience, both for the views from the top and for the insights it

After numerous false starts, it was decided to **murder** Lorenzo and his brogher Giuliano whilst they attended Mass in the cathedral. The date set was Sunday, April 26, 1478. Montesecco, however, now refused "to add sacrilege to murder", so Lorenzo's murder was delegated to two embittered priests, Maffei and Bagnone, whereas Giuliano was to be dispatched by Francesco de' Pazzi and **Bernardo Baroncelli**, a violent Pazzi sidekick deeply in debt to the family. Salviati, meanwhile, accompanied by an armed troop, was to seize control of the Palazzo della Signoria.

It all went horribly wrong. Giuliano was killed in a crazed frenzy, his skull shattered and his body rent with nineteen stab wounds, but Lorenzo managed to escape, fleeing wounded to the Duomo's new sacristy, where he and his supporters barricaded themselves behind its heavy bronze doors. Across the city, Salviati was separated from his troops, thanks to newly installed secret doors and locks in the Palazzo della Signoria, and soon arrested.

Apprised of the plot, a furious mob dispensed summary justice to several of the conspirators: Salviati's troops were massacred to a man, whilst Salviati and Francesco de' Pazzi were hanged from a window of the Palazzo della Signoria. Of the latter execution, Poliziano, the eminent humanist, noted that "as the archbishop rolled and struggled at the end of his rope, his eyes goggling in his head, he fixed his teeth into Francesco de' Pazzi's naked body". Maffei and Bagnone, the bungling priests, were castrated and hanged. Baroncelli escaped to Constantinople but was extradited and executed. Montesecco was tortured, but given a soldier's execution in the Bargello. Jacopo's end was the most sordid. Having escaped Florence, he was recaptured, tortured, stripped naked, and hanged alongside the decomposing Salviati. He was then buried in Santa Croce, but exhumed by the mob, who blamed heavy rains on his evil spirit. His corpse was dragged through the streets, tipped in a ditch, and finally propped up outside the Pazzi palace, where his rotting head was used as door knocker. Eventually the putrefying body was thrown in the Arno, fished out, flogged and hanged again by a gang of children, and finally cast back into the river.

offers into Brunelleschi's engineering genius (see box, p.78). Be prepared for the queue that usually stretches from the entrance, on the north flank of the nave; it does, however, move fairly briskly. Also be ready for the 463 lung-busting steps. Claustrophobics should note that the climb involves some very confined spaces.

After an initial ascent, you emerge onto a narrow gallery that runs around the interior of the dome, with a dizzying view down onto the maze-patterned pavement of the nave. It's also the best vantage point from which to inspect the seven **stained-glass roundels**, designed by Uccello, Ghiberti, Castagno and Donatello, below Vasari's *Last Judgement* fresco. Beyond the gallery, you enter the more cramped confines of the dome itself. As you clamber up between the inner and outer shells, you can observe many ingenious features of Brunelleschi's construction: the ribs and arches, the herringbone brickwork, the wooden struts that support the outer shell – even the hooks and holes left for future generations of repairers. From the base of the white marble lantern that crowns the dome, the views across the city are breathtaking.

The Campanile

The **Campanile** (daily 8.30am–7.30pm; €6) – the cathedral's bell tower – was begun in 1334 by Giotto during his period as official city architect and *capo*

Brunelleschi's dome

Since Arnolfo di Cambio's scale model of the Duomo collapsed under its own weight some time in the fourteenth century, nobody has been sure quite how he intended to crown his achievement. In 1367 Neri di Fioraventi proposed the construction of a magnificent **cupola** that was to span nearly 43m, broader than the dome of Rome's Pantheon, which had remained the world's largest for 1300 years, and rise from a base some 55m above the floor of the nave – taller than the highest vaulting of any Gothic cathedral. Just as radical was Fioraventi's decision to dispense with flying buttresses, regarded as ugly vestiges of the Gothic barbarism of enemy states such as France and Milan.

There was just one problem: nobody had worked out how to build the thing. Medieval arches were usually built on wooden "centring", a network of timbers that held the stone in place until the mortar was set. In the case of the Duomo, the weight of the stone would have been too great for the timber (the entire dome is thought to weigh some 33,000 tonnes), and the space to be spanned was too great for the measuring cords that would be needed to guide the masons – any cord strung across the church would sag and stretch too much for accuracy. A committee of the masons' guild was set up to solve the dilemma. One idea was to build the dome from pumice. Another was to support the dome on a vast mound of earth that would be seeded with thousands of coins; when the dome was finished, the mound would be cleared by inviting Florence's citizens to excavate the money.

After years of bickering the project was thrown open to competition. A goldsmith and clockmaker called **Filippo Brunelleschi** presented the winning scheme, defeating Ghiberti in the process – revenge of sorts for Ghiberti's triumph seventeen years earlier in the competition to design the Baptistery doors (see p.80). Doommongers, Ghiberti among them, criticized Brunelleschi at every turn, eventually

maestro (head of works) in charge of the Duomo. By the time of his death three years later, the base, the first of five eventual levels, had been completed. Andrea Pisano, fresh from creating the Baptistery's south doors, continued construction of the second storey (1337–42), probably in accordance with Giotto's plans. Work was rounded off by Francesco Talenti, who rectified deficiencies in Giotto's original calculations in the process: the base's original walls teetered on the brink of collapse until he doubled their thickness. When completed, the bell tower reached 84.7m, well over the limit set by the city in 1324 for civic towers, the building of which had long been a means of expressing aristocratic or mercantile power.

These days a climb to the summit is one of the highlights of any Florentine trip, though it's worth first taking in the tower's decorative **sculptures and reliefs** (most are now copies, the originals being in the Museo dell'Opera del Duomo). As it moved up the tower, the decoration was intended to mirror humanity's progress from original sin to a state of divine grace, a progress facilitated by manual labour, the arts and the sacraments, and guided by the influence of the planets and the cardinal and theological virtues. Thus the first storey is studded with two rows of bas-reliefs; the lower register, in hexagonal frames – some designed by Giotto, but all executed by Pisano and pupils – illustrates the Creation and Arts and Industries, while in the diamond-shaped panels of the upper register are allegories of the Seven Planets, Seven Sacraments and Seven Virtues. A century or so later Luca della Robbia added the Five Liberal Arts (Grammar, Philosophy, Music, Arithmetic and Astrology) on the north face. Further works in the second-storey niches by Pisano were eventually replaced by Donatello and Nanni di Bartolo's figures of the Prophets, Sibyls, Patriarchs and Kings (1415–36).

forcing the authorities to employ both rivals. An exasperated Brunelleschi feigned illness and resigned. Ghiberti, left to his own devices, found himself baffled, and in 1423 Brunelleschi was invited to become the dome's sole "inventor and chief director".

The key to Brunelleschi's success lay in the construction of the dome as two masonry shells, each built as a stack of ever-diminishing rings. Secured with hidden stone beams and enormous iron chains, these concentric circles formed a lattice that was filled with lightweight bricks laid in a herringbone pattern that prevented the higher sections from falling inward. Brunelleschi's relentless inventiveness extended to a new hoist with a reverse gear, a new type of crane, and even a boat for transporting marble that was so ungainly it was nicknamed *Il Badalone* (the Monster).

The dome's completion was marked by the **consecration** of the cathedral on March 25, 1436 – Annunciation Day, and the Florentine New Year – in a ceremony conducted by the pope. Even then, the topmost piece, the lantern, remained unfinished, with many people convinced the dome could support no further weight. But once again Brunelleschi won the day, beginning work on the dome's final stage in 1446, just a few months before his death. The whole thing was finally completed in the late 1460s, when the cross and gilded ball, both cast by Verrocchio, were hoisted into place.

Today it is still the largest masonry dome in the world. Only the gallery around the base remains incomplete – abandoned with just one face finished after Michelangelo compared it to "cages for crickets". This criticism aside, Michelangelo was awestruck: gazing on the cupola he is supposed to have said: *Come te non voglio, meglio di te non posso* ("Similar to you I will not, better than you I cannot").

The parapet at the top of the tower is a less lofty but in many ways more satisfying viewpoint than the cathedral dome, if only because the view takes in the Duomo itself. Be warned, though, that there are 414 steps to the summit – and no lift.

The Baptistery

Florence's **Baptistery** (Mon–Sat noon–7pm, Sun & first Sat of month 8.30am–2pm; €3) stands immediately west of the Duomo, whose geometrically patterned marble cladding mirrors that of the smaller, older building. Generally thought to date from the sixth or seventh century, the Baptistery is the oldest building in Florence, first documented in 897, when it was recorded as the city's cathedral before Santa Reparata. Though its origins lie buried in the Dark Ages, no building better illustrates the special relationship between Florence and the Roman world.

The Florentines were always conscious of their **Roman** ancestry, and for centuries believed that the Baptistery was a converted Roman temple to Mars, originally built to celebrate the defeat of Fiesole and the city's foundation. This belief was bolstered by the interior's ancient granite columns, probably taken from the city's old Roman Capitol (other columns from this site found their way to San Miniato). Further proof was apparently provided by traces of an ancient pavement mosaic, remains now thought to belong to an old Roman bakery. But if the building itself is not Roman, its exterior marble cladding – applied in a Romanesque reworking between about 1059 and 1128 – is clearly classical in inspiration, while its most famous embellishments, the gilded

bronze doors, mark the emergence of a more scholarly, self-conscious interest in the art of the ancient world.

The south doors

Responsibility for the Baptistery's improvement and upkeep lay with the Arte di Calimala, the most powerful of Florence's guilds. It was they who initiated the building's eleventh-century revamp, and they who in the 1320s turned their attention to the exterior, and in particular to the question of a suitably majestic entrance. In this they were stung into action by arch-rival Pisa, whose cathedral was not only famous for its bronze portals, but whose craftsmen had recently completed some celebrated bronze doors for the great cathedral at Monreale in Sicily.

The arrival of Andrea Pisano in Florence in 1330 offered the chance of similar glories. Within three months the Pisan sculptor had created wax models for what would become the Baptistery's **south doors**. (They were originally placed in the east portal, but were displaced when Ghiberti's "Gates of Paradise" – see below – were finished.) Over the next eight years the models were cast in bronze, probably with the assistance of Venetian bell-makers, then Italy's most accomplished bronzesmiths. Twenty of the doors' 28 panels, installed in 1339, form a narrative on the life of St John the Baptist, patron saint of Florence and the Baptistery's dedicatee; the lowest eight reliefs depict Humility and the Cardinal and Theological Virtues. The figures above the portal – the Baptist, Salome and executioner – are copies of late-sixteenth-century additions; the originals are in the Museo dell'Opera del Duomo.

The north doors

Some sixty years of financial and political turmoil, and the ravages of the Black Death, prevented further work on the Baptistery's other entrances until 1401. That year a competition was held to design a new set of doors, each of the six main entrants being asked to create a panel showing the Sacrifice of Isaac. The doors were to be a votive offering, a gift to God to celebrate the passing of another plague epidemic.

The judges found themselves equally impressed by the work of two young goldsmiths, Brunelleschi and **Lorenzo Ghiberti** (both winning entries are displayed in the Bargello). Unable to choose between the pair, it appears that the judges suggested that the two work in tandem. Brunelleschi replied that if he couldn't do the job alone he wasn't interested – whereupon the contract was handed to Ghiberti, leaving his rival to stomp off to study architecture in Rome. Ghiberti, barely 20 years old, was to devote much of the next 25 years to this one project, albeit in the company of distinguished assistants such as Masolino, Donatello and Paolo Uccello. His fame rests almost entirely on the extraordinary result.

His **north doors** (1403–24) show a new naturalism and classicized sense of composition, copying Pisano's 28-panel arrangement while transcending its traditional Gothic approach: the upper twenty panels depict scenes from the New Testament, while the eight lower panels describe the Four Evangelists and Four Doctors of the Church.

The east doors

The north doors, while extraordinary, are as nothing to the sublime **east doors** (1425–52), ordered from Ghiberti as soon as the first set was finished. The artist would spend some 27 years on the new project, work which he pursued, in his own words, "with the greatest diligence and greatest love". These doors have long been known as the "Gates of Paradise", supposedly because Michelangelo once remarked that they were so beautiful they deserved to be the portals of heaven. However, it's more likely that the name came about because these doors face the cathedral – the space between a cathedral and its baptistery was known as the *Paradiso*, because the sacrament of baptism put its recipient on the threshold of paradise.

The doors have just ten panels, a departure from both previous sets of doors, while their enclosing squares abandon the Gothic diamond or quatrefoil frame. Unprecedented in the subtlety of their casting, the **Old Testament scenes** – the Creation, the Ten Commandments, the Sacrifice of Isaac, and so on – are a primer of early Renaissance art, using rigorous perspective, gesture and sophisticated groupings to intensify the drama of each scene. Ghiberti's power of compression and detail is such that several narratives are often woven into a single scene. The sculptor has also included an understandably self-satisfied self-portrait in the frame of the left-hand door: his is the fourth head from the top of the right-hand band – the bald chap with the smirk. The gorgeous golden doors now in place are reproductions; the original panels are exhibited in the Museo dell'Opera del Duomo.

The pair of pitted **marble columns** to the side of the east doors were presented by the city of Pisa in the twelfth century, and would have been slotted into the walls had they not turned out to be too weak to bear any substantial weight. Another marble column, just north of the Baptistery, is decorated with bronze branches and leaves to commemorate a miracle of January 429 AD, brought about by the body of St Zenobius, Florence's first bishop; as the corpse was being carried from San Lorenzo into Santa Reparata it brushed against a barren elm here, which thereupon sprang into leaf.

The interior

The Baptistery **interior** is stunning, with its black-and-white marble cladding and miscellany of ancient columns below a blazing **mosaic ceiling**. Mosaics were not a Florentine speciality – in the centuries to come they would give way to fresco, but in the thirteenth century they were the predominant decorative medium. Encouraged by the interest surrounding the restoration of mosaics then taking place in the early Christian basilicas of Rome and Ravenna, the city was keen to match its rivals, principally Venice.

The earliest mosaics (1225) lie above the square apse, and depict the Virgin and John the Baptist. Above them, a wheel of prophets encircles the Lamb of God. The main vault is dominated by a vast figure of Christ in Judgement, flanked by depictions of Paradise and Hell. Just to the left of the monstrous, man-eating Lucifer, the poet Virgil (in a white cloak) can be seen leading Dante (in black) through the Inferno. These figures were a later insertion, added after the poet's death during something of a frenzy of recognition. The other five sections of the octagonal ceiling depict Biblical scenes, beginning above the north doors with the Creation, and proceeding through the stories of Joseph and John the Baptist towards the Crucifixion and Resurrection, seen above the south doors.

The interior's semi-abstract **mosaic pavement** also dates from the thirteenth century. The empty octagon at its centre marks the spot once occupied by the huge font in which every child born in the city during the previous twelve months would be baptized on March 25 (New Year's Day in the old Florentine calendar). When a child was born, a coloured bean was dropped into an urn in the Baptistery: black for a boy, white for a girl – a system which allowed the birth rate to be calculated.

To the right of the altar lies the **tomb of Baldassare Cossa**, the schismatic Pope John XXIII, who was deposed in 1415 and died in Florence in 1419. At the time of his death he was a guest of his financial adviser and close friend, Giovanni di Bicci de' Medici, the man who established the Medici at the political forefront of Florence. It was through Pope John that Giovanni became chief banker to the Papal Curia, a deal that laid the foundations of the Medici fortune: for years over half the Medici's profits would come from just two Rome-based banks. The monument, draped by an illusionistic marble canopy, is the work of Donatello and his pupil Michelozzo.

The Museo dell'Opera del Duomo

In 1296 a body called the Opera del Duomo, literally the "Work of the Duomo", was created to oversee the maintenance of the Duomo. Since the early fifteenth century its home has been the building behind the east end of the cathedral at Piazza del Duomo 9, which now also houses the **Museo dell'Opera del Duomo** (Mon–Sat 9am–7.30pm, Sun 9am–1.40pm; €6), a repository of the most precious and fragile works of art from the Duomo, Baptistery and Campanile. As an overview of the sculpture of Florence the museum is second only to the Bargello. Incidentally, you can see the stonemasons of the present-day Opera at work in their studio at Via dello Studio 23a, on the south side of the Duomo.

The ground floor

Beyond the ticket office, rooms devoted to sculpture from the Baptistery (mostly works by Tino da Camaino) and the Duomo's lateral doors precede the museum's **courtyard**, a site thick with historical associations despite its ultra-modern makeover: it was here that much of Michelangelo's *David* was sculpted. Now glazed over, the courtyard is home to all eight of Ghiberti's panels from the "Doors of Paradise", sharing the space with the graceful *Baptism of Christ* (1502–25), by Andrea Sansovino and assistants.

The largest room on this floor is a large hall devoted to the original sculptures of the cathedral's west front, foremost among which are works by the cathedral's first architect, **Arnolfo di Cambio** (and his workshop), including an eerily glass-eyed *Madonna and Child*; all were rescued from Arnolfo's quarter-finished cathedral facade which was pulled down by Ferdinand I in 1587. Equally striking is the sculptor's vase-carrying figure of *St Reparata*, one of Florence's patron saints, a work long thought to be of Greek or Roman origin. Also noteworthy is the ramrod-straight statue of *Boniface VIII*, whose corruption earned him a place in Dante's *Inferno*, which was partly written during Boniface's pontificate. Along the entrance wall are four seated figures of the Evangelists, also wrenched from the facade: Nanni di Banco's *St Luke* and **Donatello**'s *St John* are particularly fine.

The room off the far end of the hall features a sequence of **marble reliefs** (1547–72) by Bacio Bandinelli and Giovanni Bandini, part of an unfinished sequence of 300 panels proposed for the choir of the cathedral. Also here is a collection of paintings from a series of altars in the cathedral, all torn from their original home in 1838 as they were considered an affront to the purity of the building. The adjoining modern **octagonal chapel** features an assembly of reliquaries which contain, among other saintly remains, the jaw of Saint Jerome and an index finger of John the Baptist. It's easy to miss the room off to the right of the **Lapidarium** (a collection of modest works in stone), which contains items removed from the cathedral's Porta della

Mandorla, including a lovely terracotta *Creation of Eve* (1410) attributed to Donatello.

The upper floor

Up the stairs on the mezzanine level stands **Michelangelo**'s anguished **Pietà** (1550–53), moved from the cathedral as recently as 1981 while restoration of the dome was in progress, but probably fated to stay here. This is one of the sculptor's last works, carved when he was almost 80, and was intended for his own tomb; Vasari records that the face of Nicodemus is a self-portrait. Dissatisfied with the quality of the marble, Michelangelo mutilated the group by hammering off the left leg and arm of Christ; his pupil Tiberio Calcagni restored the arm, then finished off the figure of Mary Magdalene, turning her into a whey-faced supporting player.

Although he's represented on the lower floor, it's upstairs that **Donatello**, the greatest of Michelangelo's precursors, really comes to the fore. The first room at the top of the stairs features his magnificent **Cantoria**, or choir-loft (1433–39), with its playground of boisterous putti. Facing it is another splendid *cantoria* (1431–38), the first-known major commission of the young Luca della Robbia (the originals are underneath, with casts replacing them in the *cantoria* itself); the earnest musicians embody the text from Psalm 150 which is inscribed on the frame: "Praise him with the sound of the trumpet; praise him with the psaltery and harp." Both lofts were dismantled and removed from their position above the cathedral's sacristies in 1688 on the occasion of the ill-fated marriage of Violante Beatrice of Bavaria to Ferdinand de' Medici, the ineffectual heir of Cosimo III. The ceremony gave the cathedral authorities the excuse to decorate the cathedral in a more fitting "modern" style, and the ensuing clearout left the *cantorie* languishing in dusty storage for some two centuries.

Around the room are arrayed the life-size figures that Donatello carved for the Campanile, perhaps the most powerful of which is the prophet Habbakuk, the intensity of whose gaze is said to have prompted the sculptor to seize it and yell "Speak, speak!" Donatello was apparently also responsible for the statue's nickname *Lo Zuccone* (the Pumpkin) – after its bald head. Keeping company with Donatello's work are four Prophets (1348–50) and two Sibyls (1342–48) attributed to Andrea Pisano, and *The Sacrifice of Isaac* (1421), a collaboration between Nanni di Bartolo and Donatello.

Donatello's later style is exemplified by the gaunt wooden figure of Mary Magdalene (1453–55), which confronts you on entering the room off the *cantorie* room. The *Magdalene* came from the Baptistery, as did the silver altarfront at the far end of the room, a dazzling summary of the life of St John the Baptist. Begun in 1366, the piece was completed in 1480, the culmination of a century of labour by, among others, Michelozzo (responsible for the central figure of *John the Baptist*), Verrocchio (the *Decapitation* to the right) and Antonio del Pollaiuolo (the *Birth of Jesus* on the left side), who was the chief creator of the silver cross atop the altar. Ranged around the walls are more reliquaries, fabrics, copes and other religious vestments, including 27 sublimely worked **needlework panels** – former vestments and altar panels from the Baptistery – produced between 1466 and 1487 by French, Flemish and Florentine artists, including members of the Arte di Calimala (one of the chief textile guilds), working to designs by Pollaiuolo. Not surprisingly, given their provenance, they portray scenes from the life of the Baptist, one of Florence's patrons and the Baptistery's dedicatee.

In the room on the other side of the *cantorie* room you'll find the **bas-reliefs** that once adorned the Campanile. Though darkened with age, their allegorical panels remain both striking and intelligible, depicting the spiritual refinement of humanity through labour, the arts and, ultimately, the virtues and sacraments. The display reproduces the reliefs' original arrangement, the key panels being the hexagonal reliefs of the lower tier, all of which – save for the last five, by Luca della Robbia (1437–39) – were the work of Andrea Pisano and his son Nino (c.1348–50), probably to designs by Giotto.

A corridor at the end of Room II leads past a mock-up of Brunelleschi's building site, complete with broken bricks, wooden scaffolding and some of the tools that were used to build the dome, many invented specifically for the purpose by the architect himself. More arresting is Brunelleschi's **death mask**, which almost – but not quite – looks out of the window at the dome just across the way.

The sequence of rooms beyond displays various proposals for completing the balcony of the drum below the cupola and the Duomo's west front, including models created by Michelangelo, Giuliano da Maiano, Giambologna, Antonio da Sangallo, Andrea Sansovino and other leading architects. The wooden model of the **cathedral lantern** is presumed to have been made by Brunelleschi as part of his winning proposal for the design of the lantern in 1436. The final room, just off the main staircase, shows plans submitted to the three competitions held in the 1860s, when Florence was briefly capital of Italy and the question of the facade standing "ignominious in faded stucco", as George Eliot put it, once more became pressing. Emilio de Fabris's winning design of 1876 is mostly remarkable for how little it differs from the other nineteenth-century Gothic pastiches.

The Museo di Firenze com'era

The top of Via del Proconsolo, just a few yards from the Museo dell'Opera del Duomo, forms a major junction with Via dell'Oriuolo, home to the **Museo di Firenze com'era** (June–Sept Mon & Tues 9am–2pm, Sat 9am–7pm; Oct–May Mon–Wed 9am–2pm, Sat 9am–7pm; €2.70). This "Museum of Florence as it used to be" is one of the city's unsung museums, but its contents and setting – in a pleasant garden-fronted palazzo – are delightful.

The story begins with a collection of models, plans and photographs of the excavation of the Piazza della Signoria that took place in the 1980s. As one would expect, a number of discoveries were made, but for want of any better ideas the piazza was simply paved over once the dig was complete. A large, somewhat speculative model of the **Roman city** stands at the far end of the room, with coloured sections showing the buildings whose locations the archeologists are sure of.

The long, vaulted main gallery stands on the other side of the entrance corridor. Maps, prints, photos and topographical paintings chart the growth of Florence from the fifteenth century to the present, and while none of the exhibits is a masterpiece, most of them are at least informative. Perhaps the most impressive item comes right at the start: a meticulous 1887 reproduction of a colossal 1472 aerial view of Florence called the *Pianta della Catena* (Chain Map), the original of which was destroyed in Berlin during World War II. It's the oldest accurate representation of the city's layout.

Almost as appealing are the twelve lunette pictures (1555) of the **Medici villas**, reproductions of which you'll see on postcards and posters across the city. They're the work of Flemish painter Justus Utens and were painted for the Medici's Villa dell'Artimino. A poignant wooden model portrays the labyrinthine jumble of the **Mercato Vecchio**, the city's ancient heart, which was demolished to make space for the Piazza della Repubblica at the end of the nineteenth century. Elsewhere, a graphic picture portrays Savonarola's execution (see p.131), and eighteenth-century Florence is celebrated in the elegiac engravings of Giuseppe Zocchi.

The Museo del Bigallo and Piazza della Repubblica

On the other side of Piazza del Duomo, at the top of Via de' Calzaiuoli, stands the **Loggia del Bigallo**, which was built in the 1350s for the Compagnia della Misericordia, a charitable organization founded by St Peter Martyr in 1244, to give aid to the sick and to bury the dead. (The Misericordia still exists: their headquarters is just across the way, with their ambulances parked outside.) By the time the loggia was built, the Misericordia was also functioning as an orphanage – the building was commissioned as a place to display abandoned babies, in the hope that they might be recognized before being given to foster parents. For most of the fifteenth century the Misericordia was united with another orphanage, Compagnia del Bigallo (from the village in which it began), hence the loggia's name. Nowadays it houses the three-room **Museo del Bigallo** (Wed–Mon 9.30am–5.30pm; €5), which contains a tiny collection of religious paintings commissioned by the two companies. As you might expect, the Madonna and Child is a dominant theme, and St Peter Martyr is present as well, but the two highlights are a remnant of a fresco painted on the outside of the loggia in 1386, showing the transfer of infants to their adoptive parents, and the *Madonna of the Misericordia*, painted by a follower of Bernardo Daddi in 1342, which features the oldest known panorama of Florence.

A minute's stroll south of the Bigallo museum you'll find the vacant expanse of **Piazza della Repubblica**. Impressive solely for its size, this square was planned in the late 1860s, when it was decided to demolish the central marketplace (Mercato Vecchio) and the tenements of the Jewish quarter in order to give Florence a public space befitting the capital of the recently formed Italian nation. The clearance had not even begun when, in 1870, the capital was transferred to Rome, and it wasn't until 1885 that the Mercato Vecchio and its disease-ridden slums were finally swept away. On the west side a vast **arch** bears the triumphant inscription: "The ancient city centre restored to new life from the squalor of centuries." The freestanding **column** is the solitary trace of the piazza's history. Once surrounded by stalls, it used to be topped by Donatello's statue of *Abundance*, and a bell that was rung to signal the start and close of trading.

Nowadays, Piazza della Repubblica is best known for the three large and expensive **cafés** that stand on the perimeter: the *Gilli*, the most attractive of the trio, founded way back in 1733 (albeit on a different site – it moved here in 1910); the *Giubbe Rosse*, once the intellectuals' café of choice (the Futurist manifesto was launched here in 1909); and the *Paszkowski*, which began business as a beer hall in the 1840s, is now a listed historic monument, and bears the suffix "Caffè Concerto", betokening the smarmy music with which it beguiles the piazza most evenings.

Piazza della Signoria and around

Whereas the Piazza del Duomo provides the focus for the city's religious life, the **Piazza della Signoria** – site of the mighty **Palazzo Vecchio** and forecourt to the **Uffizi** – has always been the centre of its secular existence.

The Palazzo Vecchio is still the HQ of the city's councillors and bureaucrats, and the piazza in front of it is the stage for major civic events and political rallies. After work hundreds of Florentines gather here for a gossip before taking the evening *passeggiata* back and forth between the Signoria and Piazza del Duomo, along the broad pedestrianized avenue of **Via dei Calzaiuoli**. Shop-lined for almost its entire length, Via dei Calzaiuoli boasts one great monument, **Orsanmichele**, a church as notable for its statuary as for the structure itself. There's one other major religious building in this area: the **Badìa Fiorentina**, the most important of several buildings in a district that has strong associations with Florence's – indeed Italy's – foremost poet, Dante Alighieri. Immediately opposite the Badìa stands the forbidding bulk of the **Bargello**, once the city's prison, now home to a superb assemblage of sculpture, plus excellent collections of enamels, ivories, glassware, silverware and other *objets d'art*. To get a full idea of the achievement of the Florentine Renaissance, a visit to the Bargello is as important as a day in the Uffizi. And as a corrective to the notion that Florence's contribution to European civilization has been limited to the arts, you might call in at the fascinating **Museo di Storia della Scienza,** which is tucked away at the back of the Uffizi.

Piazza della Signoria

The piazza took on a public role in 1307, when a small area was laid out to provide a suitable setting for the Palazzo Vecchio, then known as the Palazzo dei Priori. All efforts to enlarge it over the next hundred years – a job sub-contracted to the Opera del Duomo, the city's largest construction company – were hampered by work on the palace and Loggia della Signoria. Contemporary accounts talk of decades when the area was little more than a rubble-filled building site, but by 1385 it was completely paved, and wheeled traffic was banned from the area (as it still is). Further restructuring occurred during Cosimo I's reordering of the Uffizi around 1560, and more alterations followed in 1871, when the medieval Loggia dei Pisani was demolished, opening up much of the square's present-day westward sweep.

The statues

Florence's political volatility is encapsulated by the piazza's array of **statues**. From left to right, the line-up starts with Giambologna's equestrian statue of **Cosimo I** (1587–94). An echo of the famous Marcus Aurelius statue in Rome, it was designed to draw parallels between the power of medieval Florence (and thus Cosimo) and the glory of imperial Rome. Three bas-reliefs at the base portray key events in Cosimo's career: becoming duke of Florence (1537); the conquest of Siena (1555); and acquiring the title Grand Duke of Tuscany (1569) from Pius V.

Next comes Ammannati's fatuous **Neptune Fountain** (1565–75), a tribute to Cosimo's prowess as a naval commander; Neptune himself is a lumpen lout of a figure, who provoked Michelangelo to coin the rhyming put-down *Ammannato, Ammannato, che bel marmo hai rovinato* ("… what a fine piece of marble you've ruined"). After a copy of Donatello's **Marzocco** (1418–20), the original of which is in the Bargello, comes a copy of the same sculptor's **Judith and Holofernes** (1456–60), which freezes the action at the moment Judith's arm begins its scything stroke – a dramatic conception that no other sculptor of the period would have attempted. Commissioned by Cosimo de' Medici, this statue doubled as a fountain in the Palazzo Medici but was removed to the Piazza della Signoria after the expulsion of the family in 1495,

The Florentine Republic

Dante compared Florence's constant political struggles to a sick man forever shifting his position in bed, and indeed its medieval history often appears a catalogue of incessant civic unrest. Yet between 1293 and 1534 – bar the odd ruction – the city maintained a **republican** constitution that was embodied in well-defined institutions. The nucleus of this structure was formed by the city's merchants and guilds, who covertly controlled Florence as early as the twelfth century and formalized their influence during the so-called **Primo Popolo** (1248–59), a quasi-democratic regime whose ten-year rule, claimed Dante, was the only period of civic peace in Florence's history. During the **Secondo Popolo** (1284), the leading guilds, the *Arti Maggiori*, introduced the **Ordinamenti della Giustizia** (1293), a written constitution that entrenched mercantile power still further and was to be the basis of Florence's government for the next two hundred and fifty years.

The rulers of this much-vaunted republic were drawn exclusively from the ranks of guild members over the age of 30, and were chosen in a public ceremony held every two months, the short tenure being designed to prevent individuals or cliques assuming too much power. At this ceremony, the names of selected guild members were placed in eight leather bags (*borse*) kept in the sacristy of Santa Croce; the ones picked from the bags duly became the **Priori** (or *Signori*), forming a government called the **Signoria**, usually comprising nine men, most of them from the *Arti Maggiori*. Once elected, the *Priori* moved into the Palazzo della Signoria, where they were expected to stay, virtually incommunicado, for their period of office – though they were waited on hand and foot, and enjoyed the services of a professional joke-teller, the *Buffone*.

Headed by the **Gonfaloniere** (literally the "Standard-Bearer"), the *Signoria* consulted two elected councils or **Collegi** – the **Dodici Buonomini** (Twelve Citizens) and **Sedici Gonfalonieri** (Sixteen Standard-Bearers) – as well as committees introduced to deal with specific crises (the Ten of War, the Eight of Security, the Six of Commerce ...). Permanent officials included the Chancellor (a post once held by Machiavelli) and the **Podestà**, a chief magistrate brought in from a neighbouring city as an independent arbitrator, and housed in the Bargello. In times of extreme crisis, such as the Pazzi Conspiracy (see box, p.76), all male citizens over the age of 14 were summoned to a **Parlamento** in Piazza della Signoria by the tolling of the Palazzo Vecchio's famous bell, known as the *Vacca* (Cow), after its deep, bovine tone. When a two-thirds quorum was reached, the people were asked to approve a **Balìa**, a committee delegated to deal with the situation as it saw fit.

All this looked good on paper but in practice the set-up was far from democratic. The lowliest workers, the **Popolo Minuto**, were totally excluded, as were the **Grandi**, or nobles. And despite the *Signoria*'s apparently random selection process, political cliques had few problems ensuring that only the names of likely supporters found their way into the *borse*. If a rogue candidate slipped through the net, or things went awry, then a *Parlamento* was summoned, a *Balìa* formed, and the offending person replaced by a more pliable candidate. It was by such means that the great mercantile dynasties of Florence – the Peruzzi, the Albizzi, the Strozzi, and of course the Medici – retained their power even when not technically in office.

to be displayed as an emblem of vanquished tyranny; a new inscription on the base reinforced the message for those too obtuse to get it. The original is in the Palazzo Vecchio.

Michelangelo's **David**, at first intended for the Duomo, was also installed here as a declaration of civic solidarity by the Florentine Republic; the original is now cooped up in the Accademia. Conceived as partner piece to the *David*, Bandinelli's **Hercules and Cacus** (1534) was designed as a personal emblem of Cosimo I and a symbol of Florentine fortitude. Benvenuto Cellini described the musclebound figure as looking like "a sackful of melons", and it's a sobering thought that the marble might well have ended up as something more inspiring. In the late 1520s, when the Florentines were once again busy tearing the Medici emblem from every building on which it had been stuck, Michelangelo offered to carve a monumental figure of Samson to celebrate the Republic's latest victory over tyranny; other demands on the artist's time put paid to this project, and the stone passed to Bandinelli, who duly vented his mediocrity on it.

The Loggia della Signoria

The square's grace note, the **Loggia della Signoria**, was begun in 1376, prompted by that year's heavy rains, which had washed out Florence's entire calendar of public ceremonies. It was completed in 1382, serving as a dais for city dignitaries, a forum for meeting foreign emissaries, and a platform for the swearing-in of public officials. Its alternative name, the Loggia dei Lanzi, comes from Cosimo I's bodyguard of Swiss lancers, who were garrisoned nearby.

Although Donatello's *Judith and Holofernes* was placed here as early as 1506, it was only in the late eighteenth century that the loggia became exclusively a showcase for sculpture. In the corner nearest the Palazzo Vecchio stands a figure that has become one of the iconic images of the Renaissance, Benvenuto Cellini's **Perseus** (1545), now back in its rightful place after a painstaking restoration. (The base is a copy, however; the original is on display in the Bargello.) Made for Cosimo I, the statue symbolizes the triumph of firm Grand Ducal rule over the monstrous indiscipline of all other forms of government. The traumatic process of the statue's creation is vividly described in Cellini's riproaring autobiography: seeing the molten bronze beginning to solidify too early, the ever-resourceful hero saved the day by flinging all his pewter plates into the

▲ The Loggia della Signoria

mix. When the bronze cooled the figure emerged from the mould missing only three toes, which were added later.

Equally attention-seeking is Giambologna's last work, to the right, **The Rape of the Sabine** (1583), conjured from the largest piece of sculptural marble ever seen in Florence, and the epitome of the Mannerist obsession with spiralling forms. The sculptor supposedly intended the piece merely as a study of old age, male strength and female beauty: the present name was coined later. The figures along the back wall are Roman works, traditionally believed to portray Roman empresses, while of the three central statues only one – Giambologna's **Hercules Slaying the Centaur** (1599) – deserves its place. The seven figures in the spandrels between the arches above depict the Virtues (1384–89), all carved to designs by Agnolo Gaddi save the head of *Faith*, which was replaced by Donatello when the original crashed to the ground.

The Palazzo Vecchio

Probably designed by Arnolfo di Cambio, the **Palazzo Vecchio** (daily 9am–7pm; Thurs closes 2pm; €6), Florence's fortress-like town hall, was begun as the Palazzo dei Priori in the last year of the thirteenth century, to provide premises for the *Priori,* the name given to the members of the ruling *Signoria*. Changes in the Florentine constitution over the years entailed alterations to the layout of the palace, the most radical coming in 1540, when Cosimo I moved his retinue here from the Palazzo Medici and grafted a huge extension onto the rear. The Medici remained in residence for only nine years before moving to the Palazzo Pitti; the "old" (*vecchio*) palace, which they left to their son, Francesco, then acquired its present name. Between 1865 and 1870, during Florence's brief tenure as capital of a newly united Italy, the palace housed the country's parliament and foreign ministry.

As for the sights, much of the palace's decoration comprises a relentless eulogy to Cosimo and his relations, propaganda that's made tolerable by some of the palace's examples of Mannerist art – among the finest pieces produced by that ultra-sophisticated and self-conscious movement. There are also frescoes by Domenico Ghirlandaio and some outstanding sculptures, not least works by Michelangelo and Donatello. It's also possible to visit hidden parts of the palace on hour-long guided **tours** known as Percorsi Segreti (see box, p.90).

The courtyard and first floor

Work on the palace's beautiful inner **courtyard** was begun by Michelozzo in 1453. The decoration was largely added by Vasari, court architect from 1555 until his death in 1574, on the occasion of Francesco de' Medici's marriage to Johanna of Austria in 1565. The bride's origin explains the otherwise puzzling presence of cities belonging to the Habsburg Empire amid the wall's painted townscapes. Vasari also designed the central fountain, though the winsome putto and dolphin (1476) at its crown are the work of Verrocchio (the present statues are copies; the originals are on the Terrazzo di Giunone on the palace's second floor). Vasari was also let loose on the **monumental staircase**, which leads to the first floor (though visitors are often directed to take a different route upstairs).

Vasari was given full rein in the huge **Salone dei Cinquecento** at the top of the stairs. It was originally built in 1495 as the meeting hall for the Consiglio Maggiore (Great Council), the ruling assembly of the penultimate republic. The chamber might have had one of Italy's most remarkable decorative schemes: Leonardo da Vinci and Michelangelo were employed to paint frescoes on opposite sides of the room, but Leonardo's work, *The Battle of Anghiari*, was abandoned (or destroyed) after his experimental technique went wrong, while Michelangelo's *The Battle of Cascina* had got no further than a fragmentary cartoon when he was summoned to Rome by Pope Julius II in 1506. Instead, the hall received six drearily bombastic murals (1563–65) – painted either by Vasari or under his direction – illustrating Florentine military triumphs over Pisa (1496–1509) and Siena (1554–55). It has generally been assumed that Vasari obliterated whatever remained of Leonardo's fresco before beginning his work, but the discovery of a cavity behind *The Battle of Marciano* has raised the possibility that Vasari instead constructed a false wall for his fresco, to preserve his great predecessor's painting. Investigations are proceeding.

The **ceiling**'s 39 panels, again by Vasari, celebrate the *Apotheosis of Cosimo I* (centre), a scene surrounded by the crests of the city's guilds and further paeans to the prowess of Florence and the Medici. (One of the Percorsi Segreti takes you into the attic above the roof, an extraordinary space where it's possible to see how Vasari pulled off the trick of suspending such a large ceiling without visible supports.) Of the **sculpture**, the highlight is Michelangelo's *Victory*, almost opposite the entrance door. Carved for the tomb of Pope Julius II, the statue was donated to the Medici by the artist's nephew, then installed here by Vasari in 1565 to celebrate Cosimo's defeat of the Sienese ten years earlier. Directly opposite, on the entrance wall, is the original plaster model of a companion piece for the *Victory*, Giambologna's **Virtue Overcoming Vice**, another artistic metaphor for Florentine military might – this time Florence's victory over Pisa. The remaining statues, the

Percorsi Segreti

The Palazzo Vecchio's various so-called **Percorsi Segreti** ("Secret Paşsageways") allow access – on guided tours only, of up to twelve people at a time – to parts of the building that are normally off limits. Most visually impressive is the trip up through the palace and into the **Attic of the Salone del Cinquecento**. From the vantage point of a balcony high above the hall, the guide describes the complex way in which Vasari created such a huge space within the medieval structure, and explains the allegorical meaning of the paintings. You are then led up into the vast attic itself, where two sets of trusses support the roof above and the ceiling below. Some of the beams are more than 20m long.

Less spectacular, but still worth it for the guide's commentary, is the route leading from the street outside up through the secret **Stairway of the Duke of Athens**. The doorway was knocked through the exterior wall of the Palazzo in 1342 as an emergency escape route for the duke, who briefly took up the reins of power here. He never in fact used the staircase, but only because his fall from grace came rather sooner than he had imagined. Another Percorso Segreto allows you inside the **Studiolo di Francesco I**, then through one of the hidden doors and up a secret little staircase to the *studiolino* or **Tesoretto** (6), Cosimo's tiny private study, which was built ten years before the *studiolo*.

Tickets cost €8 (including admission to the Palazzo Vecchio); tours take place every day between 10am and 5pm in Italian, French and/or English, and last roughly 75 minutes. Exactly what language the tours are conducted in depends on demand, but there's usually at least one English-language party for each Percorso every day. Places must be reserved in advance, either at the office next to the Palazzo Vecchio ticket desk or by phone, on ☏055.276.8224 or 055.276.8558.

masterpiece of sixteenth-century artist Vincenzo de' Rossi, portray the **Labours of Hercules** and are yet another example of Florentine heroic propaganda: the innocuously classical Hercules is also one of Florence's many civic symbols.

From the Salone del Cinquecento, a roped-off door allows a glimpse of the strangest room in the building, the **Studiolo di Francesco I** (5). Designed by Vasari towards the end of his career and decorated by no fewer than thirty Mannerist artists (1570–74), this windowless cell was created as a retreat for the introverted son of Cosimo and Eleanor. Each of the miniature bronzes and nearly all the paintings reflect Francesco's interest in the sciences and alchemy: the entrance wall pictures illustrate the theme of Earth, while the others, reading clockwise, signify Water, Air and Fire. The outstanding paintings are the two that don't fit the scheme: Bronzino's portraits of the occupant's parents, facing each other across the room. The oval paintings on the panels at the base hinted at the presence of Francesco's most treasured knick-knacks, which were once concealed in the compartments behind; the wooden structure is actually a nineteenth-century re-creation, though the paintings are original.

Much of the rest of this floor is still used by council officials, though if the seven rooms of the **Quartiere di Leone X** and **Sala dei Dugento** are open (they rarely are), don't miss the opportunity. The latter, in particular, is outstanding: Benedetto and Giuliano da Maiano, excellent sculptors both, were responsible for the design (1472–77) and for the fine wooden ceiling; the tapestries (1546–53) were created to designs by Bronzino, Pontormo and others.

The second floor

Steps lead from the Salone to the **second floor**, passing an intriguing fireworks fresco (1558) showing Piazza della Signoria during the celebrations for the feast of St John the Baptist. Turn left at the top of the stairs and you enter the **Quartiere degli Elementi**, one of the floor's three distinct suites of rooms. All five salons here are slavishly devoted to a different member of the Medici clan. Persevere, though, if only to enjoy the city **views** from the Terrazza di Saturno and Verrocchio's original *Putto and Dolphin* statue on the Terrazzo di Giunone.

Return to the stairs and head straight on and you cross a gallery with views down into the Salone. Immediately afterwards come the **Quartiere di Eleonora di Toledo**, the private apartments of Cosimo I's wife. The first room, the **Camera Verde**, has some charming wildlife on its ceiling, but the star turn is the tiny and exquisite **Cappella di Eleonora**, vividly decorated by Bronzino in the 1540s. The wall paintings show scenes from the life of Moses, episodes probably intended to draw parallels with the life of Cosimo. In the *Annunciation* that flanks the *Deposition* on the back wall, Bronzino is said to have used Cosimo and Eleonora's eldest daughter as the model for the Virgin.

Those who find all this Mannerist stuff unhealthily airless can take refuge in the more summery rooms which follow. The **Sala dell'Udienza**, originally the audience chamber of the Republic, boasts a stunning gilt-coffered ceiling by Giuliano da Maiano. The Mannerists reassert themselves with a vast fresco sequence (1545–48) by Cecchino Salviati, a cycle widely considered to be this artist's most accomplished work.

Giuliano was also responsible, with his brother Benedetto, for the intarsia work on the doors and the lovely doorway that leads into the **Sala dei Gigli**, a room that takes its name from the lilies (*gigli*) that adorn most of its surfaces – the lily is the emblem of Saint Zenobius and of the Virgin, both patron saints of Florence. The room has another splendid ceiling by the Maiano brothers, and a wall frescoed by Domenico Ghirlandaio with Sts Zenobius, Stephen and Lorenzo (1481–85) and lunettes portraying *Six Heroes of Ancient Rome*. The undoubted highlight here, however, is Donatello's original **Judith and Holofernes** (1455–60), removed from Piazza della Signoria.

Two small rooms are attached to the Sala dei Gigli: the **Cancelleria**, once Machiavelli's office and now containing a bust and portrait of the oft-maligned political thinker, and the lovely **Sala delle Carte**, formerly the Guardaroba (Wardrobe), the repository of Cosimo's state finery. Now it is decorated with 57 maps painted in 1563 by the court astronomer Fra' Ignazio Danti, depicting what was then the entire known world. One of the maps, in the far right-hand corner, conceals a door to a hidden staircase.

A door leads out from the second floor onto the broad balcony of the Palazzo Vecchio's **tower**. The views are superb, if not as good as those enjoyed from the cell in the body of the tower above, which was known ironically as the Alberghinetto (Little Hotel); such troublemakers as Cosimo de' Medici and Savonarola were once imprisoned here. The final section of the museum, just before the exit – devoted to second-rate pictures once owned by the American collector Charles Loeser – seems something of an afterthought, and is often closed.

The Uffizi

Florence can prompt an over-eagerness to reach for superlatives; in the case of the **Galleria degli Uffizi**, the superlatives are simply the bare truth: this is the finest picture gallery in Italy. So many masterpieces are collected here that it's

Uffizi practicalities

The Uffizi is open **Tuesday to Sunday from 8.15am to 6.50pm**; in high summer and at festive periods it sometimes stays open until 10pm. After the Vatican this is the busiest museum in the country, with more than one and a half million visitors each year, so during peak season you've almost no chance of getting in without paying the €4 surcharge for booking a ticket **in advance**. For next-day tickets, there's a reservations desk that opens at 8.15am at Door 2, and has an allocation of just 200. For reservations further in advance, go to Door 3, or call the Firenze Musei line on ⓣ055.294.883, or reserve through the Firenze Musei website, or call at the Orsanmichele ticket office (see p.71 for more information). Even if you have bought an advance ticket, get there half an hour before your allotted admission time, because the queue is often enormous and very slow-moving.

Full-price **tickets** cost €6.50 but EU citizens aged 18–25 pay half price and entry is free to under-18s and over-65s; there are, however, frequent special exhibitions, during which the full price is raised to €10. You should be aware that it's very rare for the whole Uffizi to be open; a board by the entrance tells you which sections are closed. In 2004 it was announced that over the next few years the Uffizi would be doubling the number of rooms open to the public, in order to show some eight hundred works usually kept in storage. This €60 million project got off to a rather inauspicious start, when excavations in preparation for the building of a new exit (a controversial high-rise canopy designed by Japanese architect Arata Isozaki) unearthed the remains of the medieval houses that were demolished in the 1560s to make way for the Uffizi. The new exit was promptly scrapped, but work on the exhibition spaces is now underway, which means that some pictures may not be on show where they appear in the following account.

not even possible to skate over the surface in a single visit. Though you may not want to emulate English historian Edward Gibbon, who visited the Uffizi fourteen times on a single trip to Florence, it makes sense to limit your initial tour to the first fifteen rooms, where the Florentine Renaissance works are concentrated, and to explore the rest another time.

The gallery is housed in what were once government offices (*uffizi*) built by Vasari for Cosimo I in 1560. After Vasari's death, work on the elongated U-shaped building was continued by Buontalenti, who was asked by Francesco I to glaze the upper storey so that it could house his art collection. Each of the succeeding Medici added to the family's trove of art treasures. The accumulated collection was preserved for public inspection by the last member of the family, Anna Maria Luisa, whose will specified that it should be left to the people of Florence and never be allowed to leave the city. In the nineteenth century a large proportion of the statuary was transferred to the Bargello, while most of the antiquities went to the Museo Archeologico, leaving the Uffizi as essentially a gallery of paintings supplemented with some classical sculptures.

Pre-Renaissance

You can take a lift up to the galleries, but if you take the staircase instead, you'll pass the entrance to the Uffizi's prints and drawings section. The bulk of this vast collection is reserved for scholarly scrutiny but samples are often on public show.

Upstairs, all the rooms lead off the statue-lined monumental corridor that runs round the building, which has a sequence of portraits of famous men high on the walls on both sides; commissioned by the Medici in the sixteenth century, the array inevitably includes plenty of images of Florence's first family. **Room 1**, housing an assembly of antique sculptures, many of which were used as a kind of source book by Renaissance artists, is often shut. The beginnings of the stylistic evolution of that period can be traced in the three altarpieces of the *Maestà* (Madonna Enthroned) that dominate **Room 2**: the *Madonna Rucellai*, *Maestà di Santa Trìnita* and *Madonna d'Ognissanti*, by **Duccio**, **Cimabue** and **Giotto** respectively. These great works, which dwarf everything around them, show the softening of the Byzantine style into a more tactile form of representation.

Painters from fourteenth-century Siena fill **Room 3**, with several pieces by Ambrogio and Pietro Lorenzetti and **Simone Martini**'s glorious *Annunciation*, the Virgin cowering from the angel amid a field of pure gold. Also in this room is Giottino's *San Remigio Pietà* (c.1360), notable both for its emotional intensity and for the alluring portrait of one of the donors – a very elegant young woman, dressed in what was then the height of fashion.

Beyond a room of Giotto-esque artists such as **Orcagna** and **Bernardo Daddi** comes a display of paintings that mark the summit of the precious style known as International Gothic. **Lorenzo Monaco** is represented by an *Adoration of the Magi* and his greatest masterpiece, *The Coronation of the Virgin* (1415). Equally arresting is the *Adoration of the Magi* (1423) by **Gentile da Fabriano**, a picture spangled with gold so thick in places that the crowns of the kings, for instance, are like low-relief jewellery. It's crammed with so much detail that there's no real distinction between what's crucial and what's peripheral, with as much attention lavished on incidentals such as a snarling leopard as on the supposed protagonists. The right-hand panel of the predella, below, was stolen by Napoleon and replaced with a copy which, unlike the rest of the painting, is not painted directly onto gold – hence the relative matt dullness of its surface. Nearby is the *Thebaid*, a beguiling little narrative that depicts monastic life in the Egyptian desert as a sort of holy fairytale; though labelled as being by the young Fra' Angelico, it's also been attributed to the now-obscure Gherardo di Jacopo Starnina, who in his time (he died around 1410) was one of Florence's major artists, and is thought to have been the master of Masolino.

Early Renaissance

Room 7 reveals the sheer diversity of early Renaissance painting. **Fra' Angelico**'s gorgeous *Coronation of the Virgin* takes place against a Gothic-like field of gold, but there's a very un-Gothic sensibility at work in its individualized depiction of the attendant throng. **Paolo Uccello**'s *The Battle of San Romano* once hung in Lorenzo il Magnifico's bedchamber, in company with its two companion pieces now in the Louvre and London's National Gallery. Warfare is the ostensible subject, but this is really a semi-abstract compendium of perspectival effects – a toppling knight, a horse and rider keeled onto their sides, the foreshortened legs of a kicking horse, a thicket of lances – creating a fight scene with no real sense of violence. The Madonna and Child in **Masolino**'s *Madonna and Child with St Anne* are thought to have been added by his pupil Masaccio, to whom the nearby tiny *Madonna and Child* is also attributed. The *Madonna and Child with Sts Francis, John the Baptist, Zenobius and Lucy* is one of only twelve extant paintings by **Domenico Veneziano**, who spent much of his life in Venice but died destitute in Florence.

Veneziano's greatest pupil, **Piero della Francesca**, is represented in **Room 8** by the paired portraits of *Federico da Montefeltro* and *Battista Sforza*, the duke and duchess of Urbino. These panels were painted two years after Battista's death; in the background of her portrait is the town of Gubbio, where she died giving birth to her ninth child and only son, Guidobaldo. A lot of space in Room 8 is given over to **Filippo Lippi**, whose *Madonna and Child with Two Angels* supplies one of the gallery's most popular faces: the model was Lucrezia Buti, a convent novice who became the object of one of his more enduring sexual obsessions. Lucrezia puts in an another appearance in Lippi's crowded *Coronation of the Virgin*, where she's the young woman gazing out in the right foreground; Filippo himself, hand on chin, makes eye contact on the left side of the picture. Their liaison produced a son, the aptly named **Filippino** "Little Philip" **Lippi**, whose *Madonna degli Otto* – one of several works by him here – is typical of the more melancholic cast of the younger Lippi's art.

The Pollaiuolo brothers and Botticelli

Lippi's great pupil, Botticelli, steals some of the thunder in **Room 9** – *Fortitude*, one of the series of cardinal and theological virtues, is a very early work by him. The rest of the series is by the brothers **Piero** and **Antonio del Pollaiuolo**, whose *Sts Vincent, James and Eustace*, one of their best paintings, is chiefly the work of Antonio; it was created for the church of San Miniato, where a copy is now on display. Antonio also painted the two sinewy images of Hercules, which show evidence of the brothers' assiduous and revolutionary study of human anatomy. This room usually contains the *Portrait of Young Man in a Red Hat*, sometimes referred to as a self-portrait by Filippino Lippi, but believed by some to be an eighteenth-century fraud.

It's in the merged **rooms 10–14** that the greatest of **Botticelli**'s creations are gathered. A century ago most people walked past his pictures without breaking stride; nowadays – despite their elusiveness – the *Primavera* and the *Birth of Venus* stop all visitors in their tracks. The identities of the characters in the **Primavera** are not contentious: on the right Zephyrus, god of the west wind, chases the nymph Cloris, who is then transfigured into Flora, the pregnant goddess of spring; Venus stands in the centre, to the side of the three Graces, who are targeted by Cupid; on the left Mercury wards off the clouds of winter. What this all means, however, has occupied scholars for decades. Some see it as an allegory of the four seasons, but the consensus now seems to be that it shows the triumph of Venus, with the Graces as the physical embodiment of her beauty and Flora the symbol of her fruitfulness – an interpretation supported by the fact that the picture was placed outside the wedding suite of Lorenzo di Pierfrancesco de' Medici.

Botticelli's most winsome painting, the **Birth of Venus**, probably takes as its source the myth that the goddess emerged from the sea after it had been impregnated by the castration of Uranus, an allegory for the creation of beauty through the mingling of the spirit (Uranus) and the physical world. The supporting players are the nymph, Cloris, and Zephyrus, god of the west wind. Zephyrus blows the risen Venus to the shore where the goddess is clothed by Hora, daughter and attendant of Aurora, goddess of dawn. A third allegory hangs close by: *Pallas and the Centaur*, perhaps symbolizing the ambivalent triumph of reason over instinct.

Botticelli's devotional paintings are generally less perplexing. *The Adoration of the Magi* is traditionally thought to contain a gallery of Medici portraits: Cosimo il Vecchio as the first king, his sons Giovanni and Piero as the other two kings, Lorenzo il Magnifico on the far left, and his brother Giuliano as the black-haired young man in profile on the right. Only the identification of Cosimo is reasonably certain, along with that of Botticelli himself, on the right in the yellow robe. In later life, influenced by Savonarola's teaching, Botticelli confined himself to devotional pictures and moral fables, and his style became increasingly severe and didactic. The transformation is clear when comparing the easy grace of the *Madonna of the Magnificat* and the *Madonna of the Pomegranate* with the more angular and agitated *Calumny*. Even the *Annunciation* (1489), painted just as Savonarola's preaching began to grip Florence, reveals a new intensity in the expression of the angel and in the twisting body of the Virgin, whose posture embodies her ambivalent reaction to the message.

Not quite every masterpiece in this room is by Botticelli. Set away from the walls is the *Adoration of the Shepherds* by his Flemish contemporary **Hugo van der Goes**. Brought to Florence in 1483 by Tommaso Portinari, the Medici agent in Bruges, it provided the city's artists with their first large-scale demonstration of the realism of Northern European oil painting, and had a great influence on the way the medium was exploited here.

Leonardo to Mantegna

Works in **Room 15** trace the formative years of **Leonardo da Vinci**, whose distinctive touch appears first in the *Baptism of Christ* by his master Verrocchio. Vasari claimed that only the wistful angel in profile was by the 18-year-old apprentice, and the misty landscape in the background, but recent X-rays have revealed that Leonardo also worked heavily on the figure of Christ. A similar terrain of soft-focus mountains and water occupies the far distance in Leonardo's slightly later *Annunciation*, in which a diffused light falls on a scene where everything is observed with a scientist's precision: the petals of the flowers on which the angel alights, the fall of the Virgin's drapery, the carving on the lectern at which she reads. In restless contrast to the aristocratic poise of the *Annunciation*, the sketch of *The Adoration of the Magi* – abandoned when

Leonardo left Florence for Milan in early 1482 – presents the infant Christ as the eye of a vortex of figures, all drawn into his presence by a force as irresistible as a whirlpool.

Most of the rest of the room is given over to Raphael's teacher, **Perugino**, who is represented by a typically placid and contemplative *Madonna and Child with Saints* (1493), and *Pietà* (1494–95). It also contains an *Incarnation* by **Piero di Cosimo**, of whom more later.

Room 18, the octagonal **Tribuna**, now houses the most important of the Medici's collection of **classical sculptures**, chief among which is the *Medici Venus*, a first-century BC copy of the Praxitelean *Aphrodite of Cnidos*. She was kept in the Villa Medici in Rome until Cosimo III began to fret that she was having a detrimental effect on the morals of the city's art students, and ordered her removal to Florence. The move clearly didn't affect the statue's sexual charisma, however: it became traditional for eighteenth-century visitors to Florence to caress her buttocks. Around the walls are hung some fascinating portraits by **Bronzino**: Cosimo de' Medici, Eleonora di Toledo, Bartolomeo Panciatichi and his wife Lucrezia Panciatichi, all painted as figures of porcelain, placed in a bloodless, sunless world. More vital is Andrea del Sarto's flirtatious *Ritratto d'Ignota* (Portrait of a Young Woman), and there's a deceptive naturalism to Vasari's portrait of Lorenzo il Magnifico and Pontormo's of Cosimo il Vecchio, both painted long after the death of their subjects.

The last section of this wing throws together Renaissance paintings from outside Florence, with some notable Venetian and Flemish works. **Signorelli** and **Perugino** – with some photo-sharp portraits – are the principal artists in **Room 19**, and after them comes a room largely devoted to **Cranach** and **Dürer**. Each has an *Adam and Eve* here, Dürer taking the opportunity to show off his proficiency as a painter of wildlife. Dürer's power as a portraitist is displayed in the *Portrait of the Artist's Father*, his earliest authenticated painting, and Cranach has a couple of acute pictures of Luther on display, one of them a double with his wife. Here you'll also find a bizarre *Perseus Freeing Andromeda* by **Piero di Cosimo**, the wild man of the Florentine Renaissance. Shunning civilized company, Piero did everything he could to bring his life close to a state of uncompromised nature, living in a house that was never cleaned, in the midst of a garden he refused to tend, and eating nothing but hard-boiled eggs. Where his contemporaries might seek inspiration in commentaries on Plato, he would spend hours staring at the sky, at peeling walls, at the pavement – at anything where abstract patterns might conjure fabulous scenes in his imagination.

A taste of the Uffizi's remarkable collection of Venetian painting follows, with an impenetrable *Sacred Allegory* by **Giovanni Bellini**, and three works attributed to **Giorgione**. A clutch of Northern European paintings includes some superb portraits by **Holbein** (notably *Sir Richard Southwell* and a self-portrait) and **Hans Memling**. In the following room – called the **Correggio** room, after the trio of pictures by the artist on show here – there's a triptych by **Mantegna** which is not in fact a real triptych, but rather a trio of exquisite small paintings shackled together. To the side of them are two other pictures by Mantegna – a swarthy portrait of Carlo de' Medici and the *Madonna of the Stonecutters*, which takes its name from the minuscule figures at work in the quarry in the background.

Michelangelo, Mannerism and Titian

Beyond the stockpile of statues in the short corridor overlooking the Arno, the main attraction in **Room 25** is **Michelangelo**'s *Doni Tondo*, the only easel painting he came close to completing. (Regarding sculpture as the noblest of the visual arts, Michelangelo dismissed all non-fresco painting as a demeaning chore.) Nobody has yet explained the precise significance of every aspect of this picture, but plausible explanations for parts of it have been put forward. The five naked figures behind the Holy Family seem to be standing in a half-moon-shaped cistern or font, which would relate to the infant Baptist to the right, who – in the words of St Paul – prefigures the coming of Christ just as the new moon is "a shadow of things to come". In the same epistle, Paul goes on to commend the virtues of mercy, kindness, humility, modesty and patience, which are perhaps what the five youths represent. **Albertinelli**'s *Visitation* tends to get upstaged by Michelangelo, but it's a lustrous and extraordinarily touching picture.

Room 26 contains **Andrea del Sarto**'s sultry *Madonna of the Harpies* and a number of compositions by **Raphael**, including his self-portrait, the lovely *Madonna of the Goldfinch* and *Pope Leo X with Cardinals Giulio de' Medici and Luigi de' Rossi* – as shifty a group of ecclesiastics as was ever gathered in one frame. The Michelangelo tondo's contorted gestures and virulent colours were greatly influential on the Mannerist painters of the sixteenth century, as can be gauged from *Moses Defending the Daughters of Jethro* by **Rosso Fiorentino**, one of the seminal figures of the movement, whose works hang in **Room 27**, along with major works by Bronzino and his adoptive father, Pontormo.

Room 28 is almost entirely given over to another of the titanic figures of sixteenth-century art, **Titian**, with nine paintings on show. His *Flora* and *A Knight of Malta* are stunning, but most eyes tend to swivel towards the *Urbino Venus*, the most provocative of all Renaissance nudes, described by Mark Twain as "the foulest, the vilest, the obscenest picture the world possesses". **Sebastiano del Piombo**'s *Death of Adonis* was reduced to little more than postage-stamp tatters by the Mafia bomb which in 1993 destroyed part of the Uffizi and killed five people; the restoration is little short of miraculous.

A brief diversion through the painters of the sixteenth-century Emilian school follows, centred on **Parmigianino**, whose *Madonna of the Long Neck* is one of the pivotal Mannerist creations. Parmigianino was a febrile and introverted character who abandoned painting for alchemy towards the end of his short life, and many of his works are marked by a sort of morbid refinement, none more so than this one. The Madonna's tunic clings to every contour, an angel

The Corridoio Vasariano

A door on the west corridor, between rooms 25 and 34, opens onto the **Corridoio Vasariano**, a passageway built by Vasari in 1565 to link the Palazzo Vecchio to the Palazzo Pitti, via the Uffizi. Winding its way down to the river, over the Ponte Vecchio, through the church of Santa Felicita and into the Giardino di Bóboli, it gives a fascinating series of clandestine views of the city. As if that weren't pleasure enough, the corridor is lined with paintings, the larger portion of which comprises a gallery of **self-portraits**, featuring such greats as Andrea del Sarto, Bronzino, Bernini, Rubens, Velázquez, David, Delacroix and Ingres. However, the corridor is currently closed for restoration, and there are plans to move the best of the paintings into the extended Uffizi galleries. The corridor used to be open two mornings per week for small-group guided tours, and in all likelihood that will be the arrangement when the restoration is completed. For the latest situation, ask at the Amici degli Amici office at the Uffizi or at one of the tourist offices.

advances a perfectly turned leg, the infant Christ drapes himself languorously on his mother's lap – prefiguring the dead Christ of the *Pietà* – while in the background an emaciated figure unrolls a scroll of parchment by a colonnade so severely foreshortened that it looks like a single column.

Rooms 31 to 34 feature a miscellany of sixteenth-century artists (look out for the El Greco) and some top-class works from Venice and the Veneto, including **Moroni**'s *Portrait of Count Pietro Secco Suardi*, **Paolo Veronese**'s *Annunciation* and *Holy Family with St Barbara*, a gathering of fine pieces by **Lorenzo Lotto** and a female nude by **Bernardino Licino** that's unusual in seeming to have no mythological pretext – the subject is not Venus, but simply a naked woman.

The seventeenth and eighteenth centuries

The Uffizi's collection of seventeenth-century art features strong work from **Van Dyck** and **Rubens**, whose *Portrait of Isabella Brandt* is perhaps his finest painting here. The most overwhelming, however, are the huge *Henry IV at the Battle of Ivry* and *The Triumphal Entry of Henry IV into Paris* – Henry's marriage to Marie de' Medici is the connection with Florence. This pair are displayed in the majestic Neoclassical Niobe Room, which takes its name from the sculptures of *Niobe and her Daughters*, Roman copies of Greek originals, which were unearthed in a vineyard in Rome in 1583.

In this section of the gallery you'll also see some superb portraits by **Rembrandt**. His sorrow-laden *Self-Portrait as an Old Man*, painted five years or so before his death, makes a poignant contrast with the self-confident self-portrait of thirty years earlier. Although there are some good pieces from **Giambattista Tiepolo**, portraits again command the attention in the adjacent room of eighteenth-century paintings, notably a brace by **Goya** and **Chardin**'s demure children.

The rooms downstairs are used for temporary exhibitions and as a showcase for Italian art of the seventeenth century. Dramatic images from Salvator Rosa, Luca Giordano and Artemisia Gentileschi make quite an impression, but the presiding genius is **Caravaggio**, with his virtuosic *Medusa* (the severed head is painted on a shield), the smug little *Bacchus*, and the throat-grabbing *Sacrifice of Isaac*. Works by lesser (but still impressive) talents show the huge influence of Caravaggio's high-contrast and high-impact art.

Orsanmichele

Looming like a fortress over Via dei Calzaiuoli, the foursquare **Orsanmichele** (Tues–Sun 10am–5pm) is the oddest church in Florence – a unique hybrid of the sacred and secular, it resembles no other church in the city, and it's not even immediately apparent which of its walls is the front. It's a major monument in itself, and its exterior was once the most impressive outdoor sculpture gallery in the city. Nowadays all of the pieces outside are replicas (most of the originals are on display in the attached museum), but copies or not, this church is one of the city's great sights.

The first building here was a small oratory secreted in the orchard or vegetable garden (*orto*) of a now-vanished Benedictine monastery. A larger church stood on the site from the ninth century: San Michele ad Hortum, later San Michele in Orte – hence the compacted form of Orsanmichele. Even after the church was replaced by a **grain market** in the thirteenth century, the place retained its religious associations. In 1300, the chronicler Giovanni Villani claimed "the lame walked and the possessed were liberated" after visiting a miraculous image of the Virgin painted on one of the market pillars.

After a fire in 1304, the building was eventually replaced by a **loggia** designed by Francesco Talenti to serve as a trade hall for the Arti Maggiori, the Great Guilds which governed the city. Between 1367 and 1380 the loggia was walled in, after which the site was again dedicated almost exclusively to religious functions, while leaving two upper storeys for use as emergency grain stores.

As far back as 1339, plans had been made to adorn each pillar of the building with a patron statue, each assigned to a different guild. In the event, only one statue was produced in sixty years – a St Stephen commissioned by the Arte della Lana. In 1408, weary of the delay, the city elders set a ten-year deadline, warning that the niches would be allocated to rival guilds if commissions remained unfulfilled. The delay was to posterity's benefit, for the statues that were eventually produced spanned the emergent years of the Renaissance.

The exterior

Beginning on the far left of Orsanmichele's Via dei Calzaiuoli flank, the first tabernacle is occupied by Ghiberti's **John the Baptist**, the earliest life-size bronze statue of the Renaissance. It was made for the Calimala, the guild of wholesale cloth importers. The adjacent niche is occupied by *The Incredulity of St Thomas* by Verrocchio, which replaced an earlier gilded statue by Donatello, *St Louis of Toulouse*, now in the Museo dell'Opera del Duomo; Giambologna's *St Luke* similarly replaced an earlier statue by Lamberti now in the Bargello.

Round the corner there's St Peter, usually attributed to Bernardo Ciuffagni, though some scholars have argued for the authorship of Brunelleschi or Donatello. He's followed by two works from Nanni di Banco: *St Philip* and his masterpiece, the so-called **Quattro Coronati**. The original Quattro Coronati were four anonymous Romans who were martyred by Diocletian; known as the Four Crowned Ones simply because the crown was a badge of martyrdom, they somehow became conflated with a group of Christian stonemasons, executed by Diocletian for refusing to carve a pagan idol – the latter group (who were actually five in number), became the patron saints of the masons' guild, sponsors of this niche. Donatello's *St George* occupies the next niche – the original is in the Bargello, as is the original accompanying bas-relief of *St George and the Dragon*.

On the church's west side stand *St Matthew* and *St Stephen*, both by Ghiberti, and *St Eligius* by Nanni di Banco; the *St Matthew*, posed and clad like a Roman orator, makes a telling comparison with the same artist's *St John*, cast just ten years before but still semi-Gothic in its sharp-edged drapery and arching lines. Earlier than either is Donatello's **St Mark**, made in 1411 when the artist was 25; the work is often considered one of the first statues of the Renaissance, a title based on the naturalism of St Mark's stance and the brooding intensity of his gaze. Pietro Lamberti's *St James* precedes the benign **Madonna della Rosa**, probably by Simone Talenti; the weakest of the sculptures, Baccio da Montelupo's *John the Evangelist*, brings up the rear.

The interior and museum

Orsanmichele's interior centrepiece is a pavilion-sized glass and marble **tabernacle** by Orcagna, the only significant sculptural work by the artist. Decorated with lapis lazuli, stained glass and gold, it frames a Madonna painted in 1347 by Bernardo Daddi as a replacement for the miraculous image of the Virgin destroyed by the 1304 fire. The brotherhood that administered Orsanmichele paid for the tabernacle from thanksgiving donations in the aftermath of the Black Death; so many people attributed their survival to the Madonna's intervention that the money received in 1348 alone was greater than the annual tax income of the city coffers. Other paintings can be seen on the pillars: devotional images of the guilds' patron saints, they can be regarded as the low-cost ancestors of the Orsanmichele statues.

The original lines of the bricked-up loggia are still clear, and the vaulted halls of the upper granaries also survive. The lower of these halls now houses the **Museo di Orsanmichele** (Mon–Sat 10am–3pm; free), entered via the footbridge from the Palazzo dell'Arte della Lana, the building opposite the church entrance. Having been restored, nearly all of the exterior statues are on show here – the main exception is the most famous of all, Donatello's *St George*, which belongs to the Bargello. From time to time exhibitions are held here, in which case an entrance fee is charged.

The Badìa Fiorentina and around

The **Badìa Fiorentina** (Florentine Abbey) is one of the most impressive churches in the centre of the city, and is also a place of special significance for admirers of **Dante**: this was the parish church of Beatrice Portinari, for whom he conceived a lifelong love as he observed her during Mass here. It was also here that Boccaccio delivered his celebrated lectures on Dante's theological epic. Nowadays the church belongs to a French monastic order called the Fraternity of Jerusalem, and tourist visits are allowed only on Monday afternoons (3–6pm).

Founded in 978 by Willa, widow of the Margrave of Tuscany, in honour of her husband, the Badìa was one of the focal buildings in medieval Florence: the city's sick were treated in a hospital founded here in 1031, while the main bell marked the divisions of the working day. The hospital also owed much to Willa's son, Ugo, who further endowed his mother's foundation after a vision of the hellish torments which awaited him by "reason of his worldly life, unless he should repent". The 1280s saw the church overhauled along Cistercian Gothic lines, probably under the direction of Arnolfo di Cambio, architect of the Duomo and Palazzo Vecchio. Later Baroque additions smothered much of the old church in 1627, though the narrow **campanile** – Romanesque at its base, Gothic towards its apex – escaped unharmed. Completed between 1310 and 1330, it remains a prominent feature of the Florentine skyline. Nowadays the church belongs to the Fraternity of Jerusalem, a French monastic order founded in the 1970s.

As you enter from Via Dante Alighieri, on the left hangs **Filippino Lippi**'s superb *Apparition of the Virgin to St Bernard*; set back to the right is the church's second highlight, the **tomb monument** to Ugo, sculpted by Mino da Fiesole between 1469 and 1481. Mino was also responsible for the nearby tomb of Bernardo Giugni and an altar frontal of the *Madonna and Child with Sts Leonard and Lawrence*. Giugni was a lawyer and diplomat, hence the figures of Justice and Faith accompanying his effigy.

A staircase leads from the choir – take the door immediately right of the high altar – to the upper storey of the **Chiostro degli Aranci** (Cloister of the Oranges), named after the fruit trees that used to be grown here. Two of its flanks are graced with a highly distinctive fresco cycle (1436–39) on the life of St Benedict, thought to be the work of Giovanni di Consalvo, a Portuguese contemporary of Fra' Angelico. A later panel – showing the saint throwing himself into bushes to resist temptation – is by the young Bronzino (1526–28).

The cloister itself (1432–38) is the work of Bernardo Rossellino, one of the leading lights of early Renaissance architecture.

The "Dante district"

Somewhat fraudulently marketed as Dante's house, the **Casa di Dante** (Tues–Sun 10am–5pm; €4) is actually a medieval pastiche dating from 1910. The museum upstairs is a homage to the poet rather than a shrine: it contains nothing directly related to his life, and in all likelihood Dante was born not on the house's site but somewhere in the street that bears his name. Numerous editions of *La Divina Commedia* are on show – including a poster printed with the whole text in minuscule type – along with copies of Botticelli's illustrations to the poem and a variety of context-setting displays.

As contentious as the Casa di Dante's claims is the story that Dante married Gemma Donati in **Santa Margherita de' Cerchi** (Mon–Sat 10am–noon & 3–5pm, Sun 10am–noon), the ancient little church up the street from the Casa di Dante on the right. Documented as early as 1032, the building does, however, contain several tombs belonging to the Portinari, Beatrice's family; the porch also features the Donati family crest, as this was also their local parish church.

Over Via Dante Alighieri from the poet's house, on Piazza San Martino, lies the tiny **San Martino del Vescovo** (Mon–Thurs & Sat 10am–noon & 3–5pm, Fri 10am–noon), built on the site of a small oratory founded in 986 that served as the Alighieri's parish church. Rebuilt in 1479, it later became the headquarters of the Compagnia di Buonomini, a charitable body dedicated to aiding impoverished better-class citizens for whom begging was too demeaning a prospect. The Buonomini commissioned from Ghirlandaio's workshop a sequence of frescoes showing various altruistic acts and scenes from the life of St Martin, and the result is as absorbing a record of daily life in Renaissance Florence as the Ghirlandaio frescoes in Santa Maria Novella.

Opposite San Martino soars the thirteenth-century **Torre della Castagna**, meeting place of the city's *Priori* before they decamped to the Palazzo Vecchio. This is one of the most striking remnants of Florence's medieval townscape, when over 150 such towers rose between the river and the Duomo, many of them over two hundred feet high.

The Bargello

The Renaissance sculpture collection of the **Museo Nazionale del Bargello** (Tues–Sat 8.15am–1.50pm; second & fourth Sun of month and first, third & fifth Mon of month, same hours; €4; longer hours and higher charge for special exhibitions), at Via del Proconsolo 4, is the richest in Italy, but the museum also devotes a vast amount of space to the decorative arts: carpets, enamels, ivories, glassware, tapestries, silverware and other *objets d'art* of the highest quality. Although they receive scant attention from most visitors, it would be easy to spend as much time on the dozen or more rooms filled with these treasures as the four rooms devoted to sculpture.

The Bargello's home, the daunting Palazzo del Bargello, was built in 1255 immediately after the overthrow of the aristocratic regime. The first of the city's public palaces, it soon became the seat of the *Podestà*, the city's chief magistrate, and the site of the main law court. Numerous malefactors were tortured, tried, sentenced and executed here, the elegant courtyard having been the site of the city's gallows and block. The building acquired its present name after 1574, when the Medici abolished the post of *Podestà*, the building becoming home to

Dante Alighieri

Dante signed himself "Dante Alighieri, a Florentine by birth but not by character", a bitter allusion to the city he served as a politician but which later cast him into exile and was to inspire some of the most vitriolic passages in his great epic poem, *La Divina Commedia* (The Divine Comedy).

The poet was born in 1265 into a minor and impoverished noble family. He was educated at Bologna and later at Padua, where he studied philosophy and astronomy. The defining moment in his life came in 1274 when he met the 8-year-old **Beatrice Portinari**, a young girl whom Boccaccio described as possessed of "habits and language more serious and modest than her age warranted". Her features were "so delicate and so beautifully formed," he went on, "and full, besides mere beauty, of so much candid loveliness that many thought her almost an angel."

Dante – just 9 at the time of the meeting – later described his own feeling following the encounter: "Love ruled my soul," he wrote, "and began to hold such sway over me … that it was necessary for me to do completely all his pleasure. He commanded me often that I should endeavour to see this so youthful angel, and I saw in her such noble and praiseworthy deportment that truly of her might be said these words of the poet Homer – *She appeared to be born not of mortal man but of God.*"

Unhappily, Beatrice's family had decided their daughter was to marry someone else – Simone de' Bardi. The ceremony took place when she was 17; seven years later she was dead. Dante, for his part, had been promised – aged 12 – to Gemma Donati. The wedding took place in 1295, when the poet was 30.

His romantic hopes dashed, Dante settled down to a military and political career. In 1289 he fought for Florence against Arezzo and helped in a campaign against Pisa. Later he joined the Apothecaries' Guild, serving on a variety of minor civic committees. In 1300 he was dispatched to San Gimignano, where he was entrusted with the job of coaxing the town into an alliance against Pope Boniface VIII, who had designs on Tuscany. In June of the same year he sought to settle the widening breach between the **Black** (anti-imperial) and **White** (more conciliatory) factions of Florence's ruling Guelph party. The dispute had its roots in money: the Whites

---

the chief of police – the *Bargello*. Torture and capital punishment were banned in 1786 (the first such abolition in Europe), though the building remained a prison until 1859.

The ground floor

You've no time to catch your breath in the Bargello: the first room to the right of the ticket office is crammed with treasures, chief of which are the work of **Michelangelo**, in whose shadow every Florentine sculptor laboured from the sixteenth century onwards. The tipsy, soft-bellied figure of *Bacchus* (1496–97) was his first major sculpture, carved at the age of 22, a year or so before his great *Pietà* in Rome. Michelangelo's style soon evolved into something less ostentatiously virtuosic, as is shown by the tender *Tondo Pitti* (1503–05), while the rugged expressivity of his late manner is exemplified by the square-jawed *Bust of Brutus* (c.1540), the artist's sole work of this kind. A powerful portrait sketch in stone, it's a coded celebration of anti-Medicean republicanism, carved soon after the murder of the nightmarish Duke Alessandro de' Medici (see p.126).

Works by Michelangelo's followers and contemporaries are ranged in the immediate vicinity; some of them would command prolonged attention in less exalted company. **Benvenuto Cellini**'s huge *Bust of Cosimo I* (1545–47), his first work in bronze, was a sort of technical trial for the casting of the *Perseus*,

contained leading bankers to the imperial powers (the Cerchi, Mozzi, Davanzati and Frescobaldi), while the Blacks counted the Pazzi, Bardi and Donati amongst their number, all prominent papal bankers. Boniface, not surprisingly, sided with the Blacks, who eventually emerged triumphant. Dante's White sympathies sealed his fate. In 1302, following trumped-up charges of corruption, he was sentenced with other Whites to two years' exile. While many of the deportees subsequently returned, Dante rejected his city of "self-made men and fast-got gain". He wandered instead between Forlì, Verona, Padua, Luni and Venice, writing much of *The Divine Comedy* as he went, before finally settling in Ravenna, where he died in 1321.

Running to more than 14,000 lines, **La Commedia** (the *Divina* was added after Dante's death) is an extraordinarily rich allegory, recounting the poet's journey through Inferno (Hell), Purgatorio (Purgatory), and Paradiso (Paradise), accompanied initially by the Roman poet Virgil (Dante was fully aware that his work would bear comparison with the greats) and then by Beatrice. Each of these three realms of the dead is depicted in 33 *canti* (a "prologue" to the Inferno brings the total up to 100), composed in a verse scheme called **terza rima**, in which lines of eleven syllables follow the rhyme scheme *aba*, *bcb*, *cdc*, *ded*, etc. This may seem an inflexible framework, but Dante employs it to achieve an amazing variety of tone, encompassing everything from the desperate abuse of the damned, through the complex theological argumentation of Purgatorio to the exalted lyricism of his vision of heaven. And the range of subject matter is astonishing too: *The Divine Comedy* is both a metaphysical epic in which the entire late-medieval view of the cosmos is encapsulated, and an incisive critique of the society in which Dante lived – a critique in which he doesn't flinch from naming names. Equally remarkable is the fact that Dante wrote his poem in the Tuscan dialect, at a time when Latin would have been regarded as the only language suitable for subjects of such seriousness. Before *La Commedia*, Tuscan was the language of the street; afterwards, it began to be seen as the language of all Italian people, from peasants to philosophers.

his most famous work. Alongside the two preparatory models for the *Perseus* in wax and bronze are displayed the original marble base and four statuettes that comprise the statue's pedestal; Perseus himself still stands in his intended spot, in the Loggia della Signoria.

Close by, **Giambologna**'s voluptuous *Virtue Overcoming Vice* or *Florence Defeating Pisa* (1575) – a disingenuous pretext for a female nude if ever there were one – takes up a lot of space, but is eclipsed by his best-known creation, the wonderful *Mercury* (1564), a nimble figure with no bad angles. Comic relief is provided by the reliably inept Bandinelli, whose coiffured *Adam and Eve* look like a grandee and his wife taking an *au naturel* stroll through their country estate. The powerfully erotic *Leda and the Swan* by **Ammannati** (1540–50) was inspired by a painting of the subject by Michelangelo that was later destroyed.

Part two of the ground floor's collection lies across the Gothic **courtyard**, which is plastered with the coats of arms of the *Podestà*. Against the far wall stand six allegorical figures by Ammannati from the fountain of the Palazzo Pitti courtyard. Of the two rooms across the yard, the one to the left features largely fourteenth-century works, notably pieces by Arnolfo di Cambio and Tino da Camaino; temporary exhibitions are often held in the room to the right.

▲ Donatello's bust of Niccolò da Uzzano, the Bargello

The first floor

At the top of Giuliano da Sangallo's courtyard **staircase** (1502), the first-floor loggia has been turned into a menagerie for Giambologna's quaint bronze animals and birds, imported from the Medici villa at Castello, just outside Florence. The nearer doorway to the right opens into the tall, Gothic **Salone del Consiglio Generale**, the museum's second key room. Here again the number of masterpieces is breathtaking, though this time the presiding genius is **Donatello**, the fountainhead of Renaissance sculpture.

Vestiges of the sinuous Gothic manner are evident in the drapery of his marble *David* (1408), but there's nothing antiquated in the **St George** (1416), carved for the tabernacle of the armourers' guild at Orsanmichele and installed in a replica of its original niche at the far end of the room. If any one sculpture could be said to embody the shift of sensibility that occurred in fifteenth-century Florence, this is it: whereas St George had previously been little more than a symbol of valour, this alert, tensed figure represents not the act of heroism but the volition behind it. The slaying of the dragon is depicted in the small, badly eroded marble panel underneath.

Also here is the sexually ambivalent bronze **David**, the first freestanding nude figure created since classical times (1430–40). A decade later the sculptor produced the strange prancing figure known as Amor-Atys, which was mistaken for a genuine statue from classical antiquity – the highest compliment the artist could have wished for. Donatello was just as comfortable with portraiture as with Christian or pagan imagery, as his breathtakingly vivid terracotta *Bust of Niccolò da Uzzano* demonstrates; it may be the earliest Renaissance portrait bust. When the occasion demanded, Donatello could also produce a straightforwardly monumental piece like the nearby *Marzocco* (1418–20), Florence's heraldic lion.

Donatello's master, **Ghiberti**, is represented by his relief of *Abraham's Sacrifice*, his entry in the competition to design the Baptistery doors in 1401, easily missed on the right-hand wall; the treatment of the theme submitted by Brunelleschi, effectively the runner-up, is hung alongside. Set around the walls of the room, **Luca della Robbia**'s simple, sweet-natured humanism is embodied in a sequence of glazed terracotta Madonnas.

The rest of this floor is occupied by a superb collection of European and Islamic applied art, with dazzling specimens of work in enamel, glass, silver, majolica and ivory: among the ivory pieces from Byzantium and medieval France you'll find combs, boxes, chess pieces, and devotional panels featuring scores of figures crammed into a space the size of a paperback. Room 9, the **Cappella di Santa Maria Maddalena**, is decorated with frescoes discovered in 1841 when the room was converted from a prison cell; long attributed to Giotto, they're now thought to be by followers.

The second floor

Sculpture resumes upstairs, with a room largely devoted to the della Robbia family, a prelude to the **Sala dei Bronzetti**, Italy's best assembly of small Renaissance bronzes. Giambologna's spiralling designs predominate, a testament to his popularity in late sixteenth-century Florence: look out for the Hercules series (Ercole, in Italian), showing the hero variously wrestling and clubbing his opponents into submission. An interesting contrast is provided by **Antonio del Pollaiuolo**'s earlier and much more violent *Hercules and Antaeus* (c.1478), which stands on a pillar nearby. Like Leonardo, Pollaiuolo unravelled the complexities of human musculature by dissecting corpses.

Also on this floor there's another roomful of della Robbias and a splendid display of bronze medals, featuring specimens from the great pioneer of this form of portable art, Pisanello. Lastly, there's a room devoted mainly to **Renaissance portrait busts**, where the centrepiece is Verrocchio's *David*, clearly influenced by the Donatello figure downstairs. Around the walls you'll find Mino da Fiesole's busts of Giovanni de' Medici and Piero il Gottoso (the sons of Cosimo de' Medici), Antonio del Pollaiuolo's *Young Cavalier* (which is probably another Medici portrait), and a bust labelled *Ritratto d'Ignoto* (Portrait of an Unknown Man) – beside Verrocchio's *Madonna and Child* – which may in fact depict Macchiavelli. Also outstanding are Francesco Laurana's *Battista Sforza* (an interesting comparison with the Piero della Francesca portrait in the Uffizi), the *Woman Holding Flowers* by Verrocchio (the first such portrait bust to show the subject's hands), and the fraught marble relief in which Verrocchio portrays the death of Francesca Tornabuoni-Pitti, from whose tomb this panel was taken.

The Museo di Storia della Scienza

Long after Florence had declined from its artistic apogee, the intellectual reputation of the city was maintained by its scientists, many of them directly encouraged by the ruling Medici-Lorraine dynasty. Two of the latter, Grand Duke Ferdinando II and his brother Leopoldo, both of whom studied with Galileo, founded a scientific academy at the Pitti in 1657. Called the Accademia del Cimento (Academy of Experiment), its motto was "Try and try again." The instruments made and acquired by this academy are the core of the **Museo di Storia della Scienza** (Mon & Wed–Fri 9.30am–5pm, Tues & Sat 9.30am–1pm; Oct–May Sat open till 5pm; €4).

Some of Galileo's original instruments are on show on the first floor, such as the lens with which he discovered the four moons of Jupiter, which he tactfully named the Medicean planets. (An enormous lodestone given by Galileo to Ferdinando II is on display by the ticket desk.) On this floor you'll also find the museum's equivalent of a religious relic – bones from one of

Galileo's fingers. Other cases are filled with beautiful Arab astrolabes, calculating machines, early telescopes, and some delicate and ornate thermometers. The most imposing single exhibit on this floor is a massive armillary sphere made in 1593 for Ferdinando I to provide a visual proof of the supposed veracity of the earth-centred Ptolemaic system.

On the floor above there are all kinds of exquisitely manufactured **scientific and mechanical equipment**, several of which were built to demonstrate the fundamental laws of physics. Dozens of clocks and timepieces are on show too, along with some spectacular electrical machines, and a huge lens made for Cosimo III, with which Faraday and Davy managed to ignite a diamond by focusing the rays of the sun. At the end there's a **medical section** full of alarming surgical instruments and anatomical wax models for teaching obstetrics, plus the contents of a medieval pharmacy, displaying such unlikely cure-alls as Sangue del Drago (Dragon's Blood) and Confetti di Seme Santo (Confections of Blessed Semen).

West of the centre: from Via dei Calzaiuoli to the Cascine

Despite the urban improvement schemes of the nineteenth century and the bombings and shellings of World War II, several of the streets immediately to the west of Piazza della Signoria retain their medieval character: an amble through streets such as Via Porta Rossa, Via delle Terme and Borgo Santi Apostoli will give you some idea of the feel of Florence in the Middle Ages, when every big house was an urban fortress. Best of these medieval redoubts is the **Palazzo Davanzati**, whose interior looks little different from the way it did six hundred years ago. Nearby, the fine church of **Santa Trìnita** is home to an outstanding fresco cycle by Domenico Ghirlandaio, while beyond the glitzy **Via de' Tornabuoni** – Florence's prime shopping street – you'll find a marvellous chapel designed by Alberti and a museum devoted to the work of Marino Marini. The exquisite ancient church of **Santi Apostoli** shouldn't be overlooked, and neither should **Ognissanti**. And if all this art is beginning to take its toll, you could take a break in the tree-lined avenues of the **Cascine** park, right on the western edge of the city centre.

From the Mercato Nuovo to Santi Apostoli

One block west of the southern end of Via dei Calzaiuoli lies the **Mercato Nuovo**, or Mercato del Porcellino (mid-Feb to mid-Nov daily 9am–7pm; mid-Nov to mid-Feb Tues–Sat 9am–5pm), where there's been a market since the eleventh century, though the present loggia dates from the sixteenth. A small group is invariably gathered round the bronze boar known as *Il Porcellino*: you're supposed to earn yourself some good luck by getting a coin to fall from the animal's mouth through the grille below his head. This superstition has a social function, as the coins go to an organization that runs homes for abandoned children.

Palazzo Davanzati

Perhaps the most imposing exterior in this district is to be seen just to the south of the market – the thirteenth-century Palazzo di Parte Guelfa, financed from the confiscated property of the Ghibelline faction and later expanded by Brunelleschi. However, for a more complete re-creation of medieval Florence you should visit the fourteenth-century **Palazzo Davanzati** in Via Porta Rossa. In the nineteenth century the palazzo was divided into flats, but at the beginning of the twentieth it was restored to something very close to the appearance it had in the 1580s, when a loggia replaced the battlements on the roof, and the Davanzati stuck their coat of arms on the front. Apart from those haute-bourgeois emendations, the place now looks much as it did when first inhabited. Virtually every room is furnished and decorated in predominantly medieval style, using genuine artefacts gathered from a variety of sources.

Nowadays the palazzo is maintained as the **Museo della Casa Fiorentina Antica**. The building was closed in 1995 for major structural repairs, an operation that was at last drawing to a close as we went to press. Pending completion of this project, only a few sections of the house are open (Tues–Sat 8.15am–1.50pm; first, third & fifth Sun of the month and second & fourth Mon of the month same hours); there's no entrance charge, but this will change when the whole palazzo is once again accessible. The description that follows gives you an idea of the interior of the museum before its closure.

The interior

The owners of this house were obviously well prepared for the adversities of urban living, as can be seen in the siege-resistant doors, the huge storerooms for the hoarding of provisions, and the private water supply. The courtyard's **well** was something of a luxury at a time when much of Florence was still dependent on public fountains: a complex series of ropes and pulleys allowed it to serve the entire house. Similarly, the palace's **toilets** were state-of-the art affairs by the standards of 1330.

An ancient staircase – the only one of its kind to survive in the city – leads to the **first floor** and the Sala Grande or **Sala Madornale**. This room, used for family gatherings, underlines the dual nature of the house: furnished in the best style of the day, it also has four wood-covered hatches in the floor to allow the bombarding of a besieging enemy. Merchants' houses in the fourteenth century would typically have had elaborately painted walls in the main rooms, and the Palazzo Davanzati preserves some fine examples of such decor, especially in the dining room or **Sala dei Pappagalli**, where the imitation wall hangings of the lower walls are patterned with a parrot (*pappagallo*) motif, while the upper walls depict a garden terrace.

Before the development of systems of credit, wealth had to be sunk into tangible assets such as the tapestries, ceramics, sculpture and lacework that alleviate the austerity of many of these rooms; any surplus cash would have been locked away in a strongbox like the extraordinary example in the **Sala Piccola**, whose locking mechanism looks like the innards of a primitive clock. There's also a fine collection of *cassoni*, the painted chests in which the wife's dowry would be stored.

Plushest of the rooms is the first-floor **bedroom**, or Sala dei Pavoni – complete with en-suite bathroom. It takes its name from the beautiful frescoed frieze of trees, peacocks (*pavoni*) and other exotic birds: the coats of arms woven into the decoration are the crests of families related to the Davizzi. The rare Sicilian linen bed cover is decorated with scenes from the story of Tristan.

The arrangements of the rooms on the upper two floors, together with their beautiful array of furniture and decoration, mirror that of the first floor. For all the splendour of the lower rooms, the spot where the palace's occupants would have been likeliest to linger is the third-floor **kitchen**. Located on the uppermost floor to minimize damage if a fire broke out, it would have been the warmest room in the house. A fascinating array of utensils are on show here: the *girapolenta*, the polenta-stirrer, is extraordinary. The leaded glass – like the toilets – would have been considered a marvel at a time when many windows were covered only with turpentine-soaked rags stretched across frames to repel rainwater.

Santi Apostoli

Between Via Porta Rossa and the Arno, on Piazza del Limbo (the former burial ground of unbaptized children), stands the church of **Santi Apostoli** (Mon–Sat 10am–noon & 4–5.30pm, Sun 4–5.30pm). A replica of an ancient inscription on the facade records the legend that it was founded by Charlemagne – it's not quite that old, but it certainly pre-dates the end of the first millennium. Probably rebuilt in the middle of that century, Santi Apostoli bears a close resemblance to the city's other Romanesque basilica, San Miniato al Monte, though side chapels were added to it in the fifteenth and sixteenth centuries. Despite these alterations, and the addition of paintings during the Counter-Reformation, Santi Apostoli still has an austere beauty quite unlike any other church in the city centre, with its expanses of bare stone wall and columns of green Prato marble. According to Vasari, it was this "small and most beautiful" building that Brunelleschi employed as his primary model for the churches of San Lorenzo and Santo Spirito.

The chief treasures of Santi Apostoli are some stone fragments from the Holy Sepulchre in Jerusalem, supposedly presented by Godfrey de Bouillon to Pazzino de' Pazzi as reward for his crusading zeal. On Holy Saturday sparks struck from these stones are used to light the flame that ignites the "dove" that in turn sets off the fireworks in front of the Duomo (see p.172). The brazier in which the holy fire is borne to the cathedral is kept in the first chapel on the left.

Piazza and Ponte Santa Trìnita

West of the Palazzo Davanzati, Via Porta Rossa runs into **Piazza Santa Trìnita** – not really a square, just a widening of the city's most expensive street, Via de' Tornabuoni. The centrepiece of the piazza is the Colonna della Giustizia (Column of Justice), raised by Cosimo I in 1565 on the spot where, in August 1537, he had heard of the defeat of the anti-Medici faction at Montemurlo. The column stands on the axis of the sleek **Ponte Santa Trìnita**, construction of which was begun in 1567 on Cosimo's orders, ten years after its predecessor was demolished in a flood – and a decade after Siena had finally become part of Florentine territory, a subjugation which the bridge was intended to commemorate. The roads on both sides of the river were raised and widened to accentuate the dramatic potential of the new link between the city centre and the Oltrarno, but what makes this the classiest bridge in Florence is the sensuous curve of its arches, a curve so shallow that engineers have been baffled as to how the bridge bears up under the strain. Ostensibly the design was conjured up by Ammannati, one of the Medici's favourite artists, but the curves so closely resemble the arc of Michelangelo's Medici tombs that it's likely the credit belongs to him.

In 1944 the Nazis blew the bridge to smithereens and a seven-year argument ensued before it was agreed to rebuild it using as much of the original material as could be dredged from the Arno. To ensure maximum authenticity in the reconstruction, all the new stone that was needed was quarried from the Bóboli gardens – where the stone for Ammannati's bridge had been cut – and hand tools were used to trim it, as electric blades would have given the blocks too harsh a finish. Twelve years after the war, the reconstructed bridge was opened, lacking only the head from the statue of *Spring*, which had not been found despite the incentive of a hefty reward. At last, in 1961, the missing head was fished from the riverbed; having lain in state for a few days on a scarlet cushion in the Palazzo Vecchio, it was returned to its home.

Santa Trìnita church

The antiquity of the church of **Santa Trìnita** (Mon–Sat 8am–noon & 4–6pm, Sun 4–6pm) is manifest in the Latinate pronunciation of its name: modern Italian stresses the last, not the first syllable. The church was founded in 1092 by a Florentine nobleman called **Giovanni Gualberto**, scenes from whose life are illustrated in the frescoes in the alcove at the top of the left aisle. One Good Friday, so the story goes, Gualberto set off intent on avenging the murder of his brother. On finding the murderer he decided to spare his life – it was Good Friday – and proceeded to San Miniato, where a crucifix is said to have bowed its head to honour his act of mercy. Giovanni went on to become a Benedictine monk and found the reforming Vallombrosan order and – notwithstanding the mayhem created on Florence's streets by his militant supporters – was eventually canonized.

The church was rebuilt between about 1300 and 1330, work being interrupted by the plague of 1348. Further rebuilding took place between 1365 and 1405, while the facade – by Buontalenti – was added in 1594. Piecemeal additions over the years have lent the church a pleasantly hybrid air: the largely Gothic interior contrasts with the Mannerist facade, itself at odds with the Romanesque front wall of the interior. Santa Trìnita's architecture is softened by a number of works of art, the best of which are Ghirlandaio's frescoes. Resist the temptation to head straight for these, however, and work round the church, beginning at the **Cappella Cialli-Sernigi**, which contains a damaged fresco and detached sinopia depicting the *Mystical Marriage of St Catherine* (1389) by Spinello Aretino, recently discovered below the frescoes in the adjoining chapel.

The next chapel, the **Cappella Bartolini-Salimbeni**, is one of only a handful in the city whose decorative scheme has remained uncorrupted by subsequent additions and changes. The frescoes (1420–25) of episodes from the *Life of the Virgin* are by Lorenzo Monaco, who also painted its *Annunciation* altarpiece. The lunette and right wall of the next chapel, the **Cappella Ardinghelli**, features Giovanni Toscani's contemporaneous frescoes of the *Pietà* (1424–25) and an unfinished altar tabernacle by Benedetto da Rovezzano (1505–13). In the sacristy, if it's open, you'll find the tomb of Onofrio Strozzi, scion of a major banking dynasty: long thought to be the work of Donatello, the tomb is now cautiously attributed to Michelozzo.

Next comes the church's highlight, the **Cappella Sassetti**, famous for its cycle of frescoes of scenes from the *Life of St Francis* (1483–86) by **Domenico Ghirlandaio**. Commissioned by Francesco Sassetti, a friend of Lorenzo il Magnifico, they were intended, in part, to rival the frescoes of Sassetti's rival, Giovanni Tornabuoni, in Santa Maria Novella, also by Ghirlandaio. These frescoes are concerned as much with a portrayal of fifteenth-century Florence as with the narrative of their religious themes. St Francis, floating in the sky, is shown bringing a child back to life in Piazza Santa Trìnita: the church of Santa

Trinita is in the background, painted as it then appeared. (Opposite the church you can see the child plummeting to his temporary death.) Above this scene, *St Francis Receiving the Rule* sets the action in Piazza della Signoria – note the Loggia della Signoria – and features (right foreground) a portrait of Sassetti between his son, Federigo, and Lorenzo il Magnifico (Sassetti was general manager of the Medici bank). On the steps below them are the humanist Poliziano and three of his pupils, Lorenzo's sons; the blond boy, at the back of the line, is Giovanni, the future Pope Leo X.

Ghirlandaio has depicted himself in the lower scene, with his hand on his hip, and is also present in the chapel's altarpiece, the *Adoration of the Shepherds* (1485) – he's the shepherd pointing to the Child and, by way of self-identification, to the garland (*ghirlanda*). A persuasive Renaissance fusion of Classical and Christian iconography, the painting sets its protagonists amid Classical columns, a Roman sarcophagus (used as the manger) and a triumphal arch transplanted from the Roman forum. The figures of the donors – Sassetti and his wife, Nera Corsi – kneel to either side; they are buried in Giuliano da Sangallo's black tombs under the side arches.

Displayed in the neighbouring **Cappella Doni** is the miraculous crucifix, formerly in San Miniato, which is said to have bowed to Gualberto. The last of the church's major works, a powerful composition by Luca della Robbia – the **tomb of Benozzo Federighi**, bishop of Fiesole – occupies the left wall of the Cappella Scali; moulded and carved for the church of San Pancrazio, it was transported here in 1896. The fine wooden **statue of Mary Magdalene**, which owes much to Donatello's *Magdalene* in the Museo dell'Opera del Duomo, was begun by Desiderio da Settignano and completed, according to Vasari, by Benedetto da Maiano.

Via de' Tornabuoni to the Cascine

In recent years **Via de' Tornabuoni** and nearby Piazza Strozzi have come to be monopolized by high-end designer stores – Versace, Ferragamo, Prada, Cavalli, Gucci and Armani all have outlets here – to the dismay of many, who see further evidence of the loss of Florentine identity in the eviction of local institutions such as the Seeber bookshop, the Farmacia Inglese and the *Giacosa* café. The last of this trio now exists in name only, as an adjunct to the Roberto Cavalli shop. Conspicuous wealth is nothing new on Via de' Tornabuoni: looming above everything is the vast **Palazzo Strozzi**, the most intimidating of all Florentine Renaissance palaces, with windows as big as gateways and embossed with lumps of stone the size of boulders. It was begun by the banker Filippo Strozzi, a figure so powerful that he was once described as "the first man of Italy", and whose family provided the ringleaders of the anti-Medici faction in Florence. He bought and demolished a dozen town houses to make space for Giuliano da Sangallo's palazzo, the construction of which lasted from 1489 to 1536. The interior is open only for special exhibitions.

The Palazzo Rucellai

Some of Florence's other plutocrats made an impression with a touch more subtlety than the Strozzi. In the 1440s Giovanni Rucellai, one of the richest businessmen in the city (and an esteemed scholar too), decided to commission a new house from Leon Battista Alberti. The resultant **Palazzo Rucellai**, two-minutes' walk from the Strozzi house at Via della Vigna Nuova 18, was the first palace in Florence to follow the rules of classical architecture; its tiers of pilasters, incised into smooth blocks of stone, evoke the exterior wall of the Colosseum. Alberti later produced another, equally elegant design for the same patron – the front of the church of Santa Maria Novella. In contrast to the feud between the Medici and the Strozzi, the Rucellai were on the closest terms with the city's de facto royal family: the **Loggia dei Rucellai**, across the street (now a shop), was in all likelihood built for the wedding of Giovanni's son to the granddaughter of Cosimo il Vecchio, and the frieze on the Palazzo Rucellai features the heraldic devices of the two families, the Medici emblem alongside the Rucellai sail.

The Museo Marino Marini and the Cappella di San Sepolcro

Round the corner from the Palazzo Rucellai stands the ex-church of San Pancrazio, deconsecrated by Napoleon, then successively the offices of the state lottery, the magistrates' court, a tobacco factory and an arsenal. It is now the swish **Museo Marino Marini** (10am–5pm; closed Tues & Sun; €4), which holds some two hundred works left to the city in Marini's will. Variations on the sculptor's trademark horse-and-rider theme make up much of the show.

Once part of the church but now entirely separate from the museum, the **Cappella Rucellai**, which was redesigned by Alberti, houses the **Cappella di San Sepolcro**, the most exquisite of his creations (June–Sept hours vary but usually Mon–Fri 10am–noon; Oct–May Mon–Sat 10am–noon & 5–5.30pm; free). Designed as the funerary monument to Giovanni Rucellai, it takes the form of a diminutive reconstruction of Jerusalem's Church of the Holy Sepulchre. Access to the *cappella* is dependent upon voluntary staff, so it's prone to unscheduled periods of closure.

Ognissanti

In medieval times one of the main areas of cloth production – the mainstay of the Florentine economy – was in the western part of the city. **Ognissanti** (daily 7.30am–12.30pm & 3.30–7.30pm), or All Saints, the main church of this quarter, stands on a piazza that might be taken as a symbol of the state of the present-day Florentine economy, dominated as it is by the five-star *Grand* and *Excelsior* hotels.

The church was founded in 1256 by the Umiliati, a Benedictine order from Lombardy whose speciality was the weaving of woollen cloth. In 1561 the Franciscans took over the church, the new tenure being marked by a Baroque overhaul which spared only the medieval campanile. The facade (1637) of the church is of historical interest as one of the earliest eruptions of the Baroque in Florence.

The young face squeezed between the Madonna and the dark-cloaked man in Ghirlandaio's *Madonna della Misericordia* (1473) – over the second altar on the right – is said to be that of Amerigo Vespucci, an agent for the Medici in Seville, whose two voyages in 1499 and 1501 would lend his name to a continent. The altar was paid for by the Vespucci, a family of silk merchants from the surrounding district, which is why other members of the clan appear beneath the Madonna's protective cloak. Among them is Simonetta Vespucci (at the Virgin's left hand), the mistress of Giuliano de' Medici and reputedly the most beautiful woman of her age – she is said to have been the model for Botticelli's *Venus*, now in the Uffizi.

The idea may not be so far-fetched, for Botticelli also lived locally, and the Vespucci and Filipepi families were on good terms. Botticelli is buried in the church, beneath a round tomb slab in the south transept, and his painting of *St Augustine's Vision of St Jerome* (1480) hangs on the same wall as the Madonna, between the third and fourth altars. Facing it is Ghirlandaio's more earthbound

St Jerome, also painted in 1480. In the same year Ghirlandaio painted the *Last Supper* that covers one wall of the **refectory**, reached through the cloister entered to the left of the church (March–June Mon, Tues & Thurs–Sun 9am–5pm; July–Feb Mon, Tues & Sat 9am–noon; free).

The Cascine

Florence's public park, the **Cascine**, begins close to the Ponte della Vittoria and dwindles away 3km downstream, at the confluence of the Arno and the Mugnone. Once the Medici dairy farm (*cascina*), then a hunting reserve, this narrow strip of green mutated into a high-society venue in the eighteenth century: if there was nothing happening at the opera, all of Florence's beau monde turned out to promenade under the trees of the Cascine. A fountain in the park bears a dedication to Shelley, who was inspired to write his *Ode to the West Wind* while strolling here on a blustery day in 1819.

Thousands of people come out here on Tuesday mornings for the colossal market beyond the former train station (which now houses an arts centre, the Stazione Leopolda), and on any day of the week the Cascine swarms with joggers, cyclists and roller-bladers. Parents bring their kids out here too, to play on the grass – a rare commodity in Florence. However, the Cascine also has a reputation as a haunt for the city's drug addicts, and it's emphatically not a place for a nocturnal stroll.

The Santa Maria Novella district

Scurrying from the train station in search of a room, or fretting in the queues for a rail ticket, most people barely give a glance to **Santa Maria Novella train station**, but this is a building that deserves as much attention as many of the city's conventional monuments. Its principal architect, Giovanni Michelucci – who died in January 1991 just two days short of his hundredth birthday – was one of the leading figures of the Modernist movement, which in Mussolini's Italy was marginalized by the officially approved pomposities of the Neoclassical tendency. Accordingly, there was some astonishment when, in 1933, Michelucci and his colleagues won the open competition to design the main rail terminal for one of the country's showpiece cities. It's a piece of impeccably rational planning, so perfectly thought-out that no major alterations were deemed necessary until very recently, when approval was given for the construction of a new terminal for the high-speed Milan–Rome rail line beneath the station. Designed by Foster Associates, it's due to open in 2011.

On the other side of the church of Santa Maria Novella – whose back directly faces the station – lies **Piazza Santa Maria Novella**. Once the venue for the wild festivities of the Palio dei Cocchi (chariot race), which was introduced by Cosimo I in 1540 and continued as an annual event until 1858, this square has for many years had a distinctly squalid undertone. Now the area is being transformed, with the repaving of the whole piazza, the development of upmarket hotels and the long-awaited opening of the **Alinari photography museum**.

The church of Santa Maria Novella

Santa Maria Novella (Mon–Thurs & Sat 9am–5pm, Fri & Sun 1–5pm; €2.50) stands on the site of the more humble Santa Maria delle Vigne, which in 1221 was handed to the Dominicans, who then set about altering the place to their taste. By 1360 the interior was finished, but only the Romanesque lower part of the **facade** had been completed. This state of affairs lasted until 1456, when Giovanni Rucellai paid for Alberti to design an elegantly classicized upper storey that would blend with the older section while improving the facade's proportions. The sponsor's name is picked out across the facade in Roman capitals (iohanes·oricellarivs …), while the Rucellai family emblem, the billowing sail of Fortune, runs as a motif through the central frieze. One other external feature is worth noting: the route into the church takes you through the cemetery, which – uniquely – is ringed by an arcade of *avelli*, the collective burial vaults of upper-class families.

Santa Maria Novella's **interior** – which was designed specifically to enable preachers to address their sermons to as large a congregation as possible – is filled with masterworks, not least a ground-breaking painting by Masaccio, a crucifix by Giotto and no fewer than three major **fresco cycles**.

The nave

Entwined around the second nave pillar on the left is a **pulpit** designed by Brunelleschi (marked 5 on our plan), notorious as the spot from which the Dominicans first denounced Galileo for espousing the Copernican theory of the heavens. The actual carving was completed by Buggiano, Brunelleschi's adopted son, who may well have advised Masaccio on the Renaissance architectural details present in the background of his extraordinary 1427 fresco of the **Trinity** (6) which is painted on the wall nearby. This was one of the earliest works in which the rules of perspective and classical proportion were rigorously employed, and Florentines queued to view the illusion on its unveiling, stunned by a painting which appeared to create three-dimensional space on a solid wall. Amazingly, the picture was concealed behind an altar in 1570 and rediscovered only in 1861. Surmounting a stark image of the state to which all flesh is reduced, the main scene is a dramatized diagram of the mechanics of Christian redemption, with the lines of the painting leading from the picture's donors, through the Virgin and the Baptist, to the crucified Christ and the stern figure of God the Father at the pinnacle.

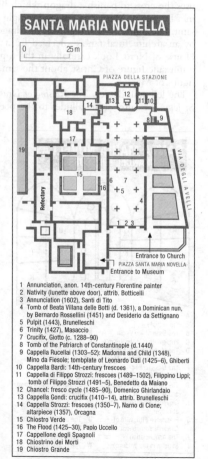

SANTA MARIA NOVELLA

0   25m

PIAZZA DELLA STAZIONE

Refectory

VIA DEGLI AVELLI

Entrance to Church
PIAZZA SANTA MARIA NOVELLA
Entrance to Museum

1 Annunciation, anon. 14th-century Florentine painter
2 Nativity (lunette above door), attrib. Botticelli
3 Annunciation (1602), Santi di Tito
4 Tomb of Beata Villana delle Botti (d. 1361), a Dominican nun, by Bernardo Rossellini (1451) and Desiderio da Settignano
5 Pulpit (1443), Brunelleschi
6 Trinity (1427), Masaccio
7 Crucifix, Giotto (c. 1288–90)
8 Tomb of the Patriarch of Constantinople (d.1440)
9 Cappella Rucellai (1303–52): Madonna and Child (1348), Mino da Fiesole; tombplate of Leonardo Dati (1425–6), Ghiberti
10 Cappella Bardi: 14th-century frescoes
11 Cappella di Filippo Strozzi: frescoes (1489–1502), Filippino Lippi; tomb of Filippo Strozzi (1491–5), Benedetto da Maiano
12 Chancel: fresco cycle (1485–90), Domenico Ghirlandaio
13 Cappella Gondi: crucifix (1410–14), attrib. Brunelleschi
14 Cappella Strozzi: frescoes (1350–7), Narno di Cione; altarpiece (1357), Orcagna
15 Chiostro Verde
16 The Flood (1425–30), Paolo Uccello
17 Cappellone degli Spagnoli
18 Chiostrino dei Morti
19 Chiostro Grande

Giotto's crucifix (7), a radically naturalistic and probably very early work (c.1288–90), now hangs in what is thought to be its intended position, poised dramatically over the centre of the nave. Hitherto, it had been hidden away in the sacristy, veiled by a layer of dirt so thick that many scholars refused to recognize it as the work of the great master; the attribution is still disputed by some.

The Cappella di Filippo Strozzi

In 1486 the chapel to the right of the chancel (11) was bought by Filippo **Strozzi**, a wealthy banker, who then commissioned Filippino Lippi to paint a much-interrupted fresco cycle (1489–1502) on the life of his namesake, St Philip the Apostle, a saint rarely portrayed in Italian art. The paintings, a departure from anything seen in Florence at the time, were completed well after Strozzi's death in 1491. Before starting the project Filippino spent some time in Rome, and the work he carried out on his return displays an archeologist's obsession with ancient Roman culture. The right wall depicts Philip's *Crucifixion* and his *Miracle before the Temple of Mars*. In the latter, the Apostle uses the cross to banish a dragon which had been an object of pagan worship in a Temple of Mars. The enraged temple priests then capture and crucify the saint. The figures swooning from the dragon's stench are almost overwhelmed by an architectural fantasy derived from Rome's recently excavated Golden House of Nero. Look carefully in the top right-hand corner and you'll see a minuscule figure of Christ, about the same size as one of the vases behind the figure of Mars.

The left wall depicts *The Raising of Drusiana* and the *Attempted Martyrdom of St John*: the latter scene alludes to the persecutions of the emperor Domitian, during which John was dipped in boiling oil in an attempt to kill him – but the Apostle emerged miraculously rejuvenated by the experience. The vaults portray Adam, Noah, Jacob and Abraham and, like the chapel's stained glass and impressive *trompe l'oeil* decoration, were also the work of Lippi. Behind the altar of this chapel is **Strozzi's tomb** (1491–95), beautifully carved by Benedetto da Maiano.

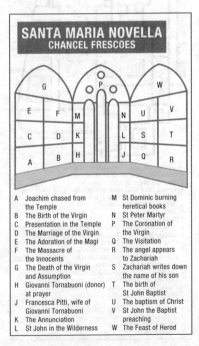

SANTA MARIA NOVELLA
CHANCEL FRESCOES

A   Joachim chased from the Temple
B   The Birth of the Virgin
C   Presentation in the Temple
D   The Marriage of the Virgin
E   The Adoration of the Magi
F   The Massacre of the Innocents
G   The Death of the Virgin and Assumption
H   Giovanni Tornabuoni (donor) at prayer
J   Francesca Pitti, wife of Giovanni Tornabuoni
K   The Annunciation
L   St John in the Wilderness
M   St Dominic burning heretical books
N   St Peter Martyr
P   The Coronation of the Virgin
Q   The Visitation
R   The angel appears to Zachariah
S   Zachariah writes down the name of his son
T   The birth of St John Baptist
U   The baptism of Christ
V   St John the Baptist preaching
W   The Feast of Herod

The chancel (Cappella Tornabuoni)

As a chronicle of fifteenth-century life in Florence, no series of frescoes is more fascinating than **Domenico Ghirlandaio's** pictures around the **chancel** and high altar (12). Ostensibly depicting scenes from the life of the Virgin (left wall) and episodes from the life of St John the Baptist, the paintings were commissioned by **Giovanni Tornabuoni**, a banker and uncle of Lorenzo de' Medici (Lorenzo the Magnificent), which explains why they are liberally sprinkled with contemporary portraits and narrative details – such as certain illustrious ladies of the Tornabuoni family being present at the births of both John the Baptist and the Virgin. Such self-glorification made the frescoes the object of special ire after they were completed, drawing the vitriol of Savonarola during his hellfire-and-brimstone sermons.

In truth, there are few frescoes in the city with such immediate charm, and none which are so self-conscious a celebration of Florence at its zenith – it's no accident that one of the frescoes on the right-hand wall includes a prominent Latin inscription (on an arch to the right) which reads: "The year 1490, when the most beautiful city renowned for abundance, victories, arts and noble buildings profoundly enjoyed salubrity and peace." Having found the inscription, you might then want to identify some of the portraits scattered around the paintings. Ghirlandaio features as a self-portrait in the scene (left wall) in which Joachim, the Virgin's father, is chased from the temple because he has been unable to have children – the painter is the figure in the right-hand group with hand on hip. In the neighbouring fresco, the young woman in the white and gold dress leading the group of women is Ludovica, Tornabuoni's only daughter, who died in childbirth aged 15: it's doubtless no accident that the scene painted in the fresco depicts the birth of the Virgin. Across the chancel, on the right wall, the **Visitation** features Giovanna degli Albizi, Tornabuoni's daughter-in-law, who also died in child-birth – she's the first of the trio of women to the right of the Virgin. The **Birth of St John the Baptist** features Tornabuoni's sister, Lucrezia, better known as the mother of Lorenzo de' Medici: she's the woman in front of the servant carrying the fruit on her head.

The Cappella Strozzi

The next chapel beyond the chancel is the **Cappella Gondi** (13), which houses Brunelleschi's crucifix, supposedly carved as a riposte to the uncouthness of Donatello's cross in Santa Croce. It is the artist's only surviving sculpture in wood. Legend claims that Donatello was so struck on seeing his rival's work that he dropped a basket of eggs.

Even more startling, however, is the great fresco cycle in the next chapel but one, the **Cappella Strozzi** (14), which lies above the level of the rest of the church at the end of the north (left) transept. Its frescoes (1350–57) were commissioned as an expiation of the sin of usury by Tommaso Strozzi, an ancestor of Filippo Strozzi, patron of the chapel across the church. The pictures are the masterpiece of Nardo di Cione, brother of the better-known Orcagna (Andrea di Cione), with whom Nardo collaborated to design the chapel's stained glass.

Orcagna alone painted the chapel's magnificent high altarpiece, *Christ Presenting the Keys to St Peter and the Book of Wisdom to Thomas Aquinas* (1357). A propaganda exercise on behalf of the Dominicans, the picture shows Christ bestowing favour on both St Peter and St Thomas Aquinas, the latter a figure second only to St Dominic in the order's hierarchy. Behind the altar, the central fresco depicts the *Last Judgement*, with Dante featured as one of the saved (in white, third from the left, second row from the top). So, too, are Tommaso Strozzi and his wife, shown being led by St Michael into paradise, with an angel helping the righteous up through a trapdoor; on the right of the altar, a devil forks the damned down into hell. The theme of judgement is continued in the bleached fresco of Dante's *Inferno* on the right wall, faced by a thronged *Paradiso* on the left.

The Museo di Santa Maria Novella

Further remarkable paintings are to be found in the spacious Romanesque conventual buildings to the left of the church of Santa Maria Novella, home to the **Museo di Santa Maria Novella** (Mon–Thurs & Sat 9am–5pm, Sun 9am–2pm; €2.70). The first set of cloisters beyond the entrance, the **Chiostro Verde**, dating from 1332 to 1350, features damaged but nonetheless remarkable frescoes of *Stories from Genesis* (1425–30) executed by Paolo Uccello and his workshop. The cloister takes its name from the green *terra verde* base pigment they used, which now gives the paintings a spectral undertone.

The windswept image of **The Flood**, the best-preserved of the cloister's frescoes, is rendered almost unintelligible by the telescoping perspective and the double appearance of the ark (before and after the flood), whose flanks form a receding corridor in the centre of the picture: on the left, the ark is rising on the deluge, on the right it has come to rest as the waters subside. In the foreground, two men fight each other in their desperation to stay alive; the chequered lifebelt that one of these men is wearing around his neck is a favourite Uccello device for demonstrating a mastery of perspective – it's a *mazzocchio*, a 72-faceted wicker ring round which a turbanned headdress was wrapped. Another man grabs the ankles of the visionary figure in the foreground – presumably Noah, though he is a much younger Noah than the hirsute patriarch leaning out of the ark on the right to receive the dove's olive branch. In the right foreground there's a preview of the universal devastation, with tiny corpses laid out on the deck, and a crow gobbling an eyeball from one of the drowned.

The Cappellone degli Spagnoli

Off the cloister opens what was once the chapterhouse of the immensely rich convent of Santa Maria, the **Cappellone degli Spagnoli**, or Spanish Chapel,

▲ The cloisters of Santa Maria Novella

which for a time was the headquarters of the Inquisition. It received its present name after Eleonora di Toledo, wife of Cosimo I, reserved it for the use of her Spanish entourage. Presumably she derived much inspiration from its majestic fresco cycle (1367–69) by Andrea di Firenze, an extended depiction of the triumph of the Catholic Church that was described by Ruskin as "the most noble piece of pictorial philosophy in Italy".

Virtually every patch of the walls is covered with frescoes, whose theme is the role of the Dominicans in the battle against heresy and in the salvation of Christian souls. The **left wall** as you enter depicts *The Triumph of Divine Wisdom*, a triumph exemplified by Thomas Aquinas, who is portrayed enthroned below the Virgin and Apostles amidst the winged Virtues and the "wise men" of the Old and New Testaments. The more spectacular **right wall** depicts *The Triumph of the Church*, or more specifically, the "Mission, Work and Triumph of the Dominican Order". At the bottom is a building supposed to be Florence's cathedral, a pinky-purple creation imagined one hundred years before the structure was completed. Before it stand the pope and Holy Roman Emperor, society's ultimate spiritual and temporal rulers. In front of them stand ranks of figures representing religious orders, among which the Dominicans are naturally pre-eminent. In particular, note St Dominic, the order's founder, unleashing the "hounds of the lord", or Domini Canes, a pun on the Dominicans' name: heretics, the dogs' victims, are shown as wolves.

Among the group of pilgrims (in the centre, just below the Duomo) are several portraits, real or imagined: Cimabue (standing in a large brown cloak); Giotto (beside him in profile, wearing a green cloak); Boccaccio (further right, in purple, holding a closed book); Petrarch (above, with a cloak and white ermine hood); and Dante (alongside Petrarch in profile, with a white cap). Above and to the right are scenes of young people dancing, hawking, playing music and engaging in other pleasures of the sort that the Dominicans so heartily condemned.

Those able to resist such abominations are shown being marshalled by a nearby friar, who hears their confession before dispatching them towards St Peter and the Gate of Paradise. Once through the gate, the blessed are shown in adoration of God and the angels with the Virgin in their midst. Foremost among those confessing is the chapel's donor, one Buonamico Guidalotti (shown kneeling), who paid for the chapel in honour of his wife, who died during the 1348 plague. The far wall shows scenes connected with the Crucifixion, while the near (entrance) wall, which is excluded from the frescoes' unified theme, contains episodes from the life of St Peter Martyr, one of the Dominicans' leading lights.

The contemporaneous decoration of the **Chiostrino dei Morti**, the oldest part of the complex, has not aged so robustly; it was closed for restoration at the time of writing. The **Chiostro Grande**, to the west, is also out of bounds, but for the more unusual reason that it is a practice parade ground for aspiring *carabinieri*. The museum adjoining the Chiostro Grande is notable chiefly for some peculiarly glamorous fourteenth- and fifteenth-century reliquary busts, containing remnants of St Ursula and Mary Magdalene, among others.

The Museo Nazionale Alinari Fotografia

Back at the start of the thirteenth century the colonnaded building that faces Santa Maria Novella across the piazza was the hospital of San Paolo, a refuge for the sick and the destitute, and also the base for the Dominicans before they moved to Santa Maria Novella. At the beginning of the fifteenth century the administration of the hospital passed to the Arte dei Giudici e Notari (the guild of judges and notaries), and it was they who enlarged the building, probably to a design by Michelozzo, whose loggia – the **Loggia di San Paolo** – is a close imitation of Brunelleschi's Spedale degli Innocenti. In the 1490s Andrea della Robbia added the attractive terracotta medallions and lunettes, further emphasizing the similarity between the two buildings. One of the lunettes depicts the momentous meeting of Saint Francis (who founded a Franciscan convent next door) and his fellow monastic reformer Saint Dominic, an event that's generally believed to have happened in Rome in 1217, but is said by local folklore to have occurred a little sooner, on this very spot.

In the 1780s the hospital was suppressed and the building became a school for impoverished girls and unmarried young women, which it remained until World War II, when it was used by the Fascists as a prison. After the war it re-opened as a state school, and now, having been handsomely restored, it's home to the **Museo Nazionale Alinari Fotografia** (Mon, Tues, Thurs, Fri & Sun 9.30am–7.30pm, Sat 9.30am–11.30pm; €9). Part of the museum is set aside for one-off photography exhibitions, but most of the space is given over to changing displays drawn from Alinari's archive of more than four million pictures, covering everything from 1840s daguerreotypes to the work of present-day photographers. The technology of the art is featured too, with a variety of cameras on show, plus stereoscopes and camera obscuras.

North of the centre: the San Lorenzo, San Marco and Annunziata districts

A few blocks from the train station and the Duomo lies the San Lorenzo district, the city's main market area, with scores of stalls encircling a vast and wonderful food hall. The racks of T-shirts, leather jackets and belts almost engulf the church of **San Lorenzo**, a building of major importance that's attached to another of the city's great draws, the **Cappelle Medicee** (Medici Chapels). While various of the Medici's most important members are buried in the main part of San Lorenzo, dozens of lesser lights are interred in these chapels, with two of the most venal being celebrated by some of **Michelangelo**'s finest funerary sculpture. The Medici also account for the area's other major sight, the **Palazzo Medici-Riccardi**, with its exquisite fresco-covered chapel, while the most celebrated of all Michelangelo's works in stone – the David – can be admired in the nearby galleries of the **Accademia**. The devotional art of Fra' Angelico fills the nearby **Museo di San Marco**, which in turn is but a stroll away from **Piazza Santissima Annunziata**, one of Florence's most photogenic squares, thanks to Brunelleschi's **Spedale degli Innocenti** and the church of **Santissima Annunziata**.

San Lorenzo

Founded in 393, **San Lorenzo** (daily 10am–5.30pm; March–Oct closes Sun 1.30pm; €3.50) has a claim to be the oldest church in Florence. For some three hundred years it was the city's cathedral, before renouncing its title to Santa Reparata, the precursor of the Duomo. By 1060 a sizeable Romanesque church had been built on the site, a building which in time became the Medici's parish church, benefiting greatly over the years from the family's munificence.

The family was in a particularly generous mood in 1419, when a committee of eight parishioners headed by Giovanni di Bicci de' Medici, founder of the Medici fortune, offered to finance a new church. **Brunelleschi** was commissioned to begin the project, starting work on the Sagrestia Vecchia (Old Sacristy) before being given the go-ahead two years later to rebuild the entire church. Construction lapsed over the next twenty years, hampered by financial problems, political upheavals and Brunelleschi's simultaneous work on the cathedral dome. Giovanni's son, Cosimo de' Medici, eventually gave the work fresh impetus with a grant of 40,000 *fiorini* (florins) – at a time when 150 florins would support a Florentine family for a year. Cosimo's largesse saved the day, but was still not sufficient to provide the church with a facade. No less a figure than Michelangelo laboured to remedy the omission, one of many to devote time to a scheme to provide a suitable frontage. None of the efforts was to any avail: to this day the exterior's bare brick has never been clad.

The interior

When you step inside the church, what strikes you first is the cool rationality of Brunelleschi's design, an instantly calming contrast to the hubbub outside. San Lorenzo was the earlier of Brunelleschi's great Florentine churches (the other is Santo Spirito) but already displays his mastery of Classical decorative motifs and mathematically planned proportions.

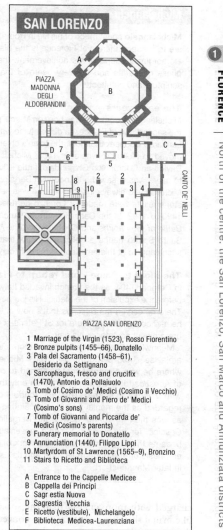

SAN LORENZO

PIAZZA MADONNA DEGLI ALDOBRANDINI

CANTO DE' NELLI

PIAZZA SAN LORENZO

1 Marriage of the Virgin (1523), Rosso Fiorentino
2 Bronze pulpits (1455–66), Donatello
3 Pala del Sacramento (1458–61), Desiderio da Settignano
4 Sarcophagus, fresco and crucifix (1470), Antonio da Pollaiuolo
5 Tomb of Cosimo de' Medici (Cosimo il Vecchio)
6 Tomb of Giovanni and Piero de' Medici (Cosimo's sons)
7 Tomb of Giovanni and Piccarda de' Medici (Cosimo's parents)
8 Funerary memorial to Donatello
9 Annunciation (1440), Filippo Lippi
10 Martyrdom of St Lawrence (1565–9), Bronzino
11 Stairs to Ricetto and Biblioteca

A Entrance to the Cappelle Medicee
B Cappella dei Principi
C Sagr estia Nuova
D Sagrestia Vecchia
E Ricetto (vestibule), Michelangelo
F Biblioteca Medicea-Laurenziana

The first work of art to catch your attention, in the second chapel on the right, is Rosso Fiorentino's **Marriage of the Virgin** (marked 1 on our plan) with its uniquely golden-haired and youthful Joseph. There's another arresting painting at the top of the left aisle – Bronzino's enormous fresco of *The Martyrdom of St Lawrence* (10) – but it seems a shallow piece of work alongside the nearby bronze pulpits by **Donatello** (2). Clad with reliefs depicting scenes preceding and following the Crucifixion, these are the artist's last works (begun c.1460), and were completed by his pupils as increasing paralysis limited their master's ability to model in wax. Jagged and discomforting,

Michelangelo

Michelangelo spent much of his life in Rome, and some of his greatest masterpieces are to be seen there, yet Florence is the place where you can best appreciate the extraordinary scope of his achievement: the city possesses creations from every phase of his life and in every genre of the visual arts he excelled in – painting, sculpture and architecture.

The early years

Michelangelo Buonarroti was born on March 16, 1475 in Caprese, in eastern Tuscany, the second son of Francesca di Neri (who was to die six years later) and Lodovico di Leonardo Buonarroti Simoni, the town's chief magistrate. One month later the family moved to Florence, where, in 1488, Michelangelo was apprenticed to the painters Davide and Domenico Ghirlandaio. Little is known about how Michelangelo learned to carve: Vasari says he trained with Bertaldo di Giovanni (a pupil of Donatello), but Michelangelo always insisted that he was self-taught. What's certain is that his first stone reliefs were made for Lorenzo de' Medici, in whose household he lived from 1490 to 1492. In the Casa Buonarroti you can see two pieces from this period: the *Battle of the Lapiths and Centaurs* and the *Madonna of the Stairs*. In the church of Santo Spirito hangs a delicate *Crucifix* that was also (almost certainly) made by Michelangelo at this time, and is his only carving in wood.

The flight to Rome – and return to Florence

In October 1494, as the French invaded Italy, Michelangelo fled Florence – a month before the expulsion of the Medici. His journey eventually took him, in 1496, to Rome. There he carved the *Bacchus* that's now in the Bargello, and by the spring of 1499 he had completed the *Pietà* for St Peter's, a work that secured his reputation as the pre-eminent sculptor of his day.

Meanwhile, Florence had become more peaceable after the overthrow of Savonarola (see box, p.130), and in 1501 Michelangelo went back to his home city, where he was promptly commissioned to create the *David*, and then a sequence of *Apostles* for the Duomo, of which only the *St Matthew* (now in the Accademia, with *David*) was started. The *Doni Tondo* – one of his very few forays into what he regarded as the menial art of easel painting – was also created during this period, as was the *Pitti Tondo*, now in the Bargello. Although his fresco of the *Battle of Cáscina*, for the Palazzo Vecchio, never advanced beyond the cartoon stage, it became the single most influential work of art in the city, with its unprecedented emphasis on the nude male form and its use of twisting figures, a recurrent motif in later Mannerist art.

charged with more energy than the space can contain, these panels are more like brutal sketches in bronze than conventional reliefs. Donatello is buried in the nave of the church, next to his patron, Cosimo de' Medici, and commemorated by a **memorial** (8) on the right wall of the chapel in the north transept, close to Filippo Lippi's 1440 altarpiece of the Annunciation (9). In the centre of the church, the **tomb of Cosimo de' Medici** (5) bears the inscription "Pater Patriae" (Father of the Fatherland) – a title once borne by Roman emperors.

The Sagrestia Vecchia

Four more leading Medici members lie buried in the **Sagrestia Vecchia** or Old Sacristy, one of Brunelleschi's earliest projects (1421–26), and the only one completed in his lifetime. Brunelleschi's biographer, Manetti, wrote that "it astounded all men both of the city and foreigners … for its new and beautiful

1505–16: Rome

In 1505 Michelangelo was called to Rome, to create a tomb for Pope Julius II. When completed in 1545, the tomb had seven instead of the planned forty statues, only three of them by Michelangelo: *Moses*, *Leah* and *Rachel*. The latter two (both 1542) were the last sculptures that Michelangelo finished; the unfinished *Slaves* in the Accademia was made for another version of the tomb. His relationship with the fiery Julius was always fractious, and in 1506 he returned to Florence. In 1508, however, he was summoned back to the Vatican to commence the most superhuman of all his undertakings – the Sistine Chapel ceiling.

Final return to Florence

In 1516, with the Sistine ceiling finished, Michelangelo returned to Florence, where in 1521 Pope Leo X contracted him to design a new sacristy for San Lorenzo church, as a Medici mausoleum. Work on this, Michelangelo's first architectural project, was interrupted frequently, and building really only began in 1523, when he was also asked to build a library – the Biblioteca Laurenziana – alongside the church. In the San Lorenzo project Michelangelo created an architectural vocabulary that was to provide the basis of Mannerist design, and he carved a remarkable group of sculptures for the sacristy.

The Medici were expelled from Florence in 1527, and Michelangelo stayed in the city to supervise the defences when it was besieged in 1530 by Emperor Charles V, who then installed the despotic Alessandro de' Medici as his puppet ruler. Once Alessandro was in place, Michelangelo's life in the city was far from easy. In 1534 he left Florence for the last time.

1534–64: Back to Rome

Michelangelo was to spend his last thirty years in Rome, where he was soon appointed architect to St Peter's, which Bramante had begun to rebuild in 1506. The colossal dome was his most spectacular addition to the architecture of the Vatican; he made a similarly profound alteration to the civic fabric of the city when he remodelled the Campidoglio in the 1540s. In 1536–41 he produced the tumultuous *Last Judgement* in the Sistine Chapel, and some time around 1540 he carved his last secular work, the *Brutus* (now in the Bargello), but the greatest sculptures of his last years are versions of the *Pietà*. One of these – an ensemble that exemplifies the quality that contemporaries termed *terribilità* ("awesome powerfulness" is an approximation) – was intended for his own tomb, and is now in Florence's Museo dell'Opera del Duomo. Michelangelo died in Rome on February 18, 1564; his body was transported to Florence, where it was borne in torchlit procession to Santa Croce.

manner. And so many people came continuously that they greatly bothered those who worked there."

The space was commissioned by Giovanni Bicci de' Medici, the principal founder of the Medici fortune, as a private chapel. On his death, Giovanni, along with his wife Piccarda, was buried beneath the massive marble slab at the centre of the chapel. Another tomb, easily missed, lies immediately to the left as you enter: the last resting place of Giovanni's grandsons, Giovanni and Piero de' Medici, it was commissioned from Verrocchio in 1472 by Lorenzo de' Medici. To the modern eye the tomb looks relatively plain, but a Florentine of the day would have been abundantly aware that it was made from the three most precious materials of antiquity – marble, porphyry and bronze.

More arresting than either of the tombs, however, is the chapel's ornamentation. Here Brunelleschi's genius was complemented by the decorative acumen of Donatello, who worked in the sacristy between 1434 and 1443, some twenty years before sculpting the pulpits in the main body of the church. He was responsible for both the cherub-filled frieze and the eight extraordinary tondos above it. The tondos' subjects are the four Evangelists and a quartet of scenes from the life of St John the Evangelist.

Two large **reliefs**, also probably by Donatello, adorn the space above the two doors on the end wall: one shows Sts Lawrence and Stephen, twin protectors of Florence, the other Sts Cosmas and Damian. These last two, twins and early Christian martyrs, were the patron saints of doctors (*medici*) and thus of the Medici, who were probably descended from doctors or apothecaries. By happy coincidence, Cosimo de' Medici, the church's chief patron, was born on the saints' feast day (27 Sept), so the two are often seen in paintings or buildings commissioned or connected with him.

Donatello was also responsible for the two bronze doors below with their combative martyrs to the left, and the *Apostles and Fathers of the Church* to the right. The chapel beyond the left door has a sublime little marble lavabo, probably by Verrocchio: many of its fantastic creatures have Medici connections – the falcon and lamb, for example, are the heraldic symbols of Piero de' Medici, who commissioned the work.

Lastly, the **stellar fresco** on the dome above the recessed altar inevitably draws your eye: opinion differs as to whether the position of the painted stars is synonymous with the state of the heavens on July 16, 1416, the birthday of Piero de' Medici, or on July 6, 1439, the date on which the union of the Eastern and Western churches was celebrated at the Council of Florence.

The Biblioteca Medicea-Laurenziana

A gateway to the left of the church facade leads through a pleasant cloister and through a doorway up to the **Biblioteca Medicea-Laurenziana** (Mon, Fri & Sat 8.30am–2pm, Tues–Thurs 8am–5pm; €3). Wishing to create a suitably grandiose home for the precious manuscripts assembled by Cosimo and Lorenzo de' Medici, Pope Clement VII – Lorenzo's nephew – asked Michelangelo to design a new Medici library in 1524. The **Ricetto** (1559–71), or vestibule, of the building he eventually came up with is a revolutionary showpiece of Mannerist architecture, delighting in paradoxical display: brackets that support nothing, columns that sink into the walls rather than stand out from them, and a flight of steps so large that it almost fills the room, spilling down like a solidified lava flow.

From this eccentric space, you're sometimes allowed into the tranquil **reading room**; here, too, almost everything is the work of Michelangelo, even the inlaid desks. Exhibitions in the connecting rooms draw on the 15,000-piece Medici collection, which includes manuscripts as diverse as a fifth-century copy of Virgil – the collection's oldest item – and a treatise on architecture by Leonardo. Note how the coffered ceiling and terracotta floor mirror each other's designs.

The Cappelle Medicee

Michelangelo's most celebrated contribution to the San Lorenzo complex forms part of the **Cappelle Medicee** (Tues–Sat 8.15am–5.50pm; first, third & fifth Sun of month and second & fourth Mon of month same hours; €6), entered from Piazza Madonna degli Aldobrandini, at the back of the church. These chapels divide into three sections: the crypt, burial place of many minor Medici; the Cappella dei Principi, housing the tombs of six of the more major Medici; and the Sagrestia Nuova, home to three major groups of Michelangelo sculpture.

Hardly any of the Medici, however humble, suffered the indignity of a modest grave. Some might have expected more, though, than the low-vaulted **crypt** of the Cappelle Medicee, home to the brass-railed tombs of many of the family's lesser lights. Most were placed here in 1791 by Ferdinand III with what appears to have been scant regard for his ancestors: one contemporary recorded how the duke had the corpses thrown together, "caring scarcely to distinguish one from the other".

After filing through the crypt, you climb steps at its rear into the larger of the chapels, the **Cappella dei Principi** (Chapel of the Princes), a morbid and dowdy marble-plated hall built as a mausoleum for Cosimo I and the grand dukes who succeeded him. The octagonal chapel took as its inspiration the floorplan of no less a building than the Baptistery, and the extent of Medici conceit was underlined by the chapel's intended centrepiece – the Holy Sepulchre of Christ, a prize that had to be forfeited when the pasha refused to sell it and an expedition sent to Jerusalem to steal it returned empty-handed. Dismissed by Byron as a "fine frippery in great slabs of various expensive stones, to commemorate rotten and forgotten carcasses", this was the most expensive building project ever financed by the Medici, and the family were still paying for it in 1743 when the last of the line, Anna Maria Luisa, joined her forebears in the basement. Scaffolding has adorned the walls since a section of cornice fell off in 2000, revealing major structural faults.

The Sagrestia Nuova

Begun in 1520, the **Sagrestia Nuova** was designed by Michelangelo as a tribute to, and re-invention of, Brunelleschi's Sagrestia Vecchia in the main body of San Lorenzo. Architectural experts go into raptures over the sophistication of the architecture, notably the empty niches above the doors, which play complex games with the vocabulary of classical architecture, but the lay person will be drawn to the three fabulous **Medici tombs** (1520–34), two wholly and one partly by Michelangelo. The sculptor was awarded the commissions by Pope Leo X – a Medici – and the pope's cousin, Cardinal Giulio de' Medici, later to become Pope Clement VII.

With your back to the entrance door, the tomb on the left belongs to **Lorenzo, duke of Urbino**, the grandson of Lorenzo the Magnificent. Michelangelo depicts him as a man of thought, and his sarcophagus bears figures of *Dawn* and *Dusk*, the times of day whose ambiguities appeal to the contemplative mind. Opposite stands the tomb of Lorenzo de' Medici's youngest son, **Giuliano, duke of Nemours**; as a man of action, his character is symbolized by the clear antithesis of *Day* and *Night*. A contemporary recorded that the sculptor gave his subjects "a greatness, a proportion, a dignity ... which seemed to him would have brought them more praise, saying that a thousand years hence no one would be able to know that they were otherwise." The protagonists were very much otherwise: Giuliano was in reality an easygoing but somewhat feckless individual, while Lorenzo combined ineffectuality with unbearable arrogance. Both died – young and not greatly lamented – of tuberculosis, combined in Lorenzo's case with syphilis.

The two principal effigies were intended to face the equally grand tombs of Lorenzo de' Medici and his brother Giuliano, two Medici who had genuine claims to fame. The only part of the project completed by Michelangelo is the **Madonna and Child**, the last image of the Madonna he ever sculpted. The figures to either side are Cosmas and Damian, which were completed to

Michelangelo's original design. Wax and clay models exist in the Casa Buonarroti and British Museum of other figures Michelangelo planned for the tomb, including allegorical figures of Heaven and Earth and statues of river gods representing the Tiber and Arno. Sketches relating to this scheme are visible behind the altar (visitors are allowed to see them, under supervision, every 30min), but the chapel was never completed as Michelangelo intended: in 1534, four years after the Medici had returned to Florence in the wretched form of Alessandro, Michelangelo decamped to Rome, where he stayed for the rest of his life.

The Palazzo Medici-Riccardi

On the edge of the square in front of San Lorenzo stands the **Palazzo Medici-Riccardi** (Thurs–Tues; €5), built for Cosimo de' Medici by Michelozzo between 1444 and 1462, supposedly after Cosimo had rejected a design by Brunelleschi on political grounds, saying "envy is a plant one should never water". With its heavily rusticated exterior, this palace was the prototype for several major Florentine buildings, most notably the Palazzo Pitti and Palazzo Strozzi, and it remained the family home and Medici business headquarters until Cosimo I moved to the Palazzo Vecchio in 1540. After 1659 the palace was greatly altered by its new owners, the Riccardi, and it now houses the offices of the provincial government. The chief attraction for tourists is the cycle of Gozzoli **frescoes** in the chapel, which a maximum of fifteen people may view at any one time.

The Gozzoli frescoes

Today all that survives of the interior of the original palace is Michelozzo's deep, colonnaded courtyard, which closely follows the new style established by Brunelleschi in the foundling hospital, and a tiny **chapel**, reached by stairs leading directly from the court. The walls of the chapel are covered by some of the city's most charming frescoes: Benozzo Gozzoli's sequence depicting *The Journey of the Magi*, painted around 1460 and recently restored to magnificent effect. The landscape scenes to either side of the altar are by the same artist.

Despite the frescoes' ostensible subject, the cycle probably portrays the pageant of the Compagnia dei Magi, the most patrician of the city's religious confraternities, whose annual procession took place at Epiphany. Several of the Medici, inevitably, were prominent members, including Piero de' Medici (Piero il Gottoso – the Gouty), who may have commissioned the pictures. It's known that several of the Medici household are featured in the procession, but putting names to these prettified faces is a problem. The man leading the cavalcade on a white horse is almost certainly Piero, while the figure behind him, in the black cloak, is probably his father, Cosimo il Vecchio. Piero's older son, the future Lorenzo il Magnifico, 11 years old at the time the fresco was painted, is probably the gold-clad young king in the foreground, riding the grey horse detached from the rest of the procession, while his brother, Giuliano, is probably the one preceded by the black bowman, to the left of Cosimo il Vecchio. The artist himself is in the crowd at the rear of the procession, his red beret signed with the words "Opus Benotii" in gold. Finally, the bearded characters among the throng might be portraits of the retinue of the Byzantine emperor John Paleologus III, who had attended the Council of Florence twenty years before the fresco was painted.

The first floor

Another set of stairs leads from the passageway beside the courtyard up to the **first floor**, where a display case in the lobby of the main gallery contains a *Madonna and Child* by **Filippo Lippi**, one of Cosimo de' Medici's more troublesome protégés. Cosimo set up a workshop for him in the Medici palace, from which he often absented himself to go chasing women. On one occasion Cosimo actually locked the artist in the studio, but Filippo escaped down a rope of bed sheets; having cajoled him into returning, Cosimo declared that he would in future manage the painter with "affection and kindness", a policy that seems to have worked more successfully.

The ceiling of the grandiloquent **gallery** glows with Luca Giordano's fresco of *The Apotheosis of the Medici* (1683), from which one can only deduce that Giordano had no sense of shame. Accompanying Cosimo III on his flight into the ether is his son, Gian Gastone (d.1737), who grew to be a man so dissolute and inert that he could rarely summon the energy to get out of bed in the morning, and was the last male Medici.

From the Mercato Centrale to the Fortezza da Basso

The **Mercato Centrale** (Mon–Sat 7am–2pm) is Europe's largest covered food hall, built in stone, iron and glass by Giuseppe Mengoni, architect of Milan's famous Galleria. Opened in 1874, it received a major overhaul a century later, reopening in 1980 with a new first floor. Butchers, *alimentari*, tripe-sellers, greengrocers, pasta stalls – they're all gathered under the one roof, and all charging prices lower than you'll readily find elsewhere in the city. Get there close to the end of the working day and you'll find some good reductions.

Each day from 8am to 7pm (except Sun) the streets around the Mercato Centrale are thronged with **stalls** selling clothing and leather goods. Most of the stuff is of doubtful quality, but this is the busiest of Florence's daily street markets, and an immersion in the haggling mass of customers can be fun.

▲ The Mercato Centrale

The Cenacolo di Fuligno

One of Florence's more obscure *cenacoli* (Last Suppers), the **Cenacolo di Fuligno**, is to be found a short distance from the market at Via Faenza 42, in the former Franciscan convent of Sant'Onofrio (Tues, Thurs & Sat 9am–noon; free, but donation requested). Discovered under layers of whitewash and grime in 1840, it was once thought to be by Raphael, then reassigned to Raphael's mentor Perugino. Latest research indicates that it was painted by a member of Perugino's workshop but designed by the master in the 1490s – the orderliness and wistful tranquillity of the scene is typical of Perugino's style, and the Apostles' poses are drawn from a repertoire of gestures which the artist frequently deployed.

The Fortezza da Basso

North of Via Faenza, the **Fortezza da Basso** was built to intimidate the people of Florence by the vile Alessandro de' Medici, who ordained himself Duke of Florence after a ten-month siege by the army of Charles V and Pope Clement VII (probably Alessandro's father) had forcibly restored the Medici. Michelangelo, the most talented Florentine architect of the day, had played a major role in the defence of the city during the siege; the job of designing the fortress fell to the more pliant Antonio da Sangallo.

Within a few years the cruelties of Alessandro had become intolerable; a petition to Charles V spoke of the Fortezza da Basso as "a prison and a slaughterhouse for the unhappy citizens". Charles's response to the catalogue of Alessandro's atrocities was to marry his daughter to the tyrant. In the end, another Medici came to the rescue: in 1537 the distantly related **Lorenzaccio de' Medici** stabbed the duke to death as he waited for an amorous assignation in Lorenzaccio's house. The reasons for the murder have never been clear but it seems that Lorenzaccio's mental health was little better than Alessandro's: in his earlier years he and Alessandro had regularly launched lecherous sorties on the city's convents, and he had been expelled from Rome after lopping the heads off statues on the Arch of Constantine. The assassination, however, had favourable consequences for the city: as Alessandro died heirless, the council proposed that the leadership of the Florentine republic should be offered to **Cosimo de' Medici**, the great-grandson of Lorenzo il Magnifico. Subsequent Medici dukes had no need of a citizen-proof fort, and the Fortezza da Basso fell into dereliction after use as a gaol and barracks.

Since 1978 there's been a vast modern shed in the centre of the complex, used for trade fairs and shows such as the Pitti Moda fashion jamborees in January and July. The public gardens by the walls are fairly pleasant, if you want an open-air spot to relax before catching a train.

The Accademia

Florence's first academy of drawing, the Accademia del Disegno, was founded in 1563 by Bronzino, Ammannati and Vasari. Initially based in Santissima Annunziata, it moved in 1764 to Via Ricasoli, and soon afterwards was transformed into a general arts academy, the Accademia di Belle Arti. Twenty years later the Grand Duke Pietro Leopoldo I founded the nearby **Galleria dell'Accademia** (Tues–Sun 8.15am–6.50pm; €6.50), filling its rooms with paintings for the edification of the students. Later augmented with pieces from suppressed religious foundations and other sources, the Accademia has an extensive collection of paintings, especially Florentine work of the fourteenth and fifteenth centuries.

The **picture galleries** which flank the main sculpture hall are quite small and generally unexciting, with copious examples of the work of "Unknown Florentine" and "Follower of …". The pieces likeliest to make an impact are Pontormo's *Venus and Cupid* (1532), painted to a cartoon by Michelangelo; a *Madonna of the Sea* (1470) attributed to Botticelli; and the painted fifteenth-century Adimari Chest, showing a Florentine wedding ceremony in the Piazza del Duomo. A cluster of rooms near the exit house gilded religious works from the thirteenth and fourteenth centuries, including an altarpiece of the Pentecost by Andrea Orcagna (c.1365).

Michelangelo's David

Commissioned by the Opera del Duomo in 1501, the **David** was conceived to invoke parallels with Florence's freedom from outside domination (despite the superior force of its enemies), and its recent liberation from Savonarola and the Medici. It's an incomparable show of technical bravura, all the more impressive given the difficulties posed by the marble from which it was carved. The four-metre block of stone – thin, shallow and riddled with cracks – had been quarried from Carrara forty years earlier. Several artists had already attempted to work with it, notably Agostino di Duccio, Andrea Sansovino and Leonardo da Vinci. Michelangelo succeeded where others had failed, completing the work in 1504 when he was still just 29.

When they gave Michelangelo his commission, the Opera del Duomo had in mind a large statue that would be placed high on the Duomo's facade. Perhaps because the finished *David* was even larger than had been envisaged, at some point it was decided that it should be placed instead at ground level, in the Piazza della Signoria. Four days and a team of forty men were required to move the statue from the workshop to the Piazza; another three weeks were needed to raise it onto its plinth. During the move the statue required protection day and night to prevent it being stoned by Medici supporters who were all too aware of its symbolism. Damage was done a few years later, in 1527, when the Medici were again expelled from the city: a bench, flung from a window of the Palazzo Vecchio by anti-Medici rioters, struck and smashed the left arm, but the pieces were gathered up and reassembled. The statue remained in its outdoor setting, exposed to the elements, until it was sent to the Accademia in 1873, by which time it had lost its gilded hair and the gilded band across its chest. Also missing these days is a skirt of copper leaves added to spare the blushes of Florence's more sensitive citizens.

Thoroughly cleaned in 2004, the *David* now occupies a specially built alcove, protected by a glass barrier that was built in 1991, after one of its toes was cracked by a hammer-wielding artist. With its massive head and gangling arms, the *David* looks to some people like a monstrous adolescent, but its proportions would not have appeared so graceless in the setting for which it was first conceived, at a rather higher altitude and at a greater distance from the public than the position it occupies in the Accademia's chapel-like space.

The Slaves

Michelangelo once described the process of carving as being the liberation of the form from within the stone, a notion that seems to be embodied by the remarkable unfinished **Slaves** (or *Prisoners*). His procedure, clearly demonstrated here, was to cut the figure as if it were a deep relief, and then to free the three-dimensional figure; often his assistants would perform the initial operation, working from the master's pencil marks, so it's possible that Michelangelo's own chisel never actually touched these stones.

Probably carved in the late 1520s, the statues were originally destined for the tomb of Julius II, intended perhaps to symbolize the liberal arts left "enslaved" by Julius's demise. The tomb underwent innumerable permutations before its eventual abandonment, however, and in 1564 the artist's nephew gave the carvings to the Medici, who installed them in the grotto of the Bóboli garden. Four of the original six statues came to the Accademia in 1909; two others found their way to the Louvre in Paris.

Close by is another unfinished work, *St Matthew* (1505–6), started soon after completion of the *David* as a commission from the Opera del Duomo; they actually requested a full series of the Apostles from Michelangelo, but this is the only one he ever began. It languished half-forgotten in the cathedral vaults until 1831.

The Museo dell'Opificio delle Pietre Dure

The **Opificio delle Pietre Dure** (Mon–Sat 8.15am–2pm, Thurs open till 7pm; €2), which occupies a corner of the Accademia building, was founded in 1588 to train craftsmen in the distinctively Florentine art of creating pictures or patterns with polished, inlaid semi-precious stones. The museum clearly elucidates the highly skilled processes involved in the creation of *pietre dure* work, and has some remarkable examples of the genre. If you want to see some more spectacular specimens, you should visit the Cappelle Medicee or the Palazzo Pitti's Museo degli Argenti. While several local workshops still maintain the traditions of this specialized art-form, the Opificio itself has evolved into one of the world's leading centres for the restoration of stonework and paintings.

The Museo di San Marco

A whole side of Piazza San Marco is taken up by the Dominican convent and church of San Marco, the former building now the home of the **Museo di San Marco** (Tues–Thurs 8.15am–1.50pm, Fri 8.15am–6pm, Sat 8.15am–7pm, also first, third & fifth Mon of month 8.15am–1.50pm, and second & fourth Sun of month 8.15am–7pm; €4). The Dominicans acquired the site in 1436, after being forced to move from their former home in Fiesole, and the complex promptly became the recipient of Cosimo's most lavish patronage. In the 1430s he financed Michelozzo's enlargement of the conventual buildings (1437–52), and went on to establish a vast library here. Abashed by the wealth he was transferring to them, the friars of San Marco suggested to Cosimo that he need not continue to support them on such a scale, to which he replied, "Never shall I be able to give God enough to set him down as my debtor." Ironically, the convent became the centre of resistance to the Medici later in the century: Girolamo **Savonarola**, leader of the government of Florence after the expulsion of the Medici in 1494, was the prior of San Marco. In 1537 Duke Cosimo expelled the Dominicans once more, reminding them that it was another Cosimo who had established the building's magnificence in the first place.

As Michelozzo was altering and expanding San Marco, the convent's walls were being decorated by one of its friars and a future prior, **Fra' Angelico**, a Tuscan painter in whom a medieval simplicity of faith was uniquely allied to a Renaissance sophistication of manner. He was born in Vicchio di Mugello, son of a wealthy landowner, some time between the late 1380s and 1400. He entered the Dominican monastery of nearby Fiesole aged around 20, where he was known as Fra' Giovanni da Fiesole. Already recognized as an accomplished artist, he flourished when he came to San Marco.

Here he was encouraged by the theologian Antonino Pierozzi – the future St Antonine – the convent's first prior and later archbishop of Florence. By the time Fra' Giovanni succeeded Pierozzi as prior, the pictures he had created for the monastery over the course of a decade and others for numerous churches in Florence and elsewhere – principally Orvieto cathedral and the Vatican – had earned him the title "the angelic painter", the name by which he's been known ever since. In 1982 he was beatified (a halfway house to sainthood), thus formalizing the name by which he had long been known, Beato Angelico, or the Blessed Angelico.

The ground floor

Immediately beyond the **entrance** lies the **Chiostro di Sant'Antonino**, designed by Michelozzo and now dominated by a vast cedar of Lebanon. Most of the cloister's faded frescoes are sixteenth-century depictions of episodes from the life of Antonino Pierozzi, Angelico's mentor. Angelico himself painted the frescoes in its four corners, of which the most striking is the lunette of *St Dominic at the Foot of the Cross*.

This weather-bleached work pales alongside the twenty or so paintings by the artist gathered in the **Ospizio dei Pellegrini**, or Pilgrims' Hospice, which lies between the cloister and the piazza. Many of the works – including several of Angelico's most famous – were brought here from churches and galleries around Florence; all display the artist's brilliant colouring and spatial clarity, and an air of imperturbable piety. On the right wall as you enter is a *Deposition* (1432–35), originally hung in the church of Santa Trìnita. Commissioned by the Strozzi family, the painting was begun by Lorenzo Monaco, who died after completing the upper trio of triangular pinnacles, and continued by Fra Angelico. At the opposite end of the room hangs the *Madonna dei Linaiuoli*, Angelico's first major public painting (1433), commissioned by the *Linaiuoli* or flax-workers' guild, for their headquarters. Halfway down the room, on the inner wall, the so-called *Pala di San Marco* (1440), though badly damaged by the passage of time and a disastrous restoration, demonstrates Fra' Angelico's familiarity with the latest developments in artistic theory. Its figures are arranged in lines that taper towards a central vanishing point, in accordance with the principles laid out in Alberti's *Della Pittura* (On Painting), published just two years before the picture was executed. The work was commissioned by the Medici as an altarpiece for the church of San Marco, hence the presence of the family's patron saints Cosmas and Damian, who can be seen at work as doctors in the small panel immediately to the right.

Back in the cloister, a doorway in its top right-hand corner opens into the **Sala del Lavabo**, where the monks washed before eating. Its entrance wall has a *Crucifixion with Saints* by Angelico, and its right wall two panels with a pair of saints, also by Angelico. The left wall contains a damaged lunette fresco of the *Madonna and Child* by Paolo Uccello, plus part of a predella by the same artist. The impressive room to the right, the **Refettorio Grande** or Large Refectory, is dominated by a large fresco of the Crucifixion by the sixteenth-century painter Giovanni Sogliani. Of more artistic interest are the rooms devoted to paintings by **Fra' Bartolomeo** and **Alesso Baldovinetti**. Note in particular Fra' Bartolomeo's suitably intense portrait of Savonarola, and his unfinished *Pala della Signoria* (1512), originally destined for the Salone dei Cinquecento in the Palazzo Vecchio.

Further round the cloister lies the **Sala Capitolare**, or Chapter House, which now houses a large conventual bell, the **Piagnone**, which was rung to summon help on Savonarola's arrest on the eve of April 8, 1498: it became

Savonarola

Girolamo **Savonarola** was born in 1452, the son of the physician to the Ferrara court. He grew up to be an abstemious and melancholic youth, sleeping on a bare straw mattress and spending much of his time reading the Bible. At the age of 23 he absconded to a Dominican monastery in Bologna, informing his father by letter that he was "unable to endure the evil conduct of the heedless people of Italy".

Within a few years, the Dominicans had dispatched him to preach all over northern Italy. Though not the most attractive of men – he was frail, with a beak of a nose and a blubbery mouth – Savonarola had an intensity of manner and of message that attracted a committed following when he settled permanently in the monastery of **San Marco** in 1489. By 1491, his sermons had become so popular that he was asked to deliver his Lent address in the Duomo. Proclaiming that God was speaking through him, he berated the city for its decadence, for its paintings that made the Virgin "look like a whore", and for the tyranny of its Medici-led government. Following the death of Lorenzo il Magnifico, the rhetoric became apocalyptic. "Wait no longer, for there may be no more time for repentance," he told another Duomo congregation, summoning images of plagues, invasions and destruction.

When Charles VIII of France marched into Italy in September 1494 to press his claim to the throne of Naples, Savonarola presented him as the instrument of God's vengeance. Violating Piero de' Medici's declaration of Tuscan neutrality, the French army massacred the garrison at Fivizzano, and Florence prepared for the onslaught, as Savonarola declaimed, "The Sword has descended; the scourge has fallen." With support for resistance ebbing, Piero capitulated to Charles; within days the Medici had fled. Hailed by Savonarola as "the Minister of God, the Minister of Justice", Charles and his vast army passed peacefully through Florence on their way to Rome.

The political vacuum in Florence was filled by the declaration of a **republican constitution**, but Savonarola was now in effect the ruler of the city. Continual decrees were issued from San Marco: profane carnivals were to be outlawed, fasting was to be observed more frequently, children were to act as the agents of

a symbol of anti-Medici sentiment ever after. Here, too, is a powerful fresco of the **Crucifixion**, painted by Angelico and assistants in 1441. At the rear of this room, entered via a passageway alongside the Chapter House, lies the **Refettorio Piccolo**, or Small Refectory, with a lustrous *Last Supper* (1480) by Ghirlandaio. This forms an anteroom to the **Foresteria**, home to the convent's former guest rooms, which is cluttered with architectural bits and pieces salvaged during nineteenth-century urban improvement schemes.

The first floor

Stairs off the cloister by the entrance to the Foresteria lead up to the first floor, where almost immediately you're confronted with one of the most sublime paintings in Italy. For the drama of its setting and the lucidity of its composition, nothing in San Marco matches Angelico's **Annunciation**. The pallid, submissive Virgin is one of the most touching images in Renaissance art, and the courteous angel, with his scintillating unfurled wings, is as convincing a heavenly messenger as any ever painted. An inscription on this fresco reminds the passing monks to say a Hail Mary as they venerate the image.

Angelico and his assistants also painted the simple and piously restrained pictures in each of the 44 **dormitory cells** on this floor, into which the

the righteous, informing the authorities whenever their parents transgressed the Eternal Law. Irreligious books and paintings, expensive clothes, cosmetics, mirrors, board games, trivialities and luxuries of all types were destroyed, a ritual purging that reached a crescendo with a colossal **"Bonfire of the Vanities"** on the Piazza della Signoria.

Meanwhile, Charles VIII was installed in Naples and a formidable alliance was being assembled to overthrow him: the papacy, Milan, Venice, Ferdinand of Aragon and the emperor Maximilian. In July 1495 the army of this Holy League confronted the French and was badly defeated. Charles's army continued northwards back to France, and Savonarola was summoned to the Vatican to explain why he had been unable to join the campaign against the intruder. He declined to attend, claiming that it was not God's will that he should make the journey, and thus set off a chain of exchanges that ended with his **excommunication** in June 1497. Defying Pope Alexander's order, Savonarola celebrated Mass in the Duomo on Christmas Day, which prompted a final threat from Rome: send Savonarola to the Vatican or imprison him in Florence, otherwise the whole city would join him in excommunication.

The people of Florence began to desert him. The region's crops had failed, plague had broken out again, and the city was at war with Pisa, which Charles had handed over to its citizens rather than return to Florence's control. The Franciscans of Florence, sceptical of the Dominican monk's claim to divine approval, now issued a terrible challenge. One of their community and one of Savonarola's would walk through an avenue of fire in the Piazza della Signoria: if the Dominican died, then Savonarola would be banished; if the Franciscan died, then Savonarola's main critic, Fra' Francesco da Puglia, would be expelled.

A thunderstorm prevented the trial from taking place, but the mood in the city had turned irrevocably. The following day, Palm Sunday 1498, a siege of the monastery of San Marco ended with Savonarola's **arrest**. Accused of heresy, he was tortured to the point of death, then **burned at the stake** in front of the Palazzo Vecchio, with two of his supporters. When the flames had finally been extinguished, the ashes were thrown into the river, to prevent anyone from gathering them as relics.

brothers would withdraw for solitary contemplation and sleep. Almost all of the outer cells of the corridor on the left have works by Angelico himself, and the marvellous **Madonna delle Ombre** (*Madonna of the Shadows*), on the wall facing these cells, is probably also by Angelico. Several of the scenes include one or both of a pair of monastic onlookers, serving as intermediaries between the occupant of the cell and the personages in the pictures: the one with the star above his head is St Dominic; the one with the split skull is St Peter Martyr, who was stabbed to death, supposedly by heretics.

At the end of the far corridor is a knot of rooms once occupied by Savonarola. These now contain various relics – a belt, a cape, a torn vest – questionably authenticated as worn by the man himself; most dubious of all is the piece of wood from his funeral pyre, which is depicted in a couple of paintings here. If you turn right at the main *Annunciation* and continue to the end of the corridor you'll come to the cells that were the personal domain of Cosimo de' Medici. The fresco of the *Adoration of the Magi* (possibly by Angelico's star pupil Benozzo Gozzoli) may have been suggested by Cosimo himself, who liked to think of himself as a latter-day wise man and gift-giving king.

On the way to these VIP cells you'll pass the entrance to **Michelozzo's Library**, built in 1441–44 to a design that exudes an atmosphere of calm study, though – as the plaque by the doorway tells you – it was here that Savonarola

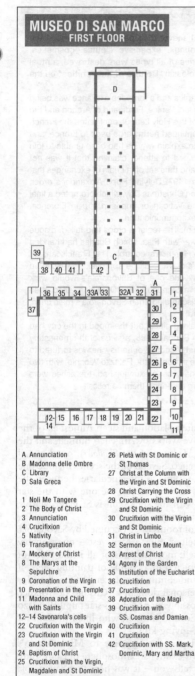

MUSEO DI SAN MARCO
FIRST FLOOR

A Annunciation
B Madonna delle Ombre
C Library
D Sala Greca

1 Noli Me Tangere
2 The Body of Christ
3 Annunciation
4 Crucifixion
5 Nativity
6 Transfiguration
7 Mockery of Christ
8 The Marys at the
   Sepulchre
9 Coronation of the Virgin
10 Presentation in the Temple
11 Madonna and Child
   with Saints
12–14 Savonarola's cells
22 Crucifixion with the Virgin
23 Crucifixion with the Virgin
   and St Dominic
24 Baptism of Christ
25 Crucifixion with the Virgin,
   Magdalen and St Dominic
26 Pietà with St Dominic or
   St Thomas
27 Christ at the Column with
   the Virgin and St Dominic
28 Christ Carrying the Cross
29 Crucifixion with the Virgin
   and St Dominic
30 Crucifixion with the Virgin
   and St Dominic
31 Christ in Limbo
32 Sermon on the Mount
33 Arrest of Christ
34 Agony in the Garden
35 Institution of the Eucharist
36 Crucifixion
37 Crucifixion
38 Adoration of the Magi
39 Crucifixion with
   SS. Cosmas and Damian
40 Crucifixion
41 Crucifixion
42 Crucifixion with SS. Mark,
   Dominic, Mary and Martha

was finally cornered and arrested in 1498. Cosimo's agents roamed as far as the Near East garnering precious manuscripts and books; in turn, Cosimo handed all the religious items over to the monastery, stipulating that they should be accessible to all, making it Europe's first public library. At the far end, a door leads through to the **Sala Greca** (usually open for guided visits on the hour), which was added to house a growing collection of manuscripts of ancient Greek texts.

San Marco church

Greatly altered since Michelozzo's intervention, the church of **San Marco** (Mon–Sat 9.30am–noon & 4–5.30pm) is worth a quick call for two works on the second and third altars on the right: a *Madonna and Saints* painted in 1509 by Fra' Bartolomeo, and an eighth-century mosaic of *The Madonna in Prayer* (surrounded by later additions), brought here from Constantinople. This had to be cut in half in transit, and you can still see the break across the Virgin's midriff.

West and north of Piazza San Marco

Within a couple of minutes' stroll west and north of **Piazza San Marco** are two little-visited art attractions, one of the city's obscurer parks, and a cluster of specialist museums. None would feature in a rushed itinerary, but the first pair in particular are worth the diversion on any high-culture point-to-point.

The Cenacolo di Sant'Apollonia

Running off the west side of Piazza San Marco, Via degli Arazzieri soon becomes Via XXVII Aprile, where the former Benedictine convent of **Sant'Apollonia** stands at no. 1

(Tues–Sun 8.15am–1.50pm; second & fourth Sun of month and first, third & fifth Mon of month same hours; free). Most of the complex has now been turned into apartments, but one entire wall of the former refectory houses Andrea del Castagno's *Last Supper*, one of the earliest uses of rigorous perspective in Renaissance art. Blood-red is the dominant tone, and the most commanding figure is the diabolic, black-bearded Judas, who sits on the near side of the table. The seething patterns in the marbled panels behind the Apostles enhance the intensity of the scene, in which the state of mind of each Apostle is distinctly delineated at the moment at which Christ announces that one of them will betray him. Painted around 1450 (which makes it the first of the city's Renaissance *cenacoli*), the fresco was plastered over by the nuns before being uncovered in the middle of the nineteenth century. Above the illusionistic recess in which the supper takes place are the faded remains of a *Resurrection, Crucifixion and Deposition* by Castagno, who also painted the lunettes of the *Crucifixion* and *Pietà* on the adjacent walls.

The Chiostro dello Scalzo

To the north of San Marco, at Via Cavour 69, is **Lo Scalzo**, the home of the Brotherhood of St John, whose vows of poverty entailed walking around barefoot (*scalzo*). The order was suppressed in 1785 and their monastery sold off, except for the **cloister** (Mon, Thurs & Sat 8.15am–1.50pm; free). This was the training ground for Andrea del Sarto, an artist venerated in the nineteenth century as a painter with no imperfections, but now regarded with slightly less enthusiasm on account of this very smoothness. His monochrome paintings of the Cardinal Virtues and Scenes from the Life of the Baptist occupied him off and on for a decade from 1511, beginning with the *Baptism*, finishing with the *Birth of St John*. A couple of the sixteen scenes – *John in the Wilderness* and *John meeting Christ* – were executed by his pupil Franciabigio in 1518, when del Sarto was away in Paris.

The Giardino dei Semplici and natural history museums

The **Giardino dei Semplici** or **Orto Botanico** (Mon, Tues, Thurs, Fri & Sun 9am–1pm, Sat 9am–5pm; €4), northeast of San Marco, was set up in 1545 for Cosimo I as a medicinal garden, following the examples of Padua and Pisa. Entered from Via La Pira, it now covers five acres, most of the area being taken up by the original flowerbeds and avenues. It's the nearest equivalent to the Bóboli gardens on the north side of the city, but unfortunately it closes at exactly the time you could use it for a midday break.

On the south side of the garden, at Via La Pira 4, you'll find the entrance to a number of **museums** administered by the university. The **Museo Botanico** (currently open only to scholars), set up for Leopoldo II of Lorraine, contains over four million botanical specimens, supplemented by plaster mushrooms and wax models of plants. Masses of rocks are on show in the **Museo di Minerologia e Litologia** (June–Sept Wed & Fri 9am–1pm; Oct–May Tues 9am–1pm & 2–5pm, Wed–Sat 9am–1pm; €6 joint ticket with the museum below), including a 150-kilo topaz from Brazil and a load of worked stones from the Medici collection – snuff boxes, little vases, a quartz boat. The **Museo di Geologia e Paleontologia** (same hours and ticket as above) is one of Italy's biggest fossil shows, featuring such delights as prehistoric elephant skeletons from the upper Valdarno and a skeleton from Grosseto once touted as the missing link between monkeys and *Homo sapiens*.

The Museo Stibbert

About 1500m north of San Marco, at Via Stibbert 26 (bus #4 from the station), is the loopiest of Florence's museums, the **Museo Stibbert** (Mon–Wed 10am–2pm, Fri–Sun 10am–6pm; compulsory guided tour €6). This rambling, murky mansion was the home of the half-Scottish, half-Italian Frederick Stibbert, who in his twenties made a name for himself in Garibaldi's army. Later he inherited a fourteenth-century house from his mother, then bought the neighbouring mansion and joined the two together, thus creating a place big enough to accommodate the fruits of his compulsive collecting. The 64 rooms contain over fifty thousand items, ranging from snuff boxes to paintings by Carlo Crivelli and a possible Botticelli.

Militaria were Frederick's chief enthusiasm, and the Stibbert **armour** collection is reckoned one of the world's best. It includes Roman, Etruscan and Japanese examples (the highlight of the whole museum), as well as a fifteenth-century *condottiere*'s outfit and the armour worn by the great Medici commander Giovanni delle Bande Nere, retrieved from his grave in San Lorenzo in 1857. The big production number comes in the great hall, between the two houses, where a platoon of mannequins is clad in full sixteenth-century gear. Also on show is the regalia in which Napoleon was crowned king of Italy.

Piazza Santissima Annunziata

Nineteenth-century urban renewal schemes spoiled many of the squares of central Florence, which makes the pedestrianized **Piazza Santissima Annunziata**, with its distinctive arcades, all the more attractive a public space. It has a special importance for the city, too. Until the end of the eighteenth century the Florentine year used to begin on March 25, the Festival of the Annunciation – hence the Florentine predilection for paintings of the Annunciation, and the prestige of the Annunziata church, which has long been the place for society weddings. The festival is still marked by a huge fair in the piazza and the streets leading off it; later in the year, on the first weekend in September, the square is used for Tuscany's largest crafts fair.

Brunelleschi began the piazza in the 1420s, with additions made later by Ammannati and Antonio da Sangallo. The equestrian **statue** of Grand Duke Ferdinand I (1608) at its centre was Giambologna's final work, and was cast by his pupil Pietro Tacca from cannons captured at the Battle of Lepanto. Tacca was also the creator of the grotesque **fountains** (1629), on each of which a pair of aquatic monkeys spit water at two whiskered sea slugs. (The mirror-image building on the other side of the piazza was designed a century later by Antonio da Sangallo and Baccio d'Agnolo.)

The Spedale degli Innocenti

The eastern flank of Piazza Santissima Annunziata is occupied by the **Spedale degli Innocenti** (Mon–Sat 8.30am–7pm, Sun 8.30am–2pm; €4). Commissioned in 1419 by the Arte della Seta, the silk-weavers' guild, it opened in 1445 as the first foundlings' hospital in Europe, and is still an orphanage today. It was largely designed by Brunelleschi (whose activity as a goldsmith, strangely, allowed him membership of the guild), and his nine-arched loggia was one of Europe's earliest examples of the new classically influenced style. (The mirror-image building on the other side of the piazza was designed a century later, by Antonio da Sangallo and Baccio d'Agnolo, as accommodation for the Servite friars who staffed the orphanage.)

Andrea della Robbia's blue-backed ceramic tondi (1487) of well-swaddled babies advertise the building's function, but their gaiety belies the misery associated with it. Slavery was part of the Florentine economy as late as the fifteenth century (it's probable that Leonardo da Vinci's mother was a slave), and many of the infants given over to the care of the Spedale were born to domestic slaves. From 1660 children could be abandoned anonymously in the *rota*, a small revolving door whose bricked-up remains are still visible at the extreme left of the facade; it remained in use until 1875.

The building within centres on two beautiful cloisters, Brunelleschi's central **Chiostro degli Uomini** (Men's Cloister) and the narrow, graceful **Chiostro delle Donne** (Women's Cloister) to the right. Stairs from the left-hand corner of the former lead up to the **museum**, a miscellany of Florentine Renaissance art that includes one of Luca della Robbia's most beguiling Madonnas and an *Adoration of the Magi* (1488) by Domenico Ghirlandaio. The latter, commissioned as the altarpiece of the building's church, features a background depicting the *Massacre of the Innocents*. The parallel of the slaughter of Bethlehem's first-born with the orphanage's foundlings, or *innocenti*, was deliberately made.

Santissima Annunziata

Santissima Annunziata (daily 7am–12.30pm & 4–6.30pm) is the mother church of the Servites, or Servi di Maria (Servants of Mary), a religious order founded by Filippo Benizzi and six Florentine aristocrats in 1234. From humble beginnings, the order blossomed after 1252, when a painting of the Virgin begun by one of the monks – abandoned in despair because of his inability to create a truly beautiful image – was completed by an angel while he slept. So many people came to venerate the image that by 1444 a new church, financed by the Medici, was commissioned from Michelozzo (who happened to be the brother of the Servites' head prior). The project, completed by Leon Battista Alberti in 1481, involved laying out the present-day Via dei Servi, designed to link Santissima Annunziata and the cathedral, thus uniting the city's two most important churches dedicated to the Madonna.

The Chiostrino dei Voti

As the number of pilgrims to the church increased, so it became a custom to leave wax votive offerings (*voti*) in honour of its miraculous Madonna. In the early days these were placed around the walls. Later they were hung from the nave ceiling. Eventually they became so numerous that in 1447 a special atrium, the **Chiostrino dei Voti**, was built onto the church. In time this came to house some six hundred statues, some of them life-sized depictions of the donor, with full-size wax horse in close attendance. The collection was one of the city's great tourist attractions until 1786, when the whole lot was melted down to make candles.

More lasting alterations to the cloister's appearance, in the shape of a major **fresco cycle**, were made in the 1510s, following the canonization of Filippo Benizzi, the Servites' founding father. Three leading artists of the day, Andrea del Sarto, Jacopo Pontormo and Rosso Fiorentino, were involved, together with several lesser painters. Some of the panels are in a poor state – all were removed from the walls and restored after the 1966 flood – but their overall effect is superb.

There are two sequences here, one depicting scenes from the life of the Virgin (an obvious theme given the church's dedication to Mary), the other portraying scenes from the life of St Filippo Benizzi. If you start to the right of the entrance to the cloister, the sequence works backwards from the Virgin's death, beginning with an **Assumption** by Rosso Fiorentino, one of his first works, painted when he was aged around 19. Alongside is Pontormo's **Visitation**, which was said to have taken some eighteen months to paint. It's followed by Franciabigio's **Marriage of the Virgin**, in which the painter is said to have taken a hammer to the Virgin's face: apparently he was angry at the monks for having secretly looked at the work before its completion, and after the artist's tantrum no one had the courage to repair the damage.

Before the next lunette comes a fine marble bas-relief of the *Madonna and Child* attributed to Michelozzo, followed by the cloister's masterpiece, Andrea del Sarto's **Birth of the Virgin**. To the right of the large church door is the same artist's **Journey of the Magi**, which includes a self-portrait in the right-hand corner. Left of the door lies Alesso Baldovinetti's **Nativity**, its faded appearance the result of poor initial preparation on the part of the artist. The sequence devoted to Filippo Benizzi begins on the next wall with Cosimo Rosselli's **Vocation and Investiture of the Saint**; the five remaining damaged panels are all the work of Andrea del Sarto.

The interior

Few Florentine interiors are as striking at first sight as Santissima Annunziata, but in order to be sure of seeing it you should visit in the afternoon: this church commands the devotion of a large congregation, and there are Masses every hour all morning. Beyond the startling first impression made by the gilt and stucco gloss that was applied in the seventeenth and eighteenth centuries, the church contains few genuine treasures. One notable exception is the ornate **tabernacle** (1448–61) immediately on your left as you enter, designed by Michelozzo to house the miraculous image of the Madonna. Michelozzo's patron, Piero di Cosimo de' Medici, made sure that nobody remained unaware of the money he sank into the shrine: an inscription reads *Costò fior. 4 mila el marmo solo* ("The marble alone cost 4000 florins"). The painting encased in the marble has been repainted into illegibility, and is usually kept covered anyway.

To the tabernacle's right lies a chapel (1453–63) originally created as an oratory for the Medici, adorned with five panels of inlaid stone depicting the Virgin's principal symbols (sun, moon, star, lily and rose) and a small picture of the *Redeemer* (1515) by Andrea del Sarto. Piero de' Medici loaned out the space to visiting dignitaries to allow them a privileged view of the Madonna.

The **Cappella Feroni**, next door, features a restrained fresco by Andrea del Castagno of *Christ and St Julian* (1455–56). The adjacent chapel contains a more striking fresco by the same artist, the *Holy Trinity and St Jerome* (1454). Now restored, both frescoes were obliterated after Vasari spread the rumour that Castagno had poisoned his erstwhile friend, Domenico Veneziano, motivated by envy of the other's skill with oil paint. Castagno was saddled with this crime until the nineteenth century, when an archivist discovered that the alleged murderer in fact predeceased his victim by four years.

Separated from the nave by a triumphal arch is the unusual **tribune**, begun by Michelozzo but completed to designs by Alberti; you get into it along a corridor from the north transept. The chapel at the farthest point was altered by Giambologna into a monument to himself, complete with bronze reliefs and a crucifix by the sculptor. The chapel to its left contains a sizeable *Resurrection* (1550) by Bronzino.

The spacious **Chiostro dei Morti** is worth visiting for Andrea del Sarto's intimate *Madonna del Sacco* (1525), over the door that opens from the north transept (you may also be able to enter the cloister from the street – the entrance is to the left of the main entrance); depicting the *Rest during the Flight into Egypt*, the picture takes its name from the sack on which St Joseph is leaning.

The Museo Archeologico

On the other side of Via della Colonna from Santissima Annunziata, the **Museo Archeologico** (Mon 2–7pm, Tues & Thurs 8.30am–7pm, Wed & Fri–Sun 8.30am–2pm; €4) houses the finest collection of its kind in northern Italy, but struggles to draw visitors for whom the Renaissance is the beginning and the end of Florence's appeal. And to tell the truth, it's not the most alluring museum in the city: it suffered terrible damage in the flood of 1966, and in some of the rooms you get the impression that the place still hasn't recovered from that disaster. Nonetheless, the new ground-floor galleries are a good space for one-off exhibitions, and the main collection is slowly being put in better order.

Its strength is its **Etruscan** collection, much of it bequeathed, inevitably, by the Medici. Most of the Etruscan finds are on the first floor, where there's a large array of funerary figures and two outstanding bronze sculptures. The first of these, the *Arringatore* (Orator), is the only known large Etruscan bronze from the Hellenistic period; made some time around 100 BC, it was discovered near Lago Trasimeno in 1566 and promptly sold to Cosimo I. Nearby is the *Chimera*, a triple-headed monster made in the fourth century BC. Showing the beast wounded in its fight with Bellerophon (it might have been part of a group that included a figure of the hero), the *Chimera* was unearthed on the outskirts of Florence in 1553.

Numerous dowdy cabinets are stuffed with unlabelled Etruscan figurines, and much of the **Egyptian collection** – the third largest such collection in Italy, after the Vatican's and the Egyptian museum in Turin – is displayed in a similarly uninspiring manner, though some of the rooms were handsomely decorated in mock-Egyptian style in the late nineteenth century. The single most remarkable object amid the assembly of papyri, statuettes and mummy cases is a Hittite chariot made of bone and wood, dating from the fourteenth century BC.

There are more Etruscan pieces on the top floor (sometimes open only to guided tours, usually hourly), but here the primary focus is on the **Greek and Roman collections**. The star piece in the huge hoard of Greek vases is the large *François Vase*, a sixth-century BC *krater* discovered in an Etruscan tomb near Chiusi in 1844s. Another attention-grabbing item is the life-size bronze torso known as the *Torso di Livorno*, probably a fifth-century BC Greek original, though some argue that it's a Roman copy. There's some debate also about the large horse's head that's on show in the same room. This fragment of a full-size statue is probably an early Hellenistic bronze from around 100 BC, but again it may be a Roman copy; what's known for certain is that it was once a feature of the garden of the Palazzo Medici, where it was studied by Donatello and Verrocchio. Also on this floor you'll see two beautiful sixth-century BC Greek *kouroi*, dubbed *Apollo* and *Apollino*, and the bronze statue of a young man known as the *Idilono di Pésaro* – yet again there's some dispute about its origins, but it's generally thought to be a Roman replica of a Greek figure dating from around 100 BC.

East of the centre: Santa Croce to Campo di Marte

The focal point of the eastern side of central Florence is the vast Franciscan church of **Santa Croce**, a building that's compelling both for its architecture and for its frescoes. The Santa Croce district was one of Florence's more densely populated areas before November 4, 1966, when the Arno burst its banks, with catastrophic consequences for this low-lying zone, which was then packed with tenements and small workshops. Many residents moved out permanently in the following years, but now the more traditional businesses that survived the flood have been joined by a growing number of new and often extremely good bars and restaurants, a transformation that's particularly noticeable around the **Sant'Ambrogio** market. In addition to the great church and its museum, the other main cultural attractions in this part of the city are the **Museo Horne**, a modest but pleasing collection of art treasures, and the **Casa Buonarroti**, a less than entirely satisfying homage to Michelangelo.

Santa Croce

Piazza Santa Croce is one of Florence's largest squares and traditionally one of its chief arenas for ceremonials and festivities. Thus when Lorenzo the Magnificent was married to the Roman heiress Clarice Orsini, the wedding was celebrated on this square, with a tournament that was as much a fashion event as a contest of skill: Lorenzo's knightly outfit, for instance, was adorned with pearls, diamonds and rubies. The square is still used as the pitch for the Gioco di Calcio Storico, a football tournament between the city's four *quartieri*; held three times in St John's week (see p.172), the game is characterized by incomprehensible rules and a level of violence which the sixteenth-century costumes do little to hinder.

▲ Piazza Santa Croce

Florence's floods

The calamity of the November 1966 flood had plenty of precedents. Great areas of the city were destroyed by a flood in **1178**, a disaster exacerbated by plague and famine. In **1269** the Carraia and Trìnita bridges were carried away on a torrent so heavy that "a great part of the city of Florence became a lake". The flood of **1333** was preceded by a four-day storm, with thunder and rain so violent that all the city's bells were tolled to drive away the evil spirits thought to be behind the tempest: bridges were demolished and the original Marzocco – a figure of Mars rather than the leonine figure that inherited its name – was carried away by the raging Arno. Cosimo I instituted an urban beautification scheme after a deluge put parts of the city under nearly twenty feet of muddy water in **1557**; on that occasion the Trìnita bridge was hit so suddenly that everyone on it was drowned, except for two children who were left stranded on a pillar in midstream, where for two days they were fed by means of a rope slung over from the bank.

It had rained continuously for forty days prior to **November 4, 1966**, with nearly half a metre of rain falling in the preceding two days. When the water pressure in an upstream reservoir threatened to break the dam, it was decided to open the sluices. The only people to be warned about the rapidly rising level of the river were the jewellers of the Ponte Vecchio, whose private nightwatchman phoned them in the small hours of the morning with news that the bridge was starting to shake. Police watching the shopkeepers clearing their displays were asked why they weren't spreading the alarm. They replied, "We have received no orders." When the banks of the Arno finally broke down, a flash flood dumped around 500,000 tonnes of water and mud on the streets, moving with such speed that people were drowned in the underpass of Santa Maria Novella train station. In all, 35 Florentines were killed, 6000 shops put out of business, more than 10,000 homes made uninhabitable, some 15,000 cars wrecked, and thousands of works of art damaged, many of them ruined by heating oil flushed out of basements.

Within hours an impromptu army of rescue workers had been formed – many of them students – to haul pictures out of slime-filled churches and gather fragments of paint in plastic bags. Donations came in from all over the world, but the task was so immense that the restoration of many pieces is still unaccomplished. Some rooms in the archeological museum, for example, have remained closed since the flood, and many possessions of the National Library are still in the laboratories. In total around two-thirds of the 3000 paintings damaged in the flood are now on view again, and two laboratories – one for paintings and one for stonework – are operating full time in Florence, developing restoration techniques that are taken up by galleries all over the world. Today, throughout the city, you can see small marble plaques with a red line showing the level the floodwaters reached on that dreadful day in 1966.

The church of **Santa Croce** (Mon–Sat 9.30am–5.30pm, Sun 1–5.30pm; €5) is the Franciscans' principal church in Florence – a rival to the Dominicans' Santa Maria Novella – and is often said to have been founded by St Francis himself. In truth it was probably begun seventy or so years after Francis's death, in 1294, possibly by the architect of the Duomo, Arnolfo di Cambio. It replaced a smaller church on the site, a building that had become too small for the vast congregations gathering to hear the Franciscans' homilies on poverty, chastity and obedience in what was then one of the city's poorest areas. Ironically, it was Florence's richest families who funded the construction of Santa Croce, to atone for the sin of usury on which their fortunes were based. Plutocrats such as the Bardi, Peruzzi and Baroncelli sponsored the extraordinary **fresco cycles** that were lavished on the chapels

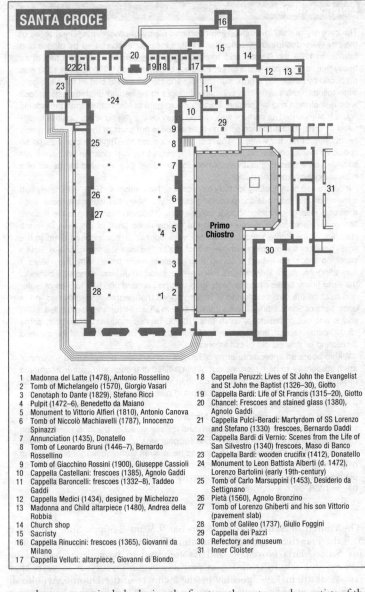

1 Madonna del Latte (1478), Antonio Rossellino
2 Tomb of Michelangelo (1570), Giorgio Vasari
3 Cenotaph to Dante (1829), Stefano Ricci
4 Pulpit (1472–6), Benedetto da Maiano
5 Monument to Vittorio Alfieri (1810), Antonio Canova
6 Tomb of Niccolò Machiavelli (1787), Innocenzo Spinazzi
7 Annunciation (1435), Donatello
8 Tomb of Leonardo Bruni (1446–7), Bernardo Rossellino
9 Tomb of Giacchino Rossini (1900), Giuseppe Cassioli
10 Cappella Castellani: frescoes (1385), Agnolo Gaddi
11 Cappella Baroncelli: frescoes (1332–8), Taddeo Gaddi
12 Cappella Medici (1434), designed by Michelozzo
13 Madonna and Child altarpiece (1480), Andrea della Robbia
14 Church shop
15 Sacristy
16 Cappella Rinuccini: frescoes (1365), Giovanni da Milano
17 Cappella Velluti: altarpiece, Giovanni di Biondo
18 Cappella Peruzzi: Lives of St John the Evangelist and St John the Baptist (1326–30), Giotto
19 Cappella Bardi: Life of St Francis (1315–20), Giotto
20 Chancel: Frescoes and stained glass (1380), Agnolo Gaddi
21 Cappella Pulci-Beradi: Martyrdom of SS Lorenzo and Stefano (1330) frescoes, Bernardo Daddi
22 Cappella Bardi di Vernio: Scenes from the Life of San Silvestro (1340) frescoes, Maso di Banco
23 Cappella Bardi: wooden crucifix (1412), Donatello
24 Monument to Leon Battista Alberti (d. 1472), Lorenzo Bartolini (early 19th-century)
25 Tomb of Carlo Marsuppini (1453), Desiderio da Settignano
26 Pietà (1560), Agnolo Bronzino
27 Tomb of Lorenzo Ghiberti and his son Vittorio (pavement slab)
28 Tomb of Galileo (1737), Giulio Foggini
29 Cappella dei Pazzi
30 Refectory and museum
31 Inner Cloister

over the years, particularly during the fourteenth century, when artists of the stature of Giotto and the Gaddi family worked here. In further contradiction of the Franciscan ideal of humility, Santa Croce has long served as the national pantheon: the walls and nave floor are lined with the **monuments** to more than 270 illustrious Tuscans, including Michelangelo, Galileo, Machiavelli, Alberti, Dante and the great physicist Enrico Fermi (though the last two are not buried here).

Of all the events that have happened at Santa Croce, none was more momentous than the **Council of Florence**, held in 1439 in an attempt to reconcile the differences between the Roman and Eastern churches. Attended by the pope, the Byzantine emperor and the Patriarch of Constantinople, the council arrived at a compromise that lasted only until the Byzantine delegation returned home. Its more enduring effect was that it brought scores of classical scholars to the city, some of whom stayed on to give an important impetus to the Florentine Renaissance.

The interior

The church's **facade** is a neo-Gothic sham which dates from as recently as 1863. The church had languished for centuries without a suitable frontage, a situation remedied when someone claimed to have discovered long-lost plans for the "original" facade; in truth the scheme was no more than a giant-sized pastiche of Orcagna's tabernacle in Orsanmichele. The vast interior is infinitely more satisfying.

Hurry towards the high altar and the Giotto-painted chapels to its right if all you want to see are the church's most famous works of art. Otherwise, take a more measured walk down the **south aisle**. Against the first pillar stands the tomb of Francesco Nori, one of the victims of the Pazzi Conspiracy, surmounted by Antonio Rossellino's lovely relief of the *Madonna del Latte* (marked 1 on our plan). Nearby is Vasari's **tomb of Michelangelo** (2); the sculptor's body was brought back from Rome to Florence in July 1574, ten years after his death, and his tomb is said to have been positioned close to the church's entrance at his own request, so that when the graves fly open on the Day of Judgement, the first thing to catch his eye will be Brunelleschi's cathedral dome.

The Neoclassical **monument to Dante** (3) is a cenotaph rather than a tomb, as the exiled poet is buried in Ravenna, where he died in 1321. Three centuries before Dante finally received this bland nineteenth-century tribute, Michelangelo had offered to carve the poet's tomb – a tantalizing thought. Against the third pillar there's a marvellous **pulpit** by Benedetto da Maiano (4), adorned with niche statuettes of the virtues and scenes from the life of St Francis.

Canova's **monument to Alfieri** (5) commemorates an eighteenth-century Italian poet and dramatist as famous for his amatory liaisons as his literary endeavours. The tomb was paid for by his mistress, the so-called Countess of Albany, erstwhile wife of Charles Edward Stuart (aka Bonnie Prince Charlie). She modelled for the tomb's main figure, an allegory of Italy bereaved by Alfieri's death. The nearby **tomb of Machiavelli** (6), carved 260 years after his death, is unexceptional save for its famous inscription: *Tanto nomini nullum par elogium* ("No praise can be high enough for so great a name"). The side-door at the end of the aisle is flanked by Donatello's gilded stone relief of the *Annunciation*.

Beyond the door is Bernardo Rossellino's much-imitated **tomb of Leonardo Bruni** (8), chancellor of the Republic, humanist scholar and author of the first history of the city – his effigy is holding a copy. Bruni, who died in 1444, was the first man of any great eminence to be buried in the church, which is a little surprising given his predominantly humanist rather than Christian beliefs. The tomb, one of the most influential of the Renaissance, makes the point: for the first time the human figure dominates, with the Madonna and Child banished to a peripheral position high in the lunette.

The Castellani, Baroncelli and Medici chapels, and the sacristy

The **Cappella Castellani** (10), at the end of the south aisle, is strikingly, if patchily, covered in frescoes by Agnolo Gaddi and his pupils. To the right are depicted the stories of St John the Baptist and St Nicholas of Bari: the latter, the patron saint of children (he's the St Nicholas of Santa Claus fame), is shown saving three girls from prostitution and reviving three murdered boys. The left wall features episodes from the lives of St John and St Antony Abbot; the latter gave away his wealth, making him a favourite of the poverty-inspired Franciscans. Also note the chapel's fine tabernacle, the work of Mino da Fiesole, and its funerary monuments, including that of the Countess of Albany.

The adjoining **Cappella Baroncelli** (11) was decorated by Agnolo's father, Taddeo, a long-time assistant to Giotto. Taddeo's cycle, largely devoted to the life of the Virgin, features one of the first night scenes in Western painting, the *Annunciation to the Shepherds*, in which the angel appears amid a blaze of light that's believed to be a representation of Halley's Comet. The main altar painting, the *Coronation of the Virgin*, may also be by Taddeo, though an increasing number of critics now attribute it to his master, Giotto.

The corridor to the right ends at the **Cappella Medici** (12), usually open only for those taking Mass. It's notable for the large terracotta altarpiece by Andrea della Robbia and a nineteenth-century forged Donatello; the chapel, like the corridor, was designed by Michelozzo, the Medici's pet architect. Finely carved wooden doors lead off the corridor into the beautifully panelled **sacristy** (15), where the highlight is a marvellous *Crucifixion* by Taddeo. The tiny **Cappella Rinuccini** (16), separated from the sacristy by a grille, is impressively covered with frescoes on the life of the Virgin (on the left) and St Mary Magdalene (on the right): the Lombard artist responsible, Giovanni da Milano, was one of Giotto's most accomplished followers.

The east chapels: Giotto's frescoes

Both the **Cappella Peruzzi** (18) and the **Cappella Bardi** (19) – the two chapels on the right of the chancel – are entirely covered with frescoes by Giotto, with some assistance in the latter. Their deterioration was partly caused by Giotto's having painted some of the pictures onto dry plaster, rather than the wet plaster employed in true fresco technique, but the vandalism of later generations was far more destructive. In the eighteenth century they were covered in whitewash, then they were heavily retouched in the nineteenth; restoration in the 1950s returned them to as close to their original state as was possible.

Scenes from the lives of St John the Evangelist and St John the Baptist cover the Peruzzi chapel, while a better-preserved cycle of the life of St Francis fills the Bardi. Despite the areas of paint destroyed when a tomb was attached to the wall, the *Funeral of St Francis* is still a composition of extraordinary impact, the grief-stricken mourners suggesting an affinity with the lamentation over the body of Christ – one of them even probes the wound in Francis's side, echoing the gesture of Doubting Thomas. The *Ordeal by Fire*, showing Francis about to demonstrate his faith to the sultan by walking through fire, shows Giotto's mastery of understated drama, with the sultan's entourage skulking off to the left in anticipation of the monk's triumph. On the wall above the chapel's entrance arch is the most powerful scene of all, *St Francis Receiving the Stigmata*, in which the power of Christ's apparition seems to force the chosen one to his knees.

Agnolo Gaddi was responsible for the design of the **stained glass** in the lancet windows round the high altar, and for all the chancel **frescoes** (20), which depict the legend of the True Cross – a complicated tale tracing the wood of the Cross from its origins as the Tree of Paradise (see p.446). The vast polyptych on the high altar is a composite of panels by several artists.

The **Cappella Bardi di Vernio** (22) was painted by Maso di Banco, perhaps the most inventive of Giotto's followers. Following tradition, the frescoes, showing scenes from the life of Saint Sylvester, portray the saint baptizing Emperor Constantine, notwithstanding the fact that Sylvester died some time before the emperor's baptism. The second **Cappella Bardi** (23) houses a wooden crucifix by Donatello, supposedly criticized by Brunelleschi as resembling a "peasant on the Cross". According to Vasari, Brunelleschi went off and created his own crucifix for Santa Maria Novella to show Donatello how it should be done.

The north aisle

As you walk back towards the entrance along the north aisle, the first pillar you pass features a ghastly nineteenth-century **monument to Leon Battista Alberti** (24), the Renaissance architect and artistic theorist whose writings did much to influence Rossellino in his carving of the Bruni tomb across the nave. The Bruni tomb in turn influenced the outstanding **tomb of Carlo Marsuppini** (25) by Desiderio da Settignano. Marsuppini's lack of Christian qualifications for so prominent a church burial is even more striking than Bruni's: he's said to have died without taking confession or communion. The tomb inscription opens with the words, "Stay and see the marbles which enshrine a great sage, one for whose mind there was not world enough."

A *Pietà* by the young Bronzino (26), a future Mannerist star, briefly disturbs the parade of tombs that follows. A surprisingly modest pavement slab marks the **tomb of Lorenzo Ghiberti** – the artist responsible for the Baptistery's marvellous doors – and his son Vittorio (27). The **tomb of Galileo** (28) is more ostentatious, though it was some ninety years after his death in 1642 that the "heretic" scientist was deemed worthy of a Christian burial in Florence's pantheon.

The Cappella dei Pazzi

The door in the south (right) aisle leads through into the church's Primo Chiostro (First Cloister), site of Brunelleschi's **Cappella dei Pazzi** (29), the epitome of the learned, harmonious spirit of early Renaissance architecture. It was commissioned in 1429 as a chapter house for Santa Croce, by Andrea de' Pazzi, a member of a banking dynasty that played a prominent role in the Pazzi Conspiracy (see box, p.76). Its exterior remained unfinished at the time of the plot, however, and it seems none of the family was ever buried here. Dogged by financial problems, the construction of the chapel was completed only in the 1470s, some thirty years after the architect's death.

Geometrically perfect without seeming pedantic, the chapel is exemplary in its proportion and in the way its decorative detail harmonizes with the design. The polychrome lining of the portico's shallow cupola is by Luca della Robbia, as is the garland of fruit which surrounds the Pazzi family crest. The frieze of angels' heads is by Desiderio da Settignano, though Luca was responsible for the tondo of *St Andrew* (1461) over the door. The portico itself may be the work of Giuliano da Maiano, while the majestic wooden doors (1472) are the product of a collaboration between the brothers Maiano, Giuliano and Benedetto. Inside, the twelve blue and white tondi of the *Apostles* are by Luca della Robbia, while the four vividly coloured tondi of the *Evangelists* in the upper roundels were produced in the della Robbia workshop, possibly to designs by Donatello and Brunelleschi.

The Museo dell'Opera di Santa Croce and the inner cloister

The recently extended **Museo dell'Opera di Santa Croce** (30), which flanks the first cloister, houses a sizeable miscellany of works of art, the best of which are gathered in the ex-refectory. Foremost of these is Cimabue's famous *Crucifixion*, very badly damaged in 1966 and now the emblem of the havoc caused by the flood. Other highlights include a detached fresco of the *Last Supper* (1333), which is considered to be the finest work by Taddeo Gaddi (end wall) and is the earliest surviving example of the many Last Suppers (*cenacoli*) dotted around the city. Also compelling are Donatello's enormous gilded *St Louis of Toulouse* (1424), made for Orsanmichele, and Bronzino's *Descent of Christ into Limbo*. Fragments of Orcagna's frescoes of *The Triumph of Death* and *Hell* (on the side walls), and Domenico Veneziano's *Sts John and Francis*, were all salvaged from Santa Croce after Vasari had carried out his supposed improvements. Elsewhere in the museum you'll find more frescoes rescued from the church, plus some excellent della Robbia ceramics.

A series of rooms sparsely filled with various damaged fragments leads you towards the spacious **Inner Cloister** (31), another late project by Brunelleschi. Completed in 1453, after the architect's death, it is the most peaceful spot in the centre of Florence, achieving its atmosphere by the slow rhythm of the narrow, widely spaced columns.

The Museo Horne

On the south side of Santa Croce, down by the river at Via dei Benci 6, stands one of Florence's more recondite museums, the **Museo della Fondazione Horne** (Mon–Sat 9am–1pm; €5). Its collection was left to the state by the English art historian Herbert Percy Horne (1864–1916), who was instrumental in rescuing Botticelli from neglect with a pioneering biography that was published in 1908. The half-a-dozen or so rooms of paintings, sculptures, pottery, furniture and other domestic objects contain no real masterpieces, but are diverting enough if you've already done the major collections. With winning eccentricity, the exhibits are labelled with numbers only and you have to carry round a key in the form of a long list, available from the ticket office.

The pride of Horne's collection was its drawings, which are now salted away in the Uffizi, though a small display is maintained in the room on the right of the **ground floor**. On the **first floor**, the highlight of Room 1 is a tiny and badly damaged panel (once part of a triptych) by Masaccio, showing *Scenes from the Life of St Julian*; nearby there's an unfinished and age-darkened *Deposition* by Gozzoli, his last documented work. The next room contains the collection's big draw, Giotto's *St Stephen* (a fragment from a polyptych), which was probably painted at around the time that Giotto was at work in Santa Croce. Room 3 has a tondo of the *Holy Family* by Beccafumi, who is also attributed with a *Drunkenness of Noah* on the **second floor**, where you'll also find minor works by Filippo and Filippino Lippi. One of the main exhibits on this storey is a piece of little artistic merit but great historical interest: a copy of part of Leonardo's *Battle of Anghiari*, once frescoed on a wall of the Palazzo Vecchio.

Casa Buonarroti and the Sant'Ambrogio district

The enticing name of the **Casa Buonarroti**, located north of Santa Croce at Via Ghibellina 70 (Wed–Mon 9.30am–2pm; €6.50), is somewhat misleading. Michelangelo Buonarroti certainly owned three houses here in 1508, and probably lived on the site intermittently between 1516 and 1525, but thereafter the properties' associations with the artist become increasingly tenuous. On Michelangelo's death, for example, they passed to his nephew, Leonardo, whose son converted them into a single palazzo, leaving little trace of the earlier houses (though he built a gallery dedicated to his great-uncle). Michelangelo's last descendant, Cosimo, left the building to the city on his death in 1858. Today the house contains a smart but low-key museum, but among the jumble of works only a handful are by Michelangelo: most were created simply in homage to the great man.

The two main treasures are to be found in the room on the left at the top of the stairs. The **Madonna della Scala** (c.1490–92) is Michelangelo's earliest known work, a delicate relief carved when he was no older than 16. The similarly unfinished *Battle of the Centaurs* was created shortly afterwards, when the boy was living in the Medici household. In the adjacent room you'll find the artist's wooden model (1517) for the facade of San Lorenzo. Close by is the largest of all the sculptural models on display, the torso of a **River God** (1524), a work in wood and wax probably intended for the Medici chapel in San Lorenzo. Other rooms contain small and fragmentary pieces, possibly by the master, possibly copies of works by him.

Sant'Ambrogio: the markets and the church

Two of Florence's markets lie within a few minutes' stroll of the Casa Buonarroti. To the north, the Piazza dei Ciompi is the venue for the **Mercato delle Pulci** or Flea Market (Mon–Sat 9am–7pm; plus same hours on last Sun of month). Much of the junk maintains the city's reputation for inflated prices, though you can find a few interesting items at modest cost – old postcards, posters and so on. Vasari's Loggia del Pesce (1567) gives the square a touch of style; built for the fishmongers of the Mercato Vecchio in what is now Piazza della Repubblica, it was dismantled when that square was laid out, and rebuilt here in 1951.

A short distance to the east, out of the orbit of most tourists, is the **Mercato di Sant'Ambrogio** (Mon–Sat 7am–2pm), a smaller, tattier but even more enjoyable version of the San Lorenzo food hall. The *tavola calda* (snacks and meals stall) here is one of Florence's lunchtime bargains, and – as at San Lorenzo – the stalls bring their prices down in the last hour of trading.

Nearby **Sant'Ambrogio** (daily 8am–12.30pm & 4–7pm) is one of Florence's older churches, having been documented in 988, though rebuilding over the centuries means that it is now somewhat bland in appearance. Inside, the most compelling feature is the Cappella del Miracolo, the chapel to the left of the high altar, and its tabernacle (1481–83) by Mino da Fiesole, an accomplished sculptor whose name crops up time and again across Tuscany. This was one of Mino's last works – he died in 1484 – making it fitting that he should be buried close by, in a pavement tomb at the chapel entrance. (Another great artist, the multi-talented Verrocchio, who died in 1488, is buried in the fourth chapel.) The narrative **fresco** (1486) alongside Mino's tabernacle alludes to the miracle that gave the Cappella del Miracolo its name. The work of Cosimo Rosselli, it describes the discovery and display of a chalice full of blood in 1230. The

Florentines believed the chalice saved them from, among other things, the effects of a plague outbreak in 1340. The painting is full of portraits of Rosselli's contemporaries, making it another of Florence's vivid pieces of Renaissance social reportage: Rosselli himself is the figure in the black beret at the extreme left of the picture.

The synagogue and Santa Maria Maddalena dei Pazzi

The enormous domed building rising to the north of Sant'Ambrogio church is the **Synagogue**; the ghetto established in this district by Cosimo I was not demolished until the mid-nineteenth century, which is when the present Moorish-style synagogue was built. It contains a museum that charts the history of Florence's Jewish population (April–Oct Sun–Thurs 10am–5/6pm, Fri 10am–2pm; Nov–March Sun–Thurs 10am–3pm, Fri 10am–2pm; €4).

West of the synagogue, on Borgo Pinti, stands the church of **Santa Maria Maddalena dei Pazzi** (Mon–Sat 9–11.50am & 5–5.20pm & 6.10–6.50pm, Sun 9–10.45am & 5–6.50pm), named after a Florentine nun who was famed for her religious ecstasies: when possessed by the holy spirit she would spew words at such a rate that a team of eight novices was needed to transcribe her inspired dictation. Such unflinching piety was much honoured in Counter-Reformation Florence: when Maria de' Medici went off to marry Henry IV of France, Maria Maddalena transmitted the news that the Virgin expected her to re-admit the Jesuits to France and exterminate the Huguenots, which she duly did.

Founded in the thirteenth century but kitted out in Baroque style, the church is not itself much of an attraction, but its chapterhouse – reached by a tortuous subterranean passageway that's accessed from the top of the right aisle – is decorated with a radiant **Perugino** fresco of the *Crucifixion* (€1). As always with Perugino, there is nothing troubling here, the Crucifixion being depicted not as an agonizing death but rather as the necessary prelude to the Resurrection.

San Salvi and Campo di Marte

Twenty-minutes' walk beyond Piazza Beccaria, east of Sant'Ambrogio (or bus #10 from the station, or #6 from Piazza San Marco), is the ex-convent of **San Salvi**, which was reopened in 1982 after the restoration of its most precious possession, the *Last Supper* by Andrea del Sarto (Tues–Sun 8.15am–1.50pm; free). As a prelude to this picture, there's a gallery of big but otherwise unremarkable Renaissance altarpieces, a gathering of pictures by various del Sarto acolytes, and the beautiful reliefs from the tomb of Giovanni Gualberto, founder of the Vallombrosan order to whom this monastery belonged. The tomb was smashed up by Charles V's troops in 1530 but they refused to damage the *Last Supper*, which is still in the refectory for which it was painted, accompanied by three del Sarto frescoes brought here from other churches in Florence.

The Stadio Comunale

As befits this monument-stuffed city, Florence's football team play in a stadium that's listed as a building of cultural significance, the **Stadio Comunale** (or **Stadio Artemio Franchi**) at **Campo di Marte** (bus #17 from the train station). It was designed by Pier Luigi Nervi in 1930, as a consequence of two decisions: to create a new football club for Florence and to stage the 1934 World Cup in Italy.

The stadium was the first major sports venue to exploit the shape-making potential of reinforced concrete, and its spiral ramps, cantilevered roof and slim central tower still make most other arenas look dreary. From the spectator's point of view, however, it's far from perfect: for instance, the peculiar D-shape of the stands – necessitated by the straight 200-metre sprint track – means that visibility from some parts of the ground is awful. But the architectural importance of Nervi's work meant that when Florence was chosen as one of the hosts for the 1990 World Cup there could be no question of simply building a replacement (as was done brilliantly at Bari), nor of radically altering the existing one (as happened at most grounds). Much of the seventy billion lire spent on the refurbishment of the Stadio Comunale was thus spent ensuring that the improvements did not ruin the clean modernistic lines, and most of the extra space in the all-seater stadium was created by lowering the pitch a couple of metres below its previous level, in order to insert another layer of seats where the track had been.

Stoked by the fans' longstanding sense of themselves as the unloved outsiders of Italian football, support at the Stadio Franchi is always intense, so **tickets** can be hard to obtain. They cost from as little as €10 and can be bought at the ground itself, or three or four days in advance from various outlets around the city, the chief of which are Box Office (see p.169) and the kiosk in Via Anselmi, off the west side of Piazza della Repubblica.

Oltrarno

Visitors to Florence might perceive the River Arno as a simple interruption in the urban fabric, but some Florentines still talk as though a ravine runs through their city. North of the river is known as *Arno di quà* ("over here"), while the other side, hemmed in by a ridge of hills that rises a short distance from the river, is *Arno di là* ("over there"). More formally, it's known as the **Oltrarno** – literally "beyond the Arno" – a terminology that has its roots in medieval times, when the district was not as accessible as the numerous bridges now make it.

Traditionally an artisans' quarter, the Oltrarno is still home to plenty of small workshops (particularly furniture restorers and leather-workers), and Via Maggio remains the focus of Florence's thriving antiques trade. The ambience is distinctly less tourist-centred here than in the area immediately across the water, and though the bars and restaurants around **Piazza Santo Spirito** and **Piazza del Carmine** attract their share of outsiders, the conversations you'll overhear are more likely to be in Italian than any other language. Which is not to say that the Oltrarno doesn't have major sights – **Palazzo Pitti**, **Santa Maria del Carmine**, **San Miniato** and **Santo Spirito** are all essential visits.

The Ponte Vecchio

The direct route from the city centre to the heart of the Oltrarno crosses the Arno via the **Ponte Vecchio**, the last in a line of bridges at the river's narrowest point that stretches back to Etruscan and Roman times. Until 1218 the crossing here was the city's only bridge, though the version you see today dates from 1345, built to replace a wooden bridge swept away by floods twelve years earlier – its name (Old Bridge) was coined to distinguish it from the Ponte alla Carraia, the bridge raised in 1218. Much later in its history the Ponte Vecchio was the only bridge not mined by the Nazis in 1944 as they retreated before the advancing American Fifth Army; Field Marshal Kesselring is said to have spared it on Hitler's express orders. Much of the rest of the city, including medieval quarters at each end of the bridge, was not so lucky: the Nazis reneged on a promise to spare the city, blowing up scores of old buildings to hamper the Allied advance.

The Ponte Vecchio has always been loaded with stores like those that are now propped over the water. Their earliest inhabitants were butchers and fishmongers, attracted to the site by the proximity of the river, which provided a convenient dumping ground for their waste. They were later joined by the tanners, who used the river to soak their hides before tanning them with horses' urine. The current plethora of jewellers dates from 1593, when Ferdinando I evicted the butchers' stalls and other practitioners of what he called "vile arts". In their place he installed eight jewellers and 41 **goldsmiths**, also taking the opportunity to double the rents. Florence had long revered the art of the goldsmith, and several of its major artists were skilled in the craft: Ghiberti, Donatello and Cellini, for example. The third of this trio is celebrated by a bust in the centre of the bridge.

Santa Felìcita

Santa Felìcita (Mon–Sat 9.30am–12.30pm & 3–6.30pm) might be the oldest church in Florence, having possibly been founded in the second century by Greek or Syrian merchants, pioneers of Christianity in the city. It's known for certain that a church existed on the site by the fifth century, by which time it had been dedicated to St Felicity, an early Roman martyr who is often shown in Renaissance paintings with her seven sons, each of whom was executed in front of her for refusing to renounce his faith (the saint herself was either beheaded or thrown into boiling oil). New churches were built on the site in the eleventh and fourteenth centuries, while in 1565 Vasari added an elaborate portico to accommodate the *corridoio* linking the Uffizi and Palazzo Pitti; a window from the corridor looks directly into the church. All but the facade was extensively remodelled between 1736 and 1739.

The interior demands a visit for the amazing **Pontormo** paintings in the **Cappella Capponi**, which lies to the right of the main door, surrounded by railings. Under the cupola are four tondi of the *Evangelists* (painted with help from his adoptive son, Bronzino), while on opposite sides of the window on the right wall are the Virgin and the angel of Pontormo's delightfully simple *Annunciation*, the arrangement alluding to the Incarnation as the means by which the Light came into the world. The low level of light admitted by this window was a determining factor in the startling colour scheme of Pontormo's almost erotic *Deposition* (1525–28), one of the masterworks of Florentine Mannerism. Nothing in this picture is conventional: the people bearing Christ's body are androgynous quasi-angelic creatures; billows of gorgeously coloured drapery almost engulf the scene; many of the figures seem to be standing in mid-air rather than on solid ground; and there's no sign of the cross, the thieves, soldiers or any of the other scene-setting devices usual in paintings of this subject – the only contextual detail is a solitary ghostly cloud. The bearded brown-cloaked figure on the right (Nicodemus) is believed to be a self-portrait of the artist.

The Palazzo Pitti

Beyond Santa Felìcita, the street opens out at Piazza Pitti, forecourt of the largest palace in Florence, the **Palazzo Pitti**. Banker and merchant Luca

Pitti commissioned the palace to outdo his rivals, the Medici. Work started around 1457, possibly using a design by Brunelleschi which had been rejected by Cosimo de' Medici for being too grand. No sooner was the palace completed, however, than the Pitti's fortunes began to decline, and by 1549 they were forced to sell out to the Medici. The Pitti subsequently became the Medici's base in Florence, growing in bulk until the seventeenth century, when it achieved its present gargantuan dimensions. Later, during Florence's brief tenure as the Italian capital between 1865 and 1870, it housed the Italian royal family.

Today the Palazzo Pitti and the pavilions of the Giardino di Bóboli contain eight museums, of which the foremost is the **Galleria Palatina**, a painting collection second in importance only to the Uffizi.

The Galleria Palatina and Appartamenti Reali

Many of the paintings gathered by the Medici in the seventeenth century are now arranged in the **Galleria Palatina** (Tues–Sun 8.15am–6.50pm; €8.50, includes admission to the Appartamenti Reali & Galleria d'Arte Moderna), a suite of almost thirty rooms on the first floor of one wing of the palace. The pictures are not arranged in the sort of didactic order observed by most galleries, but are instead hung as they would have been in the days of their acquisition, three deep in places, with the aim of making each room pleasurably varied. The best thing to do is wander at random until a picture takes your fancy. The big names just keep on coming, and the highlights are many, so you'll need hours to see the collection properly.

The current itinerary takes you straight through into the suite containing mostly less famous works, though some individual paintings are well worth seeking out, notably: **Fra' Bartolomeo**'s *Deposition*; a tondo of the *Madonna and Child with Scenes from the Life of St Anne* (1452) by **Filippo Lippi**; his son Filippino's *Death of Lucrezia*; a *Sleeping Cupid* (1608) by **Caravaggio**; and **Cristofano Allori**'s sexy *Judith and Holofernes*, for which Allori himself, his

▲ Palazzo Pitti

mother and his mistress provided the models for the principal characters. Also in this section are the Corridoio del Volterrano, which houses mainly Florentine works of the seventeenth century, and the Corridoio della Colonna, which has a Flemish theme.

In the second and more captivating part of the gallery, **Andrea del Sarto** is represented in strength, his seventeen works including a beautifully grave *Annunciation*. Even more remarkable is the Pitti's collection of paintings by his great contemporary, **Raphael**. When Raphael settled in Florence in 1505, he was besieged with commissions from patrons delighted to find an artist for whom the creative process involved so little agonizing. In the next three years he painted scores of pictures for such people as Angelo Doni, the man who commissioned Michelangelo's *Doni Tondo*, now in the Uffizi. Raphael's portraits of Doni and his wife, Maddalena (1506–7), display an unhesitating facility and perfect poise; if Maddalena's pose looks familiar, incidentally, it's because it's copied directly from Leonardo's *Mona Lisa*. Similar poise illuminates Raphael's splendidly framed 1515 *Madonna della Seggiola*, or Madonna of the Chair, which for centuries was Italy's most popular image of the Virgin: nineteenth-century copyists had to join a five-year waiting list to study the picture. According to Vasari, the model for the famous *Donna Velata* (Veiled Woman), in the Sala di Giove, was the painter's mistress, a Roman baker's daughter known to posterity as La Fornarina.

The assembly of paintings by the Venetian artist **Titian** (fourteen in all) includes a number of his most trenchant portraits. The lecherous and scurrilous Pietro Aretino – journalist, critic, poet and one of Titian's closest friends – was so thrilled by his 1545 portrait that he gave it to Cosimo I; Titian painted him on several other occasions, sometimes using him as the model for Pontius Pilate. Also here are likenesses of Philip II of Spain and the young Cardinal Ippolito de' Medici (1532), and the so-called *Portrait of an Englishman* (1540), who scrutinizes the viewer with unflinching sea-grey eyes. Nearby is the same artist's sensuous and much-copied *Mary Magdalene* (1531), the first of a series on this theme produced for the duke of Urbino. In the same room, look out for Rosso Fiorentino's recently restored *Madonna Enthroned with Saints* (1522), and the gallery's outstanding sculpture, Canova's *Venus Italica*, commissioned by Napoleon as a replacement for the *Venus de' Medici*, which he had whisked off to Paris.

Much of the rest of the Pitti's first floor comprises the **Appartamenti Reali**, the Pitti's state rooms. They were renovated by the dukes of Lorraine in the eighteenth century, and then by Vittorio Emanuele when Florence became the country's capital, so the rooms display three distinct decorative phases. The gallery leads straight through into the apartments, and after Raphael and Titian it can be difficult to sustain a great deal of enthusiasm for such ducal elegance, notwithstanding the sumptuousness of the furnishings.

The other Pitti museums

On the floor above the Palatina is the **Galleria d'Arte Moderna** (Tues–Sun 8.15am–6.50pm; joint ticket with Galleria Palatina), a chronological survey of primarily Tuscan art from the mid-eighteenth century to 1945. Most rewarding are the products of the Macchiaioli, the Italian division of the Impressionist movement; most startling, however, are the sculptures, featuring sublime kitsch such as Antonio Ciseri's *Pregnant Nun*.

The **Museo degli Argenti** (Nov–Feb 8.15am–4.30pm; March 8.15am–5.30pm; April, May, Sept & Oct 8.15am–6.30pm; June–Aug 8.15am–7.30pm; closed first & last Mon of month; joint ticket with Museo delle Porcellane,

Galleria del Costume and Giardino di Bóboli €7), entered from the main palace courtyard, is a museum not just of silverware but of luxury artefacts in general. The lavishly frescoed reception rooms themselves fall into this category: the first hall, the Sala di Giovanni da San Giovanni, shows Lorenzo de' Medici giving refuge to the Muses; the other three ceremonial rooms have *trompe l'oeil* paintings by seventeenth-century Bolognese artists. As for the exhibits, the least ambivalent response is likely to be aroused by Lorenzo the Magnificent's trove of antique vases, all of them marked with their owner's name. With many of the pieces, though, you might well be torn between admiring the skills of the craftsman and deploring the ends to which those skills were employed; by the time you reach the end of the jewellery show on the first floor, you'll have lost all capacity to be surprised or revolted by seashell figurines, cups made from ostrich eggs, portraits in stone inlay, and the like. One-off exhibitions are sometimes held here, which can affect the ticket price and opening hours.

Visitors without a specialist interest are unlikely to be riveted by the other Pitti museums that are currently open. In the Palazzina della Meridiana, the eighteenth-century southern wing of the Pitti, the **Galleria del Costume** (same hours and ticket as Museo degli Argenti) provides the opportunity to see the dress that Eleonora di Toledo is wearing in Bronzino's famous portrait of her (in the Palazzo Vecchio). The well-presented if esoteric collection of porcelain, the **Museo delle Porcellane**, is located on the other side of the Bóboli garden (same hours and ticket as Museo degli Argenti), while the **Museo delle Carrozze** (Carriage Museum) has been closed for years and will almost certainly remain so for the foreseeable future, to the chagrin of very few.

The Giardino di Bóboli

The delightful formal garden of the Palazzo Pitti, the **Giardino di Bóboli** (same hours and ticket as Museo degli Argenti), takes its name from the Bóboli family, erstwhile owners of much of this area, which was once a quarry; the bedrock here is one of the sources of the yellow sandstone known as *pietra forte* (strong stone) that gives much of Florence its dominant hue. Carefully shaped into a rough, boulder-like texture, this stone was also used to "rusticate" the Palazzo Pitti's great facade. When the Medici acquired the house in 1549 they set to work transforming their back yard into an enormous 111-acre garden, its every statue, view and grotto designed to elevate nature by the judicious application of art.

Work continued into the early seventeenth century, by which stage this steep hillside had been turned into a maze of statue-strewn avenues and well-trimmed vegetation. Opened to the public in 1766, it is the only really extensive area of accessible greenery in the centre of the city, and can be one of the most pleasant spots for a midday picnic or coffee. It's no place to seek solitude, however: some five million visitors annually, more than at any other Italian garden, take time out here. (If the queues at the main entrance are too daunting, walk about three hundred metres further along the main road, the Via Romana, where you'll find another, invariably quieter, entrance.)

Aligned with the central block of the palazzo, the garden's **amphitheatre** was designed in the early seventeenth century as an arena for Medici entertainments. The site had previously been laid out by Ammannati in 1599 over an earlier stone quarry as a garden in the shape of a Roman circus. For the wedding of Cosimo III and Princess Marguerite-Louise, cousin of Louis

XIV, twenty thousand guests were packed onto the stone benches to watch a production that began with the appearance of a gigantic effigy of Atlas with the globe on his back; the show got under way when the planet split apart, releasing a cascade of earth that transformed the giant into the Atlas mountain. Such frivolities did little to reconcile Marguerite-Louise to either Florence or her husband, and after several acrimonious years this miserable dynastic marriage came to an effective end with her return to Paris, where she professed to care about little "as long as I never have to set eyes on the grand duke again".

Of all the garden's Mannerist embellishments, the most celebrated is the **Grotta del Buontalenti** (1583–88), to the left of the entrance, beyond Giambologna's much-reproduced statue of Cosimo I's favourite dwarf astride a giant tortoise. Embedded in the grotto's faked stalactites and encrustations are replicas of Michelangelo's *Slaves* – the originals were lodged here until 1908. Lurking in the deepest recesses of the cave (which is usually opened on the hour) is Giambologna's *Venus Emerging from her Bath*, leered at by imps.

Another spectacular set piece is the fountain island called the **Isolotto**, which is the focal point of the far end of the garden; from within the Bóboli the most dramatic approach is along the central cypress avenue known as the **Viottolone**, many of whose statues are Roman originals. These lower parts of the garden are its most pleasant – and least visited – sections. You come upon them quickly if you enter the Bóboli by the little-used Porta Romana entrance.

Casa Guidi and La Specola

Within a stone's throw of the Pitti, at the junction of Via Maggio and Via Romana, you'll find the home of Robert Browning and Elizabeth Barrett Browning, the **Casa Guidi** (April–Nov Mon, Wed & Fri 3–6pm; free, but donations welcome). It's something of a shrine to Elizabeth, who wrote much of her most popular verse here (including, naturally enough, *Casa Guidi Windows*) and died here. Virtually all of Casa Guidi's furniture went under the hammer at Sotheby's in 1913, and there's just a piano and an oil painting left, but two of the three rooms still manage to conjure up something of the spirit.

There's more to enjoy on the third floor of the university buildings at Via Romana 17, in what can reasonably claim to be the strangest museum in the city. Taking its name from the telescope (*specola*) on its roof, **La Specola** (Mon, Tues, Thurs, Fri & Sun 9am–1pm, Sat 9am–5pm; €4) is a tripartite museum of zoology. One section, comprising the country's largest collection of skeletons, is open to the public only on Saturday mornings. Of the other parts, the first is conventional enough, with ranks of shells, insects and crustaceans, followed by a veritable ark of animals stuffed, pickled and desiccated, including a hippo given to Grand Duke Pietro Leopardo which used to reside in the Bóboli garden. Beyond some rather frayed-looking sharks lie the exhibits everyone comes to see, the **Cere Anatomiche** (Anatomical Waxworks). Wax arms, legs and internal organs cover the walls, arrayed around satin beds on which wax cadavers recline in progressive stages of deconstruction, each muscle fibre and nerve cluster moulded and dyed with scarcely believable precision. Most of the six hundred models – and nearly all of the amazing full-body mannequins – were made between 1775 and 1791 by one Clemente Susini and his team of assistants, and were intended as teaching aids, in an age when medical ethics and refrigeration techniques were not what they are today.

In a separate room towards the end, after the obstetrics display and a few zoological models, you'll find the grisliest section of La Specola, a trio of tableaux that were moulded in the late seventeenth century by **Gaetano Zumbo**, a cleric from Sicily who was one of the pioneers of the art of anatomical waxworks. Whereas Susini's masterpieces were created to educate, these were made to horrify, and to horrify one man in particular: the hypochondriacal Cosimo III, a Jesuit-indoctrinated bigot who regarded all genuine scientific enquiry with suspicion. Enclosed in tasteful display cabinets, they depict Florence during the plague: rats teasing the intestines from green-fleshed corpses, mushrooms growing from the mulch of fleshly debris, and the pink bodies of the freshly dead heaped on the suppurating semi-decomposed. A fourth tableau, illustrating the horrors of syphilis, was damaged in the 1966 flood, and now consists of a loose gathering of the deceased and diseased. In the centre of the room lies a dissected waxwork head, built on the foundation of a real skull; it's as fastidious as any of Susini's creations, but Zumbo couldn't resist giving the skin a tint of putrefaction, before applying a dribble of blood to the mouth and nose.

Santo Spirito

Designed in 1434 as a replacement for a thirteenth-century church, **Santo Spirito** (Thurs–Tues 9.30am–12.30pm & 4–6pm) was one of Brunelleschi's last projects, a swansong later described by Bernini as "the most beautiful church in the world". The church is so perfectly proportioned that nothing could seem more artless, yet the plan is extremely sophisticated: a Latin cross with a continuous chain of 38 chapels round the outside and a line of 35 columns running without a break round the nave, transepts and chancel. The exterior wall was originally designed to follow the curves of the chapels' walls, creating a flowing, corrugated effect. As built, however, the exterior is a plain, straight wall, and even the main facade remained incomplete, covered today by a simple plastering job. Inside the church, only the Baroque baldachin, about as nicely integrated as a jukebox in a Greek temple, disrupts the harmony.

A fire in 1471 destroyed most of Santo Spirito's medieval works, including famed frescoes by Cimabue and the Gaddi family, but as a result, the altar paintings in the many chapels comprise an unusually unified collection of religious works, most having been commissioned in the aftermath of the fire. Most prolific among the artists is the so-called **Maestro di Santo Spirito**, but the best paintings are in the transepts. In the south transept is **Filippino Lippi's** *Nerli Altarpiece*, an age-darkened Madonna and Child with saints (second chapel from the left of the four chapels on the transept's south wall). The Nerli were the family who commissioned the chapel and the painting, the donors Tanai and Nanna dei Nerli being portrayed amidst the saints; their Florentine home, the Palazzo dei Nerli near Porta San Frediano, is depicted in the background.

Across the church, in the north transept, is an unusual *St Monica and Augustinian Nuns* (1460–70), probably by Verrocchio or Francesco Botticini, that's virtually a study in monochrome, with black-clad nuns flocking round their black-clad paragon; it's in the second chapel on the right wall as you stand with your back to the high altar.

A door in the north aisle leads through to Giuliano da Sangallo's stunning vestibule and **sacristy** (1489–93), the latter designed in imitation of Brunelleschi's Pazzi chapel. The meticulously planned proportions and soft grey-and-white tones create an atmosphere of extraordinary calm that is only disrupted by the exuberantly botanical carvings of the capitals, some of which were designed by Sansovino. Hanging above the altar is a delicate wooden crucifix, attributed to **Michelangelo**. It's known that the young Michelangelo was commissioned by the monks of Santo Spirito to make a crucifix for the church in the early 1490s, and several scholars believe that this sculpture – discovered in Santo Spirito in 1963 – is the work in question; others, though, think it was made half a century later by one Taddeo Curradi.

The Chiostro dei Morti and the Cenacolo di Santo Spirito

A glass door at the far end of the vestibule, usually locked, gives out onto the **Chiostro dei Morti**, the only cloister in the complex that is still part of the Augustinian monastery. The 1471 fire destroyed much of the rest of the monastery, with the exception of its refectory (entered to the left of the main church, at Piazza Santo Spirito 29), which is now the home of the **Cenacolo di Santo Spirito** (Sat: April–Oct 9am–5pm; Nov–March 10.30am–1.30pm; €2.20), a one-room collection comprising an assortment of carvings, many of them Romanesque, and a huge fresco of *The Crucifixion* (1365) by Orcagna and his workshop.

Santa Maria del Carmine

Nowhere in Florence is there a more startling contrast between exterior and interior than in **Santa Maria del Carmine**, a couple of blocks west of Santo Spirito in Piazza del Carmine. Outside it's a drab box of shabby brick; inside – in the frescoes of the **Cappella Brancacci** (Mon & Wed–Sat 10am–5pm, Sun 1–5pm; €4) – it provides one of Italy's supreme artistic experiences. The chapel is barricaded off from the rest of the Carmine, and visits are restricted to a maximum of thirty people at a time, for just fifteen minutes. The time limit is strictly enforced in high season, but tends to become more flexible as the crowds ebb away. At the time of writing tickets could be obtained only by reserving in advance on ☏055.276.8224; this system is so cumbersome, however, that it surely will be replaced by something less visitor-repellent – ask the tourist office about the current situation.

The Cappella Brancacci

The **Cappella Brancacci** frescoes were commissioned in 1424 by Felice Brancacci, a silk merchant and leading patrician figure, shortly after his return from a stint in Egypt as the Florentine ambassador. The decoration of the chapel was begun in the same year by **Masolino** (1383–1447), fresh from working as an assistant to Lorenzo Ghiberti on the Baptistery doors. Alongside Masolino was Tommaso di Ser Giovanni di Mone Cassai – known ever since as **Masaccio** (1401–28), a nickname meaning "Mad Tom".

Two years into the project Masolino was recalled to Budapest, where he was official painter to the Hungarian court. Left to his own devices Masaccio began to blossom. When Masolino returned in 1427 the teacher was soon taking lessons from the supposed pupil, whose grasp of the texture of the real world, of the principles of perspective and of the dramatic potential of the biblical texts they were illustrating far exceeded that of his precursors. In 1428 Masolino was called away to Rome, where he was followed by Masaccio a few months later. Neither would return to the chapel. Masaccio died the same year, aged just 27, but, in the words of Vasari, "all the most celebrated sculptors and painters since Masaccio's day have become excellent and illustrious by studying their art in this chapel." (Michelangelo used to come here to make drawings of Masaccio's scenes, and had his nose broken on the chapel steps by a young sculptor whom he enraged with his condescension.) Some fifty years later the paintings were completed by **Filippino Lippi**, whose copying skills were such that his work was only recognized as distinct from that of his predecessors in 1838.

The small scene on the left of the entrance arch (marked 1 in our plan) is the quintessence of Masaccio's art. Plenty of artists had depicted the **Expulsion of Adam and Eve** before, but none had captured the desolation of the sinners so graphically: Adam presses his hands to his face in bottomless despair, Eve raises her head and screams. The monumentalism of these stark naked figures – whose modesty was preserved by strategically placed sprigs of foliage prior to the restoration – reveals the influence of Donatello, who may have been involved in the planning of the chapel. In contrast to the emotional charge and sculptural presence of Masaccio's couple, Masolino's almost dainty **Adam and Eve** (6),

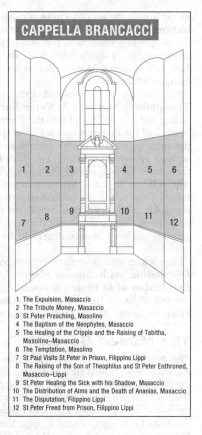

CAPPELLA BRANCACCI

1 The Expulsion, Masaccio
2 The Tribute Money, Masaccio
3 St Peter Preaching, Masolino
4 The Baptism of the Neophytes, Masaccio
5 The Healing of the Cripple and the Raising of Tabitha, Masolino–Masaccio
6 The Temptation, Masolino
7 St Paul Visits St Peter in Prison, Filippino Lippi
8 The Raising of the Son of Theophilus and St Peter Enthroned, Masaccio–Lippi
9 St Peter Healing the Sick with his Shadow, Masaccio
10 The Distribution of Alms and the Death of Ananias, Masaccio
11 The Disputation, Filippino Lippi
12 St Peter Freed from Prison, Filippino Lippi

on the opposite arch, pose as if to have their portraits painted.

St Peter is chief protagonist of all the remaining scenes. It's possible that the cycle was intended as propaganda on behalf of the embattled papacy, which had only recently resolved the long and bitter Great Schism, during which one pope held court in Rome and another in Avignon. By celebrating the primacy of St Peter, the rock upon whom the Church is built, the frescoes by implication extol the apostolic succession from which the pope derives his authority.

Three scenes by Masaccio are especially compelling. First off is the **Tribute Money** (2), most widely praised of the paintings and the Renaissance's first monumental fresco. The narrative is complex, with no fewer than three separate events portrayed within a single frame. The central episode shows Christ outside the gates of Capernaum being asked to pay a tribute owing to the city. To the left, St Peter fetches coins from the mouth of a fish in order to pay the tribute, Christ in the central panel having pointed to where the money will be found. The third scene, to the right, depicts Peter handing over the money to the tax official.

Masaccio's second great panel is **St Peter Healing the Sick with his Shadow** (9), in which the shadow of the stern and self-possessed saint (followed by St John) cures the infirm as it passes over them, a miracle invested with the aura of a solemn ceremonial. The third panel is the **Distribution of Alms and Death of Ananias** (10), in which St Peter instructs the people to give up their possessions to the poor. One individual, Ananias, retains some of his wealth with the knowledge of his wife, Sapphira. Rebuked by Peter, Ananias dies on the spot, closely followed by a similarly castigated Sapphira.

Filippino Lippi's work included the completion of Masaccio's **Raising of Theophilus's Son and St Peter Enthroned** (8), which depicts St Peter raising the son of Theophilus, the Prefect of Antioch (apparently after he'd been dead for fourteen years). The people of Antioch, suitably impressed by the miracle, build a throne from which St Peter can preach, shown as a separate episode to the right. The three figures to the right of the throne are thought to be portraits of Masaccio, Alberti and Brunelleschi, who made a trip to Rome together. Masaccio originally painted himself touching Peter's robe, a reference to the enthroned statue of Peter in Rome, which pilgrims touch for good luck. Lippi considered the contact of the artist and saint to be improper and painted out the arm; at the moment, his fastidious over-painting has been allowed to remain, but you can clearly see where the arm used to be.

Lippi left another portrait in the combined scene of **Sts Peter and Paul in Disputation with Simon Magus before Nero** (11) and the adjacent **Crucifixion of St Peter**: the central figure looking out from the painting in the trio right of the crucifixion is Botticelli, the painter's teacher, while Filippino himself can be seen at the far right.

The Museo Bardini

The best way to reach the Bardini museum from the Ponte Vecchio and elsewhere in the Oltrarno is to take Via de' Bardi, known in the Middle Ages as the Borgo Pitiglioso – the "miserable" or "flea-bitten" street. Part way down the street on the left, beyond the small Piazza di Santa Maria Soprarno, you'll pass the tiny church of **Santa Lucia dei Magnoli**, founded in 1078. Pop inside if you're lucky enough to find it open: the first altar on the left has a panel of St Lucy by the Sienese master Pietro Lorenzetti.

The **Museo Bardini**, which stands at the end of the street at Piazza de' Mozzi 1, is like the Museo Horne just across the Arno, in that it was built around the bequest of a private collector. Whereas Horne was a moderately well-off connoisseur, however, his contemporary **Stefano Bardini** (1836–1922) was once the most important art dealer in Italy. His tireless activity, at a time when Renaissance art was relatively cheap and unfashionable, laid the cornerstone of many important modern-day European and American collections. Determined that no visitor to his native city should remain unaware of his success, he ripped down a church that stood here and built a vast house for himself, studding it with fragments of old buildings. Doorways, ceiling panels and other orphaned pieces are strewn all over the place: the first-floor windows of the main facade, for instance, are actually altars from a church in Pistoia. Musical instruments, carvings, ceramics, armour, furniture, carpets, paintings – Bardini snapped them all up, and bequeathed the whole lot to the city. Displays are spread over a couple of floors and some twenty rooms, though only the more precious exhibits are fully labelled. For several years the museum has been *in restauro*, a process that is allegedly soon to be concluded; the following is a summary of the place as it was before its closure.

On the **ground floor**, Tino da Camaino's *Charity* stands out, but the most interesting items are upstairs. Room 10 is a display of funerary monuments arranged as if in a crypt, with an enamelled terracotta altarpiece attributed to Andrea della Robbia. Beyond several rooms of weapons, three pieces in Room 14 also grab the attention: a polychrome terracotta of the *Madonna and Child* by Donatello; an extraordinarily modern-looking stucco, mosaic and glass relief of the *Madonna dei Cordai* (1443), also probably by Donatello; and a terracotta *Madonna and Child with St John* by Benedetto da Maiano. Room 16 has some lovely *cassoni* (painted chests) and several of the museum's many depictions of the Madonna and Child, a subject with which Bardini appears to have been obsessed. Other highlights of the final rooms include some gorgeous carpets, Domenico Beccafumi's *Hercules at the Crossroads between Vice and Virtue*, Michele Giambono's *St John the Baptist*, a painted relief in terracotta from the workshop of Jacopo della Quercia, a *St Michael* by Antonio del Pollaiuolo and a beautiful terracotta *Virgin Annunciate*, an anonymous piece from fifteenth-century Siena.

When the museum reopens, the top floor will house the **Galleria Corsi**, a collection of no fewer than seven hundred paintings, dating from the fourteenth to the nineteenth century, donated to the city in 1937 by Fortunata Carobbi Corsi.

The Giardino Bardini and Villa Bardini

Close to the Museo Bardini, at Via de' Bardi 1r, is an entrance to the **Giardino Bardini** (same hours and ticket as the Giardino di Bóboli), which was opened to the public for the first time in 2007. The garden occupies the slope that was formerly the olive grove of the **Palazzo dei Mozzi**, a colossal house built in the late thirteenth century by the Mozzi family, at that time one of the richest families in Florence. After Stefano Bardini bought the property in 1913 he set about creating a semi-formal garden which has now been restored to the appearance he gave it, with a neo-Baroque staircase and terraces dividing the fruit-growing section from the miniature woodland of the "*bosco inglese*". At the summit of the garden, reached by a lovely long pergola of wisteria and hortensia, a colonnaded belvedere gives a splendid view of the city.

If you're coming from the Bóboli gardens you can enter the garden at the top, from Costa di San Giorgio, where you'll find the **Villa Bardini** (daily 10am–4pm; closed first and last Mon of month; €5), which was built as the Villa Manadora and extended by Stefano Bardini. Having been thoroughly restored, the villa now houses two somewhat non-essential collections. One is dedicated to Pietro Annigoni (1910–88), a vehemently anti-Modernist painter who was best known for his unchallenging portraits of luminaries such as Pope John XXIII, the Shah of Iran and Queen Elizabeth II, the other to the clothes created by Roberto Capucci (b. 1930), a designer dubbed the "Givenchy of Rome" by his admirers.

From San Niccolò to San Miniato

Beyond the Museo Bardini, Via San Niccolò swings past **San Niccolò sopr'Arno** (daily 8.30–10am & 5.30–7pm), another of this quarter's interesting little churches. Restoration work after the 1966 flood uncovered several frescoes underneath the altars, but none is as appealing as the fifteenth-century fresco in the sacristy; known as *The Madonna of the Girdle*, it was probably painted by Baldovinetti. In medieval times the church was close to the edge of the city, and two of Florence's fourteenth-century gates still stand in the vicinity: the diminutive **Porta San Miniato**, set in a portion of the walls, and the huge **Porta San Niccolò**, overlooking the Arno. From either of these gates you can begin the climb up to San Miniato: the path from Porta San Niccolò weaves up through **Piazzale Michelangelo**, with its replica David and bumper-to-bumper tour coaches; the more direct path from Porta San Miniato offers a choice between the steep Via del Monte alle Croci or the stepped Via di San Salvatore al Monte, both of which emerge a short distance uphill from Piazzale Michelangelo.

San Miniato al Monte

One of the finest Romanesque structures in Tuscany, **San Miniato al Monte** (daily: summer 8am–7.30pm; winter 8am–noon & 3–6pm) is also the oldest surviving church building in Florence after the Baptistery. Its brilliant multi-coloured facade lures hordes of visitors up the hill from Oltrarno, and the church and its magnificent interior and works of art more than fulfil the promise of its distant appearance. The **walk** up to San Miniato has some steep sections; if you don't fancy the climb, take **bus** #12 or #13 as far as Piazzale Michelangelo and then continue on foot.

The church's dedicatee, **St Minias**, was Florence's first home-grown martyr. Possibly a Greek merchant or the son of an Armenian king, he originally left home to make a pilgrimage to Rome. Around 250 he moved to Florence, where he became caught up in the anti-Christian persecutions of the Emperor Decius. Legend has it that after martyrdom by decapitation – close to the site of Piazza della Signoria – the saintly corpse was seen to carry his severed head over the river and up the hill to this spot, an area where he'd previously lived as

▲ San Miniato al Monte

a hermit: a shrine was subsequently erected on the slope. The hill, known as **Mons Fiorentinus**, was already the site of several pagan temples and a secret oratory dedicated to Peter the Apostle. A chapel to Miniato is documented on the site in the eighth century, though construction of the present building began in 1013. Initially run as a Benedictine foundation, the building passed to the Cluniacs until 1373, and then to the **Olivetans**, a Benedictine offshoot, who reside here to this day, and sell their famous liquors, honeys and tisanes from the shop next to the church.

The exterior

San Miniato's gorgeous marble **facade** alludes to the Baptistery in its geometrical patterning, and, like its model, the church was often mistaken for a structure of classical provenance during the later Middle Ages. The lower part of the facade is possibly eleventh-century, while the angular upper levels date from the twelfth century onwards, and were financed in part by the Arte di Calimala (cloth merchants' guild), the body responsible for the church's upkeep from 1288: their trademark, an eagle clutching a bale of cloth, perches on the roof. The mosaic of Christ between the Virgin and St Minias dates from 1260. The original **bell tower** collapsed in 1499 and was replaced in the 1520s by the present campanile, still unfinished. During the 1530 siege of Florence it was used as an artillery post, thus attracting the attention of enemy gunners. Michelangelo, then advising on the city's defences, had it wrapped in woollen mattresses to protect it from cannonballs.

The interior

With its choir raised on a platform above the large crypt, the sublime **interior** of San Miniato is like no other in the city, and its general appearance has changed little since the mid-eleventh century. The main additions and decorations in no way spoil its serenity, though the nineteenth-century recoating of the marble columns is a little lurid: the columns' capitals, however, are Roman and Byzantine originals removed from older buildings. The intricately patterned panels of the **pavement** are dated 1207; some claim the zodiac and strange beast motifs were inspired by Sicilian fabrics, others that they are of Byzantine origin, introduced into Italy through trade and the Crusades.

The lovely tabernacle, or **Cappella del Crocefisso**, which dominates the middle of the nave, was designed in 1448 by Michelozzo, and is one of the few works commissioned by Piero de' Medici, or Piero il Gottoso (the Gouty), during his brief tenure as head of the Medici dynasty. The marble medallion to the rear and other parts of the work are adorned with Piero's motto (*Semper*) and several Medici symbols – the eagle holding three feathers and a diamond ring, the latter a symbol of durability and toughness. The chapel originally housed the miraculous crucifix associated with St Giovanni Gualberto (see p.109), which was moved to Santa Trìnita in 1671. Today it contains painted **panels** by Agnolo Gaddi depicting the *Annunciation*, *Stories of the Passion* and *Sts Giovanni Gualberto and Miniato* (1394–96). Maso di Bartolomeo crafted the twin eagles (1449), symbols of the Calimala, to stress that while Piero was the work's sponsor, the guild was responsible for overseeing all stages of its construction. The terracotta in the barrel vault is by Luca della Robbia.

Steps either side of the Cappella lead down to the **crypt**, the oldest part of the church, where the original high altar still contains the bones of St Minias. The vaults, supported by 36 wonderfully mismatched pillars, contain gilt-backed frescoes (1341) of the saints, martyrs, prophets, virgins and Evangelists by Taddeo Gaddi.

Back in the main body of the church, steps beside the Cappella del Crocefisso lead to the raised **choir** and **presbytery**, where there's a magnificent Romanesque **pulpit** and screen dating from 1207. The odd totem-like figures supporting the lectern may represent three of the four Evangelists or, possibly, humanity placed in a middle state between the animal world (the lion) and the divine (the eagle). The great **mosaic** in the apse was created in 1297, probably by the same artist who created the facade mosaic, as their subjects are identical – Christ Pantocrator enthroned between the Virgin and Saint Minias. Off the presbytery lies the **sacristy**, whose walls are almost completely covered in a superlative fresco cycle devoted to the life of St Benedict by Spinello Aretino (1387).

Back in the lower body of the church, off the left-hand side of the nave, the **Cappella del Cardinale del Portogallo**, dating from a few years after the Cappella del Crocefisso, is one of the masterpieces of Renaissance chapel design and a marvellous example of artistic collaboration. Completed in 1473, it was built as a memorial to Cardinal James of Lusitania, who died in Florence in 1459, aged just 25. Aside from that of Minias himself, this is – remarkably – the church's only tomb.

The chapel's basic design was the work of Antonio di Manetto (or Manetti), a pupil and biographer of Brunelleschi, who borrowed heavily from his master's work in San Lorenzo's Sagrestia Vecchia. The **tomb** itself was carved by Antonio and Bernardo Rossellino; their elder brother Giovanni oversaw the chapel's construction after Manetto's death. Antonio Rossellino's tondo of the Madonna and Child keeps watch over the deceased. The chapel's architectural and sculptural work was followed in 1466 by carefully integrated frescoes and **paintings**: an *Annunciation* (to the left) and the *Evangelists* and *Doctors of the Church* by Alesso Baldovinetti (lunettes and beside the arches). Antonio and Piero del Pollaiuolo produced the **altarpiece** depicting the cardinal's patron saint, St James, with Sts Vincent and Eustace: the present picture is a copy, the original being in the Uffizi. The ceiling's tiled decoration and four glazed terracotta medallions, perhaps the finest such work in the city, were provided by Luca della Robbia. All the decorative details were carefully designed to complement one another and create a unified artistic whole. Thus Rossellino's tondo of the *Madonna and Child*, for example, echoes the round windows of the walls; the colours in Baldovinetti's *Annunciation* deliberately echo the tones of the surrounding porphyry and serpentine inlays; and the curtain held aside by angels on the cardinal's tomb is repeated in a similar curtain half-shielding the altar.

From the Forte di Belvedere to San Leonardo in Arcetri

The **Forte di Belvedere**, standing on the crest of the hill above the Bóboli garden, was built by Buontalenti on the orders of Ferdinando I between 1590 and 1595, ostensibly to protect the city, but in fact to intimidate the grand duke's subjects. The urban panorama from here is superb, and ambitious exhibitions are often held in and around the shed-like palace in the centre of the fortress, as are occasional summer evening film screenings. The city's Museo delle Arme (Arms and Armour Museum) is also due to open here, at some unspecified point in the future.

In the past it has sometimes been possible to get up to the fort from the Bóboli gardens, but if you want to be certain of getting in, approach the fort from the **Costa di San Giorgio**, a lane which you can reach by backtracking slightly from the Museo Bardini, or pick up directly from the rear of Santa Felìcita. Look out for the villa at no. 19, home to Galileo between 1610 and 1631.

East from the Belvedere stretches the best-preserved section of Florence's fortified **walls**, paralleled by Via di Belvedere. South of the Belvedere, Via San Leonardo leads past olive groves to the church of **San Leonardo in Arcetri** (daily 10am–noon in theory, but rarely open), site of a beautiful thirteenth-century pulpit brought here from a church now incorporated into the Uffizi. Dante and Boccaccio are both said to have preached from the spot.

Eating, drinking, nightlife and shopping

For a small city, Florence has plenty of big-city attractions: scores of **cafés** and **restaurants**, a full calendar of cultural events and a lot of chic **shops** to give focus to the evening *passeggiata*. The main problem is one of identity, in a city whose inhabitants are heavily outnumbered by outsiders from March to October. Restaurant standards are often patchy and prices pitched at whatever level the tourists can bear, while many of the locals swear there's scarcely a single genuine Tuscan place left in the Tuscan capital – an exaggeration, of course, but a reflection of a general feeling that too much has been lost to tourism. Yet the situation is nowhere near as bad as some reports would have it, and if anything it's been improving in recent years, with the appearance of several stylish and good-value restaurants, alongside some superb **bars**. As for **nightlife**, the university and the influx of language students keep things lively, and seasonal events such as the *Maggio Musicale* maintain Florence's standing as the hub of cultural life in Tuscany.

Restaurants

In Italian gastronomic circles, **Florentine cuisine** is accorded as much reverence as Florentine art, a reverence encapsulated in the myth that French eating habits acquired their sophistication in the wake of Catherine de' Medici's marriage to the future Henry II of France. In fact, Florentine food has always been characterized by modest raw materials and simple technique: steak (*bistecca*), tripe (*trippa*) and liver (*fegato*) are typical ingredients, while grilling (*alla fiorentina*) is a favoured method of preparation. In addition, white beans (*fagioli*) will feature on most menus, either on their own, garnished with liberal quantities of local olive oil, or as the basis of such dishes as *ribollita*.

161

Snacks and food shops

If you want to put together a picnic, an obvious place to shop is the **Mercato Centrale** by San Lorenzo church (Mon–Sat 7am–2pm), where everything you could possibly need can be bought under one roof: bread, ham, cheese, fruit, wine, ready-made sandwiches. The **Mercato Sant'Ambrogio** over by Santa Croce (same hours) is smaller but of comparable quality. Every district has its **alimentari**, which in addition to selling the choicest Tuscan produce will often make sandwiches to order. For the choicest local produce, you can't beat these three *alimentari*: 'Ino, very close to the Uffizi at Via de' Georgofili 3–7r; Mariano, near Santa Maria Novella at Via del Parione 19r; and Olio e Convivium, at Via Santo Spirito 4, in Oltrarno. Nearly all wine bars sell bottles to take away, but you'll get a far better selection at a specialist shop such as Millesimi, at Borgo Tegolaio 35r, or Obsequium, at Borgo San Jacopo 17 – both in Oltrarno. Chocoholics should check out Vestri, at Borgo degli Albizi 11r, which offers deliciously thick chocolate to drink (hot or cold depending on the season) and a mouth-watering array of chocolate products, including ice cream.

For a hearty sit-down lunchtime snack, each of the two markets has an excellent **tavola calda**, serving meatballs, pasta, stews, soups and sandwiches: *Nerbone* (Mon–Sat 7am–2pm) in the Mercato Centrale, and *Tavola Calda da Rocco* (same hours), in the Mercato di Sant'Ambrogio. If you really want to go native, you could join the throng of office workers around the tripe stall in Piazza dei Cimatori, between the Duomo and Piazza della Signoria (Mon–Fri 8.30am–8.30pm; closed four weeks July/Aug). Its speciality is the local delicacy called *lampredotto*: hot tripe served in a bun with a spicy sauce. The stall also sells wine, so you can wash the taste away should you realize you've made a horrible mistake. There's a similar operation – *Da Sergio e Pierpaolo* – parked outside the *Cibrèo* restaurant in Via de' Macci, close to the Sant'Ambrogio market (Mon–Sat 7.15am–3pm).

Bear in mind that meals – not just snacks – are served in many Florentine bars and cafés, so if you fancy a quick bite to eat rather than a full-blown restaurant meal, take a look at the "Cafés and bars" and "Wine bars" listings below.

Restaurants, cafés and bars in central Florence are marked on the **map** on pp.66–67, while more outlying places are shown on the map on pp.58–59.

City Centre

Antico Fattore Via Lambertesca 1–3r ☎055.288.975. Simple Tuscan dishes dominate the menu here, and the soups are particularly good. The nearest thing you'll find to a genuine trattoria near the Uffizi (mains €10–14), though it's a tad grander than it used to be before the refurbishment that was needed after the 1993 Uffizi bombing, which badly damaged the place. Mon–Sat 12.15–3pm & 7.15–10.30pm; closed Aug.

Oliviero Via delle Terme 51r ☎055.240.618. *Oliviero* has a welcoming and old-fashioned feel – something like an Italian restaurant of the 1960s – and the menu, though predominantly Tuscan, includes dishes from other regions of Italy. Fresh fish, when available, features strongly – something of a rarity in Florence. Expect

to pay upwards of €50, without wine – reasonable for cooking of this calibre. Mon–Sat 7pm–midnight; closed Aug.

West of the centre

Il Contadino Via Palazzuolo 71r. Small, popular place with simple black-and-white interior and fascinating large photos of old Florence on the walls. Fast and friendly service, shared tables (no booking), and very cheap but good food. There's no written menu: the four or so choices for each course are recited rapidly. Three-course lunch and dinner menu costs a mere €10. Mon–Fri noon–9.30pm.

Marione Via della Spada 27r ☎055.214.756. Simple, good-value Tuscan cooking, at prices that are a pleasant surprise for this location, a stone's throw from Via Tornabuoni. Mains from just €6.

Daily noon–3pm & 7–11.30pm. Closed first two weeks of Aug.

North of the centre

🏃 **Da Mario** Via Rosina 2r ☎ 055.218.550. Located very close to the Mercato Centrale, *Da Mario* has probably been packed out every lunchtime since the Colsi family started running the place in 1953. For earthy Florentine cooking at very low prices, there's nowhere better. It's just a pity it isn't open in the evenings. Mon–Sat noon–3.30pm; closed most of Aug.

🏃 **Zà-Zà** Piazza del Mercato Centrale 26r ☎ 055.210.756. In business for more than thirty years, *Zà-Zà* is one of the best of several *trattorie* close to the Mercato Centrale. In recent years it has raised its profile to the extent that booking is virtually obligatory in summer. The interior is dark, stone-walled and brick-arched, with a handful of tables – though in summer there are plenty more tables on the outside terraces. There's usually a set-price menu for around €15 with a choice of three or four pastas and mains; otherwise you'll pay around €30 per head. The omelette with a creamy truffle sauce is exquisite and the mixed antipasti are generous. Daily 11am–11pm; closed Aug.

East of the centre

🏃 **Baldovino** Via San Giuseppe 22r ☎ 055.241.773. This superb place, run by an imaginative Scottish couple, is renowned for its pizzas (made in a wood-fired oven), but the main menu, which changes monthly, is full of good Tuscan and Italian dishes, with mains around €12–17 – although you pay the usual premium for the succulent *bistecca alla fiorentina*. Portions are very generous. *Baldoria* – the bistro offshoot of *Baldovino*, across the street – is also very good. April–Oct daily 11.30am–2.30pm & 7–11.30pm; rest of year closed Mon.

🏃 **Cibrèo** Via de' Macci 118r ☎ 055.234.1100. Fabio Picchi's restaurant – which has now spawned a café, trattoria and a canteen-cum-theatre – is the first Florentine port-of-call for many foodies, having achieved fame well beyond the city. The recipe for success is simple: superb food with a creative take on Tuscan classics, in a tasteful dining room with friendly and professional service. You'll need to book days in advance for a table in the main part of the restaurant, but next door there's a small, somewhat spartan and sometimes overly busy trattoria (*Cibreino*) where the food is virtually the same (though the menu is smaller), no bookings are taken and the prices are much

lower: around €15 for mains, as opposed to €35 in the restaurant. Both *Cibrèo* and *Cibreino* are open Tues–Sat 12.30–2.30pm & 7–11.15pm; closed Aug.

Enoteca Pinchiorri Via Ghibellina 87 ☎ 055.242.777. No one seriously disputes the *Pinchiorri*'s claim to be Florence's best restaurant, certainly not the Michelin, who've given it three of their coveted rosettes. The food is as magnificent as the plaudits suggest, but the ceremony that surrounds its presentation might strike you as excessive (jackets are compulsory for men), and the prices are exorbitant – you could easily spend in excess of €300 per person, excluding wine, though there are two fabulous eight-course set menus for €225 per person. The wine list has no equal in Italy, with some 150,000 bottles lying in the *Pinchiorri* cellars; bottles start at about €60, rising beyond €20,000 for a 1945 Pétrus. Tues & Wed 7.30–10pm, Thurs–Sat 12.30–2pm & 7.30–10pm; closed Aug & Dec 15–27.

🏃 **Il Pizzaiuolo** Via de' Macci 113r ☎ 055.241.171. The Neapolitan pizzas here are among the best in the city. Other dishes and wines also have a Neapolitan touch, as does the atmosphere, which is friendly and high-spirited. Booking's a good idea, at least in the evening. The kitchen stays open until a little after midnight. Mon–Sat 12.30–3pm & 7pm–1am; closed Aug.

🏃 **Ora d'Aria** Via Ghibellina 3c/r ☎ 055.2001.699. This stylish venture offers a high-quality mix of the traditional and the innovative, with an unusual emphasis on fish and seafood dishes. The tasting menus (from €50) are very good value; à la carte, main courses are around €30. The cool, pale and spacious dining room is one of the most relaxing in the city as well. Mon–Sat 7.30–11.30pm.

Osteria de' Benci Via de' Benci 13r ☎ 055.234.4923. A modern, busy and reasonably priced *osteria*, with café-bar attached. The interior is pretty and pleasant – tables have paper tablecloths and you eat off chunky ceramic plates – and there's a friendly atmosphere. Outdoor tables in summer attract big crowds. The moderately priced menu offers well-prepared standards, plus creative Tuscan cuisine. The strawberry risotto is an unexpectedly delicious starter (€9) and the *goloso* and *piccante* steaks are very good. Restaurant open Mon–Sat 1–2.45pm & 7.30–10.45pm; café-bar open 8am–midnight.

Osteria Caffè Italiano Via Isola delle Stinche 11–13r ☎ 055.289.368. The high, vaulted ceilings lend a medieval touch to this café, wine bar and restaurant, but the clientele are à la mode Florentine – smart but relaxed. The cuisine is typically Tuscan – lots of beef, veal and wild boar – and first-rate; expect to pay upwards of €40 per head. Pizzas are served in a tiny annexe at number 19r, while round the corner, at Via della Vigna Vecchia 4r, you'll find *Sud*, a bistro offshoot with a southern Italian menu. All are open Tues–Sun; *Caffè Italiano* is open 10am–1am, whereas the other two are open for lunch and dinner sittings.

Oltrarno

All'Antico Ristoro di Cambi Via Sant'Onofrio 1r ☎055.217.134. Run by the same family since the 1940s, this rough-and-ready trattoria is particularly good for meaty Florentine standards such as wild boar and steak, and has a very good wine list. It's vast, but nonetheless gets packed on a Saturday night, when even the large terrace fills up. Main dishes from around €10. Mon–Sat noon–10.30pm.

Alla Vecchia Bettola Viale Lodovico Ariosto 32–34r ☎055.224.158. Located on a major traffic intersection a couple of minutes' walk from the Carmine, this place – with its long marble-topped tables – has something of the atmosphere of an old-style drinking den, which is what it once was; nowadays it boasts a good repertoire of Tuscan meat dishes, with mains from €10 and an excellent choice of wines by the glass too. Tues–Sat noon–2.30pm & 7.30–10.30pm.

Beccofino Piazza degli Scarlatti 1r ☎055.290.076. A sleek and austerely stylish venture from the owners of *Baldovino* (see p.163), *Beccofino* was once one of the city's most fashionable restaurants. It's lost some of its lustre recently, but it's still worth its place on anyone's roster of Florence's gastronomic highlights. Prices are in the region of €15–22 for *secondi*, which is reasonable for the quality – the chef has worked for Gordon Ramsay and at the *Enoteca Pinchiorri*. If you'd like to test the waters first, have a drink at the attached wine bar. Tues–Sun 7–11.30pm.

Borgo Antico Piazza di Santo Spirito 6r ☎055.210.437. The spartan chic of *Borgo Antico*'s white tile and pink plaster decor reflects the increasingly trendy character of this once sleazy piazza, and there's no Oltrarno restaurant trendier than this place. It's usually very crowded and very noisy, though in summer the tables outside offer relative quiet. Choose from pizza or a menu of Tuscan standards at reasonable prices (€13–18). The salads are good, and there's often a selection of fresh fish and seafood pastas. Servings – on the restaurant's famously huge

plates – are generous to a fault. Daily noon–midnight.

Il Santo Bevitore Via Santo Spirito 64–66r ☎055.211.264. The Holy Drinker is an airy and stylish "gastronomic *enoteca*" with a small menu (around €30 for a meal without drinks) to complement its enticing wine list. Daily 12.30–2.30pm & 7.30–11.30pm. Closed three weeks in Aug.

I Tarocchi Via dei Renai 12r ☎055.234.3912. There are a few simple dishes on the menu, but this is essentially a pizzeria – and one of the best in the city. Tues–Fri 12.30–2.30pm & 7pm–1am, Sat & Sun 7pm–1am.

La Casalinga Via del Michelozzo 9r ☎055.218.624. Located in a side-street off Piazza di Santa Spirito, this long-established family-run trattoria serves up some of the best low-cost Tuscan dishes in town (€10 for a *secondo*). No frills – paper tablecloths, so-so house wine by the carafe and brisk service – but most nights it's filled with regulars and a good few outsiders. By 8pm there's invariably a queue. Mon–Sat noon–2.30pm & 7–10pm; closed three weeks in Aug.

Osteria Antica Mescita San Niccolò Via San Niccolò 60r ☎055.234.2836. This genuine old-style Oltrarno *osteria* has a small menu of robust and well-prepared Florentine staples (*ribollita, lampredotto*) at around €10; there's also a good lunchtime buffet for a mere €10. The downstairs dining room was formerly a crypt of the adjacent church of San Niccolò. Mon–Sat 12.30–3pm & 7pm–1am; closed Aug.

Osteria Santo Spirito Piazza di Santo Spirito 16r/ Via Sant'Agostino ☎055.238.2383. Run by the owners of the *Borgo Antico*, this informal and modern *osteria* serves hearty Tuscan dishes with contemporary flair, and at good prices: pasta dishes from €6, mains from €12, and there's a lunchtime set menu at a mere €12. In summer you can eat outdoors on the piazza. Daily 12.30–2.30pm & 8pm–midnight.

Pane e Vino Piazza di Cestello 3r ☎055.247.6956. *Pane e Vino* began life as a bar, so it's no surprise that the wine list is excellent and well priced, with bottles from around €15. The ambience is stylish yet relaxed and the menu small and consistently excellent (*secondi* €15–20), featuring two very enticing set menus (€35 and €45). Small TV screens in the dining area show the chefs beavering away in the kitchen, producing some of the best food in town – the ravioli with asparagus in a lemon cream melts in your mouth. Mon–Sat 8pm–midnight; closed two weeks in Aug.

Quattro Leoni Via dei Vellutini 1r/Piazza della Passera ☏055.218.562. Occupying a three-roomed medieval interior, this is a young, relaxed place with wooden beams and splashy modern paintings strung across the rough stone walls. In summer you can also eat alfresco under vast canvas umbrellas in the tiny Piazza della Passera – one of the most appealing outdoor eating venues in the city. It's popular with visiting stars – Dustin Hoffman and Sting feature on the walls, and Anthony Hopkins ate here while filming *Hannibal*. You can eat very well for around €40 a head. Noon–2.30pm & 7–11pm; closed Wed lunch.

Sabatino Via Pisana 2r ☏055.225.955. Right by Porta San Frediano, this old-fashioned, long-running family *osteria* is not a gourmet venue, but it's absolutely authentic and ridiculously cheap (main courses from just €5). Mon–Sat noon–3pm & 7pm–midnight; closed Aug.

Cafés and bars

As elsewhere in Italy, the distinction between Florentine bars and cafés can be tricky to the point of impossibility, as almost every café serves alcohol and almost every bar serves coffee. The distinction between bars and clubs is getting vaguer too, with many of Florence's hotter bars now aiming to keep the punters on the premises all night, by serving free snacks with the *aperitivi* (usually from about 7pm–9/10pm) before the music kicks in – either live or (more often) courtesy of the in-house DJ. Bars where **music** is the main attraction are reviewed in "Nightlife" (see p.168), but at many of the places listed below you'll get good sounds too. There's one category of bar that's quite distinct from cafés, and that's the **enoteca** or wine bar – see p.167 for these.

City Centre

Astor Caffè Piazza del Duomo 20r. From its modest street-front opposite the northeast corner of the Duomo you wouldn't guess that this was the hottest spot on the piazza, but inside you'll find a glitzy and spacious three-storey set-up. Food is served in the upstairs restaurant, in the basement you get DJs playing anything from hip-hop to Brazilian music most nights, and in the ground-floor bar you sip cocktails with the city's gilded youth. Daily noon–2am.

Caffè Gilli Piazza della Repubblica 36–39r. Founded in 1733, this most appealing of this square's expensive cafés moved to its present site in 1910. The lavish *belle époque* interior is a sight in itself (though there are rumours of an imminent modernization), but most people choose to sit on the big outdoor terrace. On a cold afternoon try the famous hot chocolate – it comes in five blended flavours: almond, orange, coffee, *gianduia* (chocolate blended with hazelnut) and cocoa. Wed–Mon 8am–midnight.

Caffè Italiano Via della Condotta 56r. Located one block north of the piazza, this is a combination of old-fashioned stand-up bar and smart café, with lots of dark wood, silver teapots and superb cakes, coffees and teas. Lunch is inexpensive and excellent, as you'd expect from a place owned by Umberto Montano, owner of the outstanding *Osteria Caffè Italiano* (see p.163). Mon–Sat 8am–8pm, Sun 11am–8pm; closed two weeks in Aug.

Robiglio Via Tosinghi 11r. Renowned for its pastries and chocolates, *Robiglio* also specializes in a hot chocolate drink that's so thick it's barely a liquid. There's another branch at Via dei Servi 112r, near Santissima Annunziata. Mon–Sat 8am–8pm.

West of the centre

Art Bar Via del Moro 4r. A fine little bar near Piazza di Carlo Goldoni. The interior looks like an antique shop, while the club-like atmosphere attracts a studenty crowd. Especially busy at happy hour (7–9pm), when the low-priced cocktails are in heavy demand. The after-hours ambience is also ideal for a laid-back nightcap. Mon–Thurs 7pm–1am, Fri & Sat 7pm–2am; closed three weeks in Aug.

Noir Lungarno Corsini 12–14r. Recently revamped in moody nocturnal tones, the bar formerly known as *Capocaccia* has been voted the Florentines' favourite night-time hang-out several times, and it remains out in front. The roomy, well-designed interior has plenty of tables and stools; there's a DJ every night; and you'll be mixing almost entirely with fashionable locals, especially later on – if you have neither youth nor beauty on your side, however, you may feel out of place. Sun brunch (12.30–3.30pm) is excellent, as is the nightly *aperitivo* buffet (7.30–10.30pm). Daily noon–2am.

Procacci Via de' Tornabuoni 64r. This famous café doesn't serve coffee, just wine and cold drinks. Its reputation comes from the extraordinary and delicious *tartufati*, or truffle-butter brioche – from Oct to Dec, when truffles are in season, the wood-lined interior of *Procacci* is a swooningly aromatic spot. Mon–Sat 10.30am–8pm; closed Aug.

Slowly Via Porta Rossa 63. This extremely trendy bar, with its neat little banquettes and candle lanterns, tends to attract a showy, beautifully dressed young crowd, who while away the hours chatting over pricey cocktails and bar snacks (the *aperitivo* buffet is one of the best in Florence). The atmosphere is pretty laid back, even when the DJ gets to work. Time will tell whether its appearance in all the designer magazines will lead to style tourists edging out the Florentines. Mon–Sat 7pm–2am.

North of the centre

Nannini Coffee Shop Via Borgo San Lorenzo 7r. The Florentine outpost of Siena's *Nannini* operation, famed for its superb coffee and tooth-wrecking *panforte*, an extremely dense and delicious cake. Daily 7.30am–7.30pm (till 8.30pm Sat).

East of the centre

Caffè Cibrèo Via Andrea del Verrocchio 5r. Possibly the prettiest café in Florence, *Caffè Cibrèo* opened in 1989, but the wood-panelled interior gives it the look of a place that's at least two hundred years older. Cakes and desserts are great, and the light meals bear the culinary stamp of the *Cibrèo* restaurant kitchens opposite (see p.163). Tues–Sat 8am–1am.

Caffèlatte Via degli Alfani 39r. The one-room *Caffèlatte* began life in the 1920s, when a milk and coffee supplier opened here. Nowadays, it's expanded to include an organic bakery, which produces delicious breads and cakes; the vegetarian brunch is excellent too. The speciality drink, as you'd expect, is *caffè latte*, served in huge bowls. Laid-back music and temporary exhibitions of paintings and photographs enhance the atmosphere. Daily 8am–midnight.

Moyo Via de' Benci 23r. A young crowd flocks to this bar every evening – the food's pretty good (come for the early-evening *aperitivo* buffet) and

the free wi-fi access is a plus, but it's the buzz that really brings them in. With *Osteria de' Benci* just down the road (see p.163), this is one of the city's sparkiest corners. Open daily noon–4pm & 8pm–2am (till 3am Fri & Sat).

Oltrarno

Caffè Ricchi Piazza di Santo Spirito 9r. The smartest of the cafés on this square. Menus change daily, and there's a good selection of cakes, ice cream and sandwiches. Summer Mon–Sat 7am–1am; winter closes 10pm. Closed two weeks in Feb & two weeks in Aug.

Caffè La Torre Lungarno Cellini 65r. This bar changes its decor every year, which is one reason it has managed to remain one of the most fashionable bars in Florence. The other is its superb location, in the shadow of the tower of the Porta San Niccolò, with lots of outdoor seating. There's live music many nights, and excellent cocktails complete the picture. Daily 10.30am–3am.

Dolce Vita Piazza del Carmine 6r. This smart and extremely popular bar-club has been going for more than a decade and has stayed ahead of the game through constant updating. Install yourself on one of the aluminium bar stools and preen with Florence's beautiful young things. Live music (often Latin or jazz) Wed & Thurs 7.30–9.30pm; *aperitivo* buffet 7.30–9.30pm, then the DJ gets to work. Tues–Sun 5pm–2am.

Plasma Piazza Ferrucci 1r. Owned and designed by a theatre director, this self-styled "cocktail bar and video gallery" is so cool it almost hurts, with fibre-optic lighting throughout, a sexy red resin bar on the lower floor, and plasma screens in the big vaulted room upstairs – where, in addition to another bar, there's also a waterfall. The sound system is state of the art as well. It's some way out of the centre, about 1500m east of Ponte Vecchio, but for many style-conscious Florentines no night is complete without at least a cocktail here. Wed–Sun 7pm–2am.

Popcafé Piazza Santo Spirito 18a/r, ⓦ www .popcafé.it. This new café has proved to be a big hit with the local boys and girls, thanks to the music (often live) and boho vibe. Another aspect of its appeal is the vegetarian food: lunch from Mon to Sat, brunch on Sun (12.30–3pm), and lashings of vegetarian snacks at the *aperitivo* buffet every eve (7.30–9.30pm). Daily noon–2am.

Il Rifrullo Via San Niccolò 53–57r. New owners have smartened and expanded this bar, which is a very nice place to unwind after the hike up to San Miniato, or for a nightcap. Lying to the east of the Ponte Vecchio–Pitti Palace route, it attracts fewer tourists than many Oltrarno café-bars. Serves delicious snacks with the early-evening *aperitivi* (when the music gets turned up), as well as more substantial dishes, and the Sun brunch is always packed out. There's a pleasant roof terrace, too. Daily 8am–2am; closed two weeks in Aug.

Zoe Via dei Renai 13. Like the neighbouring *Negroni*, *Zoe* is perennially popular for summer evening drinks, but it attracts lots of young

Florentines right through the day: 8am–noon is breakfast time, lunch is noon–3pm, then it's "Aperitif" from 6–10pm, when the "American Bar" theme takes over (the Crimson Zoe cocktail is notorious). It also does good snacks and simple meals, there's a DJ in the back room, and – like *Negroni* – it's something of an art venue too. Mon–Thurs 8am–1.30am, Fri & Sat 8am–2am, Sun 6pm–1am.

Wine bars

As you'd expect in a city that lies close to some of the best vineyards in the country, Florence has plenty of bars dedicated to the **wines** of Chianti and other Tuscan producers. At one end of the scale there's the endangered species known as the **vinaio** (see box), which consists of little more than a niche with a few shelves of generally workaday wines, plus a counter of snacks. At the opposite pole there's the **enoteca**, which is a wine-bar-cum-restaurant; all *enoteche* have vast wine menus, but in some cases the kitchen has come to play so large a role in the operation that the place is now more a restaurant than a bar, which is why you'll find some *enoteche* listed in our restaurant section.

City Centre

Cantinetta dei Verrazzano Via dei Tavolini 18–20r. Owned by Castello dei Verrazzano, a major Chianti vineyard, this wood-panelled place near Orsanmichele is part-bar, part-café and part-bakery, making its own excellent pizza, focaccia

and cakes. A perfect spot for a light lunch or an early-evening drink. July & Aug Mon–Sat 8am–4pm; Sept–June Mon–Sat 8am–9pm.

Casa del Vino Via dell'Ariento 16r. Located a few yards south of the Mercato Centrale, and passed by hordes of

---

Vinai

The *vinaio* was once a real Florentine institution. Customers at these tiny seat-less places would typically linger for no more than a couple of minutes – long enough to down a tumbler of wine and exchange a few words with the proprietor. The number of *vinai* has declined markedly in recent years; the following are the notable survivors.

L'Antico Noè Volta di San Piero 6r. A long-established stand-up wine bar, tucked into an uninviting little alley to the north of Santa Croce. Mon–Sat noon–3pm & 7pm–midnight.

All'Antico Vinaio Via dei Neri 65r. Though recently revamped, this place – located between the Uffizi and Santa Croce – preserves much of the rough-and-ready atmosphere that's made it one of Florence's most popular wine bars for the last hundred years. Also serves coffee, rolls and pasta. Mon–Sat 8am–10pm; closed three weeks late July & early Aug.

I Fratellini Via dei Cimatori 38r. This minuscule, dirt-cheap bar is somehow clinging on in the immediate vicinity of the high-rent Via dei Calzaiuoli. Serves decent panini and local wines. Mid-June to Aug Mon–Fri 8am–5pm; Sept to mid-June daily 8am–8pm.

Quasigratis Piazza del Grano 10. Little more than a window in a wall at the back of the Uffizi, and it doesn't say *Quasigratis* ("Almost free") anywhere – just "Vini". Serves rolls and other snacks, and wine in tiny glasses called *rasini*. Daily 10am–11pm; closed Jan & Feb.

Gelaterie

Devotees of Italian **ice cream** will find that Florence offers plenty of opportunities to indulge: the city has several superb *gelaterie*, and some would claim that *Vivoli* is one of the top purveyors in the country.

Carabé Via Ricasoli 60r. Wonderful Sicilian ice cream made with Sicilian ingredients as only they know how. Also serves a variety of cakes. May–Oct daily 9am–1am; Nov–April daily 9am–8pm, but closed mid-Dec to mid-Jan.

Gelateria dei Neri Via dei Neri 20–22r. Small place in contention for the best ice cream in town. Close to the Uffizi but away from the crowds. The range of flavours is fantastic – fig and walnut, Mexican chocolate (very spicy), rice – and they also have some non-dairy ice cream. Daily 11am–midnight.

Grom Via del Campanile. Founded in Turin in 2003, Grom is a retro-styled but very slick operation, concocting fabulous gelati from top-quality ingredients gathered from all over Italy. The house speciality is Crema di Grom, made from organic eggs, soft *meliga* biscuits and Ecuadorian chocolate. Daily: April–Oct 10.30am–midnight, Nov–March 10.30am–11pm.

Perchè No! Via de' Tavolini 19r. Superb *gelateria*, in business since the 1930s; go for the classic *crema*, the chocolate or the gorgeous pistachio. Mon & Wed–Sun 11am–11pm, Tues noon–8pm; closed Nov.

Vivoli Via Isola delle Stinche 7r. Operating from deceptively unprepossessing premises in a side-street close to Santa Croce, this café has long been rated one of the best ice-cream-makers in Florence. Tues–Sun: summer 7.30am–midnight; winter 7.30am–9pm. Closed two weeks in Aug.

---

tourists daily – yet probably visited by only a handful. Patrons are mostly Florentines, who pitch up for a drink, a chat with owner Gianni Migliorini and an assault on various panini, *crostini* and saltless Tuscan bread and salami. Mon–Fri 9.30am–5.30pm, Sat 10am–3.30pm; closed Aug.

Zanobini Via Sant'Antonino 47r. Like the *Casa del Vino*, its rival just around the corner, this is an authentic Florentine bar, whose feel owes much to the presence of locals and traders from the nearby Mercato Centrale. Offers acceptable snacks, but most people are simply here for a chat over a glass of wine. Mon–Sat 8am–2pm & 3.30–8pm.

Oltrarno

Fuori Porta Via del Monte alle Croci 10r
℡055.234.2483. If you're climbing up to San Miniato you could take a breather at this superb and justly famous *enoteca–osteria*. There are over four hundred wines to choose from by the bottle, and an ever-changing selection by the glass, as well as grappas and malt whiskies. Cheese and cold meats are available, as well as pasta dishes and salads, all very elegantly presented. There's a summertime terrace and large dining area, but it's still wise to book if you're coming here to eat. Mon–Sat 12.30–3.30pm & 7pm–12.30am; closed two weeks in mid-Aug.

Le Volpi e L'Uva Piazza dei Rossi 1r. This discreet, friendly little *enoteca* does good business by concentrating on the wines of small producers and providing tasty cold meats and snacks to help them down (the selection of cheeses is tremendous). At any one time you can choose from at least two dozen different wines by the glass. In summer the shady terrace is a pleasant refuge from the heat. Mon–Sat 11am–9pm.

Nightlife and cultural events

Florence has something of a reputation for catering primarily to the middle-aged and affluent, but like every university town it has its pockets of **nightlife**, not to mention the added buzz generated by thousands of young tourists. Details of the city's club and live music venues are given below, but for up-to-the-minute **information** about what's on, call in at the tourist office in Via Cavour or at Box Office, northwest of the train station at Via Alamanni 39 (℡055.210.804; Mon 3–7.30pm, Tues–Sat 10am–7.30pm), which has tickets for most events (credit cards not accepted). Otherwise, keep your eyes peeled for advertising posters, or pick up the monthly *Firenze Spettacolo*, which has an English section as well as a map of places open after midnight.

Clubs

Florence has a decent **club** scene, even if clubs in Italy often don't resemble their equivalents in London or other big cities: most Florentines aren't in clubs to dance or drink – they're there to see and be seen, and dress up to the nines. Foreigners are a different matter, and one or two – mostly central – clubs have a slightly more sweaty and familiar atmosphere as a result.

Faced with a low income from the bar (Italians don't go in for UK-style binge-drinking), most clubs charge a fairly stiff **admission** – €15–25 for the bigger and better-known places – though this often includes a drink. Prices at the bar after that are usually quite steep. Some clubs operate a system where you're given a card on entry that gets stamped every time you buy a drink; if by the end of the night you haven't spent a specified amount, you have to pay a charge before the bouncers will let you out. Alternatively, the card may be used just to keep tabs on your drinks, with the bill settled at the end of the evening. Payment always has to be in cash.

In addition to the places listed below, plenty of **temporary clubs** spring into existence in the summer months, often as open-air venues on the edge of town, in spots such as Piazza della Libertà and the Cascine. From June to the beginning of September keep an eye out for posters and flyers, or check the listings in *Firenze Spettacolo*.

One other thing to bear in mind is that in recent years more and more of Florence's trendier bars have taken to employing DJs later in the evening, and serving complimentary snacks with drinks before that (usually from about 7–9/10pm), to lure the customers in. Locals head to bars such as *Noir* or *Dolce Vita* (see p.165 & p.166) quite early, fill up at the free *aperitivo* buffet, then stick around for the music. So for the complete picture, check the "Bars" section (see p.165), as well as what's listed below.

(see p.165 & p.166) ... (see p.165)

Gay and lesbian Florence

Florenzer was, during the seventeenth century at least, German slang for gay, and the city remains, for the most part, tolerant towards gay and lesbian visitors. The leading gay bar is **Crisco**, a short distance east of the Duomo at Via Sant'Egidio 43r (℡055.248.0580; Mon, Wed, Thurs & Sun 11pm–3am, Fri & Sat 10pm–6am), but the ambience can be a bit heavy for some tastes. **Piccolo**, Borgo Santa Croce 23r (℡055.200.1057; daily 8pm–2.30am), has a more chilled-out atmosphere and draws a mixed gay and lesbian crowd, as does the stylish **Y.A.G. B@r**, also near Santa Croce at Via de' Macci 8r (℡055.246.9022; daily 8pm–3am). The key bar-club is the pioneering **Tabasco**, which has been going for more than 35 years at Piazza Santa Cecilia 3r (℡055.213.000; Tues–Sun 10pm–6am). For lesbian contacts, check the noticeboard at the women's bookshop Libreria delle Donne, Via Fiesolana 2b (Mon 3.30–7.30pm, Tues–Sat 9.30am–1pm & 3.30–7.30pm).

West of the centre

Central Park Via Fosso Macinante 2, Parco delle Cascine ☎055.353.505 One of the city's biggest and most commercial clubs, with adventurous, wide-ranging and up-to-the-minute music on several dance floors from DJs who know what they're doing and have access to a superb sound system. A card system operates for drinks, and the first drink is included in the admission – around €20–25 after midnight, usually free before. Summer Tues–Sat 11.30pm–4.30am; winter Fri & Sat same hours.

Meccanò Viale degli Olmi 1/Piazzale delle Cascine ☎055.331.371. People flock here for a night out from across half of Tuscany. The place is labyrinthine, with a trio of lounge and bar areas, and a huge and invariably packed dance floor playing mostly house. In summer, when the action spills out of doors, you can cool off in the gardens bordering the Cascine. The €15–20 admission includes your first drink. Summer Tues–Sat 11.30pm–4am; winter Thurs–Sat same hours; closed Nov & two weeks in Aug.

Yab Via Sassetti 5r ☎055.215.160. This long-established basement club (full name: You Are Beautiful) has been popular for years, and is known throughout the country for Monday's Yabsmoove – Italy's longest-running hip-hop night. Thurs is deep house night. On other nights it doesn't have the most up-to-the-minute playlist in the world, but still offers probably the most relaxed and reliable night's clubbing in central Florence. You're given a card and pay on leaving if you've spent less than €15 at the bar. Mon, Tues & Thurs–Sat 9pm–4am; closed June–Sept.

East of the centre

Blob Club Via Vinegia 21r ☎055.211.209. A favourite with Florentine students, possibly on account of its free admission and the 6–10pm happy hour. Seating upstairs, bar and tiny dance floor downstairs, but don't expect to do much dancing – later on, especially on weekend nights, *Blob* gets packed to the rafters with a very happy and very drunken crowd. Quieter in the summer months. Daily 6pm–4am.

Doris Via de' Pandolfini 26r ☎055.246.6775. Recently given a cool and stylish overhaul, *Doris* is one of the best clubs in central Florence. The bar is open 7–10pm for drinks and snacks, with the club kicking into action from 11.30pm till 4am. Admission €10. Closed Mon.

Full-Up Via della Vigna Vecchia 25r ☎055.293.006. Situated close to the Bargello, this club has been going so long it's become something of an institution. Best nights are usually Thurs (hip-hop) and Fri (house). *Aperitivi* from 10.30pm each night; the music begins an hour later. Non-Italian students get in free. Tues–Sat 10.30pm–4am. Closed June–Sept.

Rex Via Fiesolana 25r ☎055.228.0331. One of the city's big night-time fixtures, a friendly bar-club with a varied and loyal clientele. Vast curving lights droop over the central bar, which is studded with turquoise stone and broken mirror mosaics. Big arched spaces to either side mean there's plenty of room, the cocktails and DJs are good, and the snacks excellent – the *aperitivi* session is 7–9.30pm. Mon & Wed–Sun 6pm–3am. Closed June–Aug.

Perètola

Tenax Via Pratese 46 ☎055.632.958, ⓦwww .tenax.org. Florence's biggest club, pulling in the odd jet-setting DJ. Given its location in the northwest of town, near the airport (there's usually a shuttle bus from the train station – otherwise, take a taxi), you'll escape the hordes of *internazionalisti* in the more central clubs. With two large floors, it's a major venue for concerts as well. Admission €20–25. Thurs–Sat 10.30pm–4am. Closed mid-May to mid-Sept.

Live music

Florence's **live music** scene isn't the hottest in Italy, but there's a smattering of venues for small-time local outfits, and a couple of big stages for visiting stars. In addition to the recommendations below, a few of the places reviewed under "Bars and cafés" and "Clubs" lay on live sessions from time to time: check listings magazines for one-off events.

West of the centre

Eskimo Via dei Canacci 12r ☎055.715.794. A small, well-established club close to Santa Maria Novella with live music every night. Its long-standing status as the prime lefty student bar is reflected in the music, which tends to be Italian solo singers or trios. The atmosphere is welcoming and you may catch the odd theatre performance or other cultural event. Entry by membership – on the door, for around €7. Daily 9pm–3am; closed June–Sept.

Loonees Via Porta Rossa 15 ☎ 055.212.249, ✆ www.loonees.it. Set up by a former biker from Birmingham, this sweltering subterranean bar is a favourite with the city's students. The music is loud right through the night, and live from Wed to Sat. Free entry. Mon–Sat 9pm–3am.

Sintetika Via Alamanni 4 ☎ 333.359.1575, ✆ www.sintetikalive.it. A new venue that primarily promotes local indie bands, but has managed to attract a few prestigious outsiders too, such as Bonnie Prince Billy. Entry by membership – €8 on the door. Days vary; usually open 11pm–4am.

North of the centre

Girasol Via del Romito 1 ☎ 055.474.948, ✆ www.girasol.it. Florence's liveliest Latin bar, located on a minor road due north of the Fortezza da Basso, is hugely popular. Rather than relying solely on salsa classes, cocktails and the usual vinyl suspects – although it does all these – the place draws in some surprisingly good live acts, with different countries' sounds each day of the week, from Brazilian bossa nova to Cuban son. Tues–Sun 7pm–2am.

East of the centre

Ambasciata di Marte Via Mannelli 2 ☎ 055.655.0786, ✆ www.ambasciatadimarte.org. This self-styled "centre for creative development" is the city's new showcase for local bands; it has a bookshop and gallery space too. It's in the Campo di Marte area, and buses #3, #6, #10, #20 and #44 go close.

Jazz Club Via Nuova de' Caccini 3 ☎ 055.247.9700, ✆ www.jazzclubfirenze.com. Florence's foremost jazz venue has been a fixture for years. The €9 "membership" fee gets you down into the medieval brick-vaulted basement, where the atmosphere's informal and there's live music most nights. Mon night is usually a jam session. Cocktails are good, and you can also snack on bar nibbles and *focaccia*. Mon–Fri 9pm–2am, Sat 9pm–3am; closed July & Aug.

Nelson Mandela Forum Viale Pasquale Paoli ☎ 055.678.841, ✆ www.mandelaforum.it. Along with the *Saschall* and *Tenax*, this 7000-capacity hall – located at Campo di Marte – is the city's main venue for big-draw mainstream acts, such as Lenny Kravitz and Zucchero. Bus #3 takes you there.

Saschall-Teatro di Firenze Via Fabrizio de André 3 ☎ 055.650.4112, ✆ www.saschall.it. Holding around 4000 people, the new and well-designed *Saschall* is used for acts that don't quite have the following to pack out the *Mandela Forum*. It's by Lungarno Aldo Moro, a couple of kilometres east of the city centre – bus #14 is the one you need.

Il Poggetto

Auditorium FLOG Via Michele Mercati 24b ☎ 055.490.437, ✆ www.flog.it. One of the city's best-known mid-sized venues, and a perennial student favourite – with a suitably downbeat look and feel – for all forms of live music (and DJs), but particularly local indie bands. It's usually packed, despite a position way out in the northern suburbs; to get there take bus #4, #8, #14, #20 or #28.

Classical music

The **Maggio Musicale**, Italy's oldest and most prestigious music festival, is the most conspicuous sign of the health of the city's classical music scene, though it should be said that the fare tends towards the conservative. In addition to this and the festival in Fiesole (see p.172), the **Amici della Musica** host a season of chamber concerts with top-name international performers from September to April, mostly in the Teatro della Pergola, occasionally in the Teatro Goldoni. The **Orchestra da Camera Fiorentina** (Florence Chamber Orchestra; ✆ www.orcafi.it) plays concerts from March to October, often in Orsanmichele, and Tuscany's major orchestra, the **Orchestra della Toscana** (✆ www.orchestradellatoscana.it), performs once or twice a month between November and May in the Teatro Verdi, often including contemporary pieces in their programmes. The Lutheran church on Lungarno Torrigiani regularly holds free chamber music and organ recitals.

Teatro Comunale Corso Italia 16 ☎ 055.213.535. Florence's main municipal theatre, out to the west of Santa Maria Novella, hosts many of the city's major classical music, dance and theatre events. It has its own orchestra, chorus and dance company, attracting top-name international guest performers.

The main season for dance and opera runs from Oct to Dec, with classical music concerts taking over from Jan until the start of the Maggio Musicale festival, when there's a rich mix of opera and concerts on offer. Chamber music and other small-scale events are held in the theatre's Teatro Piccolo.

Teatro Goldoni Via Santa Maria 15 ℡055.210.804. This exquisite little eighteenth-century theatre, located a little way past the Palazzo Pitti, is occasionally used for chamber music and opera performances, but lately it has hosted more dance productions than anything else.

Teatro della Pergola Via della Pergola 18 ℡055.226.4353, ⓦwww.pergola.firenze.it. The beautiful little Pergola was built in 1656 and is Italy's oldest surviving theatre – Verdi's *Macbeth* was first performed here. From Oct to April it plays host to chamber concerts, small-scale operas, and some of the best-known Italian theatre companies.

Teatro Verdi Via Ghibellina 99–101 ℡055.212.320, ⓦwww.teatroverdifirenze.it. Home to the Orchestra della Toscana, this is another of the city's premier music venues.

Music festivals

Estate Fiesolana ⓦwww.estatefiesolana.it. Slightly less exclusive than the Maggio Musicale, concentrating on chamber music, orchestral music and jazz. It's held in Fiesole every summer, usually from mid-June to late Aug or early Sept. Films and theatre are also featured, and most events are held in the open-air *Teatro Romano*.

Maggio Musicale Fiorentino ⓦwww .maggiofiorentino.com. The highlight of Florence's cultural calendar and one of Europe's leading festivals of opera and classical music; confusingly, it isn't restricted to May (*maggio*), but lasts for a couple of months from late April or early May. Events are staged at the Teatro Comunale, the Teatro della Pergola, the Palazzo dei Congressi, the Teatro Verdi and occasionally in the Bóboli gardens. Information and tickets can be obtained from the Teatro Comunale.

Florence's festivals

Florence's main cultural festivals are covered in the "Classical Music" section what follows is a rundown on its more folkloric events.

Scoppio del Carro

The first major folk festival of the year is Easter Sunday's Scoppio del Carro (Explosion of the Cart), when a cartload of fireworks is hauled by six white oxen from the Porta a Prato to the Duomo; there, during the Gloria of the midday Mass, the whole lot is set off by a "dove" that whizzes down a wire from the high altar. The origins of this incendiary descent of the Holy Spirit lie with Pazzino de' Pazzi, leader of the Florentine contingent on the First Crusade. On getting back to Florence he was entrusted with the care of the flame of Holy Saturday, an honorary office which he turned into something more festive by rigging up a ceremonial wagon to transport the flame round the city. His descendants continued to manage the festival until the Pazzi conspiracy of 1478, which of course lost them the office. Since then, the city authorities have taken care of business.

Festa del Grillo

On the first Sunday after Ascension Day (forty days after Easter), the Festa del Grillo (Festival of the Cricket) is held in the Cascine park. In amongst the stalls and the picnickers you'll find people selling tiny wooden cages containing crickets, which are then released onto the grass – a ritual that may hark back to the days when farmers had to scour their land for locusts, or to the tradition of men placing a cricket on the door of their lovers to serenade them.

St John's Day and the Calcio Storico

The saint's day of John the Baptist, Florence's patron, is June 24 – the occasion for a massive fireworks display up on Piazzale Michelangelo, and for the final of the

Cinema

In Italy the vast majority of English-language films are dubbed, but **Odeon Original Sound**, Via de' Sassetti 1 (℡055.214.068; closed Aug), screens films in their original language (*versione originale*) once a week, generally on Monday, for most of the year, plus Tuesday and Thursday in summer. This is the only cinema still in operation in the centre of Florence, but in summer there are often **open-air screens** at the Forte Belvedere and the Palazzo dei Congressi (near the train station). See *Firenze Spettacolo* or the listings pages of *La Nazione* for the latest screenings.

Florence and Fiesole have a few small **film festivals**, notably the **Premio Fiesole ai Maestri del Cinema** (July/Aug), in which the films of a single director are screened in Fiesole's Roman theatre, and the somewhat earnest **Festival dei Popoli** (two weeks in Nov or Dec), run by an academic institution concerned with documentary film.

Shopping

Florence is known as a producer of luxury items, notably gold jewellery and top-quality leather goods. The whole Ponte Vecchio is crammed with goldsmiths (most of them catering strictly to the financial stratosphere), but the city's premier shopping thoroughfare is **Via de' Tornabuoni**, where you'll find not only an array of expensive jewellery and shoe shops but also

Calcio Storico on Piazza Santa Croce. Played in sixteenth-century costume to perpetuate the memory of a game played at Santa Croce during the siege of 1530, this uniquely Florentine mayhem is a three-match series, with two matches in early June preceding the bedlam of June 24. Each of the four historic quarters fields a team of 27 players, with Santa Croce in green, San Giovanni in red, Santa Maria Novella in blue and Santo Spirito in grossly impractical white. The prize for the winning side is a calf, which gets roasted in a street party after the tournament and shared among the four teams and the inhabitants of the winning quarter. The Calcio Storico has been undergoing something of a crisis since the 2006 event, when the semi-final between Santa Croce and Santo Spirito became so violent that the game was stopped. The 2007 event was then cancelled, and revisions to the rules are now being introduced – under the traditional "rules", virtually any method of tackling short of outright murder was permitted.

Festa delle Rificolone

The Festa delle Rificolone (Festival of the Lanterns) takes place on the Virgin's birthday, September 7, with a procession of children to Piazza Santissima Annunziata, where a small fair is held. Each child carries a coloured paper lantern with a candle inside it – a throwback to the days when people from the surrounding countryside would troop by lantern light into the city for the Feast of the Virgin. The procession is followed by a parade of floats and street parties.

Festa dell'Unità

October's Festa dell'Unità is part of a nationwide celebration run by the Italian communists. Florence's is the biggest event after Bologna's, with loads of political stalls and restaurant marquees. Box Office (see p.169) will have details of venues.

▲ The Calcio Storico, Piazza Santa Croce

the showrooms of Italy's top fashion designers: Prada, Gucci, Armani and Dolce&Gabbana are all here, as well as the country's main outlets for the top three Florentine fashion houses – Pucci, Roberto Cavalli and Ferragamo. Younger and more left-field designers tend to cluster in and around Via Matteo Palmieri (not far from Santa Croce), while for cheap and cheerful stuff there's the plethora of street stalls around the San Lorenzo market. If you want everything under one roof, there's also a handful of **department stores**. Marbled paper is another Florentine speciality, and, as you'd expect in this arty city, Florence is also one of the best places in the country to pick up **books** on Italian art, architecture and culture. For **food** shops see the box on p.162.

Books and maps

Edison Piazza della Repubblica 27r. This US-style operation is arranged on four floors, with English-language books at the top; the stock is impressive, as are the opening hours. Mon–Sat 9am–midnight, Sun 10am–midnight.

Feltrinelli Via de' Cerretani 30r. This branch of the Feltrinelli chain, a short distance west of the Duomo, is best for Italian titles, maps and guides. Mon–Fri 9am–7.30pm, Sat 10am–8pm, Sun 10.30am–1.30pm & 3.30–7.30pm.

Feltrinelli International Via Cavour 12–20r. Bright and well staffed, this has a good stock of English and other foreign-language books, plus newspapers, videos, posters, cards and magazines. Mon–Sat 9am–7.30pm.

McRae Via de' Neri 32r. Not far from Santa Croce, this small bookshop has one of the finest collections of English-language books in town: guides, cookery books, literature and art are all covered. Daily 9am–7.30pm.

Paperback Exchange Via delle Oche 4r. Located just a few metres south of the Duomo, this shop always has a good stock of English and American books, with the emphasis on Italian-related titles and secondhand stuff; also exchanges secondhand books and has informative and friendly staff. Mon–Fri 9am–7.30pm, Sat 10am–7.30pm.

Clothing

Ferragamo Via de' Tornabuoni 14r, ⓦwww
.salvatoreferragamo.it. The one Florentine designer
whose name is known far and wide, Salvatore
Ferragamo emigrated to the US at the age of 14
and became the most famous shoemaker in the
world. Managed by his widow and children,
Ferragamo now produces ready-to-wear outfits,
but the company's reputation still rests on its
beautiful shoes. The shop, occupying virtually the
entire ground floor of a colossal palazzo on Piazza
Santa Trinita, is unbelievably grandiose, and even
has a shoe museum. Mon–Sat 10am–7.30pm.
Luisa at Via Roma Via Roma 19–21r, ⓦwww
.luisaviaroma.com. A long-standing fixture at this
address, with a host of different labels every
season. Mon–Sat 10am–7.30pm, Sun 11am–7pm.

Poncif Borgo Albizi 35r. Florentine design tends to
be somewhat conservative, but the clothes and
costume jewellery at Poncif – the work of a variety
of youngish talents – are both elegant and contemporary. Mon 3.30–7.30pm, Tues–Thurs 10am–
1.30pm & 3.30–7.30pm, Fri & Sat 10am–7.30pm.

🏃 **Raspini** Via Por Santa Maria 70r & Via
Roma 25r, ⓦwww.raspini.com. Florence's
biggest multi-label clothes shop, with a good stock
of diffusion lines. These are the two main branches;
there's a third at Via de' Martelli 5–7r. Leftovers
from previous seasons are sold at big discounts at
Raspini Vintage at Via Calimaruzza 17r, very close
to the Via Por Santa Maria branch. Mon 3.30–
7.30pm, Tues–Sat 9.30am–7.30pm, plus last Sun
of month 10am–7pm.

Department stores

Coin Via dei Calzaiuoli 56r, ⓦwww.coin.it. Central,
clothes-dominated chain store. Quality is generally

high, though styles are fairly conservative except for
one or two youth-oriented franchises on the ground

Markets

Cascine The biggest of all Florence's markets happens on Tuesday morning (8am–
1pm) at the Cascine park near the banks of the Arno (bus #1, #9, #12 or #17c), where
hundreds of stallholders set up an alfresco budget-class department store. Fewer
tourists make it out here than to San Lorenzo, so prices are keener. Clothes (some
secondhand) and shoes are the best bargains, though for even cheaper wares, you
should check out the stalls at Piazza delle Cure, just beyond Piazza della Libertà (bus
#1 or #7; Tues 8am–1pm).

San Lorenzo An open-air warehouse of cheap clothing in Piazza di San Lorenzo, the
San Lorenzo market is as well organized as a shopping mall: huge waterproof
awnings ensure that the weather can't stop the trading, and some of the stallholders
even accept credit cards. You'll find plenty of leather jackets, T-shirts and other
cheap clothes. For anything pricey, try to haggle. (Daily 8am–7pm)

Mercato Centrale Europe's largest indoor food hall is situated in Piazza del Mercato
Centrale, at the heart of the stall-filled streets around San Lorenzo, and is well worth
a sightseeing and people-watching visit whether you intend to buy anything or not.
Its popularity as a tourist sight has pushed prices up, but it's still unbeatable for
picnic supplies. (Mon–Sat 7am–2pm)

Mercato Nuovo Just to the west of Piazza della Signoria (and also known as the
Mercato del Porcellino), this is the main emporium for straw hats, plastic *David*s and the
like. (Mid-Feb to mid-Nov daily 9am–7pm; mid-Nov to mid-Feb Tues–Sat 9am–5pm)

Mercato delle Pulci A flea market stacked with antiques and bric-a-brac is pitched
near the Sant'Ambrogio food market, in Piazza dei Ciompi. Mon–Sat 9am–7pm. More
serious antique dealers swell the ranks on the last Sunday of each month (same
hours). On the second Sunday of each month there's a smaller flea market on Piazza
Santo Spirito, from 8am to 6pm.

Mercato di Sant'Ambrogio Big, cheap market in Piazza Ghiberti, near Santa Croce,
with food stalls in the central hall, as well as cheap clothes and leather. (Mon–Sat
7am–2pm)

floor. Also a good place for linen and other household goods. Mon–Sat 10am–8pm, Sun 11am–8pm.
La Rinascente Piazza della Repubblica 1, ⓦwww .rinascente.it. Like Coin, La Rinascente is part of a

countrywide chain, though this store is a touch more upmarket than its nearby rival. Sells clothing, linen, cosmetics, household goods and other staples. Mon–Sat 10am–9pm, Sun 10.30am–8pm.

Jewellery

Alessandro Dari Via San Niccolò 115r, ⓦwww .alessandrodari.com. Goldsmith Alessandro Dari produces jewellery that combines remarkable craftsmanship with a sort of neo-Baroque New Age fantasy, in which motifs such as spiders, butterflies, musical instruments and imaginary animals frequently recur. The showroom-cum-workshop – converted from a sixteenth-century loggia in which cloth used to be dyed – is pretty spectacular in itself. Mon–Sat 9.30am–1.30pm & 4–7.30pm.

Dettagli per donzelle, comari e sognatori Borgo degli Albizi 40r. Funky, brightly coloured handmade jewellery and accessories at reasonable prices. Mon 3.30–7.30pm, Tues–Sat 10am–7.30pm.
Moltissimo Via Matteo Palmieri 27r. Inventive jewellery and accessories made from non-precious materials, though there's a dash of silver in some of the pieces. You could pick up a bracelet or a pair of earrings here for around €20. Mon–Sat 10.30am–7.30pm.

Music

Alberti Via de' Pucci 16r & Borgo San Lorenzo 45–49r. Founded in 1873, this is the city's leading supplier of domestic hi-fi, DVDs, records and CDs. The Borgo San Lorenzo store is good for opera, classical and jazz, while the Via de' Pucci shop (a couple of blocks east) concentrates on

contemporary music (dance, rock, etc). Mon 3.30–7.30pm, Tues–Sat 9am–7.30pm.
Ricordi Media Store Via Brunelleschi 8–10r. The city's biggest general CD store, just off Piazza della Repubblica. Mon–Sat 9am–7.30pm, plus Sept–June last Sun of month 3.30–7.30pm.

Paper and stationery

Giulio Giannini e Figlio Piazza Pitti 36r, ⓦwww.giuliogiannini.it. Established in 1856, this paper-making and book-binding firm has been honoured with exhibitions dedicated to its work. Once the only place in Florence to make its own marbled papers, it now offers a wide variety of diaries, address books and so forth as well.

Mon–Sat 10am–7.30pm, Sun 10.30am–6.30pm.
Il Torchio Via de' Bardi 17. A marbled paper workshop using manufacturing techniques known only to the owner. Desk accessories, diaries, albums and other items in paper and leather are also available. Mon 2.30–7pm, Tues–Sat 10am–1.30pm & 2.30–7.30pm.

Perfume and toiletries

Farmacia Santa Maria Novella Via della Scala 16, ⓦwww.smnovella.it. Occupying the pharmacy of the Santa Maria Novella monastery, this sixteenth-century shop was founded by Dominican monks as an outlet for their potions, ointments and herbal remedies. Many of these are still available, including distillations of flowers and herbs, together with face-creams, shampoos, and other, more esoteric products. The shop's as famous for its wonderful interior as for its

products, which are sold worldwide. Mon–Sat 9.30am–7.30pm, Sun 10.30am–6.30pm; closed Sun in Feb & Nov.
Spezieria Erborista Palazzo Vecchio Via Vacchereccia 9r. A celebrated old shop, selling its own natural remedies and a range of unique perfumes, such as Acqua di Caterina de' Medici. July & Aug Mon–Fri 9am–7.30pm, Sat 9am–5pm; Sept–June Mon–Sat 9.30am–7.30pm, first & last Sun of month 1.30–7pm.

Prints and photos

Alinari Largo Alinari 15, ⓦwww.alinari.com. Founded in 1852, this is the world's oldest

photographic business. Owners of the largest archive of old photographs in Italy, they will print any image you choose from their huge catalogue. They also publish books, calendars, posters and cards. Mon–Fri 9am–1pm & 2–6pm; closed two weeks in mid-Aug.

Giovanni Baccani Via della Vigna Nuova 75r. You'll see prints and engravings in shops across Florence, but nowhere is the selection as rich as at

Baccani, a beautiful old shop (established in 1903) that's crammed with all manner of prints, frames and paintings. Prices range from a few euros to wallet-busting sums. Mon 3.30–7.30pm, Tues–Sat 9am–1pm & 3.30–7.30pm; July closed Sat afternoons; closed first three weeks in Aug.

Shoes and accessories

Il Bisonte Via del Parione 31–33r, ⓦwww .ilbisontefirenze.com. Beautiful and robust bags, briefcases and accessories, many of them made from *vacchetta*, a soft cowhide which ages very nicely. Mon–Sat 9.30am–7pm.

Bologna Piazza San Giovanni 13–15r5. Probably the best-known shoe shop in the city; trendy men's and women's footwear at relatively sane prices. Mon–Sat 9.30am–7.30pm, Sun 3–7pm.

Cellerini Via del Sole 37r, ⓦwww.cellerini.it. Bags, bags and more bags. Everything here is made on the premises under the supervision of the firm's founders, the city's premier exponents of the craft; bags don't come more elegant or durable. Summer Mon–Fri 9am–1pm & 3–7pm, Sat 9am–1pm; winter Mon 3–7pm, Tues–Sat 9am–1pm & 3–7pm.

🏃 **Madova** Via Guicciardini 1r. The last word in gloves – every colour, every size, every style. Prices range from around €35 to €100. Mon–Sat 9.30am–7.30pm.

🏃 **Saskia** Via di Santa Lucia 22–24r. Trained in Hamburg and Florence, Vivian Saskia

Wittmer produces exquisite and durable made-to-measure shoes in classic designs. Her workshop, located near Ognissanti, specializes in men's footwear, but makes a few designs for women too. Mon–Sat 9am–1pm & 3.30–7.30pm.

Scuola del Cuoio Via San Giuseppe 5r, ⓦwww .scuoladelcuoio.com. This academy for leatherworkers – located at the back of Santa Croce church – sells bags, jackets, belts and other accessories at prices that compare very favourably with the shops. You won't find any startlingly original designs here, but the quality is very high and the staff are knowledgeable and helpful. Mon–Sat 9.30am–6pm, Sun 10am–6pm.

🏃 **Sol Gabriel** Via Matteo Palmieri 6r, ⓦwww .solgabriel.com. As a change from all that Florentine leather, here's a shop that makes beautiful bags from all sorts of fabrics; at least three different materials go into every bag (cotton, vinyl and silk are favourites), every one is unique, and most cost under €100. Tues–Sat 10.30am–1.30pm & 2.30–7pm.

Listings

Banks and exchange Florence's main bank branches are on or around Piazza della Repubblica, but exchange booths (*cambio*) and ATM machines (*bancomat*) can be found across the city. Banks generally open Mon–Fri 8.20am–3.35pm, though some are open longer hours and some are closed for an hour in the middle of the day.

Bike, scooter & moped rental Alinari, Via Zanobi 38r ☏055.280.500, ⓦwww.alinarirental.com; Florence by Bike, Via San Zanobi 120–122r ☏055.488.992, ⓦwww.florencebybike.it (they also do repairs).

Bus information City buses are run by ATAF ☏800.424.500, ⓦwww.ataf.net. See p.178 for information on tickets and routes.

Consulates UK, Lungarno Corsini 2 ☏055.284.133; US, Lungarno Amerigo Vespucci 38 ☏055.239.8276.

Doctors The Tourist Medical Service is a private service used to dealing with foreigners; they have doctors on call 24hrs a day on ☏055.475.411

(ⓦwww.medicalservice.firenze.it), or you can visit their clinic at Via Lorenzo il Magnifico 59 (Mon–Fri 11am–noon & 5–6pm, Sat 11am–noon). Note that you'll need insurance cover to recoup the cost of a consultation, which will be at least €50. Florence's central hospital is on Piazza Santa Maria Nuova.

Internet access Internet Train (ⓦwww.internettrain .it) has seven outlets in the city, including Via de Benci 36r, Via Guelfa 54/56r, Via Porta Rossa 38r and Piazza Stazione 14 – they're open Mon–Sat 10am–midnight, Sun 3–11pm. The tourist office has a full list of current internet points.

Laundry There's a concentration of self-service *lavanderie* (around €3–4 for a complete wash) around the station and San Lorenzo districts; Wash & Dry is at Via della Scala 52–54r (daily 8am–10pm).

Left luggage Santa Maria Novella station by platform 16 (daily 6am–midnight; around €4 for first 5hrs, then less than €1 per hr).

Lost property Lost property handed into the city or railway police ends up at Via Circondaria 17b

(Mon–Sat 9am–noon; ☎ 055.367.943; bus #23 to Viale Corsica). There's also a lost property office at Santa Maria Novella station, on platform 16 next to left luggage.

Pharmacies The Farmacia Comunale, on the train station concourse, is open 24hr, as is All' Insegna del Moro, Piazza San Giovanni 20r, on the north side of the Baptistery, and Farmacia Molteni, Via dei Calzaiuoli 7r. All pharmacies display a roster in their window, showing the nearest pharmacy that's open through the night on that particular day; from midnight to 8.30pm these pharmacies (but not the trio of 24hr places) impose a surcharge of around €3.

Police Emergency ☎ 112 or 113. To report a theft or other crime, go to the Carabinieri at Borgo Ognissanti 48 (open 24hr), or the city police, at Via Pietrapiana 50r (Mon–Fri 8.30am–7.30pm, Sat closes 1.30pm) – you're likelier to find an English speaker at the latter.

Post office The main central post office is near Piazza della Repubblica at Via Pellicceria 3 (Mon–Sat 8.15am–7pm); the poste restante section is through the door immediately on the left as you enter. If you're having mail sent to you poste restante, make sure it's marked for Via Pellicceria, otherwise it will go to Florence's biggest post office, at Via Pietrapiana 53–55 (Mon–Fri 8.15am–7pm, Sat 8.15am–12.30pm).

Toilets Public toilets are usually open 10am–6pm daily and cost €0.50–60; otherwise, for the price of a coffee, you can use the facilities of any bar.

Travel details

Trains

Florence to: Arezzo (hourly; 1hr); Assisi (11 daily; 2hr 35min); Borgo San Lorenzo (hourly; 70min); Empoli (every 30min; 35min); Foligno (11 daily; 2hr 55min); Livorno (12 daily; 1hr 30min); Lucca (every 30min; 1–2hr); Pisa airport (6 daily; 70–90min); Pisa central (every 30min; 60–80min); Pistoia (every 20–30min; 40–55min); Prato (every 20–30min; 20–30min); Siena (via hourly connection at Empoli; 1hr 20min); Viareggio (hourly; 1hr 30min–2hr 25min).

Buses

Buses to destinations outside the city depart from the bus station at Via Santa Caterina da Siena, immediately west of the train station, or from the stands on the east side. Of the companies operating intertown buses from Florence, only SITA publishes a reliable timetable.

CAP Largo Fratelli Alinari 9 ☎ 055.214.637. Buses to Borgo San Lorenzo, Impruneta, Montepiano and Prato.

CAT Via Fiume 2 ☎ 055.283.400. Buses to Anghiari, Arezzo, Caprese, Città di Castello, Figline Valdarno, Incisa Valdarno and Sansepolcro.

CLAP Piazza Stazione 15 ☎ 055.283.734. Buses to Lucca and Lucca province.

COPIT Piazza Santa Maria Novella ☎ 055.215.451. Buses to Abetone, Pistoia, Poggio a Caiano and Vinci.

Lazzi Piazza Stazione 1 ☎ 166.845.010. Buses to Abetone, Calenzano, Cerreto Guidi, Empoli, Forte dei Marmi, Incisa Valdarno, Livorno, Lucca, Marina di Carrara, Marina di Massa, Montecatini Terme, Montevarchi, Pescia, Pisa, Pistoia, Pontassieve, Pontedera, Prato, Signa, Tirrenia, Torre del Lago and Viareggio.

SITA Via Santa Caterina da Siena 15 (Tuscany routes ☎ 055.483.651, national routes ☎ 055.214.721). Buses to: Barberino di Mugello (17 daily; 40min); Bibbiena (8 daily; 2hr 15min); Castellina in Chianti (1 daily; 1hr 35min); Certaldo (4 daily; 1hr 40min); Gaiole (2 daily Mon–Fri; 2hr); Greve (around 30 daily; 1hr 5min); Poggibonsi (10 daily; 1hr 20min); Pontassieve (12 daily; 50min); Poppi (9 daily; 2hr 5min); Radda in Chianti (1 daily Mon–Sat; 1hr 40min); San Casciano (14 daily; 40min); Siena (12 express services daily; 1hr 15min; also 9 stopping services); Volterra (6 daily; 2hr 25min).

2

Around Florence

CHAPTER 2 # Highlights

* **Fiesole** Escape Florence's crowds by taking a quick trip up the hill to Fiesole. See p.181

* **Medici villas** Explore the country houses of Florence's pre-eminent family. See p.185

* **Greve in Chianti** Situated in the midst of the country's most famous vineyards, Greve is perhaps the nicest town in Chianti. See p.193

* **Prato** A handsome medieval centre lurks within Prato's palisade of factories. See p.202

* **Pistoia** Off the tourist trail, but well worth a day's investigation for some remarkable sculptures. See p.207

* **San Vivaldo** This "Jerusalem in Tuscany" is one of the region's most beguiling treasures. See p.221

* **Certaldo** The quintessential hill-town: tiny and perfectly preserved. See p.222

▲ Ospedale del Ceppo, Pistoia

Around Florence

aving paid their respects to the sights of Florence, most people doing a Tuscan tour set off for another of the big-league towns, such as Siena or Pisa, leapfrogging the city's immediate surroundings. Yet there's a lot to be gained by lingering a few days in this area, either using Florence as a base, or staying at a couple of the smaller places within the city's orbit.

Inside the boundaries of Greater Florence, city buses run to the village of **Fiesole** – once Florence's keenest rival – and to many of the **Medici villas**, countryside retreats now all but engulfed by the suburbs. Further afield but readily accessible by train, the busy commercial centre of **Prato** and quiet provincial capital of **Pistoia** each make fine day-trips, with their medieval buildings and Florentine-inspired Renaissance art – and either could be used as a springboard for exploring some of the more obscure corners of Tuscany.

West of Florence, an industrialized stretch of the Arno valley leads to **Empoli**, the point of access for a number of upland attractions: **Vinci** (Leonardo da Vinci's village), the imperial settlement of **San Miniato** and the hill-towns of **Castelfiorentino** and **Certaldo**. To the north and south of Florence lie two rural regions that require independent transport for proper investigation: the **Mugello**, the wooded and agricultural area around the upper valley of the Sieve river; and **Chianti**, Italy's premier wine region and expatriate settlement.

The places covered in this chapter lie on or very near several of the principal **routes through Tuscany**, and can easily be visited on a journey between major centres. Three of these routes radiate from Florence: to Pisa (via Empoli); to Lucca (via Prato and Pistoia); and to Siena (via Chianti). The first two can be done by train or bus, the third by bus only. The fourth route – from Empoli to Siena via Castelfiorentino and Certaldo – is again possible by train or bus, though if you intend stopping off at San Gimignano, which is really the point of this trip, only the bus will do.

Fiesole

The hill-town of **FIESOLE**, which spreads over a cluster of hills above the Mugnone and Arno valleys some 8km northeast of Florence, is conventionally described as a pleasant retreat from the crowds and heat of summertime Florence. Unfortunately, its tranquillity has been so well advertised that in high season it's now hardly less busy than Florence itself; you'd probably also need paranormal sensitivity to detect much climatic difference between the two on an airless August afternoon.

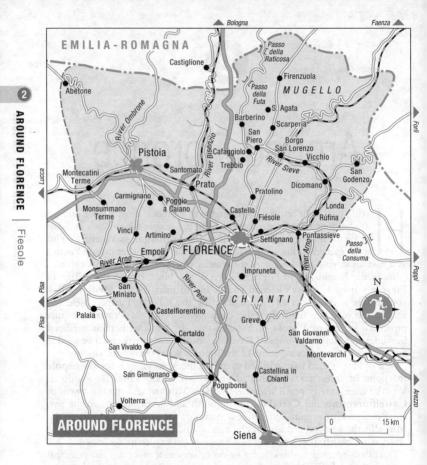

That said, Fiesole offers a grandstand view of the city, has something of the feel of a country village, and bears many traces of its history – which is actually lengthier than that of Florence. First settled in the Bronze Age, then later by the Etruscans, and then absorbed by the Romans, it rivalled its neighbour until the early twelfth century, when the Florentines overran the town. From that time it became a satellite, favoured as a semi-rural second home for wealthier citizens such as the ubiquitous Medici.

Fiesole is an easy hop from central Florence: **bus** #7 makes the half-hour journey from Santa Maria Novella train station to Fiesole's central Piazza Mino da Fiesole three times an hour.

The Town

When the Florentines wrecked Fiesole in 1125, the only major building spared was the **Duomo** (daily: summer 7.30am–noon & 3–6pm; winter 7.30am–noon & 2–5pm), on the edge of Piazza Mino. Subsequently, nineteenth-century restorers managed to ruin the exterior, which is now notable only for its lofty campanile. The most interesting part of the bare interior is the raised choir: the altarpiece is a polyptych, painted in the 1440s by Bicci di Lorenzo, and the Cappella Salutati, to the right, contains two fine pieces carved around the same time by Mino da Fiesole – an altar frontal of the *Madonna and Saints* and the tomb of Bishop Salutati. Fiesole's patron saint, St Romulus, is buried underneath the choir in the ancient crypt. Behind the Duomo at Via Dupré 1, the **Museo Bandini** (Oct–March Thurs–Mon 10am–6pm; April–Sept Wed–Mon 10am–7pm; joint ticket, valid one day, covering all Fiesole's museums €13) possesses a collection of glazed terracotta in the style of the della Robbias, the odd piece of Byzantine ivory work and a few thirteenth- and fourteenth-century Tuscan pictures, none of them inspiring.

Across the road from the museum are the town's other museums: the **Teatro Romano** and the **Museo Archeologico** (same times and ticket as Museo Bandini). Built in the first century BC, the 3000-seat theatre was excavated towards the end of the nineteenth century and is in such good repair that it's used for performances during the Estate Fiesolana festival in July and August (see p.172). Parts of the site may be closed as excavation work continues. Most of the exhibits in the site's small **museum** were excavated in this area, and encompass pieces from the Bronze Age to Roman occupation.

Fiesole's other major churches, Sant'Alessandro and San Francesco, are at the top of the steep Via San Francesco, which runs past the **Oratorio di San Jacopo** (Sat & Sun 10am–7pm; same ticket as the museums), a little chapel containing a fifteenth-century fresco and some ecclesiastical treasures. A little further up, a terrace offers a knockout view of Florence. **Sant'Alessandro** (summer Mon–Sat 9am–6pm, Sun 10am–1pm & 2–6pm; winter Mon–Sat 9am–5pm, Sun 10am–4pm) was founded in the sixth century on the site of Etruscan and Roman temples; repairs have rendered the outside a white-washed nonentity, but the beautiful *marmorino cipollino* (onion marble) columns of the basilical interior make it the most atmospheric building in Fiesole. Again, restoration has not improved the Gothic **San Francesco** (daily: April–Sept 9am–noon & 3–7pm; Oct–March closes 6pm), which occupies the site of the acropolis: the interior is a twentieth-century renovation, but the tiny cloisters are genuine. The church itself contains an *Immaculate Conception* by Piero di Cosimo (second altar on the right), and below the church is a small museum featuring material gathered mainly by missions to the Far East, much of it from China, as well as a piece of Etruscan

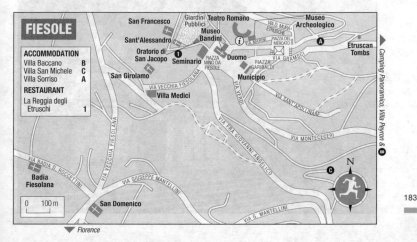

wall. From the front of San Francesco a gate opens into a wooded public park, the most pleasant descent back to Piazza Mino.

If you want to wring every last drop of historical significance from Fiesole, you could follow the signposts from here up the hill to the east of the Teatro, to the ruins of a couple of **Etruscan tombs** from the third century BC.

To San Domenico

The most enjoyable excursion from Fiesole is a wander down the narrow Via Vecchia Fiesolana, which passes the **Villa Medici** built for Cosimo il Vecchio by Michelozzo – on its way to the hamlet of **SAN DOMENICO**. Fra' Angelico was once prior of the Dominican monastery at this village and the church retains a *Madonna and Angels* by him, in the first chapel on the left; the chapterhouse also has a Fra' Angelico fresco of *The Crucifixion* (ring at no. 4 if you find the church closed).

Five-minutes' walk northwest from San Domenico stands the **Badìa Fiesolana** (Mon–Fri 8.30am–6.30pm), Fiesole's cathedral from the ninth century to the eleventh. Cosimo il Vecchio had the church altered in the 1460s, a project which kept the magnificent Romanesque facade intact while transforming the interior into a superb Renaissance building.

The Villa Peyron

Garden aficionados shouldn't miss out on the **Villa Peyron** (April–Oct daily 10am–1pm & 3–7pm; Nov–March 10am–3.30pm; €10) at Bosco di Fontelucente, 2.5km east of Fiesole (from Fiesole take bus #47). The villa itself isn't open to the public, but the garden – comprising a sequence of formal terraces surrounded by a woodland park – is a delight. Laid out by Paolo Peyron in the 1930s, it's fed by the waters of the Fontelucente spring, hence the plethora of fountains and the pair of miniature lakes, one of which is landscaped in quasi-Japanese style. Fine views of Florence add a nice garnish to the experience.

▲ The Badia Fiesolana

Practicalities

Fiesole's **tourist office** (March–Oct Mon–Sat 9am–6pm, Sun 10am–1pm &
2–6pm; Nov–Feb Mon–Sat 9am–5pm, Sun 10am–4pm; ⊤055.598.720) is at
Via Portigiani 3/5, next to the entrance to the archeological site. **Accommodation** on a tight budget is a problem. The charming one-star *Villa
Sorriso*, Via Gramsci 21 (⊤055.59.027; ⓔinfo@albergovillasorriso.com; ❷), is
the cheapest option close to the centre; the other low-cost option, the nine-
room *Villa Baccano*, is 2km farther out, at Via Bosconi 4 (⊤055.59.341,
ⓦwww.villabaccano.it; ❷). At the other end of the scale, Fiesole boasts one of
Tuscany's most sybaritic hotels, the astronomically expensive *Villa San Michele*
at Via Doccia 4 (⊤055.567.8200, ⓦwww.villasanmichele.orient-express
.com; ❾). Occupying a former monastery that was designed in part by
Michelangelo, it's surrounded by gorgeous parkland, offering terrific views,
and has a great restaurant. Doubles are not much under €1000, but online
deals sometimes bring the price down to less than €600 – not bad for a once-
in-a-lifetime kind of place. Fiesole's **campsite**, *Camping Panoramico*, at Via
Peramondo 1 (⊤055.559.069, ⓦwww.florencecamping.com), is a 120-pitch
three-star site with a bar, restaurant, pool and supermarket.

The best **restaurant** in central Fiesole is *La Reggia degli Etruschi*, Via San
Francesco 18 (⊤055.59.385; closed Tues) – the food is fabulous, as are the views
from its dining rooms and terraces.

The Medici villas

Many of the finest country houses of the Florentine hinterland were, predictably enough, built for the **Medici**. The earliest of these were primarily intended
as fortified refuges to which the family could withdraw when the political
temperature in the city became a little too hot. In time, as the family grew more
secure, the houses became somewhere to show off the humanistic culture of the
Medici. In the sixteenth and seventeenth centuries, with the Medici established
as unchallenged rulers of Florence, the villas became more ostentatious, as if to
express the might of the dynasty through their sheer luxuriousness. The land
they were built on later became a valuable asset: when Florence's importance as
a manufacturing centre was diminished, the Medici were able to divert some
resources into agriculture.

Not every Medici villa is described in this section, just the ones that are easily
accessible on a day-trip from Florence and whose interior or grounds are open
to the public. The villas at Trebbio, Cafaggiolo and Cerreto Guidi are described
later in this chapter (see p.200 & p.217). This section also includes a few sights
which can be visited on an excursion to one of the houses – the church at
Carmignano, for example, with its remarkable Pontormo altarpiece.

Villa Medicea La Petraia

The **Villa La Petraia** was adapted from a medieval castle in the 1570s and
1580s by Buontalenti, working to a commission from the future Grand Duke
Ferdinando I (bus #28 from Santa Maria Novella train station – ask the
driver to set you down near the villa). Only the watchtower of the fortress
was retained, to serve as a high-rise belvedere above the simple two-storey
house. The **interior** (daily: June–Aug 8.15am–7.30pm; April, May & Sept
8.15am–6.30pm; March & Oct 8.15am–5.30pm; Nov–Feb 8.15am–4.30pm;

closed second & third Mon of month; free) was altered in turn by Vittorio Emanuele II, who glassed over the interior courtyard to convert it into a ballroom. Its walls are covered by a seventeenth-century fresco cycle glorifying the Medici and the Knights of St Stephen, a pseudo-chivalric order founded by Cosimo I to rid the Tuscan coast of pirates. The suffocating style of the House of Savoy tends to prevail in the villa's apartments, though this is offset by the occasional sixteenth-century tapestry or painting. There is also Giambologna's bronze statue of *Venus*, now transplanted indoors from the fountain on the upper terrace of the garden.

Laid out in geometrical order, in half-hearted imitation of the Castello estate, the garden isn't much to get excited about, but the **park** behind the villa to the east is glorious, with its ancient cypress trees.

Villa Medicea di Castello

From Villa La Petraia, follow Via della Petraia past Villa Bel Riposo (where Carlo Lorenzini wrote *Pinocchio*) to the Baroque Villa Corsini, from where Via di Castello leads to the **Villa di Castello**. This house was bought in 1477 by Lorenzo and Giovanni de' Medici, second cousins of Lorenzo il Magnifico, and the principal patrons of Botticelli; the *Birth of Venus* and the *Primavera* both used to hang here. Wrecked after the expulsion of the Medici, it was rebuilt for Cosimo I, and is now the headquarters of the Accademia della Crusca, the society charged since 1585 with maintaining the purity of the Italian language.

The society doesn't allow visitors into the house, but that's no great hardship, as its Pontormo and Bronzino frescoes perished a long time back, and the villa's fame rests entirely on its **gardens** (same hours as Villa La Petraia; free), which were laid out by Tribolo for Cosimo and continued by Buontalenti, who also redesigned the house. Had the full scheme been carried out, more than fifty sculptural tableaux would have represented the Seasons, the Virtues, the landscapes of Tuscany and, of course, the triumphs of the Medici. Even in a state of semi-completion, Castello's gardens were astonishing (delighted by their labyrinths, sculptures, fountains and myriad water tricks, Montaigne judged them to be the best in Europe). Of the surviving eccentricities, the outstanding set pieces are Ammannati's colossal shivering figure of *January*, the triple-bowled fountain topped by the same sculptor's *Hercules and Antaeus*, and the Grotto degli Animali by Giambologna and his school – a man-made cave against the walls of which are stacked a menagerie of plaster birds and animals. (The bronze originals of many of these are on show in the Bargello in Florence.)

Villa Medicea di Careggi

Originally a fortified farmhouse, the **Villa di Careggi**, 5km northwest of central Florence, came into the possession of the Medici in 1417 and was altered by Michelozzo for Cosimo il Vecchio in the 1430s. It was the old man's favourite home: he brought his private library out here and hung the walls with paintings by his protégés. Cosimo died here, too, as did his son Piero and grandson Lorenzo il Magnifico, with whom the house is particularly associated, as it was here that his academy of Platonic scholars used to meet. Bus #14C runs from Florence train station to the villa, or you can follow the signposts and walk from Villa La Petraia.

Low-slung and blank-faced, Careggi is not a gracious building, its one amusing touch being a fresco in one of the garden loggias: it depicts a man being thrown down a well, demonstrating the fate of the doctor whose incompetence was alleged to have resulted in the death of Lorenzo. The villa is now a nurses' residence, and the interior can be viewed only by appointment (☎055.794.9501; visits Mon–Fri 9am–6pm, Sat 9am–noon), although the extensive surrounding gardens and woodland can be explored freely.

Poggio a Caiano and around

For the most complete picture of what life was like in the Medici villas in the family's heyday, you should make the trip to the **Villa Medici di Poggio a Caiano** (same hours as La Petraia; €2), 18km northwest of Florence, on the crest of the main road through the village of **POGGIO A CAIANO**. A COPIT bus heads to the village from Florence train station (every 30min; takes 30min), or you could take the CAP bus #M from Prato.

Lorenzo il Magnifico bought a farmhouse on this site in 1480 and commissioned Giuliano da Sangallo to rebuild it as a classical rural palace – the only architectural project instigated by Lorenzo that has survived, and the first Italian house to be built specifically as a place of country leisure. Raised on a kind of arcaded podium, it is the most elegant of the Medici villas and its impact is enhanced by later additions: the entrance loggia, for instance, was commissioned by Lorenzo's son Giovanni, the future Pope Leo X, and the curving double stairway was added in the eighteenth century. The house was often used to accommodate guests of state before they made ceremonial entrance into Florence: Charles V stayed here, and it was at Poggio a Caiano that Eleanor of Toledo was introduced to her future husband, Cosimo I.

You enter the villa through the basement, where the plush **games room** and private **theatre** hint at the splendour to come. Upstairs, the focal point is the double-height **salone** which Sangallo created out of the courtyard between the two main blocks, and which Vasari pronounced the most beautiful room in the world. Its sixteenth-century frescoes include del Sarto's *Caesar Receiving Egyptian Tribute* (the giraffe shown in the background was a gift to Lorenzo from the Sultan of Egypt), Franciabigio's *Triumph of Cicero* (a reference to Cosimo il Vecchio's return from exile) and, best of the lot, Pontormo's gorgeous *Vertumnus and Pomona*, the perfect evocation of a sun-stunned Tuscan afternoon. Also on this floor is a reconstruction of the salon from the Villa Topaia built by Cosimo III at Castello and since destroyed. This was set among orchards, and the literal-minded Cosimo duly ordered scores of horticultural **paintings** to fill the house; the Dutch still-lifes are like ideal fruit stalls, each variety of grape, peach and apple assiduously numbered and labelled. Other such painted images from La Topaia are scattered throughout the main floor.

Many of the rooms were redecorated in the nineteenth century, but one that escaped was the **apartment of Bianca Cappello**, wife of Francesco I and inspiration of many a romantic tale. Born into an upper-class Venetian family, she fled her native city with a young man, whom she quickly dumped to become Francesco's mistress. Banned from the city by Francesco's first wife, she remained an outcast even after she had become his second, being blacklisted by many of Florence's elite. In October 1587 both she and her husband died here on the same day – perhaps poisoned, perhaps victims of a particularly virulent virus.

In Lorenzo's time the grounds of Poggio a Caiano were far more extensive than they are today, and included a farm and a hunting estate; in the eighteenth century the **gardens** (same hours) were converted into an English-style landscape, now containing some magnificent old trees.

Carmignano

Some 5km west of Poggio a Caiano, the church of **San Michele** (daily: May–Sept 7.30am–6pm; Oct–April 7.30am–5pm) in the village of **CARMIGNANO** contains one of Pontormo's most celebrated paintings, *The Visitation*. Created in the early 1530s, it's as unusual an interpretation of a common theme as his great *Deposition* in Florence: attended by two stunned-looking handmaidens, Mary and Elizabeth seem to be clutching each other in a state of anxious amazement. There's a fairly regular CAP **bus** service to Carmignano from Poggio (taking 10–20min, depending on whether it goes via Comeana; see below).

Villa di Artimino

Some of the buses from Poggio a Caiano to Carmignano take a circuitous route via Comeana, 3km south, where a couple of large **Etruscan tombs** dating from the seventh century BC have been excavated (Thurs–Sat 9am–1pm; free). A few of these bus services then loop through the walled village of **ARTIMINO**, another 3km on.

The **Villa di Artimino** is known as La Ferdinanda after Grand Duke Ferdinando I, for whom Buontalenti designed the house as a hunting lodge, with no intervening garden to smooth the transition from civilization to nature. Unlike most of the other Medici villas it's still in a rural setting, and has superb views towards Florence in one direction and west along the Arno in the other. A white rectangular block with details picked out in grey *pietra serena*, the house has the appearance of a rather dandified fortress, and its most distinctive external feature has earned it the nickname "the villa of the hundred chimneys". The villa is now a hotel-cum-conference centre, and the paintings of the various Medici villas that once hung here are now on show in Florence's Museo di Firenze com'era. In the basement, however, there's a museum of Etruscan finds from the Comeana tombs (April–Oct Mon, Tues & Thurs–Sat 9.30am–12.30pm, Sun 10am–noon; €4).

While you're here, take a look at the village church of **San Leonardo**, which was put together in the twelfth century from stones recovered from an Etruscan necropolis.

Pratolino and Monte Senario

Nothing remains of Francesco I's favourite villa at **Pratolino**, 12km north of Florence (bus #25), except for its huge park (April–Sept Fri & Sun 10am–7.30pm; March & Oct Sun 10am–6pm; free) – and even this is but a shadow of its former self. The mechanical toys, trick fountains and other practical jokes that Buontalenti installed here were the most ingenious ever seen, and required so much maintenance that there was a house in the grounds just for the court plumbers. The only surviving pieces are a couple of fountains, a little temple by Buontalenti, and Giambologna's immense *Appennino*, a shaggy man-mountain who gushes water. Nonetheless, the park – known as the **Parco Demidoff**, after the nineteenth-century owners of the estate – is still one of the most pleasant green spaces within easy reach of Florence.

If you're travelling under your own steam, you could take an eight-kilometre diversion northeast off the main road into the Mugello to **Monte Senario**, a monastery established by the seven founder members of the Servite order in 1233. The complex is impressive, with a gilded Rococo basilica and hermitages scattered up the hill, but the architecture is less rewarding than the views of Mugello from the terrace.

Chianti

Ask a sample of middle-class northern Europeans to define their idea of paradise and the odds are that a hefty percentage will come up with something that sounds a lot like **Chianti**, the territory of vineyards and hill-towns that stretches between Florence and Siena (who contested ownership of much of this region until Siena's final capitulation in 1557). To the outsider, it can seem that every aspect of life in Chianti is in perfect balance: the landscape is the sort of harmoniously varied terrain beloved of painters evoking any mythical Golden Age; the climate for most of the year is balmy, and rarely too grim even in the pit of winter; and on top of all this there's the **wine**, the one Italian vintage that's familiar to just about everyone.

The British, and others from similarly ill-favoured zones, long ago took note of Chianti's charms, and the rate of immigration has been so rapid since the 1960s that the region is now popularly known as "Chiantishire". With up to a million visitors a year, tourism has overtaken wine to become the region's most important cash crop, and has helped push property prices beyond the reach of the local population – thus altering the tone of certain parts irreparably. Although foreign residents still account for only five percent of Chianti's 45,000 inhabitants and tourist handouts still talk of the unsullied charm of Chianti's medieval hamlets, many of these villages are places where history has become a commodity and where newly varnished shutters remain closed for much of the off-season. There is, nonetheless, much to enjoy in Chianti – quiet back roads, hundreds of acres of woodland, and of course the vineyards.

Buses from Florence and Siena connect with the main Chianti towns, but the best way to really get to know the region is **by car**. Your own transport allows you to roam the quieter recesses of the hills and visit any of the eight hundred wine producers to sample the local product: every village mentioned below has wine tastings on offer within a few hundred metres of the main street. There's basically a choice of two main roads to follow through Chianti: the old Florence-to-Siena road (**N2**) along the western edge of the region, or the so-called **Chiantigiana** road (**SS222**), through the Chianti heartland.

Hotels in Chianti are rarely inexpensive, but this is prime **agriturismo** territory, with scores of farms offering rooms or apartments (or even self-contained mini-villas), generally for a minimum period of one week, which for an extended stay can provide a good-value alternative to hotel accommodation. There are already far too many agriturismi in Chianti to list here, and with every passing month a new operation starts up, but you can find a good choice of properties at: ⓦwww.agriturismo.net; ⓦwww.agriturismo.it; and ⓦwww.chiantishire.org/agriturismi.htm. The Chiantishire website, despite its dreadful name, is a good source of information on the area.

Western Chianti

A stretch of *superstrada* connects Florence to Siena along the western edge of Chianti, but to get some sense of the character of the land it's better to opt for the older **N2** road, which takes in a few of the major Chianti towns en route. Apart from being a far more diverting drive, it's actually not that much slower: even with a few stops on the way (to explore the **Certosa di Galluzzo** or visit a wine house), you could reach San Gimignano or Siena comfortably in a half-day drive from Florence.

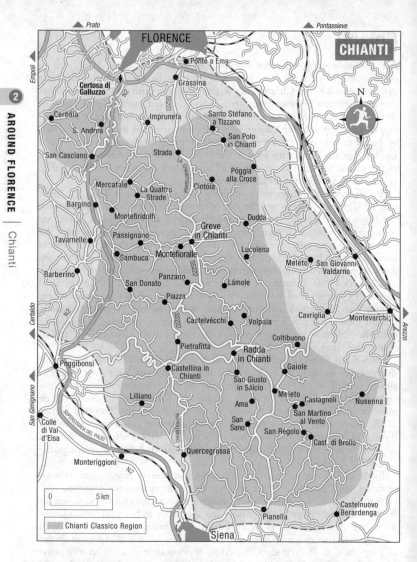

The Certosa di Galluzzo

On the city side of the Autostrada del Sole, beyond Poggio Imperiale, the N2 sweeps by the Carthusian monastery of the **Certosa di Galluzzo** (Tues–Sun 9am–noon & 3–6pm, Sun 3–6pm; winter closes 5pm; free, but donation expected), founded in the fourteenth century by the Florentine banker Niccolò Acciaioli. Bus #37 runs here from Florence train station, so it can easily be included as an excursion from the city.

The Certosa (or charterhouse) is now occupied by Cistercian monks, one of whose number shows visitors round the enormous complex. Its main architectural attraction is the **Chiostro Grande**, with its tondi of prophets and saints by Andrea and Giovanni della Robbia and their workshop. One of the eighteen monks' cells adjoining this cloister is visitable – it's the typical Carthusian arrangement, with three rooms and its own patch of garden. Beyond, the tour reaches the **Palazzo degli Studi**, now a picture gallery, though built as a study centre by the well-educated Acciaioli, who counted Boccaccio and Petrarch among his friends. The Certosa was once so rich that it owned over five hundred works of art, most of which were carried off by Napoleon. The best of those that remain are the five lunette scenes of the Passion, painted for the Chiostro Grande by Pontormo between 1522 and 1525; he and his pupil Bronzino took refuge here from a plague outbreak in the city. In the **church** itself, down in the crypt of the lay brothers' choir, there are the tombs of the monastery's founder and his descendants, including a beautiful slab originally thought to have been by Donatello, now attributed to Francesco da Sangallo.

In nearby **Bottai**, at Via San Cristofano 2, there's the *Camping Internazionale Firenze* **campsite** (☏055.237.4704, ⊛www.florencecamping.com), which also has four-berth bungalows (around €30 per person per night), a pool, kitchen facilities, a play area and internet access.

Sant'Andrea and San Casciano in Val di Pesa

South of the Certosa, the N2 passes to the east of **Sant'Andrea in Percussina**, where Machiavelli alleviated the boredom of exile by writing *The Prince*, the manual of statecraft that he hoped, in vain, would seal his rehabilitation. A house has been identified as his residence and is open to visitors by appointment, but contains nothing of interest.

SAN CASCIANO IN VAL DI PESA, 17km south of Florence, is the first real town on the N2 road. In fact, with a population of a little over 15,000, it is the only place in Chianti that is really more than an extended village. It is also home to one of the slickest commercial operations in Tuscany, the six-hundred-year-old **Antinori wine house**, as well as one of Chianti's most interesting churches, **Santa Maria del Prato**, which stands by the one surviving gateway in the town walls. The church was built in the early fourteenth century and contains some beautiful works of art from the same period, notably a Crucifix by Simone Martini, an altarpiece of the Madonna and Child by Ugolino di Nerio, and a pulpit carved by a pupil of Andrea Pisano.

The best place **to stay** in the vicinity is the spectacular ⚘ *Villa Il Poggiale*, set amid a cypress grove about 3km west of San Casciano at Via Empolese 69 (☏055.828.311, ⊛www.villailpoggiale.it; ❻); rebuilt in the sixteenth century and discreetly decorated in the style of the early nineteenth century, the villa is a beautiful and spacious building, and has a **restaurant** and outdoor pool.

Bargino and further south

Back on the N2 south of San Casciano, you pass the **Castello di Bibbione** – home of the Buondelmonte family, who triggered the Guelph versus Ghibelline battles – before coming into **BARGINO**, from where it's a short diversion east to the impressively fortified village of **Montefiridolfi**, whose castle once belonged to the sons of Ridolfo Buondelmonte (*figli di Ridolfo*).

South of Bargino, the N2 rolls into **TAVARNELLE VAL DI PESA**, which expanded as an agricultural centre in the nineteenth century. There's a reasonable **restaurant** here, *La Fattoria* at Via del Cerro 11 (☏055.807.0000; closed Mon lunch & all Tues), and, 300m from the bus stop, one of two **hostels** in Chianti, the HI *Ostello del Chianti*, Via Roma 137 (☏055.805.0265, ⊛www.ostellionline.org; open March 15–Oct 31 only), which has 82 beds, from €15 per night.

About 2km beyond lies the more ancient **BARBERINO VAL D'ELSA**, site of one of the rare **campsites** in Chianti, *Semifonte*, at Via Ugo Foscolo 4

Chianti wines

Chianti became the world's first officially defined wine-producing area in 1716, the year Cosimo III drew the boundaries within which vineyards could use the region's name on their product. Modern Chianti dates from the 1860s when Bettino Ricasoli, the second prime minister of unified Italy, established the classic formula for the wine at his estate at Brolio, based on **Sangiovese** – central Italy's predominant red grape. White *Malvasia bianca* grapes were another component of Ricasoli's recipe, but since 1995 Chianti growers have been allowed to produce wines with no white grapes in the mix.

There was a time when Chianti was synonymous with low-grade wine, and had an image that was symbolized by the squat straw-covered bottle known as a *fiasco* – indeed, by the 1950s the reputation of Chianti had sunk so low that it was suggested that many vineyards should be returned to pasture. Given the wide area over which Chianti is produced, it can never be a consistent wine, but the overall quality is nowadays far higher than used to be, and the kitschy *fiasco* is no longer used by serious producers, whose number has burgeoned since Chianti became a **Denominazione d'Origine Controllata e Garantita (DOCG)** in 1984. The area's total output is now about 100 million litres per annum, making it Italy's highest-volume DOCG by far.

The wine-growing area is split into seven classified **regions**, of which the most highly regarded are Chianti Classico and Chianti Rúfina. Many Chiantis are fine when young, though the better wines take at least four years to mature; the best recent vintages are 1997, 1999, 2001, 2004 and 2006, but one to avoid is 2002 – this was the worst Chianti summer in living memory, with torrential rain that rotted the vines all over the region.

The Chianti districts

Chianti Classico The original delineated district (see map, p.190), accounting for a third of the Chianti produced. In 1924 Chianti Classico took as its trademark the black cock (*Gallo Nero*) that was once the heraldic symbol of the baronial alliance called the Lega di Chianti.

Chianti Colli Aretini From the hills on the east side of the Arno valley, to the north of Arezzo. Tends to be lighter than Classico and is best drunk young.

Chianti Colli Fiorentini From the area immediately south and east of Florence, and along the Arno and Pesa valleys. Good quaffing wine and staple *rosso* of many a restaurant in Florence.

Chianti Colli Senesi The largest Chianti zone, split into three distinct districts: around Montalcino, around Montepulciano, and south of the Classico region east of San Gimignano. Variable quality, with the name of the producer all-important.

Chianti Colline Pisane The lightest Chianti comes from this region, southeast of Pisa, around Casciana Terme.

Chianti Montalbano From the hills west of Florence and south of Pistoia, these wines are usually soft and scented.

Chianti Rúfina The lower Sieve valley, northeast of Florence, produces some of the most refined and longest-living Chiantis. Not to be confused with the big Chianti producer Ruffino.

(☎055.807.5454, ⓦwww.semifonte.it). A beautiful Romanesque church, the **Pieve di Sant'Appiano**, parts of which date back to the tenth century, is a few kilometres southwest of the village (well signposted); due south, on the main road, is the major town of Poggibonsi (see p.364), hub for buses to San Gimignano and Siena.

The Chianti heartland

There's no better way to experience the village life of Chianti than to drive along the **Chiantigiana** road (**SS222**), which cuts right across the hills from Florence to Siena, connecting with a tangle of minor roads that traverse the most unspoilt parts of the region. If you put your foot down, its twists and turns can be negotiated in only a little more time than the major N2 road to the west, but this is more of a route to dawdle along, taking turnings on a whim and dropping by at any vineyard that takes your fancy. If you want to see the best of Chianti in a single day, devise an itinerary that takes in **Greve** and **Radda**, two of the region's most alluring little towns.

Santa Caterina d'Antella and Impruneta

As you leave Florence on the SS22, the access road for the Chiantigiana, a short detour just before the *autostrada* brings you to the village of **Ponte a Ema**. One kilometre beyond, at Rimezzano, the church of **Santa Caterina d'Antella** has a fine cycle of scenes from the life of St Catherine of Siena, painted by Spinello Aretino in 1387, immediately prior to his work at San Miniato al Monte (see p.160).

Another rewarding detour, this time just south of the *autostrada*, presents itself at **Grássina**. Take a right turn here and, after 9km of winding road, you arrive at **IMPRUNETA**. The handsome **Collegiata** here, restored after heavy bomb damage in 1944, was founded in the eleventh century to house a miraculous icon of the Madonna and Child dug up in a nearby field and said to have been painted – as these things often are – by St Luke. It's housed in one of a pair of matching chapels by Michelozzo, the second of which contains an alleged fragment of the True Cross; both have lovely enamelled terracotta decoration by Luca della Robbia. Impruneta has long been a centre of the **terracotta** industry, and holds a big fair in October on the main square.

Greve and around

Go east rather than west at Grássina and you'll come to **Santo Stefano a Tizzano**, with its Romanesque church and contemporaneous Castello di Tizzano, a producer of good wines but best known for its olive oil. About 2km further is **San Polo in Chianti**, where a major iris festival, the Festa del Giaggiolo, held in mid-May, celebrates the crop of Florence's floral emblem.

From San Polo a minor road reconnects with the Chiantigiana near **Strada in Chianti**. The turn-off southeast from Strada to Dudda is overlooked by the mighty Castello di Mugnana, which once protected this stretch of road down into the Arno valley and is now the headquarters of a massive wine estate.

For casual oenophiles, perhaps the best target is **GREVE**, 10km south on the Chiantigiana from Strada. The venue for Chianti's biggest **wine fair** (the Rassegna del Chianti Classico, usually held during the first week in Sept), this is a town with wine for sale on every street: two of the best outlets are the *Enoteca di Gallo Nero*, Piazzetta Santa Croce 8, and the *Cantina di Greve in Chianti*, at Piazza delle Cantine 6, which claims to have the biggest selection of Chianti Classico wines in the whole region.

Though razed to the ground in 1325 by Castruccio Castracani (the ruler of Lucca), by the fifteenth century Greve had re-established itself as a thriving mercantile town, focused on the funnel-shaped **Piazza Matteotti**, where a Saturday-morning market is still held today. Its irregular arcades are explained by the fact that various merchants paid for the construction of their own stretches of colonnade. The statue in the centre is of Giovanni da

Verrazzano, the first European to see what became Manhattan; he was born in the nearby Castello di Verrazzano. Other than the piazza, the Greve townscape has just one feature that might be classified as a sight: the **Museo d'Arte Sacra di San Francesco**, at Via San Francesco 4 (April–Sept Thurs & Fri 10am–1pm, Sat & Sun 4–8pm; Oct–March Thurs & Fri 10am–1pm, Sat & Sun 3.30–6.30pm; €3), a minor museum where the chief exhibit is a painted terracotta *Lamentation*, created in the 1530s, and thus one of the last examples of a genre that originated with Luca della Robbia more than a century earlier.

As the chief town of the Gallo Nero region, Greve is equipped with an efficient **tourist office**, tucked into a corner of Piazza Matteotti at Via delle Capanne 11 (Mon–Fri 10.30am–2pm & 3–6pm; ☎055.854.5243), which can give information on vineyards, accommodation in local farmhouses and trekking in Chianti. A couple of three-star **hotels** on Piazza Matteotti offer comfortable accommodation: the *Del Chianti* at no. 86 (☎055.853.763, ⊛www .albergodelchianti.it; ❸) and the more characterful ⚑ *Da Verrazzano* at no. 28 (☎055.853.189, ⊛www.albergoverrazzano.it; ❹). For travellers on a tight rein, there's the *Villa San Michele*, perched on top of the highest hill in the Florentine portion of Chianti, at Via Casole 42 (☎055.851.034, ⊛www.villasanmichele.it) in Lucolena, 9km east of Greve (no public transport); in addition to a small dormitory (beds €18 per night), it has double rooms (❷) and three apartments for two people (€80 per night), plus a **restaurant** and bar. More centrally, *Da Verrazzano* has an extremely good restaurant (closed Mon & mid-Jan to mid-Feb), with full meals at around €40 and a terrace overlooking the piazza. Alternatively, the *Gallo Nero*, just off the piazza at Via Cesare Battisti 6 (closed Thurs), is a perfectly acceptable bar-trattoria-pizzeria.

Montefioralle and the Badìa a Passignano

Five-minutes' drive from Greve, west up a steep zigzagging road, lies the much-restored hamlet of **MONTEFIORALLE**, where a single elliptical street – Via di Montefioralle – encompasses a few tower houses and a pair of Romanesque churches. This street has a simple but superb **trattoria**, the ⚑ *Taverna del Guerrino* (☎055.853.106; summer open daily for dinner, Thurs–Sun for lunch; winter open Thurs–Sun for lunch and dinner). A kilometre to the west of Montefioralle, at Via San Cresci 31–32 in Mezzuola, you'll find one of the best hotels in Chianti – the *Villa Bordoni* (☎055.884.0004, ⊛www.villabordoni .com; ❼), a magnificent country house that was rescued from dereliction by David and Catherine Gardner, owners of the restaurants *Baldovino* and *Beccofino* in Florence. Each of the ten bedrooms and suites is uniquely and beautifully furnished, and the restaurant is good as well; a pool and open-air fitness pavilion complete the package.

Continuing west from Montefioralle, the road passes the vestiges of the castle of Montefili, whose owners were benefactors of the **Badìa a Passignano** (⊛www.Badìa-a-passignano.com), situated a few kilometres on towards the N2. A monastery was founded here towards the end of the ninth century, then in 1049 was re-dedicated to the Vallombrosan order, whose founder, St Giovanni Gualberto, died here in 1073 and is buried in the abbey church of San Michele. It became one of the wealthiest religious houses in Tuscany, but is now occupied by just a handful of Vallombrosan monks, who on Sunday afternoons (usually 3pm) allow visitors to explore the site. A painting by Alessandro Allori and a bust of Giovanni Gualberto are on display, but the highlight is the refectory fresco of the *Last Supper*, painted in 1476 by Davide and Domenico Ghirlandaio.

Panzano

About 8km south of Greve along the Chiantigiana, the town of **PANZANO** overlooks a circle of hills known as the Conca d'Oro (Golden Valley) because of their sun-trap properties; the resultant wines can be sampled at the *Enoteca del Chianti Classico*, Via Giovanni da Verrazzano 8. Signposted down a branch road, the Romanesque **Pieve di San Leolino**, 1km south of the village, is one of the oldest churches in Chianti, and traces its origins to the first Christian settlers; the most notable of its paintings is a *Madonna with Sts Peter and Paul*, created in the mid-thirteenth century.

Panzano is best known, however, as the home of the **Antica Macelleria Cecchini**, perhaps the most famous butcher's shop in the country, though it compares to ordinary butcher's shops in the same way as a Ferrari relates to a Fiat – it even has a downstairs room for wine tastings, art shows and concerts. In existence at Via XX Luglio 11r for 250 years, it's run by Dario Cecchini, a charismatic and eloquent champion of Tuscan carnivorous cuisine and Chianti traditions in general. He's recently opened a terrific **restaurant** opposite the shop – called *Solociccia* ("only meat"), it has sittings at 7pm and 9pm from Thursday to Saturday, and at 1pm on Sunday (reservations compulsory; ☎055.852.727). There's no menu: you pay €30 per person and you get what you're given; the price excludes wine, which you're encouraged to bring along. Dario has recently announced plans to open a Tuscan fast-food place as well, selling burgers which of course will be the best in Italy. Panzano also has a very nice three-star **hotel**, the *Villa Sangiovese* (☎055.852.461; ⓦwww .villasangiovese.it; open March 17–Dec 15; ❹); located on Piazza Bucciarelli, it has an excellent restaurant too (closed Wed).

Castellina

The summit of the next main hill, 15km south, is occupied by well-heeled **CASTELLINA IN CHIANTI**, which formerly stood on the front line of the continual wars between Florence and Siena. The walls, fortress and the covered walkway known as the **Via delle Volte** – a kind of gallery looking

▲ Vineyards near Panzano

east from underneath the town (it was originally open, but houses were later built over it) – all bear testimony to an embattled past. Traces of a more distant era can be seen at the **Ipogeo Etrusco di Montecalvario** (open daylight hours; free), a complex of subterranean sixth-century BC Etruscan burial chambers, carved into the summit of a small hill that's five-minutes' walk north of the village. The area's distant history is illuminated in the **Museo del Chianti Senese** (Thurs–Tues 10am–1pm & 3.30–6.30pm; €5), which also gives you access to the town's tower, but neither the Etruscans nor Castellina's one sizeable church – the neo-Romanesque San Salvatore (notable only for a single fifteenth-century fresco and the mummified remains of the obscure St Fausto) – are what brings in the tourists. Wine is of course Castellina's primary attraction, as is evident from the power-station bulk of the **wine co-operative** on the main road; the local vintages (and olive oil) can be sampled at several places in town.

The very helpful Castellina **tourist office** is at Via Ferruccio 40 (daily 9am–1pm & 2.30–6.30pm; ☎0577.741.392). Pick of the **hotels** in town is the three-star ⚔ *Palazzo Squarcialupi*, which occupies the upper floors of a vast fifteenth-century palazzo at Via Ferruccio 22 (☎0577.741.186, ⓦwww .palazzosquarcialupi.com; ❹); the rooms are large and well-furnished, and there's a sauna in the basement and a pool in the garden, which commands a wonderful view. Another good three-star, the rustic *Colle Etrusco Salivolpi*, is located at Via Fiorentina 89, a short distance northwest of Castellina on the road to San Donato (☎0577.740.484, ⓦwww.hotelsalivolpi.com; ❹); surrounded by a beautiful garden, it has an outdoor pool and large timber-ceilinged bedrooms. The two best **restaurants** in Castellina are *La Torre*, an unspoilt and well-priced trattoria at Piazza del Comune 15 (☎0577.740.236; closed Fri), and *Il Gallopapa*, at Via delle Volte 16 (☎0577.742.939; closed Mon), which has a range of excellent and imaginative set menus from €50 to €75 per person, excluding drinks.

Radda and around

The best of Chianti lies east of Castellina and the Chiantigiana, in the less domesticated terrain of the **Monti del Chianti** – the stronghold of the Lega di Chianti, whose power bases were Castellina itself and the two principal settlements of this craggy region, Radda and Gaiole. The nearer of these, the ancient Etruscan-founded town of **RADDA IN CHIANTI**, became the league's capital in 1384, and the imprint of the period is perhaps stronger here than anywhere else in Chianti. The street plan of this minuscule but historic centre is focused on Piazza Ferrucci, where the frescoed and shield-studded Palazzo Comunale faces a church raised on a high platform. Neither is an outstanding building on its own, but taken together they form an impressive ancient core that gives Radda its appeal.

The **tourist office** lurks behind the church, on the corner of Piazza del Castello (Mon–Sat 10am–1pm & 3–7pm, Sun 10.30am–12.30pm; ☎0577.738.494). There are no low-cost **hotels** in Radda but stylish accommodation is on offer at the three-star *Podere Le Vigne* (☎0577.738.640; ⓦwww .tuscany.net/vigne; ❹), a converted farm located a kilometre outside Radda, just off the road between Radda and the hamlet of Villa a Radda. In addition to the rooms at the former farm, *Le Vigne* has some plainer (and much cheaper) but still very pleasant accommodation in the centre of Radda, and there's a good restaurant at the main site, where you'll pay around €40 for a meal. At Via Roma 33 you'll find the *Palazzo Leopoldo* (☎0577.735.603, ⓦwww.palazzoleopoldo.it; ❻), which was founded as a pilgrims' hostel, then converted into a magnificent town house prior to becoming an extremely elegant four-star hotel, with a very good restaurant. At the top of the range is the elegant *Relais Vignale*, which occupies a nicely converted seventeenth-century manor house on the edge of the village at Via Pianigiani 9 (℡0577.738.012, ⓦwww.vignale.it; ❼); it has a pool in the garden, a wine bar in the cellars, and a restaurant that's a touch pricier than *Le Vigne* (℡0577.738.094; daily March–Nov). You can eat cheaply and well at the *Da Michele* trattoria-pizzeria (closed Mon) – it's at the end of the car park below the town walls, and is signposted off the main road.

About 7km north of Radda lies the unspoilt village of **Volpaia**, which from the tenth to the sixteenth century was an important military lookout over the valley of the Pesa. The medieval donjon still stands, but the most interesting structure is the deconsecrated **Commenda di Sant'Eufrosino**, designed by Michelozzo, and now used as a *cantina* and exhibition space by the Castello di Volpaia wine estate (ⓦwww.volpaia.it).

South of Radda

The same distance south of Radda is **Ama**, once a fortification on the southern edge of Florentine territory. Round the village are ranged the vineyards of one of Chianti's first-rank wine estates, **Castello di Ama**, which offers tastings throughout the year, except in August. A little further south, in **San Sano**, you'll find the extremely pleasant *Hotel San Sano* (℡0577.746.130, ⓦwww.sansanohotel.it; closed Nov–March; ❼), which occupies a heavily restored thirteenth-century fortress. About 5km south of San Sano, at Pievasciata (on the minor road parallel to the N408), you'll come across the **Chianti Sculpture Park**, an intriguing initiative where artists from a great range of cultures (India, Zimbabwe, Colombia and Japan are all represented) have been commissioned to create site-specific open-air work (April–Oct Tues–Sun 10am–sunset; €7.50; ⓦwww.chiantisculpturepark.it).

Badìa a Coltibuono

On a hill six kilometres east of Radda stands the **Badìa a Coltibuono**. This Vallombrosan abbey (see p.442) was founded on the site of an eighth-century hermitage, and its church of San Lorenzo, built in 1050, is one of Tuscany's finest Romanesque buildings. The monastic complex is now owned by one of the biggest wine estates in the region, whose vintages are served at the famous Badìa a Coltibuono **restaurant**, adjoining the abbey (℡0577.749.424, ⓦwww.coltibuono.com; Nov–April closed Mon; also closed Jan to early March) – a meal here will cost in the region of €50 per head. The Badìa is also celebrated for its lavish residential cookery courses, detailed on its website, and since 2005 – when it began marketing itself as Italy's first "wine resort" – has been offering **accommodation** in eight beautifully converted monastic cells (❻). There are some good **walks** laid out through the oak and pine woods on the surrounding slopes.

Gaiole and Brolio

Modern times have caught up with the third of the Lega di Chianti triad, **GAIOLE**, 5km south of Coltibuono. Now a brisk market town, it has a **wine co-operative** at Via Mulinaccio 10 which offers splendid tasting opportunities, as does the *Enoteca Montagnani*, Via Bandinelli 13–17, which has a superlative range of Chianti Classico. The most impressive sights in the immediate area are the ruins of the **Castello di Vertine**, occupying the heights 3km west of the village, and the fortified village of **Barbischio**, up a winding little road to the east. Devotees of military ruins could follow the signposted Strada dei Castelli from Gaiole, an itinerary of half a dozen fortresses between Spaltena (1km) and Vistarenni (6km).

A couple of kilometres south of Gaiole, the towers of the **Castello di Meleto** (⊛www.castellomeleto.it) peer from behind a screen of cypresses over the road leading to **Castagnoli**. Meleto was founded by the monks of Coltibuono, but by 1269 it was in the hands of the Ricasoli family, who built its massive fortifications in the fifteenth century. The highlights of the guided tour (Mon–Sat at 11.30am, 3pm & 4.30pm, Sun 11.30am, 4.30pm & 5pm) are the delicate eighteenth-century theatre and the visit to the *cantina*, where you can sample the Meleto estate's olive oil, wine or food (the price of the tour varies according to which option you choose). Meleto has **accommodation** too, ranging from B&B (from ❹) to seven-bed agriturismo apartments (up to €2000 per week).

The busiest Chianti *cantina* is that of the **Castello di Brolio** (⊛www.ricasoli .it), just outside the nearby village of **Brolio**. The building passed to the Ricasoli family as far back as the twelfth century, and was the object of frequent tussles between the Florentines and the Sienese. Demolished by the Sienese army, it was rebuilt in the sixteenth century, then converted in the nineteenth century into a colossal mock-medieval country residence by the vinicultural pioneer **Baron Bettino Ricasoli**, who allegedly moved here in order to keep his attractive young wife away from her admirers in Florence. The castle's garden and the baron's apartments can be visited on a tour of the house (daily 10am– noon & 3–6pm; €3), but a far more rewarding experience is to buy some Castello di Brolio wine at the estate's *enoteca* (Mon–Sat 9am–6pm, plus Sun 11am–7pm in summer), or sample it as an accompaniment to a meal in the excellent but expensive *Osteria del Castello* **restaurant** (☏0577.747.277; closed Thurs). High-quality food at a lower price is provided by *Il Carlino d'Oro*, alongside the church in the neighbouring village of San Règolo (☏0577.747.136) – expect to pay around €30 a head.

The Mugello

For every hundred tourists who give over a day to the vineyards of Chianti, perhaps one will give a few hours to the **MUGELLO** (⊛www .mugellotoscana.it), the lush region on the Tuscan side of the Apennine ridge separating the province from Emilia-Romagna. Like Chianti, this is a benign, humanized sort of landscape, with nothing that will take your breath away – but it's easier to avoid the crowds here, even though it's a favourite weekend hangout of the Florentine bourgeoisie. Its celebrated olive groves and vineyards are concentrated in the central Mugello basin, formed by the Sieve and its tributary valleys; elsewhere the vegetation is principally oak, pine and chestnut forest, interspersed with small resorts whose customers tend to be short-stay vacationers from the city. The fringes of the eastern part of the Mugello lie inside the Parco Nazionale delle Foreste Casentinesi – for more on this national park, see p.456.

As with Chianti, you'll need your own transport to see anything much. Three main roads run from Florence: the Via Bologna (**N65**), which passes Pratolino on its way to the Passo della Futa; the **N302** direct to Borgo San Lorenzo; and the **N67/551**, which winds up to Borgo San Lorenzo along the Sieve. By public transport, there's a choice between the Sieve valley **train** line to Borgo San Lorenzo (nearly all of these Faenza-bound trains depart from Campo di Marte station rather than Santa Maria Novella), or SITA and CAP **buses** along

The Mugello's local museums

Like the Casentino, the Mugello has a network of **small museums** devoted to the traditional way of life and the culture of the region, most of them open at weekends only. The best of the museums affiliated to this *Sistema Museale in Mugello e Valdisieve* – such as the one in Reggello – are covered in the main part of the guide. Others that you might want to take a look at, should you find yourself close by, are listed below.

Borgo San Lorenzo: Museo della Manifattura Chini (Chini ceramics museum); Museo della Civiltà Contadini (museum of rural traditions)

Firenzuola: Museo della Pietra Serena (stonework museum); Museo del Paesaggio Storico dell'Appennino (Apennine historical landscape museum); Museo Storico-Etnografico (museum of local history)

Palazzuolo: Museo delle Genti di Montagna (mountain people's museum); Museo Archeologico Alto Mugello (archeological museum)

Pelago: Museo d'Arte Sacra (sacred art museum)

Rúfina: Museo della Vite e del Vino (vine and wine museum)

Scarperia: Museo dei Ferri Taglienti (knife museum); Museo di Vita Artigiana e Contadina (museum of rural and artisan life); Raccolta di Arte Sacra (sacred art collection)

the same route; buses run from Borgo San Lorenzo to the western and northern parts of the Mugello.

Southern Mugello

The Sieve flows into the Arno at the unprepossessing town of **PONTASSIEVE**, which makes its money from the **Rúfina wine district** immediately to the north. From here the N70 clambers over the **Passo della Consuma**, then drops south into the Casentino, towards Poppi (see p.456). The N67 trails the valley through the moderately industrialized area up to Rúfina, then on through **Dicomano**, where it veers off towards Forlì (in Emilia-Romagna), passing through the Alpe di San Benedetto. The main settlement in this part of the Mugello is **San Godenzo**, which boasts an eleventh-century abbey and not a lot else.

Hugging the course of the Sieve beyond Dicomano, the N551 runs on through **VICCHIO**, the birthplace of Fra' Angelico. Unsurprisingly, the village makes the most of the Angelico connection, but the **Museo di Arte Sacra e Religiosità Popolare Beato Angelico** (open Sun: June 15–Sept 15 10am–noon & 3.30–6.30pm; rest of year 10am–noon & 3–6pm; €3) is a context-setting exercise rather than a celebration of the man himself, and doesn't contain anything that's likely to excite greatly, though the array of workaday religious artefacts is very well displayed. The best place to stay in the vicinity of Vicchio is the parkland-girdled, four-star **hotel** *Villa Campestri*, 6km south of the village at Via di Campestri 19–22 (℡055.849.0107, ⓦwww.villacampestri.it; ❼), which has a good restaurant and – in the cellars – Italy's first *oleoteca*, where hotel guests can sample and learn about the region's finest olive oils. There are two good **campsites** in the vicinity: *Vecchio Ponte*, at Via Costoli 16 (℡055.844.8306; June–Sept), and *Residence Park Valdisieve* in Caldeta, midway between Vicchio and Dicomano (℡055.844.256; June–Sept).

Next stop along the main road is another exalted birthplace, **Vespignano**, where **Giotto** was born in around 1266. His career started, so the story goes, when Cimabue happened to pass by the spot where the boy was tending his father's flock; Giotto was drawing a picture of one of the sheep on a stone, and Cimabue was so astonished by the shepherd's proficiency that he immediately took him on as an apprentice. The bridge where the crucial encounter is said to have occurred is a few hundred metres out of Vespignano and is well signposted. The farmhouse in which Giotto was actually born – the **Casa di Giotto** (same hours as Beato Angelico museum; free) – is 1km off to the north; as with the homes of Leonardo and Michelangelo, this has value only as a pilgrimage site.

Borgo San Lorenzo and northern Mugello

With a population of 15,000 or so, **BORGO SAN LORENZO** is the giant of the Mugello towns, with industrial plots and tracts of new housing spreading further with each year – improved rail connections with Florence have given an added boost to the town in recent years. Substantially rebuilt after a massive earthquake in 1919, it has just one major building, the **Pieve di San Lorenzo**, an eleventh-century foundation that was renovated in the sixteenth century but still retains its irregularly hexagonal Romanesque tower. This isn't the most photographed sight in town, though – that honour goes to the ghastly statue of *Fido* in Piazza Dante, a memorable example of monumentalized sentimentality. The **tourist office**, in the Villa Pecori Giraldi, Via P. Togliatti (Tues–Sun 10am–1pm & 3.30–6.30pm; ☎055.845.6230), is the main office for the whole of the Mugello, and has details of plentiful *agriturismi*.

San Piero a Sieve and the Medici villas

The N551 continues up the Sieve from Borgo San Lorenzo to **SAN PIERO A SIEVE**, where it crosses the N65 coming up from Florence. San Piero's Romanesque church, spoiled by an eighteenth-century facade, houses a beautiful terracotta font, possibly by Luca della Robbia; its other main monument is the Medici fortress overlooking the town, built by Buontalenti in 1571. Other than that, San Piero is fairly nondescript, but the Mugello landscape is at its best here, with farmland foregrounding the slopes of tree-crested conical hills, so campers might want to make use of the all-year **campsite**, *Mugello Verde* (☎055.848.511, @www.florencecamping.com), 2km west of the town, at Via Massorondinaio 39.

The Medici were originally from Mugello, and the environs of San Piero contain two rough-hewn villas which encapsulate something of the flavour of the period when the family secured its political ascendancy. Near Novoli, an unsurfaced road runs west from the Via Bologna to the Medici castle of **Trebbio**, whose fortified tower peeps over a cordon of cypresses from the top of its hill. This fourteenth-century castle was converted into a country abode by Michelozzo in 1461 and became a particular favourite with Giovanni delle Bande Nere and his branch of the Medici clan: it was from here that Giovanni's son, Cosimo, rode down to Florence to assume power after the assassination of Alessandro de' Medici. Parts of the estate have now been converted into holiday apartments, while the produce of the Trebbio vineyards and olive groves can be sampled and bought at the castle's shop.

A short distance north, right on the Via Bologna, lies the villa of **Cafaggiolo**, which like Trebbio was a fortress converted for less bellicose use by Michelozzo. When Cosimo il Vecchio set about consolidating the family fortune through land acquisition in their ancestral domain, one of his first ventures was to buy this estate, which comprised the castle and tracts of land for hunting and agriculture. It was at Cafaggiolo that Cosimo's immediate descendants Lorenzo il Magnifico and his brother grew up, and Lorenzo's own children – Piero, Giovanni (Pope Leo X) and Giuliano – were taught here by such luminaries as Ficino, Poliziano and Pico della Mirandola. In those days the house would have had a more robust appearance than it does now: alterations in the nineteenth century did away with the surrounding walls, the moat, the drawbridge and one of its towers. The interior (now home to a cooking school) can be seen only on guided tours (summer Wed & Fri–Sun 2.30–6.30pm, Sat & Sun 10am–12.30pm; winter Sat & Sun 10am–12.30pm & 2.30–6.30pm; €5).

Barberino di Mugello and the Passo della Futa

North of Cafaggiolo the gradient of the road gets pretty savage as it begins the climb to Passo della Futa; a less strenuous loop goes through the main market town of western Mugello, **BARBERINO DI MUGELLO**. In the early fourteenth century this became a Florentine border post, and in later years Michelozzo picked up some work here too, giving the main square its loggia – the **Loggie Medicee**, naturally; the neighbouring Palazzo Pretorio and the Castello dei Cattani are the only other buildings to catch the eye.

Barberino has a good two-star **hotel**, *Il Cavallo*, Viale della Repubblica 7 (℡055.841.8144, ⓦwww.albergocavallo.it; ❹), with a fine **restaurant** attached. Outside Barberino, at Via Santa Lucia 24/a in Monte di Fo, is the well-equipped all-year *Sergente* **campsite** (℡055.842.3018, ⓦwww.campingilsergente.it).

From where the Barberino loop rejoins Via Bologna it's an unrelenting haul up to the **Passo della Futa**, from whose 900-metre vantage all of the Mugello's valleys and ridges are visible. This isn't the highest point on the Mugello's road network – Passo della Raticosa, 13km on, is a few metres higher – but it provides easily the best views.

Bosco ai Frati, Scarperia and beyond

The secluded monastery of **Bosco ai Frati**, reached by taking a left turn off the N503 immediately north of San Piero (it's a rough 4km track), traces its roots back to a community of Greek monks who arrived here in the seventh century. In the early eleventh century the settlement was abandoned, but two centuries later St Francis established his order here. One of the earliest Franciscan saints, Bonaventure, was the prior at Bosco ai Frati; a man of exemplary modesty, he refused to put on the cardinal's attire brought to him by a papal delegation until he'd finished washing up his brothers' pots and pans. The tree where the outfit was hung is still there.

Cosimo il Vecchio sank a lot of money into this monastery, hiring Michelozzo to redesign the complex in the plainest early Renaissance style; in the tiny museum attached to Michelozzo's porticoed **church** (daily 8.30am–7pm) is the most remarkable work of art in the Mugello: a pain-racked *Crucifix*, probably carved by Donatello for the Medici, and certainly donated to the monastery by them.

Beyond the turning for Bosco ai Frati, the N503 continues to **SCARPERIA**, a centre for the cutlery industry. Sitting on a platform of rock above a valley 5km from San Piero, it's essentially a one-street town, laid out by the Florentines after they turned it into their chief military base in the region in 1306. The **Palazzo dei Vicari**, built in the same year along the lines of Florence's Palazzo Vecchio, has a rash of coats of arms on the outside, and extensive frescoes on the inside. None of its churches is remarkable, though one of them bears an unusual dedication, to Our Lady of the Earthquakes. If you're perplexed by crowds around the town, they're on their way to the **motor-racing track** on the eastern outskirts; built in the 1970s, it's best known as Italy's grand prix motorbike circuit.

A small road climbs northwest to the tiny village of **Sant'Agata**, where the Romanesque parish church contains some beautiful inlaid panels from a dismantled twelfth-century pulpit, and a tabernacle by Giovanni della Robbia. The N503 becomes a switchback after this turnoff, swooping through the region known as Mugello's "Little Switzerland" to the hill resort of **Firenzuola**, which was rebuilt after a fierce battle in 1944 and has few blandishments.

Prato

Taking its name from the meadow (*prato*) where the ancient settlement's great market used to be held, **PRATO** has long been a commercial success and is now the second-largest city in Tuscany, after Florence. It's been Italy's chief textile centre since the early Middle Ages, and even though recession has damaged exports, it still produces three-quarters of all the woollen cloth sold from Italy, with some 8000 local companies being involved in the production and marketing of textiles. It might not feature on a list of the most attractive places in the region, but its long-time wealth has left a fair legacy of buildings and art, including an unequalled collection of paintings by **Filippo Lippi**, whose frescoes adorn the beguiling **Duomo**.

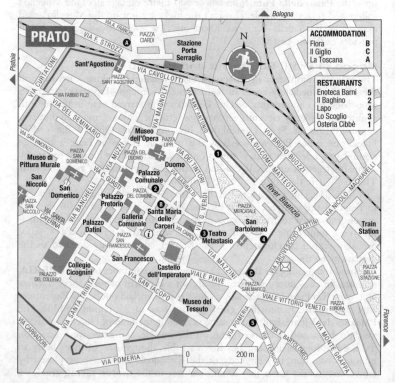

A close Florentine connection goes back to 1350, when the self-governing *comune* of Prato was besieged by its neighbour, which by then was becoming alarmed at the economic threat of Prato's cloth mills. The year after, Florence bought the titles to the town from its Neapolitan rulers, thus sealing their union. Thereafter, political events in the capital were mirrored here, a relationship that was to cost Prato dear after Savonarola's example led the Pratese to join him in rejecting the Medici. Under the direction of Leo X, the imperial army sacked Prato in 1512 as a warning to the rebellious Florentines. Two days of slaughter and pillage ensued, recorded by historian Guicciardini: "Nothing would have escaped the avarice, lust and cruelty of the invaders had not the Cardinal de' Medici placed guards at the main church and saved the honour of the women who had taken refuge there. More than two thousand men died, not fighting … but fleeing or crying for mercy." A more pacific relationship was soon established, and Florence limited its bullying to the imposition of quotas on Prato's factories. Today the balance has shifted: while Prato is fairly self-sufficient, Florence struggles to find some alternative to a service-based economy.

Arrival, information and accommodation

Buses from Florence run direct to Piazza del Duomo; if you're arriving by **train**, it's basically a question of following your nose to the city centre – cross the Ponte della Vittoria over the Bisenzio river, and Viale Vittorio Veneto leads you through the walls at Piazza San Marco. Prato's **tourist office** (Mon–Sat 9am–1.30pm & 2.30–7pm, Sun 10am–1pm; ℡0574.24.112, Ⓦwww.prato.turismo .toscana.it) is opposite the Carceri church in Piazza delle Carceri.

Hotels

Most of Prato's hotels are featureless concrete blocks catering for business visitors, but there's a handful of places in the historic centre offering decent accommodation at good prices.

Flora Via Cairoli 31 ℡0574.33.521, Ⓦwww .hotelflora.info. The 31-room *Flora* occupies a handsome nineteenth-century palazzo very close to the Piazza del Comune. It may not be a contender for any shortlist of hip Tuscan hotels, but this well-run three-star is the pick of central Prato's accommodation. ❺
Il Giglio Piazza San Marco 14 ℡0574.37.049, Ⓦwww.albergoilgiglio.it. This little two-star, tucked against the city walls, has been offering simple and functional rooms for forty years now, and the

styling hasn't changed greatly in the interim. All rooms are en suite and a/c, however, and the prices are low. ❷
La Toscana Piazza Ciardi 3 ℡0574.28.096, Ⓦwww.hoteltoscana.prato.it. Founded back in the nineteenth century, the eighteen-room *Toscana* is today a modest, tidy and bland two-star hotel. High-season doubles are about €10 pricier than at the *Giglio* – otherwise, location and history are pretty well the only things that distinguish them. ❸

The City

The historic centre remains enclosed within its hexagon of grey stone walls, making orientation very straightforward. At the centre of the hexagon lie the two most important squares, **Piazza del Duomo** and **Piazza del Comune**; on the east side, the castle guards the gate at Piazza San Marco, which is a short distance south of the huge market square; on the west side, the main art gallery – the **Museo di Pittura Murale** – is the chief focus.

The Castello area

Walking from the train station, if you turn left at the far side of Piazza San Marco (where the traffic swirls around a large Henry Moore sculpture), you'll

▲ Piazza del Duomo, Prato

pass under the **Cassero**, a fortified corridor built in the middle of the fourteenth century to link the castle to the city walls; the entrance to it is on Viale Piave (daily 10am–1pm & 4–7pm; free). A short distance beyond, in Via Santa Chiara, you'll come to the former Campolmi factory, a huge nineteenth-century textile mill that has been converted into a very impressive home for the **Museo del Tessuto** (Mon & Wed–Fri 10am–6pm, Sat 10am–2pm, Sun 4–7pm; €6, free on Sun; @www.museodeltessuto.it). Tracing the city's literal rise from rags to riches, the museum also displays a collection of more than five thousand fabrics from all over the world, ranging right back to the third century. It's a venue for one-off exhibitions on textile- or fashion-related themes, too.

Five-minutes' walk away stands the city's signature building, the white-walled **Castello dell'Imperatore** (Wed–Mon 9am–1pm & 4–7pm; €2.50, or joint ticket with Museo dell'Opera del Duomo & Museo di Pittura Murale €6.50), built in the 1230s for Emperor Frederick II as a base for his representative in the city and as a way-station for imperial progresses between Germany and his domains in southern Italy and Sicily. The castle is heavily restored and empty except for the rooms used for temporary exhibitions, but you can wander around the ramparts for views over the old city and its industrial suburbs.

Round the back is Prato's major Renaissance monument, Giuliano da Sangallo's church of **Santa Maria delle Carceri** (daily 7am–noon & 4–7pm), built to honour a miraculous talking image of the Virgin that was painted on the walls of the gaol here – hence the name "Mary of the Prisons". With its perfect proportions and uncluttered lines, the church is a rather severe demonstration of the correctness of the Brunelleschian style, though the exterior makes a decorative gesture towards the Romanesque with its half-completed bands of green and white marble. The interior – lightened by Andrea della Robbia's tondi of the Evangelists and ceramic frieze – is designed so that on the exact anniversary of the moment at which the Virgin spoke (3.18pm on July 15) a beam of light shines through the top of the cupola and strikes the centre of the altar.

Twin-coloured marble cladding also features on the facade of the thirteenth-century church of **San Francesco** (daily 8am–noon & 4–7pm), which presents

The Teatro Metastasio and Centro Pecci

Prato can boast one of Italy's most famous theatres and one of its most innovative centres for the visual arts. The magnificent **Teatro Metastasio**, at Via Cairoli 59 (☎0574.608.501, ⊛www.metastasio.net), began life in 1830 as a privately owned venture, but in the 1930s the city took it over, and since a major overhaul in the 1960s it's developed into a top-flight venue for concerts (both classical and jazz) and theatre productions. Art exhibitions and other cultural events are organized year-round by the **Centro per l'Arte Contemporanea L. Pecci** (Wed–Mon 10am–7pm; €5; ⊛www .centropecci.it), 2km southeast of the centre in Viale della Repubblica (reached by bus from Viale Pieve, close to the Castello). It has a good collection of postwar art, featuring such names as Kapoor, LeWitt, Pistoletto and Kounellis, and its one-off shows are usually exciting.

its back to the far side of the square. Inside are a couple of fine monuments: on the left wall of the single aisle you'll find Bernardo Rossellino's worn-down tomb of Gemignano Inghirami, and set into the floor near the high altar is the slab of Francesco di Marco Datini, Prato's most celebrated citizen. The subject of Iris Origo's classic study, *The Merchant of Prato*, Datini became one of Europe's richest men through his dealings in the cloth trade, and played a crucial role in the rationalization of accounting methods: on his death, his offices were found to contain tens of thousands of scrupulously kept ledgers, all inscribed "To God and profit". Off the cloister, the Cappella Migliatori has lovely frescoes of *The Lives of St Anthony Abbot and St Matthew* and *The Crucifixion*, painted in the 1390s by Niccolò di Pietro Gerini.

Datini's house, **Palazzo Datini** (Mon–Sat 9am–12.30pm; free), is a couple of minutes from the church, on the junction of Via Rinascelda and Via Ser Lapo Mazzei. Built in the 1390s, this is now home to the city archives and the Ceppo, a charity established by Datini himself. The barely legible fresco sketches on the facade – which were heavily retouched in 1910 – show scenes from his life; the ground floor of the interior is also frescoed, mostly with fleur-de-lys ceilings and engagingly cack-handed hunting scenes, though there's a more than competent *St Christopher* at the foot of the stairs, another work by Niccolò di Pietro Gerini.

Piazza del Comune and Piazza del Duomo

A short distance north of here, Datini is commemorated with a statue and bronze reliefs at the centre of the trim little **Piazza del Comune**. Inevitably, he crops up again amongst the myriad portraits of local worthies in the **Quadreria Palazzo Comunale** (free by appointment – call ☎0574.616.220). Across from the Palazzo sits the huge medieval **Palazzo Pretorio**, whose museum, the **Museo Civico**, has been undergoing restoration for many years; in the meantime, its contents have been transferred to the Museo di Pittura Murale (see p.206).

The wide and lively Piazza del Duomo, a couple of blocks further in, forms an effective space for the Pisan-Romanesque facade of the **Duomo** (Mon–Sat 7.30am–7pm, Sun 7.30am–noon & 3–7pm), distinguished by another Andrea della Robbia terracotta over the portal and by Donatello's and Michelozzo's beautiful **Pulpit of the Sacred Girdle**. This unique addition was constructed for the ceremonial display of the girdle of the Madonna, a garment allegedly dropped into the hands of the ever-incredulous apostle Thomas at her Assumption. The girdle (or *Sacro Cingolo*) was supposedly bequeathed by Thomas to a priest, one of whose descendants married a crusader from Prato, who in turn brought it back to his home town in 1141. Replicas have replaced the Donatello reliefs of gambolling children, the originals now being housed in the cathedral museum. The girdle itself is displayed five times a year: on Easter Sunday, May 1, August 15, September 8 and Christmas Day.

The story is detailed in the chapel immediately left of the main entrance in Agnolo Gaddi's fresco cycle of *The Legend of the Holy Girdle* (1392–95) – though sadly it's all but invisible behind the grating, as is the Madonna and Child carved by Giovanni Pisano in 1317. Close by, in the left aisle, is another fine piece of stonework, a chalice-shaped pulpit by Antonio Rossellino and Mino da Fiesole.

Filippo Lippi's famous frescoes, around the high altar, were completed over a period of fourteen years (1452–66) and depict the lives of John the Baptist and St Stephen. These are marvellously sensuous paintings in which even the Baptist's wilderness looks quite enticing, a whisked-up landscape like a confectioner's fantasy. Lippi's characteristic tenderness is much in evidence too, notably in the attendants kissing the feet of the dead St Stephen, and in the scene depicting John taking his leave of his parents. High drama, however, was not his forte: in the *Feast of Herod* the decapitation seems like a regrettable incident that needn't ruin the party. There's a scandalous story to the creation of these pictures: during the period of their creation, Lippi – himself a friar, at least in name – became so besotted with a young nun named Lucrezia Buti that he abducted her as she was preparing to attend the ceremony of the girdle. Later to become the mother of Filippino Lippi, Lucrezia is said to have been the model for the dancing Salome. Her lover is also believed to have depicted himself among the superb gallery of portraits around the body of St Stephen: it's most likely that he's the third mourner from the right.

After several years of restoration, the Lippi cycle is now once again on show (Mon–Sat 10am–5pm, Sun 3–5pm; €3). Your ticket also gives you access to the scenes from the lives of the Virgin and St Stephen in the chapel to the right of the high altar. Some believe – though studies of the underpainting have cast doubt on the attribution – that these were begun by Paolo Uccello in 1435, a year before he was called away to Florence to paint the Hawkwood monument in the Duomo, having finished just the vault and the lunettes of *The Birth of the Virgin*, *The Birth of St Stephen* and *The Stoning of St Stephen*; the lower part of the chapel was painted by Andrea di Giusto.

Housed alongside the Duomo, around the cloister of the bishop's palace, the **Museo dell'Opera del Duomo** (Mon & Wed–Sat 9.30am–12.30pm & 3.30–6.30pm, Sun 9.30am–12.30pm; €4, or joint ticket with Castello and Museo di Pittura Murale €6.50) contains the Donatello panels from the great pulpit; they are badly cracked and stained by exhaust fumes but their sculpted putti make a sprightly contrast with the lumbering little lads on Maso di Bartolomeo's tiny silver Reliquary for the Sacred Girdle, the museum's other main treasure. Also on show is Filippino Lippi's plucky *St Lucy*, unperturbed by the gigantic sword lodged in her neck, and the magnificent painting that Filippo Lippi produced to demonstrate his suitability for the fresco commission, *The Death of Jerome*. A doorway on the far side of the cloister opens into the Duomo's frescoed crypt; beside the altar is the head of one of the city's main wells, which – as the inscription records – was choked with corpses by the invaders of 1512.

Museo di Pittura Murale

A five-minute walk west of the Duomo, in the ex-monastery adjoining the mainly fourteenth-century church of San Domenico, the **Museo di Pittura Murale**

(Wed–Mon 9am–1pm, Fri & Sat also 3–6pm; €4, or joint ticket with Museo dell'Opera del Duomo and Castello €6.50) currently houses one of the town's star attractions – Filippo Lippi's *Madonna del Ceppo*. The painting contains portraits of the five men who financed the picture; Datini coughed up more than the other four, so he's the one depicted large-scale. Among the other Lippi pieces on show is a tender *Nativity with Sts George and Vincent Ferrer*: the Madonna and Christ were probably modelled on Lucrezia and Filippino. There are works by Filippino here as well, plus – among a variety of fourteenth-century altarpieces – a predella by Bernardo Daddi narrating the story of the Girdle of the Madonna. The rest of the display features a hotchpotch of minor frescoes, culled mostly from churches in and around Prato.

Eating and drinking

Unpretentious Prato has several good and inexpensive **restaurants**, most of which are on or near the market square. While you're in town, you might want to sample the Prato speciality, the *biscotto di Prato*, a very hard yellow biscuit, made a touch less resistant by dipping in wine or coffee. The best outlet for these and other pastries is *Antonio Mattei*, which has been in existence at Via Ricasoli 22 (close to Piazza San Francesco) since 1858.

Enoteca Barni Via Ferrucci 22 ☎0574.607.845. An excellent family-run restaurant/wine bar, where you'll spend in the region of €40–50 a head. Closed lunch Sat & Sun.

Il Baghino Via dell'Accademia 9 ☎0574.27.920. A longstanding local favourite, serving Prato speci-alities in a traditional atmosphere. Closed Sun eve & Mon lunch.

Lapo Piazza Mercatale 141 ☎0574.23.745. One of two very good trattorie on the city's largest square. Closed Sun.

Lo Scoglio Via Verdi 42 ☎0574.22.760 The best pizza in Prato – and inexpensive fish dishes too. Closed Mon.

Osteria Cibbè Piazza Mercatale 49 ☎0574.60.759. Like *Lapo* at the opposite end of the piazza, this is a good, no-nonsense trattoria, catering predominantly for locals. Closed Sun.

Pistoia

The provincial capital of **PISTOIA** is one of the least visited cities in Tuscany, an unjustified neglect for this quiet, well-preserved medieval settlement at the base of the Apennines. Just 35 minutes or so by train from Florence (about the same by bus), it is an easy and enjoyable day-trip – and also forms an attractive approach to Lucca and Pisa, with both of which it has strong architectural links. In terms of art attractions, its appeal lies in a sequence of Romanesque churches and medieval sculptures and one of the masterpieces of the della Robbia workshop.

The town's **Roman** forerunner, Pistoria, was where Catiline and his fellow conspirators against the republic were finally run to ground; the town went on to earn itself a reputation as a lair of malcontents. It was a Ghibelline city until its conquest by the Guelph city of Florence in 1254, whereupon it allegedly brought about the **division** of the Guelphs into the Black and White factions. According to the folkloric version, one Pistoiese child injured another while playing with a sword; the miscreant's father sent him to apologize, whereupon the father of the injured party chopped the offender's hand off, telling him, "Iron, not words, is the remedy for sword wounds." The city promptly polarized into the Neri and the Bianchi camps (taking the names from

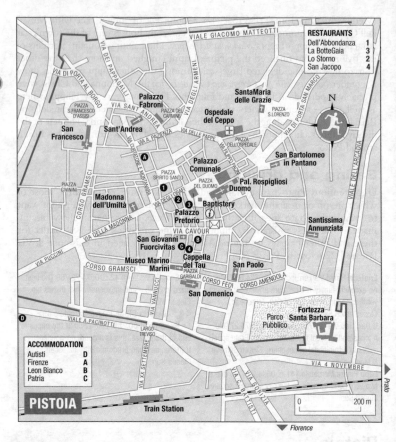

RESTAURANTS
Dell'Abbondanza	1
La BotteGaia	3
Lo Storno	2
San Jacopo	4

ACCOMMODATION
Autisti	D
Firenze	A
Leon Bianco	B C
Patria	C

PISTOIA

Train Station

0   200 m

▼ Florence

ancestors of the two parties), and by some osmotic process these battle names were taken up in Florence. Such was Pistoia's reputation for mayhem, Dante found it entirely appropriate that this should have been the home of Vanni Fucci, a thuggish factional leader whose exploits included stealing the silver from the cathedral; he's encountered in the *Inferno*, enmeshed in a knot of snakes and cursing God.

Except for a brief spell at the start of the fourteenth century, when Castruccio Castracani held the city for Lucca, Pistoia remained a **Florentine** fief, yet for centuries the mythology of murderous Pistoia endured, and Michelangelo spoke for many when he referred to the Pistoiese as the "enemies of heaven". It's fitting that, according to one school of thought, the word **pistol** should be derived from this violent town; meaning "from Pistoia", a *pistole* was originally a dagger, but the name was transferred to the first firearms made here in the sixteenth century. These days, Pistoia maintains its industrial tradition with a large rail plant, but is better known for the acres of garden nurseries on the slopes around.

The liveliest time to be in Pistoia is July, for the **Luglio Pistoiese**, a month-long programme of concerts and events (including the Pistoia Blues music festival featuring major international jazz and blues artists), and culminating in the Giostra dell'Orso (see box, p.212).

Arrival, information and accommodation

The **train station** and adjacent **bus stops** are just a couple of minutes' walk south of the historic centre: Viale XX Settembre points the way through the city walls. Pistoia's central **tourist office** is at Piazza del Duomo 4 (Mon–Sat 9am–1pm & 3–6pm, Sun 10am–1pm & 3–6pm; ☎0573.21.622, ⊛www .comune.pistoia.it).

As with Prato, the city's low tourist profile means a shortage of **accommodation**, but there are three decent options in the city centre, plus another on the fringes. The only time of year when hotel rooms might be in short supply is during the July festival (see box, p.212).

Hotels

Autisti Viale Pacinotti 43 ☎0573.21.771. This clean and friendly place is Pistoia's only one-star. The location isn't great (it's out on the southern stretch of the city's ring-road), but a double room is some €40 cheaper than any other place in Pistoia. ❶

Firenze Via Curtatone e Montanara 42 ☎0573.231.141, ⊛www.hotel-firenze.it. The twenty-room *Firenze* is Pistoia's only two-star, and it offers good value for money – all bedrooms have a/c and en-suite bathroom, and are brightly turned-out. ❸

Leon Bianco Via Panciatichi 2 ☎0573.26.675, ⊛www.hotelleonbianco.it. The thirty-room *Leon Bianco* is a long-established and inexpensive three-star, right in the heart of the city. It would benefit from a dash of renovation, but for every guest who finds it dowdy, another might find it homely. ❹

Patria Via Crispi 6–8 ☎0573.25.187, ⊛www .patriahotel.com. Like the nearby and very similar *Leon Bianco*, the chief selling points of the three-star *Patria* are its centrality and low prices. ❹

The City

The interesting part of the city begins one block north of Largo Treviso, at the junction with the centre's widest avenues, Corso Gramsci and Corso Fedi. Just follow your nose and you'll come to **Piazza del Duomo**, where the main monuments and museums are concentrated; the other main sights are just a few minutes' walk away – **San Giovanni Fuorcivitas** to the south, the **Ospedale del Ceppo** and **Sant'Andrea** to the north, and **San Bartolomeo** to the east.

Around Piazza Garibaldi

Turn right onto Corso Fedi for Piazza Garibaldi, where you'll find the thirteenth-century church of **San Domenico** (daily 7.30am–noon & 4.30–6pm, Sun closes 8pm), rebuilt in the 1970s after terrible damage during the war. Scraps of medieval frescoes remain inside, but the most arresting feature is the Rossellino brothers' tomb of the teacher Filippo Lazzari, on the right near the door. In the cloister (entered from the aisle) there are remnants of a fresco of *The Journey of the Magi* by Benozzo Gozzoli, who died of the plague in Pistoia and is buried here.

Opposite San Domenico, the **Cappella del Tau** (Mon–Sat 9am–1pm; free), or Sant'Antonio Abate, preserves a chaos of mainly fourteenth-century frescoes

Pistoia's museums

Entry to each of Pistoia's **museums** is €3.50, except for the Palazzo Fabroni, which costs €6. For €6.50 you can buy a joint ticket for the Museo Marini and the museums of the Palazzo Comunale (which contains a couple of collections that are counted as one) and Palazzo Rospigliosi (three collections counted as one). Also available is an €8 ticket that covers Palazzo Fabroni plus any two museums, and a €10 ticket for all three plus the Fabroni.

depicting the Creation (in the vault), the life of St Anthony Abbot, and the story of the sacred girdle (see p.205). Next door, in the Palazzo del Tau, is the **Museo Marino Marini** (Mon–Sat: April–Sept 10am–6pm; Oct–March 10am–5pm; €3.50, or joint ticket), showing a selection of work by Pistoia's most famous modern son. Marini found an early influence in the realism of Etruscan sarcophagi, expressed in the sculptures of horses and riders that he churned out throughout his life; in the 1940s he diversified into portraiture – subjects here include Thomas Mann, Henry Miller and Marc Chagall.

On the same side of the Cappella del Tau, a couple of minutes' walk east, looms the late thirteenth-century facade of **San Paolo**; the front of greenish stone with dark green and white inlays is topped by a statue of St James, possibly by Orcagna.

San Giovanni Fuorcivitas and Madonna dell'Umiltà

All streets north from Piazza Garibaldi link with Via Cavour, now the main street of the city's inner core but once the settlement's outer limit – as the name of the majestic **San Giovanni Fuorcivitas** (Saint John Outside the Walls) proclaims. The church (daily 7.30am–noon & 5–6.30pm) was founded in the eighth century, but rebuilt between the twelfth and fourteenth centuries, when it received the dazzling green-and-white flank that serves as its **facade**. Rather than being the focal point of the wall, the doorway is just a brief interruption in the infinitely repeatable pattern of the triple arcade and bands of contrasting marble, a colour scheme echoed in the oratory across the alleyway (now a shop). The **interior** is just as remarkable, as this is one of three Pistoia churches distinguished by pulpits that rank among the finest examples of the sophistication of Tuscan sculpture in the thirteenth century. The **pulpit** was carved in 1270 by a pupil of Nicola Pisano, whose son, Giovanni, executed the cardinal and theological virtues on the holy water stoup. On the opposite side of the church is a life-size terracotta *Visitation*, probably by Luca della Robbia.

From here, a turn up Via Roma is the quickest way into the central square, but if you want to make sure you don't miss any of Pistoia's architectural sights, follow the westward arc of Via Cavour into Via Buozzi until you come to **Madonna dell'Umiltà** (daily 7.45am–noon & 4–7pm). This handsome colossus was designed by a pupil of Bramante and finished off by Vasari with a dome so heavy that the walls had to be reinforced to prevent the church from collapsing.

Piazza del Duomo

The direct path from Via Cavour to Piazza del Duomo crosses the market square, Piazza della Sala. A marginally more long-winded alternative is to walk through the minuscule Piazza San Leone, a few blocks east; this was the centre of the ancient Lombard settlement, and its stocky tower was later the bolt-hole of Vanni Fucci.

The medieval complex of the **Piazza del Duomo** is a superb and slightly eccentric ensemble, reversing the normal priorities of the Italian central square: the ornate baptistery lurks in a recess off one corner and the Duomo faces it, turning its sparsely adorned side to the open space and leaving the huge campanile and monolithic civic buildings to take the limelight. There's something odd about the expanse of the piazza too, as if it were conceived for a town considerably larger than present-day Pistoia. Once a year, though, the square is packed to capacity for the **Giostra dell'Orso**, Pistoia's answer to the medieval shenanigans of Siena's Palio.

The Duomo

If you've come from Pisa or Lucca, the style of Pistoia's **Duomo**, the Cattedrale di San Zeno (daily 8am–12.30pm & 3.30–7pm), will be immediately familiar, with its tiered arcades and distinctive Pisan-Romanesque decoration of striped black and white marble. Set into this soberly refined front is a tunnel-vault portico of bright terracotta tiles by Andrea della Robbia, creator also of the *Madonna and Child* above the door.

The **interior** has an outstanding array of sculptural pieces, one of which is part of the entrance wall – a marvellous font designed by Benedetto da Maiano, showing incidents from the life of the Baptist. Close by, on the wall of the right aisle, is the monument to Dante's friend, the diplomat, teacher and poet Cino da Pistoia; it is said that Boccaccio is one of the pupils to whom he's shown lecturing in the bottom panel.

Just beyond this monument is the **Cappella di San Jacopo** (€2), now incorporated into the cathedral museum, which boasts one of the richest pieces of silverwork to be seen in Italy, the **Altarpiece of St James**. Weighing almost a ton and populated with 628 figures, it was begun in 1287 and completed in the fifteenth century, when Brunelleschi cast the two half-figures of prophets on the left-hand side. The length of time taken on the work is clear if you compare the scenes on the front with the bolder figures in the scenes from the life of St James on the left-hand flank, where an extra suppleness and vitality is evident. The artist responsible for these latter panels was a certain Leonardo di Ser Giovanni, who immediately after completing them was given the commission to begin another remarkable piece of silverwork – the altarpiece now in Florence's Museo dell'Opera del Duomo.

In the chapel to the left of the high altar is Antonio Rossellino's bust of Bishop Donato de' Medici, and the so-called *Madonna di Piazza*, begun by Verrocchio and finished by Lorenzo di Credi; Verrocchio, with his workshop, was also responsible for the flurried tomb of Cardinal Forteguerri, in the left aisle by the door.

The Duomo's adjacent **Campanile** was originally a Lombard watchtower, then was spruced up with Romanesque arcades in the twelfth century and a Gothic turret in the sixteenth; the swallowtail crenellations near the summit give away the town's old Ghibelline loyalties. On Saturdays and Sundays the campanile is often open for guided tours, usually at 11am, noon, 4pm and 5pm; the tourist office will have the latest details.

Around Piazza del Duomo

Similarly you have to book at the tourist office in order to see inside the partly clad Palazzo dei Vescovi, now home of the small **Museo di San Zeno** (guided tours Tues, Thurs & Fri at 8.30am, 10am, 11.30am & 3.30pm, plus Fri at 2.30pm & 4.45pm; €3.60), where the chief exhibit is Ghiberti's reliquary of St James. The basement has an even more modest archeological collection, with relics from the Roman settlement.

Opposite is the dapper Gothic **Baptistery** (Tues–Sun 10am–6pm), designed by Giovanni Pisano and completed in the mid-fourteenth century by Cellino di Nese, creator of the Duomo's monument to Cino da Pistoia. Commercial art shows sometimes fill the space around the font.

Though its interior is closed to the public, you can take a look at the courtyard of the **Palazzo del Podestà** (or Palazzo Pretorio), the law-court building to the side of the baptistery. From the stone benches half-sheltered by the portico the Pistoian judges used to pronounce sentences notorious for their severity; a grimly humorous speciality was to sentence the guilty to be elevated to the ranks of the nobility – thus depriving them of any civic rights under the town's republican constitution.

On the far side of the square, the flaking pale limestone facade of the **Palazzo Comunale** bears a small basalt head that may be a portrait of the Moorish king of Mallorca whom the Pistoiese defeated in the twelfth century; local folklore prefers to interpret it as the image of a man who betrayed the city to the army of Castruccio Castracani in 1315, which is about the time the head was mounted here (though in all likelihood it went up several years before the city fell). The building contains the **Museo Civico** (April–Sept Tues & Thurs–Sat 10am–6pm, Wed 4–7pm, Sun 11am–6pm; Oct–March Tues & Thurs–Sat 10am–5pm, Wed 3–6pm, Sun 11am–5pm; €3.50, or joint ticket), where the customary welter of run-of-the-mill medieval and Renaissance pieces is counterweighted by an impressive showing of Baroque hyperactivity – including a couple of hideous battle scenes by the evidently disturbed Ciccio Napoletano. Attached to the museum is a display devoted to Pistoia-born architect **Giovanni Michelucci**, featuring models and photographs of his major buildings, and some 900 of his drawings.

The Palazzo Rospigliosi, in Ripa del Sale (down the right-hand side of the Palazzo Comunale), houses the combined **Museo Diocesano**, **Museo Rospigliosi** and **Museo del Ricamo** (Tues–Sat 10am–1pm & 3–6pm, plus same hours on second Sun of month; €3.50, or joint ticket), where much of the space is occupied by chalices, censers, crosses, miscellaneous ecclesiastical accoutrements, mediocre paintings and various pieces of furniture, many of them bequeathed by Pope Clement IX, another illustrious native of Pistoia, who occupied the papal throne from 1667 to 1669. The last museum of the trio is a two-room showcase for some remarkably elaborate embroidery, a skill for which Pistoia's artisans were long renowned.

The Giostra dell'Orso

The earliest forerunner of the **Giostra dell'Orso** was a peculiar ritual mentioned in a chronicle of 1300. On March 10 of that year, the feast day of Santa Francesca Romana, a dozen knights fought a ceremonial battle against a bear dressed in the town's coat of arms. The precise form of this joust changed many times over the following centuries but some version of it was fought every year until 1666, when it seems suddenly to have been abandoned. In 1947 it was revived in more humane form and now takes place on July 25, feast of the city's patron, St James. It forms the centrepiece of the festival season known as the *Luglio Pistoiese* (Pistoia July).

The fun begins with a procession of around three hundred standard-bearers, trumpeters, knights, halberdiers and assorted costumed extras from the Porta Lucchese to the Piazza del Duomo. These characters represent the villages around Pistoia, the city's crafts and trades, and the four districts of the historic centre. Each of these four districts is represented in the joust by three knights, their regalia bearing the heraldic emblems of the Lion, the Stag, the Griffon and the Dragon. Having led the procession into the arena laid out on the piazza, the knights are separated into pairs, who then ride against each other around the track, scoring points by hitting the two highly stylized "bears" set on bales on opposite sides of the circuit. Points are awarded according to which parts of the target are hit with the lance, and at the end of the day two prizes are awarded – to the highest-scoring district and the highest-scoring knight.

The *giostra* is always a sell-out; to be sure of tickets, contact the tourist office at least a month in advance (℡0573.21.622; ℗www.giostradellorso.it).

▲ All dressed up for the Giostra dell'Orso

The northern quarters

At the back of the Palazzo Comunale, Via Pacini is the obvious route to take to explore the northern part of the city. Across this road, on Piazza San Bartolomeo, is the **Abbazia di San Bartolomeo in Pantano** (St Bartholomew in the Swamp), named after the marshy ground on which it was raised in the eighth century. The semi-complete façade is as appealing as any of the city's more polished fronts, and inside (daily 8.30am–noon & 4–6pm) there's the earliest of Pistoia's trio of remarkable pulpits. Executed in 1250 by Guido da Como, and reconstructed from its dismantled parts, it's far less sophisticated than the other two, comprising a rectangular box whose principal scenes are filled with figures arrayed in level ranks like a crowd in a stadium.

The most photographed feature of the Pistoia townscape is not a church but a hospital in a square at the end of Via Pacini – the **Ospedale del Ceppo**, which takes its name from the hollowed-out tree stump (*ceppo*) in which alms were traditionally collected. Established in the thirteenth century, it was embellished in the fifteenth with a portico like the one Brunelleschi designed for the Innocenti in Florence. Emblazoned along its length is the feature that makes it famous, Giovanni della Robbia's painted terracotta frieze of the *Theological Virtues* and the *Seven Works of Mercy*. Completed in the early sixteenth century, it is a startlingly colourful panoply of Renaissance types and costume: pilgrims, prisoners, the sick, the dead.

A couple of minutes' walk over to the west, at Via Sant'Andrea 18, stands **Palazzo Fabroni** (Mon–Sat noon–6pm, Sun 2–6pm; €6, or joint ticket), a recently opened venue for one-off exhibitions which also houses a permanent collection of modern art, based on work from the Museo Civico's collection and augmented with pieces bought from or donated by various Italian artists; it's a moderately engaging assembly, but the special events are generally of greater interest. The street takes its name from the twelfth-century church of **Sant'Andrea** (daily 8am–12.30pm & 3–6.30pm), which has a typically Pisan façade with a pair of Romanesque lions and a panel of *The Journey of the Magi* stuck onto it. The murky and corridor-slim aisle contains the third and greatest of the pulpits; carved in 1297 by Giovanni Pisano, it is based on his father's design for the Pisa baptistery pulpit and only marginally less elaborate than his own slightly later work in Pisa cathedral. It shows scenes from the life of Christ and the Last Judgement, the figures carved in such deep relief that they seem to be surging out of a limitless depth. Giovanni was the first to appreciate the glory of his achievement; Nicola Pisano had boasted of being the greatest living sculptor, and Giovanni's inscription brags that he has now surpassed his father. The church also has a second piece by Giovanni – the Crucifix mounted on the wall of the right aisle.

The plainest of the city's churches, the Franciscans' **San Francesco al Prato** (daily 7.30am–noon & 4–6.30pm), is a little further to the west, on the edge of one of the main bus terminals. Tattered fourteenth-century frescoes are preserved in the single nave, and some healthier specimens adorn the chapels at the east end, where there's a fine *Triumph of Augustine* in the chapel to the left of the high altar. To the side of the church there's an unusual memorial to Aldo Moro, the Italian prime minister killed by the Red Brigades on May 7, 1978; the bronze plaques are imprinted with the newspaper headlines from the day his body was found.

Fattoria di Celle

Some 4km east of Pistoia at Santomato, the **Fattoria di Celle** holds a remarkable private art collection, established in 1982 to give Italy an international forum for contemporary art comparable to such centres as the Kröller-Müller in the Netherlands. Everything here, in the rooms and park of the Villa Celle, could be described as environmental art: the large-scale outdoor pieces are conceived as interactions with the natural world, while the smaller installations inside take their cue from the enclosing space of the rooms.

Artists from all over Europe and the United States have contributed to the **sculpture park**, devising a variety of responses to its woodlands and grassy slopes, and to the wider cultural environment of Tuscany. A labyrinth of polished green and white marble by Robert Morris, for example, recalls the Romanesque churches of the region, and is so perfectly placed on the gradient of the hill that it seems to be a single mass of stone until you come to the entrance. In hi-tech contrast, Dennis Oppenheim's massive contraption of steel towers, immovable pulleys and functionless wires looks like a visual pun on the ski-lifts of the winter resorts north of Pistoia. Most of the installations date from the inaugural year, but new pieces are being commissioned all the time, maintaining the Fattoria di Celle's status as one of the most vital art centres in the country.

The centre is open for guided tours only (May–Sept Mon–Fri) and visitors must first write for an appointment, to Fattoria di Celle, 51030 Santomato di Pistoia (ⓔ goricoll@tin.it; ⓕ 0573.479.486).

Eating and drinking

There are several excellent **places to eat** in the centre of Pistoia, with four of the top recommendations to be found very close to Piazza del Duomo.

Dell'Abbondanza Via Dell'Abbondanza 10 ⓣ 0573.368.037. A superb and homely trattoria, with main courses around €15. The menu is classic Tuscan, and features quite a few offal-based dishes. Closed all Wed & Thurs lunch.
La BotteGaia Via del Lastrone 4 ⓣ 0573.365.602. A good-value *osteria* (around €30 a head), very

close to Piazza della Sala, with an enticing *menù degustazione*, main courses from €10 and a terrific wine list. Closed Sun lunch & Mon.
Lo Storno Via del Lastrone 8 ⓣ 0573.26.193. This welcoming and busy *osteria* serves robust local dishes at similar prices to *La BotteGaia*. Closed Sun.

San Jacopo Via Crispi 15 ☎ 0573.27.786. The style of *San Jacopo* is a bit more staid than the places listed above, but the food is inexpensive and of consistently good quality. Closed Sun eve & all Mon.

Montecatini and Monsummano

Known as the **Valdinievole** (Valley of Mists), the area to the west of Pistoia is a region of subterranean streams and springs that now harbours one of Italy's main concentrations of **spa towns**. As with the German spas, such resorts as a rule don't have the same aura of social exclusivity as they do in Britain, but the two big centres of the Valdinievole, **Montecatini Terme** and **Monsummano Terme**, are nonetheless unlikely to tempt you to linger overnight, though you might want to stop for a couple of hours just to sample the peculiar pseudo-*belle époque* ambience. As long as you're not passing through some time between November and Easter, that is, because in winter these places are comatose. Florence-to-Viareggio trains stop at Montecatini, but Monsummano is only really worth a call if you're driving.

Montecatini Terme

No spa in Italy has a glossier reputation than **MONTECATINI TERME**, as can be gauged from the fact that the likes of Gucci and Gianfranco Ferre find it profitable to maintain outlets here – and it was in Montecatini that Fellini filmed the spa scenes in *8½*. A leafy grid of indistinguishable apartment blocks and villas, where it seems to be eternally siesta time, surround the central **Parco delle Terme**, where each of the nine sulphate springs is encased in its own separate building. Fronting the piazza at the edge of the park is the pompous **Terme Leopoldine**, a shrine to the healing properties of mud baths. North of this is the **Tettuccio**, discovered in the fourteenth century but not exploited to the full until Grand Duke Leopoldo I gave it the works in the eighteenth. Inside, Art Nouveau paintings and ceramics create a suitably sybaritic environment in which to compose your letters in the spa café or imbibe the acrid water. Across the way, the Palladian home of the **Regina** spring suggests more astringent regimes, while at the back of the park, the mock-medieval **Torretta** embodies the straightforwardly escapist element of all spa resorts. All these spas are open from May to October; there's one establishment, the hybrid Neo-Renaissance-Modernist **Excelsior**, that's open all year.

The non-thermal delights of Montecatini can all be sampled by following Viale Diaz, which curves round the north side of the park. Here, across the road from the Regina spa, you'll find the **Accademia d'Arte** (Mon–Sat 3–6pm; free), a mishmash of gifts from illustrious guests such as Verdi, who composed *Otello* while staying in Montecatini, refining the score on the piano that's kept here. Ten-minutes' walk beyond is the relatively unkempt verdure of **Le Panteraie**, a wooded park with a swimming pool and deer reserve.

Halfway between the gallery and the woods is the only inexpensive way of having fun in Montecatini, the **funicular** to Montecatini Alto, a few hundred metres above the spa (April–Oct daily every 30min); if you drive, it's a five-kilometre haul. The original Montecatini settlement here offers excellent views, especially of Monsummano, and in summer the tiny Piazza Giusti becomes a pleasant outdoor extension of its cafés and *pizzerias*. If you want to get out of the sun for a while, there's the stalactite-heavy **Grotta Maona** (April–Oct daily

9am–noon & 2–6pm; €5), a couple of kilometres below Montecatini Alto; it's the only cave in Italy that contains two separate springs.

The **tourist office**, at Viale Verdi 66 (Mon–Sat 9am–12.30pm & 3–6pm; plus Sun 9am–noon in summer; ☎0572.772.244, ⦿www.termemontecatini.it), has full details of Montecatini's plentiful **accommodation** options, predominantly top-bracket, but with plenty of one-star hotels too. The office also has details of the treatments at offer at the various spas.

Monsummano Terme

Montecatini's sister spa, **MONSUMMANO TERME**, a few kilometres southeast, has its own speciality: the steam cave. The family of the poet Giuseppe Giusti – who was born here in 1809 – set the business in motion when they discovered a flooded cave filled with mineral-saturated steam. Divided into chambers tagged Inferno, Purgatorio and Paradiso, the **Grotta Giusti** (⦿www .grottagiustispa.com), on the eastern outskirts, is still the town's big draw – half luxury hotel, half medical centre. Competition is provided by the artificial **Grotta Parlanti** to the north, whose vapours are allegedly no less efficacious. The old town of **Monsummano Alto**, 3km from the centre up a relentlessly steep and narrow road, is now little more than a twelfth-century church and a few very ruined castle ruins; the panorama is spectacular, though.

Empoli and around

The **N67**, tracking the Arno west of Florence, is as dispiriting as the road that follows the river to the east. Busy and slow, it's strung with drab towns, industrial sites, megastores and warehouses, and – apart from a handful of attractions in **Empoli** – is only worth bothering with for the diversions to be found off it. The most popular of these, by far, are to be found in **Vinci**, birthplace of Leonardo, but the diminutive hill-town of **San Miniato** is a more substantial attraction.

Empoli

The manufacturing town of **EMPOLI**, purveyor of glass and raincoats to the nation, is a major junction of road and rail routes between Florence, Pisa, the coast and Siena, and thus might well be a place you'll find yourself passing through.

If you have some spare time for a quick look around, head for the central **Piazza Farinata degli Uberti**, named after the commander of the Ghibelline army of Siena which defeated the Florentine Guelphs at Montaperti in 1260; he's revered not for his military prowess, but for his advocacy at the "parliament of Empoli", when he dissuaded his followers from wrecking Florence. The green and white **Collegiata**, on the square, might have been founded as far back as the fifth century; its lower portion is the most westerly example of Florentine Romanesque architecture, the top a nineteenth-century imitation, reconstructed after bomb damage in World War II.

Adjacent is the **Museo Collegiata**, entered from Piazzetta della Propositora (Tues–Sun 9am–noon & 4–7pm; €3, or joint ticket with the Museo Leonardiano in Vinci and the ceramics museum in nearby Montelupo €6). Highlights of the collection of sculpture and painting are a couple of triptychs by Lorenzo Monaco, a small *Maestà* attributed to Filippo Lippi, a superb

Masolino *Pietà*, sculptures by Bernardo Rossellino and Mino da Fiesole, and Lorenzo di Bicci's *St Nicholas of Tolentino Saving Empoli from the Plague*, featuring a view of the town in the 1440s. The museum also possesses an item relating to one of Tuscany's stranger Easter rituals, a winged mechanical donkey that used to perform a version of Florence's incendiary dove ceremony, the donkey being propelled from the Collegiata tower down to Piazza Farinata degli Uberti, where it would ignite a pile of fireworks. (Nowadays a papier-mâché beast performs the role.) The museum ticket also gives you access to the adjacent church of **Santo Stefano** (Tues–Fri 9am–noon), where you can see the remnants of frescoes by Masolino and a marble *Annunciation* by Bernardo Rossellino.

Close by, at Piazza della Vittorio 15, stands the birthplace of Empoli's most famous native of recent times, the great composer-pianist Ferruccio Busoni (1866–1924). The town commemorates him with a series of concerts from October to May, but the house's small museum is not open to casual visitors.

If you're keen on Pontormo's paintings, you might want to drive out to the hamlet of **Pontorme**, on the outskirts of Empoli on the road to Florence. This was the birthplace of the artist baptized as Jacopo Carrucci, and the parish church of San Michele retains a couple of pictures by him, a *St John the Evangelist* and a *St Michael*.

Cerreto Guidi

From the time of Cosimo I to the end of the dynasty, the Medici administered their estates in this northern part of Tuscany from the villa at **CERRETO GUIDI** (daily 8.15am–7pm, closed second & third Mon of month; free), 8km northwest of Empoli and served by COPIT bus. Having converted this former castle into something more domestic, and having commissioned Buontalenti to build the huge approach ramps that remain the villa's most distinctive feature, the clan set about making it the focus of rural life in the Empoli district: they instituted a weekly fair here, with compulsory attendance for the local peasants. The villa is a plain box of a house and the church that Cosimo built next door is similarly austere – though there's a good view from the top of the ramps, with Frederick II's tower at San Miniato (see p.220) standing out in the middle distance. Unless you're a bloodsports enthusiast, in which case the Cerreto Guidi hunting museum may be of interest, the main point of visiting the interior is to see the gallery of Medici portraits. One section is entitled "Unhappy marriages among the descendants of Cosimo I" and includes a likeness of Cosimo's daughter Isabella, murdered here by her husband in 1576 for her infidelity; the Medici hitmen caught up with her alleged lover in Paris the following year.

Vinci

Sitting on the southern slopes of Monte Albano, 11km north of Empoli, **VINCI** is set amid a rolling swathe of vineyards and olive groves. The landscape is not what draws people along the road between Empoli and Pistoia, however – it's the village's association with **Leonardo da Vinci**, who in April 1452 was born in the nearby hamlet of Archiano and baptized in Vinci's church of Santa Croce.

Vinci itself is a torpid place but preserves a mighty thirteenth-century castle, the **Castello dei Conti Guidi**, which houses the main part of the **Museo Leonardiano** (daily 9.30am–7pm; Nov–Feb closes 6pm; €5, or joint ticket with the Museo Collegiata in Empoli and the Montelupo ceramics museum €6) – the ticket office is in the smaller part of the museum, the Palazzina Uzielli, in Via Rossi. Opened on the five-hundredth anniversary of Leonardo's birth, the museum is dedicated to Leonardo the inventor and engineer rather than Leonardo the artist, with a large and fairly imaginative display of models – tanks, water cannon, flying machines, looms and gear mechanisms – all reconstructed from his notebook drawings, which are reproduced alongside the relevant contraptions. Too much space is devoted to Leonardo's more whimsical jottings – half a room is given over, for example, to a mock-up of his skis for walking on water – but high production values prevail throughout. Avoid the museum on a Sunday, when it can feel as if half the population of Tuscany has turned up.

Leonardo's **birthplace** (same hours; free) is in **ANCHIANO**, some 2km farther north into the hills, a pleasant walk past fields of poppies. The house was owned by his father, a Florentine clerk called Ser Piero; Leonardo's mother is generally believed to have been either a *contadina* (peasant girl) or an Arab slave, but the only things that are known for certain are that her name was Caterina and she didn't marry his father, possibly because Ser Piero was already betrothed. Within eight months of his son's birth Ser Piero had married the sixteen-year-old daughter of a Florentine notary, and soon afterwards Caterina was married to a man who went by the name of Accattabriga, who may have been a soldier. (Meaning something like "trouble-maker", Accattabriga was a common nickname among mercenaries.) Placard-size captions and a couple of reproduction drawings are pretty well all there is to see inside the house.

San Miniato

The strategic hill-top site of **SAN MINIATO**, more or less equidistant between Pisa and Florence, has been exploited since the era of Augustus, when the Roman settlement of Quarto was founded here. A Lombard town succeeded it, and at the end of the tenth century Otto I made this an outpost of the Holy Roman Empire. A later emperor, Frederick II, gave the town its landmark fortress, and the imperial connection led to the nickname San Miniato dei Tedeschi ("of the Germans"). Today it's a brusque little agricultural town, good for a couple of hours' break of journey, but unlikely to tempt you to give it longer.

The train station and main, predominantly modern, part of town – **San Miniato Basso** – are sited down in the valley. From here it's a steep four-kilometre climb to **San Miniato Alto**, the old quarter. A minibus does the run to San Miniato Alto from the train station, depositing you just below the walls in Piazzale Dante Alighieri, which is also the place to park.

Beyond the town gate, a right turn leads to **Piazza del Popolo**, where a plan of the town is displayed outside the tourist office. At the top end of the square is the much rebuilt church of **San Domenico**, which contains the fine tomb of a Florentine doctor named Giovanni Chellini. Carved by one Pagno di Lapo Portigiani, it's modelled on the tomb of Leonardo Bruni in Florence's Santa Croce.

From here Via Conti rises to the **Piazza della Repubblica**, jazzed up by seventeenth-century *sgraffiti* on the long facade of the seminary, part of whose ground floor is a row of restored fourteenth-century shops, a rare survival. Opposite the seminary, a flight of steps rises to the **Prato del Duomo**, where a tower of the imperial fortress now houses a hotel. Next door, the **Palazzo** dei Vicari dell'Imperatore is a relic of the time when San Miniato was the seat of the vicars of the Holy Roman Empire: Countess Matilda of Tuscia, daughter of one of these vicars, was born here.

The red-brick **Duomo**, dedicated to St Genesius, the patron saint of actors, is hacked-about Romanesque, with an interior of Baroque gilding and marbling. Next door, the tiny **Museo Diocesano** (Tues–Sun: April–Sept

HONOR ADOLESCENTIS
MODESTIA
GEMMA MORVM
VERECVNDIA
S. AMBROSIO

▲ Seminary, San Miniato

10am–7pm, Oct–March 10am–5pm; €2.50) has a *Crucifixion* by Filippo Lippi and a terracotta bust of Christ by Verrocchio. At the back of the Duomo, the ponderous Santuario del Crocifisso was built to house a Crucifix that was thought to have played a part in saving the town from the plague of 1637; the Crucifix is still there, but the sanctuary is rarely open.

From the Prato del Duomo it's a short walk up to the tower of the **Rocca** (daily: April–Sept 10am–7pm, Oct–March 10am–5pm; €2.50), which was rebuilt by Frederick II and restored after damage in World War II; the main point of the climb is the stupendous panoramic view (on a clear day) of the surrounding countryside. Dante's *Inferno* perpetuates the memory of Pier della Vigna, Frederick's treasurer, who was imprisoned and blinded here, a fate that drove him to suicide by jumping from the tower – as the inscription at its foot records.

Below the tower, on the opposite side from the Duomo, stands the church of **San Francesco**, occupying the site where the Lombards dedicated the chapel to San Miniato that gave the town its name. The church was altered by the Franciscans, who were given the property after Francis himself had visited the town, and traces of their Romanesque building can still just about be discerned through the later Gothic.

Practicalities

The **tourist office** is in Piazza del Popolo (summer daily 9am–1pm & 4–7.30pm; winter Mon–Sat 10am–1pm & 3–6.30pm; ☎0571.418.739). The tower of the Prato del Duomo is now occupied by the three-star *Miravalle* **hotel** (☎0571.418.075, ⓦwww.albergomiravalle.com; ❸), San Miniato's best place to stay, with marvellous views and a good **restaurant** attached.

San Miniato boasts a rich cultural calendar between the months of May and October, with a good choice of **concerts** and **exhibitions**, both in the village itself and in outlying areas. There's a monthly **antiques market** in the Loggiata di San Domenico (first Sun of month). On the first Sunday after Easter, this area around the Rocca is packed with competitors in the national **kite-flying championships**, which compete with a flower festival held on the same day.

South of Empoli

The **N429** road and Empoli–Siena **train** line, which head south between Empoli and San Miniato, provide an easy and direct approach to San Gimignano and Siena. Along the way are two interesting, if modest, hill-town attractions: **Castelfiorentino**, home to some delightful Gozzoli frescoes, and **Certaldo**, where Boccaccio spent his last years.

Castelfiorentino

A fief of the bishops of Florence from the twelfth century onwards, **CASTELFIORENTINO** remained in the city's orbit through most of its uneventful history. Today it's a fairly large urban centre, with light industry and block housing spreading out in the modern, lower quarter of town, across the river Elsa.

From the **train station** – where you'll find the **tourist office** at Via Ridolfi 1 (Mon–Sat: summer 9am–12.30pm & 3.30–7.30pm, winter 10am–noon & 4–6pm; ☎0571.629.049, ⓦwww.comune.castelfiorentino.fi.it) – you can see the expansive Piazza Gramsci straight ahead. It's flanked by cafés, bars and the only central **hotel**, the three-star *Lami* at no. 82–83 (T0571.64.076, Wwww .albergolami.it; ❷). Best of a dozen or so **restaurants**, most grouped around Piazza Gramsci, is *La Magona*, Via Ridolfi 10 (closed Sun & Aug).

The Town

To look around the **Castello** – the old, upper town – head up the stairs at the corner of Piazza Gramsci, by the Teatro del Popolo, and you'll reach a patch of garden square, to either side of which runs Via dei Tilli.

Turn left and you come to the **Biblioteca Comunale** (summer Tues, Thurs & Sat 4–7pm, Sun 10am–noon & 4–7pm; winter Tues, Thurs & Sat 3–6pm, Sun 10am–noon & 3–6pm; €2.60), where frescoes by **Gozzoli** are displayed on the top floor, having been detached from a pair of local sanctuary chapels. To the left of the gallery entrance is a complete reconstruction of the Madonna della Tosse tabernacle, including a frescoed *trompe l'oeil* altarpiece and side-wall scenes of the death and assumption of the Virgin, their landscapes studded with cypress trees and rolling Tuscan hills. More fragmentary but more interesting are the flood-damaged frescoes and sinopie from the Tabernacle of the Visitation. These again depict episodes from the life of the Virgin, and of her parents, Joachim (Gioacchino) and Anne, the best of them full of genre detail of everyday fifteenth-century life. Both sets of frescoes were painted in the 1480s, late in Gozzoli's career, possibly during periods when the plague had hit Florence.

Turn right from the garden square along Via dei Tilli, and you come to the main **Piazza del Popolo**, flanked by the Collegiata of San Lorenzo – built on Lombard foundations – and a nineteenth-century Municipio. The stepped street above the piazza leads to the summit of the town, marked by the Romanesque **Pieve di Santi Ippolito e Biagio** (currently closed for restoration). A plaque in the facade records that it was here, in 1197, that the Tuscan League was formed by Florence, Volterra, Lucca, San Miniato and Siena, to defend the cities against "any emperor, king, or prince" – Castelfiorentino's only real episode in the limelight, and is commemorated by a plaque on the facade.

Down in the **lower town**, east of Piazza Gramsci (left as you face the station and river), a small park gives onto the Baroque church of **Santa Verdiana**, adjacent to which there's a museum (Sat 4–7pm, Sun 10am–noon & 4–7pm; €3) displaying paintings from churches in the town and region, including works by Duccio, Taddeo Gaddi and Gozzoli. Many of these panels came from nearby **San Francesco** (Fri 5–6pm), which has fragmentary fourteenth-century frescoes of the *Life of St Francis*; as is so often the case in these parts, the church claims foundation by St Francis himself. St Verdiana – the local patron saint – was his contemporary and was ordained into the order by him; she is generally depicted with a couple of serpents whose lives she saved, in a pause between other miracles.

San Vivaldo

If you have your own transport and feel like a rambling, fourteen-kilometre cross-country drive down to San Gimignano, follow the road southwest of Castelfiorentino, through either the quiet little hill-town of Montaione or the minor spa of Gambassi Terme (which has the lovely Romanesque **Pieve a Chianni** on its outskirts), to the village of **SAN VIVALDO**. Some time around 1300, a hermit by the name of Vivaldo Stricchi – later Saint Vivaldo – withdrew to a wooded hill here, where he is said to have made himself a cell inside a chestnut tree. After his death a Franciscan monastery developed on the site, and in the early sixteenth century they transformed the surrounding slopes into the **Sacro Monte** (daily 10am–7pm; free), an array of around thirty small chapels, each corresponding to a site in or around Jerusalem that has associations with the life of Christ. This "Jerusalem in Tuscany" was intended to provide the faithful with an approximation of the experience of a pilgrimage to the Holy Land, and the project was backed by the highest of authorities – Pope Leo X granted indulgences to anyone who came here. Clustered on the slope below the monastery, the eighteen surviving chapels contain remarkably dramatic terracotta tableaux, depicting events from the Annunciation to Pentecost.

Certaldo

Even without its Boccaccio connection, **CERTALDO** would justify a visit. A tiny but very striking hill-town – all red-brick towers, battlements and mansions – it is visible for miles along the Elsa valley, and itself has views out to San Gimignano. For a spell in the twelfth century, its rulers, the Alberti dukes of Prato, controlled a domain stretching north to the Arno, but subsequent domination by Florence and incursions by Siena led to its assuming a more modest role. Nowadays its lower town, built along the N429, is a prosperous place, making its money from wine and agriculture, as well as glass, brick and pasta factories. In late July or early August the town holds the atmospheric **Mercantia festival**, which features various medieval-themed events, all illuminated by torches and candles. There's also a **cultural festival** in September, the first Sunday of which is the feast of Santa Giulia della Rena, when emigrants from the town traditionally return for a reunion.

You're not allowed to drive into the old town – **Certaldo Alto** – unless you're staying overnight up there. Arriving by bus or train, you'll find yourself close to the central Piazza Boccaccio in the **lower town**, from where you can either walk up the steep Vicolo Signorini or take the funicular (daily: summer 7am–midnight; winter 7am–10pm; every 15min).

Certaldo Alto

Certaldo's upper town is little more than a single street, predictably dubbed **Via Boccaccio**, which stretches from the western side (where the funicular arrives) to the archetypally Tuscan town hall, or Palazzo Vicariale.

Halfway along the street stands the **Casa del Boccaccio** (daily: summer 9.30am–7pm; winter 9.30am–4.30pm; €3, or joint ticket with Palazzo Vicariale and Museo d'Arte Sacra €6). This is quite likely to have been the house in which the poet spent the last twelve years of his life – in very modest circumstances, despite a considerable reputation – but scholars continue to dispute quite which towered house Boccaccio specified in his will. Not only is the attribution uncertain, the house contains no direct links with Boccaccio: indeed it contains nothing of any great antiquity, other than a case of medieval shoes. Instead, all you get are photos of portraits of the writer, illustrations of scenes from the *Decameron* and various editions of his masterpiece, in the original and in translation.

More interesting is the church of **Sts Michele e Jacopo**, a short distance further up the street, which Boccaccio attended and where he was buried. A simple marble diamond on the floor of the nave marks his grave, above a mock-medieval funerary slab, which replaces the tomb destroyed in 1783: the burghers of Certaldo – having concluded, as the author did, that the *Decameron* was an ungodly work – ripped up the tombstone and scattered his ashes. Byron, who came to pay his respects a few years later, was scandalized:

... even his tomb
Uptorn must bear the hyena bigot's wrong;
No more amidst the meaner dead find room.

Byron's verses had an effect, prompting the Marquise Lenzoni – a straggler from the Medici family – to buy up and restore the Boccaccio house and arrange the **monument** on the left-hand wall of the church, which comprises a sixteenth-century bust and a slab bearing the lines the poet wrote as his own epitaph. The church's other notable features are a trio of pieces from the workshop of Andrea della Robbia, a fourteenth-century Sienese fresco of the *Madonna and Child*, and the tomb of Certaldo's patron saint, Giulia della Rena, who spent thirty years in a walled-up cell beside the sacristy, and at whose death in 1367 all the bells of Certaldo are said to have spontaneously begun to ring. The small **Museo d'Arte Sacra**, off the church's cloister (same hours as Casa del Boccaccio; €2.60, or joint ticket €6), is a typical small-town collection of humdrum paintings and ecclesiastical applied art.

As you'll see from a long way off, the **Palazzo Vicariale** (same hours as Casa del Boccaccio; €3, or joint ticket €6) is blazoned with coats of arms (including further examples from the della Robbia workshop) that attest to its use as the governor's residence, after the demise of its original owners, the Alberti. Inside, the arcaded courtyard displays further coats of arms and a fragmentary array of frescoes, many either painted or repainted at the end of the fifteenth century. To the right as you enter, the room in which the law court convened is dominated by a fresco of Doubting Thomas, attributed to Gozzoli. Cells for minor felons adjoin this room; serious offenders were dispatched to the grim, almost windowless dungeons at the rear of the courtyard, next to the women's prison. Among the graffiti etched by the prisoners you'll find a diagram of the sun, each beam signifying a day spent confined. Upstairs lie the more spacious chambers of the governor and his

Boccaccio

Giovanni Boccaccio was born, according to the account he gave his friend Petrarch, in Paris, probably in 1313. The son of a banker from Certaldo, he returned fairly early in his childhood to Tuscany. As a youth he rejected the banking career planned by his family, instead going to study in Naples, where he fell in love with Fiammetta, an illegitimate princess and the inspiration for numerous of his sonnets. He returned to Florence reluctantly, after the collapse of his father's business, and there – as well as in Milan and Avignon, where he served as a diplomat – he wrote his major works, including the **Decameron**. Completed in 1353, the *Decameron* is set during the Black Death, which had recently devastated much of Tuscany, and is narrated by ten characters, each of whom tells ten stories during the two weeks they spend taking refuge from the epidemic in a villa in Fiesole; the vast majority (if not all) of Boccaccio's one hundred tales were borrowed from existing sources, and the *Decameron* has in turn been quarried by innumerable writers, including such disparate figures as Luther, Molière and Keats.

Aged around 50, Boccaccio met a monk who so impressed him with a vision of his death that he decided to reject his worldly excesses of old and retire to Certaldo. The rest of the years here were spent producing learned volumes on geography, the vanity of human affairs, and mythology, and preparing lectures on Dante. He died on December 21, 1375.

servants, again with the odd faded fresco. These rooms are used on and off for special exhibitions, often with a Boccaccian theme.

Back downstairs, a door from the magistrates' hall opens onto a walled garden that gives you a wonderful view from its parapet. On the far side of the garden is the entrance to the deconsecrated church of **San Tommaso e Prospero**, which was used as a storeroom from the eighteenth century, then restored after World War II. It contains a miscellany of frescoes and sinopie, the most notable being the *Deposition* that forms the focus of Gozzoli's Tabernacle of the Condemned, which was moved here from the local chapel for which it was created.

Practicalities

The **tourist office** is in the lower town, at Viale Fabiani 5 (daily: summer 9am–1pm & 3.30–7pm, winter 10am–noon & 3.30–5.30pm; ☎0571.656.721). There are two good **hotel–restaurants** up in Certaldo Alto. The two-star *Il Castello*, Via della Rena 6 (☎0571.668.250, ⓦwww.albergoilcastello.it; closed Nov; ④), occupies an appealingly dowdy old mansion at the western end of Via Boccaccio; it has a splendid garden overlooking the lower town, and offers straightforward and good-value food (restaurant closed Tues). The menu at the ⚔ *Osteria del Vicario*, Via Rivellino 3 (☎0571.668.228, ⓦwww.osteriadelvicario.it; ④), by the Palazzo Vicariale, is somewhat more expensive (around €45; restaurant closed Wed) and more refined: the rooms are a touch cosier too – five of them are in the same thirteenth-century monastic building as the restaurant, four are in a neighbouring house (these have splendid views) and a further six are located in a third building, 100m away. An excellent **campsite**, *Toscana Colliverdi* at Via Marcialla 349 (☎0571.669.334; ⓦwww.camping.it/toscana/colliverdi), is a short distance east in the village of Marcialla, on the very edge of the Chianti hills.

Travel details

Trains

Empoli to: Castelfiorentino (hourly; 20min); Certaldo (hourly; 30min); Florence (every 30min; 25min); Pisa (every 30min; 25min); Poggibonsi (hourly; 40min); Siena (hourly; 1hr).
Florence to: Borgo San Lorenzo (every 2hr; 1hr); Empoli (every 20min; 35min); Montecatini (hourly; 50min); Pistoia (every 20–30min; 40–55min); Prato (every 20–30min; 20–30min).
Pistoia to: Florence (every 20–30min; 40–55min); Lucca (hourly; 45min); Montecatini (hourly; 15min); Viareggio (hourly; 1hr 15min).
Prato to: Florence (every 20–30min; 20–30min); Lucca (hourly; 1hr); Montecatini (hourly; 30min); Pistoia (every 20–30min; 15min); Viareggio (hourly; 1hr 30min).

Buses

Borgo San Lorenzo to: (SITA) San Piero a Sieve, Scarperia, Barberino di Mugello and other villages in the Mugello.

Castelfiorentino to: (SITA) Empoli, Florence, Certaldo and Volterra.
Empoli to: (COPIT) Cerreto Guidi and Vinci (from outside train station); (SITA) Castelfiorentino and Certaldo (from Piazza della Vittoria).
Florence to: (ATAF) La Petraia, Careggi, Pratolino and Fiesole; (SITA) Castellina in Chianti, Greve, Radda in Chianti, Gaiole, Barberino di Mugello, Certaldo, Pontassieve, Borgo San Lorenzo and San Casciano; (Lazzi) Cerreto Guidi, Empoli, Incisa Valdarno, Montecatini Terme, Prato, Pistoia and Pontassieve; (CAP) Borgo San Lorenzo, Impruneta and Prato; (COPIT) Pistoia and Poggio a Caiano.
Montecatini Terme to: (Lazzi) Monsummano, Pescia, Collodi, Pistoia, Prato, Florence, Pisa and Livorno.
Pistoia to: (Lazzi) Montecatini, Prato, Florence, Lucca, Pisa and Viareggio; (COPIT) Montecatini, Poggio a Caiano, Empoli and Vinci.
Prato to: (Lazzi) Montecatini, Pistoia, Florence, Lucca, Pisa and Viareggio; (CAP) Florence, Siena, Barberino and Mugello.

Lucca and northern Tuscany

CHAPTER 3 # Highlights

* **Romanesque churches**
  Found across the region,
  but especially in Lucca, the
  most urbane of Tuscan towns.
  See p.228

* **Lucca's walls** Walk or
  cycle the fortifications that
  completely encircle the old
  city. See p.236

* **Villa Reale** The best of
  several villas and gardens
  around Lucca. See p.240

* **Walking in the Alpi Apuane**
  Long and short walks in these
  dramatic mountains that rise

just behind the Riviera della
Versilia. See p.246

* **Carrara** Fascinating centre
  of Tuscany's marble-mining
  region. See p.247

* **Barga** A delightful Garfagnana
  village, with a fine cathedral
  and a rich cultural and
  gastronomic heritage.
  See p.252

* **The Orecchiella** A verdant
  patchwork of valleys and
  mountains in the Garfagnana,
  with excellent hiking.
  See p.255

▲ The church of San Michele in Foro, Lucca

3

Lucca and northern Tuscany

Northern Tuscany is one of the province's least-known regions. Very few non-Italians holiday on its resort-lined coast, the so-called Riviera della Versilia, and fewer still penetrate inland to the mountains of the Alpi Apuane or the remote hills and valleys of the Garfagnana and Lunigiana. The one city on the Tuscan sightseeing trail is Lucca – and even there tourism, strangely, is very much a secondary consideration.

Lucca's proximity to Pisa – half an hour by road or rail – makes it an excellent first or last Tuscan stop if you're flying in or out of that city's airport. Even if you're not, Lucca is well worth an overnight stay or a day-trip from Florence (the train takes around an hour). Contained within vast, park-lined walls, it's an urbane, affluent place, with as rewarding an ensemble of Romanesque churches as any you'll find in Italy.

For a quick break by the sea, the sands of the **Riviera della Versilia** are pleasant enough, and easily reached from Lucca. Though there is often little to distinguish the resorts, where the beaches are usually staked out by private operators, the towns of **Viareggio** and **Forte dei Marmi** have their moments – Viareggio during February's carnival, when it mounts Italy's most amazing procession of floats, and in high summer, when it's the first-choice resort for many Florentines having a day out by the sea. And from this coast it is a simple matter to explore the jagged peaks of the **Alpi Apuane**, which run parallel to the sea for some 40km. The mountains are best known for the **marble quarries** around **Carrara**, but head beyond these and you will find yourself amid steep forested valleys, threaded by a network of clearly marked **footpaths**. Many of these can be trekked in a day from their village trailheads, though there are longer trails and accommodation refuges if you fancy something more strenuous. More important still, the area is well mapped, not always the case in Italy.

Equally easy to visit from Lucca is the **Garfagnana**, a lovely rural enclave that focuses on the **Serchio valley** and is flanked by the eastern slopes of the Apuane on one side and the more rounded mountains of the **Orecchiella** on the other. Plenty of trails strike off into these upland regions, each of which is protected by a regional nature reserve. **Castelnuovo di Garfagnana** is the only town of any size, a good base for excursions to the hills or a visit to nearby **Barga**, the one outstanding medieval centre. North of the Serchio is one of the

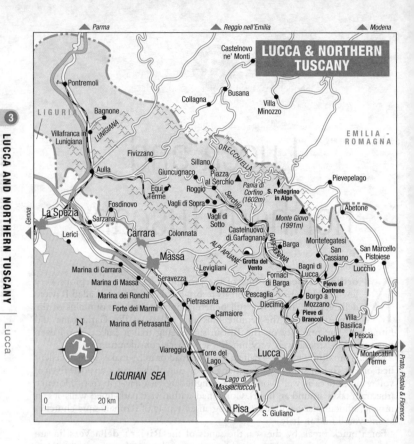

most marginalized areas of Tuscany, the **Lunigiana**, a wild and unspoilt region of rocky, forested landscape peppered with castles and tiny hamlets.

By virtue of their microclimates and a position that puts them at a meeting point of Alpine and Mediterranean vegetation zones, the Apuane and Orecchiella constitute one of the finest **floral** zones in the country: two-thirds of Italy's known species grow here, and in late spring the upland meadows are carpeted with flowers. Besides these and a wide variety of fungi, the reserves here abound in often spectacular **wildlife** such as wolves, red deer and golden eagles. At least 165 bird species have been reported, some 85 of them breeding here, including kestrels, buzzards and sparrowhawks.

Lucca

LUCCA is the most graceful of Tuscany's provincial capitals, set inside a ring of Renaissance walls fronted by gardens and huge bastions. It's quiet without being dull, absorbs its tourists with ease, has a peaceful, self-contained historic centre and offers a range of good restaurants. Henry James's eulogy – "a place overflowing with everything that makes for ease, for plenty, for beauty, for interest and good example" – still holds true. Lucca is a delightful town in which to wander at random: it's one of the few places in Tuscany where many locals ride bikes, and as a result much of the old centre is refreshingly free of traffic. The city is reputed to have once had seventy churches, and even today you can hardly walk for five minutes without coming upon a small piazza and marble-fronted church facade. Most were built obliquely to the grid of streets, so you rarely confront a church head on, but rather as a sudden apparition as you enter a square.

Lucca lies at the heart of one of Italy's richest agricultural regions ("half-smothered in oil and wine and corn and all the fruits of the earth," James wrote) and has prospered since the Romans, whose gridiron orthodoxy is still obvious in the layout of the streets. Under the **Lombards** it was the capital of Tuscia (Tuscany), though its heyday was between the eleventh and fourteenth centuries, when banking and the silk trade brought wealth and, for a time, political power. In a brief flurry of military activity Lucca lost its independence to Pisa in 1314, but regained it under the command of a remarkable adventurer, **Castruccio Castracani**, who went on to forge an empire covering much of western Tuscany. Pisa and Pistoia both fell to the Lucchesi, and but for Castracani's untimely death from malaria, Florence might have followed. In subsequent centuries the city remained largely independent – if fairly inconsequential – until passing to **Napoleon** (and rule by his sister, Elisa Baciocchi), the Bourbons, and, just short of Italian unification, to the Grand Duchy of Tuscany.

Today the city is reckoned among the wealthiest in Tuscany, a prosperity gained largely through **silk** that was produced here by scores of small family businesses, and on the region's high-quality **olive oil** and other produce. There is, too, a tradition of decorum, traceable to eighteenth- and nineteenth-century court life; up until the turn of the twentieth century, smart Italian families sent their daughters to Lucca to pick up the better manners presumed to prevail here.

Arrival, information and accommodation

The **train station**, with exchange facilities, is on Piazza Ricasoli, a short way outside the walls to the south. **Buses** arrive just inside the western stretch of walls, in Piazzale Giuseppe Verdi, while **city buses** leave from the same piazza and Corso Garibaldi.

The main **tourist office** is at Piazza Santa Maria 35 in the north of the town (daily: April–Sept 9am–7pm; Oct–March 9am–5pm; ☎0583.919.931); there's another at Piazzale Verdi (daily: April–Oct 9am–7pm; Nov–March 9am–6pm; ☎0583.583.150). A vast **antiques market** takes place on the third weekend of the month in and around Piazza San Martino.

Though Lucca isn't a major stop on the tourist trail, its limited **accommodation** always seems in demand: it's wise to book ahead at any time of year. There are very few hotels within the city walls so you might consider staying in a more central private room or B&B, or the hostel.

Hotels

A Palazzo Busdraghi Via Fillungo 170 ☎0583.950.856, ⓦwww.apalazzobusdraghi.it. An intimate and central four-star hotel, with only seven rooms, all furnished with fine antiques; one of the rooms even boasts a wardrobe owned by Puccini. ❼

Alla Corte Degli Angeli Via degli Angeli 23 ☎0583.469.204, ⓦwww.allacortedegliangeli.com. A bright, airy and colourful four-star hotel situated inside the medieval walls. Rooms are romantic, with exposed wooden beams and period furniture and fittings. ❸–❹

Diana Via del Molinetto 11 ☎0583.492.202, ⓦwww.albergodiana.com. A two-star hotel whose excellent position and keen prices make up for the slightly dated and austere rooms. ❸

La Romea Vicolo delle Ventaglie 2 ☎0583.464.175, ⓦwww.laromea.com. This welcoming three-star hotel in a fourteenth-century building, run by a

ACCOMMODATION

Alla Corte Degli Angeli	C
A Palazzo Busdraghi	B
Casa Alba	D
Centro Storico	F
Diana	N
La Romea	I
La Torre	G
Melecchi	L
Noblesse	K
Ostello San Frediano	A
Piccolo Hotel Puccini	H
San Frediano	E
Stipino	M
Universo	J

young couple, is 30m from the Guinigi Tower, and has only five pretty and intimate rooms. ❹
Melecchi Via Romana 37 ☎0583.950.234, ⓦwww.hotelmelecchi.it. A decent if bland modern two-star with ten en-suite rooms and private parking, situated a couple of blocks outside the walls. ❷
Noblesse Via Sant'Anastasio 23 ☎0583.440.275, ⓦwww.hotelnoblesse.it. Lucca's long-term lack of a five-star hotel has been remedied by this thirteen-room gem at the heart of the old city, a converted eighteenth-century palazzo over three

floors with period furniture, antiques, Persian rugs and a warm, intimate atmosphere. ❾
Piccolo Hotel Puccini Via di Poggio 9 ☎0583.55.421, ⓦwww.hotelpuccini.com. Friendly, central three-star with fourteen rooms. It's very close to San Michele, and the prices are competitive, so is an obvious first choice – and thus definitely needs booking. Private parking for an extra €15. ❸
Stipino Via Romana 95 ☎0583.495.077, ⓦwww .hotelstipino.com. Adequate two-star hotel with 21 rooms, some with private bathrooms, but some of the keenest prices in the city. ❷

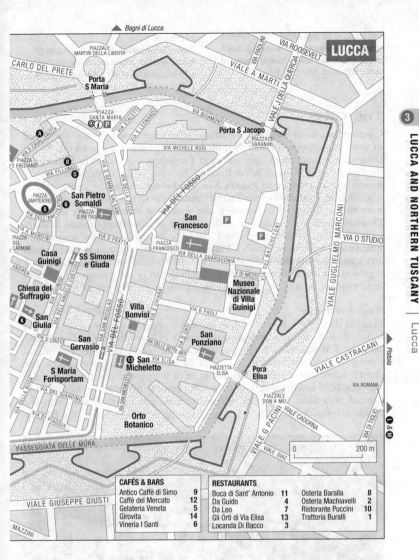

▲ Bagni di Lucca

LUCCA

▶ Pistoia

▶ **⑬** & **⑭**

CAFÉS & BARS	
Antico Caffè di Simo	9
Caffè del Mercato	12
Gelateria Veneta	5
Girovita	14
Vineria I Santi	6

RESTAURANTS			
Buca di Sant' Antonio	11	Osteria Baralla	8
Da Guido	4	Osteria Machiavelli	2
Da Leo	7	Ristorante Puccini	10
Gli Orti di Via Elisa	13	Trattoria Buralli	1
Locanda Di Bacco	3		

Universo Piazza del Giglio 1 ☏ 0583.954.854, ⓦ www.universolucca.com. Lucca's not-so-grand grand old hotel: a three-star with sixty rooms that lacks atmosphere, made up for by its location bang on the central Piazza Napoleone. **⑤**

Private rooms

Casa Alba Via Fillungo 142, second floor ☏ 0583.495.361, ⓦ www.casa-alba.com. Five clean, pleasant rooms (doubles and singles) with or without private bathroom on Lucca's main street, just north of Piazza Anfiteatro. **②**

Centro Storico Corte Portici 16 ☏ 0583.490.748, ⓔ centrostorico@tin.it. Six rooms in a conveniently located hotel, four with bathroom, located on a courtyard just northwest of Piazza San Michele. **②–④**

La Torre Via del Carmine 11 ☏ 0583.957.044, ⓦ www.roomslatorre.com. Five pleasant double rooms with or without bathroom; located off Piazza del Carmine south of Piazza Anfiteatro. Has two other outlets, *Torre 2* and *Torre 3*, at Via della Columbaia and Via Sant'Andrea (same contact details) with similarly good rooms. **③–⑤**

San Fredriano Via degli Angeli ☎ 0583.469.630, ⓦ www.sanfrediano.com. Six rooms, including singles and doubles with a choice of private and shared bathrooms. ❸

Hostel
Ostello San Frediano Via della Cavallerizza 12 ☎ 0583.469.957, ⓦ www.ostellionline.org. Conveniently located HI hostel just within the walls, with a midnight curfew. Dorm beds €19.

The City

Confined within its walls, Lucca is an easy place to get your bearings. The centre of town is ostensibly **Piazza Napoleone**, a huge expanse carved out by the Bourbons to house their administration. From here the main **Via Fillungo** – the "long thread" – heads north through the heart of the medieval city. You're most likely to gravitate to **Piazza San Michele**, home to the church of San Michele, the apotheosis of the Pisan-Romanesque style. From here, you might want to potter around the streets to the west, or push immediately on to the **Duomo**, another Romanesque gem, with one of Italy's most sublime funerary sculptures. Further east, the Fosso ("ditch") cuts off the quarter around **San Francesco**, while to the north is **Piazza Anfiteatro**, built over the old Roman arena, and **San Frediano**, the third of the city's trio of outstanding churches. A trip to Lucca is not complete without strolling part of the panoramic and tree-lined promenade atop the **walls**, accessed from almost any part of the city.

San Michele

Head to the historical heart of Lucca and you come to the site of the Roman forum, now the square surrounding the church of **San Michele in Foro** (daily: summer 7.40am–noon & 3–6pm; winter 9am–noon & 3pm–5pm; closed during services; free), which has one of Tuscany's most exquisite facades. The church is first mentioned in 795, but most of the present structure dates from between 1070 and the middle of the twelfth century (you can see the date 1143 marked on a pillar on the left side of the main portal's triumphal arch). The building is unfinished, however, money having been diverted to the **facade**,

▲ Lucca

begun in the thirteenth century; funds ran out before the body of the church could be raised to the standard of the facade. The effect is wonderful, the upper loggias and the windows fronting air, like the figure of the archangel at their summit. Its Pisan-inspired intricacy is a triumph of eccentricity, mirrored in many of Lucca's churches. Each of its myriad columns is different – some twisted, others sculpted or candy-striped. The impressive twelfth-century **campanile** is the city's tallest.

It would be hard to match the facade's bravura architectural display, and the **interior** barely tries. On the rear wall is a statue of the *Madonna and Child* by local sculptor Matteo Civitali, previously on the facade. Italians flock for spiritual regeneration to the second altar on the left, the so-called *Rifugio dei Peccatori* (Refuge of Sinners). On the opposite altar is a modest terracotta *Madonna and Child* by Andrea della Robbia; the best work of art is a beautifully framed painting of *Sts Jerome, Sebastian, Roch and Helena* by **Filippino Lippi**, at the end of the right-hand nave. Look out also for the organ, marvellously painted with intricate fleurs-de-lys.

The western quarter

The birthplace and family home of Giacomo Puccini, the **Casa di Puccini** (Ⓦ www.puccini.it), is in Corte San Lorenzo 9, off Via di Poggio, very close to San Michele – where the composer's father and grandfather both played the organ. Today the house is a school of music, and maintains a small museum (closed at the time of writing) containing the Steinway on which he wrote *Turandot*, as well as scores, photographs, and even his overcoat.

A short way west of San Michele is **San Paolino**, where Puccini cut his teeth as organist. A dull Baroque church, begun in 1522, it was built over a vast Roman edifice, possibly a temple, and founded in honour of Lucca's first bishop and patron saint, St Paulinus, whose remains are kept behind the high altar. Some third-rate eighteenth-century frescoes are his only memorial. South of San Paolino, tucked behind the Palazzo Ducale, is **San Romano**, a big, blunt Romanesque hall, probably founded in the eighth century and adapted and enlarged after 1281 in a bizarre hotchpotch of styles; it would be one of the city's more interesting churches if the restoration started in 1987 had actually shown any real progress. At the moment the whole place is sadly dilapidated.

North of San Paolino is the **Museo Nazionale di Palazzo Mansi**, Via Galli Tassi 43 (Tues–Sat 8.30am–7.30pm, Sun 8.30am–1.30pm; €4, or joint ticket with Museo Guinigi €6.50). This seventeenth-century building is worth seeing for its magnificently over-the-top Rococo decor; from a vast, frescoed music salon, you pass through three drawing-rooms hung with seventeenth-century Flemish tapestries to a spectacularly gilded bridal suite. Rooms 11–14 in the far wing house the **Pinacoteca Nazionale**, an eclectic grouping of pictures whose real highlights are a Pontormo portrait, possibly of Alessandro de' Medici (see p.648 for the dirt on this sensitive youth); Bronzino's portrait of Cosimo I; two male portraits by Tintoretto; and works by the Sienese Mannerists Beccafumi and Rutilio Manetti. Also worth seeing is the section that traces the development of Lucca's important **textile** industry, in particular its silks and damasks.

Duomo di San Martino

It needs a double-take before you realize why the **Duomo di San Martino** (mid-March to Oct Mon–Fri 9.30am–5.45pm, Sat 9.30am–6.45pm, Sun 9–10.45am & noon–5pm; rest of year Mon–Fri closes 4.45pm, Sun 6pm; free) looks slightly odd. The building is fronted by a severely asymmetric facade, its right-hand arch and loggias squeezed by the bell tower, which was already in place from an earlier building. Nonetheless, the building sets the tone for Lucca's other Romanesque churches, and little detracts from its overall grandeur, created by the repetition of tiny columns and loggias and by the stunning **atrium**, whose bas-reliefs are some of the finest sculptures in the city.

It's worth looking closely at these carvings, some dated as early as the fifth century, which were executed by a variety of mainly Lombard artists, most of them unknown. Part of the sculpture is attributed to **Nicola Pisano**, and may well be his first work after arriving in Tuscany from Apulia. His are probably the offerings around the left-hand door: the *Deposition* (in the lunette), *Annunciation*, *Nativity* and *Adoration of the Magi*. Other panels display a compendium of subjects: a symbolic labyrinth, a Tree of Life (with Adam and Eve at the bottom and Christ at the top), dragons, bears, a bestiary of grotesques, and the months of the year with their associated activities – December has a particularly graphic pig-sticking. The panels of the *Life of St Martin* (1204–10), between the doors, are the masterpiece of the architect, **Guidetto da Como**, responsible for the upper facade's three tiers of arcades. Walk along the flanks of the building to take in the ornate apse and transepts, as well as the extraordinary patterns of arches and marbles in the bricked-up side walls. One of the greatest of the exterior sculptures, a group depicting *St Martin on Horseback with the Beggar* by an unknown early fourteenth-century Lombard sculptor, has been removed inside the church, and stands at the rear right against the west wall.

The interior

The Duomo's **interior** is best known for the contribution of **Matteo Civitali** (1435–1501), who gave up his job as a barber to become a sculptor in his mid-thirties. He's represented here by a couple of water stoups near the entrance, the pulpits and several tombs and altars – notably the tomb of Pietro da Noceto, secretary to Pope Niccolò V (right wall of the south transept); the tomb of Domenico Bertini, to the left of the preceding tomb on the transept's adjoining wall; and the altar of San Regolo, on the chancel wall immediately right of the apse.

Civitali's most famous work is the **Tempietto**, the gilt and marble octagon encountered halfway down the church. Some fanatically intense acts of devotion are performed in front of it, directed at the **Volto Santo** (Holy Face), Lucca's most famous relic. A cedarwood Crucifix with bulging eyes, it's said to be a true effigy of Christ carved by Nicodemus, an eyewitness to the Crucifixion, but is probably a thirteenth-century copy of an eleventh-century copy of an eighth-century original. Legend has it that the *Volto Santo* came to Lucca of its own volition in 782, first journeying by boat from the Holy Land, and then brought by oxen guided by divine will – a story similar to the ecclesiastical sham of St James's bones at Santiago di Compostela in Spain. As at Santiago, the icon brought considerable power to the local church: it may be no coincidence that it appeared during the bishopric of Anselmo di Baggio, who was later elevated to the papacy. The effigy attracted pilgrims from all over Europe and inspired devotion in all who heard of it: King William Rufus of England used to swear by it ("Per sanctum vultum de Lucca!"), London merchants kept a copy of it, and in France a certain St Vaudeluc was conjured into existence from a corruption of *saint vault de Lucques*, the French name for the icon.

Elsewhere in the church the works of art are of less disputed origin. The finest of them is the **Tomb of Ilaria del Carretto** (1407–10), housed in the **sacristy** entered midway down the south nave (mid-March to Oct Mon–Fri 9.30am–5.45pm, Sat 9.30am–6.45pm, Sun 9.30am–10.45pm; Nov to mid-March Mon–Fri

9.30am–4.45pm, Sat 9.30am–6.45pm, Sun noon to 6pm; €2, or €6 with Museo della Cattedrale and church of San Giovanni). Considered the masterpiece of Sienese sculptor Jacopo della Quercia, it consists of a dais and the sculpted body of Ilaria, second wife of Paolo Guinigi, one of Lucca's medieval big shots. In a touching, almost sentimental gesture, the artist has carved the family dog at Ilaria's feet, a symbol of fidelity. Also within the sacristy is a superb *Madonna Enthroned with Saints* by **Domenico Ghirlandaio**.

Other pictorial highlights of the cathedral include a *Madonna and Child* in the enclosed chapel to the left of the high altar in the north transept, painted in 1509 by **Fra' Bartolommeo**. In the main part of the Duomo, the first chapel on the left has a *Presentation of the Virgin* by Alessandro Allori (1598), and the third altar on the right a *Last Supper* (1592) by **Tintoretto**.

Around the Duomo

Occupying a converted twelfth-century building across Via Arcivescovato from the cathedral is the **Museo della Cattedrale** (mid-March to Oct daily 10am–6pm; Nov to mid-March Mon–Fri 10am–2pm, Sat & Sun 10am–5pm; €4, or €6 with the cathedral sacristy and San Giovanni). The museum's four floors are home to a collection of ecclesiastical and other ephemera interspersed with the occasional artistic gem. Room I has a collection of illustrated miniatures, while Room II on the floor above houses a reliquary from Limoges decorated with stories from the life of St Thomas à Becket; an ivory diptych from Constantinople dated 506; and – one of the highlights – the *Croce dei Pisani*, an ornate crucifix probably commissioned by Paolo Guinigi after 1408. Room VII contains sculpture from the cathedral, most notably a large statue of St John the Evangelist by Jacopo della Quercia.

On the north side of the square stands the large basilica of **Santi Giovanni e Reparata** (same hours; €2.50, or joint ticket with cathedral sacristy and Museo della Cattedrale €6), Lucca's cathedral until 715. Rebuilt many times, it preserves a lion-flanked carved Romanesque portal, saved during restructuring of the facade in 1589. Inside, excavations have uncovered a tangle of architectural remains, embracing a wide range of much earlier buildings on the site. Earliest fragments include first-century Roman villa mosaics (columns in the present nave are mostly Roman in origin), parts of the original fourth-century church pavement, an eighth-century baptistery with fine 1393 ceiling, and traces of a ninth-century Carolingian church and crypt of San Pantaleone.

North to San Frediano

North of the Duomo, **Via Fillungo** cuts through Lucca's luxury shopping district, a tight huddle of streets and alleys where medieval fragments and bricked-up loggias compete with Art Nouveau-style shop fronts and lunchtime and early-evening throngs. Amid the crowds it's easy to miss the gorgeous facade of **San Cristoforo**, the deconsecrated church at the southern end; inside, the left-hand wall is completely covered in writing – the names of Lucca's dead in the two world wars. Further on is the **Torre delle Ore**, the city's clock tower since 1471; then at no. 58 there's the famous *Caffè di Simo*, a bar worth the price of a drink just for the early twentieth-century ambience. Beyond, the street branches into a warren of lanes that lead to **Piazza San Frediano**.

San Frediano

The church of **San Frediano** (Mon–Sat 8.30am–noon & 3–5.30pm, Sun 9–11.30am & 3–5.30pm; closed during services; free) is again Pisan-Romanesque, built between 1112 and 1147 on the site of a sixth-century basilica of San

Vincenzo but orientated back to front (west-facing), probably because the old entrance would have been blocked by the new set of medieval city walls nearby. In place of the characteristic multiple loggias of Lucca's other great facades is a magnificent thirteenth-century mosaic of *The Ascension* with the apostles gathered below.

The **interior** lives up to the facade's promise – a delicately lit, hall-like basilica, with subtly varied columns and capitals and some fine treasures. Immediately facing the door is one of the best, the **Fonte Lustrale**, a huge twelfth-century piece executed by three different craftsmen. The first, an unknown Lombard, carved the stories of Moses on the outer slabs of the basin, including a superb *Crossing of the Red Sea*, with the Egyptian soldiers depicted as medieval knights. The second, one Maestro Roberto, added the Good Shepherd and six prophets on the other two basin slabs, their enframing arches showing a clear Byzantine influence. To the third sculptor, an unknown Tuscan, is owed the decoration of the Apostles and the Months on the cup above the basin and the beautiful fantasy masks from which the water is disgorged. Set behind the font is an *Annunciation* attributed to Matteo della Robbia, festooned with trailing garlands of ceramic fruit.

A figure of St Bartholomew by Andrea della Robbia is to be found lower down to the left, close to the left-hand of the two chapels behind the font, the Cappella Fatinelli, which houses the "incorrupt" body of **St Zita** (died 1278). A Lucchese maidservant, Zita achieved sainthood from a fortuitous white lie: she used to give bread from her household to the poor and when challenged one day by her boss as to the contents of her apron, replied "only roses and flowers" – into which the bread was duly transformed. She is commemorated on April 27 by a flower market outside the church and by the Lucchesi freeing her of her finery and bringing her out to touch.

Moving to the top of the church, note the wonderful twelfth-century Cosmati marble **pavement** of the presbytery, while on the left are fragments of the

Around the walls

Climbing up at any of the bastions, some of which are signposted, you can follow the four-kilometre circuit of the **city walls**, either on bike or on foot. The mid-afternoon shutdown is perhaps the best time to walk their broad promenade, which is lined with plane, lime, ilex and chestnut trees. Bikes can be rented from a cluster of outlets around the tourist office in Piazza Santa Maria.

Construction of the walls started around 1500, prompted by the need to replace medieval ramparts rendered inadequate by advances in weapon technology. By 1650 the work was completed, with eleven bastions to fortify walls that were 30m wide at the base, 12m high and surrounded by moats 35m across. There were originally just three gates. Perhaps the best feature, from the present-day perspective, was the destruction of all trees and buildings within a couple of hundred metres of the walls, creating a green belt of lawns that has shielded the old town from the ugliness that's sprouted on the outside.

Ironically, having produced a perfect set of walls, Lucca was never called on to defend them. The only siege was against the floodwaters of the River Serchio in 1812, when the gates were sealed against the deluge that had flooded the countryside. Napoleon's sister and city governor, Elisa Baciocchi, one of the last people allowed in, had to be winched over the ramparts by crane. Marie Louise of Bourbon, her successor, had the walls transformed to their present garden aspect, arranging them, as the local tourist handout puts it, "with unparalleled good taste and moderation".

original tomb of San Frediano, an Irish monk who is said to have brought Christianity to Lucca in the sixth century. Moving back down the left (north) nave from the high altar, the first chapel, the **Cappella Trenta**, contains a superb carved altarpiece with niche statues of the Madonna, Child and Saints by Jacopo della Quercia; the worn pavement tombs of the chapel's donors, Lorenzo Trenat and his wife, are also by della Quercia.

The best **frescoes** in the city adorn the Cappella di Sant'Agostino, the next chapel but one: **Amico Aspertini**'s *The Arrival of the Volto Santo* and *The Baptism of St Augustine* on the left wall, and *The Miracle of St Frediano* on the right, the last depicting the River Serchio in flood being diverted by the saint's crib. Dating from the early sixteenth century, the murals are painted in a style that is much influenced by the realism of Flemish and German painters. The large fresco of the *Madonna and Child* on the right of the entrance door is also by Aspertini, while the nearby statue *Virgin Annunciate* is by Matteo Civitali.

Palazzo Pfanner

Just west of San Frediano is the **Palazzo Pfanner**, Via degli Asili 33 (April–Oct Thurs–Tues 10am–6pm; garden or palace €3, garden and palace €4.50; Ⓦ www .palazzopfanner.it), whose interesting rear loggia and gardens dotted with statues are also visible from the city walls, as is another fine church, **Sant'Agostino**. The palazzo occasionally hosts temporary exhibitions.

Piazza Anfiteatro and around

East of San Frediano is the remarkable **Piazza Anfiteatro**, aerial shots of which feature in just about all of Lucca's tourist literature. A ramshackle circuit of medieval buildings, as yet unprettified, it incorporates elements of the Roman amphitheatre that once stood here. Much of the original stone was carted off in the twelfth century to build the city's churches, while parts of the old structure were used as a medieval prison and salt warehouse, but arches and columns can still be seen embedded in some of the houses, particularly on the north side of the outer walls. Medieval slums used to occupy the centre of the arena, but these were cleared in 1830 on the orders of the Bourbon ruler, Marie Louise.

A couple of blocks east is **San Pietro Somaldi**, its delicate facade dating from 1248, this time stone on the lower levels, topped with two tiers of Pisan marbling and tiny columns. Above the lovely **portal** is a good carved frieze executed by Guido da Como in 1203, *Jesus Giving the Keys to St Peter*, and the customary pair of lions, common symbols for the Resurrection in medieval art – after the belief that cubs, when born, lay dead for three days until a male lion brought them to life by breathing in their faces. The church's interior is white-washed and blank, save for a sumptuous detached fresco of the *Assumption* on the right wall, and an uncredited fifteenth-century work above the first left-hand altar.

Torre Guinigi

The **Torre Guinigi** (daily: June–Sept 9am–midnight; Nov–Feb 9.30am–5pm; March 9am–5pm; April 9.30am–9pm; May & Oct 10am–6pm; €3.50), south of San Pietro in Via Sant'Andrea, is the strangest sight in Lucca's cityscape. This battlemented tower, attached to the fifteenth-century **Casa Guinigi**, town house of Lucca's leading family, is surmounted by an ancient holm oak whose roots have grown into the room below. You can climb the 44-metre tower, entering on Via Sant'Andrea, for a close-up of the tree and easily the best view over the city. The adjacent fortress, which has some wonderful austere medieval details, fronts a startling number of streets.

The eastern quarter

The city's canal and parallel road, the **Via del Fosso**, mark the entry to Lucca's more lacklustre eastern margins. The most attractive part of this quarter is the **Orto Botanico** (daily: mid-March to April & mid-Sept to Nov 10am–5pm; May–June 10am–6pm; July to mid-Sept 10am–7pm; rest of year open by reservation; €3) at the southern end of Via del Fosso, an extensive patch of green laid out in 1820 that neatly complements the ramparts. The rarer exhibits include medicinal plants, a sequoia, gingko tree, camphor tree and a cedar of Lebanon planted at the garden's opening.

Further north is the church of **San Francesco**, fronted by a relatively simple facade and adjoining a crumbling brick convent. The inside of the church is a vast empty barn, relieved only by a delicate rose window, some lovely inlaid choir stalls and fine but damaged Florentine fresco fragments to the right of the high altar depicting the Marriage and Presentation of the Virgin.

Across the street from San Francesco is the much-restored **Villa Guinigi**, built to supplement the family's medieval town house. It's now home to Lucca's major museum, the **Museo Nazionale di Villa Guinigi** (Tues–Sat 8.30am–7.30pm, Sun 8.30am–1.30pm; €4, or combined ticket with Palazzo Mansi €6.50), an extremely varied collection of painting, sculpture, furniture and applied arts. The lower floor is mainly sculpture and archeological finds, with numerous Romanesque pieces and works by della Quercia and Matteo Civitali. Upstairs, the gallery moves on to paintings, with lots of big sixteenth-century canvases, and more impressive works by early Lucchese and Sienese masters, as well as fine Renaissance offerings from artists such as Fra' Bartolommeo.

Eating and drinking

As a wealthy, gastronomic centre, Lucca has some high-quality **restaurants**. Local specialities often feature *zuppa di farro*, a thick soup of *farro*, an ancient variety of grain grown in the Garfagnana; other dishes include roast mountain goat (*capretto*) and puddings based on chestnut flour, such as *castagnaccio*.

For sixty types of bread, rolls or delicious *focaccia* (freshly baked every two hours) head for Forno Amedeo Giusti, Via Santa Lucia 18–20. La Cacioteca, Via Fillungo 242, sells a wide variety of cheeses, and two places on Piazza San Michele are worth a call: Pizzeria Pellegrini (no. 25), for excellent pizza by the slice, and Pasticceria Taddeucci (no. 34), partly for its cakes (the aniseed and raisin *buccellato* is the traditional favourite), partly for its 1881 wood-panelled and mosaic-tiled interior. Caniparoli in Via San Paolino is a wonderful chocolate shop.

Restaurants

Buca di Sant'Antonio Via della Cervia 3 ☎0583.55.881. Lucca's finest restaurant has been around for over two hundred years and still retains some of its old-world charm. Excellent service, top-quality meat or fish menu and delicious house pasta and desserts such as *semifreddo Buccellato*. Around €30 a head. Closed Sun eve & Mon; booking essential.

Da Guido Via Cesare Battisti 28 ☎0583.467.219. A small locals' hangout and more like an extended bar than a restaurant, this is one of the cheapest places in town for basic Lucchese nosh. Closed Sun.

Da Leo Via Tegrimi 1 ☎0583.492.236, ⓦwww .trattoriadaleo.it. A good-value, family-run place near Piazza San Michele which preserves the authentic look and feel of an old-fashioned trattoria. Closed Sun eve.

Gli Orti di Via Elisa Via Elisa 17 ☎0583.491.241. Popular pizzeria/trattoria with wonderful risottos and some vegetarian dishes. Open evenings only; closed Wed.

Da Guido-Locanda Di Bacco Via San Giorgio 36 ☎0583.493.136. This restaurant with lovely wood-panelled interior does quality food at good prices. Specialities include salt cod with chickpeas.

Osteria Baralla Via Anfiteatro 5 ☎0583.440.240.
Something of an institution in Lucca, this traditional
osteria serves simple local food in a pair of
wonderfully rustic dining rooms. Occasional live
music. Closed Sun.

Osteria Machiavelli Via Cesare Battisti 28
☎0583.467.219. A great family-run place with a
jovial air of controlled chaos, fantastic food and
unbeatable prices of around €15 for two courses.
Closed Sun.

Ristorante Puccini Corte San Lorenzo 1
☎0583.316.116, ⓦwww.ristorantepuccini.com.
Another of Lucca's top-notch restaurants, with a
welcoming interior, excellent service and imaginative seafood menu. Closed Wed eve & Tues.

Trattoria Buralli Piazza Sant'Agostino 10
☎0583.950.611. Traditional trattoria with a wide
choice of home-style local cooking and a selection
of wines from the Lucchesi hills. Closed Tues & Wed.

Cafés and bars

Antico Caffè di Simo Via Fillungo 58.
Lucca's famous century-old café, with

original Art Nouveau-style furnishings and delicious
cakes and pastries, as well as a few simple hot
dishes for €6–8. Closed Mon.

Caffè del Mercato Piazza San Michele. The most
alluring of the bars around the main piazza, particularly as the church keeps it nice and shady
throughout lunch.

Gelateria Veneta Via Vittorio Veneto 74.
This *gelateria* has been serving some of Lucca's
best ice cream since 1927 and is open
conveniently late. Closed mid-Jan to mid-Feb &
Tues in winter.

Girovita Piazza Antelminelli 2. With tables outside
in the quiet piazza opposite the cathedral, trendy
Girovita is the place to come for a lengthy
afternoon coffee or an *aperitivo*. Closed Mon.

Vineria I Santi Via dell'Anfiteatro 29a. Inventive,
well-prepared dishes, such as goose-liver paté with
marmalade, accompany the wine list at this bar,
which has tables outside on a small piazza behind
the amphitheatre. Closed Wed.

Listings

Banks and exchange Change facilities at the
train station (daily 6am–9pm) plus many banks and
numerous ATMs throughout the town.

Bike rental The tourist office in Piazzale Verdi; Cicli
Bizzarri (☎0583.496.031) or Biciclette Poli
(☎0583.493.787, ⓦwww.biciclettepoli.com), either
side of the tourist office in Piazza Santa Maria.

Buses CLAP (☎0583.587.897) and Lazzi
(☎0583.584.876) operate out of Piazzale G. Verdi
and run an extensive network in the region and to
Florence, Pisa and La Spezia. See "Travel details"
(p.260) for routes.

Hospital Campo di Marte, Via dell'Ospedale
☎0583.9701.

Internet access At the tourist office at Piazza
Santa Maria; from €3.50 per 15min.

Lost property At the *Comune*, Ufficio Economato,
Via Cesare Battisti 10 ☎0583.4422.

Police Questura, Viale Cavour 38 ☎0583.4551.

Post office Via Vallisneri 2 (Mon–Fri 8.15am–6pm,
Sat 8.30am–12.30pm).

Taxis Piazza Napoleone ☎0583.492.691, railway
station ☎0583.494.989, Piazza Santa Maria
☎0583.494.190.

East of Lucca

As with Florence's hinterland, Lucca's surroundings are dotted with
outstanding **villas**, built by wealthy merchants as retreats from the rigours of
city life, or simply as an indulgence on the part of aristocratic landowners.
Some of these started life as simple country houses, others had grandiose
ambitions from the word go; most have been repeatedly altered since their
construction. Many involved the leading architects of their day, either in the
construction of the villas themselves, or in the design of the magnificent
gardens that accompanied them.

Three of the villas – **Villa Reale**, **Villa Mansi** and **Villa Torrigiani** (also
known as the Villa di Camigliano) – lie within a ten-kilometre radius of Lucca
to the northeast; they can all be reached in a hour or so by bike. Slightly
further afield is the **Villa Garzoni** at **Collodi**, which competes for attention

with the **Parco di Pinocchio**, an attraction advertised on roadside hoardings all over Tuscany.

Villa Reale

By general consent, the **Villa Reale** at **Marlia** is the most beautiful of the villas close to Lucca. Access is via the SS445 from Lucca to Barga, turning off to Marlia after 8km; a less direct but better-signposted route takes the SS435 for Montecatini Terme, with a left turn after 7km, also signed for the villa.

The Villa Reale's life as a country house started with the destruction of a fortress on this site in the fourteenth century, its first gardens being laid out a century later. The present Neoclassical look dates from 1806, when Napoleon's sister, Elisa Baciocchi, compelled the Orsetti family to sell up. Having ousted the owners, she and her personal architect, Morel, set about a radical remoulding of the villa and garden, completely refurbishing the interior and planning an English park complete with huge monumental lake. Some of the garden's most important earlier fixtures were respected, though Napoleon's downfall and Elisa's subsequent eviction undoubtedly saved other older components from destruction. Sadly, the vigour of court life at the Villa Reale also vanished with Elisa. The violinist Paganini had been employed as resident composer; he was later known to claim his playing had caused his patroness to swoon with ecstasy.

Only the **garden** is open to the public, and only on guided tours (March–Oct Tues–Sun hourly 10am–noon & 2–6pm; also open public hols that fall on Mon; Nov–Feb by appointment only ℡0583.30.108; €7). Its most striking aspect is the sweeping lawn that runs from the house down to the lake, a feature of the original layout that was enlarged under the Baciocchi regime. To its left, set deep in the woods, is the **Grotto of Pan**, an elaborate two-storey hideaway with mosaic floor, much trailing greenery and a ceiling of stone plants and flowers. The hidden fountains that once sprayed the unwary are regrettably no longer working. To one side of the lawn, an avenue of ilex trees leads to the heart of the original garden, centred on a trio of **garden rooms**, which become progressively more confined. The first has a collection of lemon trees and a pool on which swans drift; the second features a high-spouting fountain; the third is a tiny and intimate "green theatre", its orchestra pit and seats all made of box and yew hedges, and edged with a variety of exotic flora.

Villa Mansi

Perhaps the least interesting of the villa quartet is the **Villa Mansi** at **Segromigno**, 5km east of Marlia (Tues–Sun 10am–1pm & 3–6pm; winter closes 5pm; ℡0583.920.096, ⓦwww.villamansi.it; €7). Originally a plain sixteenth-century country house, the villa was enlarged in 1635 by Muzio Oddi and expanded many times in subsequent centuries. The harmonious late-Renaissance facade remains, much adorned with statuary and flanked by two pavilions joining the three-arched portico. The **garden** has suffered more brutal treatment. The few early sections that remain intact are the best: the French-inspired eastern part, with its star-shaped avenues and irregular arrangement of fountains and basins; and the western part, laid out between 1725 and 1732 by the Sicilian architect Filippo Juvarra – the man who refashioned Turin. At the beginning of the nineteenth century much of Juvarra's geometric work was replaced by haphazard borrowings from English garden design. Innovations by the present owners have continued the garden's dubious development.

Villa Torrigiani

At **Camigliano**, 2km from the Villa Mansi, the **Villa Torrigiani**, or Villa di Camigliano (daily: March to first Sun in Nov 10am–noon & 3–7pm, ⓣ0583.928.041; garden and villa €10, garden only €8), was built for the Buonvisi family in the sixteenth century, and transformed almost entirely by Alfonso Torrigiani in the eighteenth century to conform with the prevailing taste for villas and gardens in the English manner. Though little from the original survives, the present ensemble is a fine example of less formal garden design. From Lucca, take the SS435 for Montecatini Terme, and fork left at Borgonuovo (11km). The villa is clearly signed from Camigliano.

A magnificent avenue of cypresses leads to the villa's stately Baroque facade, adorned with a similar surfeit of statuary to the Villa Mansi's; Oddi was probably the architect here, too. The **interior** has been slightly diminished by a spate of thefts, but there's still a wealth of furniture and some odd points of passing interest. The extravagantly decorated central hall and the elliptical staircase are outstanding, both products of the eighteenth-century modifications.

The **gardens**, and larger park alongside, are complex and beautiful affairs, noted above all for their *giochi d'acqua* (water games). Intended to drench unsuspecting visitors with hidden sprays and fountains activated by the owner, or by the pressure of footsteps on levered flagstones, these tricks were especially popular with Mannerist gardeners, but in fact were first used in Roman times. The devices here, initiated by the fun-loving Marquis Niccolò Santini – Lucca's ambassador to the court of Louis XIV – are among the finest examples still functioning. They're all contained in the **Garden of Flora**, a sunken garden to the east of the villa – all that has survived the garden's eighteenth-century anglicization. The Marquis would first herd his guests into the garden from an upper terrace, whereupon they would find their path blocked by a wall of spray. Attempting to retreat back down the beautiful pebble-mosaic path, they would discover that this too was now awash with water. Seeking sanctuary on the roof of the Temple of Flora, a small cupola-topped grotto, they would blunder into the biggest soaking of all, as water gushed from the domed roof, from the four statues set in the walls (representing the four winds), and, as if this weren't enough, shot up from the floor as well. In 1985, frosts damaged some of the underground piping, but the gardeners occasionally provide impromptu demonstrations of the temple's aquatic surprises.

Collodi and around

When, in 1881, Carlo Lorenzini published the first instalment of the children's book that was to make him famous, he used the pen-name Carlo Collodi, in honour of his mother's birthplace, a small town 15km east of Lucca. And so, whereas other Tuscan towns are devoted to a patron saint, **COLLODI** has dedicated itself to a living puppet with an erectile nose – **Pinocchio**. To English-speakers reared on the Disney version, it's difficult to appreciate the reverence accorded Pinocchio in his homeland, where the tale's moral simplicity and exemplary Tuscan prose ensures it a massive following. It's indicative of *Pinocchio*'s standing that an Italian national newspaper poll once shortlisted the book as a contender for the title of "Greatest Novel of All Time", and that actor-director Roberto Benigni lavished so much attention on his 2002 film version that it ended up being the most expensive film ever made in Italy.

Created in the 1950s, the **Parco di Pinocchio** (daily March–Oct 9am–sunset; ⓦwww.pinocchio.it; €10) honours the famous book with statues of its characters, a sequence of mosaics depicting moments from Pinocchio's life, and various tableaux scattered around the paths that wind through the park. The monsters and mazes are fun without any background knowledge, but you'll need to have read the book in order to get the most from the park – and to field questions should you be visiting with infatuated children. Pinocchio's importance to the nation can be gauged from the fact that Michelucci – architect of Florence's train station and several prestigious churches – was commissioned to design the **restaurant** and **museum** near the entrance. There's also a very inviting toy shop ready to hook the kids as you leave.

Overshadowing the Pinocchio park, the vast **Villa Garzoni** evolved from a castle that stood here in the days before Lucca surrendered this region to Florence. The house took on its present form in the second half of the seventeenth century, but it was towards the end of the following century that it acquired the magnificent formal **garden** (daily: April–Oct 9am–sunset; Nov–March 9am–noon & 2pm–sunset; €6) that makes this one of Italy's finest villas. Access is usually through a gate on the main road, but the garden was designed to be entered through the wood adjoining the villa, so that the visitor would emerge from the wilderness into this precisely orchestrated landscape. Maximizing the theatrical possibilities of the steep slope, it deploys the full resources of the Baroque garden: circular fountains, topiary animals, patterns of flowers and coloured stones, a water staircase, a zigzagging cascade of steps and terraces, and terracotta figures in every corner.

One of the most dramatically sited Romanesque churches in Tuscany is a short distance north of Collodi at **Villa Basilica**, a tiny village clinging to a ridge below Monte Pietra Pertusa; follow the main road for 3km, then keep an eye out for a sharp left turn. It's a sternly unadorned building, made attractive by the backdrop of woods and terraces.

Pescia and Castelvecchio

The medium-sized town of **PESCIA**, 8km west of Montecatini Terme (see p.215), is Italy's top producer of cut flowers, boxing around three million lilies, carnations, gladioli and other blooms per day at the height of the season.

Split by the Pescia river, the town has two distinct zones: the left bank forms the ecclesiastical quarter, the right is the secular and commercial district. The **Duomo**, rebuilt Baroque but with a fourteenth-century campanile, takes second slot to **San Francesco** in Via Battisti – reached by walking towards the river from the cathedral and turning right before the bridge. Here Bonaventura Berlinghieri's panel *Six Scenes from the Life of St Francis* (third altar on the right), painted nine years after Francis's death, provides what's publicized as the most accurate surviving portrait of the saint, but is in truth a routinely stylized image. On the other side of the nave, the Cappella Cardini was added to the Gothic church by the architect known simply as Buggiano, employing the style of his adoptive father, Brunelleschi. The nearby oratory of **Sant'Antonio Abbate** has a *Deposition* that's an outstanding specimen of thirteenth-century woodcarving. Over on the right bank, at one end of the elongated Piazza Mazzini, the church of **Madonna di Piè di Piazza** is another worthy creation by Buggiano. At the other end of the square stands the bemedalled **Palazzo dei Vicari**, Romanesque home of the local council. The only reason to hang around in Pescia is to sample the town's edible specialities – asparagus and a questionable stew known as *cioncia*, made from ox's muzzle; *Cecco*, Via Forti 84 (℡0572.477.955; closed Mon) is an excellent, moderately priced **restaurant**.

About 13km upstream from Pescia – past the paper mills that keep the town's second industry going – stands the strange **Pieve San Tommaso** in the village of **Castelvecchio**. Founded in the eleventh century, it bears a frieze of ghoulish faces on the facade and apse, suggesting a strong pagan undertow to the Christian piety of this area. Inside are some wonderfully carved capitals and a gloomy crypt that intensifies the threatening aura of the grimacing heads.

The Riviera della Versilia

The northern coast of Tuscany is known, somewhat hyperbolically, as the **Riviera della Versilia**. The beach resorts that run unbroken between **Viareggio** and **Forte dei Marmi** offer Italian beach culture in all its glory. Much of the sand is leased to the virtually indistinguishable *stabilimenti*, who in turn charge admission to their strips and rent out chairs and umbrellas; there are free public beaches (*spiaggia pubblica*), too, at regular intervals. For a swim and some sun in cheerfully crowded conditions, this coast is not as bad as it's usually painted: the water may be cleaner elsewhere but it's not filthy, and the sand is immaculately groomed. Bus and train links to all points are excellent, especially in the summer, when you can move up and down the coast with more ease than anywhere else in Tuscany.

Viareggio

The best town on the coast, **VIAREGGIO** is also Tuscany's biggest seaside resort, with an air of elegance lent mainly by the long avenue of palms that runs the length of its seafront promenade. A modest collection of Art Nouveau-style frontages – designed by the father of Italian Art Nouveau, Galileo Chini – adds to the sense of refinement, though for the most part the buildings are old-style seaside hotels. In the early part of last century, the town's reputation for exclusivity was well deserved; these days all that's left is the high prices. The excellent **beaches** are all private, charging €20 and upwards for admission – except for the free stretch between Viareggio and Torre del Lago – and in summer the few hotels that aren't full usually hold out for *pensione completa*. You may prefer to join the majority and cram into the train for a day-trip: this is what many Florentines do – in summer, special early-morning trains from the city are packed with raucous *ragazzi*.

Viareggio's main focus is its promenade, the **Passeggiata Margherita** along Viale Regina Margherita, the broad thoroughfare that runs along the seafront for 3km. Most of the Art Nouveau fronts are crowded together around the town's best-known spot, the *Gran Caffè Margherita*, close to the start of the *passeggiata* near the marina. Across the marina and distinct from the town, the **Viale dei Tigli** is a beautiful avenue of lime trees that stretches 6km south, giving access to various beaches and most of the town's campsites.

Carnevale at Viareggio

The only time Viareggio hits national headlines is during its three-week **Carnevale** (mid-Feb/early March), one of the liveliest in Italy. Each Sunday there's a parade of colossal floats, or *carri*, bearing lavishly designed papier-mâché models of politicians and celebrities. The "Cittadella del Carnevale" to the north of Viareggio has been designed as a home for the vast hangars in which the artists construct their imaginative creations and also boasts a theatre and multimedia museum. You can visit all year round; contact the Fondazione Carnevale, Piazza Mazzini 22 (℡0584.962.568, ⓦwww.viareggio.ilcarnevale.com) for further details.

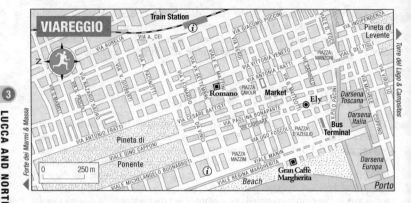

Practicalities

Viareggio's **train station**, ten-minutes' walk back from the seafront, has a summer-only **tourist office** (April–Sept Mon–Sat 9am–1pm & 3.30–7pm; ☎0584.46.382), supplementing the main tourist office in town, Viale Carducci 10 (Mon–Sat 9am–2pm & 3–7.30pm, Sun 9am–1pm, plus 3–7.30pm in July & Aug; ☎0584.962.233, ⓦwww.aptversilia.it). **Buses** stop near the centre at Piazza d'Azeglio and Piazza Mazzini. Vaibus have an office in Piazza d'Azeglio for tickets and information (☎0584.30.996). A series of kiosks at the Pineta di Ponente, north of the centre, have **bikes for rent**.

The town has over a hundred one-star **hotels**, many near the tourist office on Viale Carducci, and along Via Vespucci and Via Leonardo da Vinci. More upmarket options are equally numerous. There are several **campsites** off Viale dei Tigli on the edge of the Parco Regionale (see opposite); the first is the *Viareggio*, Via Comparini 1 (☎0584.391.012, ⓔcampingviareggio@tin.it; April–Sept), after about 1km.

Restaurant prices are considerably over the odds – especially on the seafront. For sublime fish and seafood cooking, make for the Michelin-starred *Romano*, Via Mazzini 120 (☎0584.31.382; closed Jan & Mon, plus lunch on Tues in July & Aug).

Torre del Lago and around

The journey south from Viareggio along Viale dei Tigli is worth it just for the lime trees; whether you press on to the hamlet of **TORRE DEL LAGO** (served by half-hourly buses #2 and #4 from Viareggio's Piazza d'Azeglio) depends on how much you value Puccini, who spent the later part of his life in a villa on the edge of the adjacent **Lago di Massaciuccoli**.

It's easy to miss the **Villa Puccini**, set back from the shore and surrounded by bars, trees and high iron railings. Visits are in guided groups of no more than eighteen people (every 30min; Tues–Sun 10am–12.30pm & 3–6.30pm; closes 6pm April & May, 5.30pm Dec–March; ⓦwww.giacomopuccini.it; €7); the rooms feature original furnishings, mementos and the piano on which Puccini bashed out many of his operas. In late July and August the **Festival Pucciniano** (ⓦwww.puccinifestival.it) presents the master's works in Torre del Lago's outdoor theatre and various other venues. It's an extremely popular show, as are the international regattas held on the lake through the summer.

The Lago di Massaciuccoli, no more than 2m deep, yet covering an area the size of Pisa, is one of the few Tuscan lagoons not lost to land reclamation. Once it supported virtually all Italy's species of aquatic bird, but many have been wiped out by pollution and hunters; Puccini himself came here to practise "my second favourite instrument, my rifle". Now the lake forms part of the **Parco Regionale di Migliarino–San Rossore** (Ⓦwww.parks.it), and is also a protected bird sanctuary; as a result there are some 80 breeding and another 65 occasional species on the lake. You can take a **boat trip** for an hour's tour around the lake (Ⓣ0584.350.252; €7).

Torre del Lago has several **campsites**, including *Bosco Verde*, Viale Kennedy 5 (Ⓣ0584.359.343, Ⓦwww.boscoverde.com; April–Sept) and the popular *Burlamacco*, Viale Marconi (Ⓣ0584.359.544, Ⓦwww.campingburlamacco. com; April–Sept). Of its **hotels**, most are on the main Viale Marconi, except for the fairly basic *Butterfly*, Belvedere Puccini 24 (Ⓣ&Ⓕ0584.341.024; ❶), right by the lake, and the more comfortable three-star *Turandot*, Viale Kennedy 27 (Ⓣ0584.341.025, Ⓦwww.hotelturandot.com; ❸), on the way to the sea. Along the seafront there are plenty of good **restaurants** and pizzerias, and a couple of **clubs** that draw crowds from as far afield as Florence.

North of Viareggio

The Versilia's ribbon development continues **north of Viareggio**, distinguishable only by a gradual shift downmarket. The town of **Pietrasanta**, 2km back from the Marina di Pietrasanta beach, is no more than a busy marble centre with one or two old buildings; it is, though, a good base from which to head up into the Alpi Apuane. Buses into the mountains leave from the terminal outside the train station, with hourly services to Seravezza (where you can change for connections to Levigliani and Stazzema), and three daily to Castelnuovo di Garfagnana. There is little reason to stay – unless you are planning some local hikes in the foothills.

Forte dei Marmi

As these places go, **FORTE DEI MARMI** is a pleasant resort, with lush, tree-lined streets and a good beach. It's a place for a swim and stroll, but there's nothing here to justify its reputation as the trendiest spot on the coast, nor the high prices in its top hotels and restaurants. Once a major port for marble from the Apuane, it's now one of the second-home capitals of Tuscany, and a retreat for writers and artists who hole up in its more isolated, tree-surrounded villas. For a few hundred metres north of the town there's a stretch of **dunes** with no development at all; it looks a tempting camping option, but local police will shift you within minutes if you try to pitch a tent. Beyond the dunes, nondescript Cinquale and Ronchi resume the corridor of beach-front commercialism.

Like Pietrasanta, though, Forte dei Marmi is a good point of access to the mountains, with **buses** to Seravezza, Levigliani, Stazzema and Farnocchia. There are services to these village and to Lucca, Viareggio and Pietrasanta from the Forte dei Marmi-Seravezza-Querceto **train station**, located 3km inland at Querceta, and also from Via Matteotti in the town. Buses also run from nearby Via Pascoli to La Spezia, Pisa, Lucca and Florence. The **tourist office**, Via Achille Franceschi 8b (April–Sept Mon–Sat 9am–1pm & 3–6pm, plus July & Aug Sun 9am–1pm; Oct–March Mon–Sat 9am–1pm, Fri & Sat also 3–7pm; Ⓣ0584.80.091), can provide details of the hundred-odd **hotels**. **Restaurants** largely cater to the well-heeled, though there are the usual seafront pizzerias. For about €80-plus you can have one of the region's finest culinary experiences at the Michelin-starred *Lorenzo*, Via Carducci 61 (℡0584.874.030; closed Jan & Mon, plus lunch in July & Aug). Fresh fish is the order of the day: "A fish has 24 virtues," says owner Lorenzo Viani, "but loses one with each hour that passes."

The Alpi Apuane

Tuscany's Versilia coast is dominated by the mountains of the **Alpi Apuane**, a forty-kilometre spread of genuinely Alpine spectacle. Now a protected Parco Regionale, they are crisscrossed by well-marked footpaths and offer huge rewards for the walker and naturalist. If you want to do more than admire the jagged knife-edge ridge of the mountains from afar, there are numerous marked trails starting from roadheads deep in the mountains; the biggest concentration of these tracks is in the peaks east of Forte dei Marmi and Pietrasanta, centred on **Pania della Croce** (1859m) and **Monte Forato** (1223m). Aside from busy,

Walks in the Apuane

For information on the Parco Regionale contact the **tourist office** and park **visitor centre**, at Via Corrado del Greco 11 in **Seravezza** (Mon–Sat 9.30am–12.30pm, plus Tues & Thurs 3.30–5.30pm; ℡0584.756.144, ⓦwww.parks.it); during the summer they organize full-day guided walks, free of charge, that you should book in advance. The detailed *Multigraphic* 1:25,000 map (available locally) marks all the main walking trails and refuges.

The main approach to the northern group of peaks, round **Pania della Croce**, is from **Levigliani**, reached by bus from Forte dei Marmi and Pietrasanta; it has a couple of two-star hotels: *Vallechiara*, Via Lambora 12 (℡&℻0584.778.054; ❷), and *Raffaello*, Via Nord 11 (℡&℻0584.778.063; ❶). A mining road runs from Levigliani towards Monte Corchia (1677m), about half of which has been removed by quarrying. You can sometimes get lifts up this far from mining lorries, although travelling on the road on the mine's working days is officially prohibited. From the top of the road, you can pick up trail #9 to the 31-bed *Rifugio Giuseppe del Freo* (2hr 30min walk from Levigliani; mid-June to mid-Sept open daily; rest of year Sat & Sun only; ℡0584.778.007; ❶). From here, the best walk leads up Pania della Croce (trail #126; 2hr 30min from the refuge).

Behind **Colonnata** village (site of many quarries, 8km inland from Carrara; the CAI trail #38 leads to a dense web of paths around Monte Rasore (1422m) and Monte Grondice (1805m). **Campo Cecina**, 18km north of Carrara on the SS446, has the all-year *Rifugio Carrara* (1320m; ℡0585.841.972, ⓦwww.caicarrara.it; ❶), and a rather more gentle selection of paths.

For the southern peaks, round **Monte Forato**, the best access point is **Stazzema**, a lovely village in its own right, with the one-star hotel *Procinto*, Via IV Novembre 21 (℡0584.777.004; ❶). The bus from Forte dei Marmi and Pietrasanta to Stazzema goes via Farnocchia, itself the starting point for some easy paths through the trees. The classic walk from Stazzema (trail #5) is a gentle climb through chestnut woods to the **Procinto**, a huge table-top crag mentioned by Dante. Below it, at 865m, is the 45-bed *Rifugio Forte dei Marmi* (early June to early Sept daily; rest of year Sat & Sun only; ℡0584.777.051; dorm bed €12). This makes a comfortable day's outing, with time to walk up to Monte Nona (1279m), drop back to the refuge for a snack, and then return to Stazzema by trails #121/#126. The refuge is also a perfect base for walks along the main ridge – for example, to the *Rifugio Giuseppe del Freo* (see above; 2hr).

modern Massa, the main town is **Carrara**, known above all else as the marble capital of Italy, characterized by huge blocks of stone littering the roadsides, fine white dust everywhere and mine-scarred rockfaces.

Thanks to their position and height, the Apuane are a perfect combination of different ecological habitats, from tundra through Alpine meadow to Mediterranean grassland. An extraordinary variety of **wild flowers** makes this one of the country's richest botanic enclaves, but the most noticeable vegetation is the immense **forests** of chestnut and beech which cover virtually all the lower slopes. These shelter some of the mountains' three hundred species of **birds**, including the golden eagle, which has recently returned to nest here; sadly, protection came too late to preserve many larger **mammals** from hunters, though you may see marmots – rare in the Apennines – on the higher, sunnier slopes.

Carrara

You can't get away from marble in **CARRARA**, a town whose very name is said to derive from *kar*, the Indo-European word for stone. Once you leave behind the sprawling factories around the station, however, the town itself is

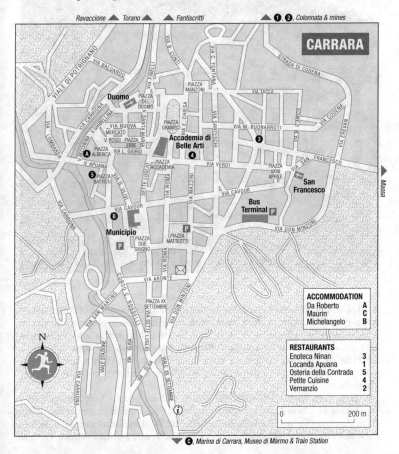

▲ Marble quarries near Carrara

a surprisingly attractive place. Set in the hills above this mess, central Carrara has a rural feel, with peeling pastel stucco on its houses, elegant side streets lined with rows of green shutters, and a couple of piazzas and a **Duomo** that would do credit to any Tuscan town. By contrast, the town's "resort", **Marina di Carrara**, is grim – more a container port than a beach. If you want the sea, it's best to drive inland to Massa, and then drop down to the coast there.

Carrara feels like a self-sufficient town, and its people have always had a reputation as a breed apart – something they preserved even under the long-term domination of the Malaspina nobles, the local medieval big shots. Before their rule, the town had developed as a trading centre poised between Tuscany, the mountains and the Ligurian coast. Roman exploitation of marble made trade with the nearby colony of Luni, over the Ligurian border, particularly brisk; something of its scale can be seen in the ruins of the colony currently being excavated there.

Today, 700,000 tonnes of stone are extracted from the Carrara area annually, making this area still the world's single largest producer of marble. Most is used – to the chagrin of many locals – not for sculpture or in building projects, but ground into dust for use in the paper industry. Huge wire saws slice into the mountains at a rate of about 8cm an hour, their 24-hour whine the bane of local residents. Environmentalists oppose the speed of extraction, but the quarry owners will fight all the way to preserve the two thousand jobs that remain, in an industry that employed as many as 14,000 men barely a century ago.

Arrival, information and accommodation

Carrara's **train station** is close to the sea and has a regular bus service to the old town. Bus connections from La Spezia and Florence arrive in Piazza Menconi in Marina di Carrara; services from more local towns use Via Don Minzoni. The **tourist office** is at Via XX Settembre 46 (Mon–Sat: April & May 9am–5pm; June–Aug 9am–1pm & 4–7.30pm; rest of year 9am–1pm & 3–5pm; ☎0585.844.136 or 0585.844.403).

Accommodation in the old town is limited to the potentially noisy two-star *Da Roberto*, Via Apuana 3/F (☎0585.70.634; ❶) and the more salubrious three-star *Michelangelo*, Corso Carlo Rosselli 3 (☎0585.777.161, ⓔhm .carrara@tin.it; ❸). There's also the one-star *Maurin*, near the station at Via Fiorino 2 (☎0585.859.385; ❶).

The town and quarries

Carrara's **old town** centres on **Piazza Alberica**, a gracious square whose beauty owes much to the hills which come down on two sides, and to the elegant colours and tone more often associated with Liguria than Tuscany. Stray blocks of marble sit at its centre, a legacy of the biennial Scolpire

---

Carrara marble

Ever-present on the Versilia coast, whether as blocks awaiting shipment or as huge snow-like scars on the mountains, **marble** has been the lifeblood of the region for over two thousand years. Marble is a metamorphic form of limestone, hardened by colossal heat and pressure. Though it takes many forms, **Carrara stone** is usually white-grey and is prized for its flawless lustre. The many other types you'll see are mostly blocks that have been imported – from as far away as Russia – to be worked by the highly rated local factories.

The **Romans** were the first to extract this stone commercially, driving pegs of fig-wood into natural faults and then soaking them until the swollen wood split the stone. In time they used scored lines and iron chisels to produce uniform blocks about two metres square – still the basic measure.

Practices remained little changed until the Renaissance, when **Michelangelo** began to visit the area. His wet nurse was from this part of Tuscany, and he claimed he became a sculptor by ingesting the marble dust in her milk; he also claimed to have introduced the art of quarrying to Carrara, a process he considered as important as sculpting itself. The *David* is sculpted from Carrara marble, and local folklore is full of Michelangelo's pilgrimages to distant corners of the mountains in search of perfect stone.

all'Aperto, a festival in which sculptors from around the world are invited to the town, given a block of marble, and left to work in the middle of the square. If you're here between late July and early October, you may get to watch them chipping away.

A short walk brings you to the eleventh-century **Duomo**, rather squashed into its piazza, but graced with a huge tower and a lovely facade built to the inevitable Pisan-Romanesque pattern. Only the intricate rose window, a superb fourteenth-century addition, departs from the norm. The interior has a severe simplicity but contains some beautiful works – a fifteenth-century **pulpit** and five appealing statues by the fourteenth-century sculptor Bergamini. The piazza's fountain, known locally as *Il Gigante* (The Giant), is an incomplete work by the lacklustre Florentine Bandinelli. Also in the square is the house where Michelangelo put up while checking out his marble supplies; nearby in Via Santa Maria are Petrarch's digs, Casa Repetti. The impressive castle on Piazza Gramsci was once a Malaspina fortress and is now the **Accademia di Belle Arti**, with a few Roman fragments and plaster casts in its courtyard.

In Via XX Settembre, 2km southwest of town on the Marina di Carrara road (and served by a bus from Via Don Minzoni), is the **Museo Civico di Marmo** (July & Aug daily 10am–8pm; May, June & Sept daily 10am–6pm; Oct–April Mon–Sat 9am–5pm; €4.50). Run as a promotional exercise by the local Chamber of Commerce, it's an impressive display that looks at the history and production of the stone – lots of photographs, examples of different types of marble, and a room devoted to rather dubious examples of marble art.

Any short trip into the interior brings you across the huge scars of the marble **quarries**, some of the most startling sights in Tuscany. A particularly accessible site is at **COLONNATA** (taking its name from a column of Roman slaves brought in to work the mines), 8km from Carrara and served in summer by eight daily CAT **buses** from Carrara's main bus terminus at Via Don Minzoni. Don't go all the way to Colonnata village, but get off at the *Visita Cave* signs by the mine; if you're driving, follow the yellow *Cava di Marmo* signs from the town up the twisting road. You'll see a huge, blindingly white marble basin, its floor and sides perfectly squared by the enormous wire saws used to cut the blocks that litter the surroundings. There are even bigger quarries farther south, notably at Monte Corchia.

Eating and drinking

There are numerous **restaurants** in Carrara, few of them tourist-oriented. For **picnic** supplies, aim for Ricci, Via Rosselli 1 (closed Wed afternoon & Sun), which preserves a wonderful Art Nouveau interior.

Enoteca Ninan Via Bartolini 3 ☎0585.74.741. An excellent little wine bar for a drink or meal. Snacks and wine by the glass are also available. Closed Mon lunch.

Locanda Apuana Via Comunale 1, Colonnata ☎0585.768.017, ⊛www.locandaapuana.com. Like *Venanzio* (see below), this restaurant is rated by the Slow Food organization. It's also excellent, and a touch cheaper. Closed Sun & Mon.

Osteria della Contrada Via Ulivi 2 ☎0585.776.961. Simple but pleasant surroundings and moderately priced regional cooking. Closed Mon.

Petite Cuisine Via Verdi 4 ☎0585.70.226. Fresh fish and seafood in a welcoming, family-owned, family-run restaurant. Closed Sun & Aug.

Venanzio Piazza Palestro 3, Colonnata ☎0585.750.062, ⊛www.ristorantevenanzio.com. For a treat, head out to Colonnata, where the Slow Food-approved *Venanzio* has attracted even the president of Italy: reckon on around €40 for what should be a sensational meal. Closed Sun eve & Thurs; booking essential.

The Garfagnana

The **Garfagnana** is the general name for the area encompassing the Serchio valley north of Lucca, one of Tuscany's least-explored yet most spectacular corners. The paucity of visitors is accounted for by the lack of any great sights – medieval **Barga** and the spa town of Bagni di Lucca are the only historic towns – but for anyone with an interest in hiking or fine scenery, there are rewards aplenty. Much of the Garfagnana is protected as a regional **nature reserve**, whose excellent on-the-ground organization has mapped and signposted a good range of walks. The best of these are on the east of the Serchio valley, up in the mountainous **Orecchiella** range. The Serchio's western flanks comprise the equally spectacular mountains of the Alpi Apuane, best reached from the coastal side (see p.246).

If you don't have your own transport, the best way to see the Garfagnana is on the **train** line which runs the entire length of the Serchio, past Barga and the region's rather lacklustre hub, **Castelnuovo di Garfagnana** – the handiest place to stay as a base for exploring. The line then cuts through the head of the valley to Aulla, centre of the Lunigiana, from where you can drop down by train to La Spezia (in Liguria), and complete a loop back to Lucca via Massa and Viareggio. Since Bagni di Lucca's train station is about 4km out of town, it's best to travel there by **bus** from Lucca. Other buses from Lucca run up and down the valley, with stops in Barga, Castelnuovo di Garfagnana and elsewhere.

The Lower Serchio valley

Although the road north up the **Serchio valley** soon leaves Lucca behind, there's something laborious about the first part of the journey, with dusty hills and patches of light industry dotting the way to Barga, 50km north. A possible detour is the **Pieve di Brancoli**, a twelfth-century abbey reached by a twisting hillside road on the east bank of the valley, 10km out of Lucca. More easily visited, with its own rail stop, is **Diecimo**, over on the west bank. Its Latin name is explained by a past as a Roman outpost, positioned ten Roman miles (17km) from Lucca. No more than a hamlet, it is dominated by a large, white Romanesque campanile, clearly visible from the river.

Some 4km on, road and rail line bypass **BORGO A MOZZANO**, which comprises a single cobbled street of medieval houses and the famous **Ponte della Maddalena** (or Ponte del Diavolo). Narrow, steep and elegant, this strange five-arched bridge was constructed in the eleventh century. According to legend it was built by the Devil in exchange for the soul of the first person to cross it; as in every European village where a version of this tale survives, the villagers outfoxed Satan by sending across an unsuspecting animal – in this case a dog. **Accommodation** includes *Pensione Gallo d'Oro*, Via del Brennero 3 (☎0583.88.380; ❶), whose seven rooms share a single bathroom, and two-star *Il Pescatore*, Via Primo Maggio 8 (☎0583.88.071, ⓦwww.ilpescatorehotel.it; ❶), with eight en-suite doubles.

Bagni di Lucca and around

Though it had been a spa for centuries, **BAGNI DI LUCCA**, 25km north of Lucca, hit the social big time only in the early nineteenth century, when the patronage of Elisa Baciocchi brought in Europe's fashionable elite. The town boasted one of Europe's first official casinos – roulette was invented here – and was graced by the presence of such luminaries as Byron, Shelley and Browning.

Today, Bagni di Lucca retains its elegance and pretty surroundings; the atmosphere is fairly subdued. A dozen reasonably priced **hotels**, spread out along the valley, cater to those who've come to soak in the salty or sulphurous waters. For some old-world charm, try the two-star *Svizzero*, Via C. Casalini 30 (T&F0583.805.315; April–Sept; ●); the one-star *Roma*, Via Umberto I 110 (T0583.87.278, Wwww.hotelromabagnidilucca.it; March–Oct; ●); or the three-star *Bridge*, 2km away in the square at Ponte a Serraglio (T0583.805.324, Wwww.bridge-hotel.it; ●). Ponte is also home to the local **tourist office**, at Via Casinò Municipale (mid-March to mid-Sept Mon–Sat 9.30am–6.30pm & 3.30–6.30pm, Sun 9.30am–12.30pm; mid-Sept to mid-March Mon & Wed–Sat 9.30am–12.30pm; T0583.805.745). The best **place to eat** in Bagni is the *Circolo Dei Forestieri*, Piazza Jean Varraud 10 (T0583.86.038; closed Mon & Tues lunch), which serves food both exquisite and inexpensive, in a beautiful building with a columned terrace.

The Lima valley

East of Bagni, the **Lima valley**, a tributary of the Serchio, rises towards the border with Emilia-Romagna. Two **buses** daily (morning and afternoon) make the run over the hills to San Marcello Pistoiese, the afternoon service continuing to the skiing and walking centre of Abetone.

In the valley itself, there are several possible rough road diversions to villages with ancient churches and spectacular mountain surroundings. **Pieve di Controne**, 3km northeast of Bagni, has a strange old church in red stone, fronted by a facade covered with odd diagonal motifs. **San Cassiano**, 7km further, has a twelfth-century church with a wonderful carved facade, three tiers of very shallow arches, and a much older and dirtier tower that cuts off half the marble-faced front. Just south of the valley, **Lucchio**, cascading down the mountainside 18km from Bagni, is crowned by a castle ruin.

Past Lucchio, you enter the province of Pistoia near **SAN MARCELLO PISTOIESE**, the business centre of these mountains. The main road north of here – a continuation of the N66 from Pistoia – leads 18km to **ABETONE**, the nearest winter-sports resort to Florence. Its six chair-lifts can cope with an hourly capacity of 14,000 people and at the height of the skiing season the system is tested to the fullest; even in summer there's often not too much space in the town's thirty-odd hotels, as thousands come up from the sweltering lowlands to revive themselves in the mountain air. As a package-tour destination Abetone isn't too bad, but it's not a place to go out of your way to see. With your own transport, you could make a more exciting approach to Abetone by taking the high mountain road from Bagni di Lucca to Montefegatesi, and then over the main ridge of the Orecchiella (impassable in bad weather and potentially dangerous at any time of year – consult the tourist office before setting out) to the dramatic **Orrido di Botri** gorge before climbing up to the pass of **Foce a Giove** (1674m).

Barga and around

The ancient hill-town of **BARGA** – poised 3.5km east of its train station on the Serchio – marks the start of the Garfagnana's best scenery, dominated by hills and incredibly lush vegetation. A couple of tempting minor roads lead into the wild country of the Orecchiella, offering stunning views over steep wooded slopes and across to the jagged profiles of the Alpi Apuane.

The old village is quiet, pretty and charming, with a flourishing cultural life (and strong Scottish ties – many of Scotland's Italian immigrants came from

▲ Barga

the village and around). It also has a long tradition of independence and a strong economic base founded on silk and, later, wool: felt hats became a speciality in the nineteenth century. It grew up originally around a Lombard castle, and was besieged by Lucca and Pisa before falling to Florence, under whose influence it remained until 1859. Where it differed from other Lucchesi strongholds was in its rule by elected council, a system it retained even under the Florentines.

The Town

Barga's **Duomo**, San Cristofano, was founded in the ninth century and expanded over the next four hundred years, with remedial work in 1920 after a severe earthquake. It stands at the village's highest point, fronted by a terrace that provides a huge panorama of rooftops, mountains and villa-spotted hills. Built in a honey-blonde stone known as *alberese di Barga*, the **facade**, probably adapted from part of the earliest church, is decorated in a shallow pattern of Lombard Romanesque-influenced reliefs and tiny arches, a delicate contrast to the **campanile**, which seems to have erupted from the tiled roof. Left of the door is a wonderful little relief of an obviously convivial feast, sculpted in 1200; on the architrave is an equally rustic harvest scene and twin lions.

Inside, the **naves** are beautifully divided by low walls of inlaid marble and overlooked by a superlative and idiosyncratic **pulpit**, widely considered one of the finest such creations prior to the pulpits of Nicola and Giovanni Pisano in Pisa, Siena and elsewhere. Probably created by the thirteenth-century sculptor Guido Bigarelli da Como (or a pupil), it consists of a huge rectangular stand, lavishly carved with scenes from the Scriptures and supported by four red marble pillars, the front pair of which are propped up by another pair of lions: one, with an inane smirk, surmounts a dragon (a symbol of evil), while the other stands on a man (a symbol of heresy) who is simultaneously stroking and stabbing the animal. The rear left pillar is supported by a grotesque dwarf, snub-nosed symbol of the pagan world. The church's other unmissable artefact is a tenth- or twelfth-century **statue** of St Christopher, looking rather like a huge wooden puppet; continuing the building's eccentric streak, the saint carries a child on one shoulder and a club the size of a small tree on the other. Around the church, you'll spot a cluster of della Robbia **terracottas** in the right chapel, **frescoes** on several pillars, a carved choir screen and two Giottesque **Crucifixes** – the overpoweringly framed example above the altar is particularly good.

Just below the Duomo to the left, the *centro storico* signs point the way to the Baroque chapel of **Santissimo Crocifisso dei Bianchi**, an oddly attractive extravagance, with a blue-gilt altar and four diversely excessive side chapels. Also worth a quick look by the cathedral is the **Museo Civico del Territorio di Barga** in the Palazzo Pretorio, Arringo del Duomo (April–Oct daily 10am–12.30pm & 2.30–5pm; rest of year by appointment; call ☏0583.724.759; €3), a collection of geological and paleological exhibits tracing the area's prehistoric background.

Grotta del Vento

From Gallicano, across the river from Barga train station, you can drive west for 9km, following the bottom of the Turrite valley, to what is rated as Tuscany's best cave, the rather commercialized **Grotta del Vento** (ⓦwww.grottadelvento.com) in **Fornovo Lasso**; arrive early to miss the crowds. From April to October, three different types of tour are available daily through the caverns and lakes of this bizarre subterranean landscape, lasting either one hour (hourly 10am–noon & 2–6pm; €7.50), two hours (11am, 3pm, 4pm & 5pm; €12), or three hours (10am & 2pm; €17). The rest of the year, all three tours run on Sundays and public holidays, while only the one-hour visit is available from Monday to Saturday.

Practicalities

It's a long haul up from Barga's **train** station to the town; coming from Lucca it's easier to use the regular **bus** (1hr 15min). All buses arrive at the Porta Reale, alongside the big car park where the road stops outside the walls. Barga's **tourist office** is at Via di Mezzo 45 (Mon–Fri 8am–2pm, Sat & Sun 10am–noon & 2.30–5pm; ☏0583.724.743, ⓦwww.barganews.com); check the website for details of the town's two small, high-quality summer **music festivals**, Barga Jazz and Opera Barga.

Several **hotels** and **restaurants** are ranged along the road north down to the Serchio at **Albiano**, a rather scrappy neighbourhood, but with good views. Aim for the three-star *Villa Libano*, Via del Sasso 6 (☏0583.723.059, ⓦwww.hotelvillalibano.com; ❷), next to the town park and with a nice restaurant with a garden terrace (open to guests only). The three-star *Alpino* is at Via Pascoli 41 (☏0583.723.336, ⓦwww.bargaholiday.com; closed Nov; ❷). Barga has several very good **places to eat**: for drinks and snacks, try the historic *Caffè Capretz*, Piazza Salvo Salvi 1 (closed Mon & part of Nov). For meals, the relaxed and Slow Food-approved *L'Altana*, Via di Mezzo 1 (☏0583.723.192; closed Wed & part of Feb), is a winner.

Castelnuovo di Garfagnana

Garfagnana's main town, **CASTELNUOVO DI GARFAGNANA**, is a disappointment, despite its mountain-ringed location. A rather featureless sprawl, it has a daytime market bustle to its centre but virtually no life after

5pm except on balmy summer evenings. However, Castelnuovo is the obvious base if you intend to explore the Orecchiella and eastern Alpi Apuane. Some of the mountain roads that radiate east and west offer astounding views for drivers, and the villages around are highly attractive. For serious hiking, it's also worth stopping in order to pick up maps and information. The only thing to see is the fourteenth-century **Rocca**, built by the Este dukes of Ferrara and best known for its former commander, the poet Ariosto, author of the romantic epic *Orlando Furioso*. By all accounts he didn't much enjoy his tour of duty in the 1520s, and mournful evocations of the area's landscape were to colour much of his later poetry. The rest of the town was badly damaged by bombing in World War II, though a lovely **terracotta** of *St Joseph and the Angels*, attributed to Verrocchio or the della Robbia family, survived on the Duomo's north wall.

Practicalities

There is a **visitor centre** at Piazza delle Erbe 1, just beyond the arch of the town's main square, Piazza Umberto I (daily: June–Sept 9am–1pm & 3–7pm; Oct–May 9am–1pm & 3.30–5.30pm; ☏0583.644.242), that offers information on trekking and tourism in the Garfagnana, as well as a booking service for hotels, agriturismi and rifugi. The **tourist office** at Via Cavalieri di Vittorio Veneto (summer Mon–Sat 9.30am–1pm & 3.30–7pm, Sun 9.30am–1pm & 3.30–6pm; winter Mon–Sat 10am–1pm & 3.30–6.30pm, Sun 10am–12.30pm; ☏0583.641.007) is mainly concerned with the town itself. For specialized **climbing** information contact the Club Alpino office (☏0583.65.577), below the car park at Via Vittorio Emanuele 3.

Most people **stay** in the three-star *Da Carlino*, Via Garibaldi 15 (☏0583.644.270, ⓦwww.dacarlino.it; ❷), up the steep street out of Piazza Umberto I, a fairly modern place with a moderately priced **restaurant** (closed Mon). For good home cooking try the excellent *Vecchio Mulino*, Via Vittorio Emanuele 12 (Tues–Sun 7.30am–8pm; ☏0583.62.192), a century-old *enoteca* with inexpensive snacks (including great panini) and simple meals: it also sells a range of wines by the bottle or glass.

There's a **campsite**, *Parco di Piella* (☏0583.62.916; caravans all year, tents April–Oct), in a wooded setting close to the train station at **Piella**, ten minutes from the centre. To get there from the station turn right, then first left up Viale della Rimembranza. Aside from this site, the only official camping area in the Garfagnana is *Monte Argegna* (☏0583.611.182, ⓦwww.toscanacampclub.com; April–Sept), near **Giuncugnano** (876m), north of the valley above Piazza al Serchio.

The Orecchiella

Though higher than the spectacular Apuane opposite, the **Orecchiella** mountains are generally tamer – but no less beautiful: rounded and thickly wooded, with steep lateral valleys and gentle grassy slopes above the treeline. The one monument of note is the monastery at **San Pellegrino**, now home to a museum of rural Garfagnana life. If you have transport, and whether you intend to hike or not, it's well worth following some of the minor roads into the mountains for a glimpse of one of the prettiest and least known of Tuscany's scenic enclaves.

Reached from Castelnuovo by a beautiful road past meadows, thatched barns and views, **CORFINO** is a small hill village (850m) which provides walkers with a choice of three **hotels**: the *Panoramico*, Via Fondo la Terra 9 (☏0583.660.161, ⓦwww.hotelpanoramico.com; March–Dec; ❷) and

Walks in the Orecchiella

If you're going in for serious **walking** in the Orecchiella, you should pick up one of the widely available *Multigraphic* 1:25,000 maps, which show all marked trails in the area.

There are three marked circular walks pioneered by *Airone*, the Italian natural history magazine, which don't involve too much planning. There's a board-plan at the park centre near Corfino, or staff can help you make sense of the routes. **Walk 1** (5hr) takes in the summit of the craggy limestone Cima Pania (1602m) and the nature reserve of the Pania di Corfino, the most important of the three special reserves in the park and a noted area for nesting birds of prey, including peregrine falcons. **Walk 2** (4hr) passes through oak and beech forest and a stretch of grassy meadow. **Walk 3** needs two days, with a choice of overnight stops: *Rifugio C. Battisti* (Ⓦwww .rifugiobattisiti.it) or *Rifugio La Bargetana* (Ⓦwww.rifugiobargentana.it). In addition to these, there are seven **Club Alpino paths** (2–3hr) in the area.

For a real challenge, there's a long-distance marked path known as **Garfagnana Trekking**, which starts and finishes at Castelnuovo and is designed to take about ten days. As well as taking in the best of the Orecchiella, five stages of this walk lead you through the Alpi Apuane. For details, ask at the park visitor centre in Castelnuovo.

An even more ambitious long-distance route, the linear **Grande Escursione Appenninica (GEA)**, runs through the Orecchiella on its 24-stage trail from Sansepolcro across the roof of Tuscany to the Passo dei due Santi above La Spezia. Contact the Club Alpino for details (Ⓦwww.cai.it).

California, Via Bagno 1 (Ⓣ0583.660.173, Ⓦwww.albergocalifornia.com; ❶), both three-stars, and the similarly priced two-star, *La Baita*, Via Prato all'Aia (Ⓣ0583.660.084, Ⓦwww.albergolabaita.com; June–Sept; ❶). The last is definitely the best: it's run by a pleasant family, with *mamma* in inspired charge of the hotel's restaurant kitchen.

It's worth heading north through the wild countryside for 7km to visit the excellent chalet-style **park centre** (July & Aug daily 9am–7pm; June & Sept Sat & Sun 10am–5pm; Ⓣ0583.619.002). It has a restaurant, bar, phones, an information and exhibition centre, a lake with nicely sited picnic spots, and a fine botanical garden. The nearby *Rifugio Isera* (Ⓣ0583.660.203, Ⓦwww .rifugioisera.it; April–Oct; ❶) has rooms and a camping area.

San Pellegrino in Alpe

From Castelnuovo, the drive 16km up a minor road northeast to **SAN PELLEGRINO IN ALPE** (1524m) offers stunning views over the steep valleys and ridges of the Orecchiella. Two daily summer **buses** from Castelnuovo take the parallel and almost equally impressive major road via Castiglione.

San Pellegrino's magnificently sited monastery is partly given over to an excellent **Museo Etnografico Provinciale**, Via del Voltone 14 (Tues–Sun: April & May 10am–1pm & 2–4.30pm; June–Sept 10am–1pm & 2–6.30pm; Oct–March 9.30am–1pm; plus Mon in July & Aug; €2.50). This unusually fascinating display of the Garfagnana's peasant traditions covers four floors, ranging over every aspect of country life.

The adjacent hamlet has a bar, a couple of run-down *pensioni*, and shops where you can buy local honey, oil, mushrooms, grappa and sweet chestnut flour, once the area's staple diet. You can find other **accommodation** on the Foce delle Radici pass at the top of the road, where there's an isolated hotel, the two-star *Lunardi*, Passo delle Radici (Ⓣ0583.649.071, Ⓦwww.albergolunardi.com; ❶). Down the parallel road towards Castiglione stands the three-star *Il Casone*

(☎0583.649.028, ⓦwww.hotelilcasone.com; ❷), perched at 1300m in a great location about 6km from the pass (ask the bus driver to drop you off).

The eastern Apuane

North of Castelnuovo di Garfagnana, the Serchio valley floor is itself not very memorable but if you have transport – or can fit in with very sparse bus services – there are several possible diversions into the **Alpi Apuane** to the west.

The most obvious is the road that climbs over the main ridge to Massa, a route covered by a morning and afternoon bus from Castelnuovo. The road is not quite the scenic backwater it appears on the map, but the early stretch, up the **Turrite valley**, is verdant and tree-lined, with good views of the vast crags of the Pania della Croce (1859m). Much of the road was widened following the opening of the hydroelectric station at Torrite, but it degenerates immediately beyond a tunnel into Massa province.

The one hamlet of consequence is **Isola Santa**. A section of the long-distance Garfagnana Trekking (GT; see box opposite) passes 100m west of the hamlet, and you can follow it north towards Lago di Vagli (about 5hr) or south for a couple of hours to the above-average bar and accommodation of *Rifugio Freo*. The best circular walk from Isola Santa is north on the GT-CAI-marked trail #145 to Monte Sumbra (1764m), and back the same way: a stiff climb but only about 8km in total.

Lago di Vagli

At Poggio, 8km from Castelnuovo, there's a choice of two roads. One runs to the high village of **Careggine** (882m), notable for little except its views. The other leads to **Lago di Vagli**, an artificial creation that submerged the village of Fabbriche, but left three others intact – Roggio, Vagli di Sotto and Vagli di Sopra. Every ten years the lake is drained and the ghost village slowly revealed – next due in 2014.

Roggio is immersed in chestnut trees; it boasts the biggest single specimen in Italy, 10m round and 26m high. It has a small one-star hotel, *La Guardia*, Piazza La Guardia (☎0583.649.121; ❶). Equally enticing, **Vagli di Sotto** sits on an arm of the lake, offering boat rental and a range of worthwhile walks (see box below).

Walks from Vagli di Sotto

Vagli di Sotto provides the starting point for a couple of excellent **walks** onto the highest ridges of the Alpi Apuane – for which the widely available *Multigraphic* map is invaluable.

The **first path** follows the road southwest up the Tambura valley, before linking with the CAI-marked trail #31; you can then follow this west to **Monte Focoletta** (1620m), or, more interestingly, east to CAI #144, which takes you to the top of **Monte Sumbra** (1764m) and then in a wide circle via the Tassetora valley back to Vagli di Sotto – a fantastic and varied day's walk (16km).

The **second path**, CAI #177, climbs to the Passo della Focolaccia (1650m), a meeting point of several other trails. The pass offers excellent views to the Apuane's highest point, **Monte Pisanino** (1947m), just to the north, and gives access to a superb ridge (trail #179) that takes you to the top of **Monte Grondilice** (1805m). From the summit you can carry on to Carrara, or north (on the GT) to the 22-bed *Rifugio Serenaia* (☎0583.610.085, ⓔdiamanti.diamanti@libero.it; April–Oct), the starting point for many more trails. The refuge is also accessible by road from the Serchio valley to the north, via Piazza al Serchio and Gramolazzo.

It has a popular three-star **hotel**, *Le Alpi*, Via Vandelli 8 (☎&ⓕ0583.664.057; April–Sept; ❷), offering somewhat average evening meals. **Vagli di Sopra**, above the lake, has a few rooms for rent. All of these villages have **trattorie** which, though small, offer excellent cooking.

The Lunigiana

Few people make it to Tuscany's northernmost tip, the **Lunigiana**. A land of rocky, forested landscape, with just two sizeable towns – **Aulla** and **Pontrémoli** – this is one of the most insular regions in Tuscany. Its isolation was ensured over centuries by its mountainous approaches, only breached in the nineteenth century by the carving out of a rail tunnel and twisting mountain road at Piazza al Serchio.

The Lunigiana's name derives from the **Luni**, an ancient tribe who proved a tough nut for the Romans to crack and were equally impervious for some centuries to Christianity. Later, numerous would-be rulers built castles to exact tolls from anyone passing through the valley – hence the tourist-board name for the area, "Land of the Hundred Castles". Many of these castles are now in private hands and many others were left in ruins after World War II, but the region still repays a visit for its scenery and self-contained atmosphere. **Train** connections are frequent, and Aulla is the hub of an extensive **bus** network.

Equi Terme, Fosdinovo and Fivizzano

The train from the Garfagnana emerges from its long tunnel at **EQUI TERME**, a tiny village that enjoys a superb scenic backdrop of crags and knife-edge peaks, sitting at the foot of the towering Il Solco canyon. The central *La Posta* **hotel**, Via Provinciale 15 (☎0585.97.937; closed Jan; ❶), has an inexpensive **restaurant** and garden; or you could try the comfortable *Hotel Terme*, Via Noceverde (☎0585.97.830, ⓦwww.hotelequiterme.com; ❷), which has a decent restaurant and a swimming pool.

Heading towards the coast from here by road, the most interesting route is via **FOSDINOVO**, a beautifully situated village that sits along a spur overlooking steep, wooded valleys. Host to Dante in 1306, the Castello della Malaspina here is certainly the best of the region's fortresses, although it is now usually closed to the public. If you want to break for a **meal**, head for the long-established and family-run *Il Cucco*, Via Cucco 26 (☎0187.68.907; closed Thurs).

FIVIZZANO – to the north, on the N63 road into Emilia – is a more substantial place, with its medieval Piazza Medicea, dominated by a Medici fountain and a retinue of Florentine *palazzi*. The village also has a fine thirteenth-century church, Sts Jacopo e Antonio, with a handful of Renaissance paintings. If you want a **room** or **meal**, an excellent choice is the central two-star *Hotel-Ristorante Giardinetto* in Via Roma 151 (☎0585.92.060; restaurant closed Mon; ❶). You might pass this way heading for the **Passo di Cerreto** (1261m), a walking and skiing centre on the Emilia-Romagna border. En route, 6km out of Fivizzano, look for the hamlet of Vendaso on the right, home to the Romanesque church of **San Paolo**.

Aulla and around

AULLA, squeezed onto a green strip at the confluence of two rivers, was almost totally destroyed in the last war and has virtually nothing of note except for the

Fortezza della Brunella, a sixteenth-century Genoese castle that testifies to the town's early strategic importance and contains a small natural history museum (Tues–Sun: March–May & Oct 9am–noon & 3–6pm; June–Sept 9am–noon & 3–7pm; Nov–Feb 9am–noon & 2–5pm; €3.50). With time on your hands, you might look into the parish church, built within the ruins of the eighth-century **San Caprasio**, an abbey that long dominated the hinterland.

Your best bet for really getting to grips with the Lunigiana is to head for some of the surrounding villages, most of which were fortified by the Malaspina nobles. Try Licciana Nardi, named after an early freedom fighter shot in 1844 while leading an uprising in southern Italy (his remains are in the big sarcophagus in the village's Piazza del Municipio), Caprigliola (6km south on the border with Liguria), Bibola or Ponzanello.

A more well-defined target is **VILLAFRANCA IN LUNIGIANA**, halfway from Aulla to Pontrémoli, again with the ruins of a Malaspina castle, but of more interest for its **Museo Etnografico** at Via dell'Antico Mulino (June–Sept Tues–Sun 9am–noon & 4–7pm; rest of year Tues–Thurs 9.30am–12.30pm, Sat & Sun 9.30am–12.30pm & 2.30–5.30pm; €3). Occupying an old mill in Via Borgo, this documents the area's rural traditions, with a special nod to the omnipresent sweet chestnut. From **BAGNONE**, 5km east, there are opportunities for walks into the remote chestnut-covered ridges of Monte Sillara (1867m) and Monte Marmagna (1851m).

Pontrémoli

PONTRÉMOLI is the Lunigiana's biggest centre and the northernmost town in Tuscany. Part is still evocatively medieval, especially the area rambling north of the **Torre del Campanone**. The tower, now the Duomo's campanile, originally formed part of a fortress built by Lucca's Castruccio Castracani in 1322 to keep the town's warring factions apart: hence its nickname, *Cacciaguerra* – "chaser-away-of-war". The **Duomo** itself is an extraordinary Baroque affair.

The town's most captivating attraction, however, is its collection of twenty or so prehistoric stele housed in the **Museo delle Statue-Stele Lunigianesi** (daily: May–Sept 9am–noon & 3–6pm; Oct–April 9am–noon & 2–5pm; €4), whose home is the Castello del Piagnaro, a bleak fourteenth-century castle. These highly stylized statues fall into three groups. The oldest date from 3000–2000 BC, and are crude rectangular blocks with just a "U" for a face, and only the suggestion of arms and trunk. The second group (2000–800 BC) have more angular heads and more detail; the last pieces (700–200 BC) are more sophisticated still, and usually have a weapon in each hand. Most stele were funerary headstones, but here it's thought they represented a pagan communion between heaven (the head), earth (the arms and their weapons) and the underworld (the buried bottom third). Those with heads missing perhaps suffered at the hands of Christians intent on doing away with idolatry.

Fifteen-minutes' walk south of the town, the small church of **Santissima Annunziata** was built to celebrate an appearance of the Virgin in 1471; it contains a trio of treasures, the most important an octagonal marble tempietto by Jacopo Sansovino, the others a fifteenth-century *Annunciation* and a Florentine altarpiece by an unknown artist.

Pontrémoli has the only **tourist office** in the Lunigiana (irregular hours ☎0187.831.180), in the central Piazza Municipio off Piazza Repubblica. Enquire here about the plentiful **accommodation** possibilities, or call at the three-star *Napoleon*, Piazza Italia 2 (☎0187.830.544, ⓦ www.hotelnapoleon.net; ❷), which has its own inexpensive **restaurant**. The local culinary speciality is a type of large pancake-like pasta, *testaroli*, available in any one of the town's top *trattorie*: *Da Bussè*, Piazza Duomo 32 (℡0187.831.371; closed Fri & Mon–Thurs eve), is best, a lovely, snug place that's been in the same family for generations. Also charming (with an Art Nouveau-style dining area), though pricier, is *Caveau del Teatro*, Via del Teatro 4 (℡0187.833.328, Ⓦwww.caveaudelteatro.it; closed Wed). It also has seven pleasant, antique-filled rooms in a tower-house (from ❸). For drinks and wonderful cakes, head for the historic *Caffè degli Svizzeri* at Piazza della Repubblica 21 (closed Mon).

Travel details

Trains

Aulla to: Castelnuovo di Garfagnana (10 daily; 1hr); Equi Terme (10 daily; 25min); Fivizzano (10 daily; 10min); Lucca (10 daily; 2hr); Pontrémoli (hourly; 25min); Villafranca in Lunigiana (hourly; 15min).
Lucca to: Aulla (10 daily; 2hr); Bagni di Lucca (10 daily; 30min); Barga (10 daily; 40min); Castelnuovo di Garfagnana (10 daily; 1hr); Equi Terme (10 daily; 1hr 30min); Fivizzano (10 daily; 1hr 50min); Florence (hourly; 1–2hr); Montecatini (hourly; 25min); Pescia (hourly; 15min); Piazza al Serchio (10 daily; 1hr 20min); Pisa (hourly; 30min); Pisa airport (4 daily; 45min); Pistoia (hourly; 40min); Prato (hourly; 1hr); Viareggio (hourly; 20min).

Buses

Aulla to: Equi Terme (6 daily; 1hr); Pontrémoli (9 daily; 20min).
Barga to: Bagni di Lucca (4 daily; 40min); Castelnuovo di Garfagnana (8 daily; 30min); Lucca (8 daily; 1hr 15min).

Castelnuovo di Garfagnana to: Barga (8 daily; 45min); Lucca (9 daily; 1hr 30min); Pietrasanta (3 daily; 1hr 45min); Vagli di Sotto (6 daily; 30min).
Lucca to: Bagni di Lucca, via Borgo a Mozzano (8 daily; 55min); Barga (11 daily; 1hr 15min); Camaiore (6 daily; 1hr); Castelnuovo di Garfagnana (9 daily; 1hr 30min); Florence (22 daily; 1hr 15min); Forte dei Marmi (9 daily; 1hr 20min); La Spezia (2 daily; 2hr 50min); Marina di Carrara (8 daily; 1hr 40min); Marina di Massa (8 daily; 1hr 30min); Massa (5 daily; 1hr 50min); Pescia (12 daily; 45min); Pietrasanta, via Viareggio (10 daily; 1hr); Pisa (hourly; 50min); Viareggio (at least hourly; 45min).
Pontrémoli to: Aulla (9 daily; 20min); Villafranca in Lunigiana (10 daily; 10min).
Viareggio to: Florence (hourly; 1hr 30min); Forte dei Marmi (hourly; 30min); Marina di Massa (hourly; 50min); Torre del Lago (every 30min; 15min).

Pisa, the central coast and Elba

CHAPTER 4 # Highlights

✻ **The Leaning Tower, Pisa** Thanks to high-tech intervention, the most famous building in Tuscany is safe for the next few centuries at least. See p.267

✻ **The Duomo, Pisa** One of the finest Romanesque churches in all of Italy. See p.269

✻ **The Baptistery, Pisa** Italy's largest baptistery, famed for its sculptures and amazing acoustics. See p.270

✻ **The Camposanto, Pisa** A tranquil, grassy cloister and beautiful frescoes make this one of the world's most impressive burial grounds. See p.270

✻ **Elba** If you need a break from all the art, head for the beaches of Elba. See p.282

✻ **Capraia** And if the crowds of Elba are too much, you can always take refuge here. See p.292

▲ The Camposanto, Pisa

4

Pisa, the central coast and Elba

Flying into Tuscany you'll most likely arrive at **Pisa**, a city which – thanks to its leaning tower – is known, at least in name, to almost every visitor to Italy. Like Lucca, a little way to the north, Pisa bears the architectural stamp of the Middle Ages, the tower being just one element of its **Campo dei Miracoli**, or Field of Miracles, Italy's most refined ensemble of medieval architecture. Since before the time of Galileo, Pisa has had one of Italy's major universities, and student life remains an important aspect of the city's strong sense of identity. It's an underrated place, seen by most outsiders on a whistle-stop trip – which means that finding accommodation is often less troublesome than in Tuscany's more overtly enticing towns. Furthermore, its excellent road and rail connections to Florence and to the north and south make it a good base for wider exploration.

The chief city of the central Tuscan coast, the port of **Livorno**, offers ferry connections and excellent seafood, but very little else. To the south, the **Costa degli Etruschi**, or Etruscan Riviera, is one of the least attractive areas of Tuscany, with its dingy resorts and drab hinterland of low hills and reclaimed swampland. However, it's not all bad: there are pockets of unspoilt sand around **Baratti**, and some beautiful areas of pine woodland (*pineta*) have been preserved at an important nature reserve at **Bólgheri**.

Close to Baratti, at the southern tip of the flatlands, **Piombino** provides the main point of embarkation for the biggest island of the Tuscan archipelago, **Elba**. Though peak-season crowds fill every hotel room on the island, Elba can be a seductive place in spring or early autumn, when it almost rivals the charm of outlying **Capraia**, a spot still remarkably little touched by tourism.

Pisa

Since the beginning of the age of the tourist brochure, **PISA** has been known for just one thing – the **Leaning Tower**. It is indeed a freakishly beautiful building, a sight whose impact no amount of prior knowledge can blunt. Yet it's just a single component of the amazing **Campo dei Miracoli**, where the Duomo, Baptistery and Camposanto complete an unrivalled quartet of medieval masterpieces. These, and a dozen or so churches and *palazzi* scattered about the town, belong to Pisa's

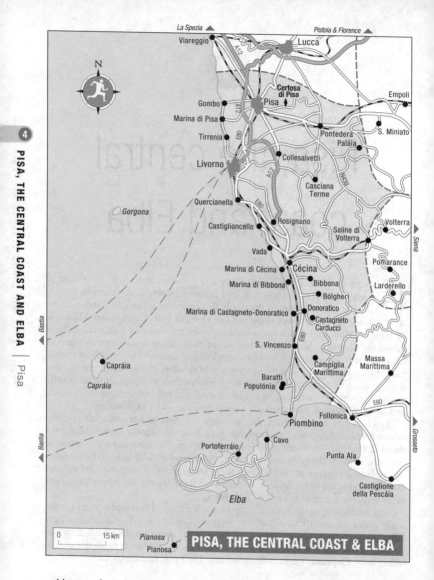

PISA, THE CENTRAL COAST & ELBA

golden age, from the eleventh to the thirteenth centuries when the city, then still a port, was one of the great powers of the Mediterranean. The **Pisan–Romanesque architecture** of this period, distinguished by its white–and–black marble facades, is complemented by some of the finest late-medieval sculpture in Italy, much of it from the workshops of Nicola and Giovanni Pisano.

The city's political zenith came in the second half of the eleventh century with a series of victories over the Saracens, whom the Pisans drove out from Corsica, Sardinia and the Balearic islands, and harassed even in Sicily. Decline set in early, however, with defeat at sea by the Genoese in 1284 followed by the silting up of the harbour. From 1406 the city was governed by Florence, whose Medici rulers re-established the University of Pisa, one of the intellectual forcing houses of the Renaissance; **Galileo**, Pisa's most famous native, was a teacher there. Subsequent centuries saw the city fade into provinciality – its state when the Shelleys and Byron took *palazzi* here, forging what Shelley termed their "paradise of exiles". The modern city has been revitalized by its airport and industrial suburbs and, of course, money from tourism.

Arrival, information and accommodation

Trains arrive at Pisa Centrale station, about 1km south of the River Arno. **Buses** from the airport and further afield come into the nearby Piazza Sant'Antonio. From either, the Campo dei Miracoli is about twenty-five-minutes' walk north (up the pedestrianized Corso Italia and across the Ponte di Mezzo), or a five-minute ride on bus #1 from outside the train station; local bus tickets are sold at a kiosk to the right out of the station. There's a **car park** outside the Porta Nuova, just west of the Campo dei Miracoli, and a free long-term car park at the airport.

There are two **tourist offices**, giving information on Pisa province as well as the city: just north of the train station, at Piazza Vittorio Emanuele 13 (Mon–Fri 9am–7pm, Sat 9am–1.30pm; ☎050.42.291, ⓦ www.pisaturismo.it); and inside the Museo dell'Opera del Duomo (see p.271).

Most people cover Pisa as a day-trip, or stay just one night, so **accommodation** is usually not too hard to find. In summer, however, it's still best to reserve in advance.

Hotels

Amalfitana Via Roma 44 ☎050.29.000, ⓕ050.25.218. Pleasant 21-room two-star, 5min walk south of the Campo dei Miracoli. ❷

Bologna Via Mazzini 57 ☎050.502.120, ⓦ www .hotelbologna.pisa.it. This smart and well-managed hotel – the best on the south side of the Arno – has 65 rooms, all of them recently refurbished to bring it up to four-star standard. ❻

Di Stefano Via Sant'Apollonia 35 ☎050.553.559, ⓦ www.hoteldistefano.pisa.it. This tidy three-star hotel, located in a quiet street just off Piazza dei Cavalieri, occupies two buildings – the better rooms are in a restored eleventh-century tower, and cost around €180 in high season. Other rooms are considerably less expensive, and online deals are frequent. ❺

Transport from Pisa airport

Pisa's **Galileo Galilei airport** (☎050.849.300, ⓦ www.pisa-airport.com), most visitors' point of entry to Tuscany, lies about 3km south of the city centre. The **drive** to Florence is straightforward (an airport slip road takes you directly onto the motorway), but the road into Pisa is so confusing that, without directions from the car-rental desk, you may well end up getting lost.

Terravision **buses to Florence** are scheduled to synchronize with incoming budget airline flights and leave from in front of the terminal; they take seventy minutes to reach Florence's Santa Maria Novella station, and tickets (€8 single) are sold at the stand right in front of you as you come out into the airport concourse. **Trains** from the airport station are cheaper (€5.40), if often slower; there are only six direct trains daily, but every thirty minutes a shuttle runs from the airport to Pisa Centrale (5min), where you can change to one of the regular services to Florence – there's rarely more than thirty minutes between trains, and the journey time is between an hour and eighty minutes. Train tickets can be bought from the office at the opposite end of the concourse from the station. Remember to validate your ticket in the platform machines before boarding. The first train from the airport to Pisa Centrale is at 6.40am, and the last departs at 10.20pm; the last train from Pisa Centrale to Florence is at 10.30pm, with services resuming at around 4am.

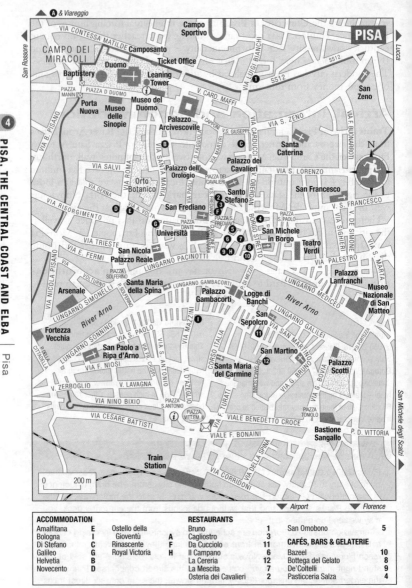

ACCOMMODATION				RESTAURANTS			
Amalfitana	E	Ostello della		Bruno	1	San Omobono	5
Bologna	I	Gioventù	A	Cagliostro	3		
Di Stefano	C	Rinascente	F	Da Cucciolo	11	CAFÉS, BARS & GELATERIE	
Galileo	G	Royal Victoria	H	Il Campano	6	Bazeel	10
Helvetia	B			La Cereria	12	Bottega del Gelato	8
Novecento	D			La Mescita	7	De'Coltelli	9
				Osteria dei Cavalieri	2	Pasticceria Salza	4

Galileo Via Santa Maria 12 ☎&⒡ 050.40.621.
Nine big – and in some cases very nicely decorated
– one-star rooms, with and without private
bathrooms; not the quietest hotel in town, but
central and good value. ②

Helvetia Via Don G. Boschi 31 ☎ 050.553.084.
Spotless and friendly one-star off Piazza

Arcivescovado offering doubles with or without
private bathroom. ②

🏃 **Novecento** Via Roma 37 ☎ 050.500.323,
ⓦ www.hotelnovecento.pisa.it. This new
three-star *residenza d'epoca* occupies a handsome
old town house, but the rooms are immaculately
modern in style. The rates are very reasonable, the

location convenient, and it has a pleasant garden as well. ⑤

Rinascente Via del Castelletto 28 ☎050.580.460, ⓦwww.pisaonline.it/hotelrinascente. This very popular one-star occupies an old *palazzo* hidden away a short distance south of Piazza dei Cavalieri – follow the signs from Via San Frediano. Shared or private bathrooms. ❷

🏃 **Royal Victoria** Lungarno Pacinotti 12 ☎050.940.111, ⓦwww.royalvictoria.it. Run by the same family since its foundation in 1837, this old-fashioned and appealingly frayed three-star is the most characterful of central Pisa's hotels – and the best value. The public rooms, with their musty engravings and antique furniture, are redolent of the place's history (there's even a music room, with piano), but if you're deterred by wobbly door-handles and patched-up ceiling frescoes, it's not the place for you. ⑤

Hostel

Ostello della Gioventù Via Pietrasantina 15, Madonna dell'Acqua ☎050.890.622, ⓦwww.pisaonline.it/albergodellagioventu. This non-HI hostel is 1km from the Campo dei Miracoli: if you don't want to walk, take bus #3 from the station or the airport. Make sure you have mosquito repellent in summer, as the hostel is right by a swamp, although it benefits from a nearby supermarket, pizzeria and burger joint. Reception opens 6pm. Dorm bed €16; bed in double room €21.

The Campo dei Miracoli

The name of the **Campo dei Miracoli** (Field of Miracles) comes from the notoriously over-excitable writer Gabriele D'Annunzio, but the label is no mere bombast – the ecclesiastical centre of Pisa is a stunning spectacle, from which the inevitable array of stalls peddling kitsch can barely detract. Nowhere else in Italy are the key religious buildings – the cathedral, baptistery and bell tower – so perfectly harmonious, and nowhere else is there so beautiful a contrast of stonework and surrounding meadow. And the mere existence of such enormous structures on this spot is remarkable in itself, because beneath the pavements and the turf lies a soggy mix of sand and silt, whose instability accounts for the angle of the Leaning Tower and the lesser tilt of its companions: take a close look at the Baptistery and you'll see that it's inclined some way off the vertical, while the facade of the Duomo is a few degrees out of true as well.

The Leaning Tower

The **Leaning Tower**, or Torre Pendente. has always been a leaning tower. Begun in 1173, it started to subside when it had reached just three of its eight storeys, but it tilted in the opposite direction to its present one. Odd-shaped stones were inserted to correct this deficiency, whereupon the tower lurched the other way. Over the next 180 years a succession of architects continued to extend the thing upwards, each one endeavouring to compensate for the angle, the end result being that the main part of the tower is slightly bent. Around 1350, Tommaso di Andrea da Pontedera completed the magnificent stack of marble and granite arcades by crowning it with a bellchamber, set closer to the perpendicular than the storeys below it, so that it looks like a hat set at a rakish angle.

By the end of the twentieth century, the tower was leaning 4.5m from the upright and nearing its limits. The collapse of a church tower in Pavia, killing four people, concentrated minds on the dangers of procrastination, and in 1990 the tower was shut to the public. Soon after the closure, ten steel bands were wrapped round the lowest section of the tower to prevent the base from buckling under the weight of the 15,000 tonnes of marble above. Various schemes aimed at arresting the effects of gravity were discussed, and in the end it was decided to place more than 900 tonnes of lead ingots at its base to counterbalance the force of the leaning stonework. In 1998, when it was clear that the weights had stabilized the structure, the project entered its second phase with a delicate drilling operation – supervised by Professor John Burland of London's Imperial College – to remove water and silt from beneath the tower's northern foundations. The resulting subsidence corrected the building's southwards tilt by ten percent, bringing it back to the angle by which it was tilting in the first half of the nineteenth century; to ensure that it stayed that way for the foreseeable future (300 years, according to Professor Burland) the foundations were strengthened and steel reinforcement bars were inserted into the walls of the tower. Eleven years and many millions of euros later, the tower was officially reopened to the public in November 2001. Now that the building has been made safe, work has begun on cleaning up the stonework – restoration is projected to continue until 2010.

▲ The Leaning Tower

Tickets for Pisa's museums and monuments

There are two **ticket offices** for the **Campo dei Miracoli** sights: on the north side of the Leaning Tower and inside the Museo delle Sinopie. **Tickets** for the Leaning Tower can be bought only from the first of these; tickets for the other five museums and monuments of the Campo dei Miracoli – the Duomo, Baptistery, Museo dell'Opera, Camposanto and Museo delle Sinopie – can be bought from either. Admission to the Duomo costs €2, except from November 1 to March 1, when it's free. Single admission to the other sights costs €5. Admission to any two sights (including the Duomo) is €6, to any four is €8.50, and to all five is €10; these combined tickets are valid for the day of issue only.

There's a separate ticket (€15) for the **Leaning Tower**; groups of thirty are allowed in for half an hour, and you should expect a long wait in high season. For an extra €2 you can pre-book your visit online at ⓦwww.opapisa.it, as long as you're making your reservation between 45 and 15 days in advance. Children under the age of 8 are not allowed into the tower.

Finally, there is also a joint €8 ticket for the Museo Nazionale di San Matteo and the Museo di Palazzo Reale, plus a €2.50 ticket for the Torre Guelfa della Cittadella Vecchia and Santa Maria della Spina. It's worth pointing out, however, that Pisa's multiple tickets are notoriously changeable.

The ascent of the tower leads you to the bell chamber up a dark and narrow spiral staircase of 294 steps, at a fairly disorientating five-degree angle. It's not for the claustrophobic or acrophobic, but you might think the steep admission fee is worth it for the privilege of getting inside one of the world's most famous and perilous buildings. The tower is **open daily**, 9am–6pm in March, 8.30am–8.30pm from April to September (8.30am–11pm from June 17 to Sept 5), 9am–7pm in October and 10am–5pm the rest of the year. Free **tours** are given in English three times daily between April and September. For details on how to **book tickets**, see the box above.

The Duomo

The **Duomo** (daily: March 10am–6pm; April–Sept 10am–8pm; Oct 10am–7pm; Nov–Feb 10am–1pm & 2–5pm; no admittance to tourists before 1pm on Sun; €2, or combined ticket; free from Nov 1 to March 1) was begun a century before its campanile, in 1064. With its four levels of variegated colonnades and its subtle interplay of dark grey marble and white stone, it's the archetype of the Pisan-Romanesque style, a model often imitated but never surpassed. Squares and discs of coloured marble are set into the magnificent facade, but the soberly graceful effect of the primary grey and white is such that you notice these other tones only when you look closely.

Inside, the impact of the crisp black-and-white marble of the long arcades – recalling Moorish architecture – is slightly diminished by the incongruous gilded ceiling, the fresco in the squashed circle of the dome, and the massive air vents that have been bunged through the upper arches. Much of the interior was redecorated, and some of the chapels remodelled, after a fire in 1595, so most of the paintings and sculpture are Renaissance or later. (The Duomo's huge bronze doors – a panoply of high-Renaissance detail – were also made after the fire, in Giambologna's workshop.)

The magnificent apse mosaic of *Christ in Majesty* is one of the survivors of the blaze. It was completed by Cimabue in 1302, the year in which **Giovanni Pisano** began to sculpt the cathedral's extraordinary **pulpit**. This was packed away after the fire, sixteenth-century Pisans evidently no longer concurring with its Latin inscription, which celebrates Giovanni as "superior to all other sculptors … incapable of creating clumsy and ungraceful figures". Only in 1926 was it rediscovered and reassembled here. The last of the great series of pulpits created in Tuscany by Giovanni and his father Nicola (the others are in Siena and Pistoia), it is a work of amazing virtuosity, the whole surface animated with figures almost wholly freed from the block. Its narrative density rewards close attention: the story of the Passion, from Judas's betrayal to the scourging of Christ, for instance, is condensed into a single panel. Unfortunately, a column obscures the view of the most tumultuous panel of all, the *Last Judgement*.

In the right transept is the mummified body of Pisa's patron saint, **Ranieri**, and (set into the east wall) the tomb of the Holy Roman Emperor **Henry VII**, who died in 1313 (aged just 38) near Siena – probably from malaria, though some said from eating a poisoned wafer at Mass. After laying Siena to waste, the pro-imperial Pisans bore the body of their hero back home, where Tino da Camaino carved this fine image. The Pisans weren't the only ones to revere the young emperor – Dante saw "alto Arrigo" as a man who could unite Italy within a new Christian empire, and in the *Divine Comedy* accorded him a throne of honour in heaven (hence the quotation from Dante below the sarcophagus). The tomb was originally placed in the centre of the transept, but was later broken up; only in 1921 were the effigy and sarcophagus placed in their current position, with other pieces of the tomb being transferred to the Museo dell'Opera del Duomo.

The Baptistery

The third building of the Miracoli ensemble, the **Baptistery** (daily: March 9am–6pm; April–Sept 8am–8pm; Oct 9am–7pm; Nov–Feb 10am–5pm; €5, or combined ticket), was begun in the mid-twelfth century by a certain Deotisalvi ("God save you"), who left his name on the column to the left of the door. Lack of money – caused mainly by Genoa's incursions into the Pisan trade network – prevented its completion in the style in which it had been started. In the second half of the thirteenth century the Gothic top storeys and attendant flourishes were applied by Nicola and Giovanni Pisano, who rounded off the job with a glorious gallery of statues – the originals of which are now displayed in the Museo dell'Opera del Duomo.

This is the largest baptistery in Italy, and the plainness of the vast interior is immediately striking, with its unadorned arcades and bare dome. The acoustics are astonishing too, as is often demonstrated by the custodian. At the centre, continuing the exotic strain of Pisan-Romanesque, is a mosaic-inlaid **font** by Guido da Como (1246), raised on stone steps for ease of immersion.

Overlooking it is Nicola Pisano's splendid **pulpit**, sculpted in 1260, half a century before his son's work in the cathedral. This was the sculptor's first major commission and – though the architectural details recall the stonework of French Gothic churches – it clearly shows the influence of classical models: the seated Virgin in the *Adoration of the Magi* is obviously derived from a Roman image, while the nude figure of Daniel (underneath the *Adoration*) is evidently Hercules under an alias. For good **views** out over the Campo dei Miracoli, climb the stairs to the upper gallery.

The Camposanto

The screen of sepulchral white marble running along the north edge of the Campo dei Miracoli is the perimeter wall of what has been called the most beautiful cemetery in the world, the **Camposanto** (same hours as Baptistery; €5, or combined ticket). According to Pisan legend, at the end of the twelfth century the city's archbishop brought back from the Crusades a cargo of soil from Golgotha, in order that eminent Pisans might be buried in holy earth. The building enclosing this sanctified site was completed almost a century later.

The Camposanto takes the form of an enormous Gothic cloister, each of whose long sides is as big as a cathedral nave. Since the fourteenth century the **arcades** have housed a large array of Roman sarcophagi, some of which were re-used for local dignitaries. Later tombs constitute a virtual encyclopedia of the various ways in which death has been accommodated, ranging from pavement slabs that record the occupant's name, dates and nothing else, to the opposite extreme, where the focus of interest is not on the deceased but on those left behind – as in the monument surmounted by a woman identified as "The Inconsolable".

However, when Ruskin described the Camposanto as one of the three most precious buildings in Italy (along with the Sistine Chapel and the Scuola di San Rocco in Venice), it was not its tombs but rather its **frescoes** that he was praising. Paintings once covered more than two thousand square metres of cloister wall, but bombs dropped by Allied planes on July 27, 1944 set the roofing on fire and drenched the frescoes in a river of molten lead, and the masterpieces of **Benozzo Gozzoli** were all but destroyed – just a few patches of his Old Testament scenes remain. Recent restoration work (the first stage of a planned restoration of all the Camposanto frescoes) has sparked a fierce dispute over a cleaning technique which, experts say, has permanently bleached the painting. Alongside is another picture that came through the bombing: a fascinating fourteenth-century **Theological Cosmograph**, showing the concentric spheres of the universe and the tripartite division of the Earth into Europe, Asia and Africa.

The most important surviving frescoes, however, are a remarkable cycle that's been put on show in a room opposite the entrance, beyond a photographic display of the Camposanto before the bombing. Some experts attribute this work to an artist called **Buonamico Buffalmacco**, though others assign it to an anonymous *Maestro del Trionfo della Morte*, the "Master of the Triumph of Death". There's also some dispute about the date: the frescoes are labelled as having been created in 1336–41, but many argue that they were painted after the Black Death of 1348, a pestilence which hit Tuscany so badly that it was known throughout Europe as the Florentine Plague. The most famous episode of the *Triumph* shows a trio of aristocratic huntsmen stopped in their tracks by a trio of coffins, the contents of which are so putrescent that one of the riders has to pinch his nose. Over to the right, squadrons of angels and demons bear away the souls of the dead, whose final resting place is determined in the terrifying *Last Judgement* and *Inferno* at the far end of the room.

The Museo dell'Opera del Duomo

A vast array of statuary from the Duomo and Baptistery, plus ecclesiastical finery, paintings and other miscellaneous pieces are displayed in the **Museo dell'Opera del Duomo** (same hours as Baptistery; €5, or combined ticket), at the southeast corner of the Campo.

The first masterpieces you encounter are the extraordinary **bronze doors** made for the Duomo by **Bonanno Pisano** (first architect of the Leaning Tower) in 1180. (Replicas are now in place at the **Portale di San Ranieri**, opposite the tower.) The panels depict the life of Christ in powerfully schematic scenes: the *Massacre of the Innocents*, for example, is represented by the smallest possible cast – Herod, one mother, one soldier and three babies. In the next room, exhibits dating from the period of the Duomo's construction illustrate the various influences at work in Pisan culture of the time. There's stonework from a Roman basilica, adapted for use in the cathedral, and items showing how Islamic influences came to filter into the city's art – notably in the marble inlays from the Duomo facade. A large bronze griffon is a more direct borrowing from Islam, having been thieved from the Middle East by a Pisan war party in the eleventh century. The most striking work, however, is from Burgundy, source of the strange painted wooden Crucifix, a gigantic figure with a tiny head and mantis-thin arms.

Sculptures by the various Pisanos are the high points of the museum, but the first pieces you encounter – Nicola and Giovanni's figures from the Baptistery – are too eroded to give much more than an approximate idea of their power. Room 7, which is given over to works by **Giovanni Pisano**, contains the most affecting statue in Pisa, the **Madonna del Colloquio**, so called because of the intensity of the gazes exchanged by the Madonna and Child. Giovanni's great contemporary, **Tino da Camaino**, monopolizes the next room, where fragments from the tomb of Emperor Henry VII are assembled; the magnificent figures of the emperor and his counsellors may have come from the tomb as well.

Nino Pisano – no relation to Nicola and Giovanni – is the subject of room 9, where his creamy marble monuments to archbishops Giovanni Scherlatti and Francesco Moricotti show the increasing suavity of Pisan sculpture in the late fourteenth century. Giovanni Pisano returns in the **treasury**, his ivory *Madonna and Child* showing a remarkable ingenuity in the way it exploits the natural curve of the tusk from which it's carved. The other priceless object here is the Pisan Cross, which was carried by the Pisan contingent on the First Crusade.

Upstairs, large altarpiece paintings take up a lot of room, none of them as impressive as the museum's remarkable examples of intarsia, the art of inlaid wood. The strangest objects on view are the two ancient parchment rolls known as **Exultets**, from the opening word of the chant on the eve of Holy Saturday. It was during this service that the cantor would unfurl these scrolls from the pulpit, so that the congregation could follow his words through the pictures painted on them. Beyond a small collection of **Roman and Etruscan** pieces, where a thin-lipped bust of Julius Caesar commands attention, the museum closes with a sequence of engravings by **Carlo Lasinio**, whose efforts were instrumental in rescuing the Camposanto from ruin at the beginning of the nineteenth century; his fastidious record of the now-lost frescoes is one of the most poignant items on show.

The Museo delle Sinopie and the city walls

On the south side of the Campo, the only gap in the souvenir stalls is the entrance to the **Museo delle Sinopie** (same hours as Baptistery; €5, or combined ticket). After the catastrophic damage wreaked on the Camposanto by the bombers, the building's restorers removed its sinopie (monochrome sketches for the frescoes). These great plates of plaster are now hung from the walls of this high-tech museum, where gantries and galleries give you the chance to inspect the painters' preliminary ideas at close range, but it's a rather scholastic enterprise.

You're not likely to get much greater reward from **taking a stroll on the small portion of the city walls** that borders the northwest corner of the Campo (March–Oct 10am–1pm & 3–6pm; €4).

The rest of the city

Within a short radius of the Campo dei Miracoli, Pisa takes on a quite different character, because very few tourists choose to explore the squares and streets of the city centre. While it's true that nothing in Pisa comes close to having the impact of the Campo, a tour of its lesser churches and other monuments could easily fill a day.

Piazza dei Cavalieri and the eastern districts

The **Piazza dei Cavalieri**, an obvious first stop after the Campo, opens unexpectedly from the narrow backstreets. Perhaps the site of the Roman forum, it was the central civic square of medieval Pisa, before being remodelled by Vasari as the headquarters of the Knights of St Stephen. This order was established by Cosimo I, ostensibly for crusading, though in reality they amounted to little more than a gang of licensed pirates, given state sanction to plunder Turkish shipping. Their palace, the sgraffiti-covered **Palazzo dei Cavalieri** (now home to the Scuola Normale Superiore, founded in 1810 by the Napoleonic regime), is fronted by a statue of Cosimo and adjoins the order's church of **Santo Stefano**, which was largely designed by Vasari and is hung with banners captured from the Turks.

On the other side of the square is the Renaissance-adapted **Palazzo dell'Orologio**, with its archway and clock tower. This was a medieval palace, in whose tower the military leader Ugolino della Gherardesca was starved to death in 1288, along with his sons and grandsons, as punishment for his alleged duplicity with the Genoese enemy – a grisly episode described in Dante's *Inferno* and Shelley's *Tower of Famine*.

Northeast from here, across the wide Piazza dei Martiri della Libertà, stands the Dominican church of **Santa Caterina**, whose Romanesque lower facade dates from the year of its foundation, 1251. Inside, there's an *Annunciation* and a tomb by Nicola Pisano, and a fourteenth-century painting of the *Triumph of Thomas Aquinas*, the ideological figurehead of the Dominicans. Nearby, in front of the **Porta Lucca** – the main northern gate of medieval Pisa – you can see the unimpressive remnants of the city's Roman baths, while tucked into the northeast corner of the city walls is the church of **San Zeno**, parts of which go back to the fifth century.

From Via San Zeno, Via Buonarroti runs south to the plain Gothic **San Francesco**, whose well-preserved frescoes include work by Taddeo Gaddi and Niccolò di Pietro Gerini. Count Ugolino and his offspring are buried in the second chapel on the right. If you continue down Via di Simone from the back of the church, you'll come out at the Museo Nazionale di San Matteo.

Borgo Stretto and the Museo Nazionale di San Matteo

Heading from Piazza dei Cavalieri towards the Arno, Via Dini swings into the arcaded **Borgo Stretto**. Pedestrianized to create a traffic-free route that extends across the river and down Corso Italia, this is Pisa's smartest street. On the west side of Borgo Stretto you'll find Pisa's **market** area (Mon–Fri mornings & Sat all day), with fruit, vegetable, fish, meat and clothing stalls filling Piazza Vettovaglie, Piazza San Ombono and the neighbouring lanes.

Past the Romanesque-Gothic facade of **San Michele** – built on the site of the Roman temple to Mars – the Borgo meets the river at the traffic-knotted Piazza Garibaldi and **Ponte di Mezzo**, the city's central bridge. A left turn along Lungarno Mediceo takes you past the **Palazzo Toscanelli** (now the city archives), which was rented by Byron in 1821–22 after his expulsion from Ravenna for seditious activities. The poet's lunatic reputation, already well-established thanks to his menagerie of horses, cats and dogs, was given a further boost when he got into a scrap with a bunch of Pisan soldiers, a contretemps that brought his brothers in exile – Shelley, Leigh Hunt and Walter Savage Landor – out onto the streets. This display of hot-blooded solidarity prompted the writer Guerrazzi to muse that he at last understood "why the English are a great people, and the Italians a clump of rags in the shop of a second-hand dealer".

A couple of doors further along the *lungarno* is the **Museo Nazionale di San Matteo** (Tues–Sat 9am–7pm, Sun 9am–2pm; €5), where most of the major works of art from Pisa's churches are now gathered. Fourteenth-century religious paintings make up most of the collection, with a Simone Martini polyptych and work by Antonio Veneziano outstanding in the early sections. Later on, there's a stash of Middle Eastern ceramics pilfered by Pisan adventurers, a panel of *St Paul* by Masaccio, Gozzoli's strangely festive *Crucifixion* and Donatello's reliquary bust of the introspective *St Rossore*. Also housed in the museum are the antique armour and wooden shields used in the annual *Gioco del Ponte* pageant (see opposite).

West of Ponte di Mezzo

The faculty buildings of Pisa's university – still one of the most important in Italy – are scattered all over the city, but the main concentration is to the west of the Ponte di Mezzo, around lively **Piazza Dante**. Immediately north of here, the bare stone nave of the eleventh-century **San Frediano** preserves some capitals from that period. West of here, off the main Via Santa Maria, lies the university's **Orto Botanico** (Mon–Sat 8.30am–1pm; free); founded in 1591, this is the oldest botanical garden in the world. At the southern end of Via Santa Maria rises Pisa's second leaning tower, the thirteenth-century campanile of **San Nicola**. Cylindrical at its base, mutating into an octagon then a hexagon, it contains a majestic spiral staircase that was Bramante's inspiration for his grand Belvedere staircase in the Vatican. Inside the church, the Crucifix in the first chapel on the left is attributed to Giovanni Pisano, while Nino Pisano is credited with the wooden *Madonna and Child* in the fourth chapel on this side. On the other side of the nave, there's a painting showing Pisa around 1400, being protected from the plague by St Nicholas of Tolentino.

Alongside San Nicola, fronting the Arno at Lungarno Pacinotti 46, is the **Museo Nazionale di Palazzo Reale** (Mon–Fri 9am–3pm, Sat 9am–1pm; €5), displaying artefacts that once belonged to the Medici, Lorraine and Savoy rulers of the city, who successively occupied the house. Lavish sixteenth-century Flemish tapestries share space with antique weaponry, ivory miniatures, porcelain and a largely undistinguished picture collection; the best-known painting, a version of Bronzino's portrait of Eleanora di Toledo, is displayed alongside a dress that belonged to her.

Further along the river, on the Lungarno Simonelli, lies the **Arsenale Mediceo**. Built by Cosimo I, it is now being converted into a home for the sixteen Roman ships which have been excavated since 1998 from the silt at nearby San Rossore, which was a port for the Roman colony at Pisa. Almost perfectly preserved in mud for two millennia, the cargo-laden fleet includes what experts believe could be the oldest Roman warship ever found.

Just west of the arsenal rises the **Torre Guelfa della Cittadella Vecchia**, or **Fortezza Vecchia** (Jan, Feb, Nov & Dec Sat & Sun 2–5pm, plus 10am–1pm on second Sun of month; March–Oct Fri–Sun 3–7pm; €2). This ancient fortress, originally built in the thirteenth century, once stood guard over Pisa's harbour but now punctuates an otherwise little-explored district; the view from the tower is spectacular.

South of the river

The more down-at-heel districts south of the Arno are popularly known as the *mezzogiorno*, the name more widely used in Italy to refer to the under-developed south of the country. On the second Sunday and the preceding Saturday of each month both banks are linked by a big street **market**, with stalls selling jewellery, candles and the like filling the lower reaches of Borgo Stretto, and furniture and general bric-a-brac around the south-bank Logge di Banchi. Formerly the city's silk and wool market, this vast and usually deserted loggia stands at the top of the main shopping street of the *mezzogiorno*, the pedestrianized Corso Italia.

East along the Lungarno Galilei, the only real sight is the octagonal **San Sepolcro**, built for the Knights Templar by Diotisalvi, first architect of the Baptistery. A short way past here is the ruined **Palazzo Scotti**, Shelley's home during the period when Byron was in residence on the other side of the river.

Along the **lungarno** to the west of the Ponte di Mezzo, the rather monotonous line of *palazzi* – mirroring those on the facing bank – is suddenly enlivened by the oratory of **Santa Maria della Spina** (March–Oct Tues–Fri 10am–1.30pm & 2.30–6pm, Sat & Sun 10am–1.30pm & 2.30–7pm; Nov–Feb Tues–Sun 10am–2pm, except second Sun of month 10am–7pm; €1.50). Founded in 1230 but rebuilt in the 1320s by a merchant who had acquired one of the thorns (*spine*) of Christ's crown, this spry little church is the finest flourish of Pisan-Gothic. Originally built closer to the water, it was moved here for fear of floods in 1871. The single-naved interior has lost most of its furnishings, but contains a trio of statues by Andrea and Nino Pisano.

Further west again, **San Paolo a Ripa d'Arno** probably occupies the site of Pisa's very first cathedral. The arcaded facade was built in imitation of the present cathedral in the twelfth century; the interior, badly damaged in World War II, has a handsome Roman sarcophagus and a finely carved capital (second on left). Behind the church is the octagonal **Cappella di Sant'Agata**, also built in the twelfth century.

San Michele dei Scalzi

Some 2km east of the centre, secreted in a residential area, stands Pisa's third leaning tower, the campanile of **San Michele dei Scalzi** – you get to it by walking along the riverbank upstream from Ponte di Mezzo. Everything in this building is severely askew: the columns in the nave lurch this way and that, the windows in the apse are all over the place, and the walls set up a drunken counterpoint to the tilt of the tower.

Eating and drinking

Pisa's proximity to the coast means that seafood is the staple of its **restaurant** menus, with *baccalà alla pisana* (dried cod in tomato sauce) and *pesce spada* (swordfish) featuring prominently. Avoid the temptation to eat at one of the plethora of places in the vicinity of the Campo dei Miracoli – aimed squarely at the tourist trade, they are generally of poor quality. It's in the backstreets, especially in the market area to the west of Borgo Stretto, that you'll find the best of the city's restaurants. Pisa doesn't have the range of **cafés and bars** that you'll find in Florence – most of the bars are fairly indistinguishable set-ups, catering for an ever-changing and impecunious student clientele.

Restaurants

Bruno Via L. Bianchi 12 ☎ 050.560.818. Simple and hearty Pisan dishes have kept this place well-regarded for years. Reckon on around €35 a head. Closed Tues.

Cagliostro Via del Castelletto 26–30 ☎ 050.575.413. Tucked away in an obscure alley parallel to Via San Frediano, *Cagliostro* is an extremely good restaurant-wine bar, offering a small but elegant menu of Pisan classics and other dishes with an innovative twist, such as Tuscan leek soup with Stilton. The dining room is spectacular too. Expect to pay about €40 per person. Closed Sun, Mon lunchtime & Tues.

Da Cucciolo Vicolo Rosselmini 9 ☎ 050.26.086. The family-run *Cucciolo* has been in business for forty years and is always reliable, offering unfussy, delicious traditional meals (with an emphasis on organic ingredients). Main courses are in the €10–15 range. Closed Sun eve & Mon.

🏃 **Il Campano** Via Domenico Cavalca 19 ☎ 050.580.585. Homemade pasta and gnocchi, and local seafood, are the draw at this first-rate *trattoria* – though they also do meaty Tuscan classics, including a 1kg Fiorentina steak (to share, of course). This may also be the only Pisan restaurant with ostrich on the menu. Extremely good selection of wines, too. Closed all Wed & Thurs eve.

La Cereria Via Pietro Gori 33 ☎ 050.20.336. Popular, unpretentious restaurant tucked away in a courtyard a short distance south of the river. Excellent seafood and pasta dishes, superb pizzas (the best in the city, some reckon) and a pleasant garden. Closed Tues.

La Mescita Via Domenico Cavalca 2 ☎ 050.544.294. This wine bar-restaurant, on the edge of the Piazza Vettovaglie market, has established a good reputation with its ever-changing Tuscan menu and excellent cellar. You'll pay around €35 per person. Closed Sat & Sun eve, Mon & three weeks in Aug.

Osteria dei Cavalieri Via San Frediano 16 ☎ 050.580.858. Outstanding quality, good prices (about €30 per person) and a pleasantly buzzy atmosphere. Their vegetarian options are excellent, which makes a pleasant change in Tuscany. Closed Sat lunch & Sun, and most of Aug.

🏃 **San Ombono** Piazza San Ombono 6 ☎ 050.540.847. This city-centre *trattoria* serves terrific, authentic Pisan home cooking, featuring dishes such as *brachette alla renaiola* – pasta in a purée of greens and smoked fish. Closed Sun & two weeks in Aug.

Cafés, bars and gelaterie

Bazeel Piazza Garibaldi 15. This stylish bar is currently Pisa's favourite hangout – the interior is cool and spacious, but when the weather's good the punters prefer the outside tables, or even the parapet overlooking the river. DJs on Fri & Sat, live music Thurs & Sun. Daily 5pm–2am.

Bottega del Gelato Piazza Garibaldi 11. In business for more than a quarter of a century, this ever-popular *gelateria* has a great range of flavours – the *Tuttobosco* (forest fruits) is gorgeous.

De' Coltelli Lungarno Pacinotti 23. Pisa's other top-rank *gelateria* has a penchant for more adventurous concoctions – anyone for seafood ice-cream? Feb–Dec daily 1pm–1am.

Pasticceria Salza Borgo Stretto 46. The best-known café-*pasticceria* in Pisa; it has a restaurant section at the back, but the food isn't as good as you'll find elsewhere. Tues–Sun 8am–8.30pm.

Around Pisa

Immediately to the east of Pisa, the one compelling detour is to the **Certosa di Pisa**, a marvellous Baroque charterhouse. This stretch of the Arno valley, however, is glum and unremittingly industrialized: **Cáscina**, about 15km east of Pisa, is notable only as the site of the Florentine victory over the Pisan army in 1364, which Michelangelo was commissioned to commemorate in his ill-fated fresco for Florence's Palazzo Vecchio; **Pontedera** is home to the Piaggio

▲ The Certosa di Pisa

factory that produces the ubiquitous Vespa scooter, and that's about all you need to know.

On the routes south towards Volterra and Siena, across the Pisan hills, only the workaday spa town of **Casciana Terme** and the thirteenth-century Roman-esque church at **Paláia** warrant as much as a mention. West of Pisa, **Marina di Pisa** and **Tirrenia** are the city's local resorts. Neither is very inspiring, but the area just inland has the **Parco Regionale di San Rossore** and the ancient church of **San Piero a Grado**.

The Certosa di Pisa

Of the thirty Carthusian monasteries left intact in Italy, none makes a more diverting excursion than the fourteenth-century **Certosa di Pisa**, set at the foot of the forested Monte Pisano near the village of **Calci**, 10km east of Pisa. A regular CPT **bus** service runs to the village from Pisa's Piazza Sant'Antonio; if you're driving, just get to the amazing Medici aqueduct – immediately visible on the eastern outskirts of the city – and follow it all the way. The monastery's **guided tour** (hourly: Tues–Sat 9am–6pm, Sun 9am–noon; €4) gives a remark-able sense of how the building related to the lives of this order.

The size of the Certosa is startling. From the frescoed central **church**, where a freestanding marble angel does service as a lectern, the tour passes through eleven other **chapels** in which Sunday Mass was apparently conducted simultaneously. Looking as fresh as the day they were decorated (they have not been restored), these are strangely sybaritic interiors – all powder blue, baby pink, pale violet and pallid green, with stucco details and *trompe l'oeil* pillars and balustrades. Floors are covered with tiles that are only paint-deep, and there's a rectangular chapel tricked out to look like an oval room with a dome.

This ballroom decor contrasts with the more conventional monasticism of the **cloister** and its cells. Each of the monks had a suite of three sparse rooms – a bedroom, a study and a workroom. Attached to every suite is a self-contained garden, walled so that the monks could maintain their soul-redeeming isolation. Their meals were served through hatches, positioned to minimize the possibility of coming face to face – except on Sundays, when conversation was permitted and all the monks ate together. From the cloister the tour progresses to the **refectory**, where frescoes of seminal moments in the history of the monastery are interspersed with images of the months and their associated crops as a reminder of the order's self-sufficiency. Nearby are the luxuriously appointed **guest rooms**, where high-born VIPs – various Medici among them – would stay for a bout of not-too-rigorous scourging of the spirit. Their private cloister features yet more *trompe l'oeil*, its windows "opening" onto the dining room and monks' cloister.

The visit is made especially absorbing by little details pointed out by the guide – like the panel with sliding wooden paddles to designate the day's duties (eg head-shaving), or, at the end of the tour, the measuring machines in the **pharmacy**. Above the gate as you leave, an inscription reads *Egredere sed non omnis* ("Leave, but not entirely"), addressed to monks who had to go out on a mission in the wider world.

Parts of the Certosa complex are owned by the University of Pisa, who have installed their **natural history** collections here (July to mid-Sept Tues–Fri 10am–7pm, Sat & Sun 10am–8pm; mid-Sept to June Mon–Sat 9am–6pm, Sun 10am–7pm; €7).

Monte Serra

If you're driving, you could make a loop down to the Arno from the Certosa by following the scenic mountain pass over **Monte Serra**. Beyond the summit, the road meanders down to the village of **Buti**, its Gothic-windowed castle looking down over the Arno valley. The descent has flattened out by the time you get to **Vicopisano**, which is built on a plump little hummock and retains four towers of its fortifications, two of which were built or rebuilt by Brunelleschi after the Florentines had conquered Pisa. In the lower part of the village is a handsome Romanesque church, fronted by a grassy piazza and backed by the Monte Pisano foothills.

West of Pisa

Some 6km west of Pisa, on the road to the coast, is the monastic complex of **San Piero a Grado** (daily 8am–7pm), allegedly founded by St Peter himself, on his way to Rome and martyrdom. The site is now in ruins except for the glorious eleventh-century basilica, a double-apsed church built from lustrous local yellow sandstone. St Peter's story is detailed in a sequence of pale fourteenth-century frescoes inside the basilica, at one end of which a section of a fourth-century oratory has been excavated, the most ancient Christian site in this part of Tuscany.

Marina di Pisa, at the end of the road, is an unobjectionable little town cursed with water made grubby by industrial waste. The view out to sea is impaired by a long breakwater parallel to the shore, a sight frequently worsened by passing tankers. These factors, combined with the usual private beach strips, don't entice. **Tirrenia**, 5km south, is a better bet, with finer sand that's separated from the road by pines and parkland. **Buses** do the half-hour run from Pisa to the resorts; both are best avoided on Sundays, when hundreds of locals nip down to the sea.

The **Parco Regionale di San Rossore** spreads over much of the coastal hinterland between Viareggio and Livorno. Its pine woods are among the densest in Tuscany, supporting populations of deer, goats and wild boar, and until World War II were also home to a herd of dromedaries, descendants of the animals placed here by Grand Duke Ferdinando II in the 1620s. Two visitor centres (℡050.989.084) offer **guided tours** on foot, bike or horseback. At the park's centre lies the village of **Gombo**, scene of the cremation of Percy Bysshe Shelley, who drowned here in 1822 and was reduced to ashes in front of his friends Lord Byron and Edward Trelawny.

Livorno

As Tuscany's third-largest city (after Florence and Prato) and Italy's second-biggest port (after Genoa), **LIVORNO** should really have more going for it than it does. Unfortunately, its docks invited blanket bombing in World War II, and the rebuilt commercial centre is not pretty.

The **Porto Mediceo** – the canal-enclosed area in which the Piazza Grande stands – is the town's most picturesque corner, and still conforms to the pentagonal plan devised for the Medici by Buontalenti in 1557. The focal point of the piazza is the **Duomo**, a postwar reconstruction of interest mainly for its doorway by Inigo Jones, whose subsequent plan for London's Covent Garden was a direct copy of the square. From here Via Grande leads down to the sea, where Sangallo's **Fortezza Vecchia** guards the bustling harbour and its tributary canals, about 100m north of central Livorno's only artwork of note, the **Quattro Mori** statue (1623) by the Carraran sculptor Pietro Tacca.

Ferries from Livorno

Dozens of **ferries** sail from Livorno daily, to **Corsica**, **Sardinia**, **Sicily** and the **Tuscan islands**. Nearly all ferries to Corsica and Sardinia leave from alongside the **Stazione Maríttima**, west of the centre behind the Fortezza Vecchia, although some (and boats to Sicily) depart from **Varco Galvani**, a long way west of town. Ferries to Capraia leave from the central **Porto Mediceo**. Check with the tourist office and the companies themselves for times and prices, and **reserve** well ahead in summer. If you're taking a car to Sardinia, note that most companies offer discount deals if you cross to Corsica and drive the 180km to the southern tip of the island – and often the subsequent ferry to Sardinia is free.

Ferry companies

Corsica Ferries/Sardinia Ferries Stazione Maríttima, Calata Carrara ℡199.400.500, ⓦwww.corsicaferries.it. To Bastia (Corsica) and Golfo Aranci (Sardinia).

Corsica Marittima Stazione Maríttima, Calata Carrara ℡0586.210.507. To Bastia, Porto Vecchio (both Corsica) and Olbia (Sardinia).

Grandi Navi Veloci (Grimaldi) Varco Galvani, Calata Tripoli, Porto Nuovo ℡06.4208.3567, ⓦwww.grimaldi-ferries.it. To Palermo (Sicily).

Moby Lines Stazione Maríttima, Calata Carrara ℡0586.899.950, ⓦwww.mobylines.it. To Bastia (Corsica), Porto Vecchio (Corsica), Olbia (Sardinia) and Barcelona.

Toremar Porto Mediceo ℡892.123 or 0586.224.511, ⓦwww.toremar.it. To Gorgona and Capraia.

To the east of the Duomo, on Via Buontalenti, the ochre **Mercato Centrale** stands at the heart of a boisterous street market. North of here lies the Venezia district, where crumbling old tenement buildings overlook the bulky **Fortezza Nuova** (daily 8am–7pm), a moated, semi-derelict recreation area ringed by quiet canals. At the end of July and beginning of August the area comes alive with the **Effetto Venezia** (Ⓦ www.effettovenezia.com), a lively street festival.

If you've time to kill in Livorno, you could visit the **Museo Civico Giovanni Fattori** (Tues–Sun 10am–1pm & 4–7pm; €4), which is devoted to Fattori and the late-nineteenth-century Macchiaioli movement, Italy's version of Impressionism; it's housed in the Villa Mimbelli, 1km south of the centre at Via San Jacopo in Acquaviva 65 (bus #1).

The **train station** is 2km east of the centre; buses #1 and #2 run from here to Piazza Grande. Most inter-town **buses** also stop here, although buses from Florence, Pisa and Lucca use Piazza Manin, a short distance south. The **tourist office** is at Piazza del Municipio (Mon–Fri 9am–1pm & 3–5pm, Sat 9am–1pm; ☏0586.204.611). Livorno's principal appeal, apart from its ferry connections, is its excellent **seafood**. The local speciality is *cacciucco*, a spicy seafood stew, traditionally made from scraps the fishermen couldn't sell.

The Costa degli Etruschi

There's little to distinguish the resorts that cling to the road south from Livorno along the so-called **Costa degli Etruschi** (Etruscan Coast). Most are remorselessly developed and edged with stony or scrubby beaches, and have an appeal only if you want to share the Italian cheek-by-jowl seaside experience. All points on the coast as far south as Follónica can be reached by **bus** or **train** from Livorno; faster Pisa–Rome expresses often stop only at Cécina, which has connections inland to Saline di Volterra, 9km from Volterra.

Quercianella to Cécina

About 13km south of Livorno, **Quercianella** is a relatively small resort that has clung onto a hinterland of scrub-covered hills and rocky headlands. The beach is pebbly, but nevertheless popular and well developed. **Castiglioncello**, the biggest of the resorts, sprawls over several small bays, some with sand, most with pebbles, and all crammed with boats and beach huts. The best beach is the fee-charging Quercetano; the bay at Caletta is one to avoid, as is Rosignano (1km south), graced as it is with a vast chemical works with outlets into the sea. Smaller **Vada**, 5km south of Rosignano, has a featureless modern centre but is preferable to Castiglion-cello, with a good beach and a long flat stretch of sand and pines to the south that shade a couple of large **campsites**, the better being the *Tripesce*, Via Cavallaggeri 88 (☏0586.788.017, Ⓦ www.campingtripesce.com; April to mid-Oct).

The town of **Cécina**, 3km inland, marks the start of the Maremma's coastal plains, and has **buses** and **trains** heading inland to Saline di Volterra (see p.376). There are fair sections of beach at **Marina di Cécina**, most freely accessible save for a patch cordoned off by the local military academy.

The Bólgheri reserve and Bibbona

South of Cécina the main road pulls back from the coast, leaving a few tracts relatively unspoilt. If you take any of the minor turnings to the sea you'll find pine forest and beaches only slightly touched by development, but the best stretch is the exquisite **Rifugio Faunistico di Bólgheri**, a nature reserve run by the World Wide Fund for Nature (visits, only available with a guide, need to be pre-booked 24hr in advance with the WWF in Piombino; ☎0565.224.361; reserve open Fri & Sat 9am–2pm, but hours may vary; €5, children €3). The entrance is off the main SS1, just south of the glorious avenue of trees that runs to Bólgheri village; take the lane that runs over the rail tracks to the sea.

Founded in 1962, this was the first private nature reserve in Italy, and is now recognized as a wildlife centre of international importance. The reserve is a microcosm of the various habitats associated with the ancient Maremma: seashore, dunes (full of rare plants), marsh and lakeland, pine groves, tracts of juniper and mixed scrub forest, *macchia*, grassland and some of the oldest stands of cypress in Italy. Such is the tranquillity of the area that even in daylight you can expect to see **boar**, **roe-buck**, **martens**, black and white **porcupines**, even **otters** – an extremely rare species in Italy. Thousands of **birds** also settle here: it's the southern limit of the lapwing and a spot for rarities like bluethroats, Blyth reed warblers, grey herons, cranes, black storks and hunters such as the osprey and lesser-spotted eagle.

The nearby resort of **Marina di Bibbona** has an immensely broad stretch of sand running for miles south from the village along a pinewood backdrop: to find privacy, just walk beyond the beach umbrellas. For a reasonable **beach hotel** with a garden, bear left on the approach road to Forte di Bibbona to the two-star *Paradiso Verde*, Via del Forte 1 (☎0565.600.022, ⓦ www.hotelparadisoverde.it; ❷).

Inland – Castagneto Carducci to Campiglia

If you're driving south from Pisa, you could take time out from the plain-induced monotony of the Via Aurelia by turning off at **Marina di Castagneto-Donoratico**, about 20km south of Cécina, for a 35-kilometre loop into the hills of the Monte Calvi nature reserve via a handful of scarcely visited medieval villages. This area is home to the Montescudaio, Bolgheri and Val di Cornia DOC wines – worth seeking out by following the **Strada del Vino degli Etruschi** wine road (ⓦ www.lastradadelvino.com) that's signposted everywhere.

CASTAGNETO CARDUCCI, 6km east of Donoratico, is renowned for two things: it was the birthplace of the poet Carducci, winner of the Nobel Prize in 1906; and it produces what is widely considered the best **olive oil** in Italy. The village is riddled with little alleyways and has a parish church filled with faded frescoes and painted terracotta saints. **Eat** at the excellent *Da Ugo*, Via Pari 3/a (☎0565.763.746; closed Mon and a period in Nov).

Beyond, the road is a rollercoaster of sea views and woods, touching **Sassetta**, a car-free maze of minute streets, beyond which the road twists down to **Suvereto**, whose thin shield of modern outskirts hides another old centre, with its thirteenth-century Palazzo Comunale and the Pisan-Romanesque church of San Giusto.

A slight detour on the return to the coast takes in **Campiglia Maríttima**, another little gem, partly spoilt by new houses and holiday homes, but with a perfect central piazza, composed of civic *palazzi* and a fine Romanesque church. The inexpensive **trattoria** opposite the train station is popular, and for excellent fish you could try the moderately priced *Il Canovaccio*, Via Vecchio Asilo 1 (☎0565.838.449; closed Tues in winter).

Populonia and the Golfo di Baratti

Perched on a high, rocky headland 5km off the coast road, **POPULONIA** was once a centre of Etruscan and Roman iron production, using ore from Elba. Now it's a tiny place looking down on the broad, half-moon bay of the **Golfo di Baratti**, with some of the best beaches for miles around. There's an impressive-looking fortress at the edge of the village, disappointing inside except for the fine views across the hills. The enterprising inhabitants of Via San Giovanni di Sotto 8 (off the main street) have opened a small private **museum** of Etruscan odds and ends (March–Nov open irregular hours; €1.50).

In the bay below, once Populonia's port, there's a cluster of houses glorified with the name of **BARATTI**, a colourful base for fishing boats, whose Etruscan roots are celebrated in an eighty-hectare **archeological park** (June–Sept Mon–Sat 10am–7pm; rest of year hours and days vary; €9 includes access to one tomb; €12 for both; ⓦwww.parchivaldicornia.it). The nicest low-cost **hotel** is the seafront *Alba* (☎0565.29.521; ❷), which has a pleasant garden.

Piombino

Ugly **PIOMBINO**, the main port of departure to Elba, is not a place to linger. The only point in passing through is to take the **ferry** (see box), in which case, if you're travelling by train, you should change at **Campiglia Maríttima** (see above), from where connecting trains run through Piombino to Piombino Maríttima. Should ferry timings oblige you to stay overnight, go for the two-star *Roma*, Via San Francesco 43 (☎0565.34.341; ❶).

Elba

Nearly 30km long and 20km across, **ELBA** is the third-largest Italian island (after Sicily and Sardinia), yet until thirty years ago it was known only for its mineral resources and as Napoleon's place of exile. Now, however, it's suffering the fate of many a Mediterranean idyll, devoured by tourism in the summer and all but deserted in the long off-season. If you come here in August, when an estimated one million visitors flood onto Elba, you'll have trouble finding a room or even space to camp. To get the most out of the island, visit in spring or late summer.

Elba has been inhabited since about 3000 BC owing to its **mineral** wealth. The Greeks named it **Aethalia** ("Sparks") after its many forges, and Roman swords were made of Elban iron. The last iron ore mine closed in 1984, but it's

---

Ferries to Elba

The main port of departure to Elba is **Piombino**, 75km south of Livorno – not a great place to stay, since it was flattened in World War II and these days makes its living from a giant steelworks. If you're arriving by **train**, you'll probably have to change at Campiglia Maríttima station, from where connecting trains run through the town to Piombino Maríttima.

At the **port**, you'll find ticket outlets for all ferry companies. Most people head to Elba's **Portoferraio**, to where Toremar and Moby ferries run every day of the year, the first around 5.50am and the last around 10.30pm (earlier and later in high summer; summer every 30min; winter every 2hr; journey time 1hr). Tickets cost about €43 one-way for a car and driver, including port taxes, €11 for additional passengers and foot passengers, tax included. If you're looking to cut costs get Toremar's cheaper ferry (about €36; foot passengers €7.30) to Rio Marina on the island's east coast. Note that you should book your return ticket from Elba as far in advance as possible in summer.

From Piombino, Toremar also serves **Rio Marina** (2–3 daily) and **Porto Azzurro** (summer 1 daily). Toremar's **additional** rapid **ferry**, or *linea veloce*, serves Portoferraio (summer 2 daily; takes 40min) and Rio Marina (summer 3 daily; 30min). Toremar's **hydrofoil**, or *aliscafo*, glides to **Cavo** (summer 5 daily; winter 3 daily; 20min) and Portoferraio (summer 4 daily; takes 30min). Fares are about €13 per person, including tax.

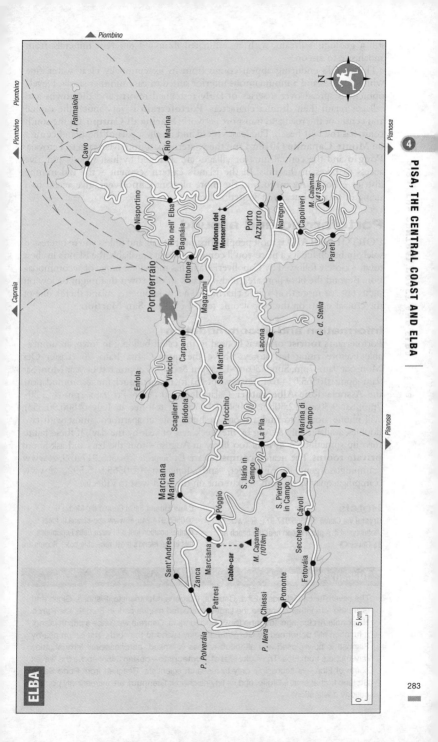

ELBA

Piombino

Piombino

Piombino

Piombino

Pianosa

Pianosa

Pianosa

Capraia

I. Palmaiola

Cavo

Rio Marina

Nisportino

Rio nell' Elba

Bagnaia

Ottone

Magazzini

Portoferraio

Enfola

Viticcio

Carpani

San Martino

Lacona

C. d. Stella

Scaglieri

Biodola

Prócchio

La Pila

Marina di Campo

Marciana Marina

Poggio

S. Ilário in Campo

S. Pietro in Campo

Cávoli

Sant'Andrea

Zanca

Marciana

Patresi

Chiessi

Pomonte

Fetováia

Seccheto

Cable-car

M. Capanne (1018m)

P. Polveráia

P. Nera

Madonna del Monserrato

Porto Azzurro

Naregno

Capoliveri

M. Calamita (413m)

Pareti

N

0 — 5 km

still a geologist's dream, with an estimated thousand different minerals, from andalusite to zircon.

The island's enduring appeal comes from its exceptionally clear water, fine white beaches and a mountainous interior suited to easy summer strolls. Development is spread over a series of fairly restrained resorts, and the towns and villages retain their distinct characters. **Portoferraio** is very much the capital and centre of the road and transport network; **Marina di Campo**, on the south coast, has the best beach. The least visited and loveliest part of the island centres on **Monte Capanne** (1018m) and the western coast from Marciana to Fetovaia. **Poggio** and the central interior villages are sheltered by lush woods and give access to hikes in the hills. In the island's eastern segment – the old mining district – **Porto Azzurro**, and the more pleasant **Capoliveri**, give access to a string of smaller but much-visited villages.

Portoferraio and around

PORTOFERRAIO is most people's first port of call, and unless you're interested solely in beach life it's a place you'll come back to: it's probably the island's liveliest town – closely followed by Capoliveri – and has the widest range of accommodation. Beyond the busy port area, it also retains an **old town** that might be low on sights but has more than a little charm, and a few kilometres inland there's one of the crucial sights on the Napoleonic trail, the villa at **San Martino**.

Information and accommodation

Portoferraio's **tourist office** is housed in the tallest building in town, an unmissable eyesore rising ten storeys above the quay, Calata Italia 26 (Easter–Oct Mon–Sat 9am–7pm, Sun 9.30am–12.30pm & 3.30–6.30pm; rest of year Mon–Sat 9am–6pm; ℡0565.914.671, ⓦwww.aptelba.it). If you're stuck for accommodation, the **Associazione Albergatori**, Calata Italia 20 (Mon–Fri 9am–1pm & 3.30–7pm, Sat 9.30am–12.30pm; ℡0565.914.754 or toll-free in Italy ℡800.90.353), will phone around to find a room, or book you an apartment (most with two doubles, available July & Aug by the week, rest of year by the day). If these fail to turn up something – as is all too likely in August – tour the bars and ask about **private rooms**. The nearest **campsites** are *La Sorgente* (℡0565.917.139, ⓦwww.campinglasorgente.it; April–Oct) and *Acquaviva* (℡0565.915.592, ⓦwww.campingacquaviva.it), both 4–5km out on the road west to Viticcio.

Hotels

Crystal Via Cairoli ℡0565.917.971, ⓦwww.hotelcrystal.it. A plush option near the beach at Le Ghiaie.⑥

L'Ape Elbana Salita Cosimo de' Medici 9 ℡0565.914.245, ⓦwww.ape-elbana.it. Ideal central position just off Piazza della Repubblica, this is the island's most venerable hotel. Rooms are

---

Tuscany's islands

The seven Tuscan islands – Elba, Capraia, Gorgona, Montecristo, Pianosa, Giglio and Giannutri – together comprise the largest protected marine park in Europe, the **Parco Nazionale Arcipelago Toscano** (ⓦwww.islepark.it). **Capraia** was once a prison island, a function still performed by **Gorgona**, the tiny island to the north. The jail on nearby Pianosa is now closed and although access is limited, an occasional ferry shuttles day-trippers from Elba. The rocky islet of **Montecristo** – poking 645m above the waves south of Elba – is accessible only to research scientists. Reached from Porto Santo Stefano further south, **Giglio**, and its tiny neighbour **Giannutri**, are increasingly popular holiday destinations.

4

rather bland: the best are the generally more spacious options overlooking the piazza. ❸ **Massimo** Calata Italia 23 ℡ 0565.914.766, Ⓦ www.elbahotelmassimo.it. Accommodation here is nothing special, but the hotel is convenient for the ferry terminal and, with 69 rooms, should have some chance of space. ❺

Villa Ombrosa Via de Gasperi 9 ℡ 0565.914.363, Ⓦ www.villaombrosa.it. A good three-star modern 38-room villa a few minutes' walk from the town centre and in a panoramic position overlooking Le Ghiaie beach. ❻

The Town

Portoferraio consists of a modern sector – where the ferries arrive – and the old Medicean **port** with its fortifications and fishing harbour. To get to the latter, turn right off the ferry along Calata Italia, past all the car parks, to the harbourside Calata Mazzini, the town's **passeggiata** parade. Midway round Calata Mazzini is the entrance to the old town, the **Porta a Mare**, from where an ampitheatre of streets rises towards the walls on the high cliffs.

The town's most obvious features are the **fortifications**, built – like Livorno's – by the Medici; you can pass an hour or so wandering around them, even though many of the main bastions are now in private hands. Most visitors walk up Via Garibaldi and make straight for Napoleon's home in exile, the **Villa dei Mulini** (Mon & Wed–Sat 9am–7pm, Sun 9am–1pm; €3; joint three-day ticket with Villa di San Martino €5). Built specifically for the ex-emperor on a site chosen for its fine views of the bay, the villa features a stunning Baroque bedroom, a library of two thousand books sent over from Fontainebleau, and various items of memorabilia – including the Napoleonic Elban flag (see box, p.286).

Villa di San Martino

Napoleon's sister Elisa bought the **Villa di San Martino** (Tues–Sat 9am–7pm, Sun 9am–1pm; €3, or joint three-day ticket with Villa dei Mulini €5), in the hills 5km southwest of Portoferraio, as a summer residence just before the emperor – who'd built it as a retreat – left the island for good. From Portoferraio, bus #1 goes to the gates.

Engulfed by a vast car park and trolleys flogging Napoleonic souvenirs, the villa is a rather chilly affair, but its drab Neoclassical facade is at least sprinkled with exuberant "N" motifs. The monograms were the idea of Prince Demidoff, husband of Napoleon's niece – and it was he who bought up the villa to create a Napoleonic museum. By all accounts, the great man himself hardly spent any time here, and the permanent exhibits are no great shakes, though special annual exhibitions are held on a Napoleonic theme. Highlight of the house is the **Sala Egizio**, with friezes outlining Napoleon's Egyptian campaign, one of his more successful. At the back of the *palazzo* is Napoleon's own modest summer retreat – in some respects he had simple tastes – which was home to the famous graffito "Ubicunque felix Napoleon" (Napoleon is happy anywhere) until 1993, when it was discovered to be a fake and consequently removed.

Eating and drinking

Portoferraio's **restaurants** are expensive and few have food to merit the prices. *L'Ape Elbana* hotel–restaurant (see p.284) has a choice of six inexpensive tourist menus. Best known of the more upmarket choices are the *Stella Marina*, Via Vittorio Emanuele II (☎0565.915.938, ⊛ www.ristorantestellamarina.com; closed Mon & a period in Jan) and *Trattoria La Barca*, Via Guerazzi 60 (☎0565.918.036; closed Wed in winter). For **bars**, pick from any of the places around Piazza della Repubblica in the heart of the old town, or Piazza Cavour – particularly *Bar Roma*, the most popular place with locals.

Eastern Elba

Eastern Elba is a distinct geographical area, comprising two tongues of land, each dominated by mountain ridges. Away from the main seaside centres of **Rio Marina** and **Porto Azzurro** the beaches are comparatively quiet, but much of the southern isthmus – Monte Calamita – was the heart of the mining industry, and is still owned by the quarrying companies. Close by, on the southern coast, **Lacona** boasts one of the island's main concentrations of campsites.

Portoferraio to Bagnaia

Heading out of Portoferraio the main road south divides, one spur going west, the other east towards Porto Azzurro. Along the latter, first stop is the spa of **San Giovanni**, where visitors pay through the nose for the privilege of wallowing in sulphurous marine mud. A few kilometres on at **Le Grotte** are the ruins of

Napoleon and Elba

Elba is indissolubly linked with **Napoleon**, even though he was exiled here for little more than nine months – from May 4, 1814 to February 26, 1815. According to island tradition, after renouncing the thrones of France and Italy by the Treaty of Fontaine-bleau, Napoleon chose Elba as his place of exile for the "gentleness of its climates and its inhabitants". In fact, he had no choice: the allies packed him off here, sweetening the pill by ordaining that Elba would be "a separate principality for his lifetime, held by him in complete sovereignty". The dethroned emperor spent the journey south doodling a new flag for his pocket-sized domain: a red diagonal on a white background – echoing the Medici banner – plus the bees of his own imperial emblem.

After a confusing episode in which his ship was shelled from Portoferraio, Napoleon came ashore to a rousing welcome, and soon set about reorganizing the island's economy and infrastructure. Some of this work might have been motivated by altruism or an inability to forgo politics, but much of what he achieved was for his own ends. The iron ore mines were revamped to supplement his income, his promised salary from Louis XVII having never materialized; the public works were to occupy and pay for the five-hundred-strong Napoleonic Guard that stuck by him. Portoferraio was given drains because the stench offended the imperial nostrils.

Some of the longer-term planning, however, undoubtedly paid dividends to the islanders: education and the legal system were overhauled, roads were built, agriculture was modernized, land was cleared, defences were repaired. These multifarious schemes suggested that Napoleon had resigned himself to his life sentence, but intrigue, rumour and unrest in France persuaded him to have another go. The day after Sir Neil Campbell, his British keeper, left for Livorno, he returned to France and the "Hundred Days" that were to culminate in his defeat at Waterloo.

▲ Cavoli beach on the island of Elba

a **Roman villa**, little more than a few stones and mosaic fragments among the gorse, but worth a stop for a great view over the sea, into which most of the building has tumbled.

Soon after comes a left turn for Rio nell'Elba (see below) and **Magazzini**, a little place with a sand and shingle beach and a couple of **hotels**: go for the three-star *Mare* (℡0565.933.069, Ⓦwww.hotelmare.org; April–Oct; ❹). For **food**, eat at the excellent *La Carretta* (℡0565.933.223; closed lunch and Wed, except in summer).

Just beyond at **Ottone** is the *Rosselba le Palme* **campsite** (℡0565.933.101, Ⓦwww.rosselbalepalme.it; mid-April to Sept), rated by many the island's best. West-facing **BAGNAIA**, a little further, is famous for its sunsets.

Nisporto to Rio nell'Elba

The route from Magazzini to Rio nell'Elba passes the old castle at **Volterraio**, once the strongest in Elba and now a silent and evocative ruin, with a great view over its desolate surroundings. It's a stiff climb from the road.

Following the twisting coast road north of Bagnaia, you'll come to the tiny twin hamlets of **NISPORTO** and **NISPORTINO**, marking the beginning of the most unspoilt beaches and coastline on Elba's north shore. You can walk into the hills behind, or take boats out to the beaches beyond the end of the road. Just about the only accommodation here is **Camping-Villaggio Sole e Mare** at Nisporto (℡0565.934.907, Ⓦwww.soleemare.it).

From Nisporto the narrow scenic road to Rio nell'Elba climbs through **La Ginestra**, 2km from the sea, where you'll find the modern and comfortable three-star *La Ginestra* (℡0565.943.181; ❸). **RIO NELL'ELBA** itself is a graceless place, though old enough in parts and rare in having apparently resisted Elba's tourist boom. From its high vantage it surveys a wild and beautiful countryside with good sea views. The town was once the capital of Elba and centre of the mining district, evidence of which can be found in the tiny **Museo dei Minerali Elbani della Gente di Rio** (April–Oct daily 10am–1pm & 4–7pm; free).

Halfway between Rio nell'Elba and Cavo is a hermitage, the Eremo di Santa Caterina and the **Orto dei Semplici Elbano** (irregular hours), a botanical garden of wild flowers from all over the Tuscan archipelago.

Cavo and Rio Marina

CAVO, on Elba's northern extremity, is a small beach resort with little on offer bar a hydrofoil link with Portoferraio. There are several **hotels**, including the waterfront *Maristella* (℡0565.949.859, ⓦwww.hotelmaristella.com; ❸), and the pleasant, mid-priced **restaurant** *La Scogliera*, with tables overlooking the beach.

The main town on Elba's east coast is **RIO MARINA**, 9km south of Cavo, a ferry terminal for connections to Piombino, Portoferraio and Porto Azzurro. Tourism and a busy harbour have replaced iron ore as the source of revenue, but this isn't one of Elba's more appealing towns. One of the island's better **restaurants**, *La Canocchia*, at Via Palestro 3 (℡0565.962.432; closed Mon in winter), is in the lower port, where options also include the very good and moderately priced fish restaurant and pizzeria, *Da Oreste la Strega*, in Piazza V. Emanuele (℡0565.962.211; closed Tues in winter).

Porto Azzurro and around

The resort of **PORTO AZZURRO** was heavily fortified by Philip III of Spain in 1603 as protection against continual raids by the French and the Austrians; today his fortress is the island's prison but you can walk around the walls and admire the inmates' artwork at a small craft shop. The town's small, pretty old quarter, closed to traffic, centres on **Via d'Alarcon**, a bustle of bars, shops and restaurants, with traditional open-front shops and balconied houses in the cobbled area near Piazza Matteotti. The best place to swim is from the rocks east of the harbour. **Boat trips** (around €20 for 3hr) run south along the coast in summer.

Accommodation is limited and lacklustre: go for the *Belmare*, Banchina IV Novembre 25 (℡0565.95.012, ⓦwww.elba-hotelbelmare.it; ❸), *Arrighi*, Via V. Veneto 18 (℡0565.95.315; closed Feb; ❷) or *Villa Italia*, Viale Italia 41 (℡0565.95.119, ⓦwww.villaitaliahotel.it; ❸).

Off the Rio Marina road to the north, at **TERRANERE**, there's a bizarre sulphurous pond, its half-stagnant waters a violent yellow contrast to the sea; the beach here is scattered with mine debris. Nearby, up an unsignposted left turn off the same road, is the **Santuario della Madonna di Monserrato**, about 1km beyond the so-called Piccolo Miniera, a tourist-trap mine reconstruction. The short walk at the end of the road brings you to the church whose chief claim to fame is its replica of the Black Madonna of Montserrat; chapel and Madonna were both commissioned in 1606 by the island's Spanish governor, who claimed this site reminded him of the holy mountain outside his native Barcelona.

East of the road between Porto Azzurro and Capoliveri, **NAREGNO** is a small resort with a good beach, though not as good as the less accessible sand to the south at Côte Piane, Liscolino and Buzzancone. None can match the village's **accommodation** possibilities, however, which include the seafront *Villa Rodriguez* (℡0565.968.423, ⓦwww.villarodriguez.it; ❹) and modern 53-room *Hotel Frank* (℡0565.968.144, ⓦwww.frankshotel.com; ❹).

Capoliveri and further south

CAPOLIVERI, 3.5km south of Porto Azzurro, is the best of the towns in eastern Elba, a prosperous centre whose close-knit streets have made few concessions to tourism. Occupying a naturally fortified spot, it's amongst the oldest settlements on the island: in Roman times its name was Caput Liberi. Its hinterland remains undeveloped, as the mining companies have not yet sold their disused plots to the hoteliers – though much of the area is thus out of bounds.

There's nothing specific to see, but **old streets** such as Via Roma, Via Cavour and Vicolo Lungo are pleasant places to roam, and there are numerous half-hidden bars in the alleyways, as well as a sprawl of outside tables in the central piazza. The town is at its busiest on Thursdays, when locals and tourists flood in for the weekly **street market**; it is also very lively in the evenings, with a reputation for being the place to go for a night out.

Capoliveri would make an ideal base for visits to the fine **beaches** at Naregno, Morcone and Innamorata. However, it's practically impossible to stay cheaply: it only has expensive **apartments** rented out by private agencies. Moderate-to-expensive **restaurants** include *Il Chiasso*, Vicolo Sauro 9 (℡0565.968.709; closed Nov–Easter, plus Tues & lunch year-round, except June–Sept), specializing in seafood, and *Osteria Summertime*, Via Roma 56 (℡0565.935.180; closed lunch on Sun; dinner only in Aug).

The much-touted local church at **Madonna delle Grazie** – another place of pilgrimage – has a school-of-Raphael altarpiece but is otherwise more or less a waste of time. It's better to continue to the trio of resorts at **Morcone**, **Pareti** and **Innamorata**. The last is the quietest and has a fine sand and shingle beach; the other hamlets have large beaches, Morcone's being more regimented than its neighbour. Parking is difficult, as is **accommodation**. Morcone has no hotels; Pareti has the *Villa Miramare* (℡0565.968.673, ⓦwww.hotelvillamiramare.it; ❸) and *Dino* (℡0565.939.103, ⓦwww.hoteldino.com; ❹).

Lacona

LACONA, well round the coast west of Porto Azzurro, is one of the island's main camping centres, and its flat foreshore is crowded with **bars** and **clubs** designed to cater to the beach crowd once the sun's gone down. The **campsites** to head for are *Il Lacona* (℡0565.964.161, ⓦwww.camping-lacona.it) or the nearby *Lacona Pineta* (℡0565.964.322, ⓦwww.campinglaconapineta.com), both set in the pine woods on the eastern arm of the Golfo di Lacona. *Stella Mare* (℡0565.964.007, ⓦwww.stellamare.it), which offers free bike rental, as well as windsurfing lessons, is on the beach a bit farther out along the headland, also amidst plenty of greenery.

Western Elba

Western Elba's road system allows for a circular tour of the area, but many people make immediately for specific targets – usually **Marina di Campo**, with its huge beach and many hotels. Upmarket alternatives are offered by the north-coast resorts of **Procchio** and **Marciana Marina**, while backpackers favour the relatively less commercialized **Énfola** area.

Fewer visitors venture inland to **Marciana**, one of Elba's most attractive villages, or explore the long sweep of the **western coast**, whose hamlets and beaches are amongst the island's most tranquil. Though the western zone tends to be rockier than the east, it's better for **walking**, the highlights being **Monte Capanne** and its surrounding ridges.

Énfola, Viticcio, Scaglieri and Biodola

For a spread of beach and a choice of campsites near Portoferraio, follow the scenic road below Monte Poppe to the headland at **Capo d'Énfola**. You pass through the hamlets of Sorgente and Punta Acquaviva (each with a campsite) before reaching **ÉNFOLA**, where the land narrows to a 75-metre-wide isthmus with beaches on both sides. The road ends at a small car park next to the *Bar Emanuel* (closed Oct–Easter), where you can get down to either strip of pebbly beach. The one daily bus from Portoferraio will drop you off at Bivio Énfola – 1km from the bar – and continue to **VITICCIO**, another spot with a dead-end road, parking area, and sand and shingle beach. Pick of the numerous **hotels** in the area is the three-star *Paradiso* at Viticcio (℡0565.939.034, ⓔparadiso@elbaturistica .it; ❺). Énfola has a shady **campsite**, *Enfola Camping* (℡0565.939.001, ⓦwww .campingenfola.it; April to mid-Oct). The popular Sansone **beach** is off the main road from Portoferraio on the right: take the track 50m before *Ristorante Tre Colonne* or ask the bus driver to stop.

From Viticcio, a footpath runs 2km round the coast to Scaglieri and Biodola, otherwise reached by a side road from the main highway out of Portoferraio. **BIODOLA** consists simply of a road, two big hotels and a superb **beach**, which inevitably gets a summer blitz of visitors. Parking is difficult, but there are no buses. Biodola's two **hotels** are very expensive, though there's a beautifully situated place two minutes from the beach, the *Casa Rosa* (℡0565.969.931, ⓔcasarosa@elbalink.it; ❻). **SCAGLIERI** is similar but a touch livelier and more picturesque, fronted by a shop, two bars, a couple of moderately priced places to **eat** and a **hotel–restaurant**, *Danila* (℡0565.969.915, ⓦwww.hoteldanila.it; April to mid-Oct; ❹).

Procchio to Marciana Marina

PROCCHIO suffers from being at a junction of main roads, the greenery of its surroundings offset by an incessant stream of summer traffic. With its shops and bars it's not a place to get away from it all, but the sea is good and the white beach excellent; access to much of the sand is free and it's large enough not to seem overcrowded. Pick of the **hotels** are the *Monna Lisa* (℡0565.907.519, ⓦwww.hotelmonnalisa.it; ❷) and the *Fontalleccio* (℡0565.907.431, ⓦwww .hotelfontalleccio.it; ❹).

Farther round the north coast, **MARCIANA MARINA** has the minor distinction of being the smallest *comune* in Tuscany, a status it's proud of, allowing only a few hotels and aiming to preserve an air of residential order away from the seafront. The traffic-filled promenade of bars, restaurants and trinket shops does nothing to lure you into staying. Even the beach, overlooked by a Pisan watchtower, is shingly and forgettable. Accommodation is largely restricted to private houses and apartments.

Poggio to Marciana

Situated 5km inland from Marciana Marina, **POGGIO** is renowned for its **Fonte di Napoleone** mineral water and a tight medieval centre whose decorated doorways and patchwork of cheerful gardens make it an attractive place to stay. The best **hotel** is *Albergo-Ristorante Monte Capanne*, Via Pini 1 (℡&ⓕ0565.99.083; ❶), in a lovely, peaceful setting. **Food** here is good, and the village claims one of the island's leading restaurants, *Publius*, Via XX Settembre 13 (℡0565.99.208; closed Dec–March & Mon, except dinner mid-June to mid-Sept), which has great views and classic Elban cooking, including *cacciucco* and wild boar with mushrooms.

It's a few steep kilometres up the mountain road from Poggio to the high and isolated village of **MARCIANA**, the oldest settlement on Elba, which is perfectly placed between great beaches (Promonte and Sant'Andrea), mountainous interior (Monte Capanne) and a modern centre for supplies (Procchio). Its **old quarter** is a delight, too, its narrow alleys, arches, belvederes and stone stairs festooned with flowers and climbing plants. There's virtually no traffic or commercial development, and with the skeletal outline of its old fortifications it feels very distinct from the rest of the island's towns.

Marciana's history is encapsulated in the small **Museo Archeologico** in Via del Pretorio (Mon–Sat: May–Nov 9.30am–12.30pm & 4–8pm, rest of year 9.30am–12.30pm & 3–7pm; €2), just below the **Fortezza Pisana**, which is closed to the public but worth the steep climb through the village for its spectacular views.

Outside the village there's a trio of interesting **churches**, the oldest of which is the twelfth-century Pisan-influenced **San Lorenzo**; now largely in ruins, it's on a track off the road to Poggio. More intriguing is the **Santuario della Madonna del Monte**, about half an hour's walk along the road curving uphill west of the village. Though it dates from the eleventh century – and was probably a pagan temple well before that – its appearance is largely sixteenth-century, the Renaissance church serving to house a stone painted by a heavenly hand with the image of the Virgin. The island's most important shrine, it's also featured on the Napoleonic trail, as the ex-emperor came here to seek spiritual solace from the monks; by all accounts he received solace of a different kind when he was joined by his Polish mistress, Maria Walewska.

The third church, the **Santuario di San Cerbone**, is passed on the **walk** to Monte Capanne (trail #1; 3hr). The track starts from the southern tip of the village, the church appearing after an hour at the junction with trail #6. San Cerbone was buried here, during a miraculous cloudburst that hid the ceremony from Lombards who had the saint's valuable remains in their sights.

If you don't want to walk up Monte Capanne, there's a popular **cable car** 1km south of the town which takes you to the top (June–Sept 10am–12.15pm & 2.30–6.30pm; Oct–May 10am–12.15pm & 2.30–5.30pm; €10 one-way, €15 return); most people choose to walk down either to Marciana or Poggio, though if you're trekking with your gear you could drop down to the coast via one of the numerous marked trails.

Marciana's **accommodation** is restricted to rented rooms and apartments. The best place to **eat** is the reasonably priced *Osteria del Noce*, Via della Madonna 14 (℡0565.901.284).

Sant'Andrea and around

The dispersed village of **SANT'ANDREA**, 6km west of Marciana, just off the coast road, is one of Elba's more fashionable retreats, with villas and hotels creeping further into the wooded hinterland each year. It's popular with divers, drawn here by what is reputedly some of the clearest sea water around Elba. **Accommodation** is at a premium, but it's not necessarily expensive, and most is discreetly set amid almost tropical vegetation. On the beach itself there's the pleasant *La Cernia* (℡0565.908.210, ⓦwww.hotelcernia.it; ❸), midway between the coast and the main road; or try *Bella Vista* (℡0565.908.015, ⓦwww.hotel-bellavista.it; ❷).

Immediately south are the hamlets of **Patresi**, **Mortaio** and **La Guardia**, rated as having the island's finest seas and still fairly unspoilt into the bargain. Cliffs drop to the sea, as they do all round this section of coast, with plenty of rock pillars and stacks for underwater enthusiasts.

The southwest coast: Chiessi to Cávoli

Further round the coast road, **Chiessi** and **Pomonte** each have a small stony beach, beautifully clear water, rocky hinterland and little commercialism. By the time you reach **Fetovaia** you're back to beach development, but the sand is superb. Fetovaia has lots of apartments and several **hotels**; try the central *Lo Scirocco* (℡0565.988.033, ⓦwww.hotellosciroccoisolaelba.it; ❹).

Further on, **Seccheto** is good for a swim from the rocks at the western end of town, or for tanning on the largely nudist stretch beyond – **le piscine** – where the water forms deep pools in the hollows of a Roman granite mine. A good place to **stay**, but away from the coast, is *Locanda dell'Amicizia* (℡0565.987.051, ℻0565.987.277; ❷), set in a peaceful spot at **Vallebuia**, in the little valley north of Seccheto. The **bar** on the main road, which can sometimes direct you to available apartments, is popular, fairly cheap and does excellent pizzas. Nearby **Cávoli** is more upmarket, with a good if crowded beach and the beachside **pensione** *Lorenza* (℡0565.987.044, Ⓦwww.hoteldelmare-lorenza.it; ❸).

Marina di Campo

Set in one of the island's few areas of plain, **MARINA DI CAMPO** was the first and is now the largest resort on Elba. The huge white **beach** is what makes the place popular: the water's clean, and there's space if you walk to the east end or out to the rockier west. There's also all the tourist frippery and nightlife you'd expect in any major seaside centre.

Pick of the numerous **hotels** are the *Santa Caterina*, Viale Elba (℡0565.976.452, Ⓔsantacaterina@elbalink.it; ❹) and the *Thomas*, Via Giannutri (℡0565.977.732, Ⓦwww.elbathomashotel.com; ❷). If you arrive early in the day you might find space at one of the three **campsites**. There are plenty of places to **eat**: the *Rosticceria Mazzarri*, Via Roma 19, has inexpensive meals and snacks; for fish, try the moderately priced *Il Cacciucco* in Piazza Cavour. For a break from the crowds you might take a bus trip out to two smaller hill-villages close by – the very pretty **Sant'Ilario in Campo** and **San Piero in Campo**, whose parish church has a hotchpotch of frescoes.

Capraia

The island of **CAPRAIA**, 30km northwest of Elba, is unspoilt, with just a couple of hotels and one road that links the small port to the old town on the hill. Its former use as a penal colony ensured that the terrain remained largely untouched, and now – despite considerable pressure from potential hoteliers – the local council have held back on commercial development, instead promoting the island's status as a **national park** to protect the natural heritage. This makes it difficult to visit, and the two hotels and single campsite come close to saturation point in summer: it's best to come slightly out of season. A Toremar **ferry** (see p.279) runs daily from Livorno throughout the year (summer Thurs & Fri twice daily).

Capraia Isola

From the tiny harbour to the town of **CAPRAIA ISOLA** – the only inhabited part of the island except the port – is a gentle walk of about 1km (there's a regular bus in summer). The island's long periods of desolation, mainly because of pirate raids, have done little for its monuments. Capraia Isola's Baroque church and convent of **Sant'Antonio** is largely ruined, and the big castle, the privately owned **Fortezza di San Giorgio**, has seen better days.

For information on wildlife, walking, accommodation and boat trips, contact the **Cooperativa Parco** (℡0586.905.071, Ⓦwww.isoladicapraia.it) or the **tourist office** (April–Sept 10am–6pm; ℡0586.905.138), both on the harbourfront Via Assunzione. **Hotels** here are the comfortable three-star *Da Beppone*, Via Assunzione 78 (℡&℻0586.905.001; ❸), and, in the upper part of

town, the smarter four-star *Il Saracino*, Via L. Cibo 30 (℡0586.905.018, Ⓦwww
.capraiaisola.info; ❻); you'll probably have to pay at least half-board in peak
periods. There are numerous private **rooms** and **apartments**; the tourist office
will call round for you, or you can just wander through town and look for the
signs. There's a single **campsite**, *Le Sughere* (℡0586.905.066; May–Sept),
behind the small church of the Assumption.

One of the best **restaurants** is *La Garitta*, Via Genova 14 (℡0586.905.230),
up near the castle; run as a bar during the day, it's an informal place, dedicated
to simple, moderately priced seafood. There are a couple of other inexpensive
places down on the harbour, best of which is *Da Beppone*.

The interior and the beaches

The scrubby, almost treeless island has a knobbly spine of 400m hills, with the
eastern slope shallow and riven with valleys, and the western coast featuring
cliffs rising almost sheer from the sea. From Capraia Isola you can easily strike
off into the uninhabited interior: tracks crisscross the whole island, but there
are four distinct and fairly obvious **walks**: to the **Torre dello Zenobito**, a
Genoese watchtower on the island's southernmost tip; to **Il Piano** and the
Pisan church of **Santo Stefano**, using the rough road south of the town; to the
lighthouse on the west coast, farther down the same track; and to the **Laghetto**,
a tarn in the hills.

Isolation has favoured the development of various indigenous animal and
vegetable species, several of them similar to species otherwise confined to
Corsica and Sardinia. These include subspecies of buzzard, sparrow, large finch
and La Marmora's warbler amongst the birds, and campion, toadflax and blue
button amongst the plants. Birds are the main natural interest, with numerous
itinerant visitors and forty resident species including peregrines, shearwaters and
up to a hundred pairs of the rare Corsican gull.

Winter storms in 1998 stripped the island's only real beach, the Cala della
Mortola, of all its sand. However, there are plenty of rocky coves and the water's
clean and clear everywhere. There's a range of small **boats** available for rent,
from canoes (around €10 per hr) to powered rubber dinghies (around €100 per
day). Both the Cooperativa Parco and Agenzia Della Rosa (℡0586.905.266,
Ⓦwww.capraiavacanze.it) run trips round the entire island (twice daily in
season). There are a couple of **diving** clubs in the port; contact the Capraia
Diving Club, Via Assunzione 100 (℡0586.905.137, Ⓦwww.capraiadiving.it), for
help and equipment rental.

Travel details

Trains

Campiglia Maríttima to: Piombino Maríttima
(hourly; 30min).
Livorno to: Campiglia Maríttima (every 30min; 1hr);
Castagneto Carducci (every 30min; 45min); Castiglioncello (every 30min; 25min); Cécina (every 30min;
35min); Florence (12 daily; 1hr 30min); Quercianella
(every 30min; 15min); Rome (hourly; 3–4hr).
Pisa to: Empoli (every 30min; 35min; change for
Volterra and Siena); Florence (every 30min;
1hr–1hr 20min); Livorno (every 20min; 15min);
Lucca (hourly; 20min); Pisa Airport (every 30min;
5min); San Rossore (every 30min; 5min).

Buses

Cécina to: Bibbona (10 daily; 20–35min); Castagneto Carducci (1 daily; 25min); Livorno (every
30min; 1hr); Saline di Volterra (6 daily; 30min).
Livorno to: Castiglioncello (every 30min; 35min);
Cecina (every 30min; 1hr); Piombino (2 daily; 1hr
30min); Pisa (hourly; 40min).

Piombino to: Campiglia Maríttima (11 daily; 30min); Donoratico (3 daily; 35min); Populonia (2 daily; 15min); Sassetta (2 daily; 1hr 15min); Suvereto (7 daily; 50min).
Pisa to: Florence (hourly via Lucca and Montecatini; 2hr 30min); Livorno (hourly; 40min); Lucca (hourly; 50min); Viareggio (hourly; 50min).

Populonia to: Baratti (4 daily; 5min).
Portoferraio to: Capoliveri (7 daily; 30min); Marciana (8 daily; 1hr); Marciana Marina (8 daily; 35min); Marina di Campo (10 daily; 30min); Porto Azzurro (10 daily; 30min); Rio nell'Elba/Rio Marina (7 daily; 50min).

The Maremma

CHAPTER 5 # Highlights

* **Massa Maríttima** Fine hill-town with a glorious Romanesque cathedral. See p.299

* **Monti dell'Uccellina** Italy's most pristine stretch of coastal scenery. See p.305

* **Marina di Alberese** The trees come right down to this unspoilt sandy beach, which has gently shelving water and views across to the Argentario. See p.307

* **Monte Argentario** Spectacular headland with chic coastal resorts. See p.311

* **Giglio** Pleasant, if popular, little island an hour offshore. See p.313

▲ Massa Maríttima

The Maremma

The **Maremma** was long Tuscany's forgotten corner, its coastal plains, marshes, forest-covered hills and wild, empty upland interior having been a place of exile and fear for much of the last five hundred years: unknown, unvisited and virtually uninhabited. "Only the wild beasts that hate the cultivated fields", wrote Dante, "make their lairs in the Tuscan Maremma." Malaria was the problem, combined with bandits in the interior and pirate attacks on the coast. With these problems eradicated, the Maremma's fortunes are changing, thanks in part to its burgeoning wine business. While it lacks historic towns such as Siena, Lucca or Arezzo – Massa Maríttima is the only town that can hold its own with the region's heavy hitters – its wonderful maritime and still-empty interior landscapes are well worth exploring.

The region was the northern heartland of the **Etruscans**, whose drainage and irrigation canals turned it into an area of huge agricultural potential. Their good work, however, was largely lost under the Romans, who abandoned much of the land and left it to revert to marsh. For years, virtually the only inhabitants were migrant charcoal burners and shepherds (who in summer abandoned the infested lowlands for the hill-villages of Amiata), and the famous *butteri* (see box below): cowboys who tend the region's oxen and horses.

Modern attempts to revive the Maremma were started in 1828 by Grand Duke Leopoldo of Tuscany, who instigated new drainage schemes to combat malaria, but real progress only began under Mussolini; the malarial mosquito was finally banished in 1950.

The butteri

The **butteri**, the Maremma's cowboys, have for centuries taken care of the region's half-feral horses and celebrated white cattle, a special breed imported from Asia for their resilience to the rigours of the Maremma climate and terrain. For most of the year, the *butteri* ride with the herds on the Maremma's grasslands, the key event of the year being the so-called *merca* in April, when the one-year-old calves and foals are rounded up, counted and branded.

You stand most chance of seeing the *butteri* on the Ombrone estuary, particularly on the road to Marina di Alberese, although from time to time they make an appearance in local festivals and special events. Such performances are nothing new: in 1911 Buffalo Bill brought a travelling troupe of cowboys to Rome, where they were trounced by the *butteri* in a series of rodeo events in the Piazza del Popolo. Today the best known of their tourist shows is the August **rodeo** in Alberese, and they also prove their skills in perhaps the most demanding equestrian arena in the world – as riders in the Siena Palio.

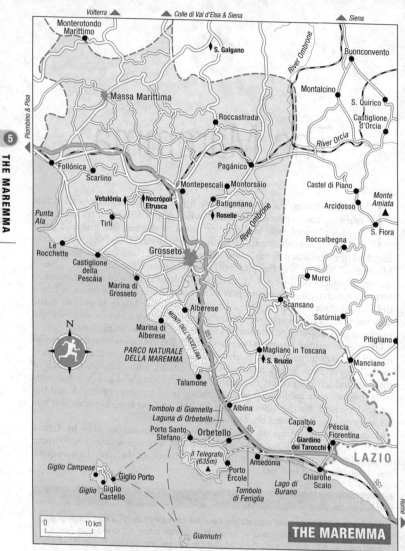

Efforts have been made to preserve the region's natural treasures, mainly in the **Monti dell'Uccellina** but also in the nature reserves at **Burano** and **Orbetello**, two of the finest birdwatching spots in the country. Inland, much of the high, rolling hill country remains pristine, still all but unvisited, though take any of the minor country lanes off the main Grosseto-to-Siena road and you'll find countryside as good as any in the region. There are plenty of seaside diversions here as well, with glorious beaches at **Marina di Alberese** and in the Uccellina, and moderately upmarket resorts at **Punta Ala** and around **Monte Argentario**.

The coast is served by the main Rome–Pisa **rail line** and the old Roman road, the Via Aurelia (SS1). To cut across country, there's a rail link from Grosseto to Siena, and a few **buses** that run inland from Grosseto, Orbetello and Massa Maríttima.

Massa Maríttima

Once the second city of the Sienese Republic and still graced with some of Siena's civic style, **MASSA MARÍTTIMA** is the finest historic town of the Maremma. Named "Massa" by the Romans – their word for a large country estate – it gained its maritime suffix in the Middle Ages, when it became the pre-eminent town of this coastal region. The sea has receded since that time and is now 20km distant across a silt-filled plain, scarcely visible from the town's hilltop.

Massa, like Volterra to the north, has long been a **mining** town, its silver, copper and other mineral reserves generating wealth since Neolithic times. In 1310 it produced Europe's first charter for the protection of miners, the *Codice Mineraio*. Sadly for Massa, its mineral riches attracted the rival attentions of Pisa and Siena, the latter finally absorbing the town in 1335. Those hundred years of glory, however, funded the building of its monuments – notably the exquisite **Duomo**. Subsequent visitations of plague and malaria, together with a downturn in mining activity, left Massa a virtual ghost town by 1737, its population reduced to just 537. Like other Maremma towns, its recovery only began with the reopening of mines and the draining of coastal marshes in the 1830s.

Arrival, information and accommodation

Intertown **buses** from Siena (2 daily), Grosseto and Larderello (for Volterra; 4 daily), as well as hourly buses from the Massa–Follonica **train station**, 19km west on the main Pisa–Rome line, stop on Via Corridoni close to Piazza Garibaldi: get off when you see the campanile of the Duomo. The **tourist office**, Via Todini 3 (Mon–Sat 9.30am–12.30pm & 3–6pm; also open Sun April–Sept 10am–1pm & June–Sept 4–7pm; ℡0566.902.756, ⓦwww.altamaremmaturismo.it), has plenty of information about agriturismi in the area, Massa's Monteregio DOC **wine** and the local **Strada del Vino** (wine trail).

Hotels

Despite Massa's popularity, there are surprisingly few **places to stay**.

Duca del Mare Piazza Dante Alighieri 1–2 ℡0566.902.284, ⓦwww.ducadelmare.it. This three-star, modern hotel on the approach to Massa makes a pleasant base. All rooms have a/c and terraces, and the décor is clean-lined and modern. There's an outdoor pool, plus a breakfast room by the garden and the chance to dine outside in summer in the restaurant. Closed mid-Jan to Feb. ❸

Girifalco Via Massetana Nord 25 ℡0566.902.177, ⓦwww.ilgirifalco.com. Two-star hotel located just outside Massa. Rooms are light and airy, and the best have fine views. Good if you're travelling with children, as there's a play area and plenty of open space. Closed mid-Nov to mid-April. ❸

Il Sole Via della Libertà 43 ℡0566.901.971, ⓦwww.ilsolehotel.it. The best hotel in town, by virtue of the fact that it is right in the centre and has good three-star facilities; closed mid-Jan to mid-Feb. ❸

La Fenice Park Hotel Corso Diaz 63 ℡0566.903.941, ⓦwww.lafeniceparkhotel.it. A big step up in price from its rival hotels, this three-star has rooms heavy on the marble, with sumptuous bathrooms and kitchenettes, plus an immaculate garden and outdoor pool. ❺

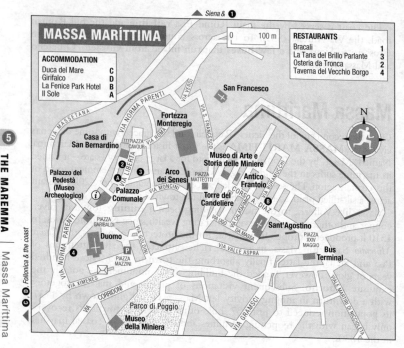

MASSA MARÍTTIMA

0   100 m

RESTAURANTS

Bracali	1
La Tana del Brillo Parlante	3
Osteria da Tronca	2
Taverna del Vecchio Borgo	4

ACCOMMODATION

Duca del Mare	C
Girifalco	D
La Fenice Park Hotel	B
Il Sole	A

The Town

An industrial estate mars the approach to Massa, and blocks of new buildings do little to improve the effect. All this is overshadowed, however, by the medieval splendour of Piazza Garibaldi in the lower, mainly Romanesque, **Città Vecchia**; it's a small, eccentric but exquisite example of Tuscan town planning, with the thirteenth-century Duomo set on broad steps at a dramatically oblique angle to the square.

The upper town, the **Città Nuova**, is more Gothic in appearance and was built largely as a residential centre. An immensely steep and picturesque lane, **Via Moncini**, connects the two; for most of the Middle Ages, the lower town was inhabited by a Pisan clan, the Todini, the upper by their Sienese rivals, the Pannochieschi.

The Duomo

The **Duomo** (daily 8am–noon & 3–7pm) is essentially Pisan Romanesque, with a few later additions blending harmoniously with the blind arches and tiny columns (most notably the extraordinary Gothic **campanile**, added in about 1400). The cathedral's dedication is to St Cerbone, the Bishop of Populonia in the sixth century. Although famous for persuading a flock of geese to follow him when he was summoned to Rome on heresy charges, Cerbone is usually depicted with a bear licking his feet, a reference to the beast he tamed when Totila the Hun threw him into a pit full of wild animals. Bas-reliefs in the architrave of the main door show scenes from the saint's life.

Inside, the bare stone walls set off some superb carvings and works of art. The most admired carvings are the thirteenth-century ones by Giraldo da Como, on the huge **baptistery** and also the quadrangular **font**. Almost as arresting are the fifteenth-century tabernacle (under the marble canopy of the baptistery), and some eleventh-century Romanesque carvings close to the entrance featuring powerful and primitive grinning faces, that are in dramatic contrast with the severe, polished Roman sarcophagus to their right. Over the altar is a large Giovanni Pisano altarpiece, and behind it the *Arca di San Cerbone*, an arch of bas-reliefs depicting the life of the saint, carved by Gori di Gregorio in 1324. Take a look, too, at the *Madonna delle Grazie* at the end of the left transept, a damaged but gorgeous Sienese work attributed to Duccio or Simone Martini. Finally, the fine little crypt has a single fresco featuring St Cerbone and St Bernardino.

The Museo Archeologico

The smaller of the two palaces on Piazza Garibaldi, the Palazzo del Podestà, contains the **Museo Civico Archeologico** and **Pinacoteca Comunale** (Tues–Sun: April–Oct 10am–12.30pm & 3.30–7pm; Nov–March 10am–12.30pm & 3–5pm; €3), where the chief exhibit is one of the finest altarpieces in Tuscany, a *Maestà* painted in 1335 by Ambrogio Lorenzetti. Vivid pink, green and tangerine illuminate the figures of Faith, Hope and Charity below the Madonna, while Cerbone and his geese lurk in the right-hand corner. The museum otherwise houses only a handful of minor paintings and some local archeological finds.

The Città Nuova

The town council has organized what it calls a "tourist itinerary", a signposted route that takes you to some very dull spots. The best thing to do is wander up to the **Città Nuova** by Via Moncini, whose tributary alleyways reveal small gardens and good views. At the end of the street, you emerge beneath an impressive but militarily useless arch, the **Arco dei Senesi**, into **Piazza Matteotti**, flanked by a segment of the town wall, and the **Torre del Candeliere** with panoramic views from the top (April–Oct Tues–Sun 10am–1pm & 3–6pm; Nov–March Tues–Sun 11am–1pm & 2.30–4.30pm; €2.50). There's also a small park, ideal for a picnic or siesta. Across Piazza Matteotti stands the **Museo di Arte e Storia delle Miniere** (April–Oct Tues–Sun 3–5.30pm, rest of year on request; €1.50), which houses a puny collection of fossils, mining equipment and archive photographs of local history. Otherwise, the only things to see up here are the church of **Sant'Agostino**, graced with simple cloisters, and the **Antico Frantoio**, Massa's oldest oil mill, at Via Populonia 3 (April–Oct Tues–Sun 10.30am–1pm, rest of year on request; €1.50).

Eating and drinking

Piazza Garibaldi has some pleasant **bars**, though its restaurants are geared towards the tourist trade. **Restaurants** include the inexpensive and excellent-value *Taverna del Vecchio Borgo*, Via Parenti 12 (⊤0566.903.950; closed for a period of mid-Jan to mid-Feb, Mon year-round, plus Sun eve in low season);

The Museo della Miniera

Inevitably, given its mining heritage, Massa boasts a **Museo della Miniera** (mining museum), housed in an underground air-raid shelter five minutes from Piazza Garibaldi off Via Corridoni (entry by guided tour only; Tues–Sun 10am–1pm & 3.30–6pm; €5). The mock-up mine has 700m of galleries and a chronological display of the area's mining methods and equipment.

Roccatederighi

Situated 15km east of Massa, **Roccatederighi** is difficult to fit into any logical itinerary, but with transport is well worth the twenty-minute journey. Perched on a needle of rock, the village has been literally carved from stone, and offers one of the finest views of the Maremma. Gird yourself for the haul up one of the impossibly steep alleys, to the rock pillars that command the area.

the recommended *La Tana del Brillo Parlante*, Vicolo del Ciambellano 4 (℡0566.901.274; closed Wed), a delightful place with just ten covers (plus seating for four outside); and the equally good ✣ *Osteria da Tronca*, Vicolo Porte 5 (℡0566.901.991; closed Wed), offering inexpensive *osteria*-style food in an atmospheric stone-wall and vaulted-ceiling setting.

Some 2km out of town to the northeast, at Via di Perolla 2, Ghirlanda, is the Michelin-starred (and very expensive) *Bracali* (℡0566.902.318; closed Mon, Tues and lunch Wed & Thurs).

Follónica and southwards

The popular, downmarket resort of **FOLLÓNICA**, which has the nearest train station to Massa Maríttima, marks something of a watershed on the Maremma coast. To the north, the flatlands drag up towards Cécina, but to the south lies a tract of relatively unspoilt, hilly countryside, a landscape similar to that of the Tuscan heartland. Pick of the mixed bag of small resorts along this stretch is **Castiglione della Pescaia**, beyond which lies a magnificent belt of classic Maremma pine forest.

Follónica itself is a large and scruffy town, its untidy beach spoilt by high-rise buildings and, at the far southern end, by factory-outlet pipes. It's very much a family resort, packed out in summer; the big, colourful Friday **market** is about the only real attraction. The **train station** is at the top of Via Matteotti, which leads straight down to the sea. If you're passing through and want an hour's sun and sea, aim for the best part of the **beach** along the stands of pines to the south, before the pipes: follow the main road for about 1km from the centre, then strike off through the trees at the garage on the left; you'll spot cars parked on the roadside.

Scarlino and Tirli

SCARLINO is invitingly situated on a steep, wooded hillside 9km east of Follónica, beyond a huge, red-striped chimney that does its best to wreck the view. The medieval village is attractive, if unexceptional, while the hills behind are dotted with fragments of castles and monasteries. It has a very friendly restaurant-pizzeria, *La Vecchia Locanda*, Piazza Garibaldi 7 (℡0566.372.99, ⓦwww.vecchialocanda.it; closed Wed), specializing in mushrooms and truffles.

Further south by minor roads through the hills is **TIRLI**, where – as in other local villages – they venerate the hermit St Guglielmo, renowned for slaying a dragon, a "rib" of which is held in the village church. There are walks into the woods behind the village, one to the ruins of **Malavalle** monastery – scene of the slaying – and to the miraculous spring of **Sant' Anna**, a point of pilgrimage on July 24.

Punta Ala and Le Rocchette

Unless you're feeling particularly flush, there's not a lot of point in making the detour to **PUNTA ALA**, a ritzy, purpose-built resort on the southern spur of the Gulf of Follónica. Beautifully situated below a castle-topped headland, it's dominated by its millionaires' marina. All but a couple of the **hotels** are four-star, as are the **campsites**, most of which are at Capo Civinini, north of the resort where the lane from the main road meets the coast.

The minor road marked on the TCI road map, between Punta Ala and **LE ROCCHETTE** to the south, is little more than a footpath: car access is from the main SS322. There's a handful of bars close to a good beach, whose tiny approach lane is chaotic in high summer. With transport, it could be a convenient point to camp, though the **campsites** have little free space in August. Try the 300-pitch *Rocchette* (℡0564.941.213, ⓦwww.rocchette.com; March–Oct).

Castiglione della Pescaia

Set among low, wooded hills that are a welcome break from the flat around Grosseto, **CASTIGLIONE DELLA PESCAIA** still affects the air of a fishing village. It does admittedly have a marina and tourist centre, but lacks Punta Ala's exclusivity, and of all the Maremma resorts, this is where you're most likely to have a good time. The bars are fun, the beach is decent, and the walled **old town** on the hill – believed to have been an Etruscan port – is a charming spot to wander, with great views from the castle. The harbourfront fish **market**, in the morning and late afternoon, is worth checking out if you're self-catering.

There's a **tourist office** at Piazza Garibaldi 6 (Mon–Fri 9am–1pm & 2–6pm, Sat 9am–5pm; ℡0564.933.678, ⓦwww.lamaremma.info). The best-sited **hotels** are on the main road north, an area still blessed with stands of umbrella pines. The best hotel is the four-star *L'Approdo*, Via Ponte Giorgini 29 (℡0564.933.466, ⓦwww.hotelapprodo.com; ❻), in a panoramic position overlooking the sea and pine woods. The modern three-star *Miramare*, Via Vittorio Veneto 35, also overlooks the sea (℡0564.933.524, ⓦwww.hotelmiramare.info; ❺). Most appealing of the cheaper places is the *Aurora*, Via Fratelli Bandiera 19 (℡0564.933.718, ⓦwww.aurora-albergo.it; ❸). The best of the local **campsites**, on the road towards Grosseto, is *Etruria* (℡0564.933.483, ⓦwww.campeggioetruria.net; May–Sept), about 1km south.

There are a lot of cheap **restaurants** and pizzerias, but standout places are the central *Romolo*, Corso Libertà 10 (℡0564.933.533, ⓦwww.daromolo.com; closed Tues & a period in Nov–Dec), with fish and local specialities, and *Il Votapentole*, Via IV Novembre 15 (℡0564.934.763; closed Mon), a tiny, simple place with room for just fourteen diners (and the same again outside in fine weather).

About 2km east of Castiglione, at the entrance to the Diaccia Botrona nature reserve, is the **Museo Multimediale della Casa Rossa Xiemenes** (Tues–Sun 4–10pm; €5). Built in 1765, this "Red House" has been restored and converted into a high-tech observation point over the reserve, which is one of the most important wetland areas in Italy. The idea is that visitors can observe the flora and fauna via three strategically positioned webcams, without disturbing the ecosystem.

South to Marina di Grosseto

The road south from Castiglione runs through a stunning woodland of **umbrella pines** (*pineta*), a small section of which is administered as a nature reserve by the World Wide Fund for Nature and has restricted access. The rest of the woodland – about twelve square kilometres in all – is accessible on foot:

you can leave your car on the roadside and walk down to the superb beaches via one of the many tracks through the trees. A **bus** service between Grosseto and Castiglione stops en route.

At first glance **MARINA DI GROSSETO** looks a dreadful place, with its gridiron streets and scattering of big, brand-new houses. As Maremma resorts go, however, it's surprisingly upbeat, and the clean, broad **beach** is backed by low-key bars and restaurants. Trees shade the open-plan residential district, giving it a touch of style.

You could get a bus out here from Grosseto for the day, though with a car or bike you'd be better off heading to the superior beaches at Marina di Alberese. The **tourist office** is on Via Grossetana (summer daily 9am–12.30pm & 4–7.30pm; winter Mon–Fri 9am–12.30pm; ☎0564.34.449).

Grosseto

Travelling by train, the chances are that you'll pass the provincial capital, **GROSSETO**, with no more than a glance, but by bus or car you'll be forced into the heart of its unappealing centre. Ringed by a factory-ridden plain, and composed mainly of characterless condominiums, this commercial metropolis was raised from the ruins of heavy bombing and now serves principally as a functional and administrative centre. Most **trains** on the main Rome–Pisa line stop at Grosseto, where you can change for Siena, or for connections to Orbetello, Cécina (for Volterra) and Follónica (for Massa Maríttima). Timetabling often leaves about an hour or so between connections – which is about all the time you need for the **old centre**, contained within a largely intact hexagon of walls commissioned by Cosimo I, after the Florentines wrested control of the city from the Sienese.

To reach the **old centre**, walk up from the station to join Via Roma, a road interrupted by an over-the-top post office and bleak piazza, both monuments to Fascist architectural endeavour. The best of what survives in Grosseto is on **Piazza Dante**, where a quirky statue shows Leopoldo II protecting Mother Maremma and crushing the serpent malaria under his foot. The **Duomo** was started in 1294, but there's virtually nothing left to suggest antiquity: the white and pink marble facade is a product of the nineteenth century, while the interior has suffered repeated and ill-advised modifications.

The best pieces from the Duomo have been transferred to the **Museo Archeologico** at nearby Piazza Baccarini (March & April Tues–Sun 9am–1pm & 4–6pm; May–Oct Tues–Sun 10am–1pm & 5–8pm; Nov–Feb Tues–Fri 9am–1pm, Sat & Sun 9am–1pm & 4–6pm; free). The upper-floor **Pinacoteca** has a handful of good Sienese paintings, notably Sassetta's *Madonna of the Cherries*, and a *Madonna and Child* attributed to Simone Martini. Most of the archeological finds are from the Etruscan settlements at Vetulonia and Rusellae, neatly arranged and well-labelled, but not likely to set the pulse racing.

The town's only other significant work is an early Crucifix by Duccio in **San Francesco**, just north of the museum, also home to a few patches of fresco. Look out for the cloisters alongside the church, distinguished by a well called the *Pozzo della Bufala* (Well of the Buffalo). From San Francesco you can have a pleasant walk round the **walls** (40min). Public gardens fill the spaces in the corner turrets, apart from one, which retains some Florentine fortifications.

Practicalities

Grosseto's **tourist office** is inconveniently far from the town centre; head north from the station, turn left at Via Abruzzi then right onto Via Monterosa 206, and it's within the concrete building on the left-hand side at no. 206 (Mon–Fri 8.30am–12.30pm & 3–6pm, Sat 8.30am–12.30pm; ☎0564.462.611). The **market** is on Thursday and draws people from all over the province.

There are several reputable **restaurants**, including the moderately priced *Buca di San Lorenzo*, Via Manetti 1 (☎0564.25.142; closed Sun & Mon). A touch more expensive is *Canapone*, Piazza Dante 3 (☎0564.24.546; closed Sun & a period in Aug), with a cheaper, pleasant offshoot next door, *Canapino*.

Monti dell'Uccellina

The hills and coastline of the **MONTI DELL'UCCELLINA** are protected as the **Parco Naturale Regionale della Maremma**, set to be upgraded to a Parco Nazionale, recognition for an area claimed to be the last virgin coastal landscape on the Italian peninsula. The "Mountains of the Little Bird" take their name from the number of birds that use these hills as a stepping-stone between Europe and North Africa.

The heart of the park is a hump of hills that rises suddenly from the plain, about 12km south of Grosseto. A breathtaking piece of countryside that combines cliffs, coastal marsh, *macchia*, forest-covered hills, pristine beaches and some of the most beautiful stands of **umbrella pines** in the country, it is a microcosm of all that's best in the Maremma – devoid of the bars, marinas, hotels, roads and half-finished houses that have destroyed much of the Italian littoral. Kept remote for centuries by malaria and impassable swamp, it's now preserved through the determination of its owners to keep the region sacrosanct. The result is an area that rewards the casual walker, birdwatcher, botanist, or anyone simply in search of a stretch of unspoilt sand.

Park practicalities

There is no public road access into the park: drivers should park near the reserve headquarters in the main square at **Alberese**. Hourly **buses** (#15, #16 & #17) run there from Grosseto station, and there's one daily **train** (in the morning) to Alberese station, 4km from the village.

Alberese's park headquarters and **visitors' centre**, in Via del del Bersagliere 4–6 (mid-June to mid-Sept daily 7.30am–6pm; rest of year hours vary; ☎0564.407.098, ⓦwww.parks.it), has details of **walks** – both guided and self-guided – and can take bookings for a three-hour night walking tour. We've detailed the pick of the marked trails below. The centre can also provide information on renting **bikes and canoes**.

Admission to the park (daily: July to Sept 7.30am–dusk; Oct–June 9am–dusk; €6) secures you a basic map and a place on an hourly bus, which runs 10km into the hills, drops you at the trailhead **Pratini** (really just a field) and leaves you to your own devices. It's about a twenty-minute stroll from Pratini to the beach. Energetic types might walk all the way from Alberese; if you want to see the wildlife at dusk (the best time) you'll have to walk back anyway, as the last bus back from Pratini departs at 5.30pm in summer, earlier in winter. You can buy bus tickets for the return journey from Alberese to Grosseto at *Bar Il Parco*, just behind the visitors' centre.

Walks in the Uccellina

Once off the bus from Alberese at Pratini, most people rush headlong along the Strada degli Olivi for the **beach**, an idyllic curving bay backed by cliffs and wooded hills; the obvious stretch is to the left, though you can trudge the beach for miles to the right, round the huge *pineta* towards the mouth of the Ombrone, Tuscany's second-longest river. Alternatively, you could choose one of the **marked trails** that crisscross each other within the park; there are more starting from Talamone (see p.308), and also several shorter trails, if you're just looking for a quick stroll.

The best of the marked routes is the circular **Trail A1** (*San Rabano*; 6km; 5hr; guided walks in summer at 8am), which starts from Pratini. The track climbs quickly to the Uccellina's main ridge (417m), with views to the coast and to Monte Amiata in the interior, reaching the abbey of San Rabano after about ninety minutes. Built in the eleventh century and abandoned five hundred years later, the church is now an ivy-covered ruin, with stone carvings littering the grass. The path then drops right, returning below the ridge to the Strada degli Olivi through evergreen woods.

Trail A2 (*Le Torri*; 5km; 3hr; guided walks in summer at 9am & 4pm; tours in English every Fri 4.30pm) starts nearer the beach and connects some of the medieval watchtowers built by the Spanish, who, with the Sienese, were the only people to bother with the area, using it as a source of cork and charcoal. Taking in several coastal habitats, it offers an extraordinary view over the **umbrella pines** on the sand bar and dunes below. These are the park's crowning glory and one of the most memorable natural sights in Tuscany – a vast canopy of emerald green that stretches almost as far as the eye can see. It's well worth dropping

---

Flora and fauna in the Uccellina

Even if you're not looking out for it, you'd have to be unlucky not to see any interesting wildlife in the protected environment of the Uccellina. An extraordinary range of species thrive here, in what is effectively a compendium of Mediterranean coastal habitats – wooded hills, olive groves, pastures, marshland, *pineta*, *macchia*, dunes, retro-dunal areas, estuary and mudflats.

The Ombrone estuary is the key target of serious birdwatchers during the spring and autumn migratory cycles, when an assortment of waders, ducks, herons and egrets can be seen. Rarities like ospreys, bee-eaters, flamingoes and even falcons and short-toed eagles can be spotted in the rockier hinterland, and you're almost guaranteed the sight of herons wheeling away from the canals, perhaps with hoopoes, shrikes, kingfishers, and the rare, brightly coloured black-winged stilt.

Other species are most likely to be encountered towards dusk, with **roe-deer** prevalent in the hills. The famous **wild boar** is an often audible inhabitant of the scrub and pine forest; an indigenous Maremma breed, it's a smaller specimen than other Italian boar, most of which are descended from bulky, Eastern European stock. The crested **porcupine**, introduced by the Romans, is also fairly common (Italy is the only place it's found outside Africa), as are badgers and foxes; it is hoped that the increasingly rare **otter** will flourish here too. In the cultivated land to the north and on the flat fringes of the estuary you'll see the semi-wild **horses** for which the Maremma is famous.

Tracking down **flora** is more a job for the specialist, though the pines and cork oaks are unmissable, as are the huge banks of rosemary bushes, purple with flowers in the late summer. The dwarf pine, Italy's only indigenous pine, has its northernmost natural limit in the park, and numerous floral rarities pepper the park's dunes, *macchia* and marshes.

▲ Umbrella pines lining the road to Alberese

down from the tower to explore the woods, where you could roam for hours, restricted only by the areas of marsh at their fringes. Many of these pines were planted (the domestic variety to be harvested for their pine nuts, the maritime ones to consolidate the dunes on the estuary).

The level **Trail A3** (*Le Grotte*; 8km; 4hr) takes in a long stretch of the woods and the canals that divide the park; although it's one of the less rewarding walks, it is quite remote and offers good chances to see wildlife. It starts near no. 2 and its ultimate destination is a group of caves, one of which (La Grotta della Fabbrica) has yielded some of the oldest human remains found in Italy.

Trail A4 (*Cala di Forno*; 12km; 6hr) is the longest, most varied, and least used of the trails, taking in hill, coast and cliff scenery, and reaching the large Cala di Forno headland that dominates the bay to the south. The return takes you along the dunes and a superb stretch of beach at Portovecchio.

Marina di Alberese to Talamone

Although located within the park, entry restrictions do not apply to **MARINA DI ALBERESE**, whose **beach** – though not as superb as that in the park proper – rates as one of the best in Tuscany. It's open all year, but there's a barrier at Spergolaia, which is closed when pressure of numbers becomes too great. You need to buy a **ticket** in advance at Piazza del Combattente in Alberese (full day €4.50, half-day €2.75). Campers, caravans and trailers are excluded, but in practice no one seems to take much notice. There's nowhere to stay and camping is prohibited.

The arrow-straight access road is a pleasure in itself, shaded by an avenue of pines, and flanked by hills, corrals of horses and fields of white oxen. Towards the sea it enters a dense *pineta*, and ends with a car park. Except for a bar and picnic area, there's no other development. The pines come right down to the beach, and in places into the sea itself, their smooth, bleached trunks creating the feel of a tropical island. The Italians, gregarious as ever, stick to the area at the end of the road, so you don't have to walk far to find solitude. The sand is clean, the sea shallow and perfect for swimming – and it's all rounded off by beautiful views to the Argentario, Giglio and the tree-covered backdrop of the Uccellina.

At the southern tip of the Uccellina, just outside the park's confines, **TALAMONE** is a fishing village and discreet summer resort. Save for a yacht-filled marina, most of its old charm remains intact. The Sienese – who never had a proper outlet to the sea – once planned to turn its hole-in-the-wall harbour into a port to rival Pisa's, but clogging weed doomed the project to failure (in the *Inferno*, Dante used this as a metaphor for pointless enterprise). The town's greatest moment came in 1860, when Garibaldi and the Thousand stopped here for three days on their way to Sicily. Talamone's sixteenth-century Spanish castle is closed to the public.

Two **walking trails** (closed 1–4pm) lead off into the hills from Talamone, making this a good base for exploring the southern edge of the park. To reach the trailhead at Caprarecce, turn right just before Talamone and continue up a dirt track for about 1km; here you'll also find a **visitors' centre** (April–Sept daily 8am–1pm). Admission to tackle these self-guided walks costs €6. **Trail T1** (2.5km; 1hr 30min) is simply a shorter version of **trail T2** (4km; 3hr); both start from Podere Caprarecce and head up through Mediterranean scrub to the Punta del Corvo, from where you can admire spectacular views of the park's southernmost coastline and Monte Argentario beyond. The trails loop back to the starting-point through holm-oak woodland.

Talamone's **tourist office** is at Piazzale del Porto (May–Sept Mon–Sat 9am–1pm & 3–7pm; ☎0564.887.410). The best hotels are the central *Telamonio*, Piazza Garibaldi 4 (☎0564.887.008, Ⓦwww.hoteliltelamonio.com; ❻) and *Baia di Talamone*, Via della Marina 23 (☎0564.887.310, Ⓦwww.hotelbaiaditalamone.it; ❺). There's also a **campsite**, *Talamone International Camping* (☎0564.887.026; April–Sept). Among the **restaurants**, try the central, popular and moderately priced *La Buca*, Via Porta Garibaldi (☎0564.887.067; closed Mon), or the more expensive *Da Flavia*, Piazza IV Novembre (☎0564.887.091; closed Tues & mid-Jan to mid-Feb), known for its fish and seafood.

Scansano and Magliano

The settlements of **Magliano** and **Scansano** offer one of the Maremma's many rewarding inland diversions. If you're spending any time in the region, Scansano is worth considering as a base, and even if you're just passing through, the enclosing walls of Magliano are a sight not to be missed. The landscape here is more inviting than most of the coast, with vineyards and woods of sweet chestnut reminiscent of Chianti – as well as excellent views of the Uccellina. Both villages are somewhat off the beaten track, with limited bus service from Grosseto; a car is therefore a distinct advantage, allowing you to visit both on a cross-country route towards Monte Amiata.

Scansano

About 25km southeast of Grosseto on the SS322, **SCANSANO** is a cramped little hill-village with fine, clear views to the ridges of the Uccellina. It is sited 500m above sea level, on a spur that pushes into an impressive wooded gorge; the end of the spur is capped in picturesque style by the bulk of the parish church.

The main road climbs into **Piazza Garibaldi**, occupied by a stern statue of the eponymous hero and several tiny *trattorie*. There's **accommodation** in the old town, entered through the arch off Piazza Garibaldi, and little more than a single street that runs the length of the spur. The mid-price option here is the two-star *Magini*, Via XX Settembre 64 (T&F0564.507.181; ❷). Alternatively, 3km out of town at Castagneta, on the SS322 to Manciano, there's the *Antico Casale di Scansano* (T0564.507.219, Wwww.anticocasalediscansano.com; ❻), but if you're planning to stay longer you might consider one of the many agriturismo options (Wwww .agriturismoinmaremma.com), for which you'll need to book in advance.

The Scansano area produces a fine DOC wine, **Morellino di Scansano** (Wwww.cantinadelmorellino.it), made from Sangiovese grapes. You can find out more about the Morellino grape and its wine at the **Museo della Vite e del Vino**, Piazza Pretorio 4 (April–Oct Tues–Sun 10am–1pm & 4–7pm; Nov–March Fri–Sun 10am–1pm & 3–6pm; free), which doubles as the town's **Museo Archeologico**. To combine wine-tasting with a **meal**, try the excellent *La Cantina*, Via della Botte 1 (T0564.507.605; closed mid-Jan to early March & all day Sun, plus Mon eve, except in Aug).

Magliano in Toscana

South of Scansano the road passes through the hamlet of Pereta – where a single huge tower crowns a fortified *borgo* and a couple of streets – before reaching **MAGLIANO IN TOSCANA**, descendant of the Etruscan town of Heba. The place today is essentially a village, its most remarkable feature an almost completely intact circle of **walls**, those on the south side dating from the thirteenth century, the rest a fifteenth-century legacy of the Sienese. The bastions are so impressive from a distance that they draw you towards the town, through the ugly estate that suddenly appears round a bend in the road. Close up, the village is a strange, crumbling mixture of old and new, with concrete houses squeezed in alongside medieval dwellings. The main **church**, in Corso Garibaldi, is a Baroque mess, but retains some well-preserved frescoes from the original building. Close by are the tiny Piazza del Popolo and the abandoned **Palazzo dei Priori**, built by the Sienese. The ghost-town atmosphere doesn't invite further exploration, but you should carry on to the end of the main street, where an arch in the walls frames a view over classic Tuscan countryside.

Nearby are the ruins of **San Bruzio**, 2km south on the road to Marsiliana. A single, bleached white stump of a tower is all that remains of this twelfth-century abbey, but it's a pleasant place, set in a large olive grove. Local legend suggests it was built on the site of a pagan temple and, more salaciously, that a tunnel connected it to the now-vanished nunnery of Sant'Anna.

There are several moderately priced **restaurants**, including the *Antica Trattoria Aurora*, Chiasso Lavagnini 12 (T0564.592.030; closed Wed & Jan–Feb) and *Ristorante Da Guido*, Via Roma 18 (T0564.592.447; closed Tues).

Orbetello

In the southwest corner of Tuscany, some 35km south of Grosseto and just before the Lazio border, **ORBETELLO** is principally distinguished by its strange location on a narrow isthmus in the middle of the **Laguna di Orbetello**. The ancient settlement of Orbetello occupied a peninsula sticking out into the lagoon; the Romans built a causeway to link the town to Monte Argentario, forming a third spit of land and dividing the lagoon in two.

Little in the place excites real attention, but it has become something of a resort, thanks to its being the gateway to the dramatic rocky outcrop of Monte Argentario; on summer weekends, it becomes a bottleneck, as cars full of tourists pile in to the Argentario's resorts. The town is a pleasant, unassuming place, graced with palm trees, the pastel-coloured remnants of its Spanish walls, and a main street – **Corso Italia** – thronged each evening with a particularly vigorous *passeggiata* and a lively **street market** on Saturdays. Orbetello was probably Etruria's leading port, though few traces remain. There's more evidence of its Hispanic past: the Spanish wrested control of the town from the papacy in 1559, establishing a military *Presidio* with Orbetello as its capital. The Spanish **fortifications** are the town's conspicuous feature and a fine example of military architecture. The elegant arsenal, Polveriera de Guzman, houses a small **archeological museum**. Nearby, the **Duomo** in Piazza della Repubblica appears promising with its lovely Gothic facade, only to disappoint with a grim Baroque interior. The town's last claim to fame was as the headquarters of Mussolini's seaplane squadrons; the surviving aircraft hangar is one of Tuscany's more bizarre architectural attractions.

Practicalities

The **train station** is 4km east at Orbetello Scalo, on the mainland edge of the lagoon, a prominent stop for trains on the Rome–Pisa line. There are connections for Siena, and slow trains to smaller stations to the north and

The Laguna di Orbetello nature reserve

Orbetello's **lagoon** offers exceptional **birdwatching**, with confirmed sightings of 200 of Italy's estimated 450 species. One reason for the variety is the relative lack of avian refuge on Italy's west coast. Another is the lagoon's modest depth (only 1m), which means an accessible mulch of fish and assorted food; there's also a variety of marsh, *macchia*, dune and reed habitats for nest-building. Even rare species are frequently sighted, and many of them are known to breed in the area. Notable are the stone curlew, osprey, black-winged stilt, bee-eater, Montagu's harrier, and – most importantly – the black-winged stilt, otherwise known to breed only in Sardinia and the Po delta. Little egrets, terns, storks and herons arrive in large numbers, glossy ibis and cranes are regular visitors, and it's not unknown for pink flamingoes to stay for the summer. Evening is the best time around the lagoon: not only is the wildlife most visible then, but the sunsets over the water and the mountains of the Argentario are fabulous.

It's possible to see wildlife from almost any point on the lagoon. In the northernmost corner, near the town of **Albinia**, the World Wide Fund for Nature has established a small **nature reserve**, L'Oasi di Protezione della Laguna di Orbetello (guided tours in Italian Sept–April Sun & Thurs 10am & 2.30pm; €5). The entrance to the reserve is off the main road 2km south of Albinia, marked by a small panda sign; the warden can sometimes be contacted at the building at the end of the track, or contact the tourist office in Orbetello for further information.

If time is tight, exploring the southern **Tombolo di Feniglia** is a good substitute for a tour of the reserve (the northern Tombolo di Giannella is less appealing, with its campsites and driveable road). Tombolo di Feniglia has one of Italy's most beautiful *pinete*, a long sandy dune covered in parasol pines, and is also protected by a small nature reserve, where you can often see roe deer. The road along it is off-limits for cars, though you can walk its whole course, dropping down to the lagoon side for great views, or to the other side for a fine beach. If you continue the walk through Ansedonia, and then along the beach south for about an hour, you'll reach the Lago di Burano.

south. Connecting buses run from the station to Orbetello's **bus terminal** just off Piazza della Repubblica; from here there are regular services to Grosseto, Porto Ercole and Porto San Stefano, as well as thrice-daily buses to Capálbio and Pitigliano.

The **tourist office** at Piazza della Repubblica 1 (Mon–Sat 10am–12.30pm & 4–7pm; ☎0564.860.447) can advise on accommodation in Orbetello and the mainland hamlets of Albinia and Ansedonia (both served by local buses). Orbetello is the nicest option, and has a fine one-star **hotel**, the central *Piccolo Parigi*, Corso Italia 169 (☎0564.867.233, ℱ0564.867.211; ❷). Most of the area's dozen or more **campsites** are on and around the lagoon and along the main SS1 Via Aurelia. The most attractive is the *Feniglia* (☎0564.831.090, ⓦwww .campingfeniglia.it), the only site on the Tombolo di Feniglia.

Orbetello's best **restaurant** is 🍴 *I Pescatori*, Via Leopardi 9 (☎0564.860.611; closed lunch & Sun in summer, Mon–Fri in winter), which maintains a good standard despite its size. For a more intimate experience, you'll find moderately priced fish dishes at the *Osteria Nochino* just off Piazza della Repubblica in Via Furio Lenzi (☎0564.860.329; dinner only).

Monte Argentario

The high, rocky terrain of **Monte Argentario** is as close to wilderness as southern Tuscany comes. The interior is mountainous, reaching 635m at its highest point, **Il Telegrafo**, and the coast is sectioned dramatically into headlands, bays and shingle beaches. Away from the villas of rich Romans, much of the area is still uninhabited scrub and woodland, badly prone to forest fires but still superb walking country. The main centres of **Porto Santo Stefano** and **Porto Ercole** once had a reputation for exclusivity, but these days they're too well known to pander solely to the top end of the market. Prices are manageable, as are the crowds, though you'll probably need to book ahead for peak periods. With your own transport you could follow the touted *gita panoramica* (**scenic drive**) around half the mountain.

Porto Santo Stefano

PORTO SANTO STEFANO is the more developed of the Argentario resorts, and also the more fashionable – which in Italy is a lot worse than just being popular. Something of the charm that first brought people here still shines through, however, despite the hotels and villas that have all but obliterated the original village. A few fishing boats still cluster in the town's smaller harbour, having relinquished the main port to the marina and its mega-yachts. You'll probably stay only as long as it takes to get a **ferry** to the island of Giglio. **Buses** run to the port from the train station at Orbetello Scalo.

The **tourist office**, Piazzale Sant'Andrea 1 (Mon–Sat: Jan–March 9am–1pm & 2–4pm; April–Dec 9am–1pm & 3–5pm; ☎0564.814.208), has information on affordable accommodation – mainly in private rooms. You'll need to book well ahead for the town's cheapest **central hotel**: the *Alfiero*, Via Cuniberti 14 (☎0564.814.067, ⓦwww.hotelalfiero.com; ❷).

Restaurants are generally swanky and overpriced, though back-street pizzerias are a more affordable option. If you're going for a blowout, *Da Siro*, Corso Umberto I 102 (☎0564.812.538; closed Mon), has quite a reputation. For a moderately priced meal, try *Il Veliero* (☎0564.812.226; closed Mon & Jan), a steep but worthwhile hike above the port at Via Panoramica 149.

Porto Ercole

On the south side of the Argentario, **PORTO ERCOLE** is more intimate than Santo Stefano, with an attractive old quarter and a fishing-village atmosphere. Though founded by the Romans, its chief historical monuments are two Spanish **fortresses** facing each other on opposing sides of the harbour, and a third one above the new town. At the entrance to the old town, a plaque on the stone gate commemorates the painter **Caravaggio**, who in 1610 keeled over with sunstroke on a beach nearby (taken to a local tavern, he soon died of a fever, and was buried in the parish church of Sant'Erasmo).

There are a couple of good **walks** from the village, the most obvious being along the Tombolo di Feniglia (see p.310). The other is to the top of **Il Telegrafo**, accessible either by road and track from the ridge that runs up from the lighthouse to the south, or on a rough road that leaves the port to the north and then runs west under the main ridge. The way is fairly open, and superb views make the haul worthwhile.

Reasonably priced **hotels** include the two-star *Conchiglia* in Via della Marina (℡0564.833.134; ❸), but if you can pay a bit more, the nicest place is the *Don Pedro*, Via Panoramico 7 (℡0564.833.914, ⓦwww.hoteldonpedro.it; ❺). And if you can pay a lot more, ⚹ *Il Pellicano* at Lo Sbarcatello, 4.5km southwest (℡0546.858.111, ⓦwww.pellicanohotel.com; closed Nov–March; ❾), is one of Italy's premier hotels, complete with pool, spa, tennis courts and a Michelin-starred **restaurant**. In town, the more moderately priced waterfront *Gambero Rosso* (℡0564.832.650; closed Wed & mid-Nov to mid-Feb) serves excellent fish; be sure to book, especially at weekends. Also worth a look is the central and more modern *Osteria dei Nobili Santi*, Via dell'Ospizio 8–10 (℡0564.833.105; closed Mon & lunch July–Sept, except public holidays).

Giglio and Giannutri

The largest of the Tuscan islands after Elba, **GIGLIO**, 15km west of Monte Argentario, is visited by an ever-increasing number of foreign tourists and is so popular with holidaying Romans that in high season you may find that there's standing-room only on the ferries. Yet it's well worth making the effort to stay on this fabulous island: the rush is fairly short-lived, most visitors are day-trippers, and few of them explore the tracks across the unspoilt interior, a mix of barren rock and reforested upland. The island is rich in **fauna** such as peregrine falcons, mouflon, kestrels and buzzards, and in **wild flowers** too: this is the only place outside North Africa to shelter wild mustard, and the sole spot in Tuscany to support the yellow flowers of artemisia. Giglio and the neighbouring islet of **GIANNUTRI** are the southernmost islands of the Parco Nazionale Arcipelago Toscano.

The island derives its name not from *giglio* (lily), but from the Roman colony Aegilium, in its day a resort for the rich and famous, a function it continued to fulfil throughout most of the Middle Ages. Granite quarries kept the economy buoyant, and Giglio stone was used to construct many medieval churches. Later, pirate incursions took the edge off its appeal, despite the miraculous defensive power of St Mamiliano's right arm, a relic hacked from a sixth-century Sicilian bishop exiled on the island of Montecristo. The limb proved effective when waved at Tunisian pirates in 1799, but less so on other occasions – notably in the twelfth century, when Barbarossa carried off most of the island's population.

Ferries to Giglio

The embarkation point for Giglio is **Porto Santo Stefano** (see p.311), served by regular buses direct from the train station at Orbetello Scalo and also from Orbetello town. Both Toremar (℡0564.810.803, Ⓦwww.toremar.it) and Maregiglio (℡0564.812.920, Ⓦwww.maregiglio.it) operate **ferries** to Giglio Porto (summer almost hourly, winter 3–5 daily; 1hr; €19 return in high summer, €15 in low season). It's usually no problem to buy your ticket from a quayside kiosk and board immediately. You should leave your **car** on the mainland; it's expensive to take it onto the island at any time of year, and in summer you need a permit. There are plenty of trustworthy parking companies on the Porto Santo Stefano waterfront that charge roughly €10 per day; parking on the street is both unsafe and lays you open to hefty fines.

Arrival, information and accommodation

Ferries (see box above) dock at **Giglio Porto**, from where there's an excellent bus service to the island's two other main villages, **Giglio Castello** and **Giglio Campese**. You can rent bikes and mopeds inexpensively in Giglio Porto. There's a **tourist office** on Via Provinciale, Giglio Porto (℡0564.809.400).

Accommodation

Giglio Porto boasts eight of the island's thirteen **hotels**. In high season, these generally offer only full board, and most are open only from June to September; the tourist office can provide details of accommodation options, including **rooms to let** around the port. Accommodation in **Giglio Castello** is limited to private rooms, such as *Affittacamere Mario Landini*, Via Contrada Santa Maria (℡0564.806.074, Ⓦwww.camerealgiglio.vze.com; summer only; ❷). **Giglio Campese** has a handful of hotels and a **campsite**, *Baia del Sole* (℡0564.804.036).

Campese Via della Torre 18 ℡0564.804.003, Ⓦwww.hotelcampese.com. Top of the range, this three-star, Mediterranean-style villa hotel with a/c rooms has been family-run for over half a century. It has a private beach, and provides a good base for watersports enthusiasts. Closed Oct–Easter. ❹

Da Ruggero Via del Saraceno 86, Giglio Porto ℡0564.809.121. A two-star hotel just a few moments from the harbour and ferry dock, but set apart in a side street so that you are away from the noise and bustle. All ten rooms have private bathrooms and balconies with sea views. ❸

Demo's Via Thaon de Revel 45, Giglio Porto ℡0564.809.235, Ⓦwww.hoteldemos.com. Pleasing modern, three-star hotel, with bright, spacious rooms right on a small beach backed with palms. Most rooms have sea views and the restaurant and bar overlook the sea and beach directly. ❺

Pardini's Hermitage Cala degli Alberi cove, Giglio Porto ℡0564.809.034, Ⓦwww.hermit.it. This small and incredibly quiet and private three-star on the sea, accessible by boat or on foot (1hr walk from Giglio Porto), is the one to go for in Giglio Porto. But it has just thirteen rooms, so book ahead. April–Sept. ❽

Giglio

Small, rock-girdled **GIGLIO PORTO** has no particular sights, but the view from the ferry is wonderful as the town draws closer, its pale-coloured houses offset by a backdrop of terraced vineyards and framed between two lighthouses. The narrow harbourfront is crammed with a mix of touristy restaurants and boat mechanics, but behind the **Torre del Saraceno**, built by Ferdinand I in 1596, you'll find a tranquil, barely visited little inlet, with the wall of a Roman eel farm visible below the waterline. As much of the land around rises sheer from the sea, the **beaches** are modest: you'll find one to the north of the port at Punta Aranella, and a couple to the south at Cala delle Canelle and Cala delle Caldane.

GIGLIO CASTELLO, perched at the highest point of the hills, up 6km of hairpins from the port, was for a long time the island's only settlement and the sole spot safe from pirate attack. Surprisingly well preserved, its maze of arches and medieval alleyways is still surrounded by thick walls. Buses stop near a vine-covered patio **bar** in the large Piazza Gloriosa, also the entrance to the granite fortress and medieval quarter. The **castle** was begun by the Pisans and completed by the Grand Duchy of Tuscany; rough paths around the walls enable you to clamber over the rocks for superb views over the island and ruins far below. For a look at St Mamiliano's miraculous arm, check out the Baroque **church**. To explore Giglio's interior, follow a minor road that winds from Castello 9km south all along the spine of the ridge to **Punta del Capel Rosso**, the southernmost tip of the island – a wild and lonely bike-ride or three-hour hike. Walking from Castello down to either Campese or Porto takes less than an hour.

At the western end of the island road is the growing resort of **GIGLIO CAMPESE**. It has the island's best **beach**, a fine stretch of sand overlooked by a Medici tower and curving for 2km from a huge phallic rock that the tourist brochures are too modest to photograph. Around the base of the tower is a modern, turreted apartment complex with a couple of restaurants, tennis courts and all manner of **watersports** facilities – including dive shops with lessons and gear to rent.

There are several quayside **restaurants** in Giglio Porto, but the food at *Demo's* hotel (see p.313) is better and comes with beach views. The best bet of all, however, is *La Paloma*, Via Umberto I 48 (☎0564.809.233; closed Mon except July & Aug), a tiny place of the old school. In **Giglio Castello**, *Da Maria* in Via Casamatta is one of the island's best moderately priced **restaurants** (☎0564.806.062, closed Wed & Jan–Feb).

Giannutri

The southernmost Tuscan island, **GIANNUTRI**, a rocky half-moon islet 15km south of Giglio, is privately owned. The few people who come do so to dive, or to visit the ruins of a **Roman villa** at Cala Maestra. Given the island's physical make-up – flat, and walkable end-to-end in two hours – it's a place for island obsessives only. **Day-trips** (€15) are run by Maregiglio (see box, p.313), with departures from Giglio Porto and, in summer, direct from Porto Santo Stefano.

South of Orbetello

South of Orbetello, most of the terrain is a drab foretaste of the expanses of Lazio, but there are several worthwhile diversions. At **Ansedonia** you can inspect one of Tuscany's few ancient Roman sites, before moving on to the important nature reserve at **Lago di Burano**. Inland **Capalbio** rates as one of the area's loveliest villages, while near **Chiarone**, which has fine beaches, is the **Giardino dei Tarocchi**, a small park of monumental sculptures that's quickly becoming both a tourist attraction and artistic talking point.

Ansedonia

ANSEDONIA crouches under a rocky crag at the end of the Tombolo di Feniglia. Peppered with holiday villas, it has a long beach and, on the hilltop above, the remains of **Cosa**, founded by the Romans in 273 BC as a frontier post against the Etruscans. It was one of their most important commercial centres in the area until its population – according to the historian Rutilius – was driven out by an army of mice. Most of the old *municipium* was devastated by the Visigoths in the fourth century, and what survived was sacked by the Sienese in 1330. Recent excavations have exposed enough of the Roman colony to suggest some idea of its former layout.

To reach the **site** (daily: May–Sept 9am–7pm, Oct–April 9am–1pm; free), leave Ansedonia on the road east, passing a couple of medieval towers (converted into houses) and the **Tagliata Etrusca**, a series of cuts into the rock believed to have been part of a system to drain the marshland. After about 1km, where the road bends sharp right, there's a signed track to Cosa off to the left. You'll find a ring of **walls** 8m high in places, the remains of a defensive cordon of eighteen towers. There's also the outline of the gridiron street plan, a **forum** (with basilica and senate discernible nearby), two **temples** and some **mosaics** and wall paintings. It's worth climbing to the top of the hill, not only to see the remains of the **acropolis**, but also for fine views across to Giannutri and Monte Argentario. Halfway up the hill is a small **Museo Archeologico** (same hours; €2), housing some of the site's finds.

Chiarone and inland

CHIARONE is nothing more than a station and a couple of bars, though its **beaches** – fifteen-minutes' walk away – are some of the best and quietest on this part of the coast, commonly regarded as enjoying the first unpolluted water north of Rome. Some 15km of unbroken sand stretch away towards Monte Argentario, with plenty of opportunities for **camping** in the dunes. Things get grubby on-shore as the summer wears on, but the gentle, shelving seabed makes for good swimming, and all it takes for solitude on the sand is a few minutes' walk.

A handful of **trains** to and from Grosseto stop at Chiarone station. There's one **hotel**, *La Palma*, Via del Chiarone 5 (☎0564.890.341, ❸www.albergolapalma .com; ❸). At the end of the road to the dunes is the beach **bar**, **restaurant** and **campsite** *Il Campeggio di Capalbio,* Via Graticciaia (☎0564.890.101, ❸www .ilcampeggiodicapalbio.it; mid-April to Sept).

The Giardino dei Tarocchi

By car from Chiarone it's possible to visit one of Italy's oddest and increasingly well-known works of modern art: **Il Giardino dei Tarocchi** (The Tarot Garden;

The Lago di Burano nature reserve

You can walk to the **Lago di Burano** along the beach from Ansedonia, or catch a slow train from Orbetello to Capalbio Scalo, less than 100m from the water. Technically a lagoon rather than a lake, Burano is a placid stretch of water, shielded from the sea by vegetation-covered dunes. Completing the scenic picture – which is captivating at dusk, with the sun behind Monte Argentario – is a superb and mysterious-looking tower, the **Torre di Burinaccio**.

Though you can walk onto the enclosing beach, access to the lagoon itself is restricted, as Burano is a protected **nature reserve**. Recognized as a wetland habitat of international significance, this and the Orbetello lagoon (see box, p.310) are together rated as the most important area for birds on Italy's west coast. The lagoon shares many of the species found in Orbetello, and for similar reasons (the lagoon here is also only 1m deep). Notable species include the bluethroat, great spotted cuckoo, great white heron and velvet scoter. The **entrance** to the reserve is on the perimeter road 500m east of the station. **Guided walks** (Sept–April Thurs & Sun 10am & 2.30pm; €5.25; ☎0564.898.829) follow the nature trail that takes in the dune, woodland and scrub habitats around the lake, stopping at the observation points en route.

April to mid-Oct daily 2.30–7.30pm; €10.50; ⓦwww.nikidesaintphalle.com), a huge set of sculptures by Niki de Saint Phalle, who died in 2002 and is most famous for the *Fontaine Stravinsky*, created with her husband Jean Tinguely outside the Pompidou Centre in Paris. The brightly coloured pieces are clearly visible from the Via Aurelia: to reach them it's a five-kilometre drive on the road from Chiarone to Pescia Fiorentina.

Using land donated by friends, the artist took almost seventeen years to complete the work (1979–1996), and the result is a truly staggering sight – a whimsical mix of Gaudí, arcane symbolism and sheer fun that children love, and which inspires bewildered admiration in adults. Each piece represents one of the Tarot's 22 major arcana, with plants and fountains forming an integral part of the scheme.

Capalbio

Stranded in empty country, the hill-village of **CAPALBIO** is virtually unknown to outsiders, though not to Rome's cultural and political elite, many of whom have homes in the locality. Most are attracted by the almost perfectly medieval interior, which at night is a deathly quiet maze of streets straight out of the Middle Ages. Views are superb, and though there's little to see apart from a few frescoes and the Aldobrandeschi fortifications, it definitely warrants a look if you're touring by car; there are also three daily **buses** from Orbetello. The **hotel** *Valle del Buttero*, Via Silone 21 (ⓣ0564.896.097, ⓦwww.valledelbuttero.it; ❸) is just below the old town. There are several **restaurants** to choose from, including the superb, moderately priced *Trattoria la Torre da Carla*, Via Vittorio Emmanuele 33 (ⓣ0564.896.070; closed Thurs & Mon–Fri in low season), in the heart of the old town.

Travel details

Trains

Grosseto to: Capalbio (hourly; 35min); Follónica (hourly; 35min; change for Massa Maríttima); Florence (8 daily via Siena; 3–4hr); Orbetello (hourly; 30min); Rome (hourly; 1hr 30min–2hr 30min); Siena (8 daily; 1hr 20min).

Buses

Follónica to: Castiglione (5 daily; 30min); Punta Ala (6 daily; 35min); Scarlino (7 daily; 30min).

Grosseto to: Castiglione della Pescaia (hourly; 45min); Florence (8 daily; 2hr 30min); Massa Maríttima (2 daily; 1hr 15min); Orbetello (3 daily; 1hr); Roccatederighi (2 daily; 1hr 10min); Scansano (4 daily; 1hr 20min); Siena (10 daily; 1hr 35min).
Massa Maríttima to: Follónica (every 45min; 10min); Grosseto (1 daily; 1hr 20min); Piombino (2 daily; 25min); Siena (2 daily; 1hr 40min).
Orbetello to: Capalbio (3 daily; 45min); Grosseto (3 daily; 1hr); Pitigliano (3 daily; 1hr); Porto Ercole (14 daily; 20min); Porto Santo Stefano (6 daily; 15min).

Siena

CHAPTER 6 # Highlights

* **The Campo** Soak up the atmosphere in Siena's scallop-shaped main square. **See p.327**

* **Museo Civico** Frescoes by Simone Martini, Ambrogio Lorenzetti and many others adorn the medieval salons of the Campo's Palazzo Pubblico. **See p.329**

* **The Palio** Siena's historic, chaotic horse race, run over three frenetic laps of the Campo. **See p.355** and *The Palio* colour section

* **The Duomo** The dazzling, art-filled cathedral features a superb fresco cycle by Pinturicchio in the Libreria Piccolomini. **See p.333**

* **Santa Maria della Scala** Once the city hospital, now a remarkable medieval monument, with frescoed halls and chapels. **See p.337**

* **Museo dell'Opera del Duomo** A treasure-chest of religious art that also gives access to Tuscany's giddiest viewpoint, atop the walls of the Duomo's abandoned new nave. **See p.342**

▲ Overview of the Campo

Siena

SIENA is the perfect counterpoint to Florence. Self-contained and still partly rural behind its medieval walls, its attraction lies in its cityscape: a majestic Gothic whole that could be enjoyed without venturing into a single museum. In its great scallop-shaped piazza, **Il Campo**, it has the loveliest of all Italian public squares; in its zebra-striped **Duomo**, a religious focus to match; and the city's whole construction, on three ridges, presents a succession of beautiful vistas over medieval cityscapes to the bucolic Tuscan countryside on all sides. It is also a place of immediate charm: airy, easy-going and pedestrianized – where Florence is cramped, busy and traffic-ridden – and is startlingly untouristed away from the few centres of day-trip sightseeing. Perhaps most important of all, the city is host to the undisputed giant of Italian festivals, the **Palio**, a bareback horse race around the Campo, whose sheer excitement and unique importance to the life of the community is reason enough to plan your holiday around one of the two race dates – July 2 and August 16.

The contrasts with Florence are extended in Siena's monumental and artistic highlights. The city's Duomo and **Palazzo Pubblico** are two of the purest examples of Italian Gothic, and the finest of the city's paintings – of which many are collected in the Palazzo's **Museo Civico** and the separate **Pinacoteca Nazionale** – are in the same tradition. Other outstanding Sienese painting remained stamped with Byzantine, Romanesque and Gothic influences long after classical humanism had transformed Florence. It is a style characterized by brilliance of colour and decorative detail and an almost exclusive devotion to religious subjects – principally the city's patroness, the Virgin. Its traditions were shaped by a group of artists working in the last half of the thirteenth century and the first half of the fourteenth: Duccio di Buoninsegna, Simone Martini and the brothers Ambrogio and Pietro Lorenzetti. The first of these was responsible for arguably the greatest of all Siena's paintings, a magnificent *Maestà*, housed in another of Siena's outstanding galleries, the **Museo dell'Opera del Duomo**. Another supreme work, the fresco cycle of Domenico di Bartolo, an artist working on the cusp of the Renaissance, fills part of **Santa Maria della Scala**, the city's hospital for some eight hundred years, now one of its premier exhibition spaces.

In its sculpture, Siena drew mainly on foreign artists: the Florentines Donatello and Ghiberti worked on the font in the **Baptistery**, while Michelangelo and Nicola and Giovanni Pisano left their mark on the Duomo.

As a provincial capital, Siena has good **transport links** with some of the finest sights and countryside of Tuscany. The city makes a good base for much of the territory covered in the following two chapters, while to the north, the wine heartland of Chianti (see p.189) extends to Florence, 78km north.

Some history

Though myth attributes its origins to Senius and Acius, sons of Remus (hence the she-wolf emblem of the city), Siena was in fact founded by the Etruscans and refounded as a Roman colony – Saena Julia – by Augustus. Over the course of the next millennium it grew to be an independent republic, and in the thirteenth and fourteenth centuries was one of the major cities of Europe. It was almost the size of Paris, controlled most of southern Tuscany and its flourishing wool industry, dominated the trade routes from France to Rome, and maintained Italy's richest banks. The city also developed a highly sophisticated civic life, with its own written constitution and a quasi-democratic council – the *comune*. It was in this great period that the city was shaped, and in which most of its art and monuments are rooted.

This golden era, when the Republic of Siena controlled a great area of central and southern Tuscany, reached an apotheosis with the defeat of a much superior Florentine army at the **Battle of Montaperti** in 1260. Although the result was reversed nine years later, shifting the fulcrum of political power towards Florence, Siena's merchants and middle classes – the so-called *Popolo Grasso* – embarked on an unrivalled urban development; from 1287 to 1355, under the rule of the **Council of Nine**, the city underwrote first the completion of the **Duomo** and then the extraordinary **Campo**, with its exuberant **Palazzo Pubblico**. Sienese bankers, meanwhile, had spread their operations throughout Europe, and with Duccio, Martini and the Lorenzettis, the city was at the forefront of Italian art.

Prosperity and innovation came to an abrupt halt with the **Black Death**, which reached Siena in May 1348. By October, when the disease had run its course, the population had dropped from 100,000 to 30,000. The city was never fully to recover (the population today is around 60,000) and its politics, always factional, moved into a period of intrigue and chaos. Its art, too, became highly conservative, as patrons looked back to the old hierarchical religious images. The chief figures in these war-ridden and anarchic years were the city's two nationally renowned saints, **Caterina** (1347–80) and **Bernardino** (1380–1444), who both exercised enormous influence, amid two further outbreaks of the plague.

As the sixteenth century opened, a period of autocratic rule under the tyrannical Pandolfo Petrucci (the self-styled Il Magnifico) brought a further military victory over Florence, but ended with the city embroiled in ever-expanding intrigues involving the Borgias, the Florentines, the papacy, the French and the empire of **Charles V**. The last proved too big to handle for the Sienese; imperial troops imposed a fortress and garrison, and then, after the Sienese had turned to the French for help to expel them, the imperial forces laid siege to the city and the surrounding countryside. The effects of the siege (1554–55) proved more terrible even than the Black Death, with the population plummeting from 40,000 to as few as 8000. The republic was over, although a band of loyalists – comprising around 700 families – took refuge at Montalcino and prolonged it there for a while, at least in name.

Two years after the siege, Philip II, Charles's successor, gave up Siena to **Cosimo I**, Florence's Medici overlord, in payment for war services, the city subsequently becoming part of Cosimo's Grand Duchy of Tuscany. This was the death knell. For sixty years the Sienese were forbidden even to operate banks, while control of what was by now an increasingly minor provincial town reverted, under Medici patronage, to the nobles.

Siena's swift decline from republican capital to little more than a market centre explains the city's astonishing state of medieval preservation. Little was built and still less demolished, while allotments and vineyards occupied the spaces between the ancient quarters, as they do today. The city also managed to escape damage

Siena's contrade

Within the fabric of the medieval city, Siena preserves its ancient division into wards, or **contrade**. These are integral to the competition of the Palio (see colour section) and sustain a unique neighbourhood identity, clearly visible as you wander around the streets. Each of the seventeen *contrade* has its own church, social centre and museum, as well as a flag and heraldic **animal motif**, after which most of them take their names. The animals – giraffe, snail, goose, porcupine, and others – can be seen all around the city on plaques and are represented in a series of modern fountains near the *contrada* churches or headquarters, in each of the city's three *terzi*:

Aquila Eagle (Città). Casato di Sotto ℡0577.288.086.
Bruco Caterpillar (Camollia). Via del Comune 44 ℡0577.44.842.
Chiocciola Snail (Città). Via San Marco 37 ℡0577.45.455.
Civetta Owl (San Martino). Piazzetta del Castellare ℡0577.285.505.
Drago Dragon (Camollia). Piazza Matteotti 19 ℡0577.40.575.
Giraffa Giraffe (Camollia). Via delle Vergini 18 ℡0577.287.091.
Istrice Porcupine (Camollia). Via Camollia 87 ℡0577.48.495.
Leocorno Unicorn (San Martino). Via di Follonico 15 ℡0577.288.549.
Lupa She-Wolf (Camollia). Via di Vallerozzi 71/73 ℡0577.270.777.
Nicchio Shell (San Martino). Via dei Pispini 68 ℡0577.49.600.
Oca Goose (Camollia). Vicolo del Tiratoio 11 ℡0577.285.413.
Onda Wave (Città). Via Giovanni Dupré 111 ℡0577.48.384.
Pantera Panther (Città). Via San Quirico ℡0577.48.468.
Selva Forest (Città). Piazzetta della Selva ℡0577.45.093.
Tartuca Turtle (Città). Via Tommaso Pendola 21 ℡0577.49.448.
Torre Tower (San Martino). Via Salicotto 76 ℡0577.222.181.
Valdimontone Ram (San Martino). Via di Valdimonte 6 ℡0577.222.590.

There were once social distinctions between the *contrade*, and although today these are blurred to the point of extinction, allegiance to one's *contrada* – conferred by birth – remains a strong element of social life. After a conventional church baptism, anyone born in a ward division is baptized for a second time in their *contrada* fountain. Subsequently, the *contrada* plays a central role in activities: for kids in the flag-twirling and drumming for the Palio and local *contrada* festivals, for adults in the social clubs – a mix of bar and dining club – and in the attendance of a herald at marriages and funerals. *Contrade* also dispense social assistance to needy members. The respect accorded to the institution of *contrade* is said to have a significant effect on the city's social cohesion. Certainly, for a city of its size, Siena has remarkably low levels of crime and drug usage. Indeed, the only violence tolerated is during the Palio, when *contrada* members may get into fights with their ancient rivals.

For an insight into the workings of the *contrade*, it is worth paying a visit to one of their **museums**, each of which gives pride of place to its displays of Palio trophies. All the museums are open to visitors during the build-up to the Palio and at other times by appointment. Each *contrada* also has its own **annual celebration**, accompanied by parades and feasts. And at almost any time of year, you'll see groups practising flag-waving and drum-rolling in the streets.

in World War II (unlike nearby Poggibonsi and other Tuscan towns); Siena was taken, unopposed, by the French Expeditionary Force on July 3, 1944.

Since the war, however, Siena has again become prosperous, partly due to **tourism**, partly to the resurgence of the **Monte dei Paschi di Siena**. This bank, founded in Siena in 1472, is one of the major players in Italian finance and in its home base is one of the city's largest employers.

Arrival and information

Most **intercity buses** arrive in the city centre on Viale Federico Tozzi, the road running alongside Piazza Gramsci, or at La Lizza nearby, but note that some stop near the church of San Domenico, while others avoid the centre altogether and terminate at the train station. Ticket offices beneath Piazza Gramsci have information on all routes. The bus company serving Siena and its hinterland is called TRA-IN (℡0577.204.246 or toll-free in Italy ℡800.570.530, ⊛www .trainspa.it).

Siena's **train station** is inconveniently sited at Piazza Fratelli Rosselli, down in the valley 2km northeast of town. Its foyer has a small train information office, exchange facilities, basic tourist information and a counter selling city bus tickets. To get into town, take just about any city bus – #3, #9 to Tozzi; #4, #7, #8, #14, #17, #77 – to Garibaldi/Sale; #10 to Gramsci. All these drop at various points on or near Piazza Matteotti or Piazza Gramsci on the northern edge of the centre. There are **taxi ranks** by the train station and on Piazza Matteotti, or taxis can be called elsewhere between 7am and 9pm by phone (℡0577.49.222). Note, however, that in Siena it's virtually impossible to book taxis in advance and you should allow plenty of time for cabs to reach you through the city's labyrinthine one-way system.

Parking can be a problem. Garages (⊛www.sienaparcheggi.com) are clearly signposted, secure and affordable, but the two biggest are misleadingly named: "Parcheggio Il Campo" is a long way from the Campo, just inside the Porta Tufi, and "Parcheggio Il Duomo" is just within Porta San Marco, nowhere near the Duomo. Street-parking outside the city walls is free; inside the walls, it can be expensive and hard to find. Follow signs to the *centro* and try to find a space at one of the following: around Piazza Gramsci; the large triangle of La Lizza (except market day, Wed 8am–2pm); opposite San Domenico in the car park alongside the stadium; off Viale Manzoni, which loops around the northeast wall of the city; or around the Porta Romana. Viale Manzoni has free parking; at the others a machine or an attendant issues tickets, usually by the hour: rates are reasonable. If you know you'll be driving in, arrange parking with your hotel in advance. You can drive through the old town alleys only in order to load or unload luggage.

Siena's main **tourist office**, Piazza del Campo 56 (Mon–Sat 9am–7pm; ℡0577.280.551, ⊛www.terresiena.it), provides hotel lists and town maps. **Guided walks** can be booked through Siena Hotels Promotion, Piazza Madre Teresa di Calcutta (℡0577.288.084, ⊛www.hotelsiena.com).

Transport from Florence

From Florence, hourly or more frequent TRA-IN **buses** bound for Siena depart from the bus station on Via di Caterina da Siena just west of the main train station; take a *Corse Rapide* or *Rapido* (about 1hr 15min; €6.50 in advance, €8 on board), as some buses (misleadingly called *Corse Dirette* or *Diretta*) are much slower and run via Colle di Val d'Elsa and Poggibonsi (1hr 35min; €4.50 in advance, €6 on board). Both services arrive at La Lizza-Piazza Gramsci. Some **trains** run direct to Siena (fastest journey 1hr 27min), but many involve changing at Empoli (about 1hr 40min). By **car**, the two cities are linked by a fast four-lane highway that starts from the Firenze Certosa junction on the A1 *autostrada*, 6km south of Florence; from central Florence, head through the Oltrarno to the Porta Romana and follow "Certosa" signs.

Accommodation

Securing a hotel room in Siena for any time between Easter and October requires booking six months in advance. If you arrive without a booking, and find that all the establishments listed below are full, make your way to the **Siena Hotels Promotion** booth (Mon–Sat 9am–8pm; winter closes 7pm; ☎0577.288.084, ⓦwww.hotelsiena.com), opposite the church of San Domenico on Piazza Madre Teresa di Calcutta. The staff are generally very helpful and can book rooms in any of the city's hotels. The city's second specialist agency, **Vacanze Senesi**, is in the tourist office at Piazza del Campo 56 (Mon–Fri 9am–7pm; ☎0577.45.900, ⓦwww.vacanzesenesi.it).

All accommodation listed below is marked on the **map** on p.324.

Hotels

🏃 **Antica Residenza Cicogna** Via dei Termini ☎0577.285.613, ⓦwww.anticaresidenzacicogna.it. A little-known B&B in a perfect, if tucked-away location. The owner is charming, and there are five en-suite rooms, all frescoed, delightfully appointed and recently restored – the "Liberty" and "Leoni" rooms are especially recommended. Breakfast is taken in an extraordinary, high-ceilinged room with colossal beams. Wi-fi available. ❸

Antica Torre Via Fieravecchia 7 ☎0577.222.255, ⓦwww.anticatorresiena.it. By far the nicest and most intimate of the three-star places: just eight smallish rooms squeezed into an old medieval tower. Top rooms have views. ❹

Bernini Via della Sapienza 15 ☎0577.289.047, ⓦwww.albergobernini.com. Nine inexpensive but rather poky one-star rooms, most en suite. ❸

Cannon d'Oro Via Montanini 28 ☎0577.44.321, ⓦwww.cannondoro.com. A stylish thirty-room two-star hotel tucked down an alleyway. Friendly and well maintained, this is the best choice among the central mid-price hotels. ❹

Centrale Via Cecco Angiolieri 26 ☎0577.280.379, ⓦwww.hotelcentralesiena.com. Seven large two-star rooms on an upper floor in a quiet street as central as the name suggests, a block north of the Campo. ❸

🏃 **Certosa di Maggiano** Via Certosa 82 ☎0577.288.180, ⓦwww.certosadimaggiano.com. This former monastery in the countryside 1km southeast of Siena offers luxurious comfort in its few tasteful rooms (€590 plus per night), and its library cloister and tranquil terrace make an alluring retreat. ❾

Chiusarelli Viale Curtatone 15 ☎0577.280.562, ⓦwww.chiusarelli.com. A pleasant old three-star villa hotel with 49 rooms and a garden, but it's on a busy street near the bus stops – ask for one of the back rooms, several of which are very large and comfortable. Also has some private parking. ❹

Duomo Via Stalloreggi 34 ☎0577.289.088, ⓦwww.hotelduomo.it. Rooms are reliable but unexceptional – apart from those with views of the Duomo – but this is nonetheless the best located of the city's three-star hotels. ❺

🏃 **Grand Hotel Continental** Via Banchi di Sopra 85 ☎0577.56.011, ⓦwww.royaldemeure.com. For years Siena had no luxury five-star hotel – until the hugely expensive restoration of this former palace. The frescoed public spaces are astounding, and there's a large covered courtyard. The best rooms are also exceptional – vast, entirely frescoed, and with stunning views of the Duomo. Other rooms are superbly appointed, but mostly lack the period details you'll see on the website. Be prepared to say goodbye to around €900 nightly, less for rooms under the eaves, or with online or tour-operator deals. ❾

La Perla Via delle Terme 25 ☎0577.47.144, ⓦwww.hotellaperlasiena.com. Regular one-star with thirteen en-suite rooms, in a very central location, two blocks north of the Campo. Curfew 1am. ❷

La Toscana Via Cecco Angiolieri 12 ☎0577.46.097, ⓕ0577.270.634. Big, well-priced three-star in an atmospheric and central location, on an alley behind Piazza Tolomei. Rooms with and without bathrooms – unusual in this category. ❸

Locanda Garibaldi Via Giovanni Dupré 18 ☎0577.284.204. A good, no-nonsense seven-room two-star (four shared bathrooms), situated above one of the city's better low-cost restaurants, just south of the Campo. Midnight curfew. ❷

🏃 **Palazzo Ravizza** Pian dei Mantellini 34 ☎0577.280.462, ⓦwww.palazzoravizza.it. This elegant three-star, located in a pleasant area near San Niccolò al Carmine, has been run by the same family since the 1920s, and has recently been renovated in a way that has freshened the

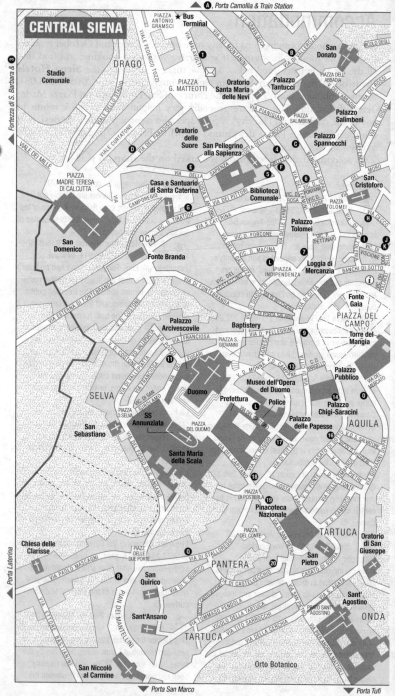

CENTRAL SIENA

▲ **A**, Porta Camollia & Train Station

Porta Camollia & Train Station

PIAZZA ANTONIO GRAMSCI
★ **Bus Terminal**

V.D. STUFASECCA

VIALE FEDERICO TOZZI

VIA MALAVOLTI

VIA DI MONTANINI

VIA DI VALLEROZZI

NICCOLÒ DEGLI

B

San Donato

PIAZZA DELL' ABBADIA

VIA DEI ROSSI

Stadio Comunale

DRAGO

VIALE DELLO STADIO

PIAZZA G. MATTEOTTI

Oratorio Santa Maria delle Nevi

Palazzo Tantucci

VIA DEI TERMINI

PIAZZA SALIMBENI

Palazzo Salimbeni

V.D. ABBADIA

VIA DEL GIGLIO

V.D. PIANIGIANI

VIALE CURTATONE

Fortezza di S. Barbara & **3**

VIALE DEI MILLE

VIA DEI PARADISO

Oratorio delle Suore

VIA DELLA SAPIENZA

San Pellegrino alla Sapienza

COSTA DELL'INCROCIATA

4

C

Palazzo Spannocchi

BANCHI DI SOPRA

VIA D. BEGHINO

D

E

5

F

VIA DEI MONTANINI

VIA DEL MORO

San Cristoforo

VIALE DEI MILLE

PIAZZA MADRE TERESA DI CALCUTTA

VIA

VIA CAMPOREGIO

Casa e Santuario di Santa Caterina

VIA DEI PITTORI

Biblioteca Comunale

VIC. D. ROSA

VIC. D. FONTANI

6

VIA D. TORRE

PIAZZA TOLOMEI

H

VIA CECCO

G

VIC. D. TIRATOIO

VIA S. CATERINA

VIA DELLE TERME

Palazzo Tolomei

VIC. P. PETTINAIO

I

J

K

VISCIONE

OCA

San Domenico

Fonte Branda

VIA DELLA GALLUZZA

VIC. D. FORCONE

VIC. D. MACINA

7

L

PIAZZA INDIPENDENZA

Loggia di Mercanzia

BANCHI DI SOTTO

VIA DI FONTEBRANDA

VIA ESTERNA DI FONTEBRANDA

VIC. DEL COSTACCIARO

VIA DIACCETO

VIA DELLA BECHERIA

VIA DI CITTÀ

i

Fonte Gaia

PIAZZA DEL CAMPO

Torre del Mangia

VIA DI PORTA SALARIA

Palazzo Arcivescovile

VIA FRANCIOSA

PIAZZA S. GIOVANNI

Baptistery

VIA D. PELLEGRINI

9

VIA D. CAMPANE

VIA DEL CASATO DI SOTTO

Palazzo Pubblico

VIA DEL MERCATO

O

11

VIA DEI FUSARI

VIA D. SAN GIROLAMO

Duomo

13

V.D. MONNA AGNESE

Museo dell'Opera del Duomo

C.D. BARGELLO

14

Palazzo Chigi-Saracini

AQUILA

SELVA

VIC. DI SAN

PIAZZA D. SELVA

San Sebastiano

SS Annunziata

Prefettura

PIAZZA DEL DUOMO

Police

VIA DEL CAPITANO

Palazzo delle Papesse

V.D.S. SALVATORE

VICOLO S. NICOLO

16

VIA DI STALLOREGGIO

Santa Maria della Scala

VIA DEL POGGIO

VIA DI CITTÀ

17

CASATO DI SOPRA

V.D. PIETRE

V.D. FONTE

VIA DELLE LOMBARDE

VIA DI SALICOTTO

Porta Laterina

18

PIAZZA DI POSTIERLA

19

Pinacoteca Nazionale

VIA SAN PIETRO

V.D. SAMBUCO

TARTUCA

Oratorio di San Giuseppe

Chiesa delle Clarisse

VIA PAOLO MASCAGNI

PIAZZ DELLE DUE PORTE

Q

VIA DI STALLOREGGIO

PIAZZA DEL CONTE

PANTERA

20

San Pietro

CASATO DI SOPRA

Sant' Agostino

R

VIA DI S. QUIRICO

San Quirico

VIA DI CASTELVECCHIO

PRATO SANT' AGOSTINO

VIA S. AGATA

PIANI DEI MANTELLINI

VIA ETTORE BASTIANINI

Sant'Ansano

VIA TOMMASO PENDOLA

VICOLO D. TARTUCA

VIA DELLA CERCHIA

ONDA

VIA PIER ANDREA MATTIOLI

TARTUCA

San Niccolò al Carmine

Orto Botanico

▼ Porta San Marco

▼ Porta Tufi

6

SIENA

324

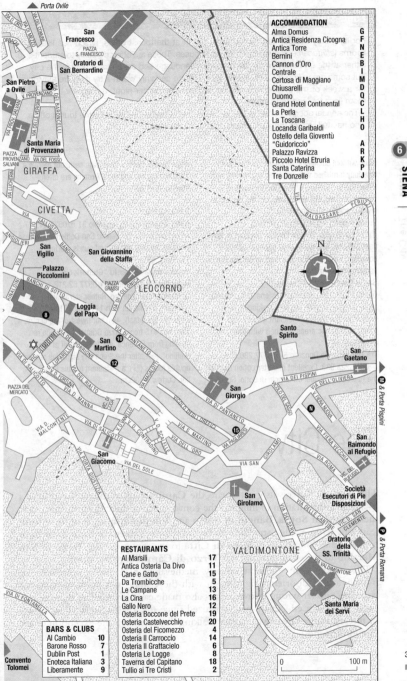

▲ Porta Ovile

San Francesco
PIAZZA S. FRANCESCO
Oratorio di San Bernardino

San Pietro a Ovile

Santa Maria di Provenzano

GIRAFFA

CIVETTA

San Vigilio

San Giovannino della Staffa

Palazzo Piccolomini

LEOCORNO

Loggia del Papa

San Martino

PIAZZA DEL MERCATO

Santo Spirito

San Gaetano

San Giorgio

San Raimondo al Refugio

San Giacomo

Società Esecutori di Pie Disposizioni

San Girolamo

Oratorio della SS. Trinità

VALDIMONTONE

Santa Maria dei Servi

Convento Tolomei

W & Porta Pispini

P & Porta Romana

N

ACCOMMODATION

Alma Domus	G
Antica Residenza Cicogna	F
Antica Torre	N
Bernini	E
Cannon d'Oro	B
Centrale	I
Certosa di Maggiano	M
Chiusarelli	D
Duomo	Q
Grand Hotel Continental	C
La Perla	L
La Toscana	H
Locanda Garibaldi	O
Ostello della Gioventù "Guidoriccio"	A
Palazzo Ravizza	R
Piccolo Hotel Etruria	K
Santa Caterina	P
Tre Donzelle	J

RESTAURANTS

Al Marsili	17
Antica Osteria Da Divo	11
Cane e Gatto	15
Da Trombicche	5
Le Campane	13
La Cina	16
Gallo Nero	12
Osteria Boccone del Prete	19
Osteria Castelvecchio	20
Osteria del Ficomezzo	4
Osteria Il Carroccio	14
Osteria Il Grattacielo	6
Osteria Le Logge	8
Taverna del Capitano	18
Tullio ai Tre Cristi	2

BARS & CLUBS

Al Cambio	10
Barone Rosso	7
Dublin Post	1
Enoteca Italiana	3
Liberamente	9

0   100 m

Long-stay accommodation

For long-stay budget accommodation, call in at the tourist office, which has lists of **rooms** (*affittacamere*) available in private houses. These are offered mainly to students, either at the university or on the numerous language and art courses held in the city, but some are willing to offer shorter lets. They're certainly worth a try if you're staying for a week or more; rates are around €25 per person per night, usually for a shared room (less for long-term lets).

The annual accommodation booklet (*Guida all' Ospitalità*) issued by the tourist office also has full lists of the agriturismo options in the area.

place without sacrificing its charm. Rooms are tastefully furnished with antiques, and paved with terracotta or parquet, with ceiling frescoes in several of them. The little garden at the back is a lovely place for afternoon tea. ❾
Piccolo Hotel Etruria Via Donzelle 3 ☏0577.288.088, ⓦwww.hoteletruria.com. A very neat two-star, and deservedly popular: advance booking for high season is a must to secure one of its thirteen rooms. ❸
Santa Caterina Via Piccolomini 7 ☏0577.221.105, ⓦwww.hscsiena.it. A nineteen-room three-star, with a/c and parking, 10min walk from the Campo. Pleasant garden and rooms and public areas adorned with fine old prints. ❻
Tre Donzelle Via Donzelle 5 ☏0577.280.358, ℉0577.223.933. Excellent one-star option right in the heart of town, just off Banchi di Sotto. Good,

clean rooms, some with private bath, but there's a 12.30am curfew and the 27 rooms are often booked solid. ❷

Hostels
Alma Domus Via Camporegio 31 ☏0577.44.177. An old pilgrim hostel behind San Domenico, with en-suite doubles, triples and quads. Curfew 11.30pm. ❶
Ostello della Gioventù "Guidoriccio" Via Fiorentina 89, Lo Stellino ☏0577.52.212, ⓦwww.ostellionline.org. Rather sterile and uninspiring HI hostel with 111 beds (€14.45, including breakfast), 4km northwest of the centre. Take bus #15 from Piazza Gramsci, or, if you're coming from Florence, ask to be let off at "Lo Stellino", just after the Siena city sign. Has several double rooms (❶), a restaurant (meals €10) and a bar. Curfew 11.30pm.

The City

The centre of Siena is its great square, the **Campo**, built at the intersection of a Y-shaped configuration of hills and the convergence of the city's principal roads, the **Banchi di Sopra**, **Banchi di Sotto** and **Via di Città**. Each of these roads leads out across a ridge, straddled by one of the city's three medieval districts, or *terzi* (literally "thirds"): the **Terzo di Città** to the southwest, the **Terzo di San Martino** to the southeast, and the **Terzo di Camollia** to the north.

This central core – almost entirely medieval in plan and appearance – is initially a little disorientating, though with the Campo as a point of reference you won't go far wrong. Movement is also made easier by the fact that the city centre has been effectively pedestrianized since the 1960s. Everywhere of use or interest in the city is within easy walking distance, with the exception of the Guidoriccio hostel.

The Campo

The Campo is the centre of Siena in every sense: the main streets lead into it, the Palio takes place around its perimeter, and in the evenings it is the natural place to gravitate towards, for visitors and residents alike. Four hundred years ago, Montaigne described it as the most beautiful square in the world – an assessment that still seems pretty fair.

With its amphitheatre curve, the Campo appears an almost organic piece of city planning. In fact, when the Council of Nine began buying up land in 1293, they were adopting the only possible site – the old marketplace, which lay at the convergence of the city quarters but was a part of none (the old Roman forum probably also occupied the site). To build on it, it was necessary to construct an enormous buttress beneath the lower half of the square, where the Palazzo Pubblico was to be raised. The piazza itself was completed in 1349, when the council laid its nine segments of paving to commemorate their highly civic rule and pay homage to the Virgin, the folds of whose cloak it was intended to symbolize.

From the start, the stage-like Campo was a focus of city life. As well as its continuing role as the city's marketplace – for livestock as well as produce – it was the scene of executions, bullfights, communal boxing matches, and, of course, the Palio. St Bernardino preached here, too, holding before him the monogram of Christ's name in Greek ("IHS"), which he urged the nobles to adopt in place of their own vainglorious coats of arms. A few did so (the monogram is to be seen on various *palazzi*), and it was adopted by the council on the facade of the **Palazzo Pubblico**, alongside the city's she-wolf symbol, which is itself a reference to Siena's legendary foundation by the sons of Remus.

At the highest point of the Campo is the Renaissance **Fonte Gaia** ("Gay Fountain"), designed and carved by Jacopo della Quercia in the early fifteenth century. Its panels are poor, nineteenth-century reproductions – some of the original marble pieces are currently being restored in the *Fienile* section of Santa Maria della Scala – but they give an idea of what was considered one of the city's masterpieces. Its conception – the Virgin at the centre, flanked by the Virtues – was a conscious emulation of the Lorenzetti frescoes on

Siena museum admission

If you're intending to visit a few different attractions, it's worth picking up a **pass** or **joint ticket** (*biglietto cumulativo*). Siena has an array of these, though they have a tendency to change from year to year. Usually they are available at any of the participating museums. All permit only a single entry to each attraction.

The **cathedral authorities** have an "Opera" pass which gives entry to the Museo dell'Opera, the Baptistery and San Bernardino for €10 (valid three days). The **civic museum authorities** have their own two-day pass, which gives entry to the Museo Civico (but *not* the Torre del Mangia), Santa Maria della Scala and the Palazzo delle Papesse, for €10. A joint ticket covering only the Museo Civico and Torre del Mangia costs €12.

Finally, there are seasonal versions of an all-encompassing, seven-day "Art Itinerary" pass – the **SIA Inverno**, or **Itinerario d'Arte Inverno** (Winter Art Itinerary; available Nov to mid-March), covering entry to the Museo dell'Opera, the Baptistery, Libreria Piccolomini, Museo Civico, Santa Maria della Scala and Palazzo delle Papesse for €14; or the **SIA Estate**, or **Itinerario d'Arte Estate** (Summer Art Itinerary; available mid-March to Oct), valid for all these plus the Oratorio San Bernardino, Museo Diocesano and the church of Sant'Agostino, for €17. Note that the Pinacoteca Nazionale is not included on any of the passes.

▲ The Palazzo Pubblico

Good and Bad Government in the Palazzo Pubblico (see below). The fountain's name comes from festivities celebrating its inauguration in 1419, the climax of a long process that began in the 1340s, when masons managed to channel water into the square.

The Palazzo Pubblico

Making no bones about its expression of civic pride, the **Palazzo Pubblico**, bristling with crenellations and glorious medieval detail, occupies virtually the entire south side of the Campo, loomed over by its giant bell tower, the **Torre del Mangia**. Built largely in the first decade of the fourteenth century, the palace's lower level of arcading is characteristic of Sienese Gothic, as are the columns separating the windows. The council was so pleased with this aspect of the design that they ordered its emulation on all other buildings on the square – and it was indeed gracefully adapted on the twelfth-century Palazzo Sansedoni on the north side.

The other main exterior feature of the Palazzo Pubblico is the **Cappella di Piazza**, a stone loggia set at the base of the tower, which the council vowed to build at the end of the Black Death in 1348. Funds were slow to materialize, however, and by 1376, when the chief mason at the cathedral turned his hand to its design, new Florentine ideas were already making their influence felt. The final stage of construction, a century later, when the chapel was heightened and a canopy added, was wholly Renaissance in concept.

The Museo Civico

In the days of the *comune*, the lower floors of the Palazzo Pubblico housed the city accounts, and the upper storeys, as today, the council. Nowadays, its principal rooms have been converted into the **Museo Civico** (daily: mid-March to Oct 10am–7pm; Nov & Feb to mid-March 10am–6pm; Dec & Jan 10am–5.30pm; €7.50, or €12 with Torre del Mangia), entered through the courtyard to the right of the Cappella di Piazza.

The museum starts on the first floor of the *palazzo*. At the top of the stairs you're directed through a disappointing, miscellaneous five-room picture collection, whose nineteenth-century hunting scenes are enough to put you off eating *cinghiale* (wild boar) for the rest of your visit. You then wind round into the **Sala del Risorgimento** (1878–90), painted with scenes commemorating Vittorio Emanuele, first king of Italy. These depict various battle campaigns, the king's coronation and his earlier meeting with Garibaldi and his army on the road to Capua, where he refused Garibaldi governorship of the Neapolitan provinces, instead inflicting a decade of martial rule.

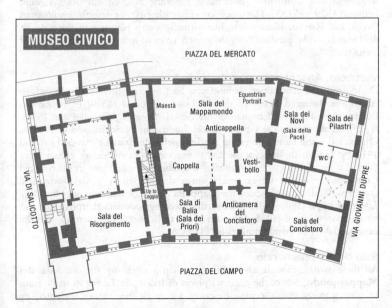

Sala di Balia

The first of the rooms of any real interest is the **Sala di Balia** (or Sala dei Priori), frescoed by Spinello Aretino and his son, Parri, in 1407 with episodes from the life of Siena-born Pope Alexander III – in particular his conflict with Frederick Barbarossa, the German Holy Roman Emperor. The story is a complex one. The pope and emperor came into dispute following Barbarossa's destruction of Milan in 1162, an event that caused the formation of a Lombard League of Italian states, supported by the Vatican and the Venetians. Barbarossa entered Rome in 1166, whereupon the pope fled to Venice (where he is depicted, disguised as a monk, but recognized by a French pilgrim). The scenes include a superbly realized naval conflict – in which the Venetians are shown capturing the emperor's son and the Germans desperately trying to rescue him – and the pope's eventual reconciliation with Barbarossa, in a procession led by the doge of Venice.

Anticamera and Sala del Concistoro

Beyond is the **Anticamera del Concistoro** (or Sala dei Cardinali). A detached fresco, *Three Saints and Donor*, attributed to Ambrogio Lorenzetti, graces the wall by the entrance door. It was transferred here in the nineteenth century and was probably once part of a much larger work depicting the *Madonna and Child*: in such pictures the donor would have been shown kneeling at the feet of the Madonna. In the centre of the left wall is a beautiful *Madonna and Child* attributed to Matteo di Giovanni, whose Madonna has the unquiet look typical of this painter: his propensity for the unsettling found expression in several grisly depictions of the *Massacre of the Innocents*, one of which is on display in the sala dei Pilastri (see p.332).

The next room is the **Sala del Concistoro**, entered via an ornate marble doorway (1448) by Bernardo Rossellino, the sculptor and architect responsible for redesigning much of the southern Tuscan town of Pienza for Pope Pius II. Mannerist star Domenico Beccafumi superbly frescoed the room's vault between 1529 and 1535. The panels are either allegories or describe events from Greek and Roman history, but, like virtually every painting in the *palazzo*, deliberately evoke parallels with the civic virtues or historical achievements of Siena itself.

Vestibolo, Anticappella and Cappella

Doors from the Anticamera behind you lead on into the **Vestibolo**, which contains a damaged fresco of the *Madonna and Child* (1340) by Ambrogio Lorenzetti and a gilded bronze of the *She-Wolf Suckling Romulus and Remus* (1429), an allusion to the city's mythical foundation by Senius, son of Remus. On the left is the more interesting **Anticappella**, decorated between 1407 and 1414 by Taddeo di Bartolo, the last major exponent of Siena's conservative Gothic style, with a vast *St Christopher* and frescoes – like those in the Sala del Concistoro – whose Greek and Roman themes reflect Siena's own civic concerns. Taddeo also frescoed the **Cappella** alongside with episodes from the *Life of the Virgin* (1407–08), work overshadowed by Sodoma's altarpiece, the vast wrought-iron screen (1435–45) – attributed to Jacopo della Quercia – and the exceptional set of inlaid choir stalls (1415–28).

Sala del Mappamondo

All these works, though, are little more than a warm-up for the **Sala del Mappamondo**, one of the great set pieces of Italian art. Taking its name from its now scarcely visible ceiling fresco of a map of the cosmos, executed by

Ambrogio Lorenzetti, the room was used for several centuries as the city's law court and contains one of the greatest of all Italian frescoes, **Simone Martini**'s fabulous and recently restored *Maestà*, a painting of almost translucent colour, which was the *comune*'s first major commission for the palace. Its political dimension is apparent in the depiction of the Christ Child holding a parchment inscribed with the city's motto of justice, and the inscription of two stanzas from Dante on the steps below the throne, warning that the Virgin will not intercede for those who betray her or oppress the poor. It is one of Martini's earliest known works, painted in 1315 at the age of 30; before this extraordinary debut not a thing is known of him. He touched up parts of the picture, following damage from damp, six years later. The richly decorative style is archetypal Sienese Gothic and its arrangement makes a fascinating comparison with the *Maestà* by Duccio (with whom Martini perhaps trained) in the Museo dell'Opera del Duomo. Martini's great innovation was the use of a canopy and a frieze of medallions which frame and organize the figures – a sense of space and hint of perspective that suggest a knowledge of Giotto's work. Martini was to experiment further in this direction, in his great cycle of the *Life of St Martin* in Assisi, painted a couple of years later.

The fresco on the opposite wall, the marvellous **Equestrian Portrait of Guidoriccio da Fogliano**, is a motif for medieval chivalric Siena, and was, until recently, also credited to Martini. Depicting the knight setting forth from his battle camp to besiege a walled hill-town (thought to be Montemassi, a village southwest of Siena near Roccastrada), it would, if it were by Martini, be accounted one of the earliest Italian portrait paintings. Art historians, however, have long puzzled over the apparently anachronistic castles: according to some, they are of a much later architectural style than the painting's supposed date of 1328. The work would also seem to be part-painted over a fresco to the right by Lippo Vanni, which is dated 1364. In the mid-1980s the waters were further muddied when, during restoration, another apparently anachronistic fresco was found – the painting now beneath the equestrian portrait showing two men in front of a castle, believed to be the one at Arcidosso in southern Tuscany; it has been variously attributed to Martini, Duccio, Pietro Lorenzetti and Memmi di Filippuccio.

The coffered figures to the right and left of the uncovered fresco beneath the equestrian portrait are a pair of saints by Sodoma dating from 1529. The other large frescoes in the room also depict Sienese military victories. Don't miss the figures on the pilasters below the latter, which from left to right are Sodoma's *Blessed Tolomei* (1533), founder of the abbey at Monte Oliveto Maggiore; *St Bernardino* (1450) by Sano di Pietro; and *St Catherine of Siena* (1461) by Vecchietta.

Sala dei Nove (Sala della Pace)

The Palazzo Pubblico's most important and interesting frescoes adorn the **Sala dei Nove** (or **Sala della Pace**) next door; these are Ambrogio Lorenzetti's **Allegories of Good and Bad Government**, commissioned in 1338 to remind the councillors of the effects of their duties, and widely considered one of Europe's most important surviving cycles of secular paintings. The walled city they depict is clearly Siena, along with its countryside and domains, and the paintings are full of details of medieval life: agriculture, craftwork, trade and building, even hawking and dancing. They form the first-known panorama in Western art and show an innovative approach to the human figure – the beautiful, reclining Peace (Pax) in the *Good Government* hierarchy is based on a Roman sarcophagus still on display in the Palazzo Pubblico. An odd detail is that the "dancing maidens" in *Good Government* are probably young men: women dancing in public, according to the historian Jane Bridgeman, would have been too shocking in medieval Siena, and the figures' short hair and slit skirts were characteristic of professional male entertainers.

The moral theme of the frescoes is expressed in a complex iconography of allegorical virtues and figures. *Good Government*, painted on the more brightly lit walls and better preserved, is dominated by a throned figure representing the *comune* (he is dressed in Siena's colours), flanked by the Virtues (Peace – from which the room takes its name – is the nonchalantly reclining figure in white) and with Faith, Hope and Charity buzzing about his head. To the left, on a throne, Justice (with Wisdom in the air above) dispenses rewards and punishments, while below her throne Concordia advises the republic's councillors on their duties. All hold ropes, symbol of agreement. *Bad Government* is ruled by the figure of Fear (or the Devil), whose scroll reads: "Because he looks for his own good in the world, he places justice beneath tyranny. So nobody walks this road without Fear: robbery thrives inside and outside the city gates." Fear is surrounded by figures symbolizing the Vices.

Ironically, within a decade of the frescoes' completion, Siena was engulfed by the Black Death – in which Lorenzetti and his family were among the victims – and the city was under tyrannical government. However, the paintings retained an impact on the citizenry: St Bernardino preached sermons on their themes.

Sala dei Pilastri and loggia

The room adjoining the Sala della Pace, the **Sala dei Pilastri** (or delle Colonne), displays panel paintings from the thirteenth to the fifteenth centuries, whose conservatism and strict formulaic composition points up the scale of Lorenzetti's achievement. Notable among them is one of the earliest Sienese masterpieces, Guido da Siena's gripping *Maestà* (1221/1260), for which Duccio repainted the Virgin's face; a fascinating picture of *St Bernardino Preaching in the Campo* by Neroccio di Bartolomeo (note how the men and women in the crowd are separated by a white cloth); and a graphically violent *Massacre of the Innocents* removed from Sant'Agostino, painted by Matteo di Giovanni – one of four he completed in the city. The stained-glass figure of St Michael in one of the windows is attributed to Ambrogio Lorenzetti.

Backtracking through the museum, it is worth climbing the stairs between the Sala del Risorgimento and Sala di Balia to the rear **loggia**, where you can enjoy a view over the Piazza del Mercato, now mainly a car park with a belvedere-like platform and a pleasant café-pizzeria and restaurant. It is here you realize how abruptly the town ends: buildings rise to the right and left for a few hundred metres along the ridges of the Terzo di San Martino and Terzo di Città, but in the centre the land drops away to a rural valley.

The Torre del Mangia

Within the Palazzo Pubblico's courtyard, opposite the entrance to the Museo Civico, is separate access to the 97-metre **Torre del Mangia** (daily: March to mid-Oct 10am–7pm; rest of year 10am–4pm; €7, or €12 with the Museo Civico). Climb the 388 steps and you have fabulous, vertigo-inducing views across the town and countryside. Built between 1338 and 1348 – the cresting was designed by Lippo Memmi – the tower takes its name from its first watchman, a spendthrift (*mangiaguadagni*) named Giovanni di Balduccio, who is commemorated by a statue in the courtyard. It was the last great project of the *comune* before the Black Death and exercised a highly civic function: its bell was rung to order the opening of the city gates at dawn, the break for lunch, the end of work at sunset and the closing of the city gates three hours later.

Piazza del Duomo

Dominating the hill on which it stands, visible from many parts of the city, Siena's mighty **Duomo** is the focus of an ensemble of art and architecture arrayed around the **Piazza del Duomo**. The southwest side of the square is occupied by the medieval complex of **Santa Maria della Scala**, Siena's main hospital for over eight hundred years and now a museum and arts complex displaying some staggering medieval frescoes. Two floors below it is the **Museo Archeologico**, a modest but well-presented collection, and part of a scheme that will see the former hospital turned into Siena's principal exhibition space. The other sides of the square continue the history of Sienese power, with the Palazzo dei Vescovi (Archbishop's Palace), the Palazzo del Magnifico built for Petrucci in 1508, and the Palazzo Granducale, erected later the same century for the Medici. More interesting than any of these, though, is the **Museo dell'Opera del Duomo**, home to Siena's single greatest work of art – Duccio's *Maestà* – and a range of other significant sculptures and paintings.

The Duomo

Few buildings reveal so much of a city's history and aspirations as Siena's **Duomo** (March–May, Sept & Oct Mon–Sat 10.30am–5.30pm, Sun 1.30–5.30pm; June–Aug Mon–Sat 10.30am–8pm, Sun 1.30–6pm; Nov–Feb Mon–Sat 10.30am–6.30pm, Sun 1.30–5.30pm; €3; €6 during the summer uncovering of the marble pavement; ⓦ www.operaduomo.siena.it). Completed to virtually its present size around 1215, the Duomo was subjected to constant plans for expansion throughout the city's years of medieval prosperity. A project at the beginning of the fourteenth century attempted to double its extent by building a baptistery on the slope below and using this as a foundation for a rebuilt nave, but the work ground to a halt as the walls gaped under the pressure. For a while, the chapter pondered knocking down the whole building and starting from scratch to the principles of the day, but eventually they hit on a new scheme to re-orientate the cathedral instead, using the existing nave as a transept and building a **new nave** out towards the Campo. Again cracks appeared, and then in 1348 came the Black Death. With the population halved and funds suddenly cut off, the plan was abandoned once and for all. The part-built extension still stands at the north end of the square, a vast structure that would have created the largest church in Italy outside Rome.

Despite all the grand abandoned plans, the Duomo is still a delight. Its style is an amazing conglomeration of Romanesque and Gothic, delineated by bands of black and white marble, an idea adapted from Pisa and Lucca – though here with much bolder and more extravagant effect. The lower part of the **facade** was designed by the Pisan sculptor Giovanni Pisano, who from 1284 to 1296 created, with his workshop, much of its statuary – the philosophers, patriarchs and prophets, now removed to the Museo dell'Opera and replaced by copies.

In the next century the **Campanile** was added, its windows multiplying at each level, as was the Gothic **rose window** above the doors. Thereafter work came to a complete halt, with the **mosaics** designed for the gables having to wait until the nineteenth century, when money was found to employ Venetian artists. Immediately above the central door, note St Bernardino's bronze monogram of Christ's name.

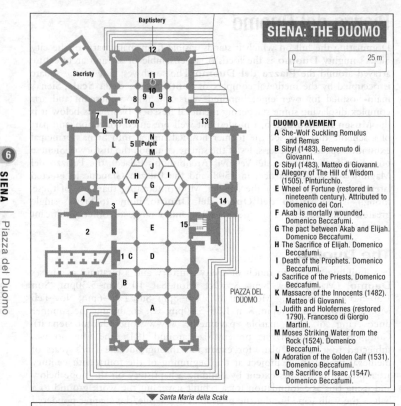

SIENA: THE DUOMO

0 ____ 25 m

Baptistery

Sacristy

Pecci Tomb

Pulpit

PIAZZA DEL
DUOMO

▼ Santa Maria della Scala

DUOMO PAVEMENT

A She-Wolf Suckling Romulus and Remus
B Sibyl (1483). Benvenuto di Giovanni.
C Sibyl (1483). Matteo di Giovanni.
D Allegory of The Hill of Wisdom (1505). Pinturicchio.
E Wheel of Fortune (restored in nineteenth century). Attributed to Domenico dei Cori.
F Akab is mortally wounded. Domenico Beccafumi.
G The pact between Akab and Elijah. Domenico Beccafumi.
H The Sacrifice of Elijah. Domenico Beccafumi.
I Death of the Prophets. Domenico Beccafumi.
J Sacrifice of the Priests. Domenico Beccafumi.
K Massacre of the Innocents (1482). Matteo di Giovanni.
L Judith and Holofernes (restored 1790). Francesco di Giorgio Martini.
M Moses Striking Water from the Rock (1524). Domenico Beccafumi.
N Adoration of the Golden Calf (1531). Domenico Beccafumi.
O The Sacrifice of Isaac (1547). Domenico Beccafumi.

SIENA DUOMO

1 Altare Piccolomini (1491). Andrea Bregno. Sculptures by Michelangelo.
2 Libreria Piccolomini. Frescoes on the life of Pope Pius II (1505–07) by Pinturicchio.
3 Flagpole from the Battle of Montaperti.
4 Cappella di San Giovanni Battista. Frescoes (1501–04) by Pinturicchio; bronze by Donatello of St John the Baptist (1457).
5 Pulpit. Nicola Pisano and assistants (1268).
6 Tomb of Bishop Pecci of Grosseto (1426–7). Donatello.
7 Tomb of Cardinal Riccardo Petroni (1314–18). Tino da Camaino.
8 Bronze candleholders (1548–50). Domenico Beccafumi.
9 Bronze candleholders (1497–99). Francesco di Giorgio Martini.
10 High altar (1532). Baldassare Peruzzi.
11 Ciborio (1467–72). Vecchietta.
12 Stained glass (1288). To a design by Duccio.
13 Cappella del Sacramento. Bas-reliefs (1425) by Domenico dei Cori.
14 Cappella Chigi (1659–62). To a design by Gian Lorenzo Bernini.
15 Tomb of Tommaso Piccolomini (1484–5). Neroccio di Bartolomeo Landi. Below: bas-reliefs of Episodes from the Life of the Virgin (1451) by Urbano da Cortona.

The pavement

The facade's use of black and white decoration is echoed by the Duomo's great marble **pavement**, or floor, which begins with geometric patterns and a few scenes outside the church and takes off into a startling sequence of 56 figurative panels within. These were completed between 1349 and 1547, with virtually every artist who worked in the city trying his hand on a design. The earliest employed a simple *sgraffito* technique, which involved chiselling holes and lines in the marble and then filling them in with pitch; later tableaux are considerably more ambitious, worked in multicoloured marble. Unfortunately, the whole effect can only be seen for about a month in August (dates vary); the rest of the year, most of the panels are rather unimaginatively protected by underfoot boarding.

The subjects chosen for the panels are a strange mix, incorporating biblical themes, secular commemorations and allegories. The most ordered part of the scheme are the ten Sibyls – mythic prophetesses who foretold the coming of Christ – on either side of the main aisle. Fashioned towards the end of the fifteenth century, when Sienese painters were still imprinting gold around their conventional Madonnas, they are totally Renaissance in spirit. Between them, in the central nave, are the much earlier *Sienese She-Wolf Suckling Romulus and Remus*, (marked A on our plan), and the *Wheel of Fortune* (E), along with Pinturicchio's *Allegory of the Hill of Wisdom* (D), a rocky island of serpents with a nude posed between a boat and the land. Moving down the nave, the central hexagon is dominated by Domenico Beccafumi's *Stories from the Life of Elijah* (F–I). Beccafumi worked intermittently on the pavement from 1518 to 1547, also designing the vast friezes of *Moses Striking Water from a Rock* (M) and *The Sacrifice of Isaac* (O). To the left of the hexagon is a *Massacre of the Innocents* (K), almost inevitably the chosen subject of Matteo di Giovanni.

It's interesting also to note the **choir stalls**, in the context of the pavement. These use intarsia techniques of a superb standard and again were made between the mid-fourteenth and mid-sixteenth centuries.

The pulpit, sculptures and chapels

The rest of the cathedral interior is equally arresting, with its zebra-stripe bands of marble, and the line of popes' heads – including several Sienese – set above the pillars. These stucco busts were added through the fifteenth and sixteenth centuries and many seem sculpted with an apparent eye to their perversity: the same hollow-cheeked scowls crop up repeatedly.

The greatest individual artistic treasure is the **pulpit** (marked 5 on our plan). This was completed by Nicola Pisano in 1268, soon after his pulpit for the Baptistery at Pisa, with help from his son Giovanni and Arnolfo di Cambio. The design of the panels duplicates those in Pisa, though they are executed with much greater detail and high relief. The carving's distance from the Byzantine world is perhaps best displayed by the statuette of the *Madonna*, whose breast is visible beneath the cloak for the first time in Italy, and by the *Last Judgement*, with its mastery of the human figure and organization of space. Come equipped with plenty of coins for lighting.

Almost all the sculpture is of an exceptional standard. Near the pulpit in the north transept are Tino di Camaino's *Tomb of Cardinal Petroni* (1314–18), a prototype for Italian tomb architecture over the next century, and, in front, **Donatello**'s bronze pavement *Tomb of Bishop Pecci* (1426). The Renaissance high altar is flanked by superb candelabra-carrying angels by Beccafumi. In the **Piccolomini Altarpiece** (1) the young **Michelangelo** also makes an appearance. He was commissioned to carve the whole series of fifteen statues here, but after completing saints Peter, Paul, Pius and Gregory in the lower niches he left for a more tempting contract in Florence – the *David*.

There are further Renaissance sculptural highlights in the two circular transept chapels. The **Cappella di San Giovanni Battista** (4) focuses on a bronze statue of the *Baptist* by Donatello, cast in 1457, a couple of years after his expressionist *Mary Magdalene* in Florence, whom the Baptist's stretched and emaciated face recalls. The frescoes in this chapel, with their delightful landscape detailing, are by Pinturicchio.

The **Cappella Chigi** (14) or Cappella del Voto, was the last major addition to the Duomo, built at the behest of Pope Alexander VII, another local boy, in 1659. It was designed by Bernini as a new setting for the *Madonna del Voto*, a thirteenth-century painting that commemorated the Sienese dedication of their city to the Virgin on the eve of the Battle of Montaperti. The style of the chapel is pure Roman Baroque, most notably seen in the four niche statues, two of which are by Bernini himself – wild, semi-clad figures of Mary Magdalene and St Jerome, the latter holding a cross in ecstasy like some 1970s rock guitarist. Outside the chapel, the walls are covered in a mass of devotional objects – silver limbs and hearts, *contrada* scarves, even the odd Palio costume and crash helmet.

Libreria Piccolomini

Midway along the nave, Pinturicchio's brilliantly coloured fresco of the *Coronation of Pius II* marks the entrance to the **Libreria Piccolomini** (2), well worth a visit for the beautiful fresco cycle within. The frescoes and library were commissioned by Francesco Piccolomini (who for ten days was Pope Pius III) to house the books of his uncle, Aeneas Sylvius Piccolomini (Pius II). They do justice to the man whom Jacob Burckhardt adopted almost as a hero in his classic *The Civilization of the Renaissance in Italy*. Pius, born at nearby Pienza in 1405, was the archetypal Renaissance man, writing poetry and the *Commentaries*, a deeply humanist work in which he enthuses over landscape, antiquity and architecture and describes the languages, customs and industries encountered on his travels.

Pinturicchio's frescoes, painted with an equal love of nature and classical decor as well as a keen sense of drama, commemorate the whole gamut of Pius's career. The cycle begins to the right of the window, with Aeneas's secular career as a diplomat: attending the Council of Basle as secretary to an Italian bishop (panel 1); presenting himself as an envoy to James II of Scotland (panel 2); being crowned poet laureate by the Holy Roman Emperor, Frederick III (panel 3); and then representing Frederick on a visit to Pope Eugenius IV (panel 4). Aeneas subsequently returned to Italy and took orders, becoming first Bishop of Trieste and then of Siena, in which role he is depicted presiding over the meeting of Frederick III and his bride-to-be, Eleonora of Portugal, outside the city's Porta Camollia (panel 5).

In 1456 Aeneas was made a cardinal (panel 6) and just two years later was elected pope (panel 7), taking the title Pius II. In political terms, his eight-year rule was not a great papacy, despite his undoubted humanism and diplomatic skill, with much of the time wasted in crushing the barons of Romagna and the Marche. The crusade he called in 1456 at Mantua (panel 8) to regain Constantinople from the Turks – who took the city in 1453 – came to nothing, and the last picture of the series (panel 10) shows his death at Ancona, where he had gone to encourage the troops. It was said that his death was brought on by grief for the failure to get the crusade off the ground, or possibly by poisoning by the troops, eager to terminate their pledge. Between these two panels is the event for which Siena most remembers him – the canonization of St Catherine.

In art history terms, Pinturicchio stands as a relatively minor figure. Originally from Perugia, he worked with Perugino in the Sistine Chapel before beginning this, his acknowledged masterpiece, in 1502. His skills lie in the brilliant colouring, the naturalistic detail – the storm scene in Aeneas's departure for Basle is one of the first in Western art – and in an easy disposition of crowds, ideal for the pageants here, and enhanced by their illusionistic placing within a series of loggias.

The library is now used to display the cathedral's **choirbooks**, illuminated by Sano di Pietro and other Sienese Gothics. At the centre of the room is displayed a Roman statue of the **Three Graces**, supposedly copied from a lost Greek work by Praxiteles. It was bought by the Piccolomini nephew and was used as a model by Pinturicchio and Raphael.

The Baptistery

The cathedral **Baptistery** (daily: March–May & Sept 9.30am–7pm; June–Aug hours vary, but usually 9am–8pm; Oct 9am–6pm; rest of year 10am–1pm & 2–5pm; €3, or €10 with joint ticket – see p.327) contains one of the city's great Renaissance works – a hexagonal font with scenes illustrating the Baptist's life. It's unusual in being placed beneath the main body of the church: to reach it, turn left out of the Duomo, follow the walls left and then take the flight of steps leading down behind the cathedral.

The cathedral chapter responsible for the **font** (1417–30) must have had a good sense of what was happening in Florence at the time, for they managed to commission panels by **Ghiberti** (*Baptism of Christ* and *John in Prison*) and **Donatello** (*Herod's Feast*), as well as by the local sculptor **Jacopo della Quercia** (*The Angel Announcing the Baptist's Birth*). Jacopo also executed the marble tabernacle above, and the summit statue of *John the Baptist* and five niche statues of the Prophets. Of the main panels, Donatello's scene, in particular, is a superb piece of drama, with Herod and his cronies recoiling at the appearance of the Baptist's head. Donatello was also responsible for two of the corner angels (*Faith* and *Hope*) and (with Giovanni di Turino) for the miniature angels on the tabernacle above.

The lavishly frescoed **walls** almost overshadow the font, their nineteenth-century overpainting having been removed after a vigorous assault by the restorers. With your back to the entrance, the best include (on the left arched vault lunette) a fresco of scenes from the life of St Anthony (1460) by Benvenuto di Giovanni, a pupil of Vecchietta; scenes from the life of Christ by Vecchietta himself (inside left wall of the central stepped chapel); and the same artist's *Prophets*, *Sibyls* and *Articles of the Creed* (the main vaults), the last a repeat of a theme he would use in Santa Maria della Scala.

Santa Maria della Scala

The complex of **Santa Maria della Scala** (daily: mid-March to Oct 10am–6.30pm; rest of year 10.30am–4.30pm; €6, or joint ticket – see p.327; ⓦwww .santamariadellascala.com), opposite the Duomo, served as the city's hospital for over eight hundred years, listing among its charitable workers St Catherine and St Bernardino. Its closure in 1995 aroused mixed feelings, for the functioning building gave a sense of purpose to the cathedral square, which won't be matched by its intended use as Siena's principal cultural and museum space. At the same time, the *comune*'s grandiose plans for the enormous building – which include a new home for the Pinacoteca Nazionale – mean that some extraordinary works are now on public view for the first time in centuries.

While some of the complex still remains off-limits, the last few years have seen the restoration and opening of the church of **Santissima Annunziata**; the **Cappella del Sacro Chiodo** with its highly acclaimed fresco cycle by Vecchietta; a beautiful Beccafumi fresco in the **Cappella del Manto**; the **Oratorio di Santa Caterina della Notte**, a finely decorated subterranean chapel used by, among others, St Catherine; and, adjacent to this, Jacopo della Quercia's original marble panels from the Fonte Gaia in the **Fienile**. Best of all, in the **Sala del Pellegrinaio**, is a vast secular fresco cycle by Domenico di Bartolo, a work now talked of as third only to the frescoes in the Duomo and Palazzo Pubblico in Siena's artistic pantheon. Siena's **Museo Archeologico** occupies the converted basement of the building.

According to legend, the hospital of Santa Maria della Scala was founded by **Beato Sorore**, a ninth-century cobbler-turned-monk who worked among orphans, a story given credence by the reputed discovery of his "tomb" in 1492. Sorore was almost certainly mythical, his name a corruption of *suore*, or nuns, who for centuries tended the sick as a part of their vocation. The hospital was probably founded by the cathedral's canons, the first written record of its existence appearing in 1090. Its development was prompted by the proximity of the **Via Francigena**, a vital trade and pilgrimage route between Rome and northern Europe, which in the early Middle Ages replaced the deteriorating Roman consular roads used previously. Its route passed below Siena's walls, giving rise to the growth of numerous rest-places (*ospedali*) where travellers and pilgrims could seek shelter and succour. Some forty of these grew up in Sienese territory alone, the most important of which was Santa Maria della Scala. Initially pilgrims were the main concern: hospital work, in the modern sense, came later: "hospitality rather than hospitalization" was the credo.

The foundation was one of the first European examples of the **Xenodochium**, literally an "abode", a hospital that not only looked after the sick but could also be used as a refuge and food kitchen for an entire town in times of famine and plague. This role made it a vital part of the city's social fabric, its importance leading to a long-running and ill-mannered tussle between lay and secular authorities. In time it passed from the cathedral canons into the hands of hospital friars, and in 1404, after an intense dispute, into the care of the *comune*, who appointed its rectors and governing body. Alms and bequests of money over the centuries kept it richly endowed, the Sienese taking to heart St Paul's stricture that charity was the most important of the three Cardinal Virtues.

Some of the donated funds were diverted away from humanitarian concerns, and into artistic and architectural commissions: as early as 1252, Siena's bishop gave permission for Santa Maria's abbot to build a **church**, the precursor of the present Santissima Annunziata. In 1335 the hospital commissioned Simone Martini and Pietro and Ambrogio Lorenzetti, the city's three leading painters, to fresco the building's facade (works that have since been lost to the elements). In 1359 it paid an exorbitant sum to acquire from Constantinople a nail used during the Passion, a piece of the True Cross, and a part of the Virgin's girdle, along with a miscellany of **saints' relics**. In 1378 it financed the setting of a stone bench along the length of the hospital's exterior, its original purpose being to provide the hospital's dignitaries with somewhere to sit during the city's interminable religious and civic ceremonies – and still much used today as a shady spot from which to view the facade of the Duomo.

Santissima Annunziata and the Cappella del Manto

To the left of the ticket desk, and also with its own door onto Piazza del Duomo, is the church of **Santissima Annunziata**, wholly within the complex of Santa Maria della Scala. Remodelled in the fifteenth century, the church is disappointingly bland, but worth a look for the high altar's marvellous bronze statue of the *Risen Christ* by Vecchietta, its features so gaunt the veins show through the skin. Vecchietta clearly understood and absorbed the new approach of Donatello, and several art historians consider this the finest Renaissance sculpture in the city. Before the church's remodelling, frescoes by Vecchietta had entirely covered its walls, a loss as tantalizing as the missing Martini and Lorenzetti frescoes on the hospital's exterior.

The other way from the ticket office leads into a small vestibule known as the **Cappella del Manto**, which contains an arresting and beautifully restored fresco of *St Anne and St Joachim* (1512), the earliest major work in Siena by the Mannerist Domenico Beccafumi. The protagonists depicted are the parents of the Virgin, whose story – popular in Tuscan painting – is told in the apocryphal gospels, biblical adjuncts reintroduced to the medieval world in the *Golden Legend* by Jacopo da Voragine. Having failed to conceive during twenty years of marriage, the pair are each told by an angel to meet at Jerusalem's Golden Gate. Here they kiss (the scene depicted in the fresco), a moment which symbolizes the Immaculate Conception of their daughter.

Sala del Pellegrinaio

From the Cappella del Manto, you turn left into a vast hall, a majestic whitewashed space typical of the "longitudinal" architectural elements introduced into Italy by French Cistercians travelling the Via Francigena, and now partly used as a bookshop. Turning immediately left again (rooms off to the right are used for temporary exhibitions) brings you into another similarly elongated space, the **Sala del Pellegrinaio**, its walls completely covered in a fresco cycle of episodes from the history of Santa Maria della Scala by Domenico di Bartolo and Vecchietta. Incredibly, this astounding space was used as a hospital ward until relatively recently.

The ward was built around 1380 and the frescoes begun in 1440, their aim being to not only record scenes from the hospital's history, but also to promote the notion of charity towards the sick and – in particular – the orphaned, whose care had been a large part of the hospital's early function. Their almost entirely **secular** content was extraordinary at the time they were painted, still some years short of the period when Renaissance ideas would allow for other than religious narratives. It's well worth taking the trouble to study the eight major panels in detail – each is full of insights into the Sienese daily life of the time – along with the two paintings on the end wall by the window. The cycle starts at the left end of the left wall and moves clockwise.

The left wall

The **first panel**, *The Dream of the Mother of Beato Sorore*, is by Vecchietta, his only contribution to the cycle. It depicts in part a dream in which the mother of Sorore, the hospital's mythical founder, foresees her son's destiny. Her vision focuses on the abandoned children of the hospital, the *gettatelli* (from *gettare*, to throw away), who are shown ascending to Paradise and the waiting arms of the Madonna. Sorore is shown twice: on the right of the painting with upraised hand receiving the first *gettatello*, and kneeling at the foot of the child-filled ladder. This ladder (*scala*) is the key to the Santa Maria della Scala, which may take its name from this part of the legend. Another version of the story suggests that a three-runged ladder, a symbol of the Trinity, was found during the hospital's construction – although the more likely explanation is that the hospital was simply built opposite the steps, or *scala*, of the Duomo. Whatever the origins, a three-runged ladder surmounted by a cross is the symbol you now see plastered all over the museum's literature and displays.

The **second panel**, *The Building of the Hospital*, depicts a mounted bishop of Siena at the head of a procession passing the hospital, which is in the process of being built, and almost running down a stonemason in the process. Note the buildings, a strange mixture of Gothic and Renaissance that bear little relation to anything in Siena, and the rector of the hospital, portrayed behind the ladder on the right doffing his hat to the visiting dignitaries. The **third panel**, the weakest of the cycle, is by Priamo della Quercia, brother of the more famous Jacopo, and shows the *Investiture of the Hospital Rector by the Blessed Agostino Novello*, the latter traditionally, but erroneously, credited as being the author of the hospital's first statute. The **fourth panel** shows one of Santa Maria's defining moments, when in 1193 Pope Celestine III gave the hospital the right to elect its own rector, thus transferring power from the religious to lay authorities. For the rest, the fresco is an excuse to portray day-to-day life in Siena – note, for example, the preponderance of oriental merchants.

The end wall

The paintings on either side of the **end wall** are late sixteenth-century works, but illustrate two fascinating aspects of the hospital's work. The vast number of orphans taken in meant that an equally large number of wet nurses, or *baliatici*, were needed to feed the infants. At one time their numbers were such that feeding took place in the vast hall now occupied by the bookshop. The pictures here show the nurses in action, and the payment for their services: in grain (on the left wall) and hard cash (on the right).

The right wall

On the long right wall, the **fifth panel**, the most famous in the cycle, shows *The Tending of the Sick*, a picture crammed with incident, notably the close scrutiny being given to a urine sample by two doctors on the left, the youth with a leg wound being washed, and the rather ominous scene on the right of a monk taking confession from a patient prior to surgery.

The **sixth panel** shows *The Distribution of Charity*, one of the hospital's main tasks, an event that takes place in the old hospital church (now replaced by Santissima Annunziata) with the central door of the Duomo just visible in the background. Bread is distributed to beggars, pilgrims and children (one of whom passes it on to his mother); at the centre an orphan puts on clothes that it has been given. In one strange vignette a child is shown trying to express milk from its mother's breast. On the left, meanwhile, the hospital's rector is shown doffing his hat, possibly to Sigismondo.

The **seventh panel** illustrates further work of the hospital, underlining the vital part it played in maintaining the social fabric of the city. It shows the reception, education and marriage of one of the female orphans, who were provided with a small grant designed to enable them to marry, stay on in the hospital or join a convent. Also included are details that suggest how the hospital not only took in children, but committed itself to caring for them over a long period. Thus the wet nurses are shown in action on the table to the left, along with scenes to suggest weaning, education and play. Bartolo also shows off his Renaissance credentials by including a wealth of extraneous detail, as well as his arcane knowledge of exotic lands, notably in the carpet under the feet of the married couple, whose dragon and phoenix symbols belong to the period of the Ming dynasty.

The final **eighth panel**, which details the feeding of the poor and the elderly, is less engaging than the rest, partly because of the awkwardly sited window, reputedly built by a nineteenth-century superintendent so that he could survey the sick from his upper-floor office without the bother of having to go down into the ward.

The Cappella del Sacro Chiodo

Some idea of what was lost in the remodelling of Santissima Annunziata can be grasped in Vecchietta's fresco cycle (1446–49) in the **Cappella del Sacro Chiodo**, so named because it once housed the nail (*chiodo*) from the Passion and other holy relics; it's also known as the **Sagrestia Vecchia**, reached through the small Cappella della Madonna beside the Sala del Pellegrinaio. Some art critics pay these frescoes more attention than the Bartolo cycle in the Sala del Pellegrinaio, but for the casual viewer they are less easy to interpret, principally because the subject matter – an illustration of the *Articles of the Creed* – requires some theological knowledge. If you can manage the Italian, however, the various panels and vaults are well described. Each lunette illustrates one or more articles, the figure of one of the Apostles to the right holding the text of the article in question, the scenes below or to the left depicting an episode from the Old Testament which embodies the article's meaning.

The frescoes are extremely unusual, partly in that they illustrate a written text – something that remained rare until much later in the Renaissance – and partly in that they revolve around the figure of Christ (depicted twice in the main vaults). The latter was a strange choice in a city dedicated to the Madonna, where virtually every work of note either eulogizes Siena itself or includes Christ only as an adjunct to the Virgin. It's thought that the choice was suggested by the "nail from the Cross" contained in the chapel, a relic with obvious relevance to the story of Christ.

Domenico di Bartolo's **high altarpiece**, the *Madonna della Misericordia* (1444), is more intelligible than much of the cycle, and shows the Madonna casting a protective cloak over various of Siena's inhabitants. This theme, a common one in Sienese and other central Italian works, derives from a vision of the Madonna experienced by a ninth-century Cistercian monk. At first painters depicted only members of the religious orders beneath the protective cloak, monks to one side, nuns to the other. At the beginning of the twelfth century members of religious confraternities were allowed protection, and a few decades later the privilege was extended to all inhabitants of a town or city. Men and women usually remained segregated, however, which makes this version – in which they're mixed – unusual. The fresco once graced the Cappella del Manto (see above), the Virgin's cloak (*manto*) having given the chapel its name. It was detached and fixed here in 1610, its side parts torn away to fit the dimensions of the new altar; in 1969, however, the discarded fragments were found and reattached.

The rest of Santa Maria della Scala

Stairs lead down to the **Fienile**, the hospital's old hayloft, now housing Jacopo della Quercia's original marble panels from the Fonte Gaia (1409–19), transferred here from the Palazzo Pubblico. With their serious state of erosion it was hard to appreciate that Jacopo della Quercia was rated by Vasari on a par with Donatello and Ghiberti, with whom he competed for the commission of Florence's Baptistery doors. Michelangelo, too, was an admirer, struck perhaps by the physicality evident in the *Expulsion of Adam and Eve*.

Adjacent is the **Oratorio di Santa Caterina della Notte**, which belonged to one of a number of the medieval confraternities who maintained oratories in the basement vaults of the hospital. It's a dark and strangely spooky place, despite the wealth of decoration; you can easily imagine St Catherine passing nocturnal vigils down here. Even if you prove immune to the atmosphere, it's worth coming down here for Taddeo di Bartolo's sumptuous triptych of the *Madonna and Child with Sts Andrew and John the Baptist* (1400).

Stairs lead down again to the lavishly decorated **Compagnia della Madonna sotto le Volte**, the oratory and meeting-room of the Società di Esecutori di Pie Diposizioni, the oldest of the lay confraternities, where you'll find a wooden crucifix said to be the one that inspired St Bernardino to become a monk.

From the small columned courtyard (**Corticella**) back on the Fienile level you enter the medieval storerooms – now used for temporary exhibitions – from where stairs lead down into the spacious labyrinth of the **Museo Archeologico**, which houses private collections from the late nineteenth century and plenty of local finds from excavation work in and around Siena, Chianti, the upper Val d'Elsa and Etruscan Murlo.

The Museo dell'Opera del Duomo

Tucked into a corner of the proposed – and abandoned – new nave of the Duomo is the impressive **Museo dell'Opera del Duomo** (daily: March–May & Sept–Oct 9.30am–7pm; June–Aug 9.30am–8pm; Nov–Feb 10am–5pm; €6; Ⓦwww.operaduomo.siena.it), which offers the bonus of fine views over Siena.

On the ground floor, in the **Galleria delle Statue**, the statuary by Giovanni Pisano (1250–1314) seems a little bizarre when displayed at eye level: the huge, elongated, twisting figures are obviously adjusted to take account of the original viewing position, which was ranged across the Duomo's facade. They are totally Gothic in conception, and for all their subject matter – philosophers from antiquity are represented alongside Old Testament prophets and other characters – show little of his father Nicola's experiment with classical forms on the cathedral pulpit. In marked contrast is Donatello's ochre-coloured *Madonna and Child*, a delicate piece in the centre of the room (removed from the door of the Duomo's south transept), alongside a bas-relief by Jacopo della Quercia of *St Anthony Abbot and Cardinal Antonio Casini*.

Upstairs, a curator admits you to the **Sala di Duccio**, curtained and carefully lit to display the artist's vast and justly celebrated **Maestà**. Originally painted on both sides, it depicts the *Madonna and Child Enthroned* (or *Maestà*) and the *Story of the Passion*. The four saints in the front rank of the main painting, the *Maestà*, are Siena's patron saints at the time, Ansano, Savino, Crescenzio and Vittore, while the ten smaller figures at the rear of the massed ranks represent ten of the Apostles. (Peter and Paul are in the second rank, accompanied by John the Baptist and other saints.) On its completion in 1311 the work was, as far as scholars can ascertain, the most expensive painting ever commissioned, and had occupied Duccio for almost four years. It was taken in a ceremonial procession from Duccio's studio around the Campo and then to a special Mass in the Duomo; everything in the city was closed and virtually the entire population attended. It then remained on the Duomo's high altar until 1505. This is one of the superlative works of Sienese art – its iconic, Byzantine spirituality accentuated by Duccio's flowing composition and a new attention to narrative detail in the panels of the predella and the reverse of the altarpiece, both now displayed to its side.

The *Maestà* – the Virgin as Queen of Heaven surrounded by her "court" of saints – was a Sienese invention, designed as a "sacrifice" to the Virgin, the city's patron (the consecration took place in 1260), a quality emphasized by the lavish use of gold. Duccio's rendering of the theme was essentially the prototype for the next three centuries of Sienese painters; his achievement, as Bernard Berenson put it, was to add "the drama of light to that of movement and expression" and a realization of the space in which action takes place.

This quality is best observed in the narrative panels, most of which have been gathered here, after the altarpiece's dismemberment in 1771 and its removal to the museum in 1887. Only a handful of panels are missing and – to quite understandable local disgust – will not be released by their owners to the city: two are in Washington, three in London's National Gallery and three in the Frick and Rockefeller collections in New York. One of the most effective of the surviving panels is the *Betrayal of Judas*, where trees relieve the main group of figures – Christ is "pointed" by the central tree – and rows of lances break the golden sky. The *Descent from the Cross*, too, is a marvellously composed image.

Also in the room is a *Madonna di Crevole*, an early work by Duccio, and Pietro Lorenzetti's triptych of the *Nativity of the Virgin*, the latter remarkable for breaking with the tradition of triptych painting by running a single scene across two of the painting's three panels. The gilded statues in the room off to the right of the *Madonna and Child with Four Saints* are attributed to Jacopo della Quercia, as is the separate statue of *St John the Baptist*. In the room behind the Sala is a fascinating nineteenth-century drawing of the cathedral pavement, providing a unified view impossible on the spot.

For the art that followed Duccio, and some that preceded him, you need to make your way upstairs again. Here you enter the **Sala di Tesoro**, featuring amid its reliquaries the head of St Galgano and a startling *Christ on the Cross* (1280), an important early work in wood by Giovanni Pisano in which Christ is shown on a Y-shaped tree growing out of the skull of Adam. The latter symbolizes the Tree of Life, or Tree of Knowledge, which grew from a sprig planted in the dead Adam's mouth and would – in the apocryphal story – eventually yield the wood used to crucify Christ (Piero della Francesca tells this story in Arezzo's fresco cycle depicting the *Story of the True Cross*; for the full story see p.446).

Beyond the Sala di Tesoro you reach the **Sala della Madonna dagli Occhi Grossi**. The work that gives its name to this room is the cathedral's original, pre-Duccio altarpiece – a stark, haunting Byzantine icon (literally the "Madonna of the Big Eyes") in the centre of the room. It occupies a special place in Sienese history, for it was before this painting that Siena's entire population came to pray before their famous victory over the Florentines at Montaperti in 1260. It was also a promise made in front of the painting prior to the battle that saw Siena dedicated to the Madonna in the aftermath of victory. Around it are grouped a fine array of panels, including works by Simone Martini, Pietro Lorenzetti and Sano di Pietro. Note the panels flanking Sano's *Madonna and Child*: one shows St Bernardino preaching in the Campo and Piazza San Francesco (the latter now home to the saint's oratory; see p.352); the other shows St Apollonia, patron saint of dentists, martyred in Alexandria in the fourth century for refusing to make sacrifices to pagan gods.

Don't miss the tiny entrance to the so-called **Panorama dal Facciatone**: this leads to steep spiral stairs that climb out of the building, up within the walls of the abandoned nave. The sensational view from the top over the city and surrounding hills is definitely worth the two-stage climb, but beware that the topmost walkway – teetering along the very summit of the abandoned nave walls – is narrow and scarily exposed.

Terzo di San Martino

Banchi di Sotto, the main thoroughfare through the **Terzo di San Martino**, leads southeast from the Campo past the imposing Renaissance buildings of **Palazzo Piccolomini, San Martino** and the **Loggia del Papa** towards the medieval Servite order's huge monastic base, **Santa Maria dei Servi**. Students outnumber tourists in this university-dominated area that ends at the south gate of the city, **Porta Romana**, but there is plenty of scope for aimless wandering through the quiet backstreets off Via Pantaneto.

Loggia di Mercanzia

Marking the start of Banchi di Sotto is the **Loggia di Mercanzia** (or Loggia dei Mercanti), designed as a tribune house for merchants to do their deals. The structure was the result of extraordinary architectural indecision by the city authorities, the chronicles recording that "on one day they build in a certain way and on the following destroy and rebuild in a different manner." It was completed in 1421 in accordingly hesitant style, with Gothic niches for the saints carved by Vecchietta and Antonio Federighi, two of the city's leading Renaissance sculptors.

Palazzo Piccolomini

Following Banchi di Sotto from the loggia, you pass the more committed Renaissance buildings of the **Palazzo Piccolomini** (at Banchi di Sotto 52) and **Loggia del Papa**, commissioned in the 1460s by Pope Pius II, the Pienza-born Aeneas Sylvius Piccolomini. Pius was the city's great Renaissance patron and an indefatigable builder. The loggia was built in 1462 by Federighi. The palace was designed by Bernardo Rossellino, architect of Piccolomini's famous "new town" of Pienza (see p.407); note the half-moon symbols, Pius's coat of arms, insinuated across much of the facade.

The Palazzo Piccolomini now houses the **Archivio di Stato**, the city's archives (guided visits Mon–Sat at 9.30am, 10.30am & 11.30am; free), an unmissable detour, but one made by probably one visitor in five hundred to the city. You're taken through corridors of archives – great bundles of vellum and leather-bound documents for each of the towns and villages in Siena's domain, each one labelled in ancient medieval script with the year in question: 1351, 1352, 1353 – a quite overwhelming amount of information for any potential historian, and most of it still unread. If you're lucky you'll also be able to pop out onto the palace's terrace, which offers a rarely seen view of the Campo.

Eventually you come to the **Museo delle Tavolette di Biccherna**, containing the city's account books, tax records (the *Gabelle*) and hallowed manuscripts dating back to the earliest days of Siena's recorded history. The chief exhibits, though, are the *Tavolette*, fascinating painted wooden panels designed as covers for civic records and accounts: what makes them more interesting still is the fact that the *comune* commissioned some of the leading painters of the day to execute the beautifully detailed vignettes. Among those employed were Sano di Pietro and Ambrogio Lorenzetti, who painted the 1344 *Gabella* with a version of his *Good Government* fresco in the Palazzo Pubblico. The paintings began with religious themes, but soon moved towards secular images of city life, providing a record of six centuries of Sienese history. Later panels were designed to be hung as pictures in the council offices, rather than mounted on the books. The city is depicted frequently in the background, protected by the Virgin and mushrooming with towers – much like San Gimignano today. Early panels include several pictures of the *camerlingo* (a duty always filled by a Cistercian monk from San Galgano) doing the audits. Later ones move into specific events: victories over the Florentines; Pius's coronation as pope (1458); entrusting the city keys to the Virgin in the Duomo (1483); the demolition of the Spanish fortress (1552); the fall of Montalcino, the Sienese Republic's last stand (1559), and the entry into Siena of Cosimo I (1560); war with the Turks (1570); and subsequent Medicean events.

San Martino

From the Palazzo Piccolomini and the Loggia, Via di Pantaneto, Via del Porrione or Via di Salicotto takes you quickly away from the bustle around the Campo towards the Porta Romana. Before setting off, however, Mannerist fans should spend a couple of minutes in the church of **San Martino**, founded in the eighth century or earlier, but now a pale Baroque shadow of its former self. The third altar on the left (north) wall features an outstanding *Nativity* (1522–24) by Domenico Beccafumi, a work painted at the same time as the artist was working on the Duomo's pavement, and one which encapsulates his passion for bizarre structures and peculiar light effects. The Virgin's strange gesture, in which she covers the infant Jesus with a veil, prefigures the Crucifixion, at which she also covers Christ's naked body.

The Palio

No Italian festival – perhaps no European festival – is as spectacular as Siena's Palio, a twice-yearly bareback horse race around the Campo. And no festival comes as loaded with history or social and cultural weight, or involves as much pageantry, intrigue and drama. But don't assume that the race is cosily preserved folklore, a jamboree for the benefit of visitors. The ninety-second, three-lap race may attract vast crowds, but at heart it remains a vital and living expression of community and civic continuity.

Drummers in the corteo storico ▲

A balcony view of the Campo ▼

Flag-twirling precedes the race ▼

The background

The Palio dates back at least to the thirteenth century and has virtually always taken place, even in times of war, plague and famine. Some elements have changed – the race was run around the city streets until the sixteenth century – but the fundamentals remain the same: races are held in honour of the Virgin on **July 2** (formerly the Feast of the Visitation) and **August 16** (the day after the Feast of the Assumption). And there are only ever ten riders, so each year the seventeen *contrade* **draw lots** to take part (losing *contrade* are guaranteed entry in the next race). The participants also draw lots for horses and starting positions.

The **jockeys** are professional outsiders, traditionally the *butteri*, or cowboys, of the Maremma (see p.297), employed according to an unreliable and shifting combination of loyalties reinforced by large cash payments and bonuses – and sometimes the threat of violence if they are treacherous. During the run-up to the races they live under the suspicions of their own *contrada* and in fear of the threats of rival *contrade*. They may be bribed to throw the race, or to whip a rival or his horse; *contrade* have been known to drug horses, and even to mount an ambush on a jockey making his way to the race.

Each *contrada* has its traditional rival, and ensuring that one's rival loses is as important as winning for oneself. The only rule of the race is that the jockeys cannot interfere with the others' reins; everything else is accepted and practised. And it's the **horse** that wins – it doesn't matter if the jockey has been thrown en route to victory.

The race

The **race** is preceded by days of pageantry. On **June 29/August 13** the horses are presented in the morning at the town hall and drawn by lot. At 7.15pm the first trial race is held in the Campo. **June 30/August 14** sees further trial races at 9am and 7.45pm. The evening race is usually followed by a concert in the Campo. Two more trial races follow on **July 1/August 15** at 9am and 7.45pm, followed by a street banquet and late-night revelry in each of the *contrade*. Restaurants also move their tables outside for these Palio nights to allow diners to enjoy the spectacle.

The day of the Palio itself – **July 2/August 16** – begins with a final trial at 9am. In the afternoon, each of the chosen *contrade* takes its horse to be blessed in its church: "Go, little horse, and return a winner" are the priest's words. It's taken as a good omen if the horse defecates in the nave. At around 5pm the town hall bell begins to ring and the **corteo storico**, a pageant of horses, riders and medieval-costumed officials, parades through the city to the Campo. The procession includes *comparse* – symbolic groups of equerries, ensigns, pages and drummers – from each of the *contrade*, who perform various *sbandierata* (flag-twirling) and athletic feats in the square. They are preceded by officials of the *comune* of Siena and representatives from all the ancient towns and villages of the Siense Republic, led by the standard-bearer of Montalcino.

Then the race, at about 7pm. At the start all the horses except one are penned between two ropes; the free one charges the group from behind, when his rivals least expect it, and the race is on. It's a hectic, violent and bizarre spectacle, and the jockeys don't even stop at the finish

▲ A horse and trainer after a trial race
▼ Horses jostle at the start of the race

▼ The main event

line but gallop at top speed out of the Campo, followed by a frenzied mass of supporters. Losers can be in danger of assault, especially if there are rumours about the match being fixed.

The aftermath

The **palio** – a silk banner with an image of the Virgin – is presented to the winning *contrada*, who then make their way to the church of Provenanzo (in July) or the Duomo (in Aug) to give thanks. Concerts and street banquets are held late into the night in each of the *contrade*. The younger *contrada* members spend the night and much of the subsequent week swaggering around town glorying in their victory, even handing out celebratory sonnets. Celebrations go on for weeks; recriminations – and thoughts of revenge – for years.

Good vantage points

Most ordinary spectators cram into the centre of the Campo free of charge (for ticketed seats, see p.355). For the **best view**, you need to have found a position by 2pm on the inner rail (preferably at the start/finish line), and to keep it for the next six hours – but you should be able to see a certain amount from anywhere within the crowd. People keep pouring in right up until a few minutes before the race, and the swell of the crowd can be overwhelming. Be aware too that you won't be able to leave the Campo for at least two hours after the race, and that toilets, shade and refreshment facilities are minimal. If you arrive late in the day, try making your way to Via Giovanni Dupré, behind the Palazzo Pubblico, from where the police usually allow people into the centre of the square an hour or so before the start of the race.

Contrada flags in the corteo storico ▲

In **Via di Salicotto** – which runs directly behind the Torre del Mangia, a couple of blocks from the Loggia del Papa – you find yourself in the territory of the Torre (tower) *contrada*. It maintains a museum at no. 76 and a fountain-square a few houses beyond. A famous sign on this street, posted in 1641, informs the citizens that the Florentine governor forbids prostitutes to operate in the neighbourhood.

Santa Maria dei Servi

Via di Salicotto or Via San Martino brings you southeast into the Valdimontone *contrada*, whose museum, fountain and parish church are in Via di Valdimontone, alongside the massive brick church and campanile of **Santa Maria dei Servi**, the Servites' monastic base. The church (closed 12.30–3pm), which is well worth the walk, is set in a quiet piazza, approached by a row of cypresses and shaded by a couple of spreading trees – good for a midday picnic or siesta. It also offers tremendous views across the city.

The Renaissance-remodelled **interior** is remarkable for a variety of top-notch paintings. The first, above the first main altar on the right (south) wall, is the so-called *Madonna di Bordone* (1261) by **Coppo di Marcovaldo**, a Florentine artist captured by the Sienese at the Battle of Montaperti and forced to paint this picture as part of his ransom for release. The next altar to the left features the *Nativity of the Virgin* (1625) by Rutilio Manetti, Siena's leading follower of Caravaggio. Two altars down, in the last altar of the left aisle, is Matteo di Giovanni's *Massacre of the Innocents* (1491), one of two versions of this episode in the church, and one of four in the city by the infanticide-obsessed Matteo. The popularity of this subject in the late fifteenth century may have been due to the much-publicized massacre of Christian children by the Saracens at Otranto in 1480. Matteo's rendition is a touch less blood-crazed than his Sant'Agostino version (moved to the Palazzo Pubblico since its restoration), but only just – certain features are common to

▲ View from Santa Maria dei Servi

both, including the powerful sense of claustrophobia and several unnecessarily perverse details, of which the most disturbing are the woman scratching the face of the soldier about to dispatch her child and the two smiling children watching the massacre from the balcony on the right.

Cheek-by-jowl violence also characterizes Pietro Lorenzetti's much earlier version of the *Massacre*, which is found on the right wall of the second chapel to the right of the high altar. (Note Herod watching the carnage from a balcony on the left.) The serene *Madonna and Child* to the right is by Segna di Bonaventura, nephew of the great Duccio. Lorenzetti is further represented by damaged frescoes of the *Banquet of Herod* and the *Death of John the Baptist*, located on the right wall of the second chapel to the left of the high altar. A fine *Adoration of the Shepherds* (1404) by one of Lorenzetti's followers, Taddeo di Bartolo, hangs in the same chapel.

Moving to the **left transept** involves a progression along a line of Sienese art history, for it contains a *Madonna della Misericordia* or *Madonna del Manto* (1436) by one of Taddeo's pupils, Giovanni di Paolo. The painting shows the Virgin sheltering a group of nuns on one side and a group of monks on the other, the latter led by Filippo Benizzi (1235–85), a Florentine general of the Servite order. Down the north aisle towards the entrance, the last altar before the rear wall contains the small but eye-catching *Madonna del Belvedere* (1363), one of only a handful of works attributed to Jacopo di Mino, a pupil of Lippo Memmi.

Porta Romana

From Santa Maria dei Servi, you're just 100m from the **Porta Romana**, the massively bastioned south gate of the city. Its outer arch has a fragmentary fresco of the *Coronation of the Virgin*, begun by Taddeo di Bartolo and completed by Sano di Pietro. If you leave the city here, and turn left along Via Girolamo Gigli, you could follow the walls north to the **Porta Pispini**, another impressive example of defensive architecture and again flanked by a fresco of the Virgin, this time a Renaissance effort by Sodoma.

Just within the Porta Romana, opposite the huge ex-convent of San Niccolò (which now houses a psychiatric hospital), is the little church of **Santuccio**, worth looking into for its seventeenth-century frescoes depicting the life of St Galgano (see p.388). In the adjacent sacristy, at Via Roma 71, are the premises of the **Società Esecutori di Pie Disposizioni** (the Society of Benevolent Works, formerly the Society of Flagellants). This medieval order, suppressed in the eighteenth century, and later refounded along more secular lines, maintains a small collection of art works (open on request: ring the bell; Mon–Fri 9am–1pm; free), including a triptych of the *Crucifixion, Flagellation and Burial of Christ* attributed to Duccio, and a semicircular tablet, with wonderful Renaissance landscape, of *St Catherine of Siena Leading the Pope Back to Rome*.

Terzo di Città

Via di Città, one of Siena's key streets, cuts across the top of the Campo through the city's oldest quarter, the **Terzo di Città**, the area around the cathedral. The street and its continuation, Via di San Pietro, are fronted by some of Siena's finest private *palazzi*, including the Buonsignori, home to the **Pinacoteca Nazionale**, Siena's main picture gallery. The district is also worth exploring for its own sake, with a variety of options taking you in loops past churches such as **Sant'Agostino** and some of the city's tucked-away corners.

Palazzo Chigi-Saracini and Palazzo delle Papesse

Walking to the Pinacoteca, you pass the **Palazzo Chigi-Saracini** at Via di Città 82, a Gothic beauty, with its curved facade and back courtyard. Although the palace is closed to the public, it houses the **Accademia Chigiana** (Ⓦ www.chigiana.it), which sponsors music programmes throughout the year and maintains a small art collection, including exceptional works by Sassetta, Botticelli and Donatello. It was from this palace that the Sienese victory over the Florentines at Montaperti was announced, the town herald having watched the battle from the tower.

Almost opposite, at Via di Città 126, is a second Palazzo Piccolomini, this one built in 1460 by Bernardo Rossellino as a residence for Pius II's sister, Caterina. Known as the **Palazzo delle Papesse**, it now houses Siena's museum of contemporary art (Tues–Sun 11am–7pm; €5, or joint ticket – see p.327; Ⓦ www.papesse .org). Its four airy floors house excellent temporary exhibits covering anything from architecture to video art, displayed in rooms, some with nineteenth-century frescoes, that still conserve many of their original Renaissance structural and decorative features.

Pinacoteca Nazionale

Via di Città continues to a small piazza, from where Via San Pietro leads left to the fourteenth-century Palazzo Buonsignori, now the home of the superb **Pinacoteca Nazionale** (Mon 8.30am–1.30pm, Tues–Sat 8.15am–7.15pm, Sun 8.15am–1.30pm; €4). Its collection is a roll of honour of Sienese Gothic painting, and if your interest has been spurred by the works by Martini in the Palazzo Pubblico or Duccio in the cathedral museum, a visit here is the obvious next step. The collection offers an unrivalled chance to assess the development of art in the city from the twelfth century through to late Renaissance Mannerism.

The main rooms are arranged in chronological order, starting on the second floor. **Room 1** begins with the earliest known Sienese work, an altar frontal dated 1215 of *Christ Flanked by Angels*, with side panels depicting the *Discovery of the True Cross*. The figures are clearly Romanesque; the gold background – intricately patterned – was to be a standard motif of Sienese art over the next two centuries. The first identified Sienese painter, Guido da Siena, makes an appearance in this room and covers the same subject in **room 2**, though the influences on his work – dated around 1280 – are distinctively Byzantine rather than Romanesque, incorporating studded jewels amid the gold. In some of his narrative panels – *Christ Entering Jerusalem*, *The Life of St Peter* and *St Clare Repelling a Saracen Attack* – his hand seems rather freer, though the colouring is limited to a few delicate shades.

Duccio di Buoninsegna (1260–1319), the dominant figure in early Sienese art, is represented along with his school in **rooms 3 and 4**. Bernard Berenson considered Duccio the last great painter of antiquity, in contrast to Giotto, the first of the moderns. The painter's advances in composition are best assessed in his *Maestà*, in the Museo dell'Opera del Duomo. Here Duccio simply shows that he "fulfilled all that the medieval mind demanded of a painter", in the words of Berenson: his dual purpose being to demonstrate Christianity to an illiterate audience and make an offering (the painting) to God. A rather more Gothic and expressive character is suggested by Ugolino di Nerio's *Crucifixion* and *Madonna* in room 4.

Sienese art over the next century has its departures from Duccio – Lorenzetti's mastery of landscape and life in the *Good and Bad Government* in the Palazzo Pubblico, for example – but the patrons responsible for commissioning works generally wanted more of the same: decorative paintings, whose gold backgrounds made their subjects stand out in the gloom of medieval chapels. As well as specifying the required materials and composition, the Sienese patrons – bankers, guilds, religious orders – would often nominate a particular painting as the model for the style they wanted.

Even within the conventions required by patrons, however, there were painters whose invention and finesse set them apart. One such was Simone Martini. Though his innovations – the attention to framing and the introduction of a political dimension – are perhaps best seen in the Palazzo Pubblico, there are several great works on show here, mainly in **room 5**, housing one of his masterpieces, the *Blessed Agostino Novello and Four of his Miracles*. Perhaps more rewarding, however, are the works by the Lorenzetti brothers, Pietro and Ambrogio, in **rooms 7 and 8**. Pietro's include a marvellous *Risen Christ*, which could almost hold company with Masaccio, and the *Carmine Altarpiece*, whose predella has five skilful narrative scenes of the founding of the Carmelite order. Attributed to Ambrogio, or, more likely, to Sassetta, are two tiny panels in room 12, *City by the Sea* and *Castles by a Lake*, which the art historian Enzo Carli claims are the first ever "pure landscapes", without any religious purpose. They are thought to have been painted on a door, one above the other.

Moving through the fourteenth century, in **rooms 9 to 11** you come to the major Sienese artists Bartolo di Fredi (1353–1410) and his pupil Taddeo di Bartolo (1362–1422). Bartolo is best known for the New Testament frescoes in San Gimignano, whose mastery of narrative is reflected in his *Adoration of the Magi*. Taddeo, painter of the chapel in the Palazzo Pubblico, has archaic elements – notably the huge areas of gold around a sketch of landscape – but makes strides in portraiture and renders one of the first pieces of dynamic action in the museum in his *Stoning of Sts Cosmas and Damian*.

These advances are taken a stage further in Sassetta's *St Anthony Beaten by Devils*, where Siena seems at last to be entering the mainstream of European Gothic art, and taking note of Florentine perspective. The influence of the patrons, however, is still prevalent in the mass of stereotyped images – gold again very much to the fore – by Giovanni di Paolo (1403–82), which fill most of **rooms 12 and 13**, and the exquisite Madonnas by Sano di Pietro (1406–81) and Matteo di Giovanni (1435–95) in **rooms 14 to 18**. It is astonishing to think that their Florentine contemporaries included Uccello and Leonardo. Subsequent rooms include some sublime works by Beccafumi, Antonio Bazzi (better known as Sodoma) and Bernardino Mei, the last an increasingly studied and admired seventeenth-century artist.

The **third floor** of the museum – not always open – presents the self-contained **Collezione Spannocchi**, a miscellany of Italian, German and Flemish works, including a Dürer, a fine Lorenzo Lotto *Nativity*, Paris Bordone's perfect Renaissance *Annunciation*, and Sofonisba Anguissola's *Bernardo Campi Painting Sofonisba's Portrait* – the only painting in the museum by a woman artist. Anguissola, who is mentioned by Vasari as a child prodigy, painted at the height of Mannerism; this work is a neat little joke, the artist excelling in her portrait of Campi, but depicting his portrait of her as a flat, stereotyped image.

Sant'Agostino and a loop to the Duomo

South of the Pinacoteca is the church of **Sant'Agostino**, open some years, closed others, where – if you are lucky – you can admire a *Crucifixion* (1506) by Perugino (second altar of the south aisle), an *Adoration of the Magi* (1518) by Sodoma and a lunette fresco of the *Madonna and Child with Saints* by Ambrogio Lorenzetti (both in the Cappella Piccolomini), and two monochrome lunette medallions by Luca

Signorelli (Cappella Bichi, south transept). The church **piazza** is a pleasant space, with a kids' playground and usually a few football games in progress. Along with the Campo, this square was the site of violent medieval football matches which were eventually displaced in the festival calendar by the Palio.

At no. 5 in the church piazza is the **Accademia dei Fisiocritici** (Mon–Wed & Fri 9am–1pm & 3–6pm, Thurs 9am–1pm; free), housing museums of zoology, geology and mineralogy – all a bit pedestrian, though with a few oddities – like terracotta models of *funghi* – to entertain botanists. Continuing the theme, you could make your way across the piazza to the **Orto Botanico** (Mon–Fri 9am–12.30pm & 2.30–5.30pm, Sat 8am–noon; free), whose herbarium is stocked with every Tuscan species.

An interesting walk from Sant'Agostino is to loop along the **Via della Cerchia**, a route that takes you past some good neighbourhood restaurants (see p.353) to the Carmelite convent and church of **San Niccolò al Carmine** (or Santa Maria del Carmine) in a predominantly student-populated section of the town. The church, a Renaissance rebuilding, contains a sensational *St Michael* by Domenico Beccafumi (midway down the south wall), painted following the monks' rejection of his more intense Mannerist version of the subject in the Pinacoteca (deemed to contain too many nudes for comfort). A hermaphrodite St Michael is shown at the centre of the crowded painting, looked down on by God, who has ordered the saint to earth to dispatch the Devil; the Devil's extraordinary face can be seen at the base of the picture. To the painting's left is a fragment of an *Annunciation* attributed to Ambrogio Lorenzetti.

If you follow the **Via del Fosso di Sant'Ansano**, north of Piazza delle Due Porte, you find yourself on a country lane, above terraced vineyards and allotments, before emerging at the Selva (wood) *contrada*'s square and **museum**, and the church of **San Sebastiano**. Climb up the stepped Vicolo di San Girolamo from here and you come out at the Duomo. Alternatively from Sant'Agostino, you could cut back to the Campo along **Via Giovanni Dupré**, where the Onda (wave or dolphin) *contrada* has its base at no. 111; to visit the **museum** you need to make an appointment at least a week in advance (℡0577.48.384). The Onda church is San Giuseppe, at the Sant'Agostino end of the street.

Terzo di Camollia

The northern **Terzo di Camollia** is flanked, to west and east, by the churches of the most important medieval orders, the **Dominicans** and **Franciscans**, vast brick piles which rear above the city's outer ridges. Each has an important association with Siena's major saints, the former with **Catherine**, the latter with **Bernardino**.

The central part of the Camollia takes in the main thoroughfare of **Banchi di Sopra**, the base of the **Monte dei Paschi** – long the city's financial power. North from here, you move into a quiet residential quarter, all the more pleasant for its lack of specific sights or visitors. To the west, interestingly detached from the old city, is the **Fortezza di Santa Barbara**.

San Domenico

The Dominicans founded their monastery in the city in 1125. Its church, **San Domenico** (daily: April–Oct 7am–1pm & 3–6.30pm; Nov–March 9am–1pm & 3–6pm), begun in 1226, is a vast, largely Gothic building, typical of the austerity of this militaristic order. The Catherine association is immediately asserted. On the right of the entrance is a kind of raised chapel, the **Cappella delle Volte**, with a contemporary portrait of her by her friend and disciple Andrea Vanni, who according to tradition captured her likeness from life during one of her ecstasies in 1414; below are steps and a niche, where she received the stigmata, took on the Dominican habit, and performed several of her miracles. The saint's own chapel, the **Cappella di Santa Caterina** (1488), is located midway down the right (south) side of the church. Its entrance arch has images of saints Luke and Jerome by Sodoma, while the marble tabernacle on the high altar (1466) encloses a reliquary containing Catherine's head (other parts of her body lie dotted across Italy). The church's highlights, however – **frescoes** by Sodoma (1526) – occupy the walls to the left and right of the altar and, respectively, depict her swooning and in ecstasy. Just to the left of the chapel, above the steps to the crypt, is a detached fresco of the *Madonna and Child, John the Baptist and Knight* by Pietro Lorenzetti.

Other notable paintings are found in some of the other chapels, especially the first to the right of the high altar, which contains a Matteo di Giovanni triptych of the *Madonna and Child with Sts Jerome and John the Baptist* and fragments of detached frescoes by Lippo Memmi and Andrea Vanni. The high altar boasts a fine marble tabernacle and two sculpted angels (1465) by the sculptor and architect Benedetto da Maiano, best known for the Palazzo Strozzi in Florence and several fine works in San Gimignano (see p.364). The second chapel to the left of the high altar houses *St Barbara, Angels and Sts Catherine and Mary Magdalene* surmounted by an *Epiphany*, considered the masterpiece of Matteo di Giovanni, though its effect is somewhat undermined by the odd eighteenth-century frescoes around it. The more appealing *Madonna and Child with Saints* (1483) opposite is by the Florentine-influenced Benvenuto di Giovanni.

Casa di Santa Caterina

St Catherine's family home, where she lived as a Dominican tertiary – of the order but not resident – is just south of San Domenico, down the hill on Via Santa Caterina. Known as the **Casa e Santuario di Santa Caterina** (daily 9am–12.30pm & 3–6pm; free), the building has been much adapted, with a Renaissance loggia and a series of oratories – one on the site of her cell. The paintings here are mostly unexceptional Baroque canvases but it is the life that is important (see box above).

Near the Santuario are the church of **Santa Caterina**, home of the Oca (goose) *contrada* – known as *gli infami* ("the infamous ones") after their record number of Palio victories – and, down in the valley, the best-preserved of Siena's several fountains, the **Fonte Branda**. Aided by the fountain's reliable water supply, this part of the city was an area for tanneries into the twentieth century. The fountain also features in Sienese folklore as the haunt of werewolves, who would throw themselves into the water at dawn to return to human form.

Monte dei Paschi di Siena and north

Between the two monastic churches lies the heart of business Siena, the **Piazza Salimbeni**, whose three interlocking *palazzi* have formed, since the fifteenth century, the head office of the **Monte dei Paschi di Siena**. Banking was at the heart of medieval Sienese wealth, the town capitalizing on its position on the Via Francigena, the "French road" between Rome and northwest Europe, and the main road between Rome and Florence and Bologna. Sienese banking families go back to the twelfth century and by the end of the thirteenth they were trading widely in France, Germany, Flanders, England and along the Danube, where they maintained networks of corresponding dealers. Activity declined after the Black Death but in the fifteenth century the Republic set up the Monte dei Paschi di Siena as a lending and charitable institution, to combat the abuses of usury. It consolidated its role under Medici rule and slowly moved into more strictly banking activities. In the twentieth century it merged with other Tuscan and Umbrian banks to become one of the key financial institutions in Italy.

There is some historical interest in the exteriors of the bank's *palazzi*: the **Spannocchi**, on the right, was the first great Renaissance palace built in Siena (1473) and the prototype for the Palazzo Strozzi in Florence, while the **Salimbeni**, in the centre, was a last flourish of Gothicism. However, to appreciate the role of the *Monte* in Siena you need to tour the building. In 1972, Pierluigi Spadolino undertook a **radical restructuring**, encasing the building's interior medieval and Renaissance features within an ultra-modern and hi-tech framework. This is a sight in itself, but it also provides a wonderful showcase for the bank's **art collection** – the bulk of which is housed in the deconsecrated church of San Donato, linked by an underground passage with the main *palazzi*. The paintings here include some of the finest Gothic works in Siena, among them an exquisitely coloured *Madonna* by Giovanni di Paolo, a *Deposition* by Sano di Pietro and a *Crucifixion* by Pietro Lorenzetti. Also displayed are a series of paintings depicting the Palio and its sixteenth-century bullfighting precursor in the Campo.

The bank sometimes exhibits its art collections during banking hours and occasionally by **appointment** only (details from the tourist office). With any luck, you will be shown the archives and major halls of the bank, as well as the paintings, and the visit ends with a trip up to the tower for a view over the Campo.

To Porta Camollia and the Fortezza

Heading north from the Piazza Salimbeni, Banchi di Sopra changes name to **Via dei Montanini** and then **Via di Camollia**, which run through the less monumental parts of the Terzo di Camollia, good for regular shopping and largely untouristed bars and restaurants.

Two churches are worth a brief look on this street, though both are only rarely open. **Santa Maria delle Nevi** contains a famous altarpiece – *Our Lady of the Snows* (1477) – by Matteo di Giovanni, while **San Bartolomeo** fronts one of the nicest *contrada* squares in the city, home of the Istrice (porcupine); the *contrada* has its museum at Via Camollia 87 (visits to be booked a week in advance:

Ⓣ0577.48.495). At the end of the street is the Renaissance **Porta Camollia**, inscribed on its outer arch "Siena opens her heart to you wider than this gate." It was here that a vastly superior Florentine force was put to flight in 1526, following the traditional Sienese appeal to the Virgin.

A short distance east of Banchi di Sopra – reached by a circuitous network of alleys – is another of the city's fountains, the **Fonte Nuova**. A further, highly picturesque fountain, the **Fonte Ovile**, is to be seen outside the Porta Ovile, a hundred metres or so beyond. Both were built at the end of the twelfth century. Near Fonte Nuova, in Via Vallerozzi, is the church of **San Rocco**, home of the Lupa (she-wolf) *contrada*; its museum is at nos. 71–73 (visits by appointment; Ⓣ0577.270.777).

Away to the west, behind the church of Santo Stefano, the gardens of **La Lizza** – taken over on Wednesdays by the town's large market – lead up to the walls of the **Fortezza di Santa Barbara** (free access). The fortress was built initially by Charles V after the siege of 1554–55, but subsequently torn down by the people, and had to be rebuilt by Cosimo I, who then moved his troops into the garrison. Its Medicean walls resemble the walls of Lucca, designed by the same architect. Occasional summer concerts are held within the fort, which is also a permanent home to the wine collections and bar of the *Enoteca Italiana* (see p.354).

San Francesco

St Bernardino, born in the year of Catherine's death, began his preaching life at the chill monastic church of **San Francesco**, across the city to the east. A huge, hall-like structure, like that of San Domenico, it has been heavily restored after damage by fire in 1655 and subsequent use as a barracks. Its remaining art works include fragmentary frescoes by Pietro and Ambrogio Lorenzetti: a *Crucifixion* (1331) by Pietro in the first chapel to the left of the high altar and two collaborative frescoes in the third chapel to the left of the high altar (the latter depicting *St Louis of Toulouse becoming a Franciscan* and the graphic *Martyrdom of Six Franciscans at Ceuta in Morocco*). There is also a glittering polyptych by Lippo Vanni of the *Madonna and Child with Four Saints* (1370) in the sacristy (entered from the right of the south transept). It's also worth hunting down the detached fresco right of the entrance door, its choir of angels part of a *Coronation of the Virgin* (1447) by Sassetta that once decorated the city's original Porta Romana. It was completed by Sano di Pietro, a pupil of Sassetta, after the master contracted a fatal chill while working outdoors on the fresco.

If you walk to the end of the right (south) aisle, you'll find the fourteenth-century **Tomba dei Tolomei**, the best of the church's many funerary monuments. It houses various scions of the Tolomei, one of Siena's grandest medieval families. The clan provided numerous of the city's bankers, as well as some of its leading churchmen, among them Bernardo Tolomei, founder of the abbey at Monte Oliveto Maggiore (see p.391). Also buried here is Pia de'Tolomei, first wife of Baldo Tolomei who came to live in Siena after his marriage to his second wife. Pia died, consumed with jealousy, in a castle in the Maremma, prompting Dante's famous reference to her in the *Purgatorio*: *Siena me fé, disfecemi Maremma* ("Siena made me, the Maremma unmade me").

Oratorio di San Bernardino and Museo Diocesano

In the piazza to the right of San Francesco as you face the church, adjoining the cloisters, is the **Oratorio di San Bernardino** (mid-March to Oct Mon–Sat 10.30am–1.30pm & 3–5.30pm; closed the rest of the year; €3, or joint ticket – see p.327). The best art works here are in the beautifully wood-panelled upper chapel: fourteen large **frescoes** by Sodoma, Beccafumi and Girolamo del Pacchia on the *Life of the Virgin*, painted between 1496 and 1518 when the former pair were Siena's leading painters. In the lower chapel are seventeenth-century scenes of the saint's life, which was taken up by incessant travel throughout Italy, preaching against usury, denouncing the political strife between the Italian city states and urging his audience to look for inspiration to the monogram of Christ. Sermons in the Campo, it is said, frequently went on for the best part of a day. Bernardino's actual political influence was fairly marginal but he was canonized within six years of his death in 1444, and remains one of the most famous of all Italian preachers. His dictum on rhetoric – "make it clear, short and to the point" – was rewarded in the 1980s with his adoption as the patron saint of advertising.

Attached to the Oratorio is the **Museo Diocesano** (same hours and tickets), which contains an array of devotional art from the thirteenth to the seventeenth centuries; the pieces are beautifully displayed, but as a collection it ranks well below the Museo dell'Opera del Duomo.

Eating and drinking

Siena feels distinctly provincial after Florence. The main action of an evening is the *passeggiata* from Piazza Matteotti along Banchi di Sopra to the Campo – and there's not much in the way of nightlife to follow. For most visitors, though, an evening in one of the city's **restaurants** provides diversion enough, while the presence of the university ensures a bit of life in the **bars**, as well as a cluster of cheaper *trattorie* alongside the restaurants.

Restaurants

Siena used to have a poor reputation for **restaurants** but over the last few years things have improved, with a range of imaginative *osterie* opening up and a general hike in standards. The only place you need surrender gastronomic ideals is for a meal out in the Campo: the posh restaurant here, *Il Campo*, isn't worth the money – though it's the one to go for if you want to eat in style in the square – which leaves a choice of routine but reasonably priced pizzerias. For cheaper meals, you'll generally do best walking out a little from the centre, west towards San Niccolò al Carmine, or north towards the Porta Camollia.

Local specialities include *pici* (noodle-like pasta with toasted breadcrumbs), *salsicce secche* (dried sausages), *finocchiona* (minced pork flavoured with fennel), *capolocci* (spiced loin of pork), *pappa col pomodoro* (bread and tomato soup), *tortino di carciofi* (artichoke omelette) and *fagioli all'uccelletto* (bean and sausage stew). The city is also famous for its **cakes and biscuits**, including the ubiquitous *panforte*, a dense and delicious wedge of nuts, fruit and honey that originated with pilgrimage journeys, *cavallucci* (aniseed, nut and spice biscuits), *copate* (nougat wafers) and *ricciarelli* (rich almond biscuits).

All restaurants listed overleaf are marked on the **map** on p.324.

Al Marsili Via del Castoro 3 ☎ 0577.47.154, ⓦ www.ristorantealmarsili.it. A large, elegant and upmarket restaurant with good local dishes (including some choice for vegetarians) and attentive service. The *risotto al limone* is worth dallying over, plus they have plenty of more exotic dishes such as guinea fowl with prunes, pine nuts and almonds. €40 buys a memorable meal.

Antica Osteria Da Divo Via Franciosa 29 ☎ 0577.286.054. A close second behind *Osteria Le Logge* for ambience, thanks to its extraordinary subterranean cellar dining rooms. Upstairs is pretty, too, and the food is well above average, with starters at €8–12 and mains at €15–24. Closed Tues.

Cane e Gatto Via Pagliaresi 6 ☎ 0577.220.751. Don't be put off by the un-Sienese Art Nouveau-style decor: this friendly restaurant serves superb Tuscan *cucina nuova*, featuring seven courses on its *menù degustazione*, or tasting menu (around €75, with a selection of wines included). Closed Thurs and lunch daily.

Da Trombicche Via delle Terme 66 ☎ 0577.288.089. A tiny, youthful, no-nonsense trattoria with a limited menu of glorified snacks – soup, cheese, salami and meat stews – accompanied by rough wine served straight from the barrel. Closed Sun.

Gallo Nero Via del Porrione ☎ 0577.284.356, ⓦ www.gallonero.it. A quirky, vaulted place, offering a Tuscan menu for around €18, or a six-course medieval menu for €27, boasting dishes such as sweet and sour duck with cheese ravioli and chicken in sweet wine with fruit. Closed Mon Nov–Feb.

La Cina Casato di Sotto 56 ☎ 0577.283.061. Quiet, affordable Chinese restaurant 150m from the Campo. The food is adequate, and makes a change from Tuscan cooking.

Le Campane Via delle Campane 6 ☎ 0577.284.035. High-quality and innovative Sienese cuisine, with an emphasis on fish and seafood, at a small, formal restaurant just below the Duomo. Set menus – meat or fish – cost around €45. Closed Mon.

Osteria Boccone del Prete Via di San Pietro 17 ☎ 0577.280.388. One of Siena's newer restaurants, near the Pinacoteca Nazionale, serving delicious *crostini*, salads and pasta dishes in a stylish setting. Closed Sun.

Osteria Castelvecchio Via di Castelvecchio 65 ☎ 0577.49.586. First-rate, pleasantly informal and moderately priced, and a good bet for vegetarians (plus plenty of meat dishes and home-made pasta too). Menus change daily. Closed Tues & July.

Osteria del Ficomezzo Via dei Termini 71 ☎ 0577.222.384. A small, simple *osteria* a touch off the tourist track with a cool, pastel interior: good value set-price menus at lunch, with innovative Tuscan food (menus change weekly), and pricier à la carte in the evening. Closed Sun.

Osteria Il Carroccio Via del Casato di Sotto 32 ☎ 0577.41.165. Just 50m from the Campo, this small *osteria* has few tables but serves up fine Tuscan food in a welcoming, informal atmosphere. Menus change weekly. Closed Wed.

Osteria Il Grattacielo Via Pontani 8 ☎ 0577.289.326. A very local *vinaio* serving wine and snacks, this minuscule café-*osteria* – ironically named "The Skyscraper" – makes a popular lunch stop for its marinated anchovies, Tuscan beans and salami.

Osteria Le Logge Via del Porrione 33 ☎ 0577.48.013. The best-looking restaurant in central Siena, occupying a fine old cabinet-lined *farmacia* off the Campo by the Loggia del Papa. Good pasta and some unusual *secondi*, but the quality of food – once exceptional – is these days merely above average. Closed Sun.

Taverna del Capitano Via del Capitano 8 ☎ 0577.288.094. A serene dining room with medieval vaulted ceiling and straight-down-the-line Tuscan cooking: *panzanella* (bread salad), *pici*, *bistecche* and the like. Reports suggest the once impeccable food and service can slip in the face of large numbers of would-be diners. Closed Tues.

Tullio ai Tre Cristi Vicolo Provenzano 1 ☎ 0577.280.608. A Sienese institution since 1830, this is the traditional neighbourhood restaurant of the Giraffa *contrada* – though its prices these days are those of a top-end establishment. A good, if smart and expensive place for a romantic meal or treat. Serves an ambitious, predominantly fish and seafood menu. Terrace tables in summer. Closed Wed.

Nightlife and entertainment

There are pleasant neighbourhood **bars** in most *contrade* and plenty of modern establishments scattered around the city for quick refreshment. The *Enoteca Italiana* (Mon noon–8pm, Tues–Sat noon–1am; ☎ 0577.288.497, ⓦ www.enoteca-italiana.it), inside the Fortezza di Santa Barbara (see p.352), is Italy's largest

Palio practicalities

It's not hard to get a view of any of the practice races or ceremonies, but for the Palio proper you need to plan ahead a little. **Tickets** for grandstand or balcony seats, ranged around the Campo, cost from €150 to €300 or more, and are sold out months before the race. To nab a seat for next year's event, contact Palio Viaggi, Piazza Gramsci 7 (☏0577.280.828, ⓦwww.palioviaggi.it). In the UK, contact Liaisons Abroad (☏020/7376 4020, ⓦwww.liaisonsabroad.com).

Most ordinary spectators crowd for free into the centre of the Campo. For the **best view** you need to have found a position by 2pm on the inner rail (ideally at the start/finish line), and to keep it for the next six hours. If you're not installed here, there's really no rush, as you'll be able to see a certain amount from anywhere within the throng. Be prepared to stand your ground: people keep pouring in right up until a few minutes before the race, and the swell of the crowd can be overwhelming. Be aware that you won't be able to leave the Campo for at least two hours after the race. Toilets, shade and refreshment facilities are minimal (which is perhaps why so little drinking goes on). If you arrive late in the day, you might try making your way to Via Giovanni Dupré, behind the Palazzo Pubblico, from where the police usually allow people into the centre of the square an hour or so before the race.

Inevitably, **hotel rooms** are extremely difficult to find at Palio time, and if you haven't booked, either reckon on staying up all night, or travelling in from a neighbouring town. The races are shown live on national **TV** and repeated endlessly all evening.

For further details on the race, see *The Palio* colour section.

national **wine collection**. Its cellar stocks every single Italian wine (almost a thousand of them), and there's a bar where you can order a glass of any of the cheaper wines, or buy any bottle. You need to head to the *Dublin Post*, uninspiringly situated on Piazza Gramsci, or *Barone Rosso*, Via dei Termini 9, for a pint of beer, the latter open in the evenings only with live music until late. Of the terrace cafés ringing the Campo, the small *Liberamente* at the corner of Casato dei Barbieri has more charm than most.

Club life is fairly limited in Siena but for a glimpse of the smart Sienese on the dance floor try *Al Cambio*, Via di Pantaneto 48 – a dark, moody place with conventional dance music and a steep entrance fee; somewhat livelier is the pub/disco *Barone Rosso* (see above), the local haunt of foreign students and Sienese army boys, with a fair selection of beers and a range of dance music.

City events and **festivals** are advertised on posters around Piazza Matteotti and in the Campo backstreets; the website ⓦwww.terresiena.it is also a good source of information. The most prestigious classical music festival – often featuring a major opera – is July and August's **Estate Musicale Chigiana**, organized by the Monte dei Paschi and Accademia Chigiana (☏0577.22.091, ⓦwww.chigiana.it), who also sponsor impressive concerts throughout the year. Other cultural events include **Siena Jazz** (☏0577.271.401, ⓦwww.sienajazz.it) in late July and August (concerts are held in venues around the city and the local area) and the modest but increasingly popular **Siena Film Festival** (☏0577.222.999, ⓦwww.sienafilmfestival.it) in September. The Siena supplement of *La Nazione* newspaper (ⓦwww.lanazione.it) has a **listings** section.

Listings

Bike rental DF Bike, some way from the centre at Via Massetana Romana 54 ℡ 0577.271.905, ⓦ www.dfbike.it; €15 daily, €85 weekly.
Hospital Loc. Le Scotte ℡ 0577.585.111.
Internet access Internet Train, Via di Città 121, and Via Pantaneto 54; MegaWeb, Via Pantaneto 132; both have long opening hours and charge around €1.50 for 15min (less for students).
Laundry Wash & Dry, Via Pantaneto 38 (daily 8am–9pm).
Left luggage At the TRA-IN bus information centre below Piazza Gramsci (daily 7am–7.45pm; €3.50 per piece for one day only). At the train station, there are self-service lockers on platform 1.
Lost property Comune di Siena, Casato di Sotto 23 (Mon–Fri 9am–12.30pm, Tues & Thurs also 3–5pm).
Market A huge weekly general market sprawls over La Lizza (Wed 8am–2pm).
Police The *Questura* is on Via del Castoro ℡ 0577.201.111.
Post office Piazza Matteotti 1 (Mon–Sat 8.15am–7pm).

Travel details

Trains

Siena to: Asciano (12 daily; 35min); Buonconvento (6 daily; 25min); Chiusi (12 daily; 1hr 35min); Empoli (hourly; 50min–1hr 20min; change for Pisa and Florence); Florence (9 daily; 1hr 40min); Grosseto (6 daily; 1hr 20min).

Buses

Siena to: Arezzo (8 daily; 1hr 30min); Asciano (3 daily; 1hr); Buonconvento (7 daily; 50min); Castellina in Chianti (7 daily; 35min); Castiglione della Pescaia (2 daily in summer; 1hr 55min); Chianciano (2 daily; 1hr 40min); Colle di Val d'Elsa (hourly; 30min); Florence (hourly; 1hr 15min); Gaiole in Chianti (5 daily; 50min); Grosseto (hourly; 1hr 25min); Monticiano (4 daily; 1hr 5min); Montalcino (7 daily; 1hr 15min); Montepulciano (5 daily; 1hr 25min); Monteriggioni (hourly; 25min); Pienza (6 daily; 1hr 15min); Poggibonsi (hourly; 45min); Radda in Chianti (5 daily; 55min); San Gimignano (10 daily; 1hr 15min); Sinalunga (2 daily; 50min).

7

The Sienese hill-towns

CHAPTER 7 # Highlights

✳ **Monteriggioni** Dante alluded to the towers of this fortified citadel, and they still lord it over the countryside today. See p.360

✳ **San Gimignano** Italy's best-known village, famous for its towers, its crowds and the stunning Collegiata, one of the most comprehensively frescoed churches in Tuscany. See p.364

✳ **Colle di Val d'Elsa** Intimate town with a medley of tiny churches and museums. See p.361

✳ **Volterra** Moody hill-town with its roots in the Etruscan era, now celebrated for its alabaster workshops. See p.375

▲ The walls of Monteriggioni

The Sienese hill-towns

Just as Siena provides a perfect antidote to Florence, so the rural **hill-towns** that cluster around the old capital of the Sienese Republic provide an intimate counterpoint to the larger towns that crowd in on the Tuscan capital. Most of Siena's satellites are more appealing than their Florentine equivalents, and benefit from surroundings that exemplify the timeless pastoral quality for which the region is renowned. **San Gimignano** is the pick of the bunch, thanks mainly to its famous towers, a vision of medieval perfection now badly compromised in summer by the huge numbers of day-trippers who crowd its warren of streets. That said, the fresco-lined Collegiata and a clutch of minor churches, not to mention one of Tuscany's best civic museums, are unmissable attractions, and well worth building an overnight stay around. **Monteriggioni**, a less well-known and thus less spoilt medieval village, is another must-see and can easily be incorporated into a visit to **Colle di Val d'Elsa**, another centuries-old enclave, but one that is often overlooked by visitors who are deterred by its unlovely outskirts. You should also try to fit **Volterra** into your itinerary; slightly cut off from the other Sienese hill-towns, it's a dramatically situated, brooding town whose Etruscan origins are never far from the surface. Known primarily for its archeological museum, it also has a fascinating art gallery and a captivating cathedral square.

From Siena to San Gimignano

Heading west from Siena, most people have San Gimignano firmly in their sights. If you have time, the best route to follow is the N2 as far as the turreted fortress-hamlet of **Monteriggioni**, then turn west to **Colle di Val d'Elsa**, whose striking medieval upper town extends along a narrow ridge. From Colle, a scenic and minor road, which walkers might try paralleling across country, runs on via Bibbiano to San Gimignano.

On **public transport**, you can stop easily enough at Colle, before catching another bus to the industrial town of Poggibonsi – and a connection from there to San Gimignano; for Monteriggioni, you can catch a bus to the turning up to the village (and hail another one on from there to Colle or back to Siena). Most

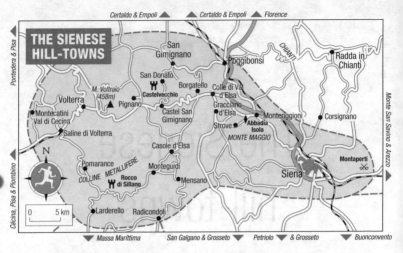

buses from Siena to San Gimignano involve a Poggibonsi connection, though there's a direct service in summer.

Note that the route north from Poggibonsi to Empoli – via Certaldo and Castelfiorentino – is covered from p.220 onwards.

Monteriggioni

The perfectly preserved walls of **MONTERIGGIONI** declare their presence for miles ahead from the N2 and the Siena–Florence *autostrada*. The citadel, begun by the Sienese in 1213, was a strategic target for any troops marching on Siena from the north and is immortalized in Dante's *Inferno*, in which he compares the fourteen towers – added during reconstruction in 1260 after the Sienese victory at Montaperti – to giants in an abyss. The verse greets you on the wall of the gate as you enter the village, which consists of a couple of dozen houses, the odd restaurant and bar and several overpriced tourist outlets. The houses give way to gardens as they near the ramparts, and an athlete could probably run the main street, from south to north gates, in about ten seconds. All of which, of course, accounts for the charm of the place, though like San Gimignano, it's severely compromised in summer by the legions of day-trippers.

You don't necessarily need a car or bike to reach Monteriggioni: the **train station** is 2km north at Castellina Scalo, about twenty-minutes' walk away. There's a small **tourist office**, Largo Fontebranda 5 (May–Oct daily 9.30am–5.30pm; Nov–April Tues–Sun 1.30–7pm; ☎0577.304.810), which has details of **private rooms**. There's a classy and very pleasant four-star **hotel**, the *Monteriggioni*, at Via I Maggio 4 (☎0577.305.009, ⓦwww.hotelmonteriggioni.net; ➐), whose twelve rooms – despite steep prices – are quickly snapped up.

Of the two moderately priced **restaurants**, *Il Pozzo* (☎0577.304.127; closed Sun eve & Mon) in Piazza Roma, the main square, is perhaps the best. Some 4km west at Via Matteotti 22 in the hamlet of Strove is the hotel *La Casalta* – worth the trip just for its excellent and moderately priced restaurant (☎0577.301.238; closed Wed, early Jan to mid-March & ten days in Nov). Midway to Strove are the outstanding Romanesque church and monastic remains of **Abbadia Isola**, originally (as the name suggests) an abbey set on an island amid marshes. If the church is closed ask for the key from the caretaker in the house to the left of the church or at the bar across the road.

Colle di Val d'Elsa

COLLE DI VAL D'ELSA, despite plentiful bus connections to Siena and San Gimignano, is not much explored. Perhaps **Colle Bassa**, the lower town, puts visitors off: paper-making, and then nail factories, have long made it a prosperous place, and today it's a sprawl of light industry and housing developments. However, the walled upper town, **Colle Alta**, is a beauty, stretching along a ridge with its one long street lined with medieval *palazzi*.

Of pre-Roman foundation, the town occupies a noted place in the annals of Florentine and Sienese rivalry, for it was at the **Battle of Colle** in 1269 that the Florentines bloodily avenged their defeat by the Sienese at the Battle of Montaperti nine years earlier. The town then vacillated between the two powers, but also retained a measure of independence, its free *comune* instigating the office of *Capitano del Popolo* in 1286, just a few years after Florence and Siena. It remained racked by factional disputes, and in 1333 voluntarily put itself under the protection of Florence. The ensuing period of relative peace enabled the town to develop its wool and paper industries, both of which made use of the abundant supplies of local water, which was channelled through the area in a series of specially built canals. Glass and paper are still local specialities.

Colle Bassa

Colle Bassa's main square, **Piazza Arnolfo**, is named after Arnolfo di Cambio, the architect of the Duomo and Palazzo Vecchio in Florence, who was born here around 1232. A block north is the town's major piece of modern architecture, the regional headquarters of the Monte dei Paschi bank, designed by Giovanni Michelucci; mixing Portakabin-like offices with open girders, it's not one of his most captivating efforts.

Just south of the piazza at Via dei Fossi 8a is the **Museo del Cristallo** (Easter–Oct Tues–Sun 10am–noon & 4–7.30pm; Nov–Easter Tues–Fri 3–7pm, Sat & Sun 10am–noon & 3–7pm; ⓦ www.cristallo.org; €3). Built on the site of an eighteenth-century glass furnace, the museum outlines the transition from Colle's traditional glass-making industry from pre-industrial pieces to 1820, the year of the first furnace, and from 1820 to the beginning of crystal production in 1963; today, Colle produces 95 percent of Italy's, and 15 percent of the world's, crystal. Virtually next door to the museum is Colle Bassa's only other worthwhile sight, the thirteenth-century church of **Sant'Agostino**, largely rebuilt by Antonio da Sangallo the Elder in 1521, three years after embarking on his masterpiece, the church of San Biagio in Montepulciano (see p.420). The second altar on the right contains a glorious *Madonna and Child with Saints* by Taddeo di Bartolo, probably a surviving panel of a triptych. The eye-catching marble tabernacle in the north aisle, the *Madonna del Piano*, is attributed to Baccio da Montelupo (1469–1535).

Colle Alta

From Piazza Arnolfo, it's a pretty steep ten-minute climb up to **Colle Alta**: follow Via San Sebastiano and then the brick-paved *costa*, which brings you out at the eastern tip of the town. If you drive or take a bus up, you're directed around a circuitous route to the west end of the ridge, by the Porta Nuova.

At the top of the *costa*, you've little choice but to follow **Via del Castello**, the centre of a three-street grid, past a scattering of tower houses; Arnolfo di Cambio was born at no. 63, in the so-called Torre di Arnolfo. Just a little further down is the small Romanesque church of **Santa Maria in Canonica**, built in the twelfth or thirteenth century, but thought to have far older origins. Its interior is notable for a stupendous late fourteenth-century tabernacle of the

Madonna and Child with Saints by Pier Francesco Fiorentino; the frame, almost as impressive as the painting, is original.

Midway along Via del Castello, the **Piazza del Duomo** opens out, flanked by the cathedral and three museums. The **Duomo**, its Romanesque origins all but obliterated by later remodelling (1603–1815), features a marble pulpit (1465) by Giuliano da Maiano, who used four pillars and capitals from a much older work to frame his bas-reliefs. His brother Benedetto was responsible for the font (1468), the two having worked together during the same period in San Gimignano. The fourth chapel on the right has a famous *Nativity* (1635), the masterpiece of Rutilio Manetti, the leading Sienese follower of Caravaggio. In the depths of the right transept stands the Cappella del Santo Chiodo, commissioned by the Piccolomini pope, Pius II, to house a nail (*chiodo*) from the Cross, the relic providing the inspiration for the beautiful tabernacle attributed to Mino da Fiesole. The nearby bronze lectern, palm branch and eagle are by Pietro Tacca, a pupil of Giambologna, whose eccentric work will be familiar if you've seen his strange fountains in Florence's Piazza Santissima Annunziata. Tacca also probably cast the impressive bronze Crucifix above the high altar, the work having been designed by Giambologna.

In the Palazzo Pretorio (1335) beside the Duomo, at Via del Castello-Piazza del Duomo 42, is the **Museo Archeologico "Ranuccio Bianchi Bandinelli"** (May–Oct Tues–Sun 10.30am–12.30pm & 4.30–7.30pm; Nov–April Tues–Fri 4.30–6.30pm, Sat & Sun 10am–noon & 4.30–7.30pm; €3). It's only of passing interest, save for the finds from the local *Tomba dei Calisna Sepu*, one of Tuscany's most important Etruscan tombs: key treasures from it are scattered in museums as far afield as Berlin. Just out of the piazza, the attractive three-room **Museo Civico e d'Arte Sacra** housed in the Palazzo dei Priori, the old bishop's palace at Via del Castello 31 (Tues–Sun 11am–6pm, but hours vary; €3), is more interesting, retaining frescoes of hunting scenes by Bartolo di Fredi. It has a fair collection of Sienese paintings gathered from local churches, with more works due to be installed here. The most interesting canvas is a *Maestà* from Abbadia Isola, once attributed to Duccio, but now given to the anonymous Maestro di Badia a Isola.

About 100m beyond Piazza del Duomo stands the **Palazzo Campana**, a Mannerist *tour de force* built in 1539 by Baccio d'Agnolo, the architect responsible for the rather less amenable Palazzo Bartolini in Florence. From here, a bridge connects the town's medieval core to its fifteenth- and sixteenth-century expansions. Off to the north stands an imposing Franciscan monastery, whose church, **San Francesco**, claims a high altarpiece (occasionally removed) of the *Madonna and Child with Four Saints* (1479) by Sano di Pietro, a painting that's more than worth the walk (ring the bell of the seminary if the church is shut). The scenes in the predella illustrate episodes from the lives of the saints depicted in the main painting (Benedict, Cyrinus, Donatus and Justina). The second panel from the left shows Cyrinus, a Croatian saint, preaching to the crowd that has come to watch his martyrdom: he's shown miraculously floating on the stone that had been tied round his neck in an attempt to drown him. Donatus, patron saint of Arezzo (his birthplace), was martyred in the fourth century, and is remembered primarily for frightening off a dragon which had been poisoning local wells: Sano shows him with his mule, bravely marching to meet the dragon emerging from its cave. The right-hand scene shows the third-century Justina, a royal princess, patron of Padua but much venerated in Pisa, being martyred on the orders of her father.

Practicalities

Inter-town **buses** from Florence, Siena, Volterra and elsewhere stop in Colle Bassa's Piazza Arnolfo. The **tourist office** is in Colle Alta at Via Francesco

Campana 43 (April–Oct Mon–Sat 10am–1pm & 2.30–7pm, Sun 10am–1pm & 3–6pm; Nov–Jan & March Mon–Sat 10am–1pm & 2.30–5pm; ℡0577.922.791, ⓦwww.comune.colle-di-val-d-elsa.si.it). Colle's busy Friday **market** spreads out from Piazza Arnolfo.

The only budget **hotel** is the 24-room, two-star *Nazionale*, in Colle Bassa just west of Piazza Arnolfo, at Via Garibaldi 20 (℡0577.920.039, ℻0577.920.168; ❷). A more upmarket option is the three-star *La Vecchia Cartiera*, just off the piazza at Via Oberdan 5–9 (℡0577.921.107, ⓦwww .chiantiturismo.it; ❺). The only hotel in Colle Alta is the three-star *Arnolfo*, Via Francesco Campana 8 (℡0577.922.020, ⓦwww.hotelarnolfo.it; ❸) – very central, although it can be noisy. Some 2km out of town, the *Hotel Villa Belvedere* (℡0577.920.966, ⓦwww.villabelvedere.com; ❺) occupies an eighteenth-century villa on the Monteriggioni road, with fifteen rooms, fine grounds, tennis courts and a pool.

Food provides a major spur to a couple of hours' exploration. In Alta, at Piazza B. Scala 11, *Da Simone* (℡0577.926.701; ⓦwww.ristorantedasimone.it; closed Mon) is a great little Tuscan restaurant with moderate prices. Otherwise, investigate the two-Michelin-starred ⁂ *Arnolfo*, Via XX Settembre 50–52a (℡0577.920.549, ⓦwww.arnolforistorante.com; closed Tues & Wed and periods in late Jan & Aug), worth the expense (starters around €25, mains €35) for a wonderful meal. Off Piazza Santa Caterina in Vicolo delle Fontanelle 4 is the *Enoteca della Fortuna* (℡0577.923.102), a wine shop with a tiny upstairs restaurant. In Bassa, try the large and beautifully converted twelfth-century mill, the *Molino il Moro* at Via della Ruota 2 (℡0577.920.862; closed Mon & lunch on Tues), for good, moderately priced local food and wine.

Casole d'Elsa

The roads south of Colle di Val d'Elsa lead into the **Colline Metallífere** (Metal Hills), dotted with geothermal energy plants (the largest are out towards Larderello) and their snaking pipelines. Other sights are few, though the countryside, as ever, is liberally sprinkled with Romanesque churches and inspiringly placed farmhouses and cypress groves.

One very pretty rural route leads through **CASOLE D'ELSA**, a village which looks inviting from a distance but yields relatively little of substantial interest. Buses also pass this way from Colle. Council offices now occupy Casole's fortress, the village's most imposing sight. An Etruscan tomb discovered nearby, reputedly one of the richest ever found, contributed some of the treasures in the attractively presented **Museo Civico e della Collegiata**, Piazza del Duomo 2 (Tues–Fri 10am–noon & 4–7pm; €3), which also has rooms devoted to painting and the decorative arts. Highlights of the latter rooms are a *Maestà* by a follower of Duccio, several works by Alessandro Casolani, a sixteenth-century artist, and a bust of Bishop Tommaso Andrei, a local cleric who died in 1303, by Gano di Fazio. The museum stands alongside the fifteenth-century Gothic **Collegiata** church (restored after war bomb damage), which holds an important *Madonna and Child* and *Massacre of the Innocents* by Andrea di Niccolò, and a *Madonna and Child* attributed to Segna di Buonaventura.

Casole's **tourist office** is at Piazza della Libertà 1 (same hours as Museo Civico; ℡0577.948.705 or 0577.949.737). A **market** is held in the piazza on the first and third Monday of the month. The stunning *Relais La Suvera* (℡0577.960.300, ⓦwww.lasuvera.it; ❾) is a sumptuous five-star hotel in the nearby hamlet of **Pievescola**. Originally a Sienese castle, it was converted into a villa by Baldassare Peruzzi during the Renaissance. With its loggia, extensive grounds, stepped terraces, antique furniture, priceless works of art, ritzy suites and beautiful rooms, it's ranked by many as Tuscany's finest hotel of its type.

Poggibonsi

POGGIBONSI, 8km east of San Gimignano, has little more than its transport links and its politics to recommend it. A serious industrial town, conspicuously ugly alongside its Tuscan neighbours, it is home to what is reputed to be Italy's reddest council. Prior to World War II, it might have looked more like Colle, but bombing left little trace of its past other than the **Castello della Magione**, a little Romanesque complex, possibly with Templar origins, consisting of a chapel and pilgrim hospice. The unfinished Medici fort at the top of the town isn't worth the slog, although the superb four-star **hotel** up here is: the *Villa San Lucchese*, Località San Lucchese 5 (T0577.937.119, Wwww.villasanlucchese .com; ⑥), is a lovely villa hotel with pool and tennis courts in a rural setting that seems a world away from the tatty town below.

San Gimignano

SAN GIMIGNANO – "delle Belle Torri" – is perhaps the best-known village in Italy, 27km northwest of Siena. Its stunning skyline of towers, built in aristocratic rivalry by the feuding nobles of the twelfth and thirteenth centuries, evokes the appearance of medieval Tuscany more than any other sight. And its image as a "Medieval Manhattan" has for decades caught the tourist imagination, helped along by its convenience as a day-trip from Florence or Siena.

The town is all that it's cracked up to be: quietly monumental, very well preserved, enticingly rural and with a fine array of religious and secular frescoes. However, from Easter until October, San Gimignano has very little life of its own – and a lot of day-trippers, who don't always respect the place: antisocial behaviour and litter are starting to become a problem. If you want to get any feel for the town, beyond the level of art treasures or quaintness, you really need to come well out of season. If you can't, then aim to spend the night here: in the evenings San Gimignano takes on a very different pace and atmosphere.

Some history

San Gimignano was probably founded by the **Etruscans** – tombs in the surrounding countryside bear witness to their presence – and later inhabited by the **Romans**. It reputedly took its name in 450 from St Gimignano, a bishop of Modena, whose intervention is supposed to have saved the settlement from the attacks of Attila the Hun. During the tenth century a feudal castle was built on the site, a stronghold that was soon surrounded by a cluster of houses, and which, by the twelfth century, had become a free *comune*. A second (surviving) set of walls was added in the middle of the thirteenth century, about the time that the town's predominantly wooden houses began to be replaced by stone structures and the first of the famous **towers**.

Wealth increased during the Middle Ages, and San Gimignano's population of 15,000 (twice the present number) prospered as a result of agricultural holdings and a position close to the Via Francigena, the ancient trade and pilgrimage route between Rome and northern Europe. In its heyday, during the fourteenth century, the town's walls enclosed five monasteries, four hospitals, public baths and a brothel. A force to be reckoned with, the town was mostly controlled by two great families, the Ardinghelli and the Salvucci – heads of the **Guelph** and

San Gimignano's first **festival** was held at the end of the 1920s, and except for a break during World War II has run just about every year since in July and August, with a series of classical concerts, plus theatre and open-air films.

These days the festival's quiet provincial air is increasingly compromised by snooty outsiders, particularly at the highlights of the event – the outdoor opera performances in Piazza del Duomo. The atmosphere remains cheerfully informal, however, with the steps of the Collegiata set aside as terracing for the town's kids. Even the official blurb exhorts you to *mettere il vestito della festa* and *cantare con la compagnia* ("put on your party clothes and sing along"). Details and tickets are available from the tourist office.

Ghibelline factions respectively. Inter-family feuds, however, had long wreaked havoc. The first conflict erupted in 1246, and for the following century there were few years of peace; whenever the town itself was united there were wars with Volterra, Poggibonsi and other nearby towns. The vendettas came to a halt only after the Black Death of 1348, which had a devastating effect both on the population and – as the pilgrim trade collapsed – on the economy. The Ardinghelli family, despite opposition from the Salvucci, applied to Florence for the town to become a part of that city's *comune*; the request was approved by only one vote, in a reflection of San Gimignano's fractious reputation.

Subjection to Florence in 1353 broke the power of the nobles, leaving San Gimignano unaffected by the struggles between aristocracy and local council that racked other Tuscan towns. The tower houses, symbolic of real control elsewhere, posed little threat and so were not torn down; today, fifteen (of an original 72) survive. The town itself, further hit by plague in 1464 and 1631, passed into a rural backwater existence. At the turn of the nineteenth century, travellers spoke of San Gimignano as "miserably poor"; it was hardly romanticized by E.M. Forster, who took the place (under the name Monteriano) as the setting for his novel *Where Angels Fear to Tread*. San Gimignano's postwar history has been one of ever-increasing affluence, through **tourism** and the production of an old-established, but recently rejuvenated, white **wine**, *Vernaccia di San Gimignano*.

Arrival and information

Most people visit San Gimignano as a day-trip from Siena. Using **public transport** you'll need to take a bus from Siena or a train or bus to Poggibonsi (40min) and then pick up one of the roughly hourly buses from the station for the twenty-minute journey to San Gimignano. There's also a fairly regular bus service from Colle Val d'Elsa.

Arriving by **bus**, you can get out either at Piazzale dei Martiri di Monte Maggio, just outside Porta San Giovanni, the south gate, or by the northern gate, Porta San Matteo. You can buy bus tickets and pick up timetables at the tourist office. The road that runs around the walls has three pay **car parks** – the simplest option for a short stay. Free parking is possible on the outskirts of town, close to Piazzale dei Martiri di Monte Maggio, but this is only worthwhile if you need a space for several days. To drive within the walls – not necessary unless you're dropping off luggage – you need to be issued with a permit from one of the hotels; the way in is through Porta San Jacopo at the northeast corner.

The helpful **tourist office** (daily 9am–1pm & 3–7pm; ☏0577.940.008, Ⓦwww.sangimignano.com) is on the south side of Piazza del Duomo.

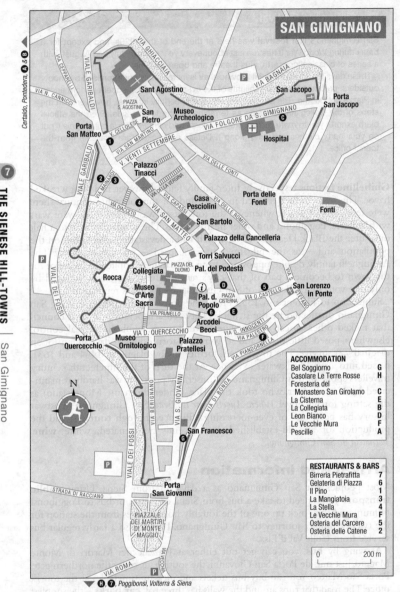

SAN GIMIGNANO

ACCOMMODATION

Bel Soggiorno	G
Casolare Le Terre Rosse	H
Foresteria del	
Monastero San Girolamo	C
La Cisterna	E
La Collegiata	B
Leon Bianco	D
Le Vecchie Mura	F
Pescille	A

RESTAURANTS & BARS

Birreria Pietrafitta	7
Gelateria di Piazza	6
Il Pino	1
La Mangiatoia	3
La Stella	4
Le Vecchie Mura	F
Osteria del Carcere	5
Osteria delle Catene	2

0   200 m

Accommodation

A crucial factor to enjoying the town is to get a room inside the walls –
which from Easter to October means booking ahead and/or arriving early
in the day. The town's main **hotels** are all expensive three-stars, but **private
rooms**, scattered around a dozen or so houses within the walls, offer a
budget alternative (doubles from around €40); most have shared bathrooms.

It's also possible to rent **apartments** by the day, but be sure to reserve ahead.

Accommodation is bookable for free through the very helpful **booking agency** Siena Hotels Promotion, located just inside the southern gate at Via San Giovanni 125 (Mon–Sat: summer 9.30am–7pm; winter 9.30am–12.30pm & 3–6pm; ☎0577.940.809, ⓦwww.sangimignano.com), which arranges rooms in hotels and private houses, apartments and agriturismo lets. The tourist office website (ⓦwww.sangimignano.com) provides details of **private rooms**. The nearest **campsite**, *Il Boschetto di Piemma* (☎0577.940.352, ⓔbpiemma@tiscalinet .it), with a bar, restaurant and pool, is in Santa Lucia, 3km downhill from Piazzale Martiri di Monte Maggio, off the Volterra road.

Bel Soggiorno Via San Giovanni 91 ☎0577.940.375, ⓦwww.pescille.it. Similar to the *Leon Bianco* in quality, price and facilities, though beware of having to take full board in summer. The 22 rooms – eight with a/c – are smallish but beautifully done. The restaurant rates quite highly, but you pay extra for breakfast. ⑤

🏃 **Casolare Le Terre Rosse** Località San Donato ☎0577.9021, ⓦwww.hotel terrerosse.com. A great choice out of town, in the hamlet of San Donato 4km to the southwest on the road to Castel San Gimignano. The three-star hotel has 42 rooms in a classic Tuscan country house in a lovely rural setting; the big pool is a summer draw. Closed Nov–Feb. ④

Foresteria del Monastero San Girolamo ☎0577.940.573, ⓕ0577.940.573. Nine rooms in a convent run by Benedictine nuns just behind Porta San Jacopo. €25 per person including breakfast, in private doubles; half price for children. ①

La Cisterna Piazza della Cisterna 24 ☎0577.940.328, ⓦwww.hotelcisterna.it. Elegant town hotel, established in 1919 and built into a medieval ensemble at the base of some of the piazza's fourteenth-century towers. It's worth paying more for a room with either a (potentially noisy) piazza outlook, or a (more restful) country-side view. ⑤

La Collegiata Località Strada 27 ☎0577.943.201, ⓦwww.lacollegiata.it. Sixteenth-century Franciscan convent 2km north of town off the Certaldo road, converted into one of Tuscany's new breed of super-expensive hotels, for very special occasions. Double rooms come in at around €520. ⑨

Le Vecchie Mura Via Piandornella 15 ☎0577.940.270, ⓔvecchiemura@tin.it. A couple of double rooms above a restaurant, but more appealing than it sounds, with welcoming owners and superb views. ①

Leon Bianco Piazza della Cisterna 13 ☎0577.941.294, ⓦwww.leonbianco.com. Tasteful three-star hotel with seventeen a/c rooms, occupying a fourteenth-century mansion in the main square. The better rooms, which have medieval features such as vaulted ceilings, look out over the square or the Val d'Elsa. The roof terrace for breakfast, drinks or lounging is a bonus. ⑤

Pescille Località Pescille, Strada Castel San Gimignano ☎0577.940.186, ⓦwww.pescille.it. A large three-star hotel ringed by vineyards and olive groves 4km north of town, with a pool and tennis courts. Rooms are restrained and suitably rustic: the best is the panoramic and eyrie-like Tower Room. Breakfast is available, but there's no restaurant. ④

The Town

San Gimignano is not much more than a village: you could walk from one end to the other in fifteen minutes, or around the walls in an hour. It deserves at least a day, however, both for the frescoes in the churches and museums, and for the surrounding countryside – some of the loveliest in Tuscany. From the fine south gate, **Porta San Giovanni** (1262) – the best place to start a tour – the *palazzo*-lined **Via San Giovanni** leads to the town's interlocking main squares, the Piazza della Cisterna and Piazza del Duomo. On the right of the street, about a hundred metres up, is the former church of **San Francesco** – a Pisan-style Romanesque building converted now, like many of the *palazzi*, to a shop selling Vernaccia and other local wines. Ignore the scrum around the tasting table and walk through to the lovely garden at the rear, where before tackling the town you can enjoy an incomparable view across the Tuscan hills.

You enter the **Piazza della Cisterna** through another majestic gateway, the **Arco dei Becci**, part of the original fortifications built before the town expanded and acquired its second set of thirteenth-century walls. The square is flanked by an anarchic cluster of towers and *palazzi*, and is named after the public cistern (1273) – still functioning – at its centre. The well was extended in 1346 on the orders of the then *Podestà*, Guccio de' Malvoli, whose coat of arms adorns one of the faces: note the rope-cut grooves, witness to centuries of use. It was in this square, and in other streets within the older inner walls, that most of the leading families had their houses.

The more austere **Piazza del Duomo** introduces further towers and civic *palazzi*. Facing the Duomo (more properly the **Collegiata**, as San Gimignano no longer has a bishop), the crenellated **Palazzo del Popolo** (or Palazzo Comunale), the town hall and home to the Museo Civico, stands to your left, the older **Palazzo del Podestà** (1239) behind you.

The Collegiata

The first church on the site of the **Collegiata** (April–Oct Mon–Fri 9.30am–7.10pm, Sat 9.30am–5.30pm, Sun 12.30–5.10pm; March & Nov–Jan Mon–Sat 9.30am–4.30pm, Sun 12.30–4.40pm; Feb religious services only; €3.50) was begun in the tenth century. Work on the present building began in the early twelfth century: it was then altered by Giuliano da Maiano in 1466. The plain facade (1239) could hardly provide a greater contrast with the **interior**, whose frescoes fill just about every available space, their brilliant colours offset by Pisan-Romanesque arcades of black and white striped marble.

The three principal **fresco cycles** fill the right and left walls, plus two short side walls which protrude from the inside wall of the facade. Beginning on this rear wall you'll find a fresco of *St Sebastian* (1465) by Benozzo Gozzoli, painted five or six years after the artist's fresco cycle in the Palazzo Medici-Riccardi in Florence (see p.124). Sebastian was often invoked during plague epidemics –

▲ Piazza della Cisterna, San Gimignano

San Gimignano's towers

The Palazzo del Popolo's **Torre Grossa** was completed in 1311, some time after a 1255 ordinance in which the *comune* decided that the town's tower-building frenzy had run its course. The **Torre della Rognosa** of the Palazzo del Podestà, which survives, was set as the maximum height (54m) for any subsequent private tower, the idea being that none should exceed the towers of the civic authorities. Looking around the skyline, it would seem that the rule was not much respected. The Salvucci clan, for example, responded at one point by building two towers in Via San Matteo, the **Torri Salvucci**, each shorter than the maximum, but arranged so close together as to make it clear that their combined height would be higher than anything conjured up by the *comune*.

To the left (northwest) of Piazza della Cisterna, beside an arch leading through to the Piazza del Duomo, are the twin Ardinghelli towers and palace; one of the Salvucci rivals rears up close by. The tower on the square's northeast flank, topping the Palazzo Cortesi, is known as the **Torre del Diavolo**, so named, according to legend, because its owner returned after a long journey convinced that it had grown taller, the only explanation for the phenomenon, he alleged, being that a DIY-inclined devil had been busy during his absence.

one had struck San Gimignano in 1464, which was the reason for Gozzoli's commission – thanks largely to his powers of recovery: he actually survived an assault with arrows – though remains the patron saint of archers: he was eventually martyred by being pummelled to death.

Either side of Sebastian, on pedestals, are two **statues** of the *Archangel Gabriel* and the *Madonna Annunciate*, carved by the Sienese sculptor Jacopo della Quercia in 1421 and given their garish painted finish by Martino di Bartolomeo five years later. In front of each statue are pillars painted with frescoes by Gozzoli of the *Annunciation* and saints Anthony, Augustine and Bernardino. These pillars anchor the side walls containing the first of the church's fresco cycles, Taddeo di Bartolo's *Last Judgement* (1410), with *Paradiso* depicted to the right, *Inferno* to the left. One of the most gruesome depictions of a customarily lurid subject, the latter offers a no-holds-barred illustration of the Seven Deadly Sins, including Bosch-like fantasies on lust and gluttony.

The church's other cycles depict scenes from the Old Testament (two tiers on the left wall) and the New Testament (two tiers on the right); in the lunettes above, scenes of the Creation above the Old Testament episodes are paralleled across the church by episodes from the Nativity. Somewhat surprisingly, the **Old Testament** and **Creation** scenes (26 in all), whose vision seems entirely medieval, were painted later, between 1356 and 1367. Created by Bartolo di Fredi, they reflect the influence of Lorenzetti's *Good and Bad Government* in Siena in their delight in narrative detail: *Abraham and Lot leading their flock towards Canaan*, for example, is a Tuscan farming scene, with appropriate landscape. They are also quirkily naturalistic – there are few odder frescoes than that of the *Drunkenness of Noah*, exposing a prominent penis in his stupor: Noah is traditionally considered to have been the first to promote agriculture and viticulture, and – more to the point – the first to have abused the products of the vine.

The cycle (which is read left to right, top to bottom) follows the story of the *Flood* with those of *Abraham and Lot* (their trip to Canaan), *Joseph* (his dream; being let down the well; having his brothers arrested and being recognized by them), *Moses* (changing a stick into a serpent before the Pharaoh; the Red Sea; Mount Sinai) and *Job* (temptation; the devil killing his herds and destroying his house; thanking God; and being consoled by friends). Above, note the fresco, perhaps the most beautiful of the entire cycle, depicting the *Creation of Eve* (fourth lunette from the left), in which Eve emerges from the rib of the sleeping Adam.

The authorship of the **New Testament** scenes (begun 1333) is disputed, with some historians now attributing them to Lippo Memmi, collaborator and brother-in-law of Simone Martini, or to a member of Memmi's workshop. Traditionally, the attribution is to Barna di Siena, another follower of Martini, possibly a pupil, who is supposed to have died in a fall from the scaffolding while at work here in the 1350s. Whatever, the scenes of Christ's Life and the Passion mark a distinct departure from Martini's style, with their interest in emotional expression. In *The Kiss of Judas* the focus of eyes is startlingly immediate, as is the absorption of all the figures in the action – St Peter thrusting into the foreground with his assault on the Roman soldier, while the other disciples gather their cloaks and flee. One of the most dramatic scenes of all is the *Resurrection of Lazarus*, in which a dumbstruck crowd witnesses the removal of a door to reveal the living Lazarus in the winding bandages of burial.

Cappella di Santa Fina

Many of the chapels of the cathedral were remodelled between 1468 and 1475 as part of Giuliano da Maiano's renovation of the church. The **Cappella di San Gimignano**, to the left of the high altar, features an altar by Giuliano's brother, Benedetto da Maiano, partly constructed from fragments of an earlier work, though both brothers reserved their best work for the **Cappella di Santa Fina**, a Renaissance masterpiece located at the top of the right (south) aisle. Giuliano designed the chapel (1468–75), while Benedetto designed its altar, marble shrine and bas-reliefs (1475), though the most eye-catching part of the ensemble, which is dedicated to San Gimignano's patron saint, is a pair of frescoes in opposing lunettes by Domenico Ghirlandaio (1475).

St Fina, the subject of the frescoes and the frieze of the shrine, was born in San Gimignano in 1238 and struck by a dreadful and incurable disease at the age of 10. She gave herself immediately to God, repented her sins (the worst seems to have been accepting an orange from a boy), and insisted on spending the agonized five years until her death lying on a plank on the floor (the idea being that she would be brought closer to Christ through increased suffering). As a result of her position, and her complete paralysis during her final days, she was tormented, among other things, by mice, which she was unable to scare away. The board, on her death, was found to be covered in flowers.

Both details appear in the fresco of the right lunette, which depicts the *Announcement of Death*, the time of Fina's demise having been vouchsafed to her by St Gregory in a vision (notice the flower-covered board and the mouse in the semi-darkness to the rear of the composition). The fresco in the opposite (left) lunette, the *Funeral of St Fina*, is said to have greatly impressed Raphael and shows the saint on her deathbed with the towers of San Gimignano in the background. Also depicted are three miracles associated with Fina: the restoration of a blind choirboy's sight; the curing of her nurse's paralysed hand; and the ringing of San Gimignano's bells by angels on the saint's death.

Ghirlandaio left a self-portrait (in the figure behind the bishop saying Mass), as well as portraits (in the figures to either side) of Davide, his brother, and Sebastiano Mainardi, his brother-in-law. Both probably assisted Ghirlandaio with the frescoes. The fresco's composition, with the dead saint surrounded by onlookers, owes much to Benozzo Gozzoli's almost identical scene painted ten years earlier in Sant'Agostino (see p.374), which in turn was influenced by Giotto's iconoclastic treatment of the *Funeral of St Francis* in Santa Croce in Florence (see p.142).

The Baptistery and Museo d'Arte Sacra

Accessed by a loggia in the same courtyard as the entrance to the Collegiata is the **Baptistery**, frescoed with an *Annunciation* by Ghirlandaio and Sebastiano Mainardi (1482). The **Museo d'Arte Sacra** (April–Oct Mon–Fri 9.30am–7.10pm, Sat 9.30am–5.10pm, Sun 12.30–5.10pm; Nov–March Mon–Sat 9.30am–4.40pm, Sun 12.30–4.40pm; €3) is housed in the old Rector's Palace off to the left of the court in Piazza Pecori. Its highlights include a *Madonna and Child* by Bartolo di Fredi, a superb wooden Crucifix, perhaps from as early as the eleventh century, several glorious illuminated choir books, and a marble bust of *Onofrio di Pietro* (1493) by Benedetto da Maiano, a work commissioned by San Gimignano's *comune* to honour Di Pietro, an eminent local scholar.

The Museo Civico and Pinacoteca

The Palazzo del Popolo, the other key component of the Piazza del Duomo, was begun in 1270, probably to a plan by Arnolfo di Cambio, born in nearby Colle di Val d'Elsa. Most of the building is devoted to the **Museo Civico**, home to an outstanding miscellany of paintings and to the **Torre Grossa**, the only one of San Gimignano's towers which you can climb (both daily: March–Oct 9.30am–7.20pm; Nov–Feb 10am–5.30pm; €5).

On entering the *palazzo* from the square you find yourself within a courtyard, built in 1323 during extension work on the palace. Its well (1360) incorporates fragments removed from local Etruscan tombs, while the stone crests around the walls represent the coats of arms of various medieval magistrates. A loggia opens on the right, from which justice and public decrees were occasionally proclaimed, hence the subject matter of its three frescoes, all of which make an allusion to justice: the left wall features an allegory (1513) by Sodoma depicting a throned magistrate flanked by the figures of Dishonesty, Prudence and Truth; in front is a *Madonna and Child* by Taddeo di Bartolo (the artist responsible for the Collegiata's *Last Judgement*) in which the Madonna is flanked by saints Gimignano and Gregory – the Child meanwhile holds a biblical inscription recommending sagacity in the administration of justice; the right wall features a chiaroscuro by Sodoma depicting St Ivo, a Breton lawyer whose pro bono legal work among the poor, widowed and orphaned saw him canonized in 1366 and made patron saint of lawyers, jurists and magistrates.

From the courtyard, stairs lead to the ticket office. The first of the museum's rooms and the *palazzo*'s public chambers, frescoed with hunting and tournament scenes, is known as the **Sala del Consiglio**, or Sala di Dante – the poet visited as Florence's ambassador to the town in 1300, making a plea here for Guelph unity. Most of the paintings displayed are fourteenth-century works, Sienese in origin or inspiration, and executed in the years before San Gimignano passed under Florentine control and influence. The room's highlight is Lippo Memmi's *Maestà* (1317), his finest work, closely modelled on Simone Martini's painting on an identical theme, completed two years previously, in Siena's Palazzo Pubblico (see p.331). San Gimignano's *Podestà* at the time, Mino de' Tolomei, is shown kneeling at the Madonna's feet, looked down on by a multitude of saints arranged in distinct rows. The fresco was enlarged at a later date, Benozzo Gozzoli having added the two saints at the extreme right and left in 1466. The fresco on the end wall shows San Gimignano's population swearing allegiance to Charles of Anjou.

Four smaller rooms on this floor are often given over to temporary exhibitions, usually easily ignored in favour of the main **Pinacoteca**, or art gallery, on the next floor. Arranged in four rooms, the **finest pictures** are in the large salon immediately on the right at the top of the stairs. On the wall on the right as you enter is a superb painted Crucifix (1260–65) by Coppo di Marcovaldo, a Florentine artist – believed to have been the teacher of Cimabue – captured by the Sienese at the Battle of Montaperti in 1260. This work, reckoned one of the masterpieces of early Tuscan painting, was probably also painted while the artist was in "captivity". The similar – but eight-metre high – *Christ* on Florence's baptistery ceiling is attributed to Marcovaldo. Panels next to each of Christ's hands depict the Madonna and St John, and the three Marys. Christ's body is flanked by six scenes from the Passion: the *Kiss of Judas, Flagellation, Crucifixion, Christ and Pilate,* the *Crown of Thorns* and the *Deposition*.

Other outstanding pictures in the room include two early tondi of the *Annunciation* (1482–83) by Filippino Lippi on the opposite end wall, with the Madonna portrayed separately in one, the Archangel Gabriel in the other; both are beautifully offset by their vast original frames. Between them is Pinturicchio's *Madonna Enthroned with Sts Gregory and Benedict* (1512), one of the last works and masterpieces of this artist. Equally arresting are two contrasting paintings of the *Madonna and Child with Saints* by Benozzo Gozzoli, both painted in 1466. The more interesting of the two shows the Madonna with John the Baptist, Mary Magdalene, St Augustine and St Martha, the last (the sister of Lazarus) being particularly venerated in Tuscany, as she is the patron saint of builders and – even more significantly – of cooks.

In the larger of the two rooms to the right, look out for the triptych by Taddeo di Bartolo depicting *Scenes from the Life of St Gimignano* (1393). It was painted when Taddeo was working on the *Last Judgement* frescoes in the Collegiata, where the painting was originally installed above the high altar. The large central panel, which shows the saint with San Gimignano on his lap, is flanked on each side with vignettes from his life. The most extraordinary is one of the four scenes on the right, in which the saint is disturbed while praying by what is euphemistically described as an urgent *"bisogno"* or need – in other words, a desperate call of nature. In answering the call he finds himself met by the Devil, whom he causes to vanish by making the sign of the Cross. The other panels on the right, which describe the saint's exorcism of the Byzantine emperor's daughter, show Gimignano being borne to Constantinople, his calming of a storm during the voyage and the eventual exorcism of the princess. The three main panels on the left depict St Severus officiating at Gimignano's burial; saving San Gimignano from Attila the Hun (the saint is seen remonstrating vigorously with Attila); and preventing a downpour of rain soaking his followers in a leaky church.

Also of interest are *Scenes from the Life of St Bartholomew* (1401) by Lorenzo di Niccolò, whose panels include the attempt to martyr the saint by flaying him alive (top right) – the operation is shown in graphic detail – and his subsequent beheading, in which bloody strips of skin hanging from the saint's body hamper the work of the exasperated executioners. The same artist was responsible for the double-sided **reliquary tabernacle** showing *St Fina and St Gregory* and *Eight Scenes from the Life of St Fina* (1402), San Gimignano's patron saint (see p.370). Fina is shown holding San Gimignano in one hand, and a bunch of violets – a symbol of humility – in the other. The scenes on one face show the mother of St Fina looking after her daughter (with a relative desperately trying to beat off hordes of mice) and the Devil casting Fina's mother down some stairs (to no ill effect); and the funeral procession during which Fina's nurse,

Beldia, miraculously recovered the use of her paralyzed hand. The panels on the other face show Fina extinguishing a fire; saving a boat in a storm; saving a builder falling from a building; and exorcising a man possessed by the Devil.

Perhaps the gallery's most enjoyable paintings, though, are the **frescoes of wedding scenes** in a small room off the stairs (straight ahead on exiting the main salon). Unique in their subject matter, they show a tournament where the wife rides on her husband's back, followed by the lovers taking a shared bath and climbing into bed: the man, remarkably, manages to retain the same red hat through all three operations. Some commentators, however, have seen the pictures in a less jolly light, describing them as allegorical scenes designed to warn men of the wiles of women. They were completed in the 1320s by Memmo di Filippuccio, the father of Lippo Memmi, who since 1303 had been working as a more or less official painter for the *comune*.

The Rocca and around

Just behind the Piazza del Duomo, a signposted lane leads to the **Rocca**, the old fortress, with its one surviving tower. It was built in 1353, to Florentine orders but at local expense, "in order to remove every cause of evil thinking from the inhabitants". A couple of centuries later, its purpose presumably fulfilled, it was dismantled by Cosimo I. Nowadays its 283-metre perimeter encloses an orchard-like public garden, with figs, olives and a well in the middle. From the ramparts, there are superb views over the countryside.

A block south of the Rocca in Via Quercecchio, the **Museo Ornitologico** (April–Sept 11am–5.30pm; €1.50) comprises the stuffed bird collections of some local worthy in the deconsecrated church near the Porta Quercecchio.

San Lorenzo in Ponte to San Iacopo

Heading away from the central squares and Via San Giovanni, the crowds quickly thin away. On Via di Castello is the Romanesque **San Lorenzo in Ponte** (1240; closed to the public at time of writing), whose brick-built interior is almost completely covered with dramatic frescoes (1413) by the little-known but accomplished Florentine Cenni di Francesco. The dramatic fragments include a *Last Judgement* on the left wall and (in the presbytery) the figures of the *Apostles, Christ and the Virgin with Angels*, and *Scenes from the Life of St Benedict*. Cenni was also responsible for the restored frescoes in the adjoining oratory, notably the entrance wall's *St Lawrence and Saints* and *Madonna and Child with Angels*, in which the Madonna's head – an earlier work – has been attributed to Simone Martini.

At the end of the street a rural lane winds down to the walls, a public well – the **Fonti** – and open countryside. The little Pisan-Romanesque church here, **San Jacopo**, has a painting of St James by Pier Francesco Fiorentino.

To Sant'Agostino

Via San Matteo leads north from Piazza del Duomo, one of the town's grandest and best-preserved streets, with quiet little alleyways branching off down to the walls. Passing a couple of mighty tower houses, the street ends at the **Porta San Matteo**, just inside which is the **Convento di Sant'Agostino** (daily: April–Oct 7am–noon & 3–7pm; Nov–March 7am–noon & 3–6pm): after the Collegiata, the most important church in San Gimignano, a large, hall-like thirteenth-century structure with several fine paintings, an impressive Renaissance altar, and an outstanding restored fresco cycle by Benozzo Gozzoli on the *Life of St Augustine*.

On the rear wall, immediately on the left as you enter by the church's side door, is the **Cappella di San Bartolo**. Framed by a draped marble curtain, it houses the remains of St Bartolo (1228–1300), yet another of San Gimignano's patron saints. Born near Pisa, he became a lay Franciscan, but at 52 contracted leprosy and was forced to retire to a leper colony, where he died twenty years later. According to legend, while he was in the colony several of his toes came off in the hands of a nun who was washing his feet. Mortified, he took the loose toes and miraculously reattached them to his foot. This is one of three miracles depicted in the predella reliefs on the magnificent altar by Benedetto da Maiano (1495). The three figures above are the *Theological Virtues*, while the frescoes to the left, by Sebastiano Mainardi, depict saints Lucy, Nicholas of Bari and Gimignano, who holds the town of San Gimignano in his arms.

On the right (south) wall are several striking frescoes, among them a *Madonna and Child with Eight Saints* (1494) by Pier Francesco Fiorentino and a figure of *Christ with the Symbols of the Passion* by Bartolo di Fredi (author of the Collegiata's Old Testament cycle), who was also responsible for the frescoes on the *Life of the Virgin* (1356) on the side walls of the chapel to the right of the high altar. The chapel's striking altarpiece, the *Nativity of the Virgin* (1523), is by Vincenzo Tamengi (1492–1530), an otherwise little-known local artist.

All paintings in the church, however, pale beside those on the walls around the high altar, a seventeen-panel fresco cycle on the **Life of St Augustine** (1463–67) by Benozzo Gozzoli, pictures which provide a superb record of life in Renaissance Italy, particularly the city life of Florence, which forms a backdrop to many of the scenes. Read from low down on the left, the first panels depict the saint – who was born in 354 in what is now Tunisia – being taken to school by his parents and flogged by his teacher, studying grammar at Carthage university and crossing the sea to Italy. The next recount his academic career: teaching philosophy and rhetoric in Rome and Milan – Gozzoli depicts the journey between the cities as a marvellously rich procession – and being received by the Emperor Theodosius. Then comes the turning point in his life, when he listens to the preaching of St Ambrose, and then, while reading St Paul's Epistle to the Romans, hears a child's voice extolling him "*Tolle, lege*" (take and read). After this, Augustine was baptized, returned to Tunisia to form a monastic community, was subsequently made bishop of Hippo and went on to become one of the fathers of the early Christian Church. Gozzoli depicts just a few crucial scenes: Augustine meeting the child whose voice he had heard; the death of his mother, St Monica; blessing the people, as bishop; confuting a heretic; having a vision of St Jerome in Paradise; and his death, a scene which almost exactly prefigures Ghirlandaio's depiction of the death of St Fina in the Collegiata.

Given the richness of the cycle, it's remarkable that the high altar's *Coronation of the Virgin* (1483) manages to hold its own. It's by Piero del Pollaiuolo, brother and collaborator of the more famous Antonio del Pollaiuolo. Moving back down the left (north) wall you come to a door leading to the **sacristy** and Renaissance **cloister** and another fresco by Sebastiano Mainardi of *San Gimignano Blessing Three Dignitaries* (1487). The effigy above is of *Fra Domenico Strambi*, the patron who commissioned the Gozzoli frescoes and Pollaiuolo altarpiece. The marble reliefs (1318) beyond, showing four half-figures of bishops, are believed to be part of the original shrine to St Bartolo, and are attributed to Tino da Camaino. The fresco fragment beyond, a *Madonna* by Lippo Memmi, is overshadowed by a large fresco of *St Sebastian*, painted by Gozzoli in 1464, the year in which plague ravaged San Gimignano.

The Museo Archeologico

Just south of Sant'Agostino is the former convent of Santa Chiara, now home to the interesting **Museo Archeologico** (April–Dec daily 11am–5.30pm;

€3.50), which boasts a large collection of local finds and details the history of the area from the Etruscans to the eighteenth century. In the same complex is a reproduction of the **Spezieria dello Spedale di Santa Fina**, one of Tuscany's oldest pharmacies, exhibiting all sorts of exotic herbal remedies and other sixteenth-century medicinal concoctions. Upstairs is the **Galleria d'Arte Moderna e Contemporanea** (same hours and ticket), showing work by nineteenth- and twentieth-century Tuscan artists and temporary exhibits.

Eating and drinking

San Gimignano isn't especially famous for its food – there are too many tourists and too few locals to ensure high standards. However, the tables set out in summer on the car-less streets and squares and the local wines still make for a beguiling evening. As an after-meal treat, drop in on the award-winning *Gelateria di Piazza*, at Piazza della Cisterna – the jovial owner creates some of the best ice cream in Tuscany. At night, San Gimignano is very much on the quiet side, with little entertainment beyond the evening *passeggiata* along Via San Giovanni and Via San Matteo. For late-night **drinking** and occasional live music head down to the *Birreria Pietrafitta*.

Birreria Pietrafitta 4km east of town on the road to Poggibonsi. This popular pub with its large shady beer garden provides welcome relief from the crowds. Wide selection of beers, wines and cocktails, as well as good panini and snacks available all day. Daily 11am–2am.

Il Pino Via San Matteo 102 ☏0577.942.225, ⓦwww.ristoranteilpino.it. San Gimignano's first-choice restaurant, with a lovely interior. Specializes in antipasti and dishes sprinkled with truffle. From €25 upwards for a full meal. Closed Thurs.

La Mangiatoia Via Mainardi 2 ☏0577.941.528. Popular restaurant with good Tuscan staples (pasta €7–9, mains €10–12) and a garden open in the summer. Closed Tues.

La Stella Via San Matteo 75 ☏0577.940.289. Well-reputed restaurant that serves produce from its own farm; often full of tourists, but still good value, with pasta dishes under €10. Closed Wed.

Le Vecchie Mura Via Piandornella 15 ☏0577.940.270. Housed in an old vaulted stable within the structure of the city walls; follow the sign off Via San Giovanni. Good atmosphere and reasonable value, with starters at €4–8, pasta from €8 and mains €10.50–12.50. Be sure to book. Closed Tues.

Osteria del Carcere Via del Castello 13 ☏0577.941.905. A relatively new and informal *osteria*, a few steps from Piazza del Duomo. Excellent hams and salami, plus Tuscan cooking with an innovative edge. Reckon on around €25–30 for three courses. Just thirty covers, so booking is advised. Closed Wed.

Osteria delle Catene Via Mainardi 18 ☏0577.941.966. A reliable place for straightforward Tuscan food. The wine list – over a hundred choices – is good, too. A good lunch will cost around €30, dinner €10–15 more. Closed Wed.

Volterra

Built on a high plateau enclosed by yellowy-grey volcanic hills, lofty **VOLTERRA** has a bleak, isolated appearance – a surprise after the pastoralism of the region around. D.H. Lawrence wrote, accurately, that "it gets all the wind and sees all the world … a sort of inland island, still curiously isolated and grim." However, its small, walled medieval core certainly merits a stop, with its cobbled and austere stone streets, dark stone *palazzi* and walled gateways. There are great views from the windswept heights, enjoyable walking, and one of the country's most important Etruscan museums.

The town lies at the heart of a mining region that yields **alabaster** (every other shop sells artefacts), as well as a variety of minerals. The mines – and the easily defended site – made it one of the largest **Etruscan** settlements, Velathri,

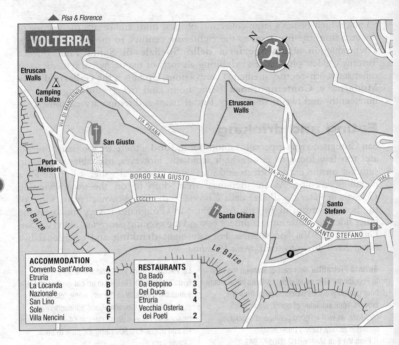

▲ Pisa & Florence

VOLTERRA

Etruscan Walls

Camping Le Balze

San Giusto

Porta Menseri

BORGO SAN GIUSTO

VIA DI MANDRINGA

VIA PISANA

Etruscan Walls

VIA PISANA

VIALE

Le Balze

VIA LECCETI

Santa Chiara

Santo Stefano

BORGO SANTO STEFANO

P

Le Balze

F

ACCOMMODATION	
Convento Sant'Andrea	A
Etruria	C
La Locanda	B
Nazionale	D
San Lino	E
Sole	G
Villa Nencini	F

RESTAURANTS	
Da Badò	1
Da Beppino	3
Del Duca	5
Etruria	4
Vecchia Osteria dei Poeti	2

and ensured its survival through the **Roman** era as Volaterrae. During the Dark Ages it became an important Lombard centre, and even sheltered the Lombard kings for a time. In the Middle Ages, however, the mines proved Volterra's downfall as the **Florentines** began to cast a covetous eye over their wealth. Florence took control of the town from 1360, and in 1472 – anxious to secure the town's alum deposits, vital for Florence's dyeing industry – crushed all pretensions to independence with a terrible siege and pillage by Lorenzo de' Medici and the Duke of Urbino, one of the three principal crimes Lorenzo confessed to Savonarola on his deathbed.

Subsequently, Volterra was a Florentine fief, unable to keep pace with changing and expanding patterns of trade and sliding into provincial obscurity. It was to remain part of the Grand Duchy of Tuscany until Italian unification in 1860. Physically, the town also began to subside, its walls and houses slipping away to the west over the **Balze** (cliffs), which form a dramatic prospect from the Pisa road. Today, Volterra occupies less than a third of its ancient extent.

Arrival and information

The nearest **train** station is 9km west at Saline di Volterra, from where CPT #790 buses shuttle into town. **Buses** arrive on the south side of the town at Piazza Martiri della Libertà, including three daily CPT #770 services from Colle di Val d'Elsa. From the piazza it's a two-minute walk to the central Piazza dei Priori, close to the Duomo and **tourist office** at Via Giusto Turazza 2 (daily: April–Oct 9am–1pm & 2–8pm; Nov–March 10am–1pm & 2–6pm; ☏0588.86.159/150, ⍈www.provolterra.it), where you can buy bus tickets. **Cars** are best parked outside the north circuit of the walls, by the Porta San Francesco or Porta Fiorentina. Best of all, if you can find a spot, is the signed, underground "Dogana" parking, convenient for the Duomo.

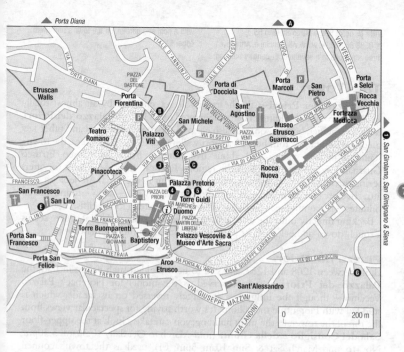

The major Volterran **festival** is the Gioco delle Contrade, a medieval tug of war held in the Piazza dei Priori at the beginning of June. The Volterra Teatro and Volterra Jazz festivals take place in July and August; the tourist office has details.

Accommodation

Ask about **apartments** and **agriturismo** stays at the tourist office, which has a free accommodation-finding service. There's a well-equipped **campsite**, *Le Balze*, 1km west of the centre at Via Mandringa (℡0588.87.880; April–Sept). It has a pool and tennis courts; riding can also be arranged.

Convento Sant'Andrea Viale Vittorio Veneto 2 ℡0588.86.028, ℮semvescovile@diocesivolterra .it. On the northeast outskirts of town; follow the road out of Porta Marcoli. There are beautiful views from the old cells, now let as private rooms with old painted brass beds – to both single travellers and couples. €18 per person in a room with private bathroom, €14 in a room with shared bathroom. ❶

Etruria Via Matteotti 32 ℡0588.87.377, ⓦwww .albergoetruria.it. Best value of the hotels proper – and located on Volterra's main street – this restored eighteenth-century building has 22 comfortable rooms and a private garden. ❷

La Locanda Via Guarnacci 24–28 ℡0588.81.547, ⓦwww.hotel-lalocanda.com. The *San Lino* had its own way for years among Volterra's top hotels, but four-star *La Locanda*, smartly converted from a

former nunnery, is now first choice, enjoying a slightly more central position. ❹

Nazionale Via dei Marchesi 11 ℡0588.86.284, ⓦwww.albergonazionale-volterra.it. In the heart of town, this three-star hotel is the inn D.H. Lawrence stayed at when researching *Etruscan Places* – the medieval *palazzo* was transformed into a hotel in 1860. Now much modernized, with 36 mostly tiny rooms, each with bathroom. ❷

San Lino Via San Lino 26 ℡0588.85.250, ⓦwww.hotelsanlino.com. Volterra's grandest hotel until the arrival of *La Locanda*, this four-star place with 43 rooms and pool is still a good bet. ❸

Sole Via dei Cappuccini 10 ℡0588.84.000, ⓦwww.hotelsolevolterra.com. A modern three-star in a quiet location outside the town walls, near the church of Sant'Alessandro. All ten rooms are en suite. ❸

Villa Nencini Borgo Santo Stefano 55 ⓣ0588.86.386, ⓦwww.villanencini.it. Attractive three-star hotel in a seventeenth-century building, with a pool and garden, on the town's northwest edge. ❸

The Town

The **Piazza dei Priori** is the heart of Volterra, enclosed by an almost totally medieval group of buildings. The battlemented town hall, or **Palazzo dei Priori**, is the eyecatcher, but the square is also close to the town's cathedral and other key medieval buildings. From here it's a short walk north to the Pinacoteca, the town's standout picture gallery, and about five minutes from the Museo Etrusco Guarnacci, home to the pick of the region's Etruscan heritage. Before (or after) seeing the museum, it makes sense to take time out in the Parco Archeologico, an attractive area of park and garden. A longer walk west – allow around fifteen minutes – is required see the Balze, Volterra's celebrated eroded cliffs.

Backing directly onto the civic power centre, Volterra's cathedral square seems a touch down-at-heel, with its partial facades and crumbling masonry.

Piazza dei Priori

Built between 1208 and 1257, and said to be the oldest such palace in Italy, the **Palazzo dei Priori** may have served as the model for Florence's Palazzo Vecchio – though the influences are largely reversed on its facade, which is studded with Florentine medallions. It's worth paying for spectacular views from the top of the tower. In the main building, you can take a look at the upper-floor **Sala del Consiglio e della Giunta** (mid-March to Oct daily 10.30am–5.30pm, Nov to mid-March Sat & Sun 10am–5pm; €1), used as the town's council chamber since 1257. Its end wall is frescoed with a huge *Annunciation* (1383) attributed to Jacopo di Cione.

Opposite the town hall is the **Palazzo Pretorio**, surmounted by the **Torre del Porcellino** (Piglet's Tower), named after the much-worn carved boar on a bracket to the right of the top window; completing the ensemble are the **Palazzo Vescovile**, or Bishop's Palace (formerly the town's granary), and a pair of tower houses, the **Buomparenti**, at the junction of Via Roma and Via Ricciarelli. Modest relatives of those of San Gimignano, the towers are linked by a passageway above the street.

The Bishop's Palace houses the rich little **Museo di Arte Sacra** (daily: mid-March to Oct 9am–1pm & 3–6pm; Nov to mid-March 9am–1pm; joint ticket with Pinacoteca e Museo Civico and Museo Etrusco €8). Displays in the first room include an Andrea della Robbia bust of *St Linus*, a Volterran who was St Peter's successor as pope; a silver reliquary bust of *St Ottaviano* by Andrea del Pollaiuolo; a fifteenth-century painted wooden tabernacle by Bartolomeo della Gatta, better known for his work around Arezzo and Cortona; and a clutch of Sienese altarpieces by Neri di Bici, Taddeo di Bartolo and Segna di Bonaventura. The second room has a gilded Crucifix by Giambologna, though the real highlights, especially for fans of Mannerism, reside in room 3, which features Rosso Fiorentino's *Madonna di Villamagna* (1521) and the *Madonna di Ulignano* (1545) by the leading local artist Daniele da Volterra.

The Duomo and its square

The **Duomo**, or Basilica di Santa Maria Assunta (consecrated in 1120), and **Baptistery** (second half of the thirteenth century) are essentially Pisan-Romanesque in style, clad in bands of black-and-white marble. Behind the baptistery, della Robbia plaques of swaddled babies signal a building that was once a foundlings' hospital. On the baptistery's exterior note the main portal, whose rounded arch contains the carved heads of Christ, the Madonna and the Apostles (1283). Inside are a water stoup fashioned from an old Etruscan funerary monument and a fine baptismal font (1502) by Andrea Sansovino.

Inside the Duomo, striped marble Romanesque aisles and a coffered Renaissance ceiling lend the building a rather makeshift appearance. Moving down the right (south) aisle you come to a chapel in the right transept with an outstanding Pisan *Deposition* (1228), its life-size figures disarmingly repainted in their original bright colours. On the right side of the choir lies the Cappella di Sant'Ottaviano, which contains the body of the eponymous saint, a sixth-century hermit whose relics saved Volterra from a plague in 1522 – he is one of the town's patron saints. The high altar, a nineteenth-century travesty, is surmounted by an exquisite tabernacle (1471) by Mino da Fiesole, who also carved the two kneeling angels flanking the high altar. In the left (north) aisle the highlights are two fifteenth-century terracotta figures in the oratory near the entrance: they depict the *Nativity* and *Adoration of the Magi*, the former graced with a painted background by Benozzo Gozzoli. Further down is a thirteenth-century Pisan pulpit, assembled in 1584 from a variety of earlier fragments. On the altar alongside is a beautiful *Annunciation* (1497), generally attributed to Fra' Bartolommeo.

Pinacoteca e Museo Civico and Ecomuseo dell'Alabastro

Paintings and sculpture gathered from Volterra's churches, including one that was swallowed up by the Balze, are displayed at the **Pinacoteca e Museo Civico**, installed in the Palazzo Minucci-Solaini, Via dei Sarti 1 (mid-March to Oct daily 9am–7pm; Nov to mid-March 8.30am–1.30pm; joint ticket with Museo d'Arte Sacra and Museo Etrusco €8). The mansion is an interesting building in its own right, part frescoed and with a multi-level cloister, possibly designed by Antonio da Sangallo.

The collections are arranged chronologically, and begin with **statuary** from the lost church of San Giusto al Bostro; there's a wonderful Romanesque capital carved from local alabaster, its mix of pagan and Christian emblems including a double-tailed mermaid and Daniel in the lions' den. The **painting** displays begin with largely Sienese works, notably Taddeo di Bartolo's polyptych of the *Madonna and Child with Saints* (1411) and the same artist's *Madonna della Rosa*, part of a dismembered polyptych, and panel of *Sts Nicola da Tolentino and Peter*. But by the fifteenth century Florence dominated art, as it did politics. Major Renaissance paintings from this period include a *Christ in Glory* (1492) with a marvellous imaginary landscape by Ghirlandaio (room X), and a *Madonna and Saints* (1491) and *Annunciation* by Luca Signorelli, one of the artist's masterpieces (room XI).

The museum's best work, however, is **Rosso Fiorentino**'s extraordinary *Descent from the Cross*, painted for the church of San Francesco in 1521. This is one of the masterpieces of Mannerism, its figures, without any central focus, creating an agitated, circular tension from sharp lines and blocks of discordant colour. The art historian Frederick Hartt saw in the work "the dilemma of a lost generation" – it was painted in the decade that culminated in the Sack of Rome – as well as virtual blasphemy in the vision of a smiling Christ and gibbering Joseph of Arimathea.

In the Torre Minucci of the same palace complex is the **Ecomuseo dell'Alabastro** (mid-March to Oct daily 11am–5pm; Nov to mid-March Sat & Sun 9am–1.30pm; €3) devoted to the local alabaster industry. The museum has details of two driving itineraries taking in points of interest connected with the industry, including two other local museums. It also has displays chronicling the industry's development, as well as objects in alabaster, including two Etruscan urns and two capitals, the latter virtually the only surviving local items in alabaster from the medieval period.

On the same street as the Pinacoteca e Museo Civico is the **Palazzo Incontri-Viti**, Via dei Sarti 41, a private residence built in about 1500; its forty-metre street frontage is attributed to Bartolomeo Ammannati. A variety of its beautifully frescoed and luxuriously furnished rooms are open to the public (April–Oct daily 10am–1pm & 2.30–6.30pm; Nov–March by appointment only at the tourist office; €4).

The Rocca, Arco Etrusco and archeological remains

South of Piazza dei Priori, Via Marchesi leads to a lush area of grass, trees and shade known as the **Parco Archeologico** (daily 10am–noon & 4–7pm; free). There's not much archeology about the place – a few odd lumps of rock, said to be part of a Roman bathhouse – but it's a beautiful part of the town to lie around for a few hours, and there's a café-bar in one corner. Overlooking the park to the east is the **Rocca**, built by the Medici after their sacking of the town; with its rounded bastions and central tower, it's one of the great examples of Italian military architecture. For the last 150 years it's been a prison for lifers and hard cases.

The first turning left off Via Marchesi, Via Porta all'Arco, runs downhill to the **Arco Etrusco**, an Etruscan gateway, third-century BC in origin, built in Cyclopean blocks of stone, with Roman and medieval surrounds; the three blackened and eroded lumps on its outer face are probably images of Etruscan gods. The gate was narrowly saved from destruction in World War II during the course of a ten-day battle between the partisans (Volterra was a stronghold) and the Nazis. A memorial commemorates the partisan losses.

If you turn north instead off Via Marchesi, and follow Via Matteotti and its continuation, Via Guarnacci, you reach the Porta Fiorentina. Just to the west of

▲ Detail of the Urna degli Sposi in Volterra's Museo Etrusco

the gate, below the road, is an area of excavations including a **Roman theatre** (now restored for use in the summer theatre festival) and a **bath complex** with mosaic floors. The **Via di Porta Diana**, straight ahead from the gate, makes for a pleasant walk, leading past the cemetery to remains of the Etruscan Porta Diana. Out beyond here tracks lead through farmland that was once a vast **Etruscan necropolis**; wandering through, you'll spot various unmarked, underground tombs.

The Museo Etrusco Guarnacci

Volterra's Etruscan legacy is represented most importantly at the **Museo Etrusco Guarnacci**, Via Don Minzoni 15 (daily: mid-March to Oct 9am–7pm; Nov to mid-March 8.30am–1.30pm; joint ticket with Museo d'Arte Sacra and Pinacoteca €8). One of Italy's major archeological museums, it consists entirely of local finds, including some six hundred **funerary urns**.

Made of alabaster, tufa and terracotta, the **urns** date from the fourth to first centuries BC – earlier tombs were lost as the cliffs fell to nothing. On their sides, bas-reliefs depict domestic events (often boar hunting) or Greek myths (usually a trip to the underworld); on the lid are a bust of the subject and symbolic flowers – one for a young person, two for middle-aged, three for elderly.

The vast collection is organized by theme, with informative notes in each room. Most of the best are arranged on the top floor and date from the "golden age" of the third and second centuries BC; past a large Roman mosaic transferred here from the baths complex outside town is the **Urna degli Sposi**, a disturbing portrait scene of a supposed husband and wife – all piercing eyes and dreadful looks. The star piece, among a number of small bronze sculptures, is the exceptional **Ombra della Sera** ("Evening Shadow"), an elongated nude which provided inspiration for the twentieth-century Swiss sculptor Alberto Giacometti. The farmer who unearthed it displayed rather less reverence: he used it as a poker for a few years.

To the Balze

To reach the Balze – Volterra's famous eroded cliffs – follow Via Riciarelli then Via di San Lino northwest from the Piazza dei Priori. This passes the church of **San Francesco**, whose adjoining Cappella della Croce di Giorno, built in 1315, contains fascinating and very early narrative frescoes (1410) of the *Legend of the True Cross* by Cenni di Francesco, an accomplished but little-known local artist. Rosso Fiorentino's famous *Descent from the Cross*, now in the Pinacoteca e Museo Civico, once stood above the high altar. From the nearby **Porta San Francesco**, follow Borgo Santo Stefano and its continuation, Borgo San Giusto, past the Baroque church and former abbey of **San Giusto**, its dilapidated but striking facade framed by an avenue of cypress trees.

At the **Balze** themselves, almost 2km west of Piazza dei Priori, you gain a real sense of the extent of Etruscan Volterra, whose old town walls drop away into the chasms. Gashes in the slopes and the natural erosion of sand and clay are made more dramatic by alabaster mines, ancient and modern. Below are buried great tracts of the Etruscan and Roman city, and landslips continue – as evidenced by the locked and ruined eleventh-century Badìa monastery ebbing away over the precipice.

Eating and drinking

As a hunting centre, Volterra's **restaurant** menus are dominated by wild boar (*cinghiale*). You see stuffed heads of the unfortunate beasts throughout town, and the meat is packaged as salamis or hams, as well as roasted in the restaurants, along with hare (*lepre*) and rabbit (*coniglio*).

Da Badò Borgo San Lazzaro 9 ☎0588.86.477. Excellent local trattoria on the SS68 Florence–Siena road run by two amiable brothers (with mother in the kitchen). Serves up delicious *crostini* and Volterran game staples such as *pappardelle alla lepre*. Closed Wed & periods in July and Sept.

Da Beppino Via delle Prigioni 13–21 ☎0588.86.051. Reliable, established and family-run restaurant in the heart of the old town, with lots of space, and some outdoor tables. Serves homemade pasta, pizzas and plenty of hunting dishes, with an emphasis on truffles and mushrooms. Closed Thurs & around mid-Nov to mid-Dec.

🏃 **Del Duca** Via di Castello 2 ☎0588.81.510. On the edge of the old centre, this small restaurant is currently the best place in town, thanks to its lovely setting (high ceilings and an impressive *cantina*), surprisingly fair prices and fine Tuscan food with a creative twist. Closed periods in late Jan & mid-Nov, plus Tues except July–Sept.

Etruria Piazza dei Priori 6 ☎0588.86.064. Best of the more expensive places: located in an old *palazzo* on the main square, with period furniture and frescoes. Despite its à la carte prices, it has inexpensive tourist menus too. Closed Wed.

🏃 **Vecchia Osteria dei Poeti** Via Matteotti 55–57 ☎0588.86.029. One of the most popular and welcoming restaurants in town – and they don't stint on portions. A central location, with one dining room and a rustic appearance that retains many features of the original medieval building. Closed Thurs.

Travel details

Trains

Poggibonsi to: Florence (hourly; 1hr 15min); Siena (hourly; 25min).
Saline di Volterra to: Cécina (8 daily; 35min; connections to Pisa and Rome).

Buses

Colle di Val d'Elsa to: Casole d'Elsa (4 daily; 20min); Florence (hourly; 1hr); Monteriggioni (hourly; 15min); Poggibonsi (hourly; 15min); Siena (hourly; 30min); Volterra (3 daily; 45min).

Poggibonsi to: Colle di Val d'Elsa (hourly; 15min); Florence (hourly; 50min); San Gimignano (every 30min; 25min); Siena (hourly; 45min).
San Gimignano to: Poggibonsi (10 daily; 25min); Siena (10 daily; 1hr 15min).
Siena to: Colle di Val d'Elsa (hourly; 30min); Florence (hourly; 1hr 15min); Monteriggioni (hourly; 25min); Poggibonsi (hourly; 45min).
Volterra to: Colle di Val d'Elsa (3 daily; 45min); Pisa (1 daily; 1hr 10min); Saline di Volterra (5 daily; 15min).

8

Southern Tuscany

CHAPTER 8

Highlights

✳ **Monte Oliveto Maggiore** A mighty monastery set amid wonderful upland countryside. See p.391

✳ **Montalcino** This perfect pocket hill-town produces some of Tuscany's finest wines. See p.394

✳ **Sant'Antimo** An austerely beautiful abbey in an idyllic pastoral setting. See p.401

✳ **Bagno Vignoni** Atmospheric village with a sulphur pool instead of a central piazza. See p.406

✳ **Pienza** Pope Pius II's town-sized monument to himself. See p.407

✳ **Montepulciano** Is there a more attractive hill-town anywhere in the country? See p.414

✳ **Pitigliano** A cliff-top hideaway in the deep south of Tuscany. See p.431

▲ Piazza Grande, Montepulciano

8

Southern Tuscany

The region **south of Siena** is Tuscany at its best: an infinite gradation of hills, trees and cultivation that encompasses the Crete Senese, the vineyards of Montepulciano and Montalcino, the Monte Amiata uplands and finally a landscape of sulphurous springs and castle-topped outcrops of tufa. The *crete*, especially, is fabulous: a sparsely populated region of pale clay hillsides, dotted with sheep, cypresses and the odd monumental-looking farmhouse.

The towns on the whole live up to this environment. **Montepulciano** is the most elegant and makes a superb base, with its independent hill-town life, acclaimed Vino Nobile wine and backdrop of Renaissance buildings. **Montalcino**, too, has appealing wines (its Brunello is regarded as Tuscany's finest vintage) and classic hill-town looks, while **Pienza** is a unique Renaissance monument, a town created by the great humanist pope, Pius II. In the south of the region, the urban highlights are **Pitigliano**, isolated on an extraordinary crag, and nearby the forgotten, half-abandoned medieval town of **Sovana**.

Monasteries are a major attraction of the area, and feature some of the greatest houses of the medieval Italian orders: Cistercian **San Galgano** and **Abbadia San Salvatore**, Benedictine **Monte Oliveto Maggiore** and **Sant'Antimo**, and Vallombrosan **Torri**. All are tremendous buildings, encompassing the best Romanesque and Gothic church architecture in Tuscany.

Equally memorable are the extraordinary sulphur springs that erupt from the rocks, or are channelled into geothermal energy, punctuating the landscape with pillars of white smoke. Several of the springs have for centuries formed the nucleus of spas. The most interesting is **Bagno Vignoni**, still with its Medicean basin in the village square. Here, and at **Bagni di Petriolo**, **Bagni San Filippo** and – most spectacularly – **Saturnia**, you can immerse yourself in open-air rock pools below warm cascades.

San Galgano and the western crete

If you have transport, the route past the abbeys of **Torri** and **San Galgano**, the sulphur spring of **Petriolo** and the villages of the western *crete* makes one of the best trips out from Siena. It could be done in a day, or alternatively with a night's stop at Buonconvento, Montalcino or one of the Murlo villages. If you're dependent on public transport, it's perhaps best to content yourself with San Galgano, which lies just off the N73 Siena–Massa Maríttima road; in a day, you could return to Siena, continue to Massa Maríttima, or stop at the village of **Palazzetto** near the abbey.

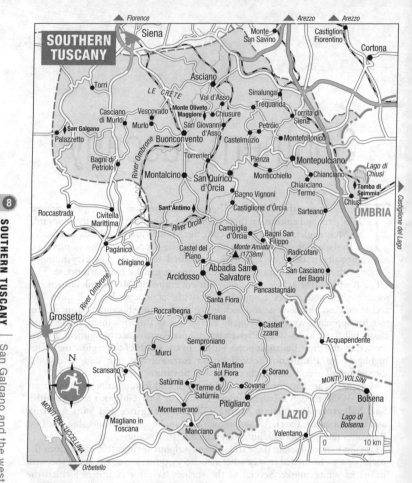

Map labels (clockwise/geographic):

▲ Florence ▲ Arezzo ▲ Arezzo

SOUTHERN TUSCANY

Siena · Monte San Mustino · Castiglion Fiorentino · Cortona

Torri · LE CRETE · Asciano · Val d'Asso · Sinalunga · Trequanda · Torrita di Siena

Casciano di Murlo · Vescovado · Monte Oliveto Maggiore · Chiusure · San Giovanni d'Asso · Petróio · Montefollónico

San Galgano · Murlo · Buonconvento · Castelmúzio · Montepulciano · Lago di Chiusi

Palazzetto · Torrenieri · Pienza · Monticchiello · Chianciano · Tomba di Scimmia

Bagni di Petriolo · Montalcino · San Quirico d'Orcia · Chianciano Terme · Chiusi

UMBRIA

Roccastrada · Civitella Marittima · Sant'Antimo · Bagno Vignoni · Castiglione d'Órcia · Sarteano

River Orcia · Campíglia d'Órcia · Bagni San Filippo · Radicófani

Paganico · Castel del Piano · Monte Amiata (1738m) ▲

Cinigiano · Arcidosso · Abbadia San Salvatore · San Casciano dei Bagni

River Ombrone · Santa Fiora · Pancastagnáio

Grosseto · Roccalbegna · Triana · Castell'zzara · Acquapendente

Semproniano

Murci · San Martino sul Fiora · Sorano · MONTI VOLSINI

Scansano · Satúrnia · Terme di Satúrnia · Sovana · Bolsena

N · Montemerano · Pitigliano · LAZIO · Lago di Bolsena

Magliano in Toscana · Manciano · Valentano

MONTI DELL'UCCELLINA

0   10 km

▼ Orbetello

Castiglione del Lago ►

Torri

Driving south from Siena, it's best to follow the N223 Grosseto road as far as the junction signposted to Brenna, Stigliano and Torri. Taking this minor road, you find yourself in the **Rosia valley**, a belt of ancient farmland increasingly marred by the expansion of a huge Bayer chemical factory, and overlooked by a series of cream-stone villages set along the wooded ridge to the south. All these villages are pastoral beauties, approached from the valley floor along cobbled roads and avenues of cypress trees, with farmyards backing onto many of the houses.

To give a focus to the trip, come on a Monday or Friday morning, when you can visit the **Monastero dei Santi Trinità e Mustiola** (Mon & Fri 9am–noon) at **TORRI**, the last of the villages, just 2km east of the Siena–Grosseto road. The monastery, founded in the eleventh century, was an important power base for the Vallombrosan order, until difficulties with the papacy led to its suppression by Pius II in 1464. It retains its Romanesque church and a magnificent three-tiered cloister, executed in panels of black and white marble. The capitals of the lower tier, in particular, are outstanding; their style and subject matter (fantastic animals and Old Testament stories) recalling the French-influenced work at Sant'Antimo (see p.401). Abandoned in the sixteenth century, the complex was bought privately in 1966. It is scarcely ever visited; note that outside the opening hours, it's kept firmly locked and nobody local has a key.

San Galgano

The **Abbazia di San Galgano**, midway between Massa and Siena, is among the greatest Gothic buildings in Italy. It is certainly the most romantic – roofless, with a grass field for a nave, patches of fresco amidst the vegetation, and panoramas of the sky, clouds and hills through a rose window. (If you have ever seen Andrei Tarkovsky's film *Nostalgia*, it will be immediately familiar from the finale, in which the director transformed the nave into a Russian landscape complete with a *dacha*.)

In the twelfth and thirteenth centuries, San Galgano – which was one of the **Cistercians**' two largest foundations in Italy – was the leading monastic power in Tuscany. Its abbots ruled over disputes between the cities, and at Siena its monks supervised the building of the Duomo and held posts as *casalinghi* (accountants) for the *comune*. The monks were a mix of Italians and French, and through them the ideas of Gothic building were imported to Italy, along with sophisticated schemes for land drainage and agriculture. As at all Cistercian houses, the monastic population included large numbers of lay brothers, who dedicated themselves to manual labour while the "choir monks" looked after the prayer and study.

The abbey

The Cistercian order built the **church** and abbey (daily 8am–8pm; Oct–April closes 6pm; free) between 1218 and 1288, at which time the complex must have looked like a small town, with its numerous workshops, dormitories and guest quarters. However, at the end of the century, during the wars between the

▲ The Abbazia di San Galgano

Tuscan cities, the English *condottiere* Sir John Hawkwood and his mercenary troops sacked the abbey, and by 1397 the abbot was San Galgano's sole occupant. During the fifteenth century it was repopulated for a while, until the papacy handed its income to a particularly profligate cardinal. The monks left and the building gradually decayed; the campanile actually collapsed during a Mass attended by villagers.

The vast church, with its seventy-metre nave and shored-up aisles, now encloses little more than a stone altar. Birds hover about the glassless windows and capitals. Outside, there are brief runs of cloister and a few conventual buildings, part-occupied by members of the Comunità Incontro who are responsible for the maintenance of the abbey and its surrounds.

The monastery commemorates **St Galgano Guidotti**, a noble from the nearby village of Chiusdino, who spent his youth in the usual saintly apprenticeship of dissipation and battles. Upon having a vision of St Michael, he renounced the life of a knight and embarked on a career as a hermit. His conviction was fortified by a kind of reversed sword-in-the-stone miracle when, during a visit from his family and fellow knights (who tried to persuade him to return to the world), he ran his sword into a rock beside his hut: it stuck fast, forming a crucifix. In 1181, at the age of 33, Galgano died, and within four years had been canonized.

The saint's hermitage was transformed into the circular **Cappella di Monte Siepi** – the building on the hill above the main abbey – between 1182 and 1185, with the **sword in the stone** forming the centrepiece. The chapel was designed as a mausoleum, but Galgano's body has been lost, though his head is preserved in the Siena cathedral museum. In the fourteenth century a Gothic second chapel was added to the original Romanesque chapel, and in the 1700s a rectory was attached, the three forming a rustic, farmhouse-like group. It is well worth the climb up the hill, as much for the views over the abbey as for the chapels themselves. The interior of the rotunda is interesting for its strange striped dome, and the side chapel has patches of frescoes by Ambrogio Lorenzetti, including a just-about-discernible image of Galgano offering the rock-embedded sword to St Michael.

Practicalities

To one side of the abbey, in the old vaulted scriptorium, is a small **tourist office** (daily: summer 10.30am–6pm; winter 10.30am–1.30pm & 3–5pm; ☎0577.756.738), which has some useful local information and sells tickets for the occasional concerts held in the abbey. Accommodation is in the village of **Palazzetto**, 4km south on the Massa road, at the *Bar-Albergo Il Palazzetto* (☎&⑤0577.751.160; ❶), which also has a good, inexpensive restaurant/pizzeria (closed Wed), as well as bar snacks.

Bagni di Petriolo and into the crete

From San Galgano, you can cut across to the N223 Siena–Grosseto road by means of a minor road that leaves the N73 at the walled village of Monticiano. The road east of Monticiano is attractive if unremarkable, twisting its way through wooded hills before finally emerging on the N223 about 20km south of Siena.

South from here, the N223 follows the River Merse before rearing into the hills by way of various viaducts. To reach the spa of **BAGNI DI PETRIOLO** you need to turn right after about 4km, then follow this road for 9km (no buses) down to a bridge beside the River Farma (a tributary of the Ombrone) and a rough enclosure of huge medieval walls. Here, on the left, is a tiny

thermal station offering treatments (April–Nov; ☎0577.757.104, ⓦwww
.termesaluteambiente.com). Just below the bridge on the left, the spa's **sulphur
springs** continue to flow freely into little rock pools before mixing with the
river. If you're going for a soak, you should leave your clothes well away from
the sulphur, and wash off afterwards with a dip in the river.

The Murlo villages

With transport, you can follow a paved track off the Petriolo road, through the
hills to **CASCIANO DI MURLO**. Scarcely more than a hamlet, Casciano has
a 29-room, three-star **hotel**, the *Mirella* (☎0577.817.667, ⓦwww.hotelmirella
.com; ❸) and a **campsite**, *Le Soline* (☎0577.817.410, ⓦwww.lesoline.it), open
year-round, located at nearby Casafranci. A fine place to break your journey, or
base yourself for a few days, Casciano is also easily reached from the N223 (it's
6km from the turning).

East of Casciano, a very high and beautiful road leads into the beginnings
of the *crete*, with hills punctuated by the occasional lake and farmhouse on
the approach to **VESCOVADO DI MURLO**. There's little reason to stop
at Vescovado, a largely modern village, but it has a hotel with swimming
pool, the three-star *Murlo*, Via Martiri di Rigosecco (☎0577.814.033,
ⓦwww.albergodimurlo.com; ❸). There's also agriturismo accommodation
at *Palazzina* (☎0577.817.776, ⓦwww.lapalazzina.com; ❸–❻), a farmhouse
between Casciano and Vescovado.

Just a couple of kilometres south of Vescovado is **MURLO** – a tiny medieval
borgo whose ring of houses forms defensive walls, enclosing the town hall and
church. Murlo is the oldest settlement in the area, and its Etruscan past is
commemorated in the **Museo Etrusco**, housed in the Castello di Murlo
(April–Sept Tues–Sun 10am–1pm & 3–7pm; March & Oct Tues–Sun 10am–1pm
& 3–5pm; Nov–Feb Tues–Fri 10am–1pm, Sat & Sun 10am–1pm & 3–5pm;
ⓦwww.comune.murlo.siena.it; €3.20). Exhibits include sphinx statues, a large
terracotta tomb frieze depicting hunting scenes, and some odd bowls, decorated
with warriors holding women whose legs form the handles.

At Vescovado or Murlo you're within easy striking distance of Buonconvento,
and near enough to Asciano, Montalcino or Siena. The Montalcino route is
lovely, as is the superbly scenic Asciano road, taking you into the heart of the
crete across sparsely populated countryside. Just off the N2, which you need to
join for a few kilometres before heading east to Asciano, there are rooms at the
Borgo Antico (☎0577.374.688, ⓦwww.hotelborgoantico.com; ❷) in the medieval
hamlet of **Lucignano d'Arbia**.

Monte Oliveto and the central crete

The heartland of the *crete* is the area southeast of Siena, around the Benedictine
monastery of **Monte Oliveto Maggiore** – arguably Tuscany's finest. The
region is studded with lonely cypresses on sun-baked clay hills, and contains all
the other classic Tuscan images. The abbey is reached easily enough by car via
Asciano or **Buonconvento**, 9km distant to the north and west, respectively;
Montalcino, too, is only 24km distant to the south and makes an excellent base
for the whole district. You can get to Asciano or Buonconvento by train or bus
from Siena, though you'll have to hitch (more promising from Buonconvento)
or hike (prettier from Asciano) the rest of the way.

Buonconvento

BUONCONVENTO is the most obvious base if you are visiting Monte Oliveto Maggiore and travelling on south. The small town looks unremittingly industrial as you approach, but once through the suburbs you come upon a perfect, walled medieval village. In its day, this was one of Siena's key outer defences, and it was here, in 1313, that Emperor Henry VII of Luxembourg, en route to besiege Siena, famously died of malaria, exhaustion or – in some versions – being fed a poisoned Host during Mass. This was a man whom Dante, among others, had seen as the saviour of Italy (Dante particularly wished the emperor to attack Florence, from which he was then exiled).

The old centre is characteristically Sienese, with its brick bastions, town hall and works of art – most of which have been removed from local churches to the excellent and little-known **Museo d'Arte Sacra della Val d'Arbia**, in the main street of the old quarter at Via Soccini 18 (mid-March to mid-Oct Tues–Sun 10am–1pm & 3–7pm; rest of the year Sat & Sun 10am–1pm & 2.30–6pm; €3.50). Pride of place in the charming museum – which on its own is worth the trouble of pulling into town – goes to a small *Madonna and Child with Angels* by Matteo di Giovanni, whose knowing Mary must surely be a portrait. Other works include a *Madonna and Child* attributed to Duccio; a *Madonna and Saints* (1470–82) and *Coronation of the Virgin* by Sano di Pietro; a lovely four-panelled *Annunciation* (1397) by Andrea di Bartolo; the curious *Madonna del Latte* by Luca di Tommè showing a breast-feeding *Madonna*; and an *Annunciation* (1490–1500) by Benvenuto di Giovanni, a Florentine-influenced work that strikes an anomalous note among the surrounding Sienese treasures.

An interesting museum, the **Museo della Mezzadria** (Tues–Sun 10am–6pm; ⓦ www.museomezzadria.it), in Piazzale Garibaldi, has varied displays devoted to the region's rural and social history. The museum occupies a superb brick-vaulted space, a late medieval granary built in and around part of the town's old walls. Numerous original objects and artefacts document an almost-vanished agrarian world, and one that most Tuscan families would have lived virtually unchanged for generations until about fifty years ago. The second floor contains part of a reconstructed *casa colonica*, the classic rural Tuscan farmhouse, offering a vivid glimpse into the life and living conditions of Tuscan peasant farmers.

These attractions aside, Buonconvento makes an enjoyable stop. You can get here easily by **train** or **bus** from Siena, Montalcino and elsewhere: there are also a couple of fast through-trains to Florence and Grosseto daily, this being one of the key stations for southern Tuscany.

Practicalities

You can get **tourist information** at Piazzale Garibaldi 2 (Tues–Sun 10am–6pm; ⓣ 0577.807.181) or in office hours at the *comune* (council office) at Via Soccini 32 (ⓣ 0577.80.971). If you need to stay – and there are worse overnight stops if you're travelling far and don't want to get tangled up in Siena – the town has two **hotels**: the *Roma*, Via Soccini 14 (ⓣ 0577.806.021, ⓕ 0577.807.284; ❶), with an inexpensive **restaurant** next door that represents a perfect piece of old-fashioned 1950s Italiana, and the three-star *Ghibellino* in Via Dante Alighieri 1 (ⓣ 0577.809.112, ⓦ www.hotelghibellino.it; ❸). The lively weekly **market** (Sat 8am–1pm) is held in Piazza Gramsci, and there's an antiques fair on the last Sunday of each month.

Alternative **accommodation** near Buonconvento is offered by the *Pieve a Salti agriturismo* (ⓣ 0577.807.244, ⓦ www.pieveasalti.it; ❸) at Pieve a Salti (signed from Buonconvento). Up in the hills, just 4km east of town, it's comfortable and welcoming, and the swimming pool has views over what seems like half of southern Tuscany. You can rent rooms for the night, or simple self-contained apartments in the rustic houses dotted across the estate. Meals are available in the cosy central house.

Monte Oliveto Maggiore

The **Abbazia di Monte Oliveto Maggiore**, 26km southeast of Siena, is sited in one of the most beautiful tracts of Sienese countryside. Approaching from Buonconvento, you climb through forests of pine, oak and cypress, and then into the olive groves that enclose the monastery. From the east, coming through Asciano or San Giovanni d'Asso, the road passes through perhaps the wildest section of all the *crete*. It all appears much as it would have to Pope Pius II, who in 1459 eulogized the woods and gardens that the monks had created from the chalk hills, and the way the russet-coloured brick buildings merged with their setting. Also preserved here is one of the most absorbing Renaissance fresco cycles that you'll find anywhere, a *Life of St Benedict* painted by Sodoma and Luca Signorelli.

The monastery had been founded a century and a half before Pius's visit by one Giovanni Tolomei. A Sienese noble, Giovanni was a major political force in Siena, who renounced all worldly goods after being struck blind and experiencing visions of the Virgin. Adopting the name Bernardo, he came with two companions to the *crete* and lived the life of a hermit. They soon drew a following in this heyday of monasticism, and within six years the pope recognized them as an order – the **Olivetans**, or White Benedictines. Attempting to recapture the simplicity of the original Benedictine rule, these first Olivetans were a remarkable group, going out in pairs during the Black Death to nurse the sick and minister to the dying in all the Sienese towns. During the Feast of the Assumption in 1348, they all met up in Siena – miraculously with no casualties – after their months of perilous work, though Bernardo died later in the year, as did many of the brothers.

The remaining monks rebuilt the order, and over the following two centuries Monte Oliveto Maggiore was transformed into one of the most powerful monasteries in the land. (Pius II had a personal reason to visit, as his relative Ambrogio Piccolomini was one of Bernardo's original companions, and in 1536, Emperor Charles V paid a call, together with a two-thousand-strong army.)

The monastery only really fell from influence with the nineteenth-century suppression of the Italian orders, and after the last war, the Italian government allowed Olivetan monks to repopulate it. They have largely restored the buildings and gardens, which they continue to maintain as a monument, supplementing their state income with a highly advanced workshop in restoring ancient books. They also produce wine, honey, olive oil and a cure-all herb liquor, *Flora di Monte Oliveto*, for sale at the monastery shop.

The monastery

At the gatehouse there is a good, moderately priced **café-restaurant**, *La Torre* (restaurant closed Tues). From the **gateway**, surmounted by a square watch-tower and niches containing della Robbia terracottas, an avenue of cypresses leads to the abbey. Off to the right, signs direct you along a walk to the **Blessed Bernardo's grotto** – a chapel built on the site where Tolomei settled as a hermit.

The **abbey** itself (daily 9.15am–noon & 3.15–5.45pm; winter closes 5pm) is a huge complex, though much of it remains off limits to visitors (guided tours take you to the library during the same hours as the abbey, except from

Nov to Feb, when it is only open at weekends). The entrance leads past the gift shop and Foresteria Monastica or **hostel**, as is the Benedictine custom (☎0577.707.652; closed Nov; **①**), to the **Chiostro Grande**, covered by frescoes of the *Life of St Benedict*, the man traditionally regarded as the founder of Christian monasticism.

Sodoma and Signorelli's Life of St Benedict

The St Benedict fresco cycle was begun by **Luca Signorelli**, a painter from Cortona who trained under Piero della Francesca before working for the papacy on the Sistine Chapel. He worked at Monte Oliveto in 1497, completing nine panels (in the middle of the series) before abandoning the work for a more stimulating commission at Orvieto Cathedral. Like much of his work elsewhere, the scenes show a passionate interest in human anatomy, with figures positioned to show off their muscularity to maximum effect.

A few years after Signorelli's departure, Antonio Bazzi (known as **Il Sodoma**), took over, painting the remaining 27 scenes between 1505 and 1508. Sodoma was from Milan and familiar with Leonardo's work, which he often emulated. How he took his nickname is unclear: Vasari suggests it was apt since "he was always surrounded by young men, in whose company he took great pleasure", though letters by Sodoma himself speak of three wives and thirty children. Whatever, the artist was a colourful figure, keeping an extraordinary menagerie of pets: "Badgers, apes, cat-a-mountains, dwarf asses, horses and barbs to run races, magpies, dwarf chickens, tortoises, Indian doves …".

Sodoma brought a sizeable contingent of these pets to Monte Oliveto, including a raven which imitated his voice, and they make odd appearances throughout his colourful, sensual frescoes – a badger is depicted at his feet in a self-portrait in the third panel. There's a notable eroticism, too, in many of the secular figures: the young men coming to join Benedict as monks, and the "evil women", seen tempting the monks in a panel towards the end of the series – these were originally nudes, before protests from the abbot. If the panels strike you as of differing quality, you might give credence to Vasari's anecdote that Sodoma complained about the money he was being paid, which the abbot subsequently raised on condition that he took more care over the remaining work, the first three historical panels of the sequence.

The **cycle** begins on the east wall, on the right of the door into the church. St Benedict, who was born in Norcia in 480, is depicted in events recorded in Gregory the Great's *Dialogues*. In the early panels he is shown leaving home to study in Rome, before withdrawing to the life of a hermit, where he experiences various tribulations and temptations before agreeing to become abbot to a group of disciples. He was an indefatigable builder of monasteries, and the next panels focus on this activity: the foundation of the twelve houses, which formed the basis of the Benedictine order, as well as depictions of various miracles to help in their construction.

The mid-sequence of the cycle depicts various attempts by an evil priest, Florentius, to disrupt the saint's work: he tries first to poison Benedict and then sends in the temptresses, before God steps in and flattens his house (the first of Signorelli's panels). The following eight scenes painted by Signorelli depict aspects of monastic life, and Benedict's trial by – and reception of – Totila, king of the Goths, before Sodoma takes over again, with the saint foretelling the destruction of Monte Cassino, the chief Benedictine house, by the Lombards. More scenes of monastic life follow, including the burial of a monk whom the earth would not accept, another monk's attempted escape (Benedict intercepts him with a serpent) and the release of a peasant persecuted by a Goth.

The rest of the monastery is inevitably overshadowed by the frescoes. The main **church** – entered off the Chiostro Grande – was given a Baroque remodelling in the eighteenth century and some superb stained glass in the twentieth. Its main treasure is the **choir stalls**, inlaid by Giovanni di Verona and others, from 1500 to 1520, with architectural, landscape and domestic scenes (including a nod to Sodoma's pets with a depiction of a cat in a window).

Back in the cloister, stairs lead up, past a Sodoma fresco of the Virgin, to the **library**, a fine Renaissance arcade lavished with carvings by Giovanni and associates. Sadly, it has had to be viewed from the door since the theft of sixteen codices in 1975. Also on view is the **refectory**, a vast room frescoed with allegorical and Old Testament figures, which gives some idea of Monte Oliveto's heyday.

Asciano

ASCIANO, 9km north of Monte Oliveto, lies on a tiny branch rail line between Siena and Grosseto that takes you through marvellous *crete* countryside. The road approach, the N438 from Siena, is still more scenic, with scarcely a hamlet amid the hills; this route is covered by one bus a day.

Of Etruscan foundation, Asciano is first mentioned in records in 715. In the ninth century it was ruled by the powerful Scialenghi counts, but in 1169 passed to Siena, which promptly ordered the destruction of the town's fortress. In 1234 it fell briefly to Florence, but was soon recaptured by the Sienese. Its most famous son is Domenico di Bartolo (1400–45), the painter responsible for the fresco cycle in Siena's Santa Maria della Scala (see p.338). The town is partially walled and shelters a glorious provincial museum. In the restored Palazzo Corboli at Corso Matteotti 120 stands the **Museo Civico Archeologico e d'Arte Sacra** (Tues–Sun 10am–1pm & 3–7pm; Nov–March closes 5.30pm; €4), which, like the museum in Buonconvento, contains an unexpected wealth of Sienese paintings and (on the second floor) the contents of the town's former Etruscan museum. It has a dozen or so works by major Sienese painters (among them Ambrogio Lorenzetti, Sano di Pietro, Taddeo di Bartolo and Matteo di Giovanni). At Via Mameli 36, the **Museo Cassioli** (open on request; ☎0577.719.510) displays paintings by local artist Amos Cassioli (1832–91).

For information visit the summer-only **tourist office** at Corso Matteotti 18 (☎0577.719.510). The town has a reasonably priced, three-star **hotel**, *Il Bersagliere*, Via Roma 39–41 (☎0577.718.715, ⓦwww.hotellapace.net; ❷), and a slightly grander, co-owned sister hotel, the three-star *La Pace* (same details; ❹), about 30m away. Local bars provide basic food, though the best **restaurant** in the vicinity is the moderately priced *La Pievina* with an excellent vegetarian menu (☎0577.718.368; closed Mon & Tues), 5.5km north along the Siena road at the hamlet of the same name.

San Giovanni d'Asso and east to Sinalunga

The next stop on the train line from Asciano – and another possible starting point to hike to Monte Oliveto – is **SAN GIOVANNI D'ASSO**, a quiet, rustic place, whose medieval past is hinted at by the presence of half a dozen churches. Romanesque San Pietro, an eleventh-century gem, is the most interesting, and there's an imposing, if extremely blunt thirteenth-century **castle**. Only ever a Sienese fiefdom, the fortress was inhabited at various times by the Buonsignori, whose Sienese palace now houses the city's Pinacoteca, and by the Salimbeni, whose dynastic seat in the city is now the headquarters of the Monte dei Paschi bank. Later it became a granary, and in time was given to Siena's Santa Maria della Scala (see p.338). The village is in truffle country, and has a recently inaugurated museum devoted to the tuber (the first in Italy), the **Museo del Tartufo** (mid-May to June Sat 2–6pm, Sun 10am–1pm & 2–6pm; July & Aug Sat & Sun 10am–1pm & 5–9pm; Sept to mid-May 10am–1pm & 2–6pm; €3; ⓦ www.museodeltartufo.it), housed in part of the castle at Piazza Gramsci 1 (you can also obtain tourist information here; ☎0577.803.101). As well as insights into truffles, the museum also offers the chance to admire some of the castle's austere but, in parts, prettily frescoed chambers.

East from San Giovanni, a fine though bus-less road meanders towards Sinalunga. The attraction here is primarily the landscape – classic Tuscan miniatures – though the road is marked out by a series of hill-top villages, most of them endowed with a castle and a smattering of medieval churches. **CASTEL-MUZIO**, 10km from San Giovanni d'Asso, was a favourite preaching ground for Bernardino of Siena, whose confraternity houses a small **Museo d'Arte Sacra** (open on request; ☎0577.665.077); the saint is also depicted in panels by Giovanni di Paolo, his close friend, and Giovanni's pupil Matteo di Giovanni, in the church of Sts Trinità e Bernardino. Close by is one of Tuscany's oldest churches – the eighth-century **Pieve di Santo Stefano** in **Cennano** – while at neighbouring **Petroio**, built on a curious circular plan, is the best **castle** in the district, a thirteenth-century brick affair where Siena's magistrates were obliged to live for a period in the thirteenth century. A few kilometres to the northeast is the **Abbadia a Sicille**, built by the Templars as a hospice on the pilgrim road to Rome. **TREQUANDA**, a slightly larger village with a couple of restaurants and bars, also preserves a good section of its castle. In the central square, the simple Romanesque parish church of **Sts Pietro e Andrea**, fronted by a brown-and-white chequered stone facade, has a fresco by Sodoma of the *Transfiguration*, and a high altarpiece of the *Madonna and Saints* by Giovanni di Paolo. The inlaid wooden urn contains the body of Bonizella Piccolomini (1235–1300), a mere beatific who never reached the heights of more illustrious family descendants such as Aeneas Piccolomini (Pope Pius II).

East of Trequanda you reach **SINALUNGA**, a modern, thriving centre with rail connections to Siena, Arezzo and Chiusi. It has one notable painting – an *Annunciation* by Benvenuto di Giovanni – in the church of **San Francesco**, sited beside the Franciscan convent at the top of an avenue of cypresses. The church should have another fine picture – a *Madonna* by Sano di Pietro – but that went missing in 1972 and has been replaced by a sad facsimile. Just out of town in the hamlet-suburb of Pieve is a pleasant **hotel**, the *Santorotto* (☎&ⓕ0577.679.012; ❶). There is further accommodation at the **spas** of Rapolano Terme and Terme San Giovanni, north of Sinalunga on the Siena road. Both are modern, upmarket places of little interest to anyone not visiting "to take the cure".

Montalcino

MONTALCINO, 37km south of Siena, is a classic Tuscan hill-town, set within a full circuit of walls and watched over by a castle of almost fairytale perfection. A quiet, immediately likeable place, affluent in an unshowy way, it is scarcely changed in appearance since the sixteenth century. It looks wonderful from below, its walls barely sullied by any modern building, and once up in the town the rolling hills, vineyards, orchards, olive groves and ancient oaks look equally

Festa del'Unità (May 8). A small palio – featuring the same horses that will appear later in the year at Siena – is held on the sports field below the fort.

Montalcino Jazz & Wine (July) in the Fortezza.

Montalcino Teatro (3rd and 4th weeks of July). An international theatre festival, presenting works in progress in the churches, Rocca, eighteenth-century Teatro degli Astrusi, and sometimes in the *crete* around the town.

Torneo della Apertura della Caccia (2nd Sun in Aug). Tournament marking the start of the hunting season that is said to have fourteenth-century origins – inspiring some of the tales in the *Decameron*. Half the town dresses up in medieval costume for parades and archery competitions (on the sports field) between the *contrade*. Street banquets complete the day.

Festa dell'Unità (mid-Aug). Ten-day festival organized by the former communist party in the pine wood above the town. Live music most nights, cheap food and wine – and usually a lot of fun.

Sagra del Tordo (last Sun in Oct). Similar events to the *Caccia* festival, but if anything even more widely touted.

lovely in turn. While there are few specific sights, the town makes an excellent base for much of southern Tuscany, lying within easy striking distance of the abbeys of Monte Oliveto and Sant'Antimo, and close to the towns of Pienza, 20km east, and Montepulciano, 11km farther.

Some history

Montalcino's origins are unknown, though it has probably been inhabited since **Paleolithic** or **Etruscan** times. No one is quite sure where its name comes from, though its coat of arms – a holm oak atop six hills – suggests that it derives from the Latin *Mons Ilcinus* (the Mount of the Holm Oak). The first reference to the town appears in 814, when it is mentioned in a list of territories ceded to the abbey of Sant'Antimo by **Louis the Pious**, the son of Charlemagne (see p.402). It was probably only permanently settled around the year 1000, colonized by fugitives fleeing Saracen attacks on the Maremma coast. The exiles' four family groups – the Borghetto, Pianello, Ruca and Travaglio – defined the four quarters or *contrade* of the town: the rival flags still hang outside the houses and they compete against each other in twice-yearly archery tournaments.

Though independent for much of its early medieval history, the town succumbed to **Sienese** rule in 1260 after the Battle of Montaperti, having previously looked to Florence for protection. Having been forced to change sides, the town eventually took its new rulers to heart. In 1526 it took just two days for its citizens to fight off a besieging army dispatched by Pope Clement VII. In 1553, over a period of four months, it withstood the attack of a combined Spanish and Medici army. The town's finest hour, however, came in 1555, when on April 21 the venerable Sienese Republic was forced, once and for all, to capitulate to the Medici. A group of Sienese exiles, supported by the French, then formed a last bastion of Sienese power in Montalcino, flying the flag of the old Republic for four years in the face of almost constant attack. Surrender was only countenanced following the treaty of Cateau Cambrésis (1559) between France and Spain. This heroic interlude is acknowledged at the Siena Palio, where the Montalcino contingent, under their medieval **banner** proclaiming "The Republic of Siena in Montalcino", still takes place of honour.

In the following centuries, the town declined to a poor, malaria-stricken village. Although the malaria was sorted out in the nineteenth century, in the 1960s Montalcino was still the poorest locality in Siena. Now the second-richest, its change in fortunes is due principally to the revival and marketing of its wines, notably the **Brunello**, which is reckoned by many the finest in Italy. The production of high-quality honey and olive oil and income from tourism also play a part.

Arrival and information

Roads up to Montalcino, perched 567m above sea level, wind through bucolic swathes of vineyards and pretty pastoral countryside (note the decorative roses

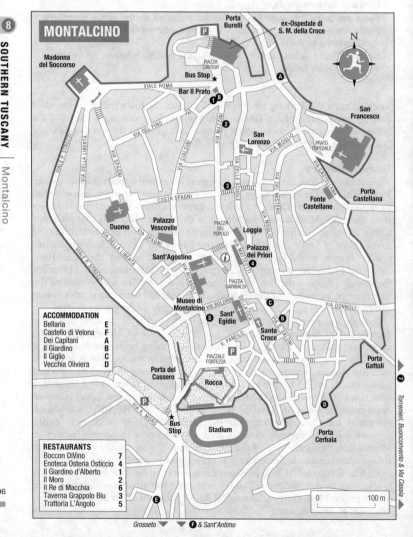

MONTALCINO

Porta Burelli
ex-Ospedale di
S. M. della Croce

N

Madonna del Soccorso

PIAZZA CAVOUR
Bus Stop
VIALE ROMA
Bar Il Prato

San Francesco

VIA DEL PINO
VIA MAZZINI
VIA DELLA LIBERTÀ
VIALE P. STROZZI

VIA CIALDINI
VIA SPAGNI

San Lorenzo
VIA DELLE SCUOLE
VIA MOGLIO
PRATO OSPEDALE
VIA CASTELLANA

COSTA SPAGNI
Fonte Castellane
Porta Castellana

Duomo
Palazzo Vescovile
PIAZZA DEL POPOLO
Loggia
VIA MATTEOTTI
Palazzo dei Priori
VIA MOGLIO

VIA SPAGNI
Sant'Agostino
VIA RICASOLI
PIAZZA GARIBALDI

VIA DELLA LIBERTÀ
VIALE P. STROZZI

Museo di Montalcino
VIA BOLDRINI
Sant'Egidio
VIA DELLA OCA
VIA S. SALONI
VIA DONNOLI

Santa Croce
V. PANFILO
PIAZZALE FORTEZZA

Porta Gattoli

Porta del Cassero
Rocca

VIA A. MORO
Bus Stop
Stadium

Porta Cerbaia

ACCOMMODATION
Bellaria	E
Castello di Velona	F
Dei Capitani	A
Il Giardino	B
Il Giglio	C
Vecchia Oliviera	D

RESTAURANTS
Boccon DiVino	7
Enoteca Osteria Osticcio	4
Il Giardino d'Alberto	1
Il Moro	2
Il Re di Macchia	6
Taverna Grappolo Blu	3
Trattoria L'Angolo	5

0   100 m

Grosseto ▼   ▼ ⓕ & Sant'Antimo

Torrenieri, Buonconvento & Via Cassia

grown at the end of many rows of vines): views to all sides are stupendous. Once up at the town, you find yourself on a road that rings the walls. Buses will stop just below the **Rocca** if you wish, but terminate in **Piazza Cavour** at the northern end of Via Mazzini, the main street: either point is convenient for Piazza del Popolo, the centre of town. If you're driving, aim to park either in the small pay **car park** by the Rocca (take the narrow road which strikes through the arch – the **Porta del Cassero** – in the castle walls) or, alternatively, use the large, free car park below the fortress (take the second turning on the right at the mini-roundabout below the Rocca).

The small **tourist office** is located just up from Piazza del Popolo at Costa del Municipio 8 (Tues–Sun 10am–1pm & 2–5.40pm; ☎0577.849.331, ⓦwww.prolocomontalcino.it). Montalcino's weekly **market** is held on Fridays (7am–1pm) in Viale della Libertà. If you need a taxi, or a car with a driver, call ☎0577.849.113.

Accommodation

Accommodation is severely limited and it's wise to book ahead at almost any time of year. There is only a handful of hotels, though if you have transport you could try one or two tempting places in the countryside nearby. The tourist office has lists of private rooms in and around town as well as at *agriturismi* in the surrounding countryside.

Bellaria Via Osticcio 19 ☎0577.848.668, ⓦwww .hotelbellariamontalcino.it. The location about 2km out of town is not ideal, but this modern, 25-room three-star is a good, family-run choice. It is a modern construction, but copies the traditional style and materials of a rural Tuscan house. ❸

🏃 **Castello di Velona** Località Castello di Velona, Castelnuovo dell'Abate, 10km south of Montalcino ☎0577.800.101, ⓦwww .castellodivelona.it. Until 2001 this twelfth-century "castle" was little more than a pile of rubble: now it is a superb twenty-room hotel, in lovely open countryside on its own hill and ringed by cypresses. Expensive, but rates drop to €210 in low season and there are often web deals. ❾

Dei Capitani Via Lapini 6 ☎0577.847.227, ⓦwww.deicapitani.it. A good, slick three-star choice, with the bonus of a small swimming pool. The 29 rooms vary, however: some are smallish and have no view; others look out over marvellous countryside. Ask to see a selection. ❹

Il Giardino Piazza Cavour 4 ☎&ⓕ0577.848.257. The cheapest hotel option in town is cheap for a reason – its rooms, a mixed bag of ten doubles, are pretty sparse, and those facing onto the piazza are likely to be a little noisy. ❶

Il Giglio Via Soccorso Saloni 5 ☎0577.848.167, ⓦwww.gigliohotel.com. A long-established hotel in a central, sixteenth-century town house that has recently been spruced up and offers pleasant, clean rooms, some with terraces. ❷

Vecchia Oliviera Via Landi 1 ☎0577.846.028, ⓦwww.vecchiaoliviera.com. Like *Dei Capitani*, a relatively new three-star hotel, but more expensive and not quite as central as its rival. However, it has a pool, its patio has excellent views, and the eleven fine rooms form part of a well-restored former olive mill close to Porta Cerbaia and the walls. Rooms, however, can suffer from noise from the road nearby. ❺

The Town

Wherever you end up, the triangular **Piazza del Popolo** lies only a few minutes' walk away. An odd little square, it is set beneath the elongated medieval tower of the **Palazzo dei Priori**, or Palazzo Comunale (1292), apparently modelled on Siena's Palazzo Pubblico. Crests of long-forgotten dignitaries dot the walls, while the statue (1564) beneath the portico, surprisingly, represents the reviled Medici ruler, Cosimo I – it was sculpted just five years after Montalcino had surrendered to the Florentines. Inside the town hall is the *Consorzio di Brunello*, which has information and an exhibition on the history and making of Montalcino's famous Brunello wine; shops the length and breadth of the town sell the stuff, most at ridiculously elevated prices.

Occupying other sides of the square are an elegant Renaissance double **loggia**, almost a reprimand in proportional architecture, and a wonderful nineteenth-century **café**, the *Fiaschetteria Italiana* (closed Thurs Nov–Feb). The café is the heart of town life and the focus, inevitably, of the passeggiata along Via Mazzini. On busy summer afternoons, however, service can be slow – not a problem if all you want to do is watch the world go by. If you've worked up a thirst, however, the **bar** to the right of the loggia, *Alle Logge di* Piazza (closed Wed), which also has outside tables, is usually quicker with liquid refreshment.

The Rocca

Following Via Mazzini's continuation, Via Matteotti, or the parallel Via Ricasoli, and curving up to the right, you emerge at the south end of town by the **Rocca** (April to last Sun in Oct daily 9am–8pm; Nov–March Tues–Sun 9am–6pm; free). It was begun in 1361 on the orders of the Sienese, but by the end of the fifteenth century the advent of artillery had left the castle all but redundant – not that this discouraged those who defended it during the 1526, 1553 and 1555 sieges. The ramparts were added by Cosimo I in 1571, together with the large Medici crest (a shield with six balls), whose present peripheral position – tucked away at the back above the road junction – is surely no accident.

Impressively intact, the walls enclose a public park and in-house **enoteca** (T 0577.849.211, W www.enotecalafortezza.it) – a reasonable place to sample some of the famed Brunello along with bread, cheese and salami (though at times it becomes hectic and uncomfortably clogged with tourists). The *enoteca* also sells tickets for access to the **ramparts** (€4, or joint ticket with Museo Civico €6) and a glimpse of the famous banner. The castle view is said to have inspired Leonardo's drawing of a bird's-eye view of the earth; the Val d'Órcia is easily made out and on a clear day you can even see Siena.

The Museo di Montalcino e Raccolta Archeologica Mediovale e Moderna

Heading north down Via Ricasoli brings you to the excellent **Museo di Montalcino e Raccolta Archeologica Mediovale e Moderna** (Tues–Sun: April–Dec 10am–6pm; Jan–March 10am–1pm & 2–5.30pm; €4.50, or joint ticket with the Rocca fortress €6) built in the former seminary of Sant'Agostino. Here the old civic and diocesan collections are featured under one roof for the first time. Like many galleries in the region, the quality of the paintings on show is out of all proportion to the size of the town. Montalcino's begins with a superb *Crucifixion* dating from the end of the twelfth century – one of the oldest pieces of Sienese art in existence. An anonymous work, it was originally hung in the abbey at Sant'Antimo. It is followed by a more mannered *Madonna and Child with Two Angels*, a lovely anonymous late-thirteenth-century work. Bartolo di Fredi has two works on show: an oddly narrow *Deposition* and a more conventional *Coronation of the Virgin*. There's also a *Madonna and Child* by Bartolo's collaborator, Luca di Tommè.

One of the gallery's most interesting works is the *Madonna dell'Umiltà* (Madonna of Humility) by Sano di Pietro, a comparatively rare subject, in which the Virgin is shown sitting or kneeling on a simple cushion rather than poised on a throne or chair. Its appearance dates from the beginning of the fourteenth century, and coincided with the ideas promulgated by the more radical wing of the Franciscan order, which advocated a return to the more rigorous and humble outlook of the first Franciscans. Two paintings by Girolamo di Benvenuto

(1470–1524) also merit a close look: an *Adoration of the Shepherds* (with ugly shepherd and fractious Child) and the more spectacular and unusual *Madonna della Cintola*. The latter concerns the Apostle Thomas, who according to legend cast doubt on the Assumption into Heaven of the Virgin (hence "doubting Thomas"). To assuage his worries he opened her tomb, which he found covered in flowers – beautifully depicted in this painting. Casting his eyes upwards, he then saw the Virgin, who removed her belt, or girdle (*cintola*), and let it fall into the hands of the kneeling Thomas. The subject was particularly popular in Tuscany – Agnolo Gaddi, for example, devoted an entire fresco cycle to the theme in Prato, which claims to have the girdle in question (see p.205).

Among the gallery's **sculptures** and miscellaneous **artefacts**, make a special point of looking for the pair of illuminated twelfth-century Bibles and the rare polychrome wooden statue *St Peter*, one of the few documented works of the sculptor Francesco di Valdambrino: it was commissioned in 1425 and given by Pius III to the town's Confraternity of St Peter. You'll also notice an almost comical *Annunciation*, an early fifteenth-century Umbro-Sienese work, in which the puppet-like Gabriel and the Virgin sport impossibly rosy cheeks and beautifully mannered hairstyles.

Churches

Walking a few paces up Via Ricasoli from the museum brings you to the church of **Sant'Agostino**, a severe Gothic-Romanesque affair begun in 1360. The barn-like single nave is dotted with patches of fresco, the most extensive of which – and with a wide variety of themes – cover the arched presbytery, and are probably the work of Bartolo di Fredi. The most interesting pictures, however, are two anonymous panels of *Scenes from the Passion*. One, on the left wall, also shows St Anthony Abbot sharing bread with a curiously attired St Augustine; the second, to the right of the side entrance, is an extraordinary and almost surreal collection of disembodied heads and symbols. Note the moon and sun, which in paintings of the Passion or Crucifixion serve, among other things, to symbolize the anguish of all creation at the death of Christ.

To the north, Via Spagni takes you past the **Duomo**, or San Salvatore, an eleventh-century Romanesque church, horrendously remodelled in Neoclassical

▲ A typical enoteca, Montalcino

style between 1818 and 1832 by an architect aptly called Fantastici; its interior is unarresting, however, save for an impressive little pyramid of reliefs in the baptistery chapel salvaged from the original church. Via Spagni continues to emerge in front of the distinctive Renaissance **Santuario della Madonna del Soccorso**, a seventeenth-century sanctuary built over an ancient chapel; its chief appeal is the sensational view from the adjoining park. Drop down Viale Roma to Piazza Cavour and pop into **Santa Maria della Croce**, a hospital founded in the thirteenth century, more recently appropriated by the local council. Just inside the main entrance is the former pharmacy, still covered in a pretty little array of original frescoes. Nearby, facing the Porta Castellana, is a medieval washhouse, the **Fonte Castellane**, and beyond it the deconsecrated church of **San Francesco**, graced with pleasant cloisters, della Robbia school terracottas and an annexe that was once a medieval hospital.

Wine and food

Sampling **Montalcino's wines** is easily done. Apart from the *enoteca* in the Rocca and the *Fiaschetteria Italiana* – which has a superb *cantina* at the back – there are half a dozen cheaper café-bars with good stocks. At Via Matteotti 31 there's the *Bar Mariuccia*, with a breathtaking view from the vast windowed terrace at the back. For bottles to take away, try the *Enoteca Les Barriques* at Via Boldrini 19, which has over 800 Tuscan wines, including the major Brunello and Rosso di Montalcino labels. *Enoteca di Piazza*, Piazza Garibaldi 1, has wines from 140 local producers, all well kept in three air-conditioned rooms. In addition to the classic Brunello and the more briefly barrel-aged Rosso di Montalcino table wine, it's worth trying some of the white Moscadelletto di Montalcino, a dessert wine produced in small quantities and at its best chilled.

Eating

Montalcino is remarkably blessed with good **restaurants**. In summer it's worth booking a table at just about any of the following places.

Boccon DiVino Località Colombaio Tozzi 201 ☏0577.848.233. 1km east of town on the Torrenieri road, this is a great wine bar and restaurant with superb views (and a lovely summer terrace). It's housed in an old rural property, and

the dining rooms have a rustic air. Food, though, is more refined – and expensive: reckon on €40 or so for a full meal. Closed Tues.
Enoteca Osteria Osticcio Via G. Matteotti 23 ☏0577.848.271, ⊛www.osticcio.com. The

Moving on

TRA-IN **buses** (☏0577.204.111, ⊛www.trainspa.it) run more or less hourly from Piazza Cavour and Viale P. Strozzi to Buonconvento and Siena via Torrenieri. At Torrenieri you can pick up one of six daily buses to San Quírico, Pienza and Montepulciano. There are four local buses daily from Montalcino to Sant'Angelo Scalo (⊛www.bargagliautolinee.it) and just one during the school term to Abbadia San Salvatore and Piancastagnaio. There's also a daily SIRA bus (☏0641.730.083) to and from Rome (it departs for Rome mid-afternoon from Piazza Cavour), useful as a direct way of getting to Pienza and Montepulciano, which it passes en route to the A1 motorway. Bus tickets are available from tobacconists around town, and from the *Bar Il Prato* on the corner of Viale Roma and Piazza Cavour.

For **rail connections** to Siena or Grosseto, head to Buonconvento, Torrenieri or to Sant'Angelo. Most services are slow, stopping numbers, but buried in the timetable are a couple of fast through trains daily to Florence (via Siena) and Grosseto (for connections to Rome and Pisa).

smartest of Montalcino's many wine bars, but worth paying a little over the odds for your glass of Brunello and light meal simply to enjoy the spectacular views over the Tuscan countryside. Closed Sun.

Il Giardino d'Alberto Piazza Cavour 1 ☎0577.849.076. Pleasant interior, with good local cooking: the chef is the owner. Closed Wed.

Il Moro Via Mazzini 44 ☎0577.849.384. A consistently reliable and no-nonsense modern trattoria with the best budget meals in town. Closed Thurs.

Il Re di Macchia Via Soccorso Saloni 21 ☎0577.846.116. Montalcino's swankiest restaurant. While the food is usually excellent, its sometimes pretentious *cucina nuova* leanings may not be to all tastes. Closed Thurs.

Taverna Grappolo Blu Via Scale di Moglio 1 ☎0577.847.150. Located in a little alley off Via Mazzini. The old stone-walled interior is cool and appealing, and the unusual pastas are excellent.

Trattoria L'Angolo Via Ricasoli 9 ☎0577.848.017. Informal and vaguely trendy little bar-trattoria just down from the Rocca, serving snack lunches and local pasta dishes. Closed Tues.

Vineyards and villages around Montalcino

As Brunello is Italy's premier wine, it seems a shame not to get out to at least one of the **vineyards**. As well as those detailed below, you can visit most others if you ask at the winegrowers' headquarters in Montalcino's Palazzo Comunale; the only period when visitors might not be welcome is at harvest time (Sept–Oct).

The **Fattoria dei Barbi** (☎0577.841.111, ⊛www.fattoriadeibarbi.it) is 7km southeast of Montalcino, signposted off to the left just after the hamlet of La Croce on the Sant'Antimo road. Its *cantina* (Mon–Fri 10am–1pm & 2.30–6pm, Sat & Sun 2.30–6pm; open until 7pm in summer) offers tasting facilities and a superb stock of vintages. Attached is a very fine **restaurant**, the ⟨ *Taverna dei Barbi* (☎0577.841.200 or 0577.847.117; closed Tues dinner and Wed except in Aug) with strictly local recipes at moderate prices – lots of *porcini*, *pici*, *papardelle* and delicious grilled pork, the *brasato al Brunello*, washed down, of course, with the Barbi's own wine.

With a third of its three thousand hectares devoted to vineyards, the **Villa Banfi** (☎0577.840.111, ⊛www.castellodibanfi.com) is Montalcino's largest and most modern wine producer. It has a moderately priced ⟨ **restaurant** (dinner only Tues–Sat) serving good-quality local cuisine (booking essential). The villa is located 18km southwest of Montalcino just outside the village of Sant'Angelo Scalo where you can get an inexpensive **pizza** at *Il Marrucheto* (☎0577.808.000) by the station.

At the halfway point on the road from Montalcino to Villa Banfi is the tiny walled village of **SANT'ANGELO IN COLLE**, set on a low hill (it can also be reached on a beautiful but partly gravel-surfaced road from Sant'Antimo). The Sienese used it as a military base against Montalcino in the mid-thirteenth century and as part of their frontier thereafter. It has some interesting frescoes inside the Romanesque church, **San Michele**, on the piazza (check out the lovely views from behind the church) and a couple of **bar-restaurants**. The one just off the piazza, *Il Pozzo* (☎0577.844.015; closed Tues), at Piazza Il Pozzo 2, is recommended for its inexpensive pasta dishes and roasts.

Sant'Antimo

It's a moot point which of Tuscany's many abbeys is the most beautiful, has the most fascinating history, or boasts the loveliest setting, but many would put the **Abbazia di Sant'Antimo** (Mon–Sat 10.15am–12.30pm & 3–6.30pm, Sun 9.15–10.45am & 3–5pm; free; ⊛www.antimo.it) near the top of their list. It's a glorious, isolated Benedictine monastery that stands comparison with the nearby foundations of San Galgano, Monte Oliveto and San Salvatore. Located a short distance from the hamlet of Castelnuovo dell'Abate, 10km south of Montalcino, and splendidly isolated in a timeless landscape of fields, olive groves and wooded hills, the abbey stood empty for some five hundred years, and is today maintained by a small group of French monks – a Cistercian offshoot known as the Premonstratensians, who celebrate Mass several times daily in haunting Gregorian chant.

There are occasional **buses** along the Sant'Antimo road from Montalcino. Alternatively, it's a pleasant country walk or feasible hitch. Additional rewards are at the moderately priced *Ristorante Bassomondo* (☎0577.835.619; closed Mon) across the road, which does wonderful *crostini*, *ribollita* and *pici*.

Mythology and history of the abbey

Tradition ascribes the foundation of the abbey to **Charlemagne**, who, while returning with his army from Rome in 781, halted in the nearby Starcia valley. Here he prayed to God, asking for relief from the disease which was crippling his army, and offering to found a church if his prayers were answered. An angel appeared, showing the emperor a herb (called *Carolina* in Italian) which he was instructed to dry and give to his men as a powder with wine. The cure worked as promised, and Charlemagne duly founded Sant'Antimo.

If this story sounds too good to be true, it is known that the abbey existed in 814, when Charlemagne's son, **Louis the Pious**, enriched it with vast tracts of land and privileges in a charter dated December 29 of that year. Other scholars suggest it may have been founded on the site of a Roman villa, or possibly by the last of the area's Lombards in about 760, the date of the foundation of the Abbadia di San Salvatore (see p.424). In fact **St Antimo** (feast day May 11) was probably a bishop martyred in Rome during the persecutions of Diocletian and Maximian (304–5 AD). Certainly it's known that in 781, the year of the abbey's supposed foundation, St Antimo's relics, along with those of St Sebastian, were given to Charlemagne by Pope Hadrian I.

Whatever the truth of Sant'Antimo's origins, the decidedly **pre-Romanesque** style of parts of the primitive church, together with documentary evidence, confirms a late eighth- or early ninth-century foundation. Over the two centuries that followed, the abbey's importance grew, thanks in part to its location close to the intersection of several of central Italy's most important medieval **trade and pilgrimage routes**. Oldest of these was a former Etruscan road linking Chiusi with Rusellae on the coast, a route which passed directly in front of the abbey (traces of the sunken lane can still be seen). This was crossed by the old Roman consular road, Via Clodia, again right in front of the abbey. The most important of the ancient roads, however, was the **Via Francigena**, which for centuries was the most important pilgrimage route between Rome and northern Europe. Countless towns and villages grew up along the route, together with numerous hospices for pilgrims: Siena – whose Santa Maria della Scala was one of the most important of these (see p.338) – and San Gimignano are just two local towns which owe their early medieval prosperity to the Via Francigena.

Sant'Antimo's heyday dates from 1118, when an enormous **bequest** allowed work to begin on the main body of the present church and a complex of monastic buildings (now largely lost). The grant's original deed – a document many hundreds of words long – was engraved in the steps of the altar, where it survives to this day. With new-found funds, the abbey authorities now had access to expertise and ideas from elsewhere in Europe, and looked for inspiration to the great Benedictine mother house at Cluny, in Burgundy, and to **French architects**, whose plans for the new church appear to have been based on the abbey church of Vignory (begun in 1050) in the Haute-Marne.

Over the years funds began to run low – hence the unfinished facade – as religious bequests increasingly found their way to new orders such as the Camaldolese and Cistercians. Worse, the rising power of Siena began to strip away the abbey's privileges and lands; in 1212, following Siena's sacking of Montalcino (then under the abbey's ownership), Sant'Antimo's abbot was forced to cede a quarter of the territory of Montalcino to the Sienese Republic. By 1293 it retained only a fifth of its original possessions, which had once made it the second richest abbey in Tuscany. **Financial problems** were soon followed by moral and spiritual decline. In 1439 Pope Eugenius IV had the abbot imprisoned for "villainy"; then in 1462, Pius II **suppressed the abbey** for good, convinced that it was beyond spiritual or financial salvation.

The abbey soldiered on for a few years under the auspices of the bishops of Siena and the newly created diocese of Montalcino, but after 1492 – when Montalcino's bishops opted to live instead in the town – it was largely **abandoned**, its buildings ransacked for stone for use in Castelnuovo and Montalcino. What remained was bought by the state in 1867.

The church

The monks' quarters aside, little remains of the plundered monastic buildings – a ruined refectory and chapterhouse are now used as barns, and accommodation for recently arrived monks. But the twelfth-century **church** itself is in excellent repair and is one of the most outstanding examples of Italian Romanesque, built in a soft, creamy stone and perfectly proportioned.

The **facade** was the last part of the church to be built, and so suffered most from the shortfall of funds. The traces of arches in the stones, and the pilasters with attached columns, suggest that a portico once provided a grander entrance: the lions which supported the portico, and symbolized the power of Satan waiting to devour the faithful, are now inside the abbey. Recent studies suggest the portal on the church of Santa Maria in nearby San Quírico d'Orcia (see p.404) was one of two portals intended for the abbey, and was perhaps given away in the light of the abbey's subsequent decline. The surviving **portal** contains a twelfth-century lintel whose Latin text alludes to one Azzo, a monk who may have been one of the original architects of the church. Otherwise the capitals, frieze and recessed, fluted arch are all lifted directly from French (Languedoc) models. Around the corner, on the left (north) wall, the little filled-in doorway and lintels survive from the earlier ninth-century church.

The interior

The French flavour becomes more marked in the lovely **interior**, whose basilican plan – with an ambulatory, and radiating chapels – is unique in Tuscany, and found elsewhere in Italy in only a handful of churches. Its presence here allowed pilgrims to walk around the apse and pray before the martyrium, the spot under the high altar which contained the relics of the saint being venerated. The **high altar** features a polychrome statue of the crucified Christ, an outstanding Romanesque work dating from the end of the twelfth century. Note the inscription on the altar steps (see opposite).

The **capitals** on the pillars of the ambulatory display some exquisite carving, a feature for which the abbey is particularly celebrated. Many are carved in lustrous alabaster, a stone which features elsewhere in the building, lending a beautifully subtle tone to the walls and sculpture. Here the carving is more Lombard than French, leading to the theory that two separate workshops – one from France (the Auvergne) and one from Lombardy (Pavia) may have worked alongside one another. Equally plausible is the idea that many of the capitals derive from the earlier Carolingian church, built before the French-inspired church of 1118.

The abbey's finest capital sits atop the second column on the right of the nave. It depicts *Daniel in the Lions' Den*, the protagonist – arms raised in prayer – a study of calm while his fellow prisoners are crushed and eaten by rampant beasts. Clearly superior to anything else in the abbey, it is the work of the so-called **Master of Cabestany**, a sculptor of French or Spanish origin whose distinctive hand has been identified in abbeys across France, Catalonia and Italy – he seems always to have worked for the Benedictines. By way of comparison, wander across to study the capital on the second column on the left, which depicts a shepherd and sheep in a far more mundane style.

The rest of the church is often closed to visitors. Areas affected include the **sacristy**, which occupies part of the ninth-century Carolingian church, entered (when open) from a door in the right aisle. It features an array of primitive black-and-white frescoes with such details as a rat looking up attentively at St Benedict, and a pair of copulating pigs. Note the stoup with Pius's Piccolomini crest at each corner. Further frescoes are to be found in some of the rooms built around the **women's gallery**, fitted out in the fifteenth century by the bishops of Montalcino: it's approached from the nave by a circular stairway, though here, too, access is often restricted.

The Val d'Órcia and Bagno Vignoni

The **Val d'Órcia** stretches from San Quírico d'Órcia down towards the border with Lazio and the lake of Bolsena. A gorgeous stretch of country, it is marked at intervals by fortresses built from the eighth century on, when the road through the valley, the **Via Francigena**, was a vital corridor north from Rome (see p.337).

The major attraction along the initial section of the valley is the remarkable Medicean sulphur baths of **Bagno Vignoni**. With transport – or enthusiasm for walking – you might strike off south from here to the region's medieval power base, the monastery of San Salvatore (see p.424). **Walkers** might also consider approaching Bagno Vignoni across country from Montalcino (a five-hour hike which would entail staying in Bagno Vignoni), or going on from Bagno Vignoni along the old gravel road to Pienza.

San Quírico d'Órcia

A rambling, part-walled village, **SAN QUÍRICO D'ÓRCIA** stands at a crossroads on the Siena-to-Bolsena road overlooking the Órcia and Asso valleys. It's quiet and appealing – an odd mix of modern and medieval – overlooked by the precarious ruins of a seventeenth-century palazzo, whose Baroque exterior frescoes are fading before your eyes. Its name comes from San Quírico a Osenna, an ancient church on the Via Francigena, though of the eponymous saint little is known except that he was martyred, probably in the fourth century. Hospitals and hospices sprang up here to accommodate

There are plenty of interesting **hikes** around San Quírico and Montalcino, in the **Parco Artistico Naturale e Culturale della Val d'Órcia**. The park information office doubles as San Quírico's tourist office, Via Dante Alighieri 33 (℡0577.897.211 or 0577.898/303, Ⓦwww.parcodellavaldorcia.com).

A moderately challenging trail runs from Bagno Vignoni out to the castle restaurant at Ripa d'Órcia and back (12km; 4hr). From 100m before the Bagno Vignoni car park, a cart-track rises through vineyards and olive groves to Rocca di Vignoni, the hamlet of Vignoni and on to Podere Bellaria, after which is a junction. One route heads right (north) to San Quírico, the other left (south) through a scenic landscape up to the Ripa d'Órcia castle. Backtracking 500m down the castle hill you'll find a signposted path leading right, down through foliage to a broken bridge over the Órcia river; don't cross, but follow the left-hand riverbank back to Bagno Vignoni.

There's an easier trail from Montalcino to San Quírico, crossing shadeless clay hills and dipping through vineyards (13km; 4hr), good for walking or cycling. From Montalcino's northern Porta Burelli, a track drops down to Gli Angeli and crosses the paved road in front of Podere La Casaccia, heading into an area of hummocks until you reach the provincial highway. Follow the road right for a few hundred metres, coming off at Podere Fiesole and heading east across clay ground to Podere Casello and Poderi Pian dell'Asso. Cross the train track and a couple of streams before climbing to Podere Belladonna and the chapel of Madonna di Riguardo. A rising and falling path covers the last 1500m into San Quírico.

pilgrims in the early Middle Ages, as they did in Siena and other settlements along the Via Francigena.

The main – and highly worthwhile – reason for stopping in the town is to look around the exceptionally pretty Romanesque **Collegiata**, with its three portals sculpted with lions and other beasts; the south door may be the work of Giovanni Pisano (or his school), while the main portal is rightly considered the finest piece of Lombard work in the region. The church was built in the twelfth century, probably on the ruins of a still older church. Inside is a delicate triptych of the *Virgin and Saints* by Sano di Pietro in the north transept, as well as a marvellous set of nine Renaissance choir stalls, whose figures and *trompe l'oeil* may have been executed to designs by Luca Signorelli. The stalls originally formed part of a larger nineteen-stall set in the Cappella del Battistero in Siena cathedral.

There's a **tourist office** at Via Dante Alighieri 33 (April–Oct daily 10am–1pm & 3.30–6.30pm; ℡0577.897.211), also the headquarters of the **Parco Artistico Naturale e Culturale della Val d'Órcia** (see box above). It provides information about the park and the Treno Natura "tourist" train line that occasionally runs through the Val d'Orcia to Monte Antico (Ⓦwww.ferrovieturistiche.it). San Quírico is a regular stop on the Siena–Buonconvento–Pienza–Montepulciano TRA-IN **bus** route, as well as a stop on the once-daily SIRA Montalcino–Rome service. It has a small two-star **hotel**, *Il Garibaldi* (℡0577.898.315; ❶), on the Via Cassia, the main road.

If you want an isolated and peaceful place to stay, **Ripa d'Órcia**, about five kilometres southwest of San Quírico at the end of a minor but perfectly passable gravelled road, has an absolutely stunning hotel, *Castello Ripa d'Órcia* (℡0577.897.376, Ⓦwww.castelloripadorcia.com; ❹), located in an isolated and ancient castle that is visible for miles around. Views from the castle are sensational, and there are lovely strolls and marked trails down to the Órcia valley and Sant'Antimo from right outside the walls.

Bagno Vignoni

Six kilometres south of San Quírico, **BAGNO VIGNONI** is scarcely even a hamlet – just a handful of buildings around a central square. The square, however, is one of Tuscany's most memorable sights, occupied by an arcaded Renaissance *piscina*. This was built by the Medici, who, like St Catherine of Siena, took the sulphur cure here. The hot springs still bubble away in the bath (which formed an amazing set in Tarkovsky's film *Nostalgia*), though they are currently out of bounds for bathing; plans to restore the *piscina* and develop the spa as a resort have so far been thwarted – thankfully – by the Siena council.

You can, however, bathe in the sulphur pools at the foot of the hillside below the village, or use the sulphur pool at the four-star *Posta Marcucci* **hotel** (☎0577.887.112, ⓦwww.hotelpostamarcucci.it; ⑥; use of pool for non-residents €10 per day), a fifteenth-century summer house erected by Pius II on the side of the piazza. The village's other hotel, the three-star *Le Terme* (☎0577.887.150, ⓦwww.albergoleterme.it; ⑨), which overlooks the *piscina*, has a marginally better restaurant. The best place to **eat**, however, is the moderately priced *Antica Osteria del Leone*, Via dei Mulini 3 (☎0577.887.300; closed Mon). Food here is Tuscan with a twist and they have several vegetarian options.

Rocca, Castiglione and Vivo d'Órcia

The **Rocca d'Órcia** (summer 10am–1pm & 3–6pm; winter Sat & Sun 10am–1pm & 2.30–6.30pm; €2), 3km south of Bagno Vignoni, is visible almost the whole way from San Quírico: from the eleventh to the fourteenth centuries this dramatic pile of a castle belonged, like almost every castle along this stretch of the Via Francigena, to the **Aldobrandeschi** family.

CASTIGLIONE D'ÓRCIA, the village below the *rocca*, is a fine-looking place, with a trio of medieval churches. In the Romanesque church of **Sts Stefano e Degna** are panels (temporarily removed to the museum in Montalcino) by Pietro Lorenzetti, Vecchietta and one attributed to Simone Martini – a hint of the wealth Castiglione must once have enjoyed. Vecchietta, incidentally, was born in the village in 1412.

Moving south towards Monte Amiata, the hamlet of **VIVO D'ÓRCIA** is another medieval treat, with beautiful walks along the river and in the woods, where you come upon the Romanesque **Cappella dell'Ermicciolo**, part of a twelfth-century Camaldolese monastery, the Eremo del Vivo, altered in 1536, reputedly by Antonio da Sangallo the Younger.

Bagni San Filippo and Radicófani

East of Vivo d'Órcia, just a few hundred metres off the N2, is the tiny spa of **BAGNI SAN FILIPPO**. Like Vignoni, this has an outdoor hot sulphur spring cascading from the rocks, as well as an unostentatious modern spa building and pool.

On the other side of the N2 from San Filippo, a road veers east into the hills to the majestically situated **Rocca** of **RADICÓFANI** (783m), which vies with the Rocca d'Órcia for the title of most imposing fortress in southern Tuscany. Clamped to a basalt outcrop, it commands the strategic heights between the Paglia and Órcia valleys. The castle is identified with one Ghino di Tacco, a fourteenth-century bandit who features in the writings of both Dante and Boccaccio. Views from the walls are stunning. Hours vary from year to year: for the latest details contact the small, summer-only tourist office at Via Renato Magi 57 (☎0578.55.684; irregular hours). Below the castle, which was devastated by an explosion in the eighteenth century, is a handsome little village, with an old Capuchin convent, a cluster of churches and the sadly dilapidated **Palazzo La Posta** – the "Great Duke's Inn", where centuries of grand tourists – including Montaigne and Charles Dickens – put up on their way to Rome. The best of the churches, the Romanesque **San Pietro**, features several good glazed terracotta works from the school of Andrea della Robbia, together with a polychrome wooden *Madonna* (second pillar on the left) by Francesco di Valdambrino. A rare sculptor, Valdambrino (1375–1435) often collaborated with the great Sienese sculptor Jacopo della Quercia, having worked with him on the panels for the Fonte Gaia, now displayed in Siena's Palazzo Pubblico. He is best known for his *St Peter* in Montalcino (see p.399).

The village remains a handy place to stay, with a modest **hotel** – *La Torre*, Via Matteotti 7 (℡0578.55.943; ●).

Pienza

PIENZA, 20km east of Montalcino, is as complete a Renaissance creation as any in Italy, conceived as a Utopian "New Town" by **Pope Pius II**, Aeneas Sylvius Piccolomini (see p.336). The site Pius chose was the village of Corsignano where he was born in 1405, the first of eighteen children of a noble family exiled from Siena in 1385 (the village, at least in part, formed part of the Piccolominis' traditional feudal domain). Archeological evidence suggests it was inhabited as early as the Bronze Age. In Roman times it was a hill-top fort of some renown, and by the thirteenth century it had a reputation as an anarchic border town: Boccaccio spoke of "Corsignan de' Ladri" ("Corsignano of the thieves") in his novel *Cecco di Fotarrigo*. Today there's little to see beyond Pius's central Renaissance piazza – the pope's death marked the end of his beloved project – though few places in Tuscany have as much immediate charm. There are also some extraordinary **views** from the walls, a scattering of good **bars and restaurants**, and a range of **accommodation** – from rooms to a fine historic hotel – if you want to stay.

Some history: Pius and Rossellino

The **construction** of Pienza began in 1459, less than a year after Pius's election to the papacy in August 1458. History rather harshly suggests the new pope wished to avenge himself on Siena – which had unjustly exiled his family – by building a city that would be both Siena's antithesis and its superior. It's also claimed Pius could not live with the shame of having come from a village as humble as Corsignano. His architect on the project was **Bernardo Rossellino**, who worked on all the major buildings here under the guidance of Leon Battista Alberti, the great theorist of Renaissance art, building and town planning.

Rossellino's commission was to build a cathedral, papal palace and town hall, but Pius instructed the various cardinals who followed his court to build their own residences too, turning the project into nothing less than a Vatican in miniature (see "Palazzo Vescovile" p.411). Astonishingly, the cathedral, the papal and bishop's palaces, and the core of the town were completed in just three years. Limited though it was, it constituted the first "Ideal City" of the Renaissance to become a reality.

After consecration of the cathedral, Pius issued a papal bull rechristening the "city" Pienza, in his own honour, and stipulating that no detail of the cathedral or palaces should be changed. The wish was fulfilled rather more easily than he

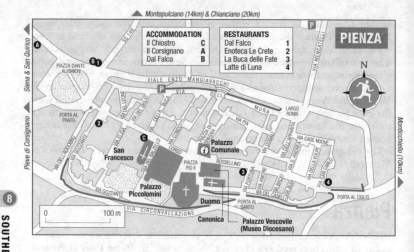

could have expected, for he died within two years, and of his successors only
Pius III, his nephew, paid Pienza any regard. The city, intended to spread across
the hill, never grew beyond a couple of blocks to either side of the main Corso,
and its population remained scarcely that of a village. Today, with a population
of 2500, it still has an air of emptiness and folly: a natural stage set, which was
used by Zeffirelli for his film of *Romeo and Juliet*.

The Town

There is no difficulty finding your way about Pienza. Roads, buses and cars
converge on the **Piazza Dante**, just outside the Porta al Murello, main
entrance gate to the papal town. From here the **Corso Rossellino** leads to
Rossellino's centrepiece, **Piazza Pio II**, enclosed by the Duomo, Palazzo
Piccolomini, Palazzo Comunale and Palazzo Vescovile, the last of these built by
one of Pius's more ambitious Vatican followers – Cardinal Borgia, the future
Pope Alexander VI. The juxtaposition of civic and religious buildings here was
deliberate, and aimed to underline the balance between Church and town
through architectural harmony. Apart from the Palazzo Comunale, based on the
medieval Palazzo Vecchio in Florence, the ensemble is entirely Renaissance in
conception. If it all seems a little cramped, it's partly because Rossellino wished
to retain the existing east–west axis of Corsignano's main street, and partly
because of Pius's insistence that his palace loggia should command a view and
that the Duomo should be flooded with light, meaning that the piazza's two key
buildings had to be orientated towards the valley to the rear. For the Duomo,
in particular, this was to have near-disastrous structural consequences.

The piazza's small well, the **Pozzo dei Cani**, sets the tone, its twin columns
and classical frieze a perfect miniature of Renaissance ambitions.

The Duomo

The **Duomo**, or Santa Maria Assunta, has one of the earliest Renaissance
facades in Tuscany, its three-tiered veneer of Istrian marble surmounted by a
vast garland of fruit enclosing Pius's papal coat of arms. The **campanile**, rocked
to its foundations by an earthquake in 1545, was virtually rebuilt in 1570.

On Pius's orders, the **interior** took inspiration from Franciscan Gothic
churches and the German *Hallenkirchen*, or hall-churches, which he had seen on

his pre-papal travels as a member of the Curia. The hall-churches, as here, were distinguished by naves and aisles of equal height. The tall **windows** were also a papal whim, designed to produce a *domus vitrea* (hall of glass), whose flood of light was intended to symbolize the age's humanist enlightenment. Pius's *Commentaries* also talk of the strangely elongated **capitals** of the nave's columns as *felici errori*, or "happy errors". Legend claims the pope found the church's earlier columns too short and insisted that Rossellino find some way of lengthening them. In fact, Rossellino deliberately introduced the capitals, partly to accentuate the nave's soaring Gothic effect, and partly to evoke parallels with similar capitals in Siena's Loggia di Mercanzia, and the Duomo, Loggia dei Lanzi, and church of San Lorenzo in Florence.

To satisfy Pius's whims, and to fit the cramped site, Rossellino had to build on sandstone with a substratum of clay. Before completion a crack appeared, and following an earthquake in the nineteenth century it has required progressively more buttressing and ties. The nave dips crazily towards the back of the church – still shifting at an estimated rate of a millimetre a year – and alarming cracks are still all too obvious, tagged by small glass ties designed to reveal further movement. At last report, however, authorities say there is no imminent danger of collapse and no need for further buttressing.

Several outstanding and contrasting **altarpieces** – the church's highlights – still fill the principal chapels, each commissioned by the pope and his architect from some of the major painters of the age. Pius's choice of artists was deliberate: each was Sienese, as was he (at least by family origin) – Rossellino, it's worth noting, was from Settignano, just outside Florence. This partisan choice, however, rather undermined Pius's Renaissance credentials, for Florentine painters by this time were far ahead of their more backward-looking Sienese counterparts. Pius's choice of each subject – the Madonna, to whom the church was dedicated – was equally considered, as was the choice of saints included in each painting. Thus St Sabina in Giovanni di Paolo's work was featured because Pius was titular head of the Basilica di Santa Sabina in Rome; St Peter appeared because he was the first pope; and saints Catherine and Bernardino achieved prominence through their Sienese connections.

The first painting, midway down the right (south) wall, is Giovanni di Paolo's *Madonna and Child with Sts Bernardino, Anthony Abbot, Francis and Sabina* with a *Pietà* above – note the Piccolomini arms at the bottom left and right of the frame. The first apse chapel features Matteo di Giovanni's *Madonna and Child with Sts Catherine of Alexandria, Matthew, Bartholomew and Lucy* with the *Flagellation* above: here, too, there's a nod to Pius in the shape of more coats of arms. The next apse contains a travertine tabernacle attributed to Rossellino, behind whose little central door is a **reliquary** containing bones alleged to be from the head of St Andrew, Pienza's patron saint. Another work by Rossellino, a vast **font**, can be seen in the crypt, along with Romanesque fragments recovered from Santa Maria, the former church near the site. The central apse – normally containing the high altar – is empty, Pius having stipulated that nothing should block the light coming from the central windows. Instead he commissioned the choir (1462), the tell-tale papal shield again appearing at the top of the central bishop's throne.

The **fourth chapel** houses a triptych of the *Assumption with Sts Agatha, Callistus, Pius I and Catherine of Siena* by **Vecchietta**, born in nearby Castiglione dell'Órcia: it's considered one of his masterpieces and is by far the finest of the church's altarpieces. The fifth chapel features Sano di Pietro's *Madonna and Child with Sts Philip, James, Anne and Mary Magdalene*.

Pius, realizing his Sienese painters lagged behind Florentine thinking, made specific requests in an attempt to bring a little Renaissance flavour to what were essentially Gothic works. Thus Sano was asked to replace the niches traditionally used in the predella (panels in the lower part of altarpieces) with a more classical frame of small pillars. The "V" arrangement of the saints around the Virgin was also new – at least in the works of Sano. Vecchietta similarly staked a claim for modernity by enclosing his *Assumption* triptych – very much a Gothic conceit – in a fixed frame that effectively made the painting a single, rather than hinged, tripartite work. Similar efforts towards a more Renaissance effect are found in the last painting, Matteo di Giovanni's *Madonna and Child with Sts Nicholas, Martin, Augustine and Jerome*, midway down the north wall. The saints here, for example, are set on different levels – compare the same artist's painting across the nave (where they are on one level) – while the Virgin's upper throne is decorated with heads whose classical inspiration is unmistakable.

Palazzo Piccolomini

Pius's residence, the **Palazzo Piccolomini**, to the right of the Duomo, was modelled on Alberti's Palazzo Rucellai in Florence, and built by Rossellino over the demolished remains of the Piccolomini's former feudal holding in the village. All three main facades are identical, novelty being provided by the imaginative addition of a triple-tiered loggia at the back, making it the first Italian building to be designed specifically to afford views over a swathe of countryside. Its cost was astronomical, Rossellino spending 50,000 gold florins, five times his allotted budget – a charge that he was liable to repay. Pius, however, accepted the expense, delighted at the building and its views.

For these views, you can walk into the superb courtyard at any time of day and through (on the left) to the original "hanging garden" behind; it has remained unchanged over the centuries and is the perfect embodiment of the Renaissance concept that gardens form an intermediary between nature and architecture. The triple-tiered loggia, with its three orders of Classical columns (Ionic, Doric and Corinthian), owes a clear debt to the great imperial buildings of ancient Rome.

For a glimpse of the splendour envisaged for Pius, however, you need to climb the steps in the courtyard to the first-floor **papal apartments** (Tues–Sun: mid–March to mid–Oct 10am–6.30pm; rest of the year 10am–4pm, but closed last two weeks of Feb & of Nov; open Mon on public holidays; €7; Ⓦwww .palazzopiccolominipienza.it), occupied until 1962 by the Piccolomini family. Guided tours conduct you to Pius II's dining room, library and music room, each filled with furniture, books, carpets and manuscripts. The highlights, though, are the papal bedroom – complete with a gloriously vulgar canopied bed – and the cavernous Sala d'Armi, filled with rows of fearsome pikes and other weapons.

Palazzo Vescovile

The **Palazzo Vescovile**, or Palazzo Borgia, to the left of the Duomo and home to the Museo Diocesano (see below), began as a single-storey Gothic palace, but was given to Roderigo Borgia by Pius on condition that he demolish it and rebuild in a more modern manner. Borgia, then a cardinal, would later become the infamous Pope Alexander VI and father four children, among them the notorious Lucrezia and Cesare Borgia. Showing the astuteness, if not the meanness, that would characterize his papacy, Borgia refrained from knocking down the palace, but saved money by altering a few superficial details and adding an extra storey. Thus on the ground floor – clearly of different vintage – you can still see the outlines of the old Gothic windows, bricked in to form tiny square windows more in keeping with Renaissance ideas. Still more visible are the holes that pockmark the upper part of the building, the legacy of a mortar bombardment during **World War II** that also knocked chunks out of the cathedral's apse. The highest marks have an even earlier vintage, having been inflicted by the artillery of Charles V and the Medici during their assault on the Sienese Republic between 1552 and 1559. How much time Borgia spent in the palace is uncertain – though the Borgia arms are clearly visible on the shield on the corner of the building. In any event, it appears he made a gift of the building in 1468, when it became the Palazzo Vescovile, or Bishop's Palace.

Museo Diocesano

Like many small southern Tuscan museums, the **Museo Diocesano**, Corso Rossellino 30 (mid-March to Oct Wed–Mon 10am–1pm & 3–7pm; Nov to mid-March Sat & Sun 10am–1pm & 3–6pm; €4.10), deserves more attention than it receives. Its star attraction is a superb thirteenth- or fourteenth-century *piviale*, or **cope**, an English work (signed *Opus Anglicanum*) of fantastically embroidered silk embellished with scenes from the life of the Virgin and St Catherine of Alexandria, together with various saints and apostles (originally the cope would also have been studded with pearls and precious stones). Tradition claims it was given to Pius by Thomas Paleologus, prince of the Peloponnese and brother of the Byzantine emperor. However, it's more likely to derive from a papal wardrobe dating from the papacy's sojourn in Avignon, where it appears in an inventory dated 1369.

The museum also contains superb tapestries, crosiers, miniatures, illuminated manuscripts, choir books with miniatures by Sano di Pietro and others – produced for Orvieto cathedral but bought by Pius – and a whole slew of top-notch **paintings**. Look out in particular for the *Madonna dell'Umiltà and Sts Elizabeth of Hungary and John the Baptist*, an anonymous work (by the "Maestro dell'Osservanza"), so-called because its Madonna is shown seated on a simple oriental carpet rather than the more usual ornate throne. Also outstanding are a famous *Madonna della Misericordia* (c.1364) by Bartolo di Fredi, his first signed and dated work; among the figures sheltered by the vermilion-robed Madonna are the Emperor Charles IV (in red cloak and crown on the right), who visited Siena in 1355 en route for Rome, together with the pope (alongside) and Charles's queen (to the left, crowned, in pink). It seems likely Siena's Council of Twelve, then in thrall to the emperor, commissioned the work to commemorate the visit.

More eye-catching still is a magnificent 48-panel painting whose tiny anonymous miniatures depict scenes from the life of Christ. It was one of only a handful of surviving "portable" paintings once used by mendicant monks as a preaching aid during their perambulations around the countryside. The picture was brought here from the castle of Spedaletto in the Val d'Órcia, together with a painting often regarded as the first Renaissance Sienese painting: Vecchietta's seminal polyptych of the *Madonna and Child with Sts Blaise, Florian, John the Baptist and Nicholas* (1462). The lunette, clearly Florentine in flavour, depicts the *Annunciation*, whose receding classical columns and three naves of equal height deliberately recall the design of the Duomo. The predella, by contrast, depicts three scenes with a more Sienese touch: the *Crucifixion*, with Siena's bare-hilled *crete* as background; the *Miracles of St Nicholas*; and the *Martyrdom of St Blaise* (for more on Blaise, see p.420).

The rest of the town

A short way down the main street from Piazza Pio II stands the church of **San Francesco**, one of two churches to survive from the original Corsignano, and the only significant medieval building remaining in Pienza. Its walls were once entirely covered in fourteenth-century frescoes, only a few of which (scenes from the life of St Francis) survive in the apse. More remains of the large Crucifix on the right, a fourteenth-century work by a follower of Duccio, and the arresting *Madonna della Misericordia* on the left, attributed to Luca Signorelli.

Be certain to take the alley to the left of the church – or those to either side of the Duomo – to gain access to Pienza's **walls**, rebuilt after being razed to the ground by the armies of the Medici and Charles V of Spain in 1559. You can see why Pius wanted his loggia, for the views from here are some of the finest from any town in Tuscany. Head east past the Duomo and you come to a lovely series of little **lanes** leading back into the village, each with impossibly twee names – notably Via dell'Amore (street of love) and Via del Bacio (street of the kiss): the names were altered from more warlike ones in the nineteenth century so as to be more in keeping with the village's Renaissance idea of itself. In the other direction a more rural lane runs out of Piazza Dante along a level ridge past public gardens.

Not to be missed is the ten-minute downhill walk from Piazza Dante (signed off the south side) to the **Pieve di Corsignano** (or San Vito), the village's original parish church, and the place where Pius was baptized. Extremely ancient, it probably dates from the tenth century, and is one of the best Romanesque churches for miles around. The cylindrical tower – used to shelter the townspeople during bandit raids – is highly unusual, as are the carvings above the main and side doors. You can get the key from the farmhouse just behind the church – leave a small tip.

Practicalities

Pienza is a pleasant place to stay, but there's not much life after dark, so it might also be considered as a day-trip from Montepulciano. TRA-IN **buses** cover the routes to Buonconvento and Siena (7 daily) and Montepulciano (9 daily); for details of times, call in at the helpful **tourist office** (℡0578.749.305, ⊛www .comunepienza.it; mid-March to Oct Mon–Sat 10am–1pm & 3–6pm or later; Nov to mid-March Sat & Sun 10am–1pm, 3–5/6pm) on the Corso in the Museo Diocesano. Among Pienza's **festivals** is the *Incontro con I Maestri dell'Arte* ("Meeting with a Master of Art"), when the work of a contemporary Italian artist is exhibited in the Palazzo Comunale over August and September.

Accommodation is limited: the *Ristorante dal Falco* at Piazza Dante 8 (☎0578.748.551; ❷) has six simple rooms, each with bathroom, but they're quickly snapped up. Much more expensive is the modern but very pleasant three-star *Hotel Il Corsignano*, Via della Madonnina 11, about 150m west of the piazza on the left (☎0578.748.501, ☜www.corsignano.it; ❹): rooms at the back have little terraces and something of a view. If you're doing Tuscany in style, or fancy a treat, the obvious choice is the three-star ☆ *Il Chiostro di Pienza*, Corso Rossellino 26 (☎0578.748.400, ☜www.relaisilchiostrodipienza.com; ❻), though it often has large groups staying. The only in-town hotel, it's an extremely chi-chi conversion – complete with frescoes, vaults and other medieval trappings – which has been infiltrated into the old cloister and buildings of a Franciscan monastery.

Among **restaurants**, the best are *Dal Falco* in Piazza Dante (closed Fri), a simple trattoria which offers superb *gnocchi* and a filling *pecorino alla griglia* (hot cheese wrapped in prosciutto), at around €23 for a full meal; and the excellent, friendly and moderately priced ☆ *Latte di Luna*, Via San Carlo 2–4 (☎0578.748.606; closed Tues & periods in Nov & Feb), blessed with a small terrace for outdoor eating and an ancient well incorporated into the old interior. Also reasonably good value is *La Buca delle Fate*, Corso Rossellino 38a (☎0578.748.272; closed Mon and periods in Jan & June), housed in part of the fifteenth-century palace of the Gonzagas and with thoroughly Tuscan country food. You can get panini and light meals at the *Enoteca le Crete* in Piazza Martiri, and there's no shortage of picnic food: Pienza is centre of a region producing **pecorino** sheep's cheese, and has gone overboard on *alimentari* and "natural food" shops.

East to Montepulciano: Monticchiello

MONTICCHIELLO, 4km east of Pienza, is a walled village with a leaning watchtower, lovely views of Pienza and a great **church** (if this is locked, you can collect a key from the house next door), which houses numerous

▲ Pecorino cheese for sale, Pienza

fourteenth-century Sienese frescoes – look out for the gargantuan *St Christopher* – and a *Madonna* by Pietro Lorenzetti. Outside the church, in the corner on the right as you stand with your back to the facade, is a tiny old-fashioned shop selling some of the most beautiful **fabrics** imaginable. They're all made by hand locally, and are exported – quietly – to all corners of the globe. As an added bonus the hamlet has a more-than-decent moderately priced **restaurant**, the *Taverna di Moranda*, Via di Mezzo 17 (℗0578.755.050, ⓦwww .tavernadimoranda.it; closed Mon and periods in Nov, Dec, Jan & Feb), run by an Italo-French couple who offer superb local food and an extensive selection of big-name local wines.

During the last week of July and the first week of August, the village puts on a now-renowned **Teatro Povero** (℗0578.755.118 or 0578.755.735, ⓦwww .teatropovero.it) featuring a play written and performed by the villagers to evoke the local folk and farming traditions – a kind of Tuscan *Archers*. It's a pleasantly informal occasion, enjoyed equally for the food at the *taverna* set up for the duration of the festival. A large exhibition space in a former granary at Piazza Nuova 1 (Tues–Sun: 10am–6pm guided tours on the hour; free) is given over to props, stage sets and audio-visual displays connected with the play and its history.

Montepulciano

One of the highest of the Tuscan hill-towns, **MONTEPULCIANO** (665m) is built along a narrow tufa ridge, with a long main street and alleys that drop away to the walls. It's a stunningly good-looking town, full of vistas, odd squares and corners, and endowed with dozens of Renaissance *palazzi* and churches, which embody the state of architecture fifty years after Bernardo Rossellino's pioneering work at Pienza. Largely forgotten in subsequent centuries, the town today makes most of its money from its wine industry, based on the famed **Vino Nobile**, though its tourist profile becomes higher with each passing year. Along with Montalcino it's perhaps the best base in southern Tuscany, with Pienza, Chiusi and Bagno Vignoni all within easy reach by car or public transport.

Some history

Montepulciano's unusually consistent array of Renaissance *palazzi* and churches is a reflection of its remarkable development after 1511, when, following intermittent alliance with Siena, the town finally threw in its lot with Florence. In

Festivals

Cantiere Internazionale d'Arte July–August; ℗0578.757.089, ⓦwww.cantiere .toscana.nu. A major international performing arts festival (especially music) founded by composer Hans Werner Henze in the 1970s. The festival makes a point of supporting young musicians, with artists and stagehands alike slumming it in the local co-operative mess rooms.

Bruscello August 14–16. The Festival of Assumption is celebrated with a sequence of masked plays and light opera in the town squares.

Bravío delle Botti Last Sunday in August. A barrel race through the streets from Sant'Agnese to the Piazza Grande, between teams from each of the town's eight *contrade*. Costume processions precede the race and a street banquet follows.

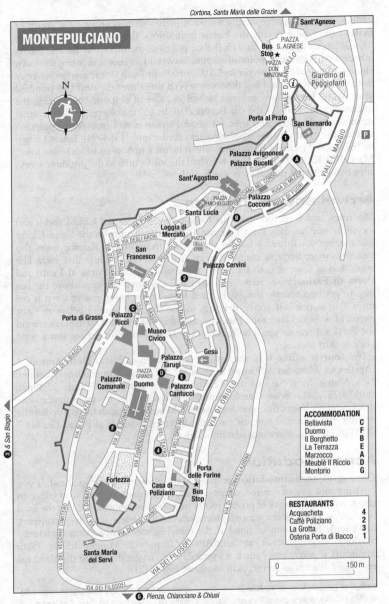

MONTEPULCIANO

Cortona, Santa Maria delle Grazie ▲

Sant'Agnese

PIAZZA
S. AGNESE

Bus
Stop ★

PIAZZA
DON
MINZONI

Giardino di
Poggiofanti

VIALE D. SANGALLO

Porta al Prato

San Bernardo

VIALE I. MAGGIO

P

Palazzo Avignonesi
Palazzo Bucelli

Sant'Agostino

PIAZZA
MICHELOZZO

Santa Lucia

VIA GRACCIANO NEL CORSO

RUGA DEL MEZZO

Palazzo
Cocconi

RUGA DI FUORI

Loggia di
Mercato

VIA PIANA

VIA DEGLI ARCHI

PIAZZA
DELL'ERBE

VIA DI VOLTAIA NEL CORSO

VIA DI ORIOLO

San
Francesco

VIA DEL PAOLINO

VIA DEL GIARDINO

Palazzo Cervini

VIA RICCI

VIA PIÈ AL SASSO

Porta di Grassi

Palazzo
Ricci

Museo
Civico

Gesù

Palazzo
Tarugi

Palazzo Comunale

PIAZZA
GRANDE

Duomo

Palazzo
Cantucci

VIA FIORENZA LA VECCHIA

VIA DI S. BIAGIO

VIA DI COLLAZZI

VIA DI S. DONATO

VIA DEL POLIZIANO

VIA DI ORIOLO

Porta
delle Farine

Bus
Stop ★

Fortezza

Casa di
Poliziano

VIA DI CIRCONVALLAZIONE

VIA DEL VECCHIO CIMITERO

Santa Maria
dei Servi

VIA DEI FILOSOFI

3 & San Biagio ◀

G, Pienza, Chianciano & Chiusi ▼

N

0   150 m

ACCOMMODATION
Bellavista	C
Duomo	F
Il Borghetto	B
La Terrazza	E
Marzocco	A
Meublè Il Riccio	D
Montorio	G

RESTAURANTS
Acquacheta	4
Caffè Poliziano	2
La Grotta	3
Osteria Porta di Bacco	1

that year the Florentines sent **Antonio da Sangallo the Elder** to rebuild the town's gates and walls, which he did so impressively that the council took him on to work on the town hall and a series of churches. The local nobles meanwhile hired him, his nephew, and later the Modena-born architect **Vignola** – a founding figure of Baroque – to work on their own *palazzi*. The work of this trio, assured in both its conception and execution, makes a fascinating comparison with Rossellino's work at Pienza.

Montepulciano was reputedly founded in the sixth century by a group of **exiles** from Chiusi fleeing the barbarian invasions, the first written allusion to *Mon Politianus* appearing in 715 (hence *poliziani*, the nickname for the town's inhabitants). A constant point of dispute between Florence and Siena, the town chose Florence as its protector in 1202 – on the grounds that it was farther away. Both cities captured and lost the town several times over the next two hundred years, while her citizens suffered several decades of despotic rule during the fifteenth century under the del Pecora clan. In 1511, however, the Florentines again assumed control, this time for good. Famous names from Montepulciano include the great classical scholar Angelo Ambrogini (1454–94), better known by his adopted name of **Poliziano**, which he took in honour of his home town. **Marcellus II** (1501–55), a pope who had the misfortune to die just three weeks after being elected pontiff, was also born here.

Arrival and information

Montepulciano is on the main **bus** route between Siena and Chiusi, and is also served by one bus daily from Florence. Its **train station** is on the Siena–Chiusi line too, but you'll need a bus for the 10km trip into town. Regular buses also link with more frequent mainline trains at Chiusi, not much farther away. The buses stop in town at both the north and south gates, the **Porta al Prato** and **Porta di Farine**; buses arrive at the latter first – climb the steps above the bus stop to get into town – though Porta al Prato at the lower end of town is the main "bus station". If you're **driving**, follow the road around below the east circuit of walls and look for a parking space; don't be tempted by the area around the Porta al Prato or you'll be ticketed. Up around the **Fortezza** is also a good place to start looking.

The **tourist office** is in the lower end of town at Piazza Don Minzoni 1 (April–Oct Mon–Sat 9.30am–12.30pm & 3–7/8pm, Sun 9.30am–12.30pm; Nov–March Mon–Sat 9.30am–12.30pm & 3–6pm, Sun 9.30am–12.30pm; ☎0578.757.341, ⊛www.prolocomontepulciano.it or www.comune.monte pulciano.si.it). Information on local wine and wine tours, and in particular the driving routes around vineyards and producers, is available at Piazza Grande 7 (☎0578.717.484, ⊛www.stradavinonobile.it).

Accommodation

Once again, **accommodation** is sparse and well worth booking ahead. If you can't get into any of our recommendations, try contacting the tourist office to check on the availability of private rooms or *agriturismo* options. Or visit the local hoteliers' website, ⊛www.montepulcianohotels.it. Unless you have transport, don't settle for a room or hotel at the outlying station area (Montepulciano–Stazione/Acquaviva), or at Sant'Albino/Terme di Montepulciano (5km southeast). If you're really stuck, it's probably best to get the bus to the bland spa resort of Chianciano Terme, 9km southeast (see p.421).

Bellavista Gabriella Massoni, Via Ricci 25 ☎0578.757.348, ⊛www.cretedisiena.com. Six well-situated private rooms, five with private bath. Four have stupendous views. No one lives here, so you must ring first, and the owner will drive up to let you in: there's a public phone in the doorway downstairs. ❶

Il Borghetto Via Borgo Buio 7 ☎0578.757.535, ⊛www.ilborghetto.it. Montepulciano's grandest three-star hotel, in a very tastefully refurbished old house off Via Gracciano nel Corso. Just eleven rooms, so be sure to book. ❹

Duomo Via San Donato 14 ☎0578.757.473, ⊛www.albergoduomo.it. A friendly welcome, thirteen spacious and comfortable rooms, three-star facilities and a nice setting off the Piazza Grande make this the town's best upmarket hotel. ❸

La Terrazza Via Piè al Sasso 16 ☏ 0578.757.440, ⓦ www.laterrazzadimontepulciano.com. Pleasant two-star rooms in an ancient house near the Duomo. ❸

Marzocco Piazza Giralomo Savonarola 18 ☏ 0578.757.262, ⓦ www.albergoilmarzocco.it. Smartest hotel in town, an elegant nineteenth-century inn with a full-size billiard table. Very courteous owners, but loses out to the Duomo on position. ❸

Meublè Il Riccio Ivana Migliorucci, Via Talosa 21 ☏ 0578.757.713, ⓦ www.ilriccio.net.

Five well-kept private double rooms, each with private bathroom, TV and phone, off Piazza Grande. ❸

Montorio Strada per Pienza 2 ☏ 0578.717.442, ⓦ www.montorio.com. A member of the "Abitare la Storia" association, whose hotels occupy historic buildings, in this case a fine country house just outside Montepulciano on the Pienza road, with a lovely garden and terraces covered with cypresses and olive trees. There are five apartments for two or four people, each with kitchen and furnished with antiques. ❺

The Town

The Prato and Farine gates are equally convenient starting points for exploring the town; our account begins at the Porta al Prato. Between the two gates runs the town's main street, the **Corso**, whose name is appended in turn to Via Gracciano, Via di Voltaia and Via dell'Opio. The town's main focus is the **Piazza Grande**, home to the **Duomo** and an ensemble of palaces. To see the town's other big sight, the Renaissance church of **San Biagio**, requires a pleasant ten-minute stroll (downhill) to the west of town.

The Corso: Porta al Prato to the Fortress

Sangallo's first commission was Montepulciano's main gate, the **Porta al Prato**, at the north end of town. Before embarking on the climb up, you should visit the church of **Sant'Agnese**, named in honour of a local Dominican abbess, Agnese Segni (1268–1317), who was canonized in 1726 and is buried in the church. The first chapel on the right contains the *Madonna di Zoccoli*, attributed to Simone Martini (or his school), while the second altar on the left features a fourteenth-century Sienese fresco of the *Madonna del Latte*. This subject, which shows a breast-feeding Madonna, is a common feature of Sienese (and Tuscan) painting of the period – the Virgin's milk, in Christian iconography, symbolizing the font of Eternal Life (many a Tuscan church in the Middle Ages claimed to have genuine drops of the Madonna's milk). The subject vanished entirely following the Council of Trent, which in a fit of Counter–Reformationary zeal banned any use of "unnecessary" nudity in the portrayal of religious characters.

Inside the Porta al Prato the **Corso** begins, the *palazzi* immediately making clear the town's allegiance to Florence. In the first square, beside the *Albergo Marzocco*, is the **Colonna del Marzocco**, a stone column bearing the heraldic lion (*marzocco*) of Florence. The original lion, now in the museum (this is an 1856 copy), was fixed to its column in 1511, when it replaced a statue of the she-wolf suckling Romulus and Remus, the symbol of Siena (according to legend the city was founded by Senius, son of Remus). Across the street further lion heads decorate the **Palazzo Avignonesi** (no. 91), probably the work of Vignola. Sangallo makes a second appearance with the **Palazzo Cocconi** (no. 70), virtually opposite the **Palazzo Bucelli** (no. 73), whose base is strikingly inset with Roman and Etruscan reliefs. These were lovingly collected in 1648 by the palace's erstwhile owner, Pietro Bucelli, whose extensive Etruscan collection – an unusual one given the classically obsessed era in which it was amassed – now resides in Florence's Museo Archeologico.

Just beyond this crop of *palazzi* is the eye-catching church of **Sant'Agostino**, designed around 1427 by the earlier Medici protégé, Michelozzo – who also carved the terracotta relief of the *Madonna and Child* above the door; within are a *Crucifixion* on the third altar on the left wall by Lorenzo di Credi and an equally good *St Bernardino* by Giovanni di Paolo on the right wall. Pride of place goes to a polychrome Crucifix on the high altar attributed to Donatello. Across the street a medieval **tower house**, a rare survival in Montepulciano, is surmounted by a *commedia dell'arte* figure of a clown, the **Pulcinella**, who strikes out the hours on the town clock; most un-Tuscan, it is said to have been put up by an exiled bishop from Naples.

About a hundred metres farther along you reach the Renaissance **Loggia di Mercato** and a fork in the road: turn right here if you want to make straight for the Piazza Grande (see below). The Corso continues to the left past further *palazzi*, including the **Palazzo Cervini**, attributed to Sangallo. Begun for the doomed Marcellus II before he became pope, it is now occupied by a bank, and has the grand civic gesture of an external courtyard. Beyond this, you pass the church of **Gesù**, remodelled in Baroque style by Andrea Pozzo (as are many other churches in the town and region), before the road turns the corner and rambles outside the town walls. Just prior to the turn – at no. 5 – is the **Casa di Poliziano**, birthplace of the Renaissance humanist and poet Angelo Ambrogini (Poliziano), who translated many of the Greek classics under the patronage of Lorenzo de' Medici, as well as teaching the Medici children.

Via di Poliziano loops outside the walls to the Gothic-fronted **Santa Maria dei Servi**, another Baroque interior job by Pozzo. Inside it's visited by devout locals eager to prostrate themselves before the much venerated *Madonna della Santoreggia*, a fifteenth-century fresco (second altar on the left). The only other attention-grabbing work is a *Madonna and Child*, oddly inserted into a larger painting (third altar on the right) by a follower of Duccio. Via di Poliziano then re-enters town by the old **Fortezza**, now partly occupied by houses. At the end of Via di San Donato, the last quiet stretch back into town, you'll find yourself in the cathedral and town hall square, Piazza Grande.

Santa Lucia, Via del Poggio and the Museo Civico

A quicker approach to Piazza Grande at the Loggia di Mercato (see above) would be to head right. A block to the north of here, a beautiful little piazza fronts the church of **Santa Lucia**, built in 1633, which has a fabulous, if damaged, *Madonna* by Luca Signorelli in a chapel on the right, though the church is rarely open. Turning instead to the south, Via del Poggio runs down to the church of **San Francesco**: note the ruined pulpit to the side of the facade, from which St Bernardino of Siena is supposed to have preached. The imposing Via Ricci takes over for the last stretch to the Piazza Grande; it is flanked on one side by the Renaissance **Palazzo Ricci**, and on the other by the Sienese-Gothic **Palazzo Neri-Orselli**.

The latter is home to the town's **Museo Civico** (April–July Tues–Sun & Sept–Oct Tues–Sat 10am–1pm & 3–7pm; Aug daily 10am–7pm; rest of the year Tues–Sun 10am–1pm & 3–6pm; €4.15), an extensive collection of small-town Gothic and Renaissance works. The courtyard contains the original Florentine *marzocco* lion removed from the Corso, while the upper-floor room opens with a series of glazed terracottas by Andrea della Robbia. The most important panel is a *St Francis*, painted by the saint's near-contemporary, Margaritone da Arezzo; the most enjoyable is Jacopo de Mino's lush *Coronation of the Virgin*.

The Piazza Grande

The **Piazza Grande**, Montepulciano's theatrical flourish of a main square, is built on the highest point of the ridge, providing the obvious site for the town's

Duomo (see below). Its most distinctive building, however, is the **Palazzo Comunale**, a thirteenth-century Gothic palace to which Michelozzo added a tower and rustication in imitation of the Palazzo Vecchio in Florence. The tower is occasionally open, offering views that on the clearest days stretch to Siena, 65km northwest.

Two of the *palazzi* on the square were designed by Sangallo. The **Palazzo Nobili-Tarugi**, by the lion and griffon fountain, is a highly innovative building, with a public loggia cut through one corner; it originally had an extension on the top floor, though this has been bricked in. More tangible pleasures await at the **Palazzo Cantucci**, one of many buildings scattered about the town that serve as *cantine* for the **wine trade**, offering *degustazione* and sale of the Vino Nobile. The lower part is by Sangallo, the upper by Baldassare Peruzzi, who was Siena's leading sixteenth-century architect.

The Duomo

Sangallo and his contemporaries never got around to building a facade for the **Duomo** (daily 9am–1pm & 3.30–7pm), whose plain brick pales against the neighbouring *palazzi*. Begun in 1680 by Ippolito Scalzi, the building was raised over an earlier church, of which the ugly fourteenth-century campanile is virtually the only reminder.

The **interior** boasts an elegant Renaissance design, and has several outstanding works of art dotted around its rather foreboding walls. The first of these are fragments of the **tomb of Bartolomeo Aragazzi** (1427–36) by the multi-talented Michelozzo, a monument which was criminally dismembered in the nineteenth century. Aragazzi was born in Montepulciano, and achieved prominence as the secretary to Pope Martin V (pontiff from 1417 to 1431), the first pope to occupy the Holy See in Rome after the Grand Schism (1378–1417) divided the papacy between Rome and Avignon. He is often described as the first "Renaissance" pope, his election coinciding with the competition to design the baptistery doors in Florence. Pope Martin was assisted in his adopted role by Aragazzi, who scoured French and German monasteries for manuscripts and oversaw the publication of classical texts by Vitruvius and others. Bas-reliefs from the tomb can now be seen at the base of the first two columns on either side of the nave (right and left), and the effigy of Aragazzi himself is mounted on the rear (west) wall to the right of the door. At the other end of the church, two of the tomb's statues surmount the high altar – which is also garlanded by putti and festoons from the tomb: two sculpted angels from the piece can be found even farther away, in London's British Museum.

Aragazzi also commissioned a painting that would be a highlight of this or any other church: **Taddeo di Bartolo's** iridescent high altarpiece of the *Assumption*, perhaps the supreme rendition of a subject that was a favourite among Siena's leading artists. The date of the painting's commission (1401) is noteworthy, for it came at a time when Montepulciano – which oscillated constantly between Florentine and Sienese domination – found itself free of Florentine rule for a brief period (1390–1404); Aragazzi's choice of a Sienese artist, and a subject dear to the Sienese, is thus revealed as an act of political as well as artistic significance. The main panels of the triptych, its predella and its gilt-turreted upper panels are crammed with detail and incident. Note, in particular, the apostles gathered around the Virgin's tomb in the main painting: Doubting Thomas is shown receiving the Madonna's girdle (see p.399), while a grief-stricken St John views her flower-decked sepulchre. Behind the latter to the right is the Apostle Thaddeus, Taddeo's namesake; the face is probably a self-portrait, an extremely unusual feature in a painting executed on the cusp of the Renaissance, when such self-advertisement would later become quite common.

Elsewhere in the church hunt out a work by Vecchietta, best known as a painter but here represented by an excellent piece of sculpture: the marble **ciborium** in the chapel to the right of the high altar. On the left (north) wall of the church, opposite the pillar of the third nave, is a poetic *Madonna del Pilastro* (Madonna of the Pillar) by Sano di Pietro. At the bottom of the north aisle, close to the main remnants of Aragazzi's tomb, the first chapel – the **Baptistery** – contains a wealth of eye-catching big-name art: the font and its six bas-reliefs (1340) are by Giovanni d'Agostino; the riot of glazed terracotta on the wall, the so-called **Altare dei Gigli** (Altar of the Lilies), is by Andrea della Robbia – it frames a relief of the *Madonna and Child* attributed to Benedetto da Maiano; and the niche statues of St Peter and John the Baptist are attributed to Mino da Camaino.

San Biagio

Antonio da Sangallo's greatest commission came in 1518, when he was invited by the town's Ricci nobles to design the pilgrimage church of **San Biagio** (daily 9am–12.30pm & 3–6/7pm) on the hillside below the town. The model for this was his brother Giuliano's design for the facade of San Lorenzo in Florence, which was never built. The Montepulciano project was more ambitious – the only bigger church project of its time was St Peter's in Rome – and occupied Antonio until his death in 1534. He lived to see its inauguration, however (in 1529), the ceremony performed by the Medici pope Clement VII. To reach the church, follow Via San Biagio out from the Porta di Grassi; it's about fifteen-minutes' walk.

The church, built over an earlier chapel to San Biagio, or St Blaise (see box below), is one of the most harmonious Renaissance creations in Italy, constructed inside and out from a porous travertine, whose soft honey-coloured stone blends perfectly with its niche in the landscape. A deeply intellectualized building, its major architectural novelty was the use of freestanding towers (only one was completed, in 1545) to flank the facade (note the tower's three orders of Classical columns – Doric, Ionic and Corinthian). Within, it is spoilt a little by extraneous decoration – a Baroque *trompe l'oeil* covers the barrel vault – but is equally harmonious. It also has superb acoustics.

Nearby, scarcely less perfect a building, is the **Canonica** (rectory), endowed by Sangallo with a graceful portico and double-tiered loggia.

San Biagio (St Blaise)

San Biagio (St Blaise in English) was an Armenian doctor who became a bishop before being called by God to abandon his worldly affairs in favour of a contemplative life in the mountains. There he lived in a cave, surrounded by wild animals who brought him food and drink, and in return were healed by him when they became sick; he's often depicted, St Francis-like, talking to the birds. He was eventually imprisoned on a charge of practising magic, and tortured by having his body scraped with a sharp-pronged instrument used to card wool. Paintings of him always show him holding such an instrument. Thus he became the patron saint of carders and textile workers, which is why he appears so frequently in Florentine and Tuscan paintings, the textile industry having been the bedrock of the region's medieval prosperity. In a more domestic vein, he is also invoked by Italians against sore throats, having once saved a child who'd had a fish bone stuck in her throat.

The main **transport** links are with Chiusi. LFI **buses** (☎0578.31.174, ⓦwww.lfi.it) run more or less every half-hour to Chianciano Terme, Chiusi and Chiusi station (plus one Siena and one to three Florence services daily). To the west, TRA-IN has seven buses daily on the circuit through Pienza, San Quírico d'Órcia, Torrenieri (change for Montalcino) and Buonconvento, with between three and five daily continuing to Siena. All buses leave from outside Porta al Prato and Porta di Farine; buy tickets from bars or shops in town, not on the bus.

If you're making a **train** connection, take a bus to Chiusi; Montepulciano's own station, 10km northeast, is a stop only for slow *regionali* or *inter-regionali* services. Local **car rental** can be arranged through Bernardini (☎0578.716.081) or Paolo Cencini (☎0330.732.723).

Eating and drinking

Vino Nobile di Montepulciano has been acclaimed since medieval times and today boasts a top-rated DOCG mark; something the townspeople have not been shy in exploiting. Montepulciano's streets are filled with wine shops selling gift sets, and local vineyards often offer tastings in the town (generally free, but usually requiring advance notice). Every restaurant can provide a range of vintages, the very cheapest of which will still set you back at least €20. The tourist office has a complete list of the town's wine outlets, and can organize a **wine-tasting** ramble for you. Some of the many places to check out include the venerable *Contucci*, Via San Donato 15 (☎0578.757.006, ⓦwww.contucci.it), which can trace the family line in Montepulciano back a thousand years, and the *Cantina Del Redi*, Via di Collazi 5 (☎0578.716.092, ⓦwww.cantinadelredi.com).

Restaurants and cafés

Acquacheta Via del Teatro 22 ☎0578.758.443, ⓦwww.acquacheta.eu. A bustling, rustic-look osteria that offers hearty, Tuscan food, including plenty of meat, sausage and salami options. Expect to pay around €20 for a couple of courses with house wine. Closed Tues.

Caffè Poliziano Via di Voltaia nel Corso 27. An 1868 tearoom restored to a classic Art Nouveau design; it serves pastries and pots of tea, while its adjoining restaurant, *Il Grifin d'Oro*, serves somewhat pricey meals (at around €25), such as *pici* (fat spaghetti) with wild boar *ragù*, and offers

great views from a small terrace. Daily 7am–midnight.

La Grotta Via di San Biagio ☎0578.757.607. Opposite San Biagio church, about 1km outside the city walls, brick-vaulted *La Grotta* serves pricey classic Tuscan cuisine in a sixteenth-century building with its own garden. Closed Wed.

Osteria Porta di Bacco Via di Gracciano nel Corso 106 ☎0578.757.948. Just inside the Porta al Prato, this quiet, characterful old stone-arched place is one of a clutch of moderately priced options, offering a set three-course menu for €12. Closed Tues.

East to Chianciano Terme and Chiusi

CHIANCIANO TERME (ⓦwww.termechianciano.it), midway between Montepulciano and Chiusi, is one of Tuscany's major spas, as evidenced by the presence of some two hundred-odd hotels. Its particular specialities are liver and bladder complaints, handy if you've overworked the Vino Nobile, though the clinic-like spa buildings aren't the usual image of a Tuscan holiday.

If you have transport, a more enjoyable route to Chiusi is the minor road that runs south just before Montepulciano's own little spa at Sant'Albino. This follows a fine, scarcely populated stretch of the Val d'Órcia down through the estates of Castelluccio and La Foce – the latter the home for many years of the

American writer Iris Origo, author of the classic *Merchant of Prato*. It was at La Foce that she hid partisans and Allied troops during the German occupation of Italy after Mussolini's fall in 1943, events recorded in her autobiography *War in Val d'Órcia*. You turn north to reach Chiusi at **SARTEANO**, a pleasant village set below a castle and within patches of Etruscan wall; it has an *Annunciation* by Domenico Beccafumi in the church of San Martino, and an excellent, inexpensive **restaurant**, *La Giara*, at Viale Europa 1 (℡0578.265.511).

Chiusi

CHIUSI, 14km southeast of Montepulciano, is useful mostly as a transport hub, with trains and buses west to Siena, south to Orvieto and Rome, and north to Montepulciano, Cortona, Arezzo and the Umbrian lake resort of Castiglione del Lago. As a target in its own right, it is only really worth a special detour for Etruscan enthusiasts: the town – known to the Etruscans as Camars – has a reasonable archeological museum and around half a dozen ancient tombs on its periphery, out towards Lago di Chiusi.

The museum and the Duomo, Chiusi's other worthwhile site, are close by each other on Via Porsenna. Chiusi's **Museo Archeologico Nazionale e Tombe Etrusche** (daily 9am–7.30pm; €4) ought to be pretty good, for the region is littered with tombs. Many of the best exhibits, however, have been spirited away to Florence and Rome and what remains is a modest collection: numerous sarcophagi, a few terracottas and the odd treasure – notably the *Gualandi Urn*. Many of the tombs in the region are in poor or dangerous condition, but one or two can be seen on request from the museum.

At the Romanesque **Duomo** there is further evidence of Chiusi's ancient past. The building itself consists almost entirely of Etruscan and Roman blocks (the interior is a mass of what appears at first sight to be mosaic work, but is in reality mock-Byzantine paintwork, created in 1915). The **Museo della Cattedrale** alongside (June to mid-Oct daily 10am–12.45pm & 4–6.30pm; rest of year Mon–Sat 10am–12.45pm, Sun 10am–12.45pm & 3.30–6pm; €2) gives access to the **Labyrinth of Porsenna** (€3, or combined ticket with Museo della Catttedrale €4), which leads you through the atmospheric tunnels of the Etruscan water-catchment system below the piazza to a huge Roman cistern and then up inside the twelfth-century campanile.

Still more of the ancient underground city can be seen in the **Museo Civico** (May–Oct Tues–Sun tours at 10.15am, 11.30am, 12.45pm, 3.15pm, 6.30pm & 5.45pm; Nov–April tours on Thurs & Fri at 10.10am, 11.10am & 12.10pm, and the same hours on Sat & Sun plus 3.10pm. 4.10pm & 5.10pm; €3), at Via Seconda Cimina 1, off the north side of Piazza XX Settembre. Atmospheric guided tours lead through 140m of Etruscan tunnel and aqueduct to a lake now some 28m below street level.

Practicalities

With time to kill in Chiusi, the best thing to do is **eat**. *Il Bucchero* (℡0578.222.092; closed Wed) at Via dei Bonci 32 is an inexpensive restaurant-pizzeria, while the *Ristorante Zaira* (℡0578.20.260; closed Mon), just up the road at Via Arunte, serves "Etruscan dishes" – boar, pigeon and the like at moderate prices.

Chiusi has a helpful **tourist office** at Piazza del Duomo 1 (Mon–Sat 9.30am–12.30pm & 3.30–7pm, Sun 9.30am–12.30pm; ℡0578.227.667). An extremely good out-of-town **hotel** is the four-star *Villa il Patriarca* at Querce al Pino (℡0578274.407, ⓦwww.ilpatriarca.it; ⑥), 4km from Chiusi. Set in fine grounds (with a pool), it is housed in a beautifully restored country villa, and has a superb, if expensive restaurant, *I Salotti* (closed Mon), that is renowned in its own right.

Monte Amiata

At 1738m, **MONTE AMIATA** is the highest point in southern Tuscany, a broad-based mountain whose hazy outline forms the backdrop to many a town and landscape in the region. A circle of towns rings its lower slopes – some historical spots, others more modern. None, with one exception, are worth a trip for their own sake, but the effect of the villages together, plus pretty streets, old castles and plenty of bucolic countryside makes this a good area to tour by car or bike for a day or so. It's also delightful walking country, refreshingly cool in summer – and there's skiing in winter.

The main centre and transport hub is **Abbadia San Salvatore**, worth a visit for its great abbey, whether you intend to venture onto the mountain or not. The town is accessible by bus from Siena (2–3 daily), Buonconvento (5 daily), Chiusi (4 daily), Arcidosso and Santa Fiora (10 daily), and Grosseto (5 daily). Avoid the "Monte Amiata" train station, on the Siena–Asciano–Grosseto line: it's a good 45km north of Abbadia San Salvatore.

Abbadia San Salvatore

There's been a settlement on the site of **ABBADIA SAN SALVATORE**, Monte Amiata's main town, since prehistoric times, though its real significance dates from the eighth century when its great abbey became the controlling centre of the Via Francigena. Its importance only waned with the rise of the Aldobrandeschi in the eleventh century. Thereafter it was contested by Orvieto and Siena, but in 1559 – along with most of southern Tuscany – fell within the orbit of the Medici's Grand Duchy of Tuscany.

Today the town is an initially disorientating modern sprawl that hides a perfect and largely self-contained **medieval quarter**. The abbey itself is actually in the modern part of the town, and best reached with Viale Roma, where buses drop off, as the starting point. From the north end of the street,

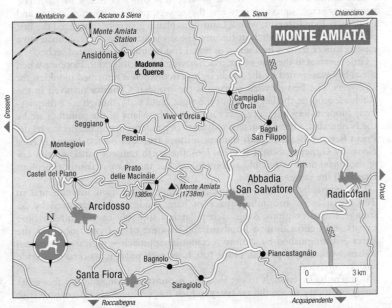

walk down Via Cavour, passing Via Mentana on the left, and take the next right, Via del Monastero.

Abbadia's **tourist office** is near the cinema, Via Adua 25 (Mon–Sat 9am–1pm & 4–6pm, Sun 9am–1pm; ☏0577.775.811, ⓦwww.amiataturismo.it). The **bus terminal** is in front of the *Bar Centrale* in Viale Roma; there's a timetable fixed to the Agenzia VAII, Viale Roma 45, which is also the place to buy tickets.

The abbey

Church tradition dates the **Abbadia San Salvatore** to 743, making it one of the oldest abbeys in Tuscany, and ascribes its foundation to King Rachis, a Lombard king who is supposed to have converted to Christianity while contemplating a Crucifix now affixed to the abbey's south wall. He was subsequently visited by an apparition of Christ as he went to do battle with the Perugians, a revelation which prompted him to take up a monastic life and found the abbey at the site of the vision. The actual story of the abbey's birth is slightly different. For a start, the Crucifix element is anachronistic, as the work dates from the twelfth century, some four hundred years after Rachis's death. Rachis himself, however, was involved in the foundation, though it appears his withdrawal into monastic isolation was forced on him, principally by leading Lombard nobles who opposed his ever-increasing leanings towards Rome. Forced to abdicate, the king symbolically awarded his crown to the pope and was succeeded by his brother, Astolfo.

The present Romanesque **church**, built in Amiata's distinctive brown trachite, was consecrated in 1036, a rebuilding programme having been instigated a year before when the abbey was at the height of its wealth and power. The present crypt (see below) dates from this period, though other parts of the building were altered during the brief tenure of the Camaldolese and later the Cistercians, who took over the abbey from the Benedictines in 1228.

Among the Cistercian additions was the triform window in the **facade**, though critics are unable to agree on the age of the two distinctive towers (one clearly unfinished), features found in very few other churches in Italy. The narrow frontage, squeezed between the towers, prepares you for a thin and immensely long **interior**, whose Latin-cross plan is generally considered the first of any Romanesque church in Tuscany. The single-naved basilica culminates in a raised chancel, framed by a series of broad and beautifully decorated arches.

Little survives in the way of art, much having been removed to Florence when the abbey was owned by the Medici – a period when it remained monkless for 157 years. The best of what remains is the wooden **Crucifix** involved in the Rachis legend (at the beginning of the right-hand wall), though it's a disquietingly modern-looking piece, and easily passed by. Many of the paintings are by the Nasini clan, a three-generation dynasty of painters born in nearby Castel del Piano (see p.428). The south transept features **frescoes** on the *Legend of King Rachis* by Giuseppe Nasini (1657–1736), the north transept panels on the *Life of the Virgin*; none is terribly accomplished, but they have a faintly ridiculous charm all the same.

The **crypt**, by contrast, is outstanding: one of the most monumental in Tuscany, it is an astounding space of bare, crude stone supported by 35 strange, fluted columns. Atop each pillar is a superbly carved lintel, whose motifs and figures show a Lombard and in some cases Byzantine hand, the latter – distinguished by a more rectangular approach – typical of northern Italian work of the period. Note, too, how each pillar is worked in a wide variety of styles.

If you're lucky enough to get into the **monastery** alongside the abbey (it's rarely open), try to see the **treasury**, which has a minute eighth-century Irish reliquary, a fine reliquary bust of Pope St Mark (1381) and an extremely rare and beautiful red silk Persian cope dating from the eighth century.

Parco Museo Minerario

The **Parco Museo Minerario** (daily: mid-June to Oct 9.30am–12.30pm & 3.30–6.30pm; rest of the year same hours Sat & Sun; €3) at Piazzale Renato Rossaro 6 is located in part of what was once one of the world's most important mercury mines, the metal having been extracted locally since the end of the nineteenth century. The only other mines of comparable significance were in Spain and Slovenia, but they, like the mines here and elsewhere around Monte Amiata, have been hit by a worldwide decline in the use of mercury. The museum building is a fine piece of industrial architecture in itself, a redoubtable nineteenth-century stone affair with a quaint tower and three rows of arched windows – the effect is more Florentine *palazzo* than factory. Inside, the museum offers numerous examples of industrial archeology, with old machines and the fittings, fixtures and tools used in the mines. Displays deal with the history of mercury mining, and there are also lots of archive photographs and other documentary material.

The Monte Amiata summit and slopes

The summit of **Monte Amiata** is accessible by road and in summer is packed out with vehicle-delivered parties, many ill-shod for the last few steps to the highest point. In July and August it has a thrice-daily bus from Abbadia San Salvatore. A number of the tatty bars at the summit rent out mountain bikes to explore the lower slopes.

At the car park is what amounts to an alpine hamlet, with bars, a handful of hotels and a short ski run – all in the shadow of a peculiar Eiffel Tower structure adapted in the form of a cross, erected in 1946 by Pope Pius XII. Alongside are a crop of radio masts, and huts selling some of the trashiest trinkets conceivable. None of this detracts from the **views**, which stretch southeast to Bolsena and west to the sea, with the nearer towns neatly delineated in a circle below. The best viewpoint is from the so-called *Madonna delle Scout*, a statue littered with the pendants of innumerable scout troops.

Amiata walking: the Anello della Montagna

Away from the summit, the woods and pathways of Amiata's **lower slopes** make up one of the region's most beautiful natural enclaves, huge forests of beech and chestnut blanketing the area and providing refuge for deer and wild boar. The mountain's extravagant greenery, so at odds with much of the surrounding countryside, derives from its volcanic origins, eruptions having formed ridges of trachite, which is fertile when broken down and also porous, allowing surface water to filter away. When the water hits the impervious volcanic rock below, it flows out in a series of **springs**, a striking feature of Amiata, whose slopes frequently echo to the sound of running water.

The combination of Amiata's lush vegetation and crisp mountain air makes it superb **walking** territory. Detailed Multigraphic and other maps have made hiking in the region a far more straightforward undertaking, and considerable effort has gone into marking the **Anello della Montagna**, a path which circles the mountain between about 900m and 1300m. With a car you can join the path from virtually any of the roads that climb from the surrounding towns; large boards mark the departure points from the road, and detail the route to either side. It's also possible, however, to walk up from the towns on paths that radiate from the main circuit: the best departure point for this approach is Abbadia San Salvatore.

The Anello's total circuit is 29km, in theory walkable in a day, though the local council has broken it into ten basic sections. It's fairly practical to walk half the route, and then take a **bus** back from Santa Fiora or Arcidosso (each have ten connections daily with Abbadia San Salvatore). The trail markings are clearly indicated on concrete posts in red, yellow and green, though they coincide with the older CAI markings of red and white stripes; either way, it's fairly hard to go wrong.

Staying on the mountain

If you want to **stay** on the mountain, the best base is **Prato Macináie** (1385m), a tree-enclosed patch of meadow and the site of one of Amiata's ski lifts (there are fourteen in all, along with twelve pistes). It's not far from the summit, but far enough to be unspoilt and away from the commercialism. The hotel, *Le Macinaie* (☎0564.959.001, ⓦwww.lemacinaie.it; ❷), fills up, so book ahead.

In a similarly pretty setting, the **Prato della Contessa** (1500m), 2km south on the summit road, has the three-star *Hotel Contessa* (☎0564.959.000, Ⓕ0564.959.002; ❷), while nearby there's *Lo Scoiattolo* (☎0564.959.003; ❶). All of these hotels have inexpensive to moderately priced **restaurants**. The nearest **campsite** is at Castel del Piano (see p.428).

Villages around Monte Amiata

If you have transport, the ring of towns around Monte Amiata is worth a little exploration. None has outstanding features but all claim a rural setting and more or less medieval centres – usually built around an Aldobrandeschi castle. Most also have a good sprinkling of hotels.

Piancastagnaio

Five kilometres south of Abbadia San Salvatore, **PIANCASTAGNAIO**, at 772m, spreads across the slopes of a mountain plateau, capped by one of the area's most impressive fortresses, a fourteenth-century Aldobrandeschi number. It has a maze of pretty streets, plus a fine Romanesque church – the twelfth-century Santa Maria Assunta. On the road outside the village, left of the main gate, the church of **Santa Maria delle Grazie** has a recently uncovered fifteenth-century fresco cycle by Nanni di Pietro. Another recently discovered cycle resides in **San Bartolomeo**, a humble Franciscan church on the Abbadia road restructured in the eighteenth century. The pictures, which depict the *Life of the Virgin*, are in the chapterhouse, off the cloister.

Santa Fiora

SANTA FIORA's craggy position drew an admiring observation from Dante as to its impregnability; its castle – of which only a tower remains – provided the feudal seat of one of the major branches of the **Aldobrandeschi**. This clan, which ruled much of southern Tuscany and the Maremma from the ninth century, had its roots in a Lombard dynasty from Lucca – the family name is an Italian corruption of "Hildebrand", testament to the family's northern German origins. In 1274 the clan divided into two main branches, one of which was installed in Santa Fiora, ruling Monte Amiata and the northern Maremma, the other in nearby Sovana, from where they controlled the coast and the southern Maremma. Santa Fiora then passed through the family's female line, and was eventually ceded by marriage to the Sforza Cesarini family, whose **palazzo**, built from the old fortress, lies alongside the Aldobrandeschi **tower**, now a clock tower overlooking a picturesque little square.

Davide Lazzeretti of Monte Labbro

Arcidosso-born **Davide Lazzeretti** (1834–78) is the most extraordinary figure that Monte Amiata – a region renowned for its mystics and seers – has thrown up: either a visionary prophet, or a crazed communist born before his time, according to greatly divergent Italian points of view. As young as 14, the boy had been marked out for great and strange things by a Franciscan monk; a vision twenty years later prompted Lazzeretti to travel to Rome, to try and interest the pope in his revelation. Scorned, he retired to a contemplative life on Monte Subiaco, in a deliberate imitation of St Benedict, who had retired to the same mountain slopes southeast of Rome 1400 years earlier.

Returning to Amiata between 1870 and 1871, Lazzeretti achieved notoriety as the founder of an ill-defined socio-religious sect, the **Jurisdavidic Church**, which as well as preaching Christianity under the banner "Long live the Republic, God and Liberty" agitated for justice and social reform amongst the peasant community which made up his following. In 1873 he was arrested, the authorities unhappy with his persuasive republican preaching, not to mention his new title: the "Messiah of Monte Amiata". In 1876 he was excommunicated, but continued to preach both in Italy and abroad, calling for a society based on co-operative principles and republican government. In time, his five thousand followers organized themselves into Italy's first **co-operative**, sharing land and animals and building a huge temple to the movement on top of Monte Labbro, south of Arcidosso. In 1877 the Church refused to allow him to continue using the temple, and in 1878 Lazzeretti met a violent end – shot, with the connivance of local landowners, by the *carabinieri* as he led an unauthorized religious procession through Arcidosso.

Repression soon dispersed the movement, which was in any case being undermined by a drift away from the land to Amiata's mercury mines. Nonetheless, Lazzeretti is remembered today as a pre-emptor of socialist and land reform movements still twenty years away at the time of his death. He is commemorated on the night of August 14, the anniversary of his death, with a huge bonfire at the largely ruined temple on Monte Labbro. Whether or not you want to pay your respects, the trip to the summit makes a fine walk or drive: a rough road takes you virtually to the top.

The village has a couple of fine churches. The **Pieve di Santa Fiora e Lucilla**, reached on Via Carolina from the square, has its walls, altar and pulpit adorned with a wide variety of topnotch terracottas (1480–90) by Andrea della Robbia and his workshop. The beautiful church, incidentally, was named after two local saints whose relics, brought here in the eleventh century, reside in the nearby priest's house. A steep, partly stepped lane leads to **Sant'Agostino**, which possesses a fine painted wooden image of the Madonna and Child attributed (dubiously) to Jacopo della Quercia, though it's been claimed for the time being by the museum in Pitigliano's Palazzo Orsini (see p.432).

Down the road you come to gardens and the oratory of **Madonna delle Nevi** – the della Robbia figures above the entrance are the local saints Fiora and Lucilla – and then to the village's nicest feature, the **Peschiera** (daily 9am in summer until sunset; in winter, contact Coop Amiata ℡0564.977.571; €1), a spring-fed lake and eighteenth-century garden surrounded by woodland and gurgling brooks. The road beyond passes evidence of Amiata's industrial side, tall chimneys signalling the thermal power plants and mercury mines that have kept the area's economic head above water.

Santa Fiora's **tourist office** is in Piazza Garibaldi (℡0564.977.036) and there are a couple of **hotels**, the three-star *Fiora*, Via Roma 8 (℡0564.977.043, ⓦwww .hotelfiora.it; ❷), and cheaper *Eden*, Via Roma 1 (℡&℻0564.977.033; ❶).

Arcidosso and Castel del Piano

West of the summit, **ARCIDOSSO** is one of the larger Amiata towns, dominated by a blunt Sienese tower, but of little other interest. It was, however, the birthplace of **Davide Lazzeretti** (see box, p.427).

More tempting on the horizon is **CASTEL DEL PIANO**, the main commercial town of this area. It doesn't really live up to the promise, though the **old centre** warrants a quick wander, with its covered market, Palazzo Pretorio and Romanesque San Leonardo. Many of its churches are lumbered with the seventeenth-century works of the Nasini, a three-generation dynasty of second-rate painters, all of whom were born in the town: their work is also found in the abbey at Abbadia San Salvatore.

Seggiano and Pescina

SEGGIANO is an old Etruscan centre, today distinguished principally by its Renaissance church of the **Madonna della Carità**, set in an olive grove just outside the village. The town's inhabitants built it as a votive offering in 1603 as thanks for deliverance from famine. They wouldn't be too impressed to see what's become of their labour of love, for the church has managed to have every one of its altarpieces stolen: grim modern paintings have taken their place. Better-educated thieves might have made for the nicely situated **Oratorio di San Rocco**, also on the village's outskirts, whose *Madonna Enthroned* (1493) by Girolamo di Domenico is by far the best of the paintings in the immediate vicinity. Nearby, also in a beautiful setting, is a tiny fortified hamlet, Potentino.

Just east of the town on the road to Pescina lies the **Giardino di Daniel Spoerri** (Easter–June Sat & Sun 4–8pm; July to mid-Sept Tues–Sun 4–8pm; mid-Sept to Oct Tues–Sun 4–7pm; €7; ⓦ www.danielspoerri.org), a fascinating sixteen-hectare sculpture garden designed by the Swiss artist to incorporate contemporary art (79 installations by forty artists) in a natural setting.

South to Saturnia and Manciano

Around 14km from Arcidosso, **TRIANA** stands on the junction of the roads west to Grosseto and south to Saturnia and Pitigliano. A perfect little fortified hamlet, it commands huge views from its castle. If you have a car, a rewarding detour off the road south is to follow the new highway to Grosseto as far as Roccalbegna. Relying on buses, however, this only really makes sense if you're making for Grosseto: two buses cover the route daily.

Roccalbegna

ROCCALBEGNA is one of the finest villages in southern Tuscany: aerial pictures of its perfect medieval streets decorate many local tourist offices, but barely hint at the rugged grandeur of its position, perched 522m up the slopes of Monte Labbro above the Albegna valley. Although the place is not on any obvious route, and visitors are few, the detour here is more than worthwhile, and there's a single **hotel** with moderately priced restaurant if you want to stay – *La Pietra*, Via XXIV Maggio (☎0564.989.019, ⓦ www .locandalapietra.it; ❷).

The **Rocca** of the town's name is obvious from afar, poised on a crag that rises almost to a pyramid above the village. Like so many in the region, it formed a defensive retreat for the Aldobrandeschi, overlords of the Maremma for several centuries. A superb walk to the top starts from the Piazza IV Novembre at the far end of the village: turn left up Salita Sasso (a yellow sign), go past the *Bar-Tabacchi* and it's then ten minutes up the winding lane and a final scramble to the fortifications. The views over the wild and rocky countryside are tremendous, though outdone by the famed vista over the village's grid of streets. The local saying *se il sasso scrocca, addio la Rocca* ("If the rock crumbles, it's goodbye to the village") seems incontrovertible from this point.

In the village, be sure to look in on the Romanesque church of **Santi Apostoli Pietro e Paolo**, noted for its medieval interior and patches of fresco, but more for a tremendous triptych of the *Madonna and Child with Sts Peter and Paul* (1340) by Ambrogio Lorenzetti. It's astonishing to find a painting here, in the middle of nowhere, by one of Siena's finest – the artist was responsible for the frescoes of *Good and Bad Government* in Siena's Palazzo Pubblico. In a touching detail, Lorenzetti has painted the Madonna affectionately clasping the Child's foot. Note too, the cherries held in the Infant's hands, symbols of Heaven, eternal life and the rewards of a righteous life. Next door to the church, up some steps in Via Campana, is the small **Oratorio del Crocifisso**, now a museum (open on request). Its high altar contains a fourteenth-century painted Crucifix (1360) by Luca di Tommè, whose presence in Roccalbegna is no accident – Lorenzetti was his main influence.

South to Saturnia

Moving south to Saturnia, there are a couple of minor places of note. After 10km you reach **SEMPRONIANO**, a crumbling half-forgotten village centred on another Aldobrandeschi castle. Its Romanesque church, Sts Vincenzo e Anastasio, has a painting of a dragon supposedly slain nearby and placed in the castle for public edification. By contrast, neighbouring Romanesque Santa Croce has a noted wooden medieval Crucifix. On a minor road 5km to the east is the virtually abandoned hamlet of **ROCCHETTE**, sited below a castle on a spur overlooking the Albegna valley. If you make the detour you'll find one of the prettiest places for miles, along with some cracking views.

Saturnia: Le Cascatelle

Word is spreading about the sulphurous hot springs at **SATURNIA**, 25km south of Triana, as the almost year-round convoys of battered Volkswagen campers and crowds of noisy Italians testify. Nonetheless, they're not that easy to find. If all you want is a dip you should initially ignore the hill-town and follow the road south towards Montemerano. A large **spa complex** (Ⓦwww.termedisaturnia.it) – with fierce admission charges, a vast pool and a five-star hotel – is signposted to the left, and about 200m on (as the road takes a sharp curve) a dirt track heads off straight, usually signalled by a cluster of cars and vans. Two-minutes' walk from here brings you to the **cascatelle**, sulphur streams and springs which burst from the ground, forming natural rock-pool jacuzzis of warm water, in which you can lie around for hours submerged up to your neck. Entrance is unrestricted and free, and even on cold days there are invariably a few people ready to indulge. The heavy pedestrian traffic means there's a bit of litter, but apart from an inexpensive bar/pizzeria there's surprisingly little commercialism.

The bubbling main pool is a bizarre sight, the water an intense turquoise, and all the more surreal if the weather is overcast and the steam rising overhead.

Practicalities

There are three daily **buses** along the road between Semproniano and Manciano: be sure to get out at the springs (*Le Terme*) and not at Saturnia village.

If you intend to **stay** near the springs, the nearest **hotel** is the excellent one-star *Albergo-Ristorante Stellata* (℡0564.602.978; ❸), in an isolated spot 1km down from the falls on the road to Manciano (it's signposted left on a dirt road).

All the other accommodation possibilities are in Saturnia village, a fairly unassuming place. Camper vans are allowed to park overnight in the more modern of the main squares, and there are a couple of **hotels** – the *Saturnia*, Via Mazzini 4 (℡0564.601.007; ❷), and *Villa Clodia*, Via Italia 43 (℡0564.601.212, ⓦ www.hotelvillaclodia.com; ❸), which is tucked away in one of the village's nicer quarters. When all's said and done, perhaps the best reason to come here is a **restaurant**, the appealing *Bacco e Cerere*, Via Mazzini 4 (℡0564.601.235; closed Wed). The service is friendly, the atmosphere intimate (room for just thirty diners) and the food – puddings especially – worth every one of the €35 it'll cost to do the job properly.

Montemerano

Midway between Saturnia and Manciano lies **MONTEMERANO**, a medieval hill-village (with modern component below) cannily fortified on two levels, its balconies and interlocked alleys decked with a more-than-usual abundance of geraniums and other hanging greenery. A fascinating church and exceptional restaurant are gradually bringing the tourists in, but for the time being it remains a pretty and all-but-undocumented little gem.

Once you've pottered around the streets – which will take only a few minutes – head for **San Giorgio**, a prettily frescoed little church full of artistic treasures. The first, on the right (south) wall, is a wooden bas-relief of the *Assumption* (1455–65) by Vecchietta, a painter who also successfully turned his hand to sculpture. Beyond it, by the door, is a faded fresco of *St Orsola*. Ahead, at the bottom of the arch beside the high altar, is the winsome and wonderfully titled *Madonna della Gattaiola* ("of the Cat-flap"), painted around 1450 by an anonymous follower of Sassetta known as the "Master of Montemerano". Originally one half of an *Annunciation* (note the Virgin's Bible, a feature of such paintings), the picture probably formed part of an organ or double-doored tabernacle; the archangel Gabriel would have occupied the second panel. It was then used as the door to a granary, probably the point at which it received the hole in the bottom right of the Virgin's cloak which led to its nickname. All this is simply a light-hearted prelude to the church's real highlights, namely a polychrome wooden statue of *St Peter* (1455–60), another work by Vecchietta (left of the high altar steps), and a glorious fifteenth-century polyptych by Sano di Pietro of the *Madonna and Child with Sts Peter, George, Lawrence and Anthony of Padua*.

For somewhere to **stay** in or around the village, the smart three-star *Oliveto* (℡0564.602.849, ⓦ www.loliveto.it; ❸) is the upmarket choice, located on the outskirts near the turn-off for Saturnia, although the pastorally situated *Villa Acquaviva* (℡0564.602.890; ❺), 2km north of Montemerano, is a definite first-choice treat, with rooms in two attractively converted buildings, surrounded by the hotel's own wine estate. The *Laudomia* (℡0564.620.013, ⓦ www.locandalaudomia .com; ❷), for centuries a coaching inn, is at Poderi di Montemerano, midway to Manciano, and has an attractive, moderately priced restaurant attached (℡0564.629.830; closed Tues).

You might be better off, however, saving money on accommodation and splashing out on a meal at the very expensive Michelin-starred **restaurant** ❧ *Da Caino*, Via Canonica 3 (℡0564.602.817, ⓦ www.dacaino.it; in winter, closed Wed & lunchtime Thurs). The coveted Michelin rosette is not the recommendation in Tuscany it might be elsewhere, but here it reflects absolutely first-class cooking. There are just 22 covers, so booking is essential, and you're looking at around €90 if you're going to stretch the chef. For less than a third of this you can eat at the moderately priced *Osteria Passaparola*, Vicolo delle Mura 21 (℡0564.602.835; closed Thurs), or the *Vecchia Osteria Cacio e Vino*, Via del Bivio 16 (℡0564.602.827), which also has handful of rooms (❶).

Manciano

MANCIANO, though hardly somewhere you'd make a special journey for, is an attractive market town 15km west of Pitigliano, with a medieval quarter grouped around a Sienese fortress, and a plentiful supply of bars in which to soak up its small-town atmosphere.

It's unlikely you'll want to stay in the town, but if stranded you'll find a handful of **hotels**, most central of which is the three-star *Rossi*, Via Gramsci 2 (℡0564.629.248, ⓦwww.hotelrossi.it; ❸).

Pitigliano and around

PITIGLIANO, the largest town in Tuscany's deep south, is best approached along the road from Manciano, to the west. As you approach, it soars above on a spectacular outcrop of tufa, with medieval buildings perched above the valley floor, and its quarters linked by the arches of an immense aqueduct. **Etruscan tombs** – some converted to storage cellars for wine – honeycomb the cliffs, a feature repeated all over the surrounding area.

Neolithic remains suggest a settlement on the site from earliest times, though it first rose to prominence as an Etruscan and later Roman town. In the early Middle Ages the town belonged to the ubiquitous **Aldobrandeschi**, who ruled it from nearby Sovana, then one of the clan's two principal southern Tuscan power bases. In 1293 it passed by marriage to the counts of **Orsini**, a major Roman family who produced three popes and countless cardinals, bishops and minor papal dignitaries. Under the clan the town became more important than Sovana, from which the bishopric was eventually transferred. Its ultimate fate (in 1608), like much of the region, was to become a part of the Grand Duchy of Tuscany.

Pitigliano was also known for its thriving **Jewish community**, which became established during the latter part of the sixteenth century, under the protection of the Orsini. In 1622, however, the Medici confined the Jews of Pitigliano to a **ghetto**, where they remained confined until 1735, when legislation introduced by the last Medici ruler, Gian Gastone, lifted the proscription against Jewish commercial activity and led to the expansion of Jewish businesses on present-day Via Zuccarelli. Before long Pitigliano was being referred to as "Little Jerusalem", and boasted a Jewish university that attracted students from around Europe. By the time of Italian Unification, around 400 of Pitigliano's 2200 residents were Jewish, but in the last decades of the nineteenth century many emigrated to Palestine, a process which accelerated after World War II – though the great majority of Pitigliano's Jews survived the Nazi occupation. Pitigliano's synagogue closed in the late 1950s, and today, in what was formerly one of the centres of Jewish learning in southern Europe, there is just a handful of Jewish residents left.

The town has today a slightly grim, occasionally sinister sort of grandeur, the result partly of its mighty fortress – dividing the upper town from the more modern lower suburb – and partly because of the tall alleys of the ghetto area.

Seen on a sunny day, though, it is a gem of small-town Italy, seemingly populated entirely by old women knitting or lacemaking. Together with the villages of **Sorano** and **Sovana** it constitutes one of the most worthwhile and neglected spots in the region.

The Town

The major entry point to the medieval town is through **Piazza Petruccioli** – host to a car park, hotel and the main bus stop, and to a small belvedere that looks along the houses and cliffs on the town's southern edge. Immediately through the gate is the high-walled and rather claustrophobic Piazza Garibaldi, and beyond it the massive **aqueduct** (1543) and **fortress**, contemporary building projects completed in the sixteenth century under Giuliano da Sangallo, along with a complex string of fortifications. Within the fortress is the Renaissance **Palazzo Orsini** and the **Museo del Medioevo e Rinascimento e Fortezza Orsini** (April–Oct Tues–Sun 10am–1pm & 2–7pm; Nov–March Fri–Sun 10am–1pm & 3–7pm; €7, includes entry to Museo Civico plus Fortezza Orsini in Sorano), begun in the thirteenth century and extended by Niccolò Orsini two centuries later. The ramp leading to the main entrance arch has a small pillar decorated with a text lauding Gian Francesco Orsini, responsible for instigating the nearby aqueduct. It also has a crest bearing the Orsini's family arms, the head of a lion and a bear (the latter is a pun: *orso* is Italian for bear); the same arms appear on the fine well in the courtyard. Inside, much of the palace has been restored, bringing new lustre to a succession of lovely Tuscan ceilings and interiors. All manner of jewellery, vestments and other ecclesiastical ephemera litter the rooms, with just valuable works of art as distraction: a wooden *Madonna and Child* attributed to Jacopo della Quercia and a painting of the *Madonna Enthroned* (1494) by Guidoccio Cozzarelli. There are also two works by Francesco Zuccarelli (1702–88), who was born in the town but worked mainly in Venice and London. The palace is also home to the five-room **Museo Civico Archeologico della Civiltà Etrusca** (Tues–Sun: April–Oct 10am–1pm & 4–7pm; Nov–March 10am–1pm & 3–6pm; €2.50, or combined ticket €7), which houses an interesting collection of vases, jewellery and trinkets unearthed in the nearby Etruscan site of Poggio Buco.

More absorbing exhibits are on show in the **Museo della Civiltà Giubonnai**, located in a series of cellars beneath the fortress which were discovered by accident during a clean-up. Some of the labyrinth had remained unseen and untouched for three hundred years; other parts had been filled with rubble during Sangallo's work on the foundations. The collection, growing all the time, centres on folk, domestic and agricultural ephemera of the Maremma. At present you need to make an appointment at the Palazzo Orsini, but the hope is to fix regular hours and admission.

The fortress backs onto **Piazza della Repubblica**, the town's elongated and beautiful main square, its symmetry accentuated by a pair of fountains and immaculately pollarded ilex trees. Wander over to the balcony for a panorama taking in the river, trees, waterfalls and the faint outline of Monte Amiata away to the north.

Beyond lies the old town proper, a tight huddle of arches, alleys and medieval streets. It consists of three main streets, merging into one at the end of the town. Take the left fork out of the square and Via Zuccarelli brings you to the former **synagogue** (Sun–Fri: June–Sept 10am–12.30pm & 3.30–6.30pm, March–May & Oct–Nov 10am–12.30pm & 3–6pm; Dec–Feb 10am–12.30pm & 3–5.30pm; closed Sat & Jewish holidays; €3), a beautifully restored little jewel. Via Zuccarelli comes to an end by the Renaissance church of **Santa Maria**, its door flanked by the arms of the Orsini family. To the left of the main door under the tower, note the twelfth-century bas-relief depicting a human figure and two winged dragons. Inside are a few patches of fresco, less interesting than the building's peculiar trapezoidal plan. Nearby, immediately outside the Porto Capisotto and the medieval ramparts, is a stretch of **Etruscan wall**. Heading back to Piazza della Repubblica, Via G. Orsini brings you to Piazza Gregorio VII and the Baroque **Duomo**, with its butter-coloured stucco facade and giant campanile, the latter a surviving portion of a much earlier Romanesque church on the site. The western end of the square features a prominent travertine pillar (1490) with another text praising the Orsini.

The third street of the grid, **Via Roma**, best encapsulates the town's provincial feel, a collection of odd, half-empty shops giving off a smell of mothballs – although some are being converted into smart tourist-orientated boutiques. Here, as elsewhere, the main pleasure is exploring the arches and alleys that lead off on either side.

Practicalities

Pitigliano's helpful **tourist office** is at Piazza Garibaldi 51 (daily: April–Oct 10.20am–1pm & 3–7pm, Nov–March 10.20am–1pm & 2–6pm; ℡0564.617.111, 🅦www.lamaremma.info). You should find room at the town's single **hotel**, the *Albergo Guastini* on Piazza Petruccioli (℡0564.616.065, 🅦www.albergoguastini .it; ❸). If the hotel is full, try one of the several rooms for rent: the tourist office carries the latest listings. An out-of-town hotel alternative is the three-star *Valle Orientina* (℡0564.616.611, 🅦www.valleorientina.it; ❸), at Località Valle Orientina, 3km from Pitigliano. Pleasantly rustic and family run, it is in a rural setting, has a swimming pool, tennis courts, natural mineral spa and offers the opportunity to rent bikes or horses.

The best **restaurants**, if you don't eat at the *Guastini*, are the inexpensive wooden-beamed *Trattoria Del Orso* in Piazza Gregorio VII or the award-winning mid-priced ✣ *Osteria Il Tufo Allegro*, Vicolo della Costituzione 1 (closed Tues). The local **wine**, Bianco di Pitigliano, hard to find elsewhere, is sold at two good-value outlets on Via Santa Chiara (off Piazza Petruccioli) and celebrated in a September **wine festival**.

There's a reasonable **bus** service (pick-up and drop-off in Piazza Petruccioli), with three departures daily to Grosseto via Manciano, five to Orbetello (via Albinia), five to Sorano and one to Semproniano via Sovana.

Sovana

Fine Etruscan tombs and pristine Romanesque architecture would place **SOVANA** firmly on the tour circuit, if only it were closer to Siena or Florence. As it is, you can explore this breathtaking, part-abandoned medieval centre in virtual solitude – save at weekends, when Romans and, increasingly, northern Europeans flock to the place.

The town dates to at least the seventh century BC, when the Etruscans took up residence. It fell to the Romans in the third century BC, later becoming a Lombard fiefdom. The town's principal monuments, though, derive from its time as the capital of the **Aldobrandeschi**, a noble clan whose domain extended over much of southern Tuscany and northern Lazio; they were said to have a castle for every day of the year. Their golden age came with the birth in Sovana in 1020 of a scion, Hildebrand, who in 1073 was to become Pope Gregory VII, a great reformer who also kept a favourable eye on family business. Decline set in during the fourteenth century, when Sovana's low-lying position made it vulnerable both to malaria and Sienese attacks, and its population and power drifted to nearby Pitigliano. Siena took control of the town in 1410, ceding power to the Grand Duchy of Tuscany in 1557. Today, Sovana's residents number just over a hundred.

The village

Sovana's main street, **Via di Mezzo**, is almost the sum of the place, a broad expanse of fishbone-patterned brick paving, laid in 1580 by Ferdinand I de' Medici and recently restored to impressive effect. Guarding its start are the ruins of the Aldobrandeschi castle, built in the eleventh century on Etruscan foundations: it fell into greater disrepair with each of its subsequent owners – the Sienese, Orsini and Medici, who tried to repopulate the place in the seventeenth century by importing 58 families from Albania.

At its end, the street swells slightly to form the **Piazza del Pretorio**, a perfect medieval ensemble dominated on the left by **Santa Maria**, one of the most beautiful churches in southern Tuscany. Built in the thirteenth century to a Romanesque-Gothic plan, it has a simple stone interior dominated by an exquisite **ciborium**, a unique piece of pre-Romanesque paleo-Christian sculpture from the eighth or ninth century. Such canopies disappeared from churches in about the thirteenth century, confirming the work's far earlier provenance. Superbly preserved early frescoes around the walls set the seal on a marvellous building.

Opposite the church is the low-arched **Loggia del Capitano**, whose stone coats of arms proclaim Medici possession, and whose arches conceal a nice bar with a handful of outdoor tables. Next to it is the thirteenth-century **Palazzo Pretorio**, home to a small **museum and gallery** (Tues–Sat 10am–1pm & 4–7pm; €3), which traces the area's history, paying particular attention to local Etruscan tombs and discoveries. Particularly illuminating are the reconstructions of how tombs might originally have looked, well worth seeing if you intend to head out and explore the necropolis (see box below). The nine stone banners here are those of the town's Sienese and Medici governors. The little pillar to the right of the main door was used to pin up public declarations.

Etruscan tombs near Sovana

All round Sovana, but especially on the road to Saturnia, **Etruscan tombs** riddle the countryside, many approached by original "sunken" Etruscan roads. Why these roads should be sunken still puzzles scholars: some believe the purpose was defensive, in that they would enable people to move unseen from town to town; others posit that they were used for moving livestock, and were cut below ground level to prevent the animals from straying. The larger graves are well marked off the road by yellow signs. The necropolis as a whole, of which the marked tombs form a tiny part, extends for miles and rates in archeological (if not tourist) terms with the graves at Tarquinia and Cerveteri. Most of the tombs date from the seventh century BC and just about every type of Etruscan grave is present, including colombari, small niches cut into the rock to take cinerary urns. What the tombs lack in paintings they often make up for with elaborate carvings.

The key tombs are the **Tomba Ildebranda** (daily: March–Oct 9.30am–dusk; Nov–Feb 10am–dusk; €7 combined ticket with Fortezza Orsini in Sorano), considered the best single tomb in Tuscany, and the Tomba della Sirena (same hours and ticket). After the tunnel on the road to Saturnia, however, you'll spot more tombs, all of which can be visited free, including the Poggio Pesca and the Pola, a couple of minutes' uphill scramble from the road.

From the square a back lane leads through gardens and olive groves to the huge **Duomo**, or Cattedrale di Sts Pietro e Paolo (closed 1–3pm), whose exterior wall and superb portal bear some of the finest Lombard-Romanesque carvings in Tuscany. The church's nucleus went up in the eighth century (the date of many of the carvings) or possibly earlier – it's known the town was a centre of a diocese in the sixth century – and was augmented in the tenth with the addition of an apse and crypt. The bare, triple-naved **interior** features some twelfth-century carved capitals, reminiscent of the Benedictine work in Sant'Antimo; the finest is that on the second pillar in the left aisle, a work which suggests the hand of Lombard masons. There are also traces of fresco, a fine Gothic font and a wonderful **crypt**, divided into five tiny naves by ancient columns, but now, sadly, closed off to the public. The urn in the main church contains the remains of St Mamiliano, a sixth-century saint who evangelized much of the region.

Beyond the Duomo you can walk down to an old town **gateway** and traces of Etruscan wall, or turn back to Piazza Pretorio along the village's modest residential street, which sports little more than a couple of shops.

Practicalities

The **tourist office** (April–Oct daily 10am–1pm & 3–8pm; Nov–March Fri–Sun 10am–1pm & 3–6.30pm; ☎0564.614.074) is at the entrance to the museum in the Palazzo Pretorio.

Sovana has two good **hotels**: opposite Santa Maria is the three-star *Taverna Etrusca* (☎0564.616.183, ⓦwww.sovana.eu; ❷), a tiny place worth booking to be sure of one of its twelve rooms. Its ⅜**restaurant** (closed Wed) is first-rate, a beautifully elegant interior scattered with covetable antique furniture, and fine food at around €35. Just off the piazza is the eight-room, one-star *Hotel Scilla* (☎0564.616.531, ⓦwww.scilla-sovana.it; ❸), whose moderately priced restaurant, *Dei Merli* (closed Tues except Aug), also has a beautiful setting, with a pergola draped in flowers and greenery.

Sorano

All the approaches to **SORANO**, 9km northeast of Pitigliano, are extraordinary: from the south the route is lined with caves and tombs cut into the hillside; from the west, the road is cut into walls of tufa. The village, visible for miles on either approach, has a decidedly weird feel, with only a fraction of the old houses still lived in. Parts of the tangled streets suggest a faded grandeur; others are desolate and derelict. Landslips are the main problem, several streets having been declared terminally uninhabitable after one big slide. Attempts to keep Sorano alive have included a policy of sponsoring ceramic workshops and various other arts and crafts businesses. The small **tourist office** on Piazza Busati (April–Oct daily 10am–1pm & 3–8pm; Nov–March Fri–Sun 10am–1pm & 3–6.30pm; ☎0564.633.099) makes a point of promoting these, and will also help if you want guidance around the wealth of Etruscan remnants in the valley.

The village is full of intriguing medieval corners, but has little in the way of specific sights. An old castle dominates the centre, and has been converted into a fine, historic three-star **hotel**, the *Della Fortezza* (☎0564.632.010, ⓦwww.hoteldellafortezza.com; ❹), entered from Piazza Cairoli. The fifteen rooms are wood-beamed and elegantly furnished with antiques, and the views are superb. Otherwise, nearby Sovana is perhaps a better overnight option, but if you wish to stay locally and pay less, you could go for the one-star *La Botte* at nearby Montorio (☎0564.638.633, ⓕ0564.638.535; ❶).

The other fortress as you enter the town is the **Fortezza Orsini** (April–Oct Tues–Sun 10am–1pm & 3–7pm; Nov–Feb Fri–Sun 10am–1pm & 3–5pm; €3, or combined ticket with local tombs and Pitigliano museums €7), a blunt and perfectly preserved piece of Renaissance military engineering. Built over an old Aldobrandeschi fort in 1552, it was often besieged but never captured.

San Quírico

From Sorano there are constant views over the wooded gorge of the River Lente, whose rushing waters echo through the streets. Down on the valley floor, tantalizing ancient tracks crisscross the countryside, linking clearly visible rock tombs, Roman wells and old watermill workings. Some 5km east is the hamlet of **SAN QUÍRICO**, to the north of which you can explore the **Rupestre di Vitozza** (April–Oct daily 10am–6pm; €2), a series of two hundred tombs, grottoes and paleo-Christian remains, and the remnants of Vitozza, San Quírico's medieval antecedent.

San Quírico has the salubrious two-star **hotel** *Agnelli* (℡0564.619.015; ❷), whose **restaurant**, *La Vecchia Fonte* (closed Mon), has a great village atmosphere and – in addition to inexpensive pizzas – serves up surprisingly good fish and seafood (bought in fresh daily). Prices are keen (around €20), making it extremely popular with locals.

Travel details

Trains

Buonconvento to: Grosseto (10 daily; 1hr); Siena (10 daily; 30min).
Chiusi-Chianciano Terme to: Asciano (10 daily; 50min); Florence (hourly; 1hr 5min–1hr 40min); Montepulciano (hourly; 15min); Siena (hourly; 1hr 30min); Sinalunga (hourly; 25min).
Siena to: Asciano (hourly; 30min); Buonconvento (10 daily; 30min); Chiusi-Chianciano Terme (hourly; 1hr 30min); Grosseto via Monte Antico (10 daily; 1hr 40min); Montepulciano (hourly; 1hr); Sinalunga (hourly; 50min).

Buses

Abbadia San Salvatore to: Arcidosso (10 daily; 45min); Buonconvento (5 daily; 1hr 10min); Chiusi (4 daily; 1hr 25min); Grosseto (3 daily; 2hr 15min); Piancastagnaio (10 daily; 15min); Santa Fiora (10 daily; 30min); Siena (2–3 daily; 2hr).
Buonconvento to: Abbadia San Salvatore (5 daily; 1hr 10min); Montalcino (9 daily; 20min); Montepulciano (7 daily; 1hr); Pienza (7 daily; 35min); Siena (6 daily; 40min); Torrenieri (6 daily; 25min).
Chiusi to: Chianciano (14 daily; 30min); Montepulciano (14 daily; 45min).

Montalcino to: Buonconvento (9 daily; 30min); Siena (6 daily; 1hr 10min); Torrenieri (10 daily; 20min).
Montepulciano to: Buonconvento (7 daily; 1hr); Chianciano (every 30min; 25min); Chiusi (every 30min; 50min); Florence (1–3 daily; 2hr); Pienza (7 daily; 20min); San Quírico d'Órcia (7 daily; 40min); Siena (5–6 daily; 90min); Torrenieri (7 daily; 50min).
Pienza to: Buonconvento (7 daily; 35min); Montepulciano (7 daily; 20min); San Quírico (7 daily; 10min); Siena (5 daily; 1hr 30min); Torrenieri (7 daily; 25min).
Pitigliano to: Albinia (6 daily; 1hr); Grosseto via Manciano (3 daily; 1hr 40min); Orbetello (5 daily; 1hr 25min); San Quírico (4 daily; 15min); Semproniano (1 daily; 45min); Sorano (5 daily; 10min); Sovana (3 daily; 10min).
San Quírico d'Órcia to: Montepulciano (7 daily; 30min); Pienza (7 daily; 10min); Siena (5 daily; 1hr 10min); Torrenieri (7 daily; 15min).
Saturnia to: Manciano (3 daily; 25min).
Sovana to: Pitigliano (3 daily; 10min); Sorano (1 daily; 15min).
Torrenieri to: Arcidosso (6 daily; 40min); Buonconvento (6 daily; 25min); Grosseto (2 daily; 1hr 20min); Montalcino (10 daily; 20min); Pienza (7 daily; 25min).

Arezzo Province

CHAPTER 9

Highlights

✳ **Arezzo** The handsome capital of the province is famed for its antiques dealers, goldsmiths and – above all – for Piero della Francesca's sublime fresco cycle. See p.443

✳ **Monterchi** This minuscule village is home to another Piero masterpiece, the *Madonna del Parto*. See p.451

✳ **Sansepolcro** A small walled town that is the third stop on the Piero trail, chiefly for the magnificent *Resurrection*. See p.452

✳ **The Casentino** The upland forests of the Casentino national park offer some of the finest walks in Tuscany. See p.454

✳ **La Verna** St Francis's mountaintop retreat, still a thriving monastery, commands wonderful views of the Apennines. See p.455

✳ **Cortona** The quintessential Tuscan hill-town: ancient, lofty and charismatic, despite the growing influx of tourists. See p.459

▲ Piero della Francesca frescoes in the basilica of San Francesco, Arezzo

Arezzo Province

Upstream from Florence, the Arno valley – the **Valdarno** – is a fairly industrialized district, with warehouses and manufacturing plants enclosing many of the small towns strung along the train line. Some of the villages up on the valley sides retain an appealing medieval square or a cluster of attractive buildings but there's no very compelling stop before you reach the provincial capital of the upper Arno region, **Arezzo**, one hour's train ride from Florence. This solidly bourgeois city has its share of architectural delights – including one of the most photogenic squares in central Italy – though the droves of foreign visitors who travel to Arezzo come to see one thing: the fresco cycle by **Piero della Francesca** in the church of San Francesco. Italians flock here in even greater numbers for antiques, traded each month on the Piazza Grande in quantities scarcely matched anywhere else in the country.

For visitors on the trail of the masterpieces of Tuscan art, there are two essential calls in the vicinity of Arezzo. The first is the modest hill-town of **Monterchi**, where della Francesca painted one of the most powerful images of the Renaissance, the pregnant *Madonna del Parto*. Two other magnificent works by the same artist are to be seen in his birthplace, **Sansepolcro**, almost on the Umbrian border to the east.

Art is far from being this province's sole attraction. In the **Casentino**, to the north of Arezzo, small hill-towns such as **Poppi** and **Bibbiena** stand above a terrain of rich farmland that's cradled by thickly wooded upland. The secluded peaks of the Casentino also harbour two of Italy's most influential monasteries, **Camáldoli** and the Franciscan sanctuary of **La Verna**, Tuscany's busiest pilgrimage site. The ancient woodlands cradling these sanctuaries have been

Getting around the province

Trains on the Florence–Rome rail line run up the Arno valley, through Arezzo and on down the Valdichiana: for Cortona the nearest station on this line is Camucia, though more services stop at the slightly more distant Teróntola. For the Casentino, there's the LFI private rail line which runs to the head of the valley from the main FS station at Arezzo. Otherwise, Arezzo and Cortona are the centres of overlapping **bus** networks, which between them cover most of Arezzo province. Note that the private FCU railway from Sansepolcro to Perugia by way of Città di Castello gives you another way into Umbria. Generally, though, a **car** is essential if you want to get to some of the region's remoter sights and back on the same day, or to get the most out of the wilder reaches.

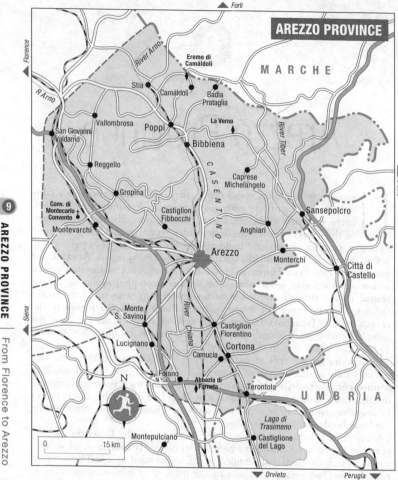

AREZZO PROVINCE

protected within the new **Parco Nazionale delle Foreste Casentinesi**, an area that extends across the surprisingly high, wild and forested border country of northern Tuscany into Emilia-Romagna.

To the south of Arezzo stretches the agricultural plain of the **Valdichiana**, where the ancient hill-town of **Cortona** is the major attraction, its steep streets forming a distinctive urban landscape and giving an unforgettable view over Lago Trasimeno and Valdichiana. It's also home to a pair of fine museums, one of which features major paintings by Fra' Angelico and locally born Luca Signorelli.

From Florence to Arezzo

If you're travelling by public transport from Florence to Arezzo there's no choice of route, as buses and trains all follow the **Valdarno**. By car, the obvious choice is between the two major roads that run roughly parallel to the river: the

Autostrada del Sole and the SS69. If you want to cover the kilometres quickly, take the former; if you want to see the few sights of the Valdarno, go for the latter, but be warned that the tarmac is clogged with lorries rumbling in and out of the industrial estates that pepper this part of the region. There is a third alternative, in the shape of the road that skirts the upland region known as the **Pratomagno**. It's a fairly testing drive, with a gear-change required every couple of hundred metres, but the views across to Chianti are gorgeous, and there's the odd Romanesque church along the way, one of them boasting a superb painting by Masaccio.

The Valdarno route

River, rail line and *autostrada* come together at the bottleneck known as Incisa Val d'Arno, 25km out of central Florence. Petrarch grew up here and some vestiges of the old town are preserved – but insufficient to make the place appealing. **Figline Valdarno**, 5km south, was the birthplace of another eminent Tuscan, Marsilio Ficino, court scholar-philosopher to Lorenzo il Magnifico. The old quarter around Piazza Ficino has a few handsome buildings and one inter-esting interior – the frescoed Collegiata di Santa Maria, which contains a fourteenth-century *Madonna* by the so-called Maestro di Figline.

SAN GIOVANNI VALDARNO, midway between Florence and Arezzo, is the most heavily industrialized but also the most rewarding town in the valley. The arcaded Palazzo Comunale is yet another design from Arnolfo di Cambio, who in the thirteenth century was put in charge of fortifying this Florentine town against the citizens of Arezzo. At the back of the *palazzo*, next to the church of Santa Maria della Grazia, the Museo della Basilica di Santa Maria

Fashion factory outlets

Tuscany is the powerhouse of the country's textile industry, and the Arno valley – in particular the area between Incisa Val d'Arno and Pontassieve – is the home of many of the factories that manufacture clothes for the top labels. Several of these factories have retail outlets alongside, in which the season's leftovers (sometimes the previous season's) are sold at discounts as high as sixty percent. The best of these shops are listed below.

Dolce e Gabbana Via Pian dell'Isola 49, località Santa Maria Maddalena, Incisa Val d'Arno ☎055.833.1300. This two-storey shed, a few kilometres north of Incisa Val d'Arno, is packed with clothes, accessories and household items from the main Dolce e Gabbana range, plus cheaper stuff from the D&G diffusion label. (Mon–Sat 9am–7pm, Sun 3–7pm)

Fendi, Loewe & Cellini Via Pian dell'Isola 66, Rignano sull'Arno ☎055.834.7155. A short distance north of Dolce e Gabbana, the Fendi/Loewe/Cellini warehouse is best for bags and other leather accessories. (Mon–Sat 10am–7pm, Sun 3–7pm)

The Mall Via Europa 8, Leccio Regello ☎055.865.7775. Located between the Fendi and Dolce e Gabbana outlets, The Mall contains separate outlets for Gucci, Bottega Veneta, Sergio Rossi, Loro Piana and Armani. Gucci is the dominant presence, with a huge range of bags, shoes, sunglasses and other accessories. (Daily 10am–7pm)

Space Levanella, Montevarchi ☎055.91.901. Located just outside Montevarchi, on a small industrial estate in the Levanella district (on the SS69), this unmarked concrete shed is the busiest of all the factory outlets, as it's stacked with clothes from the ineffably stylish Prada label, as well as items from the scarcely less trendy Jil Sander and Helmut Lang, both of which are subsidiaries of Prada. Also on sale is a good selection from Miu Miu, Prada's mid-priced diffusion range. (Mon–Sat 9.30am–7.30pm, Sun 10am–7pm)

della Grazia (summer Mon, Tues, Fri & Sat 10am–12.30pm & 4–7pm, Sun 4–7pm; winter opens and closes 30min earlier; €3) in Piazza Masaccio houses a Fra' Angelico *Annunciation* painted for the Convento di Montecarlo, plus a beautiful version of the same subject by his more obscure contemporary, Jacopo del Sellaio. Also on show is a *Madonna and Child with Four Saints*, attributed to Masaccio, born here in 1401. His house, the Museo Casa Masaccio at Corso Italia 83, is used for exhibitions, often of top-drawer contemporary art. The Gothic church of San Francesco, at right angles to Santa Maria, is blotched with frescoes as well.

In the Pliocene era the Valdarno was a vast lake, its shores patrolled by troops of prehistoric elephants. Fossil remnants of these colossal beasts are the pride of **MONTEVARCHI**, where they are installed at Via Poggio Bracciolini 36–38 in the Museo Paleontologico (Tues–Sat 10am–12.30pm & 4–6pm, Sun 10am–12.30pm; €4); around 1500 other exhibits keep them company. In the centre of town in Via Isidoro del Lungo, the sacristy of the Collegiata di San Lorenzo has been converted into a small Museo di Arte Sacra (Tues, Thurs & Sat 10am–noon; €2), where the main exhibit is a little chapel covered in ceramics by Andrea della Robbia.

This might not seem reason enough to stop on the way to Arezzo; beyond Montevarchi, there's no reason at all, unless, that is, you have time to take a meandering diversion off the SS69 into the southeastern corner of the Chianti hills. If you do, you should arm yourself with a large-scale road map and follow the road to **Mercatale Valdarno**, then take the turning for Bucine; from this road you can reach the fortified hill-top eyrie of **San Leolino**, which gives fabulous views. From there, strike east for the highlight of this diversion, the completely unspoiled medieval village of **Civitella**, with its magnificent ruined thirteenth-century castle. From here, it's just 8km to the *autostrada*, to the southwest of Arezzo.

The Pratomagno

The most famous place on the wooded east bank of the Arno is **VALLOM-BROSA**, whose abbey is the mother foundation of the Vallombrosan order, established in 1038 by the Florentine Giovanni Gualberto (see p.109). After Giovanni was canonized in 1193 this abbey became extremely influential, and by the fifteenth century it was administering wide tracts of Tuscan territory. Much rebuilt since those days, it now resembles a fortified villa and impresses mainly by its location, pillowed against the fir-covered hills. Part of the complex is still occupied by Vallombrosan monks, and part by a forestry school; the former can be visited (daily: summer 6am–noon & 3–7pm; winter 9am–noon & 3–6pm), but there's nothing engrossing inside, and neither is the adjoining church of great interest.

Milton once stayed at the abbey and in *Paradise Lost* he compared the throng of demons in hell to the "autumn leaves that strow the brooks/In Vallombrosa". Though the forests have dwindled in the intervening centuries, they are still extensive, as you'll appreciate if you go for a **walk** through the forests from the tiny resort of **Saltino**, the next village after Vallombrosa along the road to Arezzo. From here paths lead up to the summit of Monte Secchieta, from where the views are amazing.

Beyond Saltino the terrain opens out, with terraces bordering the road as it snakes down to **REGGELLO**, a diffused and characterless place much praised by connoisseurs of Tuscan olive oil. A kilometre to the south, the Romanesque **Pieve of San Pietro a Cascia** is worth a stop for the **Museo d'Arte Sacra** "**Masaccio**" (Tues & Thurs 3–7pm, Sat & Sun 10am–noon & 3–7pm; €3).

Opened to mark the six hundredth anniversary of the birth of Masaccio, who was born in nearby San Giovanni Valdarno in 1401, this tiny museum houses the earliest known work by the artist, the *San Giovenale Triptych*, which was painted in 1422. A ground-floor room is devoted to background information on the triptych, while the other rooms are given over to miscellaneous documents, furnishings and minor artworks, including some from Ghirlandaio's pupils, but in essence this is a gallery devoted to one masterpiece.

More Romanesque architecture appears at **Pian di Scò**, 10km on, where there's an eleventh-century *pieve*. **Castelfranco di Sopra**, 2km farther, was yet another town fortified by Arnolfo di Cambio but the street plan and one gate are virtually the only traces of his handiwork; its most attractive feature is a much restored thirteenth-century *badìa* on the main road. Another 10km brings you to **Loro Ciuffenna**, where ranks of new apartments form an unflattering prelude to a small medieval quarter down by the Ciuffenna river; a Romanesque tower and bridge form the core. The bridge – the Ponte Vecchio – is one of the seven that gave the old Pratomagno pilgrimage route its name, the Setteponti.

The most interesting church in this part of the Arno valley comes a couple of kilometres on, in the hamlet of **Grópina**, which is reached by taking a steep and sharp left turn just outside Loro. Here the parish church of **San Pietro** (daily 10am–noon & 3–5pm) has some of the finest Romanesque carving in Tuscany, dating from the early thirteenth century. The capitals depict knights, fighting animals and various standard motifs, but you'll have to travel a long way to find anything quite like the pulpit, with its knotted columns and rows of alarmed-looking figures with upraised arms.

The last place of any interest before Arezzo is **Castiglion Fibocchi**, whose central patch – now enclosed by light industry (clothing and fur factories, mostly) – has changed little in appearance since the Middle Ages, though no monument in particular stands out.

Arezzo

Maecenas, the wealthy patron of Horace and Virgil, was born in **AREZZO** and it's still a place with the moneyed touch, thanks in large part to its jewellers and goldsmiths, who are so numerous that the city has the world's largest gold manufacturing plant. Topping up the coffers are the proceeds of Arezzo's antiques industry: in the vicinity of the Piazza Grande there are shops filled with museum-quality furniture, and every month the **Fiera Antiquaria** turns the piazza into a vast showroom. Though Arezzo is nowadays making more of an effort to market itself to visitors (as is reflected in the improving quality of its accommodation), this is still very much a self-sufficient city.

Occupying a site that controls the major passes of the central Apennines, Arezzo was one of the most important settlements of the Etruscan federation. It maintained its pre-eminence under Roman rule, and was a prosperous independent republic in the Middle Ages until, in 1289, its Ghibelline allegiances brought about a catastrophic clash with the Guelph Florentines at Campaldino (see p.457). Arezzo temporarily recovered from this reversal under the leadership of **Bishop Guido Tarlati**, whose bellicosity eventually earned him excommunication. However, subjugation came about in 1384, when Florence paid the ransom demanded of Arezzo by the conquering army of Louis d'Anjou. When the French departed, the city's paymaster was left in power.

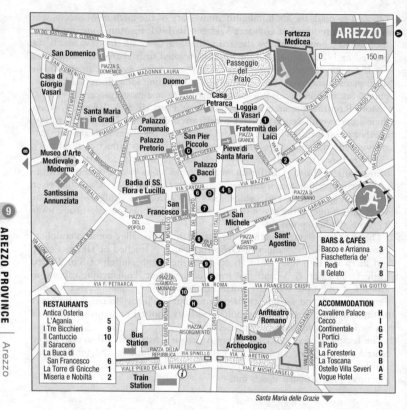

Santa Maria delle Grazie ▼

Even as a mortgaged political power, Arezzo continued to be a major cultural force. Already renowned as the birthplace of the man known as Guido d'Arezzo or Guido Monaco (c.991–1050), who is widely regarded as the inventor of modern musical notation, Arezzo was brought further prestige by Petrarch (1304–74), and then by the writer Pietro Aretino (1492–1556) and the artist-architect-biographer Giorgio Vasari (1511–74). Yet it was an outsider who gave Arezzo its greatest monument – **Piero della Francesca**, whose frescoes for the church of San Francesco belong in the same company as Masaccio's cycle in Florence and Michelangelo's in Rome.

Arrival, information and accommodation

The main **tourist office** is on the edge of the **train station** forecourt, at Piazza della Repubblica 28 (summer Mon–Sat 9am–1pm & 3–6.30pm, Sun 9am–1pm; winter closed Sun, except first Sun of month; ☎0575.377.678, ⓦwww.apt.arezzo.it); the helpful staff have masses of information on Arezzo and its province. Bus services into Arezzo all terminate by the train station. There are car parks by the train station and the archeological museum, but you'll more easily find spaces in the new car park outside the northern stretch of the city walls (near San Domenico), in the streets to the south of the rail line, or near Santa Maria delle Grazie.

Accommodation is not plentiful at any time of year, and almost impossible to come by on the first weekend of every month, because of the antiques fair; in addition the town is booked solid at the end of August and beginning of September, when the *Concorso Polifonico Guido d'Arezzo* and the *Giostra del Saracino* follow in quick succession (see box, p.448). Geared primarily to commercial visitors, Arezzo's hotels are generally rather functional – but recently, as the city has begun to make more of an effort to market itself to tourists, the situation has improved a little. At the time of going to press, the city's youth hostel, the *Ostello Villa Severi* (some way north of the centre at Via Francesco Redi 13), was closed for rebuilding; check the tourist office website for the latest information.

Hotels

Cavaliere Palace Via della Madonna del Prato 83 ☎0575.26.836, ⊛www.cavalierehotels.com. Formerly a one-star, now renamed and rebuilt as a 27-room four-star, this is one of the better hotels in central Arezzo. ❺

Cecco Corso Italia 215 ☎0575.20.986, ⊛www .hotelcecco.com. Very central 42-room two-star, above a restaurant of the same name; spacious if slightly institutional in feel. Rooms without private baths cost almost €20 less than the rest. ❷

Continentale Piazza Guido Monaco 7 ☎0575.20.251, ⊛www.hotelcontinentale.com. Large old three-star with restaurant right on the hub of the lower town. The rooms tend to be characterless, but there are excellent views from the roof terrace. ❹

I Portici Via Roma 18 ☎0575.403.132, ⊛www .hoteliportici.com. This sizeable town house has recently been converted into a very comfortable old-style four-star hotel, with just five doubles, one single and a couple of suites. ❼

Il Patio Via Cavour 23 ☎0575.401.962, ⊛www.hotelpatio.it. Another small,

welcoming and not overly expensive new four-star, 1min stroll from San Francesco. As with *I Portici*, the decor reflects Arezzo's love of antiques, but *Il Patio* wears the style with more panache. ❼

La Foresteria Via Bicchieraia 32 ☎&ℱ0575.370.474. The nicest budget accommodation in central Arezzo, *La Foresteria* comprises a dozen unfussy and well-decorated rooms in the former convent of the church of San Pier Piccolo. No credit cards. ❷

La Toscana Via M. Perennio 56 ☎&ℱ0575.21.692. One-star with seventeen rooms (nearly all with private bathroom) on the main road coming in from the west; it's no-one's idea of a romantic retreat, but if you're counting every euro it's a choice between this and the hostel. ❶

Vogue Hotel Via Guido Monaco 54 ☎0575.24.361, ⊛www.voguehotel.it. The new four-star *Vogue* has 26 rooms, each uniquely styled, but all with a sleek, modern look that makes a refreshing change from the retro atmosphere favoured by the city's other higher-end hotels. ❻

The Town

There are two distinct parts to Arezzo: the **older quarter**, at the top of the hill, and the businesslike **lower town**, much of which remains hidden from day-trippers, as it spreads behind the train station and the adjacent bus terminal. From the station forecourt, go straight ahead for Via Guido Monaco, the traffic axis between the upper and lower town. The parallel **Corso Italia**, now pedestrianized, is the route to walk up the hill.

San Francesco – Piero della Francesca's church

Off to the left of the Corso, on Via Cavour, not far from its summit, stands the building everyone comes to Arezzo to see: the basilica of **San Francesco** (summer Mon–Fri 9am–7pm, Sat 9am–6pm, Sun 1–6pm; winter Mon–Fri 9am–6pm, Sat & Sun 9am–5.30pm). Built in the 1320s, the shabby brick basilica earned its renown in the early 1450s, when the Bacci family commissioned **Piero della Francesca** to continue the decoration of the choir. The project had been started by Bicci di Lorenzo, who had painted only the *Evangelists* (in the

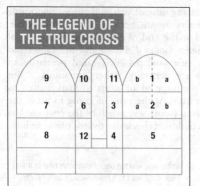

THE LEGEND OF THE TRUE CROSS

1a. Adam announces his death and implores Seth, his son, to seek the oil of mercy from the Angel of Eden.

1b. Instead the Angel gives Seth a sprig from the Tree of Knowledge, which is planted in the dead Adam's mouth.

2a. Solomon orders a bridge to be built from a beam fashioned from the tree that grew from Adam's grave. The Queen of Sheba, visiting Solomon, kneels in prayer before the bridge, sensing the holiness of the wood.

2b. The Queen of Sheba foresees that the beam will later be used to crucify a man, and that the death will bring disgrace to the Jews; she tells Solomon of her prophecy.

3. Solomon orders the beam to be buried.

4. The Emperor Constantine has a vision of the Cross, hearing a voice that declares: Under this sign shall you be victorious.

5. Constantine defeats the rival emperor Maxentius, and then is baptized. The figure of Constantine — the first emperor to rule Byzantium — may be a portrait of John Paleologus, the penultimate Byzantine emperor, who had been in Florence in 1439 to attend the Council of Florence.

6. The Levite Judas, under torture, reveals to the servants of St Helena — mother of Constantine — the burial place of the three crosses from Golgotha.

7. The crosses are excavated; the true Cross is recognized when it brings about a man's resurrection. Arezzo — serving as Jerusalem — is shown in the background.

8. The Persian king Chosroes, who had stolen the Cross, is defeated by the Emperor Heraclius. On the right he kneels awaiting execution; behind him is visible the throne into which he had incorporated the Cross.

9. Heraclius returns the Cross to Jerusalem.

10. Isaiah.

11. Jeremiah.

12. The Annunciation.

vault) and part of the *Last Judgement* (on the arch outside the chapel) before he died. For the wall paintings, Piero's patrons nominated a subject with rather fewer dramatic possibilities, but which suited the contemplative personality of the artist perfectly.

The theme chosen was **The Legend of the True Cross**, a story in which the physical material of the Cross forms the link in the cycle of redemption that begins with humanity's original sin. The literary source for the cycle, the *Golden Legend* by Jacopo de Voragine, is a very convoluted story, and the way the episodes are arranged adds to the opacity, as Piero preferred to organize the scenes according to the precepts of symmetry rather than in chronological order: thus the two battle scenes face each other across the chapel, rather than coming where the story dictates. Smaller-scale symmetries are present in every part of the work: for example, the retinue of the Queen of Sheba appears twice, in mirror-image arrangement, and the face of the queen is exactly the same as the face of the Empress Helena. This orderli-ness, combined with the pale light and the statuesque quality of the figures, create an atmosphere that's unique to Piero, and a sense of each incident as a part of a greater plan.

Our plan is a basic guide to the events depicted. The images of the *Annunciation* and two prophets on the window wall (Isaiah – painted by one of Piero's assistants – to the left; Jeremiah to the right) have nothing to do with the legend, but relate to the theme of the redemptive significance of the Cross, a point underlined by the cruciform plan of the *Annunciation*, which in turn echoes the plan of the *Vision of Constantine* on the other side of the window, where the tent pole and the rim of the tent form a cross.

Damp has badly damaged areas of the chapel and some bits have peeled away, partly as a result of Piero's notoriously slow method of working (the frescoes occupied most of his time from 1452 and 1466), but most of the rest has emerged in magnificent condition after a decade's restoration work. You can see the frescoes from the nave of the church, but you need to get closer to really appreciate them, and you're not allowed any closer than the altar steps unless you've bought a **ticket** (€6). Visits are limited to 25 people at time (same hours as the church) and to thirty minutes per group. You are encouraged to book tickets in advance by phone or online (℡0575.352.727; ⓦ www.apt.arezzo.it). However, you can make a reservation in person at the ticket office beside the church, and even in high season you may not have to wait long before getting in; in winter there's rarely any wait at all.

The Pieve di Santa Maria and Piazza Grande

Further up the Corso from San Francesco stands one of the finest Romanesque structures in Tuscany, the twelfth-century **Pieve di Santa Maria** (daily: summer 8am–1pm & 3–7pm; winter 8am–noon & 3–6pm). Its arcaded facade, elaborate yet severe, belongs to a type associated more with Pisa and western Tuscany, and is doubly unusual in presenting its front to a fairly narrow street rather than to the town's main square. Dating from the 1210s, the lively carvings of the months over the portal are the most notable adornment of the exterior. The campanile, known locally as "the tower of the hundred holes", was added in the fourteenth century. The oldest section of the chalky grey **interior** is the raised sanctuary, where the altarpiece is Pietro Lorenzetti's *Madonna and Saints* polyptych, painted in 1320. The unfamiliar saint on the far left, accompanying Matthew, the Baptist and John the Evangelist, is St Donatus, the second bishop of Arezzo, who was martyred in 304. His relics are in the crypt, encased in a beautiful gold-and-silver bust made in 1346 by local goldsmiths known only as Pietro and Paolo.

Opposite the Pieve, occupying the fourteenth-century Palazzo del Capitano del Popolo, the **Casa-Museo Ivan Bruschi** (Tues–Sun 10am–1pm & 3–7pm; €4) commemorates the man who started Arezzo's antiques fair. Bruschi's collection of sculptures, armour, books and miscellaneous *objets d'art* are nicely displayed in a simulated jumble, but it's a museum to leave until you've seen the rest of the city's sights.

The steeply sloping **Piazza Grande**, on the other side of the Pieve, is generally a peaceful spot, but it really comes alive for the *Fiera Antiquaria* and – more raucously – for September's Giostra del Saracino. A diverting assortment of buildings encloses the space, with the wooden balconied apartments on the east side facing the apse of the Pieve, the Baroque Palazzo dei Tribunali and the **Palazzetto della Fraternità dei Laici**, which has a Renaissance upper storey and a Gothic lower. The upper level is adorned by a relief of the *Madonna della Misericordia* and niche statues, all carved by Bernardo Rossellino in 1434; below, there's a lunette fresco of the *Pietà* by Spinello Aretino, dating from the 1370s, while the beautiful loggia and cornice across the top of the palazzo date from 1460 and are the work of Giuliano da Settignano. The piazza's northern edge is formed by the arcades of the **Loggia di Vasari**, occupied by shops that in some instances still retain their original sixteenth-century stone counters.

The Duomo and around

At the highest point of the town rises the large and unfussy **Duomo** (daily 6.30am–12.30pm & 3–6.30pm), whose harmonious appearance belies the protracted process of its construction. Begun in 1278, it was virtually finished by the start of the sixteenth century, but the campanile dates from 1859 and the facade from 1914.

The stained-glass windows, a rarity in Italy, were made around 1520 by Guillaume de Marcillat, an Arezzo-based Frenchman who also contributed some frescoes to San Francesco; they let in so little light that his other contributions to the interior – the paintings on the first three bays of the nave – are virtually impossible to see. Off the left aisle, separated from the nave by a huge screen, the Cappella della Madonna del Conforto has terracottas by the della Robbia family, but the best of the building's artworks lie further down the aisle. Just beyond the organ is the **tomb of Bishop Guido Tarlati** (died 1327), head of the *comune* of Arezzo during its resurgence in the early fourteenth century; the monument, plated with marble reliefs showing scenes from the militaristic bishop's career, was possibly designed by Giotto. The small fresco nestled against the right side of the tomb is **Piero della Francesca**'s *Magdalene*, his only work in Arezzo outside San Francesco. In the chapel closest to the *Magdalene* lies Pope Gregory X, who died in Arezzo in 1276; a plaque on the wall invites you to consider his remarkable life, which overlapped with the lives of many other remarkable individuals, such as St Thomas Aquinas and St Bonaventure (who both taught him in Paris), St Francis, St Dominic, the Emperor Frederick II, Dante and Marco Polo.

Arezzo's festivals

Arezzo's premier folkloric event is the **Giostra del Saracino**, which was first recorded in 1535 and is nowadays held in the Piazza Grande on the first Sunday in September. The day starts off with various costumed parades; at 5pm the action switches to the jousting arena in the piazza, with a procession of some 300 participants leading the way. The piazza is the junction of the four quarters of the city and the sides of the square are decked with flags to mark their affiliations. Each quarter is represented by a pair of knights on horseback, who do battle with a wooden effigy of a Saracen king. In one hand it holds a shield marked with point scores, a bit like a dartboard; in the other it has a cat-o'-three-tails which swings round when the shield is hit, necessitating nifty evasive action from the rider. A golden lance is awarded to the highest-scoring rider. In the days immediately preceding the joust you'll see rehearsals taking place, and in recent years the event has become so popular that a reduced version of the show is now held on the penultimate Saturday of June; check at the tourist office for information.

The musical tradition that began with Guido d'Arezzo is kept alive chiefly through the international choral competition that bears his name: the **Concorso Polifonico Guido d'Arezzo**, held in the last week of August. The less ambitious **Pomeriggi Musicali** is a season of free concerts held in various churches, museums and libraries; on average there's one concert a week from mid-January to June.

The **Fiera Antiquaria** takes over the Piazza Grande on the first Sunday of each month and the preceding Saturday. The most expensive stuff is laid out by the Vasari loggia, with cheaper pieces lower down the square and in the side streets.

The small and overpriced **Museo Diocesano** (Mon & Wed–Sun 10am–1pm & 2–6pm; €5), alongside the Duomo, won't make anyone's day, but the **Passeggio del Prato**, which extends from the east end of the Duomo to the **Fortezza Medicea**, is a good place to take a picnic. Cosimo I's fortress here was demolished in the eighteenth century, leaving only the ramparts.

From San Domenico to the Badìa

A short distance north of the Duomo you'll come across the church of **San Domenico** (daily 8am–7pm), constructed mostly in the late thirteenth century but with a Gothic campanile. Inside there are tatters of fifteenth- and sixteenth-century frescoes on the walls, while above the high altar hangs a dolorous Crucifix by Cimabue (1260), painted when the artist would have been about 20.

From here signs point the way to the **Casa di Giorgio Vasari** (Mon & Wed–Sat 8.30am–7pm, Sun 8.30am–1pm; €2) at Via XX Settembre 55, designed by the biographer-architect-painter. Born in Arezzo in 1511, Giorgio Vasari was taught to paint by his distant relative Luca Signorelli, and went on to become court painter, architect and general artistic supremo to Cosimo I. His major contribution to Western culture, however, is his *Lives of the Most Excellent Italian Architects, Painters and Sculptors*, the first attempt to relate artists' work to their social context, and a primary source for all histories of the Renaissance. The industrious Vasari frescoed much of his house with portraits and mythological characters, a decorative scheme that makes this one of the brashest domestic interiors in Tuscany. Portraits include his wife as the muse of conjugal love (in the Chamber of Apollo) and Michelangelo and Andrea del Sarto (in the Chamber of Fame). Work by other minor artists are strewn all over the place, proof that Giorgio was far from the most inept painter of his day.

At the foot of the hill, at Via San Lorentino 8, the fifteenth-century Palazzo Bruni-Ciocchi houses the **Museo d'Arte Medievale e Moderna** (Tues–Sun 8.30am–7pm; €4), containing a collection of paintings by local artists and majolica pieces from the thirteenth to the eighteenth centuries, generously spread over three floors. Highlights are the first floor's medieval and Renaissance paintings by the likes of Spinello Aretino, Luca Signorelli and Bartolomeo della Gatta; ceramics cognoscenti will revel in the five rooms containing works from Deruta, Gubbio, Faenza and other major Italian centres of production.

If you follow Via Cavour from the Museo d'Arte, a huge Baroque tower soon signals the presence of the hulking **Badìa di Santi Flora e Lucilla** (Mon–Sat 8am–noon & 4–7pm, Sun 7am–12.30pm). The interior was extensively remodelled by Vasari, who also contributed the monstrous main altarpiece, designed as a monument to his family.

The Museo Archeologico and Santa Maria delle Grazie

Nearly all the principal sights are in the upper part of Arezzo. One exception is the **Museo Archeologico** (daily 8.30am–7.30pm; €4), which occupies part of an abandoned Olivetan monastery built into a wall of the town's Roman amphitheatre, to the east of the station on Via Margaritone. The remains of the amphitheatre (entrance free) amount to little more than the base of the perimeter wall, largely because Cosimo I used the site as a quarry for the fortress up by the Duomo. More impressive are the museum's marvellously coloured coralline vases; produced here in the first century BC, they show why Arezzo's glassblowers were renowned throughout the Roman world as consummate craftsmen.

Ten-minutes' walk away, south of the city centre at the end of Viale Mecenate, stands Arezzo's most exquisite church, **Santa Maria delle Grazie** (daily 8am–7pm). In the sixth century BC the Etruscans held fertility rites here, beside a spring in the midst of the woods that covered this area. At the instigation of St Bernardino the site was purged of its pagan associations by the plugging of the spring and the construction of the church, which still has a Carmelite convent attached. Fronted by a tiny pine-ringed meadow that's flanked by a pair of arcades, the church is entered through a delicate portico built by Benedetto da Maiano in the 1470s. The church is essentially a single room, containing little more than a few seats and an altarpiece by Parri Spinello, painted on the instructions of St Bernardino; the beautiful marble and terracotta altar that encases it was created by Andrea della Robbia.

Eating and drinking

Arezzo's **restaurants** are of a generally high standard, and you'll find some nice **cafés** around piazzas Guido Monaco, Grande and San Francesco, and along Corso Italia. For picnic provisions you can't do better than *Sbarbacipolle*, at Via Garibaldi 120.

Antica Osteria L'Agania Via Mazzini 10 ☎0575.25.381. A very good and informal trattoria with a welcoming atmosphere and local dishes (special emphasis on truffles and mushrooms in season), at around €35 per head; it draws much of its clientele from the antiques dealers. Closed Mon & part of June.

Bacco e Arrianna Via Cesalpino 10. A terrific *enoteca* very close to San Francesco, with delicious food too. Closed Mon & July.

Il Gelato Via de' Cenci 24. The best *gelateria* in town. Summer 11am–midnight; winter 11am–8pm; closed Wed.

Fiaschetteria de' Redi Via de' Redi 10. Busy little *osteria* with a superb range of vintages and decent simple meals. Closed Mon.

I Tre Bicchieri Piazzetta Sopra i Ponti 3–5 ☎0575.265.57. A classy and imaginative restaurant, with a notably extensive wine list. You'll pay in the region of €40–50 per head. Closed Wed.

Il Cantuccio Via Madonna del Prato 76 ☎0575.26.830. Good-value food (meals around €30 per person) served in a pleasant vaulted cellar. The home-made pasta dishes are particularly delicious. Closed Wed.

Il Saraceno Via Mazzini 6 ☎0575.27.644. Family-run trattoria, founded in 1946, with a good wine cellar and menus of traditional Aretine specialities (notably duck) at around €35 per head; good wood-oven pizzas too. Closed Wed & part of Jan.

La Buca di San Francesco Via San Francesco 1 ☎0575.23.271. Though it's right next to the main tourist attraction in Arezzo, this place is a genuine mid-range Tuscan trattoria: it's been in business since 1929, and the subterranean interior preserves parts of an Etruscan-Roman pavement and medieval frescoes. Closed Mon eve, Tues & two weeks in July.

La Torre di Gnicche Piaggia San Martino 8. ☎0575.352.035. Perfect for a simple and inexpensive meal, washed down with a glass from a huge selection of local Colli Aretini and other Italian wines. Closed Wed & two weeks in Jan.

Miseria e Nobiltà Via Piaggia di San Bartolomeo 2 ☎0575.21.245. With its enticing pan-Italian menu and medieval vaulted dining room, this very stylish (but not expensive) restaurant is one of the best in town. Closed Mon & lunch daily.

To Sansepolcro: the Piero trail

Arezzo is the springboard for one of Tuscany's most rewarding art itineraries: the Piero della Francesca trail, which extends east of the city to **Monterchi** and **Sansepolcro** (the artist's birthplace), and continues via Perugia, where you'll find a stunning Piero altarpiece in the main art gallery. (The trail then reaches beyond the region covered in this guide, going through Urbino and on to Rimini.) There's no train link between Arezzo and Sansepolcro, the sole rail approach to Sansepolcro being the private FCU Terni–Perugia line. The SITA **bus** company runs nearly twenty services a day from Arezzo to Sansepolcro, nearly all of which continue to Città di Castello for train connections to Perugia; five stop at Monterchi at convenient times for a visit. Otherwise, the nearest regular stop to Monterchi is Le Ville, 2km to the west, from where the buses veer away through **Anghiari**. Drivers should note that the route through this area is becoming quicker with the construction of a highly conspicuous and thus controversial new *autostrada* from Arezzo to Sansepolcro.

Monterchi – the Madonna del Parto

The farming village of **MONTERCHI** is 25km east of Arezzo, and for the last few kilometres of the journey the roadsides bear signs for the **Madonna del Parto** – surely the only painting in Tuscany to be signposted as if it were a town. The fresco was painted around 1467 for a cemetery chapel that stands on the outskirts of Monterchi, and remained hidden under plaster for centuries before its rediscovery in 1889 – by which time the *St Lucy* and the *Pietà* that Piero also painted here had both been lost.

In 1993 the fresco was moved from the chapel to an ex-primary school on Via della Reglia, to undergo major restoration, and there it has remained, despite the mutterings of many who feel its former home to be more appropriate. The *Madonna* is now the focal point of a permanent **exhibition** (Tues–Sun 9am–1pm & 2–7pm; winter closes 6pm; €3) recounting the technical details of the fresco's restoration, and also that of the San Francesco cycle in Arezzo. The picture is still an object of veneration, and the museum is cleared when local pregnant women come to pray to the Virgin.

Despite the restoration, the colours of the *Madonna del Parto* lack the freshness of the Arezzo cycle, but even if it were bleached to black and white this would be a potent picture. Two attendant angels draw back the flap of a small pavilion to reveal the pregnant Virgin, who places her hand on the upper curve of her belly, her eyes downcast as if preoccupied with a foreknowledge of the child's life. Images of the pregnant Mary began to appear in Tuscan art in the 1330s (the first major *Madonna del Parto* was painted for the church of San Francesco di Paola in Florence by Taddeo Gaddi, around 1335), a date which has led Renzo Manetti, a Florentine writer and architect, to propose that these pictures should be read as references to a "hidden truth" that was known only to members of the Knights Templar. Proceeding from the facts that the Templars were suppressed in 1312 and that Florence was a major centre for the sect, Manetti argues that della Francesca's fresco (almost the last *Madonna del Parto* to be painted) is perhaps indicative of his Templar sympathies. Others have dismissed his theory as just another exercise in conspiratorial mumbo-jumbo, along the lines of the *Da Vinci Code*. Whether this *Madonna del Parto* is a piece of coded propaganda or what it plainly appears to be – a meditation on the mystery of the Incarnation – it's incontestable that few other artists of the Renaissance produced anything comparable to its beautiful gravity.

Anghiari and Caprese Michelangelo

Most buses from Arezzo to Sansepolcro call at **ANGHIARI**, an agricultural and textile-producing hill-town set amid fields of sunflowers and tobacco, with a lucrative side-line in furniture restoration – the town has a renowned training centre for specialists in the craft, and hosts an antiques fair on the third Sunday of each month, as well as a huge annual crafts market in late April. Anghiari's diminutive historic centre of narrow streets, stepped alleyways and tunnels commands a fine view across the upper Tiber towards Sansepolcro. It was on this ground, on June 29, 1440, that the Florentine army defeated the Milanese troops of Filippo Maria Visconti, an engagement that became the subject of perhaps the most famous lost artwork of the Renaissance: Leonardo da Vinci's fresco in Florence's Palazzo Vecchio. There's a small exhibition relating to the battle, in the Palazzo del Marzocco on Piazza Mameli (daily 9am–7pm; €2). On the same piazza, the imposing Palazzo Taglieschi is home to the **Museo Statale** (Tues–Sat 8.30am–7pm, Sun 9am–1pm; €2), a well-displayed collection of mostly unexceptional artworks and domestic items, but with one outstanding piece: a painted wooden *Madonna* by Jacopo della Quercia. The Child that was once perched on her knee has been displayed separately since the sculpture was restored, as the restorers believe it may not have been carved at the same time.

Michelangelo, effectively Leonardo's competitor in the decoration of the Palazzo Vecchio, was born 17km north of Anghiari in the place that now carries the name **CAPRESE MICHELANGELO**; it was just plain Caprese before being renamed in honour of the prodigious son of the town's chief magistrate and his wife. The ancient village is perched high on a cliff overlooking the car park, bus stop (with regular services from Anghiari) and the remarkably inexpensive three-star *Buca di Michelangelo* **hotel–restaurant** (℡0575.793.921, Ⓦ www.bucadimichelangelo.it; ❷). The castle and Michelangelo's supposed birthplace, the Casa del Podestà, have been converted into a **Museo Michelangiolesco** (daily: summer 9.30am–6.30pm; winter 9.30am–4.30pm; €3); a few bits of Renaissance furniture and a load of plaster casts create the undernourishing experience that's typical of these shrines to great Tuscan artists.

Sansepolcro

The SITA bus from Arezzo takes an hour to get to **SANSEPOLCRO**, an unassuming place that makes its way in the world as a manufacturer of lace and, more lucratively, pasta. If the walled *centro storico* within the industrial and commercial belt were a bit more substantial it could make a lot more money out of tourism; as it is, thousands of people come here each year to see **Piero della Francesca**'s paintings, then leave a couple of hours later. There really isn't much more to the place than these pictures, but it's a relaxing and good-looking small town, and has a couple of fine restaurants too.

Born here at some time around 1420, Piero spent much of his life in the backwater of what was then the village of Borgo San Sepolcro; a three-year sojourn in Florence was probably his longest continuous absence. Patrons in Ferrara, Rome and Urbino called upon his services, even though his creative process was so painstaking that on one occasion his father had to apologize to a client for Piero's slowness. He returned to Sansepolcro in the 1470s, having abandoned painting as his eyesight failed. Most of his last twenty years were devoted to working on his treatises *On Perspective in Painting* and *On the Five Regular Bodies*, in which he propounded the geometrical rules that he deemed essential to an accurate representation of the world, and extolled the human form as the exemplar of perfect proportion.

The Museo Civico

The **Museo Civico**, at Via Niccolò Aggiunti 65 (daily: June 15–Sept 15 9.30am–1.30pm & 2.30–7pm; rest of year 9.30am–1pm & 2.30–6pm; €6), houses a sizeable collection of pictures, including work by Pontormo, Signorelli and Santi di Tito, but there's only one focus of attention here, and that's Piero della Francesca.

A couple of minor della Francescas are hung in the vicinity of the **Madonna della Misericordia**, his earliest known painting and the epitome of his graceful solemnity. It was created in the 1440s, soon after he had been made a member of Sansepolcro's governing council, a position he was to hold for the rest of his life. Tiny panels surround the central image of the Madonna, a conventional and antiquated format that was specified by his patrons, the charitable Compagnia della Misericordia. There's no conventional fragility about this Madonna, though: compassionate and all-capable, she protects her worshippers with a cape as solid as a wall. The hooded man at her feet is wearing the uniform of the Misericordia, a sinister garb still worn by members of the modern Misericordia when bearing a body to a funeral.

The **Resurrection**, in the next room, was painted for the adjoining town hall, probably in the early 1450s, and moved here in the sixteenth century. Aldous Huxley once dubbed this "the greatest painting in the world", a piece of hyperbole that may well have saved the painting from obliteration. In 1944 the British Eighth Army was ordered to bombard Sansepolcro, but an officer recalled Huxley's article and delayed the attack in the hope that the Germans would withdraw – which they did. Much of the picture's power comes from its unique emphasis on the Resurrection as a physical event: muscular and implacable, Christ steps onto the edge of the tomb – banner in hand – as if it were the rampart of a conquered city. The strange landscape in the background – with leafless trees on one side and reborn foliage on the other – was the starting point for Kenneth Clark's description, which pinpoints a pre-Christian strand to the painting's significance: "This country god, who rises in the grey light while humanity is asleep, has been worshipped ever since man first knew that the seed is not dead in the winter earth, but will force its way upwards through an iron crust."

The rest of the town

Sansepolcro's newest museum, the **Aboca Museum**, is a few doors down from the Museo Civico at Via Niccolò Aggiunti 75 (daily: April–Sept 10am–1pm & 3–7pm; Oct–March 10am–1pm & 2.30–6pm; €8). Spread over two storeys of an imposing mansion, this is Italy's only museum dedicated to the history of herbal medicine, and it's extremely well done, with rooms full of nicely displayed old equipment, ceramics and books; there's even a reconstructed seventeenth-century laboratory. It's nonetheless a somewhat recondite collection, and expensive too.

Round the corner you'll find the Romanesque-Gothic **Duomo** (daily 7.30am–noon & 3.30–6.30pm). The main feature of the plain facade is a rose window that's glazed with thin panels of alabaster, as are the other windows, giving the interior a pleasantly warm gloom. Inside, the chapel to the left of the chancel houses a mighty tenth-century Crucifix known as the *Volto Santo*, depicting Christ as a robed patriarch. (The crown and gown with which this Crucifix is dressed for November's Feast of the Redeemer are usually on show in the Museo Civico.) Nearby, on the wall of the left aisle, hangs an *Ascension* by Perugino.

One other church merits a look – **San Lorenzo** (daily 9am–1pm & 3–7pm; shorter hours in winter), on Via Santa Croce, where the main altarpiece is a *Deposition* by the Mannerist painter Rosso Fiorentino, painted within half a century of della Francesca's last works but seeming to belong to another world.

Practicalities

If you decide to stay, you should be able to find space in at least one of the town's half-dozen **hotels**. Top recommendation is the three-star ✣ *Fiorentino*, which has been in business at Via Luca Pacioli 60 since 1807 (☎0575.740.350, ⓦ www.albergofiorentino.com; ❷); the rooms are small and functional, but the hotel has friendly owners, its location cannot be beaten (the other three-stars are outside the walled centre), and it has a very good **restaurant** (closed Fri), in which you can expect to pay around €35. Another excellent place to eat is the family-run 🍴 *Da Ventura*, Via Niccolò Aggiunti 30 (☎0575.742.560; closed Sun eve & Mon), in the same price range as the *Fiorentino*; it also has inexpensive accommodation upstairs (Ⓦwww.albergodaventura.it; ❷).

Just about the only time you'll have difficulty in finding a room is the second Sunday in September, the date of the **Palio della Balestra**, the return leg of the crossbow competition against the archers of Gubbio. The shoot-out is preceded by some very flashy flag-hurling, whose practitioners – clad in costumes inspired by Piero's paintings – show off their skills at various other times of the year as well. For details, call in at the **tourist office** on Piazza Garibaldi (daily: April–Oct 9.30am–noon & 2–7pm; Nov–March 10am–noon & 2–6pm; ☎0575.730.231).

North of Arezzo: the Casentino

North of Arezzo, beyond the factories, lies the lush upper valley of the Arno, a thoroughly agricultural area known as the **Casentino**, whose unshowy little towns see few tourists, even though a large part of the area has now been designated a national park, and efforts are being made to direct visitors towards the various museums dedicated to the traditions of the Casentino (see box below). From Bibbiena to Pratovecchio the valley is a broad green dish, ruffled by low hills and bracketed by the peaks of the Pratomagno on one side and on the other by the ridge between the Arno and the Tiber. Thick woodland of oak, beech and pine covers much of the upper slopes, the remnant of the forest that used to coat much of the Casentino. During the Medici centuries the timber

The EcoMuseo del Casentino

The Casentino is littered with tiny museums, which together are referred to as the EcoMuseo del Casentino – the Casentino Environmental Museum. Usually consisting of just a couple of rooms of tools, furniture and photographs, and in several cases open only for a few hours at the weekend, or by request (see Ⓦwww.ecomuseo.casentino.toscana.it), none of them is likely to make a rewarding target for a day's excursion, but all are worth a look if you happen to be passing. The list is as follows:

Capolona Museo dell'Aqua (water museum)

Castel Fococagno Centro di Documentazione Rurale (centre for rural heritage)

Castel San Niccolò Museo della Civiltà Castellana (museum of castle heritage)

Cetica Museo del Carbonaio (charcoal burners' museum)

Chitignano Museo del Contrabbando e Polvere da Sparo (museum of smuggling and gunpowder)

Partina Museo Archeologico del Casentino (archeological museum)

Poppi Centro di Documentazione di Storia Locale (centre for documentation of local history)

Raggiolo Museo della Castagna (chestnut museum)

Stia Museo del Bosco e della Montagna (museum of forests and mountains)

Subbiano Museo della Civiltà Contadina (museum of rural culture)

Talla Museo della Musica (museum of music)

from here supplied the shipyards of Pisa, Livorno and Genoa, as well as the building sites of Tuscany.

Florence did not always have territorial rights in this region. From the eleventh century the northern part of the Casentino was ruled by the **Guidi** dynasty of Poppi, who kept control from a string of castles – their ruins still litter the hills. In the Middle Ages Arezzo, landlord of the southern Casentino, brawled constantly with Florence for possession of this lucrative valley. After Florence bested the Aretines at the battle of Campaldino, the traditionally Ghibelline Guidi counts recognized the authority of the Guelph victors, and were in return allowed to maintain their power base here, though within a century or so the Florentines had ousted them completely. The seclusion of the higher ground fostered a strong monastic tradition as well, and the communities at **Camáldoli** and at **La Verna** continue to be important centres for their respective orders.

By **public transport**, the best target for a day-trip from Arezzo is **Poppi**; it's connected to the city by bus and by the private LFI **train** line which shares the state FS station in Arezzo. There are fourteen trains daily (five on Sun, when services may be replaced by a bus): journey time is 55 minutes. To strike into the hills and to visit the monasteries of La Verna and Camáldoli requires a car, unless you want to stay overnight; buses do run from Bibbiena to Badìa Pratáglia, Camáldoli and Chiusi della Verna (the nearest stop to the monastery of La Verna), but they are too infrequent to make a round trip feasible in a day.

Bibbiena

The chief commercial town of the Casentino is **BIBBIENA**, a place swathed in straggling development, much of it connected with tobacco production. In the moderately attractive inner quarter, the main sight is the church of **San Lorenzo**, a fifteenth-century building that contains a fair quantity of terracotta from the della Robbia workshops. At the top end of town, close to Piazza Tarlati – its name a sign of its links with Arezzo (see p.443) – the oddly shaped church of **Santi Ippolito e Donato** has a fine altarpiece by Bicci di Lorenzo. Once you've seen these, there's no reason to hang around.

La Verna

In 1213 a pious member of the Guidi clan, Count Orlando, donated to **St Francis** and his closest followers a plot of land at **LA VERNA** (Ⓦ www.santuariolaverna .org), 23km east of Bibbiena, just inside the modern boundaries of the national park. It was at this hermitage, on September 14, 1224, that Francis received the stigmata from a vision of the crucified Christ, a badge of sanctity never previously bestowed.

Francis's mountain-top sanctuary rapidly grew into a monastic village, whose ten chapels are connected by a network of corridors, cloisters, dormitories and stone pathways. Nowadays tens of thousands of pilgrims come here annually, some of them staying in the guesthouse adjoining the monks' quarters, most coming to pay an hour's homage at the site of the miracle, or merely out of curiosity. Unlike at the basilica at Assisi, however, secular sightseers don't obscure the purpose of the place. The sanctuary is open every day from 6am to 8.30pm, though in winter the road is sometimes closed by snow.

Relics of the saint – his walking stick, belt, drinking glass – are displayed in the fifteenth-century **basilica**, where there's a glorious *Ascension* by Andrea della Robbia, whose other masterpieces are the focal points of the Chiesa delle Stimmate (built on the spot where Francis received the stigmata) and the

Parco Nazionale delle Foreste Casentinesi

One of Italy's newest national parks, the **Parco Nazionale delle Foreste Casentinesi** (Ⓦwww.parks.it/parco.nazionale.for.casentinesi) encompasses a vast area that spans Tuscany and Emilia-Romagna, and has been created to conserve the region's terrain and wildlife, as well as the historic monuments of La Verna and Camáldoli. The tourist office in Arezzo (see p.444) makes a good place to start if you want to plan a trip, but the park **headquarters** is in Pratovecchio, at Via G. Brocchi 7 (Mon–Thurs 8am–1pm & 3–5pm, Fri 8am–1pm; ☏0575.50.301). Within Tuscany there are other **visitor centres** (usually open Sat & Sun) at Parco I Maggio in Chiusi della Verna (☏0575.532.098), at Via della Rota 8 in Castagno d'Andrea (7km southeast of San Godenzo, in the Mugello; ☏055.837.5125), at Parco del Lago in Londa (also in the Mugello, 7km southeast of Dicomano; ☏055.835.1202), and at Via Nazionale 14a in Badía Prataglia (☏0575.559.477). The last is open virtually all year, whereas the others are open only in spring and summer.

Though you get good views from the roads between these villages and over the border into Emilia-Romagna, to get to grips with the wilderness you need to **walk**. The forests are criss-crossed by dozens of paths and tracks, most of them marked on the SELCA 1:25,000 map *Carta Escursionistica-Parco Nazionale delle Foreste Casentinesi, Monte Falterona, Campigna*, which is available from the park centres and local bookshops.

Badía Prataglia, 12km northeast of Bibbiena and 10km east of Camáldoli, has no great attractions in itself, other than its Romanesque parish church, but it's a good base for the Parco Nazionale, as it's the starting point of several trails, has one of the park's main visitor centres, and has plentiful **accommodation** (though many hotels here are closed in Nov and Dec). The most comfortable option is the three-star *Bosco Verde*, Via Nazionale 8/10 (☏0575.559.017, Ⓔhotel.boscoverde@badiaprataglia.it; ❷), which has a **restaurant**.

Cappella di Santa Maria degli Angeli. Halfway along the corridor leading to the Stimmate – a walkway painted with modern scenes of the story of St Francis – a small door opens into a gash in the crag, where Francis used to sleep on a bed of stone. (According to Franciscan orthodoxy, the rocks at La Verna split apart at the moment of Christ's death.) The route also passes the marginally more comfortable cell in which St Anthony of Padua stayed in 1230. The Sasso Spicco, reached by a flight of steps near the corridor, was Francis's preferred place of meditation.

A path through the forest above the sanctuary leads to the summit of **La Penna** (1283m), from where there's a panorama of the Casentino meadows in one direction and the savage serrations of the Apennines in the other. The drive from La Verna to Sansepolcro is a fabulous descent into the upper Tiber valley; the valley itself, however, is a mess of light industry and quarries.

Poppi

POPPI, 6km north of Bibbiena and plainly visible from there, amounts to not much more than a couple of tiny squares and a narrow arcaded main street, but it is lent a monumental aspect by the Casentino's chief landmark, the **Castello dei Conti Guidi** (March 15–June 30, Sept & Oct daily 10am–6pm; July & Aug daily 10am–7pm; rest of year Thurs–Sun 10am–5pm; €4). Built for the Guidi lords in the 1270s, it is based closely on Florence's Palazzo Vecchio and it's likely that Arnolfo di Cambio was one of the architects here as well. The deep courtyard, with its wooden landings and beautiful staircases, is the most attractive piece of secular architecture in the Casentino – the stone caryatid at the head of the stairs is a portrait of Count Simone di Battifolle, for whom the castle was built, and whose ghost is said to haunt the place. In the cellars there's a display on warfare and fortifications in the era of the Guidi, featuring a teeming model of the battle of Campaldino, plus a dismembered knight under the floorboards for added impact; under the stairs you'll find the castle dungeon. Upstairs, a fine old library has changing displays of books and manuscripts, and the top-floor chapel is frescoed with scenes from the life of the Virgin, John the Baptist and John the Evangelist, painted in the 1330s by Taddeo Gaddi. You get a fine view from the windows on this storey, but the best vantage point is the summit of the **tower** (€2), a 104-step ascent.

At the upper end of Via Cavour (the main street) stands the domed **Oratorio del Madonna contro il Morbo**, raised in the sixteenth century to give thanks to Mary for – as the name tells you – delivering the town from plague. At its lower end, the street climaxes at the magnificent twelfth-century **Badìa di San Fedele** (daily 10am–noon & 3–7pm), which contains an array of paintings by some obscure sixteenth-century artists, and the splendid reliquary bust of St Torello, a Vallombrosan monk who was born in Poppi in 1202 and spent the last six decades of his life immured in a cell in this church.

Tiny Poppi has just two **hotels**, the better of which, right by the castle at Piazza della Repubblica 6, is the plain, homely and inexpensive three-star *Casentino* (☎0575.529.090, ⓦwww.albergocasentino.it; ❷), which has a nice courtyard garden, a bar and a very popular restaurant (closed Wed). The ten-room *San Lorenzo* (☎0575.520.176; ⓦwww.poppi-sanlorenzo.com; ❷), which has a sauna and health centre in the cellar, is furnished with contemporary cast-iron furniture, and has good views over the valley. There's also another excellent **restaurant** in town: the *Antica Cantina*, Via Lapucci 2 (☎0575.529.844; closed Mon, plus Tues in winter).

A short distance north of Poppi is the site of the **Battle of Campaldino**, where on June 11, 1289 the Florentine Guelphs defeated the Arezzo Ghibellines to establish Florence's pre-eminence in the power struggles of Tuscany. Warfare in Italy during this era was chiefly conducted by relatively small

▲ Poppi emerging from the morning mist

companies of hired troops, who would typically hold a town to ransom and then, maybe after a bit of skirmishing, depart with their cash. Pitched battles on the scale of Campaldino were a rarity: some 22,000 men fought here, and nearly 2000 of them were killed. One who survived was Dante, then 24 years old. A column, where the road splits, marks the battle site.

Camáldoli

One of the best bases for the national park is **CAMÁLDOLI**, just over 15km northeast of Poppi, where in 1012 San Romualdo (or St Rumbold) founded an especially ascetic order of the Benedictines. Notwithstanding the severity of its order, this sylvan retreat became a favourite with non-monastic penitents, so much so that a second site was opened up to accommodate visitors and to administer the woodlands that Romualdo had been granted. This lower complex has been much rebuilt and the only point of interest is its sixteenth-century pharmacy, which now sells herbal products.

On summer weekends lots of people come out here for strolls through the forest up to the **Eremo**, the heart of the monastery – which is around 3km away, up the mountain. These days both men and women can visit, but no one is allowed near the living quarters, except to take a peek at Romualdo's cell. More strenuous walks are possible from the Eremo (the country to the north is very wild), or from Camáldoli village itself – paths worth considering are those to Badìa Prataglia (to the east) and Poggio Muschioso (to the west).

Pratovecchio and Stia

PRATOVECCHIO, the birthplace of Paolo Uccello, retains some attractive old arcaded streets, but the major attractions are outside the town, on a narrow little lane to the west of the main road. The **Pieve di Romena**, though patched up a few times since its foundation in the twelfth century, is a wonderfully preserved Romanesque church, with splendid capitals and a beehive-shaped sacristy. An inscription on the first column to the right identi-fies the sculptor as the parish priest, Albericus; on the second pillar on the left another states that the work was completed during a famine in 1152. Close by are the precarious but still intimidating ruins of the **Castello di Romena** (closed to the public), built by the Guidi counts and once the mightiest castle in the Casentino. Dante was a guest here, and in the *Inferno* he mentions one of its former tenants, Adamo da Brescia, whose counterfeit coins wreaked such havoc with the local economy that the enraged Florentines roasted him alive. If you're in town and looking for a bite to **eat**, be certain to drop into *L'Osteria di Giovanni*, Via Roma 57 (closed Tues): Giovanni's speciality, a sandwich made from local ham smoked over a fire of juniper wood, makes a delicious snack.

The LFI rail line finishes 2km on at **STIA**, the nearest town to the source of the Arno, which rises to the north on Monte Falterona. The hills around Stia are dotted with natural springs, and in the town's park – the Parco del Palagio Fiorentino – a modern spa complex has been built around the Fonte di Calce-donia, a long-established source that nowadays provides one of Italy's best-known bottled mineral waters. The porticoed Piazza Tanucci is the heart (and summit) of the medieval town, where the steep roofs give the place an alpine feel. Stia's chief monument, the Romanesque **Santa Maria Assunta**, houses a *Madonna* by Andrea della Robbia and a triptych by Bicci di Lorenzo. Stia has a couple of reasonably priced **hotels**: the handsome three-star *Falterona*, on Piazza Tanucci (℡0575.550.4569; ⓦwww.albergofalterona.it; ➌), and the two-star *Foresta*,

Via Roma 27 (☎0575.550.650, ⓦwww.fattorialaforesta.it; ③). The *Falterona* has a decent **restaurant**.

At Stia the road divides: to the west of Monte Falterona one branch passes another Guidi fortress and the frescoed church of Santa Maria delle Grazie on its way to the Sieve valley (see p.199); the other, to the east, crosses the Passo la Calla then drops down into Emilia-Romagna.

South of Arezzo: the Valdichiana

Travelling south from Arezzo you enter the **Valdichiana**, prosperous agricultural country that nurtures the Chianina breed of cattle, source of the best Florentine *bistecca* – though the Chianina is far rarer than it used to be, and much *bistecca* now comes from Spanish herds. As with the Maremma, this former swampland was first drained by the Etruscans, whose work was allowed to unravel in medieval times, when the encroaching marshes drove the farmers of the region back up to the hill-towns. Only in the nineteenth century, with the reclamation schemes of the Lorraine dukes of Tuscany, did the Valdichiana become fertile again. It's an underwhelming landscape, but its flatness does mean that the towns on its flanks – of which **Cortona** is the most inspiring – have very long sight-lines.

In contrast to the Casentino, **public transport** is quite good. Frequent Rome-bound trains from Florence and Arezzo run down the valley, most of them stopping at Camucia or Teróntola (or both), the access points for Cortona. Buses from Arezzo serve the intervening villages, while services from Cortona cover routes across the valley.

Cortona

From the valley floor, a five-kilometre road winds up through terraces of vines and olives to the hill-town of **CORTONA**, whose heights survey a vast domain: the Valdichiana stretching westwards, with Lago Trasimeno visible over the low hills to the south. The steep streets of Cortona are more or less untouched by modern building: limitations of space have confined almost all later development to the lower suburb of Camucia, which is where the approach road begins. Even without its monuments and art treasures, this would be a good place to rest up, with decent hotels, excellent restaurants and an amazing view at night, with the villages of southern Tuscany twinkling like ships' lights on a dark sea. In recent years, though, Cortona's tourist traffic has increased markedly, in the wake of Frances Mayes' *Under the Tuscan Sun* and *Bella Tuscany*, books that continue to entice coachloads of her (mainly American) readers to the place where Mayes realized the expat dream of the good life in the land of life-affirming Latins.

Folklore has it that Cortona was founded by Dardanus, later to establish the city of Troy and give his name to the Dardanelles. Whatever its precise origins, there was already a sizeable Umbrian settlement here when the **Etruscans** took over in the eighth century BC. About four hundred years later it passed to the **Romans** and remained a significant Roman centre until its destruction by the Goths. By the eleventh century it had become a free *comune*, constantly at loggerheads with Perugia and Arezzo; in 1258 the **Aretines** destroyed Cortona, but the town soon revived under the patronage of Siena. It changed hands yet again at the start of the fifteenth century, when it was appropriated by the Kingdom of Naples and then sold off to the **Florentines**, who never let go.

Arrival and information

Cortona is easily visited as a day-trip from Arezzo, but in many ways it's the more pleasant of the two places in which to spend the night. There are hourly LFI **buses** between the two towns, and stopping **trains** from Arezzo call at Camucia–Cortona station, from where a shuttle (roughly every 30min) takes ten minutes to run up to the old town; buy tickets at the station bar. Florence–Rome trains stop at Teróntola, 10km south, which is also served by a shuttle roughly every hour (25min to Cortona's Piazza Garibaldi); Teróntola is the station to get off at if you are approaching from Umbria. The centre is closed to all but essential traffic, so if you're driving you should use one of the free **car parks** on the periphery – they are all well signposted.

The **tourist office** at Via Nazionale 42 (May–Sept Mon–Sat 9am–1pm & 3–7pm, Sun 9am–1pm; Oct–April Mon–Sat 9am–1pm & 3–6pm; ☏0575.630.352, ⓦwww.cortonaweb.net) can help with accommodation.

Accommodation

Cortona is inundated with tourists in high season: if you're thinking of visiting any time between Easter and late September, you'd be well advised to book your **accommodation** in advance.

Il Falconiere San Martino a Bocena ☏0575.612.679, ⓦwww.ilfalconiere.com. Located 3km away on the SS71 towards Arezzo, this intimate four-star has nineteen rooms, all of them beautifully presented (some frescoed), and two pools: one in the luscious garden, the other amid the hotel's vineyards and olive groves. The restaurant is justly celebrated, and residential cookery courses are offered. Doubles start at a little under €300 and go up to just under €600 for the best suite. ❽

Italia Via Ghibellina 5 ☏0575.630.254, ⓦwww .planhotel.com. A decent three-star, occupying a renovated fifteenth-century house, with 26 rooms and a panoramic breakfast terrace. It's not the most attractive hotel in Cortona, but the location – very near Piazza della Repubblica – makes the price more than reasonable. ❹

Ostello San Marco Via G. Maffei 57 ☏0575.601.392, ⓦwww.cortonahostel.com. Clean and spacious eighty-bed HI hostel in an old monastery in the heart of town, with fantastic views from the dormitories and friendly management. Dorm beds €14; doubles and family rooms available (€18 per person). Open mid-March to mid-Oct; reception open daily 7–10am & 3.30pm–midnight.

Sabrina Via Roma 37 ☏0575.630.397, ⓔinfo @cortonastorica.com. With just eight rooms,

Cortona's other three-star is considerably smaller than the *Italia*, and somewhat cheaper as well. The breakfasts are excellent and it has a nice family atmosphere. ❸

San Luca Piazza Garibaldi 2 ☏0575.630.460, ⓦwww.sanlucacortona.com. The four-star *San Luca* is a somewhat functional sixty-bedroom modern building, but many of its rooms have lovely views over the Valdichiana. Its prices are low for a four-star too. ❹

🏃 **San Michele** Via Guelfa 15 ☏0575.604.348, ⓦwww.hotelsanmichele.net. The most expensive and luxurious in-town choice, this handsome 43-room four-star has been converted from a rambling medieval town house. The rooms are a generous size, even if the decor is rather routine. ❺

🏃 **Villa Marsili** Via Cesare Battisti 13 ☏0575.605.252, ⓦwww.villamarsili.net. This capacious four-star – occupying an eighteenth-century villa – looks unexceptional from the outside, but the rooms are nicely furnished with antiques, and command a very photogenic view of the valley. Prices are very good as well – in high season it's sometimes possible to pick up a room for a little over €100, though you're likelier to pay in the region of €150–200. ❻

The Town

The bus terminus is in **Piazza Garibaldi**, from where the only horizontal street in town (and thus the venue for the *passeggiata*), Via Nazionale, leads into Piazza della Repubblica, where the tall staircase of the squat, castellated Palazzo Comunale is the grandstand from which the *ragazzi* appraise the world as it

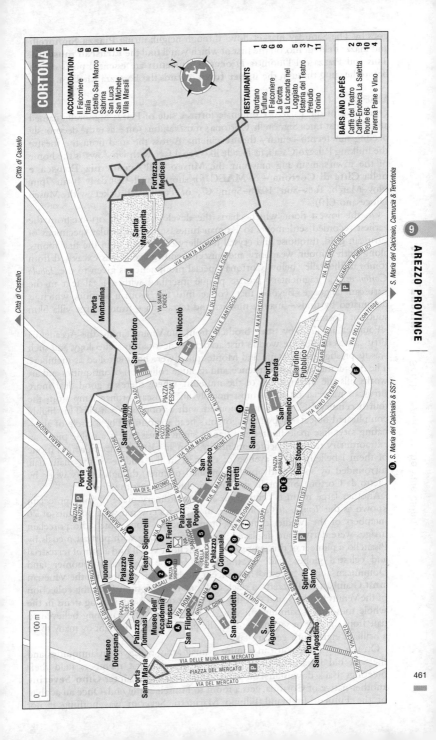

CORTONA

Città di Castello ▲
Città di Castello ▲

Fortezza Medicea

Santa Margherita

Porta Montanina

▶ S. Maria del Calcinaio, Camucia & Teróntola
▶ S. Maria del Calcinaio & SS71

San Cristoforo

San Niccolò

VIA SANTA MARGHERITA
VIA DELL'ORTO DELLA CERA
VIA SANTA CROCE
VIA DELLE SANTUCCE

Sant'Antonio

PIAZZA PESCAIA

VIA DEL SALVATORE
VICOLO B.'A. PERAZZI
PIAZZA POZZO TONDO
VIA G. MAFFEI

San Marco

VIA S. NICCOLÓ

Porta Berada

San Domenico

Giardino Pubblico

VIA S. MARGHERITA
VIALE CESARE BATTISTI
VIA GINO SEVERINI
VIALE GIARDINI PUBBLICI
VIA DELLE CONTESSE
VIA DEL CROCEFISSO

▶ G. S. Maria del Calcinaio & SS71

Porta Colonia

VIA DI S. ANTONIO
VIA DEL SALVATORE
VIA S. MARIA NUOVA
VIA S. MARCO

San Francesco

VIA BERRETTINI
VIA G. MAFFEI MONETTI
VIA G. MAFFEI

Palazzo del Popolo
Palazzo Ferretti

PIAZZA GARIBALDI ★
Bus Stops

Duomo

Palazzo Vescovile

Teatro Signorelli

Pal. Fierli

PIAZZA S. G. MAFFEI
VIA SANTUCCI
PIAZZA SIGNORELLI

Palazzo Comunale

PIAZZA DELLA REPUBBLICA

VIA NAZIONALE
VIA COPPI

Spirito Santo

VIALE CESARE BATTISTI
VIA S. SEBASTIANO

Museo Diocesano
Palazzo Tommasi

Porta Santa Maria

PIAZZA DEL DUOMO

Museo dell' Accademia Etrusca

San Filippo

VIA CASALI
VIA ROMA
VIA GHIBELLINA
VIA GUELFA
VIA GRINI

San Benedetto

VIA DEL GIARDINO

S. Agostino

Porta Sant'Agostino

VIA DELLE MURA ETRUSCHE
VIALE DELLE MURA ETRUSCHE
VIA DELLE MURA DEL MERCATO

PIAZZA DEL MERCATO
VIA DEL MERCATO

BORGO S. VINCENZO

P (parking symbols throughout)

N (compass)

0 — 100 m

goes by. The Saturday market flows through neighbouring **Piazza Signorelli** and Piazza del Duomo, on the first of which you'll find the **Etruscan museum**. This and Piazza del Duomo's **Diocesan museum** are essential ports of call before heading through the **upper town** towards the Fortezza Medicea.

MAEC

One flank of the Palazzo Comunale forms a side of Piazza Signorelli, named after the artist Luca Signorelli, Cortona's most famous son – as is the decorously peeling nineteenth-century theatre-cinema. Across the road from the theatre the hulking Palazzo Casali, its facade like a rockface with windows, is the home of the town's main big museum, the **Museo dell'Accademia Etrusca e della Città di Cortona** – or **MAEC**, for short (April–Oct daily 10am–7pm; Nov–March Tues–Sun 10am–5pm; €7, or combined ticket with Museo Diocesano €10).

On the lowest floor, which charts the development of Cortona from the earliest recorded settlements to Roman times, some spectacular specimens of Etruscan gold, turquoise and crystal jewellery catch the eye in the first rooms, along with armour, weaponry and miscellaneous grave goods excavated from tombs in the valley below Cortona. Special prominence is given to the *Tabula Cortonensis*, a fragmentary bronze plaque inscribed with a legal text in the Etruscan language. Beyond that, you're into the Roman section, which is dominated by finds – mainly mosaics and terracotta – from a large villa 5km south of Cortona.

Founded in 1727 by three brothers from the Venuti family, the Accademia Etrusca was one of the world's first academies devoted to archeology, and such was its prestige that Voltaire and Montesquieu were both enrolled as members. The Accademia is still in existence, and its huge collection of antiquities and art works fills the upper floors of the museum, where there's a good deal more Etruscan material on show, most notably an Etruscan bronze lamp from the fourth century BC, which is honoured with a room all to itself. This highly complicated object – showing a gorgon's head surrounded by a circle of alternating satyr-like male figures and female sirens – was cast as a single piece, an extraordinary technical achievement. Etruscan and later bronze figurines (none of them labelled) fill an avenue of cabinets in the middle of the main hall, surrounded by some fairly undistinguished pictures, though there's work by Pietro da Cortona, Signorelli and Pinturicchio amongst the dross.

Another large room is centred on an extraordinary piece of frilly porcelain known as the *Tempio di Ginori*; made in 1737, it's covered with portraits of 76 members of the Medici clan. The bronze medals from which the porcelain images were derived are displayed in a wall case, along with portrait medals by Pisanello, a pioneer of this genre. Also on this floor you'll find a pair of terrestrial and celestial globes made in the 1710s by the eminent astronomer (and Dominican abbot) Silvestro Moroncelli, a clutch of pictures by the Venetian artist Giambattista Piazzetta, a stack of Roman inscriptions from the collection of the Venuti brothers, and – at the end – one of the most alluring items in the whole museum: a painting, on slate, of the Muse Polimnia. Long believed to date from the first or second century, the picture is now thought by many to be a brilliant eighteenth-century fake.

On the top floor you can admire a small array of Egyptian antiquities and the vast old library of the Academy, where the first members held their meetings. Back downstairs, on a mezzanine level, the painter **Gino Severini**, another native of Cortona, gets a room to himself at the end. Once an acolyte of the Futurist firebrand Filippo Marinetti, Severini was nothing if not versatile, as you'll see in this small collection, where jagged quasi-Cubist prints hang alongside some very conventional portraits, including his best-known image, *Maternity* – the sort of thing that Marinetti would have consigned to the flames.

The Duomo and Museo Diocesano

Via Casali links Piazza Signorelli with Piazza del Duomo, where the **Duomo** (daily 8.30am–12.30pm & 3–6.30pm) stands hard up against the city walls. Raised on the ruins of a pagan temple, it was rebuilt in the sixteenth century, but retains elements of its Romanesque precursor in its flaking facade; the interior is rather chilly and grey, but there's a Pietro da Cortona *Nativity* on the third altar on the left, and a possible Andrea del Sarto (an *Assumption*) to the left of the high altar.

The church that used to face the Duomo now forms part of the **Museo Diocesano** (same hours as MAEC; €5, or combined ticket with MAEC €10), a tiny but high-quality collection of Renaissance art plus a fine Roman sarcophagus, carved with fighting centaurs. Predictably Luca Signorelli features strongly, though only two works – *Lamentation* (1502) and *The Communion of the Apostles* (1512) – are unequivocally his: seven others are attributed to him and his school. Outstanding paintings from Sassetta, Bartolomeo della Gatta and Pietro Lorenzetti are also on show, but none of these measures up to Fra' Angelico, represented by a *Madonna, Child and Saints* and an exquisite *Annunciation*, painted when he was based at Cortona's monastery of San Domenico.

The upper town

To get the full taste of Cortona take Via Santucci from Piazza della Repubblica and then clamber along Via Berrettini, at the near end of which stands the crusty and ancient church of **San Francesco** – designed by St Francis's disciple Brother Elias, this was the first Franciscan church to be built outside Assisi after Francis' death. It's been *in restauro* for many years, but if you find it open you may see a Byzantine ivory reliquary for a piece of the True Cross on the high altar (behind which Brother Elias is buried), and on the third altar on the left an *Annunciation* by the man the street is named after, Pietro Berrettini, otherwise known as Pietro da Cortona. (He was born at no. 33, further up the hill.) This is Pietro's last work, and was left unfinished; the best of his art is in Rome, where he and Bernini were two of the most influential figures in the creation of Roman Baroque. At the time of writing the picture had been removed to MAEC, but it should return when the builders have finished.

A further work by Signorelli is to be found in the church of **San Niccolò** (daily 9am–noon & 3–7pm; closes 5pm in winter; €1 minimum donation expected), signposted just beyond Piazza della Pescaia. It's a frail little church with a delicate portico and a fine wooden ceiling that's sagging with age. Signorelli's high altarpiece is a standard which he painted on both sides: a characteristically angular *Entombment* on the front and a *Madonna and Saints* on the back – revealed by a neat hydraulic system that swivels the picture away from the wall, as the sacristan who lets you into the building will demonstrate.

From Piazza della Pescaia, a steep path leads to the neo-Romanesque **Santa Margherita** (daily: summer 8am–noon & 3–7pm; winter 9am–noon & 3–6pm). Built to honour the town's patron saint, **Saint Margaret of Cortona**, it was begun in 1297, the year of her death, but was remodelled so extensively in the nineteenth century that the only part of the original structure that's left is the rose window of the facade. The daughter of a local farmer, Margaret seems to have been a spectacularly beautiful young woman who led a wild life before becoming the servant and lover of a lord whose castle was near Montepulciano. When she was 27 years old he was murdered, and soon afterwards Margaret underwent a drastic conversion: she took vows as a Franciscan nun and devoted herself to helping the poor and sick of Cortona, for whom she founded a hospital close to the site of the church. So intense was her relationship with the Almighty that the townspeople would pack into San Francesco to observe her delirious behaviour at Mass: "She became ashen pale, her pulse ceased, she froze, her throat was so affected by hoarseness that she could scarcely be understood when she returned to her senses," one witness recorded. Her tomb (1362), with marble angels lifting the lid of her sarcophagus, is now mounted on the wall to the left of the chancel; it's unoccupied, as her mummified body lies in a glass coffin at the high altar. The main altarpiece, Signorelli's *Lamentation*, has been removed to the Museo Diocesano, but in the chapel to the right of the chancel you can see a thirteenth-century Crucifix that is said to have spoken to Margaret on a number of occasions, when it was hanging in San Francesco.

The **Fortezza Medicea**, at the summit of the town, is sometimes used as an exhibition space in summer, and the area in front of it is good ground for a picnic, offering superb views over ruined Etruscan and Roman walls towards Trasimeno. You could descend to Piazza Garibaldi by the stepped Via Crucis, where the Stations of the Cross are represented by mosaics by Severini.

San Domenico and Santa Maria del Calcinaio

The last church to check out is **San Domenico** (daily 3–6pm), a half-minute's walk from Piazza Garibaldi. Completed in 1438, it has a fine high altarpiece by Lorenzo di Niccolò Gerini (*Coronation of the Virgin*), yet another Signorelli (*Madonna and Child with Saints*) and a dilapidated fresco by Fra' Angelico in the lunette above the main door, but it's hard to see behind its screen of protective glass.

Below the piazza, the middle distance is occupied by the perfectly proportioned – though severely eroded – Renaissance church of **Santa Maria del Calcinaio** (summer Mon–Sat 4–7pm & Sun 10am–12.30pm; winter Mon–Sat

▲ Cortona

3–5pm & Sun 10am–12.30pm). The masterpiece of Giorgio di Martini, it was begun in 1484 to enshrine a miraculous image of Mary that a lime-burner (*calcinaio*) had unearthed at the tannery here (lime was used in the tanning process). Another Tuscan church of this vintage – Santa Maria delle Carceri in Prato – was built for similar reasons, but the sheer number of pilgrims who flocked to Cortona made it impossible for the architect to employ the fashionable central-plan design used in Prato. Hence this highly refined compromise: classical detailing applied to an old-fashioned and capacious cruciform church. Inside, the miraculous Madonna is still displayed on the high altar.

Just past Santa Maria, signs direct you farther down the hill to the **Tanella di Pitagora** – a well-preserved Etruscan chamber tomb that's fancifully identified with the Greek mathematician Pythagoras. In fact it was constructed for a wealthy family by the name of Cuso, who are cited in the *Tabula Cortonensis*.

Eating and drinking

For a town of its size, Cortona has an abundance of good restaurants. Nearly all the places to eat and drink are within a very short distance of Piazza della Repubblica.

Restaurants

Dardano Via Dardano 24 ☎0575.601.944. An excellent, unpretentious, inexpensive and very popular trattoria – it's full to bursting most nights. Closed Wed.

Fufluns Via Ghibellina 1–3. If a pizza is all you need, this spacious and bustling place is the first choice. Closed Tues.

Il Falconiere San Martino a Bocena ☎0575.612.679, ⓦwww.ilfalconiere.com. The Michelin-awarded restaurant of the *Falconiere* hotel uses ingredients that are produced on the hotel's own land. It's expensive (around €70 per person), but worth every euro. Closed three weeks in Jan.

La Grotta Piazzetta Baldelli 3 ☎0575.630.271. Much like *Dardano*, *La Grotta* is a straight-down-the-line trattoria, albeit with a slightly higher percentage of tourists among the clientele. Closed Tues.

La Locanda nel Loggiato Piazza Pescheria 3–4 ☎0575.630.575. This place offers a small, high-quality and meat-centric menu, at around €35 a head; the loggia, overlooking Piazza della Repubblica, is the nicest dining spot in the centre of town. Closed Wed.

Osteria del Teatro Via Maffei 5 ☎0575.630.556. Occupying the entire lower floor of a rambling old mansion, this is a good-naturedly busy (sometimes frantic) place, featuring delicious homemade pastas on a meat-heavy menu; portions are generous and prices

more than fair – the bill should be around €35 per person. Closed Wed & mid-Nov to mid-Dec.

Preludio Via Guelfa 11 ☎0575.630.104. The food is invariably good and prices surprisingly moderate (around €30) in this smartly turned-out restaurant. Closed Mon, and lunchtime in winter.

Tonino Piazza Garibaldi 1 ☎0575.630.500. Good antipasti and a wonderful panoramic view from the terrace are the chief attractions of the dependable *Tonino*. Closed Mon evening, plus all day Tues in winter.

Bars and cafés

Caffè del Teatro On the terrace of the Teatro Signorelli. On summer evenings this is a favourite night-time hangout, with live music some weekends. Closed Mon.

Caffè-Enoteca La Saletta Via Nazionale 26–28. A glossy café-cum-wine shop, which also does simple meals.

Route 66 Via Nazionale 78. This self-styled "music bar" attracts the youngest crowd in town – the soundtrack is usually loud, and there are occasional DJ nights. It does food too, but it's not the nosh that makes it popular. Open Tues–Sun till 3am.

Taverna Pane e Vino Piazza Signorelli 27. A good choice if you're after a quick lunch or a light evening meal: the menu offers various types of bruschetta, a wide selection of salamis and cheeses, plus a few more substantial dishes – and the wine list runs to some 900 different vintages. Closed Mon.

Castiglion Fiorentino

Looming high above the road and railway 12km north of Cortona are the walls and massive tower of **CASTIGLION FIORENTINO** – known as Castiglion

Aretino until Arezzo became a Florentine possession in 1384. The fortified old town is so far above the train station that it makes more sense to visit by bus; the half-hourly bus from Arezzo to Cortona bowls through here thirty minutes into its one-hour journey, stopping right outside the walls in Piazza Matteotti.

From here the Corso Italia rises to the elegant Piazza del Municipio, the navel of the *centro storico*. There's a modest art gallery, the **Pinacoteca Comunale**, a short distance up the hill behind the Municipio, in Via del Passero (April–Oct Tues–Sun 10am–12.30pm & 4–6.30pm; Nov–March Sat & Sun 10am–12.30pm & 3.30–6pm; €3, or €5 with archeological museum), with works by Taddeo Gaddi and two fine paintings by Bartolomeo della Gatta. In the neighbouring library is the equally modest **archeological museum** (same hours; €3, or €5 with Pinacoteca), where the chief exhibit is a reconstructed fragment of an Etruscan temple. On the same ticket you can visit the excavations of the Etruscan walls underneath the summit of the hill, from which rises the **Torre del Cassero** (May–Sept Sun 10am–12.30pm & 4–6.30pm; €1.50), Castiglion Fiorentino's landmark tower, built to the orders of Arezzo's pugnacious Bishop Tarlati.

Opposite the Palazzo Comunale is a handsome **loggia** – supposedly designed by Vasari – which forms a picture-frame for the hills to the east. Look to the right through the loggia and you'll see the town's major church, the **Collegiata**, which has a *Holy Family* by Lorenzo di Credi to the right of the high altar. The adjoining **Pieve** – which is being converted into a small museum of sacred art – has a Signorelli fresco of the *Deposition*.

Some 4km south of here, the eleventh-century castle of **Montecchio Vesponi** jabs up from the horizon. Commanding a great sweep of the valley, this property was acquired in 1384 by the fearsome *condottiere* Sir John Hawkwood (he of the fresco in Florence's Duomo), and is the only one of his numerous ill-gotten residences to survive intact. It's still in private hands.

Farneta, Foiano and Lucignano

About 10km west of Cortona, in the middle of the valley, stands the ancient Benedictine **Abbazia di Farneta**. Built largely with stone plundered from a nearby Roman temple dedicated to Bacchus, this beautifully plain building first appeared in local records in 1014, but may have been founded as far back as the eighth century, by the Lombards. Once the most powerful religious house in the Valdichiana, it had fallen into disrepair by 1937, when a remarkable priest by the name of Monsignor Sante Felici arrived here. Over the course of the next sixty years he almost single-handedly stripped the abbey of the eighteenth-century accretions that had defaced the Romanesque structure, and also excavated the ancient **crypt**, an operation that yielded numerous archeological and paleontological discoveries, including the bones of prehistoric elephants, hippos and rhinos. An engagingly ramshackle little museum used to occupy part of the neighbouring house, but repeated robbery attempts necessitated the transfer of its most precious artefacts to Cortona's MAEC (see p.462), while the most spectacular of Monsignor Felici's fossils are now on show in Florence's museum of paleontology. At the time of writing, the Abbazia was closed for structural repairs; when it reopens, it will probably have the same hours as before. (Daily 9am–1pm and 2–4pm).

FOIANO DELLA CHIANA, 4km west of the abbey, sometimes bills itself as "La Città di Carnevale", because it was here, in the 1860s, that allegorical floats were first produced for carnival parades, thereby inaugurating a form of folk art that nowadays is best represented by the Viareggio carnival. Other than at carnival, however, workaday Foiano is far from the most alluring small town in Tuscany. The weathered brick fortifications of the old centre are mildly impressive, and devotees of the art of the della Robbia dynasty might want to take a look at the examples of their output in the churches of **San Michele Arcangelo**, **Santa Maria della Fraternità** and the **Collegiata**, the last of which also houses the last painting by Luca Signorelli. If none of these appeal, you'd best press on a further 8km to **LUCIGNANO**.

This trim and perfectly preserved little town is laid out in a pattern of concentric ellipses, encircling the medieval Palazzo Comunale and the **Collegiata**, an unexceptional church that's given a touch of panache by the double semicircular staircase leading to its door. Round the back, the **Museo Comunale** (summer Mon & Thurs–Sun 10am–1pm & 2.30–5.30pm; €3) contains a couple of lesser works by Signorelli and the most arresting artefact on this side of the Valdichiana, an amazing fourteenth-century gilded reliquary known as the *Albero di Lucignano*, or *Albero d'Oro*, for its tree-like shape. Made in Arezzo between 1350 and 1470, it stands 2.5m high and has branches of coral leafed with crystal, enamels and miniature paintings. Thirteenth- and fourteenth-century frescoes, some of them by Bartolo di Fredi, decorate the adjacent church of **San Francesco**. And that's about it, apart from the inevitable Medici fortress on the hill to the north, but Lucignano is an attractive and restful place to stay for a night – or even longer, as it's perfectly placed, midway between Arezzo and Siena. A family-run **hotel-trattoria**, *Da Totó*, occupies a converted monastery on Piazza del Tribunale (T 0575.836.763, W www.trattoriatoto.it; ❸). The best place to stay, however, is *Il Cassero* (T 0575.836.260, W www.ilcassero-tuscany.com; ❹), a six-apartment *residenza d'epoca* adjoining the village's tower; the proprietors are extremely welcoming, and guests have the use of a pool a short distance outside the village walls. Tiny it may be, yet Lucignano has two superb places to eat, both on Via Matteotti: 🍴 *Il Goccino*, at no. 88–90 (T 0575.836.707; closed Mon); and 🍴 *La Rocca*, at no. 15–17 (T 0575.836.775; closed Tues & Jan), which also has accommodation next door at no.13 (T 0575.836.175; ❷).

Monte San Savino

On the opposite side of the Valdichiana from Cortona rises **MONTE SAN SAVINO**, now a busy market town, once a contentious border post between the territories of Florence, Siena and Arezzo; it was razed in 1325 on the orders of Bishop Tarlati of Arezzo. The town retains a slightly decrepit mix of medieval and Renaissance monuments, but it is not one of Tuscany's more seductive hill-towns. Should you want to explore it, however, there are regular trains from Arezzo to the station in the lower town, from where there's the usual bus shuttle; buses from Cortona also periodically cross the valley.

The town was the birthplace of **Andrea Sansovino**, now best remembered as the mentor of Jacopo Sansovino, a crucial figure in Venice's artistic history, who took his teacher's surname. Terracotta was one of Andrea's preferred media – the town remains a major producer of majolica – and some of his best ceramics altarpieces are in the church of **Santa Chiara**, which stands in Piazza Gamurrini. Virtually next to the church stands the fourteenth-century Sienese castle known as the **Cassero**, which houses a small tourist office, has a modest **Museo Civico** that's largely given over to ceramics (Sat & Sun 9am–noon & 3–6pm; €1.60), and stages occasional art exhibitions.

Continuing down the narrow main street from Piazza Gamurrini you'll pass the **Loggia dei Mercanti**, a collaboration between Sansovino and Antonio da Sangallo the Elder – architect of the Palazzo Comunale opposite. Beyond the Palazzo Pretorio lies the small central square, Piazza di Monte, on both of whose churches Sansovino left a mark. He designed the now crumbling portal of **San Giovanni**, and added the cloister to the fourteenth-century **Sant'Agostino**, which contains some fifteenth-century frescoes and an altarpiece by Vasari.

Should you want to stay, the best **hotel** in town is the three-star *Sangallo*, Piazza Vittorio Veneto 16 (☎0575.810.049, ⓦwww.sangallohotel.it; ②).

Travel details

Trains

Arezzo to: Assisi (12 daily; 1hr 35min); Bibbiena (hourly; 50min); Bolzano (5 daily; 7hr 30min); Camucia-Cortona (hourly; 20min); Chiusi (hourly; 1hr); Florence (hourly; 1hr); Foligno (every 2hr; 1hr 50min); Monte San Savino (12 daily; 25min); Orvieto (7 daily; 1hr 20min); Perugia (every 2hr; 1hr 15min); Poppi (Mon–Sat hourly, Sun 5 services; 1hr); Rome (hourly; 1hr 40min); Terni (1 direct daily; 2hr 35min); Teróntola (hourly; 25min); Trento (5 daily; 7hr); Udine (5 daily; 7hr); Venice (5 daily; 5hr 10min); Verona (5 daily; 5hr 15min).

Buses

Arezzo to: Bibbiena & La Verna (1 daily – change at Bibbiena for Poppi & Camaldoli); Città di Castello (at least 12 daily; 1hr 30min); Cortona (hourly; 1hr); Sansepolcro (17 daily, some via Monterchi, most via Anghiari; 1hr); Siena (5 daily Mon–Fri).

Bibbiena to: Badia Prataglia (8 daily Mon–Sat; 40min); Camáldoli (4 daily Mon–Sat 40min); Chiusi Verna (3 daily Mon–Sat; 50min).

Cortona to: Arezzo (hourly; 50min); Castiglione del Lago (7 daily; 1hr); Chianciano (4 daily, changing for Montepulciano; 1hr).

⑩

Perugia and northern Umbria

CHAPTER 10

Highlights

* **Corso Vannucci, Perugia** Umbria's best *passeggiata*, with some wonderful people-watching. See p.478

* **Collegio del Cambio, Perugia** Medieval chamber decorated with outstanding frescoes by Perugino. See p.481

* **Galleria Nazionale dell'Umbria, Perugia** The region's finest collection of medieval and Renaissance art. See p.482

* **Città di Castello** The Pinacoteca Comunale and Museo Diocesano hold paintings by Raphael, Signorelli, Rosso Fiorentino and others. See p.499

* **Palazzo dei Consoli, Gubbio** A majestic medieval palace, with sweeping views from its belvedere. See p.509

* **Funicular ride, Gubbio** A dizzying six-minute ride over woods and crags into the mountains. See p.515

* **Parco Regionale del Monte Cucco** Wonderful mountain scenery with some great hiking. See p.517

▲ The Fontana Maggiore, Piazza IV Novembre, Perugia

Perugia and northern Umbria

Perugia makes for a distinctly uncharacteristic introduction to Umbria. The home of Buitoni pasta and Perugino chocolate, it's a place whose historic core is hidden within a ring of initially off-putting industrialized suburbs, and whose big-city feel, universities and famous summer jazz festival make it wholly different from its bucolic, hill-town neighbours. If you've come to Umbria for the rural experience, you may be tempted to bypass Perugia altogether. Its medieval heart, however, demands at least a day's exploration, two sights alone making the trip more than worthwhile: the **Palazzo dei Priori**, justifiably hyped as one of the greatest public palaces in Italy, and the **Galleria Nazionale dell'Umbria**, which boasts the region's best collection of Umbrian art. And if actually staying in the city doesn't appeal, its highlights can easily be taken in on day-trips from Assisi, Montefalco or other nearby towns.

West of Perugia lies the placid, if unspectacular, **Lago Trasimeno**, a popular magnet for campers and one of the few places in the region where you can put your feet up on a beach. Its nicest town is **Castiglione del Lago**, with brasher **Passignano** the main camping and after-hours resort.

North of Perugia is a moderately pretty and pastoral region centred on the upper reaches of the **Tiber valley**. Road and rail routes follow the river's course, useful mainly for onward forays into Tuscany and the Marche – in particular to Sansepolcro or Urbino for the paintings of Piero della Francesca. Unheralded **Città di Castello** is the only worthwhile Umbrian port of call, a captivating

Getting around the region

Perugia is one of the key transport hubs for the region, with direct **trains** from Assisi, Spello, Foligno (for Gubbio and Spoleto), Terni, Narni, Todi, Città di Castello and Teróntola (for Orvieto). A couple of fast trains run direct to Perugia from both Florence and Rome, as do more regular trains from Teróntola on the main Florence–Rome line. The private FCU train line runs throughout the region, from Sansepolcro in the north, through Città di Castello, Perugia and on to Todi (see p.612) and Terni (see p.601). A fast **road** connects Perugia to the A1 Autostrada del Sole, with quick links on to Todi, Assisi, Spello and Foligno. **Buses** run to most major centres and many minor ones. For public transport details, see p.518.

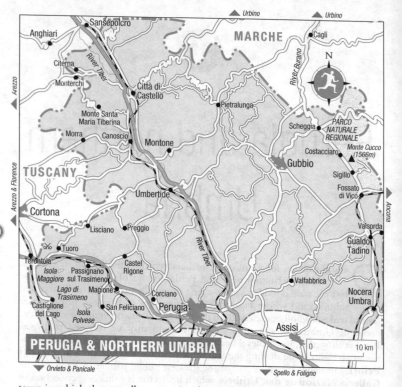

town in which the art gallery contains the region's only painting by Raphael, an artist apprenticed to Perugino, Umbria's pre-eminent Renaissance painter.

East of the Tiber, minor roads climb through swathes of attractively barren country to **Gubbio**, one of Italy's medieval gems and – given Assisi's increasing commercialism – the region's least spoiled hill-town. Much in the town merits comparison with Siena, not least its overbearing civic palace, the **Palazzo dei Consoli**, a magnificent piece of medieval bluster. Churches and galleries abound, and the honeycomb of old streets is riddled with things of interest. Moving east, you come up against the first foothills of the Apennines, their slopes home to the earthquake-shattered, half-forgotten hill-town of **Gualdo Tadino**. The mountains behind – **Monte Cucco** in particular – boast the area's best scenery and opportunities for some straightforward hiking.

Perugia and Lago Trasimeno

PERUGIA is a place of some style – at least in its old centre – and a city proud of its big-league attractions, its chocolate, its university for foreigners and its football team. In terms of sights, Perugia's interest is essentially medieval, despite its considerable Etruscan heritage. In addition to the **Palazzo dei Priori**, home to the **Galleria Nazionale** and the Perugino-painted **Collegio del Cambio**, there is the **Duomo** and a full quota of memorable churches. A drink on the **Corso Vannucci**, Perugia's central street, reveals a buzz you won't find elsewhere in the region, a sense of dynamism embodied by the cosmopolitan **Università Italiana per Stranieri**, created by Mussolini to improve the image of Italy abroad; now privately run, it's the country's largest language school. This same dynamism remains evident in Perugia's above-average number of film screenings, concerts and miscellaneous cultural events, and is highlighted further at July's **Umbria Jazz** (ⓦwww.umbriajazz.com), Italy's foremost jazz festival, whose stars have included Miles Davis, Stan Getz and Wynton Marsalis. Also hugely popular is the **Eurochocolate festival** (ⓦwww.eurochocolate.com) in October, when Perugians flee the city in the face of the crowds of outsiders who come for this vast fair, in which hundreds of booths offer chocolate in every conceivable form.

To the west of Perugia is Lake Trasimeno, Italy's fourth largest lake, an intermittently pretty body of water, fringed by low hills and farming country. Castiglione del Lago is the most appealing of several small towns on its shores, thanks to a handful of small beaches, an attractive waterfront and historic centre, and a decent choice of hotels and restaurants.

Some history

Perugia's command of the Tiber and its major routes has made it the region's main player throughout a long history – albeit not quite as long as early chroniclers made out when they claimed to have traced its foundation to Noah. The easternmost of the twelve key cities of the **Etruscan** federation, Perusia, as it was called, was conquered by **Rome** in 309 BC, later taking the wrong side in the civil war that followed the death of Julius Caesar. Allying itself with Mark Antony, it suffered a debilitating siege at the hands of his opponent Octavius, later the emperor Augustus. It might have survived the ordeal but for the actions of Gaius Cestius, one of the city's less stout defenders, who set fire to his house in a panic-stricken funk. The ensuing conflagration destroyed the city, and Augustus rebuilt it as Augusta Perusia.

The city's passage through the Dark Ages is obscure, though legend claims it was besieged by Totila in 547 and saved from destruction by its bishop, St Ercolano (Herculanus). By 592 it had been absorbed into the **Lombard** Duchy of Spoleto, later emerging as a papal vassal and finally, around 1140, as an independent *comune*.

Medieval Perugia was evidently a hell of a place to be. "The town had the most warlike people of Italy," wrote the historian Sismondi, "who always preferred Mars to the Muse." Male citizens played a game – for pleasure – in which two teams, wearing beaked helmets and clothes stuffed with deer hair, stoned each other mercilessly until the majority on one side was dead or wounded. Children were encouraged to join in to promote "application and aggression". In 1265 Perugia was also the birthplace of the **Flagellants**, who within ten years had half of Europe whipping itself into a frenzy before the movement was declared heretical. In addition to some hearty scourging, they took to the streets on moonlit nights, wailing, singing dirges and clattering human bones together – all as expiation for the wrongs of the world.

Using its economic muscle and numerous short-lived alliances, the city built up a huge power base, peaking with its **conquest of Siena** in 1358. Around this time the *Priori* (members of the ten leading guilds), noble families and papal agents began vying for control, plunging Perugia into a period when, according to one chronicler, "perfect pandemonium reigned in and about the city". Individual *condottieri* rose briefly from the chaos, the key figures being Biondo Michelotti – stabbed to death in 1398, after five years in power – and the oddly named Braccio Fortebraccio (Arm the Strong Arm), whose eight years of rule brought short-lived stability. The Oddi nobility ran the town until 1488, when the colourful but demented **Baglioni** took over. Their story is the stuff of soap

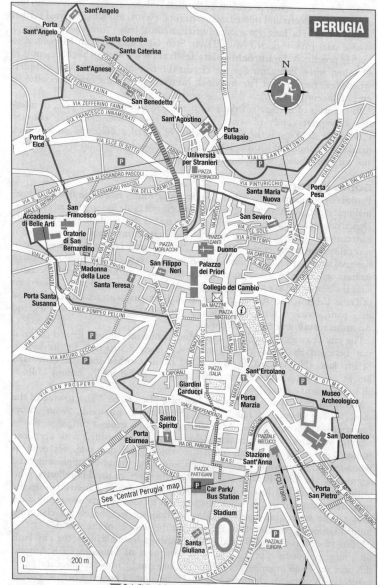

Sant'Angelo

Porta
Sant'Angelo

Santa Colomba

Santa Caterina

Sant'Agnese

VIA ZEFFERINO FAINA

CORSO GARIBALDI

VIA BENEDETTA

San Benedetto

VIA ZEFFERINO FAINA

VIA FRANCESCO INNAMORATI

VIA DEL BULAGAIO

Sant'Agostino

N

Porta
Elce

VIA ELCE DI SOTTO

VIA FABRETTI

Porta
Bulagaio

Università
per Stranieri

PIAZZA
FORTEBRACCIO

VIALE SANT'ANTONIO

CORSO BERSAGLIERI

VIALE BRUNAMONTI

VIA PINTURICCHIO

Porta
Pesa

VIA E. DAL POZZO

VIA S. GALIGANO

VIALE Q. ANTINORI

VIA ALESSANDRO PASCOLI

VIA ALESSANDRO PASCOLI

VIA DELL'EREMITA

Santa Maria
Nuova

Accademia
di Belle Arti

San Francesco

VIA DEL ROSCETTO

San Severo

VIA DEL SOLE

VIA BONTEMPI

Oratorio
di San
Bernardino

VIA AQUILONE

VIA S. PAOLO

VIA S. FRANCESCO

VIA A. FABRETTI

VIA U. ROCCHI

VIA C. BATTISTI

VIA BARTOLO

PIAZZA
MORLACCHI

PIAZZA
DANTI

Duomo

VIA CARTOLARI

VIA G. ALESSI

Madonna
della Luce

Santa Teresa

VIA DELLA SPOSA

VIA DEI PRIORI

San Filippo
Neri

Palazzo
dei Priori

VIA DELL'ORSO

Collegio del Cambio

Porta Santa
Susanna

VIALE Q. ANTINORI

VIALE POMPEO PELLINI

VIA MAZZINI

PIAZZA
MATTEOTTI

ℹ

VIA QUATTORDICI SETTEMBRE

VIA TANCREDI RIPA DI MEANA

VIA P. COLOMBATA

VIA ARTURO CECCHI

VIA DELL'URSO

CORSO VANNUCCI

V. CAPORALI

PIAZZA
ITALIA

VIA BAGLIONI

VIA OBERDAN

VIA MARZIA

Sant'Ercolano

Museo
Archeologico

Giardini
Carducci

Porta
Marzia

VIA MARCONI

San Domenico

VIA SAN PROSPERO

Santo
Spirito

Porta
Eburnea

VIALE INDEPENDENZA

VIA DEL PARIONE

PIAZZALE
BELLUCCI

Stazione
Sant'Anna

VIA DEL BULAGAIO

VIA F. DI LORENZO

VIA ENRICO DAL POZZO

VIA MASI

FCU Trains

CORSO CAVOUR

BORGO VENTI GIUGNO

Porta
San Pietro

VIA DEL FILOSOFI

VIALE ROMA

VIA XX SETTEMBRE

PIAZZA
PARTIGIANI

See 'Central Perugia' map

Car Park/
Bus Station

Stadium

VIALE XX SETTEMBRE

VIA F. DI LORENZO

VIA MARCONI

PIAZZALE
EUROPA

Santa
Giuliana

VIA CACCIATORI DELLE ALPI

VIA FRATELLI PELLAS

0   200 m

▼ Train Station & Campsites

San Pietro ▶

opera: complicated vendettas, incestuous marriages, hearts torn from bodies and eaten, and any number of people murdered on their wedding nights. After one episode was settled with a hundred murders, the bloodied cathedral had to be washed down with wine and reconsecrated. One Baglioni, Malatesta IV, assigned the defence of Florence in 1530, famously sold his services to the enemy, earning the title "world's greatest traitor".

When the last Baglioni, the wimpish Ridolpho, bungled an assassination of the papal legate, it was a cue for the papacy to step in. **Pope Paul III**, one of the more powerful and peculiar pontiffs, razed the Baglioni palaces in 1538, then entered the city demanding that all its nuns line up and kiss his feet. Thus refreshed, he built the Rocca Paolina, a huge fortress that guaranteed church supremacy for three centuries. During the nineteenth-century unification of Italy, Perugia's liberation from the papacy was particularly violent, with numerous citizens massacred by Swiss Guards sent to bolster Church control. Liberation from the Nazis in 1944, courtesy of the British Eighth Army, was considerably less bloodthirsty.

Arrival and information

Arriving by **air** you'll land at the Aeroporto Regionale Umbro Sant'Egido (℡075.592.141), 12km east of the centre. Bus shuttles (€3.50) run to Piazza Italia between 4.40pm and 9.45pm. Arriving by **train**, you'll find yourself well away from the *centro storico* at Piazza Vittorio Veneto: it's too far to walk from here – it's all uphill on busy roads – but the centre is an easy bus ride away. Take a bus from outside the station – it's a ten-minute hop to Piazza Italia or Piazza Matteotti, both equally convenient (the bus stop lists the destinations). You can buy a bus **ticket** (€1 for unlimited journeys in 1hr 10min) from the station newsagent or a booth on the left of the forecourt as you exit the station; paying on board costs €1.50, and you must have the right change. The private FCU rail line between Sansepolcro, Perugia and Terni (℡075.572.9121, ⓦwww.fcu.it) comes into the more central **Stazione Sant'Anna**, in the southern part of town near the Piazza dei Partigiani bus terminal, the point of arrival for out-of-town **buses** (for contact details, see p.49). To reach the centre, cross the main road outside the terminal for the ramp leading to the *scala mobile* (escalator) to Piazza Italia.

The *centro storico* is closed to traffic at most times – and even when open is almost impossible to navigate. Your best bet is to follow the signs for Piazza dei Partigiani in the south, where there's a large covered **car park**. From here you can jump on a *scala mobile* through the subterranean Via Baglioni Sotteranea to Piazza Italia. Another good option, in the west, is the car park in Viale Pompeo Pellini, connected by escalators to Via dei Priori. If you're driving in from the north, try the car park in Viale Sant'Antonio.

There's a **tourist office** in the Loggia dei Linari on the east side of Piazza Matteotti at no. 18 (May–Sept Mon–Sat 8.30am–6.30pm, Sun 9am–1pm; Oct–April Mon–Sat 8.30am–1.30pm & 3.30–6.30pm, Sun 9am–1pm; ℡075.572 8937 or 075.573.6458, ⓦwww.umbria2000.it). A private office, Infotourist Point, on the northeastern corner of Piazza Partigiani (Mon–Fri 9am–1pm & 2.30–6.30pm, Sat 9am–1pm; ℡075.573.2933), is a good source of information on tours (ⓦwww.guideinumbria.com).

Accommodation

Perugia has plenty of **accommodation**, though you should book ahead as some of the cheapest places may be taken up by long-stay students; book, too,

CENTRAL PERUGIA

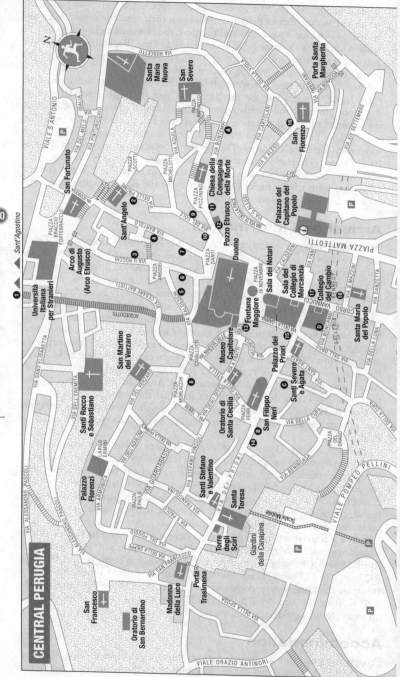

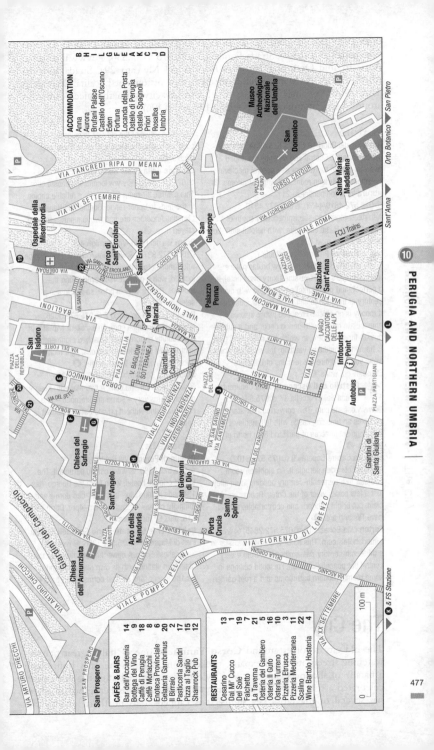

ACCOMMODATION

Anna	B
Aurora	H
Brufani Palace	I
Castello dell'Oscano	L
Eden	G
Fortuna	F
Locanda della Posta	E
Ostello di Perugia	A
Ostello Spagnoli	K
Priori	C
Rosalba	J
Umbria	D

CAFÉS & BARS

Bar dell'Accademia	14
Bottega del Vino	9
Caffè di Perugia	18
Caffè Mortacchi	8
Enoteca Provinciale	6
Gelateria Gambrinus	20
Il Birraio	2
Pasticceria Sandri	17
Pizza al Taglio	15
Shamrock Pub	12

RESTAURANTS

Cesarino	13
Dal Mi' Cucco	1
Del Sole	19
Falchetto	7
La Taverna	21
Osteria del Gambero	5
Osteria Il Gufo	16
Osteria Turreno	10
Pizzeria Etrusca	3
Pizzeria Mediterranea	11
Scalino	22
Wine Bartolo Hosteria	4

during the July jazz festival, when rates will likely be raised. Perugia has two **campsites** – *Il Rocolo*, Strada Fontana 1n (☎075.517.8550, ⓦwww.ilrocolo.it; April to mid-Oct), and *Paradis d'Été*, Via del Mercato 29a, Strada Fontana (☎075.517.3121; March–Oct), both 5km west of town at Località Colle della Trinità, but you may prefer to travel into the city from the nicer campsites around Lago Trasimeno (see p.493, p.495 and p.496).

Hotels

Anna Via dei Priori 48 ☎075.573.6304, ⓦwww .albergoanna.it. Central and recently revamped two-star on the fourth floor of a central medieval townhouse; fourteen rooms, all with bathrooms. ❷

Aurora Viale Indipendenza 21 ☎075.572.4819/4453, ⓕ075.572.4819. A thirteen-room two-star immediately south of Piazza Italia. Basic and clean, with helpful staff, but on a very busy road. ❸

Brufani Palace Piazza Italia 7 ☎075.573.2541, ⓦwww.brufanipalace .com. Perugia's only five-star luxury class hotel, in a perfect (and panoramic) position and with over a century of tradition to call on, is the obvious choice if money is no object. Frescoed public spaces, immaculate rooms with period decor and a subterranean fitness centre, in which the swimming pool is framed by medieval vaulting; transparent panels allow you to admire the remains of the city's Etruscan-era walls. ❾

Castello dell'Oscano Località Cenerente, Strada della Forcella 37 ☎075.584.371, ⓦwww.oscano.com. This converted four-star hotel occupies an amazing castle with full medieval trappings set in acres of parkland 8km north of Perugia. ❼

Eden Via Cesare Caporali 9 ☎075.572.8102, ⓦwww.hoteleden.perugia.it. An eighteen-room two-star in a thirteenth-century building in an alley just a few paces west of the Corso. Rooms are plain, but bright, modern and comfortable, and all have TVs and a/c. ❸

Fortuna Via Bonazzi 19 ☎075.572.2845, ⓦwww .umbriahotels.com. This spick-and-span two-star in a thirteenth-century *palazzo* benefits from a very central but peaceful location. Frescoed ceilings in some rooms, modern bathrooms and a roof garden

with good views of the old city. In summer, consider paying the extra €30 or so for an a/c double. ❸

Locanda della Posta Corso Vannucci 97 ☎075.572.8925, ⓦwww.locandadellaposta.com. This central, 39-room four-star is a reliable choice in the mid- to upper-range. Goethe and Hans Christian Andersen are just two luminaries to have stayed here. ❻

Priori Via dei Priori–Via Vermiglioli 3 ☎075.572.3378, ⓦwww.hotelpriori.it. First-choice mid-range hotel, tastefully fitted out and well located, with a great terrace overlooking the rooftops. Rooms vary in price, so ask to see a selection. ❸

Rosalba Piazza del Circo 7 ☎075.572.0626, ⓦwww.hotelrosalba.com. An excellent two-star in a beautifully restored and detached eighteenth-century villa with eleven spacious, light rooms (though ceilings are low in some). ❷

Umbria Via Boncambi 37 ☎075.572.1203, ⓦwww.hotel-umbria.com. A two-star with keen prices; rooms vary – some are cramped – and come with and without private bath. Breakfast is poor. ❷

Hostels

Ostello di Perugia Via Bontempi 13 ☎075.572.2880, ⓦwww.ostello.perugia.it. The town's original hostel, 2min from the Duomo, has 134 beds in four-, six- and eight-bed dorms and a midnight curfew. Closed 9.30am–4pm. Dorm beds €15, plus €2 for sheets.

Ostello per la Gioventù Mario Spagnoli Località Pian di Massiano ☎075.501.1366, ⓦwww .umbriahostels.org. A newer hostel down near the main train station, with its own restaurant and space for 186 in four- and six-bed dorms. Dorm beds €16.

The City

The old city revolves around **Corso Vannucci**, one of Italy's great people-watching streets, its broad expanse packed from dawn to the early hours with a parade of shoppers, students and style-makers. Named after the city's most celebrated artist, Pietro Vannucci, better known simply as Perugino, the street has several of the city's key sights. It is capped at its northern end by the

Piazza IV Novembre – home to the **Duomo**, the **Palazzo dei Priori** and the **Fontana Maggiore** – and in the south by **Piazza Italia**, jumping-off point for the city's southern quarters. The twisting medieval alleys off the Corso are initially disorientating, but by dividing the city into western, northern and southern sections you soon get to grips with the layout. **West of the Corso** (see p.484), Via dei Priori curves downhill through a slice of the old city, culminating in the **Oratorio di San Bernardino**, one of Perugia's prime pieces of sculpture. **East of the Corso** (see p.485) there are a couple of diversions – not least an impressive Etruscan well and Raphael fresco – in the fine medieval quarter beyond Piazza Danti. Both routes meet up at Piazza Fortebraccio, access point for the city's **northern quarters** (see p.486), which hold few sights as such, but make a pleasant place for a stroll. Perugia's other highlights are grouped along Corso Cavour in the **southern quarters** (see p.487): **San Domenico**, Umbria's largest church, the region's **archeological museum** and the tenth-century basilica of **San Pietro**.

You can **walk** everywhere, although you'll cover a fair bit of ground in the course of a day's sightseeing – particularly if you take in sights at the extreme northern and southern ends of town. You should also be prepared for **steep climbs** between Perugia's many levels: lifts and escalators help out only occasionally.

The Fontana Maggiore

The **Fontana Maggiore** has quite a pedigree: it was designed in 1277 by Fra' Bevignate, the Silvestrine monk who had a hand in shaping Orvieto's cathedral, and sculpted by the father-and-son team of Nicola and Giovanni Pisano, possibly with help from Arnolfo di Cambio. It was installed to receive the water from the town's new aqueduct, a five-kilometre affair designed by a leading hydraulic engineer of the age, the Venetian Boninsegna. However, as the chronicler Bonazzi observed, "beasts, barrels and unwashed pots and unclean hands were forbidden the use of the water, and indeed it was guarded with such jealous care that it seemed as though the people of Perugia had built their fountain for the sake of beauty only".

The **sculptures** and **bas-reliefs** on the two polygonal basins were part of a carefully conceived decorative scheme designed to illustrate the city's glory and achievements. By some canny calculation none of them line up directly, encouraging you to walk around the fountain chasing a point of repose that never comes. The lower basin has 25 double reliefs, twelve showing the *Labours of the Months*, together with the appropriate sign of the zodiac – December's pigsticking is particularly graphic. The remaining reliefs include a lion and griffon,

Perugia's medieval symbols; four double panels depicting the Liberal Arts; scenes from the Old Testament (note the relief of the large lion and smaller lion being beaten, an allegory expounding the virtues of punishment); and reliefs portraying Roman scenes and two of Aesop's fables. Most of the 24 upper basin statues are by Giovanni Pisano and depict a wide range of characters, among them saints, Old Testament heroes and a variety of allegorical figures representing Victory, Theology and the like. Giovanni also completed the three figures in the basin, believed to represent the three Cardinal Virtues – Faith, Hope and Charity.

The Palazzo dei Priori

The northern end of the Corso is dominated by the gaunt bulk of the **Palazzo dei Priori**, with its majestic Gothic doorway, rows of trefoil windows (from which convicted criminals were thrown to their deaths) and businesslike Guelph crenellations. Often cited as Italy's most impressive civic palace (it's certainly one of the largest), it was begun in 1293 by two local architects and completed in 1443, its impressive effect deriving as much from its sheer bulk as the harmonious beauty created by the buildings around it. Four separate sights are hidden within its precincts: the **Sala dei Notari**, **Sala del Collegio della Mercanzia**, **Collegio del Cambio** and – the star turn – the **Galleria Nazionale dell'Umbria**. All are worthwhile, but orientation within the *palazzo* can be a little confusing; it's easiest to tackle them in the order given below.

Sala dei Notari

The **Sala dei Notari** (daily 9am–1pm & 3–7pm; Oct–May closed Mon; free), the medieval lawyers' meeting hall, is entered via the fan-shaped steps opposite the Duomo. It's an obvious point of reference, its doorway topped by copies of a bronze Guelph lion and Perugian griffon (the originals are in the Galleria Nazionale; see p.482). Once thought to be Roman, the figures were probably made in 1274 or 1281, making them among the first pieces of large-scale casting in medieval Italy. Latest research, however, suggests the body of the griffon, at least, may be Etruscan, the wings having been added during the thirteenth-century casting. The chains below, according to tradition, were snatched from the gate and gallows of Siena during a raid in 1358. The triple-arched **loggia** is thought to be a remnant of San Severo, a church demolished to make way for the palace in the thirteenth century.

The Sala is one of the oldest parts of the *palazzo*, dating from the late 1290s – about the same time as the civic palaces in Florence and Siena were being raised. It's a tremendous space, overarched by superb vaulting. Before the lawyers got their hands on it, it was used as a meeting place for the townspeople in times of crisis and decision. Its celebrated **frescoes**, however, were substantially repainted in the nineteenth century, the net result being little more than flashes of colour, fancy flags and swirls. They represent the arms of various *podestà*, or magistrates of the city, from 1297 to 1424, infinitely duller than the hard-to-see thirteenth-century frescoes of scenes from Aesop's Fables and the Old Testament which adorn the upper arches.

Sala del Collegio della Mercanzia

The **Sala del Collegio della Mercanzia** (March–Oct & 20 Dec–6 Jan Tues–Sat 9am–1pm & 2.30–5.30pm, Sun 9am–1pm; rest of year Tues, Thurs & Fri 8am–2pm, Wed & Sat 8am–5pm, Sun 9am–1pm, though winter openings variable; €1.50, or joint ticket with Collegio di Cambio €5.50) is hidden behind an inconspicuous door at no. 15, further down the Corso side of the *palazzo* (right of the main portal). Since 1390 it has been the seat of the merchants' guild – the city's most important, and a body that survives as a charitable institution to this day. At first glance it amounts to little, but at close quarters the room reveals intricately inlaid wooden panelling, breathtaking fifteenth-century work that is considered some of Italy's finest.

The Collegio del Cambio

The **Collegio del Cambio**, a few doors down at Corso Vannucci 25 (Mon–Sat 9am–12.30pm & 2.30–5.30pm, Sun 9am–12.30pm; joint ticket with Collegio della Mercanzia €5.50), was the hall of the town's money-changers, a guild (founded in 1259) that survives as a charitable body to this day. **Frescoes by Perugino** cover its walls; these are not only considered his masterpieces, but also reckoned one of the best-preserved Renaissance schemes in the country. The bankers' guild awarded the commission in 1496, about the same time as Perugino was approached to fresco part of the Duomo in Orvieto, an undertaking eventually executed by Luca Signorelli. The city's bankers were determined to have paintings commensurate with their own sense of self-importance, and to this end probably paid Perugino – then at the peak of his powers – more than was on offer in Orvieto. This most likely explains the painter's mysterious disappearance from that city after just five desultory days of work in the cathedral.

Having paid their money, the bankers were determined to impose upon the painter their **theme** of choice; Francesco Maturanzio, a leading humanist theorist, was brought in as consultant, and proposed a fusion of classical and Christian culture, painting Christian icons alongside figures of classical myth. Though not an unusual Renaissance conceit, the vigour and uncompromising way in which the themes are yoked together created a distinctly curious juxtaposition. The thesis intended to suggest that there was unity in variety, and that human perfection, expressed by classical art, was obtainable through Christ's example.

Whatever the metaphysical intent, the frescoes certainly succeed aesthetically, unified by Perugino's melancholy tone, idealized and soft-focus figures and mellow landscapes. The paintings cover virtually all the walls and ceiling vaults of the single room, part of which – probably the prophets and sibyls on the right-hand wall (behind the ticket desk) – was allegedly painted by Perugino's pupil **Raphael**, then only about 13 years old. Up on the door-side wall there's a famous bust and unremarkable self-portrait of the master, looking on with sour-faced disapproval – ironically, the only element disturbing the frescoes' beautiful evenness of tone.

The ceiling vaults illustrate the main gods of the classical world: Apollo on his chariot at the centre; Saturn, Jupiter and Mars above the Corso wall; Mercury, Venus and Diana towards the window. Right of the window are portraits of famous Greeks and Romans, real and mythical, with the allegorical figures of Prudence and Justice joined by Cato (symbol of Wisdom), and with Socrates and Trajan, among others, below. The end wall, farthest from the entrance, introduces the Christian strand, with a *Nativity* and the *Transfiguration*, cleaned after having been blackened by smoke from the room's former oil lamps. The right-hand wall shows God amongst the angels, with sibyls to the right and men to the left: Isaac, Moses, Daniel (possibly a portrait of Raphael), David, Jeremiah and Solomon. The lovely little chapel to the rear, the **Cappella di San Giovanni Battista**, is smothered in a frescoed *Life of John the Baptist* (1513–18) by Giovanni di Paolo – like Raphael, a former pupil of Perugino.

The Galleria Nazionale dell'Umbria

The **Galleria Nazionale dell'Umbria** (Tues–Sun 8.30am–7.30pm; €6.50; Ⓦ www.gallerianazionaleumbria.it), on the fourth floor of the palace complex, is the region's main repository of Umbrian art. Its entrance is through the opulent doorway on the Corso; having pushed past harassed Perugians on their way to do battle with council bureaucracy, you might well find the small lift isn't working, in which case you have to clamber up the stairs, a route once taken by nobles on horseback. Dust has now settled on a long restoration project, which has turned the gallery into one of central Italy's best. Be certain to follow the gallery's prescribed itinerary: after passing through the rotonda, make for room 2 straight ahead and left. Free guides in several languages are usually available just beyond the ticket office. Note that some paintings may be moved: the gallery seems to be in a constant state of flux, and plans are in hand to extend the exhibition space across the palace's lower floors. In past years there has been special summer **late opening** (mid-June to mid-Sept until 11pm).

The gallery traces the entire chronology of the Umbrian art canon, from its Byzantine-influenced roots, its parallel development with the Sienese in the thirteenth and fourteenth centuries, through to its late fifteenth-century golden age when Perugia became the main focus of endeavour. The region's premier painters, **Perugino** and **Pinturicchio**, are predictably well covered, as are their imitators, and artists who worked in a late-Renaissance vein and fall outside the confines of the Umbrian school.

Early Umbrian and Sienese schools

Some of the gallery's finest moments have nothing to do with indigenous painters. This is particularly true of early rooms, where the **Sienese** largely hold sway. Amongst a welter of anonymous works, the first highlight is a large *Crucifixion* by the so-called Maestro di San Francesco, one of the gallery's earliest pieces, and painted by the anonymous hand believed to be responsible for some of the superlative frescoes in the nave of the Lower Church in Assisi's Basilica di San Francesco. Also look out for an outstanding *Madonna and Angels* by **Duccio** (1304–08), its static beauty the obvious model for many of the Umbrian works that follow. Other named Sienese masters include Bartolomeo da Siena, Domenico di Bartolo and Taddeo di Bartolo, the last responsible here for three altarpieces, including a *Pentecost* that displays a radical approach to composition, at odds with the more conservative Umbrians to come.

In acknowledging the increasing influence of Tuscan painters on Umbrians as the fifteenth century progressed, the gallery almost allows a pair of paintings by outsiders to steal the show. One is an astounding triptych by **Fra' Angelico**, the *Madonna and Child with Angels and Saints*. Radiant with the painter's gorgeous swathes of blue, it was painted in 1437 for Perugia's church of San Domenico. The other is more extraordinary still: **Piero della Francesca**'s sensational polyptych of the *Madonna and Child and Sts Anthony of Padua and John the Baptist with Sts Francis and Elizabeth of Hungary*, executed for Perugia's Sant'Antonio convent church around 1460, about the time of his *Arezzo* cycle. It's full of eccentric compositional nuances, particularly in the small *Annunciation* hinged to the top of the main painting, in which a mannered succession of arches around the Virgin recedes into a blank wall. The predella depicts miracles performed by the saints in the main painting.

Dozens of anonymous early fifteenth-century Umbrian works follow, amounting in many cases to no more than a surfeit of the religious iconography that fills Umbrian paintings without the redeeming dulcet qualities of the Sienese. The better of the Umbrians are Matteo da Gualdo and **Niccolò Alunno**, the latter represented by a *gonfalone*, or painted banner, a genre later to become the special preserve of Perugian painters. Alunno's banner hangs next to a similar work by **Benedetto Bonfigli**, an important mid-period Umbrian painter, who is also represented by a superb *Annunciation and St Luca*; more significantly, he decorated the palazzo's chapel between 1454 and 1480 with surviving fragmentary episodes from the life of Ercolano and Louis of Toulouse, Perugia's patron saints. The frescoes provide a detailed picture of aspects of fifteenth-century Perugia – walls, towers and monuments – that have now largely vanished.

Perugino and the Renaissance

Heralded by a bevy of Perugian contemporaries – talked of by his contemporaries in the same breath as Michelangelo and Leonardo da Vinci – **Perugino** marks the apotheosis of the Umbrian school. About a dozen sublime works here encapsulate his immense output. The loveliest painting is probably the *Madonna della Consolazione* (1496–98), a work whose imagery and bravura technique underline just how much Raphael, Perugino's pupil, would take from his master. Almost equally fine are two earlier pieces painted around 1475, a *Pietà* and an *Adoration of the Magi*.

The second-ranked Umbrian, and Perugino's occasional collaborator, **Pinturicchio**, is not so well represented, save for the gargantuan *Pala di Santa Maria dei Fossi* (1495), widely considered one of the masterpieces of the Umbrian canon. This aside, however, there is little to compare with the artist's frescoes of Spello's Santa Maria Maggiore (see p.545) or the works in Siena's Libreria Piccolomini (see p.336). Other rooms contain perfectly good works by followers of Perugino; names to look out for are Sinibaldo Ibi, Giannicola di Paolo and Eusebio di San Giorgio, all fluent interpreters of Perugino's merging of Umbrian and Florentine traditions. The rest of the gallery ploughs a remorseless course through seventeenth- to nineteenth-century Umbrian offerings, most of them large, gloomy canvases.

The Duomo

Piazza IV Novembre is backed by the plain-faced **Duomo**, or **Cattedrale di San Lorenzo** (Mon–Sat 7am–12.45pm & 4–7.45pm, Sun 7am–1pm & 4–7pm; free). There's been a church on this site for a thousand years, but the cornerstone for the present building was laid in 1345, though the Black Death (1348) almost immediately interrupted subsequent construction. Most of the building was completed late in the following century and even then the facade, which is in the lovely pink stone of most local towns, was left unfinished. Taking a pragmatic approach to the problem, the Perugians stole the marble facing intended for Arezzo's cathedral, though a subsequent hammering from Arezzo brought about its shame-faced return.

To the left of the portal on the building's southern flank is a bronze statue (1555) of Pope Julius III by Vincenzo Danti, and to the right an unfinished **pulpit** built for the roving St Bernardino of Siena, who was something of a hit with the Perugians. It was here that he preached a Bonfire of the Vanities, urging women to burn their wigs and everyone else to give up books, fine clothes and general good times. To the left are remains of the Loggia Fortebraccio (1423), taken from the house of the city's one-time ruler.

The Baroque **interior** is imposing enough, though short on artworks. Its pride and joy is the Virgin's "wedding ring", a novel relic, housed in the

Cappella del Santo Anello (first chapel on the left). An unwieldy piece of agate, said to change colour according to the character of the person wearing it, the ring was stolen by the Perugians from Chiusi in 1473 and encased in a series of fifteen boxes, fitted like Russian dolls; it's brought out for public edification once a year on July 30. Embedded in the wall nearby are fragments of an altar by Agostino di Duccio (1473); next to them is a lovely painting by Berto di Giovanni showing 1520s Perugia in the background, with a small lunette above by Giannicola di Paolo.

In the right aisle, the first chapel, closed by an iron screen, contains a widely admired *Deposition* painted in 1569 by Barocci, apparently under the influence of poison administered by a jealous rival. More toxin-related mementos are contained in the transepts, where urns hold the ashes of Pope Martin IV, who died in the city after eating too many eels, and Urban IV, who was reputedly poisoned with *acquetta*, an imaginative little brew made by rubbing arsenic into pork fat and distilling the resultant ooze. The most conspicuous piece of art is the *Madonna delle Grazie* attributed to Giannicola di Paolo, on the third pillar of the right nave. Easily recognized by its tinselly votive offerings, it's supposed to have miraculous powers, and mothers still bring their newly baptized children to kneel before it.

The Museo Capitolare della Cattedrale di San Lorenzo

Through the cathedral sacristy (or if it's closed, through a courtyard to the left of the entrance) are the cloisters and **Museo Capitolare**, or Museo dell'Opera del Duomo (Tues–Sun 10am–1pm & 2.30–5.30pm; €3.50), inaugurated in 1923 on the four hundredth anniversary of Perugino's death. It is a rich treasury scattered through 26 rooms with some fine examples of the miniatures for which medieval Perugia was renowned, as well as a *Madonna and Saints* (1484) by Luca Signorelli, and works by Umbrian and Sienese masters such as a fine triptych by Meo da Siena, panels by Andrea Vanni and a *Pietà* by Bartolomeo Caporali. Despite the listed opening hours, note that you often have to ring the bell at the cathedral chapterhouse for entry.

West of the Corso: Via dei Priori to San Francesco

The steeply sloping **Via dei Priori**, if you're to believe the medieval chroniclers, was a conduit for almost constantly flowing rivers of blood from those killed in the vendettas and intrigues for which Perugia was famous. The side streets, too, have associations with Perugia's gory past, notably **Via della Gabbia**, the first street down on the right, where there once hung a large iron cage used to imprison thieves and wayward clergymen. You can still make out long spikes on some of the lower walls of the street, used for the heads of executed criminals.

Just beyond, on the left, is the little church of **Santi Severo e Agata** (daily 8am–1pm & 3–7pm), which was built between 1219 and 1314 on the site of an earlier chapel and retains a sense of its austere Romanesque origins. Inside, a *Crucifixion* dominates the altar wall, possibly from the earlier structure, discovered during restoration work in 1911. There are good fragments of two fourteenth-century Umbrian school fresco cycles on the west and north walls, the latter – *Scenes from the Life of San Severo* – the more intelligible. **San Filippo Neri**, further down on the right, is a Baroque church worth a look for its high altarpiece, a painting of the *Immaculate*

Conception (1662) by Pietro da Cortona, a local star who would go on to make his name in Rome and Florence.

Further down still is the rarely open **Santi Stefano e Valentino**, a lovely little thirteenth-century church on the right with fragments of frescoes; it puts the ugly **Santa Teresa** opposite to shame. Nearby is the unmissable 46-metre **Torre degli Sciri**, one of the few medieval towers (they reputedly numbered seven hundred) to have survived.

Near the end of Via dei Priori comes **Madonna della Luce** (1513–19), dominated by a vault frescoed by G.B. Caporali and an altarpiece by Tiberio d'Assisi, both accomplished followers of Perugino. The tiny chapel takes its name ("Madonna of the Light") from an incident in 1513, when a young barber swore so profusely on losing at cards that a Madonna in a wayside shrine closed her eyes in horror, and kept them closed for four days. The miracle inspired celebrations, processions and the building of this new church. Immediately to the left, the **Porta Trasimena**, or Arco di San Luca, has been one of the principal entrances to the city since Etruscan times.

Bearing right beyond the Madonna della Luce brings you to a welcoming patch of grass, often frequented by students from the art school next door, and conveniently placed for admiring Agostino di Duccio's colourful **Oratorio di San Bernardino** (daily 9am–1pm & 3.30–6pm; winter closes 5.30pm; free). Its richly embellished facade is far and away the best piece of sculpture in the city, an odd but appealing mix of bas-reliefs and coloured marble, commissioned in 1457 by the city's magistrates in gratitude to St Bernardino for trying to bring peace to Perugia. The detail of the carving warrants a close look, especially the lower frieze depicting the Bonfire of the Vanities – a pile of Perugian wigs, books and hosiery elicited by the saint's preaching. The church interior is infrequently open, but contains the tomb of Fra' Angelo, who ordered the oratory's construction, and a high altar fashioned from a fourth-century Christian sarcophagus. Alongside is what's left of **San Francesco**, Bernardino's lodging in the city, and in its time Perugia's most sumptuous church. Started just four years after Francis's death in 1226, it's been laid low by earthquakes and landslips, though the curiously jumbled facade is still just about standing and the interior is often used as a concert hall. From San Francesco, Via Alessandro Pascoli leads east to Piazza Fortebraccio (see p.486).

East of the Corso

Piazza Danti, the pleasant little square behind the Duomo, is the scene of a weekend flower and terracotta **market** and site of a third-century BC **Pozzo Etrusco**, or Etruscan well, entered at no. 18 (April & Aug daily 10am–1.30pm & 2.30–6pm; May–July, Sept & Oct Tues–Sun 10am–1.30pm & 2.30–6.30pm; rest of year Tues–Sun 11am–1.30pm & 2.30–5pm; €2.50, includes admission to San Severo & Museo delle Mura e delle Porte Urbiche), well worth the few minutes it takes to see. Little in the dim, ancient alley that drops to the entrance hints at the scale of the structure, a massive affair that dramatically illustrates the engineering and technical skills of its Etruscan builders. Its 430,000-litre capacity was sufficient to supply the entire city – water still gathers here from moisture-bearing strata – and was at least 35m deep: the precise depth is impossible to ascertain because of debris at the bottom of the shaft.

Close by is the church of **San Severo** (same hours and ticket as Pozzo Etrusco), the chief sight of this district; take Via Bontempi off the square, then the tiny stepped Via Raffaello curving left, and the church is straight ahead in Piazza Raffaello. Legend claims it was built on the site of a pagan temple to the sun – the spot is east-facing and the town's highest point – which gave its name to the Porta Sole district of the Etruscan city. There would once have been five such districts, spreading down from the temple to five corresponding gates in the outer wall. Most of the church is a Baroque rehash, grafted onto a building that dates from 1007, though one chapel was spared – a survivor that contains one of **Raphael**'s first complete works, a *Holy Trinity and Saints* (1505–8 and 1521), probably painted shortly before (or just after) he settled in Florence in 1505. The fresco, as often in paintings of the Trinity, is on three levels, though the upper level – God the Father – is missing. Notice the figure of Christ, whose nudity echoes the nudity of the heroes of Classical art, and which shows the young Raphael's assimilation of new Renaissance notions. The painter was summoned to Rome to work in the Vatican and never completed the picture: in a poignant piece of artistic irony, the lower panels, depicting *Six Saints*, were painted in 1521 by Perugino, then in his dotage, a year after the death of his erstwhile pupil. Perugino's work shows him at his most stilted, an artist who found a winning formula from which he never moved on, even in old age: Raphael's debt to his master is obvious, but even as a fledgling talent in this fresco he demonstrates his more dynamic approach, not least in the arrangement of his figures: where Perugino's saints stand in a line, face on, Raphael's figures are arranged facing out or sideways, creating a more dramatic compositional effect.

From San Severo, it's easy to continue to Piazza Fortebraccio by way of **Santa Maria Nuova**, a sprawling and much knocked-about church recently restored more or less to its original Gothic appearance (to reach it, return to Via Bontempi and turn left downhill). Its main point of interest is the *gonfalone* (banner) in the second chapel on the right; created in 1472 by Bonfigli, it features a view of Perugia under attack from divine thunderbolts. Via Pinturicchio continues to Piazza Fortebraccio.

The northern quarters

The **northern quarters** of the *centro storico* start at **Piazza Fortebraccio**, ten-minutes' walk downhill from Piazza IV Novembre, and a similar distance from San Francesco and Santa Maria Nuova. The first route follows Perugia's oldest street, the 2500-year-old **Via Ulisse Rocchi**; the second passes the modern university buildings and goes under the famous raised walkway of **Via del Acquedotto**. However, the best way to see this part of the city is actually to use this walkway – the views are great and there's no traffic. It can be picked up off Via Baldeschi just north of Piazza IV Novembre, or from just southwest of Piazza Fortebraccio. By following its continuation, Via del Fagiano, you can walk, if you wish, as far as the midway point of Corso Garibaldi near Sant'Agnese. Failing that, walk north from Piazza Fortebraccio and use it as part of your route back to the city centre from **Sant'Angelo**, the best of the rather lacklustre sights in the northern quarters: the church is well worth the walk, if only to have a picnic or snooze in its grounds.

Piazza Fortebraccio and Sant'Agostino

Unlovely **Piazza Fortebraccio** is dominated by the **Arco di Augusto**, or Arco Etrusco, a massive gateway whose lowest section represents one of the few remaining monuments to Etruscan Perugia. It dates from the second century BC, when it was the main entrance to the city. The upper arch and bulwarks were added by the Romans when they recaptured the city in 40 BC; under the arch you can still see the letters spelling out its new name, Augusta Perusia – the first part immodestly large, the latter considerably smaller. The top-storey loggia is a sixteenth-century addition. On the western side of the square, housed in the Palazzo Gallenga, is the **Università Italiana per Stranieri**, founded in 1925 and now a favourite of foreigners studying Italian art, language and culture.

A short walk north along Corso Garibaldi brings you out to the half-defunct church of **Sant'Agostino** (Mon–Sat 7.30am–12.30pm & 3.30–6.30pm, Sun 7.30am–12.30), originally Romanesque, now botched Baroque, and filled with wistful signs explaining which paintings (fine works by Perugino and others) used to hang in the church before they were spirited to France by light-fingered Napoleonic troops. The missing pictures have been replaced with poor modern art. The church, however, is not entirely ruined: there's a beautiful **choir** (1502), probably based on drawings by Perugino, and patches of fresco in the second and third chapels of the north (left-hand) wall, giving a tantalizing idea of what the place must once have been like. Better still is the fresco *Madonna delle Grazie* attributed to Giannicolo di Paolo in the glassed-off first chapel on the south wall. Adjoining the church is the fifteenth-century **Oratorio di Sant'Agostino**, its ludicrously ornate ceiling erupting in gilt, stucco and chubby plaster cherubs. It's entered from the piazza; the sacristan should open up if you ask.

Sant'Angelo

At the end of Corso Garibaldi, tucked into the northern corner of the walls, is the circular **Sant'Angelo** (Tues–Sun 9.30am–noon & 3.30pm–dusk), founded in the fifth century as a temple to St Michael the Archangel. One of the oldest churches in Umbria – Spoleto's San Salvatore just pips it for antiquity – it was probably built on the site of a Roman temple, its two rings of pillars deriving from an earlier building (there was once a third set, removed to build the church of San Pietro; see p.489). Further evidence of a pagan predecessor lurks in the high altar, which is cobbled together from Roman fragments. The church is beautifully plain, its Baroque additions having been stripped away. The setting, too, is delightful, a grassy and tranquil retreat, the shade of the walls and cypresses providing a favourite siesta spot.

Virtually alongside the church is the **Museo delle Porte e delle Mura Urbiche** (April & Aug daily 10am–1pm & 2.30–6pm; May–July, Sept & Oct Tues–Sun 10am–1.30pm & 2.30–6pm; Nov–March 11am–1.30pm & 2.30–5pm; €2.50, includes admission to Pozzo Etrusco & San Severo). Housed in the Porta Sant'Angelo, built in the fourteenth century, it is the largest of Perugia's medieval gateways. The small museum details the history of the city's walls, gateways and other fortifications, but its real draw is the superb view from the top of the gate's tower.

The southern quarters

Perugia's other highlights are conveniently clustered along **Corso Cavour** in the southern side of town, the busy main road out of town towards Assisi, which you can reach by walking down from **Piazza Italia** across Via Baglioni and the stepped alley off Via Oberdan under the Arco di Sant'Ercolano.

En route, you'll pass the strange octagonal church of **Sant'Ercolano** (now a war memorial), raised between 1297 and 1326 on the spot where the head of Perugia's first bishop miraculously reattached itself after it had been removed by the Goths. A little southwest of this is the **Porta Marzia** (daily 8am–7pm), a superb Etruscan archway above an entrance to **Via Baglioni Sotteranea**, part of an extraordinary complex of submerged medieval streets that can also be accessed from the escalators on the southwest side of Piazza Italia and from Piazza Partigiani. The streets' houses, built over Etruscan ruins, now form part of the foundations for Piazza Italia above, but were once part of the **Rocca Paolina**, a colossal sixteenth-century papal fortress designed by Sangallo, the remains of which can best be seen coming up on the escalators from Piazza Partigiani (or down from the west side of Piazza Italia). Taking in ten churches and four hundred houses, the Rocca was connected by tunnels to strategic points throughout the city. It was pulled down at Unification, using dynamite and bare hands, by what appears to have been every man, woman and child in the city – and even then the process took thirty years. Trollope, watching the demolition, wrote that "few buildings have been laden with a heavier amount of long-accumulated hatred". Within the Rocca's old confines is **La Rocca Paolina e La Città** (April & Aug daily 10am–1.30pm & 2.30–6pm; May–July, Sept & Oct Tues– Sun 10.30am–1.30pm & 2.30–6pm; Nov–March Tues–Sun 11am–1.30pm & 2.30–5pm; €1), with modest displays divided into four chronological groups, documenting the fortress's history.

San Domenico

The unmissable landmark on Corso Cavour is **San Domenico**, which, at 122m in length, is Umbria's biggest church. Its unfinished exterior has an attractively melancholy air, with pigeons nesting and grass growing on the pinkish marble, but the interior (begun in 1305) collapsed in the sixteenth century to be replaced by a vast, cold Baroque conversion (1632).

Like Sant'Agostino, however, it's full of hints of past beauties. In the fourth chapel on the right, the Cappella della Madonna del Voto, is a superb **carved arch** by Agostino di Duccio (1459), a fragment of the original church spoilt only by nineteenth-century frescoes and a doll-like Madonna. On the right wall of the first chapel to the right of the high altar is the **tomb of Benedict XI**, another pope who died in Perugia – this time from eating poisoned figs – after ruling for just eight months in 1304. He left to posterity one of the greatest Gothic carvings of its kind in Italy, an elegant and well-preserved piece by one of the period's leading sculptors – Giovanni Pisano, Lorenzo Maitani or Arnolfo di Cambio; nobody knows which, although it's modelled on the tomb of Cardinal de Braye in Orvieto, one of Arnolfo's most influential works (see p.632). Some of the marble work is missing, picked out by troops when a Napoleonic cavalry regiment was billeted in the church. In the next chapel to the right are extensive patches of fresco, another good choir, and – a welcome splash of colour – some impressive stained-glass windows (1411), the largest in Italy after those of Milan's cathedral. Also worth hunting out is the *gonfalone* (painted banner) by **Giannicola di Paolo** in the third chapel in the south transept. It was painted as a votive offering after the plague of 1494 and shows Christ above with the people of Perugia and a view of the city below flanked by saints Dominic and Catherine of Siena. The right wall of the left-most chapel in the north transept has an interesting **fresco of St Sebastian** in which, for once, the saint is not depicted riddled with arrows: the painting instead shows the archers preparing to fire.

It is possible to view **Le Soffitte di San Domenico**, the church's imposing vaults and lofts, which contain works by Giovanni Pisano and Carlo Maderno. Guided visits (Sat & Sun only) are by prior appointment on ☏075.573.1635.

The Museo Archeologico Nazionale dell'Umbria

Housed in San Domenico's cloisters is the **Museo Archeologico Nazionale dell'Umbria**, Piazza Giordano Bruno 10 (Mon 2.30–7.30pm, Tues–Sun

8.30am–7.30pm; €4; the hard-to-find ticket office is on the first floor of the cloister). Before being hammered by Augustus, Perugia was a big shot in the twelve-strong Etruscan federation of cities, which is why the city has one of Italy's most extensive Etruscan collections. The museum has recently undergone a major overhaul, and is definitely worth a visit: there's far more here than the usual run of Etruscan urns and funerary monuments. Particularly compelling are the **Carri Etruschi di Castel San Marino**, some quite exquisite sixth-century BC bronze chariots; a witty collection of eye-opening artefacts devoted to fashion and beauty in the Etruscan era; and a series of bronze helmets and shields. The bewildering **Bellucci Collection** is a private hoard of charms and amulets through the ages: everything from the obvious – lucky horseshoes – to stranger and often more sinister charms such as snakeskins, dried animals, feathers and odd scraps of wool. The exhibits span several thousand years and form a unique and oddly poignant picture of fears and superstitious hopes across the millennia. Other parts of the museum are still in the process of being updated.

San Pietro

Further south on Corso Cavour, through the double-arched Porta San Pietro (1147), is the tenth-century basilica of **San Pietro**, the city's first cathedral and still the most beautiful and idiosyncratic of its churches. Advertised by a rocket-shaped bell tower visible for miles around (rebuilt in 1463), it's tangled up in a group of buildings belonging to the university's agricultural department; the entrance is through a doorway in the far left-hand corner of the first courtyard off the road.

The **interior** comes as a shock. Few churches, even in Italy, are so sumptu-ously decorated, every inch of space being covered in gilt, paint or marble. The effect is appealing, and in the candlelit gloom the church actually feels like a sacred place. That so much of the Romanesque building survives is due to events at Unification, when the church's Benedictine monks sided with the townspeople in their revolt against papal control. Loyalty to the cause of libera-tion was not forgotten, and when the religious houses were broken up a year later, San Pietro was allowed to keep its patrimony.

The interior's finest single component is the extraordinary **choir** (1526), which has been called the greatest in Italy. All the woodwork here is superb: look out also for the intricately gilded side-pulpits. As for the **paintings**, there's a *Pietà* by Perugino between the first and second altars on the left, three works by Vasari in the Cappella del Sacramento, and a much-praised depiction of *Christ on the Mount* by Guido Reni (located on the left wall of the Cappella Ranieri); the eleven eye-catching frescoes around the upper walls are by a disciple of Veronese. The baffling fresco on the rear wall is a genealogical tree of the Benedictines, collecting together the most eminent members of the order. The best pictures of all are five saints by Perugino and a possible Raphael, gathered in the **sacristy**; ask the sacristan to let you in.

The Orto Botanico

If you've walked this far, you might want to push on a touch further down the road beyond San Pietro to rest up in the shady and attractive **Orto Botanico**, founded in 1768, at Borgo XX Giugno 74 (Mon–Fri 8am–5pm; free). The gardens divide into two: the medieval section is entered from the church courtyard, with the larger botanical section accessed from a gate just across the road.

Eating, drinking and entertainment

Perugia's cuisine is rewarding. While a plethora of fast-food and snack bars cater for the student market, there are several good mid-range **restaurants** and a couple of top-notch ones. There is a covered **food market**, the Mercato Coperto (Mon–Sat 7.30am–1pm), off Piazza Matteotti. An open-air **general market** (Tues & Sat 8am–1pm) operates on the Scala di Sant'Ercolano, near the church of the same name. You can buy other picnic supplies from Giuliano at Via Danzetta 1, a small alley off the east side of the Corso just north of Piazza della Repubblica.

There are also plenty of places to **drink**, including the inevitable rash of Irish pubs, but the city's most popular **clubs** are in the suburbs; ask at the tourist office for the latest hotspots. Several places lay on **live music**: one of the longest-established is the **Contrappunto Jazz Club**, Via Scortici 4a (closed Mon), open until 2am. The only real in-town club is the sleek **Velvet Fashion Café**, Viale Roma 20 (closed Mon & Tues; ☎075.572.1321, ⓦwww.velvetfashioncafe.com), which offers smart dining, drinking and occasional live music.

Perugia is strong on events, with films, theatre and concerts packing a page or so each day in the **listings** of the local *Corriere dell'Umbria* newspaper. Posters around the city, in particular near the university on Piazza Fortebraccio, give details of concerts and English-language films.

Restaurants

Cesarino Piazza IV Novembre 4–5 ☎075.572.8974. A very central trattoria-pizzeria that has been around for over thirty years, though sadly it's been modernized a touch recently. Booking is advised, as it attracts students, visitors, locals, Perugia's first-team footballers and politicians alike. Around €25, less for pizzas. Closed Wed.

Dal Mi' Cucco Corso Garibaldi 12 ☎075.573.2511. A variety of set-price menus are available here: the restaurant, as the old local dialect name suggests, presents traditional Perugian dishes. Good value at around €13. Closed Mon.

Del Sole Via Oberdan 28 ☎075.573.5031, ⓦwww.ristorantesole.it. Two large dining rooms under ancient vaults and a terrace with a fine view for summer dining. Food is classic Umbrian (great antipasti), and a full meal should come in at no more than €30. Closed Mon.

Falchetto Via Bartolo 20 ☎075.573.1775, ⓦwww.ilfalchetto.it. Central, reliable restaurant in a simple medieval setting; food is adequate but service can be slapdash. Reasonably priced if you stick to the basics. Closed Mon.

La Taverna Via delle Streghe 8 ☎075.572.4128. Tucked away in a small alley, a serious restaurant that often claims the highest rating in the Italian foodie guides that count. Serves a mixture of regional and one-off inventive dishes, plus heavyweight desserts. Wines are overpriced,

though, and when the place is full service and food can occasionally suffer. From €30. Closed Mon & late July.

🏃 **Osteria del Gambero** Via Baldeschi 9 ☎075.573.5461, ⓦwww.osteriadelgambero .it. Don't be put off by the English menus: this is a great place that's been in business since 1989 and has picked up a clutch of awards for its traditional cooking. The interior is simple and tasteful; three *degustazione* menus are priced at €25 (vegetarian), €27 (regional specialities) and €29 (fish and seafood) with wine. Otherwise €20–25. Closed Sun.

Osteria Il Gufo Via della Viola ☎075.573.4126. The best sort of *osteria*: relaxed atmosphere, old marble tables, open kitchen, and traditional regional cooking with the odd dash of innovation. Just 35 covers, with a few tables on the tiny piazza outside in summer. From €20. Closed Sun, Mon and a period in Aug & Sept.

🏃 **Osteria Turreno** Piazza Danti 16 ☎075.572.1976. This *tavola calda* has been in business for several generations and it shows: the handful of hot dishes each lunchtime are simple but well prepared and very fairly priced. You can buy food to take away or sit outside, at one of a handful of tables by the counter, or in the larger (and rather hidden) seating area to the rear. From €5; for €10 you can get meat, veg, salad, a hunk of bread and a soft drink. Lunch only; closed Sat.

Pizzeria Etrusca Via Ulisse Rocchi 31 ☎075.572.0762. Located on the hill down to

Piazza Braccio Fortebraccio, this is a no-nonsense pizzeria whose keen prices make it popular with students.

Pizzeria Mediterranea Piazza Piccinino 11–12 ☎075.572.1322. A stylish pizzeria with simple medieval stone walls, a wood-fired oven and pretty brick vaults. From €8.

Scalino Via Sant'Ercolano 2 ☎075.572.5372. An authentic and old-fashioned pizzeria and trattoria staffed by venerable women and patronized almost entirely by locals. It has a fabulous brick-vaulted dining room and very reasonable prices.

Wine Bartolo Hosteria Via Bartolo 30 ☎075.571.6027. Any old-style *osteria* that earns the approval of the Slow Food movement is usually a reliable choice, and this is no exception. The cosy, bottle-lined dining room accommodates just forty diners, so book ahead. Menus change according to season, but you can always be assured of excellent Umbrian dishes (and first-class Umbrian wines) that aren't afraid of the odd exotic touch, and prices that shouldn't top €25–30 for a full meal, excluding wine.

Cafés and bars

Bar dell'Accademia Via dei Priori 52. A good place for a break on a street with several cafés and restaurants. It has a great spread of pastries, and plenty of seating room.

Bottega del Vino Via del Sole 1. A wine bar and shop which offers wine by the glass or bottle, along with snacks. Mon–Sat 7pm–1am.

Caffè di Perugia Via Mazzini 10 ☎075.573.1863. A pleasantly smart setting with superb thirteenth-century vaulted ceiling. All the café staples, plus a restaurant with simple meals, a pizzeria-grill and a wine bar, the last a good early-evening retreat. Closed Tues.

Caffè Morlacchi Piazza Morlacchi 8 ☎075.572.1760. Smart but student-oriented bar with occasional live music. Closed Sun.

Enoteca Provinciale Via Ulisse Rocchi 16–18. Close to the Duomo, this wineshop-cum-bar is the best place to indulge in local wines; it also does excellent snacks and has a vast selection of wines to buy by the bottle. Mon 4.30–8.30pm, Tues–Sat 10.30am–2.30pm & 4.30–10pm.

Gelateria Gambrinus Via Bonazzi 3 ☎075.573.5620. Queues from this ice-cream parlour off the Corso often stretch onto the nearby Piazza della Repubblica, especially at the height of the Sunday *passeggiata*. A great choice of flavours and very generous scoops.

Il Birraio Via delle Prome 18. There's no mistaking the beer bias of this odd, modern place, the entrance to which is lined with the copper tanks and vats of an in-house microbrewery. Tues–Sun 5pm–2am.

Pasticceria Sandri Corso Vannucci 32. The most atmospheric café in Perugia – turn-of-the-century Viennese style with lots of brass, wood panels and frescoed ceilings. Worth at least a cake and a cappuccino just to gaze at the interior. Closed Mon.

Pizza al Taglio Via dei Priori 3. This hole-in-the-wall place a few steps from the Corso does a roaring trade in takeaway pizza by the slice.

Shamrock Pub Piazza Danti 18. Predictable but conveniently central Irish pub and restaurant in an alley almost next to the Pozzo Etrusco.

Listings

Banks and exchange Foreign exchange is handled by most of the banks on Corso Vannucci.

Books and newspapers La Libreria, Via Oberdan 52 (Mon–Sat 10am–8pm, Sun 11am–1pm & 4–8pm), has maps, guides and English-language titles. For English newspapers, try the stands along the Corso.

Bus enquiries ASP ☎075.573.1707 or 075.751.145, ⓦwww.apmperugia.it; SIT ☎0743.212.211; ATC ☎0744.402.900; Sulga ☎800.099.661.

Car rental Avis: airport ☎075.692.9346/9796, Piazza Vittorio Veneto 7 (train station) ☎075.500.0395; Hertz: Piazza Vittorio Veneto 4 (train station) ☎075.500.2439.

Emergencies For first aid, call ☎075.578.3422; for an ambulance, call ☎113 or 075.691.9480.

The hospital is at Via Bonacci Brunamonti (☎075.60.81 or 075.57.81).

Pharmacies Farmacia San Martino, Piazza Matteotti 26 (☎075.572.2335) is a late-night pharmacy.

Phones Booths inside the post office are open until 11.45pm; the Telecom Italia offices in Via Marconi, Corso Cavour and Corso Vannucci are open 8.30am–10pm.

Police (Questura) ☎075.50.621.

Post office Piazza Matteotti (Mon–Fri 10am–5.30pm, Sat 10am–2pm).

Study courses Contact the Università Italiana per Stranieri ☎075.57.461, ⓦwww.unistrapg.it.

Taxis Radio Taxi ☎075.500.4888; Piazza Italia ☎075.573.6092; Corso Vannucci ☎075.572.1979; train station ☎075.501.0800.

Lago Trasimeno

The most tempting option near Perugia – whose surroundings are generally pretty bleak – is the reed-fringed **Lago Trasimeno**. An ideal spot to hole up for a few days and swim (if you don't mind murky water), it is the biggest stretch of water on the Italian peninsula and the fourth largest in Italy overall (after Garda, Maggiore and Como), though at times is in danger of drying up completely. With demands on water from agriculture and increased silting, the lake's greatest depth is no more than 7m (average 4.9m) – hence its bath-warm temperature in the summer. It's mostly clean, however, largely because the tourist and fishing industries are the area's economic bread and butter: banks of weed occasionally drift in during the summer, but they're peremptorily taken care of by the council and dumped on the shore. Note that the lake is also easily accessible from, and provides a base for visits to, Cortona (see p.459).

People have lived on or close to Trasimeno's shores since Paleolithic times, though its greatest historical fame dates from 217 BC, when the Romans suffered one of the worst defeats in their history at the hands of **Hannibal** (see p.494). Its strategic position meant that numerous castles and fortified villages grew up on its shores and in the hills around, predecessors of present-day towns such as Castiglione del Lago. Attempts to regulate the fluctuating water level date back to Roman times, and a number of serious proposals have been put forward to drain the lake altogether. These remained largely in abeyance for much of the late Middle Ages, when the (then) wooded shores were exploited for hunting, and again in the nineteenth century, when the marshy surrounds became a breeding ground for malarial mosquitoes.

These days the main drawback to Trasimeno is its popularity: in high season the lake is covered with speedboats, yachts and windsurfers. If you're after relative seclusion, steer clear of the northern shore – recently opened up by Perugia's *autostrada* spur – and head instead for the stretches south of Magione and Castiglione, though even here, foreign number-plates are in ever greater

▲ Boats in the harbour at Passignano, Lago Trasimeno

Boats on Lago Trasimeno

Boats run roughly twelve times a day throughout the year from **Passignano**'s landing-stage in front of Piazza Garibaldi to the **Isola Maggiore** – either directly (Sun only; 25min) or via **Tuoro** (Mon–Sat; 35min). Boats also shuttle between Passignano and Tuoro (summer up to 8 daily; 20min), and Passignano and **Castiglione del Lago** (summer Sat & Sun 2 daily; 40min). Boats run to the Isola Maggiore from Castiglione del Lago, but with reduced services outside summer (May–Sept 6–8 daily; Oct–April Sat & Sun 6–8 daily; 30min). To reach **Isola Polvese**, there are boats year-round from both Passignano (1 daily; 55min) and San Feliciano on the eastern shore (around 9 daily; 10min), about 12km from Passignano.

Typical **ticket prices** are €6 return for the trip from Passignano to Isola Maggiore; €4.80 return from Tuoro to Isola Maggiore; €4.80 return from San Feliciano to the Isola Polvese; and €6.60 return from Castiglione del Lago to Isola Maggiore. For more information, contact APM-Navigazione (☎075.506.781, ⊛www.apmperugia.it – click on "orari" and then "Navigazione del Trasimeno").

evidence. Be warned that **unofficial camping** is not as easy as it looks: commercial sites have grabbed the best spots and much of the remaining shoreline is marshy. If you're just passing through, probably the best option is to settle down for a long fish lunch at one of the lakefront restaurants in Castiglione, or take a **boat trip** from Passignano, Tuoro or Castiglione to the Isola Maggiore, one of the three islands on the lake.

Passignano

The lake's most accessible point is **PASSIGNANO**, a newish and reasonably attractive resort strung out along the northern shore and served by hourly trains from Perugia and Teróntola (near Cortona). Popular with Italians, the town in summer is often one big traffic jam, Sundays being especially bad. In the evenings, though, it's an enjoyable place as people come flooding in from the surrounding campsites, livening up the bars, discos and fish restaurants. The waterfront strip is the chief focus, and there's plenty going on in the web of streets behind as well. Bar two dull Renaissance churches and a bit of a castle, there's nothing much to see: you can skip the town in the daytime unless it's to catch a boat.

The **tourist office** is at Piazza Trento e Trieste 6 (June–Sept Mon–Sat 10am–12.30pm & 4–7pm, Sun 10am–12.30pm; Oct–May Fri & Sat 3–6.30pm, Sun 10am–12.30pm; ☎075.827.635). There are around a dozen **hotels**, most in the upper bracket. The least expensive options are the one-stars *Florida*, Via II Giugno 2 (☎075.827.228; ❶), and *Del Pescatore*, Via San Bernardino 5 (☎075.829.6063, ⓔdelpescatore@libero.it; ❶). Just 1km north of town in a quiet spot among olives and oaks is the three-star *Hotel Cavalieri*, Via delle Ginestre (☎075.829.292, ⓦwww.hotelcavalieri.it; ❸). Some of the 35 rooms have lovely lake views, as does the dining terrace of its *La Sosta dei Templari* restaurant (closed Tues), and there's also an outdoor pool. The main **campsites** are in the nearby hamlet of San Donato, notably the *Europa* (☎075.827.405, ⓦwww.camping-europa.it; April–Sept).

Passignano has plenty of simple **pizzerias** and cheap **restaurants**. If you want to eat fish, make for the *Cacciatori da Luciano*, Via Nazionale 11 (☎075.827.210; closed Wed – except during summer – & Nov). Otherwise, the best local restaurant is *La Darsena*, 3.5km east at Via Perugina 52 in San Donato (☎075.829.331; closed Wed Nov–March); it gets away from the area's obsession with fish (though this is still available), and has three-star hotel rooms (❶).

Tuoro sul Trasimeno

The rambling hill-village of **TUORO SUL TRASIMENO**, 4km west of Passignano and a three-kilometre walk from the Trasimeno battlefield, is a quiet but decidedly dull little place giving road access into the desolate, beautiful mountains north of the lake – the best scenery within easy reach of Perugia.

The SPNT boat company office, on the waterfront at Pontile di Tuoro, Punta Navaccia, is also home to a seasonal **tourist office** (June–Aug daily 9am–1pm & 4–7pm; ☎075.827.157), which has information on two **walking itineraries** around the battlefield: the *Esterno* (16km) concentrates more on the area's scenery, while the *Interno* (8km) takes you through the Valle della Battaglia itself – not terribly exciting, even when you've managed to find its start, which is vaguely signed 1km from Tuoro as a right turn as you drive west on the minor road towards Cortona (the right turn is a long, straight, tree-lined road). That said, the various observation platforms along the route give an excellent idea of the lie of the land, though it's hard to reconcile the tranquil farm country in front of you with a scene of mass

Hannibal and the Battle of Lago Trasimeno

On the shore west of Passignano is the spot where the Romans suffered the most traumatic defeat in their history, on June 24, 217 BC, at the hands of Hannibal. The Carthaginian leader was headed for Rome, having already crossed the Alps and won a sweeping victory at Placentia – though by this stage only one of his famous elephants was still alive. He was accompanied by a battle-hardened army of around 40,000, and was met by a Roman force of some 25,000 men under the consul **Flaminius** (responsible for the Via Flaminia), close to an amphitheatre of hills above the lake – a location, said the historian Livy, that was "formed by Nature for an ambush".

Things might have gone better for Flaminius if he'd heeded the omens that piled up on the morning of battle. First he fell off his horse, then the legionary standards had to be dug from the mud, then – and this should have been the clincher – the sacred chickens refused their breakfast. (Poultry accompanied all Roman armies in the field, their behaviour or the look of their innards at moments of crisis being interpreted as communications of the will of the gods.) Hannibal lured Flaminius into a masterful ambush, ranging his men in the hills above the amphitheatre under the cover of early-morning mist. Meanwhile he sent a small detachment over the hills to the rear of the amphitheatre, allowing Flaminius to see them, thus tricking the Roman commander into thinking he had seen the tail end of Hannibal's army vacating the basin. Thus duped, Flaminius abandoned his marshy position on the lakeshore in favour of the amphitheatre's drier ground. As he marched into the trap Hannibal's men poured down the surrounding slopes, creating havoc among the Roman soldiers – who were marching in a non-battle formation – many of whom barely had time to draw their swords. The only escape lay in a muddy retreat back to the lakeshore, where they were mercilessly pursued and hacked down by Hannibal's men. Two entire legions (16,000 men) were killed, including the hapless commander, run through with a lance. The slaughter lasted for three hours. Hannibal, for his part, is thought to have lost just 1500 men.

Hannibal's sappers had orders to bury the dead where they fell, and recently 113 mass graves, or *ustrina* – deep stone-lined pits with lids – have been discovered. Scientific dating of the remains tallies exactly with the date of the battle. You can follow a poorly waymarked **walk** and **drive** (see above) around the battlefield area, which begins off the minor lakeside road about 1km west of Tuoro.

slaughter. A permanent memorial to the carnage exists in the place names of two local hamlets, **Sanguineto** (Place of Blood), which you pass on the battlefield tour, and **Ossaia** (Place of Bones), which lies northwest just below Cortona.

Accommodation is restricted to a single **hotel**, the eight-room *Volante Inn*, Via Sette Martiri 52 (℡075.826.107, Ⓔvolanteinn@libero.it; ❶); in the nearby hamlet of Punta Navaccia is the *Punta Navaccia* **campsite**, Via Navaccia 4 (℡075.826.357, Ⓦwww.puntanavaccia.it; April–Sept).

Castel Rigone

CASTEL RIGONE, 8km east of Passignano, is the outstanding – virtually the only – village in the mountains above the lake. If you have time you can make a neat little driving tour of the area by taking the road north out of Tuoro to Lisciano (13km), then cutting southeast to Castel Rigone via Pian di Marte and Trecine (20km). Castel Rigone itself is a faintly odd little village with superb views and a small, geranium-strewn medieval centre. Most of its incumbents are pensioners, here for the bracing climate and fresh air. There are two smart, rather staid **hotels**, the better of which is the *Relais La Fattoria*, Via Rigone 1 (℡075.845.322, Ⓦwww.relaislafattoria.com; ❸), occasionally cited for its **restaurant**, which in reality isn't up to much. A little outside the village is the Renaissance church of **Madonna dei Miracoli**, much lauded but not worth a special visit and somewhat out of place in the overall medieval context.

Castiglione del Lago

CASTIGLIONE DEL LAGO cuts a fine silhouette from other points on the lake, jutting into the water on a fortified promontory. It's a friendly, unpretentious place that can hold your attention for a couple of days – longer if all you want to do is crash out on one of its modest but pleasant **beaches**. Dotted around the promontory (the best swimming is on the south side), they get extremely busy in summer. It's easy to reach Castiglione by road and rail, though a lot of the fast trains on the Rome–Florence line no longer stop here, so you'll probably end up taking a slower train from Chiusi or Teróntola.

There's little in the town to head for, despite its Etruscan and Roman origins, though the largely sixteenth-century **castle**, or Rocca del Leone (mid–March to April, Sept & Oct 9.30am–1pm & 3.30–7pm; May & June 10am–1.30pm & 4–7.30pm; July & Aug 10am–1.30pm & 4.30–8pm; Nov to mid-March Sat, Sun & public holidays 9.30am–4.30pm; €2.60, or €6.20 for the "Museo Aperto" ticket that gives access to the Palazzo della Corgna and museums in Panicale, p.497, and Città della Pieve, p.634), is well preserved, particularly its strange fortified passageway, part of a defensive scheme that in the thirteenth century made it one of Europe's impregnable fortresses. Its design has been attributed to Frate Elias, a controversial Franciscan monk (see p.526) who may have been responsible for the Basilica di San Francesco in Assisi. The ticket also lets you into the ducal **Palazzo della Corgna** (same hours) in Piazza Gramsci, full of large rooms with ceilings covered in frescoes of Classical subjects. Machiavelli once stayed here, as did Leonardo da Vinci (in 1503), who made a drawing of the town's fortifications. The castle ramparts offer good views of the lake, and there's a stage for outdoor summer events. You might also hunt down the church of **Santa Maria Maddalena** at the western end of Via Vittorio Emanuele, where the main left altar has a fine *Madonna and Child* by Eusebio di San Giorgio, a follower of Perugino.

Practicalities

The main **tourist office** for the Trasimeno region is in Castiglione's main square, at Piazza Mazzini 10 (Mon–Fri 8.30am–1pm & 3.30–7pm, Sat 9am–1pm & 3.30–7pm, Sun 9am–1pm & 4–7pm; ℡075.965.2484 or 075.965.2738, ℮info@iat.castiglione-del-lago.pg.it); they have on their books plenty of **agriturismo** choices in the surrounding countryside, a lot of reasonable if characterless **rooms** in private houses, and **apartments** to rent on a weekly basis.

Hotel prices have shot up to capitalize on the town's increasing popularity: the top-priced places are the pleasant, family-run three-star *Duca della Corgna*, Via Bruno Buozzi 143 (℡075.953.238, ⓦwww.hotelcorgna.com; ❸), with the three-star *Trasimeno*, Via Roma 174 (℡075.965.2494, ⓦwww.hotel-trasimeno .it; ❸), hot on its heels. The atmospheric *Miralago*, Piazza Mazzini 6 (℡075.951.157, ⓦwww.hotelmiralago.com; ❸), has views of the lake behind. Out of town, in Petrignano, 14km to the northwest, the loveliest choice is ⚔ *Alla Corte del Sole* (℡075.968.9008, ⓦwww.cortedelsole.com; ❻), a superb eighteen-room country retreat with fabulous views, pool, orangerie and sixteenth-century period rooms. Most of the **campsites** are some way north or south; the most highly rated is *Badiaccia*, Via Trasimeno I, 91, Località Badiaccia (℡075.965.9097, ⓦwww.badiaccia.com).

Aside from the summer-only **restaurants** on the promenade, the place to eat game, fish fresh from the lake and other dishes is *L'Acquario*, Via Vittorio Emanuele II 69 (℡075.965.2432; closed Wed; winter also closed Tues). Another good option is *La Fontana* in the *Miralago* hotel (see above), which in summer has tables in a garden at the rear with pleasant lake views. A lovely place for a light meal, snack or glass of wine is *Vinolento*, Via del Forte 75 (℡075.952.5262, ⓦwww.vinolento.it; closed Mon), in a medieval setting with a beautifully frescoed ceiling. The town's lively **market** is on Wednesdays.

Isola Maggiore and Isola Polvese

Regular boats (see p.493) from Passignano, Tuoro and Castiglione make the trip out to **Isola Maggiore**, one of Trasimeno's three islands – a fun ride if you don't mind the crowds. There's a single village of about one hundred people, traditionally known for its lacemaking, and a pretty **walk** round the island's two-kilometre perimeter: follow the quaint brick-paved street from the landing stage to the twelfth-century church of San Salvatore at the top and the path continues beyond. The island is famous for a visit by St Francis in 1211, a forty-day sojourn during which he consumed just half a loaf of bread; a chapel marks the point of his disembarkation, and there's a small Franciscan monastery on the southeast shore. The best outing – and another lovely walk – is through the olive groves to the church of **San Michele Arcangelo** (irregular hours, but should be open Sat, Sun & public holidays 10am–1pm & 2.30–6pm; €2), sited at the island's highest point; the twelfth-century building is decorated with frescoes and has a *Crucifixion* painted by Bartolomeo Caporali in 1460. It forms part of a small island "museum itinerary", or **Percorso Museale di Isola Maggiore**, which also includes the small **lace museum**, the Museo del Merletto (same hours and ticket as San Michele), housed in the Palazzo delle Opere Pie; a **museum of island life**, the Centro di Documentazione sull'Isola Maggiore (housed in the Casa del Capitano del Popolo); and the Romanesque-Gothic church of **San Salvatore**, begun in 1155 during the time of Federico I (better known as

Barbarossa), whose effigy you can see on the facade (interior open by appointment only: ☎075.825.4233). The island's single **hotel** is the two-star *Da Sauro*, at the village's northern limit, Via G. Guglielmi 1 (☎075.826.168; ❸); book ahead, whether it's for a room or for a table in the adjoining and equally popular fish **restaurant** (closed Nov–Feb). Alternatively, once everyone's gone home you might discreetly pitch a tent.

Boats also run to the tiny **Isola Polvese**, on which stands the 98-bed *Fattoria Il Poggio* (☎075.965.9550, ⓦwww.fattoriaisolapolvese.com; €17, plus €10 for lunch or dinner; March–Oct; ❶), with dorm beds, rooms and apartments for rent. It's not far from the jetty, where there is a map showing its location: the owners will generally meet guests and help with luggage. There's no public access to **Isola Minore**, the privately owned third island.

Panicale and around

The low hills south of Lago Trasimeno make a good scenic backdrop. With your own transport, you could take a detour to **PANICALE**, 5km south of the shore, a village of Etruscan origins which gave birth to the pioneering painter Tommaso Fini, better known as Masolino da Panicale (1383–1440), the master of Masaccio. It's a quiet place for lunch or a stopover, and also breaks your journey if you're walking some of Trasimeno's marked trails. The streets offer picture-postcard views of the lake, plus an easily missed Perugino painting, the *Martyrdom of St Sebastian* (1505) in the church of **San Sebastiano** (guided tours during opening hours of the tourist office), outside the walls in Viale Belvedere, off Piazza Vittoria. In 2005, restorers discovered a fresco here of the *Madonna Enthroned with Angels*, tentatively attributed to Raphael, Perugino's pupil. Apart from a tiny medieval core, there's little else to the place, save a small museum of religious relics, the **Museo degli Arredi Sacri** in Via Roma (guided tours during tourist office hours), and the modest **Museo del Tulle** (June–Aug daily 10am–12.30pm & 4.30–7pm; rest of year by appointment during tourist office hours), a museum in the church of Sant'Agostino devoted to local lace and tulle production.

Panicale's **tourist office** is at Piazza Umberto I 69 (daily 10am–12.30pm & 3.30–7pm; closed Sun Nov–Easter; ☎075.837.8017). There are two **hotels**, the one-star *Masolino*, Via Roma 7 (☎075.837.180/151, Ⓕ075.837.151; ❶), and the three-star *Le Grotte di Boldrino*, Via Virgilio Ceppari 43 (☎075.837.161, ⓦwww.grottediboldrino.com; ❷); the latter, its spacious rooms well furnished with antiques, is built into part of the old medieval walls and surrounded by a garden. The hotel **restaurant** offers both pizzas and full meals, though the quality can be erratic. Also within striking distance of Panicale is the fine *Villa di Monte Solare*, located 14km by road east in the hamlet of Colle San Paolo, at Via Montali 7 (☎075.832.376, ⓦwww.villamontesolare.com; ❺), a lovely 24-room house set amidst olives, vines and woodlands with rooms that retain original features such as massive fireplaces, frescoes, antique brickwork and period furniture; meals are also available and there are tennis courts, riding facilities and a pool.

On the map, the main SS220 road below Panicale between Perugia and Città della Pieve looks a good touring proposition; in fact it's a laborious route, spotted by light industry and the odd factory chimney. The only point of interest is the **Santuario di Mongiovino**, a Renaissance temple high above the road, 7km south of Panicale, which looks a good deal more impressive from afar than it does close up.

Northern Umbria

Moving north from Perugia you have two principal options. The most immediately tempting is the thirty-kilometre journey to **Gubbio**, which is among the best-preserved medieval towns in central Italy. This is easily accomplished as a day-trip by car or bus from Perugia, but there's enough in the town and the countryside beyond to warrant an overnight stay, especially if you want to explore the wild upland countryside further east, the best of which is protected by the **Parco Naturale del Monte Cucco**, a mountain park with some excellent hiking trails. Other towns in the remote northeast of the region are rare, and only hilltop **Gualdo Tadino** merits attention – though not a special visit – the only other town in the area, Nocera Umbra, having been left little more than a ghost town by the 1997 earthquakes.

The second option from Perugia is to follow the course of the River Tiber (Tevere) towards **Sansepolcro**, an obvious option if you're heading towards eastern Tuscany or on the trail of Piero della Francesca (see p.450). The river's reaches north of Perugia are pretty and pastoral, and mostly lack the light industry that blights the Valle di Spoleto and stretches of the Tiber further south. However, there is little of major note to see, though if you have time you could take in two artistic diversions at **Montone** and **Morra**, with a fine little art gallery and frescoes by Luca Signorelli respectively. The highlight of the area is **Città di Castello**, an unheralded and relatively little-visited town that may not be in quite the same league as Gubbio, but is definitely worth a stop for its pristine medieval centre, outstanding art and trio of fascinating museums.

By **car**, you could combine the region's major towns by visiting Gubbio and then heading west on the SS219 road to pick up the SS3bis road north to Città di Castello at Umbertide, a largely modern town with a small medieval core. **Public transport** connections are slow and infrequent between these two centres, making Città di Castello best seen by rail on the FCU from Perugia if you're without transport.

North from Perugia

The highlight of the area immediately north of Perugia is the abbey of **Santa Maria di Valdiponte** at **MONTELABATE**, on the east side of the valley 16km from Perugia. This monastic foundation once controlled twenty castles in the area, and similar abbeys administered great swathes of the land between Gubbio and the Tiber. Built between the twelfth and fourteenth centuries, the church itself is of rather less interest than the cloisters – which are medieval perfection – and the various artistic treasures, including frescoes by Fiorenzo di Lorenzo and Bartolomeo Caporali.

Umbertide

Bombed to the edge of oblivion in World War II, **UMBERTIDE** is now a light-industrial town relieved by a tiny, captivating medieval centre. Artistic attractions are limited to the **Palazzo Comunale** – the best Baroque conversion in Umbria – and a tremendous *Deposition* by Luca Signorelli in the **Museo Comunale di Santa Croce**, just outside the old walls in Piazza San Francesco

(June–Sept Fri–Sun 10.30am–1pm & 4–6.30pm; Oct–May Fri–Sun 10.30am–1pm & 3–5.30pm; €3.50).

Monte Corona (693m), 6km south of Umbertide, is topped by the **Badìa di San Salvatore**, a good-looking twelfth-century monastery ravaged by a sixteenth-century interior conversion.

Montone and Morra

The castle of Civitella Ranieri rises invitingly northeast of Umbertide, but it's privately owned. More worthwhile is the hill-village of **MONTONE**, 6km north, which harbours a surprisingly good collection of paintings and early medieval sculpture in the **Museo Comunale di San Francesco** (April–Sept Fri–Sun 10.30am–1pm & 3.30–6pm; Oct–March Sat & Sun 10am–1pm & 3–5.30pm; €3.50) in Via San Francesco, housed in the fifteenth-century Gothic former church of San Francesco. It has some beguiling frescoes from as early as the eleventh century, the best of which are in the apse and depict *Scenes from the Life of St Francis* (1422–23) by Antonio Alberti. The most interesting painting is a *gonfalone* (banner) by Bartolomeo Caporali, the *Madonna del Soccorso* (1481), with a view of fifteenth-century Montone in the foreground.

There's a small **tourist office** in the *comune* at Via San Francesco 1 (Mon–Fri 10.30am–2pm; ☎075.930.6427). If you need to **stay**, head for the two-star *Fortebraccio*, Via dei Magistrati 11 (☎075.930.6138, ✉aloigi@libero.it; ❷) or the *Locanda del Capitano*, Via Roma 5–7 (☎075.930.6521, ⓦwww.ilcapitano.com; closed Feb; ❸), just eight rooms in a fine medieval building with a good restaurant (closed Mon) and a veranda for outdoor summer dining. If you're heading east to Gubbio, you might stop off at **Campo Reggiano**, 11km east of Umbertide, for a look at its tiny eleventh-century church and crypt of San Bartolomeo.

West off the main routes towards Città di Castello, accessed via a turnoff at Trestina towards Castiglion Fiorentino, is the village of **Morra**, with a little-known but superb fresco cycle by Luca Signorelli in the **Oratorio di San Crescentino** (visit with custodian daily 9am–12.30pm & 3–6.30pm; free).

Città di Castello

Umbria's northernmost town, **CITTÀ DI CASTELLO**, is a relatively little-visited spot whose more than passable *centro storico* is a touch spoilt by the industry on its outskirts – mainly tobacco-processing plants, the town being one of Italy's leading producers. On either side of the valley floor, green wooded hills provide a pleasant backdrop, concealing one of Umbria's larger concentrations of rented villas and farmhouses. At the town's southern edge lies the **Pinacoteca Comunale**, the main artistic reason – along with an excellent diocesan museum – for visiting the town. The old centre is also a pleasant enough place to spend a night, particularly if you devote an evening to sampling the local Colli Altotiberini wines, or happen to catch one of the burgeoning number of festivals. The **tourist office**, in the Logge Bufalini just off Piazza Matteotti (Mon–Sat 9am–1pm & 3.30–6.30pm, Sun 10am–1pm; ☎075.855.4922, ✉info@iat.citta-di-castello.pg.it), deals with the whole Upper Tiber region and can provide details of the town's internationally renowned **Festival delle Nazioni** (Festival of Chamber Music; late Aug & early Sept; ⓦwww.festival nazioni.com). The equally well-known **Mercato del Tartufo** – a truffle show and market – is held every November. Piazza Gabriotti is the site of the regular

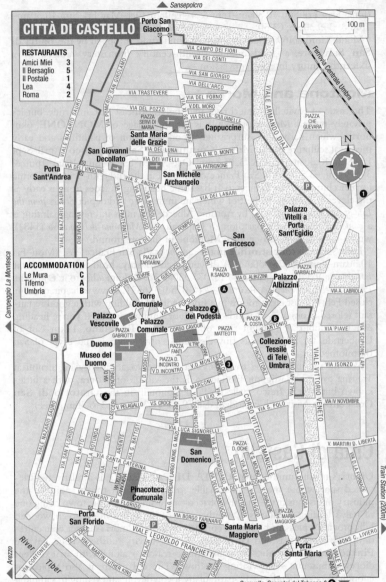

Garavelle, Seccatoi del Tabacco & **5**

market (Thurs & Sat), while Piazza Matteotti has a large monthly **flea market**, the Fiera del Rigattiere (third Sun of month 8am–8pm).

Access is by direct **train** on the private FCU line from Perugia or Terni to the south, or from Sansepolcro to the north; the station is just outside the walls to the southeast, five-minutes' walk from the centre. Alternatively, you could take a mainline FS train to Arezzo and pick up an ACT bus to Città di Castello, whose **bus station** is in Piazza Garibaldi, on the eastern edge of the *centro storico*. There are **car parks** around the city walls, one of the most convenient being that on Viale Nazario Sauro in the west, linked by a path to the piazza in front of the Duomo.

Accommodation

The town doesn't have many places to stay, but what it does have is good. If you want more flexibility than a hotel, note that the *Residenza Antica Canonica*, near the Duomo, on Via San Florido 23 (℡075.852.3298; ⓦwww.umbriaholidays .net; ❷), offers good-value **apartments**. The nearest **campsite**, the pleasant *Montesca* (℡075.855.8566, ⓦwww.lamontesca.it; May–Sept), is at La Montesca, 1km west.

Le Mura Via Borgo Farinario 24 ℡075.852.1070, ⓦwww.hotellemura.it. Three-star *Le Mura* is in a renovated rural house near the Pinacoteca. Bathrooms are rather small for the price, but there's an appealing little garden with fountain. ❷

Palazzo Terranova Loc. Ronti Vocabolo ℡075.857.0083, ⓦwww.palazzoterranova .com. This sublime but expensive country retreat is 2.5km north of town. It has just ten individually designed rooms, arranged in a seventeenth-century villa at the end of a wonderful long drive. The rustic restaurant, with beamed ceilings, is also first-rate. ❾

Tiferno Piazza Raffaello Sanzio 13 ℡075.855.0331, ⓦwww.hoteltiferno.it. The town's best hotel is the central, four-star *Tiferno*, housed in a former sixteenth-century nobles' palace. The public spaces are wonderful: spacious and full of antiques and period and contemporary art, with a large fireplace and beamed ceilings; the rooms are a little more functional and modern. ❹

Umbria Via dei Galanti 4 ℡075.855.4925, ⓦwww.hotelumbria.net. A modern one-star hotel in an excellent position. Rooms are bright and clean, and with little in the way of adornment. ❷

The Pinacoteca Comunale

The **Pinacoteca Comunale** (Tues–Sun: April–Oct 10am–1pm & 2.30–6.30pm; Nov–Feb 10am–12.30pm & 3–6pm; March 10am–12.30pm & 3–6pm; €6), towards the south of the walled town at Via della Cannoniera 22, is housed in the Palazzo Vitelli alla Cannoniera, one of four surviving palaces in Città di Castello formerly owned by the Vitelli, the town's erstwhile overlords. One of the region's more prepossessing buildings, the *palazzo* was built for Alessandro Vitelli between 1521 and 1532 by Sangallo the Younger and Pier Francesco da Viterbo, and decorated with some beautiful sgraffito by Vasari on the garden facade. Inside, the painted stairwells and period furniture complement the paintings, recently restored sixteenth-century frescoes by Cola dell'Amatrice on the stairs and in the first-floor *Salone* being some of the most striking. Not all the *palazzo*'s former guests, however, had time to appreciate the high-class fittings: Laura, one of the Vitelli women, was wont to throw her rejected lovers to their deaths from the windows.

The **gallery** spreads over two floors. One of the highlights is *The Martyrdom of St Sebastian* (1497–8) by **Luca Signorelli** (active in and around the town between 1474 and 1500), the painter of Orvieto's extraordinary fresco cycle (see p.628) and another in Morra, near Città di Castello (see p.499). More compelling still is the damaged but still ravishing processional standard by

Full-price **tickets** to the Pinacoteca or Museo del Duomo allow varying reductions on the admission to Città di Castello's other key sights, namely the Collezione Burri in the Palazzo Albinizzi and Via Pierucci; the Collezione Tessile; and the folk museum in Garavelle.

Raphael, the *Creation of Eve* and *Sts Roch and Sebastian*. It was painted in about 1503 as a votive offering following an epidemic, Roch and Sebastian being two saints traditionally invoked against the plague. Raphael spent about five years in Umbria and the region once had many works by him. Today the only pieces in Umbria entirely by him are the standard here and the panel in the church of San Severo in Perugia: many of the others were removed to France by Napoleon. A marvellous thirteenth-century *Maestà* by the anonymous Maestro di Città di Castello is also finally ensconced in the gallery, having been backwards and forwards to Florence for restoration since 1969. Other works include **Sienese** and later **Venetian** paintings, among them outstanding pieces by Antonio Vivarini and his brother-in-law Giovanni d'Alemagna (the two often worked in collaboration), as well as versions of the *Madonna and Child* by Spinello Aretino, Neri di Bicci and Andrea di Bartolo. The sculptural high spot is provided by the *Reliquary of St Andrew* (1420), which is graced with two gilded bronze statuettes by the workshop of Lorenzo Ghiberti. There are also ceramics from the **della Robbias**, a lovely sacristy cupboard (1501) in poplar and walnut, and a miscellaneous sculpture collection distinguished by a fourteenth-century marble relief, the *Baptism of Christ*.

The Duomo and the Museo del Duomo

Many of Città di Castello's buildings have lost their medieval aspect to later facades, most notably the rather odd-looking **Duomo** (Mon–Sat 7.30am–12.30pm & 3.30–7.30pm), whose half-finished Baroque frontage was begun in 1632 and abandoned some fifteen years later. By 580 the church had already been rebuilt at least once, and further versions followed in the eleventh and fourteenth centuries, and again in 1458, when the building had to be reconstructed virtually from the ground up after an earthquake. Something of its chequered construction history can be seen in the wonderful round **campanile**, which combines an eleventh-century base with a newer Gothic upper level, and in the Gothic lines of the **north portal**, whose carvings include two fine panels, *Mercy* and *Justice* (1339–59). The heavily reworked interior promises little, though if you're lucky enough to find the **sacristy** open (door on the right), take a look at its small annexe containing a handful of paintings.

The excellent **Museo del Duomo** is entered to the right of the cathedral's dog's-dinner of a facade at Piazza Gabriotti 3a (Tues–Sun 10am–1pm & 3–6.30pm; €6). The museum is arranged over two main floors: pride of place on the ground floor, in Sala I, goes to the **Tesoro di Canoscio**, a hoard of paleo-Christian silverware comprising nine plates, eleven spoons and five miscellaneous pieces – some of them beautifully engraved – turned up in the nearby hamlet of Canoscio in 1935 by a farmer ploughing his fields. They were probably made in Constantinople around the sixth century and might have been used to celebrate the Eucharist.

In the adjoining Sala II is an almost equally valuable – and visually more striking – *paliotto*, or **gilded altar-relief**, reputedly presented to Città di Castello by Pope Celestine II in 1142. Of quite exquisite detail, the work shows Christ surrounded by symbols and scenes from his life, running from left to right in two orders. The upper order comprises the *Annunciation*, *Visitation*, *Nativity* (note the comical donkey), *Adoration of the Magi*, *Flight from Egypt* (first panel bottom left), *Arrest of Christ at Gethsemane* and the *Crucifixion* with three saints; below are the four symbols of the Evangelists. In the same room is a superb **Sienese crozier**, dated 1324 and worked in mind-boggling detail: note the tiny statuettes of the Virgin and Child and a kneeling bishop in the curl of the crook at the top of the octagonal shaft.

The rest of the ground floor and part of the **upper floor** display religious ephemera such as reliquaries, chalices and crosses spanning some six centuries, plus documents and maps of local buildings. At the top of the stairs, a processional cross contains tiny relics, among them a bone belonging to St Catherine of Siena. Elsewhere upstairs, the early rooms feature a series of good if unexceptional paintings, among them an *Annunciation* by the local painter Francesco da Tiferno (active 1490–1510), a *Madonna* (1492) by the school of Luca Signorelli, and a picture of *St Floridus* (1412), the sixth-century bishop of Città di Castello who rebuilt the Duomo in 580. This sequence is interrupted in **Sala VII** where there are five exceptional paintings. These include the *Madonna and Child with St John* by Pinturicchio, two paintings of angels by Giulio Romano and – the highlight – *Christ in Glory* (1528–30) by Mannerist superstar **Rosso Fiorentino**, with the figures of the Virgin Mary and her mother, St Anna, on the right, and Mary of Egypt and Mary Magdalene on the left. This would be an exceptional painting were it in the Uffizi or a gallery of similar stature, so it is a treat to find it here. It even warranted comment from Vasari, who thought the figures and items pictured were some of the "strangest things in the world", though in every other respect he considered the work outstanding.

The rest of the town

The third of the town's triumvirate of museums is the fascinating **Collezione Tessile di Tele Umbra**, just off the main Piazza Matteotti at Via Sant'Antonio 3 (Tues–Sat 10am–noon & 3.30–5.30pm, Sun 10.30am–1pm & 3–6pm, Nov–March Sun closes 5.30pm; €3.50). The museum is annexed to a not-to-be-missed small textile workshop set up in 1908 by the Franchetti, a local aristocratic family determined to provide employment and keep alive the centuries-old traditions of linen-making in the region; it's still in operation and looks much as it must have done almost a century ago. The museum traces the history of textiles in the Upper Tiber valley, though in many ways it is less interesting than the **workshop** (Wed–Sat 10am–noon & 3.30–6pm; Oct–March closes 5.30pm; €1 in addition to museum ticket), which still employs local women and still – almost uniquely in Italy – uses traditional hand-worked looms. A small shop sells products made in the workshop.

Palaces

Just east of the Duomo, in Piazza Gabriotti, lies Città di Castello's old civic heart, dominated by the **Palazzo Comunale** (or Palazzo dei Priori), whose unfinished sandstone bulk was begun in 1322 by Angelo da Orvieto, the architect partly responsible for Gubbio's more impressive Palazzo dei Consoli (see p.509). Opposite rises the **Torre Comunale**, or Torre Civica, seat of the town's medieval prison, which can be climbed for some nice views over the rooftops. A graceful fourteenth-century loggia leads out of the square to the **Palazzo del Podestà** (finished 1368), again by Angelo da Orvieto, though much of the medieval work has been obscured by seventeenth-century additions.

You can extend your knowledge of the town's palace architecture by visiting Piazza Garibaldi and the **Palazzo Vitelli a Porta Sant'Egidio**, built in 1540 for Paolo Vitelli, possibly to a design by Vasari, the attribution appearing likely in view of Vasari's involvement with the Palazzo Vitelli alla Cannoniera (Pinacoteca Comunale, see p.501). Its garden frontage provides its best aspect, an outlook that would be improved were the grotto, garden and statues in front of it to be tidied up. The palace now belongs to a bank, but you'll catch a glimpse of the interior if you attend one of the many concerts held here during the summer season.

The Burri collection

The fifteenth-century **Palazzo Albizzini** (Tues–Sat: 9am–12.30pm & 2.30–6pm; Sun 10.30am–12.30pm & 3–6pm; €6), on Piazza Garibaldi, houses a collection of paintings donated to the town by the local-born **Alberto Burri** (1915–95), a modern artist of international standing, whose work was at the forefront of postwar avant-gardism. Larger paintings and sculptures are displayed in the **Seccatoi del Tabacco** (same ticket and hours, but closed mid-Nov to Feb; ⓦ www.fondazioneburri.org), colossal buildings on Via Pierucci on the southern edge of town once used to dry tobacco. They're worth visiting for their own sake and provide a breathtaking display space for Burri's work.

Churches

None of Città di Castello's churches can be said to set pulses racing, but taken together they offer a worthwhile medley of miscellaneous treasures. **San Domenico**, a gloomy Gothic affair built between 1271 and 1424, might once have been more tempting, but its Signorelli *Madonna* has been snapped up by the Pinacoteca, while the Raphael *Crucifixion* which once adorned its east nave now resides in London's National Gallery. In their absence you must make do with a set of lovely inlaid choir stalls (1435) and several fifteenth-century patches of local and Sienese fresco. **Santa Maria delle Grazie** (rebuilt in 1587) is almost equally tantalizing, for its main treasure, a painting of the *Madonna delle Grazie* (1456) – the only documented work of Giovanni di Piamonte, also known as a collaborator of Piero della Francesca – is kept hidden in a cupboard on the church's north side and only exhibited on February 2 and August 26. Worthy of interest, though, is a fresco of *The Dormition of the Virgin*, attributed to the Gubbian master Ottaviano Nelli. **San Francesco**, situated on Piazza Raffaello Sanzio, dates from 1273, though its interior bears the all too obvious marks of an eighteenth-century restoration. It, too, once boasted a Raphael (which is now in Milan's Brera gallery), but now all of note is an altarpiece by Vasari, located in the Cappella Vitelli (also by Vasari) off the north aisle. Finally, **San Giovanni Decollato**, in Via Sant'Andrea, has frescoes that show the influence of Luca Signorelli, while the nearby **San Michele Archangelo** (Via Sant'Angelo) contains a high altarpiece by Raffaellino del Colle (1480–1566), an accomplished artist active locally in Citerna, Gubbio and elsewhere.

South of the centre

About 2km south of Città, in the hamlet of Garavelle, is one of Umbria's best folk museums, the recently extended and restored **Centro delle Tradizioni Popolari** (Tues–Sun: April–Oct 8.30am–12.30pm & 3–7pm; Nov–March 8.30am–12.30pm & 2–6pm; €5). Situated in Via Marchese Cappelletti, it comprises an eighteenth-century farmhouse, preserved with all the accoutrements of daily life – pots, pans, furniture and so forth, plus a range of exhibits covering wine-making, weaving and carpentry. There's even a blacksmith's forge.

Eating and drinking

🏃 **Amici Miei** Via del Monte 2 ☎ 075.855.9904. Nicely located in a vaulted cellar, this is the best-value of the town's restaurants; closed Wed.

Il Bersaglio Via V.E. Orlando 14 ☎ 075.855.5534. Located 200m southeast of the walls, *Il Bersaglio* is

known for its truffle dishes; it's cosy inside, and there is usually the option of at least one *degustazione* menu. Closed Wed & two weeks in July.

🏃 **Il Postale** Via Raffaele de Cesare ☎ 075.852.1356. With grander and more

The great outdoors

There's plenty to take home from a visit to Tuscany and Umbria, but some of your most enduring memories will probably be of the regions' sublime scenery. In the popular imagination, much of the landscape is a pastoral patchwork of low hills, vineyards and wooded valleys, but the reality is rather different. The variety of landscape is extraordinary, from the clay hills of the Sienese crete and brooding uplands around Volterra to the high peaks of the Alpi Apuane and the pristine maritime landscapes of the Maremma.

The Alpi Apuane ▲

The crete near Siena ▼

From high peaks to coastal plains

High mountain scenery is a feature of eastern Umbria, where the Sibillini range tops 2400m, just a little higher than the almost equally dramatic Alpi Apuane and Orecchiella peaks of northwest Tuscany. In northeast Tuscany, the broad sweep of the Apennines contains the Foreste Casentinesi, a high, wild upland of ancient woodlands, while in the region's opposite corner, close to the coast, the Maremma is a glorious medley of hills, pristine beaches, pine forests and a variety of marine habitats. Nearby is the Parco Nazionale Arcipelago Toscano, comprising the islands of Elba, Giglio, Capraia, Gorgona, Pianosa, Giannutri and Montecristo – the largest marine park in Europe.

Throughout both regions there are also smaller, anomalous landscapes. In Umbria these include the dulcet Lago Trasimeno, the steep-sided Valnerina valley east of Spoleto, the imposing whaleback mountain of Monte Subasio above Assisi, and the cave-riddled slopes of Monte Cucco northeast of Gubbio. In Tuscany the range is even greater, from the coastal habitats of Bólgheri, Lago di Burano and Laguna di Orbetello to the lonely volcanic peak of Monte Amiata in the south. Most distinctive of all is the crete near Siena: a region of bare clay hills and ridges that make up one of Italy's defining landscapes.

Flora

The flora of Tuscany and Umbria is often exceptional, and spring carpets of flowers – particularly on upland meadows – can be breathtaking. The prime times are late April and May (later in the mountains), and the best areas in Tuscany are the Orecchiella and Alpi Apuane, at the meeting point of Alpine and Mediterranean vegetation zones. In Umbria, the Martani hills, Monte Subasio and the Piano Grande are blanketed in orchids, fritillaries and countless other flowers in May and June. In olive groves and on hillsides all manner of common plants thrive: poppies, primroses, violets, grape hyacinth, cyclamen, irises, cistus and many more. Specially adapted marine species can be found in the reserves of the Maremma.

Cypresses and **umbrella pines** are the icons of the Tuscan countryside, while oak forests blanket many of the interior hills, in Chianti in particular. Elsewhere there are large tracts of virgin forest, especially in the Casentino around Camáldoli, filled with oak, beech and pines, many of them huge ancient specimens. **Sweet chestnut** dominates in the Orecchiella and Alpi Apuane, rolling unbroken across mile after mile of the lower hills. On the higher hills, notably in the Sibillini, there are clumps of high **beech forest**, the predominant tree of the Apennines and of limestone in general. Coastal areas, especially in the Monti dell'Uccellina, have preserved the classic profiles of Mediterranean *macchia*: dwarf trees (usually oak), and a scrub of laurel, broom, lentisk, heather and fragrant plants.

▲ Classic Tuscan countryside

▼ Poppy field, Castiglione D'Orcia

Top five walks

▸▸ Stazzema to the Procinto;
see p.246.
▸▸ Le Torri Trail, Monti dell'Uccellina;
see p.306.
▸▸ Bagno Vignoni to Ripa d'Orcia;
see p.405.
▸▸ Sentieri Natura, Foreste Casentinesi;
see p.456.
▸▸ Forca Canapine to Castelluccio
across the Piano Grande; see p.595.

Wildlife

Tuscany and Umbria host an interesting array of **birds**. Coastal areas offer the richest pickings, and in particular the reserves set aside to protect them: Lago di Burano, Laguna di Orbetello and the Monti dell'Uccellina. These closely connected areas draw numerous migrant birds, many of them extremely rare. Inland, you can still see hoopoes, doves, woodpeckers and run-of-the-mill wrens, thrushes and starlings. Mountain areas boast a few hawks and buzzards, and even golden eagles.

Of the larger mammals in the area, the **wild boar** is best known, found through much of Tuscany and now spreading into Umbria. In the Maremma there is an indigenous breed, smaller than the boar of Eastern European origin common elsewhere, and shy and difficult to spot. **Porcupines**, though also elusive creatures, are common, and you often find quills on country walks. **Roe deer** have been reintroduced into the reserves at Bólgheri and the Monti dell'Uccellina; elsewhere they've been hunted to extinction.

A hoopoe, Giglio ▲

A wolf, the Valnerina ▼

Wolves drift into the Valnerina from their heartlands in the Abruzzo mountains to the south. There are at least 150 to 200 specimens in Italy, all protected – in theory. Elsewhere, you may see **smaller mammals** – hares, rabbits, foxes and weasels – though these too have been much depleted by the hunters' guns. Wilder upland areas are seeing the return of the **wild cat**, but numbers are tiny, and the chance of seeing them minimal. **Snakes**, and the viper in particular, are common, particularly around abandoned farmland – of which there's plenty.

elevated cuisine than the other options in town is the one-Michelin-star *Il Postale*, where you'll need to spend at least €50 per person to get the best of the creative cooking. Closed Mon, lunch on Sat & dinner on Sun Oct–May.

Lea Via San Florido 28 ⊤075.852.1678. A locals' favourite, a short way south of the cathedral, this is a good old-fashioned sort of trattoria, with regional cooking and fair prices. Closed Mon.

Roma Via Mario Angeloni 2 ⊤075.855.3560. For simple meals or pizzas, a few steps from Piazza Matteotti. Closed Sun.

Around Città di Castello

Beyond Città di Castello you have a choice of three routes: striking **east** towards Urbino and the Marche, or pressing on into Tuscany, either by heading **north** towards Sansepolcro or **west** towards Arezzo. All are accessible by train or bus from Città di Castello, though only drivers are likely to want to stop en route.

Towards Sansepolcro

North along the Sansepolcro road, 1km east of Lama, you can see faint remains believed to have been a villa owned by Pliny. Some 5km beyond, **San Giustino** is a more or less modern settlement, save for the **Castello Bufalani**, a thirteenth-century castle partly converted by Vasari into a splendid villa. Visits are at the discretion of the owners; enquire at the tourist office in Città di Castello. By a quirk of fate, Cospaia, a huddle of houses on the hill outside, was a tiny independent republic until 1826, though there are no visible reminders of its past glories. Sansepolcro (see p.452) lies 5km north of San Giustino.

Monte Santa Maria Tiberina and Citerna

One of the nicest drives out of Città di Castello is to the picture-perfect village of **MONTE SANTA MARIA TIBERINA**, atop a hill about 8km west on a minor road. It came under the sway of the Margraves del Colle, descendants of the Franks, in the tenth century, and remained under their control until 1815, having survived as an independent duchy. Until this time it could declare war, strike its own coins and was apparently one of only three places in Europe where duels could legally be fought to the death. Today it's sleepy and pristine, with little to see save a parish church with a fine font and some superb views.

Head west on the SS221 out of Città di Castello and you hit **CITERNA**, a perfect fortified hilltop village whose powerful wooded position attracted attention as late as 1944, when the Nazis destroyed its strategically important castle (leaving only the present little tower). The town dates from Roman times, was rebuilt after barbarian depredations in the seventh and eighth centuries, and achieved high renown in 1849 when Giuseppe Garibaldi, hero of Italian Unification, spent three days here after the unsuccessful Roman uprising of 1848. Today its neat brick houses are spick and span, despite a massive earthquake in 1917 and damage inflicted during both world wars. The fine local church, **San Francesco**, built in 1316 and revamped in 1508, has a grand assortment of gilded wooden altars; a late (1522–23), faded niche fresco by Luca Signorelli and assistants, *Madonna and Child with Sts Francis and Michael* (second altar on the right); and the outstanding and extravagantly framed sixteenth-century painting *Madonna and St John the Evangelist* by Raffaellino del Colle (left transept). The busy *Deposition* (1568) in the choir is by the otherwise obscure Alessandro Forzorio from Arezzo. Citerna's **hotel** is the 25-room, three-star *Sobaria*, Via della Pineta 2 (⊤075.859.2118, Ⓔhotelsobaria@libero.it; ❷). From Citerna it's a short hop into Tuscany to see Piero della Francesca's *Madonna del Parto* at Monterchi (see p.451).

Gubbio

High, remote **GUBBIO** has the most beautiful medieval appearance of the northern Umbrian towns – indeed it is so well preserved that some Italian guides and the local tourist blurb describe it as the Umbrian Siena. It's not quite that, but the streets are all attractive rosy-pink stone, the monuments worth visiting, and the medieval nooks and crannies as endearing as any in Italy. In many ways it has become the region's loveliest town to explore, since visitor numbers and tacky commercialism have increasingly compromised Assisi's charms. Better still, the countryside around is gorgeous – the forest-covered mountains of the Apennines rearing up behind and the waters of the Camignano gorge running through the town itself (in winter at least). A broad and largely unspoilt plain – bar a cement works to the north – stretches out in front of the town.

Gubbio is attracting ever-greater numbers of visitors, and on summer mornings the streets can be very busy. Come even slightly off-season, however, or stay the night, and you'll see it in a different and much more appealing light.

Some history

Local folklore insists that Gubbio was one of the first five towns built after the Great Flood. It was actually founded by the **Umbrians** around the third or fourth century BC, and may even have been their political and religious capital, later passing to the **Etruscans**, for whom it marked the easternmost limit of their territorial ambitions. Several bronze slabs, the **Eugubine Tablets** – now in the Museo Civico – survive as memorials to both cultures, some of the most important archeological finds of their type (see p.511). The **Romans** followed, building the colony of Iguvium at the edge of the plain, where a sprinkling of monuments and the gridiron plan of their streets survive to this day. Barbarian raids subsequently saw Gubbio's focus move up the hillside, whose steep terraced slopes form the town's present-day heart.

In the medieval period, Gubbio maintained a strategic importance as the pivotal town between Rome and Ravenna, its *comune* achieving a status that rivalled Perugia. According to contemporary chroniclers, the population grew to 50,000 – twice its present number – the town's wealth and size providing not only the wherewithal to build its vast civic palaces, but also the impulse towards artistic and cultural innovation. Umbria's first school of **painting** developed here, as did a **ceramic** tradition that continues today. Gubbio remained in the Duchy of Urbino until 1624, then became part of the **Papal States**, perhaps one reason why it still feels a town apart, not properly a part of Tuscany, Umbria or the Marche.

Arrival and information

APM has roughly hourly **buses** to Gubbio (fewer on Sun) from Perugia, plus three buses daily from Umbertide (there are also once-daily direct buses to both Rome and Florence). The nearest **train station** is at Fossato di Vico, 19km south on the Rome–Foligno–Ancona line, from where buses shuttle to Gubbio (Mon–Sat 10 daily, 6 on Sun). Gubbio's main **bus stops** are near the medieval heart of the old town in Piazza Quaranta Martiri. The newsagent on the south side of the piazza sells bus tickets and maps, including detailed CAI (Club Alpino Italiano) maps, invaluable if you plan to walk in the nearby hills or the Monte Cucco park (see p.517). By **car**, you'll most likely approach on the meandering cross-country SS298 from Perugia. Except on Tuesdays, when it's the site of the town's weekly **market**, you can **park** at Piazza Quaranta Martiri;

pay at the "Easy Gubbio–Cassa Parcheggio" office a short way up Via della Repubblica on the left. Alternative parking is off Viale del Teatro Romano, close to San Domenico, or in Via del Cavarello near Porta Romana.

There's a **tourist office** at Piazza Odersi 6, off the central Corso Garibaldi (Mon–Fri 8.30am–1.45pm & 3.30–6.30pm, Sat 9am–1pm & 3.30–6.30pm, Sun 9.30am–12.30pm; winter afternoon hours slightly shorter; ☎075.075.922.0693, ✉info@iat.gubbio.pg.it).

Accommodation

You shouldn't have any problem finding a **place to stay** in Gubbio, though the place gets busy. The tourist office has details of **rooms** to let out of town, as well as more than fifty **agriturismo** options dotted around the countryside nearby; there's some great accommodation, for example, in Vallingegno, 14km south, including **apartments** in a converted abbey, the *Abbazia di Vallingegno* (☎075.920.158; ⓦwww.abbaziadivallingegno.com; ❷). *Città di Gubbio* (☎075.927.2037, ✉info@gubbiocamping.com; April–Sept) is a hundred-pitch **campsite** with a pool in a good setting in Ortoguidone, 3.5km south off the Perugia road.

Hotels

Biagiotti Via Piccardi 12 ☎075.927.6108. Five rooms and one apartment, all with private bathrooms; a good standby if the slightly more expensive – but better – rooms of *Residenza Le Logge* almost opposite are full. Daily and weekly deals available. ❶

Bosone Palace Via XX Settembre 22 ☎075.922.0668, ⓦwww.mencarelligroup.com. This old-world three-star, full of frescoes, medieval vaults and antiques in its common areas, offers a touch of traditional style. Rooms are comfortable enough, but a little tired. You may be obliged to take half-board, but rates are reasonable. ❹

Dei Consoli Via dei Consoli 59 ☎075.927.3335. One of the best locations – in an atmospheric street – and recently revamped, turning nine formerly plain two-star rooms into four-star offerings. Best are the quieter rooms away from the street. ❹

Gattapone Via G. Ansidei 6/Via Beni 11 ☎075.927.2489, ⓦwww.mencarelligroup.com. First choice mid-range option; a renovated three-star hotel in a quiet medieval building, with spacious rooms (though bathrooms are small) and a peaceful garden. Light sleepers may be disturbed by the bells of San Giovanni nearby. ❸

Grotta dell'Angelo Via Gioia 47 ☎075.927.1747, ⓦwww.grottadellangelo.it. Reliable two-star in a quiet side-street, with a good, inexpensive restaurant; all rooms are en suite, at prices a little lower than the *Locanda del Duca*. ❶

Locanda del Duca Via Piccardi 1 ☎075.927.7753. The town's only one-star, with seven rooms. Overlooks the river, and has a reasonable restaurant with a picturesque terrace.

Note that for virtually the same price, you can stay in the good rooms at *Residenza Le Logge* on the same street. ❷

Locanda del Gallo Frazione Santa Cristina ☎075.922.9912, ⓦwww.locandadelgallo.it. Located in peaceful countryside 21.5km from town off the main road to Perugia, this is an intimate twelfth-century aristocratic house that fully retains its old medieval appearance – the rather misplaced Oriental furnishings are the only incongruous note. There's a pool too. ❹

Park Hotel ai Cappuccini Via Tifernate ☎075.9234, ⓦwww.parkhotelaicappuccini.it. Major-league hedonism (swimming pool, sauna, garden, gym), in an elegantly converted seventeenth-century monastery. The downside is the pleasant but out-of-town parkland setting, the size (85 rooms and lots of conference facilities) and the price, though off-season rates are more affordable. ❾

🏃 **Relais Ducale** Via Montefeltro–Via Galeotti 9 ☎075.922.0157, ⓦwww.relaisducale .com. The best upmarket choice. Three converted medieval houses, in a faultless position between Piazza Grande (from where it's signed) and the cathedral, with a lovely terrace and 26 glorious (and varied) rooms decorated with traditional simplicity and elegance. ❻

Residenza Le Logge Via Piccardi 7–9 ☎075.927.7574, ✉residenzalelogge@virgilio.it. Very appealing rooms (some sleeping four) in a quiet medieval street just off busy Piazza Quaranta Martiri, but well away from its bustle. Clean, comfortable and nicely presented: there's even a small garden. Weekly rates are also available. ❶

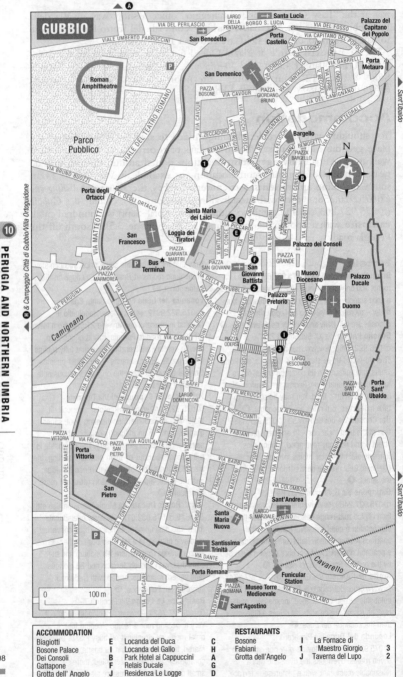

GUBBIO

Roman Amphitheatre

Parco Pubblico

& Campeggio Città di Gubbio/Villa Ortoguidone

VIA DEL PERILASCIO

LARGO DELLA PENTAPOLI

BORGO S. LUCIA

Santa Lucia

VIA DEL FOSSO

Palazzo del Capitano del Popolo

VIALE UMBERTO PARRUCCINI

San Benedetto

Porta Castello

VIA CAPITANO DEL POPOLO

Porta Metauro

VIA DEL TEATRO ROMANO

San Domenico

PIAZZA BOSONE

VIA CAVOUR

VIA BORROMEO

VIA POPOLO

VIA LOGGE

VIA GABRIELLI

VIA N. VANUCCI

VIA ONGARO

VIA LEPRE

VIA BECCILI

VIA DELLA CAMIGNANO

Sant'Ubaldo

PIAZZA GIORDANO BRUNO

VIA CAMIGNANO

VIA CAVOUR

V. ZECCADORO

V. PERUGINI

VIA TOCCHI MOSCA

VIA FELICITI

Bargello

REMOSETTI

PIAZZA BARGELLO

VIA DELLA CATTEDRALE

V. BENAMATI

VIA TONDI

VIA ANTONINI

VIA TONDI

VS. FULLININO

VIA DELLA ZECCA

VIA DEI CONSOLI

Porta degli Ortacci

V. DEGLI ORTACCI

V. CRISTINI

B

VIA DEI CONSOLI

VIA GALEOTTI

Santa Maria dei Laici

C **D**

E

VIA PICCARDI

VIA BALDASSINI

GATTAPONE

VIA MATTEOTTI

San Francesco

Loggia dei Tiratori

PIAZZA QUARANTA MARTIRI

VIA BATTUTA

VD. CONCE

VIA BENI

F

San Giovanni Battista

PIAZZA SAN GIOVANNI

Palazzo dei Consoli

PIAZZA GRANDE

Museo Diocesano

Palazzo Ducale

LARGO PIAZZA MARMOREA

Bus Terminal

VIA PERUGINA

VIA MAZZATINI

VIA DELLA REPUBBLICA

2

Palazzo Pretorio

G

VIA XX SETTEMBRE

VIA MONTEFELTRO

Duomo

VIA S. UBALDO

Camignano

VIA MASSARELLI

VIA GIOIA

CORSO GARIBALDI

VIA ANSIDEI

VIA SAVELLI DELLA PORTA

PIAZZA ODERSI

I

3

LARGO VESCOVADO

Porta Sant'Ubaldo

PIAZZA SANT' UBALDO

Sant'Ubaldo

VIA CARIOLI

(i)

VIA PICCOTTI

VIA BALDINI

J

VIA A. SAFFI

VIA PALMERUCCI

VIA DE MONTE

VIA CAMPO DI MARTE

VIA REPOSATI

VIA FORNICA

VIA MAZZINI

VIA MENGHINI

VIA BENUCCI

LARGO DOMENICONI

V. RISCACCIANTI

V. ALESSANDRINI

VIA APPENNINO

VIA MONTELLO

VIA MAFFEI

VIA CONCOLTI

CORSO GARIBALDI

VIA FABIANI

STRADA SAN GEROLAMO

PIAZZA VITTORIA

VIA FALCUCCI

PIAZZA SAN PIETRO

VIA AQUILANTE

VIA CANTILMAGGI

VIA MARINELLA

VIA BARBI

VIA SAVELLI DELLA TORTA

VIA SPERELLI

VIA XX SETTEMBRE

Porta Vittoria

VIA ARMANNI

VIA BONCOMPAGNI

VIA FRANCARINI

VIA MARIONI

VIA NELLI

VIA COLOMBONI

VIA CAMPO DEL MARTE

San Pietro

VIA PONTE AVELLANA

Santa Maria Nuova

LARGO S. MARZIALE

VIA APPENNINO

Sant'Andrea

VIA PIAVE

P

Santissima Trinità

VIA DEL CAVARELLO

VIA DANTE

Cavarello

Porta Romana

PIAZZA ROMANA

VIA PISACANE

VIA G. DEVITO

Museo Torre Medioevale

Funicular Station

VIA SAN GEROLAMO

PIAZZA ROMANA

Sant'Agostino

N

0   100 m

ACCOMMODATION				RESTAURANTS			
Biagiotti	**E**	Locanda del Duca	**C**	Bosone	**I**	La Fornace di	
Bosone Palace	**I**	Locanda del Gallo	**H**	Fabiani	**1**	Maestro Giorgio	**3**
Dei Consoli	**B**	Park Hotel ai Cappuccini	**A**	Grotta dell'Angelo	**J**	Taverna del Lupo	**2**
Gattapone	**F**	Relais Ducale	**G**				
Grotta dell' Angelo	**J**	Residenza Le Logge	**D**				

The Town

Piazza Quaranta Martiri makes an obvious place to start a tour of Gubbio; it was named after forty innocent citizens murdered by the Nazis in 1944 as a reprisal for partisan attacks in the surrounding hills; the fighting around Gubbio as the Allies advanced north was especially tough, the battle for the town taking three weeks. After taking in **San Francesco** and its fresco cycles you should head into the medieval town proper, where the vast **Palazzo dei Consoli** houses the town's museum and picture gallery, and then wander the short distance to the adjoining **Duomo**, **Museo Diocesano** and **Palazzo Ducale**, the last based on the Montefeltros' famous palace in Urbino. A lane behind the Duomo – the route taken by competitors during the famous Corsa dei Ceri (see box, p.511) – leads up to **Monte Ingino**, a hilltop eyrie which offers lovely views and plenty of picnic and strolling opportunities. Alternatively, you could take in the streets around **San Domenico** and then head east to Porta Romana, where a panoramic funicular also runs up Monte Ingino.

San Francesco and around

In Piazza Quaranta Martiri, slightly stranded from the medieval heart of town, is the town's finest church, Gothic **San Francesco**, possibly designed by Fra' Bevignate, the brains behind Perugia's Fontana Maggiore. Within the recently restored interior is an engaging if faded cycle of **frescoes** painted around 1410 by Ottaviano Nelli (c.1375–c.1444), leading light of the Gubbian school. Ranged around the chapel to the left of the apse, the seventeen panels comprise *Scenes from the Life of the Virgin*. High up in the apse you can just make out early thirteenth-century frescoes showing *Christ Enthroned with Saints*, while the chapel to the right of the apse has still more frescoes, this time fourteenth-century *Scenes from the Life of St Francis*. A small chapel in the sacristy is reputedly the room in which St Francis slept when he visited Gubbio, a sojourn that included his famous taming of a wolf that had been terrorizing the town. The simple cloisters beyond still cling to a few fourteenth-century frescoes.

Opposite the church is the distinctive fourteenth-century **Loggia dei Tiratori** (Weavers), Italy's best surviving example of this now rare type of building. Wool was stretched out in the shade of its arches to dry and shrink evenly away from the heat of the sun. The little church to its left is the often-locked **Santa Maria dei Laici**, built in the fourteenth century but altered to dull effect three centuries later. Behind the loggia, Via Piccardi leads just north of a small square containing the church of **San Giovanni Battista**, restored to its thirteenth-century state and distinguished by an oddly elongated campanile. Just off to the east, Via Baldassini contains the **Casa di Sant'Ubaldo**, the former home of one of Gubbio's patron saints. Ubaldo, born in Gubbio in 1100, became a bishop and earned his saintly spurs by helping defend the town from Barbarossa in 1155: he's buried in the basilica bearing his name on Monte Ingino.

The Palazzo dei Consoli

Bearing east into the medieval town, along Via della Repubblica, centre-stage is taken by the austere **Palazzo dei Consoli**, a superb building whose crenellated outline and campanile dominate the countryside for miles around. Its western face is particularly impressive, vast buttressing supporting a building that rises almost 100m from the base of the foundations to the tip of the campanile. The plain **facade** is disturbed only by a triple-paired window motif that's unique to Gubbio and repeated elsewhere in the town, by a lovely doorway, and by a hole at the top right-hand corner – made to

▲ The Palazzo dei Consoli, Gubbio

hold the cage, or *gogna* (from *vergogna,* meaning "shame"), in which criminals were incarcerated. The little lunette above the door features the *Madonna and Child with John the Baptist and Ubaldo*.

An overbearing gesture of civic pride, the Palazzo dei Consoli took the place of the previous civic headquarters in Via Ducale, which had been embarrassingly overshadowed by a symbol of religious power, the Duomo; this previous headquarters was subsequently lost beneath the foundations of Montefeltro's

Palazzo Ducale. Work began on the Palazzo dei Consoli in 1321, probably to the plans of the eminent Gubbian architect Matteo Gattapone. Angelo da Orvieto (active 1334–52), fresh from civic palaces in Città di Castello, may have designed the doorway and its flanking Gothic windows. Construction took a couple of hundred years, during which time vast tracts of the medieval town were levelled, mostly to accommodate the huge **Piazza Grande** (or Piazza della Signoria), a windswept belvedere with excellent views, and a suitable setting for this colossal building and for the lesser, unfinished **Palazzo Pretorio** opposite, built to the same Gattapone design.

The Museo Civico

The cavernous barrel-vaulted Salone dell'Arengo, where the council officers discussed their business, now accommodates a **Museo Civico** (daily: April–Sept 10am–1pm & 3–6pm; Oct–March 10am–1pm & 2–5pm; closed May 15; €5). Much of this consists of coins and sculptures, scattered like a medieval jumble sale in the main hall, but one of its adjoining rooms off to the left also contains Umbria's most important archeological find, the **Eugubine Tablets**.

Discovered in 1444 by an illiterate shepherd – who twelve years later was conned by the *comune* into swapping the priceless treasure for a worthless piece

---

The Corsa dei Ceri

The vigil of the feast day of Ubaldo, Gubbio's patron saint, the **Corsa dei Ceri** (May 15) is little known outside Italy, but in Tuscany and Umbria ranks second only to Siena's Palio in its exuberance and bizarre pageantry. The rules and rigmarole of the nine-hundred-year-old ceremony are mind-boggling, but in essence begin with an early-morning Mass and a **procession** through the packed streets of the vast wooden **ceri** (candles), removed from Ubaldo's Monte Ingino basilica. Each is dedicated to a particular saint – **Ubaldo**, **Anthony** and **George**. At 10.30am another procession makes its way to the Piazza Grande, where an hour later the four-metre-high *ceri* are raised by members of the town's three traditional confraternities: the builders (represented by St Ubaldo), the artisans (St George) and the peasants (St Anthony). A statue of the relevant saint tops each column.

There follows yet another procession through the streets to show the *ceri* to the townspeople (and TV crews from across Italy). The pillars are then dumped until 4.30pm while all concerned adjoin for a gut-busting fish lunch in the Palazzo dei Consoli. Yet another procession ensues, during which the clergy are finally allowed to participate, a journey that takes the *ceri* through just about every last corner of the town.

Back in the Piazza Grande, at 6pm the mayor brandishes a white banner to signal the beginning of a **race**, the climax of the day, which involves carrying the *ceri* back up to the hilltop Basilica di Sant'Ubaldo. No sooner has the race begun than there's a stop at the Porta del Monte. It then resumes up the steep path to the basilica, each confraternity being allowed ten official carriers who have to be replaced every ten minutes – but without stopping. "Race" is something of a misnomer, however, for the *cero* of Ubaldo always wins, the other teams having to ensure they're in the basilica before the leaders shut the doors. The *ceri* are then left in the basilica, and the saints brought down in a candlelit procession. Thereafter there's more celebration and a good deal of drinking.

A scholarly debate rages over the origins of the event, generally cited as either a secular feast commemorating the day in 1155 when Ubaldo talked Barbarossa out of flattening Gubbio, or a hangover from some pagan fertility rite. These days the Church claims it as its own, though judging by the very phallic *ceri* and the roar that goes up when they're raised to the vertical in Piazza Grande, there's something more than Christian jubilation going on.

of land – the tablets consist of seven bronze slabs, four of which probably date from about 200 BC, and three from around 100 BC. They are the most significant extant record of the Umbrian language, believed to have been a vernacular tongue without standard written characters. The bastardized Latin and Etruscan of their texts aimed at producing a phonetic transliteration of the dialect, using the main languages of the day. Gubbio was close to the shrine of the so-called Apennine Jove, a major pagan deity visited by pilgrims from all over Italy, and it's thought the tablets were the work of Roman and Etruscan priests taking advantage of the established order to impose new religious cults in a region where their languages weren't understood. The ritual text – the most important to have survived from antiquity – comprises a prayer divided into stanzas, a list of Gubbio's enemies, and a series of instructions for conducting services and the art of divination from sacrificed animals and the flight of birds. Most importantly, they suggest Romans, Etruscans and Umbrians achieved some sort of coexistence, refuting a long-held belief that succeeding civilizations wiped out their predecessors.

Also worth hunting out in the museum are several key examples of Gubbio's **ceramic tradition**. Its greatest exponent, Maestro Giorgio Andreoli, was born in 1498, and distinguished himself by discovering gold and ruby glazes, the latter – *riverbero* – a colour you rarely see in ceramics as it's extremely difficult to achieve. Two works by Giorgio – *Circe* and the *Fall of Phaeton* – are on show in the Sala della Loggetta, from which a corridor leads to Room IV of the Pinacoteca.

The Pinacoteca and the Museo Archeologico

The **Pinacoteca** (same hours and ticket as Museo Civico) is housed in five wonderful medieval rooms at the top of a steep flight of steps on the *palazzo*'s second floor. Though the paintings aren't anything special, they trace the development of the Gubbian School, one of central Italy's earliest; names to look out for are Guido Palmerucci and Mello. Sienese artists are also represented, notably by Rutilio Manetti, the city's leading follower of Caravaggio, and there's a lovely *Crucifix* by the Maestro di San Francesco (best known for his work in the Basilica di San Francesco in Assisi). Don't miss the tremendous views over the Piazza Grande and the lower town from the palace's loggia, entered from the gallery.

The same ticket also allows you into the **Museo Archeologico** on the palace's lower floor, entered separately at the rear of the palace (the entrance is signed at the junction of Via dei Consoli and Via Gattapone). This is a rather patchy miscellany, with a Byzantine sarcophagus and a collection of Roman and Umbrian bronzes, carvings and other displays.

The Duomo

A couple of streets east of the Palazzo dei Consoli, the rather plain thirteenth-century Gothic **Duomo** (usually daily 9am–6pm, except during services) is redeemed by a fine interior. Immediately noticeable is the strange arched ceiling, a Gubbian speciality known as "wagon vaulting", in which the ten arches are gracefully curved, apparently to emulate the meeting of hands in prayer. There are some fine twelfth-century stained-glass windows, a glitzy Baroque chapel and a wealth of **frescoes** and **panel paintings**. Key works include *Adoration of the Shepherds* by Eusebio di San Giorgio (sixth niche on the north wall), a student of Pinturicchio; the adjoining altarpiece *Santa Maria Maddalena* (1521) by Timoteo Vito; and a painting next door by Sinibaldo Ibi, *Madonna and Child with Sts Ubaldo and Sebastian* (1507). In the last niche on the north wall is a beautifully restored picture of St Ubaldo with a lovely green background by the Gubbian painter Benedetto Nucci (1515–87). The **presbytery** contains a superb choir dating from 1549 – sadly, roped off – while the altar (a Roman sarcophagus) conceals the relics of saints Mariano and Giacomo, martyred in 259 in what is now Algeria. Back down the south wall towards the church entrance, the outstanding painting is a *Deposition* by Dono Doni, to the left of which is a good fragment of a fresco of *St Sebastian*. Off this side of the church is the gaudy **Cappella del SS Sacramento**, built on the orders of Alessandro Sperelli, a seventeenth-century bishop of Gubbio, who is buried inside.

The Museo Diocesano

A few paces down from the Duomo stands the modest but well-presented **Museo Diocesano** (daily: April–Oct 10am–7pm; Nov–March 10am–6pm; €4), housed in the old canons' palace. Its prize exhibit is a florid Flemish cloak – parts of which were stolen in 1990 – presented to the cathedral by Pope Marcellus II, a former bishop of Gubbio, in 1555: extravagantly embroidered, it portrays scenes from the Passion. There are also a number of frescoes removed from the crypt of the church of Santa Maria dei Laici and other fifteenth-century murals, as well as the interesting *Madonna in Glory*; this painting had long been attributed to Guiduccio Palmerucci, considered Gubbio's earliest documented fourteenth-century painter, but recent restoration has revealed a new signature, *Opus Melli Eugubii* ("a work by Mello di Gubbio", a previously unknown artist).

The Palazzo Ducale

Opposite the Duomo – and overshadowing it – is the **Palazzo Ducale** (Tues–Sun 8.30am–7pm; €2), built in 1470 over an earlier Lombard palace and the twelfth-century Palazzo Comunale by Federigo da Montefeltro, the renowned duke of Urbino, and designed as a scaled-down copy of his palace in that town. The architect of the two buildings was probably the same man, Dalmatian-born Luciano Laurana, selected by Federigo after he'd failed to find a suitably bold Florentine designer. The calm Renaissance **courtyard** sets the tone, close to which a stone staircase leads down to a series of vaulted store-rooms and excavations that have revealed the remains of four earlier buildings on the site. Among them are fragments from the tenth century and remnants of the former Palazzo Comunale.

As in Urbino, many of the rooms of the main palace appeal as much for their measured architectural calm as for any paintings or furniture. Most are virtually empty, however, and the result is frankly dull, though the views make some amends. The **duke's study** (off room 2) was left bare after its intarsia wood panelling was stripped in the nineteenth century (it found its way to the Metropolitan Museum in New York). The stone-carved windows and doorways are superb, however, as are the fireplaces and terracotta floors. The central **Salone** offers lovely views of the Palazzo dei Consoli and contains a fireplace that must have worked wonders during Gubbio's mountain-cold winters.

The northern quarters

Wandering the streets around town you'll soon come across examples of **Porte della Morte** ("Doors of Death") – narrow, bricked-up doorways wedged into the facades of medieval town houses, a conundrum found only in Gubbio, Assisi and southern France. The party line has it they were cut to carry a coffin out of the house and then, having been tainted by death, sealed up – a nice theory, and very Italian, but to judge by the constricted stairways behind the doors, their purpose was probably defensive: the main door could be barricaded, leaving the more easily defended passageway as the only entrance. Gubbio's best examples are in Via dei Consoli. There are dozens of similar picturesque odds and ends around Gubbio's streets, which lend themselves to a slow ramble. Some of the best are in the north: the lanes around San Domenico, and especially along the banks of the Camignano, are the most tempting. Via Baldassini, below Piazza Grande, is also worth a stroll.

En route to these points from Piazza Grande, the **Bargello** – built in 1302 as the medieval police station – in Via dei Consoli is worth tracking down, as it's one of the town's more attractive medieval buildings. Furthermore, the adjoining **Fontana dei Matti** (Fountain of the Mad) was once Gubbio's prime water source but is now undistinguished, save for the tradition that anyone walking round it three times will wind up deranged. There's usually someone about wondering whether to give it a go; you qualify for a *patente da matto* ("licence of madness") if you make the run and are simultaneously soaked with water by three locals. Via dei Consoli is home to most of Gubbio's **ceramic shops**, together with Officina Libris, a shop selling paper and leather-bound books, at no. 39.

From here you can head east towards the funicular (see opposite) or drop down to look into the nearby church of **San Domenico** (closed at the time of writing for long-term restoration), distinguished by a fine intarsia lectern, or take in the impressive fifteenth-century **Palazzo Beni** and Palazzo del Capitano del Popolo, the latter home to an odd little private museum of modern sculpture and medieval torture instruments.

Following the walls anticlockwise back to the Piazza Quaranta Martiri, you could detour to the **Anfiteatro Romano** (daily: April–Sept 8.30am–7.30pm; Oct–March 8am–1.30pm; free). Built in the first century AD, it's one of the largest in the Roman world, at 112m in diameter. It retains its seats and much of the lower arcades – the arena providing the setting for a summer festival of Shakespeare and classical drama. Current excavations are uncovering more remains.

The southern quarters

A path near the Duomo zigzags up Monte Ingino, but the panoramic way up is to take the highly recommended funicular (see opposite). En route to the base station at Porta Romana – walk part of the way on **Corso Garibaldi** for a good view of the large eighteenth-century statue of St Ubaldo at the street's end – you can take in Ottaviano Nelli's masterpiece, the winsome *Madonna del Belvedere* (1413) in the deconsecrated **Santa Maria Nuova**, together with patches of fresco left by his pupils (if the church is shut, try the custodian at Via Dante 66). Little **Sant'Andrea** nearby, probably of eleventh-century foundation and recently restored, is also worth a passing look. Porta Romana itself has a small museum, the **Museo della Ceramica a Lustro e della Torre Medioevale** (daily: June–Sept 9am–1pm & 3.30–8pm; Oct–May 10.30am–1pm & 3.30–7pm; €2.50), devoted to local ceramics and displays on the mechanics of defending a medieval gateway.

Just outside the walls, the thirteenth-century **Sant'Agostino** is notable for its apse, which is smothered in 26 Nelli frescoes of *Scenes from the Life of St Augustine* (1420); there's a light on the right (south) side alongside a glass casket containing the waxy image of Beato Pietro of Gubbio. The entire church was once frescoed, and tantalizing fragments remain dotted around the walls: the sixth arch-cum-chapel on the right has a particularly good fresco by a follower of Nelli; the third arch has a painting by Nelli and his workshop showing the Madonna with saints, angels and purged souls; and on the north wall the fifth altar features an anonymous *Madonna del Soccorso* (1485) with various Augustinian saints.

Monte Ingino

You can walk to **Monte Ingino** (827m), one of the mountains above Gubbio, from Porta Sant'Ubaldo near the Duomo (a stiff climb) or drive there from Porta Metauro in the north. The most entertaining way to reach the top, however, is courtesy of the six-minute **funicular** from Porta Romana (July & Aug Mon–Sat 8.30am–7.30pm, Sun 8.30am–8pm; June & Sept Mon–Sat 9.30am–7pm, Sun 9am–7.30pm; April & May Mon–Sat 10am–6.30pm, Sun 9.30am–7pm; Oct daily 10am–6pm; March Mon–Sat 10am–5.30pm, Sun 9.30am–6pm; Nov & Dec Thurs–Tues 10am–5pm; €5 return). It has open ski-lift type cages holding two people, and affords ample time to admire the view – and to study your cage's welding and bolts, which are all that lie between you and oblivion. Beware the off-season break for lunch (March–May & Oct–Dec daily, June Mon–Sat closed 1.15–2.30pm).

Once you're atop Monte Ingino, the views and a bar are the main attractions. Even better vistas are at hand if you climb up to the **Rocca**. The **Basilica di Sant'Ubaldo**, five minutes from the top station, is not of great interest, though it's revered for the body of the town's patron saint, whose missing three fingers were hacked off by his manservant as a religious keepsake. Inside, you can't miss the big wooden pillars, or *ceri* (candles), featured in Gubbio's annual *Corsa dei Ceri* (see box, p.511).

Eating

Gubbio offers some fine small-town cooking. Cheaper **restaurants** can be found at the northern end of Via dei Consoli, and for picnic supplies there's a **supermarket** at Via Nicola Vantaggi, plus a good bakery at Via dei Consoli 27 and a fruit and vegetable store two doors below that.

Bosone Via XX Settembre 22 ☎075.922.0688. Thanks to its garden, the restaurant of the *Bosone* hotel is the nicest place to eat outdoors in the summer. Prices are little over the average for the town, at around €12 for mains. Closed Wed except June–Sept.

Fabiani Piazza Quaranta Martiri 26a/b ☎075.927.4639, ⓦwww.ristorantefabiani.it. Fine, friendly place, with several dining rooms set in part of the elegant Palazzo Fabiani, with an attractive terrace for summer dining. Good value (meals from around €30), given the quality of the cooking. Closed Tues.

Grotta dell'Angelo Via Gioia 47 ☎075.927.3438. Annexed to the *Grotta dell'Angelo* hotel (see p.507), offering very tasty and reasonably priced basic

meals in a wonderful dining room or a delightful garden in the summer. Closed Tues.

La Fornace di Maestro Giorgio Via Maestro Giorgio 2 ☎075.922.1836. Vaguely modish and usually less costly upmarket rival to the *Taverna del Lupo*. Attractive period dining rooms sited in the converted workshop of one of Gubbio's medieval master ceramacists. Full meals come in around €40 and the wine list offers 500 choices. Closed Tues and a period in Feb.

Taverna del Lupo Via Ansidei 21 ☎075.927.4368, ⓦwww.mencarelligroup.com. A smart and long-established place in an attractive medieval setting, well worth a splurge (mains around €18) for its classic Umbrian dishes and excellent truffle risotto. Closed Mon.

Gualdo Tadino

The main centre east of Gubbio is **GUALDO TADINO**, a hill-town that takes its name from the German *Wald* (wood), a throwback to the days of the Holy Roman Empire and Italy's northern European rulers ("Tadino" was only tagged on in 1833). It occupies the site of ancient **Tadinum**, a Roman staging post on the Via Flaminia, and lies close to the site of the battlefield at which Narses, a eunuch and renowned Byzantine general, killed Totila and won a famous victory over the Goths in 552. Later it was the birthplace of **Matteo da Gualdo** (1435–1513), an accomplished but little-known painter (at least outside Umbria) whose works crop up in Assisi, Trevi and Spoleto, as well as in his home town.

Today, the town, which sprawls over the lower slopes of the Apennines, has the remote outpost feel of other eastern Umbrian towns. But while the medieval centre is a touch bleak, with little of substance to see, it's quiet and atmospheric, and makes a good base for exploring the beautiful Monte Cucco region (see opposite). Economic well-being flows from the town's renowned **ceramics**, best seen during a big summer exhibition devoted to the craft. The town was badly hit by the 1997 earthquake; accessibility and opening times of all sites remain erratic for the foreseeable future. The town is best seen as part of a day-trip that might also take in the mountains to the east and north. It's an easy trip by **bus** from Gubbio, and three buses run daily from Foligno (Mon–Sat); **trains** from Assisi, Foligno or Spoleto are frequent, and there's a shuttle bus from the train station to the old centre.

The Town

The Gothic **Duomo** (1256), also known as San Benedetto, is located in the central Piazza Martiri della Libertà, and boasts a three-tiered facade, a fine carved doorway and a rose window; the interior, though, was done to death in the nineteenth century. The little fountain on the building's Corso Italia flank is attributed to Antonio da Sangallo the Elder. Opposite the cathedral is the **Palazzo Comunale**, of eighteenth-century vintage, and close by is the nicely restored **Palazzo del Podestà**. Various works of art left to the cathedral over the years are hidden from public view owing to lack of funds and the high probability they'll be lifted by thieves.

Similar worries prevailed in the town's art gallery, which is closed indefinitely, though most of its works have been moved to the **Museo Civico** (June–Sept Tues–Sun 10.30am–1pm & 4–7pm; April & May Thurs–Sun 10.30am–1pm & 3.30–6pm; Oct–March Sat & Sun 10.30am–1pm & 3–6pm; €3), housed in the imposing Rocca Flea in Via della Rocca, a fine-looking fortress reconstructed by Emperor Frederick II. It's arranged in three sections, including an antiquarium with archeological finds from the town and its surroundings; a section devoted to ceramics, for centuries the town's economic lifeblood; and a picture gallery, the real reason for a visit. Most of the gallery exhibits are by Matteo da Gualdo, mercilessly lampooned by nineteenth-century critics for his "incorrect drawing", though his brilliant colouring has since restored him to critical favour. However, Matteo's paintings, together with a Sienese *Coronation of the Virgin* by Sano di Pietro, are eclipsed by a sublime polyptych (1471) by **Niccolò Alunno**, whom Berenson described as "the first painter in whom the emotional, now passionate and violent, now mystic and ecstatic, temperament of St Francis's countrymen was revealed".

The church of **San Francesco**, if open (call ☎075.915.021 for information), is also pictorially rewarding. Deconsecrated, its airy interior is used for temporary exhibitions, and features frescoes on the *Life of St Julian* (1469) by the school of Ottaviano Nelli (above the west door), a lunette with a damaged *Madonna* (high on the south wall), and a large painted Crucifix in the apse by a follower of the Maestro di San Francesco (see p.528). On the north side of the church also look out for part of a Roman sarcophagus flanked by two winged figures representing Victory, and the unmissable raised fourteenth-century pulpit. Among the apse frescoes is a *Crucifixion* by **Matteo da Gualdo**, who also left a *Madonna and Child with St Francis* in the third arch on the left and another *Madonna and Child* on the pillar between the first and second chapels: the last is the artist's oldest known work. There's another bright Matteo triptych – the *Madonna and Child with Sts Sebastian and Roch* – in the church of **Santa Maria dei Raccomandati** in Piazza XX Settembre, close by. If the paintings of Matteo appeal, it's worth driving to the hill-village of **San Pellegrino**, 6km northwest off the SS219 Gubbio road, where the church of San Facondino (note the tenth-century tower) has several of his frescoes and a triptych (1465) by Giovanni di Camerino, recovered after its theft.

Parco Regionale del Monte Cucco

Some of Umbria's best upland scenery is to be found in the mountains east and north of Gualdo on the border with the Marche, much of it protected by the **Parco Regionale del Monte Cucco**. Where this area really scores is in its organized trails and backup for outdoor activities of every kind; if you want to don walking boots without too much fuss, this is the area to do it – and the chances are you won't meet another soul all day. Access is easy, with **buses** from Gualdo to Valsorda and from Perugia, Gualdo, Gubbio and Assisi to Costacciaro.

The southernmost base for exploration of the park is the resort of **Valsorda** (1000m), 8km northeast of Gualdo. Regular buses run from Gualdo to the village, which is a launching pad for easy hill walks and is a reasonably scenic, if developed, spot in its own right. You can tackle the straightforward trek up **Serra Santa** (1421m), on a track of motorway proportions carved out by pilgrims over the years. From the summit you could then drop into the spectacular **Valle del Fonno** gorge and follow it down to Gualdo. Paths follow the main ridge from Valsorda north and south, and it's feasible to walk all the way to Nocera Umbra.

To get closer to the heart of the mountains, head north from Gualdo past **Fossato di Vico**, a hill-town with the eleventh-century Romanesque San Pietro, and the small Cappella della Piaggiola, which contains some fine frescoes by the school of Ottaviano Nelli. Beyond Fossato the road passes through **Sigillo** and then, 3km further on, **Costacciaro**, a town that looks rather as if it has tried to attract tourists and failed: it is a centre of sorts for the park's outdoor pursuits and access point for the **Grotta di Monte Cucco**, at 922m the fifth-deepest cave system in the world. The cave was explored as early as 1889, but has only recently been opened up by the hundreds of cavers that flock here from all over Europe; over 40km of galleries have now been charted. Above, the huge, bare-sloped Monte Cucco (1566m) is the main playground for walkers.

Practicalities

For **information**, head to the park's administrative office, at Via Matteotti 52 in Sigillo (℡075.917.7326, Ⓦwww.parks.it/parco.monte.cucco), or to the Centro Escursionistico Naturalistico Speleologico in Costacciaro (Calcinaro 7a; ℡075.917.0400, Ⓦwww.cens.it). Unusually for Italy, reasonable **maps** are available: the 1:50,000 *Kompass #665 Assisi–Camerino* covers the area around Gualdo, and there's a special trail map that you may be able to pick up in Sigillo or Costacciaro; newsagents and bookshops sometimes stock it.

The **hotel** *Monte Cucco di Tobia* (☎075.917.7194, ⓦ www.albergomontecucco
.it; Easter–Oct; ❶) is a fabled mountaineers' and cavers' hangout in the Val di
Ranco east of Sigillo. In Sigillo, the only hotel is the three-star *Dominus*, Via
Matteotti 55 (☎075.917.9074, ⓦ www.dominushotel.it; ❷). Both have **restaurants** (*Monte Cucco's* 200-seat place is closed Mon). The nearest **campsite** for the
park is *Rio Verde* (☎075.917.0138, ⓦ www.campingrioverde.it; Easter–Sept; ❶) at
Fornace, 3km north of Costacciaro. It also offers bungalows for two and four
people at €20 per person (€25 July & Aug). Camping is prohibited within the
park, but elsewhere you'll have few problems finding a discreet pitch for a tent.
At Valsorda, perched at 1010m is the forty-pitch one-star campsite *Valsorda*
(☎075.913.261; June–Sept).

Travel details

Trains

Città di Castello to: Perugia (hourly; 50min);
Sansepolcro (hourly; 20min).
Fossato di Vico (for Gubbio) to: Foligno (9–13
daily; 45min); Gualdo Tadino (8–11 daily; 10min);
Nocera Umbra (8–11 daily; 20min); Orte (10 daily;
1hr 55min); Rome (10 daily; 2hr 40min); Spoleto
(10 daily; 1hr 15min); Terni (10 daily; 1hr 30min).
Perugia to: Assisi (hourly; 25min); Città di Castello
(hourly; 50min); Deruta (hourly; 30min); Florence
(6 daily; 2hr 15min); Foligno (hourly; 40min – for
connections to Spoleto, Fossato di Vico, Terni, Narni
and Orte); Passignano (hourly; 30min); Sansepolcro
(hourly; 1hr 40min); Spello (hourly; 35min); Terni
(hourly; 1hr 50min); Teróntola (hourly; 40min – for
6 connections daily to Rome and Siena); Todi
(hourly; 50min).

Buses

Città di Castello to: Rome Tiburtina (1 daily; 3hr
15min); Rome Fiumicino airport (Mon–Sat 1 daily;
3hr 50min); Todi (Mon–Sat 1 daily; 2hr).

Gubbio to: Florence (Mon–Sat 1 daily; 2hr 30min);
Fossato di Vico train station, continuing to Gualdo
Tadino and Nocera Umbra (Mon–Sat 10 daily, 6 on
Sun; 30min); Perugia (Mon–Sat 10 daily, 4 on Sun;
1hr 10min); Rome (1 daily; 2hr 40min); Umbertide
(3 daily; 50min).
Perugia to: Ascoli Piceno (1–4 daily; 3hr); Assisi
(3–12 daily; 30min); Castiglione del Lago (Mon–Sat
7–9 daily; 1hr 15min); Chiusi (Mon–Sat 5 daily;
1hr 45min); Città della Pieve (Mon–Sat 5 daily;
1hr 30min); Florence (1 daily; 2hr); Gualdo Tadino
(Mon–Sat 6 daily, 2 on Sun; 1hr 25min); Gubbio
(Mon–Sat 10 daily, 4 on Sun; 1hr 10min); Nocera
Umbra (Mon–Sat 1 daily; 1hr 20min); Norcia
(1 daily; 2hr 50min); Orvieto (1 daily; 2hr 25min);
Passignano (Mon–Sat 7 daily; 1hr 10min); Rome
(2–6 daily; 2hr 30min); Rome Fiumicino airport
(1–3 daily; 3hr); Siena (3–7 daily; 1hr 30min);
Spello (Mon–Sat 4 daily; 55min); Spoleto (Mon–Sat
1 daily; 1hr 20min); Todi via Deruta (Mon–Sat
3–7 daily; 1hr 15min); Torgiano (Mon–Sat 7 daily;
30min).

11

Assisi and the Vale of Spoleto

CHAPTER 11

Highlights

* **Basilica di San Francesco, Assisi** One of Italy's great buildings, and the burial place of St Francis. See p.526

* **Tempio di Minerva, Assisi** An excellently preserved first-century temple front. See p.536

* **Spello** Charming hill-town, whose church of Santa Maria Maggiore hosts a fresco cycle by Pinturicchio. See p.543

* **Monte Subasio** Great walks and drives on the mountain above Assisi, with spectacular views and superb spring flowers. See p.548

* **Bevagna** Captivating village, known for its medieval main square and fine Romanesque churches. See p.551

* **Montefalco** Home of the outstanding Sagrantino Passito wine, plus a major fresco cycle by Benozzo Gozzoli. See p.554

* **Trevi** The most spectacularly sited of the Umbrian hill-towns. See p.558

▲ Carving on the portal of the church of San Michele, Bevagna

Assisi and the Vale of Spoleto

The **Vale of Spoleto**, the broad plain between Perugia and Spoleto, is Umbria's historic and spiritual heartland: a sweep of countryside that is beautiful in parts and has a majestic focus in **Assisi**. Birthplace of St Francis, Italy's premier saint, this hill-town has been an object of pilgrimage for over seven hundred years, now attracting a staggering five million or more visitors annually. It has also long emerged from the trauma of the 1997 earthquake, which brought the town to worldwide prominence when part of the famous Basilica di San Francesco collapsed, killing four.

Quieter hill-towns are just around the corner. **Spello**, the most accessible, remains just ahead of the tourist boom – though the visitors have arrived – and features more art treasures in the shape of Pinturicchio's frescoes in the church of Santa Maria Maggiore. Nearby **Bevagna**, like Spello an outpost on the Roman Via Flaminia, is a tiny, wall-enclosed village locked around a central square that's almost without equal in Umbria. Lording it over the vale is **Montefalco**, a windblown hive of medieval streets that is home to yet another superb fresco cycle – this one by the Tuscan Benozzo Gozzoli – and one of the province's strangest attractions, a quartet of mummified holy corpses. Across the valley is **Trevi**, relatively little visited, but in the throes of a renaissance and perhaps the most perfectly situated of all Italian hill-towns.

Foligno, the regional capital, has a limited appeal but is useful for accommodation and as a transport hub. The main **rail** link from Rome to Ancona passes through Foligno, from where there are connections to Spoleto, Terni and Narni to the south, Nocera and Gualdo Tadino to the north, and a branch line spur that runs to Teróntola via Spello, Assisi and Perugia. **Buses** radiate from Foligno to the local villages, and there are frequent connections between Perugia, Assisi and further south. **Road** journeys are quick thanks to the dual carriageway (SS3) between Perugia and Foligno.

Assisi

ASSISI would be an irresistible target even without its great Basilica and Franciscan sideshow. Visible for miles around, it sits enticingly beneath the whaleback slopes of Monte Subasio, the prominent castle and pink-stoned medieval houses lording it over the Vale of Spoleto. Millions come as an act of faith, but a substantial number visit simply to see the sublime paintings in the **Basilica di San Francesco**, where frescoes by **Giotto** and **Pietro Lorenzetti** comprise one of the greatest monuments of Italian art. Yet for all the coach parties of pilgrims, both religious and secular, Assisi just about remains a town with an uncompromised identity – as an overnight stay, after the car parks have cleared, will reveal. At close quarters, the tacky tourist paraphernalia and religious kitsch are offset by tranquil backstreets, geranium-filled windowboxes and buildings in the muted, rosy stone that distinguishes all the vale's towns. With sufficient enthusiasm you can see almost all the sights in a day, but be warned: this is the third most visited pilgrimage site in Italy (after St Peter's in Rome and Padre Pio's shrine in Puglia).

Assisi's **history** is not all tied to the Franciscan masthead. Founded by the **Umbrians** – in contrast to Perugia's Etruscan heritage – the town later

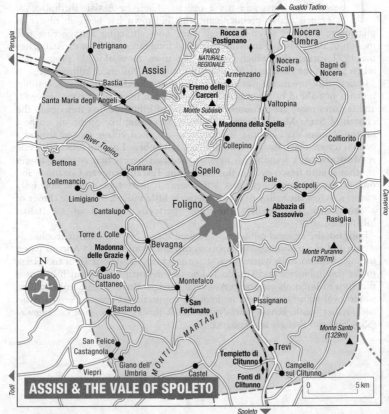

ASSISI & THE VALE OF SPOLETO

0   5 km

achieved prominence as Asisium, a **Roman** *municipium*. Thereafter invaders passed it over, attracted by the richer pickings of Perugia, but in the end it fell under the control of that city's monstrous **Baglioni** family. These were characters, said one Franciscan historian, "who did not shudder to murder men, cook their flesh, and give it to the relations of the slain to eat in their prison dungeons". Plague, famine and eventually Church control turned the town into a moribund backwater. However, Francis's elevation to the status of national saint in 1939 managed to reverse its economic decline, and today religious and other tourism has made this a very prosperous town indeed.

Arrival and information

There are roughly hourly **trains** from Foligno (via Spello) and from Teróntola (via Perugia, which is only thirty minutes away) to Assisi's station, located in the modern suburb of Santa Maria degli Angeli, 5km southwest of the old town. Roughly half-hourly buses from the station (tickets from the station kiosk) take twenty minutes to reach **Piazza Unità d'Italia** below the Basilica or **Piazza Matteotti**, some by way of Largo Properzio, south of the Basilica di Santa Chiara – from where there's an unreliable escalator to the gateway at Porta Nuova. Both squares are less than five-minutes' walk from the heart of the medieval town, **Piazza del Comune**. The town slopes steeply from the Basilica di San Francesco in the west to Piazza Matteotti in the east, so wherever you arrive or stay, you can be faced with a climb.

The main **bus terminal** is in Piazza Matteotti. Long-distance Sulga buses (☎075.500.9641, ⓦ www.sulga.it) to Florence, Rome, Milan and Naples use Piazza San Pietro, at the other end of town. Note that Perugia airport (see p.475) is actually roughly equidistant between Perugia and Assisi, or about 15km from the latter.

Parking in central Assisi is virtually impossible. It's best to leave cars at the underground car park in Piazza Matteotti or in Piazza Unità d'Italia. There are hundreds of free spaces up by the Rocca, a long walk to the Basilica, and by the cemetery off Viale Albornoz on the road from Porta San Giacomo. Other fringe car parks are located outside Porta Nuova and Porta Moiano. Orange **minibuses** A and B provide connecting services around the town, though distances are short and it's easiest to walk; tickets are sold at shops and newsagents displaying an ASP or *Comune di Assisi* sign.

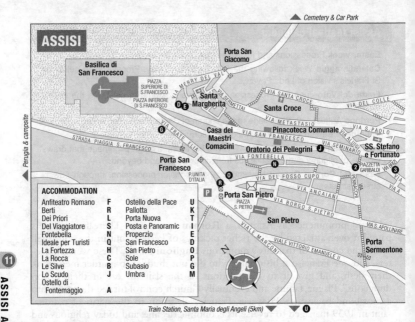

ASSISI

Basilica di
San Francesco

PIAZZA
SUPERIORE DI
S.FRANCESCO

PIAZZA INFERIORE
DI S.FRANCESCO

Porta San
Giacomo

VIA MERRY DEL VAL

VIA SAN SPAGNETTI
Santa
Margherita

D E

VIA SANTA CROCE

Santa Croce

VIA DEL COLLE

VIA METASTASIO

VIA S. PAOLO

VIA FRATE ELIA

Casa dei
Maestri
Comacini

G

STRADA PIAGGIA S. FRANCESCO

Porta San
Francesco

P.UNITA
D'ITALIA

VIA SAN FRANCESCO

Pinacoteca Comunale

VIA S. ALTIGO

VIA SEMINARIO

SS. Stefano
e Fortunato

Oratorio dei Pellegrini

J

PIAZZETTA
GARIBALDI

2

3

VIA FONTEBELLA

N

VIA A

VIA A A

PINACCHI

O

VIA DEL FOSSO CUPO

P

Porta San Pietro

R

PIAZZA
S. PIETRO

VIA ANCAIANI

VIA BORGO S. PIETRO

San Pietro

VIA S. APOLLINARE

VIALE MARCONI

VIALE VITTORIO EMANUELE II

Porta
Sermentone

Perugia & campsite ◀

Perugia ◀

ACCOMMODATION

Anfiteatro Romano	F	Ostello della Pace	U
Berti	R	Pallotta	K
Dei Priori	L	Porta Nuova	T
Del Viaggiatore	S	Posta e Panoramic	I
Fontebella	N	Properzio	E
Ideale per Turisti	Q	San Francesco	D
La Fortezza	H	San Pietro	O
La Rocca	C	Sole	P
Le Silve	B	Subasio	G
Lo Scudo	J	Umbra	M
Ostello di Fontemaggio	A		

N

The **tourist office** is at the western end of Piazza del Comune (April–Oct Mon–Sat 8am–2pm & 3–6.30pm, Sun 10am–1pm & 2–7pm, but Sun hours vary; Nov–March Mon–Sat 8am–2pm & 3–6pm, Sun 9am–1pm; ☎075.812.534 or 075.813.8680, ⓔinfo@iat.assisi.pg.it), and there are usually **summer information offices** in Largo Properzio near Porta Nuova (☎075.816.766), with lots of accommodation information, at Santa Maria degli Angeli (☎075.812.479), and at the train station (☎075.813.499).

Accommodation

There are getting on for a hundred **hotels** in Assisi, though advance booking is still highly advisable, and essential if you plan to visit over Easter or during the Festa di San Francesco (Oct 3–4) or Calendimaggio (the week after the first Tues in May). The tourist office can provide full accommodation lists, including *agriturismi* and **rooms** for rent (ask for the *extralberghieri*), and will make reservations for you; try to avoid the cheaper places in San Pietro Campagna, Santa Maria degli Angeli and the grim little village of Bastia, 4km out.

The tourist office carries a list of many dozens of often extraordinarily cheap **pilgrim hostels** (*Case Religiose di Ospitalità*), usually open to both women and men and requiring booking in advance. Most offer singles and doubles and sometimes a couple of dorm rooms. Costs are around €20–25 per person, depending on whether rooms have private bathrooms and how many people are sharing. Virtually all provide breakfast for an extra couple of euros, plus very reasonable half- and full-board options.

There's a two-star **campsite** attached to the *Fontemaggio* hostel (see p.526), open all year and with full services; the *Internazionale Assisi*, Via San Giovanni in Campiglione 110 (☎075.813.710, ⓦwww.campingassisi.it; April to mid-Oct),

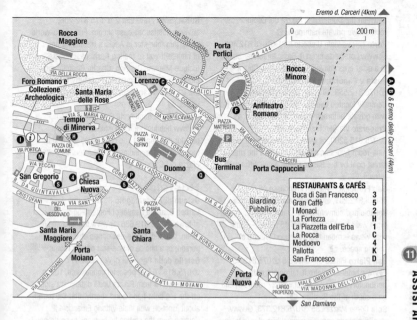

Eremo d. Carceri (4km)

0   200 m

RESTAURANTS & CAFÉS
Buca di San Francesco	3
Gran Caffè	5
I Monaci	2
La Fortezza	H
La Piazzetta dell'Erba	1
La Rocca	C
Medioevo	4
Pallotta	K
San Francesco	D

San Damiano

is three-star but in not such a pleasant setting, 3km west of Assisi on the SS147 to Bastia.

Hotels

Anfiteatro Romano Via Anfiteatro Romano 4 ℡075.813.025, ℻075.815.110. Good-value one-star hotel, in one of the most pleasant parts of town. Seven rooms, en suite and not. ❶

Berti Piazza San Pietro 29 ℡075.813.466, ⓦwww.hotelberti.it. Two-star with a/c rooms located in a quiet piazza, handy for the Basilica. ❸

Dei Priori Corso Mazzini 15 ℡075.812.237, ⓦwww.assisi-hotel.com. Rates vary considerably between rooms at this three-star, 34-room hotel, but expect to pay €115 for a standard high-season double. ❷–❺

Del Viaggiatore Via Sant'Antonio 14 ℡075.816.297, ⓦwww.albergodelviaggiatore .com. Small, personal, eleven-room two-star above a decent restaurant in the web of streets between Santa Maria Maggiore and Piazza del Comune. ❷

Fontebella Via Fontebella 25 ℡075.812.456, ⓦwww.fontebella.com. By far the most elegant and intimate of Assisi's smart hotels, despite its three-star rating. Try for a room on one of the top two floors for views over the rooftops and the Vale of Spoleto. ❼

Ideale per Turisti Piazza Matteotti 1 ℡075.813.570, ⓦwww.hotelideale.it. Follow signs south from Piazza Matteotti a short way outside the

walls to reach this slightly outlying but very reasonable eleven-room two-star hotel. All rooms have private bathroom. Hotel parking is a bonus. ❸

La Fortezza Vicolo della Fortezza 19b ℡075.812.418, ⓦwww.lafortezzahotel.com. Friendly two-star with just seven rooms in a perfect central position just off Piazza del Comune: the restaurant is also excellent. ❷

La Rocca Via di Porta Perlici 27 ℡&℻075.812.284. A fifteen-room one-star beyond the Duomo at the very end of Via di Porta Perlici. Quiet and with fine views from some rooms; most with own bath. ❶

Le Silve Caparrocchie, near Armenzano ℡075.801.9000, ⓦwww.lesilve.it. This delightful hotel in lovely countryside 10km east of Assisi on the slopes of Monte Subasio makes an excellent, if expensive, alternative to staying in town. A traditional, converted rural house (parts of which date back to the tenth century), it offers a swimming pool, tennis and riding. ❻

Lo Scudo Via San Francesco 3 ℡&℻075.813.196. A small sign outside a pretty medieval house signals this well-placed seven-room one-star; despite its modest rating, all rooms have private bathrooms and you're at the heart of the action. ❷

Pallotta Via San Rufino 6 ℡075.812.307, ⓦwww .pallottaassisi.it. Small two-star in a good location

525

between the Duomo and Piazza del Comune; all rooms have private bathroom. ❷

Porta Nuova Viale Umberto I, 21 ☎075.812.405, ⓦwww.hotelportanuova.it. Basic three-star standby in a quiet area above Basilica di Santa Chiara. ❸

Posta e Panoramic Via San Paolo 17–19 ☎075.812.558, ⓦwww.hotelpostaassisi.it. Centrally located two-star with fourteen rooms (all with private bathroom) west of the Duomo. ❶

Properzio Via San Francesco 38b ☎075.815.5200, ⓦwww.hotelproperzio.it. Simple nine-room two-star, handily placed on the main street right by the Basilica, with a delightful roof terrace. ❷

San Francesco Via San Francesco 48 ☎075.812.281, ⓦwww.hotelsanfrancescoassisi.it. Reliable and conveniently situated three-star just 1min walk from the Basilica; 45 rooms – some with views – mean there's a good chance of finding space. ❹

San Pietro Piazza San Pietro 5 ☎075.812.452, ⓦwww.hotel-sanpietro.it. Large but rather perfunctory three-star hotel with 37 rooms by the gate south of the Basilica. ❹

Sole Corso Mazzini 35 ☎075.812.373, ⓦwww.assisihotelsole.com. Functional two-star hotel in a convenient position 1min walk from the Basilica di Santa Chiara. Also has an annexe at Corso Mazzini 20. Rooms vary in price, so ask to see a range. ❷

Subasio Via Frate Elia 2 ☎075.812.206, ⓦwww.hotelsubasioassisi.com. Full of old-world style, this four-star is Assisi's traditional hotel of choice if you're feeling flush: past guests include Marlene Dietrich, Charlie Chaplin and Elizabeth Taylor. Surprisingly unstuffy for all that; the 61 rooms vary considerably, but most have views. ❻

Umbra Vicolo degli Archi 6 ☎075.812.240, ⓦwww.hotelumbra.it. An excellent and very popular mid-market choice, with 25 three-star rooms almost immediately off the southern edge of Piazza del Comune. ❹

Hostels

Ostello di Fontemaggio Strada Eremo delle Carceri 8, at the hamlet of Fontemaggio, 2km east of town ☎075.813.636, ⓦwww.fontemaggio.it. Clean, ten-bed, single-sex dorms at €20 per person; or a choice of one-star private rooms.

Ostello della Pace Via di Valecchie 177 ☎075.816.767. In peaceful countryside, 10min walk downhill from Piazza Unità d'Italia. It's signed off the big right-hand bend shortly after the round-about junction with Viale Vittorio Emanuele II. Coming from the station by bus, ask to be dropped at "Villa Guardi": the hostel is signposted from here. Dorm beds €16, plus half- and full-board deals.

The Basilica di San Francesco

The **Basilica di San Francesco** is a major site of worldwide Catholic pilgrimage, and its cycle of paintings by Giotto has long been considered one of the turning points in Western art, moving from the Byzantine world of iconic saints and Madonnas to one of humanist narrative.

The construction of the Basilica is in two tiers, with the **Upper Church** placed above the **Lower Church**. This posed enormous engineering problems, which were solved by the use of massive arched buttressing that effectively propped up the western end of the town. One of the wonders of early medieval architecture, its creator remains unknown: all the original drawings were burnt in a raid by the Perugians. Most historians presume it to have been the work of Lombard masons, who would have drawn their inspiration from the Gothic churches of southern France. As one of the earliest examples of Italian Gothic, the Basilica exerted great architectural influence, its single-naved Upper Church becoming a model for countless Franciscan churches around the country.

The history of the Basilica

The Basilica was conceived, shortly after Francis's death, by the man who had taken over the running of the order a decade or so earlier, one **Elias of Cortona**. Elias, one of the saint's earliest disciples, served as vicar-general of the Franciscans until 1239, presiding over a series of bitter disputes and schisms, until he was deposed and excommunicated. In the early years of the post-Francis order, however, he ran things very much his way, capitalizing on the saint's popular appeal to build the Franciscans into a powerful force, and raising the money to make the founder's Basilica one of the great Christian shrines. To the horror of the more ascetic and zealous followers of the saint – to whom Francis himself was allied in his final years – Elias set about a massive fundraising project, selling religious indulgences across Europe. The "fundamentalist" wing argued that the indulgences were a corruption, and the Basilica's proposed magnificence at odds with Francis's preference for smaller churches. They pointed out, too, that Francis's choice of **burial site** was intended as a gesture of humility: he had picked one of the most despised spots of medieval Assisi, known as the Colle del Inferno, where criminals were taken for execution. It was to no avail. The burial site was rechristened Colle del Paradiso and a building more ambitious than any in Italy was begun.

While **construction** of the Basilica proceeded, the **political background** became increasingly murky, the strangest twist coming on the day of Francis's canonization. Elias by this time had fallen out with the papacy, which was organizing the ceremony, and as the saint's hearse proceeded through the streets of Assisi, he and a posse burst onto the scene and seized the body. Ignoring the anger of the crowd and the indignation of the papal entourage, they hurried the coffin into the Lower Church and bolted the doors behind them. Prompted perhaps by the fear that his master's remains would be stolen or desecrated (medieval relics had enormous financial and spiritual value), Elias had decided to bury Francis in a **secret tomb** deep within the Basilica. The episode gave rise to a myth, recycled by Vasari, that a vast hidden church had been built below the Basilica, far greater in beauty and grandeur than the churches above. Inside this sealed chamber it was believed the body of the "almost alive saint" hovered above the altar awaiting his call to heaven. The tomb remained undiscovered, or at least unreached, until a two-month search in 1818.

The **1997 earthquakes** could have been catastrophic for the Basilica. In fact, the damage was relatively minor. What is poignant and ironic is that the Basilica's builders were aware of the problems posed by Umbria's seismic history, and had designed the building to withstand tremors: part of the vaults in the Upper Church collapsed only because tonnes of rubble had accumulated in the hollow ceiling space over the centuries, which generations of restorers had been too lazy to clear. The strengthened and revamped foundations will now withstand, it is hoped, earthquakes of anything up to a most unlikely 12 on the Richter scale.

The Lower Church

The sombre **Lower Church** is the place to begin if you want to follow the architectural and artistic chronology of the shrine. Its convoluted floor plan and

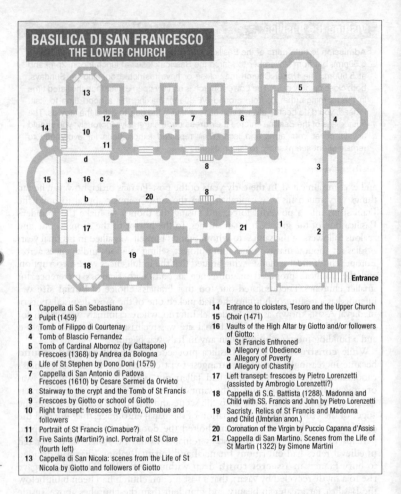

BASILICA DI SAN FRANCESCO
THE LOWER CHURCH

1 Cappella di San Sebastiano
2 Pulpit (1459)
3 Tomb of Filippo di Courtenay
4 Tomb of Blascio Fernandez
5 Tomb of Cardinal Albornoz (by Gattapone)
  Frescoes (1368) by Andrea da Bologna
6 Life of St Stephen by Dono Doni (1575)
7 Cappella di San Antonio di Padova
  Frescoes (1610) by Cesare Sermei da Orvieto
8 Stairway to the crypt and the Tomb of St Francis
9 Frescoes by Giotto or school of Giotto
10 Right transept: frescoes by Giotto, Cimabue and
   followers
11 Portrait of St Francis (Cimabue?)
12 Five Saints (Martini?) incl. Portrait of St Clare
   (fourth left)
13 Cappella di San Nicola: scenes from the Life of St
   Nicola by Giotto and followers of Giotto

14 Entrance to cloisters, Tesoro and the Upper Church
15 Choir (1471)
16 Vaults of the High Altar by Giotto and/or followers
   of Giotto:
   a St Francis Enthroned
   b Allegory of Obedience
   c Allegory of Poverty
   d Allegory of Chastity
17 Left transept: frescoes by Pietro Lorenzetti
   (assisted by Ambrogio Lorenzetti?)
18 Cappella di Maestro S.G. Battista (1288). Madonna and
   Child with SS. Francis and John by Pietro Lorenzetti
19 Sacristy. Relics of St Francis and Madonna
   and Child (Umbrian anon.)
20 Coronation of the Virgin by Puccio Capanna d'Assisi
21 Cappella di San Martino. Scenes from the Life of
   St Martin (1322) by Simone Martini

low-lit vaults are intended to create a mood of calm and meditative introspection; the natural light has been augmented by fairly discreet spotlighting – a concession that has altered the atmosphere, but also makes it possible to study the frescoes and intricate decoration that cover every surface.

The main nave

The highlights span a century of continuous artistic development. Important but somewhat stilted early works by Byzantine-influenced artists line the walls of the main nave, many credited to the mysterious **Maestro di San Francesco**, the anonymous hand that crops up elsewhere in Umbria. These are the oldest frescoes in the Basilica (1253), the *Scenes from the Passion* (right wall) and *Episodes from the Life of St Francis* (left wall). Faded in places, they have also been partly obliterated by the subsequent opening up of the side chapels, a necessity forced on the Franciscans by the need to accommodate the growing number of pilgrims visiting Assisi.

Don't overlook the church's minor works, notably the little *Madonna Enthroned* (1422) by the Gubbian artist Ottaviano Nelli (on the left as you enter, just right of the Cappella di San Sebastiano), or the **Tomb of Cardinal Albornoz** (marked 5 on our plan), built as a temporary resting place for the Spanish firebrand responsible for reinforcing papal power in Umbria. He rebuilt and regarrisoned the castles of Assisi, Narni and Spoleto, among others, and was rewarded for his pains with a tomb in the Basilica. The tomb is the work of **Matteo di Gattapone**, the architect responsible for Spoleto's Ponte delle Torri and Gubbio's Palazzo dei Consoli, projects conceived on a far greater scale.

The Cappella di San Martino

Simone Martini's frescoes in the **Cappella di San Martino** (21), the first chapel on the left as you enter the nave, are among the Lower Church's highlights. He worked here in the mid-1310s, shortly after painting the great *Maestà* in Siena, and was given completely free rein: every detail, even the floor and stained glass, came under his control. The panels on the underside of the arch as you enter the chapel were probably painted in 1317. They show eight saints, and were painted to honour St Louis of Toulouse, who had just been sanctified; he is the red-robed figure in the upper left panel, flanked by saints Francis, Anthony and Clare.

In the interior chapel, a far more distinct and insular space than much of the Lower Church, is a complete fresco cycle of the life of **St Martin of Tours**. The father of monasticism in France, Martin was venerated as far afield as Ireland and Africa; here, however, he is featured partly as a sop to the Franciscan friar who commissioned the chapel (the friar had been made cardinal with the title of San Martino ai Monti). The ten-panel cycle starts on the left-hand wall and moves clockwise around the chapel, the lowest four panels representing scenes from the secular part of Martin's life up to and including his conversion, the remaining four wall frescoes and two painted ceiling vaults treating the period after his conversion. Martin was born in 315 in what is now Hungary and brought up in Italy at Pavia. The key event of his conversion – and the first depicted in the cycle – came as a young officer at Amiens, when he gave half his cloak to a beggar, a figure he was later led to recognize as Christ. To the right is the *Dream of St Martin*, in which Christ and angels appear to the saint, a panel that mingles secular and sacred iconography amid a panoply of courtly emblems. This trait is continued in the next panel on the right-hand wall, *St Martin is Knighted*, an out-and-out evocation of life at court without religious iconography of any kind. To its right is *St Martin Renounces his Weapons*: "I am Christ's soldier; I am not allowed to fight." Here too, Martini seems to reserve his finest painting for the background – the tents, spears, lances and costumes of the Roman camp and Emperor Julian.

The narrative moves to the second tier back on the left-hand wall, starting with the *Miracle of the Resurrected Child*, another episode never before depicted in Italian art, in which Martin, transported presumably by artistic licence to Siena (the city's Palazzo Pubblico is in the background), raises a child from the dead before its mother and an expectant crowd. Alongside is the *Meditation*, with the saint moved to distraction by contemplation of the Divine, and unmoved by the acolytes trying to direct his attention to the Mass. Round to its right is the *Miraculous Mass*, an unusual subject portrayed here for the first time. Martin has again given a cloak to a beggar, and is about to celebrate Mass when angels appear to present him with a beautifully embroidered piece of material. The next fresco, the *Miracle of Fire*, is damaged, though the sense of the scene is clear: a tongue of flame is forced down the throat of Emperor Valentinian for refusing to give Martin an audience.

The uppermost level depicts two self-explanatory scenes, the saint's death and burial, both distinguished by the exquisite detail of the saint's robes, and by the architectural details that correspond to the moods of the episodes – severe, bare-walled and geometrical around the scene of death, and more ornate in the Gothic chapel that hosts the funeral.

The right transept

Cenno di Pepo, popularly known as **Cimabue** (c.1240–1302), was the first great named artist to work on the Basilica. Vasari's *Lives of the Artists* opens with an account of him, in which he is described as the father of Italian painting, and an obsessive perfectionist, often destroying work with which he was not completely happy. He probably painted in the transepts of the Upper Church between 1270 and 1280, and was active in the Lower Church some time later. His major painting in the Lower Church – where much of his work was later overpainted – is in the **right transept** (right wall), the over-restored *Madonna, Child and Angels with St Francis*, a work that survives from the church's earlier decorative scheme (1280). Ruskin described this painting as the noblest depiction of the Virgin in Christendom. It includes the famous portrait of St Francis, which you'll already have seen plastered all over the town. Next to it, the *Crucifixion* has been attributed to **Giotto**, as have – though with less certainty – the scenes on the end wall and vaults depicting the *Childhood of Christ*. To the left are a half-length *Madonna and Child* and pair of saints, while on the side wall is a set of five saints, all the work of **Simone Martini**. One of the figures – another image much duplicated around town – is believed to be **St Clare**, founder of the women's chapter of the Franciscans (see box, p.538). The painting shows a clear attempt at the depiction of emotion, the use of light and shade to add verisimilitude to figures, and the creation of a coherent three-dimensional sense of space – all steps on the path trodden with equal certainty by Giotto and Martini's Sienese contemporary, Pietro Lorenzetti.

The vaults over the altar

The question of **Giotto**'s involvement in the Basilica has been at the centre of one of Italy's greatest art history controversies. Certain twentieth-century historians opined that Giotto had never painted in Assisi at all. Some still hold this view, though the modern consensus is that Giotto was indeed responsible for the bulk of the paintings in the Upper Church, executed from about 1295. Authorship in the Lower Church is more dubious, and credit for the allegorical frescoes in the **vaults over the altar** – some of the church's most beautiful and complex – has been taken from Giotto and given to nameless assistants. The same goes for the *Life of Mary Magdalene* cycle (c.1309) in the **Cappella della Maddalena**, the third chapel on the right, as well as the right transept's *Childhood of Christ* (see above). In the hothouse atmosphere of the Basilica during its decoration, however, co-operative efforts must have been commonplace: definitive attributions are all but impossible.

The left transept

Pietro Lorenzetti is represented by a beautiful series of works in the **left transept** (17). Recent criticism sees the *Six Scenes of the Passion*, on the ceiling of the left-hand transept, as his earliest surviving works, probably painted on a visit to Assisi in about 1314. Restrained, static pieces, they betray the influence of Duccio, an impulse shrugged off when the artist returned to the Basilica in the years 1324–25 and 1327–28. By this time he had absorbed the lessons of Giotto, bringing them to bear on the *Passion of Christ* in the left transept, a cycle he had probably started on his visit ten years earlier.

The frescoes portraying scenes leading up to Christ's crucifixion are comparatively weak. The *Last Supper*, however, in which Christ and the apostles are crowded into a curious hexagonal loggia, reveals a treatment of light and shadow hardly matched during the fourteenth century. The moon and stars light the sky, while to the left is a kitchen illuminated by light from a fire, in which servants unconcernedly scrape food into a dog's bowl – a fine incidental detail paralleled by the two chattering servants to the left of Christ, who are quite oblivious to events before them. The only illumination at the table is from the haloes of Christ and the apostles, a deliberate juxtaposition of material and spiritual light.

Three other panels stand out in the cycle: the *Entombment*, *Crucifixion* and *Deposition*. Dominating almost an entire wall, the *Crucifixion* shows an amazing sense of drama, with Christ raised high above a crowd of onlookers, and closer study reveals carefully observed nuances of character in the crowd. These natural touches recur in the faces of the *Deposition*, less immediately striking but still amongst Lorenzetti's masterpieces for its bold and simple composition. The upper portion of the Cross is completely missing, leaving just the broad horizontal and huge amounts of vacant space, all focusing on the figure of Christ, his limbs bent with rigor mortis.

Lorenzetti also painted in the chapel beyond, the **Cappella di San Giovanni Battista** (18), where he left the frescoed triptych of the *Madonna and Child with Sts Francis and John the Baptist*. The central panel of stained glass here is attributed to Jacopo Torriti, one of the largely unsung but important Roman artists to have frescoed parts of the Upper Church.

The tomb of St Francis

Before leaving the Lower Church, drop down to the crypt (8) and the **tomb of St Francis**, a spot that remained hidden until 1818. The present tomb, rebuilt in the 1920s, honours Francis's desire for a humble burial, replacing a more elaborate tabernacle raised in the excitement of discovery. Above the main altar is the simple stone coffin that contains the body; at the four corners of the central canopy are the bodies of Francis's earliest key companions, the beatific Leone, Rufino, Masseo and Angelo.

There's a short account of the tomb's fascinating history and discovery tacked to the stone walls.

The Museo del Tesoro

The well-presented **Museo del Tesoro e Collezioni F.M. Perkins** (April–Oct Mon–Sat 9.30am–5pm; donation expected) is entered from doors in the transept behind the main altar (14). It contains a rich collection of paintings, including 55 masterpieces from the Frederick Mason Perkins Collection, a bequest from an American philanthropist which includes work by Fra' Angelico, Pier Francesco Fiorentino, Luca Signorelli and Masolino. It's also particularly strong on the Sienese, with paintings by Pietro Lorenzetti, Segno di Bonaventura, Bartolo di Fredi and Taddeo di Bartolo. The museum's own original collection contains works by Benozzo Gozzoli and little-known Umbrians like Lo Spagna, Bonfigli and Dono Doni. The remainder of the gallery is crammed with copes, vestments, silverware, reliquaries and the like, given to the Franciscans over the centuries. Pride of place goes to a tapestry of St Francis (1479) and an altar front (1478), both presented by Pope Sixtus IV, the latter with figures by Antonio del Pollaiuolo, together with a series of thirteenth-century Tuscan and Umbrian crucifixes.

The Upper Church

The **Upper Church** is a completely different architectural, aesthetic and emotional experience, its airy Gothic plan intended to inspire celebration rather than contemplation. It feels less a church than a gallery for Giotto's dazzling *Life of St Francis* frescoes, rightly regarded – notwithstanding the odd doubt as to its attribution – as one of the greatest of all Italian fresco cycles. Few signs of earthquake damage remain, save a couple of completely bare vaults, striking memorials to the events of 1997 amid the colour on all sides.

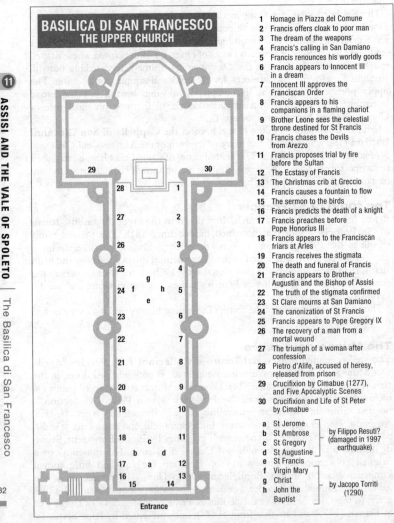

BASILICA DI SAN FRANCESCO
THE UPPER CHURCH

1 Homage in Piazza del Comune
2 Francis offers cloak to poor man
3 The dream of the weapons
4 Francis's calling in San Damiano
5 Francis renounces his worldly goods
6 Francis appears to Innocent III in a dream
7 Innocent III approves the Franciscan Order
8 Francis appears to his companions in a flaming chariot
9 Brother Leone sees the celestial throne destined for St Francis
10 Francis chases the Devils from Arezzo
11 Francis proposes trial by fire before the Sultan
12 The Ecstasy of Francis
13 The Christmas crib at Greccio
14 Francis causes a fountain to flow
15 The sermon to the birds
16 Francis predicts the death of a knight
17 Francis preaches before Pope Honorius III
18 Francis appears to the Franciscan friars at Arles
19 Francis receives the stigmata
20 The death and funeral of Francis
21 Francis appears to Brother Augustin and the Bishop of Assisi
22 The truth of the stigmata confirmed
23 St Clare mourns at San Damiano
24 The canonization of St Francis
25 Francis appears to Pope Gregory IX
26 The recovery of a man from a mortal wound
27 The triumph of a woman after confession
28 Pietro d'Alife, accused of heresy, released from prison
29 Crucifixion by Cimabue (1277), and Five Apocalyptic Scenes
30 Crucifixion and Life of St Peter by Cimabue

a St Jerome
b St Ambrose
c St Gregory
d St Augustine
} by Filippo Resuti? (damaged in 1997 earthquake)

e St Francis
f Virgin Mary
g Christ
h John the Baptist
} by Jacopo Torriti (1290)

Entrance

Giotto's Life of St Francis

Giotto's *Life of St Francis* cycle starts from the **far right-hand side** of the nave. Although critics haven't reached a consensus on the date of the frescoes, most believe they are early works, painted with assistants some time around 1296, when Giotto was 29. The style and peripheral narrative content of the last four frescoes has led to their being attributed to the so-called Maestro di Santa Cecilia, who may also have overpainted parts of the first panel.

Giotto was by far the most important artist to work in the Basilica. Dante immediately recognized his supremacy, and in a famous passage (intended to illustrate the hollowness of earthly glory) wrote: "Cimabue thought to lord it over painting's field. And now his fame is obscured and the cry is Giotto." It seems that Giotto got the commission on the prompting of Cimabue, and that some test pieces in the Lower Church persuaded the friars that Giotto was up to the task of decorating the upper part of the Basilica. Like many writers and artists of the age, Giotto was a member of the lay **Franciscan Tertiaries**. His frescoes reveal a profound sympathy for the spirit of St Francis and show an almost total rejection of the artistic language of the Byzantines, whose remote icons were highly inappropriate for Francis's very human message. The cycles are full of the natural beauty that moved the saint to profound joy, and the figures are mobile and expressive – aspects of Giotto's art typified by the famous panel **The Sermon to the Birds** (marked 15 on our plan). More than any other, this fresco crystallizes the essence of Franciscan humility, with the flock addressed as an indivisible part of God's creation and attending to the saint as distinct from them solely by virtue of the power of speech.

Giotto's narrative genius cuts straight to the heart of the matter, as seen in the very first panel, **The Homage in Piazza del Comune** (1), in which the universality of Francis's appeal is evoked in a single act of tribute. Moreover, the frescoes display a wealth of everyday detail that made them accessible to the ordinary people of his age. The first people to look at **Francis Offering his Cloak to a Poor Man** (2) would have recognized the world in which it is set as the one they themselves inhabited: the backdrop includes a detailed view of Assisi from the Porta Nuova, along with the Benedictine abbey on Monte Subasio, now vanished. This attention to the tone and substance of the real world, to its textures and solidity, makes the art of Giotto as revolutionary as Francis's message to the medieval Church.

The choir and the other frescoes

The **choir** is a second focal point. Its 105 inlaid stalls – completed in the fifteenth century – are of immense intricacy and delicacy, most of them depicting famous Franciscans or episodes from their lives. The central throne is a papal seat, the only one in the country outside St Peter's in Rome. Behind the throne, and in the **left (north) transept**, are frescoes by Giotto's probable master, **Cimabue**. These suffered during the ceiling collapse, but were already almost ruined from the oxidation of badly chosen pigments, though this transept's *Crucifixion* remains an impressive composition, its dynamism an obvious departure from static Byzantine order. Giotto and Duccio may have helped on the painting as pupils.

Running around the church immediately above Giotto's Franciscan panels is another much damaged though virtually complete cycle, *Scenes from the Old and New Testaments*. Vasari believed these scenes were by Cimabue, though today they are attributed to artists of the Roman school – **Torriti**, **Rusuti** and **Pietro Cavallini** – who were working in the church around the same time. Before coming to Assisi all three had worked primarily in mosaic, a traditional

▲ Franciscan friars in the lower courtyard of the Basilica di San Francesco

Byzantine medium, but in the Basilica they turned to fresco, moving, like Cimabue, with cautious innovation towards a freer interpretation of old themes. The *Four Doctors of the Church* in the vaults (Sts Jerome, Ambrose, Gregory and Augustine), especially, shows a narrative sense absent in earlier art: cloaks are left thrown over chairs, books lie open as if half-read. The Doctors, moreover, are depicted as characters in their own right, distinct individuals rather than the symbolic representatives of artistic convention. The 1997 earthquake dislodged the *St Jerome* fresco, which is currently being pieced back together.

To the Piazza del Comune

Southeast from the Basilica, **Via San Francesco** heads off along the ridge of medieval Assisi towards the Piazza del Comune. To each side steep and often stepped alleyways lead down to city gates and peripheral churches, of which **San Pietro** most rewards the diversion. The lanes north and east of Via San Francesco – in particular **Via Metastasio** – are peaceful and attractive; secreted away in them is a medley of little **churches**, notably Santa Margherita and Santa Croce. None is any great shakes artistically, but all make pretty diversions. Take this route, however, and you will miss the **Pinacoteca Comunale**, which might seem insignificant after the Basilica, but contains several interesting frescoes and one or two paintings of which any gallery would be proud.

San Pietro

Wonderfully restored to its Romanesque-Gothic state, **San Pietro** is a peaceful antidote to the crowds of the Basilica above it. Grass and benches outside offer views over the Vale of Spoleto and of the fine, two-tiered facade – pink below, creamy-white above – with its three huge rose windows. Originally Benedictine, the church dates from the thirteenth century, though it may have been founded as long ago as the second century. The bare interior, mainly Romanesque, also shows the first hints of Gothic in its gently pointed arches and in the ceiling, supported by strange curved vaulting.

The Oratorio dei Pellegrini

At Via San Francesco 11, the **Oratorio dei Pellegrini** (daily 9am–noon & 3–6pm; free) is an exquisite fifteenth-century building that served as part of a hospice for visiting pilgrims. The interior is covered in fetching frescoes, some by the local sixteenth-century artist Matteo da Gualdo, beginning with a faded sample outside under the wooden-eaved exterior. Inside he was responsible for the murals on the altar wall, the vault and side walls being the work of another local artist, Pierantonio Mezzastris. Painted in 1477, the pictures illustrate *Scenes from the Life of St James*, including the comical *Miracle of the Two Hens*, an episode in which the saint restored two dead chickens to life so they could testify to the innocence of a falsely accused pilgrim. Another shows the *Miracle of the Hanged Man*, in which the saint supports an apparently dead man until his parents find him alive. Two scenes on the left wall represent episodes from the life of St Anthony Abbot, distributing alms and receiving camels that have brought him and his fellow monks food; the *Three Saints* on the inner face are attributed to Perugino or L'Ingegno, one of his followers. If people are at prayer here – and they often are – you may have to content yourself with a glimpse of the paintings through the glass door.

Close by, at no. 14, is Assisi's finest medieval town house, the headquarters of the masons' guild, known as the **Casa dei Maestri Comacini** (a disproportionate number of the Basilica's builders hailed from Como). A short way beyond the hospice on the right is the arched portico of **Monte Frumentario**, a thirteenth-century hospital – one of the first in Italy. It adjoins the **Fontano di Corletta**, whose inscription warns that the penalty for washing your smalls in the water was one *scudo* and the surrender of your laundry.

The Pinacoteca Comunale

Almost opposite the Oratorio dei Pellegrini in the Palazzo Vallemani is the excellent **Pinacoteca Comunale** (daily: March–May & Sept–Oct 10am–5pm;

June–Aug 10am–6.30pm; Nov–Feb 10.30am–1pm & 2–5pm; €3.50, or joint ticket with Foro Romano & Rocca Maggiore €5) – well worth the admission, not least for the wonderful paintings moved here on a semi-permanent basis from earthquake-ravaged Nocera Umbra, including the impressive *Immaculate Conception of the Virgin* (1495–1505) by Matteo da Gualdo. This is complemented by many detached frescoes rescued from churches and other buildings around Assisi, among them important works by the Gubbian artist Ottaviano Nelli. Look out for the wonderfully strange fresco by an unknown fourteenth-century Umbrian painter of San Giuliano mistakenly killing his parents, having returned home and mistaken them for his wife and her lover – the artist clearly enjoyed painting the quite unnecessarily graphic and gaping wounds. All the displays are helped by good English commentaries, and more works of art are due to be moved to restored medieval rooms on other floors.

Piazza del Comune

Piazza del Comune was built over either the site of the Roman forum or an important sacred area – theories differ. It's a stunning medieval square, lined with plenty of pricey bars from which to people-watch. The tourist office (see p.524) is here, part of the impressive Neo-Gothic former post office, a frescoed mock medieval hall complete with vaulted ceilings.

The piazza is dominated by the **Tempio di Minerva** (Mon–Sat 7.15am–noon & 2–7pm, Sun 8.30am–noon & 2–7pm; free), six Corinthian columns and a pediment from a first-century Roman temple – perfectly preserved and dazzlingly restored. It's as good as any classical monument in Italy, and was the only thing Goethe wanted to see in Assisi. The writer was moved to hyperbole on seeing it – "the first complete classical monument I have seen … so perfect in design… I cannot describe the sensations which this work aroused in me, but I know they are going to bear fruit for ever." He didn't bother with the Basilica, calling it a "Babylonian pile". While the temple is great from the outside, the church behind is a seventeenth-century conversion whose lack of interest has been redeemed by a fine restoration of its Baroque interior, which uncovered parts of the original pavement and massive wall and terracing to the rear.

Outside, the temple frieze contains reference to two brothers, Gneo Cesio Tirone and Tito Cesio Prisco, who helped finance the temple. It had a chequered history, not least in the early Middle Ages, when it was in such a parlous state that is was described in records as a *casolino* – a little house – and in the thirteenth century, when it passed to the *comune*, who made the lower area a prison and the upper one a council chamber.

To the left of the temple stands the **Palazzo del Capitano del Popolo**, completed in 1282 – though various cod medieval adornments were added in 1927 – and the Torre del Popolo, built in 1305. Note the measures at the base of the tower, which record standard sizes for stones and other building materials as they were in 1348. On the opposite side of the piazza, the much-restored **Palazzo Comunale** once contained the Pinacoteca Comunale, the sign for which remains, since it forms part of a historic building and as such apparently cannot be removed.

South of the piazza, you might pay quick homage to St Francis's supposed birthplace, a spot commemorated by the unremarkable **Chiesa Nuova** (daily 6.30am–noon & 2.30–6pm; free) – built on land owned by Francis's father at the expense of Philip III of Spain – and a piazza boasting two prominent bronze statues (1984) of Francis's parents.

Foro Romano e Collezione Archeologica

The **Foro Romano e Collezione Archeologica**, entered just off Piazza del Comune at Via Portica 2 (same hours as Pinacoteca Comunale; €3.50, including admission to Pinacoteca, or joint ticket with Pinacoteca and Rocca Maggiore €5), is unlikely to divert unless you're interested in archeology and Assisi's Roman heritage. It's housed in the crypt of the defunct church of San Niccolò, documented as early as 1097 but demolished in 1926 to make way for the ersatz-medieval post office building. A passage from the museum runs under Piazza del Comune, where excavations are in progress to uncover the Roman remains here without disrupting the piazza above; at present it's rather hard to make any sense of the underground maze, which scholars now believe is not the old Roman forum (as was long believed), but a religious sanctuary linked to the surviving Tempio di Minerva; the forum, it's now thought, may have occupied the present-day site of the Duomo. Dotted around the area are parts of statues and pillars, busts, urns and other Roman and Etruscan fragments, all given added lustre by their strange subterranean setting.

The Duomo, Santa Chiara and the Rocca

Just south of the Piazza del Comune, the Franciscan trail continues with important stops at the **Duomo** and **Santa Chiara**, while up in the northeast corner of the walls a sweep of park leads to the **Rocca Maggiore**, the best-preserved castle in Umbria, with fine views over the city and beyond.

The Duomo

As you emerge from the narrow streets east of Piazza del Comune, you're met by the captivating sight of the **Duomo**, or San Rufino (daily 7.30am–12.30pm & 2.30–7pm; free), with its typically three-tiered Umbrian facade. Its Roman-esque **portal** is a superb piece of carving, guarded by two red marble lions and framed by lilies, leaves, faces, birds, winged crocodiles and a pair of griffons. Look in the lunette for the child being suckled, and its two dour parents. Alongside is a huge, stolid **campanile**, managing somehow to fit into the overall scheme of the church.

According to tradition the first church on the site was built around 412, ostensibly to house the bones of St Rufinus, Assisi's first bishop, martyred some 170 years earlier. Another, better-documented building was raised around 1029 by Bishop Ugone, from which the crypt and present campanile survive. Yet another church – more or less the one that survives today – was begun in 1140 and consecrated in 1253. Off the right (south) nave, there's the small **Museo Diocesano**, or **Museo della Cattedrale** (mid-March to July & Sept to mid-Oct Thurs–Tues 10am–1pm & 3–6pm; Aug daily 10am–6pm; mid-Oct to mid-March Thurs–Tues 10am–1pm & 2.30–5.30pm; €3), with a handful of good paintings, including a 1470 work by Niccolò Alunno, and an atmospheric **crypt**, the **Cripta di San Rufino** (same hours & ticket), or Basilica Ugoniana, entered outside down steps to the right of the facade, which contains fragments from these earlier churches. The area was not discovered until 1895, and features remnants of very early frescoes, parts of a Roman wall and conduit and a third-century Roman sarcophagus used as Rufinus's original tomb. Local tradition has it that Bishop Ugone had wanted to bury Rufinus in Santa Maria Maggiore, then the town's cathedral, but the townspeople had argued for the new church. There apparently ensued a literal tug-of-war with the saint's coffin, the bishop and his cohorts pulling one way, the locals the other. The latter clearly triumphed, though the tale is probably more a parable of the ascendancy of the lay city councils of the time than anything else.

Inside, the main point of interest is the **font** used to baptize St Francis, St Clare and (possibly) the future emperor Frederick II, apparently born prematurely in a nearby village. It's at the near end of the church on the right, fronted by Romanesque statues of a lion and winged ox. Opposite, the beginning of the left aisle contains a little door, which leads to an impressive **Roman cistern**, recent research having led scholars to believe that the cathedral square – rather than Piazza del Comune – was the site of the town's original Roman forum. Various **glass panels** were let into the floor during post-quake restoration to offer insights into the building's earlier incarnations, but they offer little of interest. The church does have a couple of offbeat sights: a terracotta Virgin (left of the altar) which burst into tears in 1494, and a stone knelt on by an angel attending Francis's baptism – he left the imprint of his knee on it. St Rufinus's remains still lie beneath the altar.

The Basilica di Santa Chiara

South of the Duomo, though most easily reached from the Piazza del Comune, is the **Basilica di Santa Chiara** (daily: Easter–Oct 8.30am–7pm; Nov–Easter 8.30am–5pm; free), the burial place of St Clare, St Francis's devoted follower. The church was begun in 1257 and consecrated in 1265, twelve years after her death. It stands on the site formerly occupied by the church of San Giorgio, where St Francis went to school, where his canonization took place, and where his body lay during construction of the Basilica. Clare, too, was buried in the church until her own resting place was completed.

The church is a virtual facsimile of the Basilica di San Francesco, with its simple facade and opulent rose window. Its engineering, however, wasn't up to

---

St Clare

St Clare (Santa Chiara) was a close early companion of St Francis and the founder of the **Poor Clares**, the Franciscan nuns. Born in 1182 into a noble family, she had a deeply religious upbringing from her mother, an education which backfired when, enraptured at the age of 17 by the preaching of Francis, she rejected her family and two offers of marriage to live with the saint. In an act of symbolic removal from the world he cut off her blonde hair, the locks of which are still visible in her basilica, and replaced her finery with a rough cassock. A year after her conversion she took her leave of Francis, and – but for the occasional vision – never saw him again until his death.

After initial opposition from the family, Clare's sister, **St Agnes**, joined her in spiritual retreat, and was later joined by her widowed mother. Other young girls from Assisi, similarly inspired by Francis's example, added to the growing community of women, which was soon installed by Francis in the church of San Damiano. In 1215 Clare obtained from Pope Innocent III the "privilege of poverty" – permission for the creation of an order of nuns to live solely on alms and without property of any kind. Over the years the Poor Clares' right to exist was frequently challenged, yet Clare (like Francis) managed to disseminate the movement throughout Europe.

She died on August 12, 1253, outliving Francis by 27 years. She was canonized two years later, and by undignified quirk is now the **patron saint of television**, awarded the honour in 1958 by Pope Pius XII in recognition of her powers: although bedridden, she was able to see and hear the rites of a Christmas service performed by Francis a kilometre away.

the same standards, and the strange buttresses were added in 1351 to prevent its collapse. Before venturing in, wander over to the edge of the piazza in front of the church for some grand views of the Vale of Spoleto and the town's rooftops. The **interior** is dark and almost bare, the result of some zealous early censorship: a seventeenth-century German bishop called Spader, afraid that the nuns might be corrupted by contact with worldly tourists, had its cycle of frescoes obliterated. Only a few patches of earlier Sienese frescoes from the original San Giorgio have survived, mostly in the transepts and cross vaults above the high altar; high in the south transept are *Scenes from the Apocalypse and Life of Christ*, and under them *The Death and Funeral of St Clare*, all the work of a close collaborator of Giotto. The scenes above the high altar, above which hangs a large thirteenth-century Crucifix, show *Scenes from the Life of St Clare*, while the two registers way up in the north transept depict *Episodes from Genesis*. The altar's *Madonna and Child* (c.1265) is probably the work of the Giottesque artist of the south transept. One of the two chapels off the right aisle, the **Oratorio del Crocifisso**, contains the Byzantine Crucifix that bowed its head and spoke to Francis in San Damiano. Alongside are various clothes and oddments that belonged to Clare and Francis, while the body of Clare herself rests in the Baroque horror of the **crypt**.

The Rocca Maggiore

11

Rising above the town, the **Rocca Maggiore** (daily 10am–dusk; Aug opens 9am; €3.50, or joint ticket with Pinacoteca and Foro Romano €5) dates back to Charlemagne, who is supposed to have raised the first defensive walls here after sacking the town. The structure surviving today, with its looming towers, turrets and parapets, owes most to Cardinal Albornoz, who arrived to assert papal authority in 1367, repairing an earlier castle that had been ravaged by repeated skirmishes with Perugia. Church governors reputedly dispensed justice by hanging criminals on the battlements or by throwing them out of a castle window into the ravine. The seductive **medieval streets** leading up to the Rocca from the Duomo are the quietest in Assisi, partly because of their distance from tourist targets, but perhaps as much due to their fierce gradients. The fortress is well worth the climb: the green surrounds provide ideal picnic territory, and you'll be rewarded with all-embracing **views** taking in Assisi, Perugia and the Vale of Spoleto across to Montefalco and the Monti Martani.

Outside the walls

The Franciscan trail leads south from Santa Chiara to **San Damiano** and, for the energetic, to a couple of sites further outside town – the **Eremo delle Carceri** (4km east) and **Santa Maria degli Angeli** in the new town around the station (5km southwest of the old town). San Damiano is well worth the short detour: in a town increasingly undermined by tacky commercialism, it retains an air of calm and dignity.

San Damiano

It was in **San Damiano** (daily 10am–12.30pm & 2–6pm; Nov–March closes 4.30pm), in 1205, that Francis received his calling to make repairs, and where he brought St Clare and her followers (see box opposite), "pouring the sweetness of Christ into her ears". Clare remained here till her death, though the nuns left seven years afterwards. After installing the Poor Clares, Francis came to San Damiano just once, towards the end of his life, when – sick and half-blind – he composed the *Canticle of the Sun*. His body rested here briefly after death, fulfilling a promise to Clare that she might see him once more.

Owned by Lord Lothian until 1983, the church now belongs to the Friars Minor, who have kept it in much the same state as it was centuries ago – a condition laid down by Lothian when he made his bequest. Lothian had inherited it in turn from descendants of Lord Ripon, a Catholic convert, who bought it in 1870 when Italy's monastic and most other religious institutions passed to the state. Alone among the places in Assisi with Franciscan associations, this one preserves something of an ideal that is recognizably Franciscan – rural and peaceful in its groves of olives, cypresses and wild flowers, with the pastoral Vale of Spoleto stretching away below. To reach it, walk down the Borgo Aretino from Santa Chiara and then follow the signs through the car park and olive grove – a very steep downhill walk of about fifteen minutes.

Signs point the way round the complex, starting outside with a fresco depicting St Roch – the saint invoked against infectious diseases – proudly displaying a plague sore. The little **balcony** above the main entrance is the point from which Clare, holding aloft the Sacrament, turned back an entire Saracen army that was pursuing Assisi's Guelphs. **Inside**, the nave of the church – which was a Benedictine foundation at least as early as 1030 – is simple and smoke-darkened, with a beautifully decrepit wooden choir and lectern. On the right-hand side is the small window where San Damiano's priest threw the money that Francis offered him to repair the church. Nearby you can see the tiny hole where the saint hid "for a month" from the wrath of his father. Beyond some stairs leading to a terrace and small garden is a vestibule with the woodwormed choir and two frescoes, one a lovely *Madonna and Child* by an unknown Giottesque artist. Up the stairs you reach the **oratory**, and then a small **dormitory**, with a cross and flowers marking the spot where Clare died. A door to the right leads to the **cloisters**, where you may catch a glimpse of the refectory, still equipped with its original table and oak benches.

The Eremo delle Carceri

All over Assisi you'll see pictures of the **Eremo delle Carceri** (daily 6.30am–dusk; closed for religious festivals; donation expected), an active monastery situated in oak woods about 6km east. It can be easily reached by road but the best approach is to follow the footpath – climbing very steeply for the first kilometre or so – from the Porta Cappuccini: outside the gate, turn left along the track of cypresses and then follow the marked path up and to the right behind the Rocca Minore (at the major fork a little way beyond, turn right; sometimes the sign's missing), then, at the top, keep going level and straight until you hit the road just above the monastery. Allow at least an hour, less coming back.

The hermitage was an early place of retreat for Francis and his followers: the saint caused the well in the courtyard to flow (as depicted by Giotto) and a cell known as the **Oratorio Primitivo** has been identified as that occupied by Francis. There's also a **chapel** containing various unlikely relics: Francis's pillow and a piece of the Golden Gate through which Jesus passed into Jerusalem. The hermitage once owned a lock of the Virgin's hair, too, and some earth from the mound that God used to create Adam, though these treasures have sadly disappeared. With some very low doors and tight corners to negotiate, the whole experience is quite claustrophobic.

On the other side of the church is a dry riverbed, once a torrent until Francis told it to hush because it was spoiling his prayers. It fills up today only when some public calamity is at hand. One of the walls here was built over the so-called *buco del diavolo*, a crevice into which Francis cast a devil by the power of prayer. An old **holm oak**, kept upright by iron stakes, is said to have shaded the saint, and to have been a spot where birds collected to hear his sermons. Beyond this point a lovely **path** ambles into the woods, with plenty of nooks and side tracks where you can escape for a siesta.

Santa Maria degli Angeli

Difficult to miss from almost any point in the Vale of Spoleto, the huge domed basilica of **Santa Maria degli Angeli** (daily 6.30am–8pm; Aug also 9–11pm) rises from the new town clustered around Assisi train station. A majestically uninspiring pile, it was built between 1569 and 1684, then rebuilt after an earthquake in 1832. Its function is to shelter the **Porzuincola** (Little Portion), the hut-cum-chapel that Francis made the centre of the earliest Franciscan movement. Stranded like a doll's house in the church's austere Baroque bowels, it has been embellished with dreadful nineteenth-century frescoes on the outside, but inside there are features claimed to be those of Francis's rough-stone hovel, as well as good fourteenth-century frescoes on the life of the saint.

Bits of the old monastery have been excavated under the **main altar**, site of the saint's death and of Clare's abrupt conversion. Buried in the chapel is Brother Cataneii, one of the earliest Franciscans. He performed so many miracles from beyond the grave, and attracted so many expectant crowds as a result, that Francis implored him in prayer, "Now that we are infected with all these people of the world, I enjoin thee by obedience to make an end of thy miracles and allow us to recover in peace." The miracles stopped. In the garden are descendants of the **rose bushes** into which Francis threw himself while grappling with some immense nocturnal temptation; their thorns obligingly dropped off after contact with his saintly flesh. They now bloom, thornless, every May, their leaves stained with the blood shed that night.

Pilgrims flock to the basilica on August 1–2 for the **Pardon of St Francis**, a visit that guarantees automatic absolution. The pardon recalls a vision of Christ that Francis experienced, when he was asked what might be best for the human soul. Francis replied: forgiveness for all who crossed the threshold of his chapel. The already vast numbers of pilgrims were swelled in the 1920s by the supposed movement of the eight-metre-high bronze Madonna on the facade.

Eating and drinking

Multilingual tourist menus proliferate in Assisi's **restaurants** and prices can be steep. In general, the medieval streets leading up from the Duomo to the Rocca are where you'll find the cheapest bars and snacks. **Cafés** and **bars** are dotted around town, with those in Piazza del Comune offering the best people-watching opportunities – and the highest prices. For something quieter, try the *Gran Caffè*, Corso Mazzini 16a: the interior is pleasant, despite the mimsy pastel frescoes and chintzy cherubs. For **ice cream** and **cakes** make for *La Bottega del Pasticceria*, Via Portica 19, a small place a few steps from Piazza del Comune that must have the most mouthwatering window display in Umbria. Pilgrim-bound Assisi has just one in-town **club**, the *Hermitage*, located under the *Hermitage* hotel, Via degli Aromatari 1.

Restaurants

Buca di San Francesco Via Brizi 1
☏075.812.204. A reputation as the best in town is sometimes belied by erratic quality, though the cooking can be outstanding. As a bonus there's a half-covered outside terrace for summer eating. Closed Mon & two weeks in July.

I Monaci Scaletta del Metastasio, Via Fontebella ☏075.812.512. Large, friendly place for pastas and pizzas from a wood-fired oven, though service and standards can be patchy; one of the few places where pizzas are available at lunchtime. Closed Wed.

La Fortezza Vicolo della Fortezza 2 ☏075.812.418. Invariably busy but friendly restaurant, with a high reputation, great food, medieval setting and reasonable prices. However, service can be very slow at busy times. Reservations essential in summer. Closed Thurs & Feb. Lunch Tues, Sat & Sun only.

La Piazzetta dell'Erba Via San Gabriele dell'Addolorata 15b ☏075.815.352. Lost in a tangle of alleys and arches a few steps from the Tempio di Minerva, this rustic and informal little place is good for simple, well-cooked meals. It's possible to eat outside in good weather. Closed Mon.

La Rocca Via di Porta Perlici 27 ☏075.812.284, ⓦwww.hotellarocca.it. Annexed to the hotel, this is a big, cheap, high-quality locals' place with reasonable food and no frills. Closed Wed.

Medioevo Via dell'Arco dei Priori 4b ☏075.813.068. Just south off the Piazza del Comune, this extremely tasteful medieval vaulted dining room is recommended if you want to dress up a touch; the excellent cooking has a vaguely "international" flavour. There's a cheaper and lighter menu at lunch. Closed Wed, Jan & three weeks in July.

Pallotta Via Volta Pinta 2 ☏075.812.649. Only just off Piazza del Comune, but a very reasonable, unpretentious and welcoming trattoria; book, or arrive before 12.30pm to be sure of getting a place for lunch. Closed Tues.

San Francesco Via San Francesco 52 ☏075.813.302. Generally good and original cooking that takes Umbrian basics as its starting point. However, service can be surly and prices can be higher than the food merits. Closed Wed & two weeks in July & Nov.

Listings

Bike rental Andrea Angelucci, Via Becchetti 31 ☏075.804.2550.

Books and maps Eredi di E. Zubboli in the southeast corner of Piazza del Comune has guides in English and some English-language titles. It also has maps, as does Assisi's oldest shop, San Vignati, about 75m away downhill at Via Portica 19.

Bus enquiries APM, for Assisi and around ☏075.573.1707, ⓦwww.apmperugia.it; SULGA, for Rome & Florence ☏075.500.9641, ⓦwww .sulga.it; SPOLETINA, for Foligno, Montefalco and Bevagna ☏0742.670.746 or 0743.212.201, ⓦwww.spoletina.com.

Car rental See Perugia "Listings" (p.491) for agencies at Perugia airport (equidistant between Perugia and Assisi). In Assisi most rentals come with a driver: contact Costantini, Viale Umberto I 40 (☏075.816.356, ⓦwww.autonoleggiocostantini.it).

Exchange ATMs outside banks in Piazza del Comune and Piazza Unità d'Italia; Banca Popolare,

Piazza Santa Chiara 19; and Banca Toscana, Piazza San Pietro 6. Numerous exchange kiosks around town.

Hospital Ospedale di Assisi, 1km southeast of Porta Nuova on Via Fuori Porta Nuova ☏075.812.824 or 075.813.9227.

Lost property At Vigili Urbani, Vicolo Volta Pinta (Mon–Sat 9am–noon; ☏075.812.820).

Markets Assisi's main market is in Piazza Matteotti (Sat mornings). Piazza Chiesa Nuova hosts an antiques market (Sat & Sun of second week of month).

Police Piazza Matteotti 3b ☏075.812.239, and Piazza del Comune ☏075.812.215.

Post office Largo Properzio 4 ☏075.81.314, and Piazza San Pietro 4 ☏075.815.178.

Travel agent Stoppini, Corso Mazzini 31 ☏075.812.597. Train and bus tickets.

The Vale of Spoleto

The **Vale of Spoleto**, or Valle Umbra, describes a graceful arc from Assisi in the north to Spoleto in the south, an almost perfectly flat crescent of land that was once the bottom of Lago Tiberino, a vast, shallow lake similar to present-day Lago Trasimeno that was eventually drained by the Romans. It has long been an important strategic route, carrying part of the Via Flaminia, a Roman consular road, an artery that either bolstered or prompted the foundation of the area's key towns and villages: **Spello**, **Bevagna**, **Foligno**, **Montefalco** and **Trevi**.

All of these places are essential points of call (with the exception of Foligno, a large and mostly modern provincial town), and all epitomize the qualities that have come to be associated with Tuscan and Umbrian hill-towns: old medieval centres, atmospheric little streets and alleys, fascinating art galleries and excellent restaurants and historic hotels. Around these villages and above the valley floor, the landscapes are hilly and pretty, but on the plain itself intensively cultivated agricultural land is spotted with the ever-increasing blight of modern housing and haphazardly planned industrial concerns. In a car you can avoid the worst of these by following country roads, but on the excellent bus or rail links that provide access to all the towns and villages be warned that you will be faced with the worst of the valley's modern development.

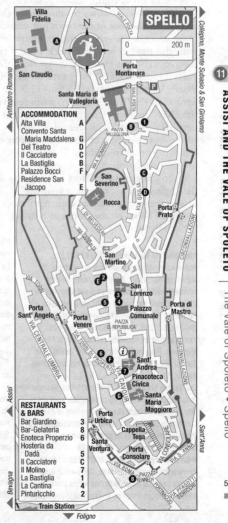

SPELLO

ACCOMMODATION
Alta Villa	A
Convento Santa Maria Maddalena	G
Del Teatro	D
Il Cacciatore	C
La Bastiglia	B
Palazzo Bocci	F
Residence San Jacopo	E

RESTAURANTS & BARS
Bar Giardino	3
Bar-Gelateria	8
Enoteca Properzio	6
Hosteria da Dadà	5
Il Cacciatore	C
Il Molino	7
La Bastiglia	1
La Cantina	4
Pinturicchio	2

Spello

Ranged impressively on broad walled terraces above the Vale of Spoleto, with the lofty slopes of Monte Subasio beyond, pink-stoned **SPELLO** offers an easily accessible taste of medieval small-town Umbria – and a major art attraction in its superlative frescoes by Pinturicchio in the church of

Santa Maria Maggiore. It also boasts a few reminders of its Roman past, when as Hispellum it served as a retirement home for pensioned-off legionaries and an important staging post on the Via Flaminia. Later it fell to the Lombards – who destroyed it – then became part of the Duchy of Spoleto. In 1238 it fell to Frederick II (who also destroyed it) and then passed under the yoke of Perugia. Once you're off the main street, the main core of the town is beautifully medieval. Today, despite its proximity to Assisi and Spoleto, it remains relatively quiet, though several new hotels and a rash of chintzy food, wine and trinket shops are testament to increasing numbers of tourists.

Arrival, information and accommodation

Regular stopping **trains** serve the town from Foligno and Perugia – check that they really do stop (the station is unstaffed, but there's a ticket machine in the waiting room) – and up to nine **buses** (Mon–Sat) on the Assisi–Foligno run drop off at the foot of the town just outside the Porta Consolare. The tortuous main street is one-way along its entire length (uphill from Porta Consolare), with the most central **car park** on the right immediately after Sant'Andrea. Alternatively you can walk down from the big car park off Via Cimitero by Porta Montanara. Call for a **taxi** on ☎0742.651.582. The **tourist office** is at Piazza Matteotti 3 (daily 9.30am–12.30pm & 3–5.30pm; Nov–March closes at 5pm; ☎0742.301.009). Spello's main **festival** is the *Infiorita* on Corpus Domini (late May or early June), when the streets are laid with carpets of minutely detailed pictorial scenes created entirely by hand from millions of flower petals. In the weeks leading up to the event you will see people everywhere patiently removing petals from stalks. There's also a festival celebrating the area's olive oil in the week before Shrove Tuesday.

Spello's **accommodation** is rarely too stretched, except in the days around the *Infiorita*. The nearest **campsite**, *Campeggio Subasio* (☎0742.801.0655, ⓦwww.campeggiosubasio.com; April to early Oct), is in Località Sportella, at a height of 840m on the slopes of Subasio.

Hotels

Alta Villa Via Mancinelli 2 ☎0742.301.515, ⓦwww.hotelaltavilla.com. Very comfortable, if rather gaudily smart, three-star hotel, several minutes' walk downhill from the old town (follow the signs from the corner of Piazza Vallegloria). ❸

Convento Santa Maria Maddalena Via Cavour 1 ☎0742.301.285. Very pleasant and low-cost rooms almost immediately opposite Santa Maria Maggiore. Ring the bell on the rather anonymous door on the side of the building facing back down the hill. ❶

Del Teatro Via Giulia 24 ☎075.301.140, ⓦwww.hoteldelteatro.it. Stung by competition from the *Alta Villa* and *Palazzo Bocci*, the owners of the *Cacciatore* opened this superbly appointed intimate three-star hotel with just eleven rooms and a pretty breakfast terrace down the road. ❹

Il Cacciatore Via Giulia 42 ☎0742.651.141, ⓦwww.ilcacciatorehotel.com. Good-value and friendly two-star hotel, with fine views from some rooms (although those on the road side are noisy).

It's worth staying here just for the superlative panoramic terrace. ❸

La Bastiglia Via dei Mollini 17 ☎0742.651.277, ⓦwww.labastiglia.com. Smallish but smart rooms in a beautifully restored mill, many of which command a view – plus a fancy restaurant that currently has a Michelin star. Some rooms can be ridiculously overpriced, but cheaper options are available out of high season. ❺

🏃 **Palazzo Bocci** Via Cavour 17 ☎0742.301.021, ⓦwww.palazzobocci.com. Tasteful four-star hotel with twenty rooms in a converted, frescoed *palazzo* just up from Santa Maria Maggiore. A definite first choice if you're doing Umbria in style. ❺

Residence San Jacopo Via Giulia 1 ☎0742.301.260, ⓦwww.residencesanjacopo.it. An excellent choice if you wish to self-cater or are travelling in a group. Ten mini-apartments are available (above the *Pinturicchio* restaurant), each with linen, TV, private bathroom and kitchen, from €60 for two people. ❸

The Town

Spello is easily explored, most of its main sights being on or just off the main street, **Via Consolare** and its continuation, **Via Cavour**, which winds through the town from the southern Porta Consolare, one of several minor monuments to the town's Roman heyday. Five minutes up the street is Spello's main draw, the church of **Santa Maria Maggiore**, with a lovely fresco cycle by Pintoricchio. More paintings and works of art feature in other of the town's churches, notably nearby **Sant'Andrea** and – further up the central street – **San Lorenzo**. Much of Spello's appeal, however, as so often in small Umbrian towns, resides in the charm of its small streets and alleys.

Porta Consolare

The **Porta Consolare** at the foot of the town is one of five Roman gates in the Augustan-era walls that still more or less enclose Spello. The gate is in a slightly sorry state, with an ancient olive tree growing from its crumbling upper reaches – a sixteenth-century fresco in the Palazzo Comunale shows the tower with its tree even then – but it still gives some idea of the glory that was Rome, and retains three original **statues**, figures removed from the town's amphitheatre that local folklore claims depict a family killed by eating poisonous mushrooms. Parts of the old Roman road are also exposed here, while to the left along Via Roma range some well-preserved stretches of the original Augustan-era walls (some of the best-preserved in Italy).

Inside the gate begins the main street, **Via Consolare–Via Cavour**, which bends and climbs steeply: it has no pavements, so beware – you're forever dodging cars. A couple of minutes' walk (you might take the rubber-surfaced alley on the left as a short cut) brings you to the odd little **Cappella Tega** (open to view behind glass), half-covered in frescoes from 1461 by Niccolò Alunno.

Santa Maria Maggiore

In 1600 Spello had some two thousand inhabitants – compared with around eight thousand today – and a staggering one hundred churches, of which 22 were dedicated to the Virgin. One of the most important of these was **Santa Maria Maggiore** (daily 8.30am–12.30pm & 3–7pm; Nov–March closes at 6pm), which celebrated both the Virgin's Birth (Sept 8) and the Assumption (Aug 15).

Begun in the twelfth century, the church was remodelled five centuries later to dull effect, the most obvious alterations being the **facade**, which was shifted forward a full nine metres, and the mundane Baroque botch visited on the interior. The facade did keep parts of the original Romanesque portal, however, some of whose fine carving has been attributed to Binello and Ridolfo, the mysterious craftsmen responsible for the strange sculptures on the churches of nearby Bevagna (see p.551). The two columns at the base of the campanile are from an earlier Roman building; Spello's main street follows exactly the course of the old Roman road, and a Roman aqueduct runs beneath it to this day.

Inside is an outstanding Roman **stoup** for holy water, fashioned from the altar tomb (AD 60) of Gaius Titienus Flaccus, a leading light of Hispellum's most important family. The dead man is shown on horseback above an inscription, while in the lower part of the stoup you can still make out a little hollow once used to store his ashes. Another similar tomb – that of a young woman – was moved from the church in the eighteenth century and now supports the cross on top of the campanile.

More fascinating are the paintings (1501) by **Pinturicchio** covering the Cappella Baglioni on the left as you enter, vast frescoes which rank with the artist's masterpieces in Siena's Libreria Piccolomini (see p.336) and Rome's Sistine Chapel and Borgia apartments. Sadly, they are behind glass: you need coins to illuminate them. The barrier also means you can't get a proper look at the chapel's **ceramic pavement** (1566), a faded testimony to the skill of Deruta's medieval craftsmen (see p.621).

The three panels are read from left to right; the ceiling vaults depict the *Four Sibyls*. The **first fresco** features the *Annunciation*, with the Virgin having just read the prophetic text from the Bible open in front of her. Below and to the right, the obvious hanging painting is a self-portrait of Pinturicchio, and under it a plaque with his name from which dangle brushes, styluses and other tools of the painter's trade. The **central fresco** on the rear wall depicts the *Adoration of the Child*, with the shepherds shown left of Christ and the Magi behind them to the left. Behind the Magi one of the group of armed men amidst the rocks bears an anachronistic detail: a shield with the Baglioni coat of arms (the chapel was commissioned by a prelate belonging to the infamous family in 1500). The painting is also remarkable for its preponderance of symbols, in particular the cross (a prefiguration of Christ's Crucifixion), the peacock (symbolizing eternal life and the incorruptibility of the flesh) and the flask of wine and bread in the bottom right-hand corner (an allusion to the Eucharist). The **final fresco**, the *Disputation in the Temple*, has rather more points of incidental narrative and decorative interest, including a portrait of Troilo Baglioni, the man who commissioned the paintings, shown in his black prioral habit at the extreme left. Alongside him stands his treasurer, with his bag of money, another pictorial reminder of who paid for the frescoes. Over on the extreme right the grisly-featured old woman is an allusion to the "Old Woman of the Cross", the central character in one of Spello's seminal medieval legends. The harridan is said to have tried to fan the mutual hatred of the inhabitants of the upper and lower town, but was vaporized before any bloody encounter could take place by the miraculous apparition of a cross above the town hall in 1346. Pinturicchio also makes an appearance, his name being picked out on the note held by the character in the prominent white headgear in the group to the right of Christ. The artist's hand can also be seen in the disturbing details in the background: the disabled beggars in front of the temple and, more macabre, the tiny figure dangling from a gibbet on the hill-top to the right of the large palm tree.

Elsewhere in the church are a couple of further paintings by Pinturicchio: in the **Cappella del Sacramento**, the chapel to the left of the apse, is a faintly etched angel holding a plaque above a little lavabo; the inscription – *Lavamini et mundi, estote* – means "Wash yourself and be pure." Beyond that, in the canon's room, is an overpainted but beautifully lyrical *Madonna and Child*. Two good late paintings by **Perugino** adorn the two pillars flanking the apse, one a *Pietà*, the other a *Madonna and Child with Sts Blaise and Catherine*. The only other worthwhile painting is a tantalizing fresco of the *Agony in the Garden* (1391) to the left of the large window at the rear of the apse. It's the work of **Cola Petruccioli**, an early Umbrian painter, and represents all that remains of a complete cycle sacrificed to the apse's blanket of whitewash in the seventeenth century.

The Pinacoteca Civica

Spello's **Pinacoteca Civica** (Tues–Sun: April–Sept 10.30am–1pm & 3–6.30pm; Oct–March 10.30am–12.30pm & 3.30–5.30pm; €2.60) is situated in the old Palazzo dei Canoncini almost beside Santa Maria Maggiore. It reopened in late 2005 after long-term restoration, but parts of the collection are still to be exhibited, and the gallery is likely to remain in a state of flux for some time. The best pieces include the wonderful polychrome wooden statue, *Madonna and Child*, an Umbrian work dating from the end of the twelfth century. Also outstanding is an extraordinary statue of the crucified Christ, its arms hinged to resemble a crude marionette. Such statues, now extremely rare, were used by religious confraternities during Holy Week celebrations: its arms would be opened or folded according to the particular religious celebration.

The gallery's vaguely open-plan arrangement makes it hard to figure out which room is which, but everything is well labelled, making it easy, for example, to track down treasures such as the superb enamelled cross (1398). The central figure depicts the Virgin. Nearby, the little diptych (1391) by Cola Petruccioli, designed as a portable preaching aid for itinerant monks, shows the *Crucifixion* on one panel and the *Coronation of the Virgin* on the other. Two of the gallery's highlights are a pair of early fifteenth-century panels of a triptych by the anonymous Maestro dell'Assunta di Amelia: *St John and the Prophet Isaiah*, and *John the Baptist and Nicholas of Bari*. The original triptych was stolen in 1970, and the main central panel – a *Madonna and Child* – has never been recovered. A similar fate befell another *Madonna and Child*, the central part of a triptych, attributed to Pinturicchio, stolen in the same year from Santa Maria Maggiore, but here the work was recovered in 2004 and is now exhibited in the gallery.

Even this happy returnee is overshadowed by a still better work, the superbly restored *Crucifixion, Virgin and Saints* by Niccolò Alunno. Nearby is a double-sided *gonfalone*, or banner, probably painted by one of Alunno's assistants. One side depicts the *Madonna della Misericordia* shielding Spello's citizens beneath her cloak, the other the *Miracle of the Cross of Spello*, the event alluded to in Pinturicchio's fresco of the *Disputation in the Temple* in Santa Maria Maggiore.

Elsewhere, look out for the double-sided *gonfalone* (1576) by Lorenzo Doni, depicting a particularly graphic *Martyrdom of St Barbara* on one side and the members of Spello's Confraternity of St Barbara on the other. Also pause in front of the five canvases by Marcantonio Grecchi, especially the *Madonna and Child with St Felix and Andrea Caccioli*; St Felix, an early bishop of Spello, is one of the town's patron saints. The painting's charm lies in the perfectly realized little portrait of Spello held by the two protagonists, the town looking much the same as it does today.

Sant'Andrea and around

A short distance uphill from the Pinacoteca lies **Sant'Andrea**, its simple thirteenth-century facade hiding a darkly atmospheric interior. Most surfaces are inexpertly painted, though the overall effect is superb, and there is another outstanding **Pinturicchio** – a *Madonna and Child with Saints* in the right transept, executed with Eusebio di San Giorgio. On the extreme right is the figure of St Lawrence, who is shown holding the black griddle on which he was roasted to death. A panel depicting this martyrdom in detail is shown as a luminous square picture rather oddly stitched into the lower half of his robes. Also look out for the two small panels close to one of the saints (Giovannino), where the painter has proudly transcribed a letter sent to him by Gentile Baglioni, the bishop of Orvieto. The vast eye-catching Crucifix hanging above the altar is by an unknown fourteenth-century Umbrian follower of Giotto.

The spread of impressive-looking decoration in the apse and elsewhere dates from the nineteenth century and may, it's thought, conceal all sorts of hidden treasures. When the large altar in the left transept was removed for cleaning, areas of important early fresco were revealed behind it, much of which, it appears, had been whitewashed following some long-forgotten plague epidemic.

Shortage of funds has as yet prevented any further investigation. In the left transept is the tomb of the Spello-born beatific **Andrea Caccioli** (1194–1254), one of the earliest followers of St Francis.

A diversion from Sant'Andrea along nearby Via Torri di Properzio (left off Via Cavour) brings you to the best remnant of Roman Spello, the perfectly preserved if slightly forlorn **Porta Venere**, possibly named after a long-vanished temple to Venus: Constantine is said to have built one of Umbria's largest shrines to the goddess in the vicinity. The imposing twin towers flanking the gate might be Roman or medieval; no one's sure.

The rest of the town

Further up Via Cavour beyond Sant'Andrea, the main **Piazza della Repubblica** is part grotesque twentieth-century, part medieval, with its arched **Palazzo Comunale** boasting a couple of fourteenth-century frescoes by local painters. Further up again, **San Lorenzo** rates as one of Umbria's more successful Baroque conversions. A mongrel of a church, it had a succession of architects who left a variety of decorative effects, some laughable, like the obviously fake marbles, others more persuasive – as with the *baldacchino*, a bronze canopy copied from Bernini's piece for St Peter's in Rome. The most arresting sight is the minutely realistic statue of St Peter the Martyr, midway down the west wall, complete with trickle of blood from the cleaver delicately planted in his head.

At the top of Spello's main street you'll probably be heartily sick of having to dodge cars, but here you can start to explore the alleys and backstreets that provide the town's typical Umbrian charm. Views from the east side of town are especially good, with lovely panoramas over the bucolic countryside below Monte Subasio. The arch almost opposite San Lorenzo leads to the highest point of the town, occupied by the **belvedere** and **Rocca** – the latter giving the only view you need of the overgrown remains of the first-century Roman amphitheatre to the west.

Beyond the walls, near the amphitheatre, is the half-collapsed twelfth-century church of **San Claudio**, which has a strange Romanesque asymmetry inside and out. It was raised from the ashes of an old Roman building on the same site. A ten-minute walk beyond – also accessible via a country lane which drops down from Piazza Vallegloria – is the little-known **Villa Fidelia** (Tues–Sun 10.30am–6pm, April–Sept closes 7pm; €3), with a beautiful garden and the

A walk over Monte Subasio

A tough but wonderful **walk** starts beyond the Rocca at the Porta Montanara. This route is worth climbing just for twenty minutes or so in order to get superb views of Spello and the Vale of Spoleto, though if you follow it the whole way you can reach Assisi (allow a full day for this) via the summit of **Monte Subasio** and/or the Eremo delle Carceri. To find the route, take the second right turn after the Porta Montanara (signposted for Collepino), walk past the olive-oil works on the right, and after 100m take the (initially surfaced) track left at the fountain. The path is marked by the *Club Alpino Italiano*: look for trail no. 50 and red spot markings which run all the way to Assisi. It's a good idea to have a detailed walking **map** to hand – try the newsagents to the right of San Lorenzo in Spello. You can **drive** on the part-gravel road from the northern end of Spello over Monte Subasio to Assisi (signed "Monte Subasio" and *La Baita*, the latter a panoramic bar-restaurant on a side road halfway up): be certain not to miss the left turn after a couple of kilometres, or you'll end up in Collepino and Armenzano. The **views** are superlative and there are sensational spreads of orchids and narcissi in late May and early June.

miscellaneous Straka-Coppa private collection of paintings, sculptures, old furniture and costumes, together with displays on the Futurists.

Eating and drinking

Spello has a good range of places to **eat**, from long-established and simple trattorias to Michelin-starred restaurants. The *Bar-Gelateria* on Via Roma opposite the Porta Santa Maria Maggiore serves up **ice cream** and sorbets just a wafer away from perfection. *Bar Giardino*, Via Garibaldi 12, with a huge grassy terrace and tables to the rear, is a wonderful spot to soak up the scenery. For **wine**, try the *Enoteca Properzio* at Via Torri di Properzio 8a. For picnic supplies, make tracks for the lovely old-fashioned Scarponi **bakery** opposite the *Teatro* hotel at Via Giulia 43 or Hispellum, a **food shop** at Via Cavour 37.

Restaurants

Hosteria da Dadà Via Cavour 47 ☏0742.301.327.
Very cheap, and good for lunch or a light meal, this is a small place with a few shared tables.
Closed Mon.

Il Cacciatore Via Giulia 42 ☏0742.651.141.
Middling food and service, but one of the great Umbrian terraces for summer eating, and a wonderful choice for lunch if the *Bastiglia*'s prices are too high. Closed Mon.

Il Molino Piazza Matteotti 6–7 ☏0742.651.305.
An upmarket option, with a pleasing medieval setting and some good food – as long you avoid the occasional unfortunate pretension to Italian nouvelle cuisine. Closed Tues.

La Bastiglia Via dei Mollini 17 ☏0742.651.277.
Spello's best restaurant is the Michelin-starred hotel dining room of *La Bastiglia*, with expensive and rarefied cooking (dining outside in summer is a treat).

La Cantina Via Cavour 2 ☏0742.651.775. A friendly local place set in a vaulted medieval town house serving plenty of regional specialities and wonderful fresh pasta, though it suffers from being rather big and unatmospheric on quiet nights.
Closed Wed.

Pinturicchio Largo Mazzini 8 ☏0742.301.003.
A cheap but first-rate option is this trattoria on the left at the top of the main street just past San Lorenzo. Closed Tues.

Foligno and around

On public transport, sooner or later you're likely to find yourself passing through **FOLIGNO**, a hub for trains and buses. Although this was the place where, in 1472, the first book was printed in Italian – three hundred copies of Dante's *Divine Comedy* – today Foligno is a largely modern place, ringed with factories and concrete sprawl, its star turns bombed during World War II. What remains is a not unpleasant provincial town, though with nothing that would merit a special visit, and certainly nothing to tempt you away from Spello, Bevagna or Montefalco.

Arrival, information and accommodation

For Foligno's **tourist office** – at Corso Cavour 126 (April–Oct Mon–Sat 10am–1pm & 4–7pm, Sun 10am–1pm; Nov–Feb Mon–Sat 10am–1pm & 3–6pm, Sun 10am–1pm; ☏0742.354.459) – and **bus station** (Porta Romana), follow Viale Mezzetti west from the **train station** to Piazzale Alunno. Piazza della Repubblica is a short walk along Corso Cavour from here. To get to Montefalco, there are infrequent buses from Porta Todi, around Via N. Sauro from Piazzale Alunno.

If hotels in Assisi and Spello are full, you may have cause to try Foligno's **accommodation** options, which are inexpensive but generally not terribly inspiring.

Hotels

Italia Piazza Matteotti 12 ☎0742.350.412,
ⓦwww.hotelitaliafoligno.com. A functional three-
star place, very centrally located immediately south
of Piazza della Repubblica. ❸

Pierantoni Via Pierantoni 23 ☎0742.342.566,
ⓔfolhostel@tiscalinet.it. A big hostel with around
two hundred dorm beds (€15–17) arranged in 39
rooms.

Valentini Via Flavio Ottaviani 19 ☎0742.353.990.
A family-run two-star just north of the train station
– surprisingly pleasant given its position. ❷

Villa Roncalli Viale Roma 25 ☎0742.391.091,
ⓕ0742.391.001. Best of the upmarket three-star
places; a smart seventeenth-century villa with
garden and pool and Foligno's top gourmet
restaurant. ❷

The Town

The town was particularly badly hit by the 1997 earthquakes – the dramatic
collapse of the Torre Comunale was broadcast worldwide – and the residue of
its medieval heritage is conveniently concentrated in the central **Piazza della
Repubblica**. The **Duomo** is the main eye-catcher, the twelfth-century Palazzo
Comunale opposite having been ruined by a Neoclassical facade at the
beginning of the nineteenth century. Unusually, the church boasts two facades,
the south frontage containing one of the most impressive portals in the region:
a riot of carving full of zodiac signs, intricate patterning and bizarre animals, as
well as a likeness of Frederick II on the left (one of only two in Italy) and a
Muslim star and crescent near the apex of the arch. The mosaics of the other
facade are a nineteenth-century afterthought. Inside, a panel by Niccolò Alunno
in the sacristy is the only feature worth seeking out.

At the western end of the piazza is the **Palazzo Trinci** (1389–1407), the
much-altered home of the Trinci, Foligno's medieval big shots and by far the
best reason to visit the town. Long-term restoration has revived a fine
courtyard, palace frescoes and painted staircase, and a small **archeological
museum** (April–Oct Tues–Sun 10am–1pm & 3–7pm; rest of the year closed
6.30pm; €6) and linked **Pinacoteca Comunale** (same hours and ticket). The
key sight is a fine fresco cycle by Gentile da Fabriano whose non-religious
themes include the story of the founding of Rome, the Seven Liberal Arts, the
Seven Ages of Man, the hours of the day, the cycle of the planets and more.
Other high points include a frescoed chapel by Ottaviano Nelli and an
Annunciation attributed to Benozzo Gozzoli. The only other monument
which hints at Foligno's former glory is **Santa Maria Infraportas**, a church
of pagan origins in which St Peter is said to have celebrated Mass. The oldest
part of the current eighth-century church is the Cappella dell'Assunta off the
left nave; the Byzantine mural behind its altar is the town's most precious
piece of art.

Eating and drinking

Cheap **pizzerias** are numerous. For coffee, drinks, snacks and light **meals**, *La
Bottega Barbanera*, Piazza della Repubblica 34 (☎0742.350.672; closed Mon),
serves tempting local dishes in charming surroundings – a former *drogheria* with
lovely old counter. Even better, and popular with locals, is the small *Il Bacco
Felice*, Via Garibaldi 73–75 (☎0742.341.019; closed Mon), set in a library-type
salon full of old bottles and books on food and wine; the attention to detail and
focus on ingredients is excellent (co-owner Tiziana has accumulated 32
different types of tomato alone for use in salads and sauces). With a similar
approach, the *Hostaria Sparafucile*, Piazzetta Duomo 30 (☎0742.342.602; closed
Wed, Oct & lunch in winter), has a great selection of wines and simple,
inexpensive local dishes, served outside in summer.

East of Foligno

Visible from afar from the Vale of Spoleto, the Benedictine **Abbazia di Sassovivo** (daily dawn to dusk; free), 6km east of Foligno, is one of the oldest monasteries in Umbria, dating from 1070. Set in wooded countryside, it also claims the region's finest medieval cloisters, with 128 variegated columns and 58 arches all decorated with mosaics and coloured marble. The church is dull, save for its eleventh-century crypt, cloister and loggia (daily 8.30am–7.30pm).

To the north, the SS77 road to Camerino threads through the beautiful **Menotre valley**, a region of small, lost villages and virgin hill country. To explore properly, you'll need transport or the will to hike (plus the invaluable Kompass *Assisi-Camerino* map #665). **PALE**, 8km east of Foligno, is the first village you'll come to. It has a castle and a stalactite-crammed cave, the **Grotta di Pale**. Paths cover the 4km to the summit of the craggy **Sasso di Pale** (958m), also accessible from Santa Lucia, 1km on from Pale. The only place of any real size in the valley is **COLFIORITO**, 25km from Foligno, in an area of Umbria that very few tourists see. Once an important Iron Age site, controlling one of the lowest Apennine passes into the Marche, Colfiorito sits at the heart of some extraordinary countryside, mostly marsh and upland plain – rather like the Valnerina – surrounded by fields of grass and mountain peaks. Green and cool in summer, the town has become something of a holiday retreat for locals and is well served by **hotels**, including the three-star *Villa Fiorita*, Via del Lago 9 (℡0742.681.326, Ⓦwww.hotelvillafiorita.com; ❸), and the small, two-star *Valico*, Via Casette di Cupigliolo (℡0742.681.385, Ⓦwww.valico.it; ❶).

Bevagna

BEVAGNA, shadowed by the Martani hills 8km southwest of Foligno, is even more serene and handsome a backwater than Spello, with a windswept central piazza of austere perfection and two of Umbria's finest Romanesque churches. An Umbrian and then an Etruscan settlement, it became Mevania under the Romans, and a staging post on the Via Flaminia (built in 220 BC) – now the Corso Matteotti, which bisects the town. Its decline dates from the building of a new spur to the Flaminia five centuries later, a road that was routed through Terni and Spoleto rather than Bevagna. After the Roman era it was sacked by Barbarossa, Frederick II, Foligno's Trinci family and, inevitably, Perugia's Baglioni. Today it has scarcely spread beyond its medieval walls, remaining miraculously unscarred by the urban blight of most nearby hill-towns.

Arrival, information and accommodation

From Foligno, five to eight **buses** daily run to Montefalco via Bevagna (four back from Montefalco), dropping off in the little square immediately to the south of San Silvestri; buy tickets in the bar secreted away in the medieval loggia on the square's eastern edge. The small and irregularly open **tourist office** (℡0742.361.667) is below the Palazzo dei Consoli's stone staircase.

From a village that until relatively recently had nowhere to stay except for an austere convent with a few rooms, Bevagna now has a disproportionate number of charming **places to stay**.

Accommodation

Il Chiostro di Bevagna Corso G. Matteotti 107
ⓣ0742.361.987, ⓦ www.ilchiostrodibevagna.com.
The most central option is this one-star in an
atmospheric renovated Dominican convent dating
from the thirteenth century, with an original cloister
where you can take breakfast in good weather. ❷
Locanda Piazza Onofri Piazza Onofri
ⓣ0742.361.926, ⓦ www.enotecaonofri.it. Good-
value mini-apartments with kitchenettes attached to
the Enoteca di Piazza Onofri (see opposite). ❸

🏃 **L'Orto degli Angeli** Via Dante Alighieri 1
ⓣ0742.360.130, ⓦ www.ortoangeli.it.
A luxurious, historic mansion, with porticoes,
beautiful gardens and the *Redibus* restaurant (see

opposite); the house has been in the same family
since 1788. ❼
Palazzo Brunamonti Corso G. Matteotti 79
ⓣ0742.361.932, ⓦ www.brunamonti.com.
A sumptuous, central aristocratic townhouse from
the seventeenth century, with period fittings,
beamed ceilings, and *trompe l'oeil* decorations.
Usually closed Jan & Feb. ❹
Pian di Boccio Località Pian di Boccio 10
ⓣ0742.360.164, ⓦ www.piandiboccio.com. If you
want to camp, or be out of town in a pleasant
agriturismo, make for *Pian di Boccio*, about 4km
southeast of the village. It has a pool, nine rustic
apartments with kitchens, a pizzeria, and plenty to
keep kids entertained. ❶

The Town

Bevagna's backstreets sooner or later converge on the pedestrianized main
square, **Piazza Silvestri**, broad and open after its shadowed surroundings.
Every member of this unimprovable arrangement is thoroughly medieval, with
the sole exception of the nineteenth-century fountain, and even that blends in
perfectly. Two churches face each other across the square, both untouched and
creaking with age. The smaller, deconsecrated **San Silvestro** is a magnificent
squat example of early Umbrian-Romanesque; its exterior bears a plaque with
the date of construction – 1195 – and the name of the builder, Binello, who
was also responsible for San Michele opposite, but of whom nothing else is
known except for his work on Spello's Santa Maria Maggiore (see p.545). Pieces
of Roman remains are woven into the facade, whose upper half is faced in pink
Subasio stone and boasts the stump of an unfinished tower. The **interior** –
which tends to be open when the rest of the town is shut – is superbly ancient
in look and feel, with a raised presbytery and sunken crypt. Look out for the
capitals of the blunt columns in the nave, which are of an Egyptian order (rather
than Doric, Ionic or Corinthian) and were perhaps copied from a Roman
temple to distant deities. Britain's Prince Charles has been instrumental in
helping raise funds to restore the church. **San Michele**, the second church,
appears more recent, perhaps owing to its rose window, punched through in the

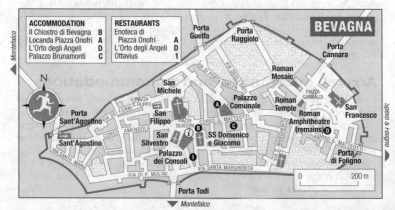

eighteenth century. It is in fact San Silvestro's contemporary and is built to a similar interior plan; its capitals are similarly eccentric, as are the magnificently surreal gargoyles over the main doorway.

The square's third component is the twelfth-century **Palazzo dei Consoli**, distinguished by a broad stone staircase. Infiltrated into it is the delightful nineteenth-century **Teatro F. Torti**, full of minuscule boxes and balconies, one of only a few surviving examples of the tiny provincial theatres that once flourished across Italy. Enquire at the Museo di Bevagna for admittance (see below). Beside is **Sts Domenico e Giacomo**, rectangular and workaday, its Baroque interior relieved only by fragments of fresco and two early wooden sculptures. The church's prime position was a gift from the *comune* to the Dominicans for help in rebuilding the town after one of its sackings. Be sure to have a look at the small cloister, reached through the church.

The church of **San Francesco** at the town's highest point claims to have the stone from which St Francis preached his famous sermon to the birds, a discourse that supposedly occurred on the road between Bevagna and Cannara (the spot is also commemorated at Assisi's Eremo delle Carceri).

Roman Bevagna

The small **Museo di Bevagna** (April–Sept daily 10.30am–1pm & 2.30–5.30/7pm; Oct–March closes Mon & at 5pm; €3.50), Corso G. Matteotti 70, devoted to the history of the village, is divided into three modest sections: archeological displays, art and history, and maps, letters and other documents. The paintings are eminently forgettable, but the medley of Roman remains – all found locally – is worth a look. None, though, compares with the impressive black-and-white **Roman mosaic** on the north side of Via Porta Guelfa (free with museum ticket: guided tours depart from museum for mosaics and theatre roughly every 20min). Laid down in the second century, it formed part of a bath complex – hence the associations of its dolphins, lobsters and other sea creatures. To the south, the pillars and half-columns of the **Roman temple** date from roughly the same period. Just to the north, **Porta Cannara**, the best preserved of the town's gates, offers access to a nice stretch of the medieval walls. Farther east on Corso G. Matteotti, be sure to explore Via dell'Anfiteatro, whose diminutive houses follow the line of the former **Roman amphitheatre**, and which gives access to a series of little tunnels that burrow mysteriously into the old under-stage area.

You can also join guided tours at the museum around the **Circuito Medievale Storie di Antichi Mestieri** (twice daily during museum opening days at 11am, plus 3.30pm April–May & Sept, 4.30pm June–Aug & 3pm Oct–March). This involves visits to four recreated workshops connected with medieval trades, namely paper-making, silk-weaving, a mint and a pharmacy.

Eating and drinking

Good eating options in Bevagna have proliferated in recent years, thanks mainly to the opening of new hotels. The gourmet **restaurant** *Redibus*, for example, attached to the hotel *L'Orto degli Angeli* (see opposite; closed Wed), is a fine place to eat in an atmospheric setting, part recovered from the former Roman ampitheatre. The simple *Enoteca di Piazza Onofri*, Piazza Onofri 1 (℡0742.361.926, ⒲www.enotecaonofri.it; closed Wed, Mon–Fri at lunch, plus a period in July & Aug), offers light meals based on traditional dishes executed with a slight twist; desserts are usually excellent (try the *soufflé al cioccolato*). A touch more expensive is the excellent *Ottavius*, Via del Gonfalone

4 (℡0742.360.555; closed Mon Nov–Feb and periods in Jan & July), wonderfully situated in an old single-vaulted medieval room; the food – great *gnocchi al Sagrantino* and succulent *filetto* – is pure Umbrian. If you have a car, consider driving to nearby Cannara (see below) to eat at the first-rate *Perbacco*. The **bar** just off Bevagna's central piazza – good for ice cream and snacks – has perhaps Umbria's most miserable service and oddest clientele.

Around Bevagna

With your own transport, you can explore the rich agricultural plain surrounding Bevagna. In the hills above the town, clearly delineated on the skyline, is the Renaissance church of **Madonna delle Grazie** (rarely open), admirable from below, but by no means worth the journey for a closer look. The most rewarding trip follows the minor road northwest towards Cannara. Some 2km out is the pretty, restored Convento dell'Annunziata, followed by the one-horse hamlet of **Cantalupo** and the tiny stone chapel of Madonna della Pia. Take a minor left turn 1km beyond and you hit **Limigiano**, a classic fortified hamlet centred on a thirteenth-century church, San Michele. At the crossroads for Cannara, a left turn leads to **Collemancio**, where 500m north of the village's public gardens are the unexcavated ruins of Urbinum Hortense, a Roman or possibly Etruscan settlement destroyed by Totila in 545. The odds and ends – traces of a temple, pavement and mosaics – merit a wander, while the views over the Vale of Spoleto are superb.

CANNARA itself, stranded mid-plain but sheltered by trees, has three churches, each with significant paintings by major Umbrian artists: **San Giovanni** sports frescoes by Lo Spagna, while **San Matteo** and **San Francesco** have works by Niccolò Alunno. The Palazzo Comunale in Piazza Umberto houses a small **gallery** with frescoes detached from local churches and archeological finds from Urbinium. You'd do well to make a point of **eating** at the exceptional *Perbacco*, Via Umberto I 14 (℡0742.720.492; dinner only; closed Mon and four weeks in July & Aug), an inexpensive *osteria* at the centre of the village. Everything served is rigorously local, with old-fashioned and sometimes robust dishes you won't find everywhere such as *zampetti con salsa verde* (pigs' trotters) and *piccione in casseruola* (pigeon casserole).

Montefalco

As you'd expect from its name, **MONTEFALCO** ("the Falcon's Mount") commands the Vale of Spoleto. The local tag of *la ringhiera dell'Umbria* ("the balcony of Umbria") may be a touch hyperbolic but the views are nonetheless majestic and past the modern suburbs lies one of the finest hill-towns in the area, a maze of tiny, cobbled streets, with an artistic heritage – including pictures by Perugino and a stunning Gozzoli fresco cycle – out of all proportion to its size.

The town was the birthplace of eight saints, good going even by Italian standards, and began life as a small independent medieval *comune* known as Coccorone. It was destroyed by **Frederick II** in 1249, his only legacy a gate named in his honour, whereafter Montefalco took its new name, supposedly after the imperial eagle of Frederick's crest. Its chief historical interest lies in a brief interlude in the fourteenth century, when the town became a refuge to Spoleto's papal governors, left vulnerable by the defection of the popes to Avignon. Their munificent presence resulted in the rich decoration of local churches and the commissioning of **Lorenzo Maitani**, who was later to work

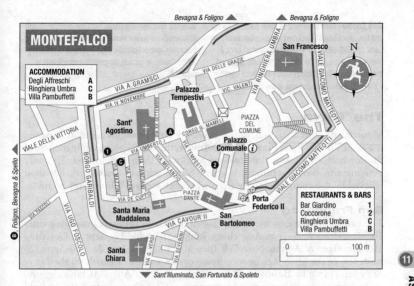

MONTEFALCO

San Francesco

N

ACCOMMODATION
Degli Affreschi	A
Ringhiera Umbra	C
Villa Pambuffetti	B

VIA DELLE GRAZIE

VIA A.GRAMSCI

Palazzo
Tempestivi

VIC. VALENTI

VIA RINGHIERA UMBRA

VIALE GIACOMO MATTEOTTI

VIA IV NOVEMBRE

Sant'
Agostino

VIA XX SETTEMBRE

CORSO G. MAMELI

PIAZZA
DEL
COMUNE

Palazzo
Comunale ℹ

VIALE DELLA VITTORIA

BORGO GARIBALDI

VIA UMBERTO I

VIC. MAZZINI

VIA PANCANI

VIA PICENA

VIA MELANZIO

VIA TEMPESTIVI

VIALE GIACOMO MATTEOTTI

VIA DE CUPPIS

PIAZZA
DANTE

Porta
Federico II

RESTAURANTS & BARS
Bar Giardino	1
Coccorone	2
Ringhiera Umbra	C
Villa Pambuffetti	B

Santa Maria
Maddalena

VIA CAVOUR II

San
Bartolomeo

VIA G. VERDI

VIA SEVERINI

Santa
Chiara

0   100 m

Foligno, Bevagna & Spello ◀ B

▼ Sant'Illuminata, San Fortunato & Spoleto

on the Duomo in Orvieto, to strengthen the town walls (still impressively intact) and to build a fortress for the exiled rulers. Power thereafter devolved to Foligno's Trinci family, to the rapacious Baglioni and eventually to the Church – a cue for several centuries of quiet decline.

Arrival, information and accommodation

Five to eight **buses** daily (Mon–Sat) from Foligno's Porta Romana, and one to three daily from Perugia (Mon–Sat) stop just outside the walls at the bottom of Via Umberto I in Viale della Vittoria. There are also connections to Bevagna. Everything is within a few minutes' walk of the main square, Piazza del Comune, home to a **tourist information** office on the south side (daily: April–Oct 8am–1pm & 2–6pm; Nov–March opens at 9am; ☎0742.378.490, ⓦwww.stradadelsagrantino.it). The office has maps and information concerned with the Strada del Sagrantino: a quartet of driving (or cycling) routes around the vineyards, estates and countryside of Montefalco. There's also an irregularly open Pro Loco office alongside the San Francesco museum (☎0742.379.598) on Via Ringhiera Umbra.

Accommodation

There's no need to spend more than a morning in Montefalco, but it's a peaceful spot to rest up, and there are a couple of appealing out-of-town options too.

Degli Affreschi Corso G. Mameli 45 ☎0742.378.150, ℻0742.378.400, ⓦwww .hoteldegliaffreschi.it. Closer to the main square and fancier than the *Ringhiera*. Residents can use the swimming pool at the ugly modern sister hotel *Hotel Nuovo Mondo*, 2km west of town on the main road. ❷

Ringhiera Umbra Corso G. Mameli 20 ☎0742.379.166, ⓦwww.ringhieraumbra.com. Tiny and quaintly old-fashioned, with a relaxed little

restaurant (closed Mon in winter) in the medieval vaulted room downstairs. ❶

Villa Pambuffetti Via Vittoria 3 ☎0742.379.417, ⓦwww.villapambuffetti .com. A marvellous four-star villa-hotel with park and pool, 100m west of town towards Foligno. Make sure you're in the main villa, not the gatehouse; the room to go for is the one in the old tower, with a 360-degree view. ❻

Villa Zuccari 8km southeast of town (beyond Turrita and the sanctuary of Madonna della Stella), near San Luca ☎0742.399.402, ⓦwww.villazuccari.com. A divine rural hotel, on the fringe of the hills adjoining the valley floor. The Zuccari family has lived here for some 400 years, though most of the present, superbly restored villa dates from the eighteenth and nineteenth centuries. Rooms have panoramic balconies and delightful period furniture, and there's a fine Italianate garden, elegant restaurant, and a pool. ❺

The Town

Montefalco's chief attraction, the ex-church of **San Francesco** and its museum, is a stone's throw from **Piazza del Comune**, the main square, while the rest of the town is little more than five-minutes' walk from end to end. The only outlying site, **San Fortunato**, is about fifteen-minutes' walk away, the stroll relieved by the comprehensively frescoed church of **Sant'Illuminata** en route.

San Francesco

The cavernous fourteenth-century church of **San Francesco** (June–Aug daily 10.30am–1pm & 3–7pm, Aug closes 7.30pm; March–May, Sept & Oct daily 10.30am–1pm & 2–6pm; Nov–Feb Tues–Sun 10.30am–1pm & 2.30–5pm; €5) hosts one of the great Renaissance fresco cycles, a series of panels on the *Life of St Francis* (1452) by **Benozzo Gozzoli**, a pupil of Fra' Angelico. His delightful cycle – which duplicates in its subjects many of Giotto's panels in Assisi – is bold in its colouring and utterly assured of its narrative, and is also of interest for its closely observed townscapes: Arezzo is depicted, as is Montefalco (visited by St Francis after his sermon to the birds). The panels completely fill the apse, with twenty medallions around them depicting famous Franciscans; underneath the

Sagrantino

Montefalco's **wines** have always been prized within Umbria, but have recently started to achieve wider fame. Their reputation rests not so much on the serviceable Rosso di Montefalco as on two powerful reds of mysterious origin, the extraordinary **Sagrantino** and **Sagrantino Passito**. Both are made from the Sagrantino grape, a variety found nowhere else in Europe. Why it should be unique to a tiny area of central Italy is a mystery: it appears in records in the nineteenth century, but experts claim a far more ancient pedigree, some saying it was imported by the Saracens, others that it was introduced by Syrian monks in the seventh century, or perhaps came from Piedmont or Catalonia. Its name may derive from its sacramental use by Franciscan communities who used to cultivate this grape.

Sagrantino is a dry red, usually made with up to five percent of the common Trebbiano Toscano. Sagrantino Passito is similar, with the important difference that it uses semi-dried or passito grapes to produce that rarest of drinks – a sweet red dessert wine. Both varieties, in the words of Italian wine guru Burton Anderson, have a remarkable "dark purple-garnet colour, rich, berry-like scent, and warm, rich full flavour". There are numerous small producers, with **Adanti** being reliable leading exponents of both varieties, their singular Rosso d'Arquata, in Anderson's words, "one of central Italy's most original and enjoyable red wines". Any of the many producers in the tiny DOC area, however, should come up trumps, especially **Caprai** at Torre di Montefalco (☎0742.378.802, ⓦwww.arnaldocaprai.it) and **Paolo Bea** at Cerrette (☎0742.378.128, ⓦwww.paolobea.com). **Antonelli**, **Benincasa** and **Rocca di Fabbri** are also first-rate. Most vineyards are open to the public (Caprai generally daily in summer, Paolo Bea and others more restricted opening). The *alimentari* and bar-*enoteca* in Montefalco's Piazza del Comune contain a superb selection of the area's wines.

main window appear Petrarch, Dante and Giotto, members of the lay tertiary order. Further work by Gozzoli fills the walls and vaults to the right, as well as the first chapel on the left (south) side of the church. The striking but cruder frescoes in the fourth, fifth and sixth chapels on this side are the work of the fifteenth-century Foligno artist Giovanni di Corraduccio.

Elsewhere are paintings by many of the leading lights of the Umbrian Renaissance, such as Perugino, Niccolò Alunno and Tiberio d'Assisi. Perugino's *Nativity* (1503) on the west wall, in particular, is worth looking out for, as Lago Trasimeno is featured in the background. Works originally commissioned for San Francesco remain *in situ*, with others housed in the excellent **Pinacoteca-Museo Civico di San Francesco** up the stairs (same hours & ticket). Look out for Francesco Melanzio's *Madonna Enthroned with Six Saints*, the work of a local Renaissance painter, and for the two panels – one by Melanzio – showing the *Madonna del Soccorso*. The story, common in Umbria though rarely painted elsewhere, concerns a young mother who, tired of her whingeing child, cries, "Would that the Devil might take you away!", whereupon the Devil appears, prompting the mother to invoke the Virgin to save her infant.

Sant'Agostino

The Augustinians' monastery and church of **Sant'Agostino** is 200m from the Franciscans' power base, across the Piazza del Comune. A simple Gothic hall, begun in 1275, it is typical of the order, designed with a view to minimizing the fripperies and maximizing the preaching space. It has a few excellent frescoes that have survived the damp – including a *Coronation of the Virgin* by Caporali (1522) – but its main interest, lending a distinctly spooky air, lies in its collection of mummies. Midway down the right nave are the first of these – the tiny bodies of **Beata Illuminata** and **Beata Chiarella**, clad in dusty muslin which only half hides their bones, skin and yellow faces. At the top of the left-hand side of the church is another dusty cadaver, propped on one elbow and looking very comfortable in a glass-fronted wardrobe. Known as the **Beato Pellegrino** (Holy Pilgrim), he apparently came to venerate Illuminata and Chiarella, fell asleep in the church in the position he's in now, and was found dead next morning against a confessional. Immediately placed in a sepulchre, he was found outside it the next day, and refused to stay put on several subsequent occasions. His body and clothes didn't decay for a hundred years. Despite this impressive behaviour, nothing was known of the character, so there was no sainthood, and he was plonked for posterity in his wardrobe.

Santa Chiara

In the church of **Santa Chiara**, five minutes from San Francesco in Via Verdi, the wizened body of St Clare of Montefalco languishes in a transparent casket high up on the altar. The saint – not to be confused with her more famous namesake at Assisi – was born in Montefalco in 1290, became a nun at the age of 6 and embarked on a series of miracles connected with the Passion of Christ. There's a small fresco cycle on her life in a chapel inside the convent (ring the bell on the door to the right of the casket and ask one of the nuns to unlock it). The nuns might also show you around the rest of the adjoining **convent**. On show is a small Crucifix enshrining three of the saint's gallstones (representing the Trinity) as well as the remains of her heart and the scissors with which the relic was hacked out of her, all of which are kept in a cupboard under her body – shared by the main church and this private chapel. The story relates that Christ appeared to Clare, saying the burden of the Cross was becoming too heavy for him; the saint replied she would help by carrying it within, and when she was opened up a cross-shaped piece of tissue was duly found on her heart. Other sights include a miraculous tree that grew from a staff planted by Christ, who appeared again to Clare in the shrubbery. The nuns believe it to be the sole wild specimen of its species in all of Europe; the berries are used to make rosaries, and are said to have powerful medicinal properties.

Sant'Illuminata and San Fortunato

Down Via Verdi from Santa Chiara is the tiny church of **Sant'Illuminata**, worth a visit for its triple-arched Renaissance portico and comprehensively frescoed interior. The standard of painting isn't always high – most works are by the obscure local man Melanzio – but the overall effect is captivating.

Keep heading out of town from here, down the avenue of horse chestnuts, then turn left at the T-junction, and a ten-minute trudge brings you out at the **Monastero di San Fortunato** (closed daily noon–4pm), set amongst ilex woods, the site home to a church since the fifth century. It has noted frescoes on the *Life of St Francis* (1512) by Tiberio d'Assisi – one of Perugino's leading disciples – in its Cappella delle Rose, to the left of the main courtyard. Gozzoli painted the very faded *Madonna and Child with Angels* over the door of the main church (the *St Sebastian* is by Tiberio), the dark fresco of St Fortunatus inside on the left altar, and the three worn tondi on the sarcophagus of St Severus in the little chapel off the right aisle. The St Fortunatus fresco once sat above the remains of Fortunatus himself, whose bones were laid out in a macabre skull-and-crossbones arrangement; at the time of writing they have been temporarily removed. The saint died in 390, and in rotting away proved rather more corruptible than Sant'Agostino's holy personages.

Eating and drinking

For something grander than the *Ringhiera*'s cosy and inexpensive **restaurant** (see p.555), try the outstanding ☂ *Coccorone*, set in a medieval building on the corner of Largo Tempestivi and Via Fabbri (☎0742.379.535; closed Wed in winter), where the chances are you'll have one of Umbria's better meals – great pasta and *crespelli* (rolled pancakes), and superlative *tiramisù*. To find it, follow the off-putting yellow signs for the "Tipical Ristorant". The restaurant in the *Pambuffetti* hotel is also good, though more formal and pricier; the dining room is a lovely glass-enclosed space with views onto the garden. This makes it great in summer, but no match in winter for the roaring wood-fire cosiness of the *Coccorone* (the fire usually burns in summer as well – it's used to grill the meats).

You might while away an hour in one of the **bars** in the main square, or try the little *Bar Giardino*, signed off the western end of Via Umberto I. The old **food shop** on Piazza del Comune has a well-priced stock of truffles, local oils and leading wines.

Trevi

Few people give **TREVI** more than an admiring glance from the train or motorway. From across the valley, the town looks merely enticing, but at closer range Trevi has the most stupendous appearance of any town in Umbria, its medieval houses perched on a pyramidal hill and encircled by miles of olive groves renowned for producing central Italy's finest oil. Its daunting inaccessibility is one of the reasons for its easygoing, old-fashioned charm; the feeling

▲ Trevi

is of a pleasant, ordinary provincial town, unspoilt but just beginning – like Spello and Montefalco before it – to feel the first effects of tourism. The town's name, incidentally, has no relation to Rome's celebrated Trevi Fountain, other than the fact that it derives, like that of the fountain, from the fact that three roads, or *tre vie*, met here. Olives aside, you might also note Trevi's peculiar black celery (*sedano nero*), in season in October, when a Thursday morning market is devoted to it.

The Town

As with most Umbrian hill-towns, Trevi's chief pleasure lies in tramping the medieval streets, which are obsessively well kept and characterized by complicated patterns of cobblestones. Roman fragments are embedded in the inner of two sets of medieval **walls**, raised when Trevi paraded as a minor independent *comune*.

The key sight is the modern **Pinacoteca Comunale**, or **Raccolta d'Arte di San Francisco** (April, May & Sept Tues–Sun 10.30am–1pm & 2.30–6pm; June & July Tues–Sun 10.30am–1pm & 3.30–7pm; Aug daily 10.30am–1pm & 3–7.30pm; Oct–March Fri–Sun 10.30am–1pm & 2.30–5pm; €4), in the former Convento di San Francesco on Largo Don Bosco, where St Francis's preaching was once interrupted by the braying of an "indomitable ass". The museum is a slick but pleasing affair, and houses a well-presented display of coins, ceramics and Roman fragments, several paintings by Umbrian masters and one outstanding work, a *Coronation of the Virgin* (1522) by Lo Spagna, removed from the church of San Martino (see p.560); it was commissioned by Trevi's medieval governors as a copy of a more famous work by the Florentine Ghirlandaio, mainly because they couldn't afford the real thing. Also look out for *Scenes from the Life of Christ* by Giovanni di Corraduccio, a fifteenth-century painter from Foligno whose frescoes are on display in Montefalco's San Francesco (see p.556). In the same complex is the **Museo della Civiltà dell'Ulivo** (same hours and ticket), a well-intentioned but not entirely successful museum devoted to the history of the olive and olive-oil production.

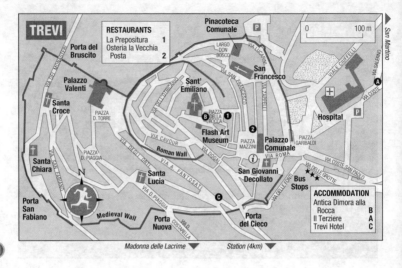

The highest point of the town is **Sant'Emiliano**, comely and recently restored twelfth-century Romanesque on the outside, Baroque horror-show within. Emilianus was an Armenian missionary and bishop of the town cut off in his prime in 302: his feast day (Jan 27) is celebrated by a procession. The only early survivors of the butchery of the building are a captivating *Altar of the Sacrament* (1522) in the second chapel on the left and frescoes by Melanzio, who was active in many villages hereabouts (notably Montefalco) at the start of the sixteenth century. Almost opposite is a very modest gallery of modern art, the **Trevi Flash Art Museum**, Via Lucarini 1 (Tues–Fri 4–7pm but hours vary; €4).

Outside the walls

A stroll north from Piazza Garibaldi, following the tree-lined Viale Ciufelli left of the hospital complex, offers a superb view of the valley and after ten minutes brings you to the conventual church of **San Martino** (most often open in the morning), site of Trevi's original parish church. It has a lunette above the door by Tiberio d'Assisi plus two pictures in the tabernacles on either side of the presbytery, *St Martin Dividing his Cloak with Beggar* by Tiberio, and a fifteenth-century *Madonna and Child with St Francis and St Antony of Padua* by Mezzastris, a local painter. In the Cappella di San Girolamo, to the left of the church, is an *Assumption and Saints* (1512) by Lo Spagna, another Spoletan artist, and *St Emilianus* by Tiberio d'Assisi.

Most noteworthy of the other peripheral churches is the battered **Madonna delle Lacrime** (undergoing long-term restoration; opening hours variable), just under 1km south of the centre on the minor road towards the Via Flaminia, home to a fine *Epiphany with Sts Peter and Paul* from 1521 (second altar on the right) by Perugino and a sweep of frescoes (1520) by Lo Spagna in the chapel of the left transept.

Practicalities

Arrive by **train**, and you have to hope for one of the rare connecting buses to the old town centre, a very steep 4km distant; **buses** from Foligno drop off in

Piazza Garibaldi, a large square on the east of town just outside the walls, also with parking. It's a half-minute stroll to the main square inside the walls, Piazza Mazzini, where there's a small and obliging Pro Loco **tourist office** at no. 6 (daily 9am–1pm & 3–6/7pm; ℡0742.781.150), and a very helpful Tourist Co-Op (Mon–Sat 8.30am–2pm; ℡0742.780.066, ⓦwww.bedandbreakfastumbria .com) beneath the Torre Comunale, which can organize **accommodation**, from rooms to villas, as well as tours and activities. Despite the afternoon closing, there's generally someone in the office most of the day. **Hotels** comprise the bland but adequate three-star *Trevi*, Via Fantosati 2 (℡0742.780.922, ⓦwww.trevihotel.net; ❸), and the newer two-star *Il Terziere*, Via Salerno 1 (℡0742.78.359, ⓦwww.ilterziere.com; ❷), outside the walls, with a pleasant garden. The best place to stay, however – and a sign of how Trevi is changing – is the central, 24-room ⚐ *Antica Dimora alla Rocca*, Piazza della Rocca 1 (℡0742.385.401, ⓦwww.hotelallarocca.it; ❹), the sort of smartly renovated historic building (in this case a sixteenth-century *palazzo*) that has appeared in most Umbrian towns in the last decade or so.

For **food**, try the *Osteria La Vecchia Posta*, Piazza Mazzini 14 (℡0742.381.690; Sept–June closed Thurs), or the half-hidden *La Prepositura*, Vicolo Oscura 2a, part of the *Antica Dimora* hotel (see above), which has lovely medieval dining areas.

South to Spoleto

As you move south from Trevi towards Spoleto (see p.565), the Vale of Spoleto becomes increasingly pockmarked with new houses and small factories. It's all the more unexpected, then, to come across the sacred **Fonti di Clitunno** (Mon–Fri: Jan, Feb, Nov, Dec, March 1 to mid-March & Oct 9am–1pm & 2–6pm; mid-March to end of March 9am–1pm & 2–6.30pm; April 1 to mid-April 9am–7.30pm; mid-April to end of April 9am–8pm; May–Aug 8.30am–8pm; Sept 1 to mid-Sept 8.30am–7.30pm; mid-Sept to end of Sept 9am–6.30pm; Sat & Sun same opening and closing time year-round but remains open all day; €2), a series of springs revered since Roman times. Originally dedicated to the oracular god Clitunnus, the springs were often used as a party venue by the likes of Caligula and Claudius, even though their major curative effect is allegedly that of removing any appetite for alcohol. Earthquakes over the years have upset many of the underground sources, so the waters aren't as plentiful as they once were, but they still flow as limpid as they did when Byron extolled "the sweetest wave of the most living crystal ... the purest god of gentle waters". There's some commercial fuss around the entrance but the springs, streams and willow-shaded lake beyond are languidly romantic, with the occasional coach party the only intrusion on weekdays; at weekends the racket is more intense. Unfortunately, the proximity of the road, with its roaring trucks and buses, comes close to ruining the springs' effect.

A few hundred metres north, and easily missed, is the so-called **Tempietto di Clitunno** (Tues–Sun 9am–dusk; free), accessible only from the road (not directly from the Fonti). It looks like a miniature classical temple, but is actually an eighth-century Christian church cobbled together with columns from the ruins of Roman temples and villas, all long vanished. Scholars until recently were fooled into thinking it a genuine piece of Roman antiquity, though Goethe was one notable dissenter from the party line. The track that runs below the facade is the remains of the original Via Flaminia. The entrance is to the side; if it's shut, try ringing the bell on the gate. Inside are some faded Byzantine frescoes, dated to the eighth century and said to be the oldest in Umbria, representing Christ, St Peter and St Paul.

Though its position above the Fonti di Clitunno is impressive enough, the main attraction of the small, fortified hamlet of **CAMPELLO** is the fact that there is nearby **accommodation** in the shape of the two-star *Fontanelle*, Via d'Elci 1 (℡0743.521.091, ⓦwww.albergofontanelle.it; ❶), in the hamlet of Fontanelle, with a **restaurant** and reasonable rooms. There are superb mountain excursions on the roads northeast of Campello: minor roads follow deep-cut valleys via Pettino and Spina into marvellous countryside, the hills on either side rising to over 1400m at Monte Maggiore and Monte Brunnette.

Travel details

Trains

Assisi to: Foligno (18–24 daily; 17min), Passignano sul Trasimeno (18–24 daily; 50min); Perugia (18–24 daily; 30min); Spello (18–24 daily; 9min); Terontola (18–24 daily; connections to Chiusi, Orvieto, Arezzo and Florence; 1hr); Tuoro sul Trasimeno (18–24 daily; 55min).

Foligno to: Assisi (18–24 daily; 17min); Fossato di Vico (for Gubbio; 9–13 daily; 45min); Gualdo Tadino (8–11 daily; 40min); Narni (12–16 daily; 1hr 10min); Passignano sul Trasimeno (18–24 daily; 1hr 5min); Perugia (18–24 daily; 40min); Rome (16 daily; 1hr 55min); Spello (18–24 daily; 9min); Spoleto (12–18 daily; 20min); Terni (12–18 daily; 55min); Teróntola (18–24 daily; connections to Chiusi, Orvieto, Arezzo and Florence; 1hr 15min); Trevi (12–16 daily; 7min); Tuoro sul Trasimeno (18–24 daily; 1hr 10min).

Buses

Assisi to: Bastia (7 daily; 15min); Cannara (4 daily; 30min); Foligno (4 daily Mon–Sat; 50min); Gualdo

Tadino (1 daily; 1hr); Norcia (1 daily Mon–Sat, from Santa Maria degli Angeli; 2hr 10min); Perugia (7–10 daily; 40min); Rome (1 daily; 3hr 30min); Santa Maria degli Angeli (every 30min; 7min); Todi (1 weekly on Fri; 90min).

Bevagna to: Foligno (5 daily Mon–Sat; 30min); Montefalco (4–5 daily Mon–Sat; 40min).

Foligno to: Assisi (4 daily Mon–Sat; 50min); Bevagna (5–8 daily Mon–Fri; 20min); Colfiorito (4 daily Mon–Sat; 55min); Giano dell'Umbria (2 daily Mon–Sat; 1hr 5min); Gualdo Tadino (3 daily Mon–Sat; 50min); Montefalco (5–8 daily Mon–Sat; 30min); Nocera Umbra (4–5 daily Mon–Sat; 30min); Norcia (1 daily Mon–Sat; 1hr 35min); Perugia (7–10 daily; 1hr 20min); Rome (2–3 daily; 3hr); Spello (11 daily Mon–Sat; 20min); Spoleto (4–8 daily; 50min); Trevi (4 daily Mon–Sat; 23min).

Montefalco to: Bevagna (4–5 daily Mon–Sat; 20–40min); Foligno (3–5 daily Mon–Sat; 30min); Perugia (1–3 daily Mon–Sat; 1hr).

12

Spoleto and the Valnerina

▲ Piazza San Benedetto, Norcia

Spoleto and the
Valnerina

astern Umbria is in many ways the most enjoyable part of the region, at least in terms of its landscapes, offering superb walking and car or cycle touring amid some of the wildest scenery in central Italy. Its main city and transport hub, **Spoleto**, is one of Umbria's more stimulating bases, its many Romanesque churches and other monuments and a year-round programme of exhibitions and concerts making it an essential feature of any itinerary.

The walking and scenery are at their best in the extreme east of the region, where the spectacular **Monti Sibillini** look down over the **Piano Grande**, a breathtaking highland plain which in spring becomes an expanse of wild flowers. There is sporadic public transport access to these areas from Spoleto and **Norcia**, a friendly town and the earthquake-prone birthplace of St Benedict, founder of Western monasticism. Equally beautiful, and a little easier to reach, are the villages of the **Valnerina**, an upland valley enclosed by mountains that arc through the region east of Spoleto. Much of the Sibillini and the upper reaches of the Valnerina are best seen using Norcia as a base.

Access to Spoleto is straightforward, as the town lies on the Rome–Ancona **train** line, with links to Terni and Narni to the south, and Foligno, Assisi and Perugia to the north. **Buses** provide feasible links for the main villages of the Valnerina, but not for the trailheads of the Monti Sibillini and Piano Grande; to get the most from the countryside you really need your own transport. If you're driving, note there's a quick road tunnel just east of Spoleto off the old minor road over the mountains to Vallo di Nera. The tunnel picks up the Valnerina road a little south of the old Vallo di Nera junction close to Sant'Anatolia di Narco.

Spoleto

"The most romantic city I ever saw," said Percy Bysshe Shelley of **SPOLETO**, a place that would demand a visit with or without its famous summer **Festival dei Due Mondi**, a contemporary arts jamboree with considerable international kudos. One of the most graceful of all Italian hill-towns, Spoleto maintains a bustling life of its own, a seductively medieval appearance and a superb assembly of museums and Romanesque monuments. Its major architectural attractions are

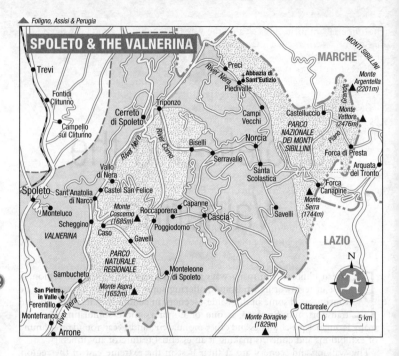

SPOLETO & THE VALNERINA

in the medieval **Upper Town**, though the largely modern **Lower Town** also boasts three major Romanesque churches. The whole is a relatively compact area and getting around is easy enough on foot – though you don't want to be trudging between the Upper and Lower towns too often in the summer heat. Road and transport links make Spoleto a natural base for exploring: even Assisi is an easy day-trip. The one drawback to the place is its ever-increasing popularity; hotels are relatively thin on the ground and, during the height of the summer festival, accommodation is tight and prices are inflated.

Some history

Of Bronze Age origin, the city was an important Umbrian centre, the vast gorge-surrounded crag at its heart an obvious point of strategic importance. Its ancient grandeur is attested to by a series of well-preserved **Roman walls**. Cicero described Spoletium, founded in 241 BC, as Rome's most renowned colony, and it was strong enough to distract and turn away **Hannibal** in 217 BC after his victory at Lago Trasimeno (see p.494) – had it not, history might have been very different, as the Carthaginian general was forced into a damaging excursion into the Marche when an all-but-defenceless Rome lay at his mercy. Strategically sited between Rome and Ravenna, Spoleto prospered while the focus of the Western Empire shifted from one to the other, though its real prominence was to come after 576 when it was established first as a **Lombard** and later as a **Frankish** dukedom. The autonomous **Duchy of Spoleto** eventually stretched to Benevento near Naples, dominating most of central Italy.

During the emergence of the city states it became "the magnificent city, defended by a hundred towers". Its fall from grace came in the shape of **Barbarossa**, who flattened the city in 1155 during an Italian sojourn to restore his imperial authority. This cleared the way for rebuilding, rapid growth and the powerful re-emergence of a quasi-democratic regime (already in existence before 1155) that saw Spoleto at the height of its powers during much of the thirteenth century. Decline and deliverance into the hands of the Church followed a century later, the humdrum years that ensued being relieved in 1499 when the nineteen-year-old **Lucrezia Borgia** was appointed governor by her father, Pope Alexander VI. Apparently she ruled well for the two years she was in nominal charge before being dispatched by her father to conclude the third of her marriages. Thereafter, Spoleto fell into obscurity until the arrival of the festival nearly fifty years ago.

Arrival and information

Fast **trains** on the Rome–Ancona or Rome–Perugia lines stop at Spoleto, and there are local links with Terni, Orte and Foligno. From the station, city buses A, B and C ("Centro") shuttle until around 8pm to **Piazza della Libertà** in the Upper Town; buy tickets (€0.80) from the station bar and newspaper stall. Most **inter-town buses**, notably from Montefalco and Perugia, are run by Spoletina (℡0743.212.211); most terminate in the Upper Town at **Piazza Carducci**, just south of Piazza della Libertà, a few in the Lower Town at Piazza Garibaldi. Buses from Norcia and the Valnerina arrive at the train station. It's difficult to **park** in the Upper Town (the likeliest slots are on Via della Rocca). There are large car parks on Via Don P. Bonilli by the stadium and Viale Cappuccini south of the Giardino Pubblico.

The **tourist office**, Piazza della Libertà 7–9 (April–Oct Mon–Fri 9am–1pm & 4–7pm, Sat & Sun 10am–1pm & 4–7pm; Nov–March Mon–Fri 9am–1pm & 3.30–6.30pm, Sat 10am–1pm & 3.30–6.30pm, Sun 10am–1pm; ℡0743.238.911, Ⓔinfo@iat.spoleto.pg.it), can provide help with accommodation and details of cultural events, as well as information on local walks, including a map for a route into the Monteluco woods, some 8km east.

Accommodation

Spoleto's **hotels** charge vastly different prices for different rooms within a single establishment: if the one you're offered seems too expensive, it's worth asking if there's anything cheaper. Several new hotels have opened in recent years, most of them superb historic properties and all in the upper price brackets. Accommodation is very hard to come by during the summer festival (see box, p.569).

There are two local campsites. *Camping Monteluco* (℡0743.220.358, Ⓦwww .campingspoleto.com; April–Sept), just behind the church of San Pietro, is pleasant but tiny (just 35 pitches). Some 10km northwest in Petrognano (hourly buses from the train station), *Il Girasole* (℡0743.51.335) is a big, flashy affair with a swimming pool nearby and tennis courts.

Hotels

Aurora Via dell'Apollinare 3 ℡0743.220.315, Ⓦwww.hotelauroraspoleto.it. Excellent and very popular mid-range three-star, in a courtyard just off Piazza della Libertà. ❸

Charleston Piazza Collicola 10 ℡0743.220.052, Ⓦwww.hotelcharleston.it. Fancy eighteen-room three-star with the bonus of a fine Upper Town location, by the church of San Domenico. ❸

Clitunno Piazza Sordini 6 ℡0743.223.340, Ⓦwww.hotelclitunno.com. The best-value mid-range three-star in the Upper Town, just west of Piazza della Libertà. There's a wide price difference among its 35 rooms. ❸

Dei Duchi Viale G. Matteotti 4 ℡0473.44.541, Ⓦwww.hoteldeiduchi.com. Comfortable, modern rooms in a hard-to-beat position just off Piazza della Libertà. The best rooms are on the upper floors, with views south to the hills. ❹

Gattapone Via del Ponte ℡0743.223.447, Ⓦwww.hotelgattapone.it. One of central Italy's nicest and most intimate four-star hotels,

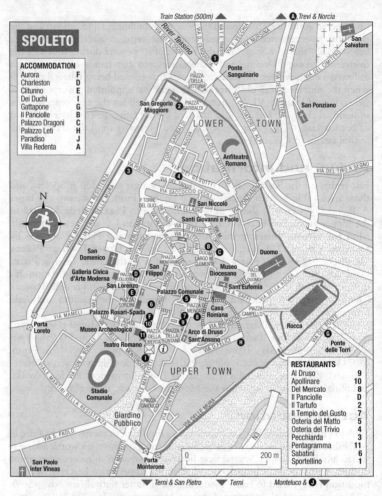

Train Station (500m) ▲   ▲ ❹ Trevi & Norcia

SPOLETO

ACCOMMODATION

Aurora	F
Charleston	D
Clitunno	E
Dei Duchi	I
Gattapone	G
Il Panciolle	B
Palazzo Dragoni	C
Palazzo Leti	H
Paradiso	J
Villa Redenta	A

LOWER TOWN

UPPER TOWN

RESTAURANTS

Al Druso	9
Apollinare	10
Del Mercato	8
Il Panciolle	D
Il Tartufo	2
Il Tempio del Gusto	7
Osteria del Matto	5
Osteria del Trivio	4
Pecchiarda	3
Pentagramma	11
Sabatini	6
Sportellino	1

0   200 m

▼ Terni & San Pietro   ▼ Terni   Monteluco & ❿ ▼

where the big-name festival performers tend to stay, with a sublime and (faint road noise apart) peaceful setting looking over to Monteluco. Splash out to enjoy views over the gorge and Ponte delle Torri. Note that there are older and newer parts of this converted country residence: the latter (the ones right off the bar area, in the south of the building) are better. **7**

Il Panciolle Via del Duomo 4 ☎&🖷0743.45.677. Seven rooms, each with private bathroom, above a nice restaurant in a quietish (road-facing rooms can suffer from noise) but convenient part of the Upper Town. A very good two-star option. **2**

🏃 **Palazzo Dragoni** Via del Duomo 13 ☎0743.222.220, 🖲www.palazzodragoni.it. As this glorious sixteenth-century converted town house is classified as a "Residenza d'Epoca",

rather than a hotel, it remains relatively unknown, so – budget permitting – you have a good chance of snapping up one of its handful of elegant rooms, which are full of frescoes, antique furniture and other period details. A definite first choice at the luxury end of the market. **7**

Palazzo Leti Via degli Eremiti 10 ☎0743.223.340, 🖲www.palazzoleti.com. The *Palazzo Leti*, another "Residenza d'Epoca", opened in 2003 and combines the romantic period splendour of the *Palazzo Dragoni* with the charm, peaceful position and great views of the nearby *Gattapone*. **6**

Paradiso Monteluco 19 ☎0743.223.082, 🖲www .albergoparadiso.net. A faded modern three-star with 21 rooms, in the wooded hills above Spoleto – fine if you don't fancy in-town options or their alternatives on the main road to Terni. It's a long twisting drive up here, however, so not that convenient for sightseeing. ❷

🏃 **Villa Milani** Località Colle Attivoli 4 ☎ 0473.225.056, ⓦ www.villamilani.com. An out-of-town treat (2.5km from the centre) in a delightful and eclectic villa that has been in the same family for generations. There are just eleven rooms, with elegant decor and precious furnishings, plus a pool and a beautiful garden. Closed for a period in Jan & Feb. ❼

Villa Redenta Via di Villa Redenta 1 ☎ 0743.224.936, ⓦ www.villaredenta.com. This Lower Town hotel, a former hostel, has 72 rooms that are inexpensive but far from convenient. From the station, walk the length of Viale Trento e Trieste, the road that stretches away from the forecourt, and turn left at the end onto Via Flaminia Vecchia; the hotel is another 7/8min walk on the left almost opposite Via delle Lettere. Bus D from Piazza della Libertà (every 30min) runs close by. ❶

The Lower Town

Spoleto's art-festival credentials are immediately established by a rather grotesque monumental **sculpture** by Alexander Calder outside the train station. A relic of the 1962 festival, it serves as a gateway to the **Lower Town**, a quarter much rebuilt after Allies-inflicted bomb damage in the last war. The area does offer a trio of outstanding **Romanesque churches**, however, as well as a handful of Roman fragments. If these don't appeal, catch the city bus from the station to Piazza della Libertà, heart of the old town, tempting from this vantage with its skyline of spires and tiled roofs and splashes of craggy countryside; the fifteen-minute walk is reasonably enjoyable too, once you're beyond the concrete of Viale Trento e Trieste. Head up Corso Garibaldi from Piazza Garibaldi for the most direct approach on foot.

San Salvatore and San Ponziano

One of Italy's oldest churches, **San Salvatore** (daily 7am–7pm; March, April, Sept & Oct closes 6pm; Nov–Feb closes 5pm) lies on the edge of the Lower Town, half-hidden in the cemetery, a faintly bizarre attraction in its own right for the glimpse it gives into the Italian way of death. Little has changed in the church since it was built by monks from the eastern Mediterranean in the fourth or fifth century, on a site probably chosen for its proximity to Christian and Neolithic catacombs. Most of the decoration and building materials are Roman and it was conceived when the only models for religious buildings were Roman temples. Not surprisingly, the end result has a distinctly pagan feel, the church's dusty, gloomy **interior** evoking an almost eerie antiquity. The walls are

The Spoleto Festival

Firmly established as Italy's leading international arts festival, the **Festival dei Due Mondi** – the Festival of the Two Worlds – came to Spoleto in 1958 when composer Gian Carlo Menotti and his advisers chose the town over thirty other contenders on account of its small venues, outstanding scenery and an artistic, historical and cultural heritage almost without equal. Menotti's original dream was to combine the best of young Italian and American talent (hence the original "Two Worlds" tag), an idea which eventually saw the birth of a sister festival in Charleston, South Carolina. Melbourne in Australia also came on board, albeit in a half-hearted way, to make it an unofficial Festival of the Three Worlds.

For information and **tickets**, visit ⓦ www.spoletofestival.it or the office at Piazza del Duomo 8 (☎ 0743.45.208); or call ☎ 800.565.600 (toll-free in Italy) or 0743.220.320. There is also a box office at Piazza della Libertà 12 (Tues–Sun 10am–1pm & 3–7pm; ☎ 0743.44.700 or 0743.46.416).

bare, the floors covered in fallen stone, the crumbling Corinthian columns are wedged awkwardly alongside one another and the arches in the nave have been filled in to prevent total collapse. The apse, ringed round with Roman friezes and capitals, is a later addition that gives the church's upper half a crowded and lopsided appearance.

Just a couple of minutes away is twelfth-century **San Ponziano**, dedicated to Spoleto's patron saint. Its Romanesque frontage promises much but delivers little inside. An admiring glance are all the place merits, unless you are lucky enough to find the interior open, when you'll have a chance to admire the **tenth-century crypt**, a fascinating structure of odd, triangular columns believed to be *metae* (turning posts) from a Roman *circo* (race-track), backed by well-preserved patches of Byzantine fresco.

San Gregorio and the Anfiteatro Romano

Across the river in Piazza Garibaldi, **San Gregorio** dates from 1069 at the latest, but parts look as if they were built yesterday, a result of restoration after years of fire, flood and earthquake damage. Its narrow, porticoed **facade** incorporates a patchwork of fragments filched from Roman remains. The pragmatic mix of materials is most obvious in the tower, its lower half built of massive Roman blocks, the upper of more refined fifteenth-century workmanship. The similarly patchworked portico was a sixteenth-century afterthought, added when the church was heightened to imitate the Duomo in the Upper Town. The **interior** commands most interest, its walls stripped back to their Romanesque state, with substantial frescoes interrupted by a series of intimidating stone confessionals. The frescoes are local fourteenth-century efforts, the best of them in the presbytery, which is raised several metres above the nave, allowing for a **crypt** supported by dozens of tiny, mismatched pillars.

Tradition has it that somewhere under the church are the bones of ten thousand Christian martyrs killed by the Romans in the **amphitheatre** close by; the chapel alongside the portico, the Cappella degli Innocenti, is the favoured candidate for their resting place. Parts of the amphitheatre are still visible in the barracks on Via dell'Anfiteatro. No one seems to mind if you walk straight into the complex, which was formerly a monastery; bear right from the main gateway for the most substantial remains. When the Romans passed on, the huge arena was cannibalized for its stone, first by Totila and then by Cardinal Albornoz for the castle in the Upper Town. What remained was adapted as a medieval shopping arcade, and later bricked up in the courtyard you see today.

The ever-ingenious Romans constructed special gutters to drain blood from the arena into the Tessino river, which ran crimson as a result. The liberal flow of Christian blood is said to have inspired the name for the Roman **Ponte Sanguinario,** now under nearby Piazza Garibaldi. It formed part of the improvements to the Via Flaminia ordered by the Emperor Augustus, remaining in use until the fourteenth century, and rediscovered in 1817. Much remains intact below the piazza, but the site has been shut for years; Spoleto's council has tried to operate regular hours (daily 10am–1pm & 3–5pm), though don't be surprised to find that all you can see is a glimpse of a single arch through closed railings.

The Upper Town

The place to head for first in the **Upper Town** is **Piazza della Libertà**, the terminus for local and inter-town buses and home to the tourist office. Orientation is difficult in the jumble of levels and twisting, narrow streets around, though everything worthwhile is a short walk from here. Shops, banks and services are mostly concentrated in **Corso Mazzini**, which runs north from the square, and in **Corso Garibaldi**, which drops down to Piazza Garibaldi. Corso Mazzini is the scene of a rumbustious *passeggiata*, Sunday's walk being a particularly fine spectacle, but for the day-to-day social heart of the town you need to make for **Piazza del Mercato**, site of the old Roman forum.

Piazza della Libertà

For an introduction to Spoleto's much-touted Roman heritage, you only have to cross **Piazza della Libertà** from the tourist office. Here you can look through the railings at the much-restored first-century **Roman theatre**, excavated in 1891 and now used for summer performances. Its past includes a grisly episode in 1319 when four hundred Guelph supporters were rounded up by the Spoletans and dumped on the stage with their throats cut; the corpses were then pushed into a pile and burnt. Today it's a trifle overshadowed by the gaudily painted buildings on all sides: the worst of these offenders, the church and convent of Sant'Agata, absorbed much of the stage area in the Middle Ages, the theatre having been damaged and half-buried over the centuries by landslips.

The conventual buildings now house a restoration centre and modest **Museo Archeologico** (daily 8.30am–7.30pm; €4), entered from just down Via Sant'Agata beyond an attractive little medieval loggia. The ticket includes admission to the **theatre**, with its extraordinary vaulted tunnel beneath the tiered seats. You then climb the steps to the museum, which opens with two small rooms, displaying among other artefacts a superb shield, rings and other fragments from a Bronze Age tomb discovered in Piazza d'Armi. Next door to the right is a longer room, graced with a fine fresco, the *Last Supper*, and a well-presented gallery of Roman portrait busts and miscellaneous statuary. A small annex at the end is devoted to the remarkable Lex Spoletina, a pair of tawny-brown Roman stone inscriptions that forbade the felling of trees in the sacred woods of Monteluco.

Piazza del Mercato

Straddling the entrance to the nearby **Piazza del Mercato** – the old forum – is the **Arco di Druso**, raised in 23 AD by the Spoletan senate to commemorate victories in Germany by Drusus, son of Tiberius and heir to the empire until his early death, courtesy of Caligula. The **walls** hereabouts, and in Via dei Felici, are the city's oldest, built in the sixth century BC by the mysterious Umbrians. Beside the arch is what's described as a **Roman temple and shop**, though you'll need a vivid imagination to see it as anything other than a ditch. However, it's well worth popping into the adjacent church of **Sant'Ansano** (daily 7.30am–noon & 3–6.30pm; Nov–March closes 5.30pm) for the crypt, entered down the stairs to the left of the high altar (where fragments of the temple have been uncovered). As well as containing more persuasive chunks of the temple than lie outside, the crude stone walls are decorated with recently restored frescoes that may date from the sixth century, a time when it was home to refugee Christian monks. The main structure dates from the twelfth century.

Nowhere do you get a better sense of Spoleto's market-town roots than in the cosy **Piazza del Mercato**. In the square, the women wash fruit and vegetables in the striking 1746 fountain (its crown embellished with an attractive clock), the men drink in the bars and swap gossip, and tourists browse the food shops. The left-hand crest of the coat of arms atop the fountain monument, built by Carlo Maderno in 1626 for Pope Urban VIII, features three bees, symbols of the

Barberini, the Roman family from which Urban hailed. The *alimentari* dotted around the square are a cornucopia of picnic provisions, with a bias towards truffles, oils and sticky liqueurs. The piazza's little open **market** runs in the mornings (Mon–Sat 8.30am–1pm), but there's almost more going on late in the evening when the outdoor tables of the main bar on the west side are the best place for in-town summer drinking.

The Duomo

It's a short walk from Piazza del Mercato to the **Duomo**, or Santa Maria Assunta (daily 7.30am–12.30pm & 3–6pm; Nov–Feb closes 5pm), whose restrained and elegant facade is one of the loveliest in Umbria. The careful balance of Romanesque and Renaissance elements is framed by a gently sloping piazza and hanging gardens, with the broad background of sky and open countryside setting the seal on the beautifully unified whole. The lovely, carving-swathed **portico**, an obvious addition, dates from 1491 and is flanked by two little external pulpits, one of which was used by the wandering St Bernardino of Siena to preach to the notoriously wayward Spoletans.

The building was consecrated in 1198, having been commissioned by Pope Innocent III to replace a seventh-century church flattened by Barbarossa. The twelfth-century **campanile** (with fifteenth- and sixteenth-century additions) borrowed much of its stone from Roman ruins, a hotchpotch technique continued in the rest of the building. Architectural details unusual in Italy add interest for the technically minded, most notably the **flying buttresses** tucked out of sight on the side walls; climb to Piazza F. Campello to the right for the best view. Strange, too, are the eight rose windows, clustered around a restored thirteenth-century mosaic of *Christ, the Virgin and St John*.

Less successful transformations were commissioned for the **interior**, where Pope Urban VIII's architect, Luigi Arrigucci, applied great dollops of Baroque midway through the seventeenth century. Urban – named Maffeo Barberini – had been bishop of Spoleto before becoming pope: his impetus and the money of a nephew, another of the town's bishops, financed the works and paid for a Bernini bust of Urban, now in the Museo Diocesano (see p.574). On the first altar on the left, behind glass, stands a brightly restored Crucifix (1187) by Alberto Sotio, the earliest documented Umbrian painter. Walking across to the right-hand side of the church, look in on the **Cappella Eroli** (1497), named after the Spoletan bishop Costantino Eroli: it features Pinturicchio's faded but beautifully lyrical *Madonna and Child with the Baptist and St Stephen*, with a depiction of Lago Trasimeno in the background. In the larger **Cappella dell'Assunta** (or Eroli) adjoining to its right are cruder but nonetheless striking frescoes by the Sicilian Jacopo Santori: that on the left wall shows another Eroli bishop, Francesco, who commissioned the chapel at the beginning of the sixteenth century, kneeling before a separate inset painting of the *Madonna*. The wall to its right has frescoes of saints – *Michael the Archangel* (with sword) and *Lucy*, a popular Spoletan saint: further right, the wall is adorned with the Eroli family shields.

Back across the church is the **Cappella delle Reliquie**, entered at the top of the left aisle. Restored in 1993, it features impressive intarsia work, vivid painted panels that depict characters from the Old Testament, and some beautifully frescoed ceiling vaults. The vaults and panels are the work of Francesco Nardini, an otherwise little-known sixteenth-century painter. On the right is an outstanding fourteenth-century polychrome wooden statue, the *Madonna and Child*. To its right, behind glass in a gaudy blue-columned frame, is a fragmentary letter in Latin, written by St Francis to Fra' Leone, one of the saint's earliest and most besotted followers (he hoarded virtually every scrap and relic associated with Francis). It is one of only two letters written by the saint to have survived and was written after Francis received the stigmata at La Verna (see p.455), by which time he was virtually blind – hence the shaky handwriting. It salutes Leone and wishes him peace (the word *pacem* is clearly visible near the beginning), urging him to follow his own conscience in matters of faith rather than constantly coming to Francis for advice.

All other works of art in the cathedral are eclipsed by the building's original **marble floor**, and by magnificent **frescoes** on the *Life of the Virgin*, painted in 1467 by **Filippo Lippi** and his assistants Fra' Diamanti and Pier Matteo. The newly restored cycle fills the domed apse, starting from the left wall with *The Annunciation* and *The Assumption of the Virgin*, the latter with portraits of the three painters to the right: Lippi is the figure with the white monk's habit over a black tunic. The cycle concludes with the *Nativity* (mostly by Matteo and Diamanti), while above spreads the most glittering scene of all, the *Coronation of the Virgin*. Note the columns and classical motifs separating the panels, many of which Lippi copied directly from old buildings around Spoleto, notably the church of San Salvatore in the Lower Town.

Lippi died shortly after the cycle's completion, the rumour being that he was poisoned for seducing the daughter of a local noble family. The Spoletan cathedral authorities, not too bothered by such moral laxity, were delighted to have someone famous to put in their cathedral, being, as Vasari put it, "poorly provided with ... distinguished men". Thus they refused to send the dead artist back to Lorenzo de' Medici, his patron, who had loaned Filippo to Spoleto, reputedly to stop his Florentine philandering. Interred in a **tomb** designed by his son Filippino Lippi, the corpse disappeared during restoration two centuries later, spirited away, according to local legend, by descendants of the compromised girl. The empty tomb is on the left wall of the right (south) transept.

Sant'Eufemia

Spoleto's most celebrated church is the twelfth-century **Sant'Eufemia** (same hours and ticket as Museo Diocesano), above Piazza del Duomo in Via Aurelio Saffi. The entrance is easily missed, as the church lies inside a courtyard complex off the street; look out for the yellow signs.

The church was probably built in honour of a local bishop, **San Giovanni**, who was martyred by the Goths and reputedly buried here in 980, on a site within both the precincts of the old **Benedictine** monastery and the archbishop's palace. Excavations have revealed that it also lies over the **Lombards'** eighth-century ducal palace, and Roman remains have been found, too. Good use was obviously made of materials from these previous buildings: one of the mismatched columns – that separating the first and second arches on the right – is carved with distinctive Lombard motifs. Many of the mismatched capitals, too, are also clearly from an earlier building. The church is unique in Umbria for its **matroneum**, a high-arched gallery above the aisles (reached from a tiny door at the beginning of the left aisle) that served the purpose of segregating the women of the congregation from the men. Rebuilding took place in the early part of the twelfth century, when northern Italian models were used as inspiration – the current structure bears a striking resemblance, for example, to the church of San Lorenzo in Verona.

Today, Sant'Eufemia is redolent with age and dank solemnity, its walls bare but for the odd patch of **fresco**, notably a *St Lucy* (1455), complete with eyes in a bowl, on the second column on the right (the church was known as Santa Lucia for several centuries). The only other frills are a stone chair and simple but stunning **altar**, both brought from the Duomo in the thirteenth century. Recently, exhibitions of modern art have begun to be installed in Sant'Eufemia, and you now have to pay to enter the church, the only saving grace being that proceeds go to worthy causes.

The Museo Diocesano

The excellent **Museo Diocesano d'Arte Sacra** (April–July, Sept & Oct Mon–Fri 10am–1pm & 3–6pm, Sat & Sun 10am–6pm; Aug daily 10am–6pm; Nov–March Mon–Fri 10am–1pm & 3–5pm, Sat & Sun 11am–5pm; €3) occupies the same courtyard as Sant'Eufemia, and displays a wealth of fascinating paintings and other artefacts culled from churches across the diocese. Most of these works – many removed after the 1979 earthquake which ravaged the Valnerina – are due to be returned to their respective churches, though the prevailing view is that they've been in Spoleto for so long that they'll probably remain in the museum.

On the wall to your right as you enter **room 1** is a thirteenth-century triptych of the *Madonna and Child*, juxtaposing three scenes from the life of Christ with a panel (bottom left) showing St Martin dividing his cloak and giving one half to a beggar (later revealed to be Christ). In **room 2**, the strange *Madonna and Child* to your left shows the Child in the brown habit and triple-knotted belt of the Franciscans. Nearby is a thirteenth-century dossal, once used as the rear wall of a confessional, hence its faded appearance and the clear evidence of its having been sawn into pieces at some point. On the wall beside the entrance is a triptych with **St Lucy** depicted to the right of the central panel's *Crucifixion*. The saint, a fourth-century martyr from Sicily, was much venerated in Spoleto and the Valnerina. She was killed for refusing to marry a high-ranking pagan Roman magistrate, the spurned official having her dragged behind two oxen and then boiled alive; on hearing that the magistrate had been captivated by the beauty of her eyes, Lucy is reputed to have torn them out and sent them to her tormentor (hence her usual depiction holding a dish containing a pair of eyes). In the next painting, also a triptych, three episodes from Lucy's life make up the predella: giving to the poor; her denunciation in front of the governor of Syracuse; and her ordeal by oxen. To its left, a triptych with saints **Sebastian** and **Catherine of Alexandria** is attributed to the same painter as the previous work, Bartolomeo da Miranda, active locally in the mid-fifteenth century. Sebastian was often invoked against plague, and this painting was probably a votive offering during an epidemic, a theory reinforced by the green of the Virgin's cloak (as opposed to the more usual blue), a colour symbolizing rebirth as well as being associated with Hope, one of the three Theological Virtues.

Room 3 features the gallery's single greatest painting, a sublime freestanding *Madonna and Child with Sts Montano and Bartholomew* (1485) by **Filippino Lippi**. It's strange enough that Lippi, a Florentine, should have painted in Umbria, and stranger still that the painting should have been commissioned for Todiano, a now almost deserted village lost in the depths of the Valnerina (see p.586). The theory is that it was commissioned by a merchant who left the village and grew wealthy as a result of trade. Bartholomew and Montano are Todiano's patron saints, the latter best known for having tamed a bear and commanded it to take the place of an ox it had devoured. The little scene in the predella shows the bear alongside an ox pulling a plough. The parallel predella scene to the right shows St Bartholomew with his skin slung over his shoulder (the saint was flayed alive). Opposite is another premier painting, *Adoration of the Child* by the Sienese Mannerist **Domenico Beccafumi**, and the room also holds another freestanding Tuscan work, **Neri di Bicci**'s *Madonna della Neve* (1464), an excellent example of a relatively common theme, the *neve* (snow) referring to the miraculous fall of snow in Rome in August which is traditionally said to have marked out the site of the city's ancient Basilica di Santa Maria Maggiore. Its presence here is explained by the strong medieval trading links between Spoleto and Rome.

Left of the Lippi painting, a door leads into **room 4**, where on your left is a *Madonna and Child with Sts Sebastian and Leonard*. Sebastian, unusually, is shown holding a clutch of arrows rather than being shot through with them, an allusion to the fact that he recovered from his ordeal by archery (he was martyred by being pummelled to death). St Leonard is rarely portrayed in central Italian art. Little is known of this sixth-century figure, other than that his faith persuaded King Clovis to grant him the right to release any prisoner he met. As a result he is the patron saint of prisoners, who would traditionally have made a votive offering of a shackle to the saint on their release – which is why he is shown in this painting holding a vast leg-iron. Other works here include an *Annunciation* and *Deposition* by Andrea da Caldaroba.

Retracing your steps, bear right through the large room beyond room 3, which – like much of the museum building – has a stupendous carved wooden ceiling. Don't let the four gloomy canvases in the far corner distract you from the large bust of Pope Urban VIII by **Gianlorenzo Bernini**, removed from the cathedral. Past rooms with vestments, a door unexpectedly opens into the upper gallery, or *matroneum*, of Sant'Eufemia, offering a wonderful view of the church.

Look out for a fascinating series of wooden statues of the Madonna and Child, as well as an unusual statue of Christ with movable arms: the arms were extended during processions on Good Friday to mark the Crucifixion, and lowered on Easter Sunday to celebrate the Resurrection. Also to come is an exquisite small *Madonna and Child*, an anonymous Florentine work, and detached frescoes, notably a *St Michael with the Devil* just visible at the bottom trying to tilt the scales in which Michael is weighing the souls of sinners and the saved.

Most entertaining of these works in limbo are numerous decorated **wooden tiles**, a series of ex-votos painted with often amusing cartoon-like depictions of sick-bed scenes and escapes from perilous (and not so perilous) episodes for which the tiles give thanks. These show events such as women being gored by bulls and a man hanging upside down from a tree and losing his hat, or a precipitous fall from a hayrick (the Virgin, as in other tiles, looks down from a cloud in the top left) and a cart falling from a bridge and hurling its inhabitants into a river.

The Casa Romana and the art galleries

Very near the Museo Diocesano, in a side-street below the Palazzo del Municipio, is the **Casa Romana** (Roman House), entered from Via Aurelio Saffi (daily: mid-March to mid-Oct 10am–8pm; mid-Oct to mid-March 10am–5.30pm, but may close 1–3pm; €2.50). This dark and atmospheric little corner contains the remains of a house fancifully believed to have belonged to Vespasia Polla, the mother of the emperor Vespasian. Bedrooms, bath and other remnants survive, including swathes of patterned black-and-white mosaic floor.

Spoleto's **Pinacoteca**, which for years was stuck away in the farthest reaches of the Palazzo del Municipio, is closed for long-term restoration and most of its works are housed in the new museum in the Rocca (see p.576).

Over the years, Spoleto's festival has attracted some high-profile contemporary artists to the town: see some of the results in the **Galleria Civica d'Arte Moderna** (Wed–Mon: mid-March to mid-Oct 10.30am–1pm & 3–7pm; mid-Oct to mid-March closes 5pm; €4) on the west of town in Piazza Collicola. The collection has works by leading Italian contemporary artists, alive and dead, including Guttoso, Burri, Dorazio and Accardi, plus foreign works from the likes of Calder (he of the railway station sculpture) and a section devoted to the glazed terracotta and other sculptures of Spoleto's own Leoncillo Leonardi (1915–68).

The Rocca

If you do nothing else in Spoleto, take the short walk out to the Ponte delle Torri, the town's picture-postcard favourite. It's best taken in as part of a circular walk around the base of the Rocca, or on the longer trek to San Pietro (see below). The **Rocca** itself is a perfectly endowed castle, with an impressive tally of towers, neatly delineated crenellations and sheer walls. It was built as one of a chain of fortresses with which the tireless Cardinal Albornoz tried to re-establish Church authority in central Italy in the years preceding the Great Schism. Later it became part-fortress, part-holiday home, with several popes staying over, most notably Julius II, sometimes accompanied by Michelangelo, Nicholas V, who fled here from the plague in 1449, and the Sienese Pius II.

The fort's main latter-day function has been as a high-security prison, testimony to the skill of its medieval builders; as many as five hundred prisoners were kept here by the papal authorities between 1817 and 1860; Slavic and Italian political prisoners were held here during the war, while more recent inmates included members of the Red Brigades and Pope John Paul II's would-be assassin, Mohammed Ali Agca. Since its demise as a prison in 1982, two decades and more of stop-start restoration kept the Rocca closed, partly as a result of the scale of the operation, partly through sheer mismanagement.

In a classic Italian fudge, areas of the complex can be seen as part of the **castle** (Tues & Wed 9am–5pm, Thurs–Sat 9am–5.45pm, Sun 9am–7pm; longer hours Tues–Sat in summer; €6, or €7.50 with museum), others as part of the long-awaited Duchy **museum** (April–Oct Tues–Sat 9am–7.30, Sun 9am–1.30pm; Nov–March Tues & Wed 9am–1.30pm, Thurs–Sat 9am–7.30pm, Sun 9am–1.30pm; €6, or combined ticket €7.50), which finally opened in 2007. Opt for the combined ticket: everything is worth seeing.

The best bits are the superb views, the imposing twin courtyards and the quite staggering scale of the building: the entrance is the castle drive on Piazza F. Campello at the top of Via Aurelio Saffi, just to the left of the large fountain, whose massive stone face marks the end of a Roman and medieval aqueduct.

Highlights of the **interior** start with the **first courtyard**, the Cortile d'Onore, an upper storey supported on vast orange-brick arches and dotted with patches of fresco. The arches are slightly different: one set belongs to Gattapone, the original designer, the other to Bernardo Rossellino, Pius II's architect in Pienza (see p.407), who worked here. An arched passage leads to a plainer courtyard beyond, the arch frescoed with six towns in the papal domain, with Spoleto obvious on the right thanks to the depiction of the Ponte delle Torri, along with Perugia (middle left) and Orvieto (far left), obvious from its cathedral. The missing patches of fresco (two of the four Cardinal Virtues also illustrated are missing) were damaged by fires lit by guards, who sheltered on duty in the passage. The **second courtyard** (used for performances in the summer festival and other events) was once the prison exercise yard: turn round to see the coats of arms above the entrance arch, which belong to Albornoz,

Urban V, Eugenius IV – also represented is the monogram of Christ and the crossed keys, symbols of the Church's temporal power, a motif repeated throughout the fortress. Some idea of the castle's past importance, and its illustrious visitors and inhabitants, can be gained from the wealth of other leading family and papal arms around the place – the Barberini bees (particularly in evidence), Medici, Borgia, Colonna, Della Rovere, Piccolomini, Visconti, Aldobrandini, Lambertini and many more. Rooms on the **upper storey** of the Cortile d'Onore are impressive more for their size and views than for any surviving frescoes or other artefacts. The exceptions are the bedroom and studio-bathroom, which have well-preserved and pretty courtly scenes from the early fifteenth century appropriate to a bedroom and riding and hunting vignettes in the studio.

The Ponte delle Torri

Within minutes of leaving the shady gardens of Piazza F. Campello you suddenly find yourself in open countryside, with a dramatic view across the Tessino gorge and south to the mountains of Castelmonte. There's an informal little bar, often blaring crackly opera favourites from tinny speakers, about 100m before the Ponte to help you enjoy the view.

This is a good point to look down on a fine stretch of the town's **walls** and the **Ponte delle Torri**, an astonishing piece of medieval engineering with a 240-metre span supported by ten vast arches, the most central ones some 76m high. The site is a notorious lovers' leap. Probably designed by the Gubbian architect Gattapone – the man responsible for Gubbio's Palazzo dei Consoli – it was planned initially as an aqueduct to bring water from Monteluco, replacing a Roman causeway whose design Gattapone borrowed and enlarged upon. In time it became part of the town's defences, providing an escape from the castle when Spoleto was under siege. The remains of what used to be a covered passageway connecting the two are still visible straggling down the hillside. It's possible to walk across the bridge, a highly recommended stroll, with obvious paths on the other side (wind up the stone steps to the right) leading left into

▲ Ponte delle Torri, Spoleto

lovely ilex woods with superb belvederes overlooking the bridge and gorge. Follow the level path for 1km or so and you bend round an arm of the gorge to emerge in peaceful olive groves.

San Pietro

Accessible on a walking route from the Ponte delle Torri is the church of **San Pietro** (daily 9–11am; to visit 3.30–6.30pm, ring the bell of the custodian in the house adjacent to the church). The facade is the thing to see, visible from the bridge; as you draw close, it reveals a series of twelfth-century **sculptures** that – with Maitani's bas-reliefs in Orvieto – constitute the finest Romanesque carving in Umbria. Partly Lombard in their inspiration, they draw on the Gospels and medieval legend for their complicated narrative and symbolic purpose. Much of the allegory is elusive, but reasonably self-explanatory panels include *A Wolf Disguised as a Friar* before a fleeing ram – a dig at dodgy monastic morals – and, particularly juicy, the *Death of a Sinner* (left series, second from the top). Here the Archangel Michael abandons the sinner to a couple of demons who bind and torture the unfortunate before bringing in the burning oil to finish him off. Compare this with the panel above, the *Death of a Just Man*, where St Peter frees the man of his chains while Michael holds his soul in his scales; the Devil, lashed by the keys of St Peter, tries to tip the scales in his favour and holds a scroll that laments *doleo quia ante erat meus* ("I mourn because he was mine before").

San Domenico to Santi Giovanni e Paolo

Among Spoleto's lesser churches, the massive monastic **San Domenico**, on the town's western margins, warrants a diversion for its colourful pink and white marble banding. Inside – in an interior of stripped-down Baroque – there are some fragments of fresco fossilized in new yellow plaster, the outstanding picture being a large, early fifteenth-century fresco on the southern right-hand wall, *The Triumph of St Thomas Aquinas*. At the back of the church to the right of the presbytery is a small room filled with crude but eye-catching early frescoes; the Cappella dei Montevecchio in the left transept enshrines the umpteenth Nail of the Cross.

A stroll away in Via Filitteria is the tiny chapel of **Santi Giovanni e Paolo**, consecrated in 1174, which has an impressive thirteenth-century fresco outside, and an interior – rarely open – but worth checking out as it is covered in superb frescoes dating from the twelfth century onwards.

Eating and drinking

Spoleto takes its **food** pretty seriously. The town lies at the heart of renowned olive oil country, the oils of its top producer, Monini, used in kitchens across Italy. These can be bought just about anywhere, but for a **picnic**, stock up at the market and food shops in the Piazza del Mercato: the little shop immediately on the left as you exit the square to the north has an excellent selection, including local wines such as Montefalco's Sagrantino Passito (see p.556), truffle paste and other more rarified products. Another good shop, at the opposite end of the square, is the old-fashioned Salumeria Padrichelli, Via Arco del Druso 22.

The best **bar** in town is the *Vincenzo* on Corso Mazzini – you'll see the big names there during the festival – but for late evenings out-of-doors make for the bar in Piazza del Mercato. On Sunday, late in the afternoon, the region's busiest *passeggiata* takes place from the bar in Piazza della Libertà, surging down Corso Mazzini.

Restaurants

Al Druso Via Arco del Druso 25 ☎ 0743.221.695.
Busy trattoria-pizzeria at the southern entrance to
Piazza del Mercato. Pizzas and basic meals at keen
prices, but no frills. Closed Mon.

Apollinare Via Sant'Agata 14
☎ 0743.223.256, Ⓦ www.ristorante
apollinare.it. Rivals *Sabatini* for the title of
Spoleto's best Upper Town restaurant. The blue
and gold upholstery is initially off-putting, but the
medieval setting is good and the welcome
friendly. The *menù degustazione* is excellent
value. Don't miss the sublime *caramello* starter –
a cheese and truffle delight. Closed Tues.

Del Mercato Piazza del Mercato 29
☎ 0743.45.325. Unexceptional but inexpensive and
convenient spot on the central square with outside
tables. Closed Thurs.

Il Panciolle Largo Muzio Clemente–Via del Duomo
3 ☎ 0743.45.677. Below the hotel of the same
name, this is a good choice for a reliable and
reasonably priced, if never over-exciting, meal of
Umbrian specialities such as *stringozzi* and fire-
grilled meats. Also known for its selection of
cheeses. Has a great outside terrace – though the
medieval interior with open fire is cosy enough.
Closed Wed.

Il Tartufo Piazza Garibaldi 24 ☎ 0743.40.236,
Ⓦ www.ristoranteiltartufo.it. Regarded by many as
the best restaurant in Spoleto, and particularly
renowned for its superlative truffle and Umbrian
dishes. Piped music, a Lower Town location and
high prices work against it, though the medieval
interior is wonderful; you can eat outdoors in
summer, and pick from a couple of *degustazione*
menus. Closed Sun at dinner, Mon and periods in
Feb & July.

Il Tempio del Gusto Via Arco del Druso 11
☎ 0743.47.121, Ⓦ www.iltempiodelgusto.com.
"The Temple of Taste'" was founded by Eros Patrizi,
a former pupil of the legendary Vissani, patron of
the eponymous restaurant near Baschi, in southern
Umbria, that for years has rated as one of Italy's
best. Standards – and the often recherché cooking
– are similar, and you'll be paying around €70 for
the works. Closed Thurs.

Osteria del Matto Vicolo del Mercato 3
☎ 0743.225.506. A good bet, if only for the charm
of the owner and the informal atmosphere. It has a
single, cosy dining room, and you can drink wine
late into the evening, or settle down for a good
light meal or snack. Lunch can be had for as little
as €6 and there are set menus at lunch and dinner
(both €16). Closed Tues.

Osteria del Trivio Via del Trivio 16 ☎ 0743.44.349.
Welcoming and rustic *osteria* that is a little north of
the historic core, and thus quieter and more
reasonably priced than the more central places.
Reckon on about €25 for a full meal of Umbrian
staples: starters and the stuffed artichokes, in
season, are excellent. Closed Tues & and a period
in Jan.

Pecchiarda Vicolo San Giovanni 1
☎ 0743.221.009. A friendly, family-run atmosphere, summer pergola and fair prices have made
this one of the town's most popular *trattorie*. The
house red is a cheap and cheerful Sangiovese
made by the owner. It's a big and far from intimate
place, however, and not too central either.

Pentagramma Via Martani 4 ☎ 0743.223.141.
This medieval vaulted dining room with its out-of-
place red-chequered tablecloths specializes in
traditional Spoletan staples at middling prices. A
relaxed and rather un-Italian bistro atmosphere, but
it needs to be busy to be enjoyable. Closed Sun eve
& Mon.

Sabatini Corso Mazzini 54 ☎ 0743.221.831. Best-
known top choice in the Upper Town, though the
Apollinare perhaps just pips it for quality of
cooking. Has a simple, elegant interior and small
garden for summer eating, serving imaginative, if
occasionally over-elaborate variations of local
dishes; just avoid the house speciality, cheese
risotto. Good wines too. Closed Mon.

Sportellino Via Cerquiglia 4 ☎ 0743.45.230.
Walking in, you feel as if you're entering someone's
home: it's a simple place with good regional
cooking to match. Go for *stringozzi*, or robust meat
dishes. Pecorino cheese to finish is excellent, and
the *antipasti* Sportellino is almost a meal in itself.
Closed Thurs & Aug.

The Valnerina

The **Valnerina** is a valley that curves in a broad arc through the east of Umbria,
rising in the mountains of the Sibillini and then following a southwesterly
course through scenery with a stark, wild beauty which is all the more dramatic
after the pastoral hill country to the west. Desolate and sparsely populated these
days, the "little valley of the Nera" was once the hub of communications

between the kingdom of Naples and the dukedom of Spoleto, and later a bone of contention between the Church and the Holy Roman Empire – which explains its liberal sprinkling of fortified villages. Today, it constitutes a self-contained area of high mountains, steep wooded valleys, lonely hamlets and vast stretches of upland wilderness. Deserted farms bear witness to a century of continuous emigration, and wolves still roam the summit ridges, half-heartedly protected by a Parco Regionale. Few parts of Tuscany or Umbria are so genuine a "forgotten corner".

There is no easy way of visiting the valley's highlights. The best approach is from Spoleto, either on the winding scenic road over the mountains that meets the valley just below Vallo di Nera or via the fast tunnel which emerges close to Sant'Anatolia di Narco. You should first head south from either point to see the **Lower Valnerina** and visit the region's main highlight, the abbey of **San Pietro in Valle**. Beyond this the valley loses most of its appeal, becoming more scrappy and built-up in the run past Ferentillo and Arrone towards Terni. A route following the Nera all the way to Terni only makes sense if you are making for Narni, Orte and the road to Rome or the north.

From San Pietro in Valle you should double back and head north – no hardship, as the scenery is delightful – picking one of three options: the slow but very scenic mountain road from Sant'Anatolia di Narco to Monteleone (and then on to Norcia via Cascia and the SS320); the direct but still striking SS396 road to Norcia from just south of Triponzo; or exploring the **Upper Valnerina**, following the SS209 valley road before diverting south towards Norcia via Preci and another fine abbey, **Sant'Eutizio**, and the pretty Val Castoriana (also easily explored using Norcia as a base).

Access to the heart of the region can be very tricky without your own transport, but there are several **bus** services daily from Spoleto east to Norcia on the quickest SS396 route, stopping at most villages along the way. In many cases you'll find a bus waiting at key junctions such as that below **Sant'Anatolia di Narco** to connect with more remote villages to the south and east.

The Lower Valnerina

East of Spoleto, the beautiful and tortuous SS395 road towards Norcia climbs and then – amidst tremendous views – drops to meet the main SS209 running along the floor of the Valnerina at the junction at the hamlet of **Piedipaterno**. This twenty-kilometre route is slow, however, so if you want to have more time to explore the valley, take the tunnel which emerges close to Sant'Anatolia di Narco to the south (see below).

To Sant'Anatolia di Narco

About 1km south of Piedipaterno lies a turnoff left to the village of **VALLO DI NERA**, a self-contained medieval ensemble perched on a hill, the type of fortified village you'll see all the way up and down the valley. In the church of **Santa Maria** in the lower part of the village (the house at no. 4 has the key if the building is shut) are minor but beautiful fourteenth-century apse frescoes. Later, but no less arresting frescoes (1536) adorn the church of **San Giovanni Battista** at the top of the village (try the priest's house next door for access if the church is shut). They're the work of the Sicilian artist Jacopo Santori (or Siculo), who also frescoed one of the Eroli chapels in Spoleto's Duomo.

Around 2km south on the main road you pass **Castel San Felice**, another picture-perfect fortified village, and a couple of kilometres further arrive at a turnoff to the less alluring **SANT'ANATOLIA DI NARCO**, continually inhabited since the eighth century BC. Take the turn left just before the village (visible on the hill above) at the noisy roadside **bar** and **hotel** *Tre Valli* (℡0743.613.385; ❶), cross the river and look for the small yellow sign 100m or so beyond on the left directing you to the little twelfth-century church of **San Felice**. Its facade bears only the bare essentials – arched doorway, rose window and two pairs of narrow windows. Lumpen red and white marble slabs floor the lovely interior, which is distinguished by a raised sanctuary, an ancient sarcophagus in the crypt, and fifteenth-century frescoes of Christ (in the apse) and the *Adoration of the Magi* (on the left wall of the nave).

From Sant'Anatolia to Monteleone

From Sant'Anatolia a sensational minor road strikes southeast to Monteleone di Spoleto, offering great **views** and cutting across the main mountain ridge. You pass the somnolent little hamlets of **CASO** and **GAVELLI** (1127m), both looking across a vast tree-covered gorge whose scale and appearance are more akin to South America than central Italy. Around 1km past Caso look out on the left for the little bell tower of **Santa Cristina** (signed), a Romanesque church with a scattering of frescoes. The church of **San Michele** in Gavelli is even better, and one of the extraordinary and unexpected artistic gems so common in Umbria. The entire interior is covered in sixteenth-century frescoes by Lo Spagna, recently restored with the aid of UK-based walking company, ATG Oxford. If the door is locked, knock at the first house on the left as you climb the lane past the church.

Off-road **walks** from higher up to nearby summits are straightforward, the best target being **Monte Coscerno** (1685m) – the peak on your left as you drive up – reputedly home to at least two pairs of golden eagles. To pick up the track drive about 1km past Gavelli, looking out for a yellow-signed lane back to Gavelli on the right. Opposite this, on the left, a stony track kicks off obliquely uphill. Simply follow this clear, broad path-cum-gravel road gently up, looking out for the one single diversion – an obvious left turn at the pass after about 45 minutes, which will take you on to the breezy open ridge to the **summit**. Continue right for a few metres on the track that starts downwards to get staggering **views** as far as Monte Vettore and the Sibillini.

Scheggino

About 3km south of Sant'Anatolia, and again laid out below a castle, **SCHEGGINO** is one of the more appealing spots in the region. Much of its charm derives from a couple of canals below the tiny and much-tidied medieval streets. A further fine incentive for stopping, especially at lunch, is an excellent ✕ **hotel**, *Albergo-Trattoria del Ponte*, Via di Borgo 17 (℡075.61.253, ℻0743.61.131; ❷). There are twelve modern two-star rooms, cool, quiet and attractive, and a four-room annexe at Via Roma 6. The hotel's **restaurant** (closed Mon & early Sept) serves the local speciality, trout and truffles, the former plucked from the ice-clear river, the latter harvested by the local Urbani family, top operators in the Italian truffle world (their factory is the yellow building on the left about 1km north of the village). Also check out the fabulous *gelateria*, part of the hotel bar. The only **campsite** for miles around is the *Valnerina* at nearby Valcasana (℡0743.61.115; June–Sept), reached by taking the road east for 1km past the trout farm just outside Scheggino. Halfway there on the left is a great outdoor public swimming pool (late June to Aug).

Abbazia di San Pietro in Valle

From Scheggino, the SS209 continues south 8km to an easily missed turning on the right immediately before the hamlet of Colleponte, signed to the

Abbazia di San Pietro in Valle (daily 10am–noon & 2–5pm; if it's closed ring at the custodian's house, signed on the left midway up the two-kilometre approach road). Set high on the hillside near a thickly wooded cleft, this is one of central Italy's finest abbeys and one of Umbria's few memorials to the Lombards' dukedom of Spoleto. The abbey buildings, which have been in private hands since 1860 (the church is a state-owned national monument), have been part-converted into a hotel, a lovely place but a development that has slightly compromised the peace of this perfect medieval ensemble.

In **Roman** times there was probably a pagan temple on the site, later replaced by a series of small hermitic communities. Meanwhile, in Spoleto, the sixth Lombard Duke of Spoleto, **Faroaldo II**, who reigned between 703 and 720, experienced a vision in which St Peter told him to found a monastery in his honour at a place in which he would discover a lone and disconsolate monk. While hunting some time later he came across a recently bereaved monk, and so duly founded an abbey, but also abdicated his throne in favour of the monastic life. At his death eight years later he was buried in the abbey, his tomb a magnificent Roman **sarcophagus** which survives to this day to the right of the high altar. The abbey became a mausoleum for many of the Spoletan Lombard dukes, the last to be buried here being Franco Vinigisio, who abdicated in 822.

The abbey was sacked by a **Saracen** raiding party in 881 and restored in 991, when a series of fortresses were built to lend it added protection. One of these, **Umbriano**, can still be seen on the opposite side of the valley; fanciful legend has it that it was the first settlement ever founded in Umbria. Thereafter the abbey became one of the most powerful religious houses in the region, controlling vast tracts of land and dominating the lives of thousands of people. In 1234 it passed from the Benedictines to the **Cistercians**, but by 1300 had become so corrupt that Boniface VIII was forced to transfer responsibility for its operation to Rome. In 1484 Innocent VIII sold its land and feudal rights to Franceschetto Cybo and his descendants, who took the title of Count of Ferentillo: it remained in their domain until 1730, passing through other minor aristocratic hands until 1860, when the church was appropriated by the newly formed Italian state and the buildings sold to the local Costanzi family, still the current owners.

The abbey ✈ **hotel** (☎0744.780.129, ⓦwww.sanpietroinvalle.it; ⑤) is a lovely place to stay, even if you can't help but feel its presence has taken something from this glorious spot. You can also stay in **SAMBUCHETO**, the hamlet at the foot of the approach road, where the nine-room *Ninfa del Nera* sits on the busy main road, Via del Monastero 3 (☎0744.780.172 ①); it also has a **restaurant**, though you'd be better advised to aim for the *Del Ponte* in nearby Scheggino (see p.581).

The church

The highlight of the complex is the **church**, much of which survives from two separate periods of building – the eighth and twelfth centuries, the earlier date probably having yielded the transept, the three apses and parts of the rough mosaic pavement behind the main altar.

As you enter via the main rear door there is a small conical **stone altar** on your right, a pagan altar dating back to the first century BC. On the left is a series of medieval and Roman fragments from the earliest buildings on the site. The rear wall has two accomplished sixteenth-century **frescoes**, *The Madonna of Loreto* and *The Madonna and Child with St Sebastian*. Out of the door immediately off the right side of the church is a faultless two-tiered **cloister**, usually decked out with a profusion of flower-filled pots; the custodian should open the door for you to see two exquisite ninth-century statues of saints Peter and Paul, flanking the portal. Moving down the church you cross a **stone division** set into the floor, flanked by two small pillars: this marked the point beyond which those who had not been baptized were forbidden to progress.

Up above, covering most of the side walls, are two breathtaking, if badly faded, **fresco cycles**. Painted in 1190, they are considered some of the most important paintings of their period in Italy, being amongst the first attempts to move away from the stylized influence of Byzantine painting; the artist is unknown. Most of these precocious pictures are biblical scenes, showing a startling sense of invention and composition, full of narrative detail and attempts at light and shade unique for their time. Those on the left-hand wall are from the Old Testament, those on the right from the New.

The **Old Testament** scenes are better preserved, and are worth studying. They are arranged in three tiers, and progress left to right from the top tier down. The **first tier** comprises the *Creation of the World*, *Creation of Adam*, *Creation of Eve* (who is shown emerging from Adam's rib, with the four Rivers of Paradise – looking like fish – at Adam's side), *Adam Naming the Animals*, *Original Sin*, *God's Warning*, and *The Expulsion from Paradise*. The **second tier** comprises the *Sacrifice of Cain and Abel*, *Cain Slaying Abel*, *God's Warning to Noah*, *The Construction of the Ark*, *Noah Giving Thanks to God*, *Abraham and the Three Angels*, *The Sacrifice of Isaac*, and *Isaac and Jacob*. Only one fresco survives of the lowest tier, its theme unclear.

The **New Testament** scenes on the opposite wall depict, in the badly faded **upper tier**, angels and Old Testament characters. The **second tier** has seven better-preserved panels, from left to right: *The Shepherds being told of Christ's Birth*, *Journey of the Magi*, *Epiphany*, *Departure of the Magi*, *Massacre of the Innocents*, *Baptism of Christ*, and the *Wedding at Cana*. The **lowest tier** has four panels that can be clearly made out: *Christ's Entry into Jerusalem*, *The Last Supper*, *The Washing of the Feet*, and *Calvary*.

The church's magnificently preserved **altar** is a still more significant artefact, being one of only a tiny handful of dated works of art anywhere in Italy of Lombard vintage – its age is obvious even from a cursory glance at the almost Celtic figures and motifs that decorate its two main faces. It was carved by Ursus, the left of the two crude figures depicted in the lower front section (his signature is still clearly visible): the other figure is Ilderico, Duke of Spoleto between 739 and 742, who commissioned the piece. To each side are well-preserved Roman **sarcophagi**, the right-hand specimen – Faroaldo's tomb – especially appealing, backed by some of the gloriously coloured Giottesque frescoes (c.1320) that dot much of the apse and shallow transepts.

In the **left transept**, look for the tiny fresco on the side wall depicting Faroaldo's vision of St Peter: the duke is shown lying in a canopied bed while his companions play dice to the right. The capitals in the apse are probably from the original Roman building on the site, likely crowning fluted columns that are now concealed under the plasterwork of subsequent centuries. Three other carved sarcophagi lie elsewhere in the church, along with odd stone fragments around the walls, including a bas-relief of a monk, brought from Syria by refugee Christians in the seventh century.

On your way out of the abbey (the route currently lies around the back of the church rather than through the cloister) take a look at the twelfth-century **campanile**, similar to the Lombard-influenced towers common in Rome and Lazio, and distinguished by fragments and reliefs salvaged from the eighth-century church.

The Upper Valnerina

The **Upper Valnerina** is the most beautiful part of the valley, the mountains higher and closer to the road, the villages more remote and less visited. If you are short of time, you can head directly to **Norcia**, the region's obvious base, but it's well worth following the river simply for the scenery, perhaps branching off to explore some of the empty upland roads above the valley's succession of small villages such as Preci and Piedvalle. Just above the latter is the area's highlight, the **Abbadia di Sant'Eutizio**, the cradle of the Benedictine movement; a visit here leaves you well placed for the short drive south to Norcia.

Preci and around

Just before **Triponzo** – an ancient hamlet whose prominent marking on the map belies its size: just a shop and a couple of houses – the SS396 heads off through a tunnel into the deep **Corno valley** on the way to Norcia, the scenery becoming increasingly wild amid steep mountains cut by tempting deserted side valleys. On this road, there are **hotels** at the hamlet of **Biselli** – the three-star *Dei Cacciatori* (℡0743.822.347, ℱ0743.822.237; closed for periods in Dec & Jan; ❷) – and 2km farther on at the larger village of **Serravalle**, the good two-star *Italia* (℡0743.822.267, ℰhotelitalia@libero.it; ❶).

In the Nera valley, 12km north of Triponzo, lies the fortified village of **PRECI**, a likeable place, despite some terrible damage in the 1997 earthquake. Aim to arrive in time for lunch at the first-rate *Il Castoro*, an inexpensive **restaurant-pizzeria** in Via Roma (℡0743.939.248; closed Thurs in winter, and a period in Nov). The **hotel** *Agli Scacchi* (℡0743.99.221, ⓦwww .hotelagliscacchi.com; ❷) has a pool but occasionally unreliable plumbing. The town also has a **park information centre** for the Parco Nazionale dei Sibillini (see p.591), the Casa del Parco, Via Madonna della Peschiera (May & June Sat & Sun 9.30am–12.30pm & 3.30–6.30pm, July & Aug daily same hours; ℡0743.937.000, ⓦwww.sibillini.net).

Nearby at the hamlet of **CASTELVECCHIO** is a beautifully sited and top-grade **hotel** and **campsite**, *Il Collaccio* (℡0743.939.084, ⓦwww.ilcollaccio .com; ❷), with a friendly, English-speaking owner, pool and riding, cycling,

---

The surgeons of Preci

Preci was once famous for its thirty families of **surgeons**, who from the twelfth to the mid-eighteenth centuries handed down their medical knowledge and hearsay from generation to generation. Over the years their patients included such luminaries as Pope Sixtus V, Sultan Mehmed the Conqueror and Elizabeth I of England. Their most notorious sideline was the castration of young boys foolish enough to show operatic potential, a spin-off that developed from the technique of using castration to prevent death from hernia – an area of expertise that the Preci surgeons picked up from their work on pigs. The methods employed were entirely empirical: if something didn't work and the patient died, another approach was tried the next time. Their only classroom was the operating table, more often than not the patient's kitchen table. Crude anaesthetic – a jug of rum or strong wine – would be administered, with boiling vinegar used as a post-operative antiseptic. Though some of Preci's surgeons gained a reputation for their skill in extracting kidney stones, most of the doctors were quacks, and when the papacy introduced more stringent licensing of medical practitioners the end of the tradition was swift: not one of Preci's sawbones was granted a licence.

tennis and hang-gliding. There are wooden chalets for rent that sleep four to six people (around €500 weekly in summer) and a farmhouse with hotel rooms (❷), as well as a cheap **restaurant** serving huge portions.

From Preci, the most direct route to Norcia continues up the valley past Piedivalle to the Forca d'Ancarano pass (see p.586). A longer alternative runs north through Visso (in the Marche), then onwards by the desolate and stunning road over the Passo di Gualdo (1496m) and through Castelluccio (see p.593).

Abbazia di Sant'Eutizio

Some 2km south of Preci, signposted off the Norcia road at Piedivalle, is the rambling monastic complex of **Abbazia di Sant'Eutizio** (irregular opening hours, but generally daily 10am–noon & 3–5pm). It was one of the cradles of the **Benedictine** movement, which helped preserve much of Western learning though the depredations of the Dark Ages. Initially the site of a Roman building, then a cemetery for hermits who had lived in the hills, it became a community that eventually controlled over a hundred churches and local castles, its domain extending as far as the Adriatic. After years of neglect and near-ruin it has been extensively restored, thanks largely to the efforts of a single monk based in Norcia. The effect is perhaps a little too tidy, but there's no denying the beauty and tranquillity of the place, nor its seminal role in the history of the Benedictines.

Its Romanesque **church**, built in 1190, has a fourteenth-century apse and gallery and, inside, a *Crucifixion* by Nicola da Siena (1461) above the high altar. The altar houses the sepulchre of St Eutizio, one of the early hermits, who was known for his missionary zeal and for his ability to induce rain; when there's a drought, locals still parade his tunic round the fields. Crawling through the specially constructed tunnel below the altar is supposed to guarantee relief from all manner of back ailments. Down in the **crypt** are a couple of vast sandstone columns, perhaps remnants of the original Roman building on the site. Steps behind the abbey church, to the right of the fountain, lead to the **caves** of the earliest monks; according to Gregory the Great, it was in these grottoes that Benedict – in conversation with Eutizio and a fellow hermit, Spes – discovered his religious vocation.

From Campi to Norcia

The road south from the Abbazia di Sant'Eutizio runs for 15km through delightful and pastoral country, the Castoriana and Nida valleys, which once made up one of the most important north-to-south trading routes in this part of the Apennines. It passes little medieval hamlets such as Piedivalle and **Campi**. Just before the latter is the church of **San Salvatore**, a double-fronted Romanesque beauty gleaming from restoration work necessitated by the 1979 earthquake that ravaged the Valnerina (the fault line runs along this valley, more or less in front of the church). It's rarely open, but the interior is smothered with frescoes by Giovanni and Antonio Sparapane, part of a fifteenth-century dynasty of painters active around Spoleto and the Valnerina.

Above is the village of **CAMPI VECCHI**, across the wooded hillside to the north; to reach it drive through Campi and keep your eyes open for the yellow sign directing you to **Sant'Andrea**, the church clearly visible at the side of the village, its portico framing one of the loveliest views in the area. The key to the church is kept by a woman in the village – with your back to the building, walk down the steps and take the lane right in the little piazza: the house is about four down on the right. The custodian may also regale you with stories of the cholera pit beneath the church and the evil princess buried under the inverted

Roman inscription on the facade, as well as show you the beautifully kept interior; leave a generous tip. She also holds the key to the chapel of **Santa Maria di Piazza**, in the same little street as her house, about 50m down on the right but so broken and well disguised you could walk past it. The vaults are covered in several superbly well-preserved and accomplished frescoes on the *Life of the Virgin*, the work of the Sparapane. Other areas of frescoes have been revealed on the whitewashed walls, but there's no money at present to pay for their restoration.

Across the valley, the villages of **Abeto** and **Todiano** appear invitingly over the woods and hilly ridges – but, though they were once stuffed with paintings and other works of art (now in Spoleto's Museo Diocesano), they've become almost completely deserted. Continuing on the road to Norcia, 4km south of Piedivalle beyond Sant'Angelo, you climb to 1008m at **Forca d'Ancarano**, a pass that affords spectacular views over surrounding mountains before the precipitous drop down to Norcia.

Norcia

Noted on the one hand as the birthplace of St Benedict – founder of Western monasticism – and on the other as one of Italy's great culinary capitals, **NORCIA** is small, walled and stolid, the only place of substance in eastern Umbria. Its air of faint desolation and low, sturdy houses are a world away from the bucolic towns to the west, a contrast explained by the constant threat of earthquakes. Thick-walled and heavily buttressed, Norcia's buildings have been compulsorily stunted since 1859, when a law forbade the raising of houses over 12.5m high. The last tremor, a particularly violent one, was in 1979; outside town you'll see ranks of temporary housing, ready for the next big one. At the same time Norcia is a prosperous and likeable place, the sort of town where everything works and everybody knows everyone else. Its streets are relieved by glimpses of the mountains, views of which unfold unexpectedly at many corners. The town can serve as the base for some good trips into the **Monti Sibillini** and **Piano Grande** (see p.591) and north to the Castoriana valley and abbey of **Sant'Eutizio** (see p.585).

Norcia has been inhabited since prehistoric times, thanks to its abundant springs, fine agricultural land and a vital position commanding one of the lowest east-to-west routes across the Apennines. Ancient Norcia was the north-ernmost town of the **Sabines**, contemporaries of the Umbrians, before becoming Nursia, a minor Roman *municipio* (290 BC). After the attentions of sixth-century barbarians, recovery took a long time to come – and when it did, **earthquakes** periodically discouraged long-term development. For five centuries before Italian Unification, though, the town was effectively a frontier post between the Papal States and the kingdom of Naples, making it a safe haven for bandits and refugees from opposing sides. Papal reaction was to build the **Castellina** in 1554, a huge, blunt fortress that dominates the town centre. Thereafter Norcia and the surrounding countryside was drained by emigration, a trend that continues today, but whose effects have been tempered by the success of its small food-processing concerns.

Arrival and information

Norcia is well served by **buses** from Spoleto, Terni, Perugia, Foligno and Assisi; they drop off at the Porta Romana, from where it's a straight walk on Corso

NORCIA

Porta San Giovanni
Sant'Antonio
Porta Romana
San Giovanni
Tempietto
Police
Oratorio di Sant' Agostinuccio
Porta Santa Lucia
Porta Palatina
Sant' Agostino
PIAZZA GARIBALDI
Palazzo Comunale
San Francesco
Porta Orientale
Castellina (Museo Civico)
PIAZZA SAN BENEDETTO
San Benedetto
Porta Ascolana
Duomo
Porta del Colle

Stadio

Hospital

ACCOMMODATION

Casa Religiosa San Benedetto	B
Da Benito	D
Grotta Azzurra	E
Ostello Norcia	C
Salicone	A

0   100 m

RESTAURANTS & BARS

Bar Vignola	3
Grotta Azzurra	E
Taverna de' Massari	1
Trattoria del Francese	2

Sertorio to the central **Piazza San Benedetto**. There's no tourist office; the offices of the *Vigili Urbani*, located under the arches of the Palazzo Comunale, often have **maps** and information, while in the southeast corner of Piazza San Benedetto and just outside the Porta Ascolana are *tabacchi* that sell **walking maps** and **guides** – handy if you're going on into the Sibillini. The hotel bar in Castelluccio (see p.593) also usually has copies, as does the excellent Geosta, an outdoor store off Corso Sertoria near the Porta Romana at Via Foscolo 10 (☎0743.828.470) with books, maps and **internet** access. There is a **park information office** for the Sibillini national park, the Casa del Parco di Norcia, at Via Solferino 22-Piazza San Benedetto (July & Aug daily 9.30am–12.30pm & 3.30–6.30pm; Sept–June Tues–Fri 9.30am–12.30pm & 3–5pm; ☎0743.817.090; ⓦwww.sibillini.net), which offers plenty of information on both the town and the mountains.

Accommodation

Norcia has become more popular with visitors in the last four or five years, but it should still be easy to find a **hotel** room without too much trouble, though the town has yet to acquire any of the stylish four- and five-star places that have opened elsewhere in Umbria.

Casa Religiosa San Benedetto Via delle Vergini 13 ☎0743.828.208. First accommodation choice on a budget; all 35 rooms have bathrooms, and there are good half- and full-board deals available. ❶

Da Benito Via Marconi 5 ☎0743.816.670, ⓦwww .hotelbenito.it. The eight rooms of the one-star *Da Benito* are adequate and central, but if you can afford the extra get a room at the *Grotta Azzurra*. ❶

Grotta Azzurra Via Alfieri 12 ☎0743.816.513,
🖳www.bianconi.com. The best, busiest and
friendliest hotel in town. A listed historic building,
it has been run by the same family for generations, and forms part of an old papal granary just a
few moments from the main square. Rooms are
clean, but rather dated, though the easy-going air
and friendly bustle of the place more than
compensate. ❹

Ostello Norcia Via Ufente 1b ☎0743.817.487 or
0349.300.2091, 🖳www.montepatino.com. Norcia's

hostel sleeps 52 people in two-, four-, five- and
ten-bed rooms. Dorm beds €15.

Salicone Viale Umbria, just outside the walls at
Porta Romana ☎0743.828.076, 🖳www.bianconi
.com. A very smart three-star hotel with some of
the best sports facilities in central Italy: all sorts of
leading soccer, volleyball, basketball and other
sports teams from across Europe have come to
train here. ❻

The Town

The main **Piazza San Benedetto** is a large, open area with something of a
High Noon atmosphere in mid-afternoon, but at other times is the lively focus
of the town's comings and goings. It's presided over by a statue of a suitably
severe and disapproving Benedict, erected in 1880 on the 1400th anniversary of
his birth and these days liberally adorned with football flags, hats and scarves
after victories by the *Azzurri* (the Italian national team) or Milan or Juventus.
In earlier centuries the square was the site of a bullring and a place of execution
for witches, traitors, adulterers and necromancers.

San Benedetto

The piazza's most arresting sight is the church of **San Benedetto**, built,
according to legend, over the house where Benedict and his sister,
St Scholastica, were born; it's more likely to have been the site of a Roman
temple, as the square itself was the site of the forum. Despite repeated post-
earthquake reconstructions, the facade – sole survivor from the 1389 original
– remains an attractive, two-tiered affair, its design typical of several churches
in the region (notably San Francesco and Sant'Agostino in Norcia itself). It
features a lovely Gothic portal, rose window, niche statues of Benedict and
Scholastica and a fourteenth-century campanile to the rear. During Norcia's
blast-furnace summers the newer arched gallery (1570) to the right provides
welcome shade, and it has a drinking fountain too. Notice also the unusual
old stone measures, used for selling or distributing wine and olive oil when
the gallery was used as a market.

On the left as you enter the church is a good restored niche **fresco** – possibly
the work of Francesco Sparapane, one of a dynasty of local fifteenth-century
painters – of *Sts Barbara and Michael*, with a *Madonna and Child* above. The only
other worthwhile painting is Filippo Napoletano's *St Benedict and Totila* (1621),
located in the left arm of the left transept. Down in the **crypt**, excavated as
recently as 1910, the little apse at the head of the left aisle is traditionally held
to be the place where Benedict and Scholastica were born. It's half-covered in
faded frescoes depicting the *Annunciation, Nativity* and other scenes. Stone
fragments of a late Roman edifice are visible closed off nearby, making this by
far the most evocative part of the church.

The Castellina

Across the square from San Benedetto is the unmissable **Castellina**, an extraordinarily gaunt fortress with no concessions to architectural subtlety. The superb
granite lions outside came originally from the crypt of San Benedetto. It was
built on the site of a Benedictine priory and Norcia's old parish church for Pope
Julius III by the usually sophisticated Vignola and now houses the town's

Truffles

Though disconcertingly turd-like in appearance, weight for weight **truffles** are one of the world's costliest foodstuffs – only saffron costs more. Norcia is one of Italy's truffle capitals, home to the fabled black truffle – *Tuber melanosporum*.

Truffles have been known, if not understood, since ancient times. They were enjoyed by the Babylonians, the Greeks and the Romans, who consumed them as much for their reputed aphrodisiac qualities as their gastronomic allure. Plutarch believed they were mud cooked by lightning; Juvenal that they were the product of thunder and rain. Pliny, bewildered by their origins, considered them Nature's greatest miracle. In the Middle Ages they were considered a manifestation of the Devil. And no wonder, for here was a plant apparently without root, branch, or stem; without leaf, fruit or flower; lacking, in fact, all visible means of growth.

Truffles' underground existence precludes photosynthesis, meaning they rely for nutrients on a symbiotic relationship with the roots of certain trees, most commonly the oak, hazel, beech and lime. Unlike a normal mushroom, their spores are spread not by the wind, but by truffle-eating animals such as rodents, deer, slugs and wild boar – and to ensure they're snuffled up, they need to advertise their presence.

And this is where the truffle's famous perfume – and dogs and pigs – come in. The fungi mature slowly, often over the course of several months, attaining their final dimensions – anything from the size of a pea to the size of a football – over a few days during the spring. Only when ripe – from about November onwards – do they give off their distinctive perfume, and only then for about ten days, thus ensuring they're snaffled up only when laden with viable spores. Thereafter they become poisonous and rot.

Pigs and truffles once went together, pigs being foremost among the sleuths inclined to nose them out (goats, foxes, ferrets and – in Russia – even bear cubs are used). Pigs love truffles – at least female ones do – for among the volatile compounds exuded by the truffle is one that resembles the musky pheromones of the wild boar. This is all well and good, but not only are sows huge and difficult to manage, they're also prone to attacks of sexual frenzy when close to a truffle. Dogs are therefore now preferred, and can be worth anything up to £2500 when trained.

There are countless **types of truffle**. Nine are edible, though only six are well known and commercialized. Four are considered a delicacy, and of these two are found in quantity around Norcia and Spoleto. Varieties mature at different depths and at different times of the year, so that April and May are the only times of the year when fresh truffles are not available. Umbria's most common type is the **tartufo nero**, gathered from a few centimetres below the ground between mid-November and mid-March. More prized is the **tartufo pregiato**, available over the same period. Rarer are the two summer and autumn **scorzone** varieties.

Many a *cavatore*, or truffle-hunter, sells either directly to a restaurant, or, more likely than not, to an agent working for Signor Urbani, king of the truffle world, whose small company, based just outside Scheggino (see p.581), a village a few kilometres from Norcia, controls 65 percent of the world's truffle trade. Truffles, after all, are big business: a kilo of white Alban truffles could be yours for around £1990; an equivalent quantity of Beluga caviar costs around £1750. Black truffles, of the type found in France and Umbria, retail at around £300 a kilo.

But why all the fuss? The fungi's perfume has been compared to leaf mould, over-ripe cheese, garlic, methane and armpits. But for enthusiasts, the appeal lies in the truffle's unique and subtle flavour. Elizabeth David, in her classic cookbook *Italian Food*, called them the "most delicious of all foods anywhere".

You'll find **food shops** all over Norcia selling truffle-related products (see box, p.591). For the real thing, however, head for the tremendous *Grotta Azzurra* **restaurant**, a temple to Umbrian cuisine (see opposite).

⑫

Museo Civico (erratic hours, but usually May–Sept Tues–Sun 10am–1pm & 4–7.30pm; phone for winter hours; ☎0743.817.030; €4). If it's open, both the building and the handful of top-quality exhibits are well worth the admission. Most of the rooms, which look down prettily onto the square, are taken up with **sculptures**, the highlights being a rare thirteenth-century *Deposition* – five figures in all – a *St Sebastian* (minus arrows) and a poignant life-size glazed terracotta *Madonna* by Andrea della Robbia. Among the **paintings** look out for a bizarre *Risen Christ* (1460) by Nicola da Siena, in which a near-naked but curiously sexless Christ is shown stepping forcefully from his marble sepulchre. There is also a lovely picture attached to a casket lid of Benedict and Scholastica, the former shown holding a painted church, as well as a beautifully restored *Madonna and Child with Saints* by Giacomo di Giovannofrio, the Virgin sitting atop a gloriously decorated throne beneath a coffered Renaissance vault.

The Duomo and the Palazzo Comunale
Almost beside the Castellina is the largely uninteresting sixteenth-century **Duomo**, its less-than-dominating position a result of comparative modernity, its forlorn interior the legacy of countless earthquakes. It does have one outstanding work, however: the **Cappella della Madonna della Misericordia**, located at the end of the north aisle and consisting of an ornate altar (1640–41) of inlaid marble whose appearance, so at odds with central Italian work of the period, has led experts to attribute it to Francesco Duquesnoy, a noted sculptor in the employ of the Neapolitan court. At the heart of the altar is an early sixteenth-century painting, probably by Francesco Sparapane, the *Madonna and Child with Sts Benedict and Scholastica*. Benedict is shown pointing to a painted miniature of Norcia, whose prominent Gothic campanile no longer exists, having collapsed in the eighteenth century.

Completing Piazza San Benedetto's ensemble is the now superbly restored **Palazzo Comunale**, oddly but beautifully multicoloured, and based around a 1492 portico and later additions which blend delightfully to create the town's most distinctive building.

The rest of the town
Five-minutes' walk north of Piazza San Benedetto is the **Tempietto**, or **Edicola** (literally "Kiosk"), one of the town's more unusual buildings. Built in 1354 by Vanni Tuzi, it's a small arched structure, decorated with bas-reliefs and open to the street on all sides. Its purpose is unknown, but it may have been commissioned in honour of San Felicianus, who evangelized Norcia, as a shrine to be used in Holy Week processions – hence the signs of the Passion which figure among its decoration; possibly it was used as a *contra pestum*, a votive offering against the plague (an epidemic ravaged much of Italy at the time that the work was built).

Beyond is an area that fell into disrepair during the Middle Ages and was taken over by shepherds from Castelluccio. Adopting it as their own, they built small houses – complete with stalls for their sheep – amidst a jumble of streets that contrasts with the central grid. Look out for the church of **Sant'Antonio Abate** – the shepherds' saint, invoked to protect their flocks – and the nearby **San Giovanni**, known for its wooden ceiling and magnificent Renaissance altar of the *Madonna della Palla*, located on the right wall; the arched and gilt marble surround frames a painting of the Madonna (1469), so-called because someone is supposed to have kicked a ball (*palla*) against the painting, causing the Virgin's expression to change miraculously at an act of such wanton sacrilege.

The church of **Sant'Agostino**, in Via Anicia, is half-filled with surprisingly accomplished and well-preserved frescoes, those on the entrance wall depicting, among other things, the grisly martyrdoms of several saints. Also make time for the tremendous wooden ceiling of the **Oratorio di Sant'Agostinuccio** just behind Piazza Palatina.

Eating and drinking

You'd be foolish not to try local specialities in Norcia's **restaurants**, the most lauded of which – in most Italian foodie guides – is the *Trattoria del Francese*, Via Riguardati 16 (℡0743.816.290; closed Fri), which in the event turns out to have a rather tatty trattoria atmosphere. You'd do far better to make for the medieval dining halls of the 🍴 *Grotta Azzurra*, Via Alfieri 12 (℡0743.816.513), complete with huge fire, suits of armour and tapestries, for probably one of the best meals you'll eat in Umbria – treat yourself to *risotto al tartufo* or *tagliolini al tartufo*, the latter the classic way to tackle a truffle, or, if finances allow, indulge in their award-winning marriage of truffle and steak, *Filetto del Cavatore* ("Fillet of the Truffle-Hunter"). For a change, try the *Taverna de' Massari*, Via Roma 13 (℡0743.816.218; closed Tues), or one of the more affordable pizzerias in the back streets (a couple are set into the walls just south of the Porta Ascolana).

The Piano Grande and the Monti Sibillini

The mountainous landscape east of Norcia is one of the most distinctive in all Italy, with its centrepiece the eerie **Piano Grande**, an upland prairie devoid of any feature outside the summer months save sheep, hang-gliders and the odd bedraggled haystack. Surrounded on all sides by the sheer and barren mountains of the **Monti Sibillini**, the Piano Grande forms a colossal amphitheatre that's often swathed in a dense, early morning mist. Gazing down on this wilderness from the remote hamlet of **Castelluccio**, it's easy to imagine the hazards for the unsuspecting traveller in past centuries. Papal rulers forbade crossing the plain during winter, and even today the bells of Castelluccio toll on gloomy days to guide shepherds across its desolation. The plain was a key set on Zeffirelli's glutinous Franciscan epic, *Brother Sun, Sister Moon*, and is also famous for being – reputedly – the world's largest football pitch, having hosted a match between two teams of a hundred players each; the home side went down by twelve goals to one.

Late spring to early summer is the best period to visit the *piano*, when it blazes with an extraordinary profusion of wild flowers. In about mid–May crocuses and narcissi bloom, giving way in early June to buttercups, wild tulips and fritillaries, followed by poppies and cornflowers in late June/early July. These are only approximate timings though, and can vary by up to two weeks. Woven into the floral carpet are rare Alpine flora, including the *Carex buxbaumi*,

▲ Paragliding in the Monti Sibillini

an Ice-Age relic discovered in 1971 and believed to be unique. On the mountains around can be found further rarities such as Apennine edelweiss (found elsewhere only in parts of Abruzzo), the martagon lily, bear's grape, Apennine potentilla and the Alpine buckthorn – but you don't need to be an expert to enjoy the startling spectacle.

Castelluccio

An isolated farming village at 1452m, **CASTELLUCCIO** is one of Italy's highest continually inhabited settlements, and the only habitation for many kilometres around. As well as its appeal as a belvedere onto the grasslands and a trailhead for **mountain walks**, the village attracts **hang-gliders**, drawn by the Sibillini's treeless slopes.

A couple of the village's bars have smartened themselves up, as has the long-established hang-gliding school, but the place has made few other concessions to tourism and the feel is of an uncompromising and bleak working village. The exception is summer, when the presence of tour buses and the like underline the fact that even this remote little outpost has finally (and sadly) succumbed to the curse of mass tourism. This said, the almost incestuously interrelated population has still dropped from 700 in 1951 to around 150 today, most of whom are migrant shepherds, many of them Sardinians or former Yugoslavs, who spend the winter months down in Norcia. The most immediately noticeable thing in the village is its **graffiti**, daubed in thick white paint on huge walls; this forms a kind of social document for the community, the pieces – often malicious and some going back generations – recording stories and myths about local people. Wander up to the **parish church**, which has a marvellous fresco cycle on the left wall describing the life of St Anthony Abbot, patron saint of shepherds and their flocks. On the arch outside the church to the right as you look down to the Piano Grande is a Fascist plaque, of a type long ago removed from other, less remote towns and villages in Italy, which salutes Il Duce, "refounder of the Italian Empire".

Practicalities

Castelluccio is served by two **buses** a week on Norcia's market day only – Thursday – currently departing Norcia's Porta Ascolana at 6.25am and 1.30pm; the return bus leaves Castelluccio at 2.20pm.

It's well worth booking **accommodation** in advance. There's only one hotel, the two-star *Sibilla* (℡0743.870.113, Ⓦwww.sibillacastelluccio.com; hotel closed in winter; ➊), an Alpine-style building in the village centre (ask for a room with views over the Piano Grande – half of them look onto the scrappy car park piazza). The *Sibilla* has a **restaurant** which, though less appealingly rustic, serves up remarkably good food. Castelluccio's shops, such as they are, have only the most basic supplies, though fruit and bread vans visit regularly – except in winter, when the place is frequently cut off by snow.

On the Norcia–Arquata road 8km south of Castelluccio, on the pass at the southern edge of the Piano Grande, is *Forca Canapine*, a huge pink building built as a hotel to serve the small "ski resort" locally. It is an excellent base for walks in all directions, or would be except for the fact that successive owners have found it hard to make it pay, and at the time of writing it was closed. Enquire at the park centre in Norcia for latest details. Rooms are plain but clean, with what must be some of the smallest bathrooms in Italy. **Camping** anywhere in the hills around is no problem; there's plenty of grassy flat ground a stone's throw from the village. Further afield, be sure to take enough water, as the limestone hills have no surface source.

The bar of the *Sibilla* and *Bar del Capitano*, on the southern edge of the village with a great belvedere over the Piano Grande, can provide **walking information** and maps and books on the area.

Walking in the Sibillini

The **Monti Sibillini** (Ⓦ www.sibillini.net) are the only really wild mountains of Tuscany and Umbria, and the most precious natural environment for many hundreds of miles. The northernmost of the big Apennine massifs, they run north–south for about 40km, their summit ridge marking both the Umbrian border and the watershed between the Adriatic and Tyrrhenian seas. In **Monte Vettore** (2476m) they have the third-highest point on the peninsula, a massive, barren mountain that rises above the Piano Grande with majestic grandeur. The Sibillini have been designated a **national park**, a status that sadly exists more on paper than on the ground, with no binding laws to stop hunting or building.

According to local tradition, the mountains were home to one of the three ancient **sibyls** – the wise women with oracular powers who were supposed to have foretold the coming of Christ. Later misogynist versions of the sibyl myth transformed them into temptresses possessed by the Devil – those lured to the sibyls' caves were doomed to remain trapped there until the Day of Judgement – which perhaps explains why these mountains have a reputation for necromancy and Satanism. By happy coincidence the code for the *Kompass* map to the area is 666, the Devil's number.

Hiking in the Sibillini is superb, whether you fancy casual day hikes or more demanding backpack ventures. Unlike the Alps or Abruzzo there are few marked paths and you're unlikely to meet many people other than shepherds. The Club Alpino Italiano (CAI) has discreetly tagged a few trails, with a view ultimately to creating a continuous path on the summit ridge.

The 1:50,000 *Kompass: Sibillini* **map** is adequate and widely available, though locally you should be able to pick up the better 1:25,000 *Montevettore* produced by *Universo* and the *Unione Italiana Sport Popolare*, or the similiar CAI map. **Paths** marked on maps do generally exist but in good weather the hills are so open (bar a few glorious beech woods) that you can wander pretty much at will, at least on the western, Umbrian side of the mountains. This is less true on the eastern flanks (in the Marche), which are dotted with dangerous crags and screes. However, around Castelluccio and the western ramparts the worst you'll have to contend with are some of the steepest grass slopes you'll ever come across. For enthusiasts or emergencies there are several **mountain huts** (marked on maps), none with services and often in a poor state.

The hikes

Castelluccio is the best base for **day hikes**, with trails leaving from the village in all directions. **Monte Vettore** via Forca di Presta (8km east of Castelluccio on the road to the Marche) is the obvious target, returning along the ridge via Quarto San Lorenzo and Forca Viola. This is a pretty tough full day's outing, which you could take at a more leisurely pace by starting at the summer-only **refuge** at *Forca di Presta* (☏ 0736.809.278, 0743.99.165 or mobile 347.087.5331; always call in advance). Sited at 1500m, the *rifugio* is a source of basic food, maps and information.

Another good walk from Forca di Presta or Castelluccio, mainly downhill through woods, takes you to **ARQUATA DEL TRONTO** in the Marche, a smallish place with two **hotels**, the better of which is *Ca' Martina*

(℡0743.99.261; ❶), on a side road just north of the village, well placed for the paths on and off the hills. The village has a park **information centre** at Frazione Borgo 6 (℡0736 809.600, Ⓦwww.sibillini.net), which also has information on the neighbouring Monti della Laga park.

A third rewarding hike is to strike across country from Castelluccio to Norcia, a route comfortably accomplished in a day, though the route-finding here requires a little more diligence: paths to the ridge (around 1800m) are straightforward, but the drop from the ridge can be a bit of scramble if you miss the path. Trails lower down, which you'll easily pick up, are much better.

For a quick and easy glimpse of the scenery **north of Castelluccio** follow the *strada bianca* (gravel road), for about twenty minutes, past the *Scuola di Volo*, round the corner into the Valle Canatra and on to the Fonte Valle Canatra. It's an all-but-level stroll which you could prolong by following the obvious cart track to the head of the lovely valley and the open plains under Monte delle Rose (1881m) – good camping territory. Another excellent, straightforward and not overly demanding walk is to leave Castelluccio on the upper *strada bianca* west and then follow the rough road and clear path along the ridges of the Piano Grande's western rim (Colle Tosto, Monte Vetica, and others), staying at *Forca Canapine* (if open; see p.593).

A more ambitious and longer hiking route is to cross over the ridge **east of Castelluccio** into the Marche, where the best-known walk runs to the **Lago di Pilato**, an idyllic spot under Monte Vettore. This is supposedly the burial place of Pontius Pilate, the story being that Pilate's body was dispatched from Rome on a cart pulled by two oxen, which traipsed through wild country and then plunged into the lake, disappearing without trace. The legend has made the lake the heart of the mountains' supposed necromantic practices; Norcians used to sacrifice animals here, and humans too, so it is said, to placate the demons and protect themselves from storms and bad weather. When the area was part of the Papal States a wall was built by the Church to prevent access to the lake, and stones inscribed with occult symbols have been found on the shores. In many recent summers the lake has all but dried up, putting in danger an endemic crustacean (*Chirocephalus marchesonii*), which used to stain the water red, a colouring anciently attributed to the blood of Pilate.

From Lago di Pilato, another superb trail runs under the main ridge along the Valle del Aso to the hamlet of **FOCE**: the combined trek from Castelluccio to the lake and then to Foce makes a perfect day's walk. The only problem is you'll have to haul yourself back over the mountains if you're returning to Castelluccio the next day, so this is a route for seasoned hikers.

Cascia and around

CASCIA, 18km south of Norcia, figures large on the map but is disappointing in actuality, only recommendable to pilgrims in search of **St Rita**. Her presence – and the stupendously ugly twentieth-century Basilica – dominates both the new and the earthquake-damaged hill-town, which was abandoned for a time in the eighteenth century. Little known elsewhere, Rita has a massive cult following in Italy, especially amongst women, for whom she is a semi-official patron saint. Every year on May 21 and 22, thousands flock here for the torchlight **Celebrazioni Ritiane**, when the saint's shrine is venerated.

Rita's **Basilica**, which contains her mummified body, is a monument to religious kitsch probably without equal – a piece of Fascist architectural brutalism that attempts to place Byzantine and Romanesque elements in a modern context, and in doing so produces a fantasy in white marble that might sit more happily in Disneyland. Your time might be better spent at the excellent **Chiesa-Museo di Sant'Antonio Abate** just outside the walls in Via Porta Leonina (mid-March to April & Sept 19 to Oct Sat & Sun 10.30am–1pm & 3–6pm; May–July & Sept 1–18 Fri–Sun same hours; Aug & Dec 24–Jan 6 daily same hours; Nov–March Sat & Sun 10.30am–1pm & 3–5pm, plus other days during special exhibitions; €3). This contains two marvellously preserved fresco cycles: the fifteenth-century, sixteen-panel cycle on the *Life of St Anthony* by the Maestro della Dormito di Terni, and *Stories of the Passion and the Life of Christ* (1461) by Nicola da Siena. The presbytery holds a precious sixteenth-century group of wooden statues depicting Tobias and the Angel.

Cascia's **tourist office**, in the central square, Piazza Garibaldi 1 (Mon–Sat 9am–1pm & 3.30–6pm; summer also Sun 8.30am–12.30pm; ☏0743.71.147, ⓔinfo@iat.cascia.pg.it), is the main office for eastern Umbria, including the Valnerina, Norcia and the Piano Grande, and so can be worth a visit for maps and pamphlets.

Roccaporena and the Corno valley

Cascia's countryside is considerably more rewarding than the town. If you want a quick taste – and to stay on the St Rita trail – the trip to Roccaporena, the saint's birthplace, admirably fits the bill. The best way to get here is to take the marked and well-worn **Sentiero-Passeggiata di Santa Rita**, a perfectly level path that contours above the Corno gorge for 6km between Cascia and the village. The track can be picked up in the centre of town through the forecourt of the *Delle Rose* hotel: drop down into the underground car park, walk through it and take the gate 100m beyond, slightly to the left when you

St Rita

St Rita, patron saint of Cascia, experienced – and survived – the kind of hardships borne by women throughout history, which is the main reason for her appeal, and also why she's sometimes known as the "saint of the impossible". Born in 1381, a poor child of aged parents, she was forced to marry at 15 and endured eighteen years of mistreatment from an alcoholic husband. Having weaned himself from the bottle and repented his past, the husband died in a brawl a few weeks later. Rita's children, for the most part wretched wasters, both died attempting to avenge their father.

Beaten, widowed and childless, Rita sensibly thought it about time she became a nun. Her knowledge of the marital bed, however, made this impossible; only a relaxation of convent rules allowed her to become an Augustinian, a development held up as one of her "impossible" miracles. No sooner had she joined than she developed a sore in the middle of her forehead, an excrescence so foul-smelling that none of the nuns would come near her. This supposedly developed when a thorn fell from a crown of thorns as she was praying to a statue of Christ, and so was regarded by her companions as a kind of stigmata. The smell abated only once – to allow her to join her companions on a week's visit to Rome to meet the pope; on their return the odour returned as virulent as ever.

Rita died in 1457, but the process of her beatification was laborious, hampered by doubts as to the veracity of her miracles, by the fact that she was a woman (and one with a past), and doubtless by the size of her grassroots support, a groundswell the papacy feared beyond their control. The proclamation of her beatification finally came in 1628, and her elevation to sainthood as late as 1900, and then only in the wake of a huge public campaign.

emerge. After 4km – you simply follow the same track all the way, with no diversions left or right – cut down to cross the river on a track that branches off right just after a ruined house and the point where a large pipe crosses the river: you'll know if you've gone too far as the track, which has been following an underground aqueduct, becomes too narrow to walk on. The last kilometre is on the road.

The surreal little village of **ROCCAPORENA** sits at the bend of a deep-sided, heavily wooded valley, dominated by a soaring vegetation-shrouded crag, the **Scoglio di Santa Rita**. Perched on the needle-point summit is a tiny chapel, tiring to reach but with magnificent views. In the village, a small but often pilgrim-thronged place devoted almost entirely to Rita, the parish church of **San Montano** has the graves of Rita's family, and is the spot where she concluded her unfortunate marriage. More people make the pilgrimage to the **Orto di Santa Rita**, site of the saint's now rather tatty garden, an unlikely spot for horticulture given its barren, cliff-edge location. It's well signed, on the valley side opposite the Scoglio, the spot marked by a modern bronze statue of the saint, on and around which are often dozens of invocations scrawled on scraps of paper. The obvious place to **stay** is the three-star *Hotel Roccaporena-Casa del Pellegrino* (☏0743.7549, ⓦwww.roccaporena.com; ❷), an institutional but spotless and comfortable pilgrims' hotel. It also has a cheap, canteen-like **restaurant**, more or less the only place in the village to eat.

The Corno valley and Monteleone

There are plenty of opportunities for **walks** into the hills from Roccaporena, particularly along the wooded arm of the **Corno valley** that makes a dog's-leg turn to the south. To pick up paths simply follow the gravel road beyond the *Casa del Pellegrino*, which climbs quickly, becoming a cart track after a couple of kilometres. East 1km into the valley, it's worth making a brief detour to the hamlet of Capanne, for its views and small fifteenth-century church. An hour's walk northwest from there, over upland, leads to the lonely **Madonna delle Stelle**, a restored monastery which you can also reach more easily from the Borgo Cerreto–Monteleone road.

MONTELEONE itself, on the only road south into Lazio, is a fine, if in parts earthquake-battered medieval village surrounded by grand hill country and noted for woodcarving and delicacies such as olives, wine and truffles. The main sight is the church of **San Francesco**, graced with an exceptional Gothic door, and scattered with artistic and archeological fragments excavated from a massive Neolithic necropolis nearby. The village is best known, however, for *farro*, a crude grain (the increasingly trendy spelt in English) that finds its way into soups – *zuppa di farro* – across the Valnerina. The Romans and Etruscans used *farro* as a staple grain, and allegedly fed it to their soldiers before they went into battle.

Travel details

Trains

Spoleto to: Arezzo (8 daily; 2hr 10min); Florence direct (8 daily; 2hr 30min–3hr); Foligno via Trevi (12–18 daily; 20min; connections for Spello, Assisi, Perugia & Teróntola); Fossato di Vico (for Gubbio; 9–13 daily; 1hr 10min); Narni (10–17 daily; 40min); Nocera Umbra (8 daily; 40min); Orte (10–17 daily; 55min; additional connections to Rome and Florence); Perugia direct (15–20 daily; 45min);

Rome (10–17 daily; 1hr 15min–1hr 45min); Terni (10–17 daily; 30min).

Buses

Note that all buses between Spoleto and Norcia and Cascia run via Sant'Anatolia di Narco; Cascia services to and from Norcia, Spoleto or Rome require a connection at Serravalle.

Cascia to: Foligno (Mon–Sat 1 direct daily; 2hr); Norcia (Mon–Sat 5–8 daily, 1 on Sun; 40min); Roccaporena (1–3 daily; 15min); Rome (Mon–Sat 2 daily, 1 on Sun; 3hr); Spoleto (Mon–Sat 5–7 daily, 3 on Sun; 1hr 5min).

Norcia to: Borgo Cerreto via Campi, Preci and Triponzo (Mon–Sat 1 daily, currently leaves 1.25pm; 1hr); Cascia (Mon–Sat 5–8 daily, 1 on Sun; 40min); Castelluccio via Forca Canapine (2 on Thurs; 50min); Perugia (Mon–Sat 1 direct daily, currently leaves 6.15am; 2hr 30min); Rome (Stazione Tibertina; Mon–Sat 2 daily, 1 on Sun; 3hr); Spoleto (Mon–Sat 5–7 daily; 3 on Sun; 55min).

Spoleto (train station or Piazza Vittoria) to: Cascia (Mon–Sat 5–7 daily, 3 on Sun; 1hr 5min); Foligno (Mon–Sat 4 daily; 50min); Monteleone (Mon–Sat 1 daily, via Caso and Gavelli; currently departs 1.05pm); Montefalco (Mon–Sat 3–4 daily; 1hr); Norcia (Mon–Sat 5–7 daily, 3 on Sun; 55min); Perugia (Mon–Sat 1 daily, via Spello and Santa Maria degli Angeli; 1hr 40min; additional connections at Foligno); Scheggino (Mon–Sat 4 daily with change at Sant'Anatolia di Narco; 40min); Terni (Mon–Sat 5 daily; 45min).

13

Orvieto and southern Umbria

CHAPTER 13

Highlights

* **Narni** A compact hill-town with an outstanding cathedral, medieval streets and Romanesque churches. See p.605

* **Amelia** This tiny hill-town is part-enclosed by some of Italy's oldest and mightiest walls. See p.610

* **Todi** A main piazza of medieval perfection: imposing palaces, a lovely cathedral and a fascinating museum. See p.612

* **Duomo, Orvieto** Umbria's most spectacular cathedral, with the finest facade in Italy and an outstanding and influential fresco cycle by Signorelli. See p.624

* **Underground Orvieto** Guided tours into the labyrinth below the town. See p.631

* **Pozzo di San Patrizio, Orvieto** This colossal well is a dazzling example of medieval engineering. See p.633

▲ Amelia

13

Orvieto and southern Umbria

S outhern Umbria features two of the region's most illustrious hill-towns – **Orvieto** and **Todi**. Each has become a little too popular for its own good, but they are essential visits, the former for Italy's richest Gothic cathedral, the latter for the atmosphere, museum, main square and stunning high-altitude location. Often bypassed in the rush to these star attractions are a number of smaller but still enjoyable centres, notably **Narni** – occupying a promontory above the River Nera – and **Amelia**, whose encircling walls are among the most redoubtable in the country.

Terni, a transport hub and the province's largest supply centre after Perugia, is the area's low spot, a grim industrial city whose most valuable role is as the southern gateway to the **Valnerina**. Roads up the valley pass the most celebrated landscape attraction in this part of Umbria, the **Cascate delle Marmore** – a partly artificial waterfall that nonetheless provides an impressive spectacle – and continue to **San Pietro in Valle**, the region's loveliest abbey.

Mainline **trains** from Terni head north to Spoleto and south to Narni, connecting with the Rome–Florence route (and Orvieto trains) at **Orte**. The Ferrovia Centrale Umbra (FCU) provides the most enjoyable ride, a private single-track line that runs from Terni to Perugia, and then on to Città di Castello and Sansepolcro. Using spartan two-carriage trains, the line fills the gaps left by the state network, rattling through lovely countryside to provide access to Todi, and to minor halts like **Deruta**, heart of the region's ceramic tradition. Good **road** links follow almost identical routes: if you're driving, the big junction with the A1 at Orte – an obvious gateway in and out of the region – offers options in all directions.

Terni

TERNI, the southernmost major town in Umbria, was the unlikely birthplace of **St Valentine**, patron saint of lovers and bishop of the town until his martyrdom in 273 – but a less romantic city would be hard to imagine. Prewar Terni formed the cradle of Italy's industrial revolution, claiming the country's first steel mill and producing the world's first viable plastic; its armaments and

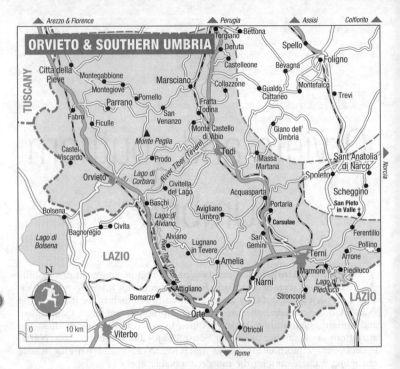

Torgiano ● Bettona
Deruta ● Spello
Città della Pieve ● Castelleone Bevagna ● Foligno
Montegabbione Marsciano Collazzone Gualdo Montefalco ● Trevi
Montegiove Pornello Cattaneo
Parrano Fratta
Fabro Ficulle San Todina
Venanzo Giano dell'
Monte Peglia Monte Castello Umbria
di Vibio
Castel Prodo Todi Sant'Anatolia
Viscardo Massa di Narco
Lago di Martana
Orvieto Corbara Spoleto
Civitella Acquasparta Scheggino
del Lago San Pieto
Baschi Portaria in Valle ✝
Bolsena Avigliano CarsualES
Lago di Umbro Ferentillo
Bagnoregio Civita Alviano Pollino
Lago di Alviano Lugnano San Terni Arrone
Bolsena in Tevere Gemini Marmore Piediluco
LAZIO Amelia Lago di
Piediluco
N Narni **LAZIO**
Bomarzo Attigliano Stroncone
Orte
0　　　10 km Otricoli
Viterbo
▼ *Rome*

steel industries made it a target for Allied bombing in 1944. During over a hundred air raids, most of the town – including the best part of its Roman and medieval heritage – was reduced to rubble. These days Terni remains an unattractive industrial town, if no longer quite the manufacturing powerhouse it was in the past, with arms and chemicals still well to the fore: the gun that allegedly shot Kennedy was made here.

To give the town credit, it does its best: the piazzas are often filled with sculpture; cultural life is rich and varied, with an offshoot of the **Umbria Jazz** festival held here around Easter; and the arrival of **film-makers** and production companies, increasingly put off by high costs in Rome, has seen the growth of Terni as a movie production centre. Much of Roberto Benigni's *Life is Beautiful*, for example, was shot in a local suburb here. The best times to be in Terni are **May Day** – celebrated with unusual vigour and a parade of floats by this committed left-wing town – and **St Valentine's Day** (Feb 14), marked by a festival, market and evening Latino disco. The **International Piano Festival** is a high-class event held in June.

Arrival, information and accommodation

Terni is a major **rail** junction, with trains running on the state network from Rome, Orte (connection-point from Orvieto and Florence), Spoleto, Foligno (connection-point from Assisi, Spello and Perugia) and Rieti. There's also the private FCU train line, which shares the main railway station, with hourly trains from Todi, Perugia, Città di Castello, Sansepolcro and stations en route. ATC **buses** leave from the forecourt near the train station to numerous local villages, and to Narni, Todi, the Cascate delle Marmore, Piediluco, Arrone, Ferentillo, Triponzo, Spoleto, Orvieto, Viterbo and Scheggino.

From the train station, head 300m along Viale della Stazione to the seventh turning on the right, for the **tourist office**, Viale Cesare Battisti 7a (Mon–Sat 9am–1pm, Tues & Fri also 3–6pm; ☎0744.423.047). The regional tourist office covering the Lower Valnerina, Narni and Otricoli is in the same building.

Hotels

Brenta Viale Brenta 12 ☎0744.283.007. Central sixteen-room one-star hotel with a restaurant. Extremely cheap but also pretty basic; not all rooms have private bathrooms. ❶
De Paris Viale Stazione 52 ☎&℻0744.58.047, ⓦwww.hotelparis.it. Large 63-room three-star hotel that offers better value than the nearby four-star *Michelangelo Palace*. The facilities are good,

but the modern rooms are somewhat soulless; very convenient for the station, however, if you're just passing through. ❸
Garden Viale Bramante 4 ☎0744.300.041, ⓦwww.gardenhotelterni.it. Not central, but top-of-the-range comfort in a modern and large four-star hotel close to the exit from the *superstrada*, with swimming pool, flower-filled balconies and all the frills. ❺

The Town

There's little to see in Terni, and what there is is usually lost amongst modern buildings. Perhaps the best reason for leaving the train station is the new **Pinacoteca Comunale "O. Metelli" e "Museo A. De Felice"** in the Neoclassical Palazzo Gazzoli, Via del Teatro Romano 13 (Tues–Sun 10am–1pm & 4–7pm; €4). Its star turns are *The Marriage of St Catherine* by Benozzo Gozzoli, the *Pala dei Francescani* by Piermatteo d'Amelia, and a *Crucifixion* by the Folignese artist Nicolò Alunno, along with works by several key moderns – Chagall, Braque, Picasso, Ernst, Kandinsky and Miró. Contemporary works are arranged in a separate section of the gallery. There's also a generous helping of canvases by Orneore Metelli (1872–1938), an impoverished shoemaker from Terni who chronicled his daily life in colourful and appealing naive paintings.

St Valentine

Terni's tourist literature treads carefully around the subject of St Valentine, talking of his "delicate tradition" – delicate, that is, because there are doubts about whether he ever existed and exactly whose body it is that pilgrims venerate in the Basilica di San Valentino, 2km south of Terni. The uncertain identity of the corpse, however, didn't stop someone stealing the saint's head as a love-token in 1986; it was found three years later, wrapped in newspaper, under a park bench at the Cascate delle Marmore.

According to the delicate tradition, Valentine was elected first bishop of Terni in 197 AD and attempted to bring converts to Christianity – then still outlawed – by encouraging the religious marriage of young people. It's also said that star-crossed lovers would turn to him for advice, drawn by his open-mindedness and his custom of giving them flowers from his garden. His most famous success was the union of Sabinus and Serapia, two lovers – he pagan, she Christian – barred from marriage by their lack of a shared faith. Valentine comforted them with the assurance that their souls would never be separated; when the young Serapia died, he converted Sabinus and thus achieved the reunion of the lovers when Sabinus died soon after. Another theory suggests the saint's feast day was the same day on which birds in Umbria were traditionally thought to mate.

Evidence of Valentine's other qualifications for sainthood is scarce, though after his martyrdom in Rome, his head is said to have rolled 93km from its place of execution. Interestingly enough, his following in Italy is considerably less than in the "unromantic" Anglo-Saxon countries.

13

The same ticket gives you admission to the Mostra Permanente di Paleontologia, Largo Liberotti (Tues, Fri & Sat 9am–1pm & 4–7pm), a very modest collection of fossils.

The greenest parts of a grey city are the gardens of its southwest quadrant around San Salvatore and the Roman amphitheatre. **San Salvatore**, off the shapeless sprawl of Piazza Europa, is the town's most interesting church, featuring a rotunda that was long believed to have been a Roman temple to the sun, but has recently been dated to the eleventh century.

Eating and drinking

Terni has a couple of top-grade **restaurants**, numerous cheap and serviceable *trattorie* and dozens of pizza-by-the-slice and fast-food outlets. *Tacitus*, Piazza Tacito, is a good local trattoria a few minutes' walk south of the station (closed Fri) – you'll pass it en route to the tourist office. For something just as good, try the tiny *La Piazzetta*, Via del Leone 34 (☏0744.58.188), with a long menu of reliable regional dishes (closed Sun and two weeks in Aug). The city's oldest **bar** is the *Pazzaglia*, Corso Tacito 10, a great source of **cakes and pastries**, including *l'amour polenta*, the house speciality.

The Lower Valnerina

Terni is the ideal point of entry for the **Lower Valnerina** and on to Norcia and the Sibillini: drive or take a bus along the SS209, which follows the valley into its upper reaches (see p.584). Buses from Terni go as far as Triponzo (see p.584), via Piedipaterno, where you could link up with bus connections on to Norcia or Spoleto. The lower valley's highlight is undoubtedly the Abbazia di San Pietro in Valle (see p.581), 18km north of the city, but on the way you'll pass a number of fine natural diversions, such as the **Marmore waterfalls**. Scenery is generally scrappy until **Ferentillo**, however – when the hills start to rise in impressive fashion – so there's an argument for simply ignoring the valley's lower reaches until you hit San Pietro.

Cascate delle Marmore

The first stop of interest in the valley comes just 6km southeast of Terni at the **Cascate delle Marmore** (access by train or buses from Terni's Piazza Dante), which at 165m are among the highest waterfalls in Europe. They were created by the Romans in 271 BC, when they diverted the River Velino into the Nera during drainage of marshlands to the south. Further channels were cut in 1400 and 1785, both with the intention of draining Rieti's plain without flooding Terni, though the falls' major boost came with the damming of nearby Lago di Piediluco in the 1930s to satisfy industrial demand for hydroelectric power. Terni's power-station complex is the largest hydroelectric plant in Italy.

Pictures of the falls in full spate adorn most Umbrian tourist offices, but what they don't tell you is that the water can be diverted through turbines at the flick of a switch, leaving a none-too-spectacular trickle. **Flow times** are notoriously variable, though in general, afternoons, summer evenings and Sunday mornings are likeliest, especially during July and August when there's an impressive *son et lumière*.

There are two **observation points**: the belvedere in Marmore village, and the SS209 road down below. A steep and frequently muddy path connects the two, starting 100m downstream of the falls, and there are swimming pools at the bottom of the cascade when the water's turned off. The green and luxuriant

13

setting, tumbling water and acres of gleaming marble add up to a spectacular show – shame about the factories around the corner.

Marmore has a **campsite**, the *Marmore*, at the nearby hamlet of Campacci (T0744.67.198; April–Sept).

Ferentillo and its mummies

FERENTILLO is rapidly becoming the **free-climbing** capital of Italy, its crags swarming at weekends as new and more difficult routes are pioneered. The village itself sprawls across two rocky hillsides, guarded by twin fourteenth-century towers, and merits a stop for one of Umbria's more grotesque ménages – a collection of mummies. These are to be found propped up in the **Museo delle Mummie** in the crypt of San Stefano on Via della Torre, signposted off the main road (daily: April–Sept 9am–12.30pm & 2.30–7.30pm; March & Oct closes 6pm; Nov–Feb 10am–12.30pm & 2.30–5pm; €3), on the east side of the Nera in the Precetto quarter. Now behind glass and viewed on guided tours – a precaution taken after a head was stolen – the corpses were simply dumped in the crypt and preserved by accident, apparently dried by their bed of sandy soil and a desiccating wind from the south-facing windows. The characters are a curious mix: two French soldiers hanged during the Napoleonic wars; a bearded dwarf; a mother who died in childbirth (the child displayed alongside her); a papal soldier, bolt upright with his gun, housed in the case of a grandfather clock; a lawyer shot in a local feud over a farm; a farmer whose gun backfired in the same feud and blasted a hole in his stomach; and a hapless Chinese couple who came to Italy in 1880 for their honeymoon and died of cholera. To round things off there's a pile of leering skulls with a mummified owl perched in their midst.

You wouldn't necessarily want to stay locally, though there is a small 25-bed **hostel**, *Il Tiglio*, Via Abruzzo (open year-round 9am–1pm & 4–7.30pm; T0744.388.1710 or 335.752.9232, Elameridianaergon@virgilio.it; dorm beds €14.50; ①). There is also a good three-star **hotel**, the eleven-room *Monterivoso*, a converted mill at Via Case Sparse 5 in the nearby hamlet of Monteriviso (T0744.780.772, Wwww.monterivoso.it; ②) – though you'd do better staying 6km north at the abbey of San Pietro (see p.581). There's a good **restaurant**, the *Piermarini*, Via della Vittoria 53a (T0744.780.714, Wwww.saporipiermarini .it; closed Sun evening, Mon and three weeks in Aug & Sept), whose interesting cooking ventures beyond the more usual Umbrian standards. Lunch needs to be booked Tuesday to Friday.

Narni

NARNI is an intimate, unspoilt hill-town that juts into the Nera valley on a majestic spur crowned by another of Cardinal Albornoz's formidable citadels. It lies half an hour by train midway between Terni and Orte; from the latter, it's a spectacular trip through a tree-filled gorge. The fortress draws an admiring glance before you see the welter of chemical works around Narni Scalo, the new town that's grown up around the station – thankfully almost invisible from the medieval centre. Old Narni's stage-set medievalism is even more complete than Perugia's or Assisi's, its quiet piazzas, Romanesque churches – notably the **Duomo** and **Santa Maria in Pensole** – and labyrinth of ancient streets and stepped passageways forming one of Italy's most congenial townscapes. There are also vestiges from the time when Narni was the Roman colony of Narnia, established in 299 BC – one of the first in Umbria – and a linchpin in Rome's defences, standing close to the Tiber valley and the undefended road to the capital. It was the birthplace in AD 32 of the Roman emperor Nerva, and of Erasmo da Narni, better known as Gattamelata (1370–1443), one of the greatest of all medieval mercenaries.

San Giovenale is the focus of Narni's main **festival**, during which a fortnight of festivities lead up to the **Corsa dell'Anello**, held on the second Sunday in May. On the Saturday evening of that weekend a torchlit procession takes place. The next day, contestants from the town's three medieval quarters compete to thrust a lance through a ring (*anello*) suspended in Via Maggiore.

Arrival and information

Buses from nearby towns as well as the station arrive at Piazza Garibaldi, where there's an ATC office for bus information and tickets and limited **parking** (there are more spaces on the approach to the square in Via Roma). Frequent **trains** from both Terni and Orte (where you can pick up connections to Orvieto on the Rome–Florence line) arrive at Narni Scalo station. From the station forecourt buses run into town; buy tickets on board or from the station news kiosk. You may have to wait, but don't be tempted into the long and tedious walk.

The **tourist office** is at Piazza dei Priori 3 (summer Mon–Fri 9.30am–12.30pm & 4–7pm, Sat 9.30am–12.30pm & 4.30–7.30pm, Sun 10am–12.30pm & 4.30–7.30pm; variable winter hours; ☎0744.715.362, ✆info@iat .narni.tr.it). Ask here for details of **Narni Sotterranea** (Underground Narni; ⓦwww.narni sotterranea.it), partly inspired by the similar excellent enterprise in Orvieto (see p.631). It involves guided tours of some of the town's ancient subterranean chambers and tunnels, notably those around San Domenico, Santa Maria Impensole and the Roman "Formina" aqueduct that brought water to Piazza Garibaldi. Tours are rather impromptu, and currently restricted to Saturdays and some Sundays, but more may be introduced, especially in summer.

Accommodation

The town has just two **hotels**; there's a **campsite** 5km south at Monte del Sole, on the road to Borgaria (℡ 0744.796.336; April–Sept).

Casa di Accoglienza Via Gattemelata 74 ℡ 0744.715.217. A cheap accommodation option is the simple *Casa di Accoglienza*, run by the nuns of Santa Anna, which has beds in double or single rooms (for men and women) at €17 per person.

Dei Priori Vicolo del Comune 4 ℡ 0744.726.843, Ⓦ www.loggiadeipriori.it. The superior of the town's hotels is this three-star option – all old-world finery – and it's very central too, with a great restaurant. ❸

Minareto Via dei Cappuccini Nuovi 32 ℡ 0744.726.343, Ⓕ 0744.726.284. The three-star *Minareto*, situated outside the walls just southeast of the Porta Ternana, is very much a no-frills option. ❶

Novelli Via della Stazione 12 ℡ & Ⓕ 0744.751.004. An alternative to a hotel in town is staying in Narni Scalo: by the station, this three-star option has had a complete renovation, which has turned it into a comfortable and inexpensive place to stay. However, its location, unless you're coming off the train, is hardly perfect. ❷

The Town

The circuitous bus route from Narni Scalo to the medieval town allows a brief view of the Roman **Ponte di Augusto**, a solitary arch built in 27 BC in the middle of the river (a second collapsed in 1855), remnant of a bridge which in its day was 30m high and spanned 160m, a product of Augustan-era renovations to the Via Flaminia. In the eighteenth century this was one of the key sights on the Grand Tour – Corot, among others, painted the scene (the picture is in the Louvre) – but now is so lost among the lower town's development that you could easily miss it completely: the best viewpoint is provided by the train from Orte, just before you pull into Narni.

Piazza Garibaldi is the town's rather oddly shaped and disjointed social hub; its ancient name, Piazza del Lago, hints at one reason for the strangeness, for the square was once a medieval cistern (or *lacus*), built over a Roman cistern fed by an aqueduct from the surrounding hills. Note the piazza's restored fountain (1527), decorated by imaginary animals. From the square, the main street, Via Garibaldi (and its continuation, Via Mazzini), leads north to the heart of the old town – still built on the old Roman grid – through an arch in the city walls, following the course of the Via Flaminia, whose construction in 220 BC set the seal on Narni's importance.

The Duomo

The Duomo, or **Cattedrale di San Giovenale** (daily 8.30am–12.30pm & 3.30–7pm; free), fronting Via Garibaldi's first bend, was built around 1047 and named after Narni's first bishop, who was buried in accordance with Roman custom outside what were then the town walls in 376. Other religious worthies buried on the site include San Cassio, interred here in 558. By the ninth century (perhaps earlier), a chapel had been built which provided the basis for the 1047 church – by then within the town's medieval borders. It was consecrated in 1145 by Pope Eugenius III and amended over the years so that it is now an intriguing mix of accretions from most centuries since. Its facade is small and unassuming, cramped by surrounding buildings and by the Lombard-influenced portico, which dates from 1492 (with later additions). The portal, laced with carvings, dates from the twelfth century.

Inside, the church has a slightly lopsided feel, owing to the addition of an outer south aisle in the fifteenth century. The extravagant Baroque altar is overshadowed by gold-leafed **pulpits** on either side of the nave and an intricate **screen** – all mainly late fifteenth-century works, but incorporating fragments of Romanesque and paleo-Christian reliefs. The Cosmati pavement is also attractive, while elsewhere parts of the original church show through, chiefly in the patches of fresco – notably a little niche *Madonna and Child* on the west (rear) wall and in the apse behind the choir. The little wooden summer **statue** (1474) representing St Anthony Abbot near the rear wall at the start of the left aisle is by the Sienese master Vecchietta, who may also have been responsible for *San Giovenale*, a painting of Narni's patron saint on the last pillar of the right aisle.

Giovenale's tomb lies in the cellar-like chapel midway down the south aisle, the extraordinary **Sacello di San Giovenale e San Cassio** (also known as the Oratorio di San Cassio). It's shielded by a Cosmatesque marble screen and pillars, possibly from the presbytery of the Romanesque church here rebuilt in 1322, and a relief of *Two Lambs Adoring the Cross*, together with two thirteenth-century niche statues of the *Pietà* and *San Giovenale*. An important piece of early Christian architecture, the chapel dates from 558; its crude, age-blackened walls contain a ninth-century **mosaic** of Christ high up on an inner wall, the oldest in the region. Inside are more Cosmati fragments and reliefs, together with the eighth- or ninth-century sarcophagus used as Giovenale's tomb: the stones beyond the tomb represent part of the original Roman wall. The tomb of Cassio and his wife, Fasta, is above the chapel entrance. The couple's remains, along with those of Giovenale, were stolen by the Tuscans in 850 and languished for a time in Lucca.

The Pinacoteca Civica

The bulk of the town's paintings and other works of art are housed in a new gallery, the **Museo della Città e del Territorio** (April–June & Sept Tues–Sun 10.30am–1pm & 3.30–6pm; July & Aug Tues–Sun 10.30am–1pm & 4.30–7.30pm; Oct–March Fri–Sun 10.30am–1pm & 3–5.30pm; €5) in the Palazzo Eroli, just south of the church of San Domenico on the left at the northern end of Via Aurelio Saffi. Years in the planning and execution, it collects work previously held in the Palazzo del Podestà and various churches around town; there is also a section devoted to the gold and silverware from the cathedral treasury. In the collection, the influence of Tuscan artists in the region is acknowledged in Benozzo Gozzoli's *Annunciation* (1451–2) and a tabernacle attributed to the school of Agostino di Duccio. One section is devoted to San Girolamo, an important former Franciscan convent 13km southeast of Narni that was once home to the town's best painting, Domenico Ghirlandaio's *Coronation of the Virgin*, commissioned for the convent in 1486 by Cardinal Eroli, a cleric who was also busy in Spoleto's cathedral (see p.572).

Piazza dei Priori

Via Garibaldi continues through a vibrant residential centre, following the line of the old Roman Cardo Maximus past Via del Campanile on the left, which provides a glimpse of the cathedral's fifteenth-century campanile (built on a Roman base). It soon emerges into the **Piazza dei Priori**, a perfect little civic square where pride of place goes to the fourteenth-century **Palazzo dei Priori** and its loggia, designed by the Gubbian Matteo Gattapone, the architect responsible for Gubbio's Palazzo dei Consoli and Spoleto's vast Ponte delle

Torri. Next to its high arches and Roman inscription is a little exterior pulpit, built for the peripatetic St Bernardino. The striking Palazzo Sacripante alongside is covered in medieval reliefs.

Opposite the Palazzo dei Priori is the **Palazzo del Podestà**, or Palazzo Comunale, cobbled together by amalgamating three town houses and adding some token decoration. The thirteenth-century Romanesque sculptures above the main door are worth a glance, as are the numerous Roman fragments of the courtyard.

The rest of the town

Beyond the piazza, Via Mazzini passes after 50m the inconspicuous but lovely church of **Santa Maria Impensole** (daily 8.30am–12.30pm & 3.30–7.30pm; free). A simple basilica, unchanged since it was built in 1175, it was located over a pagan place of worship that in turn was the site of a cemetery and then a Roman-era house with two still extant cisterns. It has an enchanting triple-arched Romanesque portico and a beautiful carved frieze around the square doorways. The interior is plain save for a few simple carvings and capitals, though interesting rooms below the nave with Roman remains are occasionally open, including one with a sixth-century tomb.

The ex-church of **San Domenico**, a slightly forlorn building a short way farther down Via Mazzini, is now home to Narni's archives and public library (Mon–Thurs 9am–1pm & 3.15–6pm, Fri 9am–1pm; free). It's worth dropping by for the wealth of medieval fresco fragments around the walls and the funerary wall monument (1494) to Gabriele Massei, crafted by followers of Agostino di Duccio. You could also try asking in the library to view the Roman **aqueduct** that lies below the building. Behind the church to the left, at the beginning of Via Aurelio Saffi, a small **garden** with fragments of an old tower offers great views down into the Nera gorge: the distinctive building way down below is the recently restored twelfth-century Benedictine **Abbazia di San Cassiano** (generally open to the public on Sun).

The northern tip of the town is graced with more gardens and good views, as well as steep little streets leading down to Via Gattamelata; no. 70 is reputedly the birthplace of the eponymous *condottiere* (mercenary). Towards the street's southern end lies the tatty, water-stained church of **Sant'Agostino**, its large, bare portal concealing an interior with a redoubtable fourteenth-century stone altar and a few medieval faded frescoes amidst half-hearted Baroque. The best fresco, to the right of the main door, is a *Madonna Enthroned with Sts Lucy and Apollonia* (1482) by the accomplished local artist Pier Matteo d'Amelia, best known as one of Fra' Filippo Lippi's two assistants on the apse frescoes in Spoleto cathedral. Also spare a moment for the fresco fragments in the apse, which depict a variety of saints.

Returning to Piazza Garibaldi and heading south takes you into a warren of little streets, worth wandering for their own sake. At the top of this quarter lies the **Rocca**, now open (guided tours only) after decades of restoration (Fri–Sun Aug–Sept 11am–1pm & 4.30–7.30pm; Sat & Sun Oct–Dec 11am–1pm & 3.30–5.30pm; €3), though opening times are liable to change. It's a massive affair, lording it over the town and surrounding country and reached by Via del Monte, a street that threads through the *terziere di Mezule*, one of the three areas into which the medieval town was divided. The castle was commissioned by Cardinal Albornoz in the 1370s and is attributed to Gattapone, responsible for the town's Loggia dei Priori; it formed a link in the chain of fortresses by which Albornoz sought to reassert papal authority across Umbria. The park around the castle is a perfect spot for a picnic and siesta.

Eating and drinking

Pizzerias and bars are gathered on Piazza Garibaldi, and there are good snacks at *Il Forno* bakery off Piazza del Popolo.

Da Sara Strada Calvese 55–7 ☎0744.796.138. In wooded, hilly country 8km south of town near the hamlet of Moricone is *Da Sara*, a typical rural trattoria with a small bar-*osteria* alongside. Prices in both are reasonable – €25 should get you three courses. Closed Wed.

Il Gattemelata Via Pozza della Comunità 4, just off Piazza Garibaldi ☎0744.717.245. A pleasantly understated place with more than usually ambitious Umbrian cooking: €30 should buy you a good meal. Closed Mon.

Il Pincio Via XX Settembre 117 ☎0744.722.241, ⓦwww.ristoranteilpincio.it. The Slow Food-recommended *Il Pincio* occupies, in part, an ancient grotto, and is run by the charming Cesare and Rita. The cooking, of course, is Umbrian, with

virtually all produce sourced locally. Without wine, expect to pay around €25 a head. Oct to mid-April closed Wed.

La Loggia Vicolo del Comune ☎0744.722.744. The longest-established restaurant in the heart of Narni's old town is this classy place, cosy with vaulted stone ceilings. Closed Mon & late July.

Monte del Grano Strada Guadamello 128 ☎0744.749.143. The best out-of-town restaurant lies 15km south in the hilltop hamlet of San Vito. It's small and has a fine reputation, so booking is usually essential; service, food and ambience all justify the prices (mains €13–18), though not all the innovative dishes are a complete success. Closed Mon & mid-Jan to mid-March; Tues–Fri eves only.

Amelia and around

AMELIA, 11km west of Narni Scalo, sits perched on top of a sugarloaf hill, its position and surrounding countryside the nicest for some distance around. The town is as delightful as its setting, enclosed by some of the oldest and mightiest **walls** in Italy. Formed from vast polygonal blocks joined without mortar, they are up to 4m wide and 8m high. Parts are known to have belonged to an Umbrian acropolis of the fifth century BC, though the Roman historian Pliny claimed the town was formed in the eleventh century BC, three centuries before Rome. The Romans took advantage of the fortifications in 90 BC when they used the town, then named Amerina, as a staging post on the Via Amerina, one of nine military roads linking Etruria to the Via Flaminia. Thereafter the town within the walls was all but destroyed by Totila, and later history followed a predictable course through rule by the nobility and slow decline.

Arrival, information and accommodation

Buses run to Amelia from Terni and Orvieto, as well as from the two nearest train stations, Narni Scalo and Orte. Beside the Porta Romana is the **tourist office**, Via Roma 4 (Tues–Sat 9.30am–12.30pm & 2.30–6.30pm, Mon & Sun 9.30am–12.30pm; Nov–March closes 5.30pm; ☎0744.981.453, ⓦwww.amelia .it). A minibus shuttle runs between here and the centre. There's also a lift from a lower car park to the upper town, letting you out near the post office.

On the main approach road, 2km from the walls, is one of two local **hotels**, the three-star *Scoglio dell'Aquilone*, Via Orvieto 23 (☎0744.982.445, Ⓔscogliodellaquilone@tiscalinet.it; ❶). The other, with a good restaurant (closed Mon except July & Aug), is the three-star *Anita*, Via Roma 31, 200m from the turnoff on the Narni road (☎0744.982.146, Ⓕ0744.983.079; ❷). There is also an excellent **youth hostel**, the *Giustiniani*, Piazza Mazzini 9, (March–Sept daily 8–10am & 4pm to midnight; ☎0744.978.673, ⓦwww .ostellogiustiniani.it; ❷), which has dorm beds at €16, two-bed rooms at €20 per person and four- and six-bed rooms at €18 per person.

The Town

Access is through one of the four original gates: the main entry is the **Porta Romana**. The walls can be seen from a small park to the left of the gate, and from the pleasant two-kilometre path that starts here and encircles the town. Immediately inside the gate stands the church of **San Francesco**, also known as Sts Filippo e Giacomo, its typically plain-faced facade relieved by a rose window of 1401. Inside, the Cappella di Sant'Antonio contains six tombs belonging to members of the Geraldini family, the clan that held sway over Amelia for long periods during the Middle Ages. One family member, Alessandro (1455–1525), achieved fame as one of the key advocates in the Spanish court of Columbus's 1492 expedition to the New World. The monuments (1477) on the top right, to Matteo and Elisabetta Geraldini, are the work of Agostino di Duccio. Next door at Piazza Augusto Vera 10 is the ex-Collegio Boccarini, with a beautiful courtyard and double loggia, home to the **Museo Archeologico di Amelia**, Piazza Augusto Vera 10 (July & Aug daily 10.30am–1pm & 4.30–7.30pm; April–June & Sept daily 10.30am–1pm & 4–7pm; Oct–March Fri–Sun 10.30am–1pm & 3.30–6pm; €4). The star exhibit is a bronze statue discovered locally in 1963 of the Roman general Nerone Claudio Druso, better known as Germanico, a nephew of Tiberius who died in mysterious circumstances in AD 17. There's also a picture gallery of paintings removed from local churches and palaces. If you're in town at the weekend, be sure to explore the Roman cisterns under Piazza Matteotti (April–Sept Sat 4.30–7.30pm, Sun 10.30am–12.30pm & 4.30–7.30pm; Oct–March Sat 3–6pm, Sun 10.30am–12.30pm & 3–6pm; €2; ☎0744.978.436, ⓦ www.ameliasotterranea.it).

From San Francesco, the spiralling Via della Repubblica draws you to **Piazza Marconi**, a lovely old square from where the stepped Via del Duomo leads steeply to the town's summit, site of a panoramic cathedral square. A small park here offers the best views. The most striking feature of the **Duomo**, a Romanesque church ruined by Baroque superfluities and nineteenth-century frescoes, is a twelve-sided **tower**, dated 1050 and claimed by some to symbolize the Apostles, by others to represent the signs of the zodiac. It's studded with Roman fragments and originally served as the town's principal civic tower. Inside, flanking the second chapel on the right are two standards reputedly won from the Turks at the Battle of Lepanto. The first chapel in the north aisle holds the *Tomb of Giovanni Geraldini* (1476) by Agostino di Duccio, and the first column on the right was the one against which St Fermina, the local patron saint, is said to have been martyred. A distinctive **octagonal chapel** is attributed to Antonio da Sangallo, its two funerary monuments to Ippolito Scalza, who played a key role during the construction of Orvieto's Duomo.

You might also investigate the uncovered frescoes and *sinopie* in **Sant'Agostino**'s sacristy in Via Cavour, thought to date back to the year 1000, showing four saints, red star motifs and floral decoration. Amelia's attraction otherwise is the typically Umbrian mix of views, medieval streets and close-at-hand countryside. You could walk the short distance to **Monte San Salvatore**, worthwhile for its views and a tiny ninth-century chapel, or head for the nearby rural church of **Madonna delle Cinque Fonti**, supposed site of a St Francis sermon.

Eating and drinking

Amelia is well served with **restaurants**. *Osteria dei Cansacchi*, Piazza Cansacchi 4 (☎0744.978.557; closed Wed), offers basic pastas and pizzas, but also more adventurous meat and fish dishes. You might also try the restaurant in the *Anita* (see p.610), or *La Tavernetta* pizzeria on Via della Repubblica in the old centre. At **Gabelletta**, 3.5km northeast on the Foce road, is *La Gabelletta*, Via Tuderte (☎0744.982.159; closed Mon & late July), a large, courteous and highly rated restaurant. Be sure to indulge in Amelia's speciality, a teeth-rotting combination of white figs, chopped nuts and chocolate known as *fichi girotti*, available from local bars.

Lugnano in Teverina

The run along the back roads between Orvieto and Amelia (possible by bus) is a treat, offering plenty of oak forests and the chance to catch one of southern Umbria's Romanesque highlights, the twelfth-century **Santa Maria Assunta** in **LUGNANO IN TEVERINA**. Fronted by an exotic, restored portico (1230), the church has finely carved twin pulpits and has somehow hung onto a triptych by Nicolò Alunno in the apse. The interior also has plenty of lovely carved capitals, a reconstructed *cantoria* and a Cosmatesque floor, while the beautifully pillared crypt features a fine sculpted screen and further Cosmati marble work.

Carsulae and around

The building of the Roman Via Flaminia from Rome to Ancona confirmed this region's importance as the crossroads of Italy; colonies along its route were to evolve into modern-day Narni, Terni, Spoleto and Spello. Some settlements, however, such as **CARSULAE**, 15km north of Terni, were abandoned after earthquakes and civil war. In its day, this particular pile of stones was known as the Pompeii of central Italy, its beauty praised by both Tacitus and Pliny the Younger. To get there, take the first junction for San Gemini Fonte on the main Todi–Terni road (ie before the tunnel heading south), and then just before San Gemini Fonte (not before plain San Gemini) take the signposted route to the ruins, the largest Roman site in Umbria.

The site (daily: April–Sept 8.30am–7.30pm; Oct–March 8.30am–5.30pm; free) is today dominated by a church, **San Damiano**, made from materials filched from the ruins; other precious marbles went to build local houses. Behind the church you can follow a long stretch of the original **Via Flaminia**, complete with grooves made by chariots, to a substantial arched gateway, built by Trajan; beyond the arch, on the left, is a large square Roman tomb. Walking back on the Flaminia, you'll see the site of the **Basilica Forense** (law courts) off to the left; behind it, across a modern lane rise the remnants of the **amphitheatre**, built in the hollow of a natural depression. Behind the arena is a **theatre**, its orchestra still impressively intact, and to its rear a spread of ruins still awaiting excavation. Back across the site, behind San Damiano and the Flaminia, are the **forum**, composed of numerous low walls, and the vague outlines of baths, a well and two temples.

Todi

TODI provides a graphic illustration of what has happened in much of Umbria over the last two decades. Once a sleepy, simple agricultural centre, it became a favoured retreat for foreign expats and Rome's arts and media types, attracted as much by the town's considerable rustic charms as its relative proximity to the Italian capital. These days the transformation is all but complete: Todi is firmly on the tourist trail and has been smartened up to within a whisker of its life. Gentrification is manifest in a scattering of estate agents, shuttered holiday homes and the revamped and decidedly high-profile **Todi Festival** – ten days of music, ballet and other arts at the beginning of September. The final straw came when an American university study proclaimed it the world's most amenable place in which to live: the few remaining unrestored farmhouses and villas were duly snapped up. Don't be put off, for the town is still unmissable, with much charm and many sights, notably an impressive **Piazza del Popolo** and the churches of **San Fortunato** and **Santa Maria della Consolazione**, though perhaps what lingers most in the memory is its position 410m up, a stunning and daunting prospect from below.

Iron Age remains suggest some three thousand years of continual habitation. Tradition has it the Umbrian town was built where an eagle dropped a table-cloth snatched from a local family – hence the eagle and cloth in the town's insignia. More certain is the **Etruscan** heritage: coins bearing the name Tutare ("border") suggest a town of some independence during pre-Roman rule, probably one of several outposts used by the Etruscans to defend their frontier along the Tiber. Necropolises all round Todi have yielded some of the finest Etruscan treasures, most of them – including a famous bronze statue of Mars – shipped off to Rome. Ancient Roman rule came (in 42 BC) and went, leaving little except a second set of walls and indistinct ruins. The town's heyday was the thirteenth century, when as a free *comune* – one of Umbria's first – it managed to annex Amelia and Terni, hold its own in skirmishes with Spoleto, Narni and Orvieto, and build a third set of walls and crop of civic palaces. The two small eaglets under the wings of the Todi eagle on some of the town's coats

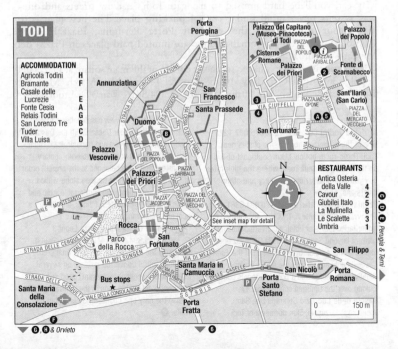

of arms represent the towns of Amelia and Terni. The **Atti** were the leading noble family, overseeing – in tandem with the Church's representatives – a period of decline interrupted only by a flicker of sixteenth-century prosperity that produced more palaces and Todi's great Renaissance church of Santa Maria della Consolazione.

Arrival, information and accommodation

Access to Todi by public transport can be a headache. The town has two **train** stations on the FCU line between Terni (33km) and Perugia (41km), but both are in the middle of nowhere and connecting buses can involve a longish wait. The Ponte Rio station, 6km east, is marginally closer, and has a more reliable shuttle minibus to the old town (Linea C; around 12 daily Mon–Sat; tickets from the station ticket office); the other station is Ponte Naia southeast of the town. Buses back to Ponte Rio station leave from Piazza Jacopone – between Piazza del Popolo and San Fortunato – fifteen minutes before each train departure. Local taxi companies can be contacted on ☎075.894.2375 and 075.894.2525.

From Perugia, **buses** are more convenient: there are around six daily (Mon–Sat, more on school days), the last return bus leaving at 5pm. Most stop in Piazzale della Consolazione (on Vioale della Consolazione) next to Santa Maria della Consolazione. From here to the centre, you can take an orange minibus (Linea A), or follow the marked footpath that strikes off Viale della Consolazione, 20m beyond the corner on the right. Buy tickets for the minibuses and long-haul buses from the unlikely-looking stall that sells nuts and snacks. Some inter-town buses – plus a once-daily service to Rome – continue to (and leave from) Piazza Jacopone. Get tickets and information from the fruit shop in the piazza.

By car, you'll be hard pressed to navigate Todi's narrow streets and one-way system, never mind find a central **parking** place. The best plan is to leave your car outside the walls at Porta Perugina, Piazzale della Consolazione or Porta Romana. There are limited paid places in Piazza del Mercato Vecchio.

Todi's **tourist office** is in the southeast corner of the main square at Piazza del Popolo 36 (April–Oct daily 10am–1pm & 4–7pm; Nov–March Mon–Sat 10am–1pm & 3–5pm, Sun 10am–1pm; ☎075.894.5416, ✉info@iat.todi.pg.it).

Accommodation

Agricola Todini Collevalenza ☎075.887.122. One of the numerous agriturismo places near Todi. Three-room option 11km southeast of Todi on the Massa Martana road, where the high rates buy you swimming, riding, archery and other diversions. ❹

Bramante Via Orvietana 48 ☎075.894.8381, ⓦwww.hotelbramante.it. This long-established but rather faded four-star hotel, a converted medieval convent beyond Santa Maria della Consolazione, had its thunder stolen by the opening of the *Fonte Cesia*. Its only advantages are easier parking, slightly airier rooms and a pool and tennis courts looking over the Umbrian countryside. ❼

Casale delle Lucrezie Contrada Due Santi, Vocabolo Palazzaccio, 5km northeast of Todi ☎075.898.7488, ⓦwww.casaledellelucrezie .com. Out of town near Duesanti (off the Dastardo road), in peaceful, green and panoramic surroundings, the *Casale* is part of a thirteenth-century monastery that once belonged to the ancient order of Lucrezian monks. The thirteen stone-walled rooms and apartments are comfortable, chic and rustic in style, with modern fittings, and there's a pool and restaurant too. ❸

Fonte Cesia Via Lorenzo Leoni 3 ☎075.894.3737, ⓦwww.fontecesia.it. Definitely the first choice in Todi if finances allow: beautiful converted *palazzo* on several levels, with excellent restaurant, good service and very comfortable rooms: the central four-star is also the only one of Todi's hotels within the walls. ❻

Relais Todini Località Collevalenza
℡075.887.182, ⓦwww.relaistodini
.com. A glorious restored thirteenth-century
hilltop castle 9km south of Todi, beautifully
appointed with just twelve rooms and period
fittings, antiques, oil paintings, pastel colour
scheme, wood and stone floors and walls.
Facilities include tennis courts and a swimming
pool. ⑥
San Lorenzo Tre Via San Lorenzo 3
℡075.894.4555, ⓦwww.sanlorenzo3.it. Very
comfortable rooms in a pleasantly and elegantly
furnished town house in the street parallel to Via
del Duomo just east of the cathedral. ④
Tuder Via Maestà dei Lombardi 13
℡075.894.2184, ⓦwww.hoteltuder.com.
Functional three-star in an uninspiring modern,
built-up district,10min walk, relatively unpleasant,
from Porta Romana. ③
Villa Luisa Via Angelo Cortesi 147
℡075.894.8571, ⓦwww.villaluisa.it. Relatively
smart, if uninspiringly modern three-star that
boasts a pleasant garden but has a far from central
location, a short distance beyond the *Tuder*. ④

The Town

All Todi's main sights are within a few minutes' walk of each other, though the
southeast part of the town around Porta Romana involves a long downhill hike,
as does the walk to **Santa Maria della Consolazione**. From the bus terminal,
the minibus drops you at the central **Piazza del Popolo**, home to the cathedral
and an outstanding **museum**; walking up via the footpath leaves you in the
municipal gardens, near the church of **San Fortunato**. Like many a hill-town,
random exploration is one of Todi's pleasures.

Piazza del Popolo

The **Piazza del Popolo** is often described as the most perfect medieval piazza
in Italy – and with full justice, even if the cars detract slightly from the overall
effect. Flanked by a range of *palazzi* housing the excellent **Museo–Pinacoteca
e Museo della Città** and a superb **Duomo**, it's enough to take the breath
away, however many other Italian hill-towns you've seen.

Elsewhere in the piazza, the restored **Palazzo dei Priori**, built between 1293
and 1337, was the seat of Todi's various rulers and is now the town hall – note
the eagle coat of arms, complete with tablecloth; if you can look like you're on
council business you should be able to peek inside. Originally the site of the

▲ Piazza del Popolo, Todi

A **joint ticket** (€6) is available for the Museo-Pinacoteca di Todi, the Cisterne Romane and the campanile of San Fortunato. However, note that this represents only a very modest saving over individual tickets.

Roman forum, the piazza is built above a surviving complex of Roman cisterns (signed off the square down a small alley). The **Cisterne Romane** (April–Oct Tues–Sun 10.30am–1pm & 2.30–6.30pm; Nov–March Sat & Sun 10.30am–1pm & 2–4.30pm; €2, or combined ticket with Museo della Città & Campanile di San Fortunato €6), are the well-preserved remains. There isn't much to see, but the cisterns' scale graphically illustrates the Romans' engineering acumen.

The best place to enjoy the piazza's street life above ground is from the **bar** down on its southwest corner, a locals' local in contrast to the smarter place midway down the piazza's western side – though the latter does a good line in sandwiches and enjoys more sunshine. Finally, for some wonderful **views** of the surrounding countryside, wander to **Piazza Garibaldi** just alongside the square. The statue here (1890) is of Giuseppe Garibaldi, while the scenically perfect cypress is supposed to have been planted to celebrate Garibaldi's visit to Todi with his wife in 1849.

The Duomo

The **Duomo** (daily: summer 8.30am–12.30pm & 3–7pm; winter 8.30am–12.30pm & 2.30–5.30pm; free), atop a broad flight of steps added in 1740, represents a merging of the last of the Romanesque and the first of the Gothic forms filtering in from France in the early fourteenth century. Construction started at the beginning of the twelfth century, on the site of a Roman temple to Apollo, and continued intermittently until the seventeenth. The square, three-tiered **facade**, recently restored, is inspired simplicity, with just a sumptuous rose window and ornately carved composite doorway (1513 and 1639) to embellish the pink weathered marble – the classic example of a form found all over Umbria and the Abruzzo. The exterior sides of the church are more complicated, and it's worth walking down adjoining side streets for glimpses of arches, windows and bulging buttresses.

The **interior** has some impressive nineteenth-century stained glass in the arched right-hand aisle, a lovely font (1507), an exquisite fourteenth-century *Madonna and Child* and, at the end of the aisle, a fetching altarpiece by Perugino's follower Giannicolo di Paolo. Nothing, however, matches the **choir**, carved with incredible delicacy and precision by a local father-and-son team between 1521 and 1530; a nice touch are the panels at floor level near the front which depict the tools used to carve the piece. The rear west wall is defaced by a dreadful sixteenth-century *Last Judgement* (derived from Michelangelo's Sistine Chapel fresco). Underground, there's a mildly interesting crypt-cum-passageway (€0.80), entered from the top of the north aisle, scattered with Roman and possibly Etruscan fragments; pay at the little wooden kiosk midway down the north (left) aisle. The little cells in the corridor were used as tombs until the nineteenth century.

The Palazzo del Capitano

The piazza's other key buildings are a trio of thirteenth-century public palaces, squared off near the Duomo in provocative fashion – the *comune*'s aim being to put one over on the Church. The **Palazzo del Capitano**, built around 1290, and the adjoining **Palazzo del Popolo**, dating from 1213 (one of Italy's earliest civic palaces), are the most prominent, thanks mainly to their external staircase, which looks like the set of a thousand B-movie swordfights.

The upper floor of the Palazzo del Capitano houses the town's superb modern museum, the **Museo-Pinacoteca e Museo della Città** (Tues–Sun: April–Oct 10.30am–1pm & 3–6pm; Nov–March 10am–1.30pm & 2.30–5pm; €3.50, or combined ticket with the Cisterne Romane & Campanile di San Fortunato €6), which brilliantly weaves an open-plan sequence of rooms into the existing medieval structure. Before entering the gallery proper, take a look at the poignant painting by the ticket desk of Todi near the Porta Romana as it

Jacopone da Todi

Fra' Jacomo dei Benedetti, known to all as **Jacopone**, was among Italy's leading medieval poets, a trenchant critic of the papacy, and the probable author of what became one of Christendom's most famous carols, the *Stabat Mater Dolorosa*. Born in Todi in 1228, he pursued the life of decadence that seems the birthright of those ultimately destined for sainthood – gambling, feasting, cavorting in fine clothes and rarely levering himself out of bed before midday. After training as a lawyer in Bologna, however, he returned to Todi a respectable attorney. Aged about 38 he married Vanna, a young, rich and deeply devout member of the Umbrian aristocracy. A year after the marriage, Vanna was attending a local festival when the platform on which she was sitting gave way. Injured, she was carried from the scene by Jacopone, who, tearing away her fine clothes, found she had been wearing a hair shirt beneath her *haute couture*. Seconds later she died in his arms.

Jacopone was inconsolable, shocked at both Vanna's death and his ignorance of her deep devotion. The experience became the catalyst for his conversion and deliberate abasement. He sold his house, gave his wealth to the poor, distanced himself from family and friends and tramped Todi's streets dressed in rags, often spending days on all fours. He appeared at a niece's wedding dressed in tar and feathers. He added soil and wormwood to his food, to make it repugnant, and demanded to be given the most menial tasks. He also requested that when he died his "grave" should be the belly of a wolf so that his "relics" would be merely excrement. Applying to join the Franciscans, who had recently been established in Todi by Francis himself, he was rejected because his behaviour was deemed too extreme; it was to be many years before they allowed him into their community.

Spurned, Jacopone wandered Umbria's countryside for a decade, deliberately remaining cold, hungry, thirsty and dirty to atone for his sins. He also began to compose the poems and *laude* (hymns) for which he was to become famous, writing 211 in all and becoming, in the words of one modern authority, "the most popular and the most inspired of the poets of the Franciscan tradition". He also wrote the influential *Donna del Paradiso*, a powerful dialogue on the grief of the Virgin at the Crucifixion. The work spread throughout Italy, and would inspire the Passion plays, some of the country's first theatrical creations since the Romans.

Jacopone also achieved considerable fame for his outspoken criticism of the papacy. Boniface VIII, one of the most vice-ridden of popes, was a regular visitor to Todi, where he had a reserved stall in the cathedral. One of his favourite tricks was to have the tongues of heretics nailed to doors. Jacopone bravely said of him: "Blasphemous tongue, that has poisoned the world,/There is no kind of ugly sin/In which you have not become infamous." He was imprisoned for his eloquence, lucky to escape with his life, and remained incarcerated for five years in the papal dungeons of Palestrina, near Rome. Only the election of Pope Benedict XI in 1303 secured his release. Returning to Todi, he joined a Franciscan convent at Collazzone, north of Todi, where he died on Christmas Day, 1306. Todi remembers him with a piazza and the vast mausoleum in the crypt of San Fortunato.

appeared in the early twentieth century: the walls are completely unsullied by modern building, the only incongruous detail a single early motor car.

The first area of the museum, the **Museo della Città**, delves into Todi's history, with lots of individually interesting paintings and artefacts. Look out in particular, in Section IV, for the large painting (1592) of Todi's patron saints and protectors (including Fortunato defending the town from the Goths) by Pietro Paolo Sensini. Todi's *Book of Martyrs* lists no fewer than 853 saints and martyrs who had some sort of connection with the town (plus 53 Servants of God): only five were elevated to the position of patron saints – Fortunato, Callisto, Cassiano, Degna and Romana. Along the wall to the left are several extremely old statues and carvings, some going back to the eighth century, opposite an eye-catching painting depicting various branches of the Benedettoni family, singled out because they were descendants of Jacopone da Todi (see box, p.617). This area's greatest oddity is the saddle of Anita Garibaldi, left behind when she passed through the town in an advanced state of pregnancy and could no longer bear the discomfort it caused her: it's rather hidden by the exit as you leave the "Museo della Città" part of the gallery.

The sections that follow are devoted to archeology, coins and medals (including an important collection of Republican and Imperial-era **Roman coins**), medallions and fabrics. In many cases the rooms are more alluring than their exhibits, particularly the lovely **salon** devoted to ceramics, which was frescoed in 1367 on the orders of the town's priors when it became their home: most of the surviving pictures date from the seventeenth to the twentieth centuries, and include portraits of illustrious Todians and a map by Sensin (1612) of the territory once controlled by the town. Numerous individual exhibits merit a closer look, none more so than the museum's star painting: the sumptuous **Coronation of the Virgin** (1507) by Lo Spagna which greets you as you walk into the picture gallery. The predella of the painting was appropriated by Napoleon in 1811 and now resides, sadly, in the Louvre.

San Fortunato

The single most celebrated site after the piazza is the enormous **San Fortunato** (summer daily 8.30am–12.30pm & 3–7pm; winter Tues–Sun 9.30am–12.30pm & 3–5pm; free), set above some half-hearted gardens a stroll south of the piazza. Its disproportionate size is testimony to Todi's medieval wealth, and the messy-looking and squat facade – an amalgam of Romanesque and Gothic – reflects the time it took to build the church (1292–1462). Lorenzo Maitani was commissioned to decorate the facade as he did Orvieto's Duomo, and the story goes that the burghers of that town, unable to stomach the prospect of a rival church, took out a contract on his life. If true, it was money spent too late, because his florid **doorway** stands good comparison with that in Orvieto, all arched swirls and carved craziness. The Annunciate angel in the niche to the left of the portico is outstanding, and has been attributed to the Sienese sculptor Jacopo della Quercia. Look out for some of the smaller details, especially the tiny figures – small jokes, you suspect, on the part of the sculptor – which are hidden in the twists of the portal's spiral columns.

The light, airy **interior**, recently highlighted by cleaning and several controversial coats of whitewash, marks the pinnacle of the Umbrian Gothic tradition of large vaulted churches. The style was based on the smaller, German-influenced "barn" churches common in Tuscany, distinguished – as here – by a single, low-pitched roof with naves and aisles of equal height. (San Domenico in Perugia is another, less successful example.) Note the grey stone brackets, added to correct the increasingly alarming lean of the supporting pilasters. The two battered stoups may date from an earlier church on the site. At the rear sits an excellent

choir (1590), heavier and with more hints of the Baroque than the one in the Duomo, as well as a few scant patches of fresco – the *Madonna* by **Masolino di Panicale** (1432) in the fourth chapel on the right is a good if somewhat battered example of this painter's rare work. The sixth chapel on this side contains further good fresco fragments of the Crucifixion and scenes from the life of St Francis from around 1340 by an unknown Umbrian follower of Giotto.

It is possible to climb the 153 steps of the church **tower** for some fine views (Tues–Sun: April–Oct 10.30am–1pm & 3–6.30pm; Nov–March 10.30am–1pm & 2.30–5pm; €1.50, or combined ticket with Museo della Città & Cisterne Romane €6); the entrance is on the north aisle. Be sure to pay homage to the **tomb of Jacopone da Todi** in the crypt, which was built in 1596 on the orders of Bishop Angelo Cesi to house this tomb and those of the town's five patron saints. Cesi was one of a family who managed to retain control of the town's clergy for decades, holding the bishopric continually from 1523 to 1606 – probably not unconnected with the fact that one of the Cesi, Paolo Emilio, managed to become Pope Paul III. The **cloisters** are outside and to the right of the church.

Note that a quiet lane leads from the right of the church into **public gardens**, full of shady nooks and narrow pathways, and an enjoyable spot for a siesta or picnic on the route to Santa Maria della Consolazione. On this western edge of town, there's also a kids' playground and a very small **Rocca** of Albornoz vintage, both far less noteworthy than the views, which are extensive, if often obscured by haze. At the gardens' western end a zigzag path cuts down to Viale della Consolazione for the church.

Santa Maria della Consolazione

Many architectural cognoscenti rate **Santa Maria della Consolazione** (daily except Tues: April–Oct 9am–1pm & 2.30–6pm; Nov–March 10am–12.30pm & 2.30–6pm; free) as one of the best Renaissance churches in Italy. Inspired by an apparition of the Virgin on the site and completed in 1607, the project was initiated a century earlier, probably by the virtually unknown Cola da Caprarola, possibly using one of Bramante's drafts from St Peter's in Rome. The church's use of alternating types of window in the cupola – known as rhythmic bays – is a Bramante trademark. Over the years, virtually every leading architect of the day had his say in the design of the church, including Sangallo, Peruzzi and Vignola. Tantalizingly, a picture from 1489 of the church was also found among the architectural drawings of Leonardo da Vinci, pre-dating Caprarola's involvement. Whatever the church's convoluted and mysterious origins, it eventually came to conform to most of the precepts articulated by Alberti, the great theoretician of Renaissance architecture: a Greek-cross floor plan (purity of form and proportion), isolation in an open piazza, a white or near-white finish (purity again), high windows (cutting off from earthly contact) and a preference for statuary (again of greater "purity" than painting).

The rest of the town

For a reminder of ancient Todi, take a look at the so-called *nicchioni* (niches) in **Piazza del Mercato Vecchio**, sited just below Piazza del Popolo; cisterns and walls aside, they constitute more or less all that's left of the Roman colony. The town's proud of them, but they don't amount to much: four slightly overgrown arches, which perhaps formed the wall of an Augustan basilica. Two-minutes' walk down from here brings you to **San Ilario** (also known as San Carlo), an ancient Lombard chapel well off the beaten track, and all too often locked to protect a fresco of the *Madonna della Misericordia* by Lo Spagna. Just beyond the church, adjoining a crumbling, flower-strewn arbour, is the **Fonte Scarna-becco** (1241), an unusual arched fountain that was Todi's lifeblood and social meeting place before piped water.

Just inside the medieval walls at Porta Romana are the churches of **San Filippo**, dull except for frescoed panels on the right-hand wall, and the more interesting **San Nicolò**, distinguished by a striking wooden ceiling, three imposing Gothic arches and two small Umbrian frescoes on the left-hand wall. You might also drop in on thirteenth-century **Santa Maria in Camuccia**, two minutes off Via Roma, recently reunited with its priceless, stolen twelfth-century wooden Madonna. Two beautifully fluted Roman columns flanking the entrance are the most substantial parts of a large collection of Roman pieces dug up from under the church; for a look at the minor pieces, chat up the resident priest – the stuff is in his quarters.

Eating and drinking

Eating out can be a memorable experience in Todi, particularly if you plump for one of the **restaurants** with views. The *Pianiggiana* is a good **bar** with outside tables, though the couple of bars in Piazza del Popolo give you more to look at.

Antica Osteria della Valle Via Ciufelli 19 ☎075.894.4848. An excellent option, in a less appealing situation than the *Umbria* but with a cosy brick-vaulted interior and creative cooking, a little way down from San Fortunato. Closed Mon.
Cavour Corso Cavour 21–23 ☎075.894.3730. A friendly, cheap in-town option, with an unfortunate tendency to piped music, but with good, basic food (including pizzas) and outside dining on a fine panoramic terrace.
Giubilei Italo Piazza Bartolomeo d'Alviano, 100m from Piazza del Popolo ☎075.894.2645. A somewhat spartan pizzeria-*rosticceria*. Closed Mon after 8pm.
La Mulinella 3km away near the sports centre, Pontenaia 29 ☎075.894.4779. South of town, locals head to this family-run place where

matriarch Irma changes the menu regularly without straying too far from regional staples. In summer, you can sit in the garden and look up to Todi. Closed Wed & part of Nov.
Le Scalette Via Le Scalette 1 ☎075.894.4422. Directly opposite the *Antica Osteria*, this restaurant offers a small panoramic terrace, cave-like stone-walled interior and less imaginative food at similar prices. Closed Mon.
Umbria Via San Bonaventura 13 ☎075.894.2737. Todi's most enjoyable restaurant for lunch; prices are rather high (€30 or over for a full meal) and service can be slow and offhand, but the panorama across what seems like half of Umbria from the outside terrace makes it all worthwhile; in season arrive early or book to be sure of an outside table. Inside, the appeal is considerably reduced. Closed Tues.

Along the Tiber valley

North of Todi, the Tiber valley broadens out to a plain, edged with low hills and dotted with light industry. It's not an area where you'll want to spend a lot of time – and most people tear through (or crawl along on the FCU train). A few of the castles, villages and Romanesque churches, however, are well worthwhile if you're in no hurry to get to Perugia.

Monte Castello di Vibio

The spectacularly sited **MONTE CASTELLO DI VIBIO** is 12km from Todi, off the N397. This eagle's nest of a village dominates the countryside, and its castle was one of a reputed 365 fortresses that formed a defensive screen around Todi. There's little to see, save extraordinary views and the usual maze of medieval alleyways. It does, however, have a lovely little 99-seat **theatre**

(Sat & Sun 10am–12.30pm & 3/3.30–5.30/6.30pm; or by appointment ⊤075.878.0307, Ⓦwww.teatropiccolo.it; free but donations welcome), built in 1808 in celebration of the French Revolution and restored in 1993. The village makes an excellent base away from the crowds, thanks to the twenty-room three-star **hotel** *Relais Il Castello*, Piazza G. Marconi 5 (⊤075.878.0560, Ⓦwww .relaisilcastello.it; ❹), superbly converted from a sixteenth-century patrician town house and with a suitably authentic-looking medieval stone-walled **restaurant**-dining room.

Deruta

DERUTA is best known for its **ceramics** – much of it handmade, hand-painted and by general consent among Italy's best. The Romans worked the local clay, but it was the discovery of distinctive blue and yellow glazes in the fifteenth century, allied with the Moorish-influenced designs of southern Spain, that put the town firmly on the map. Some fifty workshops traded as far afield as Britain, and pieces from Deruta's sixteenth-century heyday have found their way into the world's major museums. Designs these days are mainly copies, with little original work; if you're serious about this sort of thing, avoid the roadside stalls and head for the workshops of the new town for the best selection and prices. The **old town** on the hill isn't particularly compelling, apart from the **Museo Regionale della Ceramica** alongside the church of San Francesco (July–Sept daily 10am–1pm & 3.30–7pm; April–June daily 10.30am–1pm & 3–6pm; Oct–March daily except Tues 10.30am–1pm & 2.30–5pm; €3). The best material is on the second floor, with ceramics from the Renaissance period: elsewhere you'll find exhibits from the Roman period to the present day.

Torgiano

TORGIANO, 8km north of Deruta, though a fairly dull town, is home to Umbria's finest wines, all of them produced by **Giorgio Lungarotti**, first of the new breed of Italian producers. A self-made man and now something of a national celebrity, he's put together an interesting and extensive **Museo del Vino** in the suitably atmospheric cellars of the Palazzo Graziani-Baglioni, Corso Vittorio Emanuele II (daily 9am–1pm & 3–7pm; Oct–March closes 6pm; €4, or joint ticket with Museo dell'Olivo €7; Ⓦwww.lungarotti.it). Early sections look at the origins of viticulture, followed by documentation relating to wine-making in the Middle Ages. Subsequent rooms are devoted to Vin Santo, commerce, the legal niceties of wine-making, cultivation, wine mythology and more, everything well labelled in English. The less persuasive **Museo dell'Olivo e dell'Olio**, Via Garibaldi 10 (same hours; €4, or joint ticket €7), traces the story of olives and local olive cultivation.

Orvieto

ORVIETO sits on a spectacular tabletop of volcanic tufa whose sheer sides fall 325m to the vine-covered valley floor – a cliff-edged remnant of the four volcanoes whose eruptions also bequeathed the soils that produce Orvieto's occasionally fine wines. Out on a limb from the rest of Umbria, the town is perfectly placed between Rome and Florence to serve as a historical picnic for tour operators, and tourists flood here in their millions in high season, drawn by the **Duomo** – one of the greatest Gothic buildings in Italy and home of some sublime frescoes by Luca Signorelli.

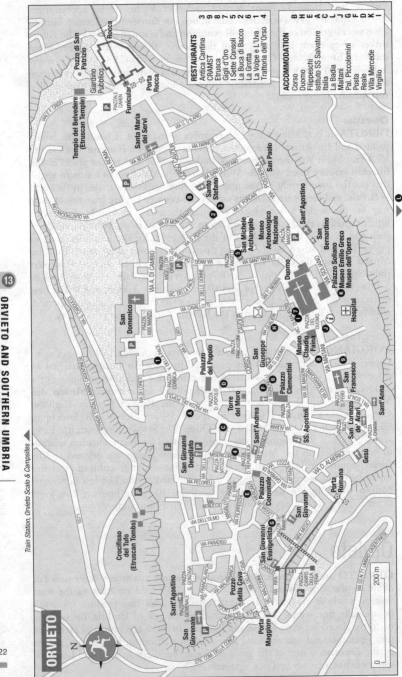

ORVIETO

N

Train Station, Orvieto Scalo & Campsites

Viterbo & Bolsena

RESTAURANTS

Antica Cantina	3
CRAMST	9
Etrusca	8
Gigli d'Oro	7
I Sette Consoli	5
La Buca di Bacco	2
La Grotta	6
La Volpe e L'Uva	1
Trattoria dell'Orso	4

ACCOMMODATION

Corso	B
Duomo	H
Filippeschi	E
Istituto SS Salvatore	A
Italia	C
La Badia	L
Maitani	J
Pal. Piccolomini	G
Posta	F
Reale	D
Villa Mercede	K
Virgilio	I

Tempio del Belvedere (Etruscan Temple)

Rocca

Pozzo di San Patrizio

Giardino Pubblico

PIAZZALE CAHEN

Funicular

Porta Rocca

Santa Maria dei Servi

VIA ROMA

VIA U. ILARIO

VIA FARNESE

CORSO CAVOUR

VIA BELISARIO

Santo Stefano

VIA SANTO STEFANO

San Paolo

VIA POSTIERLA

Sant'Agostino

VIA DI MONTEMERE

VIA D. PERTICHE

San Michele Arcangelo

VIA S. PORCARI

VIA S. ANGELO

PIAZZA MARCONI

San Bernardino

Museo Archeologico Nazionale

Palazzo Soliano
Museo Emilio Greco
Museo dell'Opera

Duomo

VIA A. DI CAMBIO

PIAZZA ANGELO DA ORVIETO

VIA ANGELO DA ORVIETO

VIC. DELLA PACE

VIA V. DELLE DONNE

San Domenico

PIAZZA XXIX MARZO

VIA CAVALLOTTI

ORTI

VIA DI LORETO

VIA D. PIAZZA

PIAZZA FRACASSINI

CORSO CAVOUR

PIAZZA FRACASSINI CAVOUR

San Giuseppe

Palazzo del Popolo

PIAZZA DEL POPOLO

Torre del Moro

V. SIGNORELLI

Palazzo Clementini

Museo Claudio Faina

Hospital

San Francesco

VIA MAITANI

VIA DEL DUOMO

VIA MAGONI

VIA DE' MAGONI

VIA DELL'ORDINAZIONE

VIA G. ALBERI

VIA DELLA PACE

PIAZZA CORSICA

STRADA STATALE UMBRO CASENTINESE

San Giovanni Decollato

PIAZZA VITOZZA

MISERICORDIA

Sant'Andrea

PIAZZA D. REPUBBLICA

SS. Apostoli

San Lorenzo de' Arari

Sant'Anna

VIA DELLA CAVA

VIA PECORELLI

VIA ALBANI

VIA SOLANA

VIA DE' MAGONI

VIA M. SOLANA

VIA SCALZA

VIA BUZI

San Francesco

Gesù

VIA D. ALBERICI

Porta Romana

VIA GARIBALDI

VIA COZZA

VIA LATTANZI

Palazzo Comunale

San Giovanni

PIAZZA DEL POPOLO

VIA LOGGIA DE' MERCANTI

VIA FILIPPESCHI

VIA BENUCCIO

VIA DELL'OLMO

VIA PARADISO

San Giovanni Evangelista

PIAZZA RANIERI

VIA RIPA MEDIA

VIA RIPA

PIAZZA CAMPO DELLA FIERA

VIA VOLSINII

Pozzo della Cava

Sant'Agostino

PIAZZA G. GONZAGA

San Giovenale

PIAZZA G. BOVENALE

VIA FRANCALANCIA

VIA MALABRANCA

VIA DELLA CAVA

VIA VOLSINII

VIA MALCORINI

Porta Maggiore

Crocifisso del Tufo (Etruscan Tombs)

SS71

SSTL

STR. COM. DELLA CONCA

VIA D. ALBERICI

STR. N 71 UMBRO CASENTINESE

SSTL

0   200 m

The city is one of the most ancient in Italy, thanks to its irresistible site. Bronze and Iron Age tribes were present before it became an **Etruscan** settlement, later named Volsinii Veteres, or Velzna, in around the ninth century BC. Eventually it became a leading member of the twelve-strong Etruscan federation, and possibly the site of the Etruscans' principal religious shrine, the Fanum Voltumnae. In 264 BC (possibly earlier), the **Romans** ravaged the town and displaced the Etruscans to present-day Bolsena, or Volsinii Novi – the place they abandoned becoming known as Urbs Vetus (the Old City), thus Orvieto. Its medieval influence was considerable, the independent *comune* challenging Florence and eventually claiming land as far as Monte Amiata in the north and to the coast at Orbetello in the west. Power and prestige remained high until the usual internecine squabbling, the **Black Death** of 1348 sounding the town's effective death knell. It passed to the Church for good a hundred years later and became something of a papal home from home: 32 popes in all stayed in the city. One of them, Gregory I, even met **Edward I** of England here on Edward's return from the Crusades.

Arrival and information

Fast **trains** on the Rome–Florence run tend to bypass Orvieto, so you may well have to change at Orte or Chiusi to a slower connecting service; from Perugia (86km), change at Teróntola. Orvieto's station is in the grim new town of Orvieto Scalo, a twisting three-kilometre drive from the old centre. From the station forecourt, a wonderful restored nineteenth-century **Bracci funicular** (Mon–Sat every 10min 7.20am–8.30pm, Sun every 15min 8am–8.30pm; €0.90) runs up to Piazza Cahen in the old town, from where it's a pleasant five- or ten-minute walk along Corso Cavour to the centre. Minibuses (free with a funicular ticket; otherwise €0.90) shuttle every few minutes from the top station to Piazza del Duomo – either direct (bus A) or via Piazza della Repubblica (bus B). After 8.30pm, buses replace the funicular. Inter-town **buses** take you to Piazza Cahen, Piazza XXIX Marzo or Piazza della Repubblica, depending on the service; some terminate at the train station. Local **taxi** companies can be contacted on ☏0763.301.903 and 0763.342.613.

Cars are prohibited in the old town at certain times, but even when they're not, finding a parking space is a tall order. There are car parks in Piazzale Cahen and off Via Roma just to the west, or you could use the big free car park on the east side of the station and take the funicular. Better still, aim to park at Campo della Fiera, below the southwest corner of the old town, where you can pick up local buses (Linea B or C) on their run from the station to Piazza della Repubblica; pedestrian lifts and escalators up to the centre (exiting near Via Garibaldi and Via Ripa Medici) also run from this point.

The **tourist office** is at Piazza del Duomo 24 (Mon–Fri 8.15am–2pm & 4–7pm, Sat & Sun 10am–7pm & 3–6pm; variable and shorter winter hours; ☏0763.341.772, ⓦwww.comune.orvieto.tr.it).

Accommodation

The tourist office has plenty of maps and information, as well as details of **private rooms** and a dozen or so **agriturismo** options nearby. The town has also seen the rapid growth of a **B&B** sector, with central rooms mostly at around €65–85, depending on the time of year. You can get details from the tourist office or on the *comune* website (click on "*dove dormire*"). There are also plenty of cheap, modern but characterless hotels in the unlovely Orvieto Scalo.

Corso Corso Cavour 343 ☎0763.342.020, ⓦwww.hotelcorso.net. A good, but relatively pricey three-star hotel, part of a fine and recently renovated medieval town house with nine bright, spacious rooms (some with panoramic terraces) in a fairly quiet and convenient position. ❸

Duomo Vicolo di Maurizio 7 ☎0763.341.887, ⓦwww.orvietohotelduomo.com. An excellent central sixteen room three-star option. In a peaceful and perfect location, one alley north of the Duomo, but the tile floors make rooms and corridors very noisy if you have heavy-footed neighbours. ❹

Filippeschi Via Filippeschi 19 ☎&ⓕ0763.343.275, ⓔalbergofilippeschi@tiscali.net. Moderately priced fifteen-room three-star in a convenient central location just west of Piazza della Repubblica. ❸

Istituto SS Salvatore Via Piazza del Popolo 1 ☎0763.342.910, ⓔistitutosansalvatore @tiscalinet.it. You can stay cheaply with the nuns in this central Dominican convent, but the minimum stay is generally two nights and there's a 10pm curfew (9pm autumn & winter). Has fifteen rooms with and without bathrooms, with doubles from €45. ❶

Italia Piazza del Popolo 13 ☎0763.342.065, ⓦwww.grandhotelitalia.it. The biggest central hotel, with 45 three-star rooms; likely to have space in an emergency. ❸

La Badia Località La Badia ☎0763.301.959, ⓦwww.labadiahotel.it. Most Umbrian towns now have a luxurious, out-of-town option: this is Orvieto's, a converted abbey 5km south on the Bagnoregio road. It's not as grand as some newer conversions, however, and could do with a revamp, especially some of the relatively austere rooms. This said, the grounds (with good views of Orvieto) are lovely, and there are all the usual smart facilities, including tennis courts and a pool. ❻

Maitani Via Lorenzo Maitani 5 ☎0763.342.012, ⓦwww.hotelmaitani.com. The most traditional and most central of Orvieto's quartet of four-star hotels – and with forty rooms there's a good chance of space. ❹

🏃 Palazzo Piccolomini Piazza Ranieri 36 ☎0763.341.743, ⓦwww.hotelpiccolomini.it. This thirty-room four-star, converted in 1997 from a sixteenth-century palace, in the manner of the Fonte Cesia in Todi or Palazzo Bocci in Spello, is one of the breed of very stylish, tasteful and refined historic hotels which the region does extremely well. ❻

Posta Via Luca Signorelli 18 ☎0763.341.909, ⓦwww.orvietohotels.it. The only inexpensive two-star choice amongst the central hotels; faded and rather charmingly old-fashioned medieval house just 2min from the Duomo, with a garden and twenty cool, quiet and pleasant rooms with and without private bathrooms. ❶

Reale Piazza del Popolo 25 ☎0763.341.247, ⓦwww.orvietohotels.it. Slightly less expensive 31-room three-star than the nearby Italia, but only if you go for one of the handful of lower-grade rooms without private bath. ❸

Villa Mercede Via Soliana 2 ☎0763.341.766, ⓔvillamercede@orvienet.it. It's harder to imagine a cheaper bed close to the cathedral than in this simple but perfectly situated twelve-room religious house, where doubles (all en suite) open to men, women and couples, are €68. Minimum stay is two days, and there is a 10pm curfew (9pm in autumn and winter). ❷

Virgilio Piazza del Duomo 5–6 ☎0763.342.325. Often celebrated for its perfect position, but in fact only a handful of the relatively modest three-star rooms actually have (side-on) views of the Duomo. And rooms looking on to the piazza are likely to be noisy on summer evenings. ❸

Campsites

Il Falcone Località Vallonganino 2a, Civitella del Lago ☎0744.950.249 or 347.274.5016, ⓔilfalcone@tin.it. A well-run two-star site with a friendly owner, overlooking Lago di Corbara. Although it's 10km or so from Orvieto, you can pick up supplies in Civitella or eat at the Bar-Pizzeria, Via Italia 16, or in the restaurant Da Crespino, Via degli Atti, Montecchio ☎0744.951.017. Open April–Sept. Another campsite on the lake, the Orvieto, was closed at the time of writing.

Scacco Matto ☎0744.950.163, ⓦwww .scaccomatto.net. Basic site, also by Lago di Corbara; take the bus for Civitella del Lago (two daily) or Narni (six daily; alight at Baschi). Has a few rooms to rent as well (❸). Open March–mid-Oct, but varies year to year.

The Duomo

The historian Jacob Burckhardt described Orvieto's **Duomo** (daily 7.30am–12.45pm & 2.30–7.15pm; March & Oct closes 6.15pm; Nov–Feb closes 5.15pm; free; the Cappella di San Brizio has different hours and an admission charge, see p.627; ⓦwww.opsm.it) as "the greatest and richest polychrome monument in the world"; Pope Leo XIII called it the "Golden Lily of Italian cathedrals", adding that on the Day of Judgement it would float to Heaven carried by its own beauty. Though the cathedral's overall effect might be a bit rich for some tastes, it rates – with Assisi's Basilica di San Francesco – as one of the two essential sights in Umbria.

The monumental **facade** of the Duomo is just the right side of overkill: a riot of columns, spires, bas-reliefs, sculptures, dazzling colour, colossal doorways and hundreds of capricious details held together by four enormous fluted pillars. Many have compared it to a painted triptych in an elaborate frame. Some 52m high and recently cleaned and overhauled, it is a stunning spectacle from the piazza, particularly at sunset or under floodlights. Most of the basic work was accomplished by **Lorenzo Maitani** (see box below), but such illustrious names as Andrea Pisano and Andrea Orcagna – responsible for much of the rose window – also had a hand in design and construction.

Construction of the Duomo

Church tradition holds that the Duomo was built to celebrate the Miracle of Bolsena, which occurred in 1263. The protagonist, a young Bavarian priest, was on a pilgrimage to Rome to shake off his disbelief in transubstantiation (the idea that the body and blood of Christ are physically present in the Eucharist). While he celebrated Mass in a church near Lago di Bolsena, blood started to drip from the Host onto the *corporale*, the white linen cloth that covers the altar, "each stain severally assuming the form of a human head with features like the Volto Santo, the face of the Saviour". The linen was whisked off to Pope Urban IV, who was holed up in Orvieto to escape the literal and political heat in Rome. He proclaimed a miracle and a year later Thomas Aquinas, then teaching in Orvieto's San Domenico, drew up a papal bull instigating the feast of Corpus Domini.

The cornerstone of the Duomo was not put in place for another 25 years (laid by Pope Nicholas IV on Nov 13, 1290) and Aquinas's bull makes no specific mention of Bolsena, so it's likely that the raising of the Duomo was as much a shrewd piece of political pragmatism as a celebration of a miracle. The papacy at the time was in retreat and the Umbrian towns – not least Orvieto – at the height of their civic expansion. Thus it seems likely that the building of this awe-inspiring cathedral, in one of the region's most powerful towns, was a piece of political muscle-flexing to remind errant citizens of the papacy's power.

It was, indeed, miraculous that the Duomo was built at all. Medieval Orvieto was so violent that at times the population considered abandoning the city altogether. Dante wrote that its family feuds were worse than those between Verona's Montecchi and Cappelli, inspiration for Shakespeare's murderous Montagues and Capulets in *Romeo and Juliet*. The building was also dogged by a committee approach to design, the plans being modified continually to accommodate changes in architectural taste. At least the site posed no problems: the city's highest point was previously home to an Etruscan temple and Orvieto's first cathedral, Santa Maria Prisca. Even today, the cathedral continues to dominate the skyline for miles around.

The architect is unknown, though it seems possible that it was Arnolfo di Cambio, designer of Florence's Duomo. At Orvieto the plan initially was for a simple and orthodox Romanesque church, but in the early years of work a local architect's extravagant departures into the Gothic brought the structure close to collapse, leading to the call-up in 1310 of the Sienese master, Lorenzo Maitani. In the course of three decades he guided the construction at its most crucial stage and produced the magnificent carvings on the facade. Though building dragged on for over three hundred years, exhausting 33 architects, 152 sculptors, 68 painters and 90 mosaicists, the final product is a surprisingly unified example of the transitional Romanesque-Gothic style.

▲ Bas-reliefs on the facade of Orvieto's Duomo

The four pillars at the base are among the highlights of fourteenth-century Italian **sculpture**. The work of Maitani and his pupils, they depict episodes from the Old and New Testaments in staggering detail: lashings of plague, famine, martyrdom, mutilation and murder. The panels read from left to right, starting with the Creation on the left-most pillar. The stories in stone here are wonderfully graphic and self-explanatory, but the delicacy of the carving, especially of the trees, which have the intricacy of coral, is extraordinary. Look in particular at the scene of Eve emerging from Adam's rib (second tier), the casting out of Adam and Eve (fourth tier) and Cain slaying Abel (fifth tier, right-hand panel), the last especially powerful. The second pillar has the stories of Abraham and David, and the third, scenes from the lives of Christ and the Virgin. Many details, it appears, were created partly to point an accusing finger at Orvieto's moral slackers, as the extraordinary fourth and final pillar makes clear, with its depictions of the Last Judgement, Hell and Paradise, and the damned packed off to eternal fire, brimstone and the company of an awful lot of snakes.

Maitani was also responsible for the four large bronzes of the symbols of the Evangelists across the first tier, and for the angels over the beautiful central **doorway**. These, however, together with the *Madonna* in the lunette, have been removed for restoration and will probably be replaced by copies: the originals are lined up for display in the Museo dell'Opera. The **mosaics**, the facade's showiest aspect, are mostly eighteenth- and nineteenth-century additions, replacements for originals nabbed by Rome. Only the four examples in the corners of Orcagna's huge **rose window** (1359) have any vintage, completed around 1388. The central bronze doors, by Emilio Greco, were made as recently as 1965, and in the best traditions of the Duomo were added after much talk and controversy.

The Cappella di San Brizio

At first, little save the colossal scale grabs your attention in the Duomo's interior – which is far less cluttered than the similar cathedral in Siena – a few snatches of fresco in the scalloped side niches, and the work immediately on your left as you enter, a heavily restored *Madonna and Child* (1425) by Gentile da Fabriano, with a very sickly-looking Jesus. However, in the right transept – the **Cappella di San Brizio** – are **Luca Signorelli**'s superlative paintings of the Last Judgement (1499–1504), one of Italy's great fresco cycles and one that had a profound influence on Michelangelo's version in the Sistine Chapel, painted forty years later. The cycle is on view again after years of restoration (April–June Mon–Sat 9am–12.45pm & 2.30–7.15pm, Sun 2.30–5.45pm; July–Aug same hours but closes 6.45pm on Sun; Nov–Feb Mon–Sat 9am–12.45pm & 2.30–5.15pm, Sun

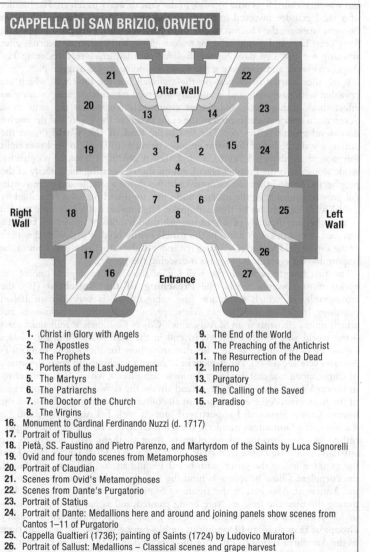

CAPPELLA DI SAN BRIZIO, ORVIETO

1. Christ in Glory with Angels
2. The Apostles
3. The Prophets
4. Portents of the Last Judgement
5. The Martyrs
6. The Patriarchs
7. The Doctor of the Church
8. The Virgins
9. The End of the World
10. The Preaching of the Antichrist
11. The Resurrection of the Dead
12. Inferno
13. Purgatory
14. The Calling of the Saved
15. Paradiso
16. Monument to Cardinal Ferdinando Nuzzi (d. 1717)
17. Portrait of Tibullus
18. Pietà, SS. Faustino and Pietro Parenzo, and Martyrdom of the Saints by Luca Signorelli
19. Ovid and four tondo scenes from Metamorphoses
20. Portrait of Claudian
21. Scenes from Ovid's Metamorphoses
22. Scenes from Dante's Purgatory
23. Portrait of Statius
24. Portrait of Dante: Medallions here and around and joining panels show scenes from Cantos 1–11 of Purgatory
25. Cappella Gualtieri (1736); painting of Saints (1724) by Ludovico Muratori
26. Portrait of Sallust: Medallions – Classical scenes and grape harvest
27. Empedocles (?) and The End of The World

2.30–5.45pm; March & Oct Mon–Sat 9am–12.45pm & 2.30–6.15pm, Sun 2.30–5.45pm; €5, also includes Museo dell'Opera & Sant'Agostino). **Tickets** are not available in the cathedral, but must be bought from the tourist office.

Several painters tackled the chapel before Signorelli. **Fra' Angelico** made a start in 1447, completing two of the ceiling's eight vaults, *Christ in Glory with Angels* (marked as 1 on our plan) and *The Prophets* (3), with the assistance of **Benozzo Gozzoli**, whose hand can be seen in the angels of the latter panel. Angelico, it appears, suggested the frescoes' central theme, the Last Judgement, but was then called to Rome to work in the Vatican, never to return. The murder of a local grandee involved in financing the project, Arigo Monaldeschi, then brought work on the Duomo to one of its periodic halts. **Perugino** popped up forty years later and disappeared for reasons unknown – never to return – after working for just five days. Signorelli saved the day, graciously restoring Fra' Angelico's work and completing the vaults according to the original plan.

Work then started in earnest on the walls, all but the lowest of which are crowded with passionate and beautifully observed muscular figures, creating an effect that's both realistic and almost grotesquely fantastic at the same time. Seven main episodes are painted in the eight panels of the vaults and the twelve floor-level groups of frescoes. The first is the **End of the World** (9) on the entrance wall, the last of the major episodes painted (1503–4). In the lower right foreground are depicted Eritrea, a sibyl, shown holding a book of prophecies, while alongside is the Prophet David, who is shown asserting the veracity of the prophecies. Behind them an earthquake brings down a temple and three youths fall prey to brigands; in the background ships are tossed on a sea convulsed by a tidal wave brought on by the earthquake. High up on the left you see the fall of the rebel angels, many of whom unleash thunderbolts of fire which fall on a terrified crowd below. A putto in the panel's centre holds a sign with the mark of the Opera del Duomo (OPSM), a reminder of the cathedral works committee responsible for commissioning and overseeing the project.

The first lunette panel on the wall left of the entrance depicts one of the cycle's most powerful works, the **Preaching of the Antichrist** (10), the iconography of which is unique (the subject itself is very rare in Italian painting). It derives from a text whose precise authorship is unknown, but which unites elements from St Augustine's *City of God*, ancient millennial texts – the world was widely expected to end in the year 1000 – and the *Golden Legend* of Jacopo de Varagine (also the inspiration for Piero della Francesca's Arezzo cycle: see p.445). The Antichrist is shown preaching and bears the image of Christ, albeit one that displays a demonic demeanour, with a devil whispering in his ear. Various historical figures stand amidst the crowd to the left and right of the Antichrist, designed to represent all colours, creeds and conditions of the human family: Signorelli has portrayed himself with Fra' Angelico behind (in the black of a Dominican monk) in the left foreground, both apparently unperturbed by the garroting taking place in front of them. Also present in the left-hand group are Dante (rear right, in profile with red hat), Cesare Borgia (on the extreme left of the group with beard, blond hair and red hat) and Pius II, the corpulent fellow in yellow behind the figure with hands on hips alongside the Antichrist. Also here is the figure of Signorelli's mistress, who jilted him during the time the frescoes were being painted, and as punishment is prominently portrayed in the foregound of the group as a prostitute taking money. Groups of Franciscan and Dominican monks can be seen to the rear and right of the Antichrist trying to calculate the precise date of the end of the world – one counts off three and a half years with his fingers, the 1290 days that the reign of the Antichrist was expected to endure. The two other group vignettes behind the monks to right and left show a false miracle and the execution of two penitents. In the background is the Temple of Solomon, while in the heavens, the Archangel Michael is seen preventing the ascension of the Antichrist and unleashing a storm of fire onto the corrupt below.

The sequence then moves to the first lunette on the right wall with the **Resurrection of the Dead** (11) summoned by the trumpets of the angels depicted on high. Signorelli here departs from convention, painting the figures emerging dramatically from the bare earth rather than from tombs, the traditional iconography employed in depictions of this scene. Note the small scratched figures at the centre of the panel, probably drawn by Signorelli to illustrate some point to the cathedral committee. The adjoining lunette on the right wall depicts **Inferno** (12), probably Signorelli's first completed fresco in the chapel.

On the altar wall right of the window is the **Punishment of the Damned**, or Purgatory (13), which in its portrayal of the damned inevitably draws on Dante's *The Divine Comedy*, but also utilizes the iconography of pagan works such as the battle scenes carved on the reliefs on Trajan's Column in Rome. Signorelli's mistress is again prominently painted, this time as the figure at the centre of the picture being carried by a flying winged devil. The panel left of the window shows the **Calling of the Saved** (14), a portrayal that includes two of Orvieto's saintly protectors, Costanzo and Brizio, at its centre; St Michael weighing the souls; and angels serenading and guiding the elected to **Paradiso** (15), the scene portrayed in the adjoining lunette on the left wall. In this last mural, Paradise's peace and harmony are symbolized by a heavenly choir of nine angel musicians and – in the centre – by two angels who scatter roses and camellias. These flowers were painted onto dry plaster, a less durable technique than the more usual practice of adding paint to wet plaster, hence their faded appearance. The altarpiece, incidentally, is the *Madonna di San Brizio*, an anonymous work held by tradition to have been painted by St Luke, but in truth probably executed towards the end of the fourteenth century.

The outstanding **frescoes and medallions** (numbered 16 to 27) on the lower parts of the walls are also by Signorelli and include portraits of Homer, Dante, Ovid, Virgil, Horace, Lucan, Empedocles and others, together with episodes from classical myth, notably Ovid's *Metamorphoses* and Dante's *Divine Comedy*. Of particular note is the *Pietà with Sts Faustino and Pietro Parenzo* (18) in the recess on the right. Vasari claimed that the figure of the dead Christ was a close portrait of Signorelli's own son, Antonio, who died from the plague in 1502 while the artist was employed on the frescoes.

Everything here has a didactic purpose, further illustrating or drawing allusions to the main theme of the frescoes above. Dante's *Divine Comedy* – which is frequently evoked – forms an obvious corollary, with its themes of salvation and damnation. Elsewhere, however, Signorelli uses Classical myth and literary figures to his own ends; Empedocles (27), for example, is shown in shocked contemplation of the end of the world, though he in fact never prophesied such an event. Some critics believe this is actually a figure of a common man who has not converted to Christianity, and looks on at the horrors that await him as one of the damned. The separate portrait of Stazio (23) is used in a similar way. The figure looks towards the chapel's high altar as if receiving spiritual illumination, but Dante writes that while the poet converted to Christianity, he kept his conversion and subsequent faith a secret. Throughout the Middle Ages the figure was therefore a symbol of salvation and also of only partial redemption – just the sort of character who would have been compromised, to say the least, come the Day of Judgement.

The Cappella del Corporale and the apse

The artistic pyrotechnics of the Cappella di San Brizio rather overshadow the opposite transept's **Cappella del Corporale**, which contains the sacred *corporale* of the Miracle of Bolsena, usually locked away in a massive, jewel-encrusted casket on the left designed in 1358 as a copy of the facade. On the chapel walls are extensive **frescoes** (1357–64) by a local artist, Ugolino di Prete Ilario, depicting episodes from the *Miracle of Bolsena* (right-hand wall) and various *Miracles of the Sacrament* (opposite). The chapel also houses (on the right) the glorious freestanding *Madonna dei Raccomandati* (1339) by the Sienese painter Lippo Memmi.

Ugolino covered the entire **apse** in frescoes (1370–84) of scenes from the *Life of the Virgin*, many of which were touched up by Pinturicchio, who was eventually kicked off the job for "consuming too much gold, too much azure, and too much wine".

The rest of the town

Nothing in Orvieto can quite live up to the Duomo, but then nor can much else in central Italy, though the piazza has a tremendous Etruscan museum, the **Museo Claudio Faina**, and a couple of other worthwhile sights. The dark tufa used as building stone around town can make parts seem a little dour during aimless exploration, particularly in poor weather, but some of the town's peripheral corners provide attractions that more than justify the walk – **San Giovenale** and the strange **Pozzo di San Patrizio** in particular. Trying to arrange a logical itinerary is difficult, but as distances are modest the walking's not too onerous – though be warned that the town drops sharply away on its western side, so expect a steep walk back to the centre from this area.

Piazza del Duomo

Beside the Duomo stands the **Palazzo Soliano**, or Palazzo dei Papi, begun for Pope Boniface VIII in 1297. For years it has been home to the **Museo dell'Opera del Duomo** (Wed–Mon: April–June & Sept–Oct 10am–6pm; July & Aug 10am–1pm & 3–7pm; Nov–March 10am–5pm; €5, includes admission to Signorelli frescoes in the duomo and church of Sant'Agostino), reopened after years of fitful restoration. Highlights of the collection include some top-notch paintings, notably a self-portrait by Signorelli, a *Madonna and Child* (1268) by the influential early Tuscan painter Coppo di Marcovaldo, and five parts of a polyptych from San Domenico by the Sienese master Simone Martini. Among the sculptures are wooden and marble Madonnas by Nino, Giovanni and Andrea Pisano, a lovely font filled with Escher-like fishes, and unfinished but important pieces by Arnolfo di Cambio.

On the ground floor of the museum is a section devoted to **Emilio Greco**, who created the Duomo's bronze doors in the 1960s (Tues–Sun: April–July 10.30am–1pm & 3.30–5.30pm; Aug–Sept 11am–5pm; rest of the year Fri–Sun 10.30am–1pm & 2.30–4.30pm; €2.50, Biglietto Cumulativo, which includes Il Pozzo di San Patrizio €5.50). On display are nearly a hundred works donated to the city by the artist. None of them is profoundly interesting unless you're a Greco enthusiast: peek through the door beyond the ticket office and you'll see enough of the exhibits to know if you want a closer look.

The Palazzo Papale, beyond the cathedral's east end, houses the unremarkable **Museo Archeologico Nazionale** (daily 8.30am–7.30pm; €3, joint ticket with Necropoli Etrusca, or Crocifisso del Tufo), which contains fourth-century BC Greek vases, two reconstructed painted tombs with their original murals and other Etruscan artefacts excavated during digs at Orvieto's own Cannicella and Crocifisso del Tufo tombs.

The Museo Claudio Faina

You're better off spending your money on the **Museo Claudio Faina** (incorporating the Museo Civico and Museo dei Ragazzi) opposite the Duomo (April–Sept daily 9.30am–6pm; Oct daily 10am–5pm; Nov–March Tues–Sun 10am–5pm; €4.50; ⓦ www.museofaina.it), a wonderful showcase for one of Italy's leading private archeological collections. It's worth the admission price simply for a view of the Duomo from the upper floor. The core of the collection is 34 vases given in the nineteenth century to Mauro Faina, a Perugian count, by Princess Maria Bonaparte, Napoleon's grandniece (the count had been a regular "visitor" to the princess's home). Over the years Faina, together with his nephew, added obsessively to the collection, which was left to the city in 1954. The exhibits spread over 22 rooms on two upper floors of the Palazzo Faina (plus a small ground-floor civic collection), arranged in a modern museum setting that would be the envy of far grander galleries.

Highlights include three vast, sixth-century BC Attic **amphorae** (room 6) attributed to Exekias, one of antiquity's finest vase painters – their presence in Orvieto testimony to the town's prosperity at the time. Also famous is the so-called **Vanth group** (rooms 11, 18 and 22), the name given to a collection of pots made locally in the last two decades of the fourth century BC. Vanth was an important female divinity associated with the Etruscan underworld, often portrayed with two serpents around each arm and, in the manner of medieval saints, with symbols such as keys, taper, mantle and scroll, the last partially unrolled to reveal the name of the goddess. As here, she was often portrayed greeting the recently deceased on their arrival in the underworld.

There are also many black *bucchero* **vases** (rooms 10, 11 and 14), so-called because at the time of their discovery they were thought to resemble vases from South America known to the Spanish as *bucaro*. The black colour was imparted in the kiln, where the firing process oxidized iron compounds in specially chosen clay. Quality declined around the fifth century BC, the result of insufficiently pure clays, a shortfall that resulted in *bucchero grigio*, or grey ware (gradually replaced by simple black–glazed pottery). A similar falling-off of quality occurred with the familiar black-figure Attic vases (rooms 11, 13 and 16), invented in Corinth around 700 BC, and made by painting a figure in black silhouette before incising detail so that the lighter-coloured clay beneath showed through. Such pottery was wildly popular throughout the Mediterranean, but no market was as large as Tyrrhenian Etruria. It was eventually replaced by Attic red-figure pottery (rooms 11, 14, 17 and 18), invented in Athens around 530 BC, in which figures and decorative details

---

Underground Orvieto

Cut into the crag below the town are the fascinating **Grotte della Rupe**, an extraordinary honeycomb of caves, wine cellars, aqueducts, quarries and tunnels used – and added to – since Etruscan times. A staggering 1200 separate caves have been found beneath Orvieto, around a third of the entire area under the town having been excavated at one time or another. Guided tours in English are run by Orvieto Underground, leaving from the tourist office (daily 11am, 12.15pm, 4pm & 5.15pm; €5.50; ⓣ 0763.344.891, 339.733.2764 or 347.383.1472, ⓦ www.orvietounderground.it); call for details or to make advance bookings (although you can just turn up and hope to get on a tour). The Pozzo della Cava, Via della Cava 26 (Tues–Sun 8am–8pm; ⓦ www.pozzodellacava.it; €3 or €2 for holders of tickets for buses, funicular, Pozzo di San Patrizio or Museo Emilio Greco), is a large smooth-sided Etruscan-era well, one of about forty found around the town. It's a slightly cynical money-making exercise but striking enough if you haven't time for the full underground tour.

were composed in the clay and the rest of the pot painted black. The museum also has a large collection of coins, bronzes and miscellaneous funerary objects.

West to San Giovenale

The tiny Romanesque **San Lorenzo de' Arari** (or dell'Ara), a short walk west of the Duomo, was built in 1291 on the site of a church destroyed by monks from nearby San Francesco because the sound of its bells got on their nerves. Four restored frescoes (1330) on the left of the nave depict traumatic scenes from the *Life of St Lawrence*, including execution by roasting, and there's a Byzantine-influenced *Christ Enthroned with Four Saints* in the apse. An Etruscan sacrificial slab rather oddly serves as the altar (*arari*) from which the church derives its name.

From nearby Piazzale Cacciatore there's a good **walk** around the city's southern walls along **Via Ripa Medici**, with views over to a prominent outcrop of rock in the mid-distance, part of the old volcanic crater. En route, stop by the excellent **Enoteca Regionale**, Via Ripa Serancia 16 (Mon–Sat 9am–1pm & 3–7pm; wine-tasting tours mid-April to mid-Sept daily 11am & 5pm, rest of year daily 4pm; check for latest times; ☏0763.393.529). To learn more, or to visit local vineyards, contact the Consorzio Tutela Vino, Corso Cavour 36 (☏0763.343.790).

Ten minutes or so farther west – with a big drop to the Porta Maggiore and a climb up again – is the ancient **San Giovenale**, set amid rustic surroundings on the western tip of Orvieto's plateau (you might also approach this part of town from Piazza della Repubblica and the northwest tangle of streets to avoid the slopes). New studies have established the previously accepted date of its foundation – 1004 – as the date of its first restoration. It's not much to look at from outside, but the musty interior is a distinctive hybrid of a church, the thirteenth-century Gothic transept, with its two pointed arches, standing rather oddly a metre above the rounded Romanesque nave. Beautiful thirteenth- and fifteenth-century **frescoes** cover all available surfaces; they include a *Tree of Life* to the right of the main door and the macabre *Calendar of Funeral Anniversaries* partly covered by the side entrance.

Make the walk worthwhile by taking in the glorious **view** from the town wall just to the west, or by following the wall-top lane (Via Volsinia II) down towards the Porta Maggiore. Otherwise, from San Giovenale back to the centre of town, Via Malabranca and Via Filippeschi are the best preserved of the medieval streets.

Piazza della Repubblica and around

Back in the heart of town, **Sant' Andrea**, in **Piazza della Repubblica**, is worth a look for its twelve-sided campanile, odd patches of fresco and pieces of Roman and Etruscan city in the crypt. For an overview of the town, climb the medieval **Torre del Moro** not far east of the church at Corso Cavour 87 (daily: March–April & Sept–Oct 10am–7pm; May–Oct 10am–8pm; Nov–Feb 10.30am–1pm & 2.30–5pm; €2.80). The bell up here is engraved with the 24 symbols of Orvieto's medieval guilds and was cast in 1316; it's been tolling every fifteen minutes ever since.

Northeast of Piazza del Popolo, **San Domenico** stands next to a Fascist-era barracks – far and away the ugliest building in the town. Half of the church, built between 1233 and 1264 (and thus Italy's first church to be dedicated to St Dominic) was sliced off during the construction of the barracks. The principal artwork is the *Tomb of Cardinal de Braye* (died 1281), a pioneering work by Arnolfo di Cambio in the Cappella Petrucci, entered via a door on the south (right) wall. This defined the format of wall tombs for the next century, showing the deceased lying on a coffin below the Madonna and Child, within an elaborate architectural framework.

The Pozzo di San Patrizio and the Rocca

Orvieto's novelty act is the huge cylindrical well known as the **Pozzo di San Patrizio** (daily: April–May & Sept 10am–5pm; June–Aug 9am–8pm; Oct–March 10am–5pm; €4.50, or €5.50 with the Emilio Greco museum), signposted beside the funicular terminus in Piazza Cahen east of the centre. Pope Clement VII commissioned it from Antonio da Sangallo the Younger two years after the Sack of Rome, which he'd been forced to flee disguised as a greengrocer. An attack on Orvieto was expected from the imperial troops, and the well was designed to guarantee the town's water supply during a siege. The attack never materialized – which was fortunate, as it took ten years of digging to hit water. It was while in Orvieto that Clement took the fateful decision not to annul Henry VIII's marriage to Catherine of Aragon.

The well is a virtuoso piece of engineering, 13m wide and 62m deep, and takes its name from a supposed resemblance to the Irish cave where St Patrick died at the ripe old age of 133. Water was brought to the surface by donkeys on two broad 248-step staircases, cannily designed in a double helix so that they never intersect. Half the well is carved from solid tufa, half is brick-lined, and the whole thing is lit by 72 strange windows cut from the spirals into the central shaft.

The direct recipient of the water from the *pozzo* was the nearby **Rocca**, built in 1364 by Cardinal Albornoz, the papal firebrand recruited to restore Church authority across central Italy. Views from the ruins are wonderful; nearby are the small but pleasant **public gardens**, one of Orvieto's few patches of green and home to the prominent remains of an Etruscan temple, the **Tempio del Belvedere**. The castle itself was built over the only stratum of travertine in the town, a robust piece of rock that escapes the landslips that strike the tufa with increasing regularity. Defoliation, the collapse of ancient sewers, the lowering of the water table and the intensification of traffic culminated in disastrous slips during 1977 and 1979, finally prompting the approval of vast funds from the European Union. Miles of tunnels and caves dating back to the Etruscans still honeycomb the rock, a labyrinth once used for quarrying, burials and the fermenting of wine; the subterranean conditions were said to be responsible for the excellence of Orvieto's vintages. Modern methods now make a drier product, better selling but less exalted than the traditional semi-sweet *abboccato*.

The Necropoli Etrusca

The **Necropoli Etrusca, or Crocifisso del Tufo** (daily 8.30am–7pm; Oct–March closes 5pm; €3, joint ticket with Museo Archeologico) – a set of sixth-century BC Etruscan tombs – are well worth a look: walk or drive down the town's approach road from Piazza Cahen (or from Porta Maggiore on the town's west side) to the small car park on the south side of the road and follow the signs. There are rows of massive and sombre stone graves (more are being excavated), though none has the grandeur or the paintings of the more famous necropolises in Tarquinia or Cerveteri. Still visible, however, are Etruscan inscriptions above the tomb entrances, thought to refer to the names of the erstwhile occupants.

Eating and drinking

Orvieto's tourist traffic once inflated prices in the town's many **restaurants**, and for years it has had fewer genuine culinary high spots than neighbouring towns. Over the past few years, however, a crop of good small **trattorie** has opened, together with a selection of excellent more upmarket places. Cheaper **pizzerias** are mostly clustered together at the very eastern end of Corso Cavour.

There are plenty of **bars**, with obvious key sites for watching the world go by in front of the Duomo and in Piazza della Repubblica, though the most prestigious bar in town, founded in 1917, is *Montanucci* at Corso Cavour 21. You can also check your **email** here (8am–midnight; closed Wed; €6.20 per hr). Also good, if only because it's quiet and you can while away a siesta in the shade of two fine trees outside, is the *Bar del Teatro* in Piazza Fracassini. For **ice cream**, the best bet is the *Gelateria Pasqualetti*, which has outlets to the left of the cathedral as you face it at Piazza del Duomo 14, and at Corso Cavour 56.

Antica Cantina Corso Cavour/Piazza Monaldeschi 18–19 ☏ 0763.344.746. One of the best places on the Corso, reasonably priced and with an old-fashioned trattoria atmosphere and food *come una volta* ("as it was in the past"). Very popular, especially at lunch. There is a handful of outside tables. Closed Wed.

CRAMST also known as *Al San Francesco*, Via Lorenzo Maitani 15/Via B. Cerretti 10 ☏ 0763.343.302. Much patronized by locals, this is a co-operatively run 400-seat affair, offering a choice between a restaurant (eve only) and less formal self-service (lunch and eve). Very good value, with pasta dishes from a few euros. Closed Sun.

Etrusca Via Lorenzo Maitani 10 ☏ 0763.444.016. A traditional-looking restaurant with a medieval vaulted dining-room – first choice in the more upmarket category with relaxed atmosphere and service and surprisingly fair prices for top-notch Umbrian specialities – reckon on about €30 for three courses. Be sure to go downstairs to see the wine cellars, carved out of solid tufa. Closed mid-Jan to mid-Feb.

Gigli d'Oro Piazza del Duomo ☏ 0763.341.903. Cooking here is hardly original, but the quality's always high: what you're paying for, though – three course start at about €40 – are elegant surroundings and the pleasure of dining in the shadow of the Duomo. Closed Wed.

I Sette Consoli Piazza Sant'Angelo 1a ☏ 0763.343.911. Highly rated by Italian restaurant guides, but the innovative food is not always successful and the dining room is a little austere (with only 35 covers). Three courses start from about €35. Fine if *La Volpe e L'Uva* (see below) is busy. Closed Wed plus Sun dinner Nov to March & a period in Feb or March.

La Buca di Bacco Corso Cavour 299–301 ☏ 0763.344.792. Almost opposite *Antica Cantina*, mildly more formal but also in the first rank of Orvieto's traditional restaurants. Closed Tues.

La Grotta Via Signorelli 5 ☏ 0763.341.348. Just off Via del Duomo and a few steps down from the hotel *Posta*, this is a good-value and friendly trattoria, offering reliable Italian staples. Closed Tues and parts of late Jan & late July.

La Volpe e L'Uva Via Ripa Corsica 1 ☏ 0763.341.612. A very good and popular trattoria offering traditional cooking – the menu, if anything, is almost too long – but great value for money, with three-course meals from about €25. A touch bigger and cheaper than *I Sette Consoli*, and an awful lot more relaxed and welcoming, although there are still only two rooms (one for non-smokers). Closed Mon, Tues (in winter) & a period in March.

Trattoria dell'Orso Via della Misericordia 16–18 ☏ 0763.341.642. This is Orvieto's oldest restaurant, and little has changed over the years, certainly not the excellent local cooking. Friendly service and a simple, snug interior with just a handful of tables. Good value for money. Closed Mon & Tues.

Around Orvieto

The environs of Orvieto are not the most compelling in Umbria. However, if you have transport and time to spare, you should definitely make for little-visited, but interesting **Città della Pieve**, perhaps en route to Montepulciano.

Città della Pieve

CITTÀ DELLA PIEVE, 41km north of Orvieto on the A1 (or 47km via the prettier, winding SS47), is best known as the birthplace of painter **Perugino**, born in 1446. Straggling impressively along its 500-metre-high ridge, the town,

13

founded by the Etruscans, consists of tiny, red-brick houses (there being no local building stone) and narrow streets, one of which, Via della Baciadonna, claims to be the narrowest in Italy – the width of a woman's kiss, the name suggests (or so narrow that you have no option but to kiss anyone you pass).

Via Garibaldi and Via Vittorio Veneto make up the main east–west axis, meeting in the linked central squares of Piazza Gramsci and **Piazza del Plebiscito**, where you'll find the seventeenth-century **Duomo**. This has a couple of late works that show Perugino in his worst light, the *Baptism of Christ* (1510) on the first altar of the north (left) aisle, and the *Madonna Enthroned with Sts Peter, Paul, Gervasio and Protasio* (1514) in the apse: the original ninth-century parish church, or *pieve* (which gave the town its name), on the site of the Duomo, was dedicated to the last two saints. The same square contains the **Torre del Pubblico**, thirteenth-century Romanesque at the base (built in travertine) and fifteenth-century Gothic higher up. Also here are the Palazzo dei Priori and, opposite the Duomo, the **Palazzo della Corgna**. which – with the church of **Sant'Agostino** and the **Oratorio di Santa Maria dei Bianchi** – have been united in a self-contained circuit known as the **Museo Aperto,** with a single-ticket admission, available from any of the relevant attractions (daily: May–Sept 9.30am–1pm & 4–7.30pm; Oct–April 10am–12.30pm & 3.30–6pm; €4), The *palazzo* contains some half-decent sixteenth-century frescoes by Salvio Savini and Pomarancio, the second another painter born in the town.

Continue down Via Roma and through Porta del Vacciano (or Romana) and 200m from the square, after passing a church on the right dedicated to Giacomo Villa, a seventeenth-century beatific, you come on your left to **Santa Maria dei Servi** (rarely open), which contains Perugino's *Deposition* (1517), an important late fresco damaged when monks erected a choir screen nearby. Greater damage was done to Città's artistic patrimony by foreigners, not least by Napoleon, who removed cartloads of the town's other Peruginos to the Louvre.

The **Oratorio di Santa Maria dei Bianchi** is reached by returning to the main Piazza del Plebiscito and continuing north on Via Pietro Vannuci. The Perugino here, *The Adoration of the Magi*, is one of his masterpieces; note Lago Trasimeno in the background. It was painted in just 29 days in 1504, perhaps, claim some critics, with the assistance of Perugino's pupil, the young Raphael. Perugino initially asked for 200 florins for the work, then said he'd be happy with half that as he was a native of the town; in the end the confraternity which owned the Oratorio (it exists to this day as a charitable institution) paid him just 75. Two letters from the artist displayed with the painting document the financial wrangling. If the building is shut, try asking at the custodian's house, Via Pietro Vannucci 42.

Practicalities

The **tourist office** is at Piazza Matteotti 1 (Mon–Sat 10.30am–12.30pm & 4–6/7pm; ℡0578.299.375). Città della Pieve makes a peaceful enough stop and has a two-star **hotel**: the *Vannucci*, Via Icilio Vanni 1 (℡0578.299.572, Ⓦwww .hotel-vannucci.com; ❸), located not far after the church of San Francesco beyond the eastern end of Via Vittorio Veneto. It has a small pool, garden and a restaurant, though the best **place to eat** in town is *Serenalla*, Via Fiorenzuola 28 (℡0578.299.683; closed Wed), a family-run place off Via Vittorio Veneto. Another hotel a touch farther out (in the same direction as the *Vannucci*: turn right at the fork after San Francesco) is the three-star *Piccolo Eden*, Via Santa Lucia 53 (℡0578.297.065; ❶), where they'll lend you a bike to run into town or explore farther afield. Four kilometres out of town, and even nicer – if more expensive

– is the *Relais dei Magi*, a stylish thirteen-room rural retreat set in broad swathes of woodland and olive groves at Località le Selve Nuove (℡0578.298.133, Ⓦwww .relaismagi.it; ❻; closed for a period between Jan & March). It has indoor and outdoor pools, sauna, Turkish bath, spa and a delightful setting.

Travel details

Trains

Narni to: Foligno (9–13 daily; 55min; connections for Assisi, Nocera Umbra, Gualdo Tadino, Fossato di Vico – for Gubbio – and Perugia); Fossato di Vico (5 daily; 1hr 45min); Gualdo Tadino (5 daily; 1hr 35min); Nocera Umbra (5 daily; 1hr 10min); Orte (12–16 daily; 15min; connections for Rome, Orvieto, Chiusi, Arezzo and Florence); Rome direct (10 daily; 1hr); Terni (12 daily; 15min).

Orvieto to: Arezzo (14–20 daily; 1hr 20min); Castiglione del Lago (14–20 daily; 40min; connections to Siena, 1hr 30min and additional connections to Castiglione del Lago, 10min); Florence (14–20 daily; 1hr 30min); Orte (14–20 daily; 40min; connections to Narni, Terni, Spoleto and Foligno); Rome (14–20 daily; 1hr–1hr 30min); Teróntola (7–10 daily; 50min; connections to Perugia).

Terni to: Foligno (18–23 daily; 40min; connections for Assisi, Nocera Umbra, Gualdo Tadino, Fossato di Vico – for Gubbio —- and Perugia); Fossato di Vico (5 daily; 1hr 30min; additional connections at Foligno); Gualdo Tadino (5 daily; 1hr 20min; additional connections at Foligno); Narni (12 daily; 15min); Nocera Umbra (5 daily; 1hr; additional connections at Foligno); Orte (12–16 daily; 30min; connections to Rome, Orvieto, Chiusi, Arezzo and Florence); Perugia Ponte San Giovanni/Sant'Anna (10–16 daily; 1hr 30min; connections at Sant'Anna for FCU services to Città di Castello and Sansepolcro; connections at Ponte San Giovanni for Trenitalia services to Teróntola and Foligno); Rome direct (12–16 daily; 50min–1hr 20min); Spoleto (12 daily; 20min); Todi (10–16 daily; 40min).

Todi to: Perugia Ponte San Giovanni/Sant'Anna (10–16 daily; 1hr 30min; connections at Sant'Anna for FCU services to Città di Castello and Sansepolcro; connections at Ponte San Giovanni for Trenitalia services to Teróntola and Foligno; 45min); Terni (10–16 daily; 40min).

Buses

Amelia to: Avigliano (3 daily Mon–Sat, 1 connecting to Todi via Dunarobba; 25min); Lugnano in Teverina (Mon–Sat 10 daily, 1 on Sun; 20min); Narni (10 daily Mon–Sat, 1 on Sun; 25min); Orvieto (5–7 daily Mon–Sat; 1hr 15min); Terni (10 or more daily Mon–Sat, 1 on Sun; 50min).

Orvieto to: Amelia (5–7 daily Mon–Sat; 1hr 15min); Bolsena (2 daily Mon–Sat; 50min); Corbara/Civitella del Lago (1 daily Mon–Sat; 50min); Lugnano in Teverina (7 daily Mon–Sat; 1hr); Narni (5 daily Mon–Sat; 1hr 40min); Perugia (1 daily; 2hr); Terni (5 daily Mon–Sat; 2hr); Todi (1 daily Mon–Sat; 1hr 30min).

Narni to: Amelia (10 daily Mon–Sat, 1 on Sun; 25min); Orvieto (5 daily Mon–Sat; 1hr 40min); Otricoli (8 daily Mon–Sat; 30min).

Terni to: Amelia (10 or more daily Mon–Sat, 1 on Sun; 50min); Cascata delle Marmore (15-plus daily Mon–Sat, 11 on Sun; 40min); Ferentillo (17 daily Mon–Sat, 12 on Sun; 40min); Lugnano in Teverina (8 daily Mon–Sat, 1 on Sun 1hr 10min); Orvieto (via Baschi, Guardea, Montecchio and Amelia; 5 daily Mon–Sat; 2hr); Piediluco (9 daily Mon–Sat, 6 on Sun; 35min); Scheggino (8 daily Mon–Sat, 5 on Sun; 50min); Todi (via Sangemini, Acquasparta or Avigliano; 3 daily Mon–Sat; 1hr).

Todi to: Deruta (3 daily Mon–Sat; 40min); Marsciano (2 daily; 30min); Orvieto (1 daily Mon–Sat; 1hr 30min); Perugia (3 daily; 1hr); Terni (3 daily Mon–Sat; 1hr).

Contexts

Contexts

The historical background: Tuscany

A comprehensive history of Tuscany in its medieval and Renaissance heyday would consist in large part of a mosaic of more or less independent histories, as each of the region's cities has a complex story to tell. In an overview such as this, fidelity to the entanglements of central Italy's past is impossible. Instead, within a broad account of the main trends in the evolution of Tuscany, we have concentrated on the city that emerged as the dominant force – Florence. The brief reviews of the other major towns – Siena, Pisa, Arezzo, Prato, Pistoia and so on – are supplemented by background given in the appropriate sections of the guide. Similarly, crucial episodes in the history of Florence and its culture – for instance, the ascendancy of Savonarola – are covered in greater detail in the chapter on that city.

Etruscans and Romans

The name of the province of Tuscany derives from the **Etruscans**, the most powerful civilization of pre-Roman Italy. There's no scholarly consensus on the origins of this people, with some experts insisting that they migrated into Italy from Anatolia at the start of the ninth century BC, and others maintaining that they were an indigenous tribe. All that's known for certain is that the Etruscans were spread thoughout central Italy from the eighth century BC, and that the centre of gravity of their domain was in the southern part of the modern province, roughly along a line drawn from Orbetello to Lago Trasimeno. Their principal settlements in Tuscany were Roselle, Vetulonia, Populonia, Volterra, Chiusi, Cortona, Arezzo and – most northerly of all – Fiesole.

It seems that the Etruscans absorbed elements of those cultures with whom they came into contact, thus their trade with Greek settlements produced some classically influenced art that can be seen at its best in Florence's archeological museum and in Cortona. The Etruscan language has still not been fully deciphered (a massive translation programme is under way in Perugia), so at the moment their wall paintings and terracotta funerary sculptures are the main source of information about them, and this information is open to widely differing interpretations. Some people have inferred an almost neurotic fear of death from the evidence of their burial sites and monuments, while others – most notably D.H. Lawrence – have on the contrary intuited an irrepressible and uncomplicated vitality.

There may have been an Etruscan settlement where Florence now stands, but it would have been subservient to their base in the hill-town of Fiesole. The substantial development of Tuscany's chief city began with the **Roman** colony of Florentia, established by Julius Caesar in 59 BC as a settlement for army veterans – by which time Romans had either subsumed or exterminated most Etruscan towns. Expansion of Florentia itself was rapid, with a steady traffic of trading vessels along the Arno providing the basis of accelerated growth in the second and third centuries AD.

This rise under the empire was paralleled by the growth of **Siena**, **Pisa** and **Lucca**, establishing an economic primacy in the north of Tuscany that has endured to the present. According to legend Siena was founded by the sons of

Remus, supposedly fleeing their uncle Romulus, while the port at Pisa was developed by the Romans in the second century BC. Lucca was even more important, and it was here that Julius Caesar, Crassus and Pompey established their triumvirate in 56 BC.

Barbarians and margraves

Under the comparative tranquillity of the Roman colonial regime, **Christianity** began to spread through the region. Lucca claims to have been the first Christian city in Tuscany – evangelized by a disciple of St Peter – though Pisa's church of San Pietro a Grado is said to have been founded by Peter himself. In Florence, the church of San Lorenzo and the martyr's shrine at San Miniato were both established in the fourth century.

This period of calm was shattered in the fifth century by the invasions of the **Goths** from the north, though the scale of the destruction in this first barbarian wave was nothing compared to the havoc of the following century. After the fall of Rome, the empire had split in two, with the western half ruled from Ravenna and the eastern from Constantinople (Byzantium). By the 490s Ravenna was occupied by the Ostrogoths, and forty years later the Byzantine emperor Justinian launched a campaign to repossess the Italian peninsula.

The ensuing mayhem between the Byzantine armies of Belisarius and Narsus and the fast-moving Goths was probably the most destructive phase of central Italian history, with virtually all major settlements ravaged by one side or the other – and sometimes both. In 552 Florence fell to the hordes of the Gothic king **Totila**, whose depredations so weakened the province that less than twenty years later the **Lombards** were able to storm in, subjugating Florence to the duchy whose capital was in Pavia, though its dukes preferred to rule from Lucca.

By the end of the eighth century Charlemagne's **Franks** had taken control of much of Italy, with the administration being overseen by imperial **margraves**, again based in Lucca. These proxy rulers developed into some of the most powerful figures in the Holy Roman Empire and were instrumental in spreading Christianity even further, founding numerous religious houses. Willa, widow of the margrave Uberto, established the Badìa in Florence in 978, the first monastic foundation in the centre of the city; her son Ugo, margrave in turn, is buried in the Badìa's church.

The hold of the central authority of the Holy Roman Empire was often tenuous, with feudal grievances making the region all but ungovernable, and it was under the imperial margraves that the notion of an autonomous Tuscan entity began to emerge. In 1027 the position of margrave was passed to the **Canossa** family, who took the title of the Counts of Tuscia, as Tuscany was then called. The most influential figure produced by this dynasty was **Matilda**, daughter of the first Canossa margrave. When her father died she was abducted by the German emperor Henry III, and on her release and return to her home territory she began to take the side of the papacy in its protracted disputes with the empire. The culmination of her anti-imperialist policy came in 1077, when she obliged the emperor Henry IV to wait in the snow outside the gates of Canossa before making obeisance to Pope Gregory VII. Later friction between the papacy, empire and Tuscan cities was assured when Matilda bequeathed all her lands to the pope, with the crucial exceptions of Florence, Siena and Lucca.

Guelphs and Ghibellines

Though Lucca had been the titular base of the imperial margraves, Ugo and his successors had shown a degree of favouritism towards **Florence**, and over the next three hundred years Florence gained pre-eminence among the cities of Tuscany, becoming especially important as a religious centre. In 1078 Countess Matilda supervised the construction of new fortifications for Florence, and in the year of her death – 1115 – granted it the status of an independent city. The new *comune* of Florence was essentially governed by a council of one hundred men, the great majority drawn from the rising merchant class. In 1125 the city's increasing dominance of the region was confirmed when it crushed the rival city of Fiesole. Fifty years later, as the population boomed with the rise of the textile industry, new walls were built around what was then one of the largest cities in Europe.

Not that the other mercantile centres of Tuscany were completely eclipsed, as their magnificent heritage of medieval buildings makes plain. **Pisa** in the tenth and eleventh centuries had become one of the peninsula's wealthiest ports and its shipping lines played a vital part in bringing the cultural influences of France, Byzantium and the Muslim world into Italy. Twelfth-century **Siena**, though racked by conflicts between the bishops and the secular authorities and between the nobility and the merchant class, was booming thanks to its cloth industries and its exploitation of a local silver mine – foundation of a banking empire that was to see the city rivalling the bankers of Venice and Florence on the international markets.

Throughout and beyond the thirteenth century Tuscany was torn by conflict between the **Ghibelline** faction and the **Guelphs**. The names of these two political alignments derive from Welf, the family name of Emperor Otto IV, and Waiblingen, the name of a castle owned by their implacable rivals, the Hohenstaufen. Though there's no clear documentation, it seems that the terms Guelph and Ghibelline entered the Italian vocabulary at the end of the twelfth century, when supporters of Otto IV battled for control of the central peninsula with the future Frederick II, nephew of Otto and grandson of the Hohenstaufen emperor Barbarossa (1152–90). Within the first few years of Frederick II's reign (1212–50), the labels Guelph and Ghibelline had changed their meaning – the latter still referred to the allies of the Hohenstaufen, but the Guelph party was defined chiefly by its loyalty to the papacy, thus reviving the battle lines drawn up during the reign of Matilda.

To muddy the waters yet further, when Charles of Anjou conquered Naples in 1266, alliance with the anti-imperial French became another component of Guelphism, and a loose Guelph alliance soon stretched from Paris to Naples, substantially funded by the bankers of Tuscany.

Ghibelline/Guelph divisions approximately corresponded to a split between the feudal **nobility** and the rising **business classes**, but this is only the broadest of generalizations. By the beginning of the thirteenth century the major cities of Tuscany were becoming increasingly self-sufficient and inter-city strife was soon a commonplace of medieval life. In this climate, affiliations with the empire and the papacy were often struck on the basis that "my enemy's enemy is my friend", and allegiances changed at baffling speed: if, for instance, the Guelphs gained the ascendancy in a particular town, its neighbours might switch to the Ghibelline camp to maintain their rivalry. Nonetheless, certain patterns did emerge from the confusion: Florence and Lucca were generally Guelph strongholds, while Pisa, Arezzo, Prato, Pistoia and Siena tended to side with the empire.

As a final complicating factor, this was also the great age of **mercenary** armies, whose loyalties changed even quicker than those of the towns that paid for their services. Thus **Sir John Hawkwood** – whose White Company was the most fearsome band of hoodlums on the peninsula – is known today through the monument to him in Florence's Duomo, but early in his career was employed by Ghibelline Pisa to fight the Florentines. He was then taken on by Pope Gregory XI, whom he deserted on the grounds of underpayment, and in the end was granted a pension of 1200 florins a year by Florence, basically as a form of protection money. Even then he was often absent fighting for other cities whenever a fat purse was waved in his direction.

Medieval Florence before the Medici

In this period of superpower manoeuvring and shifting economic structures, city governments in Tuscany were volatile. The administration of Siena, for example, was carried out by various combinations of councils and governors and in 1368 its constitution was redrawn no fewer than four times. However, Florence provides perhaps the best illustration of the turbulence of Tuscan politics in the late Middle Ages.

In 1207 the city's governing council was replaced by the **podestà**, an executive official who was traditionally a non-Florentine, in a semi-autocratic form of government that was common throughout the region. It was around this time, too, that the first **arti** (guilds) were formed to promote the interests of the traders and bankers, a constituency of ever-increasing power. Then in 1215 Florence was riven by a feud that was typical of the internecine violence of central Italy at this period. On Easter Sunday one **Buondelmonte de' Buondelmonti**, on his way to his wedding, was stabbed to death at the foot of the Ponte Vecchio by a member of the Amidei clan, in revenge for breaking his engagement to a young woman of that family. The prosecution of the murderers and their allies polarized the city into those who supported the *comune* – which regarded itself as the protector of the commercial city against imperial ambitions – and the followers of the Amidei, who seem to have politicized their personal grievances by aligning themselves against the *comune* and with the emperor.

These Ghibellines eventually enlisted the help of Emperor Frederick II to oust the Guelphs in 1248, but within two years they had been displaced by the Guelph-backed regime of the **Primo Popolo**, a quasi-democratic government drawn from the mercantile class. The *Primo Popolo* was in turn displaced in 1260, when the Florentine army marched on Siena to demand the surrender of some exiles who were hiding out in the city. Though greatly outnumbered, the Sienese army and its Ghibelline allies overwhelmed the aggressors at **Montaperti**, after which the Sienese were prevented from razing Florence only by the intervention of Farinata degli Uberti, head of the Ghibelline exiles.

By the 1280s the balance had again moved back in favour of Florence, where the Guelphs were back in control – after the intervention of Charles of Anjou – through the **Secondo Popolo**, a regime run by the *Arti Maggiori* (Great Guilds). It was this second bourgeois administration that definitively shifted the fulcrum of power in Florence towards its bankers, merchants and manufacturers – whereas in Siena, the second richest city in Tuscany, the feudal families retained a stranglehold for far longer. Agitation from the landed nobility of the countryside around Florence had been a constant fact of life until the *Secondo Popolo*, which in 1293 passed a programme of political reforms known as the *Ordinamenti della Giustizia*, excluding the nobility from government and investing power in the **Signoria**, a council drawn from the *Arti Maggiori*.

CONTEXTS | The historical background: Tuscany

Strife between the virulently anti-imperial "Black" and more conciliatory "White" factions within the Guelph camp marked the start of the fourteenth century in Florence, with many of the Whites – Dante among them – being exiled in 1302. Worse disarray was to come. In 1325 the army of Lucca under **Castruccio Castracani** defeated the Florentines and was about to overwhelm the city when the death of their leader took the momentum out of the campaign. Then in 1339 the Bardi and Peruzzi banks – Florence's largest – both collapsed, mainly owing to the bad debts of Edward III of England. The ultimate catastrophe came in 1348, when the **Black Death** destroyed as many as half the city's population.

However, even though the epidemic hit Florence so badly that it was generally referred to as the Florentine Plague, its effects were equally devastating throughout the region, and did nothing to reverse the economic – and thus political – supremacy of the city. Florence had subsumed Pistoia in 1329 and gained Prato in the 1350s. In 1406 it took control of Pisa and thus gained a long-coveted sea port, and five years later Cortona became part of its territory. From this time on, despite the survival of Sienese independence into the sixteenth century, the history of Tuscany increasingly becomes the history of Florence.

The early Medici

A crucial episode in the liberation of Florence from the influence of the papacy was the so-called **War of the Eight Saints** in 1375–78, which brought Florence into direct territorial conflict with Pope Gregory XI. This not only signalled the dissolution of the old Guelph alliance, but had immense repercussions for the internal politics of Florence. The increased taxation and other economic hardships of the war provoked an uprising of the industrial day-labourers, the **Ciompi**, on whom the wool and cloth factories depended. Their short-lived revolt resulted in the formation of three new guilds and direct representation for the workers for the first time. However, the prospect of increased proletarian presence in the machinery of state provoked a consolidation of the city's oligarchs and in 1382 an alliance of the city's Guelph party and the **Popolo Grasso** (the wealthiest merchants) took control of the *Signoria* away from the guilds, a situation that lasted for four decades.

Not all of Florence's most prosperous citizens aligned themselves with the *Popolo Grasso*, and the foremost of the well-off mavericks were the **Medici**, a family from the agricultural Mugello region whose fortune had been made by the banking prowess of Giovanni Bicci de' Medici. The political rise of his son, **Cosimo de' Medici**, was to some extent due to his family's sympathies with the *Popolo Minuto*, as the members of the disenfranchised lesser guilds were known. With the increase in public discontent at the autocratic rule of the *Signoria* – where the Albizzi clan were the dominant force – Cosimo came to be seen as the figurehead of the more democratically inclined sector of the upper class. In 1431 the authorities imprisoned him in the tower of the Palazzo Vecchio and two years later, as Florence became embroiled in a futile and domestically unpopular war against Lucca, they sent him into exile. He was away for only a year. In 1434, after a session of the *Parlamento* – a general council called in times of emergency – it was decided to invite him to return. Having secured the military support of the Sforza family of Milan, Cosimo became the pre-eminent figure in the city's political life, a position he maintained for more than three decades.

Cosimo il Vecchio – as he came to be known – rarely held office himself, preferring to exercise power through backstage manipulation and adroit investment. His extreme generosity to charities and religious foundations in Florence was no doubt motivated in part by genuine piety, but clearly did no harm as a public relations exercise – even if it didn't impress the contemporary who recorded that his munificence was due to the fact that "he knew his money had not been over-well acquired".

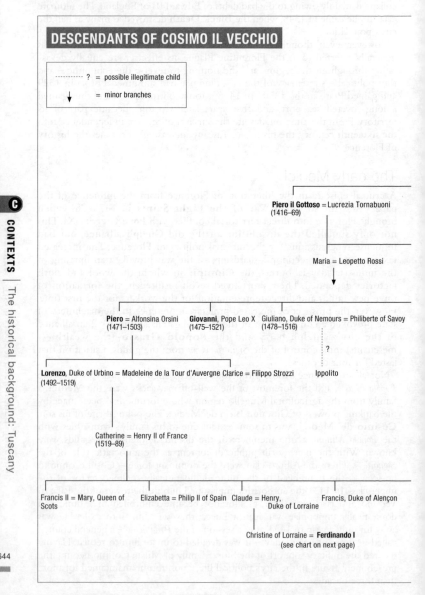

DESCENDANTS OF COSIMO IL VECCHIO

--------- ? = possible illegitimate child

↓ = minor branches

Piero il Gottoso = Lucrezia Tornabuoni
(1416–69)

Maria = Leopetto Rossi
↓

Piero = Alfonsina Orsini   **Giovanni**, Pope Leo X   Giuliano, Duke of Nemours = Philiberte of Savoy
(1471–1503)   (1475–1521)   (1478–1516)

            ?

Lorenzo, Duke of Urbino = Madeleine de la Tour d'Auvergne   Clarice = Filippo Strozzi   Ippolito
(1492–1519)

Catherine = Henry II of France
(1519–89)

Francis II = Mary, Queen of   Elizabetta = Philip II of Spain   Claude = Henry,   Francis, Duke of Alençon
Scots   Duke of Lorraine

Christine of Lorraine = **Ferdinando I**
(see chart on next page)

Dante, Boccaccio and Giotto in the first half of the fourteenth century had established the literary and artistic ascendancy of Florence, laying the foundations of Italian humanism with their emphasis on the importance of the vernacular and the dignity of humanity. Florence's reputation as the most innovative cultural centre in Europe was strengthened during the fifteenth century, to a large extent through Medici patronage. Cosimo commissioned work from Donatello, Michelozzo and a host of other Florentine artists, and

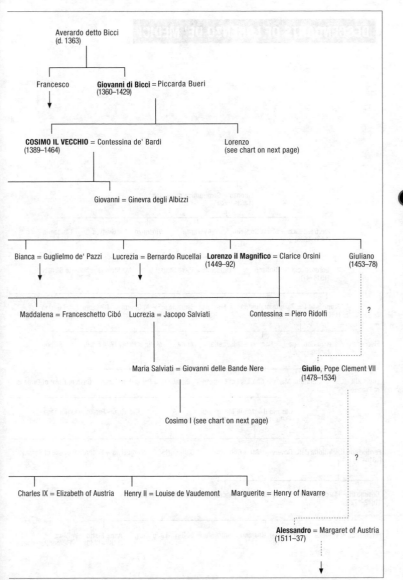

took advantage of the 1439 Council of Florence – a conference of the Catholic and Eastern churches – to foster scholars who were familiar with the literatures of the ancient world. His grandson **Lorenzo il Magnifico** (who succeeded Piero il Gottoso, the Gouty) continued this literary patronage, promoting the study of the classics in the Platonic academy that used to meet at the Medici villas. Other Medici were to fund projects by Botticelli, Michelangelo, Pontormo – in fact, most of the seminal figures of the Florentine Renaissance.

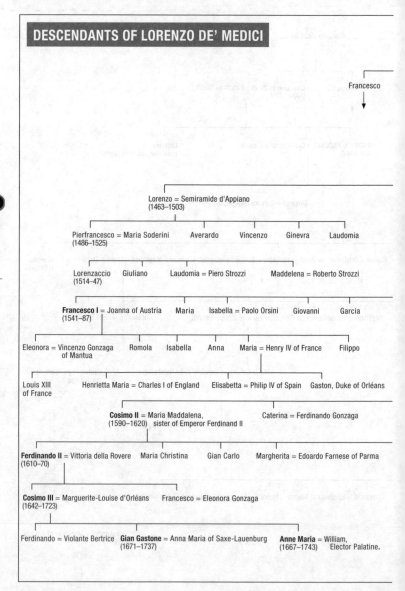

DESCENDANTS OF LORENZO DE' MEDICI

Francesco

Lorenzo = Semiramide d'Appiano
(1463–1503)

Pierfrancesco = Maria Soderini   Averardo   Vincenzo   Ginevra   Laudomia
(1486–1525)

Lorenzaccio   Giuliano   Laudomia = Piero Strozzi   Maddelena = Roberto Strozzi
(1514–47)

Francesco I = Joanna of Austria   Maria   Isabella = Paolo Orsini   Giovanni   Garcia
(1541–87)

Eleonora = Vincenzo Gonzaga   Romola   Isabella   Anna   Maria = Henry IV of France   Filippo
of Mantua

Louis XIII   Henrietta Maria = Charles I of England   Elisabetta = Philip IV of Spain   Gaston, Duke of Orléans
of France

Cosimo II = Maria Maddalena,   Caterina = Ferdinando Gonzaga
(1590–1620)   sister of Emperor Ferdinand II

Ferdinando II = Vittoria della Rovere   Maria Christina   Gian Carlo   Margherita = Edoardo Farnese of Parma
(1610–70)

Cosimo III = Marguerite-Louise d'Orléans   Francesco = Eleonora Gonzaga
(1642–1723)

Ferdinando = Violante Bertrice   **Gian Gastone** = Anna Maria of Saxe-Lauenburg   **Anne Maria** = William,
(1671–1737)   (1667–1743)   Elector Palatine.

Lorenzo il Magnifico's status as the *de facto* ruler of Florence was even more secure than that of Cosimo il Vecchio, but it did meet one stiff challenge. While many of Florence's financial dynasties were content to advise and support the Medici, others – notably the mighty Strozzi clan – were resentful of the power now wielded by their fellow businessmen. In 1478 one of these disgruntled families, the Pazzi, conspired with Pope Sixtus IV, who had been riled by Lorenzo's attempt to break the papal monopoly of alum mining. This **Pazzi**

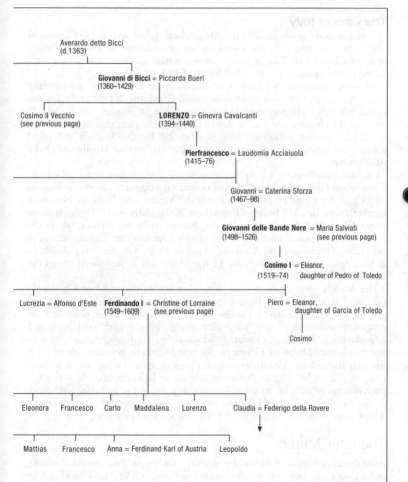

Conspiracy resulted in an assault on Lorenzo and his brother Giuliano during Mass in the Duomo; Lorenzo was badly injured and Giuliano murdered, an outcome that only increased the esteem in which Lorenzo was held. Now that the plot had failed, Sixtus joined forces with the ferocious King Ferrante of Naples to launch a war on Florence, and excommunicated Lorenzo into the bargain. Taking his life in his hands, Lorenzo left Florence to persuade Ferrante to leave the alliance, a mission he somehow accomplished successfully, to the jubilation of the city.

The wars of Italy

Before Lorenzo's death in 1492 the Medici bank failed, and in 1494 Lorenzo's son Piero was obliged to flee following his surrender to the invading French army of Charles VIII. This invasion was the commencement of a bloody half-century dominated by the so-called **Wars of Italy**.

After the departure of Charles's troops, Florence for a while was virtually under the control of the inspirational monk **Girolamo Savonarola**, but his career was brief. He was executed as a heretic in 1498, after which the city continued to function as a more democratic republic than that of the Medici. In 1512, however, following Florence's defeat by the Spanish and papal armies, the Medici returned, in the person of the vicious **Giuliano, Duke of Nemours**.

Giuliano's successors – his equally unattractive nephew Lorenzo, the Duke of Urbino, and Giulio, illegitimate son of Lorenzo il Magnifico's brother – were in effect just the mouthpieces of Giovanni de' Medici (the Duke of Nemours' brother), who in 1519 became **Pope Leo X**. Similarly, when Giulio became **Pope Clement VII**, he was really the absentee ruler of Florence, where the family presence was maintained by the ghastly **Ippolito** (the illegitimate son of the Duke of Nemours) and **Alessandro** (acknowledged by the Duke of Urbino as his illegitimate son, but believed by most historians to have been in fact the son of Pope Clement VII).

The Medici were again evicted from Florence in the wake of Charles V's pillage of Rome in 1527, Pope Clement's humiliation by the imperial army providing the spur to eject his deeply unpopular relatives. Three years later the pendulum swung the other way: after a siege by the combined papal and imperial forces, Florence capitulated and was obliged to receive Alessandro, who was proclaimed **Duke of Florence**, the first Medici to bear the title of ruler. Though the sadistic Alessandro lost no opportunity to exploit the immunity that came from his title, in the wider scheme of Italian politics he was a less powerful figure than his ancestors. Tuscany was becoming just one more piece in the vast jigsaw of the Habsburg empire, a superpower far more interventionist than the medieval empire of Frederick II could ever have been.

The later Medici

After the assassination of Alessandro in 1537, power passed to another **Cosimo**, not a direct heir but rather a descendant of Cosimo il Vecchio's brother. The emperor Charles V, now related to the Medici through the marriage of his daughter to Alessandro, gave his assent to the succession of this seemingly pliable young man – indeed, without Habsburg consent it would not have happened. Yet it turned out that Cosimo had the clear intention of maintaining Florence's role as the regional power-broker, and he proved immensely skilful at judging just how far he could push the city's autonomy without provoking the imperial policy-makers.

Having finally extinguished the subversive threat of the Strozzi faction at the battle of **Montemurlo**, Cosimo went on to buy the territory of Siena from the Habsburgs in 1557, giving Florence control of all of Tuscany with the solitary exception of Lucca. Two years later Florentine hegemony in Tuscany was confirmed in the Treaty of Cateau-Cambrésis, the final act in the Wars of Italy. Soon after, though, the new Habsburg emperor, Philip II, installed a military outpost in the Orbetello area to keep Tuscany under scrutiny.

Imperial and papal approval of Cosimo's rule was sealed in 1570, when he was allowed to take the title **Cosimo I, Grand Duke of Tuscany**. In European terms Tuscany was a second-rank power, but by comparison with other states on the peninsula it was in a very comfortable position, and during Cosimo's reign there would have been little perception that Florence was drifting inexorably towards the margins of European politics. It was Cosimo who built the Uffizi, extended and overhauled the Palazzo Vecchio, installed the Medici in the Palazzo Pitti, had the magnificent Ponte Santa Trìnita constructed across the Arno and commissioned much of the public sculpture around the Piazza della Signoria.

Cosimo's descendants were to remain in power until 1737, and aspects of their rule continued the city's intellectual tradition: the Medici were among Galileo's strongest supporters, for example. Yet it was a story of almost continual if initially gentle economic decline, as bad harvests and recurrent epidemics worsened the gloom created by the shift of European trading patterns in favour of northern Europe. The half-century reign of **Ferdinando II** had scarcely begun when the market for Florence's woollen goods collapsed in the 1630s, and the city's banks simultaneously went into a terminal slump. The last two male Medici, the insanely pious **Cosimo III** and the drunken pederast **Gian Gastone** – who was seen in public only once, vomiting from the window of the state coach – were fitting symbols of the moribund Florentine state.

To the present

Under the terms of a treaty signed by Gian Gastone's sister, Anna Maria de' Medici, Florence passed in 1737 to the **House of Lorraine**, cousins of the Austrian Habsburgs. The first Lorraine prince, the future Francis I of Austria, was a more enlightened ruler than the last Medici had been and his successors presided over a placid and generally untroubled region, doing much to improve the condition of Tuscany's agricultural land and rationalize its production methods. Austrian rule lasted until the coming of the French in 1799, an interlude that ended with the fall of **Napoleon**, who had made his sister Elisa Baciocchi Grand Duchess of Tuscany.

After this, the Lorraine dynasty was brought back, remaining in residence until the last of the line, Leopold II, consented to his own deposition in 1859. Absorbed into the new **Kingdom of Italy** in the following year, Florence became the **capital** in 1865, a position it held until the beginning of 1871, when Rome – having at last become part of the otherwise united country – took over the role.

Italy's unpopular entry into World War I cost thousands of Tuscan lives, and the economic disruption that followed was exploited by the regime of Benito **Mussolini**. The corporate Fascist state of the 1920s did effect various improvements in the infrastructure of the region, but Mussolini's alliance with Hitler's Germany was to prove a calamity. In 1943, as the Allied landing at Monte Cassino was followed by a campaign to sweep the occupying German forces out of the peninsula, Tuscany became a battlefield between the Nazis and the

partisans. The districts around Monte Amiata and the Val d'Órcia sheltered particularly strong partisan groups, and many of the province's hill-towns had their resistance cells, as numerous well-tended war memorials testify.

Yet, as elsewhere in Italy, the loyalties of Tuscany were split, as is well illustrated by the case of Florence, an ideological centre for the resistance but also home to some of Italy's most ardent Nazi collaborators. Wartime Florence in fact produced one of the strangest paradoxes of the time: a Fascist sympathizer in charge of the British Institute and a German consul who did so much to protect suspected partisans that he was granted the freedom of the city after the war.

Although most of the major monuments of Tuscany survived the war – sometimes as a result of pacts between the two sides – there was inevitably widespread destruction. Grosseto, Pisa and Livorno were badly damaged by Allied bombing raids, while Florence was wrecked by the retreating German army, who bombed all the bridges except the Ponte Vecchio and blew up much of the medieval city near the banks of the Arno.

Postwar Tuscany

Tuscany is a prosperous and conservative region that in the past has tended to return right-of-centre members of parliament. On a local level, however, left-wing support is high, partly as a consequence of the Italian communist party's record in the war and subsequent work on land reform. The communists were effectively excluded from national government by the machinations of the now-defunct Christian Democrat party (which, like the old Socialist party, was undone by the corruption scandals of the early 1990s), but the newer left-leaning parties that have emerged over the past couple of decades have projected as the grassroots opposition to the centralization and corruption of Roman politics. It's a strategy that has been particularly successful in Tuscany, which has clung onto an image of itself as a state within the state. Since the 1970s the town halls of the region have been governed predominantly by communist-led coalitions, forming the heartland of the so-called "red belt" of central Italy.

Despite migration from the land in the 1950s and 1960s, the **economy** of Tuscany has been adroitly managed. The labour-intensive vineyards, olive groves and farms continue to provide a dependable source of income, boosted by industrial development in the Arno valley and around Livorno and Piombino. Production of textiles, leather goods and jewellery have brought money into Prato, Florence and Arezzo, while wine has brought untold prosperity to previously moribund towns such as Montalcino and Montepulciano. But **tourism** plays an uncomfortably large and ever-increasing part in balancing the books of these and other historic centres. This is a mixed blessing, sheer weight of numbers in places such as Florence, Siena and San Gimignano (and many others) overburdening an already creaking infrastructure and – worse – undermining the charm and damaging the historic and artistic treasures that attract visitors in the first place.

The historical background: Umbria

A lthough the history of Umbria overlaps with that of Tuscany in the eras of the Etruscans and the Romans, the emergence of self-governing cities marks a divergence between the economically dynamic Tuscan region and landlocked, more inward-looking Umbria. As with the summary of Tuscan history, what follows is but a sketch of what is an immensely complex story, more details of which are to be found in the accounts of the various Umbrian towns.

Pre-Roman Umbria

Over 1500 years before the birth of Christ, a large-scale migration of primitive tribes from central Europe and the east brought permanent settlers to the marshy lowlands around Terni and Perugia. As time went by, these tribes started to move away from the plains in favour of the uplands around Norcia, giving rise to the first of the **hill-towns** that were eventually to dominate the entire region.

By the eighth century BC these peoples were absorbed by the larger and more sophisticated tribes that followed them from the north. These gradually formed themselves into three distinct groups: the Samnites, the Latins (who later became the Romans), and the **Umbrians**. All three had common cultural roots, spoke dialects of a shared language, and between them occupied all but the southernmost tip of the Italian peninsula. The Umbrians' own territory extended far beyond the region's present boundaries, including the best part of what is now Tuscany and the Marche – a vast area for a people of whom almost nothing is known. Only the Eugubine Marbles found near Gubbio yield any clues as to the religion or language of what was clearly a cogent civilization. Other than these, the Umbrians' only memorials are the walls still standing, more or less intact, in a dozen-odd cities in the region.

When the **Etruscans** began to encroach on these cities, their predominantly agricultural inhabitants retreated quietly into the mountains and carried on life much as they had done before. In time they started to trade and intermarry with their new neighbours and the two cultures became more or less indistinguishable. By 700 BC Etruscan influence in Umbria extended as far east as the Tiber, and in some isolated cases – Gubbio for example – some way beyond it. All aspects of their life point to a sophisticated and ordered social set-up, with a political system formed around a confederation of cities, of which two – Perugia and Orvieto – were situated in what is now Umbria.

Roman Umbria

The first time Umbria appears in **Roman** records is in 309 BC, the occasion being Perugia's defeat at the hands of the Roman consul Fabius. The battle marked the beginning of the end for the Etruscan cities, and though some continued to cling to independence, by the second century BC most had become reluctant allies of the Romans. Any vestiges of autonomy were stripped away when Perugia was defeated a second time, a consequence of the power struggle that followed the murder of Julius Caesar in 44 BC. This effectively amounted to a confrontation between the consul Mark Antony, his brother

Lucius, and **Octavius**, Caesar's great-nephew. In 40 BC the dispute reached crisis point, and while Antony was preoccupied with Cleopatra in Egypt, Octavius succeeded in harrying Lucius from Rome. Lucius, unhappily for the citizens of Perugia, decided to take refuge within their walls – an action that resulted in the city's destruction at the hands of Octavius.

Octavius went on to proclaim himself **Emperor Augustus**, and with this proclamation the Imperial Age began. Under his rule, Umbria continued to enjoy a period of prosperity that had begun with the opening of the **Via Flaminia** in 220 BC. The new road linked Rome to the Adriatic coast and to the cities of the north, and gave Umbria immense strategic importance. It superseded the Tiber as the focal point of the region and brought in its wake a massive increase in trade and prosperity: colonies were built from scratch or on the sites of Umbrian and Etruscan settlements, land was drained and roads constructed. Umbria – named as such for the first time – became a unified and thriving province.

Early Christianity and the barbarian invasions

Christianity spread quickly in Umbria, thanks mainly to Roman lines of communication. By the first century AD towns such as Spoleto and Foligno had become bishoprics, and within two hundred years most towns had Christian communities. As religious practice increasingly adhered to the monastic pattern established in the eastern Mediterranean, it was in Umbria's remote countryside, however, rather than its cities, that Christianity found its most enduring home. The first recorded **monastery** was founded at Monteluco, near Spoleto, by Julian, a Syrian from Antioch. From such beginnings was born the extraordinary religious and monastic tradition in Umbria that was to culminate with St Francis, nearly a millennium later.

St Benedict, the most significant of Umbria's early saints, was born in Norcia in 480 AD, within a few years of the deposition of the last Roman Emperor, and at the very moment that the first barbarian invaders from the north were turning towards Italy. The order he founded and the rule he drew up to guide its members were of incalculable importance in ensuring the survival of Western culture in the tumult that followed the fall of Rome. The rule aimed to move men to a perfect love of God through a combination of prayer, study and work, thus ensuring that countless monks were quietly working, studying and preserving aspects of learning that might otherwise have vanished for good.

As the **Goths** and **Huns** plundered the country, Umbria succumbed to the consequences of plague and famine. The only order in these desperate times came from the clergy, who began to take over the civic functions formerly carried out by the Roman state. Bishops took it upon themselves to become generals, frequently instigating resistance to the invaders. While on the face of things their achievements seemed negligible, in that virtually every Umbrian city was razed to the ground, they won increasing respect for themselves and the Church they represented.

After the death of their leader, Totila, at Gualdo Tadino, the Goths were replaced by the Lombards, who by 571 had established three principalities in Italy, the central one of which contained most of Umbria and had Spoleto as its capital. This Dukedom of Spoleto was to achieve great importance throughout central Italy, despite being cut off from the Lombard kingdom centred on Pavia to the north by a narrow corridor of territory controlled by the Byzantines – a ribbon of land running from the Adriatic to Rome, including Narni, Amelia, Terni and Perugia. This buffer-state remained a thorn in the

Lombards' side for three hundred years, though in Umbria it had the effect of guaranteeing the Dukedom of Spoleto considerable independence of action, a habit that in the coming years would be a hard one to break. The Lombards generally adopted the manners and customs of the local people, establishing an order which brought a short-lived increase in artistic and commercial initiative. Acknowledging the increasing growth of Christianity, they built monasteries alongside those of the Benedictines.

In 754 the growing power of the papacy as a force in Italian politics was illustrated by Pope Stephen III's appeal to the **Franks** to rid Italy of the Lombards. The Franks took up the invitation, first under Pepin the Short, and then under his more famous son, **Charlemagne**. By 800 the Lombards and Byzantines had both been driven out of the country.

Between the empire and the papacy

The papacy received great tracts of land from Charlemagne, who in return demanded that Pope Leo III crown him emperor of the new **Holy Roman Empire**. Peace reigned while Charlemagne lived, but the harmony between papacy and empire disappeared within a few years of his death. The divisions amongst his successors and their preoccupations in northern Europe again left much of Italy prey to invasion and conflict. The papacy was no healthier, weakened by the rival claims of powerful families; with no central authority, it was not long before the whole country reverted once more to chaos.

The anarchy of the next few years set the tone of events for centuries to come. Many towns and old Roman centres, such as Carsulae (near Todi), unsuited to the rigours of constant invasion and siege, were either abandoned or destroyed, to be replaced by **fortified villas** and **castles**, for which the region's hilly terrain was ideal. Around these fortresses developed independent and self-sufficient communities, creating a pattern of isolated, ambitious hilltowns, each with an eye on the territory of its neighbour.

Throughout this period Italy was the scene of a complicated, confused and constantly shifting conflict between the parties of the empire and the papacy, the **Guelphs** and **Ghibellines** (see p.739). As elsewhere, Umbrian towns frequently switched their allegiances, exacting new measures of independence from whomever ruled them at the time, in exchange for promises of loyalty. Yet of all its cities, only Perugia ever really came to merit attention on a national scale. It had become a free *comune* in 1139, owing its wealth to trade links with Rome and the burgeoning economic power of Florence, and was soon the prime mover in any machinations that affected the region as a whole.

Occasionally, however, the Umbrians were distracted from their squabbles by events taking place in the world at large. In 1152, for example, the truce between the empire and the papacy produced by the Concordat of Worms was shattered by the election of a new and ambitious emperor: Frederick Hohenstaufen. His determination to reassert the power of the empire in Italy spelt doom for the Umbrian cities, who soon had cause to fear the man better known by his Italian nickname of **Barbarossa**. As he marched south, some towns, such as Assisi, took his side while others, such as Perugia, tried to stand up to him; the majority – of which Spoleto was the most notable example – were partly or completely destroyed.

Like Charlemagne before him, Barbarossa was unable to ensure the survival of the authority he had imposed on the empire. After his death Pope Innocent III set about exploiting the anti-imperialist feeling aroused in Italy by the ferocity of his campaigns, and to ally it with the collective guilt at the capture of Jerusalem by the infidel Saladin in 1187, hoping thereby to resurrect papal fortunes. When he came to Umbria, however, he met with little success, cities such as Perugia and Spoleto being quite happy to accept new powers of autonomy, but turning obstructive when papal governors were sent to oversee them.

Medieval comunes and war lords

In 1308 the papacy moved to Avignon, and the outlook for the Church grew even more bleak from 1387 until 1417, when Europe was divided in its support for rival popes in Rome and France. The power vacuum that resulted from this **Great Schism** was the single most important factor in allowing the development of democratic comunes in central Italy. At the same time, the influence of the older noble families was eclipsed by the emergence of a mercantile class, brought to prominence by the increase and diversification of trade. With the influx of new money and new men, secular building took place on an unprecedented scale, giving the rapidly expanding cities the appearances that they have largely retained to the present day.

Liberal and sophisticated constitutions were drawn up to administer the new towns, of which **Spoleto**'s, instituted at the end of the thirteenth century, serves as a typical example. Originally civic issues were decided by a show of hands in the *arringo*, a general assembly of all adult males convoked in the central piazza. By 1296, when a new constitution was drawn up, the size of the population had made such an arrangement impracticable, and the role of the *arringo* was reduced to a body that could express opinions, but no longer take decisions. The legislative function was taken over by a General Council elected from the twelve parishes that made up Spoleto's administrative districts. Final executive and judicial power lay with the **podestà**, a kind of troubleshooter elected for a year and often brought in from outside the city – as in Tuscany. He was answerable to the **capitano del popolo**, a police chief and appeals judge who was also responsible for the day-to-day running of the administration. Below him were a host of elected minor officials, all of whom were, in the manner of contemporary Italian bureaucracy, constrained by rigid job specifications.

The theory was reasonable, but the practice was often rather different. First, the cities spent so much time arguing with their neighbours that their administrations were obliged to be almost constantly prepared for war. Second, towns were plagued by continual dissent from within as Guelphs and Ghibellines fought each other, most of them citing their allegiances to distant authority merely as an excuse to wipe out local rivals and seize power. Citizens soon came to realize that a strong executive was the only means to combat such disorder, and began to accept the domination of forceful individuals, usually the heads of the strongest **noble families** of the moment, or the person who could muster the largest private army – in most cases one and the same man.

At about the same time, other powerful individuals began to figure in Umbria's affairs: the **condottieri**, or itinerant private soldiers hired to fight battles on behalf of their citizens. Most of them were English or French refugees from the Hundred Years' War, or German and Swiss stragglers from the imperial armies. Some were astute enough to form themselves into efficient bands and soon found in Umbria a healthy market for their services. The cities were losers in every way in these contracts, wasting money on unreliable allies while property was destroyed and land plundered. Added to this, there was the everyday chaos produced by warring noble families, whose disputes were often settled in bloodshed worthy of Jacobean tragedy. Taking into account the normal range of calamities, such as plague and famine, which could strike the medieval world at any time, life in Umbria should have been intolerable.

But against this background of violence and suffering, the artistic and intellectual life of the region went from strength to strength. The same subtle changes being wrought throughout northern Italy that were to culminate in the **Renaissance** were also taking place in Umbria. In religion, St Francis had almost single-handedly revitalized man's relations to the divine. In painting, Cimabue, Giotto and their followers had introduced a naturalism that left behind the stilted beauty of the Byzantines. A university was founded in Perugia as early as 1308, and the first edition of Dante's *Divine Comedy* was printed not in Florence, but in Foligno.

Papal consolidation and the Risorgimento

Gradually the infighting exhausted the cities, and the **papacy** – which out of choice or necessity had largely stood back from the centuries of bloody disorder – seized the opportunity to exert its power. One by one the cities fell: Spoleto in 1354 to the crusading Cardinal Albornoz; Foligno in 1439, when the ruling Trinci family surrendered to soldiers of Pope Euginius V; Spello in 1535, after 150 years of despotic rule; and Gubbio in 1624, handed over to Urban VIII by the last of the ruling Montefeltro.

The old civic administrations were replaced by papal governors and for the two centuries before Unification Umbria slumbered under the rule of the Church. Although order was restored, peace and papal rule were no guarantee of prosperity. The isolation that had once served the region so well now began to tell against it. Absentee landlords – amongst whom the papacy figured large – collected rents but took little interest in land management, so that the soil deteriorated and with it the agriculture on which Umbria depended. Such industry as existed was agriculture-based and so shared in its stagnation, and in any case it was cut off from the prosperous markets to the north by poor communications. To anyone surveying the Umbrian scene at the end of the eighteenth century it would have seemed as if very little had changed in almost five hundred years.

Matters improved somewhat in the upheaval that followed the French Revolution and the rule of **Napoleon**, when the French organized the region into two districts and tried to encourage economic growth. In the more liberal atmosphere of the times, a more free-thinking class of merchants emerged, which the return of papal rule after Napoleon's death could do little to repress. By the time of the battle for the Unification of Italy, this spirit had found broader and more popular support, and Umbria welcomed **Garibaldi**'s troops into Perugia on September 11, 1860.

Unfortunately, when trade barriers between the regions were abolished the Umbrian economy was subjected to the rigours of free competition, with which it was ill-equipped to deal. Traditional craft and agricultural industries crumbled in the face of industrialization in the north. Private wealth remained idle, or was invested in the north, while the state failed to make the improvements to the region's infrastructure that might have halted the agricultural decline.

Umbria in the twentieth century

In the first years of the twentieth century the Italian economy as a whole was on an upswing, and for a while things began to look up for Umbria as well, with light industry appearing in the region for the first time. But this flicker of prosperity came to an abrupt end when the small **Banca di Perugia**, which had been largely responsible for funding the new investments, was swallowed by the Banca Commerciale, which preferred to invest in the more profitable and less risky ventures in the north.

Where the capital went, the people went too. Although in 1911 half the region's population was illiterate, they did not need education to know that their future lay outside Umbria. Thousands **emigrated** to America or to the new factories of Turin and Germany, leaving a population at home who increasingly saw socialism as the answer to the region's ills. By 1919, Umbria's scattered left-wing parties commanded 48 percent of the vote and had established control of many local and regional councils. Hopes of reform, however, were quickly dashed by the rise of Mussolini, even if the preparations for war did put some energy into the regional economy.

World War II left Umbria relatively unscathed until the German retreat up the peninsula, when the key strategic corridors – between Lago Trasimeno, Perugia and Orvieto – made it the seat of bitter fighting. Resistance groups were active in the hills above the main valleys, with the area around Gubbio seeing particularly intense partisan activity.

Postwar emigration rates were higher than ever. Only when central government devolved more power to the regions did Umbria begin to prosper. Political control by now was in the hands of the Communist Party, which carefully directed funds at co-operative ventures and projects appropriate to the region's special needs, with transport, agriculture and latterly tourism as the main priorities. Road and rail links at last provided an economic lifeline to Rome and the north.

Finally, and perhaps most importantly, the last few decades have seen the birth of what can only be described as a new pride and enthusiasm in Umbria. There is still poverty and there are still problems but there is also a powerful sense of vigour and community which seems determined to overcome them. It is a spirit that even the most casual visitor cannot fail to notice, manifestly obvious in the region's extraordinary range of cultural events, the diversity and skill of its craftspeople, the Umbrians' own obvious pride in their countryside and their heritage, and a host of more minor signs that at last point to progress.

A directory of artists and architects

Agostino di Duccio (1418–81). Born in Florence, Agostino served as a mercenary before turning to sculpture. Having possibly studied with Jacopo della Quercia, he carved the altarpiece for Modena cathedral then returned to Florence in 1442. His masterpiece is the Tempio Malatestiano in Rimini, on which Alberti and Piero della Francesca also worked. The best example in this region of his marble relief work, with its emphasis on linear grace, is the Oratorio di San Bernardino in Perugia. He returned to Florence briefly in the 1460s, a period during which he spoiled the marble block that was to become Michelangelo's *David*.

Alberti, Leon Battista (1404–72). Born illegitimately to a Florentine exile, probably in Genoa, Alberti was educated in Padua and Bologna. One of the most complete personifications of the Renaissance ideal of universal genius, he was above all a writer and theorist: his *De Re Aedificatoria* (1452) was the first architectural treatise of the Renaissance, and he also wrote a tract on the art of painting, *Della Pittura*, dedicated to his friend Brunelleschi. His theory of harmonic proportions in musical and visual forms was first put into practice in the facade of Santa Maria Novella in Florence, while his archeological interest in classical architecture found expression in the same city's Palazzo Rucellai, his first independent project. Even more closely linked to his researches into the styles of antiquity is the miniature temple built for the Rucellai family in the church of San Pancrazio. His other buildings are in Mantua and Rimini.

Albertinelli, Mariotto (1474–1515). A colleague of Fra' Bartolommeo in the workshop in San Marco, Albertinelli abandoned painting to be an innkeeper. His best work is the Uffizi *Visitation*.

Alunno, Nicolò (1430–1502). The greatest of the purely Umbrian painters before Perugino, Alunno was probably the pupil of the Venetian Carlo Crivelli, whose bright colouring and precise contours are a feature of his work. Emotionally more intense than Perugino, he usually rejects the conventional dulcet pastoralism of Umbrian art for a bleaker landscape such as that around Gubbio and Foligno.

Ammannati, Bartolomeo (1511–92). A Florentine sculptor-architect, much indebted to Michelangelo, Ammannati is best known for his additions and amendments to the Palazzo Pitti and for the graceful Ponte San Trinita (though in all likelihood this was largely designed by Michelangelo). He created the fountain in the Piazza della Signoria, with some assistance from his pupil Giambologna, and the Bargello contains some of his pieces made for the Bóboli gardens.

Andrea del Sarto (1486–1530). The dominant artist in Florence at the time of Michelangelo and Raphael's ascendancy in Rome. He made his name with frescoes for two Florentine churches in the San Marco district – the Scalzo and Santissima Annunziata. For a period in the 1510s he was in France, and the received wisdom is that his talent did not develop after that. However, two of his other major works in Florence date from after his return – the *Last Supper* in San Salvi and the *Madonna* *del Sacco* in the cloister of the Annunziata. His major easel painting is the *Madonna of the Harpies* in the Uffizi.

Arnolfo di Cambio (c.1245–1302). Pupil of Nicola Pisano, with whom he worked on sculptural projects in Bologna, Siena and Perugia before going to Rome in 1277. The most important of his independent sculptures are the pieces in Florence's Museo dell'Opera del Duomo and the *Tomb of Cardinal de Braye* in San Domenico in Orvieto. The latter defined the format of wall tombs for the next century, showing the deceased lying on a coffin below the Madonna and Child, set within an elaborate architectural framework. However, Arnolfo is best known as the architect of Florence's Duomo and Palazzo Vecchio, and various fortifications in central Tuscany, including the fortress at Poppi.

Bandinelli, Baccio (1493–1560). Born in Florence, Bandinelli trained as a goldsmith, sculptor and painter. He perceived himself as an equal talent to Michelangelo and to Cellini, his most vocal critic. Despite manifest shortcomings as a sculptor, he was given prestigious commissions by Cosimo I, the most conspicuous of which is the *Hercules and Cacus* outside the Palazzo Vecchio. Other pieces by him are in the Bargello.

Beccafumi, Domenico (1484/6–1551). The last great Sienese painter, Beccafumi was in Rome during the painting of the Sistine Chapel ceiling and Raphael's *Stanze*. He returned to Siena in 1513, when his work showed tendencies that were to become prevalent in Mannerist art – contorted poses, strong lighting, vivid artificial coloration. His decorative skill is especially evident in his illusionist frescoes in the Palazzo Pubblico and the pavement of the Duomo.

Benedetto da Maiano (1442–97). Florentine sculptor, best known for his portrait busts in the Bargello and the pulpit in Santa Croce.

Botticelli, Sandro (c.1445–1510). Possibly a pupil of Filippo Lippi, Botticelli was certainly influenced by the Pollaiuolo brothers, whose paintings of the *Virtues* he completed. The mythological paintings for which he is celebrated – including the *Birth of Venus* and *Primavera* – are distinguished by their emphasis on line rather than mass, and by their complicated symbolic meaning, a reflection on his involvement with the Neo-Platonist philosophers whom the Medici gathered about them. In the last decade of his life his devotional pictures became almost clumsily didactic – a result, perhaps, of his involvement with Savonarola and his followers.

Bronzino, Agnolo (1503–72). The adopted son of Pontormo, Bronzino became the court painter to Cosimo I. He frescoed parts of the Palazzo Vecchio for Eleanor of Toledo, but his reputation rests on his glacially elegant portraits.

Brunelleschi, Filippo (1377–1446). Trained as a sculptor and goldsmith, Brunelleschi abandoned this career after his failure in the competition for the Florence Baptistery doors. The main product of this period is his contribution to the St James altarpiece in Pistoia. He then devoted himself to the study of the building techniques of the Classical era, travelling to Rome with Donatello in 1402. In 1417 he submitted his design for the dome of Florence's Duomo, and all his subsequent work was in that city – San Lorenzo, the Spedale degli Innocenti, Cappella Pazzi (Santa Croce) and Santa Spirito. Unlike the other great architect of this period, Alberti, his work is based on no theoretical premise, but rather on an empiricist's admiration for the buildings of Rome. And unlike Alberti he oversaw every stage of construction, even devising machinery that would permit the raising of the innovative structures he had planned.

Buonarroti, Michelangelo (1475–1564). See box, p.120.

Buontalenti, Bernardo (c.1536–1608). Florentine architect, who began as a military architect to the papacy. Much of his later output was for the court of the Medici – the grotto of the Bóboli gardens, the gardens of the villa at Pratolino and tableaux for court spectaculars. Less frivolous work included the Fortezza del Belvedere, the facade of Santa Trìnita, the villa Artimino and the fortifications at Livorno.

Castagno, Andrea (c.1421–57). The early years of Castagno's life are mysterious, and the exact year of his birth is not known. Around 1440 he painted the portraits of some executed rebels in the Bargello, a job that earned him the nickname "Andrea of the Hanged Men". In 1442 he was working in Venice, but a couple of years later he was back in Florence, creating stained glass for the Duomo and frescoes for Sant'Apollonia. His taut sinewy style is to a large extent derived from the sculpture of his contemporary Donatello, an affinity that is especially clear in his frescoes for Santissima Annunziata. Other major works in Florence include the series of *Famous Men and Women* in the Uffizi and the portrait of *Niccolò da Tolentino* in the Duomo – his last piece.

Cellini, Benvenuto (1500–71). Cellini began his career in Rome, where he fought in the siege of the city by the imperial army in 1527. His sculpture is greatly influenced by Michelangelo, as is evident in his most famous large-scale piece, the *Perseus* in the Loggia della Signoria. His other masterpiece in Florence is the heroic *Bust of Cosimo I* in the Bargello. Cellini was an even more accomplished goldsmith and jeweller, creating some exquisite pieces for Francis I, by whom he was employed in the 1530s and 1540s. He also wrote a racy *Autobiography*, a fascinating insight into the artistic world of sixteenth-century Italy and France.

Cimabue (c.1240–1302). Though celebrated by Dante as the foremost painter of the generation before Giotto, very little is known about Cimabue – in fact, the only work that is definitely by him is the mosaic in Pisa's Duomo. He is generally given credit for the softening of the hieratic Byzantine style of religious art, a tendency carried further by his putative pupil, Giotto. Some works can be attributed to him with more confidence than others; the shortlist would include *The Madonna of St Francis* in the lower church at Assisi, the *Passion* cycle in the upper church, the *Maestà* in the Uffizi and the crucifixes in Santa Croce (Florence) and San Domenico (Arezzo).

Civitali, Matteo (1436–1501). Probably self-taught sculptor from Lucca, where all his important work is to be found.

Daddi, Bernardo (c.1290–1349). A pupil of Giotto, Daddi combined the solidity of his master's style with the more decorative aspects of the Sienese style. His work can be seen in the Uffizi and Santa Croce in Florence.

Desiderio da Settignano (c.1428–64). Desiderio continued the low relief technique pioneered by Donatello in the panel for the Orsanmichele *St George*, and carved the tomb of Carlo Marsuppini in Santa Croce, Florence. Better known for his exquisite busts of women and children, a good selection of which are on show in the Bargello.

Donatello (c.1386–1466). A pupil of Ghiberti, Donatello assisted in the casting of the first set of Florence

Baptistery doors in 1403, then worked for Nanni di Banco on the Duomo. His early marble *David* (Bargello) is still Gothic in its form, but a new departure is evident in his heroic *St Mark* for Orsanmichele (1411) – possibly produced after a study of the sculpture of ancient Rome. Four years later he began the intense series of prophets for the Campanile, and at the same time produced the *St George* for Orsanmichele, the epitome of early Renaissance humanism, featuring a relief that is the very first application of rigorous perspective in Western art.

In the mid-1420s Donatello started a partnership with Michelozzo, with whom he created the tomb of Pope John XXIII in the Florence Baptistery, a refinement of the genre initiated by Arnolfo di Cambio. He went to Rome in 1431, possibly with Brunelleschi, and it was probably on his return that he made the classical bronze *David* (Bargello), one of the first nude statues of the Renaissance period. Also at this time he made the *cantoria* to be placed opposite the one already made by Luca della Robbia, the pulpit for Prato cathedral (with Michelozzo) and the decorations for the old sacristy in Florence's church of San Lorenzo – the parish church of his great patrons, the Medici.

After a period in Padua – where he created the first bronze equestrian statue since Roman times – he returned to Florence, where his last works show an extraordinary harshness and angularity. The main sculptures from this period are the *Judith and Holofernes* (Palazzo Vecchio), the *Magdalene* (Museo dell'Opera del Duomo) and the two bronze pulpits for San Lorenzo.

Duccio di Buoninsegna (c.1255–1318). Though occupying much the same pivotal position in the history of Sienese art as Giotto does in Florentine art, Duccio was a less revolutionary figure, refining the stately Byzantine tradition rather than subverting its conventions. One of his earliest works was ordered by Florence's church of Santa Maria Novella – the *Maestà* now in the Uffizi – but the bulk of his output is in his home city. Despite frequent ructions with the civic authorities, for refusing to do military service among other transgressions, in 1308 he received his most prestigious assignment, the painting of a *Maestà* for Siena's Duomo. The polyptych no longer exists in its original form, but most of the panels are now in Siena's Museo dell'Opera del Duomo. This iconic image of the Madonna, with its rich use of gold and decorative colour, was to profoundly influence such painters as the Lorenzettis and Simone Martini, while the small scenes on the back of the panels reveal a less frequently acknowledged mastery of narrative painting.

Fra' Angelico (1387/1400–55). Born in Vicchio, Fra' Angelico joined the Dominican order in Fiesole, near his home town, and later entered their monasteries in Cortona and Foligno. His first authenticated painting dates from the mid-1420s, but the first one that can be definitively dated is a *Madonna* he produced for the linen guild of Florence in 1433. Three years later the Dominicans took over the San Marco monastery in Florence, and soon after he embarked on the series of frescoes and altarpieces now displayed in the museum there. In the mid-1440s he was called to Rome to work on the Vatican, after which he worked at Orvieto, served for three years as prior of the monastery in Fiesole, and returned to Rome around 1452, where he died.

Fra' Bartolommeo (c.1474–1517). Fra' Bartolommeo's earliest known work is the Raphael-influenced *Last Judgement* painted for the San Marco monastery in Florence in 1499. The following year he became a monk there, then in 1504 became head of the workshop, a post previously occupied by Fra' Angelico. In 1514 he was in Rome, but according to Vasari was discouraged by Raphael's fame. The works he later produced in Florence had an influence on High Renaissance art, with their repression of elaborate backgrounds and anecdotal detail, concentrating instead on expression and gesture.

Francesco di Giorgio Martini (1439–1501/2). Sienese painter, sculptor and architect, whose treatise on architectural theory was circulated widely in manuscript form; Leonardo had a copy. Employed for a long period by Federico da Montefeltro – also a patron of Piero della Francesca – he probably designed the loggia for the Palazzo Ducale in Urbino and the church of San Bernardino. The church of Santa Maria degli Angeli in Siena and the Palazzo Ducale in Gubbio might be by him; the one Tuscan building that was certainly designed by him is Santa Maria del Calcinaio in Cortona, one of the finest early Renaissance structures in Italy.

Gaddi, Taddeo (d.1366). According to tradition, Taddeo Gaddi worked with Giotto for 24 years, and throughout his life barely wavered from the precepts of his master's style. His first major independent work is the cycle for the Cappella Baroncelli in Santa Croce, Florence. Other works by him are in Florence's Uffizi, Accademia, Bargello and Museo Horne. **Agnolo Gaddi** (d.1396), Taddeo's son, continued his father's Giottesque style; his major projects were for Santa Croce in Florence and the Duomo of Prato.

Gentile da Fabriano (c.1370–1427). Chief exponent of the International Gothic style in Italy, Gentile da Fabriano came to Florence in 1422, when he painted the gorgeous *Adoration of the Magi* now in the Uffizi. In 1425 he went on to Siena

and Orvieto, where the intellectual climate was perhaps more conducive than that in the Florence of Masaccio; he finished his career in Rome.

Ghiberti, Lorenzo (1378–1455). Trained as a goldsmith, painter and sculptor, Ghiberti concentrated on the last discipline almost exclusively after winning the competition to design the doors for Florence's Baptistery. His first set of doors are to a large extent derived from Andrea Pisano's earlier Gothic panels for the building, yet his workshop was a virtual academy for the seminal figures of the early Florentine Renaissance, Donatello and Uccello among them. The commission took around twenty years to complete, during which time he also worked on the Siena Baptistery and the church of Orsanmichele in Florence, where his Baptist and St Matthew show the influence of classical statuary. This classicism reached its peak in the second set of doors for Florence's Baptistery (the Gates of Paradise) – taking the innovations of Donatello's low relief carving to a new pitch of perfection. The panels occupied much of the rest of his life but in his final years he wrote his *Commentarii*, the main source of information on fourteenth-century art in Florence and Siena, and the first autobiography by an artist.

Ghirlandaio, Domenico (1449–94). The most accomplished fresco artist of his generation, Ghirlandaio was the teacher of Michelangelo. After a short period working on the Sistine Chapel with Botticelli, he came back to Florence, where his cycles in Santa Trinita and Santa Maria Novella provide some of the most absorbing documentary images of the time, being filled with contemporary portraits and vivid anecdotal details.

Giambologna (1529–1608). Born in northern France, Giambologna – Jean de Boulogne – arrived in Italy in the mid-1550s, becoming the most influential Florentine sculptor after Michelangelo's death. Having helped Ammannati on the fountain for the Piazza della Signoria, he went on to produce a succession of pieces that typify the Mannerist predilection for sculptures with multiple viewpoints, such as the *Rape of the Sabines* (Loggia della Signoria) and the *Mercury* (Bargello). His workshop also turned out scores of reduced bronze copies of his larger works; the Bargello has an extensive collection.

Giotto di Bondone (1267–1337). It was with Giotto's great fresco cycles that religious art shifted from being a straightforward act of devotion to the dramatic presentation of incident. His unerring eye for the significant gesture, his ability to encapsulate moments of extreme emotion and his technical command of figure modelling and spatial depth brought him early recognition as the greatest artist of his generation – and even as late as the sixteenth century artists were studying his frescoes for their solutions to certain compositional problems. Yet, as with Cimabue, the precise attribution of work is problematic. In all probability his first major cycle was the *Life of St Francis* in the upper church at Assisi, though the extent to which his assistants carried out his designs is still disputed. The Arena chapel in Padua is certainly by him, as are large parts of the Bardi and Peruzzi chapels in Santa Croce in Florence. Of his attributed panel paintings, the Uffizi *Maestà* is the only one universally accepted.

Gozzoli, Benozzo (1421–97). Though a pupil of Fra' Angelico, Gozzoli was one of the more worldly artists of the fifteenth century, with a fondness for pageantry that is seen to most impressive effect in the frescoes in Florence's Palazzo Medici-Ricardi. His celebrated cycle in Pisa's Camposanto was all but destroyed in World War II; his other surviving fresco cycles include the *Life of St Francis* in Montefalco and the *Life of St Augustine* in San Gimignano.

Guido da Siena (active mid-thirteenth century). Guido was the founder of the Sienese school of painters, but his life is one of the most problematic areas of Siena's art history. A signed painting by him in the Palazzo Pubblico is dated 1221, but some experts think that the date may have been altered, and that the work is from the 1260s or 1270s – a period when other pictures associated with him are known to have been painted.

Leonardo da Vinci (1452–1519). Leonardo trained as a painter under Verrocchio, and it is said that his precocious talent caused his master to abandon painting in favour of sculpture. Drawings of landscapes and drapery have survived from the 1470s, but the first completed picture is the *Annunciation* in the Uffizi. The sketch of the *Adoration of the Magi*, also in the Uffizi, dates from 1481, at which time there was no precedent for its fusion of geometric form and dynamic action. Two years later he was in the employment of Lodovico Sforza of Milan, remaining there for sixteen years. During this second phase of his career he produced the *Lady with the Ermine* (Kraków), the fresco of the *Last Supper* and – probably – the two versions of *The Virgin of the Rocks*, the fullest demonstrations to date of his so-called sfumato, a blurring of tones from light to dark. Innumerable scientific studies and military projects engaged him at this time, and he also made a massive clay model for an equestrian statue of Francesco Sforza – never completed, like so many of his schemes.

When the French took Milan in 1499 Leonardo returned to Florence, where he devoted much of his time to anatomical researches. It was during this second Florentine period that he was commissioned to paint a fresco of the *Battle of Anghiari* in the main hall of the Palazzo Ducale, where his detested rival Michelangelo was also set to work. Only a fragment of the fresco was completed, and the innovative technique that Leonardo had employed resulted in its speedy disintegration. His cartoons for the *Madonna and Child with St Anne* (Louvre and National Gallery, London) also date from this period, as does the most famous of all his paintings, the Louvre's *Mona Lisa*, the portrait of the wife of a Florentine merchant. In 1506 he went back to Milan, thence to Rome and finally, in 1517, to France. Again, military and scientific work occupied much of this last period – the only painting to have survived is the *St John*, also in the Louvre.

Lippi, Filippo (c.1406–69). In 1421 Filippo Lippi was placed in the monastery of the Carmine in Florence, just at the time Masaccio was beginning work on the Cappella Brancacci there. His early works all bear the stamp of Masaccio, but by the 1430s he was becoming interested in the representation of movement and a more luxuriant surface detail. The frescoes in the cathedral at Prato, executed in the 1450s, show his highly personal, almost hedonistic vision, as do his panel paintings of wistful Madonnas in patrician interiors or soft landscapes – many of them executed for the Medici. His last work, the *Life of the Virgin* fresco cycle in Spoleto, was probably largely executed by assistants.

Lippi, Filippino (1457/8–1504). The son of Filippo completed his father's work in Spoleto – aged

about 12 – then travelled to Florence, where his first major commission was the completion of Masaccio's frescoes in Santa Maria del Carmine (c.1484). At around this time he also painted the *Vision of St Bernard* for the Badìa, which shows an affinity with Botticelli, with whom he is known to have worked. His later researches in Rome led him to develop a self-consciously antique style – seen at its most ambitious in Santa Maria Novella.

Lippo Memmi (d.1357). Brother-in-law of Simone Martini, Lippo Memmi was his assistant on the Uffizi *Annunciation*. His major work is the *Maestà* in the Palazzo Pubblico in San Gimignano, and he may also have been responsible for the dramatic New Testament frescoes in the Collegiata of the same town.

Lorenzetti, Ambrogio (active 1319–47). Though Sienese, Ambrogio spent part of the 1320s and 1330s in Florence, where he would have witnessed the decoration of Santa Croce by Giotto and his pupils. He's best known for the *Allegory of Good and Bad Government* in the Palazzo Pubblico, which shows painting being used for a secular, didactic purpose for the first time. The Uffizi *Presentation of the Virgin* highlights the difference between Ambrogio's inventive complexity and the comparative simplicity of his brother's style (see below). There's a fine altarpiece by him in Massa Maríttima as well.

Lorenzetti, Pietro (active 1306–48). Brother of Ambrogio, Pietro Lorenzetti was possibly a pupil of Duccio's in Siena. His first authenticated work is the altarpiece in Arezzo's Pieve di Santa Maria (1320); others include frescoes in Assisi's lower church, in which the impact of Giotto is particularly noticeable, and the *Birth of the Virgin* in Siena's Museo dell'Opera del Duomo, one of the best demonstrations of his skill as a narrative painter. It's probable that both the Lorenzettis died during the Black Death.

Lorenzo Monaco (1372–1425). A Sienese artist, Lorenzo Monaco joined the Camaldolese monastery in Florence, for which he painted the *Coronation of the Virgin*, now in the Uffizi. This and his other earlier works are fairly conventional Sienese-style altarpieces, with two-dimensional figures on gold backgrounds. However, his late *Adoration of the Magi* (Uffizi), with its fastidious detailing and landscape backdrop, anticipates the arrival of Gentile da Fabriano and fully fledged International Gothic.

Lo Spagna (1450–1528). Possibly of Spanish origin – hence the name – Lo Spagna spent much of his life in Umbria. Like many of his contemporaries he came under the influence of Raphael, who spent at least five of his formative years in the region.

Maitini, Lorenzo (c.1270–1330). Sienese architect and sculptor, Maitini was the only local artist to challenge the supremacy of the Pisani. In 1310 he was made supervisor of Orvieto's Duomo, for which he designed the biblical panels of the facade – though it's not certain how much of the carving was actually by Maitini. Virtually nothing else about him is known.

Martini, Simone (c.1284–1344). The most important Sienese painter, Simone Martini was a pupil of Duccio but equally influenced by Giovanni Pisano's sculpture and the carvings of French Gothic artists. He began his career by painting a fresco counterpart of Duccio's *Maestà* in the city's Palazzo Pubblico (1315). Soon after he was employed by Robert of Anjou, King of Naples, and there developed a sinuous, graceful and courtly style. In the late 1320s he was back in Siena, where he probably produced the portrait of Guidoriccio

da Fogliano – though some experts doubt its authenticity. At some point he went to Assisi, where he painted a cycle of *The Life of St Martin* in the lower church. In 1333 he produced a sumptuous *Annunciation* for the Siena Duomo; now in the Uffizi, this is the quintessential fourteenth-century Sienese painting, with its immaculately crafted gold surfaces and emphasis on fluid outline and bright coloration. In 1340 Martini travelled to the papal court of Avignon, where he spent the rest of his life. It was at Avignon that he formed a friendship with Petrarch, for whom he illustrated a magnificent copy of Virgil's poetry.

Masaccio (1401–28). Born just outside Florence, Tomasso di se Giovanni di Mone Cassai – universally known as Masaccio – entered the city's painters' guild in 1422. His first large commission was an altarpiece for the Carmelites of Pisa (the central panel is now in the National Gallery in London), which shows a massive grandeur at odds with the International Gothic style then being promulgated in Florence by Gentile da Fabriano. His masterpieces – the *Trinity* fresco in Santa Maria Novella and the fresco cycle in Santa Maria del Carmine – were produced in the last three years of his life, the latter being painted in collaboration with Masolino. With the architecture of Brunelleschi and the sculpture of Donatello, the Carmine frescoes are the most important achievements of the early Renaissance.

Maso di Banco (active 1340s). Maso was perhaps the most inventive of Giotto's acolytes, and his reputation depends chiefly on the cycle of the *Life of St Sylvester* in Santa Croce, Florence.

Masolino da Panicale (1383–1447). Masolino was employed in Ghiberti's workshop for the production of the first set of baptistery doors, and the semi-Gothic early style of Ghiberti conditioned much of his subsequent work. His other great influence was the younger Masaccio, with whom he worked on the Brancacci chapel.

Michelangelo (1475–1564). See box, p.120.

Michelozzo di Bartolommeo (1396–1472). Born in Florence, Michelozzo worked in Ghiberti's studio and collaborated with Donatello before turning exclusively to architecture. His main patrons were the Medici, for whom he altered the villa at Careggi and built the Palazzo Medici, which set a prototype for patrician mansions in the city. He later designed the Villa Medici at Fiesole for the family, and for Cosimo de' Medici he added the light and airy library to the monastery of San Marco. In the Alberti-influenced tribune for the church of Santissima Annunziata, Michelozzo produced the first centrally planned church design to be built in the Renaissance period.

Mino da Fiesole (1429–84). Florentine sculptor, perhaps a pupil of Desiderio da Settignano, Mino is known chiefly for his tombs and portrait busts; there are examples of the former in Fiesole's Duomo and the Badìa in Florence, and of the latter in the Bargello.

Nanni di Banco (c.1384–1421). A Florentine sculptor who began his career as an assistant to his father on the Florence Duomo, Nanni was an exact contemporary of Donatello, with whom he shared some early commissions: Donatello's first *David* was ordered at the same time as an *Isaiah* from Nanni. The finest works produced in his short life are his niche sculptures at Orsanmichele (especially the *Four Saints*) and the relief above the Duomo's Porta della Mandorla.

Nelli, Ottaviano (active 1400–44). The artist who brought the International Gothic style to Umbria; his intricate and glittering paintings can be seen in Foligno, Assisi and Gubbio.

Odersi, or Oderigi (1240–99). The founder of the Umbrian school, little is known of Odersi except that he was a friend of Giotto and worked mainly in Gubbio. A handful of his miniatures survive, though Dante called him *l'onor d'Agobbio* ("the pride of Gubbio") and stuck him in Purgatory as punishment for an obsession with art that left him no time for anything else.

Orcagna, Andrea (c.1308–68). Architect-sculptor-painter, Orcagna was a dominant figure in the period following the death of Giotto, whose emphasis on spatial depth he rejected – as shown in his only authenticated panel painting, the Strozzi altarpiece in Santa Maria Novella. Damaged frescoes can be seen in Santa Croce and Santo Spirito, but Florence's principal work by Orcagna is the massive tabernacle in Orsanmichele. Orcagna's brothers Nardo and Jacopo di Cione were the most influential painters in Florence at the close of the fourteenth century: the frescoes in the Strozzi chapel are by Nardo.

Perugino (1445/50–1523). Born Pietro di Cristoforo Vannucci in Città della Pieve, Perugino was the greatest Umbrian artist. Possibly a pupil of Piero della Francesca, he later trained in Florence in the workshop of Andrea Verrocchio, studying alongside Leonardo da Vinci. By 1480 his reputation was such that he was invited to paint in the Sistine Chapel, filling the east wall with his distinctive gently melancholic figures; today only one of Perugino's original three panels remains. In 1500 he executed his greatest work in Umbria, a fresco cycle commissioned by the bankers' guild of Perugia for their Collegio di Cambio. This was probably the first occasion on which he was assisted by his pupil Raphael – and the moment his own career began to wane. Vasari claimed that he was "a man of little or no religion, who could never bring himself to believe in the immortality of the soul", and the production-line altarpieces that his workshop later turned out were often lacking in genuine passion. Yet he was still amongst the most influential of the Renaissance painters, the catalyst for Raphael and mentor for a host of Umbrian artists. In Tuscany he is best seen in the Uffizi and in the church of Santa Maria Maddalena dei Pazzi.

Piero della Francesca (1410/20–1492). Piero was born in Borgo Sansepolcro, on the border of Tuscany and Umbria. In the late 1430s he was in Florence, working with Domenico Veneziano, and his later work shows the influence of such Florentine contemporaries as Castagno and Uccello, as well as the impact of Masaccio's frescoes. The exact chronology of his career is contentious, but much of his working life was spent in his native town, for which he produced the *Madonna della Misericordia* and the *Resurrection*, both now in the local Museo Civico. Other patrons included Sigismondo Malatesta of Rimini and Federico da Montefeltro of Urbino, of whom there's a portrait by Piero in the Uffizi. In the 1450s he was in Arezzo, working on the fresco cycle in the church of San Francesco, the only frescoes in Tuscany that can bear comparison with the Masaccio cycle in Florence. He seems to have stopped painting completely in the early 1470s, perhaps to concentrate on his vastly influential treatises on perspective and geometry, but more likely because of failing eyesight.

Piero di Cosimo (c.1462–1521). One of the more enigmatic figures of the High Renaissance, Piero di Cosimo shared Leonardo's scholarly interest in the natural world but turned his knowledge to the production of allusive mythological paintings. There are pictures by him in the Uffizi, Palazzo Pitti, Museo degli Innocenti and Museo Horne.

Pietro da Cortona (1596–1669). Painter-architect, born Pietro Berrettini, who with Bernini was the guiding force of Roman Baroque. The style was introduced to Florence by Pietro's ceiling frescoes in the Palazzo Pitti. His last painting is in his home town.

Pinturicchio (1454–1513). Born Bernardino di Betto in Perugia, Pinturicchio was taught by Perugino, with whom he collaborated on the painting of the Sistine Chapel. His rich palette earned him his nickname, as well as Vasari's condemnation for superficiality. Most of his work is in Rome but his last commission, one of his most ambitious projects, was his *Life of Pius II* for the Libreria Piccolomini in Siena.

Pisano, Andrea (c.1290–1348). Nothing is known of Andrea Pisano's life until 1330, when he was given the commission to make a new set of doors for the Florence Baptistery. He then succeeded Giotto as master mason of the Campanile; the set of reliefs he produced for it are the only other works definitely by him (now in the Museo dell'Opera del Duomo). In 1347 he became the supervisor of Orvieto's Duomo, a job later held by his sculptor son, Nino.

Pisano, Nicola (c.1220–84). Born somewhere in the southern Italian kingdom of the emperor Frederick II, Nicola Pisano was the first great classicizing sculptor in pre-Renaissance Italy; the pulpit in Pisa's Baptistery (1260), his first masterpiece, shows clearly the influence of Roman figures. Five years later he produced the pulpit for the Duomo in Siena, with the assistance of his son **Giovanni** (c.1248–1314) and Arnolfo di Cambio. Father and son again worked together on the Fonte Gaia in Perugia, which was Nicola's last major project. Giovanni's more turbulent Gothic-influenced style is seen in two other pulpits, for San Andrea in Pistoia and for the Pisa Duomo. The Museo dell'Opera del Duomo in Siena has some fine large-scale figures by Giovanni, while its counterpart in Pisa contains a large collection of work by both the Pisani.

Pollaiuolo, Antonio del (c.1432–98) and **Piero del** (c.1441–96). Though their Florence workshop turned out engravings, jewellery and embroideries, the Pollaiuolo brothers were known mainly for their advances in oil-painting technique and for their anatomical researches, which bore fruit in paintings and small-scale bronze sculptures. The influences of Donatello and Castagno (Piero's teacher) are evident in their dramatic, often violent work, which is especially well represented in the Bargello. The Uffizi's collection of paintings suggests that Antonio was by far the more skilled artist.

Pontormo, Jacopo (1494–1556). Born near Empoli, Jacopo Carrucci – better known as Pontormo after his native village – was successively a pupil of Leonardo da Vinci, Piero di Cosimo and Andrea del Sarto, and became a crucial figure in the evolution of the hyper-refined Mannerist style. It was through del Sarto that he received one of his earliest independent commissions, for The Visitation in the atrium of Santissima Annunziata in Florence, where del Sarto had already completed several frescoes. Begun when Pontormo was only 20, The Visitation displays an eccentric quality – notably in the foreground figure of the sunbathing boy – that was always to be characteristic of him, and evidently appealed to many: in the early 1520s he was hired by the Medici to decorate part of their

villa at Poggio a Caiano, then executed a Passion cycle for the Certosa, to the south of the city, after which he painted what is generally regarded as his masterpiece: the Deposition in Santa Felicita. The major project of his later years, a fresco cycle of the Last Judgement, painted in the chancel of San Lorenzo, has been totally destroyed, but other paintings by him can be seen in the Uffizi, at Carmignano and at Sansepolcro..

Quercia, Jacopo della (1374–1438). A Sienese contemporary of Donatello and Ghiberti, della Quercia entered the competition for the Florence Baptistery doors which Ghiberti won in 1401. The first known work by him is the tomb of Ilaria del Carretto in Lucca's Duomo. His next major commission was a fountain for Siena's main square, a piece now reassembled in the loggia of the Palazzo Pubblico; before that was finished (1419) he had begun work on a set of reliefs for Siena's Baptistery, a project to which Ghiberti and Donatello also contributed. From 1425 he expended much of his energy on reliefs for San Petronio in Bologna – so much so, that the Sienese authorities ordered him to return some of the money he had been paid for the baptistery job.

Raphael (1483–1520). With Leonardo and Michelangelo, Raphael (Raffaello) Sanzio forms the triumvirate whose works define the essence of the High Renaissance. Born in Urbino, he joined Perugino's workshop some time around 1494 and within five years was receiving commissions independently of his master. From 1505 to 1508 he was in Florence, where he absorbed the compositional and tonal innovations of Leonardo; many of the pictures he produced at that time are now in the Palazzo Pitti. From Florence he went to Rome, where Pope Julius II set him to work on the papal apartments

C

(the Stanze). Michelangelo's Sistine ceiling was largely instrumental in modulating Raphael's style from its earlier lyrical grace into something more monumental, but all the works from this more rugged later period are in Rome.

Robbia, Luca della (1400–82). Luca began as a sculptor in conventional materials, his earliest achievement being the marble *cantoria* (choir gallery) now in the Museo dell'Opera del Duomo in Florence, typifying the cheerful tone of most of his work. Thirty years later he made the sacristy doors for this city's Duomo, but by then he had devised a technique for applying durable potter's glaze to clay sculpture and most of his energies were given to the art of glazed terra-cotta. His distinctive blue, white and yellow compositions are seen at their best in the Pazzi chapel in Santa Croce, the Bargello, and at Impruneta,

What is the Renaissance?

In the middle of the sixteenth century Giorgio Vasari coined the term *Rinascenza* (rebirth) to designate the period that stretched from around 1300 (when Giotto was active) to the time of Michelangelo. In the late nineteenth century the term "Renaissance" entered general usage, largely thanks to the writings of Jacob Burckhardt, whose book *The Civilization of the Renaissance in Italy* (published in German in 1860, and in English translation in 1878) is perhaps the single most influential study of the subject. To historians of this period, the Renaissance was often seen as a singular and all-pervasive phenomenon, in which the rediscovery of ancient classical culture gave impetus to a regeneration of European civilization after the intellectual impoverishment of the Middle Ages. It was characterized by its focus on humanity, and the epicentre of this explosion of humanist art and scholarship was Florence.

While nobody doubts that many of the artists, writers and patrons of Renaissance Italy believed themselves to be participants in the creation of a new society, it's debatable that "Renaissance values" reached deeply into the lives of most ordinary people. For the general populace, life continued to be "medieval" long after their masters had taken to reading Plato. Not only was a peasant's existence as harsh as ever, but there can have been few more dangerous periods in Italian history than the so-called "High Renaissance". From 1494 to 1559 the peninsula was an almost continuous battleground for the major powers of Europe, and at the end of this period, with Habsburgs as the dominant force, most of the Italian city-states were reduced to the ranks of bit-players.

The problem of beginnings

Locating the beginnings of the Italian Renaissance is a problematic business. Giotto (1267–1337) is often taken as a starting point, and when his paintings are compared to the art of the "Gothic" era, it does seem as if he introduced a new realism and drama to European art. His great contemporary Dante (1265–1321), who presents Giotto as an innovator in the *Divine Comedy*, appears modern in his use of vernacular Tuscan rather than Latin. On the other hand, the stern theology of Dante's master-piece strikes us as belonging to a distinctly pre-modern world.

Dante's immediate successors, Petrarch (1304–1374) and Boccaccio (1313–75) – both of them Tuscans – certainly feel more modern than he does. Petrarch's love poetry, his collecting of classical manuscripts and his appreciation of landscape for itself might be described as manifestations of a Renaissance spirit. Similarly, Boccaccio's *Decameron* has a claim to be the first example of modern prose fiction. And yet in the visual arts it can seem that in the century after Giotto painting didn't change enough to support the idea that his work initiated an unstoppable process. It wasn't until Masaccio's frescoes in the Brancacci chapel, painted a hundred years after Giotto's in Santa Croce, that Italian art could be said to have taken its next leap forward.

just outside Florence. The best work of his nephew, **Andrea della Robbia** (1435–1525), who continued the lucrative terracotta business, is at the Spedale degli Innocenti in Florence and at the monastery of La Verna. **Giovanni della Robbia** (1469–1529), son of Andrea, is best known for the frieze of the Ceppo in Pistoia.

Rossellino, Bernardo (1409–64). An architect-sculptor, Rossellino worked with Alberti and carried out his plans for the Palazzo Rucellai in Florence. His major architectural commission was Pius II's new town of Pienza. As a sculptor he's best known for the monument to Leonardo Bruni in Santa Croce – a derivative of Donatello's tomb of John XXIII in the baptistery. His brother and pupil Antonio (1427–79) produced the tomb of the Cardinal of Portugal in Florence's San Miniato al Monte, and a number of excellent

The case of Florence

If it's impossible to say exactly where and when the Renaissance begins, there's no doubt that the high culture of Florence (and most of Italy) in 1500 was radically different from that of 1300. Furthermore, Florence in the fifteenth century nurtured more of these "avant garde" figures than any other city in Italy. But what were the circumstances that made Florence the pre-eminent centre of creativity?

A primary factor was the city's wealth. Buoyed by revenues from banking and manufacture, the Florentine upper classes had plenty of surplus cash with which to fund the accumulation of libraries and art collections. Competing against each other in displays of educated taste, clans such as the Strozzi, the Medici, the Rucellai and the Tornabuoni were furthering a Florentine self-image that can be traced back at least as far as Giovanni Villani (1275–1348), author of a twelve-volume history of the city (written in Tuscan), in which he wrote that Florence, "the daughter and offspring of Rome, is on the increase and destined to do great things."

Even before Villani, Florence had something of a humanist tradition. Dante's teacher, Brunetto Latini (c.1210–94), for instance, studied Aristotle and Cicero, wrote in the vernacular (both Italian and French) and with his *Livre du trésor* produced what might be called the first encyclopedia. A century later, Florence's university invited Manuel Chrysoloras (c.1350–1415) to travel from Constantinople to teach Greek – the first time for seven hundred years that the language had been taught in Italy. Chrysoloras translated Plato and Homer, wrote about the monuments of Rome and Byzantium, and numbered among his pupils Leonardo Bruni – chancellor of the Florentine Republic, author of the *History of the Florentine People* and books on Dante, Petrarch and Boccaccio, translator of Plato and Aristotle, and the first scholar to define his work as *studia humanitatis*.

In 1439 the Council of Florence – convened to forge a reconciliation between the Roman and Eastern churches – brought a host of classical scholars to the city, some of whom remained in Florence, to be joined after 1453 by others who fled from Constantinople following its conquest by the Turks. These refugees further enriched an environment in which developed so many great artists and such prodigious philosopher scholars as Marsilio Ficino, Poliziano and Pico della Mirandola, all of whom were members of the Medici court.

But while Botticelli's *Birth of Venus* or Michelangelo's *David* unarguably embody something new, Renaissance philosophy was essentially an elaboration of the work of ancient thinkers – of Plato in particular. For all their learning, Ficino and the rest produced nothing to equal the originality of medieval philosophers such as Thomas Aquinas or Duns Scotus.

portrait busts (Bargello).

Rosso Fiorentino (1494–1540).
Like Pontormo, Rosso Fiorentino
was a pupil of Andrea del Sarto, but
went on to develop a far more
aggressive, acidic style than his
colleague and friend. His early
Deposition in Volterra (1521) and the
roughly contemporaneous *Moses
Defending the Daughters of Jethro*
(Uffizi) are typical of his extreme
foreshortening and tense deployment
of figures. After a period in Rome
and Venice, he eventually went to
France, where with Primaticcio he
developed the distinctive Mannerist
art of the Fontainebleau school.

Sangallo, Antonio da, the Elder
(1455–1534). A Florence-born
architect, Antonio da Sangallo the
Elder produced just one major
building, but one of the most influential of his period – San Biagio in
Montepulciano, based on Bramante's
plan for St Peter's in Rome. His
nephew, **Antonio the Younger**
(1485–1546), was also born in
Florence but did most of his work in
Rome, where he began his career as
assistant first to Bramante then to
Peruzzi. He went on to design the
Palazzo Farnese, the most spectacular
Roman palace of its time. In Tuscany
his most important building is the
Fortezza da Basso in Florence.

Giuliano da Sangallo (1445–1516),
sculptor, architect and military
engineer, was the brother of Antonio
the Elder. A follower of Brunelleschi,
he produced a number of buildings
in and around Florence – the Villa
Medici at Poggio a Caiano, Santa
Maria delle Carceri in Prato (the first
Renaissance church to have a Greek-
cross plan) and the Palazzo Strozzi,
the most ambitious palace of the
century.

Sassetta (c.1392–1450). Sassetta was
basically a conventional Sienese
painter, though his work does show
the influence of International Gothic.
Works by him are on show in Siena,
Assisi and the Uffizi.

Signorelli, Luca (1450–1523).
Though a pupil of Piero della
Francesca, Signorelli is more indebted
to the muscular drama of the
Pollaiuolo brothers and the gestural
vocabulary developed by Donatello.
In the early 1480s he was probably
working on the Sistine Chapel with
Perugino and Botticelli, but his most
important commission came in 1499,
when he was hired to complete the
cycle begun by Fra' Angelico in
Orvieto's Duomo. The emphasis on
the nude figure in his *Last Judgement*
was to greatly affect Michelangelo.
Shortly after finishing this cycle he
went to Rome but the competition
from Raphael and Michelangelo
drove him back to his native
Cortona, where he set up a highly
proficient workshop. Works are to be
seen in Cortona, Arezzo, Monte
Oliveto, Perugia, Sansepolcro and in
the Uffizi and Museo Horne in
Florence.

Sodoma, Il (1477–1549). After
training in Milan (where he became
familiar with the work of Leonardo
da Vinci) and Siena, Giovanni
Antonio Bazzi was taken to Rome
by the Sienese banker Agostino
Chigi in 1508. Having failed to make
much of an impact there (he began
work on the papal apartments but
was replaced by Raphael), he
returned to Siena, where he married
in 1510. Though Siena was his base
for the rest of his life, his work took
him to various Italian cities, notably
Florence, Lucca, Pisa and Volterra; his
major creation in Tuscany is his
fresco cycle at the monastery of
Monte Oliveto Maggiore, begun
immediately before his sojourn in
Rome. Vasari states that the nickname
by which he's always known came
about because he "loved small boys
more than was decent", but it's
possible that it was a joke of Bazzi's
own devising – and it seems unlikely

that he would have received as many church commissions as he did if his proclivities were as Vasari said.

Spinello Aretino (active 1370s–1410). Probably born in Arezzo, Spinello studied in Florence, possibly under Agnolo Gaddi. He harks back to the monumental aspects of Giotto's style – thus paradoxically paving the way for the most radical painter of the next generation, Masaccio. His main works are in Florence's church of San Miniato al Monte and Santa Caterina d'Antella, just to the south of the city.

Uccello, Paolo (1396–1475). After training in Ghiberti's workshop, Uccello went to Venice, where he worked on mosaics for the Basilica di San Marco. He returned to Florence in 1431 and five years later was contracted to paint the commemorative portrait of Sir John Hawkwood in the Duomo. This *trompe l'oeil* painting is the first evidence of his interest in the problems of perspective and foreshortening, a subject that was later to obsess him. After an interlude in Padua, he painted the frescoes for the cloister of Santa Maria Novella (c.1445), in which his systematic but non-naturalistic use of perspective is seen at its most extreme. In the following decade he painted the three-scene sequence *Battle of San Romano* (Louvre, London National Gallery and Uffizi) for the Medici – his most ambitious non-fresco paintings, and similarly notable for their strange use of foreshortening.

Vasari, Giorgio (1511–74). Born in Arezzo, Vasari trained with Luca Signorelli and Andrea del Sarto. He became the leading artistic

impresario of his day, working for the papacy in Rome and for the Medici in Florence, where he supervised (and partly executed) the redecoration of the Palazzo Vecchio. His own house in Arezzo is perhaps the most impressive display of his limited pictorial talents. He also designed the Uffizi gallery and oversaw a number of other architectural projects, including the completion of the massive Madonna dell'Umiltà in Pistoia. He is now chiefly famous for his Tuscan-biased *Lives of the Most Excellent Painters, Sculptors and Architects*.

Veneziano, Domenico (1404–61). Despite the name, Domenico Veneziano was probably born in Florence, though his preoccupation with the way in which colour alters in different light conditions is more of a Venetian concern. From 1439 to 1445 he was working on a fresco cycle in Florence with Piero della Francesca, a work that has now perished. Only a dozen surviving works can be attributed to him with any degree of certainty and only two signed pieces by him are left – one of them is the central panel of the so-called *St Lucy Altar* in the Uffizi.

Verrocchio, Andrea del (c.1435–88). A Florentine painter, sculptor and goldsmith, Verrocchio was possibly a pupil of Donatello and certainly his successor as the city's leading sculptor. A highly accomplished if sometimes over-facile craftsman, he ran one of Florence's busiest workshops, whose employees included the young Leonardo da Vinci. In Florence his work can be seen in the Uffizi, Bargello, San Lorenzo, Santo Spirito, Orsanmichele and Museo dell'Opera del Duomo.

Books

Most of the books recommended below are currently in print, and those that aren't shouldn't be too difficult to track down on websites such as ⓦwww .abebooks.com or ⓦwww.alibris.com. Titles that are currently out of print in both the US and UK are marked o/p. ⚑ symbol indicates titles that are especially recommended.

Travel books and journals

Charles Dickens *Pictures from Italy*. The classic mid-nineteenth-century Grand Tour, recording the sights of Emilia, Tuscany, Rome and Naples in measured and incisive prose.

Wolfgang Goethe *Italian Journey*. Revealing for what it says about the tastes of the time – Roman antiquities taking precedence over the Renaissance.

Edward Hutton *Florence*; *Country Walks About Florence*; *The Valley of the Arno*; *A Wayfarer in Unknown Tuscany*; *Siena and Southern Tuscany*; *Cities of Umbria*; *Assisi and Umbria Revisited*; *The Cosmati* (all o/p). A Tuscan resident from the 1930s to 1960s, Hutton was nothing if not prolific. Some of his prose adds a new shade to purple, but his books, between them, cover almost every inch of Tuscany and Umbria and are packed with assiduous background on the art and history.

Henry James *Italian Hours*. Urbane travel pieces from the young James; perceptive about particular monuments and works of art, superb on the different atmospheres of the great Italian cities.

D.H. Lawrence *Sketches of Etruscan Places*. Published posthumously, these are Lawrence's provocative musings on Etruscan art and civilization – which he considered more or less ideal ("ripe with the phallic knowledge", etc).

Mary McCarthy *The Stones of Florence*. Written in the mid-1960s, *Stones* is a mix of high-class reporting on the contemporary city and anecdotal detail on its history – one of the few accounts that doesn't read as if it's been written in a library.

H.V. Morton *A Traveller in Italy*. Morton's leisurely and amiable books were written in the 1930s, and their nostalgic charm has a lot to do with their enduring popularity. But this title – recently reissued – is also packed with learned details and marvellously evocative descriptions.

Iris Origo *War in the Val d'Orcia*. A stirring account of Origo's activities in the last war, hiding partisans and Allied troops on her estate near Montepulciano.

History and society

General

Harry Hearder *Italy: A Short History*. The best one-volume survey of the country from prehistory to the present.

Giuliano Procacci *History of the Italian People*. A comprehensive if dense history of the peninsula, charting the development of Italy as a nation state and giving a context for the story of Tuscany and Umbria.

Medieval

Adrian House *Francis of Assisi*. A much-needed modern biography that brings to life a saint who is respected by Christians and non-believers alike. House doesn't dodge difficult issues, such as Francis's relationship with St Clare or the possible causes of his stigmata, and provides an entertaining account of his early, apparently dissolute, life.

Iris Origo *The Merchant of Prato*. Based on the massive documentation of Francesco di Marco Datini's business empire, this is a wonderfully lively re-creation of domestic life in fourteenth-century Tuscany.

Frances Stonor Saunders *Hawkwood: Diabolical Englishman*. Fascinating study of the rapacious mercenary captain whose private army terrorized vast tracts of Italy in the late fourteenth century, in the wake of the miseries of the Black Death. More than an excellent biography, this book is a vivid reconstruction of a hellish period of Italian history.

Florence and the Renaissance

Gene A. Brucker *Renaissance Florence*. Concentrating on the years 1380–1450, this brilliant study of Florence at its cultural zenith uses masses of archival material to fill in the social, economic and political background to its artistic achievements.

Jacob Burckhardt *The Civilization of the Renaissance in Italy*. A pioneering nineteenth-century classic of Renaissance scholarship – the book that did more than any other to form our image of the period.

J.R. Hale *Florence and the Medici*. Scholarly yet lively, this covers the full span of the Medici story from the foundation of the family fortune to the calamitous eighteenth century. Vivid in its re-creation of the various personalities involved, it also presents a fascinating picture of the evolution of the mechanics of power in the Florentine state.

Christopher Hibbert *The House of Medici: its Rise and Fall*. More anecdotal than Hale's book, this is a gripping read, chock-full of heroic successes and squalid failures. His *Florence: The Biography of a City* is yet another excellent production, packed with illuminating anecdotes and fascinating illustrations – unlike most books on the city, it's as interesting on the political history as on the artistic achievements, and doesn't grind to a standstill with the fall of the Medici.

Mary Hollingsworth *Patronage in Renaissance Italy* (o/p). The first comprehensive English-language study of the relationship between artist and patron in *quattrocento* Italy's city-states. A salutary corrective to the mythology of self-inspired Renaissance genius.

George Holmes *Florence, Rome and the Origins of the Renaissance*. Magnificent – and costly – portrait of the world of Dante and Giotto, with especially compelling sections on the impact of St Francis and the role of the papacy in the political and cultural life of central Italy.

Michael Levey *Florence: A Portrait*. An often illuminating analysis of the city's history, and its artistic history in particular, with snippets and details missed by other accounts.

Luaro Martines *April Blood: Florence and the Plot Against the Medici*. A thorough and engrossing account of the most notorious conspiracy in Florentine history.

Paul Strathern *The Medici: Godfathers of the Renaissance*. Like Hibbert's book, this is a pacy and well-researched narrative of Florence's most famous family, but gives a little more space to the various luminaries (Michelangelo, Galileo etc) who were drawn into their orbit.

Siena, Assisi and Perugia

Edmund G. Gardner *The Story of Siena*; Margaret Symonds & L. Duff Gordon *The Story of Perugia* and *The Story of Assisi*. Published in Dent's "Medieval Towns" series in the 1920s, these pocket encyclopedias contain lots of anecdote and historical detail you won't find elsewhere.

Judith Hook *Siena: A City and its History* (o/p – but available in Siena). This superb study of the city and its art concentrates on the medieval heyday but also takes the story through to the present, and includes a good analytical section on the Palio.

Contemporary Italy

Paul Ginsborg *Italy and its Discontents*. If you want to understand contemporary Italy's baffling mixture of dynamism and ideological sterility, this book – lucidly argued and formidably well-informed – is an essential read. There is no better book on the subject.

Tobias Jones *The Dark Heart of Italy*. Written during a three-year period in Parma, and comprising essays dealing with aspects of modern Italian society, from the legal and political systems to the media and football. An affectionate but clear-eyed corrective to the sentimentalizing claptrap perpetrated by so many English and American expats.

Douglas Preston, with Mario Spezi *The Monster of Florence*. Between 1974 and 1985 the area around Florence was terrorised by Italy's most notorious serial killer. The crimes were truly monstrous, but Preston describes them without prurience, and much of this gripping book is devoted to the still unfinished hunt for the murderer – a tale of vainglorious and incompetent investigators, deranged conspiracy theorists and incredible "witnesses".

Charles Richards *The New Italians*. An affectionate and very well-informed survey of modern Italy, with plenty of vivid anecdotes that illustrate the tensions within a culture that is at once deeply traditional yet at the same time enthralled by the trappings of modernity.

Art and architecture

Charles Avery *Florentine Renaissance Sculpture* (o/p). Dependable introduction to the milieu of Donatello and Michelangelo.

Michael Baxandall *Painting and Experience in Fifteenth-Century Italy*. Invaluable analysis, concentrating on the way in which the art of the period would have been perceived at the time.

Malcolm Bull *The Mirror of the Gods: Classical Mythology in Renaissance Art*. Scores of illustrious academics have devoted themselves to decoding the meaning of the multitude of Renaissance artworks that are derived from classical mythologies, and Malcolm Bull is here arguing that most of them have been barking up the wrong tree. He contends that there is no coherent philosophy underlying this use of pagan imagery, and that such art was marginal – and not in an entirely negative sense. A provocative, exciting and demanding study.

Rona Goffen *Renaissance Rivals.* It's a truism that the cultural history of Renaissance Italy is to a large extent a history of competition – between artists, between individual patrons and between the various city states. However, Rona Goffen's masterly book is revelatory in its analysis of the depth and the complexity of the antagonisms involved in the production of high art in this period. She illuminates a world in which painters, sculptors and architects were ceaselessly endeavouring to supersede their contemporary rivals and the exemplars of the ancient world.

Richard Goy *Florence: the City and its Architecture.* Goy's superb book uses multiple perspectives to illuminate the architecture of Florence: the first section summarizes the city's development up to the unification of Italy; part two looks at the influence of the two chief "nuclei of power" – the Church and the State; part three analyses the fabric of the city according to building type (*palazzi*, churches, fortifications, etc); and the final section looks at the changes that Florence has undergone in the last century and a half. Encompassing everything from the Baptistery to the football stadium, and magnificently illustrated, this is a clear first choice.

J.R. Hale (ed.) *Concise Encyclopaedia of the Italian Renaissance* (o/p). Exemplary reference book, many of whose summaries are as informative as essays twice their length; covers individual artists, movements, cities, philosophical concepts, the lot.

Frederick Hartt & David Wilkins *History of Italian*

Renaissance Art. If one book on this vast subject can be said to be indispensable, this is it. In view of its comprehensiveness and the range of its illustrations, it's a bargain.

Michael Levey *Early Renaissance* (o/p). Precise and fluently written account from former director of the National Gallery, and well illustrated; probably the best introduction to the subject. Levey's *High Renaissance* (Penguin, o/p) continues the story in the same style.

Peter Murray *The Architecture of the Italian Renaissance.* Begins with Romanesque buildings and finishes with Palladio – useful both as a gazetteer of the main monuments and as a synopsis of the underlying concepts.

Diana Norman *Painting in Late Medieval and Renaissance Siena.* This concise and well-illustrated book explicates the evolution of Sienese art from the thirteenth century to the middle of the sixteenth, finishing with the work of Beccafumi, the last Sienese painter of any magnitude.

John Shearman *Mannerism* (o/p). The self-conscious art of sixteenth-century Mannerism is one of the most complex topics of Renaissance studies; Shearman's brief discussion analyses the main currents, and never succumbs to oversimplification or pedantry.

Giorgio Vasari *Lives of the Artists.* Penguin's two-volume abridgement is the fullest available translation of Vasari's classic (and highly tendentious) work on his predecessors and contemporaries. Includes essays on Giotto, Brunelleschi, Leonardo and Michelangelo. The first real work of art history, and still among the most revealing books on Italian Renaissance art. Oxford University Press publishes a newer and briefer one-volume selection.

Individual artists

James A. Ackerman *The Architecture of Michelangelo*. A concise, scholarly and highly engaging survey, which will make you see Michelangelo's architecture with fresh eyes.

Charles Avery *Giambologna*. This is the best survey of the career of the pre-eminent sculptor of the Mannerist period, an artist who can be seen as the successor of Michelangelo and precursor of Bernini. Avery's book is admirably comprehensive (every single sculpture is covered) and beautifully illustrated, with plenty of detailed close-ups of the major pieces and fascinating examples of the clay models that Giambologna created while sketching out his ideas.

Luciano Bellosi *Duccio: The Maestà*. This superb production aims to present "a very direct experience of Duccio di Buoninsegna's master-piece", and it does just that, with page after page of the highest quality details from the greatest of all Sienese paintings. The analytical essay that precedes the reproductions is a useful introduction to the work, but essen-tially this is a book to contemplate rather than read.

Bruce Cole *Giotto and Florentine Painting 1280–1375* (o/p). Excellent introduction to the art of Giotto and his immediate successors.

Ludwig Goldscheider *Michelangelo: Paintings, Sculpture, Architecture*. Virtually all monochrome reproductions, but an extremely good pictorial survey of Michelangelo's output, covering everything except the drawings.

Anthony Grafton *Leon Battista Alberti*. A fascinating study of one of the central figures of the Renaissance, Grafton's book illuminates every aspect of Alberti's astonishingly versatile career, which encompassed not just the visual arts and architecture, but also music, law, science and literature. Invaluable, not just as a portrait of an amazing man, but as an introduction to the whole culture of *quattrocento* Italy.

James Hall *Michelangelo and the Reinvention of the Human Body*. A provocative and frequently brilliant study of Michelangelo, arguing for the essential modernity of Michelangelo's unprecedented emphasis on the male nude. Not all of Hall's observations are wholly convincing, but on almost every page there's an insight that will make you look afresh.

Anthony Hughes *Michelangelo*. This was one of the first titles in Phaidon's "Art & Ideas" series, a project which aims to present well-illustrated overviews of the work of individual artists and art movements, written by scholars but in a style that's accessible to all. *Michelangelo* is a superb adver-tisement for the series, giving a clear narrative while delineating the social and cultural milieu, and explaining clearly the key issues of style, technique and intepretation.

Ross King *Brunelleschi's Dome*. The tale of one of the most remarkable feats of engineering in European history – the design and construction of the dome of Florence's cathedral. King is good on the social and intel-lectual atmosphere, and has a thriller writer's sense of pace.

Marilyn Aronberg Lavin *Piero della Francesca*. Another title in Phaidon's "Art & Ideas" project, this is the best English-language intro-duction to this most elusive of major Renaissance artists. Lavin is perhaps the world's leading authority on the subject, but this overview is perfectly pitched for the general reader, and benefits from having been published after the restoration of the Arezzo cycle, so its illustrations are uniquely accurate.

Charles Nicholl *Leonardo: The Flights of the Mind*. Leonardo left more than 7000 pages of manuscript notes, and Nicholl's dazzling biography is founded on an intensive study of these largely unpublished writings. The result is a book which is both a highly persuasive portrait of this elusive genius, and a compendious reconstruction of the milieu in which he worked.

Jeffrey Ruda *Fra Filippo Lippi*. Ruda's monograph is a fine achievement, combining a biographical study of the most wayward of early Renaissance masters with a consistently illuminating analysis of the paintings, which are reproduced in gorgeous large-format colour plates.

John White *Duccio: Tuscan Art and the Mediaeval Workshop* (o/p). The fullest study of the Sienese master available in English, concentrating on his art in the context of medieval workshop practices.

Alison Wright *The Pollaiuolo Brothers: the Arts of Florence and Rome*. As painters, sculptors and goldsmiths, the Pollaiuolo brothers ran one of the busiest workshops in fifteenth-century Florence. Wright's book is a thorough and superbly illustrated study of the business of art production, as well as giving an unimprovable guide to the brothers' highly varied and innovative output.

Literature

Dante Alighieri *The Divine Comedy*. No work in any other language bears comparison with Dante's poetic exegesis of the moral scheme of God's creation: in late medieval Italy it was venerated both as a book of almost scriptural authority and as the ultimate refinement of the vernacular Tuscan language. There are numerous translations; John D. Sinclair's prose version (published in three volumes by Oxford University Press) has the huge advantage of presenting the original text opposite the English, and has exemplary notes. Newcomers to Dante will get a lot out of *Dante in English*, an excellent Penguin anthology of English-language translations, as well as poetry influenced by Dante.

Ludovico Ariosto *Orlando Furioso*. Barbara Reynolds has done a fine job in this two-volume verse translation of Italy's chivalric epic (published by Penguin), set in Charlemagne's Europe. Oxford University Press produces a one-volume prose translation.

Giovanni Boccaccio *The Decameron*. Set in the plague-racked Florence of 1348, Boccaccio's assembly of one hundred short stories is a fascinating social record as well as a constantly diverting and often smutty comedy.

Benvenuto Cellini *Autobiography*. Shamelessly egocentric record of the travails and triumphs of the sculptor and goldsmith's career; one of the freshest literary productions of its time. There are two good translations – one from Penguin and one from Oxford University (under the title *My Life*).

Niccolo Machiavelli *The Prince*. A treatise on statecraft which actually did less to form the political thought of Italy than it did to form foreigners' perceptions of the country; yet there was far more to Machiavelli than the *Realpolitik* of *The Prince*, as is shown by the selection of writings included in Viking's superb anthology *The Portable Machiavelli*.

Petrarch (Francesco Petrarca) *Selections from the Canzoniere*. Often

C

CONTEXTS | Books

described as the first modern poet, by virtue of his preoccupation with worldly fame and secular love, Petrarch wrote some of the Italian language's greatest lyrics. This slim selection from Oxford University Press at least hints at what is lost in translation.

Leonardo da Vinci *Notebooks*. This Oxford University Press selection gives you a fascinating miscellany of speculation and observation from the universal genius of Renaissance Italy; essential to any understanding of the man.

Tuscany and Umbria in English fiction

Michael Dibdin *Ratking*. Crime time in Perugia. Best of the Italy-set books of an author who sometimes tries a little too hard to underline just how much he knows about the country.

George Eliot *Romola*. Weighty tale of fifteenth-century Florence; researched to the hilt, but will probably remain the great unread Eliot novel.

E.M. Forster *Where Angels Fear to Tread* and *Room with a View*. The settings are, respectively, San Gimignano and Florence, the milieu uptight Edwardian English society in Forster's two perfectly formed Italian novels.

Magdalen Nabb *Death in Spring-time*, *Death in Autumn*, and many other titles. Florence is the locale for many of Nabb's brilliant thrillers, based on a good knowledge of the city's low life and the Sardinian shepherds who dabble in a spot of kidnapping in the hills.

Michael Ondaatje *The English Patient*. At the close of World War II, a badly burned English aviator sees out his days in a wrecked Tuscan villa, attended by a cast of characters who come from widely differing backgrounds yet all think and speak in high-flown lyrical language. Some find Ondaatje's prose hypnotic, others find it portentous.

Barry Unsworth *After Hannibal*. Unsworth lives in Umbria, which is where this black comedy is set. Where lesser writers resort to rose-tinted fantasies, Unsworth evokes the reality of expat existence.

Special interest

Stefano Ardito *A Piedi in Umbria* (Edizione Iter). One of a series of hiking guides by the doyen of Italian backpackers.

Antonio Arrighi and Roberto Pratesi *A Piedi in Toscana* (Edizione Iter, 2 vols). Useful route guides for walkers, with basic maps. Widely available in Italy.

Hugh Johnson *Tuscany and its Wines* (Mitchell Beazley). Johnson's knowledge of his subject is sound, and the photographs almost qualify as oeno-porn.

Elizabeth Romer *The Tuscan Year: Life and Food in an Italian Valley* (Orion; North Point). An engaging mix of recipes and background on countryside traditions.

Language

Language

Italian

The ability to speak English confers prestige in Italy, and there's often no shortage of people willing to show off their knowledge, particularly in the main cities and resorts. However, in more remote areas you may find that no one speaks English at all.

Wherever you are, it's a good idea to master at least a little Italian, a task made easier by the fact that your halting efforts will often be rewarded by smiles and genuine surprise. In any case, it's one of the easiest European languages to learn, especially if you already have a smattering of French or Spanish, which are extremely similar to Italian grammatically.

Pronunciation

Easiest of all is the **pronunciation**, since most words are spoken exactly as they're written, and usually enunciated with exaggerated, open-mouthed clarity. The only difficulties you're likely to encounter are the few consonants that are different from English.

c before e or i is pronounced as in **ch**urch.

ch before e or i is hard, as in **c**at.

sci pronounced as in **sh**eet.

sce pronounced as in **sh**elter.

g is soft before e or i, as in **g**eranium; hard before h, as in **g**arlic.

gn as in o**ni**on.

gl is softened (the g is silent), as in sta**lli**on.

h is not aspirated, as in honour.

When **speaking to strangers**, the third person is the polite form (ie *Lei* instead of *Tu* for "you"); using the second person is a mark of disrespect. It's also worth remembering that Italians don't use "please" and "thank you" half as much as we do: it's all implied in the tone, though if you're in any doubt, err on the polite side.

All Italian words are **stressed** on the penultimate syllable unless a stress mark – ´ or ` – denotes otherwise. Note that the ending *-ia* or *-ie* counts as two syllables, hence *trattoria* is stressed on the i. Generally, in the text we've added stress marks whenever it isn't immediately obvious how a word should be pronounced, though these are omitted in Italian. **Accents** look similar to stress marks – generally ` – but they have the function of altering a word's final vowel sound, as in *città* or *caffè*, and can never be dropped.

Italian words and phrases

Basics

good morning	buongiorno	good night	buonanotte
good afternoon/ evening	buonasera	hello/goodbye (informal)	ciao

goodbye (formal)	arrivederci	Canadian/	canadese/nuova
yes	sì	New Zealand	zelandese
no	no	Australian (m/f)	australiano/a
please	per favore	Mr ...	Signor ...
thank you	(molte/mille) grazie	Mrs ...	Signora ...
(very much)		Miss ...	Signorina ...
you're welcome	prego	good/bad	buono/cattivo
alright/that's OK	va bene	big/small	grande/píccolo
excuse me	mi scusi	cheap/expensive	económico/caro
(apology)		early/late	presto/tardi
excuse me	permesso	hot/cold	caldo/freddo
(in a crowd)		near/far	vicino/lontano
sorry	mi dispiace	quickly/slowly	velocemente/
How are you?	Come stai?		lentamente
(informal)		slowly or quietly	piano
How are you?	Come sta?	with/without	con/senza
(formal)		more/less	più/meno
I'm fine	bene	enough, no more	basta
Do you speak	Parla inglese?	wait a minute!	aspetta!
English?		here/there	qui/là
I don't understand	Non ho capito	today	oggi
I don't know	Non lo so	tomorrow	domani
I'm here on holiday	Sono qui in	day after tomorrow	dopodomani
	vacanza	yesterday	ieri
I live in ...	Abito a ...	now	adesso
I'm ...	Sono ...	later	più tardi
English/Scottish	inglese/scozzese	in the morning	di mattina
Welsh/Irish	gallese/irlandese	in the afternoon	nel pomeriggio
American (m/f)	americano/a	in the evening	di sera

Questions

Where?	Dove?	How much does	Quant'è?
Where is/are ...?	Dov'è ...?/Dove	it cost?	
	sono ...?	Is it ...?/Is there ...?	È ...?/C'è ...?
When?	Quando?	What time does it	A che ora
What?	Cosa?	open/close?	apre/chiude?
Why?	Perchè?	What's it called	Come si chiama in
What is it?	Cos'è?	in Italian?	italiano?
How much/many?	Quanto/Quanti?	What time is it?	Che ore sono?

Accommodation

I'd like to book a	Vorrei prenotare una	Do you have rooms	Avete cámere libere?
room	cámera	free?	
I have a booking	Ho una prenotazione	a single/	una cámera singola/
Is there a hotel	C'è un albergo qui	double room	doppia
nearby?	vicino?		

Do you have a room ...	Ha una cámera ...
for one person	per una persona
for two/three people	per due/tre persone
for one night	per una notte
for two/three nights	per due/tre notti
for one week	per una settimana
for two weeks	per due settimane
with a double bed	con un letto matrimoniale
with twin beds	a due letti
with a shower/bath	con doccia/bagno
with a balcony	con balcone
hot/cold water	acqua calda/fredda
Could I see the room?	Potrei vedere la cámera?
Could I see another room?	Potrei vedere un'altra cámera?

How much is it?	Quanto costa?
Is breakfast included?	È compresa la prima colazione?
half/full board	mezza pensione/ pensione completa
Do you have anything cheaper?	Ha niente che costa di meno?
I'll take it	La prendo
Can we camp here?	Possiamo fare il campeggio qui?
Is there a campsite nearby?	C'è un campeggio qui vicino?
tent	tenda
cabin	cabina
youth hostel	ostello per la gioventù
porter	facchino
lift	ascensore
key	chiave

Travel and directions

bus	autobus/pullman
bus station	autostazione
train	treno
train station	stazione ferroviaria
ferry	traghetto
hydrofoil	aliscafo
ship	nave
ferry terminal	stazione maríttima
port	porto
A ticket to ...	Un biglietto a ...
one-way	solo andata
return	andata e ritorno
Can I book a seat?	Posso prenotare un posto?
What time does it leave?	A che ora parte?
When is the next train to ...?	Quando parte il prossimo treno per ...?
Do I have to change?	Devo cambiare?
Where does it leave from?	Da dove parte?
What platform does it leave from?	Da quale binario parte?
How many kilometres is it?	Quanti chilometri sono?
How long does it take?	Quanto ci vuole?

What number bus is it to ...?	Che número di autobus per ...?
How do I get to ...?	Per andare a ...?
How far is it to ...?	Quant'è lontano a ...?
Can you give me a lift to ...?	Mi può dare un passaggio a ...?
left/right	sinistra/destra
go straight ahead	sempre diritto
turn left/right	gira a sinistra/destra
Can you tell me when to get off?	Mi può dire quando devo scendere?
Next stop please	La prossima fermata, per favore
bicycle	bicicletta
hitchhiking	autostop
on foot	a piedi

Driving

car	macchina
Where's the road to ...?	Dov'è la strada a ...?
parking	parcheggio
no parking	divieto di sosta/sosta vietata
one-way street	senso único
no entry	senso vietato
slow down	rallentare
road closed	strada chiusa/guasta

no through road	vietato il transito	crossroads	incrocio
no overtaking	vietato il sorpasso	speed limit	limite di velocità

Signs

entrata/uscita	entrance/exit	suonare il campanello	ring the bell
ingresso líbero	free admission	acqua potabile	drinking water
aperto/chiuso	open/closed	signori/signore	gents/ladies toilet
chiuso per restauro	closed for restoration	bagno	WC
chiuso per férie	closed for holidays	líbero/occupato	vacant/engaged
tirare/spingere	pull/push	arrivi/partenze	arrivals/departures
non toccare	do not touch	dogana	customs
perícolo	danger	binario	platform
attenzione	beware	cassa	cash desk
avanti	go or walk	affítasi	to let
alt	stop	pronto soccorso	first aid
guasto	out of order		
vietato fumare	no smoking		

Numbers

1	uno	19	diciannove
2	due	20	venti
3	tre	21	ventuno
4	quattro	22	ventidue
5	cinque	30	trenta
6	sei	40	quaranta
7	sette	50	cinquanta
8	otto	60	sessanta
9	nove	70	settanta
10	dieci	80	ottanta
11	undici	90	novanta
12	dodici	100	cento
13	tredici	101	centuno
14	quattordici	110	centodieci
15	quindici	200	duecento
16	sedici	500	cinquecento
17	diciassette	1000	mille
18	diciotto	5000	cinquemila

Restaurants

I'd like to reserve a table	Vorrei riservare una távola	C'è carne dentro?	Is there meat in it?
Have you a table for two?	Avete una távola per due?	I'd like ...	Vorrei ...
		It's good/delicious	È buono/buonissimo
I'd like to order	Vorrei ordinare	The bill, please	Il conto, per favore
I'm a vegetarian (m/f)	Sono vegetariano/a	Is service included?	Il servizio è incluso?

Italian menu reader

Meals and courses

colazione	breakfast	zuppe/minestre	soups
pranzo	lunch	secondi	main courses
cena	dinner	contorni	vegetables
antipasti	starters	dolci	desserts
primi	first courses	menù degustazione	tasting menu

General terms

cameriere	waiter	maionese	mayonnaise
menù/lista	menu	marmellata	jam (jelly)
lista dei vini	wine list	olio	oil
coltello	knife	olive	olives
forchetta	fork	pane	bread
cucchiaio	spoon	pane integrale	wholemeal bread
senza carne	without meat	panna	cream
coperto	cover charge	patatine	crisps (potato chips)
servizio	service charge	patatine fritte	chips (french fries)
aceto	vinegar	pepe	pepper
aglio	garlic	pizzetta	small cheese and tomato pizza
biscotti	biscuits	riso	rice
burro	butter	sale	salt
caramelle	sweets	uova	eggs
cioccolato	chocolate	zucchero	sugar
frittata	omelette		
grissini	breadsticks		

Cooking terms

affumicato	smoked	al Marsala	cooked with Marsala wine
arrosto	roast	Milanese	fried in egg and breadcrumbs
ben cotto	well done		
bollito/lesso	boiled	pizzaiola	cooked with tomato sauce
brasato	braised		
cotto	cooked	al puntino	medium (steak)
crudo	raw	ripieno	stuffed
al dente	firm (not overcooked)	al sangue	rare (steak)
aí ferri	grilled without oil	allo spiedo	on the spit
fritto	fried	surgelato	frozen
grattuggiato	grated	in úmido	steamed/stewed
alla griglia	grilled		

L

LANGUAGE | Italian menu reader

Pizzas

calzone	folded pizza
capricciosa	literally "capricious"; topped with whatever they've got in the kitchen, usually including baby artichoke, ham and egg
cardinale	ham and olives
frutta di mare	seafood; usually mussels, prawns and clams
funghi	mushrooms; the tinned sliced variety, unless it specifies fresh (*funghi freschi*)
margherita	cheese and tomato
marinara	tomato, anchovy and olive oil
napo/napoletana	tomato
quattro formaggi	"four cheeses", usually including mozzarella, fontina and gruyère
quattro stagioni	"four seasons"; the toppings split into four separate sections, usually including ham, green pepper, onion and egg.

Antipasti

antipasto misto	mixed cold meats and cheeses
caponata	mixed aubergine, olives, tomatoes
caprese	tomato and mozzarella salad
crostini	mixed chicken liver canapés
insalata di mare	seafood salad
insalata di riso	rice salad
insalata russa	Russian salad (diced vegetables in mayonnaise)
melanzane alla parmigiana	aubergine (eggplant) in tomato and Parmesan cheese
peperonata	green and red peppers stewed in olive oil
pomodori ripieni	stuffed tomatoes
prosciutto	ham

pinzimonio	raw seasonal vegetable in olive oil, with salt and pepper
prosciutto di cinghiale	cured wild boar ham
salame toscano	pork sausage with pepper and cubes of fat
salsicce	pork or wild boar sausages

Tuscan antipasti

crostini di milza	minced spleen on pieces of toast
donzelle/donzelline	fried dough balls
fettuna/bruschetta	garlic toast with olive oil
finocchiona	pork sausage flavoured with fennel

Umbrian antipasti

prosciutto di Norcia	cured ham from Norcia
salame mezzafegato	sausage spiced with a mixture of pine nuts, pork liver, candied orange, sugar and raisins
schiacciata	flat bread baked with olive oil, or flavoured with onions or cooked greens
torta al testo	unleavened bread baked on a stone slab

Primi

Soups

brodo	clear broth
minestrina	any light soup
minestrone	thick vegetable soup
pasta fagioli	pasta soup with beans
pastini in brodo	pasta pieces in clear broth
stracciatella	broth with egg

Pasta

cannelloni	large tubes of pasta, stuffed
farfalle	literally "butterfly"-shaped pasta
fettucine	narrow pasta ribbons
gnocchi	small potato and dough dumplings
maccheroni	tubular spaghetti
pasta al forno	pasta baked with minced meat, eggs, tomato and cheese
penne	smaller pieces of rigatoni
rigatoni	large, grooved tubular pasta
risotto	cooked rice dish, with sauce
spaghettini	thin spaghetti
tagliatelle	pasta ribbons (another word for fettucine)
tortellini	small rings of pasta stuffed with meat or cheese
vermicelli	"little worms" (very thin spaghetti)

Pasta sauce (salsa)

amatriciana	tomato and cubed pork
arrabbiata	spicy tomato sauce with chillies
bolognese	tomato and meat
burro	butter
carbonara	cream, ham and beaten egg
funghi	mushrooms
panna	cream
parmigiano	Parmesan cheese
peperoncino	olive oil, garlic and fresh chillies
pesto	basil and garlic sauce
pomodoro	tomato sauce
ragù	meat sauce
vóngole	clam and tomato sauce

Tuscan primi

acquacotta	onion soup served with toast and poached egg
cacciucco	fish stew with tomatoes, bread and red wine
carabaccia	onion soup
garmugia	soup made with fava beans, peas, artichokes, asparagus and bacon
gnocchi di ricotta	dumplings filled with ricotta and spinach
minestra di farro	wheat and bean soup
minestrone alla fiorentina	haricot bean soup with red cabbage, tomatoes, onions and herbs
panzanella	summer salad of tomatoes, basil, cucumber, onion and bread
pappa al pomodoro	tomato soup thickened with bread
pappardelle	wide, short noodles, often served with hare sauce (con lepre)
pasta alla carrettiera	pasta with tomato, garlic, pepper, parsley and chilli
penne strasciate	pasta in meat sauce
ribollita	winter vegetable soup, based on beans and thickened with bread
risotto nero	rice cooked with cuttlefish (in its own ink)
zuppa di fagioli	bean soup

manfrigoli	rustic pasta made from emmer, a coarse type of wheat introduced into the region by the Romans
minestra di farro	tomato, wheat and vegetable soup

pici/stringozzi/ ceriole	thread-like spaghetti, usually served with garlicky tomato sauce
spaghetti alla norcina	spaghetti with an oily sauce of black truffles, garlic and anchovies
umbrici	large, heavy noodles

Secondi

Meat (carne)

agnello	lamb
bistecca	steak
cervello	brain
cinghiale	wild boar
coniglio	rabbit
costolette	chops
cotolette	cutlets
fagiano	pheasant
faraona	guinea fowl
fegatini	chicken livers
fégato	liver
involtini	meat slices, rolled and stuffed
lepre	hare
lingua	tongue
maiale	pork
manzo	beef
ossobuco	shin of veal
pernice	partridge
pancetta	bacon
pollo	chicken
polpette	meatballs
rognoni	kidneys
salsiccia	sausage
saltimbocca	veal with ham
spezzatino	stew
tacchino	turkey
trippa	tripe
vitello	veal

Fish (pesce) and shellfish (crostacei)

acciughe	anchovies
anguilla	eel
aragosta	lobster
baccalà	dried salted cod
calamari	squid
céfalo	mullet
cozze	mussels
dentice	dentex
gamberetti	shrimps
gámberi	prawns
granchio	crab
merluzzo	cod
óstriche	oysters
pesce spada	swordfish
polpo	octopus
sardine	sardines
sgombro	mackerel
sogliola	sole
tonno	tuna
triglie	red mullet
trota	trout
vóngole	clams

Tuscan secondi

árista	roast pork loin with garlic and rosemary
asparagi alla fiorentina	asparagus with butter, fried egg and cheese
baccalà alla livornese	salt cod with garlic, tomatoes and parsley
bistecca alla fiorentina	thick grilled T-bone steak
cibreo	chicken liver and egg stew
cieche alla pisana	small eels cooked with sage and tomatoes, served with Parmesan
lombatina	veal chop

peposo	peppered beef stew
pollo alla diavola/ al mattone	chicken flattened with a brick, grilled with herbs
scottiglia	stew of veal, game and poultry, cooked with white wine and tomatoes
spiedini di maiale	skewered spiced cubes of pork loin and liver, with bread and bay leaves
tonno con fagioli	tuna with white beans and raw onion
trigile alla livornese	red mullet cooked with tomatoes, garlic and parsley
trippa alla fiorentina	tripe in tomato sauce, served with Parmesan

Umbrian secondi

anguilla alla brace	grilled eel
anguilla in úmido	eel cooked with tomatoes, onions, garlic and white wine

frittata di tartufi	black truffle omelette
gobbi alla perugina	deep-fried cardoons (like artichokes) with meat sauce
lepre alle olive	hare cooked with herbs, white wine and olives
palombe/palombacci	woodpigeon, usually spit-roasted
pollo in porchetta	chicken cooked in the same way as suckling pig
porchetta	suckling pig cooked in a wood oven with fennel, garlic, mint and rosemary
regina in porchetta	Lago Trasimeno carp, cooked as above
salsiccia all'uva	pork sausage cooked with grapes
tegamaccio	freshwater-fish stew with white wine and herbs

Vegetables (contorni) and salad (insalata)

asparagi	asparagus
basílico	basil
capperi	capers
carciofi	artichokes
carciofini	artichoke hearts
carote	carrots
cavolfiore	cauliflower
cávolo	cabbage
cetriolo	cucumber
cipolla	onion
fagiolini	green beans
finocchio	fennel
funghi	mushrooms
insalata mista	mixed salad
insalata verde	green salad
melanzane	aubergine (eggplant)

orígano	oregano
patate	potatoes
peperoni	peppers
piselli	peas
pomodori	tomatoes
radicchio	chicory
spinaci	spinach
zucchini	courgettes

Tuscan contorni

fagioli all'olio	white beans served with olive oil
fagioli all'uccelletto	white beans cooked with tomatoes, garlic and sage
frittata di carciofi	fried artichoke flan

Sweets (dolci), fruit (frutta), cheese (formaggi) and nuts (noce)

amaretti	macaroons
ananas	pineapple
anguria/coccómero	watermelon
arance	oranges
banane	bananas
cacchi	persimmons
ciliégie	cherries
fichi	figs
fichi d'India	prickly pears
fontina	northern Italian cooking cheese
frágole	strawberries
gelato	ice cream
gorgonzola	a soft blue cheese
limone	lemon
macedónia	fruit salad
mándorle	almonds
mele	apples
melone	melon
mozzarella	soft white cheese
nespole	medlars
parmigiano	Parmesan cheese
pecorino	strong hard sheep's cheese
pere	pears
pesche	peaches
pinoli	pine nuts
provolone	strong hard cheese
ricotta	soft white sheep's cheese
torta	cake, tart
uva	grapes
zabaglione	dessert made with eggs, sugar and Marsala wine
zuppa inglese	trifle

Tuscan dolci

brigidini	anise wafer biscuits
buccellato	anise raisin cake
cantucci/cantuccini	small almond biscuits, served with Vinsanto wine
castagnaccio	unleavened chestnut-flour cake containing raisins, walnuts and rosemary
cenci	fried dough dusted with powdered sugar
frittelle di riso	rice fritters
meringa	frozen meringue with whipped cream and chocolate
necci	chestnut-flour crêpes
panforte	hard fruit, nut and spice cake
ricciarelli	marzipan almond biscuits
schiacciata alla fiorentina	orange-flavoured cake covered with powdered sugar, eaten at carnival time
schiacciata con l'uva	grape- and sugar-covered bread dessert
zuccotto	sponge cake filled with chocolate and whipped cream

Umbrian dolci

cialde	paper-thin sweet biscuits
fave di morte	almond biscuits
pinoccate	pine nut biscuits
serpentone/torcolato	almond and dried fruit dessert in the shape of a coiled snake (torcolo)

Drinking essentials

aperitivo	pre-dinner drink
digestivo	after-dinner drink
vino rosso	red wine
vino bianco	white wine
vino rosato	rosé wine
spumante	sparkling wine

secco	dry	cioccolato caldo	hot chocolate
dolce	sweet	latte	milk
birra	beer	frappé	milkshake made with ice cream
litro	litre	frullato	milkshake
mezzo	half-litre	ghiáccio	ice
quarto	quarter-litre	granita	iced drink with coffee or fruit
Salute!	Cheers! (toast)		
acqua minerale	mineral water	limonata	lemonade
naturale/liscia	still	aranciata	orangeade
frizzante/con gas	sparkling	spremuta	fresh fruit juice
bicchiere	glass	succo di frutta	concentrated fruit juice with sugar
bottiglia	bottle		
tazza	cup	soda	soda water
caffè	coffee	tónico	tonic water
tè	tea		

Travel
store

D: Rough Guide
DIRECTIONS for
short breaks

Available from all good bookstores

ROUGH GUIDES Complete Listing

For more information go to www.roughguides.com

ROUGH GUIDES

Visit us online

www.roughguides.com

Information on over 25,000 destinations around the world

BROADEN YOUR HORIZONS

NOTES

A Rough Guide to Rough Guides

Published in 1982, the first Rough Guide – to Greece – was a student scheme that became a publishing phenomenon. Mark Ellingham, a recent graduate in English from Bristol University, had been travelling in Greece the previous summer and couldn't find the right guidebook. With a small group of friends he wrote his own guide, combining a highly contemporary, journalistic style with a thoroughly practical approach to travellers' needs.

The immediate success of the book spawned a series that rapidly covered dozens of destinations. And, in addition to impecunious backpackers, Rough Guides soon acquired a much broader and older readership that relished the guides' wit and inquisitiveness as much as their enthusiastic, critical approach and value-for-money ethos.

These days, Rough Guides include recommendations from shoestring to luxury and cover more than 200 destinations around the globe, including almost every country in the Americas and Europe, more than half of Africa and most of Asia and Australasia. Our ever-growing team of authors and photographers is spread all over the world, particularly in Europe, the USA and Australia.

In the early 1990s, Rough Guides branched out of travel, with the publication of Rough Guides to World Music, Classical Music and the Internet. All three have become benchmark titles in their fields, spearheading the publication of a wide range of books under the Rough Guide name.

Including the travel series, Rough Guides now number more than 350 titles, covering: phrasebooks, waterproof maps, music guides from Opera to Heavy Metal, reference works as diverse as Conspiracy Theories and Shakespeare, and popular culture books from iPods to Poker. Rough Guides also produce a series of more than 120 World Music CDs in partnership with World Music Network.

Visit www.roughguides.com to see our latest publications.

Rough Guide travel images are available for commercial licensing at www.roughguidespictures.com

Rough Guide credits

Text editor: Natasha Foges and Lucy Ratcliffe
Layout: Pradeep Thapliyal
Cartography: Alakananda Roy
Picture editor: Sarah Cummins
Production: Rebecca Short
Proofreader: Margaret Doyle
Cover design: Chloë Roberts
Photographer: Chris Hutty, Roger d'Olivere Mapp, Michelle Grant, James McConnachie and Dylan Reisenberger
Editorial: London Ruth Blackmore, Andy Turner, Keith Drew, Edward Aves, Alice Park, Lucy White, Jo Kirby, James Smart, Róisín Cameron, Emma Traynor, James Rice, Emma Gibbs, Kathryn Lane, Christina Valhouli, Monica Woods, Mani Ramaswamy, Alison Roberts, Harry Wilson, Lucy Cowie, Helen Ochyra, Joe Staines, Peter Buckley, Matthew Milton, Tracy Hopkins, Ruth Tidball; **New York** Andrew Rosenberg, Steven Horak, AnneLise Sorensen, Ella Steim, Anna Owens, Sean Mahoney, Paula Neudorf; **Delhi** Madhavi Singh, Karen D'Souza, Lubna Shaheen
Design & Pictures: London Scott Stickland, Dan May, Diana Jarvis, Mark Thomas, Chloë Roberts, Nicole Newman, Emily Taylor; **Delhi** Umesh Aggarwal, Ajay Verma, Jessica Subramanian, Ankur Guha, Sachin Tanwar, Anita Singh, Nikhil Agarwal

Production: Vicky Baldwin
Cartography: **London** Maxine Repath, Ed Wright, Katie Lloyd-Jones; **Delhi** Rajesh Chhibber, Ashutosh Bharti, Rajesh Mishra, Animesh Pathak, Jasbir Sandhu, Karobi Gogoi, Swati Handoo, Deshpal Dabas
Online: **London** George Atwell, Faye Hellon, Jeanette Angell, Fergus Day, Justine Bright, Clare Bryson, Áine Fearon, Adrian Low, Ezgi Celebi, Amber Bloomfield; **Delhi** Amit Verma, Rahul Kumar, Narender Kumar, Ravi Yadav, Debojit Borah, Rakesh Kumar, Ganesh Sharma, Shisir Basumatari
Marketing & Publicity: **London** Liz Statham, Niki Hanmer, Louise Maher, Jess Carter, Vanessa Godden, Vivienne Watton, Anna Paynton, Rachel Sprackett, Libby Jellie, Laura Vipond; **New York** Geoff Colquitt, Nancy Lambert, Katy Ball; **Delhi** Ragini Govind
Manager India: Punita Singh
Reference Director: Andrew Lockett
Operations Manager: Helen Phillips
PA to Publishing Director: Nicola Henderson
Publishing Director: Martin Dunford
Commercial Manager: Gino Magnotta
Managing Director: John Duhigg

Publishing information

This seventh edition published June 2009 by
Rough Guides Ltd,
80 Strand, London WC2R 0RL
345 Hudson St, 4th Floor,
New York, NY 10014, USA
14 Local Shopping Centre, Panchsheel Park,
New Delhi 110017, India
Distributed by the Penguin Group
Penguin Books Ltd,
80 Strand, London WC2R 0RL
Penguin Group (USA)
375 Hudson Street, NY 10014, USA
Penguin Group (Australia)
250 Camberwell Road, Camberwell,
Victoria 3124, Australia
Penguin Group (Canada)
195 Harry Walker Parkway N, Newmarket, ON,
L3Y 7B3 Canada
Penguin Group (NZ)
67 Apollo Drive, Mairangi Bay, Auckland 1310,
New Zealand

Cover concept by Peter Dyer.

Typeset in Bembo and Helvetica to an original design by Henry Iles.

Printed and bound in China.

© Jonathan Buckley, Mark Ellingham and Tim Jepson, 2009

No part of this book may be reproduced in any form without permission from the publisher except for the quotation of brief passages in reviews.

712pp includes index

A catalogue record for this book is available from the British Library.

ISBN: 978-1-84836-067-9

The publishers and authors have done their best to ensure the accuracy and currency of all the information in **The Rough Guide to Tuscany & Umbria**, however, they can accept no responsibility for any loss, injury, or inconvenience sustained by any traveller as a result of information or advice contained in the guide.

1 3 5 7 9 8 6 4 2

Help us update

We've gone to a lot of effort to ensure that the seventh edition of **The Rough Guide to Tuscany & Umbria** is accurate and up to date. However, things change – places get "discovered", opening hours are notoriously fickle, restaurants and rooms raise prices or lower standards. If you feel we've got it wrong or left something out, we'd like to know, and if you can remember the address, the price, the hours, the phone number, so much the better.

Please send your comments with the subject line "**Rough Guide Tuscany & Umbria Update**" to ⓔ mail@roughguides.com. We'll credit all contributions and send a copy of the next edition (or any other Rough Guide if you prefer) for the very best emails.

Have your questions answered and tell others about your trip at
ⓦ community.roughguides.com

Acknowledgements

Tim Jepson would like to thank Duncan and Amanda Baird, Marella Caracciolo, Michael Sheridan and Yasmin Setha, as well as Nicholas Harrison for extra updating.

Readers' letters

Thanks to all those readers of the sixth edition who took the trouble to write in with their amendments and suggestions. Apologies for any misspellings or omissions.

Chris Alborough, Linda Baker, Juliet Brennan & Michael Rowe, Kay Burtenshaw, Nicole Fiore, Erica Gabrielle Foldy & Jane Sumner, Lars Holm, Jenny Howard, I Johnson, Sandy Le Mole, Kamin Mohammadi, Deborah Siegel, P K Starling, Ken Thomson, Sheelagh Watford, Nigel and Edyth Watt, Evelyn Wrin.

Photo credits

All photos © Rough Guides except the following:

SMALL PRINT

Selected images from our guidebooks are available for licensing from:
ROUGHGUIDESPICTURES.COM

Index

Map entries are in colour.

I INDEX

O

INDEX

Map symbols

maps are listed in the full index using coloured text

----	International boundary	🅿	Car park
---	Chapter division boundary	♦	Point of interest
--··	Regional boundary	@	Internet access
▬▬	Motorway	ⓘ	Tourist office
═══	Road	⊠	Post office
▬▬	Pedestrianized street	✈	Airport
▥▥▥	Steps	★	Bus stop
▬•▬	Railway	✡	Synagogue
= = =	Tunnel	🏛	Monument
-----	Footpath	♜	Castle
——	River	⊞	Hospital
----	Ferry	⚱	Church (regional maps)
——	Town wall	⊞	Church (town maps)
Ѧ	Campsite	▮	Building
⌃⌃	Mountains	▭	Market
▲	Mountain peak	⊞⊞	Christian cemetery
⊠—⊠	Gate		Park/forest
◉	Accommodation		Beach
▣	Restaurant